How to access the supplemental web study guide

We are pleased to provide access to a web study guide that supplements your textbook, *Foundations of Sport and Exercise Psychology, Sixth Edition.* The web study guide includes activities that allow students to watch video clips of coach–athlete interactions, sport psychology consultants using techniques and tools with their clients, and experts discussing research and practice; activities that allow for self-assessment; and activities that help students reflect on their own personal journey in the field.

Accessing the web study guide is easy!
Follow these steps if you purchased a new book:

1. Visit **www.HumanKinetics.com/FoundationsOfSportAndExercisePsychology**.

2. Click the <u>sixth edition</u> link next to the corresponding sixth edition book cover.

3. Click the Sign In link on the left or top of the page. If you do not have an account with Human Kinetics, you will be prompted to create one.

4. If the online product you purchased does not appear in the Ancillary Items box on the left of the page, click the Enter Key Code option in that box. Enter the key code that is printed at the right, including all hyphens. Click the Submit button to unlock your online product.

5. After you have entered your key code the first time, you will never have to enter it again to access this product. Once unlocked, a link to your product will permanently appear in the menu on the left. For future visits, all you need to do is sign in to the textbook's website and follow the link that appears in the left menu!

→ Click the Need Help? button on the textbook's website if you need assistance along the way.

How to access the web study guide if you purchased a used book:

You may purchase access to the web study guide by visiting the text's website, **www.HumanKinetics.com/FoundationsOfSportAndExercisePsychology**, or by calling the following:

800-747-4457 . . . . .U.S. customers
800-465-7301 . . . . .Canadian customers
+44 (0) 113 255 5665 . . . . European customers
08 8372 0999 . . . . Australian customers
0800 222 062 . . . . .New Zealand customers
217-351-5076 . . . . .International customers

For technical support, send an e-mail to:
support@hkusa.com . . . . U.S. and international customers
info@hkcanada.com . . . . Canadian customers
academic@hkeurope.com . . . . European customers
keycodesupport@hkaustralia.com . . . . . Australian and New Zealand customers

HUMAN KINETICS
The Information Leader in Physical Activity & Health

09-2014

FOUNDATIONS OF SPORT AND EXERCISE PSYCHOLOGY

SIXTH EDITION

Robert S. Weinberg, PhD
Miami University

Daniel Gould, PhD
Michigan State University

Human
Kinetics

Library of Congress Cataloging-in-Publication Data

Weinberg, Robert S. (Robert Stephen), author.
 Foundations of sport and exercise psychology / Robert S. Weinberg, Daniel Gould. -- Sixth edition.
   p. ; cm.
 Includes bibliographical references and index.
 I. Gould, Daniel, 1952- author. II. Title.
 [DNLM: 1. Sports--psychology. 2. Exercise--psychology. QT 260]
 GV706.4
 796.01--dc23
                              2014001380

ISBN: 978-1-4504-6981-4 (print)

The web addresses cited in this text were current as of April 2014, unless otherwise noted.

Acquisitions Editor: Myles Schrag; **Developmental Editor:** Amanda S. Ewing; **Managing Editors:** Casey A. Gentis and Anne Cole; **Copyeditor:** Amanda M. Eastin-Allen; **Indexer:** Bobbi Swanson; **Permissions Manager:** Dalene Reeder; **Graphic Designer:** Nancy Rasmus; **Graphic Artist:** Denise Lowry; **Cover Designer:** Keith Blomberg; **Photograph (cover):** © Human Kinetics; **Photographs (interior):** © Human Kinetics, unless otherwise noted; **Photo Asset Manager:** Laura Fitch; **Photo Production Manager:** Jason Allen; **Art Manager:** Kelly Hendren; **Associate Art Manager:** Alan L. Wilborn; **Art Style Development:** Joanne Brummett; **Illustrations:** © Human Kinetics, unless otherwise noted; **Printer:** Courier Companies, Inc.

Printed in the United States of America   10   9   8   7   6   5   4   3   2   1

The paper in this book was manufactured using responsible forestry methods.

Human Kinetics
Website: www.HumanKinetics.com

United States: Human Kinetics, P.O. Box 5076, Champaign, IL 61825-5076
800-747-4457
e-mail: humank@hkusa.com

Canada: Human Kinetics, 475 Devonshire Road Unit 100, Windsor, ON N8Y 2L5
800-465-7301 (in Canada only)
e-mail: info@hkcanada.com

Europe: Human Kinetics, 107 Bradford Road, Stanningley, Leeds LS28 6AT, United Kingdom
+44 (0) 113 255 5665
e-mail: hk@hkeurope.com

Australia: Human Kinetics, 57A Price Avenue, Lower Mitcham, South Australia 5062
08 8372 0999
e-mail: info@hkaustralia.com

New Zealand: Human Kinetics, P.O. Box 80, Torrens Park, South Australia 5062
0800 222 062
e-mail: info@hknewzealand.com

E6197

CONTENTS

TO THE INSTRUCTOR

Sport and exercise psychology has significantly changed our lives and the lives of many athletes, coaches, and other sport and exercise professionals with whom we have worked and trained over the years. We have felt enriched by our studies in this field, and we want to give something back to our field by writing this comprehensive, introductory text on sport and exercise psychology. In the first five editions, our goal was to create a book for introductory sport and exercise psychology classes that bridged up-to-date research and practice, capturing the best of what we had learned from coaches, scholars, exercisers, sports medicine and health care personnel, and athletes. We have followed this general orientation in our sixth edition.

Since our first five editions, we have received a great deal of feedback from teachers and students indicating that we have been successful in reaching our goal. We have been pleased that our book has helped fill a void in the teaching of sport and exercise psychology. But as with any academic text, there is always room for improvement and updating, hence our decision to write a sixth edition. In this edition, we have held to the basic goals and objectives of our first five editions and have tried also to incorporate the insightful comments and suggestions we have received in order to make this sixth edition an even better text. But because faculty and students appeared to like our basic orientation and the design of the text, we decided not to make "wholesale changes," although changes were most certainly made.

For example, we have updated every chapter with the latest research and practice in sport and exercise psychology. This included updating the references to include more contemporary sources. In some cases these changes were extensive because the research and subsequent implications for best practice have developed significantly. In other chapters the changes are less dramatic because those particular areas have not grown or altered significantly in the past several years. We also have presented even more contemporary practical examples, case studies, and anecdotes to help students understand various theories, concepts, and research. In-depth questions are provided after each chapter as opportunities for students to think more critically about applying the material, leading from research to practice. In this latest edition, we have again used four colors, which makes the material come to life even more and foster easier reading and comprehension.

We have also spent a lot of time on improving the ancillary package to help instructors provide the best learning environment for their students. The ancillaries explained next accompany this book. To access these ancillaries, visit www.HumanKinetics.com/FoundationsOfSportAndExercisePsychology:

- **Presentation Package Plus Image Bank.** The presentation package has more than 1,000 slides based on the material in the book. In addition, more than 50 slides include key figures and tables from the text, and more than 100 slides link to the new instructor videos (see below for more discussion on this new ancillary). While we have streamlined the subject matter, we purposely did not cut a lot of content from previous editions of the slides. Not all instructors teach using all chapters in the book, and some instructors spend more time on particular chapters than others. Therefore, we didn't want to cut content from the Presentation Package when we know it is used. Feel free to modify the slides as needed so that they fit your needs. The image bank (which is new to the sixth edition) includes all the figures and tables from the book, separated by chapter. These items can be added to the presentation package, student handouts, and so on.
- **Test Package.** The test package has more than 780 multiple choice questions to choose from, based on text material. The questions have been updated to reflect the new content added to the text.
- **Chapter Quizzes.** New to the sixth edition are chapter quizzes. These learning management system (LMS)-compatible, ready-made quizzes can be used to measure student learning of the most important concepts for each chapter.

Two hundred forty questions (ten questions per chapter) are included in multiple choice format.

- **Instructor Guide.** The instructor guide provides instructors with a sample course outline for organizing lectures and chapters. It also includes additional class exercises, and a detailed class outline highlights key material to discuss for each text chapter. The instructor guide also lists each chapters' web study guide activities and highlights whose activities that are supported by video, most all of which is to this edition.

- **Instructor Videos.** New to the sixth edition is a library of online video clips that instructors can use during their in-person class lectures or online courses. Clips include interviews with leading experts in the field, demonstrations of sport and exercise psychology techniques, and interviews with coaches, athletes, and exercisers. More than 70 unique video clips are included and correspond with most of the 24 chapters of the text. All of the video clips from the web study guide are included here, too. Thus, a total of 122 videos are available in this one ancillary. Links to these videos are included in the Presentation Package, too. (Note: You must have an Internet connection in order to view this streaming video content.)

- **Web Study Guide.** The web study guide includes exercises, audio files, and video segments that bring to life and reinforce the most salient points discussed in the text and help engage today's learner, who has grown up using technology. We have retained most of the exercises from the fifth edition and even added a few new ones, as well as more video content.

Students will receive free access to the web study guide when they purchase a new copy of the text. Included in the study guide's features are audio and video interviews with top sport psychologists speaking about their research and topics from specific chapters. In addition, there are exercises that can be completed in or out of class and sample psychological inventories. This web study guide is meant to supplement and complement what is in the text and help the material come alive. We encourage instructors to integrate this online material into their courses as they see fit.

When you finish teaching the course, we would like to hear from you regarding your thoughts on the book. We wrote this textbook for students, but instructors are in an excellent position to give feedback to help better meet the needs of students in the future. (Earlier feedback helped us immensely in revising the first five editions.) We hope you will enjoy teaching sport and exercise psychology as much as we continue to.

The study of human behavior is at once complex and important, and thus it has intrigued people for many years. This book focuses on human behavior in certain types of situations—namely sport and exercise settings. In essence, it examines what motivates people, what angers them, and what scares them; how they regulate their thoughts, feelings, and emotions; and how their behaviors can become more effective.

Perhaps you want to be a physical educator, a coach, a fitness instructor, an athletic trainer or sports medicine professional, or even a sport psychologist. Or maybe you are simply curious about how people behave in sport and exercise settings and why they behave in these ways. In any case, *Foundations of Sport and Exercise Psychology* has been designed to meet your need for information. It will, we hope, provide you with an overview of sport and exercise psychology, bridge the gap between research and practice, convey fundamental principles of professional practice, and capture some of the excitement of the world of sport and exercise.

Your Road Map to Understanding Sport and Exercise Psychology

Most of you do not get into a car to begin a long trip without a destination in mind and a plan to get there. You pick a specific place and use a road map or GPS device to find the best, most enjoyable route.

Ironically, though, some students read textbooks with no plan and no educational destination (other than getting the next day's assignment completed on time). Failing to set a goal and plan of study with your textbooks is much like driving without a destination and road map or GPS: You spend a lot of time driving aimlessly.

Your understanding of sport and exercise psychology will come easier if you set a plan and keep a goal in mind while reading this text. It is our goal to provide you with the most up-to-date and relevant knowledge and information within the field of sport and exercise psychology. However, we want to bring you this knowledge in a manner that you find user-

friendly and can thus easily implement it into your daily personal and professional lives. We do not feel that your journey will be complete until you are able to take this information and use it in everyday life. You can use this introduction as a road map to achieve two goals: (a) a better understanding of sport and exercise psychology and (b) an understanding of how to use or apply sport and exercise psychology knowledge.

This book has seven parts:

1. Beginning Your Journey
2. Learning About Participants
3. Understanding Sport and Exercise Environments
4. Focusing on Group Processes
5. Improving Performance
6. Enhancing Health and Well-Being
7. Facilitating Psychological Growth and Development

Although these parts and their chapters work well when read in order, your instructor may elect to change the order to fit your particular class. That's okay, because we have designed each chapter to stand alone, without depending on knowledge from the previous chapters. The lone exception to this guideline is chapter 1, which we recommend should always be read first, especially if this is your introduction to the field. If it helps, think of the chapters as individual stops on a path that completes a journey. Each individual stop (chapter) is necessary to create a path that leads you to a destination, but you can choose to skip certain stops, linger at a stop for only a short time, or start the path from the opposite end. All of the stops are necessary to complete the path, but you don't have to "visit" at each stop to reach the end of the path.

The practical set up of each chapter will help you move through the text in whatever order your professor assigns. The model in this introduction will help you tie together the specifics into a coherent whole. In it you'll see eight stops—points of interest—on your journey to understanding sport and exercise psychology. Part I, Beginning Your Journey, is where

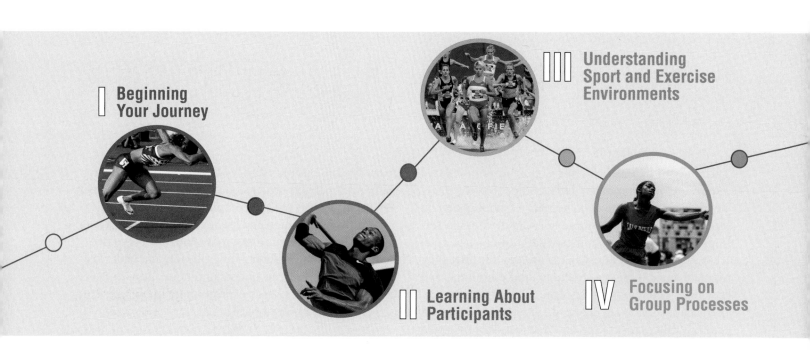

I Beginning Your Journey

II Learning About Participants

III Understanding Sport and Exercise Environments

IV Focusing on Group Processes

you prepare for the journey. In chapter 1 you are introduced to the field of sport and exercise psychology, its history, and its contemporary directions and likely paths for the future. You will also learn how closely research and practice are linked and how you can make that connection even stronger.

The next stop on your journey is part II, Learning About Participants. Effective teaching, coaching, and training rest on understanding the psychological makeup of the people you work with—what makes them tick! Hence, the three chapters in this part focus on individuals, whether they are exercisers, athletes, rehabilitation clients, or physical education students. This material will help you understand people in terms of their personalities, motivational orientations, achievement motivation, competitiveness, and anxiety levels.

You must also consider the situations or environments in which people function. For this reason part III, Understanding Sport and Exercise Environments, examines major environmental influences affecting sport and exercise participants. You will learn about competition and cooperation and how feedback and reinforcement influence people.

The fourth stop on your journey is part IV, Focusing on Group Processes, which focuses on the workings of groups. Most teachers, coaches, and exercise leaders work with groups, so it is critical to understand team dynamics, group cohesion, leadership, and communication. Topics such as group cohesion, social loafing, group structure, and leadership styles are included in this section.

Enhancing individual performance is a mainstay of sport and exercise psychology. For this reason part V, Improving Performance, is one of the longest stops on our journey, consisting of six chapters. Here you will learn how to develop a psychological skills training program to regulate arousal, use imagery to improve performance, enhance self-confidence, set effective goals, and strengthen concentration.

Part VI, Enhancing Health and Well-Being, introduces you to the joint roles of psychology and physical development in motivating people to exercise, enjoying the benefits of exercise, treating athletic injuries, and aiding rehabilitation. You will find critical information here about combating substance abuse, eating disorders, exercise addiction, and overtraining.

One of the most important functions that sport and exercise professionals have is helping people with their psychological growth and character development. Part VII, Facilitating Psychological Growth and Development, concludes the text with discussions of three special issues: children in sport, aggression, and character development.

The book ends with a short section we have aptly called Continuing Your Journey. Here, we reinforce the research-to-practice orientation of the text. After studying the seven parts of the book you will have not only an excellent idea of what sport and exercise psychology involves but also specific knowledge of how to use the information effectively.

A map or GPS does little good if it's not used. This is also true of the model we have created. So, before you read a chapter, see where it fits into the overall

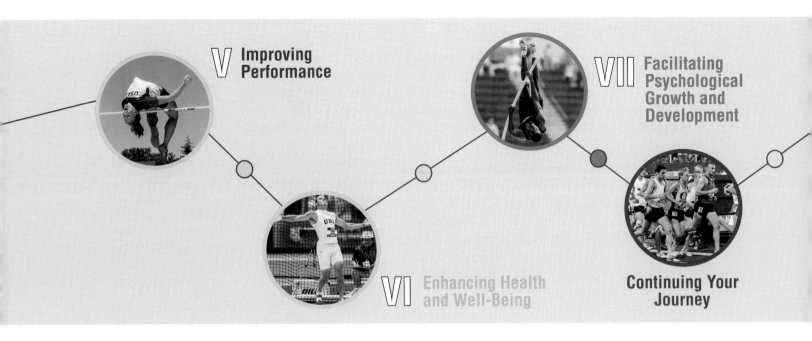

V Improving Performance

VII Facilitating Psychological Growth and Development

VI Enhancing Health and Well-Being

Continuing Your Journey

journey. And as you read each chapter, ask yourself these questions:

1. What can I do as a professional to use this information effectively?
2. What personal and situational considerations will influence how I will use and modify this information?
3. Will my primary goal in using this information be to help participants enhance performance, develop and grow personally, or a combination of these objectives?
4. How can I integrate this information and derive efficient, effective strategies for practice?

Assistance for Your Journey

We have tried to make this book user-friendly in several ways, both through features in the textbook as well as through an online resource.

Textbook Features

There are many items in the textbook that will help you identify and retain key information. Key points in each chapter summarize information that is crucial to remember. Here's an example of a key point:

> **KEY POINT**   Sport and exercise psychology is the scientific study of people and their behaviors in sport and exercise activities and the practical application of that knowledge.

Sidebars highlight new research, case studies, and research-to-practice examples. Case studies are identified by this icon:

At the end of each chapter, you'll find Learning Aids—a chapter summary, a list of key terms, review questions, and critical thinking questions—that will let you know if you have a thorough grasp of the chapter's content and that will give you an opportunity for in-depth analysis of important topics.

Web Study Guide

The web study guide (WSG) is also a valuable resource to use as you go through the book. The WSG was specifically developed to help students understand the material and concepts in this edition. The WSG includes activities to help make the material in the text come alive and give you a chance to reflect on the concepts in depth. We have interviewed some of the top sport psychologists in the world so that you can either hear or see them talk about their work, research, and how they relate to the material in the text. You'll also be able to view video clips and complete interactive self-assessments. Throughout the book you'll see callouts to these different types of WSG activities:

Journey: Each part opener contains an audio or video activity that asks an open-ended, thought-provoking question to help you to further explore the phase of your journey through the field of sport psychology that you are learning about.

Listen: In these activities, you are directed to watch or listen to an audio or video interview. You'll then have a chance to record your comments on what you've heard in a downloadable document and submit it to your instructor, if requested.

View: These activities direct you to watch a video showing sport psychology consultants in action, whether talking directly with an athlete, demonstrating an exercise, or discussing an important topic. For many of the activities, you'll then have a chance to record your comments on what you've seen in a downloadable document and submit it to your instructor, if requested.

Discover: Throughout each chapter, you're directed to activities that ask you to complete self-assessments or apply concepts you learned about in the text to real-world situations. Many of these activities provide you with a downloadable document that provides a framework for you to record your responses. If your instructor assigns an activity as homework, you can save the document and then submit it electronically or print the document and turn it in by hand.

You can access the activities by going to www. HumanKinetics.com/FoundationsOfSportAnd ExercisePsychology. In some cases, your instructor might offer these activities in some other format. If your instructor has you access the activities through a learning management system (LMS), follow the instructor-provided instructions. We hope you find this WSG informative, interesting, and enjoyable—just another way to enhance the learning and appreciation of the material presented in this textbook. Begin your WSG experience by completing these first three activities:

eBook available at your campus bookstore or HumanKinetics.com

VIEW In Introduction Activity 1, Dr. Dan Gould, one of the coauthors of this text, introduces you to the field of sport and exercise psychology.

DISCOVER To assess your current level of knowledge about sport and exercise psychology, take the short quiz in the WSG (see Introduction Activity 2).

DISCOVER Complete Introduction Activity 3 to consider the roles and responsibilities of professionals in kinesiology and the sport sciences.

ACKNOWLEDGMENTS

The sixth edition of this book would not have been possible if not for the tireless work of countless dedicated sport and exercise psychologists throughout the world. It is because of their research, writing, and consulting that the field has advanced so far in recent years, and it is for this reason that we acknowledge all their efforts.

We would also like to recognize the teachers, coaches, sports medicine specialists, and athletes with whom we have had the opportunity to consult. Indeed, they have taught us a great deal about sport and exercise psychology.

We would like to thank the staff at Human Kinetics for helping make this book possible. In particular, special thanks to acquisitions editor Myles Schrag, developmental editor Amanda Ewing, and managing editor Casey Gentis for their careful attention to detail with all the changes necessary in such a large revision. Dan would also like to thank Nori Pennisi for all her help editing and organizing materials for this edition of the book.

Finally, we would like to acknowledge our families. In particular, Dan would like to thank his wife, Deb, and sons, Kevin and Brian. Bob would like to thank his mom and dad (who passed away after the completion of the fourth edition), his brother, Randy, his children, Josh and Kira, and most recently, Elaine. They all deserve a great deal of thanks for their unconditional support. So, thanks everybody.

PART I

Beginning Your Journey

Where do you fit in the field of sport and exercise psychology?

In this beginning section, we focus on getting you, the future sport and exercise science practitioner, started on your journey to understanding sport and exercise psychology. First, to inform you of the nature of sport and exercise psychology, we describe what this ever-growing field involves. Chapter 1 introduces you to the field, details some of its history, and defines its current status. Here we describe what sport and exercise psychologists do, discuss orientations to studying the field, and present the field's future directions and opportunities. Because bridging science and practice is an important concept, the chapter also introduces the main ways in which knowledge is gained in sport and exercise psychology, emphasizing the importance of teaming scientific and practical knowledge to allow you to better assist students, athletes, and exercisers psychologically. This information might also help you decide whether you want to pursue a career in sport and exercise psychology.

VIEW Dr. Dan Gould introduces part I of the text in the Introduction activity.

JOURNEY This activity asks you to record your expectations as you begin your journey in exercise and sport psychology.

LISTEN Go to part I of the web study guide to meet the following experts in the field: Dan Gould, PhD; Diane L. Gill, PhD; and Rainer Martens, PhD. In this activity, you'll hear or see the experts discussing the evolution of sport and exercise psychology.

Welcome to Sport and Exercise Psychology

After reading this chapter, you should be able to

1. describe what sport and exercise psychology is,
2. understand what sport and exercise psychology specialists do,
3. know what training is required of a sport and exercise psychologist,
4. understand major developments in the history of sport and exercise psychology,
5. distinguish between scientific and professional practice knowledge,
6. integrate experiential and scientific knowledge,
7. compare and contrast orientations to the field, and
8. describe career opportunities and future directions in the field.

Jeff, the point guard on the high school basketball team, becomes overly nervous in competition. The more critical the situation, the more nervous he becomes and the worse he plays. Your biggest coaching challenge this season will be helping Jeff learn to manage stress.

Beth, fitness director for the St. Peter's Hospital Cardiac Rehabilitation Center, runs an aerobic fitness program for recovering patients. She is concerned, however, because some clients don't stick with their exercise programs after they start feeling better.

Lisa majors in kinesiology and knows she wants to pursue some type of health-related career, such as going to graduate school and becoming an orthopedic doctor, physician's assistant, or physical therapist. Although she loves the biological sciences, she wonders what role psychological factors play in preventative medicine, especially as they relate to holistic wellness and using physical activity as medicine.

Mario has wanted to be a physical educator for as long as he can remember. He feels frustrated now, however, because his high school students have so little interest in learning lifelong fitness skills. Mario's goal is to get the sedentary students motivated to engage in fitness activities.

Patty is the head athletic trainer at Campbell State College. The school's star running back, Tyler Peete, has achieved a 99% physical recovery from knee surgery. The coaches notice, however, that in practices he still favors his formerly injured knee and is hesitant when making cutbacks. Patty knows that Tyler is physically recovered but that he needs to regain his confidence.

Tom, a sport psychologist and longtime baseball fan, just heard about his dream position, a consulting job. The owners of the Chicago Cubs, fed up with the team's lack of cohesion, have asked him to quickly design a training program in psychological skills. If Tom can construct a strong program in the next week, he will be hired as the team's sport psychology consultant.

If you become a coach, an exercise leader, a health care provider, a physical educator, an athletic trainer, or even a sport psychologist, you also will encounter the kinds of situations that Jeff, Beth, Lisa, Mario, Patty, and Tom face. Sport and exercise psychology offers a resource for solving such problems and many other practical concerns. In this chapter you will be introduced to this exciting area of study and will learn how sport and exercise psychology can help you solve practical problems.

Defining Sport and Exercise Psychology

Sport and exercise psychology is the scientific study of people and their behaviors in sport and exercise contexts and the practical application of that knowledge (Gill & Williams, 2008). Sport and exercise psychologists identify principles and guidelines that professionals can use to help adults and children participate in and benefit from sport and exercise activities.

> **KEY POINT** Sport and exercise psychology is the scientific study of people and their behaviors in sport and exercise activities and the practical application of that knowledge.

Most people study sport and exercise psychology with two objectives in mind: (a) to understand how psychological factors affect an individual's physical performance and (b) to understand how participation in sport and exercise affects a person's psychological development, health, and well-being. They pursue this study by asking the following kinds of questions:

Objective A: Understand the effects of psychological factors on physical or motor performance

- How does anxiety affect a basketball player's accuracy in free-throw shooting?
- Does lacking self-confidence influence a child's ability to learn to swim?
- How does a coach's reinforcement and punishment influence a team's cohesion?
- Does imagery training facilitate recovery in injured athletes and exercisers?
- How does a health care provider's communication style influence a patient's adherence to home rehabilitation exercise schedule and recovery?

Objective B: Understand the effects of physical activity participation on psychological development, health, and well-being

- Does running reduce anxiety and depression?
- Do young athletes learn to be overly aggressive from participating in youth sports?
- Does participation in daily physical education classes improve a child's self-esteem?
- Does participation in college athletics enhance personality development?
- Does physical therapy influence a wounded warrior's physical health as well as help him or her create a more optimistic view of the future?

Sport psychology applies to a broad population base. Although some professionals use sport psychology to help elite athletes achieve peak performance, many other sport psychologists are concerned more with children, persons who are physically or mentally disabled, seniors, and average participants. More and more sport psychologists have focused on the psychological factors involved in exercise and health, developing strategies for encouraging sedentary people to exercise or assessing the effectiveness of exercise as a treatment for depression. To reflect this broadening of interests, the field is now called sport and exercise psychology. Some individuals focus only on the exercise- and health-related aspects of the field.

> **KEY POINT** Sport and exercise psychologists seek to understand and help elite athletes, children, persons who are physically or mentally disabled, seniors, and average participants achieve maximum participation, peak performance, personal satisfaction, and development through participation.

VIEW Activity 1.1 helps you understand the objectives of sport and exercise psychology.

Specializing in Sport Psychology

Contemporary sport psychologists pursue varied careers. They serve three primary roles in their professional activities: conducting research, teaching, and consulting (figure 1.1). We discuss each of these briefly.

Research Role

A primary function of participants in any scholarly field is to advance the knowledge in the field by conducting

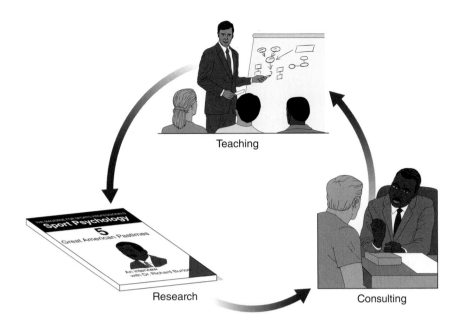

Teaching

Research

Consulting

FIGURE 1.1 The roles of sport and exercise psychologists.

research. Most sport and exercise psychologists in a university conduct research. They might, for example, study what motivates children to be involved in youth sport, how imagery influences proficiency in golf putting, how running for 20 minutes four times a week affects an exerciser's anxiety levels, or what the relationship is between movement education and self-concept among elementary physical education students. Today, sport and exercise psychologists are members of multidisciplinary research teams that study problems such as exercise adherence, the psychology of athletic injuries, and the role of exercise in the treatment of HIV. Sport psychologists then share their findings with colleagues and participants in the field. This sharing produces advances, discussion, and healthy debate at professional meetings and in journals (see "Leading Sport and Exercise Psychology Organizations and Journals").

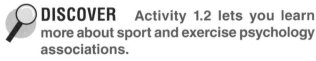 **DISCOVER** Activity 1.2 lets you learn more about sport and exercise psychology associations.

Teaching Role

Many sport and exercise psychology specialists teach university courses such as exercise and health psychology, applied sport psychology, and the social psychology of sport. These specialists may also teach such courses as personality psychology or developmental psychology if they work in a psychology department, or courses such as motor learning and control or sport sociology if they work in a sport science program.

Consulting Role

A third role is consulting with individual athletes or athletic teams to develop psychological skills for enhancing competitive performance and training. Olympic committees and some major universities employ full-time sport psychology consultants, and hundreds of other teams and athletes use consultants on a part-time basis for psychological skills training. Some sport psychologists now work with the military to help prepare troops for peak performance, and others work with surgeons to help them perfect their surgical skills. Many sport psychology consultants work with coaches through clinics and workshops.

Some sport and exercise psychologists now work in the fitness industry, designing exercise programs that maximize participation and promote psychological and physical well-being. Some consultants work as adjuncts to support a sports medicine or physical therapy clinic, providing psychological services to injured athletes.

Distinguishing Between Two Specialties

In contemporary sport psychology, a significant distinction exists between two types of specialties: clinical sport psychology and educational sport psychology.

Next we discuss the distinction between these two specialties and the training needed for each.

Clinical Sport Psychology

Clinical sport psychologists have extensive training in psychology, so they can detect and treat individuals with emotional disorders (e.g., severe depression, suicidal tendencies). Clinical sport psychologists are licensed by state boards to treat individuals with emotional disorders and have received additional training in sport and exercise psychology and the sport sciences. Clinical sport psychologists are needed because, just as in the normal population, some athletes and exercisers develop severe emotional disorders and require special treatment (Brewer & Petrie, 2014; Proctor & Boan-Lenzo, 2010). Eating disorders and substance abuse are two areas in which a clinical sport psychologist can often help sport and exercise participants.

> **KEY POINT** Clinical sport and exercise psychologists treat athletes and exercisers who have severe emotional disorders.

Educational Sport Psychology

Educational sport psychology specialists have extensive training in sport and exercise science, physical education, and kinesiology; and they understand the psychology of human movement, particularly as it relates to sport and exercise contexts. These specialists often have taken advanced graduate training in psychology and counseling. They are not trained to treat individuals with emotional disorders, however, nor are they licensed psychologists.

A good way to think of an educational sport psychology specialist is as a "mental coach" who, through group and individual sessions, educates athletes and exercisers about psychological skills and their development. Anxiety management, confidence development, and improved communication are some of the areas that educational sport psychology specialists address. When an educational sport psychology consultant encounters an athlete with an emotional disorder, he or she refers the athlete to either a licensed clinical psychologist or, preferably, a clinical sport psychologist for treatment.

> **KEY POINT** Educational sport psychology specialists are "mental coaches" who educate athletes and exercisers about psychological skills and their development. They are not trained to work with individuals who have severe emotional disorders.

Both clinical and educational sport and exercise psychology specialists must have a thorough knowledge of both psychology and exercise and sport science (figure 1.2). In 1991, the AASP began a cer-

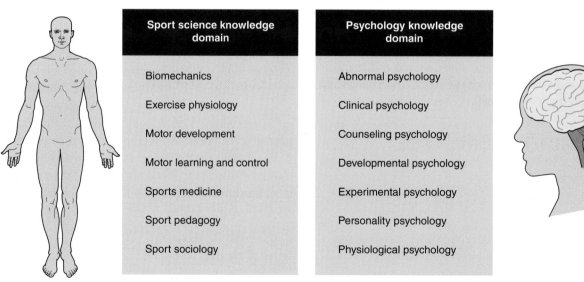

Sport and Exercise Psychology

Sport science knowledge domain	Psychology knowledge domain
Biomechanics	Abnormal psychology
Exercise physiology	Clinical psychology
Motor development	Counseling psychology
Motor learning and control	Developmental psychology
Sports medicine	Experimental psychology
Sport pedagogy	Personality psychology
Sport sociology	Physiological psychology

FIGURE 1.2 The relationship of knowledge in the sport science and psychology domains to the field of sport and exercise psychology.

Leading Sport and Exercise Psychology Organizations and Journals

Organizations

- *Association for Applied Sport Psychology (AASP)*—The sole purpose of this organization is to promote research and practice in applied sport and exercise psychology. Special interest groups focus on a variety of topics, including health psychology, intervention-performance enhancement, and social psychology.

- *American Psychological Association (APA) Division 47—Exercise and Sport Psychology*—One of almost 50 divisions in the APA (the largest professional psychology organization in the United States), this organization emphasizes both research and practice in sport and exercise psychology.

- *European Federation of Sport Psychology (FEPSAC)*—Begun in 1968, this organization promotes scientific, educational, and professional efforts in Europe. It hosts a conference once every four years, organizes congresses and courses, and publishes position statements.

- *International Society of Sport and Exercise Psychology (ISSP)*—Begun in 1965, this organization is devoted to promoting research, practice, and the development of sport and exercise psychology throughout the world.

- *North American Society for the Psychology of Sport and Physical Activity (NASPSPA)*—One of the oldest organizations focusing on the psychological aspects of sport and physical activity, this organization focuses on research in motor development, motor learning and control, and social psychology and physical activity.

Journals

- *International Journal of Sport Psychology*—Begun in 1970, this is the official journal of the International Society of Sport Psychology. It is aimed at enhancing theoretical and practical knowledge in the science of physical activity, exercise, and sport.

- *International Review of Sport and Exercise Psychology*—This journal publishes critical reviews of the research literature in sport and exercise psychology.

- *Journal of Applied Sport Psychology*—Begun in 1989, this is the official journal of the AASP. It publishes applied sport psychology research and professional practice articles.

- *Journal of Sport Psychology in Action*—This journal does not publish original research. Rather, it is an applied journal that promotes the application of scientific knowledge to the practice of sport, exercise, and health psychology.

- *Journal of Sport and Exercise Psychology*—This journal publishes basic and applied sport and exercise psychology research studies. Begun in 1979, it is one of the oldest and most respected research journals in the field.

- *Sport, Exercise and Performance Psychology*—Started in 2012 and one of the newest journals in the field, this is the official journal of Exercise and Sport Psychology Division 47 of the American Psychological Association. It publishes papers that focus on sport, exercise, and performance psychology.

- *The Psychology of Sport and Exercise*—Begun in 2000, this journal provides a forum for scholarly reports in sport and exercise psychology broadly defined.

- *The Sport Psychologist*—This journal, begun in 1987, publishes both applied research and professional practice articles that facilitate the delivery of psychological services to coaches and athletes.

- *Sport and Exercise Psychology Review*—This journal publishes articles on all aspects of sport psychology and focuses particularly on the training of sport psychologists and the practice of sport and exercise psychology.

tified consultant program. To qualify for certification as sport and exercise consultants, people must have advanced training in both psychology and the sport sciences. This requirement protects the public from unqualified individuals professing to be sport and exercise psychologists.

Reviewing the History of Sport and Exercise Psychology

Today, sport and exercise psychology is more popular than ever before. It is a mistake, however, to think that this field has developed only recently. Modern sport psychology dates back to the 1880s (Kornspan, 2012), and references to psychology can be traced back to the ancient Olympic Games (Kremer & Moran, 2008). The history of sport psychology mirrors the history of other fields such as psychology, physical education, and kinesiology. In addition, the field has been influenced by larger sociocultural developments such as growth of the Olympic movement, women's liberation efforts, and the popularity of professional sport (Gould & Voelker, 2014).

The history of sport psychology falls into six periods, which are highlighted here along with some specific individuals and events from each period. These various periods have distinct characteristics and yet are interrelated. Together they contributed to the field's development and growing stature.

Period 1: Early Years (1893–1920)

NORMAN TRIPLETT

In North America, sport psychology began in the 1890s. For example, Norman Triplett, a psychologist from Indiana University and a bicycle racing enthusiast, wanted to understand why cyclists sometimes rode faster when they raced in groups or pairs than when they rode alone (Triplett, 1898). First, he verified that his initial observations were correct by studying cycling racing records. To test his hunch further, he also conducted an experiment in which young children were to reel in fishing line as fast as they could. Triplett found that children reeled in more line when they worked in the presence of another child. This experiment allowed him to make more reliable predictions about when bicycle racers would have better performances.

Another early pioneer was E.W. Scripture, a Yale psychologist who was interested in taking a more scientific data-based approach to the study of psychology, as much of the psychology in these early years was introspective and philosophical (see Kornspan, 2007a, for an in-depth examination of his work). Scripture saw sport as an excellent way to demonstrate the value of this "new" scientific psychology, and with his students he conducted a number of laboratory studies on reaction and muscle movement times of fencers and runners as well as transfer of physical training. Scripture also discussed early research examining how sport might develop character in participants. Most interesting was the fact that Scripture worked closely with William Anderson of Yale, one of the first physical educators in America. This demonstrates that those in the fields of physical education and psychology worked together to develop sport psychology.

While Triplett and Scripture were part of the "new psychology" movement that focused on using experimental laboratory methods and measurement to gain knowledge, others were interested in the field from a more philosophical perspective. Most notable was Pierre de Coubertin, the founder of the modern Olympic Games (Kornspan, 2007b). Coubertin wrote extensively on the psychological aspects of sport and organized two early Olympic Congresses that focused on psychology as it could be related to sport in this time period.

In these early years, psychologists, physical educators, and other interested parties were only beginning to explore psychological aspects of sport and motor skill learning. They measured athletes' reaction times, studied how people learn sport skills, and discussed the role of sport in personality and character development, but they did little to apply these studies. Moreover, people dabbled in sport psychology but no one specialized in the field.

Highlights of Period 1

- 1893: E.W. Scripture conducts data-based studies of athletes at Yale, examining reaction and movement times as well as transfer of physical training.

- 1897: Norman Triplett conducts the first social psychology and sport psychology experiment, studying the effects of others on cyclists' performances.

- 1897: Second Olympic Congress debates psychological effect of sport on youths.

- 1899: E.W. Scripture of Yale describes personality traits that he believes can be fostered via sport participation.

- 1903: Third Olympic Congress focuses on sport psychology.
- 1903: G.T.W. Patrick discusses the psychology of play.
- 1914: R. Cummins assesses motor reactions, attention, and abilities as they pertain to sport.
- 1918: As a student, Coleman Griffith conducts informal studies of football and basketball players at the University of Illinois.

Period 2: The Development of Laboratories and Psychological Testing (1921–1938)

COLEMAN GRIFFITH

This time period in the history of sport and exercise psychology has been characterized by the development of sport psychology laboratories in Germany, Japan, Russia, and the United States and increased psychological testing (Kornspan, 2012). Coleman Griffith was the first North American to devote a significant portion of his career to sport psychology, and today he is regarded as the father of American sport psychology (Kroll & Lewis, 1970). A University of Illinois psychologist who also worked in the department of physical welfare (physical education and athletics), Griffith developed the first laboratory in sport psychology, helped initiate one of the first coaching schools in America, and wrote two classic books, *Psychology of Coaching* and *Psychology of Athletics*. He also conducted a series of studies on the Chicago Cubs baseball team and developed psychological profiles of such legendary players as Dizzy Dean. He corresponded with Notre Dame football coach Knute Rockne about how best to psych teams up and questioned Hall of Famer Red Grange about his thoughts while running the football. Ahead of his time, Griffith worked in relative isolation, but his high-quality research and deep commitment to improving practices remain an excellent model for sport and exercise psychologists. During this time period, psychologists also began to test athletes, assessing such things as reaction times, concentration, personality, and aggression. For exam-

ple, baseball immortal Babe Ruth was brought to the Columbia University Psychological Laboratory to be tested (Fuchs, 2009).

Highlights of Period 2

- 1920: Robert Schulte directs a psychological laboratory at the German High School for Physical Education.
- 1920: The first sport psychology department is begun by P.A. Rudik in Moscow at the State Institute of Physical Culture.
- 1921: Schulte publishes *Body and Mind in Sport*.
- 1921–1931: Griffith publishes 25 research articles about sport psychology.
- 1925: Schulte publishes *Aptitude and Performance Testing for Sport*.
- 1925: University of Illinois research-in-athletics laboratory is established; Griffith is appointed director.
- 1926: Griffith publishes *Psychology of Coaching*.
- 1928: Griffith publishes *Psychology of Athletics*.

Period 3: Preparation for the Future (1939–1965)

FRANKLIN HENRY

Franklin Henry at the University of California, Berkeley, was largely responsible for the field's scientific development. He devoted his career to the scholarly study of the psychological aspects of sport and motor skill acquisition. Most important, Henry trained many other energetic physical educators who later became university professors and initiated systematic research programs. Some of his students became administrators who reshaped curriculums and developed sport and exercise science or the field of kinesiology as we know it today.

Other investigators from 1939 to 1965, such as Warren Johnson and Arthur Slatter-Hammel, helped lay the groundwork for future study of sport psychology and helped create the academic discipline of exercise and sport science. Applied work in sport psychology was still limited; however, by the end of the era this was beginning to change.

One individual doing applied work during this era was Dorothy Hazeltine Yates, one of the first women in the United States to both practice sport psychology and conduct research. Yates consulted with university boxers, teaching them how to use relaxation and positive affirmations to manage emotions and enhance performance (Kornspan & MacCracken, 2001). Yates developed the technique, called the relaxation-set method, during World War II when she consulted with a college boxing team with considerable success. She later taught a psychology course exclusively for athletes and aviators. Like many of today's sport psychologists, Yates was interested in scientifically determining whether her interventions were effective, and she published an experimental test of her technique with boxers (Yates, 1943). Although she did her work in relative isolation, Yates' research on practice orientation was especially impressive.

Another individual doing applied work was David Tracy, who was hired to work with the St. Louis Browns, a professional baseball team (Kornspan & MacCracken, 2001). His work was widely publicized and is credited with bringing attention to sport psychology (Kornspan, 2009).

Highlights of Period 3

- 1938: Franklin Henry assumes a position in the department of physical education at the University of California, Berkeley, and establishes a graduate program in the psychology of physical activity.
- 1943: Dorothy Yates works with college boxers and studies the effects of her relaxation-training intervention.
- 1949: Warren Johnson assesses precompetitive emotions of athletes.
- 1951: John Lawther writes *Psychology of Coaching.*
- 1965: First World Congress of Sport Psychology is held in Rome.

Period 4: Establishment of Academic Sport Psychology (1966–1977)

By the mid-1960s, physical education had become an academic discipline (now called kinesiology or exercise and sport science) and sport psychology

had become a separate component in this discipline, distinct from motor learning. Motor learning specialists focused on how people acquire motor skills (not necessarily sport skills) and on conditions of practice, feedback, and timing. In contrast, sport psychologists studied how psychological factors—anxiety, self-esteem, and personality—influence sport and motor skill performance and how participation in sport and physical education influences psychological development (e.g., personality, aggression).

BRUCE OGILVIE

Applied sport psychology consultants also began working with athletes and teams. Bruce Ogilvie of San Jose State University was one of the first to do so, and he is often called the father of North American applied sport psychology. Concurrent with the increased interest in the field, the first sport psychology societies were established in North America.

Highlights of Period 4

- 1966: Clinical psychologists Bruce Ogilvie and Thomas Tutko write *Problem Athletes and How to Handle Them* and begin to consult with athletes and teams.
- 1967: B. Cratty of UCLA writes *Psychology of Physical Activity.*
- 1967: First annual NASPSPA conference is held.
- 1974: Proceedings of the NASPSPA conference are published for the first time.

Period 5: Multidisciplinary Science and Practice in Sport and Exercise Psychology (1978–2000)

From the mid-1970s to 2000, tremendous growth in sport and exercise psychology took place both in North America and internationally. The field became more accepted and respected by the public. Interest in applied issues characterized this period, as did the growth and development of exercise psychology as a specialty area for researchers and practitioners. Sport and exercise psychology also separated from the related exercise and sport science specializations of motor learning and control and motor development. More and better research was conducted, and this research was met with increased respect and acceptance in related fields such as psychology. Alternative forms of qualitative and interpretive research emerged and became better accepted as the

DOROTHY HARRIS

period came to a close. Specialty journals and conferences in the area were developed, and numerous books were published. Both students and professionals with backgrounds in general psychology entered the field in greater numbers. Training in the field took a more multidisciplinary perspective as students took more counseling- and psychology-related course work. The field wrestled with a variety of professional practice issues such as defining training standards for those in the area, developing ethical standards, establishing licensure, and developing full-time positions for the increasing numbers of individuals entering the field.

In this period, Dorothy Harris, a professor at Pennsylvania State University, advanced the cause of both women and sport psychology by helping to establish the PSU graduate program in sport psychology. Her accomplishments included being the first American and the first female member of the International Society of Sport Psychology, the first woman to be awarded a Fulbright Fellowship in sport psychology, and the first female president of the North American Society of Sport Psychology and Physical Activity. Harris broke ground for future women to follow at a time when few women were professors in the field.

Highlights of Period 5

- 1979: *Journal of Sport Psychology* (now called *Sport and Exercise Psychology*) is established.
- 1980: The U.S. Olympic Committee develops the Sport Psychology Advisory Board.
- 1984: American television coverage of the Olympic Games emphasizes sport psychology.
- 1985: The U.S. Olympic Committee hires its first full-time sport psychologist.

- 1986: The first applied scholarly journal, *The Sport Psychologist,* is established.
- 1986: AASP is established.
- 1987: APA Division 47 (Sport Psychology) is developed.
- 1988: The U.S. Olympic team is accompanied by an officially recognized sport psychologist for the first time.
- 1989: *Journal of Applied Sport Psychology* begins.
- 1991: AASP establishes the "certified consultant" designation.

Period 6: Contemporary Sport and Exercise Psychology (2001–Present)

Today sport and exercise psychology is a vibrant and exciting field with a bright future. However, some serious issues must be addressed. Later in this chapter you will learn about contemporary sport and exercise psychology in detail, but some of the key developments are highlighted here.

Highlights of Period 6

- 2000: The journal *Psychology of Sport and Exercise* is developed and published in Europe.
- 2003: APA Division 47 focuses on sport psychology as a specialized proficiency area.
- 2013: International Society of Sport Psychology Conference in China has more than 700 participants from 70 countries.
- Concerns emerge about the best ways to prepare and educate students.
- Exercise psychology flourishes, especially in university environments, driven by external funding possibilities and its utility in facilitating wellness and holding down health care costs.
- Strong, diverse, and sustained research programs are evident around the world.
- Interest in applied sport psychology continues to increase.

Focusing on Sport and Exercise Psychology Around the World

Sport and exercise psychology thrives worldwide. Sport psychology specialists work in more than 70 countries. Most of these specialists live in North

America and Europe; major increases in activity have also occurred in Latin America, Asia, and Africa in the past decade.

AVKSENTY PUNI

Sport psychologists in Japan, Russia, and Germany began working at about the time Coleman Griffith began his work at the University of Illinois. The pioneering work of Russian sport psychologist Avksenty Puni has recently been disseminated to English-speaking audiences and provides a fascinating glimpse of this individual's 50-year career (Ryba, Stambulova, & Wrisberg, 2005; Stambulova, Wrisberg, & Ryba, 2006). Puni's theorizing on psychological preparation for athletic competition focusing on realistic goals, uncompromising effort, optimal emotional arousal, high tolerance for distractions and stress, and self-regulation was groundbreaking and far ahead of what was being done in North America at the time. His work demonstrates the importance of looking outside one's borders for sport psychology knowledge.

The ISSP was established in 1965 to promote and disseminate information about sport psychology throughout the world. The ISSP has sponsored 12 World Congresses of Sport Psychology—focusing on such topics as human performance, personality, motor learning, wellness and exercise, and coaching psychology—that have been instrumental in promoting awareness of and interest in the field. Since 1970, the ISSP has also sponsored *International Journal of Sport Psychology.*

FERRUCCIO ANTONELLI

Credit for much of the international development of sport psychology goes to Italian sport psychologist Ferruccio Antonelli, who

Women in Sport and Exercise Psychology

When one looks at the history of sport and exercise psychology, the absence of women is striking. This is not uncommon in the history of many sciences, and multiple factors account for this absence. Historically, women were not given the same equal opportunities as their male counterparts, and women who were involved often had to overcome prejudices and other major obstacles to professional advancement. Also, women's contributions have often been underreported in scientific history.

Kornspan and MacCracken (2001) identified the important research, teaching, and intervention work Dorothy Hazeltine Yates completed in the 1940s, and the work of Dorothy Harris has also been acknowledged. Vealey (2006), in providing a comprehensive history of the evolution of sport and exercise psychology, also uncovered some previously ignored contributions of female pioneers in the field. Finally, Krane and Whaley (2010) and Whaley and Krane (2012) conducted a study of eight U.S. women who greatly influenced the development of the field over the past 30 years. These included Joan Duda, Deb Feltz, Diane Gill, Penny McCullagh, Carole Oglesby, Tara Scanlan, Maureen Weiss, and Jean Williams. These women shared a number of characteristics (e.g., driven, humble, competent, passionate about the field) and helped shape the field by mentoring countless male and female students, producing top-notch lines of research, and providing caring, competent leadership (Krane & Whaley, 2010). They also faced numerous challenges in their trailblazing efforts, such as overcoming department politics and sexism (Krane & Whaley, 2010). However, their "quiet competence" prevailed, and these outstanding women contributed greatly to the history of U.S. sport and exercise psychology.

Contributions of women to sport and exercise psychology are not limited to the United States. Women from around the world, such as Russian Natalia Stambulova, German-born Dorothea Alfermann, and Spaniard Gloria Balague, have made important contributions to the field for multiple decades. Most notable is Ema Geron of Bulgaria, who published books in the area and played a major leadership role in the formation of the European Federation of Sport Psychology. She was the first president of the organization, serving from 1969 to 1973.

One thing is clear: Although they may not be given the credit they deserve, women have greatly contributed to the development of sport psychology and exercise psychology and are helping drive major advances in the field today.

was both the first president of the ISSP and the first editor of *International Journal of Sport Psychology*. Sport and exercise psychology is now well recognized throughout the world as both an academic area of concentration and a profession. The prospect of continued growth remains bright.

Bridging Science and Practice

Reading a sport and exercise psychology textbook and actually working professionally with exercisers and athletes are very different activities. To understand the relationship between the two you must be able to integrate scientifically derived textbook knowledge with practical professional experience. We will help you develop the skills to do this so you can better use sport and exercise psychology knowledge in the field.

Scientifically Derived Knowledge

Sport and exercise psychology is above all a science. Hence, it is important that you understand how scientifically derived knowledge comes about and how it works; that is, you need to understand the **scientific method**. Science is dynamic—something that scientists do (Kerlinger, 1973). Science is not simply an accumulation of facts discovered through detailed observations but rather is a process, or method, of learning about the world through the systematic, controlled, empirical, and critical filtering of knowledge acquired through experience. When we apply science to psychology, the goals are to describe, explain, predict, and allow control of behavior.

Let's take an example. Dr. Jennifer Jones, a sport psychology researcher, wants to study how movement education affects children's self-esteem. Dr. Jones first defines self-esteem and movement education and determines what age groups and particular children she wants to study. She then explains why she expects movement education and self-esteem to be related (e.g., the children would get recognition and praise for learning new skills). Dr. Jones' research is really about prediction and control: She wants to show that using movement education in similar conditions will consistently affect children's self-esteem in the same way. To test such things, science has evolved some general guidelines for research:

• The scientific method dictates a **systematic approach** to studying a question. It involves standardizing the conditions; for example, one might assess the children's self-esteem under identical conditions with a carefully designed measure.

• The scientific method involves **control** of conditions. Key variables, or elements in the research (e.g., movement education or changes in self-esteem), are the focus of study, and other variables are controlled (e.g., the same person doing the teaching) so they do not influence the primary relationship.

• The scientific method is **empirical**, which means it is based on observation. Objective evidence must support beliefs, and this evidence must be open to outside evaluation and observation.

• The scientific method is **critical**, meaning that it involves rigorous evaluation by the researcher and other scientists. Critical analysis of ideas and work helps ensure that conclusions are reliable.

Theory

A scientist's ultimate goal is a **theory**, or a set of interrelated facts that present a systematic view of some phenomenon in order to describe, explain, and predict its future occurrences. Theory allows scientists to organize and explain large numbers of facts in a pattern that helps others understand them. Theory then turns to practice.

One example is the **social facilitation theory** (Zajonc, 1965). After Norman Triplett's first reel-winding experiment with children (see "Reviewing the History of Sport and Exercise Psychology"), psychologists studied how the presence of an audience affects performance, but their results were inconsistent. Sometimes people performed better in front of an audience and other times they performed worse. Zajonc saw a pattern in the seemingly random results and formulated a theory. He noticed that when people performed simple tasks or jobs they knew well, having an audience influenced their performance positively. However, when people performed unfamiliar or complex tasks, having an audience harmed performance. In his social facilitation theory, Zajonc contended that an audience creates arousal in the performer, which hurts performance on difficult tasks that have not been learned (or learned well) and helps performance on well-learned tasks.

KEY POINT A theory is a set of interrelated facts presenting a systematic view of some phenomenon in order to describe, explain, and predict its future occurrences.

Zajonc's theory increased our understanding of how audiences influence performance at many levels (e.g., students, professionals) and in many situations (e.g., sport, exercise). He consolidated many seemingly random instances into a theory basic enough for performers, coaches, and teachers to remember and to apply in a variety of circumstances. As the saying goes, nothing is more practical than a good theory!

Of course, not all theories are equally useful. Some are in the early stages of development and others have already passed the test of time. Some theories have a limited scope and others have a broad range of application. Some involve few variables and others involve a complex matrix of variables and behaviors.

◉ VIEW Activity 1.3 has you design your own research study and experiment in sport and exercise psychology.

Studies Versus Experiments

An important way in which scientists build, support, or refute theory is by conducting studies and experiments. In a **study**, an investigator observes or assesses factors without changing the environment in any way. For example, a study comparing the effectiveness of goal setting, imagery, and self-talk in improving athletic performance might use a written questionnaire given to a sample of high school cross country runners just before a race. The researchers could compare techniques used by the 20 fastest runners with those used by the 20 slowest runners. The researchers would not change or manipulate any factors but rather would simply observe whether faster runners reported using particular mental skills (e.g., imagery). The researchers would not know whether the goal setting, imagery, and self-talk caused some runners to go faster or whether running faster stirred the runners to set more goals. Studies have lim-

🗒 Coming Off the Bench: A Sport Psychology Consulting Case Study

Jerry Reynolds was referred to Ron Hoffman, Southeastern University sport psychology consultant, at the end of his freshman year of varsity basketball. Jerry had had a successful high school career, lettering in three sports and starting every basketball game. On a full scholarship at Southeastern, Jerry worked harder than anyone else on the team and improved his skills. Still, he did not make the starting five. In the second half of the season's first contest, Coach Johnson put Jerry into the game. As he moved to the scorer's table and awaited the substitution whistle, Jerry found that he was much more nervous than ever before. His heart was pounding and he could not shut off the chatter in his mind. He entered the game and had a disastrous performance. He threw the ball away several times, picked up two silly fouls, and failed to take an open shot. Coach Johnson took Jerry out. After the game, Jerry's coaches and teammates told him it was just nerves and to relax. But Jerry could not relax, and a pattern of high anxiety and deteriorating performance ensued. After a few more disasters, Jerry rode the bench for the remainder of the season.

Jerry hesitated to see a sport psychologist. He did not think he was mentally ill, and he was somewhat embarrassed about the idea of seeing a "shrink." Much to Jerry's surprise, Dr. Hoffman was a regular guy who talked a lot like a coach, so Jerry agreed to meet with him every couple of weeks.

Working with Dr. Hoffman, Jerry learned it was common to experience anxiety when making the transition from high school to college ball. After all, 90% of the players he had defeated in high school were no longer competing. Hoffman also pointed out that after Jerry had started for 3 years in high school, it was no surprise that he had a hard time adjusting to coming off the bench and entering a game cold. He was experiencing a new kind of pressure, and his response to the pressure—his nervousness—was to be expected.

Dr. Hoffman taught Jerry how to relax by using a breathing technique called centering. He taught Jerry to control negative thoughts and worries by stopping them with an image and replacing them with more positive affirmations. Jerry developed a mental preparation routine for coming off the bench, including stretches to keep loose and a procedure to help him focus as he waited at the scorer's table.

Jerry practiced these psychological techniques extensively in the off-season and refined them during early-season practices and scrimmages. After he was able to come off the bench without falling apart, he worked on taking open shots and quickly resumed playing to his full potential.

That season Jerry accomplished his goal of coming off the bench and helping the team with a solid performance. He did not quite break into the starting lineup, but Coach Johnson expressed his confidence in Jerry by using him in tight situations. Jerry felt happy to be contributing to the team.

ited ability to identify what scientists call causal (cause and effect) relationships between factors.

KEY POINT Determining causal relationships is the main advantage that conducting experiments has over conducting studies.

An **experiment** differs from a study in that the investigator manipulates the variables along with observing them and then examines how changes in one variable affect changes in others. Runners might be divided into two equal groups. One, called the **experimental group**, would receive training in how to set goals and use imagery and positive self-talk. The other, called the **control group**, would not receive any psychological skills training. Then, if the experimental group outperformed the control group (with other factors that might affect the relationship being controlled), the reason, or cause, for this would be known. A causal relationship would have been demonstrated.

DISCOVER Activity 1.4 asks you to abstract a sport and exercise psychology research study.

Any method of obtaining knowledge has strengths and limitations. The scientific method is no different in this regard. The major strength of scientifically derived knowledge is that it is reliable; that is, the methodology is systematic and controlled and scientific findings are consistent or repeatable. Also, the scientists are trained to be as objective as possible. One of their goals is to collect **unbiased data**—data or facts that speak for themselves and are not influenced by the scientist's personal feelings.

On the negative side, the scientific method is slow and conservative because reliability must be judged by others. It also takes time to be systematic and controlled—more time than most practitioners have. A breakthrough in science usually comes after years of research. For this reason, it's not always practical to insist that science guide all elements of practice.

Sometimes scientific knowledge is **reductionistic**. That is, because it is too complex to study all the variables of a situation simultaneously, the researcher may select isolated variables that are of the most critical interest. When a problem is reduced to smaller, manageable parts, however, our understanding of the whole picture may be compromised or diminished.

Another limitation of science is its overemphasis on **internal validity**. That is, science favors the extent to which the results of an investigation can be attributed to the treatment used. A study is usually judged by how well the scientists conform to the rules of scientific methodology and how systematic and controlled they were in conducting the study. Too much emphasis on internal validity can cause scientists to overlook external validity, or whether the issue has true significance or utility in the real world. If a theory has no **external validity**, its internal validity doesn't count for much. Finally, scientific knowledge tends to be conservative.

Professional Practice Knowledge

Professional practice knowledge refers to knowledge gained through experience. Perhaps, for example, you spend a lot of time helping exercisers, athletes, and physical education students enhance their performance and well-being, and in the process you pick up a good deal of practical understanding or information. Professional practice knowledge comes from many sources and ways of knowing, including these:

- Scientific method
- Systematic observation
- Single case study
- Shared public experience
- Introspection (examining your thoughts or feelings)
- Intuition (immediate understanding of knowledge in the absence of a conscious, rational process)

Although exercise leaders, coaches, and certified athletic trainers ordinarily do not use the scientific method, they do use theoretically derived sport and exercise principles to guide their practice.

For example, volleyball coach Theresa Hebert works with the high school team. She develops her coaching skills in a variety of ways. Before the season begins, she reflects (uses **introspection**) on how she wants to coach this year. During team tryouts she uses **systematic observation** of the new players as they serve, hit, and scrimmage. Last season, she remembers, the team captain—a star setter—struggled, so Coach Hebert wants to learn as much about her as possible to help her more this year. To do this, the coach talks with other players, teachers, and the setter's parents. In essence, the coach conducts a **case study**. When she and her assistant coaches compare notes on their scouting of the next opponent, **shared public experience** occurs. Coach Hebert often uses

intuition also—for example, she decides to start Sarah over Rhonda today, the two players having similar ability, because it feels right to her. Of course, these methods are not equally reliable; however, in combination they lead to effective coaching. Like her players, Coach Hebert sometimes makes mistakes. But these errors or miscalculations also become sources of information to her.

Professional practice knowledge is guided trial-and-error learning. Whether you become a physical therapist, coach, teacher, exercise leader, or certified athletic trainer, you will use your knowledge to develop strategies and then evaluate their effectiveness. With experience, an exercise and sport science professional becomes more proficient and more knowledgeable in practical ways.

Professional practice knowledge has major strengths and limitations. This practical knowledge is usually more holistic than scientifically derived knowledge, reflecting the complex interplay of many factors—psychological, physical, technical, strategic, and social. And unlike science, professional practice knowledge tends to absorb novel or innovative practices. Coaches, teachers, exercise leaders, and trainers enjoy using new techniques. Another plus is that professionals can use practical theories immediately because they do not have to wait for the theories to be scientifically verified.

On the downside, professional practice can produce fewer and less precise explanations than science can. Professional practice is more affected by bias than is science and thus is less objective. Practical knowledge tends to be less reliable and definitive than scientifically based knowledge. Often a teacher knows a method works but does not know why. This can be a problem if the teacher wants to use the method in a new situation or revise it to help a particular student. Table 1.1 summarizes the strengths and limitations of both scientifically derived knowledge and professional practice knowledge.

Integration of Scientific and Professional Practice Knowledge

The gap you may sense between reading a textbook and pursuing professional activities is part of a larger division between scientific and professional practice knowledge. Yet bridging this gap is paramount because the combination of the two kinds of knowledge is what makes for effective applied practice.

There are several causes for this gap (Gowan, Botterill, & Blimkie, 1979). Until recently, few opportunities existed to transfer results of research to professionals working in the field: physical educators, coaches, exercise leaders, athletes, exercisers, and trainers. Second, some sport and exercise psychologists were overly optimistic about using research to revolutionize the practice of teaching sport and physical activity skills. Although basic laboratory research was conducted in the 1960s and 1970s, little connection was then made to actual field situations (external validity). The gap must be closed, however, and practitioners and researchers must communicate to integrate their worlds.

Taking an Active Approach to Sport and Exercise Psychology

To effectively use sport and exercise psychology in the field requires actively developing knowledge. The practitioner must blend the scientific knowledge of sport and exercise psychology with professional practice knowledge. Reading a book such as this, taking a course in sport and exercise psychology, or working (as a teacher, coach, or exercise leader) is simply not enough. You must actively integrate scientific knowledge with your professional experiences and temper these with your own insights and intuition.

TABLE 1.1 Strengths and Limitations of Scientifically Derived Knowledge and Professional Practice Knowledge

Source of knowledge	Strengths	Limitations
Scientifically derived	• Highly reliable • Systematic and controlled • Objective and unbiased	• Reductionistic, conservative, often slow to evolve • Lack of focus on external validity (practicality)
Professional practice	• Holistic • Innovative • Immediate	• Less reliable • Lack of explanations • Greater susceptibility to bias

To take an active approach means applying the scientific principles identified in subsequent chapters of this book to your practice environments. Relate these principles to your own experiences as an athlete, exerciser, and physical education student. In essence, use the gym, the pool, or the athletic field as a mini-experimental situation in which you test your sport and exercise psychology thoughts and understanding of principles. Evaluate how effective these ideas are and in what situations they seem to work the best. Modify and update them when needed by keeping current regarding the latest scientific findings in sport and exercise psychology.

In using this active approach, however, you must have realistic expectations of the research findings in sport and exercise psychology. Most research findings are judged to be significant based on probability. Hence, these findings won't hold true 100% of the time. They should work or accurately explain behavior the majority of the time. When they do not seem to predict behavior adequately, analyze the situation to identify possible explanations for why the principle does or does not work and, if the findings are theoretically based, consider the key components of the theory behind the original predictions. See if you need to consider overriding personal or situational factors at work in your practice environment.

Recognizing Sport and Exercise Psychology as an Art

Psychology is a social science. It is different from physics: Whereas inanimate objects do not change much over time, human beings do. Humans involved in sport and exercise also think and manipulate their environment, which makes behavior more difficult (but not impossible) to predict. Coach "Doc" Counsilman (Kimiecik & Gould, 1987), legendary Olympic swim coach and key proponent of a scientific approach to coaching, best summed up the need to consider individuality when he indicated that coaches coach by using general principles—the science of coaching. The art of coaching enters as they recognize when and in what situations to individualize these general principles. This same science-to-practice guiding principle holds true in sport and exercise psychology. Interestingly, some investigators (Brown, Gould, & Foster, 2005) have begun to study contextual intelligence (the ability of individuals to understand and read the contexts in which they work) and its development, which has implications for better understanding how we learn the art of professional practice.

> **KEY POINT** The science of coaching focuses on the use of general principles. The art of coaching is recognizing when and how to individualize these general principles.

Choosing From Many Sport and Exercise Psychology Orientations

Some coaches believe that teams win games through outstanding defense, other coaches believe that teams win through a wide-open offensive system, and still others believe that wins come through a

Learn more about sport and exercise psychology by accessing these websites:

- American Alliance for Health, Physical Education, Recreation and Dance
- Association for Applied Sport Psychology
- North American Society for the Psychology of Sport and Physical Activity
- Division 47 of the American Psychological Association
- European Federation of Sport Psychology
- American Sport Education Program
- Coaching Association of Canada

structured and controlled game plan. Like coaches, sport psychologists differ in how they view successful interventions. Contemporary sport and exercise psychologists may choose from many orientations to the field, three of the most prevalent being psychophysiological, social–psychological, and cognitive–behavioral approaches.

Psychophysiological Orientation

Sport and exercise psychologists with a **psychophysiological orientation** believe that the best way to study behavior during sport and exercise is to examine the physiological processes of the brain and their influences on physical activity. These psychologists typically assess heart rate, brain wave activity, and muscle action potentials, determining relationships between these psychophysiological measures and sport and exercise behavior. An example is using biofeedback techniques to train elite marksmen to fire between heartbeats to improve accuracy (Landers, 1985). Hatfield and Hillman (2001) provided a comprehensive review of the research in the area. A number of researchers are starting to examine the effects of physical activity, especially aerobic exercise, on brain functioning using electroencephalograms and neuroimaging measures (Hillman, Erickson, & Kramer, 2008). Results are very exciting because they show that physical activity has a number of positive effects on brain functioning.

KEY POINT Psychophysiological sport and exercise psychologists study behavior through its underlying psychophysiological processes occurring in the brain.

Social–Psychological Orientation

Using a **social–psychological orientation**, sport and exercise psychologists assume that behavior is determined by a complex interaction between the environment (especially the social environment) and the personal makeup of the athlete or exerciser. Those taking the social–psychological approach often examine how an individual's social environment influences her behavior and how the behavior influences the social–psychological environment. For example, sport psychologists with a social–psychological orientation might examine how a leader's style and strategies foster group cohesion and influence participation in an exercise program (Carron & Spink, 1993).

KEY POINT People with a social–psychological orientation focus on how behavior is determined by a complex interaction between the environment and one's personal makeup.

Cognitive–Behavioral Orientation

Psychologists adopting a **cognitive–behavioral orientation** emphasize the athlete's or exerciser's cognitions or thoughts and behaviors and believe that thought is central in determining behavior. Cognitive–behavioral sport psychologists might, for instance, develop self-report measures to assess self-confidence, anxiety, goal orientations, imagery, and intrinsic motivation. The psychologists then would see how these assessments are linked to changes in an athlete's or an exerciser's behavior. For example, groups of junior tennis players who were either burned out or not burned out were surveyed using a battery of psychological assessments. Burned-out tennis players, compared with non-burned-out players, were found to have less motivation. They also reported being more withdrawn, had more perfectionist personality tendencies, and used different strategies for coping with stress (Gould, Tuffey, Udry, & Loehr, 1996a). Thus, links between the athletes' thoughts and behaviors and the athletes' burnout status were examined.

KEY POINT A cognitive–behavioral orientation to sport and exercise psychology assumes that behavior is determined by both the environment and cognition; thoughts and interpretation play an especially important role.

DISCOVER Activity 1.5 lets you learn from someone in the field.

Understanding Present and Future Trends

Now that you have learned about the field of sport and exercise psychology, including its history, scientific base, and orientations, you need to understand the significant current and future trends in the area. We briefly discuss these trends.

1. Consulting and service opportunities are more plentiful than ever, and more sport psychologists are helping athletes and coaches achieve their goals. Exercise psychology has opened new service opportunities

Ethical Standards for Sport and Exercise Psychologists

Sport psychology is a young profession, and only recently have its organizations—such as the Association for Applied Sport Psychology and the Canadian Society for Psychomotor Learning and Sport Psychology—developed ethical guidelines. These guidelines are based on the more general ethical standards of the American Psychological Association (2002), and at their core is the general philosophy that sport psychology consultants should respect the dignity and worth of individuals and honor the preservation and protection of fundamental human rights. The essence of this philosophy is that the athlete's or exerciser's welfare must be foremost in one's mind.

The AASP ethical guidelines outline six areas (general principles):

1. *Competence.* Sport psychologists strive to maintain the highest standards of competence in their work and recognize their limits of expertise. If a sport psychologist has little knowledge of team building and group dynamics, for example, it would be unethical to lead others to believe that he does have this knowledge or to work with a team.

2. *Integrity.* Sport and exercise psychologists demonstrate high integrity in science, teaching, and consulting. They do not falsely advertise, and they clarify their roles (e.g., inform athletes that they will be involved in team selection) with teams and organizations.

3. *Professional and scientific responsibility.* Sport and exercise psychologists always place the best interests of their clients first. For instance, it would be unethical to study aggression in sport by purposefully instructing one group of subjects to start fights with the opposing team (even if much could be learned from doing so). Those conducting research are also responsible for safeguarding the public from unethical professionals. If a sport psychologist witnesses another professional making false claims (e.g., that someone can eat all she wants and burn off all the extra fat via imagery), the sport psychologist is ethically bound to point out the misinformation and to professionally confront the offender or report him to a professional organization.

4. *Respect for people's rights and dignity.* Sport psychologists respect the fundamental rights (e.g., privacy and confidentiality) of the people with whom they work. They do not publicly identify persons they consult with unless they have permission to do so. They show no bias on the basis of such factors as race, sex, and socioeconomic status.

5. *Concern for welfare of others.* Sport psychologists seek to contribute to the welfare of those with whom they work. Hence, an athlete's psychological and physical well-being always comes before winning.

6. *Social responsibility.* Sport and exercise psychologists contribute to knowledge and human welfare while always protecting participants' interests. An exercise psychologist, for instance, would not offer an exercise program designed to reduce depression to one group of experimental participants without making the same program available to subjects in the control group at the end of the experiment. Offering the treatment to the experimental group only would not be socially responsible and, indeed, would be unethical.

for helping people enjoy the benefits of exercise. For these reasons, applied sport and exercise psychology will continue to grow in the years to come (Cox, Qui, & Liu, 1993; Murphy, 2005a). In addition, with sport psychology as its core, performance psychology—in which sport psychology principles are applied to other high-performance areas such as business, the performance arts, medicine, and the military—is beginning to emerge as an area of interest.

2. There is greater emphasis on counseling and clinical training for sport psychologists. Accompany-ing the increased emphasis on consulting is a need for more training in counseling and clinical psychology (Peterson, Brown, McCann, & Murphy, 2012). Individuals who want to assume a role in sport and exercise consulting will have to understand not only sport and exercise science but also aspects of counseling and clinical psychology. Graduate programs have been developed in counseling and clinical psychology, with an emphasis in sport and exercise psychology.

3. Ethics and competence issues are receiving greater emphasis. Some problems have accompanied

the tremendous growth in sport and exercise consulting (Murphy, 1995; Silva, 2001). For example, unqualified people might call themselves sport psychologists, and unethical individuals might promise more to coaches, athletes, and exercise professionals than they can deliver. That is, someone with no training in the area might claim to be a sport psychologist and promise that buying his imagery app will make an 80% free-throw shooter out of a 20% shooter. This is why the AASP has begun a certification program for sport and exercise psychology consultants and why in 2006 the APA recognized sport psychology as proficiency in psychology. Ethical standards for sport psychology specialists have also been developed (see "Ethical Standards for Sport and Exercise Psychologists"). Physical education, sport, and exercise leaders should become informed consumers who can discriminate between legitimate, useful information and fads or gimmicks. They must also be familiar with ethical standards in the area.

4. Specializations and new subspecialties are developing. Knowledge in sport psychology has exploded. Today's sport psychologists cannot be experts in every area that you will read about in this text. This has led to the separation of sport psychology as defined here and motor learning or motor control (the acquisition and control of skilled movements as a result of practice) as separate sport science areas. In addition, subspecializations in sport and exercise psychology are emerging (Rejeski & Brawley, 1988; Singer, 1996). Exercise psychology is the most visible growth area. However, other new specializations that are attracting considerable interest include youth life skills development through sport (see chapter 11) and the psychology of performance excellence (applying sport psychology performance-enhancement principles to other settings such as music, arts, and business [see Hays, 2009]). We expect this trend toward specialization to continue.

5. Tension continues to exist between practitioners of academic and applied sport psychology. This textbook is based on the philosophy that sport psychology will best develop with an equal emphasis on research and professional practice. However, some tension exists between academic (research) and applied sport psychology consultants, each group believing that the other's activities are less crucial to the development of the field. Although such tension is certainly undesirable, it is not unique. Similar disagreement exists in the broader field of psychology. Sport psychologists must continue working to overcome this destructive thinking.

6. Qualitative research methods are now accepted. The 1990s reflected a change in the way sport and exercise psychologists conduct research. Although traditional quantitative research is still being conducted, many investigators have broadened the way they do research by using qualitative (nonnumeric) methods, which entail collecting data via observation or interviews. Instead of analyzing numbers or ratings statistically, researchers analyze the respondents' words and stories or narration for trends and patterns. This has been a healthy development for the field.

7. Applied sport psychologists have more work opportunities than ever but only limited chances at full-time positions. On one hand, they have more opportunities to work with teams and consult with athletes. On the other hand, although increasing, not enough full-time consulting positions exist. Furthermore, a person needs advanced graduate training to become a qualified sport psychology specialist. Hence, people should not expect to quickly obtain full-time consulting positions with high-profile teams and athletes simply on the basis of a degree in sport psychology.

8. Sport and exercise psychology has become a recognized sport science of considerable utility and is receiving increased attention and recognition all around the world. Many universities now offer sport and exercise psychology courses, and some graduate programs include up to five or six courses. Research and professional resources are increasingly available to students. However, we believe that the greatest gains are still to come. Physical education teachers, coaches, fitness instructors, and certified athletic trainers have increasing access to information about sport and exercise psychology. With this up-to-date information, physical activity professionals will make great strides toward achieving their various goals.

9. A number of leaders in the general field of psychology have embraced a positive psychology movement (e.g., Seligman & Csikszentmihalyi, 2002). This movement emphasizes the need for psychologists to focus more on the development of positive attributes such as optimism, hope, and happiness in individuals, as opposed to focusing the majority of attention on people's deficits (e.g., depression). Sport and exercise psychologists have been practicing positive performance for some time, which has opened up new opportunities. For example, leading sport psychologists such as Graham Jones, Jim Loehr, Austin Swain, Shane Murphy, and Steve Bull have taken what they learned in sport to the business

world, teaching businesspeople how to enhance their psychological skills and work performance. Similarly, sport psychologist Kate Hays (Hays, 2002, 2009) has helped elite performance artists such as dancers and musicians develop the psychological skills needed for top performance.

10. The importance of embracing the globalization of sport and exercise psychology is paramount for contemporary students of the field and will increase in years to come. New knowledge and best practices are rapidly being developed in a host of European, Asian, and South American countries. Examining sport psychology across cultures allows us to understand which principles generalize across cultures and which are culturally bound. To understand contemporary sport and exercise psychology, a global perspective is essential and will only grow in importance.

11. Multidisciplinary research is increasing. Sport and exercise psychologists will work with experts from other kinesiology subdisciplines (e.g., exercise physiology and biomechanics) and with individuals from other disciplines (e.g., engineering, social work, and nursing) to study big issues facing society, such as overcoming the obesity epidemic or enhancing posi-tive youth development. Researchers are discovering that real world problems have multiple causes and that no one field alone can address them.

12. As technology develops at record pace and changes all aspects of our lives, sport psychologists are learning how to use these technologies to facilitate their efforts. That might involve using virtual reality to train performers, using neuroimaging to unlock the mysteries of the brain and exercise's influence on it, using computer games to enhance physical activity, or consulting online.

13. As our world becomes seemingly smaller and more connected, more emphasis in contemporary sport psychology is being placed on studying cultural diversity and examining how groups such as men and women, baby boomers and generation Xers, or those from different ethnic cultures are both similar and unique. Greater emphasis is also being placed on increasing understanding, facilitating inclusion, and embracing diversity.

VIEW Activity 1.6 has you predict the future of sport and exercise psychology.

Sport Psychology–Business Link

A number of sport psychology specialists have been transferring what they learned in sport to the world of business. Here are two examples:

• Noted sport psychologist Jim Loehr (Loehr & Schwartz, 2001) has drawn a parallel between top executives and world-class athletes. He teaches some of America's top executives to be more effective by becoming corporate athletes who reach ideal performance states by learning to better develop and manage their physical, emotional, mental, and spiritual capacities.

• The Lane4 Management Group is a worldwide consulting group started by sport psychology specialist Graham Jones and Olympic swimming champion Adrian Moorhouse. Using lessons learned in high-performance sport, Lane4 associates help major corporations, business teams, and individual executives achieve and sustain high performance through interactive workshops, team development events, organization performance assessments, and senior executive coaching. Topics often addressed by Lane4 associates include leadership development, stress management, confidence, focus, team building, team performance enhancement, teamwork, and one-to-one executive coaching and consulting (Jones, 2002).

LEARNING AIDS

SUMMARY

1. **Describe what sport and exercise psychology is.**

   Sport and exercise psychology is the scientific study of the behavior of people engaged in sport and exercise activities and the application of the knowledge gained. Researchers in the field have two major objectives: (a) to understand how psychological factors affect a person's motor performance and (b) to understand how participating in physical activity affects a person's psychological development. Despite enormous growth in recent years, sport psychology dates back to the early 1900s and is best understood within the framework of its six distinct historical periods.

2. **Understand what sport and exercise psychology specialists do.**

   Contemporary sport and exercise psychologists engage in different roles, including conducting research, teaching, and consulting with athletes and exercisers.

3. **Know what training is required of a sport and exercise psychologist.**

   Not all sport and exercise psychology specialists are trained in the same way. Clinical sport and exercise psychologists are trained specifically in psychology to treat athletes and exercisers with severe emotional disorders, such as substance abuse or anorexia. Educational sport psychology specialists receive training in exercise and sport science and related fields; they serve as mental coaches, educating athletes and exercisers about psychological skills and their development. They are not trained to assist people with severe emotional disorders.

4. **Understand major developments in the history of sport and exercise psychology.**

   Sport and exercise psychology has a long and rich history dating back more than 100 years. Its history falls into six periods. The first period, the early years (1893–1920), is characterized by isolated studies. During the second period (1921–1938), sport psychology laboratories and psychological testing took place at a number of locations around the world. In the United States, Coleman Griffith became the first American to specialize in the area. The third period, preparation for the future (1939–1965), is characterized by the field's scientific development attributable to the educational efforts of Franklin Henry. During the establishment of the academic discipline (1966–1977), sport and exercise psychology became a valued component of the academic discipline of physical education. The fifth period, multidisciplinary science and practice (1978–2000), is characterized by tremendous growth as the field became more accepted and respected by the public. Interest in applied issues and the growth and development of exercise psychology were evident. Training in the field took a more multidisciplinary perspective, and the field wrestled with a variety of professional practice issues. The final period of contemporary sport and exercise psychology (2001–present) has been distinguished by continued growth worldwide, considerable diverse research, and interest in application and consulting. Exercise psychology flourishes.

5. **Distinguish between scientific and professional practice knowledge.**

   Sport and exercise psychology is above all a science. For this reason you need to understand the basic scientific process and how scientific knowledge is developed. Scientific knowledge alone, however, is not enough to guide professional practice. You must also understand how professional practice knowledge develops.

6. **Integrate experiential and scientific knowledge.**

   Scientific knowledge must be integrated with the knowledge gained from professional practice. Integrating scientific and professional practice knowledge will greatly benefit you as you work in applied sport and exercise settings.

7. **Compare and contrast orientations to the field.**

   Several approaches can be taken to sport and exercise psychology, including the psychophysiological, social–psychological, and cognitive–behavioral orientations. Psychophysiological sport psychologists study physiological processes of the brain and their influence on physical activity. Social–psychological sport psychologists focus on how complex interactions between the social environment and personal makeup of the athlete or exerciser influence behavior. Cognitive–behavioral sport psychologists examine how an individual's thoughts determine behavior.

8. **Describe career opportunities and future directions in the field.**
Although there are more career opportunities today than ever before, only limited numbers of full-time consulting positions are available. Sport and exercise psychology is flourishing and has much to offer those interested in working in sport and physical activity settings. Trends point to such future directions as an increased interest in psychological skills training and applied work, more counseling and clinical training for sport psychologists, increased emphasis on ethics and competence, increased specialization, some continuing tension between academic and applied sport psychologists, more qualitative research, and the need to take a global perspective.

KEY TERMS

sport and exercise psychology	unbiased data
clinical sport psychologists	reductionistic
educational sport psychology specialists	internal validity
scientific method	external validity
systematic approach	professional practice knowledge
control	introspection
empirical	systematic observation
critical	case study
theory	shared public experience
social facilitation theory	intuition
study	psychophysiological orientation
experiment	social–psychological orientation
experimental group	cognitive–behavioral orientation
control group	

REVIEW QUESTIONS

1. What is sport and exercise psychology, and what are its two general objectives?
2. Describe the major accomplishments of the six periods in the history of sport and exercise psychology. What contributions did Coleman Griffith and Franklin Henry make to sport and exercise psychology?
3. Describe three roles of sport and exercise psychology specialists.
4. Distinguish between clinical and educational sport psychology. Why is this distinction important?
5. Define science and explain four of its major goals.
6. What is a theory and why are theories important in sport and exercise psychology?
7. Identify the strengths and limitations of scientifically derived knowledge and professional practice knowledge. How does each develop?
8. Describe the gap between research and practice, why it exists, and how it can be bridged.
9. Why does a need exist for certification in contemporary sport and exercise psychology?
10. Identify and briefly describe the six major ethical principles in sport and exercise psychology.
11. Why do contemporary sport psychologists need to take a global perspective?

CRITICAL THINKING QUESTIONS

1. Describe the active approach to using sport and exercise psychology.
2. You are interested in investigating how self-confidence is related to recovery from athletic injury. Design both a study and an experiment to do so.
3. Think of the career you would like to pursue (e.g., sport and exercise psychology, coaching, certified athletic training, sport journalism). Describe how the knowledge and the practice of sport psychology can affect you in that career.

PART II

Learning About Participants

Are successful athletes distinguished by certain key personality characteristics? What motivates people to participate in physical activity? Why are some people so motivated to achieve competitive success, whereas others dread the mere thought of competition? How does one "psych up" for optimal performance without psyching out?

These are some of the important questions addressed at the first stop on our journey to understanding sport and exercise psychology. This part of the book focuses on personal factors—personality characteristics, individual orientations, and emotions—that affect performance and psychological development in sport, physical education, and exercise settings. It is important for practitioners to know about these factors because they can lead to important changes in the behavior of exercisers, athletes, teachers, and coaches.

Personality, discussed in chapter 2, is important to understand because to work effectively with students, athletes, patients, and exercisers, you need to know what makes them tick as individuals. The information in this chapter will help you better understand the psychological makeup of those you will work with.

Chapter 3 focuses on the various theories and underpinnings of motivation. A person-by-situation interactional model of motivation is presented and used to help you understand motivation in a variety of physical activity contexts (although this part focuses on the participants, the next part focuses on the environment that makes for a perfect interaction). Achieve-ment motivation, goal orientations, and attributions (three explanations used to account for behavior) are also discussed, along with the situational factor of motivational climate. The information in this chapter will help you understand why some people are go-getters, whereas others seem to lack motivation. You'll learn how situational factors influence participant motivation. Most important, you will learn effective strategies for enhancing a person's level of motivation.

Chapter 4 examines arousal and anxiety. Here you'll learn the definition and types of anxiety as well as what is involved in the stress process. In addition, we discuss why students and athletes become uptight and how anxiety and arousal influence performance—why do athletes sometimes psych up for a big game and sometimes become psyched out? You'll also learn to identify major sources of stress that affect participants in sport and exercise.

VIEW Dr. Dan Gould introduces part II of the text in the Introduction activity.

JOURNEY This activity asks you to reflect on the personality type and motivation level that a sport or exercise participant might have in a setting you work in.

LISTEN Go to part II of the web study guide to meet the following experts in the field: Robin Vealey, PhD; Joan Duda, PhD; and Robert C. Eklund, PhD, FACSM. In this activity, you'll hear the experts discussing understanding sport and exercise participants.

Personality and Sport

After reading this chapter, you should be able to

1. describe what makes up personality and why it is important,
2. discuss major approaches to understanding personality,
3. identify how personality can be measured,
4. assess personality tests and research for practicality and validity,
5. understand the relationship between personality and behavior in sport and exercise,
6. describe how cognitive strategies relate to athletic success, and
7. apply what you know of personality in sport and exercise settings to better understand people's personalities.

Thousands of articles, many of them written during the 1960s and 1970s, have been published on aspects of sport personality (Ruffer, 1976a, 1976b; Vealey, 1989, 2002). This voluminous research demonstrates how important researchers and practitioners consider the role of personality to be in sport and exercise settings. Researchers have asked, for example, what causes some students to be excited about physical education classes while others don't even bother to dress for class. Researchers have questioned why some exercisers stay with their fitness program but others lose motivation and drop out, whether personality tests should be used to select athletes for teams, and whether athletic success can be predicted by an athlete's personality type.

DISCOVER Activity 2.1 helps you identify why understanding personality is important for sport and exercise science professionals.

Defining Personality

Have you ever tried to describe your own personality? If you have, you probably found yourself listing adjectives, such as *funny, outgoing, happy,* or *stable.* Maybe you remembered how you reacted in various situations. Is there more to personality than these kinds of attributes? Many theorists have attempted to define personality, and they agree on one aspect: uniqueness. In essence, personality refers to the characteristics—or blend of characteristics—that make a person unique. One of the best ways to understand personality is through its structure. Think of personality as divided into three separate but related levels (figure 2.1): a psychological core, typical responses, and role-related behavior (Hollander, 1967; Martens, 1975).

KEY POINT Personality is the sum of the characteristics that make a person unique. The study of personality helps us work better with students, athletes, patients, and exercisers and work more effectively with coworkers.

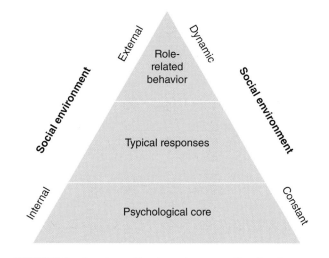

FIGURE 2.1 A schematic view of personality structure.

Adapted, by permission, from R. Martens, 1975, *Social psychology and physical activity* (New York: Harper & Row), 146. Copyright 1975 by Rainer Martens.

Psychological Core

The most basic level of your personality is called the **psychological core**. The deepest component, it includes your attitudes and values, interests and motives, and beliefs about yourself and your self-worth. In essence, the psychological core represents the centerpiece of your personality and is "the real you," not who you want others to think you are. For example, your basic values might revolve around the importance of family, friends, and religion in your life.

Typical Responses

Typical responses are the ways we each learn to adjust to the environment or how we usually respond to the world around us. For example, you might be happy-go-lucky, shy, and even-tempered. Often your typical responses are good indicators of your psychological core. That is, if you consistently respond to social situations by being quiet and shy, you are likely to be introverted, not extroverted. However, if someone observed you being quiet at a party and from that evidence alone concluded that you were introverted, that person could well be mistaken—it may have been the particular party situation that caused you to be quiet. Your quietness may not have been a typical response.

Role-Related Behavior

How you act based on what you perceive your social situation to be is called **role-related behavior**. This behavior is the most changeable aspect of personal-

ity: Your behavior changes as your perceptions of the environment change. Different situations require playing different roles. You might, on the same day, play the roles of student at a university, coach of a Little League team, employee, and friend. Likely you'll behave differently in each of these situations; for example, you'll probably exert more leadership as a coach than as a student or employee. Roles can conflict with each other. For example, a parent who is coaching her child's soccer team might feel a conflict between her coaching and parenting roles.

DISCOVER Activity 2.2 helps you recognize the structure of your own personality.

Understanding Personality Structure

As shown in figure 2.1, the three levels of personality encompass a continuum from internally driven to externally driven behaviors. To simplify this, compare your levels of personality to a chocolate-covered cherry. Everyone sees the outside wrapper (role-related behavior), those who go to the trouble to take off the wrapper see the chocolate layer (typical responses), and only the people interested or motivated enough to bite into the candy see the cherry center (psychological core).

The psychological core is not only the most internal of the three levels and the hardest to get to know; it is also the most stable part of your personality. It remains fairly constant over time. On the other end of the continuum are the most external, role-related behaviors, which are subject to the greatest influence from the external social environment. For example, you might always tell the truth because being truthful is one of your core values. But your behavior might vary in some areas, such as being aloof in your role as a fitness director and affectionate in your role as a parent. Usually your responses lie somewhere in between, however, because they result from the interaction of your psychological core and role-related behaviors.

Both stability and change are desirable in personality. The core, or stable, aspect of personality provides the structure we need to function effectively in society, whereas the dynamic, or changing, aspect allows for learning.

As coaches, physical educators, certified athletic trainers, health care professionals, and exercise leaders, we can be more effective when we understand the different levels of personality structure that lie beyond the role-related behaviors particular to a situation. Getting to know the real person (i.e., the psychological core) and that person's typical modes of response produces insight into the individual's motivations, actions, and behavior. In essence, we need to know what makes people tick to choose the best way to help them. It's especially helpful to understand more about people's individual core values (i.e., psychological core) when we work with them in the long term, such as over a season or more.

Studying Personality From Five Viewpoints

Psychologists have looked at personality from several viewpoints. Five of the major ways of studying personality in sport and exercise have been called the psychodynamic, trait, situation, interactional, and phenomenological approaches.

Psychodynamic Approach

Popularized by Sigmund Freud and neo-Freudians such as Carl Jung and Erik Erikson, the **psychodynamic approach** to personality is characterized by two themes (Cox, 1998). First, it places emphasis on unconscious determinants of behavior, such as what Freud called the *id,* or instinctive drives, and how these conflict with the more conscious aspects of personality, such as the *superego* (one's moral conscience) or the *ego* (the conscious personality). Second, this approach focuses on understanding the person as a whole rather than identifying isolated traits or dispositions.

The psychodynamic approach is complex; it views personality as a dynamic set of processes that are constantly changing and are often in conflict with one another (Vealey, 2002). For example, those taking a psychodynamic approach to the study of personality might discuss how unconscious aggressive instincts conflict with other aspects of personality, such as one's superego, to determine behavior. Special emphasis is placed on how adult personality is shaped by the resolution of conflicts between unconscious forces and the values and conscience of the superego in childhood. For example, Gaskin, Andersen, and Morris (2010) used a psychodynamic approach to study the sport and physical activity experiences of a

young man with cerebral palsy. They found that sport helped address this individual's sense of inferiority that resulted from social isolation in his childhood. At the same time, however, his success in sport did not totally compensate for his feelings of inferiority and in some ways allowed him to avoid some challenges (e.g., developing romantic relationships) that young adults must face. Thus, this individual's present functioning could be explained by conflicts and unresolved childhood issues, and although sport served a positive role in his life, it allowed him to unconsciously avoid other important issues.

Although the psychodynamic approach has had a major effect on the field of psychology, especially clinical approaches to psychology, it has had little effect on sport psychology. Swedish sport psychologist Erwin Apitzsch (1995) urged North Americans to give more attention to this approach, however, pointing out the support that it receives in non-English studies of its value in sport. Apitzsch has measured defense mechanisms in athletes and uses this information to help performers better cope with stress and anxiety. Specifically, he contends that athletes often feel threatened and that they react with anxiety. As a defense against their anxiety, athletes display various unconscious defense mechanisms, such as maladaptive repression (the athletes freeze or become paralyzed during play) or denial of the problem. When inappropriate defense mechanisms are used, the athletes' performance and satisfaction are affected. Through psychotherapy, however, athletes can learn to effectively deal with these problems.

Strean and Strean (1998) and Conroy and Benjamin (2001) heeded Apitzsch's call to give more attention to the psychodynamic approach. Besides overviewing the approach, Strean and Strean (1998) discussed how psychodynamic concepts (e.g., resistance) can be used to explain athlete behavior—not just maladaptive functioning of athletes, but normal personality as well. Gaskin, Andersen, and Morris (2009, 2010) also published several case studies demonstrating how a psychodynamic approach can help in understanding deep and often unconscious issues such as poor self-image, identification with people who do not have disabilities, and compliance that may arise in those with physical disabilities. Finally, Conroy and Benjamin (2001) discussed and presented examples of the use of a structural analysis method of social behavior to measure psychodynamic constructs through case study research. This is important because a major weakness of the psychodynamic approach has been the difficulty of testing it.

Another weakness of the psychodynamic approach is that it focuses almost entirely on internal determinants of behavior and gives little attention to the social environment. For this reason, many contemporary sport psychology specialists do not adopt the psychodynamic approach. Moreover, it is unlikely that most sport psychology specialists, especially those trained in educational sport psychology, will become qualified to use a psychodynamic approach. However, Giges (1998) indicated that although specialized training is certainly needed to use the psychodynamic approach in a therapeutic manner, an understanding of its key concepts can help us understand athletes and their feelings, thoughts, and behaviors.

Finally, the key contribution of this approach is the recognition that not all the behaviors of an exerciser or athlete are under conscious control and that at times it may be appropriate to focus on unconscious determinants of behavior. For example, a world-class aerial skier had a particularly bad crash; when he recovered, he could not explain his inability to execute the complex skill he was injured while performing. He said that in the middle of executing the skill he would freeze up "like a deer caught in headlights." Moreover, extensive cognitive–behavioral psychological strategies (described later in this chapter), which have been successfully used with other skiers, did not help him. The athlete eventually was referred to a clinical psychologist, who took a more psychodynamic approach to the problem and had more success.

Trait Approach

The **trait approach** assumes that the fundamental units of personality—its traits—are relatively stable. That is, personality traits are enduring and consistent across a variety of situations. Taking the trait approach, psychologists consider that the causes of behavior generally reside in the person and that the role of situational or environmental factors is minimal. Traits are considered to predispose a person to act a certain way regardless of the situation or circumstances. If an athlete is competitive, for example, he will be predisposed to playing hard and giving his all regardless of the situation or score. However, at the same time, a predisposition does not mean that the athlete will always act this way; it simply means that the athlete is *likely* to be competitive in sport situations.

KEY POINT The trait approach, which dominated the early study of personality, does not consider the particular situations that might also influence an individual's behavior.

The most noted of the trait proponents in the 1960s and 1970s include Gordon Allport, Raymond Cattell, and Hans Eysenck. Cattell (1965) developed a personality inventory with 16 independent personality factors that he believed describe a person. Eysenck and Eysenck (1968) viewed traits as relative, the two most significant traits ranging on continuums from introversion to extroversion and from stability to emotionality. Today, the Big 5 model of personality is most widely accepted (Allen, Greenless, & Jones, 2013; Gill & Williams, 2008; Vealey, 2002). This model contends that five major dimensions of personality exist: neuroticism (nervousness, anxiety, depression, and anger) versus emotional stability, extraversion (enthusiasm, sociability, assertiveness, and high activity level) versus introversion, openness to experience (originality, need for variety, curiosity), agreeableness (amiability, altruism, modesty), and conscientiousness (constraint, achievement striving, self-discipline). These five dimensions have been found to be the most important general personality characteristics that exist across individuals; most other more specific personality characteristics fall within these dimensions (McRae & John, 1992). Moreover, it is hypothesized that individuals possessing different levels of these characteristics will behave differently. For example, people high in conscientiousness would be more motivated toward order, self-discipline, and dutifulness, whereas those high on neuroticism would generally be vulnerable and self-conscious. The Big 5 model of personality has been shown to be of some use in understanding why different exercise interventions are appropriate for people with different personality characteristics (Rhodes, Courneya, & Hayduk, 2002). A meta-analysis or statistical review of 35 independent studies also showed that the personality traits of extraversion and conscientiousness were positively correlated with physical activity levels, whereas neuroticism was negatively related to physical activity (Rhodes & Smith, 2006). Researchers have also begun to test the Big 5 model of personality in sport (Piedmont, Hill, & Blanco, 1999; Wann, Dunham, Byrd, & Keenan, 2004). For example, in a study of sports fans, Wann and colleagues (2004) found that identifying with a local team (and receiving social support from others) was positively related to psychological well-being as measured by the Big 5 subscales of extroversion, openness, and conscientiousness. Today, a number of sport and exercise psychology researchers are examining the influence of Big 5 personality characteristics, such as conscientiousness and extraversion (Demulier, Le Scanff, & Stephan, 2013; Lochbaum et al., 2010; Merritt & Tharp, 2013; Singley, Hale, & Russell, 2012), and other characteristics, such as hardiness (Sheard & Golby, 2010), on both psychological states and behavior. Summarizing much of this literature in a comprehensive review, Allen and colleagues (2013) concluded that personality is related to long-term athletic success. According to Allen and colleagues, good evidence shows that athletes have higher levels of extraversion than do nonathletes and that athletes who play high-risk sports and team sports score higher on extraversion and lower on conscientiousness than do athletes who play low-risk sports and individual sports.

Regardless of the particular view and measure endorsed, trait theorists argue that the best way to understand personality is to consider traits that are relatively enduring and stable over time. However, simply knowing an individual's personality traits will not always help us predict how that person will behave in a particular situation. For example, some people anger easily during sport activity, whereas others seldom get angry. Yet the individuals who tend to get angry in sport may not necessarily become angry in other situations. Simply knowing an individual's personality traits does not necessarily help us predict whether she will act on them. A person's predisposition toward anger does not tell you what specific situations will provoke that response. Note, however, that Allen and colleagues (2013) have indicated that sport personality research has stagnated and has not kept pace with developments in general psychology. This suggests that traits have some utility in predicting behavior across a number of situations.

Situation Approach

Concerns with the trait approach to studying personality motivated some researchers to focus on the situation or environment that might trigger behaviors rather than on personality traits. The **situation approach** argues that behavior is determined largely by the

The trait approach assumes that personality traits are enduring and consistent across a variety of situations. An athlete is likely to behave the same regardless of the situation.

The Paradox of Perfectionism

Perfectionism has been the most widely studied personality characteristic in sport and exercise psychology over the past decade. Perfectionism is a personality style characterized by setting extremely high standards of performance, striving for flawlessness, and a tendency to be overly critical in evaluating one's performance (Flett & Hewitt, 2005). Investigators have differentiated between self-oriented perfectionism (the degree to which an individual sets extremely high personal standards and stringently self-evaluates relative to those standards), socially prescribed perfectionism (the degree to which one perceives that significant others hold them to extremely high standards and base their approval on meeting those standards), and other-oriented perfectionism (the degree to which one holds others to extremely high standards) (Appleton, Hall, & Hill, 2010; Dunn, Dunn, & McDonald, 2012). Investigators have also developed a sport-specific measure that assesses four dimensions: personal standards, concern over mistakes, perceived parental pressure, and perceived coach pressure (Dunn, Craft, & Dunn, 2011).

The multidimensional nature of perfectionism has led to some interesting findings. **Maladaptive perfectionism** (a focus on high standards accompanied by a concern over mistakes and evaluation by others) has been found to be associated with excessive exercise (e.g., Flett & Hewitt, 2005; Flett, Pole-Langdon, & Hewitt, 2003), poor performance (Stoeber, Uphill, & Hotham, 2009), and athlete burnout (Appleton, Hall, & Hill, 2009). However, **adaptive perfectionism** (a focus on high standards but not excessively worrying about making mistakes or about how others evaluate one's performance) has been found to be associated with better learning and performance (Stoeber et al., 2009) and more adaptive goal patterns (e.g., Stoll, Lau, & Stoeber, 2008). Thus, depending on the specific components characterizing one's perfectionistic personality, perfectionism can lead to both highly positive and extremely negative consequences. Other interesting findings derived from the literature on sport psychological perfectionism include the following:

- Perfectionistic standards do not automatically undermine performance and with the right goal focus can lead to optimal performance.
- Perfectionistic standards become debilitating when their attainment is needed for self-validation.
- Perfectionism is thought to be especially negative in times of failure.
- Extreme perfectionists with an ego orientation and low perceptions of ability will have debilitating effects, high levels of stress, motivational problems, and burnout.
- Perfectionists are at greater risk if they have poor coping skills.
- Certain types of perfectionism predispose people to engage in certain thought and behavioral processes that influence their exercise.
- Perfectionistic demands emanate from within individuals themselves or from others.
- A relationship exists between a child's levels of perfectionism and his or her parents' levels of perfectionism. Children whose parents model their own perfectionism or provide conditional approval of the child's attempts at achievement are more likely to have perfectionistic tendencies.
- Adaptive perfectionism is related to approach motivation, whereas maladaptive perfectionism is related to avoidance motivation.

From an applied perspective, investigators suggest that it is important for those working in sport to help athletes and exercisers distinguish between a healthy commitment to high performance standards and unhealthy strivings (e.g., negative reactions to imperfections, fear of failure) associated with maladaptive perfectionism. This requires that the athlete not overly link his or her self-worth to performance and reduce any irrational sense of importance placed on performance (Hill, Hall, & Appleton, 2010). Finally, if individuals are characterized by extreme perfectionism, seeing a sport psychologist may be warranted.

situation or environment. It draws from social learning theory (Bandura, 1977a), which explains behavior in terms of observational learning *(modeling)* and social reinforcement *(feedback)*. This approach holds that environmental influences and reinforcements shape the way you behave. You might act confident, for instance, in one situation but tentative in another, regardless of your particular personality traits. Furthermore, if the influence of the environment is strong enough, the effect of personality traits will be minimal. For example, if you are introverted and shy, you still might act assertively or even aggressively if you see someone getting mugged. Many football players are gentle and shy off the field, but the game (i.e., the situation) requires them to act aggressively. Thus, the situation would be a more important determinant of their behavior than their particular personality traits would be.

Although the situation approach is not as widely embraced by sport psychologists as the trait approach, Martin and Lumsden (1987) contended that you can influence behavior in sport and physical education by changing the reinforcements in the environment. Still, the situation approach, like the trait approach, cannot truly predict behavior. A situation can certainly influence some people's behavior, but other people will not be swayed by the same situation.

Interactional Approach

The **interactional approach** considers the situation and person as codeterminants of behavior—that is, as variables that together determine behavior. In other words, knowing both an individual's psychological traits and the particular situation is helpful in understanding behavior. Not only do personal traits and situational factors independently determine behavior, but at times they interact or mix with each other in unique ways to influence behavior. For example, a person with a high hostility trait won't necessarily be violent in all situations (e.g., as a frustrated spectator at a football game in the presence of his mother). However, when the hostile person is placed in the right potentially violent situation (e.g., as a frustrated spectator at a football game with his roughneck friends), his violent nature might be triggered. In that particular situation, violence might result (e.g., he hits an opponent-team fan who boos his favorite player).

KEY POINT Situations alone are not enough to predict behavior accurately—an individual's personality traits must also be considered.

Researchers using an interactional approach ask these kinds of questions:

- Will extroverts perform better in a team situation and introverts in an individual (i.e., nonteam) situation?
- Will highly motivated people adhere to a formal exercise program longer than exercisers with low motivation?
- Will self-confident children prefer competitive sport and youngsters with low self-confidence prefer noncompetitive sport situations?

The vast majority of contemporary sport and exercise psychologists favor the interactional approach to studying behavior. Bowers (1973) found that the interaction between persons and situations could explain twice as many behaviors as traits or situations alone could. The interactional approach requires investigating how people react individually in particular sport and physical activity settings.

For example, Fisher and Zwart (1982) studied the anxiety that athletes showed in different basketball situations—before, during, and after the game (e.g., "The crowd is very loud and is directing most of its comments toward you; you have just made a bad play and your coach is criticizing you"). Given these situations, the athletes were asked to report to what degree they would react (e.g., get an uneasy feeling, enjoy the challenge). Results revealed that the athletes' reactions to each basketball situation were colored by their particular mental and emotional makeup. Thus, Jeff, who is usually anxious and uptight, may choke before shooting free throws with a tied score, whereas Pat, who is laid back and less anxious, might enjoy the challenge. How would you react?

Phenomenological Approach

Although most contemporary sport and exercise psychologists adopt an interactional approach to the study of personality, the phenomenological approach is the most popular orientation taken today (Vealey, 2002). Like the interactional view, the **phenomenological approach** contends that behavior is best determined by accounting for both situations and personal

Interactional Approach to a Case of Low Self-Esteem

Two women enroll in an exercise class. Maureen has high self-esteem, and Cher has low self-esteem. The class is structured so that each participant takes a turn leading the exercises. Because she is confident in social situations and about how she looks, Maureen really looks forward to leading the class. She really likes being in front of the group, and after leading the class several times she has even given thought to becoming an instructor. Cher, on the other hand, is not confident about getting up in front of people and feels embarrassed by how she looks. Unlike Maureen, Cher finds it anxiety provoking to lead class. All she can think about are the negative reactions the class members must be having while watching her. Although she really likes to exercise, there is no way she wants to be put in the situation of having to get up in front of class again. Not surprisingly, Cher loses interest in the class and drops out.

characteristics. However, instead of focusing on fixed traits or dispositions as the primary determinants of behavior, the psychologist examines the person's understanding and interpretation of herself and her environment. Hence, an individual's subjective experiences and personal views of the world and of herself are seen as critical.

Many of the most prominent contemporary theories used in sport psychology fall within the phenomenological framework. For example, self-determination theories of motivation such as cognitive evaluation theory (discussed in chapter 6), achievement goal theory (discussed in chapter 3), social cognitive theories such as Bandura's self-efficacy (discussed in chapter 14), and much of the recent research focusing on cognitive characteristics associated with athletic success (discussed later in this chapter) fall within the phenomenological approach.

In summary, these five approaches or viewpoints to understanding personality differ in several important ways. First, they vary along a continuum (figure 2.2) of behavioral determination ranging from the view that behavior is determined by a person's internal characteristics (e.g., psychodynamic theories) to the view that behavior is determined by the situation or environment (e.g., situation approach). Second, they vary greatly in terms of assumptions about the origins of human behavior—whether behavior is determined by fixed traits or by conscious or subconscious deter-

minants and how important a person's active interpretation of himself and his environment is. Although all these viewpoints have played an important role in advancing our understanding of personality in sport and physical activity, the interactional and phenomenological views are most often stressed today and form the basis of much of this text.

Measuring Personality

When research is conducted appropriately, it can shed considerable light on how personality affects behavior in sport and exercise settings. Psychologists have developed ways to measure personality that can help us understand personality traits and states. Many psychologists distinguish between an individual's typical style of behaving *(traits)* and the situation's effects on behavior *(states)*. This distinction between psychological traits and states has been critical in the development of personality research in sport. However, even though a given psychological trait predisposes someone to behave in a certain way, the behavior doesn't necessarily occur in all situations. Therefore, you should consider both traits and states as you attempt to understand and predict behavior.

KEY POINT We should consider both situations and psychological traits in order to understand and predict behavior.

| Psychodynamic | Trait | Interactional | Phenomenological | Situation |

Internally determined   Environmentally determined

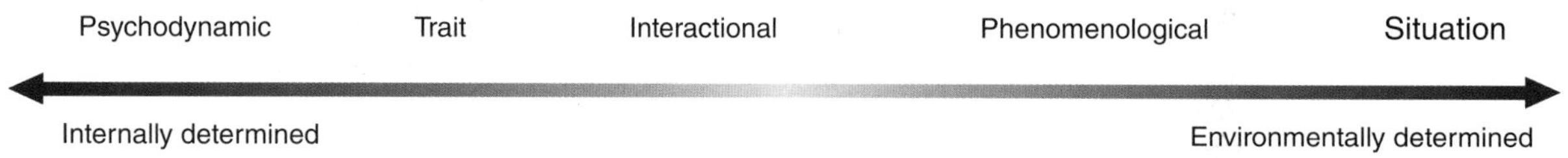

FIGURE 2.2 Continuum of behavioral determination.
Data from Vealey 2002.

Trait and State Measures

Look at the sample questions from trait and state measures of confidence (Vealey, 1986). They highlight the differences between trait and state measures of confidence in a sport context. The Trait Sport Confidence Inventory asks you to indicate how you "generally" or typically feel, whereas the State Sport Confidence Inventory asks you to indicate how you feel "right now," at a particular moment in time in a particular situation.

Situation-Specific Measures

Although general scales provide some useful information about personality traits and states, **situation-specific measures** predict behavior more reliably for given situations because they consider both the personality of the participant and the specific situation (interactional approach). For example, Sarason observed in 1975 that some students did poorly on tests when they became overly anxious. These students were not particularly anxious in other situations, but taking exams made them freeze up. Sarason devised a situationally specific scale for measuring how anxious a person usually feels before taking exams (i.e., test anxiety). This situation-specific scale could predict anxiety right before exams (state anxiety) better than a general test of trait anxiety could.

KEY POINT We can predict behavior better when we have more knowledge of the specific situation and the ways individuals respond to particular types of situations.

 DISCOVER Activity 2.3 allows you to measure your trait sport confidence.

Sport-Specific Measures

Now look at some of the questions and response formats from the Test of Attentional and Interpersonal Style (Nideffer, 1976b) and the Profile of Mood States (McNair, Lorr, & Droppleman, 1971). Notice that the questions do not directly relate to sport or physical activity. Rather, they are general and more about overall attentional styles and mood.

KEY POINT Sport-specific measures of personality predict behavior in sport settings better than do general personality tests.

Until recently, almost all of the trait and state measures of personality in sport psychology came from general psychological inventories that did not specifically reference sport or physical activity. Sport-specific tests provide more reliable and valid measures of personality traits and states in sport and exercise contexts. For example, rather than test how anxious you are before giving a speech or going out on a date, a coach might test how anxious you are before a competition (especially if excess anxiety proves detrimental to your performance). A sport-specific test of anxiety assesses precompetitive anxiety better than a general anxiety test does. Psychological inventories developed specifically for use in sport and physical activity settings include

---

Trait Sport Confidence Inventory

Think about how self-confident you are when you compete in sport. Answer the following three questions based on how confident you *generally* feel when you compete in your sport. Compare your self-confidence with that of the most self-confident athlete you know. Please answer (circle number) as you really feel, not how you would like to feel.

	Low			Medium			High		
1. Compare your confidence in your ability to execute the skills necessary to be successful with that of the most confident athlete you know.	1	2	3	4	5	6	7	8	9
2. Compare your confidence in your ability to perform under pressure with that of the most confident athlete you know.	1	2	3	4	5	6	7	8	9
3. Compare your confidence in your ability to concentrate well enough to be successful with that of the most confident athlete you know.	1	2	3	4	5	6	7	8	9

State Sport Confidence Inventory

	Low			Medium			High		
1. Compare the confidence you feel right now in your ability to execute the skills necessary to be successful with that of the most confident athlete you know.	1	2	3	4	5	6	7	8	9
2. Compare the confidence you feel right now in your ability to perform under pressure with that of the most confident athlete you know.	1	2	3	4	5	6	7	8	9
3. Compare the confidence you feel right now in your ability to concentrate well enough to be successful with that of the most confident athlete you know.	1	2	3	4	5	6	7	8	9

- the Sport Competition Anxiety Test, which measures competitive trait anxiety (Martens, 1977);
- the Competitive State Anxiety Inventory-2, which measures precompetitive state anxiety (Martens, Burton, Vealey, Bump, & Smith, 1982); and
- the Trait–State Confidence Inventory, which measures sport confidence (Vealey, 1986).

Some tests have been developed for particular sports. These inventories can help identify a person's areas of psychological strength and weakness in that sport or physical activity. After gathering the results, a coach can advise players on how to build on their strengths and reduce or eliminate their weaknesses. An example of a sport-specific test is the Tennis Test of Attentional and Interpersonal Style (Van Schoyck & Grasha, 1981).

Fluctuations Before and During Competition

Feelings change before and during a competition. Usually states are assessed shortly before (within 30 minutes of) the onset of a competition or physical activity. Although a measurement can indicate how someone is feeling at that moment, these feelings might change during the competition. For example, Matt's competitive state anxiety 30 minutes before playing a championship football game might be very high. But once he takes a few good hits and gets into the flow of the game, his anxiety might drop to a moderate level. In the fourth quarter, Matt's anxiety might increase again when the score is tied. We need to consider such fluctuations when evaluating personality and reactions to competitive settings.

Test of Attentional and Interpersonal Style

Using the following scale, please indicate the answer that most closely fits the way you see yourself.

0 = Never   **1** = Rarely   **2** = Sometimes   **3** = Frequently   **4** = Always

_____ I get caught up in my thoughts and become oblivious to what is going on around me.

_____ I have difficulty clearing my mind of a single thought or idea.

_____ It is easy for me to direct my attention and focus narrowly on something.

_____ At stores, I am faced with so many choices that I cannot make up my mind.

_____ I am good at rapidly scanning crowds and picking out a particular person or face.

Profile of Mood States

The following is a list of words that describe feelings people have. Indicate how you have been feeling this past week, including today.

0 = Never   **1** = Rarely   **2** = Sometimes   **3** = Frequently   **4** = Always

_____ Energetic   _____ Full of pep   _____ Confused

_____ Fatigued   _____ Tense   _____ Annoyed

Sample Items From the Tennis Test of Attentional and Interpersonal Style

Please check the answer that most closely fits the way you see yourself. Use the following scale:

0 = Never   **1** = Rarely   **2** = Sometimes   **3** = Frequently   **4** = Always

_____ When playing tennis, I find myself distracted by the sights and sounds around me.

_____ When playing doubles, I am aware of the movements and positions of all the players on the court.

_____ I am good at quickly analyzing a tennis opponent and assessing strengths and weaknesses.

_____ At stores, I am faced with so many choices that I cannot make up my mind.

_____ When playing tennis, I get anxious and block out everything.

Consider Traits and States to Understand Behavior

Terry is a confident person in general; he usually responds to situations with higher confidence than Tim, who is low trait-confident. As a coach you are interested in how confidence relates to performance, and you want to know how Tim and Terry are feeling immediately before a swimming race. Although Tim is not confident in general, he swam on his high school swim team and is confident in his swimming abilities. Consequently, his state of confidence right before the race is high. Conversely, although Terry is highly confident in general, he has had little swimming experience and is not even sure he can finish the race. Thus, his state confidence is low right before the race. If you measured only Tim's and Terry's trait confidence, you would be unable to predict how confident they feel before swimming. On the other hand, if you observed Tim's and Terry's state confidence in a different sport—baseball, for example—their results might be different.

This example demonstrates the need to consider both trait and state measures when investigating personality. State and trait levels alone are less significant than the difference between a person's current state level and trait level. This difference in scores represents the effect of situation factors on behavior. Terry's and Tim's state anxiety levels differed because of experience in swimming (a situational factor).

Using Psychological Measures

The knowledge of personality is critical to success as a coach, teacher, health care professional, or exercise leader. You may be tempted to use psychological tests to gather information about the people whom you want to help professionally. Bear in mind, however, that psychological inventories alone cannot actually predict athletic success, and they have sometimes been used unethically—or at least inappropriately—and administered poorly. Indeed, it isn't always clear how psychological inventories should be used! Yet it is essential that professionals understand the limitations and the uses and abuses of testing in order to know what to do and what not to do.

You want to be able to make an informed decision—that is, to be an informed consumer—on how (or whether) to use personality tests. These are some important questions to consider about psychological testing:

- Should psychological tests be used to help select athletes for a team?
- What qualifies someone to administer psychological tests?
- Should coaches give psychological tests to their athletes?
- What types of psychological tests should be used with athletes?
- How should psychological tests be administered to athletes?

In 1999, the American Psychological Association and the National Council on Measurement in Education provided seven helpful guidelines on the use of psychological tests. We explain these guidelines briefly in the following sections.

> **KEY POINT** All psychological tests contain a degree of measurement error; use caution when interpreting their results.

Know the Principles of Testing and Measurement Error

Before you administer and interpret psychological inventories you should understand testing principles, be able to recognize measurement errors, and have well-designed and validated measures. Not all psychological tests have been systematically developed and made reliable. Making predictions or drawing inferences about an athlete's or exerciser's behavior and personality structure on the basis of these tests would be misleading and unethical. Test results are not absolute or irrefutable.

Even valid tests that have been reliably developed may have measurement errors. Suppose you wish to measure self-esteem in 13- to 15-year-old physical education students. You choose a good test developed for adults because no tests have been developed specifically for youngsters. If the students do not fully understand the questions, however, the results will not be reliable. Similarly, if you give a test developed on a predominantly white population to African American and Hispanic athletes, the results might be less reliable because of cultural differences. In these situations, a researcher should conduct pilot testing with the specific population to establish the reliability and validity of the test instrument.

People usually want to present themselves in a favorable light. Sometimes they answer questions in what they think is a socially desirable way, a response style known as "faking good." For example, an athlete may fear letting her coach know how nervous she gets before competition, so she skews her answers on a precompetitive anxiety test in an attempt to appear calm, cool, and collected.

Know Your Limitations

The American Psychological Association recommends that people administering tests be aware of the limitations of their training and preparation. However, some people do not recognize the limits of their knowledge, or they use and interpret test results unethically, which can be damaging to the athletes. For instance, it is inappropriate to use personality inventories developed to measure psychopathology (abnormality, such as schizophrenia or manic depression) to measure a more normal increase in anxiety. Furthermore, it is inappropriate to give physical education students a clinical personality test.

> **KEY POINT** Individuals need special training (e.g., certification, course work) in psychological assessment to be qualified to interpret results from personality tests.

Do Not Use Psychological Tests for Team Selection

Using only psychological tests to select players for a team is an abuse because the tests are not accurate enough to be predictive. For example, determining whether an athlete has the "right" psychological profile to be a middle linebacker in football or a point guard in basketball on the basis of psychological tests alone is unfair. Some psychological tests may have limited use, but they must be considered in conjunction with physical performance measures, coach evaluations, and the actual levels of play.

Using personality inventories alone to select athletes for a team or to cut them from a team is an abuse of testing that should not be tolerated. When psychological tests are used as part of a battery of measures to help in the athlete-selection process, three key conditions should always be kept in mind (Singer, 1988). First, the particular test must be a valid and reliable measure. Second, the user must know what personality characteristics are key for success in the sport of interest and the ideal levels of those characteristics needed. Third, the user should know how much athletes can compensate in some characteristics for the lack of others.

Include Explanation and Feedback

Before they actually complete tests, athletes, students, and exercisers should be told the purpose of the tests, what they measure, and how the tests are going to be used. Athletes should receive specific feedback about the results to allow them to gain insight into themselves from the testing process.

Assure Athletes of Confidentiality

It is essential to assure people that their answers will remain confidential in whatever tests they take (and to ensure that this confidentiality is maintained!). With this assurance, test takers are more likely to answer truthfully. When they fear exposure, they may fake or falsify their answers, which can distort the findings and make interpretation virtually useless. Students in a physical education class might wonder if a test will affect their grades, and in these circumstances they are more likely to exaggerate their strengths and minimize their weaknesses. If you do not explain the reasons for testing, test takers typically become suspicious and wonder whether the coach will use the test to help select starters or weed out players.

Take an Intraindividual Approach

It is often a mistake to compare an athlete's psychological test results with the norms, even though in some cases such a comparison might be useful. Athletes or exercisers might seem to score high or low in anxiety, self-confidence, or motivation in relation to other people, but the more critical point is how they are feeling relative to how they usually feel (an **intraindividual approach**). Use this psychological information to help them perform better and enjoy the experience more, but relative to their own standards, not the scores of others.

Dos and Don'ts in Personality Testing

Do

- Inform participants about the purpose of the personality test and exactly how it will be used.
- Allow only qualified individuals who have an understanding of testing principles and measurement error to give personality tests.
- Integrate personality test results with other information obtained about the participant.
- Use sport- and exercise-specific tests whenever possible, giving these tests in consultation with a sport psychologist.
- Use both state and trait measures of personality.
- Provide participants with specific feedback concerning the results of the test.
- Compare individuals against their own baseline levels rather than against normative information.

Don't

- Do not use clinical personality tests that focus on abnormality to study an average population of sport and exercise participants.
- Do not use personality tests to decide who makes a team or program and who doesn't.
- Do not give or interpret personality tests unless you are qualified to do so by the American Psychological Association or another certifying organization.
- Do not use personality tests to predict behavior in sport and exercise settings without considering other sources of information, such as observational data and performance assessments.

Take the example of assessing an exerciser's motivation. It isn't as important to know whether the individual's motivation to exercise is high or low compared with that of other exercisers as much as how it compares with competing motivations that particular exerciser has (e.g., being with his family or carrying out his job responsibilities).

Understand and Assess Specific Personality Components

A clear understanding of the components of personality provides you with some perspective for using and interpreting psychological tests. For example, to measure someone's personality, you would certainly be interested in her psychological core. You would select specific types of tests to gain an accurate understanding of the various aspects of her personality. To measure more subconscious and deeper aspects of personality, you could use a projective test, for example. **Projective tests** usually include pictures or written situations, and the test takers are asked to project their feelings and thoughts about these materials. Hence, someone might be shown a photo of an exhausted runner crossing a finish line at the end of a highly contested cross country race and then be asked to write about what is happening. A high-achieving, confident person might emphasize how the runner made an all-out effort to achieve his goal, whereas a low achiever might project feelings of sorrow for losing the race in a close finish.

Projective tests are interesting, but they are often difficult to score and interpret. Consequently, sport psychologists usually assess personality in sport by looking at typical responses invoked by the actual situation they are interested in. For instance, coaches want to know more than whether an athlete is generally anxious—they also want to know how the athlete deals with competitive anxiety. So a test that measures anxiety in sport would be more useful to a coach or sport psychologist than would a test that measures anxiety in general. Likewise, a test that measures motivation for exercise would be more useful to an exercise leader than a general motivation test would be.

Focusing on Personality Research

The research from the 1960s and 1970s yielded few useful conclusions about the relationship of personality to sport performance. In part these meager results

stemmed from methodological, statistical, and interpretive problems, which we discuss later. Researchers were divided into two camps. Morgan (1980) described one group as taking a credulous viewpoint; that is, these researchers believed that personality is closely related to athletic success. The other group, he said, had a skeptical viewpoint and argued that personality is not related to athletic success.

Neither the credulous nor the skeptical viewpoint appears to have proved correct. Rather, some relationship exists between personality and sport performance and exercise involvement, but it is far from perfect. That is, although personality traits and states can help predict sport behavior and success, they account for only some of the behavior and may not be as precise as hoped. For example, the fact that some Olympic long-distance runners exhibit introverted personalities does not mean that a long-distance runner needs to be introverted to be successful. Similarly, although many successful middle linebackers in football have aggressive personalities, other successful middle linebackers do not.

We now turn our focus to the research on personality, sport performance, and sport preference. But remember that personality alone doesn't account for behavior in sport and exercise. Some caution is needed in interpreting the findings of personality research because an attribution or assumption of cause-and-effect relationships between personality and performance was a problem in many of the early studies.

Athletes and Nonathletes

Try to define an athlete. It isn't easy. Is an athlete someone who plays on a varsity or interscholastic team? Someone who demonstrates a certain level of skill? Who jogs daily to lose weight? Who plays professional sports? Who plays intramural sports? Keep this ambiguity in mind as you read about studies that have compared personality traits of athletes and nonathletes. Such ambiguity in definitions has weakened this research and clouded its interpretation.

KEY POINT No specific personality profile has been found that consistently distinguishes athletes from nonathletes.

One large comparative study of athletes and nonathletes tested almost 2,000 college males using Cattell's personality inventory, which measures 16 personality factors or traits (Schurr, Ashley, & Joy,

1977). No single personality profile was found that distinguished athletes (defined for the study's purposes as a member of a university intercollegiate team) from nonathletes. However, when the athletes were categorized by sport, several differences did emerge. For example, compared with nonathletes, athletes who played *team* sports exhibited less abstract reasoning, more extroversion, more dependency, and less ego strength. Furthermore, compared with nonathletes, athletes who played *individual* sports displayed higher levels of objectivity, more dependency, less anxiety, and less abstract thinking.

Hence, some personality differences appear to distinguish athletes and nonathletes, but these specific

Traits that are desirable for sport—such as independence and assertiveness—are not specific to either men or women. All good athletes must possess these personality traits.

differences cannot yet be considered definitive. Schurr and colleagues (1977) found that team-sport athletes were more dependent, extroverted, and anxious but less imaginative than individual-sport athletes. Of course, it's possible that certain personality types are drawn to a particular sport, rather than that participation in a sport somehow changes one's personality. The reasons for these differences remain unclear.

Female Athletes

As more women compete in sport, we need to understand the personality profiles of female athletes. In 1980, Williams found that successful female athletes differed markedly from the normative female in terms of personality profile. Compared with female nonathletes, female athletes were more achievement oriented, independent, aggressive, emotionally stable, and assertive. Most of these traits are desirable for sport. Apparently, outstanding athletes have similar personality characteristics regardless of whether they are male or female.

> **KEY POINT** Few personality differences are evident between male and female athletes, particularly at the elite level.

Positive Mental Health and the Iceberg Profile

After comparing personality traits of more successful athletes with those of less successful athletes using a measure called the Profile of Mood States (POMS), Morgan developed a **mental health model** that he reported to be effective in predicting athletic success (Morgan, 1979b, 1980; Morgan, Brown, Raglin, O'Connor, & Ellickson, 1987). Basically, the model suggests that positive mental health as assessed by a certain pattern of POMS scores is directly related to athletic success and high levels of performance.

Morgan's model predicts that an athlete who scores above the norm on the POMS subscales of neuroticism, depression, fatigue, confusion, and anger and below the norm on vigor will tend to pale in comparison with an athlete who scores below the norm on all of these traits except vigor, instead scoring above the norm on vigor. Successful elite athletes in a variety of sports (e.g., swimmers, wrestlers, oarsmen, and runners) are characterized by what Morgan called the **iceberg profile**, which reflects positive mental health.

The iceberg profile of a successful elite athlete shows vigor above the mean of the population but tension, depression, anger, fatigue, and confusion below the mean of the population (figure 2.3a). The profile looks like an iceberg in that all negative traits are below the surface (population norms) and the one positive trait (vigor) is above the surface. In contrast, less successful elite athletes have a flat profile, scoring at or below the 50th percentile on nearly all psychological factors (figure 2.3b). According to Morgan, this reflects negative mental health.

> **KEY POINT** Morgan's mental health model proposes that successful athletes exhibit greater positive mental health than less successful (or unsuccessful) athletes exhibit.

Performance Predictions

Morgan (1979b) psychologically evaluated 16 candidates for the 1974 U.S. heavyweight rowing team using the POMS, correctly predicting 10 of the 16 finalists. Success with this and similar studies led Morgan to conclude that more successful athletes exhibit the iceberg profile and more positive mental health than those who are less successful. You might think that these impressive statistics mean you should use psychological tests for selecting athletes for a team. However, as you will later read, most sport psychologists vehemently oppose using psychological tests for team selection and, in fact, Morgan did not think the test should be used for selection purposes. Personality testing is far from perfect (only 10 of 16 rowers were correctly predicted), and use of testing for selection might mean that athletes will be unfairly and erroneously selected for or cut from a team.

> **KEY POINT** Tests can help identify an athlete's psychological strengths and weaknesses, and this information can be used to develop appropriate training in psychological skills.

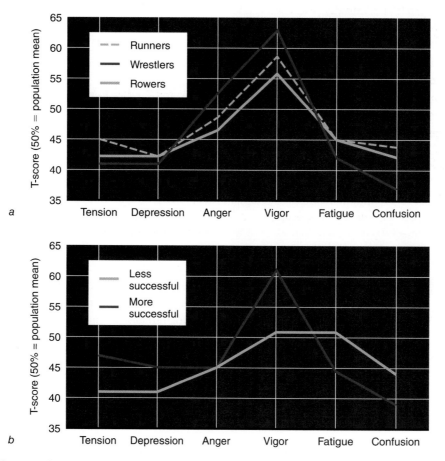

FIGURE 2.3 (a) Iceberg profiles for elite wrestlers, distance runners, and rowers. (b) Psychological profiles of more and less successful elite athletes.

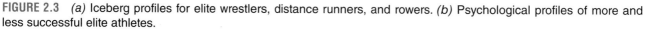

Adapted, by permission, from W. Morgan, 1979, *Coach, athlete and the sport psychologist* (Toronto: University of Toronto School of Physical and Health Education), 185. By permission of W. Morgan.

Although Morgan's mental health (iceberg profile) model is still supported in the literature (Raglin, 2001b), it has received some criticism in recent years (Prapavessis, 2000; Renger, 1993; Rowley, Landers, Kyllo, & Etnier, 1995; Terry, 1995). Renger (1993), for instance, believed that results had been misinterpreted. According to Renger, evidence was insufficient to conclude that the profile differentiates athletes of varying levels of ability; instead, it distinguished only athletes from nonathletes. Similarly, Rowley and colleagues (1995) conducted a statistical review (called a **meta-analysis**) of all the iceberg profile research and found that the profile did indeed differentiate successful from less successful athletes but accounted for a very small percentage (less than 1%) of their performance variation. Rowley and colleagues warned that the evidence does not justify using the instrument as a basis of team selection and that users must be careful to protect against social desirability effects (e.g., participants "faking good" to impress their coaches). Terry (1995) also warned that the POMS is not a test for "identifying champions," as Morgan had originally proposed in his iceberg profile model of mental health. At the same time, according to Terry, this does not imply that the test is useless. He indicated that optimal mood profiles are most likely sport dependent; therefore, mood changes in athletes should be compared with the athletes' previous mood levels and not with large-group norms. Drawing on research and his experience in consulting with athletes, Terry recommended that the POMS test be used in the following ways:

- To monitor the athlete's mind-set
- To catalyze discussion during one-on-one sessions
- To improve one's mood over time
- To identify problems early
- To monitor the mood of team officials and support staff
- To monitor training load (see chapter 21 for more details)
- To monitor an athlete during the acclimatization process
- To identify overtrained athletes (also see chapter 21)
- To monitor an athlete during rehabilitation from overtraining (also see chapter 21)
- To monitor emotional responses to injury (see chapter 19 for more details)

- To predict performance (but not for athlete selection)
- To individualize mental training

Thus, iceberg profile research clearly has implications for professional practice. However, the recent criticisms of this research have shown that it is not possible to realistically select teams or accurately predict major variations in athletic performance on the simple basis of giving a personality measure. Personality data of this type, however, have some useful purposes. Such data can help sport psychologists discover the kinds of psychological traits and states associated with successful athletes, and once these psychological factors are understood, athletes can work with sport psychologists and coaches to develop psychological skills for improving performance. For example, psychological skills training (see chapters 11–16) can help exercisers and athletes cope more effectively with anger and anxiety.

In summary, personality tests are useful tools that help us better understand, monitor, and work with athletes and exercisers. They are not magical instruments that allow us to make sweeping generalizations about individuals' behaviors and performances.

Exercise and Personality

Sport psychologists have investigated the relationship between exercise and personality. We briefly review the relationship between exercise and two personality dispositions: type A behavior and self-concept.

Type A Behavior

The type A behavior pattern is characterized by a strong sense of urgency, an excess of competitive drive, and an easily aroused hostility. The antithesis of the type A behavior pattern is called type B. Initially, a link was found between type A behavior and increased incidence of cardiovascular disease. Later, it was suspected that the anger–hostility component of the type A construct is the most significant disease-related characteristic. Although the causes of type A behavior have not been conclusively determined, considerable evidence points to the sociocultural environment, such as parental expectations of high standards in performance, as the likely origin (Girdano, Everly, & Dusek, 1990).

Early efforts to modify type A behavior through exercise interventions have had mixed results. One positive study showed that a 12-week aerobics program not only was associated with reductions in type

A behavior but also helped participants significantly reduce cardiovascular reactivity to mental stress (Blumenthal et al., 1988). Thus, changing type A behavior patterns through exercise could result in positive health benefits.

> **KEY POINT** Type A behavioral patterns apparently can be altered through exercise, and this can reduce the risk of cardiovascular disease.

Self-Concept

Exercise appears to also have a positive relationship with self-concept (Biddle, 1995; Marsh & Redmayne, 1994; Sonstroem, 1984; Sonstroem, Harlow, & Josephs, 1994). Sonstroem (1984) suggested that these changes in self-concept might be associated with the *perception* of improved fitness rather than with actual changes in physical fitness. Although studies so far have not proved that changes in physical fitness produce changes in self-concept, exercise programs seem to lead to significant increases in self-esteem, especially with subjects who initially show low self-esteem. For example, Martin, Waldron, McCabe, and Yun (2009) found that girls participating in the Girls on the Run program had positive changes in their global self-esteem and in appearance, peer, physical, and running self-concepts.

> **KEY POINT** Exercise and increased levels of fitness appear to be associated with increases in self-esteem, especially among individuals initially low in self-esteem.

Parallel to the sport personality research, the exercise and self-concept research has shown that it is best to think of self-concept or self-esteem not only as a general trait (global self-esteem) but also as one that includes numerous content-specific dimensions, such as social self-concept, academic self-concept, and physical self-concept. As you might expect, research shows that exercise participation has the greatest effect on the physical dimension of self-concept (Fox, 1997; Marsh & Sonstroem, 1995; Spence, McGannon, & Poon, 2005). This relationship is discussed further in chapter 17.

DISCOVER Activity 2.4 tests your knowledge of sport and exercise personality research.

Examining Cognitive Strategies and Success

Although some differences are evident among the personality traits and dispositions of athletes and exercisers, researchers have not been satisfied with the utility of the information thus far. For this reason many contemporary investigators have adopted the phenomenological approach to studying personality and turned from studying traditional traits to examining mental strategies, skills, and behaviors that athletes use for competition and their relationship to performance success (Auweele, Cuyper, Van Mele, & Rzewnicki, 1993; Gould & Maynard, 2009; Vealey, 2002).

One of the first studies to take this approach was an investigation by Mahoney and Avener (1977) of gymnasts competing for berths on the U.S. men's gymnastics team. The authors found that the gymnasts who made the team coped better with anxiety, used more internal imagery, and used more positive self-talk than those who didn't make the team.

> **KEY POINT** Olympic medalists, unlike nonmedalists, internalize their strategies to the extent that they react automatically to adversity.

Smith, Schutz, Smoll, and Ptacek (1995) developed and validated a measure of sport-specific psychological skills, the Athletic Coping Skills Inventory-28 (ACSI). The ACSI yields an overall score of an athlete's psychological skills as well as scores on seven subscales, which include the following:

- Coping with adversity
- Peaking under pressure
- Goal setting and mental preparation
- Concentration
- Freedom from worry
- Confidence and achievement motivation
- Coachability

Smith and colleagues examined the relationship between the overall scale and subscale scores and athletic performance in two studies. In the first study (Smith et al., 1995), 762 high school male and female athletes representing a variety of sports completed the ACSI. They were classified as underachievers (those who had a coach's talent rating that was higher than their actual performance ratings), normal achievers (those whose ratings were equal to their actual performance), and overachievers (those who were rated by their coaches as performing above their talent level). The study showed that, compared with the other groups, the overachieving athletes had significantly higher scores on several subscales (coachability, concentration, coping with adversity) as well as higher total scale scores. These results show that psychological skills can assist athletes in getting the most out of their physical talent.

The sample in the second study (Smith & Christensen, 1995) was a quite different group of athletes: 104 minor league professional baseball players. Scores on the ACSI were related to such performance measures as batting averages for hitters and earned run averages for pitchers. Interestingly, as with the high school athletes from the first study, expert ratings of *physical* skills did not relate to ACSI scores. Moreover, psychological skills accounted for a significant portion of performance variations in batting and pitching, and these skills contributed even more than physical ability. (Remember that these were all highly skilled and talented athletes, so this does not mean that physical talent is unimportant.) Finally, higher psychological skill scores were associated with player survival or continued involvement in professional baseball 2 and 3 years later. Thus, performance in elite sport appeared to be clearly related to mental skills.

A third study using the ACSI was conducted with Greek athletes (basketball, polo, and volleyball) at both the elite and nonelite levels (Kioumourtzoglou, Tzetzis, Derri, & Mihalopoulou, 1997). It revealed a number of differences, most notably that the elite athletes all showed superior ability, compared with the nonelite controls, to cope with adversity. The elite athletes were also better at goal setting and mental preparation.

Although Smith and colleagues (1995) acknowledged that the ACSI is a useful measurement tool for research and educational purposes, they warned that it should not be used for team selection. They argued that if athletes think the ACSI is being used for selection purposes, they are likely to knowingly give answers that will make themselves look good to coaches or to unwittingly give certain responses in hopes that they will become true.

In-Depth Interview Techniques

Researchers have also attempted to investigate the differences between successful and less successful athletes by taking a **qualitative approach** (a growing methodological trend in the field, as mentioned in chapter 1). In-depth interviews probe the coping strategies that athletes use before and during competition. The interview approach provides coaches, athletes, and sport psychologists with much more in-depth personality profiles of an athlete than do paper-and-pencil tests. For example, all 20 members of the 1988 U.S. Olympic freestyle and Greco-Roman wrestling teams were interviewed. Compared with nonmedalist wrestlers, Olympic medal winners used more positive self-talk, had a narrower and more immediate focus of attention, were better prepared mentally for unforeseen negative circumstances, and had more extensive mental practice (Gould, Eklund, & Jackson, 1993).

Mental Strategies Used by Successful Athletes

- To enhance confidence, successful athletes practice specific plans for dealing with adversity during competition.
- They practice routines for dealing with unusual circumstances and distractions before and during a competition.
- They concentrate wholly on the upcoming performance, blocking out irrelevant events and thoughts.
- They use several mental rehearsals before competition.
- They don't worry about other competitors before a competition and focus instead on what is controllable.
- They develop detailed competition plans.
- They learn to regulate arousal and anxiety.

One wrestler described his ability to react automatically to adversity:

" Something I've always practiced is to never let anything interfere with what I'm trying to accomplish at a particular tournament. So, what I try to do is if something is [maybe going] to bother me . . . completely empty my mind and concentrate on the event coming up . . . . My coping strategy is just to completely eliminate it from my mind, and I guess I'm blessed to be able to do that. (Gould, Eklund, & Jackson, 1993) "

Medalists seemed able to maintain a relatively stable and positive emotional level because their coping strategies became automatic, whereas nonmedalists had more fluctuating emotions as a consequence of not coping well mentally. Take the following example of a nonmedalist Olympic wrestler:

" I had a relaxation tape that seemed to give me moments of relief . . . . It got to the point where what you would try to do was not think about wrestling and get your mind on other things. But inevitably . . . you would bind up and get tight, [your] pulse would pick up, and your palms and legs and hands or feet [would be] sweating. You go through that trying to sleep, and I would resort to my relaxation tape. I don't think I coped very well with it really. (Gould, Eklund, & Jackson, 1993) "

Mental Plans

Mental planning is a large part of cognitive strategies. Some additional quotes from Olympic athletes may help further explain the benefits and workings of the mental strategies mentioned by the wrestlers just quoted (Orlick & Partington, 1988):

" The plan or program was already in my head. For the race I was on automatic, like turning the program on cruise control and letting it run. I was aware of the effort I was putting in and also of my opponent's position in relation to me, but I always focused on what I had to do next. "

" Before I start, I focus on relaxing, on breathing calmly. I feel activated but in control since I'd been thinking about what I was going to do in the race all through the warm-up. I used the period just before the start to clear my mind, so when I did actually start the race all my

thoughts about what I would be doing in the race could be uncluttered. "

" I usually try to work with my visualization on what is likely I'm going to use. Different wrestlers have different moves, you know. They always like to throw a right arm spin or something, and I'll visualize myself blocking that and things like that. "

Olympic athletes learn a systematic series of mental strategies to use before and during competition, including refocusing plans. Thus, they come prepared mentally not only to perform but also to handle distractions and unforeseen events before and during the competition (Gould & Maynard, 2009; Orlick & Partington, 1988). These mental plans especially help athletes whose sense of control (a personality trait) is low; the plans allow them to feel more in control regardless of situational influences. Figure 2.4 provides an example of a detailed refocusing plan for a Canadian Olympic alpine skier.

This skier's refocusing plan to meet the demands of the situation shows how important it is to study both an athlete's personality profile and his or her cognitive strategies and plans. In this way, coaches can continually structure practices and training environments to meet the situation and maximize performance and personal growth.

VIEW Activity 2.5 helps you better comprehend how cognitive strategies influence athletic performance.

Identifying Your Role in Understanding Personality

Now that you have learned something about the study of personality in sport and exercise settings, how can you use the information to better understand the individuals in your classes and on your teams? Later chapters explore the practical aspects of changing behaviors and developing psychological skills. In the meantime, use these guidelines to help you better understand the people with whom you work now and to consolidate what you have learned about personality structure.

1. *Consider both personality traits and situations.* To understand someone's behavior, consider both the person and the situation. Along with understanding personality, always take into account the particular situation in which you are teaching or coaching.

Situation	Strategy
Hassles and distractions	Use adrenaline and anger as positives instead of letting them bring me down.
	Let coaches or other personnel rectify the problem.
Delay in start	Relax, think of anything and everything that makes me happy.
Loss of ideal focus in race run	Think of the course in "sections" and deal with a mistake as a mistake in the previous "section;" when entering the "new section," a refocusing occurs.
	Think of and deal with the remainder of the course as previously rehearsed.
Mistake in race run	Deal with the mistake as I would a loss of focus.
	Go for the future, not the past.
Poor performance—first run	Think of the second run with a "nothing-to-lose" attitude.
Poor performance—final run	Determine what went wrong and why.
	Learn from the mistake, train, and see the mistake dissolve mentally and physically.
	Make the poor performance a challenge to defeat.

FIGURE 2.4   Refocusing plan for an Olympic alpine skier.

Adapted, by permission, from T. Orlick, 1986, *Coaches training manual to psyching for sport* (Champaign, IL: Human Kinetics), 30. By permission of T. Orlick.

2. *Be an informed consumer.* To know how and when to use personality tests, understand the ethics and guidelines for personality testing. This chapter has provided some guidelines. As a professional, it will be your responsibility to understand the dos and don'ts of personality testing.

3. *Be a good communicator.* Although formal personality testing can disclose a great deal about people, so can sincere and open communication.

Asking questions and being a good listener can go a long way toward establishing rapport and finding out about an individual's personality and preferences. A more detailed discussion of communication is presented in chapter 10.

4. *Be a good observer.* Another good way to gain valuable information about people's personalities is to observe their behavior in different situations. If you combine your observation of an individual's behavior with

open communication, you'll likely get a well-rounded view and understanding of his or her personality.

5. *Be knowledgeable about mental strategies.* A constellation of mental strategies facilitates the learning and performance of physical skills. Be aware of these strategies and implement them appropriately in your programs, selecting them to benefit an individual's personality.

Nature Versus Nurture and Gravitation Versus Change

Given recent advances in genetic research and testing, the question of whether personality is determined genetically (by nature) or through the environment (by nurture) is highly relevant to sport and physical activity professionals. Although this issue has not been studied in sport and exercise psychology per se, general psychological research shows both that personality has a genetic base (up to 60%) and that it is influenced by learning. Both extreme positions regarding nature versus nurture, then, are false. Genetics and the environment determine one's personality. Moreover, some research suggests that although we may be genetically predisposed to have certain characteristics, our environment influences whether and how much we manifest these characteristics. In sport and exercise psychology, then, we focus primary attention on learning and environmental influences because sport and exercise science professionals can influence personality development regardless of the role of genetics in personality.

A second critical question addressed in personality research focuses on the notion of whether certain individuals gravitate to specific sports because of their personality characteristics (the gravitation hypothesis) or whether one's personality changes as a result of participation in sport and physical activity (the change hypothesis). Although some evidence exists for both notions, neither has been convincingly demonstrated, most likely because both have an element of truth.

LEARNING AIDS

SUMMARY

1. **Describe what makes up personality and why it is important.**

   Personality refers to the characteristics or blend of characteristics that makes individuals unique. It comprises three separate but related levels: a psychological core, the most basic and stable level of personality; typical responses, or the ways each person learns to adjust to the environment; and role-related behaviors, or how a person acts based on what she perceives the situation to be. Role-related behavior is the most changeable aspect of personality. Understanding personality will help you improve your teaching and coaching effectiveness.

2. **Discuss major approaches to understanding personality.**

   Five major routes to studying personality in sport and exercise are the psychodynamic, trait, situation, interactional, and phenomenological approaches. The psychodynamic approach emphasizes the importance of unconscious determinants of behavior and of understanding the person as a whole. It has had little impact in sport psychology. The trait approach assumes that personality is enduring and consistent across situations and that psychological traits predispose individuals to behave in consistent ways regardless of the situation. In contrast, the situational approach argues that behavior is determined largely by the environment or situation. Neither the trait nor the situational approach has received widespread support in the sport psychology literature. Most researchers take an interactional approach to the study of sport personality, which considers personal and situational factors as equal determinants of behavior. The phenomenological approach focuses on a person's understanding and subjective interpretation of himself and his environment versus fixed traits. This highly held view is also consistent with the interactional view in that behavior is believed to be determined by personal and situational factors.

3. **Identify how personality can be measured.**

   To measure personality, an interactional approach should assess both psychological traits (an individual's typical style of behaving) and states (the situation's effects on behaviors). Although general personality scales provide some useful information about personality states and traits, situation-specific measures (e.g., sport-specific measures) predict behavior more reliably.

4. **Assess personality tests and research for practicality and validity.**

   Although useful, psychological tests alone have not proved to be accurate predictors of athletic success. And when they are used, they must be used ethically. Users of personality tests must know the principles of testing and measurement error, know their own limitations relative to test administration and interpretation, avoid using tests alone for team selection, always give athletes test explanations and feedback, assure athletes of confidentiality, take an intraindividual approach to testing, and understand and assess specific personality components.

5. **Understand the relationship between personality and behavior in sport and exercise.**

   Exercise has been found to enhance self-concept, especially the physical component of one's self. Type A behavior has been shown to be an important personality factor influencing wellness. Although some personality differences have been found through comparison of athletes with nonathletes and comparison of athletes from different sports, the most interesting and consistent findings come from comparisons of less successful athletes with more successful athletes exhibiting more positive mental health. These results, however, have limited application.

6. **Describe how cognitive strategies relate to athletic success.**

   In recent years researchers have turned their attention away from measuring traditional traits and toward examining cognitive or mental strategies, skills, and behaviors that athletes use. Successful athletes, compared with their less successful counterparts, possess a variety of psychological skills. These include arousal regulation and management, high self-confidence, better concentration and focus, feelings of being in control and not forcing things, positive imagery and thoughts, commitment and determination, goal setting, well-developed mental plans, and well-developed coping strategies.

7. **Apply what you know of personality in sport and exercise settings to better understand people's personalities.**

   As a professional in sport and exercise, you need to gather information about the personalities of people with whom you work. Specifically, consider both personality traits and situations, be an informed consumer, communicate with athletes, observe your subjects, and be knowledgeable about mental strategies.

KEY TERMS

psychological core	adaptive perfectionism	projective tests
typical responses	situation approach	mental health model
role-related behavior	interactional approach	iceberg profile
psychodynamic approach	phenomenological approach	meta-analysis
trait approach	situation-specific measures	qualitative approach
maladaptive perfectionism	intraindividual approach	

REVIEW QUESTIONS

1. Discuss the three levels of personality, including the stability of the different levels.

2. Compare and contrast the psychodynamic, situation, trait, interactional, and phenomenological approaches to personality. Which approach is most common among sport psychologists today? Why?

3. Compare and contrast state and trait measures of personality. Why are both needed for a better understanding of personality in sport?

4. Why are sport-specific personality inventories more desirable than general psychological inventories for measuring personality in sport and exercise? Name examples of both sport-specific and general personality measures.

5. Discuss four important guidelines for administering psychological tests and providing feedback from the results of these tests.

6. Discuss the research comparing the personalities of athletes and nonathletes and male and female athletes. Do athletes versus nonathletes and male versus female athletes have unique personality profiles?

7. Discuss Morgan's mental health model and the iceberg profile as they relate to predicting athletic success. Can athletic success be predicted from psychological tests? Explain.

8. What personality factors are related to exercise behavior?

9. Compare and contrast the cognitive strategies of successful athletes with those of less successful athletes.

CRITICAL THINKING QUESTIONS

1. Should psychological tests be used for team selection? Explain your answer.

2. What is your role in understanding personality? When might you consider using personality tests? Discuss other ways to assess participants' personalities.

3

Motivation

After reading this chapter, you should be able to

1. define motivation and its components,
2. describe typical views of motivation and whether they are useful,
3. detail useful guidelines for building motivation,
4. define achievement motivation and competitiveness and indicate why they are important,
5. compare and contrast theories of achievement motivation,
6. explain how achievement motivation develops, and
7. use fundamentals of achievement motivation to guide practice.

Dan is a cocaptain and center on his high school football team. His team does not have outstanding talent, but if everyone gives maximum effort and plays together, the team should have a successful season. When the team's record slips below .500, however, Dan becomes frustrated with some of his teammates who don't seem to try as hard as he does. Despite being more talented than he, these players don't seek out challenges, are not as motivated, and often give up in the presence of adversity. Dan wonders what he can do to motivate some of his teammates.

Like Dan, teachers, coaches, and exercise leaders often wonder why some individuals are highly motivated and constantly strive for success whereas others seem to lack motivation and avoid evaluation and competition. In fact, coaches frequently try to motivate athletes with inspirational slogans: "Winners never quit!" "Go hard or go home!" "Give 110%!" Physical educators also want to motivate inactive children, who often seem more interested in playing computer games than volleyball. Exercise leaders and physical therapists routinely face the challenge of motivating clients

to stay with an exercise or rehabilitation program. Although motivation is critical to the success of all these professionals, many do not understand the subject well. To have success as a teacher, coach, or exercise leader requires a thorough understanding of motivation, including the factors affecting it and the methods of enhancing it in individuals and groups. Often the ability to motivate people, rather than the technical knowledge of a sport or physical activity, is what separates the very good instructors from the average ones. In this chapter, we introduce you to the topic of motivation.

Defining Motivation

Motivation can be defined simply as the direction and intensity of one's effort (Sage, 1977). Sport and exercise psychologists can view motivation from several specific vantage points, including achievement motivation, motivation in the form of competitive stress (see chapter 4), and intrinsic and extrinsic motivation (see chapter 6). These varied forms of motivation are all parts of the more general definition of motivation. Hence, we understand the specifics of motivation through this broader, holistic context, much as a football coach views specific plays from the perspective of a larger game plan or offensive or defensive philosophy. But what exactly do these components of motivation—**direction of effort** and **intensity of effort**—involve?

- The direction of effort refers to whether an individual seeks out, approaches, or is attracted to certain situations. For example, a high school student may be motivated to go out for the tennis team, a coach to attend a coaching clinic, a businesswoman to join an aerobics class, or an injured athlete to seek medical treatment.

- Intensity of effort refers to how much effort a person puts forth in a particular situation. For instance, a student may attend physical education class (approach a situation) but not put forth much effort during class. On the other hand, a golfer may want to make a winning putt so badly that he becomes overly motivated, tightens up, and performs poorly. Finally, a weightlifter may work out 4 days a week like her friends yet differ from them in the tremendous effort or intensity she puts into each workout.

> **KEY POINT** Motivation is the direction and intensity of effort.

Although for discussion purposes it is convenient to separate the direction of effort from the intensity of effort, for most people direction and intensity of effort are closely related. For instance, students or athletes who seldom miss class or practice and always arrive early typically expend great effort during participation. Conversely, those who are consistently tardy and miss many classes or practices often exhibit low effort when in attendance.

Reviewing Three Approaches to Motivation

Each of us develops a personal view of how motivation works, our own model on what motivates people. We are likely to do this by learning what motivates *us* and by observing how other people are motivated. For instance, if someone has a physical education teacher she likes and believes is successful, she will probably try to use or emulate many of the same motivational strategies that the teacher uses.

Moreover, people often act out their personal views of motivation, both consciously and subconsciously. A coach, for example, might make a conscious effort to motivate students by giving them positive feedback and encouragement. Another coach, believing that people are primarily responsible for their own behaviors, might spend little time creating situations that enhance motivation.

Although thousands of individual views exist, most people fit motivation into one of three general orientations that parallel the approaches to personality discussed in chapter 2. These include the trait-centered orientation to motivation, the situation-centered orientation, and the interactional orientation.

Trait-Centered View

The **trait-centered view** (also called the **participant-centered view**) contends that motivated behavior is primarily a function of individual characteristics. That is, the personality, needs, and goals of a student, athlete, or exerciser are the primary determinants of motivated behavior. Thus, coaches often describe an athlete as a "real winner," implying that this individual has a personal makeup that allows him to excel in sport. Similarly, another athlete may be described as a "loser" who has no get-up-and-go.

Some people have personal attributes that seem to predispose them to success and high levels of motivation whereas others seem to lack motivation, personal goals, and desire. However, most of us would agree that we are in part affected by the situations in which we are placed. For example, if a teacher does not create a motivating learning environment, student motivation will consequently decline. Conversely, an excellent leader who creates a positive environment will greatly increase motivation. Thus, ignoring environmental influences on motivation is unrealistic and is one reason sport and exercise psychologists have not endorsed the trait-centered view for guiding professional practice.

Situation-Centered View

In direct contrast to the trait-centered view, the **situation-centered view** contends that motivation level is determined primarily by situation. For example, Brittany might be really motivated in her aerobic exercise class but unmotivated in a competitive sport situation.

Probably you would agree that situation influences motivation, but can you also recall situations in which you remained motivated despite a negative environment? For example, maybe you played for a coach you didn't like who constantly yelled at and criticized you, but still you did not quit the team or lose any of your motivation. In such a case, the situation was clearly not the primary factor influencing your motivation level. For this reason, sport and exercise psychology specialists do not recommend the situation-centered view of motivation as the most effective for guiding practice.

Interactional View

The view of motivation most widely endorsed by sport and exercise psychologists today is the participant-by-situation **interactional view**. Interactionists contend that motivation results neither solely from participant factors (e.g., personality, needs, interests, and goals) nor solely from situational factors (e.g., a coach's or teacher's style or the win–loss record of a team). Rather, the best way to understand motivation is to examine how these two sets of factors interact (figure 3.1).

> **KEY POINT** The best way to understand motivation is to consider both the person and the situation and how the two interact.

Sorrentino and Sheppard (1978) studied 44 male and 33 female swimmers in three Canadian universities, testing them twice as they swam a 200-yard freestyle time trial individually and then as part of a relay team. The situational factor that the researchers assessed was whether each swimmer swam alone or as part of a relay team. The researchers also assessed a personality characteristic in the swimmers—their affiliation motivation, or the degree to which a person sees group involvement as an opportunity for social approval versus social rejection. The objective of the study was to see whether each swimmer was oriented more toward social approval (i.e., viewing competing with others as a positive state) or toward rejection (i.e., feeling threatened by an affiliation-oriented activity, such as a relay, in which she might let others down) and how their motivational orientation influenced their performance.

As the investigators predicted, the approval-oriented swimmers demonstrated faster times swimming in the relay than when swimming alone (figure 3.2). After all, they had a positive orientation toward seeking approval from others—their teammates. In contrast, the rejection-threatened swimmers, who were overly concerned with letting their teammates down, swam faster alone than when they swam in the relay.

From a coaching perspective, these findings show that the four fastest individual swimmers would not necessarily make the best relay team. Depending on the athletes' motivational orientation, some would perform best in a relay and others would perform best individually. Many experienced team-sport coaches agree that starting the most highly skilled athletes does not guarantee having the best team in the game.

The results of the swimming study clearly demonstrate the importance of the interactional model of motivation. Knowing only a swimmer's personal characteristics (motivational orientation) was not the best way to predict behavior (the individual's split time) because performance depended on the situation (performing individually or in a relay). Similarly, it would be a mistake to look only at the situation as the primary source of motivation because the best speed depended on whether a swimmer was more approval oriented or rejection threatened. The key, then, was to understand the interaction between the athlete's personal makeup and the situation.

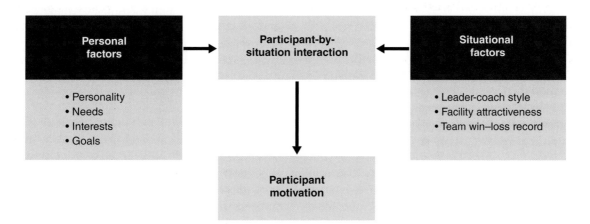

FIGURE 3.1 Participant-by-situation interactional model of motivation.

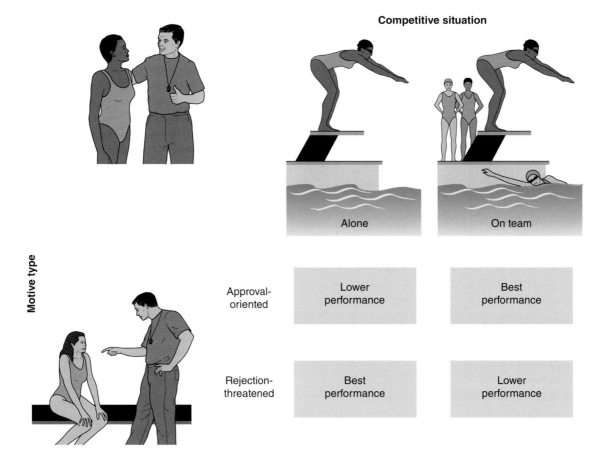

FIGURE 3.2 The interaction of two types of competitive situations (performing alone or on a relay team) and swimmer's approval orientation (approval oriented versus rejection threatened) on swimming performance.

DISCOVER Activity 3.1 helps you better appreciate motivation and major views of motivation.

Building Motivation With Five Guidelines

The interactional model of motivation has important implications for teachers, coaches, trainers, exercise leaders, and program administrators. Some fundamental guidelines for professional practice can be derived from this model.

Guideline 1: Consider Both Situations and Traits in Motivating People

When attempting to enhance motivation, consider both situational and personal factors. Often when working with students, athletes, or clients who seem to lack motivation, teachers, trainers, coaches, or exercise leaders immediately attribute this lack to the participant's personal characteristics. "These students don't care about learning," "This team doesn't want it enough," or "Exercise is just not a priority in these folks' lives"—such phrases ascribe personal attributes to people and, in effect, dismiss the poor motivation or avoid the responsibility for helping the participants develop motivation. At other times, instructors fail to consider the personal attributes of their students or clients and instead put all the blame on the situation (e.g., "This material must be boring" or "What is it about my instructional style that inhibits the participant's level of motivation?").

In reality, low participant motivation usually results from a combination of personal and situational factors. Personal factors do cause people to lack motivation, but so do the environments in which people participate. In fact, in the past decade motivation researchers have placed increased attention on the motivational climates that surround athletes and exercisers. Often it may be easier for an instructor to change the situation or create a certain kind of environment than to change the needs and personalities of the participants. The key, however, is not to focus attention only on the personal attributes of the participants or only on the situation at hand but to consider the interaction of these factors.

KEY POINT   To enhance motivation, you must ana-lyze and respond not only to a player's personality but also to the interaction of personal and situational characteristics. Because motivations may change over time, you should continue to monitor people's motives for participation even months after they've begun.

Guideline 2: Understand People's Multiple Motives for Involvement

Consistent effort is necessary in order to identify and understand participants' motives for being involved in sport, exercise, or educational environments. This understanding can be obtained in several ways.

VIEW   Activity 3.2 lets you use your own experiences to identify the major motives for sport and exercise participation.

Identify Why People Participate in Physical Activity

Researchers know why most people participate in sport and exercise, and this is important because practitioners consider motives to be very important in influencing individual and team performance (Theodorakis & Gargalianos, 2003). Motives are also seen as critical in influencing exercise participation and adherence to injury rehabilitation protocol (see chapters 18 and 19). After reviewing the literature, Gill and Williams (2008) concluded that children have a number of motives for sport participation, including skill development and the demonstration of competence as well as challenge, excitement, and fun. Adult motives are similar to those of youths, although health motives are rated as more important by adults and competence and skill development less important. For example, Wankel (1980) found that adults cited health factors, weight loss, fitness, self-challenge, and feeling better as motives for join-ing an exercise program. Their motives for continuing in the exercise program included enjoyment, the orga-nization's leadership (e.g., the instructor), the activity type (e.g., running, aerobics), and social factors. It has also been found that motives change across age groups and that older adults' motives are less ego

oriented than younger adults' (Steinberg, Grieve, & Glass, 2000). Moreover, research has found that the exercise behavior of male college students is more motivated by intrinsic factors such as strength and competition whereas that of female college students is more motivated by extrinsic factors such as weight management and appearance (Egli, Bland, Melton, & Czech, 2011).

Taking a more theoretical approach, psycholo-gists Edward Deci and Michael Ryan (1985, 2000) developed a general theory of motivation called self-determination theory. This theory contends that all people are motivated to satisfy three general needs: the need to feel competent (e.g., "I am a good runner"), autonomous (e.g., a pitcher loves to decide what pitches to throw and to have the fate of the game in his or her hands), and social connectedness or belonging (e.g., a soccer player loves to be part of the team). How these motives are fulfilled leads to a continuum of motivation ranging from amotivation (no motiva-tion) to extrinsic motivation to intrinsic motivation. This continuum of motivated behavior, especially the distinction between intrinsic and extrinsic motivation and the advantages of self-determined motivation, is discussed in more depth in chapter 6. What is important to understand now is that the athletes, exercisers, or patients you work with have the three general motivational needs of competence, autonomy, and connectedness or relatedness. The more you can provide for these needs, the greater a participant's motivation will be.

What motivates you to participate in sport and physical activity? As you think about what motivates you and others, remember these points:

• *People participate for more than one reason.* Most people have multiple motives for participation. For example, you may lift weights because you want to tone your body. Yet lifting weights also makes you feel good, plus you enjoy the camaraderie of your lift-ing partners. Thus, you lift for more than one reason.

• *People have competing motives for involve-ment.* At times people have competing motives. For instance, a person may want to exercise at the club after work *and* to be with his family. As a coach, teacher, or exercise leader, you should be aware of such conflicting interests because they can affect participation.

• *People have both shared and unique motives.* Although it is possible to identify why people usually participate in sport and exercise, motives for participation vary greatly and can be unique to each individual. For example, Dwyer (1992) assessed college students' motives for participation and obtained results similar to those for young athletes: The most important motives for participation were fitness, fun, excitement and challenge, and improving skills. However, the college students rated friendship, achievement status, and team factors as less important—findings that vary from those in the youth sports literature. Thus, many of us would cite physical fitness, fun, and friendship as major motives for sport participation. However, some of us might have motives that are more individual, such as parental pressure or needing something to do. Still others might have highly idiosyncratic motives, such as the need to physically dominate others or the experience of calmness they actually derive from competition. Hence, people have both shared and unique motives for participation.

• *Sex differences in motivation.* Some sex differences exist in motivations for involvement. For example, Sirard, Pfeiffer, and Pate (2006) studied motivational factors associated with sport participation in more than 1,600 middle school children. Findings showed that having fun was the highest-rated

motive for all the children. When motives were compared across sexes, girls cited social and skill benefits, competition, and fitness as major motives whereas boys emphasized competition, social benefits, and fitness most often. The authors concluded that middle school boys have a greater attraction to the competitive aspects of sport whereas girls have a greater attraction to the social aspects. The conclusions of this study are restricted to the age group sampled; however, they emphasize the importance of recognizing that although males and females may share many common motives for involvement in sport and physical activity, important differences may be evident.

• *Cultural emphasis affects motives.* Although many motives for sport and physical activity involvement are common across cultures, some are given more emphasis. Kim, Williams, and Gill (2003), for example, found that U.S. and Korean middle school students differed in their motivation: U.S. youngsters were more intrinsically motivated than their Korean counterparts. They also suggested that participants from Asian countries are more interdependence oriented whereas North Americans are more independence oriented. In another study, Yan and McCullagh (2004) found that American, Chinese, and Chinese American youths differed in their

Many factors influence a person's motivation to participate in sport. How does the motivation of these athletes differ from your motivation?

motives for sport and physical activity participation. Specifically, American youths were motivated primarily by competition and the need to improve; Chinese youths were more involved for social affiliation and wellness; and Chinese American youths participated because of travel, equipment use, and having fun. As most contemporary societies are becoming more culturally diverse, coaches, exercise leaders, and physical educators must become familiar with and recognize important cultural differences in participant motives.

Observe Participants and Continue to Monitor Motives

Because people have such a diverse range of motives for sport and exercise participation, you need to be aware of your students', athletes', or exercisers' motives for involvement. Following these guidelines should improve your awareness:

1. Observe the participants and see what they like and do not like about the activity.

2. Informally talk to others (e.g., teachers, friends, and family members) who know the student, athlete, or exerciser and solicit information about the person's motives for participation.

3. Periodically ask the participants to write out or tell you their reasons for participation.

Continue to monitor motives for participation. Research has shown that motives change over time. For instance, the reasons some individuals cited for beginning an exercise program (e.g., health and fitness benefits) were not necessarily the same motives they cited for staying involved (e.g., social atmosphere of the program; Wankel, 1980). Consequently, continuing to emphasize fitness benefits while ignoring the social aspect after people have begun the exercise program is probably *not* the most effective motivational strategy.

Guideline 3: Change the Environment to Enhance Motivation

Knowing why people become involved in sport and exercise is important, but this information alone is insufficient to enhance motivation. You need to use what you learn about your participants to structure the sport and exercise environment to meet their needs.

Provide Both Competition and Recreation

Not all participants have the same desire for competition and recreation. Opportunities for both need to

be provided. For example, many park district directors have learned that although some adult athletes prefer competition, others do not. Thus, the directors divide the traditional competitive softball leagues into competitive and recreational divisions. This choice enhances participation rates by giving people what they want.

> **KEY POINT** To enhance motivation, structure teaching and coaching environments to meet the needs of all participants.

Provide Multiple Opportunities

Meeting participant needs isn't always simple. Structuring a situation to enhance motivation may mean constructing an environment to meet multiple needs. For example, elite performers demand rigorous training and work at a very intense level. Some coaches mistakenly think that world-class athletes need only rigorous physical training, but the truth is that elite athletes often also want to have fun and enjoy the companionship of their fellow athletes. When coaches pay more attention to the motives of fun and fellowship along with optimal physical training, they enhance motivation and improve their athletes' performance.

Adjust to Individuals in Groups

An important but difficult component of structuring sport and exercise environments is individualizing coaching and teaching. That is, each exerciser, athlete, and student has her unique motives for participation, and effective instructors must provide an environment that meets these diverse needs. Experienced coaches have known this for years. Legendary football coach Vince Lombardi (for whom the Super Bowl trophy is named), for example, structured his coaching environment to meet the needs of individual athletes (Kramer & Shaap, 1968). Lombardi had a reputation as a fiery, no-nonsense coach who was constantly on his players' backs. All-pro guard Jerry Kramer, for instance, has said that Lombardi always yelled at him. (But Coach Lombardi was also clever: Just when Kramer was discouraged enough to quit because of the criticism, Lombardi would provide some much-needed positive reinforcement.) In contrast to the more thick-skinned Kramer, all-pro quarterback Bart Starr was extremely self-critical. The coach recognized this and treated Starr in a much more positive way than he treated Kramer. Lombardi understood that these two players had different personalities and needs, which required a coaching environment flexible enough for them both.

Individualizing is not always easy to accomplish. Physical educators might be teaching 6 classes of 35 students each, and aerobics instructors might have classes with as many as 100 students in them. Without assistants it is impossible to structure the instructional environment in the way Lombardi did. This means that today's instructors must be both imaginative and realistic in individualizing their environments.

Of course, a junior high school physical educator cannot get to know his students nearly as well as a personal trainer with one client or a basketball coach with 15 players on the team. However, the physical educator could, for example, have students identify on index cards their motives for involvement ("What do you like about physical education class? Why did you take the class?"), assess the frequency with which various motives are mentioned, and structure the class environment to meet the most frequently mentioned motives. If more students indicated they preferred noncompetitive activities to traditional competitive class activities, the instructor could choose to structure class accordingly. The instructor also might offer options in the same class and have half the students play competitive volleyball on one court and the other half play noncompetitive volleyball on a second court.

Guideline 4: Influence Motivation

As an exercise leader, physical educator, or coach, you have a critical role in influencing participant motivation. A survey of physical educators who were all coaches showed that 73% of them considered themselves and their actions to be very important motivational factors for their athletes (Theodorakis & Gargalianos, 2003). At times your influence may be indirect and you won't even recognize the importance of your actions. For example, a physical educator who is energetic and outgoing will, on personality alone, give considerable positive reinforcement in class. Over the school year her students come to expect her upbeat behavior. However, she may have a bad day and, although she does not act negatively in class, she may not be up to her usual cheeriness. Because her students know nothing about her circumstances, they perceive that they did something wrong and consequently become discouraged. Unbeknownst to the teacher, her students are influenced by her mood (figure 3.3).

FIGURE 3.3 "She was pretty upset with us tonight. I wonder what we did wrong?"

You too will have bad days as a professional and will need to struggle through them, doing the best job you can. The key thing to remember is that your actions (and inaction) on such days can influence the motivational environment. Sometimes you may need to act more upbeat than you feel. If that's not possible, inform your students that you're not quite yourself so that they don't misinterpret your behavior.

Guideline 5: Use Behavior Modification to Change Participants' Undesirable Motives

We have emphasized the need for structuring the environment to facilitate participant motivation because the exercise leader, trainer, coach, or teacher usually has more direct control over the environment than over the motives of individuals. This does not imply, however, that it is inappropriate to attempt to change a participant's motives for involvement.

A young football player, for example, may be involved in his sport primarily to inflict injury on others. This player's coach will certainly want to use behavior modification techniques (see chapter 6) to change this undesirable motivation. That is, the coach will reinforce good clean play, punish aggressive play intended to inflict injury, and simultaneously discuss appropriate behavior with the player. Similarly, a cardiac rehabilitation patient beginning exercise on a doctor's orders may need behavior modification from her exercise leader to gain intrinsic motivation to exercise. Using behavior modification techniques to alter participants' undesirable motives is certainly appropriate in some settings.

Making Physical Activity Participation a Habit: Long-Term Motivation Effects

Karin Pfeiffer and colleagues (2006) took a very different approach to understanding physical activity motivation. These investigators examined whether participation in youth sports predicts the levels of adult involvement in physical activity. Assessing females across three time periods (8th, 9th, and 12th grades), they found that sport participation in the 8th and 9th grades predicted physical activity participation in the 12th grade. This suggests that requiring a habit of being physically active at a young age influences motivation for being active later in life. Although future studies need to further verify this important finding, this topic is a key area of future research given the current obesity crisis facing many nations.

KEY POINT Use behavior modification techniques to change undesirable motives and strengthen weak motivation.

Developing a Realistic View of Motivation

Motivation is a key variable in both learning and performance in sport and exercise contexts. People sometimes forget, however, that motivation is not the only variable influencing behavior. Sportswriters, for instance, typically ascribe a team's performance to motivational attributes—the extraordinary efforts of the players; laziness; the lack of incentives that follows from million-dollar, no-cut professional contracts; or a player's ability (or inability) to play in clutch situations. A team's performance, however, often hinges on nonmotivational factors, such as injury, playing a better team, being overtrained, or failing to learn new skills (Gould, Guinan, Greenleaf, Medbery, & Peterson, 1999). Besides the motivational factors of primary concern to us here, biomechanical, physiological, sociological, medical, and technical–tactical factors are significant to sport and exercise and warrant consideration in any analysis of performance.

KEY POINT As a leader, you are critical to the motivational environment and you influence motivation both directly and indirectly.

Some motivational factors are more easily influenced than others. It is easier for an exercise leader to change his reinforcement pattern, for instance, than it is for him to change the attractiveness of the building. (This is not to imply that cleaning up a facility is too time-consuming to be worth the trouble. Consider, for example, how important facility attractiveness is in the health club business.) Professionals need to consider what motivational factors they can influence and how much time (and money) it will take to change them. For example, a study by Kilpartrick, Hebert, and Bartholomew (2005) showed that people are more likely to report intrinsic reasons for participating in sport (e.g., challenge and enjoyment) and extrinsic reasons for taking part in exercise (e.g., appearance and weight). Because intrinsic motivation is thought to be a more powerful predictor of behavior over the long run, they suggest that exercise leaders who are interested in facilitating an active lifestyle may want to place more emphasis on sport involvement rather than simply focusing on increasing the amount of exercise time.

Understanding Achievement Motivation and Competitiveness

Throughout the first part of the chapter we have emphasized the importance of individual differences in motivation. In essence, individuals participate in sport and physical activity for different reasons and are motivated by different methods and situations. Therefore, it is important to understand why some people seem so highly motivated to achieve their goals (like Dan in the football example at the beginning of the chapter) and why others seem to go along for the ride. We start by discussing two related motives that influence performance and participation in sport achievement: achievement motivation and competitiveness.

What Is Achievement Motivation?

Achievement motivation refers to a person's efforts to master a task, achieve excellence, overcome obstacles, perform better than others, and take pride in exercising talent (Murray, 1938). It is a person's

Breathing Life Into the Gym: A Physical Educator's Plan for Enhancing Student Motivation

Kim is a second-year physical education teacher. The school she teaches at is pretty run down and is scheduled to be closed in the next 5 years, so the district doesn't want to invest any money in fixing it up. During the first several weeks of class, Kim notices that her students are not very motivated to participate.

To determine how to motivate her students, Kim examines her own program. She realizes she is using a fairly standard program based on the required curriculum and begins to think of ways to modernize the routine. First, she notices that the gym itself is serviceable but dingy with use and age.

Kim realizes that student motivation would likely improve if the facility was revamped, but she also knows that renovation is unlikely, so she decides to take improvement into her own hands. First, she cleans up the gym and gets permission to take the old curtains down. Next, she brightens the gym by backing all the bulletin boards with color and hanging physical fitness posters on the walls. She also thanks the custodian for helping her get rid of those old curtains and asks if he can change his cleaning schedule so the gym gets swept up right after lunch.

Of course, Kim realizes that improving the physical environment is not enough to motivate her students. She herself must also play an important role. She reminds herself to make positive, encouraging remarks during class and to be upbeat and optimistic. She also asks the students what they like and dislike about gym class. Students tell her that fitness testing and exercising at the start of class are not much fun. However, these are mandated in the district curriculum. (Besides, many of her students are couch potatoes and badly need the exercise!)

Kim works to make the fitness testing a fun part of a goal-setting program, in which each class earns points for improvement. She tallies the results on a bulletin board for students to see. The "student of the week" award focuses on the one youngster who makes the greatest effort and shows the most progress toward his fitness goal. Exercising to contemporary music is also popular with students.

Through talking to her students, Kim is surprised to learn of their interest in sports other than the old standards, such as volleyball and basketball. They say they'd like to play tennis, play golf, and swim. Unfortunately, swimming and golfing are not possible because of the lack of facilities, but Kim is able to introduce tennis into the curriculum by obtaining rackets and balls through a U.S. Tennis Association program in which recreational players donate their used equipment to the public schools.

Looking back at the end of the year, Kim is generally pleased with the changes in her students' motivation. Sure, some kids are still not interested, but most seem genuinely excited. In addition, the students' fitness scores have improved over those of previous years. Finally, her student-of-the-week program is a big hit, especially for those hard-working students with average skills who are singled out for their personal improvement and effort.

orientation to strive for task success, persist in the face of failure, and have pride in accomplishments (Gill, 2000).

Not surprisingly, coaches, exercise leaders, and teachers have an interest in achievement motivation because it includes the precise characteristics that allow athletes to achieve excellence, exercisers to gain high levels of fitness, and students to maximize learning.

Like the general views of motivation and personality, views of achievement motivation in particular have progressed from a trait-oriented view of a person's need for achievement to an interactional view that emphasizes more changeable achievement goals

and the ways in which these affect and are affected by the situation. Achievement motivation in sport is popularly called competitiveness.

What Is Competitiveness?

Competitiveness is defined as "a disposition to strive for satisfaction when making comparisons with some standard of excellence in the presence of evaluative others" (Martens, 1976, p. 3). Basically, Martens views competitiveness as achievement behavior in a competitive context, with social evaluation as a key component. It is important to look at a situation-specific achievement orientation: Some people who are highly oriented toward achievement in one setting (e.g., competitive sport) are not in other settings (e.g., math class).

Martens' definition of competitiveness is limited to situations in which one is evaluated by, or has the potential to be evaluated by, knowledgeable others. Yet many people compete with themselves (e.g., trying to better your own running time from the previous day) even when no one else evaluates the performance. The level of achievement motivation would bring out this self-competition, whereas the level of competitiveness would influence behavior in socially evaluated situations. For this reason, we discuss achievement motivation and competitiveness together in this chapter.

Effects of Motivation

Achievement motivation and competitiveness deal not just with the final outcome or the pursuit of excellence but also with the psychological journey of getting there. If we understand why motivation differences occur in people, we can intervene positively. Thus, we are interested in how a person's competitiveness and achievement motivation influence a wide variety of behaviors, thoughts, and feelings, including the following:

- Choice of activity (e.g., seeking out opponents of equal ability to compete against or looking for players of greater or lesser ability to play with)

- Effort to pursue goals (e.g., how often you practice)

- Intensity of effort in the pursuit of goals (e.g., how consistently hard you try during a workout)

- Persistence in the face of failure and adversity (e.g., when the going gets tough, do you work harder or take it easier?)

Identifying Four Theories of Achievement Motivation

Four theories have evolved over the years to explain what motivates people to act: need achievement theory, attribution theory, achievement goal theory, and competence motivation theory. We consider each of these in turn. A fifth, self-determination theory, is discussed in chapter 6 because it also explains how reinforcement influences motivation.

Need Achievement Theory

Need achievement theory (Atkinson, 1974; McClelland, 1961) is an interactional view that considers both personal and situational factors as important predictors of behavior. Five components make up this theory: personality factors or motives, situational factors, resultant tendencies, emotional reactions, and achievement-related behaviors (figure 3.4).

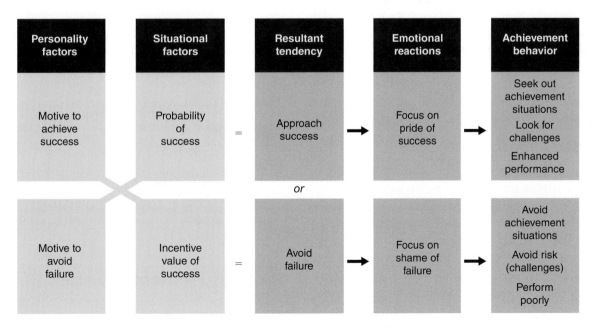

FIGURE 3.4 Need achievement theory.

Personality Factors

According to the need achievement view, each of us has two underlying achievement motives: to achieve success and to avoid failure (see figure 3.4). The motive to achieve success is defined as "the capacity to experience pride in accomplishments," whereas the motive to avoid failure is "the capacity to experience shame in failure" (Gill, 2000, p. 104). The theory contends that behavior is influenced by the balance of these motives. In particular, high achievers demonstrate high motivation to achieve success and low motivation to avoid failure. They enjoy evaluating their abilities and are not preoccupied with thoughts of failure. In contrast, low achievers demonstrate low motivation to achieve success and high motivation to avoid failure. They worry and are preoccupied with thoughts of failure. The theory makes no clear predictions for those with moderate levels of each motive (Gill, 2000).

Situational Factors

As you learned in chapter 2, information about traits alone is not enough to accurately predict behavior. Situations must also be considered. You should recognize two primary considerations in need achievement theory: the **probability of success** in the situation or task and the **incentive value of success**. Basically, the probability of success depends on whom you compete against and the difficulty of the task. That is, your chance of winning a tennis match would be lower against Venus Williams than against a novice. The value you place on success, however, would be greater because it is more satisfying to beat a skilled opponent than it is to beat a beginner. Settings that offer a 50-50 chance of succeeding (e.g., a difficult but attainable challenge) provide high achievers the most incentive for engaging in achievement behavior. However, low achievers do not see it this way because losing to an evenly matched opponent might maximize their experience of shame.

Resultant Tendencies

The third component in need achievement theory is the **resultant tendency** or **behavioral tendency**, derived by considering an individual's achievement motive levels in relation to situational factors (e.g., probability of success or incentive value of success). The theory is best at predicting situations in which the chance of success is 50-50. That is, high achievers seek out challenges in this situation because they enjoy competing against others of equal ability or performing tasks that are not too easy or too difficult.

Low achievers, on the other hand, avoid such challenges, instead opting either for easy tasks where success is guaranteed or for unrealistically hard tasks where failure is almost certain. Low achievers sometimes prefer very difficult tasks because no one expects them to win. For example, losing to LeBron James one-on-one in basketball certainly would not cause shame or embarrassment. Low achievers do not fear failure—they fear the negative evaluation associated with failure. A 50-50 chance of success causes maximum uncertainty and worry and thus increases the possibility of demonstrating low ability or competence. If low achievers cannot avoid such a situation, they become preoccupied and distraught because of their high need to avoid failure.

Emotional Reactions

The fourth component of the need achievement theory is the individual's emotional reactions, specifically how much pride and shame she experiences. Both high and low achievers want to experience pride and minimize shame, but their personality characteristics interact differently with the situation to cause them to focus more on either pride or shame. High achievers focus more on pride, whereas low achievers focus more on shame and worry.

Achievement Behavior

The fifth component of the need achievement theory indicates how the four other components interact to influence behavior. High achievers select more challenging tasks, prefer intermediate risks, and perform better in evaluative situations. Low achievers avoid intermediate risk, perform worse in evaluative situations, and avoid challenging tasks by selecting tasks so difficult that they are certain to fail or tasks so easy that they are guaranteed success.

KEY POINTS
- Achievement motivation is the tendency to strive for success, persist in the face of failure, and experience pride in accomplishments. Achievement motivation in sport and exercise settings focuses on self-competition whereas competitiveness influences behavior in socially evaluative situations.
- High achievers select challenging tasks, prefer intermediate risks, and perform better when they are being evaluated. Low achievers avoid challenging tasks, avoid intermediate risks, and perform worse when they are being evaluated.

Significance of Need Achievement Theory

These performance predictions of the need achievement theory serve as the framework for all contemporary explanations for achievement motivation. That is, even though more recent theories offer different explanations for the thought processes underlying achievement differences, the behavioral predictions of high and low achievers are basically the same. The most important contribution of need achievement theory is its task preference and performance predictions.

Attribution Theory

Attribution theory focuses on how people *explain* their successes and failures. This view, originated by Heider (1958) and extended and popularized by Weiner (1985, 1986), holds that literally thousands of possible explanations for success and failure can be classified into a few categories (figure 3.5). These most basic attribution categories are **stability** (a factor to which one attributes success or failure is either fairly permanent or unstable), **locus of causality** (a factor is either external or internal to the individual), and **locus of control** (a factor either is or is not under the individual's control).

Attributions as Causes of Success and Failure

A performer can perceive his success or failure as attributable to a variety of possible reasons. These perceived causes of success or failure are called attributions. For example, you may win a swimming race and attribute your success to

- a stable factor (e.g., your talent or good ability) or an unstable factor (e.g., good luck),

- an internal cause (e.g., your tremendous effort in the last 50 meters) or an external cause (e.g., an easy field of competitors), and

- a factor you can control (e.g., your race plan) or a factor out of your control (e.g., your opponents' lack of physical conditioning).

Or, you may drop out of an exercise program and attribute your failure to

- a stable factor (e.g., your lack of talent) or an unstable factor (e.g., the terrible instructor),

- an internal cause (e.g., your bad back) or an external cause (e.g., the exercise facility being too far from your home), and

- a factor you can control (e.g., your lack of effort) or a factor out of your control (e.g., the cost of the program).

Historically, attribution theory has been used to describe individuals' sport or exercise behavior. However, investigators have also begun to examine team attributions—that is, reasons or explanations for team performance (Allen, Coffee, & Greenlees, 2012; Shapcott, Carron, Greenlees, & Hakim, 2010). This is an important development because team attributions are being found to influence a number of important cognitive (e.g., expectations and choices), affective (e.g., emotions), and behavioral (e.g., approach or avoidance) responses of groups.

Why Attributions Are Important

Attributions affect expectations of future success or failure and emotional reactions (Biddle, Hanrahan, & Sellars, 2001; McAuley, 1993b). Attributing performance to certain types of stable factors has been

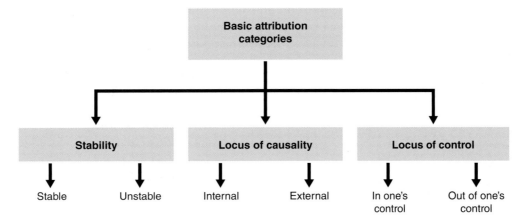

FIGURE 3.5 Weiner's basic attribution categories.

linked to expectations of future success. For example, if Susie, an elementary physical education student, ascribes her performance success in gymnastics to a stable cause (e.g., her high ability), she will expect the outcome to occur again in the future and will be more motivated and confident. She may even ask her parents if she can sign up for after-school gymnastics. In contrast, if Zach attributes his performance success in tumbling to an unstable cause (e.g., luck), he won't expect it to occur regularly and his motivation and confidence will not be enhanced. He probably wouldn't pursue after-school gymnastics. Of course, a failure also can be ascribed to a stable cause (e.g., low ability), which would lessen confidence and motivation, or to an unstable cause (e.g., luck), which would not.

> **KEY POINT** How performers explain or attribute their performance affects their expectations and emotional reactions, which in turn influence future achievement motivation. Attribution theory focuses on how individuals explain their successes and failures.

Attributions to internal factors and to factors in our control (e.g., ability, effort) rather than to external factors or factors outside our control (e.g., luck, task difficulty) often result in emotional reactions such as pride and shame. For example, a lacrosse player will have more pride (if successful) or shame (if unsuccessful) if she attributes her performance to internal factors than she would if she attributes it to luck or an opponent's skill (table 3.1).

VIEW Activity 3.3 tests your understanding of attribution theory.

Achievement Goal Theory

Both psychologists and sport and exercise psychologists have focused on achievement goals as a way of understanding differences in achievement (Duda & Hall, 2001; Dweck, 1986; Maehr & Nicholls, 1980; Nicholls, 1984; Roberts, 1993). According to the **achievement goal theory**, three factors interact to determine a person's motivation: achievement goals, perceived ability, and achievement behavior (figure 3.6). To understand someone's motivation, we must understand what success and failure mean to that person. The best way to do that is to examine a person's achievement goals and how they interact with that individual's perceptions of competence, self-worth, or ability.

Outcome and Task Orientations

Holly may compete in bodybuilding because she wants to win trophies and have the best physique of anybody in the area. She has adopted an **outcome goal orientation** (also called a **competitive goal orientation** or **ego orientation**) in which the focus is on comparing herself with and defeating others. Holly feels good about herself (has high perceived ability) when she wins but not so good about herself (has low perceived ability) when she loses.

Sarah also likes to win contests, but she primarily takes part in bodybuilding to see how much she can improve her strength and physique. She has adopted a **task goal orientation** (also called a **mastery goal orientation**) in which the focus is on improving relative to her own past performances. Her perceived ability is not based on a comparison with others.

For a particular situation, some people can be both task and outcome oriented. For example, a person

TABLE 3.1 Attributions and Achievement Motivation

Attributions	Psychological result
Stability factors	**Expectancy of future success**
Stable	Increased expectation of success
Unstable	Decreased expectation of success
Causality factors	**Emotional influences**
Internal cause	Increased pride or shame
External cause	Decreased pride or shame
Control factors	**Emotional influences**
In one's control	Increased motivation
Out of one's control	Decreased motivation

FIGURE 3.6 Three key factors in the achievement goal approach.

might want to win the local turkey trot but also set a personal best time for the race. However, according to researchers in achievement goal orientation, most people tend to be higher on either task or outcome orientation.

Value of a Task Orientation

Sport psychologists argue that a task orientation more often than an outcome orientation leads to a strong work ethic, persistence in the face of failure, and optimal performance. This orientation can protect a person from disappointment, frustration, and a lack of motivation when the performance of others is superior (something that often cannot be controlled). Because focusing on personal performance provides greater control, individuals become more motivated and persist longer in the face of failure.

KEY POINT An outcome goal orientation focuses on comparing performance with and defeating others, whereas a task goal orientation focuses on comparing performance with personal standards and personal improvement. It is best to adopt a task orientation, which emphasizes comparisons with your own performance standards rather than with the performances of others.

Task-oriented people also select moderately difficult or realistic tasks and opponents. They do not fear failure. And because their perception of ability is based on their own standards of reference, it is easier for them to feel good about themselves and to

demonstrate high perceived competence than it is for outcome-oriented individuals to do so.

Problems With Outcome Orientation

In contrast to task-oriented individuals, outcome-oriented people have more difficulty maintaining high perceived competence. They judge success by how they compare with others, but they cannot necessarily control how others perform. After all, at least half of the competitors must lose, which can lower a fragile perceived competence. People who are outcome oriented and have low perceived competence demonstrate a low or maladaptive achievement behavioral pattern (Duda & Hall, 2001). That is, they are likely to reduce their efforts, cease trying, or make excuses. To protect their self-worth they are more likely to select tasks in which they are guaranteed success or are so outmatched that no one would expect them to do well. They tend to perform less well in evaluative situations (see "Setting Outcome Goals and One Skier's Downfall").

Social Goal Orientations

Most goal orientation research has focused on task or outcome goal orientations. However, contemporary investigators have also identified social goal orientations as determinants of behavior (Allen, 2003; Stuntz & Weiss, 2003). Individuals high in a social goal orientation judge their competence in terms of affiliation with the group and recognition from being liked by others. Hence, in addition to judging their ability relative to their own and others' performances, they would be motivated by the desire for social connections and the need to belong to a group. Social goal orientations are important because they have been shown to be related to participant enjoyment, intrinsic motivation, and competence (Stuntz & Weiss, 2009). Thus, defining success in terms of social relationships has positive motivational effects.

Entity and Incremental Goal Perspectives

Elliott and Dweck (1988), Dweck (1999), and Elliott (1999) proposed that, similar to task and outcome goals, achievement behavior patterns are explained by how participants view their ability. According to these researchers, participants who are characterized by an **entity view** adopt an outcome goal focus, where they see their ability as fixed and unable to be changed through effort, or an **incremental focus**, where they adopt a task goal perspective and believe they can change their ability through hard work and effort. Research shows that physical activity participants who adopt an entity focus are characterized by maladaptive motivation patterns (e.g., negative self-thoughts and feelings; Li & Lee, 2004). Jowett and Spray (2013) also found that although elite British track and field athletes felt that natural ability was certainly evident in their high-level performance, overall they adopted an incremental view of ability in which they believed that general ability in athletics is malleable rather than fixed and that building on it is possible. These beliefs about ability were influenced by their upbringing, their transition from junior to senior sport, the motivation climate in which they trained and competed, coaching, and the initial success they had in sport.

Approach Versus Avoidance Achievement Goals

Another component of achievement goal theory deals with the approach and avoidance dimension of goals (Elliott, 1999). Researchers contend that in addition to outcome and mastery goal orientations, people's views of competence are characterized by either approach goals, where the athlete or exerciser focuses on achieving competence (e.g., working out because of a desire to look good or perform well), or avoidance goals, where the athlete or exerciser focuses on avoiding incompetence (e.g., working out because one does not to want to look bad or fail at something). Thus, an individual can be mastery approach oriented (e.g., "I want to improve my personal best running time"), mastery avoidance oriented (e.g., "I don't want

to run slower than my personal best time"), outcome approach oriented (e.g., "I want to win the race and beat her"), or outcome avoidance oriented (e.g., "I don't want to lose to her"). Recent research has shown that approach goals (both mastery and outcome) are positively related to the physical activity levels of university students (Lochbaum, Podlog, Litchfield, Surles, & Hillard, 2013). Other studies have also found that approach and avoidance goals are related to physical activity motivation (Moreno, Gonzales-Cutre, Scilica, & Spray, 2010; Nien & Duda, 2008; Wang, Liu, Lochbaum, & Stevenson, 2009). This research suggests that practitioners in sport and exercise should target approach goals rather than avoidance goals.

Importance of Motivational Climate

In recent years, sport psychologists have studied how goal orientations and perceived ability work together to influence motivation of physical activity participants as well as how the social climate influences one's goal orientations and motivation level (Duda, 2005; Ntoumanis & Biddle, 1999). Some psychologists contend, for example, that the social climates of achievement settings can vary significantly in several dimensions. These include such things as the tasks that learners are asked to perform, student–teacher authority patterns, recognition systems, student ability groupings, evaluation procedures, and times allotted for activities to be performed (Ames, 1992).

Research has revealed that in a motivational climate of mastery or task goal orientation, there are more adaptive motivational patterns, such as positive

---

▨ Setting Outcome Goals and One Skier's Downfall

After years of hard work, Dave becomes a member of the U.S. ski team. He has always set outcome goals for himself: becoming the fastest skier in his local club, winning regional races, beating archrivals, and placing at nationals. Unfortunately, he gets off to a rocky start on the World Cup circuit. He had wanted to be the fastest American downhiller and to place in the top three at each World Cup race, but with so many good racers competing it has become impossible to beat them consistently. To make matters worse, because of his lowered world ranking Dave skis far back in the pack (after the course has been chopped up by the previous competitors), which makes it virtually impossible to place in the top three.

As Dave becomes more frustrated by his failures, his motivation declines. He no longer looks forward to competitions; he either skis out of control, focused entirely on finishing first, or skis such a safe line through the course that he finishes well back in the field. Dave blames his poor finishes on the wrong ski wax and equipment. He does not realize that his outcome goal orientation, which had served him well at the lower levels of competition where he could more easily win, is now leading to lower confidence, self-doubt, and less motivation.

attitudes, increased effort, and effective learning strategies. In contrast, a motivational climate of outcome orientation has been linked with less adaptive motivational patterns, such as low persistence, low effort, and attribution of failures to (low) ability (Ntoumanis & Biddle, 1999).

Most important, researchers have found that motivational climates influence the types of achievement goals participants adopt: Task-oriented climates are associated with task goals and outcome-oriented climates are associated with outcome goals (Duda & Hall, 2001). Coaches, teachers, and exercise leaders, then, play an important role in facilitating motivation through the psychological climates they create.

Competence Motivation Theory

A final theory that has been used to explain differences in achievement behavior, especially in children, is competence motivation theory (Weiss & Chaumeton, 1992; Weiss & Ambrose, 2008). Based on the work of developmental psychologist Susan Harter (1988), this theory holds that people are motivated to feel worthy or competent and, moreover, that such feelings are the primary determinants of motivation. **Competence motivation theory** also contends that athletes' perceptions of control (feeling control over whether they can learn and perform skills) work along with self-worth and competence evaluations to influence their motivation. However, these feelings do not influence motivation directly. Rather, they influence affective or emotional states (e.g., enjoyment, anxiety, pride, and shame) that in turn influence motivation. It is also important to recognize that one's competence differs across domains (e.g., academic, physical, social).

If a young soccer player, for example, has high self-esteem, feels competent, and perceives that he has control over the learning and performance of soccer skills, then efforts to learn the game will increase his enjoyment, pride, and happiness. These positive affective states will in turn lead to increased motivation. In contrast, if an exerciser has low self-esteem, feels incompetent, and believes that personal actions have little bearing on increasing fitness, then negative affective responses will result, such as anxiety, shame, and sadness. These feelings will lead to a decline in motivation.

Considerable research has demonstrated the link between competence and motivation (Weiss, 1993; Weiss & Ambrose, 2008). Specifically, feedback and reinforcement from others and various motivational

orientations (e.g., goal orientations and trait anxiety) influence feelings of self-esteem, competence, and control. Wong and Bridges (1995) tested this model using 108 youth soccer players and their coaches. The researchers measured perceived competence, perceived control, trait anxiety, and motivation as well as various coaching behaviors. As you might expect, they found that trait anxiety and coaching behaviors predicted perceived competence and control, which in turn were related to the players' motivation levels. Hence, young athletes' perceptions of competence and control are critical determinants of whether they will strive toward achievement. Thus, enhancing perceived competence and control should be primary goals of professionals in exercise and sport science.

What Theories of Achievement Motivation Tell Us

To compare how these four theories explain achievement motivation, table 3.2 summarizes major predictions from each, showing how high and low achievers differ in terms of their motivational orientation and attributions, the goals they adopt, their perceived competence and control, their task choices, and their performance. We next discuss how a person's achievement motivation and competitiveness develop.

Developing Achievement Motivation and Competitiveness

Is achievement motivation learned? At what age do children develop achievement tendencies? Can sport and exercise professionals influence and motivate children toward certain kinds of achievement?

Achievement motivation and competitiveness are believed to develop in three stages (Scanlan, 1988; Veroff, 1969). These stages are sequential—that is, you must move through one stage before progressing to the next (figure 3.7). Not everyone makes it to the final stage, and the age at which people reach each stage varies considerably. The three stages are as follows:

1. *Autonomous competence stage.* In this stage, which is thought to occur before the age of 4 years, children focus on mastering their environment and on self-testing. For example, Brandon is a preschooler who is highly motivated to learn to ride his tricycle, and he couldn't care less that his sister Eileen can

TABLE 3.2   What Theories of Achievement Motivation Tell Us

	High achiever	Low achiever
Motivational orientation	High motivation to achieve success Low motivation to avoid failure Focuses on the pride of success	Low motivation to achieve success High motivation to avoid failure Focuses on shame and worry that may result from failure
Attributions	Ascribes success to stable and internal factors within one's own control Ascribes failure to unstable and external factors outside one's own control	Ascribes success to unstable and external factors outside one's own control Ascribes failure to stable and internal factors within one's own control
Goals adopted	Usually adopts an incremental or task goal Typically adopts approach goals	Usually adopts outcome or entity goals Typically adopts avoidance goals
Perceived competence and control	Has high perceived competence and believes that achievement is within one's own control	Has low perceived competence and believes that achievement is outside one's own control
Task choice	Seeks out challenges and able competitors and tasks	Avoids challenges; seeks out very difficult or very easy tasks and competitors
Performance conditions	Performs well in evaluative conditions	Performs poorly in evaluative conditions

ride better than he can. He rarely compares himself with others and focuses instead on self-referenced standards.

2. *Social comparison stage.* In the social comparison stage, which begins at about the age of 5 years, a child focuses on directly comparing his performance with that of others. Children seem preoccupied with asking, "Who is faster, bigger, smarter, and stronger?"

3. *Integrated stage.* The integrated stage involves both social comparison and autonomous achieve-

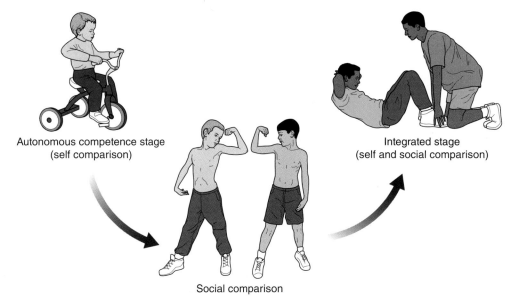

Autonomous competence stage (self comparison)

Social comparison

Integrated stage (self and social comparison)

FIGURE 3.7   Three stages in the development of achievement motivation.

Tips for Guiding Achievement Orientation

- Consider the interaction of personal and situational factors in influencing achievement behavior.
- Emphasize task or mastery goals and downplay outcome goals. Create a mastery motivational climate.
- Monitor and alter your attributional feedback.
- Assess and correct inappropriate participant attributions.
- Help participants determine when to compete and when to focus on individual improvement.
- Enhance perceptions of competence and control.

ment strategies. The person who fully masters this integration knows when it is appropriate to compete and compare herself with others and when it is appropriate to adopt self-referenced standards. This stage, which integrates components from the previous two stages, is the most desirable. There is no typical age for entering this stage.

Importance of Distinguishing Between Stages

Recognizing the developmental stages of achievement motivation and competitiveness helps us better understand the behavior of people we work with, especially children. Thus, we will not be surprised when a preschooler is not interested in competition or when fourth and fifth graders seem preoccupied with it. An integrated achievement orientation, however, must ultimately be developed, and it is important to teach children when it is appropriate or inappropriate to compete and compare themselves socially.

Influencing Stages of Achievement Motivation

The social environment in which a person functions has important implications for achievement motivation and competitiveness. Significant others can play an important role in creating a positive or negative climate. Parents, teachers, and coaches all play especially important roles. Teachers and coaches directly and indirectly create motivational climates. They define tasks and games as competitive or cooperative, group children in certain ways (e.g., picking teams through a public draft in which social comparison openly occurs), and differentially emphasize task or outcome goals (Ames, 1987; Roberts, 1993).

As professionals we can play significant roles in creating climates that enhance participant achievement motivation. For example, Treasure and Roberts (1995) created both task and outcome motivational climates in a study of a youth soccer physical education class by randomly assigning the children to either a task or ego-oriented climate. They found that after 10 sessions of having players participate in each climate, players who performed in the mastery climate focused more on effort, were more satisfied, and preferred more challenging tasks compared with those who performed in the outcome motivational climate. In another study, Gershgoren, Tenenbaum, Gerhgoren, and Eklund (2011) randomly assigned youth soccer players and their parents to different parental feedback conditions and examined the effects of parental feedback on players' goal orientations and performance on a penalty kick task. Findings revealed that players who received task-oriented feedback from their parents perceived the motivational climate to be more mastery oriented and become more task-oriented and less ego-oriented while performing. Similarly, Pensgaard and Roberts (2000) examined the relationship between motivational climate and stress in Olympic soccer players and found that a perception of a mastery climate was related to reduced stress. Hence, the motivational climate created by parents, teachers, and coaches influences achievement motivation and other important psychological states (e.g., stress).

Using Achievement Motivation in Professional Practice

Now that you better understand what achievement motivation and competitiveness involve and how they develop and influence psychological states, you can draw implications for professional practice. To help you consolidate your understanding, we now discuss some methods you can use to help the people you work with.

A coach must understand what motivates his athletes. The tactics used to motivate this athlete may be very different from the tactics used to motivate her teammates.

Recognize Interactional Factors in Achievement Motivation

You now know that the interaction of personal and situational factors influences the motivation that particular students, athletes, and exercisers have to achieve. What should you watch for to guide your practice? Essentially, you assess

- the participants' stages of achievement motivation,
- their goal orientations,
- attributions they typically make about their performances, and
- situations they tend to approach or avoid.

Let's take two examples. Jose performs well in competition, seeks out challenges, sets mastery-oriented approach goals, and attributes success to stable internal factors such as his ability. He also adopts an incremental approach where he believes hard work leads to achievement. These are desirable behaviors, and he is most likely a high achiever. Felix, on the

other hand, avoids competitors of equal ability, gravitates toward extreme competitive situations (where either success or failure is almost certain), focuses on outcome goals, becomes tense in competitions, and attributes failure to his low ability (or attributes success to external, unstable factors, such as luck). Felix is also characterized by an entity view of achievement where he views his abilities as fixed and in many ways nonmalleable. Because of this, Felix demonstrates maladaptive achievement behavior and will need your guidance.

Felix's may even be a case of **learned helplessness**, an acquired condition in which a person perceives that his or her actions have no effect on the desired outcome of a task or skill (Dweck, 1980). In other words, the person feels doomed to failure and believes that nothing can be done about it. The individual probably makes unhelpful attributions for failure and feels generally incompetent (see "Recognizing a Case of Learned Helplessness").

Emphasize Task Goals

There are several ways to help prevent maladaptive achievement tendencies or rectify learned helpless states. One of the most important strategies is to help people set task goals and downplay outcome goals. Society emphasizes athletic outcomes and student grades so much that downplaying outcome goals is not always easy. Luckily, however, sport and exercise psychologists have learned a great deal about goal setting (see more in chapter 15).

Focus on Approach Goals

Emphasize task goals as well as approach goals with students, athletes, and exercisers. Do not emphasize avoidance goals, and make an effort to intervene if students are voicing avoidance goals.

Monitor and Alter Attributional Feedback

In addition to downplaying outcome goals and emphasizing task or individual-specific mastery goals, you must be conscious of the attributions you make while giving feedback. It is not unusual for teachers, coaches, or exercise leaders to unknowingly convey subtle but powerful messages through the attributions that accompany their feedback. Adults influence a child's interpretations of performance success—and

▨ Recognizing a Case of Learned Helplessness

Johnny is a fifth grader in Ms. Roalston's second-period physical education class. He is not a very gifted student, but he can improve with consistent effort. However, after observing and getting to know Johnny, Ms. Roalston has become increasingly concerned. He demonstrates many of the characteristics of learned helplessness that she became familiar with in her university sport psychology and sport pedagogy classes.

- Johnny seldom tries new skills, usually opting instead to go to the back of the line.
- When Johnny does try a new skill and fails in his first attempt, he asks why he should even try because he's no good at sport.
- His reaction to initial failure is embarrassment and decreased effort.
- He feels so bad about his physical competence that he just wants to get out of the gym as quickly as possible.

Johnny has all the characteristics of learned helplessness. Ms. Roalston remembers that learned helplessness is not a personality flaw—it is not Johnny's fault. Rather, it results from an outcome goal orientation; maladaptive achievement tendencies; previous negative experiences with physical activity; and attributions of performance to uncontrollable, stable factors, especially low ability. Equally important, learned helplessness can vary in its specificity—it can be specific to a particular activity (e.g., learning to catch a baseball) or can be more general (e.g., learning any sport skill). Ms. Roalston knows that she can help Johnny overcome learned helplessness by giving him some individual attention, repeatedly emphasizing mastery goals, and downplaying outcome goals. Attributional retraining, or getting Johnny to change his low-ability attributions for failure, will also help him. It will take some time and hard work, but she decides that a major goal for the year is to help get Johnny out of his helpless hole.

future motivation—by how they give feedback (Biddle et al., 2001; Horn, 1987). For example, notice how this physical educator provides feedback to a child in a volleyball instructional setting:

" **You did not bump the ball correctly. Bend your knees more and contact the ball with your forearms. Try harder—you'll get it with practice.** "

The coach not only conveys instructional information to the young athlete but also informs the child that he can accomplish the task. The instructor concludes the message by stating that persistence and effort pay off. In contrast, consider the effects of telling that same child the following:

" **You did not bump the ball correctly! Your knees were not bent and you did not use your forearms. Don't worry, though—I know softball is your game, not volleyball.** "

Although well-meaning, this message informs the young athlete that she will not be good at volleyball

so she shouldn't bother trying. Of course, you should not make unrealistic attributions (e.g., telling an exerciser that with continued work and effort she will look like a model when in fact her body type makes this unlikely). Rather, the key is to emphasize mastery goals by focusing on individual improvement and then to link attributions to those individual goals (e.g., "I'll be honest: You'll never have a body like Tyra Banks or Kate Upton, but with hard work you can look and feel a lot better than you do now").

When you work with children, attributing performance failure to their low effort may be effective only if they believe they have the skills they need to ultimately achieve the task (Horn, 1987). If Jimmy believes that he is totally inept at basketball, telling him that he didn't learn to dribble because he did not try will not increase his achievement motivation—it may only reinforce his low perception of ability. Do not make low-effort attributions with children under the age of 9 unless you also reassure them that they have the skills needed to accomplish the task. The child must believe he has the skills necessary to perform the task.

Assess and Correct Inappropriate Attributions

We need to monitor and correct inappropriate or maladaptive attributions that participants make of themselves. Many performers who fail (especially those with learned helplessness) attribute their failure to low ability, saying things such as "I stink" or "Why even try? I just don't have it." They adopt an entity perspective to defining ability. Teaching children in classroom situations to replace their lack-of-ability attributions with lack-of-effort attributions helped them alleviate performance decrements after failure—this strategy was more effective than actual success (Dweck, 1975)! Moreover, attribution retraining that focuses on creating positive emotional states and expectations after success and avoiding low-ability attributions after failure has been shown to be effective in sport and physical education contexts (Biddle et al., 2001). If you hear students or clients make incorrect attributions for successful performances, such as "That was a lucky shot," correct them and indicate that hard work and practice—not luck—made the shot successful. Especially important is the need to correct participants when they make low-ability attributions after failure. Get them to change from statements such as "I stink; why even try? I will never get it" to "I'll get it if I just hang in there and focus on what my coach said to do." You have an important responsibility to ensure that participants use attributions that will facilitate achievement motivation and efforts.

 VIEW   Activity 3.4 helps you learn to empower athletes.

KEY POINT   Teaching children in classroom situations to replace lack-of-ability attributions with lack-of-effort attributions helped alleviate performance decrements after failure.

Determine When Competitive Goals Are Appropriate

You are also responsible for helping participants determine when it is appropriate to compete and when it is appropriate to focus on individual improvement. Competing is sometimes a necessity in society (e.g., to make an athletic team or to gain admission to a selective college). At times, however, competing against others is counterproductive. You wouldn't encourage a basketball player to not pass off to teammates who have better shots or a cardiac rehabilitation patient to exceed the safe training zone in order to be the fastest jogger in the group.

The key, then, is developing judgment. Through discussion you can help students, athletes, and exercisers make good decisions in this area. Society emphasizes social evaluation and competitive outcomes so much that you will need to counterbalance by stressing a task (rather than an outcome) orientation. Talking to someone once or twice about this issue is not enough. Consistent, repeated efforts are necessary to promote good judgment about appropriate competition.

Attributional Guidelines for Providing Instructor Feedback

Do

- In the case of student or client failure, emphasize the need to try harder and exert effort. However, link such attributions to individual goals and capabilities.
- In the case of student or client success, attribute success to ability.
- In the case of student or client success, attribute success to high effort.

Don't

- In the case of student or client failure, don't make low-ability attributions signifying that personal improvement is unlikely.
- In the case of student or client success, don't attribute success to luck.
- In the case of student or client success, don't attribute success to easiness of task.
- In general, don't make insincere or false attributions of any kind.

Adapted from American College of Sports Medicine 1997.

KEY POINT Make consistent and repeated use of achievement motivation strategies.

Enhance Feelings of Competence and Control

Enhancing perceived competence and enhancing feelings of control are critical ways to foster achievement motivation in physical activity participants, especially children (Weiss, 1993). You can do this by keeping practices and competitions fun and focused on achievement and by matching participant skills and abilities. Instructors can enhance competence by using appropriate feedback and reinforcement and by helping create individualized challenges and goals for participation (see chapters 6 and 15, respectively). Maximizing the *involvement* of all participants is critical for enhancing competence. Chapter 14 discusses additional means of enhancing competence.

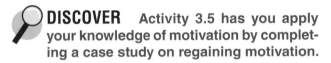 **DISCOVER** Activity 3.5 has you apply your knowledge of motivation by completing a case study on regaining motivation.

LEARNING AIDS

SUMMARY

1. **Define motivation and its components.**
   Motivation can be defined as the direction and intensity of effort. The direction of effort refers to whether an individual seeks out, approaches, or is attracted to certain situations. The intensity of effort refers to how much effort a person puts forth in a particular situation.

2. **Describe typical views of motivation and whether they are useful.**
   Three views of motivation include the trait-centered view, the situation-centered view, and the interactional view. Among these models of motivation, the participant-by-situation interactional view is the most useful for guiding professional practice.

3. **Detail useful guidelines for building motivation.**
   Five fundamental observations, derived from the interactional view of motivation, make good guidelines for practice. First, participants are motivated both by their internal traits and by situations. Second, it is important to understand participants' motives for involvement. Third, you should structure situations to meet the needs of participants. Fourth, recognize that as a teacher, coach, or exercise leader you play a critical role in the motivational environment. Fifth, use behavior modification to change participants' undesirable motives. You must also develop a realistic view of motivation: Recognize that other factors not related to motivation influence sport performance and behavior and learn to assess whether motivational factors may be readily changed.

4. **Define achievement motivation and competitiveness and indicate why they are important.**
   Achievement motivation refers to a person's efforts to master a task, achieve excellence, overcome obstacles, perform better than others, and take pride in exercising talent. Competitiveness is a disposition to strive for satisfaction when making comparisons with some standard of excellence in the presence of evaluative others. These notions are important because they help us understand why some people seem so motivated to achieve and others seem simply to go along for the ride.

5. **Compare and contrast theories of achievement motivation.**
   Theories of achievement motivation include the need achievement theory, the attribution theory, the achievement goal theory, and the competence motivation theory. Together these theories suggest that high and low achievers can be distinguished by their motives, the tasks they select to be evaluated on, the effort they exert during competition, their persistence, and their performance. High achievers usually adopt mastery (task) and approach goals and have high perceptions of their ability and control. They attribute success to stable, internal factors such as high ability and attribute failure to unstable, controllable factors such as low effort. They are characterized by an incremental view of achievement. Low achievers, on the other hand, usually have low perceived ability and control, judge themselves more on outcome goals, focus on avoidance goals, and attribute successes to luck or ease of the task (external, uncontrollable factors). They attribute failure to low ability (an internal, stable attribute). Low achievers are also characterized by an entity view of achievement.

6. **Explain how achievement motivation develops.**

   Achievement motivation and its sport-specific counterpart, competitiveness, develop through stages that include an autonomous stage when the individual focuses on mastery of her environment, a social comparison stage when the individual compares herself with others, and an integrated stage when the individual both focuses on self-improvement and uses social comparison. The goal is for the individual to reach an autonomous, integrated stage and to know when it is appropriate to compete and compare socially and when instead to adopt a self-referenced focus of comparison.

7. **Use fundamentals of achievement motivation to guide practice.**

   Parents, teachers, and coaches significantly influence the achievement motivation of children and can create climates that enhance achievement and counteract learned helplessness. They can best do this by (a) recognizing interactional influences on achievement motivation, (b) emphasizing individual task goals and downplaying outcome goals, (c) monitoring the attributions made by those with whom you work and providing appropriate attributional feedback, (d) teaching participants to make appropriate attributions, (e) discussing with participants when it is appropriate to compete and compare themselves socially and when it is appropriate to adopt a self-referenced focus, and (f) facilitating perceptions of competence and control.

KEY TERMS

motivation
direction of effort
intensity of effort
trait-centered view (participant-centered view)
situation-centered view
interactional view
achievement motivation
competitiveness
need achievement theory
probability of success
incentive value of success
resultant tendency (behavioral tendency)

attribution theory
stability
locus of causality
locus of control
achievement goal theory
outcome goal orientation (competitive goal orientation, ego orientation)
task goal orientation (mastery goal orientation)
entity view
incremental focus
competence motivation theory
learned helplessness

REVIEW QUESTIONS

1. Explain the direction and intensity aspects of motivation.
2. Identify three general views of motivation. Which should be used to guide practice?
3. Describe five fundamental guidelines of motivation for professional practice.
4. What are the primary motives people have for participating in sport? What are their primary motives for participating in exercise activities?
5. In what ways does achievement motivation influence participant behavior?
6. Explain and distinguish four theories that explain achievement motivation.
7. What are attributions? Why are they important in helping us understand achievement motivation in sport and exercise settings?
8. Distinguish between an outcome (competitive) and a task (mastery) goal orientation. Which should be most emphasized in sport, physical education, and exercise settings? Why?
9. Identify the three stages of achievement motivation and competitiveness. Why are these important?
10. Discuss how a teacher's or coach's attributional feedback influences participant achievement. What is learned helplessness? Why is it important?

CRITICAL THINKING QUESTIONS

1. List at least three ways to better understand someone's motives for involvement in sport and physical activity.
2. Design a program that eliminates learned helplessness in performers. Indicate how you will foster an appropriate motivational climate.

Arousal, Stress, and Anxiety

After reading this chapter, you should be able to

1. discuss the nature of stress and anxiety (what they are and how they are measured),
2. identify the major sources of anxiety and stress,
3. explain how and why arousal- and anxiety-related emotions affect performance, and
4. compare and contrast ways to regulate arousal, stress, and anxiety.

Jason comes to bat in the bottom of the final inning with two outs and two men on base. With a hit, his team will win the district championship; with an out, his team will lose the biggest game of the season. Jason steps into the batter's box, his heart pounding and butterflies in his stomach, and has trouble maintaining concentration. He thinks of what a win will mean for his team and of what people might think of him if he does not deliver. Planting his cleats in the dirt, Jason squeezes the bat, says a little prayer, and awaits the first pitch.

If you're involved in athletics, you have probably faced the elevated arousal and anxiety of situations such as Jason's. Consider the following quote from Bill Shankly, former manager of Liverpool Football Club, regarding the importance of winning and losing in competitive sport:

" **Some people think football is a matter of life and death. I don't take that attitude. I can assure them it is much more serious than that. (Shankly, 1981)** "

Although pressure is all too real in military and emergency services settings, where life and death can truly rest on one's decisions, coping skills, and eventual performance (e.g., Janelle & Hatfield, 2008), success and failure in competitive sport—especially at high levels—can also produce extreme anxiety. History is replete with athletes who have performed exceedingly well under pressure (see chapter 11 for a discussion of mental toughness) and those who have performed exceedingly poorly (see chapter 16 for a discussion of choking). It is no surprise that the relationship between competitive anxiety and performance has been one of the most debated and investigated topics in sport psychology (for reviews, see Hanton, Neil, & Mellalieu, 2008, 2011). Sport and exercise psychologists have long studied the causes and effects of arousal, stress, and anxiety in the competitive athletic environment and other areas of physical activity. Many health care professionals are interested in both the physiological and psychological benefits of regular exercise. Does regular exercise lower stress levels? Will patients with severe anxiety disorders benefit from intensive aerobic training and need less medication? Consider how stress provoking learning to swim can be for people who have had a bad experience in water. How can teachers reduce this anxiety?

Defining Arousal and Anxiety

Although many people use the terms *arousal, stress,* and *anxiety* interchangeably, sport and exercise psychologists find it important to distinguish among them. Psychologists use precise definitions for the phenomena they study in order to have a common language, reduce confusion, and diminish the need for long explanations.

Arousal

Arousal is a blend of physiological and psychological activity in a person, and it refers to the intensity dimensions of motivation at a particular moment. The intensity of arousal falls along a continuum (figure 4.1) ranging from not at all aroused (i.e., comatose) to completely aroused (i.e., frenzied; see Gould, Greenleaf, & Krane, 2002). Highly aroused individuals are mentally and physically activated; they have increased heart rates, respiration, and sweating. Arousal is not automatically associated with either pleasant or unpleasant events. You might be highly aroused by learning that you have won $10 million. You might be equally aroused by learning of the death of a loved one.

Anxiety

In a general sense, **anxiety** is a negative emotional state characterized by nervousness, worry, and apprehension and associated with activation or arousal of the body. (Although anxiety is perceived as negative or unpleasant, it does not necessarily affect performance negatively; this is discussed later in the chapter.) In sport settings, anxiety refers to "an unpleasant psychological state in reaction to perceived stress concerning the performance of a task under pressure" (Cheng, Hardy, & Markland, 2009, p. 271). Anxiety has a thought component (e.g., worry and apprehension) called **cognitive anxiety**. It also has a component called **somatic anxiety**, which is the degree of physical activation perceived. In addition to the distinction between cognitive and somatic anxiety, it is important to distinguish between state and trait anxiety.

> **KEY POINTS**
> - Arousal is a general physiological and psychological activation that varies on a continuum from deep sleep to intense excitement.
> - Anxiety is a negative emotional state in which feelings of nervousness, worry, and apprehension are associated with activation or arousal of the body.

State Anxiety

At times we refer to anxiety as a *stable* personality component; other times we use the term to describe a *changing* mood state. **State anxiety** refers to the ever-changing mood component. It is defined more formally as an emotional state "characterized by subjective, consciously perceived feelings of apprehension and tension, accompanied by or associated with activation or arousal of the autonomic nervous system" (Spielberger, 1966, p. 17). For example, a player's level of state anxiety changes from moment to moment during a basketball game. She might have a slightly elevated level of state anxiety (feeling somewhat nervous and noticing her heart pumping) before tip-off, a lower level once she settles into the pace of the game, and then an extremely high level (feeling very nervous, with her heart racing) in the closing minutes of a tight contest.

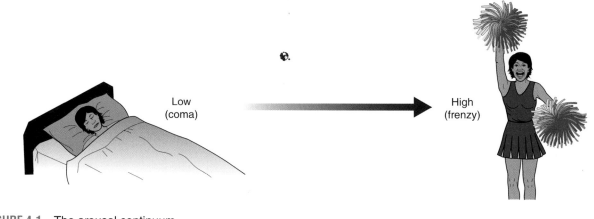

Low
(coma)

High
(frenzy)

FIGURE 4.1 The arousal continuum.

Cognitive state anxiety concerns the degree to which one worries or has negative thoughts, whereas **somatic state anxiety** concerns the moment-to-moment changes in perceived physiological activation. Somatic state anxiety is not necessarily a change in one's physical activation but rather one's perception of such a change. Recent research also suggests that there is a **perceived control** or regulatory component of state anxiety; that is, the degree to which one believes one has the resources and ability to meet challenges is an important component of state anxiety as well (Cheng, Hardy, & Markland, 2009).

> **KEY POINT** State anxiety is a temporary, ever-changing emotional state of subjective, consciously perceived feelings of apprehension and tension associated with activation of the autonomic nervous system.

Trait Anxiety

Unlike state anxiety, **trait anxiety** is part of the personality, an acquired behavioral tendency or disposition that influences behavior. In particular, trait anxiety predisposes an individual to perceive as threatening a wide range of circumstances that objectively may not actually be physically or psychologically dangerous. The person then responds to these circumstances with state anxiety reactions or levels that are disproportionate in intensity and magnitude to the objective danger (Spielberger, 1966, p. 17).

For instance, two field-goal kickers with equal physical skills may be placed under identical pressure (e.g., to kick the winning field goal at the end of the game) yet have entirely different state anxiety reactions because of their personalities (i.e., their levels of trait anxiety). Rick is more laid back (low trait-anxious) and does not perceive kicking the game-winning field goal as overly threatening. Thus, he does not have more state anxiety than would be expected in such a situation. Ted, however, is high trait-anxious and consequently perceives the chance to kick (or, in his view, to miss) the winning field goal as very threatening. He has tremendous state anxiety—much more than we would expect in such a situation.

Finally, like state anxiety, trait anxiety has different components. For example, the Sport Anxiety Scale originally developed by Smith, Smoll, and Schutz (1990) and updated and extended to young athletes (the Sport Anxiety Scale-2; SAS-2) (Smith, Smoll, Cumming, & Grossbard, 2006) is one of the more widely used measures in the field and breaks trait anxiety down into three components as well as a total score. The three components include somatic trait anxiety (e.g., the degree to which one typically perceives heightened physical symptoms such as muscle tension), cognitive trait anxiety (e.g., the degree to which one typically worries or has self-doubt), and concentration disruption (e.g., the degree to which one typically has concentration disruption during competition). See figure 4.2 for a summary of the interrelationships among arousal, trait anxiety, and state anxiety.

> **KEY POINT** Trait anxiety is a behavioral disposition to perceive as threatening circumstances that objectively may not be dangerous and to then respond with disproportionate state anxiety. People with high trait anxiety usually have more state anxiety in highly competitive, evaluative situations than do people with lower trait anxiety.

Measuring Arousal and Anxiety

Sport and exercise psychologists measure arousal, state anxiety, and trait anxiety in various physiological ways and through psychological measures. To measure arousal they look at changes in these physiological signs: heart rate, respiration, skin conductance (recorded on a voltage meter), and biochemistry (used to assess changes in substances such as catecholamines). These psychologists also look at how people rate their arousal levels using a series of statements (e.g., "My heart is pumping," "I feel peppy") and numerical scales ranging from low to high. Such scales are referred to as **self-report measures** of arousal and anxiety.

To measure state anxiety, psychologists use both global and multidimensional self-report measures. In the global measures, people rate how nervous they feel using **self-report scales** from low to high. Summing the scores of individual items produces a total score. The multidimensional self-report measures are used in about the same way, but people rate how worried (cognitive state anxiety) and how physiologically activated (somatic state anxiety) they feel, again using self-report scales ranging from low to high. Subscale scores for cognitive and somatic anxiety are obtained by summing scores for items representing each type of state anxiety. Sport-specific scales that measure state anxiety in sport have been developed to better predict one's anxiety state in competitive sport settings. One example is the widely used Competitive State Anxiety

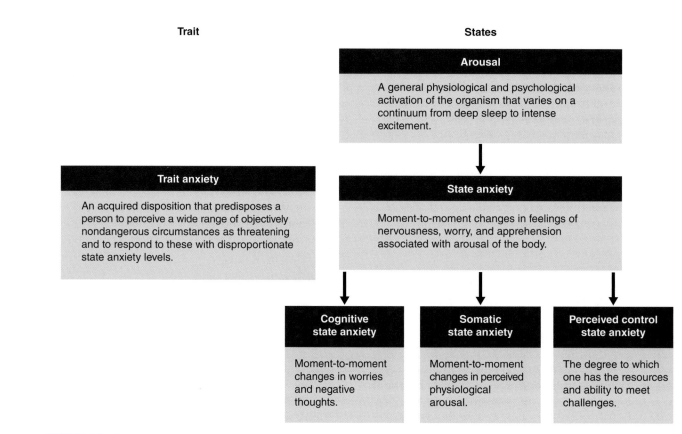

Trait

States

Arousal

A general physiological and psychological activation of the organism that varies on a continuum from deep sleep to intense excitement.

Trait anxiety

An acquired disposition that predisposes a person to perceive a wide range of objectively nondangerous circumstances as threatening and to respond to these with disproportionate state anxiety levels.

State anxiety

Moment-to-moment changes in feelings of nervousness, worry, and apprehension associated with arousal of the body.

Cognitive state anxiety

Moment-to-moment changes in worries and negative thoughts.

Somatic state anxiety

Moment-to-moment changes in perceived physiological arousal.

Perceived control state anxiety

The degree to which one has the resources and ability to meet challenges.

FIGURE 4.2 The interrelationships among arousal, trait anxiety, and state anxiety.

Emotions and Sport and Exercise Psychology

Although the focus of this chapter is on arousal and anxiety, it is important to note that many sport and exercise psychologists have begun to study various emotions in athletes and exercisers. For example, in chapter 17 we examine how participation in physical activity influences a range of participant emotions such as depression, anxiety, and pleasure; later in this chapter we discuss how arousal- and anxiety-associated emotions are related to athletic performance. Think about it. You get frustrated if you make a mistake or get pleasure from performing well while playing your favorite sport. You also feel less anxious after you exercise or less frightened by some challenge facing you. Emotions are everywhere in sport and exercise settings. A challenge that sport psychologists face in studying emotions is defining them and differentiating them from related phenomena such as moods and feeling states. Gill and Williams (2008) indicate that **emotions** are complex phenomena, "short-lived feeling states that occur in response to events" that one has. They comprise both physiological and psychological components and unfold as a process rather than a static episodic event. Conversely, Jones (2012) proposes that mood is a more enduring state, less intense than an emotion, in which the individual does not know the causes of feelings. Despite these distinctions, the boundaries between mood and emotion are often blurred, especially when a person is unable to distinguish between feelings triggered in response to specific events (emotions) and those already present as part of an underlying mood state.

The leading researcher in this field, psychologist Richard Lazarus (2000), defined emotion as "an organized psychophysiological reaction to ongoing relationships with the environment, most often, but not always, interpersonal or social," involving subjective experiences, observable actions or impulses to act, and physiological changes. Finally, emotions can be both positive (e.g., pleasure) and negative (e.g., shame). Common emotions include anger, anxiety, fright, guilt, shame, sadness, envy, jealousy, happiness, pride, relief, hope, love, gratitude, and compassion (Lazarus, 2000). As we move through this book, you will learn about how many of these emotions influence or are influenced by participating in sport and physical activity.

Inventory-2 (CSAI-2) (Martens, Vealey, & Burton, 1990), displayed here.

Psychologists also use global and multidimensional self-reports to measure trait anxiety. The formats for these measures are similar to those for state anxiety assessments; however, instead of rating how anxious they feel right at that moment, people are asked how they typically feel. Sport-specific trait anxiety scales have been developed; one example is the SAS-2 mentioned earlier (Smith et al., 2006). To better understand the differences among cognitive state anxiety, somatic state anxiety, and trait anxiety in sport, complete the sample questions from the CSAI-2 and SAS-2 self-report scales.

DISCOVER   Activity 4.1 measures your trait and state anxiety.

A direct relationship exists between a person's levels of trait anxiety and state anxiety. Research has consistently shown that those who score high on trait anxiety measures also have more state anxiety in highly competitive, evaluative situations. This relationship is not perfect, however. A highly trait-anxious athlete may have a tremendous amount of experience in a particular situation and therefore not perceive a threat and the corresponding high state anxiety. Similarly, some highly trait-anxious people learn coping skills to help reduce the state anxiety they experience in evaluative situations. Still, generally speaking, knowing a person's level of trait anxiety is usually helpful in predicting how that person will react to competition, evaluation, and threatening conditions.

To make matters more complex, we know from anecdotal reports as well as research (e.g., Butt, Weinberg, & Horn, 2003) that anxiety can fluctuate throughout competition. For example, we often hear football players say that they felt very anxious before competition but settled down after the first hit. (Interestingly, it appears that somatic anxiety levels decrease rapidly when competition starts but that cognitive anxiety levels change throughout competition.) Others in soccer have reported that they did not feel anxious throughout a game but that their anxiety level went "sky high" when they had to take a penalty kick at the end of the game. Future measures need to assess these changes in anxiety, although it is difficult to do so during a competition. One possible strategy is to retrospectively measure changes in anxiety. Research has indicated that athletes are quite good at assessing

Competitive State Anxiety Inventory-2

Following are several statements that athletes have used to describe their feelings before a competition. For the purposes of this exercise, think of a competition in which you have participated. Read each statement and then circle the appropriate number to the right of the statement to indicate how you felt at that moment. There are no right or wrong answers. Don't spend too much time on any one statement, but choose the answer that best describes your feelings at that particular time.

Statement	Not at all	Somewhat	Moderately so	Very much so
1. I am concerned about this competition.	1	2	3	4
2. I feel nervous.	1	2	3	4
3. I feel at ease.	1	2	3	4
4. I have self-doubts.	1	2	3	4
5. I feel jittery.	1	2	3	4
6. I feel comfortable.	1	2	3	4
7. I am concerned that I may not do as well as I could in this competition.	1	2	3	4
8. My body feels tense.	1	2	3	4
9. I feel self-confident.	1	2	3	4

Sport Anxiety Scale-2 (SAS-2): A Measure of Trait Anxiety

Following are several statements that athletes have used to describe their thoughts and feelings before or during competition. Read each statement and then circle the number to the right of the statement that indicates how you usually feel before or during competition. Some athletes feel they should not admit to feeling nervous or worried, but such reactions are actually quite common, even among professional athletes. To help us better understand reactions to competition, we ask you to share your true reactions. There are no right or wrong answers. Do not spend too much time on any one statement.

Statement	Not at all	Somewhat	Moderately so	Very much so
1. My body feels tense.	1	2	3	4
2. I worry that I will play badly.	1	2	3	4
3. I cannot think clearly during the game.	1	2	3	4
4. My stomach feels upset.	1	2	3	4
5. It is hard to concentrate on the game.	1	2	3	4
6. I worry that I will let others down.	1	2	3	4

their state anxiety levels after the fact (Hanin & Syrja, 1996). For example, athletes could be asked within an hour of finishing a game about how they felt at different times throughout the game.

Defining Stress and Understanding the Stress Process

Stress is defined as "a substantial imbalance between demand (physical and/or psychological) and response capability, under conditions where failure to meet that demand has important consequences" (McGrath, 1970, p. 20). It is a process or a sequence of events that will lead to a particular end. According to a simple model that McGrath proposed, stress consists of four interrelated stages, which are depicted in figure 4.3: environmental demand, perception of demand, stress response, and behavioral consequences. Here we briefly describe these stages.

KEY POINT Stress occurs when a substantial imbalance exists between the physical and psychological demands placed on an individual and that person's response capability under conditions in which failure to meet the demand has important consequences.

Stage 1: Environmental Demand

In the first stage of the stress process, some type of demand is placed on an individual. The demand might be physical, such as when a physical education student has to execute a newly learned volleyball skill in front of the class, or psychological, such as when parents are pressuring a young athlete to win a race.

Stage 2: Perception of Demand

The second stage of the stress process is the individual's perception of the physical or psychological demand. People do not perceive demands in exactly the same way. For instance, two eighth graders may view having to demonstrate a newly learned volleyball skill in front of the class quite differently. Maya may enjoy the attention of being in front of the class, whereas Issaha may feel threatened. That is, Issaha perceives an imbalance between the demands placed on him (having to demonstrate in front of the class) and his ability to meet those demands. Maya perceives no such imbalance or perceives it only to a nonthreatening degree.

A person's level of trait anxiety greatly influences how that person perceives the world. Highly trait-anxious people tend to perceive more situations—especially evaluative and competitive ones—as threatening than lower-trait-anxious people do. For this reason trait anxiety is an important influence in stage 2 of the stress process.

Stage 3: Stress Response

The third stage of the stress process is the individual's physical and psychological response to a perception of the situation. If someone's perception of an imbalance between demands and his response capability causes him to feel threatened, increased state anxiety results, bringing with it increased worries (cognitive state anxiety), heightened physiological activation (somatic state anxiety), or both. Other reactions, such as changes in concentration and increased muscle tension, accompany increased state anxiety as well.

Stage 4: Behavioral Consequences

The fourth stage is the actual behavior of the individual under stress. If a volleyball student perceives an imbalance between capability and demands and feels increased state anxiety, does performance deteriorate? Or does the increased state anxiety increase intensity of effort, thereby improving performance?

The final stage of the stress process feeds back into the first. If a student becomes overly threatened and performs poorly in front of the class, the other children may laugh; this negative social evaluation becomes an additional demand on the child (stage 1). The stress process, then, becomes a continuing cycle (figure 4.3).

Implications for Practice

The stress process has a number of implications for practice. If a corporate fitness specialist is asked by her company's personnel director to help develop a stress management program for the company's employees, for example, stage 1 of the model suggests that she should determine what demands are placed on the employees (e.g., increased workloads, unrealistic scheduling demands, hectic travel schedules). An analysis of stage 2 might lead her to question who is experiencing or perceiving the most stress (e.g., individuals in certain divisions or with certain jobs, or those with certain personality dispositions). Stage 3 would call for studying the reactions the employees are having to the increased stress: somatic state anxiety, cognitive state anxiety, or attention–concentration problems. Stage 4 analysis would focus on the subse-

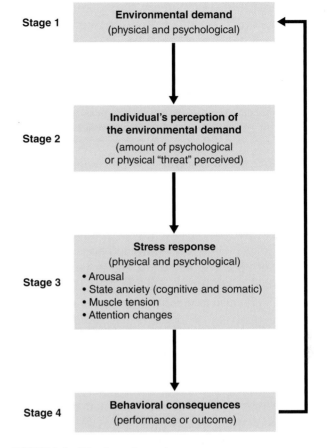

FIGURE 4.3 The four-stage stress process.

quent behavior of employees feeling increased stress, such as greater absenteeism, reduced productivity, or decreased job satisfaction. By understanding this stress cycle, the fitness director can target her efforts to reduce stress. She might suggest physical activity (most likely in stage 3) or other means of stress management (e.g., time management seminars, restructured work schedules). She now has a better grasp of the specific causes and consequences of stress, which allows her to design more effective stress management activities.

Identifying Sources of Stress and Anxiety

There are thousands of specific sources of stress. Exercise psychologists have also shown that major life events such as a job change or a death in the family, as well as daily hassles such as an auto breakdown or a problem with a coworker, cause stress and affect physical and mental health (Berger, Pargman, &

Weinberg, 2007). In athletes, stressors include performance issues such as worrying about performing up to capabilities, self-doubts about talent, and team selection; environmental issues such as financial costs, travel, and time needed for training; organizational issues such as coaching leadership and communication; physical danger; negative personal rapport behaviors of coaches; and relationships or traumatic experiences outside of sport, such as the death of a family member or negative interpersonal relationships (Dunn & Syrotuik, 2003; Noblet & Gifford, 2002; Woodman & Hardy, 2001a). McKay, Niven, Lavallee, and White (2008) recently concluded that athletes experience a core group of stress or strain sources that include competitive concerns, pressure to perform, lifestyle demands, and negative aspects of personal relationships. Gould, Udry, Bridges, and Beck (1997a) also found that injured elite athletes had psychological (e.g., fear, shattered hopes and dreams), physical, medical- or rehab-related, financial, and career stress sources along with missed opportunities outside the sport (e.g., inability to visit another country with the team).

Researchers have also examined sources of stress for coaches; these include such issues as communicating with athletes, recruiting, the pressure of having so many roles, and a lack of control over their athletes' performance (Frey, 2007). Furthermore, stress sources in officials include controversial calls, confrontations with coaches, difficulties working with a partner official, and physical abuse (Dorsch & Paskevich, 2007; Voight, 2009). Finally, parental pressure (especially with young athletes) has been a traditional source of stress, although a recent study found that the climate in which the pressure is perceived can alter its effects (O'Rourke, Smith, Smoll, & Cumming, 2011). Specifically, researchers found that high pressure in a highly ego motivational climate (i.e., focus on outcome) increased perceptions of anxiety but high pressure in a highly mastery motivational climate (i.e., focus on improvement) decreased perceptions of anxiety. The many specific sources of stress for those participating in sport and physical activity contexts fall into some general categories determined by both situation and personality.

DISCOVER Activity 4.2 helps you identify potential stress sources you may encounter in your sport and exercise science career.

Situational Sources of Stress

Two common sources of situational stress exist. These general areas are the importance placed on an event or contest and the uncertainty that surrounds the outcome of that event (Martens, 1987b).

Event Importance

In general, the more important the event, the more stress provoking it is. Thus, a championship contest is more stressful than a regular-season game, just as taking college boards is more stressful than taking a practice exam. Little League baseball players, for example, were observed each time they came to bat over an entire baseball season (Lowe, 1971). The batters' heart rates were recorded while they were at bat and their nervous mannerisms on deck were observed. How critical the situation at bat was in the game (e.g., bases loaded, two outs, last inning, close score) and how important the game was in the season standings were both rated. The more critical the situation, the more stress and nervousness the young athletes exhibited.

> **KEY POINT** The more important an event, the more stress provoking it will be. The greater the degree of uncertainty an individual feels about an outcome or others' feelings and evaluations, the greater the state anxiety and stress.

The importance placed on an event is not always obvious, however. An event that may seem insignificant to most people may be very important for one particular person. For instance, a regular-season soccer game may not seem particularly important to most players on a team that has locked up a championship. Yet it may be of major importance to a particular player who is being observed by a college scout. You must continually assess the importance participants attach to activities.

Uncertainty

Uncertainty is a major situational source of stress; the greater the uncertainty, the greater the stress. Often we cannot do anything about uncertainty. For example, when two evenly matched teams are scheduled to compete, there is maximum uncertainty but little can or should be done about it. After all, the essence of sport is to put evenly matched athletes and teams together. However, at times teachers, coaches, and sports medicine professionals create unnecessary uncertainty by not informing participants of things such as the starting lineups, how to avoid injury in learning high-risk physical skills (e.g., vaulting in gymnastics), or what to expect while recovering from a serious athletic injury. Trainers, teachers, and coaches should be aware of how they might unknowingly create uncertainty in participants.

Uncertainty is not limited to the field or the gym. Athletes and exercisers can have stress as a result of uncertainty in their lives in general. For example, a study of Australian football players found that uncertainties about one's career, one's future after football, relocation, and work and nonwork conflicts were major stress sources (Noblet & Gifford, 2002). Similarly, a retired person who exercises might be stressed because of economic uncertainty resulting from volatility in the stock market. Therefore, teachers, coaches, and trainers need to understand uncertainty that may be going on in a client's or athlete's life outside of sport and exercise.

Personal Sources of Stress

Some people characterize particular situations as important and uncertain and view them with greater anxiety than other people do. Two personality dispositions that consistently relate to heightened state anxiety reactions are high trait anxiety and low self-esteem (Scanlan, 1986). A third important anxiety disposition in the context of exercise is social physique anxiety.

Trait Anxiety

As previously discussed, trait anxiety is a personality factor that predisposes a person to view competition and social evaluation as more or less threatening. A highly trait-anxious person perceives competition as more threatening and anxiety provoking than a lower trait-anxious person does. In fact, research shows that individuals with high trait anxiety have a cognitive bias to pick out more threat-related information in the same situation than their peers with low trait anxiety do.

> **KEY POINT** High trait anxiety and low self-esteem are related to heightened state anxiety reactions in athletes.

Self-Esteem

Self-esteem is also related to perceptions of threat and corresponding changes in state anxiety. Athletes with low self-esteem, for example, have less confidence and more state anxiety than do athletes with high self-esteem. Strategies for enhancing self-confidence are important means of reducing the amount of state anxiety that individuals experience.

Social Physique Anxiety

Social physique anxiety is a personality disposition defined as "the degree to which people become anxious when others observe their physiques" (Hart, Leary, & Rejeski, 1989). It reflects people's tendency to become nervous or apprehensive when their body is evaluated (Eklund, Kelley, & Wilson, 1997). Compared with people without this kind of anxiety, people with high social physique anxiety report experiencing more stress during fitness evaluations and experiencing more negative thoughts about their bodies. It has also been found that a negative relationship exists between social physique anxiety and exercise behavior and perceived physical ability (Hausenblas, Brewer, & Van Raalte, 2004) and that social physique anxiety is related to need satisfaction, physical activity motivation, and behavior (Brunet & Sabiston, 2009). People with high social physique anxiety, then, are likely to avoid fitness settings or struggle with motivation when they participate because they fear how others will evaluate their physiques. Females in particular are susceptible to social physique anxiety because today's culture places a tremendous emphasis on the body and female attractiveness (Roper, 2012). An encouraging finding is that physical activity interventions can reduce social physique anxiety in participants (Hausenblas et al., 2004). For example, if you can reduce people's social physique anxiety by having them exercise in less revealing shorts and T-shirts instead of tight-fitting clothes, you can increase their participation in physical activity (Crawford & Eklund, 1994).

Connecting Arousal and Anxiety to Performance

One of the most compelling relationships that sport and exercise psychologists study is the relationship (positive or negative) between arousal, anxiety, and emotional states on one hand and performance on the other. Most of us recognize readily enough when our nerves make us feel vulnerable and out of control. But how exactly do physiological arousal and psychological arousal function to the advantage of one person and the detriment of another? How does it happen that even

Can the uniforms popular with a sport discourage participation? Can they lead to anxiety?

in our own performance on a single afternoon, we can notice fluctuations in anxiety levels and their effects?

Sport and exercise psychologists have studied the relationship between anxiety and performance for decades. They haven't reached definitive conclusions, but they have illuminated aspects of the process that have several implications for helping people psych up and perform better rather than psych out and perform poorly. Some 60 years ago, researchers concentrated on drive theory, which was later used in the 1960s and 1970s to explain social facilitation. In the past quarter-century psychologists have found the inverted-U hypothesis more convincing, and still more recently they have proposed some variations and newer hypotheses, including the concepts of zones of optimal functioning, multidimensional anxiety theory, the catastrophe phenomenon, reversal theory, and the anxiety direction and intensity view. We discuss each of these briefly.

Drive Theory

Psychologists first saw the relationship between arousal and performance as direct and linear (Spence & Spence, 1966). According to this view, called **drive theory**, as an individual's arousal or state anxiety increases, so too does her performance. The more

psyched up an athlete becomes, for example, the better that individual performs. Most athletes, of course, can also remember situations in which they became overly aroused or overly anxious and then performed more poorly. Little scholarly support exists for the drive theory (Mellalieu, Hanton, & Fletcher, 2006).

You may recall the social facilitation theory (the example of a theory we used in chapter 1). Zajonc (1965) observed a pattern in the seemingly random way in which people sometimes performed better in front of an audience and other times performed worse. His observation was that the presence of an audience had a positive effect when people performed tasks that they knew well or that were simple, whereas their performance suffered when they performed less familiar or more complex tasks. Zajonc's social facilitation theory contended that an audience creates arousal in the performer, which hurts performance on difficult tasks that are not yet learned but helps performance on well-learned tasks.

KEY POINT Social facilitation theory predicts that the presence of others helps performance on well-learned or simple skills and inhibits or lessens performance on unlearned or complex tasks.

An audience need not be present for social facilitation to occur. The theory refers more broadly to the effects of the presence of others on performance, including coaction (two people performing simultaneously). Zajonc (1965) used drive theory to show that the presence of others increases arousal in the performer and that this increased arousal (drive) increases or brings out the performer's dominant response (the most likely way to perform the skill). When people perform well-learned or simple skills (e.g., sit-ups), the dominant response is correct (positive performance) and the increased arousal facilitates performance. When people perform complex or unlearned skills (e.g., a novice golfer learning to drive a golf ball), the presence of others increases arousal and more often causes their dominant response to be incorrect (poorer performance). Thus, social facilitation theory predicts that an audience (i.e., coaction or the presence of others) inhibits performance on tasks that are complex or have not been learned thoroughly and enhances performance on tasks that are simple or have been learned well.

The implications are that you would want to eliminate audiences and evaluation as much as possible in learning situations. For example, if you were teaching a gymnastics routine, you would not want to expose youngsters to an audience too soon. It is critical to eliminate or lessen audience and coaction effects in learning environments to make them as arousal free as possible. However, when participants are performing well-learned or simple tasks, you might want to encourage people to come watch.

Although the drive and social facilitation theories explain how an audience can hurt performance when one is learning new skills, they do not explain so well how an audience affects a person's performance of well-learned skills. These theories predict that as arousal increases, performance increases in a straight line. If this were true, we would expect highly skilled athletes to consistently excel in all high-pressure situations. Yet nervousness and choking in the clutch occur even at the elite level. For this reason, we can only conclude that on well-learned skills, an audience may sometimes enhance performance and at other times inhibit it. The views presented next will give you a better understanding of how increased arousal or anxiety influences performance on well-learned tasks. In addition, "Home-Court Advantage: Myth or Reality" discusses what sport psychology researchers have learned about the home-field advantage—a topic

related to both audience effects and the relationship between anxiety and performance.

Inverted-U Hypothesis

Dissatisfied with the drive theory, most sport psychologists turned to the **inverted-U hypothesis** to explain the relationship between arousal states and performance (Landers & Arent, 2010). This view holds that at low arousal levels, performance will be below par (figure 4.4); the exerciser or athlete is not psyched up. As arousal increases, so too does performance—up to an optimal point where best performance results. Further increases in arousal, however, cause performance to decline. This view is represented by an inverted U that reflects high performance with the optimal level of arousal and lesser performance with either low or very high arousal.

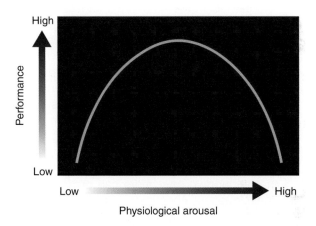

FIGURE 4.4 The inverted U showing the relationship between arousal and performance.

Most athletes and coaches accept the general notions of the inverted-U hypothesis. After all, most people have experienced underarousal, optimal arousal, and overarousal. However, despite the acceptance of the hypothesis in general and recent evidence supporting its predictions on relatively simple tasks (Landers & Arent, 2010), it has come under criticism (Gould & Udry, 1994; Mellalieu et al., 2006). Critics rightly question the shape of the arousal curve, ask whether optimal arousal always occurs at the midpoint of the arousal continuum, and question the nature of the arousal itself. In essence, the inverted U has taken us as far as it can, but now we need more explicit explanations. Hence, sport psychologists have begun to explore other views, hoping to more specifically understand the arousal–performance relationship.

Home-Court Advantage: Myth or Reality

One way spectators influence performance is by providing support and encouragement for the home team. In fact, in many sports, teams battle throughout the season for the best record so that they can have the home-court advantage during the play-offs. Do teams really win more at home than on the road?

Research has shown that teams actually do win more at home and that the advantage is fairly small in football and baseball but quite large in basketball and hockey. Because the latter two sports are played in intimate indoor sites, compared with the more open outdoor stadiums of baseball and football, it may be that the proximity of the fans to the action and the noise level they generate in enclosed facilities enhance players' performance. The continual flow of activity in hockey and basketball might also make it easier for a crowd to get emotionally involved and thus play a part in motivating and arousing the players. The increased level of involvement is reflected in elevated noise levels and emotional outbursts, such as sustained booing of referees or opposing coaches.

Despite the evidence supporting the home-court advantage during the regular season, other findings have indicated that this advantage might be lost in the play-offs and championship games. In fact, the home court might even become a disadvantage. For example, in a study of baseball World Series games played from 1924 to 1982, Baumeister and Steinhilber (1984) found that in series that went at least five games, the home team won 60% of the first two games but only 40% of the last two games. In the 26 series that have gone to a final and deciding seventh game, the home team won only 38% of the time. To test the generalizability of these results, the researchers conducted a similar analysis on professional basketball. Home teams won 70% of the first four games. However, the home team's winning percentage was 46% during the fifth and sixth games and dropped to a dismal 38% for the deciding seventh game.

Thus, the home-court advantage turned to a disadvantage as games became more critical and the pressure mounted. Game statistics were gathered to determine how and why this occurred. In both baseball and basketball, the visiting teams' performance remained fairly consistent throughout the series. However, the home teams' performance significantly decreased as games became more critical, producing more errors in baseball and lower foul shooting in basketball. In essence, home teams were choking under pressure instead of getting a lift from their fans. Researchers argue that supportive spectators can create expectations for success, which in turn can increase self-consciousness in athletes, causing them to think too much instead of simply playing and performing automatically, as is characteristic of highly skilled athletes. This results in a "championship choke."

However, the success of home teams in basketball appears to have shifted over the years. Specifically, from 1984 to 1994 the home team won 18 consecutive seventh and deciding games during the National Basketball Association (NBA) play-offs. In addition, when focusing just on game 7 of the NBA finals, the home team won 15 and lost only 3. It's possible that coaches and athletes have become more knowledgeable about putting too much pressure on themselves in critical games, thus reducing self-consciousness and letting the emotion of hometown fans carry them to victory.

So, looking at the research in this area in general, what is the bottom line? Home-field advantage or disadvantage?

- During the regular season, a clear home-field advantage exists for both professional and amateur team sports and dates back almost 100 years.

- The home-field advantage occurs for both team and individual sports and for both male and female athletes.

- Researchers propose that a home-field disadvantage exists during play-offs, but the evidence supporting this concept in sport is mixed. Leading group dynamics researchers Carron, Hausenblas, and Eys (2005) concluded that the jury is still out on the home-field disadvantage in championship games. They noted, however, that nonsport research supports the idea of choking in a championship as a result of performer self-consciousness.

- Athletes bound for play-offs should have well-developed strategies for coping with anxiety in order to prevent negative attentional effects that interfere with performance.

Individualized Zones of Optimal Functioning

Yuri Hanin, a noted Russian sport psychologist, presented an alternative view called the **individualized zones of optimal functioning (IZOF)** model. Hanin (1980, 1986, 1997) found that top athletes have a zone of optimal state anxiety in which their best performance occurs. Outside this zone, poor performance occurs.

Hanin's IZOF view differs from the inverted-U hypothesis in two important ways. First, the optimal level of state anxiety does not always occur at the midpoint of the continuum but rather varies from individual to individual. That is, some athletes have a zone of optimal functioning at the lower end of the continuum, some in the midrange, and others at the upper end (figure 4.5). Second, the optimal level of state anxiety is not a single point but a bandwidth. Thus, coaches and teachers should help participants identify and reach their own specific optimal zone of state anxiety. However, despite the support that exists for the IZOF model, it has been criticized for its lack of explanation of why individual levels of anxiety may be optimal or detrimental for performance (Woodman & Hardy, 2001b).

The IZOF model has good support in the research literature (e.g., Gould & Tuffey, 1996; Hanin, 2007). In addition, Hanin (1997, 2000, 2007) expanded the IZOF notion beyond anxiety to show how zones of optimal functioning use a variety of emotions and other psychobiosocial states, such as determination, pleasantness, and laziness. He concluded that for best performance to occur, athletes need individualized optimal levels not only of state anxiety but of a variety of other emotions as well. The IZOF view also contends that there are positive (e.g., confident, excited) and negative (e.g., fearful, nervous) emotions that enhance performance and positive (e.g., calm, comfortable) and negative (e.g., intense, annoyed) emotions that have a dysfunctional influence on performance. This development is important because it recognizes that a given emotion (e.g., anger) can be positively associated with performance for one person but negatively associated with performance for another. A major coaching implication of the IZOF model, then, is that coaches must help each individual athlete achieve the ideal recipe of positive and negative emotions needed by that athlete for best performance.

> **KEY POINT** A person's zone of optimal functioning may be at the lower, middle, or upper end of the state anxiety continuum.

Multidimensional Anxiety Theory

Hanin's IZOF hypothesis does not address whether the components of state anxiety (somatic and cognitive anxiety) affect performance in the same way. These state anxiety components are generally thought to influence performance differentially; that is, physiological arousal (somatic state anxiety) and worry (cognitive state anxiety) affect performers differently. Your heart racing or pounding and your mind reiterating negative predictions, for instance, can affect you differently.

Multidimensional anxiety theory predicts that cognitive state anxiety (worry) is negatively related to performance; that is, increases in cognitive state

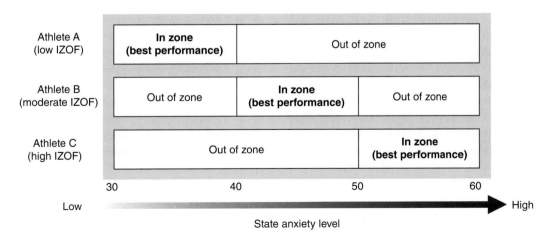

FIGURE 4.5 Individualized zones of optimal functioning (IZOF).

anxiety lead to decreases in performance. But the theory predicts that somatic state anxiety (which is physiologically manifested) is related to performance in an inverted U and that increases in anxiety facilitate performance up to an optimal level, beyond which additional anxiety causes performance to decline. Although studies have shown that these two anxiety components differentially predict performance, the precise predictions of multidimensional anxiety theory have not been consistently supported (Arent & Landers, 2003; Gould, Greenleaf, & Krane, 2002; Mellalieu, Hanton, & Fletcher, 2006). One reason for this lack of support is the prediction that cognitive anxiety always has a detrimental effect on performance. As noted earlier in this chapter, the effect of cognitive anxiety (as well as somatic anxiety) on performance appears to be determined by a performer's interpretation of anxiety, not just the amount or type of anxiety (Jones & Swain, 1992). Consequently, multidimensional anxiety theory has little support with respect to its performance predictions and is of little use in guiding practice.

Catastrophe Phenomenon

Hardy's catastrophe view addresses another piece of the puzzle. According to his model, performance depends on the complex interaction of arousal and cognitive anxiety (Hardy, 1990, 1996). The **catastrophe model** predicts that physiological arousal is related to performance in an inverted-U fashion, but only when an athlete is not worried or has low cognitive state anxiety (figure 4.6a). If cognitive anxiety is high (i.e., the athlete is worrying), however, the increases in arousal

at some point reach a kind of threshold just past the point of optimal arousal level, and afterward a rapid decline in performance—the catastrophe—occurs (figure 4.6b). Therefore, physiological arousal (i.e., somatic anxiety) can have markedly different effects on performance depending on the amount of cognitive anxiety one is experiencing. Moreover, amid high worry, performance deteriorates dramatically once overarousal and the catastrophe occur. This is different from the steady decline predicted by the inverted-U hypothesis, and recovery takes longer.

The catastrophe model predicts that with low worry, increases in arousal or somatic anxiety are related to performance in an inverted-U manner. With great worry, the increases in arousal improve performance to an optimal threshold, beyond which additional arousal causes a catastrophic or rapid and dramatic decline in performance. In low-worry situations, arousal is related to performance in a traditional inverted-U fashion. However, overall performance is not as elevated as in the high-worry situation. Finally, under conditions of great worry, high levels of self-confidence allow performers to tolerate higher levels of arousal before they hit the point where they have a catastrophic drop in performance (Hanton, Neil, & Mellalieu, 2008).

Figure 4.6b shows that under conditions of high cognitive anxiety as physiological arousal increases, performance also increases until an optimal arousal level is reached (marked a on the curve). After that point, however, a catastrophic decrease in performance occurs; the performer drops down to a low level of performance (marked b on the curve). Once the athlete

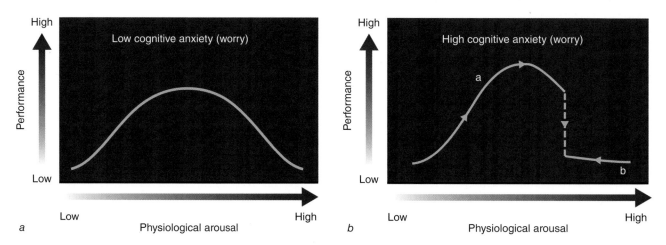

FIGURE 4.6 Catastrophe theory predictions: *(a)* arousal–performance relationship under low cognitive state anxiety; *(b)* arousal–performance relationship under high cognitive state anxiety.

is at that part of the curve, he would need to greatly decrease his physiological arousal before being able to regain previous performance levels. The catastrophe model predicts, then, that after a catastrophic decrease in performance, the athlete must (a) completely relax physically, (b) cognitively restructure by controlling or eliminating worries and regaining confidence and control, and (c) reactivate or rouse himself in a controlled manner to again reach the optimal level of functioning. Doing all this is no easy task, so it is understandably very difficult to quickly recover from a catastrophic decrease in performance.

Finally, figure 4.6 shows that an athlete's absolute performance level is actually higher under conditions of high cognitive anxiety than under conditions of low cognitive anxiety. This shows that cognitive anxiety or worry is not necessarily bad or detrimental to performance. In fact, this model predicts that you will perform better with some worry, provided that your physiological arousal level does not go *too* high (i.e., a little bit of stress heightens an athlete's effort and narrows attention, giving the individual an edge over other performers). Performance deteriorates only under the combined conditions of high worry plus high physiological arousal.

Although some scientific support exists for the catastrophe model, it is very difficult to scientifically test (Hardy, 1996; Woodman & Hardy, 2001b) and, to date, evidence for it is equivocal (Mellalieu, Hanton, & Fletcher, 2006). Still, you can derive from it an important message for practice, namely that an ideal physiological arousal level isn't enough for optimal performance; it is also necessary to manage or control cognitive state anxiety (worrying).

Reversal Theory

Kerr's application of **reversal theory** (Kerr, 1985, 1997) contends that the way in which arousal affects performance depends basically on an individual's interpretation of his arousal level. Joe might interpret high arousal as a pleasant excitement, whereas Jan might interpret it as an unpleasant anxiety. She might see low arousal as relaxation, whereas Joe sees it as boring. Athletes are thought to make quick shifts—"reversals"—in their interpretations of arousal. An athlete may perceive arousal as positive one minute and then reverse the interpretation to negative the next minute. Reversal theory predicts that for best performance, athletes must interpret their arousal as *pleasant excitement* rather than as unpleasant anxiety.

Reversal theory's key contributions to our understanding of the arousal–performance relationship are twofold. First, reversal theory emphasizes that one's interpretation of arousal—not just the amount of arousal one feels—is significant; second, the theory holds that performers can shift or reverse their positive or negative interpretations of arousal from moment to moment. Reversal theory offers an interesting alternative to previous views of the arousal–performance relationship. However, few have tested the theory's predictions, so firm conclusions cannot be made about the scientific predictions.

> **KEY POINT** How a performer interprets arousal influences performance.

Anxiety Direction and Intensity

For many years, most researchers assumed that anxiety had only negative effects on performance. English sport psychologist Graham Jones and colleagues (Jones, 1995; Jones, Hanton, & Swain, 1994), however, showed that an individual's interpretation of anxiety symptoms is important for understanding the anxiety–performance relationship. People can view anxiety symptoms either as positive and helpful to performance (facilitative) or as negative and harmful to performance (debilitative). To fully understand the anxiety–performance relationship, you must examine both the intensity of a person's anxiety (how much anxiety the person feels) and its direction (his interpretation of that anxiety as facilitative or debilitative to performance). Jones and colleagues contended that viewing anxiety as facilitative leads to superior performance, whereas viewing it as debilitative leads to poor performance.

Jones (1995) also developed a model of how **facilitative anxiety** and **debilitative anxiety** come about (figure 4.7). Specifically, some stressor occurs in the environment, such as running in the finals at the state track meet. How much stress a runner will have depends on individual factors such as her trait anxiety or self-esteem. Most important, whether the resulting state anxiety is perceived as facilitative or debilitative depends on how much control the athlete perceives. If the runner feels in control (e.g., that she can cope with the anxiety and that running a certain time in the race is possible), then facilitative anxiety will result. However, if she believes that there is no way she can run a competitive time and that she can't cope with the pressure, debilitative anxiety occurs.

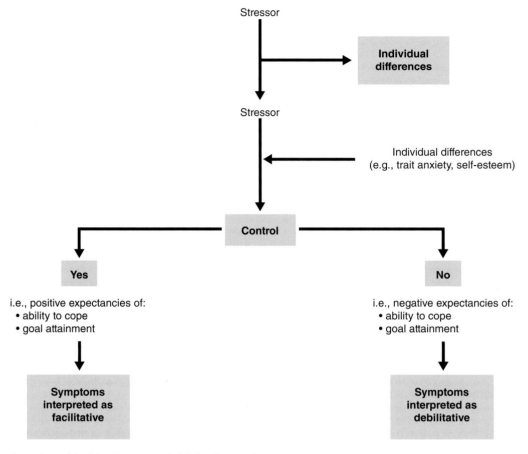

FIGURE 4.7 Jones' model of facilitative and debilitative anxiety.

Adapted from G. Jones, 1995, "More than just a game: Research developments and issues in competitive anxiety in sport," *British Journal of Psychology* 86: 449-478. Adapted with permission from the British Psychological Society. © The British Psychological Society.

The athlete's **perception of control** relative to coping and goal attainment is critical, then, in determining whether state anxiety will be viewed as facilitative or debilitative.

Sport psychologists have already found some support for this association between how anxiety is perceived and performance level. For example, good performances on the balance beam have been associated with gymnasts interpreting cognitive anxiety as facilitative (Jones, Swain, & Hardy, 1993). Similarly, elite swimmers have reported both cognitive and somatic anxiety as more facilitative and less debilitative than have nonelite swimmers (Jones & Swain, 1992). In addition, researchers (Hanton & Jones, 1999a,b; Wadey & Hanton, 2008) found that elite swimmers were able to consistently maintain a facilitative interpretation of anxiety, especially through using psychological skills such as goal-setting, imagery, and self-talk. In essence, performers can be trained to effectively use their anxiety symptoms in a produc-

tive way and to develop a rational appraisal process in relation to their experiences during competition (Hanton, Thomas, & Mellalieu, 2009).

Although these results suggest that using relaxation techniques (see chapter 12) to reduce the intensity of anxiety may not always be appropriate, athletes should learn a repertoire of psychological skills to help interpret anxiety symptoms as facilitative. Furthermore, Nicholls and colleagues (2012) suggest that the interpretation of anxiety as facilitating may not be what enhances performance per se; rather, they argue that the positive emotion of excitement might enhance performance. Whereas most previous studies measured only the construct of anxiety, they measured both anxiety and excitement in their study. Future studies should assess other positive emotions (e.g., excitement, happiness, hope, pride) along with anxiety and other negative emotions (e.g., shame, sadness, guilt, anger) to determine what has the greatest influence on performance.

It is also important to note that a range of personal and situational variables may influence the directional response (see Hanton, Neil, & Mellalieu, 2008, for a review). Some of these personal factors include trait anxiety, neuroticism, extraversion, achievement motivation, hardiness, self-confidence, sex, coping strategies, and psychological skills. The situational variables that influence the interpretation of anxiety include competitive experience, skill level, goal attainment, expectations, sport type, and performance. The individual difference variable that has most consistently determined whether anxiety is interpreted as facilitative or debilitative has been skill level. Specifically, elite performers interpret their anxiety symptoms as more facilitative and report higher levels of self-confidence than their nonelite counterparts do. Studies have revealed that these elite athletes maintain a facilitative perspective as well as high levels of confidence through rationalizing thoughts and feelings before competing via the combined use of such psychological skills as self-talk, imagery, and goal setting (Hanton, Neil, & Mellalieu, 2011).

In summary, how an athlete interprets the direction of anxiety (as facilitative or debilitative) has a significant effect on the anxiety–performance relationship. Athletes can learn psychological skills that allow them to interpret their anxiety as facilitative. It follows that coaches should try to help athletes view increased arousal and anxiety as conditions of excitement instead of fear. Coaches should also do everything possible to help athletes develop perceptions of control through enhancing confidence and through psychological skills training.

Frequency of Anxiety

Compared with direction of anxiety, frequency of anxiety has received little attention in the sport psychology literature. It seems intuitive that the frequency with which athletes have anxiety symptoms (especially ones that are interpreted as debilitating) is an important component of the anxiety response and its effect on performance. Along these lines, Thomas, Hanton, and Maynard (2007) demonstrated that the frequency of cognitive and somatic anxiety symptoms increased as competition approached. More specifically, in another study the same researchers found that athletes who viewed anxiety as facilitative had lower frequencies of cognitive anxiety and higher frequencies of self-confidence throughout the precompetition period than did athletes who viewed their anxiety as debilitating (Thomas, Maynard, & Hanton, 2004). From a coaching perspective, a coach would want to know how often an athlete feels anxiety symptoms, not just how intense the symptoms are and how they are interpreted. For example, a soccer player may rarely have anxiety symptoms but does so when he is chosen to take a penalty kick. Knowing both how frequently and in what situations a player has anxiety that would be debilitative is helpful for coaches in choosing to play certain players in certain situations.

Significance of Arousal–Performance Views

There is certainly no shortage of arousal–performance views—there are so many that it is easy to get confused. So let's summarize what these views tell us regarding practice. The IZOF, multidimensional anxiety, catastrophe, reversal, and direction and intensity views offer several guidelines (Hanton, Neil, & Mellalieu, 2011; Hardy, Jones, & Gould, 1996; Mellalieu, Hanton, & Fletcher, 2006; Woodman & Hardy, 2001b):

1. Arousal is a multifaceted phenomenon consisting of both physiological activation and an athlete's interpretation of that activation (e.g., state anxiety, confidence, facilitative anxiety). We must help performers find the optimal mix of these emotions for best performance. Moreover, these optimal mixes of arousal-related emotions are highly individual and task specific. Two athletes participating in the same event may not have the same optimal emotional arousal level, and a person's optimal emotional arousal level for performing a balance beam routine would be quite different from the optimal arousal level for a maximum bench press in power weightlifting.

2. Arousal and state anxiety do not necessarily have a negative effect on performance. The effects can be positive and facilitative or negative and debilitative, depending largely on how the performer interprets changes. In addition, self-confidence and enhanced perceptions of control are critical to facilitating heightened arousal as positive (psyching up) as opposed to negative (psyching out).

3. Some optimal level of arousal and emotions leads to peak performance, but the optimal levels of physiological activation and arousal-related thoughts (worry) are not necessarily the same!

4. Both the catastrophe and reversal theories suggest that the interaction between levels of physiological activation and arousal-related thoughts appears to be more important than absolute levels of each. Some people perform best with relatively low optimal arousal and state anxiety, whereas others perform their best with higher levels.

5. An optimal level of arousal is thought to be related to peak performance, but it is doubtful that this level occurs at the midpoint of the arousal continuum. Excessive arousal likely does not cause slow, gradual declines in performance but rather "catastrophes" that are difficult to reverse.

6. Strategies for psyching up should be used with caution because it is very difficult for athletes to recover once they have a performance catastrophe.

7. Athletes should have well-practiced self-talk, imagery, and goal-setting skills for coping with anxiety. They must also perceive performance goals to be truly attainable.

Why Arousal Influences Performance

Understanding why arousal affects performance can help you regulate arousal, both in yourself and in others. For instance, if heightened arousal and state anxiety lead to increased muscle tension in Nicole, a golfer, then progressive muscle relaxation techniques may reduce her state anxiety and improve performance. Thought control strategies, however, may work better for Shane, another golfer, who needs to control excessive cognitive state anxiety.

At least two things explain how increased arousal influences athletic performance: (a) increased muscle tension, fatigue, and coordination difficulties, and (b) changes in attention, concentration, and visual search patterns.

Muscle Tension, Fatigue, and Coordination Difficulties

Many people who have great stress report muscle soreness, aches, and pains. Athletes who have high

© Picture Alliance/Photoshot

Optimal levels of arousal and anxiety lead to peak performance.

levels of state anxiety might say, "I don't feel right," "My body doesn't seem to follow directions," or "I tensed up" in critical situations. Comments like these are natural: Increases in arousal and state anxiety cause increases in muscle tension and can interfere with coordination.

For example, some highly trait-anxious and lower trait-anxious college students were watched closely as they threw tennis balls at a target. As you might expect, the higher trait-anxious students had considerably more state anxiety than the lower trait-anxious participants had (Weinberg & Hunt, 1976). Moreover, electroencephalograms monitoring electrical activity in the students' muscles showed that increased state anxiety caused the highly anxious individuals to use more muscular energy before, during, and after their throws. Similarly, in a study of novice rock climbers traversing an identical route under high-height versus low-height conditions, participants had increased muscle fatigue and blood lactate concentrations when performing in the high-anxiety height condition (Pijpers, Oudejans, Holsheimer, & Bakker, 2003). Thus, these studies show that increased muscle tension, fatigue, and coordination difficulties contributed to the students' and athletes' inferior performances under high-stress conditions.

KEY POINT Increased arousal and state anxiety cause increased muscle tension and fatigue and can interfere with coordination.

Attention, Concentration, and Visual Search Changes

Increased arousal and state anxiety also influence athletic performance through changes in attention, concentration, and visual search patterns (Janelle, 2002; Williams & Elliott, 1999; Wilson, 2010). First, increased arousal narrows a performer's attentional field (Landers, Wang, & Courtet, 1985). For example, Joe is a goalie in ice hockey and needs to maintain a broad but optimal focus of attention as three opponents break into his end of the ice. If he becomes preoccupied with Tim, who has the puck, and does not attend to the other players on the periphery, Tim will simply pass off to a teammate on the wing for an easy score. Under normal conditions, Joe can maintain his optimal attentional focus (figure 4.8a), but if he is underaroused (figure 4.8b) his attentional focus may be too broad, taking in both task-relevant (e.g., the opposing players)

and irrelevant (e.g., the crowd) cues. When he has excessive levels of arousal and state anxiety, however, his attentional focus narrows too much and he is unable to survey the entire playing surface (figure 4.8c). One athlete who had severe anxiety problems put it this way: "When the pressure is on, it's like I'm looking through the tube in a roll of toilet paper." In psychological terms, increased arousal causes a narrowing of the attentional field, which negatively influences performance on tasks requiring a broad–external focus.

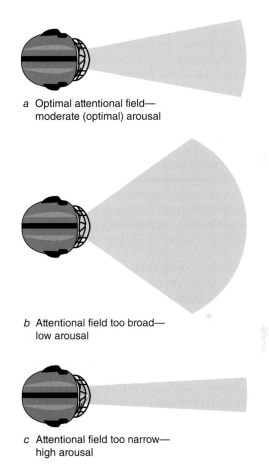

a Optimal attentional field—
moderate (optimal) arousal

b Attentional field too broad—
low arousal

c Attentional field too narrow—
high arousal

FIGURE 4.8 Attentional narrowing under conditions of high arousal.

When arousal is increased, performers also tend to scan the playing environment less often. For example, Tony is a wrestler who has high levels of arousal and state anxiety. He becomes preoccupied with executing one move on an opponent and does not visually or kinetically scan the opponent's total body position for other potential opportunities. Thus, Tony's performance deteriorates as he scans less often, and potential scoring opportunities consequently go undetected.

Arousal and state anxiety also cause changes in attention and concentration levels by affecting attention style (Nideffer, 1976a). Athletes must learn to shift their attention to appropriate task cues (see chapter 16). For example, a quarterback in football needs to shift from a broad–external span when surveying the field for open receivers to a narrow–external focus when delivering a pass. Each individual also has a dominant attention style. Increased arousal can cause performers to shift to a dominant attention style that may be inappropriate for the skill at hand.

Increased arousal and state anxiety also cause athletes to attend to inappropriate cues. For instance, most athletes perform well-learned skills best when they fully concentrate on the task. Unaware of their levels of concentration, they perform on automatic pilot or in a "flow zone" (see chapter 6). Unfortunately, excessive cognitive state anxiety sometimes causes performers to focus on inappropriate task cues by "worrying about worrying" and becoming overly self-conscious (Beilock & Gray, 2007). This, in turn, affects optimal concentration. In addition, Hatzigeorgiadis and Biddle (2001) showed that three types of thoughts are tied to cognitive interference for athletes: performance worries, situation-irrelevant thoughts, and thoughts of escape.

> **KEY POINT** Arousal and state anxiety narrow one's attentional field, decrease environmental scanning, and cause a shift to the dominant attentional style and to inappropriate cues.

Research has also shown that visual cues are differentially identified and processed when performers are anxious. In studying karate participants, for example, Williams and Elliott (1999) showed that increased anxiety influences attention via changes in visual search patterns. Janelle (2002) also showed that increased anxiety is associated with alterations in gaze tendencies and eye fixations. Wilson, Vine, and Wood (2009) conducted an interesting study using basketball free-throw shooting. Shooters performed under conditions of either high or low threat of evaluation, and their efficiency of eye gaze (the final visual fixation on the target before physical movement) was assessed. As expected, participants in the high-stress condition shot less well and had a significant reduction in the "quiet eye" period just before the shot. (Longer fixations are better.) This shows that anxiety influences performance by disrupting the visual attention of shooters. However, quiet eye training

has been shown to increase performance (Wilson, 2010).

Finally, the complexity of the way anxiety influences sport performance is reflected in processing efficiency theory (Hill, Porter, & Quilliam, 2013; Wilson, 2008, 2010; Woodman & Hardy, 2001b). This theory contends that increased anxiety interferes with working memory resources. In the short run, this does not negatively influence performance because the athlete makes up for the deficits caused by the anxiety by increasing his effort. However, as anxiety increases, the benefits of increased effort are often outweighed by the reduced attentional capacity (processing inefficiency) that comes with heightened anxiety. Thus, anxiety may initially result in increased performance because of increases in effort, but the attentional deficits will overcome any increases in effort when the anxiety gets high enough.

What all these studies show, then, is that the relationship between increased anxiety and attention or thought control is a key mechanism for explaining the arousal–performance relationship.

Applying Knowledge to Professional Practice

You can integrate your knowledge of arousal, stress, and anxiety by considering its implications for professional practice. Five of the most important guidelines are to

1. identify the optimal combination of arousal-related emotions needed for best performance;
2. recognize how personal and situational factors interact to influence arousal, anxiety, and performance;
3. recognize the signs of increased arousal and anxiety in sport and exercise participants;
4. tailor coaching and instructional practices to individuals; and
5. develop confidence in performers to help them cope with increased stress and anxiety.

Identify Optimal Arousal-Related Emotions

One of the most effective ways to help people achieve peak performance is to increase their awareness of how arousal-related emotions can lead to peak performances (see chapter 12 for specific techniques).

Once this is accomplished, teaching athletes various psychological strategies (e.g., using imagery and developing preperformance routines) can help them regulate arousal.

Think of arousal as an emotional temperature and arousal-regulation skills as a thermostat. The athlete's goals are to identify the optimal emotional temperature for his best performance and then to learn how to set his thermostat to this temperature—either by raising (psyching up) or lowering (chilling out) his emotional temperature. For example, a study by Rathschlag and Memmert (2013) found that athletes can induce emotions and that certain emotions such as anger and happiness can lead to increased performance, whereas sadness and anxiety can lead to decreased performance.

Recognize the Interaction of Personal and Situational Factors

Like other behaviors, stress and anxiety can best be understood and predicted by considering the interaction of personal and situational factors (figure 4.9). For instance, many people mistakenly assume that the low trait-anxious athlete will always be the best performer because she will achieve an optimal level of state anxiety and arousal needed for competition. In contrast, the assumption is that the highly trait-anxious athlete will consistently choke. But this is not the case.

Where the importance placed on performance is not excessive and some certainty exists about the outcome, you might expect a swimmer with high trait anxiety to have some elevated arousal and state anxiety because he is predisposed to perceive most competitive situations as somewhat threatening. It seems likely that

he would move close to his optimal level of arousal and state anxiety. In contrast, a competitor with low trait anxiety may not perceive the situation as very important because she does not feel threatened. Hence, her level of arousal and her state anxiety remain low and she has trouble achieving an optimal performance.

In a high-pressure situation, in which the meet has considerable importance and the outcome is highly uncertain, these same swimmers react quite differently. The higher trait-anxious swimmer perceives this situation as even more important than it is and responds with very high levels of arousal and state anxiety: He overshoots his optimal level of state anxiety and arousal. The low trait-anxious swimmer also has increased state anxiety, but because she tends to perceive competition and social evaluation as less threatening, her state anxiety and arousal will likely be in an optimal range. The interaction of personal factors (e.g., self-esteem, social physique anxiety, and trait anxiety) and situational factors (e.g., event importance and uncertainty) is a better predictor of arousal, state anxiety, and performance than either set of these factors alone.

Recognize Arousal and State Anxiety Signs

The interactional approach has several implications for helping exercise and sport participants manage stress. Chief among these implications is the need to identify people who are experiencing heightened stress and anxiety. This is not easy to do. Coaches, for example, have been found to be inaccurate predictors of their athletes' anxiety levels. Hanson and Gould (1988) found that only one in four college cross-country coaches accurately read their athletes' state and trait

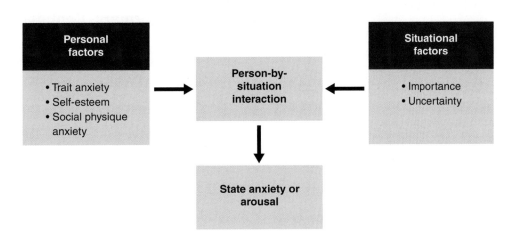

FIGURE 4.9 Interactional model of anxiety.

anxiety levels. Coaches who could accurately read the anxiety levels did not think it was an easy task; rather, they worked hard to learn about their athletes.

> **KEY POINT** To accurately detect an individual's anxiety level, you must know the various signs and symptoms of increased stress and anxiety.

You can more accurately detect a person's anxiety levels if you are familiar with the signs and symptoms of increased stress and anxiety:

- Cold, clammy hands
- Need to urinate frequently
- Profuse sweating
- Negative self-talk
- Dazed look in the eyes
- Increased muscle tension
- Butterflies in stomach
- Feeling ill
- Headache
- Cotton (dry) mouth
- Being constantly sick
- Difficulty sleeping
- Inability to concentrate
- Consistently performing better in noncompetitive situations

Although no specific number or pattern of symptoms characterizes a high level of stress, people who have high levels of state anxiety often exhibit several of the signs listed. The key is to notice changes in these variables between high- and low-stress environments (e.g., when a normally positive athlete becomes negative).

One of the best (although often overlooked) ways to understand what people are feeling is to ask them! Encourage your participants to talk freely about their feelings with you. Be empathic by trying to see things from their perspectives (i.e., thinking of how you would feel in their situation at their level of experience). This allows you to associate specific behavioral patterns with varying levels of stress and anxiety and to better read people's anxiety levels.

 **DISCOVER** Activity 4.3 identifies your signs and symptoms of increased anxiety.

Tailor Coaching Strategies to Individuals

Individualize teaching, exercise, and coaching practices. At times arousal and state anxiety levels need to be reduced, at other times maintained, and at still other times facilitated (see chapter 12 for specific strategies). The teacher or coach should recognize when and in whom arousal and state anxiety need to be enhanced, reduced, or maintained.

For example, if a student or athlete with high trait anxiety and low self-esteem must perform in a highly evaluative environment, the teacher or coach would best de-emphasize the importance of the situation and instead emphasize the performer's preparation. A pep talk stressing the importance of the situation and of performing well would only add stress and increase arousal and state anxiety beyond an optimal level. Someone with moderate levels of trait anxiety and self-esteem may be best left alone in the same highly evaluative situation. This individual's arousal and state anxiety would probably be elevated but not excessive. However, an athlete with very low trait anxiety and high self-esteem may need a pep talk to *increase* arousal before performing in a nonthreatening environment.

> **KEY POINT** Sometimes arousal and state anxiety need to be reduced, at other times maintained, and at still other times facilitated.

Instructors who have students or clients with high social physique anxiety should encourage these exercisers to wear clothes that cover their bodies. Instructors can also minimize social evaluation of physiques by creating settings that eliminate observation by passersby.

Develop Performers' Confidence

One of the most effective methods of helping people control their stress and anxiety is to assist them in developing their confidence and perceptions of control. Highly confident people who believe in both their performance abilities and their ability to cope with stress have less state anxiety. Moreover, when they do have anxiety, they tend to interpret their increased anxiety as facilitative versus debilitative. Two important strategies for enhancing confidence are to foster a positive environment and to instill a positive orientation to mistakes and losing. (See chapter 14 for some other excellent strategies.)

One major source of stress is uncertainty, which often results when athletes or students participate in negative practice environments. For instance, some coaches harp on mistakes that players make, yelling and screaming all through practice. Then, on game day, these same coaches say how confident they are in their athletes' abilities. After hearing so much negative feedback in practice, the athletes may not believe what the coach says on game day. A productive approach for facilitating confidence is to create a positive practice environment. Give frequent and sincere encouragement. That way, when athletes encounter stressful environments, they will have confidence in their abilities to meet the demands of the situation.

Foster a positive, productive orientation to mistakes and even to losing. When individuals make mistakes, they typically become frustrated and often overly aroused and anxious. This leads to unproductive attention changes and increased muscle tension, which further deteriorate performance. It is useful to teach people to view mistakes in a more productive light. Just as legendary UCLA basketball coach John Wooden did with his players, good sport psychologists teach performers to view mistakes not as bad or evil but as building blocks to success (Smoll & Smith, 1979). No performer is happy to make mistakes, but getting upset only makes a mistake a complete mistake. Instead, one should try to gain at least a partial success by staying cool and learning from the mistake: Use it as a building block to success. Mastering this strategy reduces anxiety, making for a more productive learning and performance environment. (See chapter 14 for more strategies for building confidence.)

LEARNING AIDS

SUMMARY

1. **Discuss the nature of stress and anxiety (what they are and how they are measured).**

   Stress, arousal, and anxiety each have distinct meanings. Stress is a process that occurs when people perceive an imbalance between the physical and psychological demands on them and their ability to respond. Arousal is the blend of physiological and psychological activity in a person that varies on a continuum from deep sleep to intense excitement. Anxiety is a negative emotional state characterized by feelings of nervousness, worry, and apprehension associated with activation or arousal of the body. It has cognitive, somatic, trait, and state components.

2. **Identify the major sources of anxiety and stress.**

   Some situations produce more state anxiety and arousal than others (e.g., events that are important and in which the outcome is uncertain). Stress is also influenced by personality dispositions (e.g., trait anxiety and self-esteem). Individuals with high trait anxiety, low self-esteem, and high social physique anxiety have more state anxiety than others.

3. **Explain how and why arousal- and anxiety-related emotions affect performance.**

   Arousal-related emotions, such as cognitive and somatic state anxiety, are related to performance. Arousal and anxiety influence performance by inducing changes in attention and concentration and by increasing muscle tension. Hanin's individualized zones of optimal functioning, Hardy's catastrophe model, Kerr's interpretation of reversal theory, and Jones' distinction between the direction and intensity of anxiety should guide practice. An optimal recipe of emotions is related to peak performance, and when performers are outside this optimal range, poor performance results. This optimal combination of emotions needed for peak performance does not necessarily occur at the midpoint of the arousal–state anxiety continuum, and the relationship between arousal and performance depends on the level of cognitive state anxiety (worry) a performer exhibits.

4. **Compare and contrast ways to regulate arousal, stress, and anxiety.**

   An interactional model of motivation should guide teachers and coaches in their efforts to help students and athletes manage arousal and state anxiety. Creating a positive environment and a productive orientation to mistakes and losing is an effective way to manage stress. Additionally, the following five guidelines for managing stress should be followed: (a) identify the optimal combination of arousal-related emotions needed for best performance; (b) recognize how personal and situational factors interact to influence arousal, anxiety, and performance; (c) recognize the signs of increased arousal and anxiety in sport and exercise participants; (d) tailor coaching and instructional practices to individuals; and (e) develop confidence in performers to help them cope with increased stress and anxiety.

KEY TERMS

arousal	trait anxiety	individualized zones of optimal
anxiety	emotions	functioning (IZOF)
cognitive anxiety	self-report measures	multidimensional anxiety theory
somatic anxiety	(self-report scales)	catastrophe model
state anxiety	stress	reversal theory
cognitive state anxiety	social physique anxiety	facilitative anxiety
somatic state anxiety	drive theory	debilitative anxiety
perceived control	inverted-U hypothesis	perception of control

REVIEW QUESTIONS

1. Distinguish between the terms *arousal, state anxiety, trait anxiety, cognitive state anxiety,* and *somatic state anxiety.*

2. Define stress and identify the four stages of the stress process. Why are these stages important? How can they guide practice?

3. What are two or three major sources of situational and personal stress?

4. What is social facilitation theory? What implications does this theory have for practice?

5. Discuss the major differences in how arousal relates to performance according to the following theories:
   - Drive theory
   - Inverted-U hypothesis
   - Individualized zones of optimal functioning
   - Multidimensional anxiety theory
   - Catastrophe model
   - Reversal theory
   - Anxiety direction and intensity view

6. Describe the major signs of increased state anxiety in athletes.

7. Discuss three practical applications from the research and theories on the arousal–performance relationship.

8. Discuss the relationship between ability and an athlete's interpretation of anxiety as facilitative or debilitative.

9. Does a home-court advantage exist in sport? Discuss the research that addresses this issue.

CRITICAL THINKING QUESTIONS

1. How might you tailor coaching strategies to individuals who are trying to deal with stress and anxiety? Give an example.

2. Discuss three implications for professional practice that you derived from the theories and scientific data in this chapter.

3. The chapter begins with the story of Jason coming to bat in a pressure situation. Given what you have learned, what can Jason do to manage his anxiety and play well? How could you help him view his anxiety as facilitative rather than debilitative?

PART III

Understanding Sport and Exercise Environments

What effect do competition and cooperation have on a person's behavior? How do feedback and reinforcement affect learning and performance?

In part II you learned how a person's psychological makeup influences that individual's behavior in physical education, sport, and exercise contexts. People do not exist in vacuums, however, and as you learned, a person-by-situation interactional model is the best way to understand behavior psychologically. When dealing with athletes and exercisers, focusing, for example, on an individual's motivation and then on the type of competitive situation they are in will help you develop the best program for both performance enhancement and enjoyment.

In part III of our journey, we focus on two major classes of situational factors that influence behavior. Chapter 5 examines the important environmental effect that competition and cooperation have on a person's behavior. Virtually everything we do as professionals in sport, teaching, and exercise settings involves competition or cooperation to some degree. In this chapter you'll read that competition and cooperation are learned behaviors; you'll also come to understand the ways in which competition and cooperation influence performance, the positive and negative effects of competitive and cooperative settings, and ways to balance competition and cooperation so that healthy development is maximized.

Chapter 6 focuses on feedback and reinforcement and their effect on learning and performance. We offer guidelines for giving feedback and reinforcement to people in sport and exercise settings, including the systematic use of reinforcement in behavioral programs. We discuss how rewards can both enhance and undermine the natural, intrinsic motivation of participants, and we present strategies for increasing intrinsic motivation. The chapter closes with a discussion of flow—an ultimate form of intrinsic motivation—and how to achieve it.

 VIEW   Dr. Dan Gould introduces part III of the text in the Introduction activity.

JOURNEY   This activity allows you to record your position on the relative emphasis that should be placed on competition and cooperation in sport and exercise.

LISTEN   Go to part III of the web study guide to meet the following experts in the field: Rainer Martens, PhD; Diane L. Gill, PhD; and Chris Harwood, PhD. In this activity, you'll hear or see the experts discussing motivation and competition.

Competition and Cooperation

After reading this chapter, you should be able to

1. understand the difference between competition and cooperation,
2. describe the process of competition,
3. detail the psychological studies of competition and cooperation,
4. discuss the social factors influencing competition and cooperation,
5. explain why competition can be both good and bad, and
6. understand how to balance competitive and cooperative efforts.

From the anecdotes former athletes tell, it is evident that competitive sport can affect participants very differently in terms of personal growth and development. For example, Hall of Fame quarterback Roger Staubach stated, "Because of athletics and my experiences in sport, I learned to handle things in business and life." In contrast, Tom House, former Major League Baseball pitcher, said, "The professional athlete is for all practical purposes terminally adolescent . . . . The longer the exposure to the professional sport environment, the further athletes drift from an ability to understand and cope with the demands of the real world." Many competitive sport participants argue that competitive sport not only can bring out cooperative efforts among teammates pursuing a common goal (think about Kevin Garnett, Ray Allen, and Paul Pierce of the Boston Celtics as they reduced their respective roles in quest of a championship) but also can help prepare a person for life. Others argue that competitive sport can produce self-centered athletes who avoid dealing with real-life issues (Manny Ramirez can certainly hit a baseball, but what will he do outside of baseball?). These critics cite the growing number of athletes who have been accused of physical or sexual abuse, substance abuse, murder, robbery, or unsportspersonlike behavior (e.g., spitting at officials, choking their coaches).

Who is right? The answer is that people on both sides of this argument may be right because virtually all sport and physical activity involves both competition and cooperation. Players cooperate with their teammates while they compete against their opponents. Sometimes competition even exists *within* a team as players battle for playing time and starting positions. Therefore, the interactions of these competitive and cooperative forces and their effects on participants are complex. Let us start by defining the terms *competition* and *cooperation*.

Defining Competition and Cooperation

The term **competition** is popularly used to refer to a variety of situations. For example, we compete against others, against ourselves, against the clock or record book, and against objects and the elements (e.g., rock climbing, white-water rafting). But in defining competition, most researchers have focused on situations in which people compete against others in organized physical activities. For example, Coakley (1994) defined competition as "a social process that occurs when rewards are given to people on the basis of how their performances compare with the performances of others doing the same task or participating on the same event" (p. 78). According to this definition, rewards in competition are limited to those who outperform others. Thus, besides being a process, competition has a reward structure, which fosters the notion that the success of one participant or team automatically causes the failure of others.

Another process in which success can be measured and performance rewarded is cooperation. **Cooperation** has been defined as "a social process through which performance is evaluated and rewarded in terms of the collective achievements of a group of people working together to reach a particular goal" (Coakley, 1994, p. 79). This definition implies that a cooperative reward structure is characterized by the mutual involvement of more than one participant. Rewards are therefore shared equally by everyone in the group, and group success depends on the collective achievement of all the participants. A team winning a championship shares in the victory, even though some of its players might have actually contributed more than other members in terms of performance. Successful, achievement-oriented, hard-working people are not necessarily competitive. They may simply combine strong achievement orientations with cooperative or individualistic orientations. In fact, cooperative people are just as likely to be successful as are competitive people. Research has indicated that competitive reward structures, although useful in relatively simple physical tasks of short duration, are less effective than cooperative reward structures for tasks that are complex and that involve solving difficult problems (Kohn, 1992).

 DISCOVER Activity 5.1 helps you define different types of competition.

We compete against many different things—other people, ourselves, and even nature.

Zuma Press/Icon SMI

Although research concerning competition now dates back more than a century (Triplett, 1898), the first concerted effort to study competition was initiated by Morton Deutsch (1949), who noted that few everyday situations are purely cooperative or competitive. Deutsch argued that most social interactions involve some kind of goal-directed behavior that rewards the person (or persons) for achieving the goal while also requiring some type of cooperative effort from everyone involved. Basketball is a good example: Each player on a team must cooperate to win the game, but players might also vie against each other for playing time and a starting position in the lineup.

Although isolated studies regarding competition and cooperation were performed in the 1950s and 1960s, no conceptual framework existed to help guide the research in this area. Fortunately, Rainer Martens (1975) developed a specific model that gave a framework to further studies of competition in sport and exercise environments. Furthermore, Martens' definition is similar to the one later developed by Coakley; in both, competition is a process. However, Martens' definition and approach to competition also focused on *social evaluation.* He argued that to maximize participants' personal development, it is critical to understand the social influences that help structure the activity environment. Thus, Martens' social evaluation approach defines competition and helps us understand the competitive process in sport.

Viewing Competition as a Process

According to Martens, competition is more than a single event; rather, it involves a process that encompasses four distinct events or stages, which are illustrated in figure 5.1. This process somewhat resembles the model of stress presented in chapter 4,

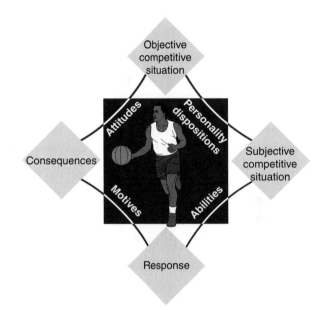

FIGURE 5.1 The competitive process.

Adapted, by permission, from R. Martens, 1975, *Social psychology and physical activity* (New York: Harper & Row), 69. Copyright 1975 by Rainer Martens.

Competition Versus Decompetition

Over the years, competition has been given a bad rap. People often focus on the negative aspects of competition, whereas cooperation is seen as a positive alternative to competition. However, Shields and Bredemeier (2009) argued that what in the past has been called the good and bad of competition is better viewed as *competition* and *decompetition.* In essence, the authors provide a novel perspective on competition that challenges traditional beliefs through a research-backed defense. They argue that partnership is the essence of competition. Although competition can be fierce and highly contested, each competitor is seen as a facilitator or enabler for the other. True competitors want well-matched opponents who will challenge them. In addition, competitors follow the spirit of the rules even if doing so results in a competitive disadvantage. Fairness to their opponents is more important than merely following the rules. This synergy enables the competitors to reach new heights of excellence, positive character development, enjoyment, and mastery that they could not achieve in isolation. In true competition, opponents strive with each other to reach excellence.

Conversely, in **decompetition**, opponents see each other as rivals, striving against each other to win the competition. Decompetitors look to beat or annihilate their opponents and do not see them as cooperators or partners. Rules for them are simply conventions, and stretching the rules in the quest for winning is not uncommon. Fairness is often shrunk to what people can get away with as long as they don't get caught. Winning is the ultimate goal, and winning is sought at all costs, including cheating, being argumentative, or playing mind games. In essence, decompetition is the opposite of competition.

which provides a good way to view the competitive process. Notice in the figure that although these stages are distinct, they also are linked to one another.

Individuals experience the competitive process differently. Therefore, the person is at the focal point of the process and can influence the relationship among the various stages. Personal attributes such as previous experience, ability, motivation, and attitudes are just some of the factors that might influence a person's responses in competition. As with any social process, each stage is influenced by the other stages as well as by such external environmental factors as feedback and external rewards. In addition, the process of competition should include the role of the socialization process and social context in determining competitive levels and orientation. Along these lines, a model developed by Eccles and Harold (1991) emphasizes that sport attitudes emerge at an early age and that differences in sex seem to be a consequence of gender socialization rather than natural aptitude.

Stage 1: Objective Competitive Situation

Martens proposed a definition of the **objective competitive situation**, stemming from social evaluation theory (Festinger, 1954), that includes a standard for comparison and at least one other person. The comparison standard can be an individual's past performance level (e.g., 4:10 in the mile run), an idealized performance level (e.g., a 4-minute mile), or another individual's performance (e.g., your main rival has run a 4:05 mile). The primary thing that distinguishes a competitive situation from other comparison situations is that the criteria for comparison are known by at least one person who is in a position to evaluate the performance.

Consider these examples with Martens' definition in mind. You go out alone for a 3-mile jog, setting a goal for yourself to run this distance in 21 minutes. (Your previous best was 22 minutes.) This would not be considered competition because only you are aware of the standard of excellence you are striving to beat. However, if you ran with a friend and told her about your goal to run 3 miles in 21 minutes, the situation would be competitive because your friend is aware of the criterion for evaluation and can evaluate your performance.

Some people argue that the first example is also competition in that you are competing against yourself. Martens would not necessarily disagree with this point of view, but he argued that to study competition scientifically, we must delimit its scope. Without another person involved to evaluate the comparison process,

almost anything might be called competition. How would one know if you were trying to run 3 miles in 21, 20, or 19 minutes? Martens stated that most activities commonly thought to be competitive are indeed covered by his definition, so we don't lose much by limiting the definition to include another person.

Stage 2: Subjective Competitive Situation

Regardless of whether people are in an objective competitive situation because they seek the situation or because circumstances place them in it, they must evaluate the situation in some way. This brings into play the next stage, the **subjective competitive situation**, which involves how the person perceives, accepts, and appraises the objective competitive situation. Here the individual's unique background and attributes become important. Such factors as perceived ability, motivation, the importance of the competitive situation, and the opponent may well influence the subjective appraisal of the competitive setting.

> **KEY POINT** Competitiveness is the personality characteristic that best predicts how people appraise the objective competitive situation.

For example, one gymnast may look forward to competing in a championship meet as a means of gaining experience, whereas another gymnast facing the same objective situation may dread the upcoming meet. Similarly, one runner in an adult fitness class may want to turn every jog into a race, whereas another seeks to avoid comparisons with other runners in the class.

Highly competitive people tend to seek out competitive situations and be more motivated to achieve in them than people with lower levels of competitiveness. Trait competitiveness alone, however, does not adequately predict how a person will respond to a particular competitive situation. Other situational variables (e.g., type of sport, coach, parents, teammates) also exert strong influences on behavior.

> **KEY POINT** The four stages of competition are (1) the objective competitive situation, (2) the subjective competitive situation, (3) the response, and (4) the consequences of the response. In an objective competitive situation, "an individual's performance is compared with some standard of excellence, in the presence of at least one other person who is aware of the criterion for comparison" (Martens, 1975).

Because competitiveness is such an important personal factor in the competitive process, let's take a closer look at it. Gill and Deeter (1988), attempting to define the term more clearly, developed the **Sport Orientation Questionnaire (SOQ)** to provide a reliable and valid measure of competitiveness. Sample questions are given in the "Sport Orientation Questionnaire (SOQ)." Using the SOQ, Gill and Deeter (1988) found three types of competitive orientations, all of which represent different subjective outcomes of a competitive situation:

- **Competitiveness** is an enjoyment of competition and desire to strive for success in competitive sport settings. A competitive person simply loves to compete and actively seeks competitive situations.
- **Win orientation** is a focus on interpersonal comparison and winning in competition. It is more important to beat other competitors than to improve on personal standards.
- **Goal orientation** is a focus on personal performance standards. The goal is to improve one's own performance, not to win the competition.

A person's competitive orientation affects how he perceives the competitive situation (see Gill, 2000, for a review). For example, athletes generally scored higher than nonathletes on all three subscales but especially on the competitive aspect of the SOQ (Gill, 1993). Athletes also vary greatly in their competitive orientations, but Gill's study suggests that more of them are oriented toward improving their own performances (goal orientation) than toward winning. This finding may seem surprising to many, but it in fact confirms the research on goal setting (Weinberg, Burton, Yukelson, & Weigand, 2000) showing that improving performance was the goal most often cited and that winning came in second. Furthermore, individuals can be high on more than one orientation. For example, research with elite athletes has revealed that they are high on both win and goal orientations (Hardy et al., 1996). Finally, researchers (Sambolec, Kerr, & Messe, 2007) have found that individuals high on competitiveness try harder and perform better on coactive tasks than do individuals low on competitiveness. Competitiveness seems to be enhanced when one is directly competing against another because the social comparison aspect

---

Sport Orientation Questionnaire (SOQ)

The following statements describe reactions to sport situations. We want to know how you usually feel about sport and competition. Read each statement and circle the number that indicates how much you agree or disagree with each statement on the scale. There are no right or wrong answers; simply answer as you honestly feel. Do not spend too much time on any one statement. Remember—choose the number that describes if you generally agree or disagree.

	Strongly agree	Slightly agree	Neither agree nor disagree	Slightly disagree	Strongly disagree
Examples of SOQ competitive items					
I am a competitive person.	1	2	3	4	5
I enjoy competing against others.	1	2	3	4	5
Examples of SOQ win orientation items					
Winning is important.	1	2	3	4	5
I hate to lose.	1	2	3	4	5
Examples of SOQ goal orientation items					
I set goals for myself when I compete.	1	2	3	4	5
Performing to the best of my ability is very important to me.	1	2	3	4	5

is amplified. Thus, coaches can play this competitive aspect up or down, depending on the athlete's goals and orientation toward competition.

Stage 3: Response

According to Martens' competitive process model, after a person appraises a situation, she decides to either approach or avoid it. The chosen **response** initiates the third stage of the model. If the decision is not to compete, then the response stops there. However, a response to compete can occur at the behavioral, physiological, or psychological level, or at all three levels. For example, at the behavioral level, you might decide what type of opponent you prefer to play: someone better than you, so you might improve; someone worse than you, so you can make sure you win; or someone equal to you, so you have a challenging competition. On a physiological level, your response might be that your heart starts to beat faster and your hands become cold and clammy. Several psychological factors, both internal and external, can also affect a person's response. Motivation, confidence, and perceived ability level are just a few of the internal factors affecting the response. Facilities, weather, time, and opponent ability are some external influences.

Stage 4: Consequences

The final stage of the competitive process results from comparing the athlete's response with the standard of comparison. **Consequences** are usually seen as either positive or negative, and many people equate positive consequences with success and negative consequences with failure. However, as we discussed earlier, the athlete's perception of the consequences is more important than the objective outcome. For example, although you might have lost the game, you might still perceive the outcome as positive if you played well and met your own standard of excellence.

These feelings of success and failure do not occur in isolation: They work their way back into the process and affect subsequent competitive events. Modifying the rules (e.g., not keeping score, allowing a player to stay at bat until he hits the ball into fair territory) or the facilities and equipment (e.g., lowering the rim in basketball; using smaller balls for basketball, volleyball, and football) can influence perceptions of success and failure. "Demonstrating the Model of Competition" gives some useful and appropriate modifications for young participants and shows how a junior high physical education teacher might apply Martens' model.

Demonstrating the Model of Competition

Mr. Davis is a physical education teacher at a junior high school. He has been teaching volleyball skills for the past few weeks, and recently the class has started to play some competitive games. Mark, who is outgoing and athletic, looks forward to the competition; he enjoys the challenge and the chance to show his classmates his skills. John, on the other hand, is shy and not very athletic. He is nervous about the competition because he is unsure of his skills and afraid of embarrassing himself. Mr. Davis is aware that Mark views competition positively, whereas John would like to avoid competition at all costs (subjective competitive situation). Mark likes to compete against people as good as or better than he is because he sees this as a challenge, whereas if John has to compete he likes to play against a weaker opponent so that he doesn't look too bad (response).

In a competition, Mark handles winning and losing very well because his self-esteem is not threatened if he plays poorly or if his team loses. In contrast, John has had a lot of failure, often receiving criticism and even ridicule for his athletic endeavors. Naturally he feels threatened and apprehensive about losing or performing poorly (consequences).

Because Mr. Davis understands this process of competition and the ways in which students differ, he structures his physical education class to meet the needs of both John and Mark. He sets up different types of learning situations and lets students choose among them. For example, on one court he sets up teams and a competition for those who seek out a challenge and enjoy the excitement of competition. On another court, the emphasis is on learning and improving skills rather than competing. On this court, students who are still unsure of themselves can learn without the pressure of competition. Mr. Davis attempts to structure his physical education class so that students enjoy themselves, acquire skill, and develop a positive feeling toward sport and physical activity.

In a subjective competitive situation, a coach might manipulate the situation by emphasizing to a gymnast the importance of the competition and of settling for nothing less than first place. Having parents and friends at the meet might also accentuate the importance of performing well, which would probably increase the pressure and anxiety the athlete feels. Conversely, the coach could focus on team cooperation and encourage the gymnasts to give each other emotional support. The coach could tell the gymnasts, "Go out and do your best—enjoy yourselves." This orientation would influence the gymnasts' subjective perception of the competitive situation.

Administrators, coaches, and parents should know how to help performers feel more successful about sport experiences. Taking a participant-centered approach by modifying rules, facilities, and equipment to provide more action, more scoring, closer games, and more personal involvement can create positive experiences for all participants.

In essence, competition is a learned (rather than innate) social process that is influenced by the social environment (including coaches, parents, friends, and sport psychologists). Competition is inherently neither good nor bad. It is simply a process, and the quality of leadership largely determines whether it will be a positive or negative experience for the participant. Thus, you should consider the many factors that can influence the relationship between the objective competitive situation, subjective competitive situation, response, and consequences of the competitive process.

KEY POINT Competition is inherently neither good nor bad. It is neither a productive nor a destructive strategy—it is simply a process.

Reviewing Studies of Competition and Cooperation

People have been competing in sport for hundreds of years, but only recently have sport psychologists systematically studied competitive and cooperative behaviors in sport. Next we review some of the classic and pioneer psychological investigations into the processes of competition and cooperation.

Triplett's Cyclists

The first experiment that addressed the effects of competition on performance was documented in 1898 by Norman Triplett (whose influence we discussed briefly in chapter 1). Triplett noted that racers showed varying performances (as measured in time) when they raced alone, with a pacer, or in competition with another racer. By consulting the records of the Racing Board of the League of American Wheelmen, he found that cyclists were faster when racing against or with another cyclist than when racing alone against the clock. Thus, for the first time, face-to-face competition against fellow competitors was shown to potentially enhance performance.

Deutsch's Puzzles

In Morton Deutsch's classic study (1949), college students were required to solve puzzle problems during a 5-week span, using both competitive and cooperative instructions. Students in the competitive condition were told that a reward (a grade in the class) would be given to the person in the group who solved the highest average number of puzzles. Students in the cooperative condition were told that they would be evaluated by their group's ranking in relation to four other groups who were also solving puzzles and would receive a reward as a team. Results revealed that students in the competitive group were self-centered, directed their efforts at beating others, had closed communication, and exhibited group conflict and mistrust. Students in the cooperative group, however, communicated openly, shared information, developed friendships, and actually solved more puzzles than their competitive counterparts. This finding has been replicated many times over the years.

One implication from Deutsch's study is that teams work together better when they have a common goal and when reaching that goal produces similar rewards for all participants. For example, if one basketball team member is most interested in the scoring title and the others are interested in winning their division, a counterproductive conflict of interests potentially exists. Consequently, coaches should make sure that all players understand their roles and strive toward common goals. Coaches can accomplish this by emphasizing the unique role and contribution of each team member. To Deutsch, the potential negative effects of competition were so destructive that in 1982 he called for a planned reduction of competitive situations in society because these often led to conflict. In fact, Deutsch (2000) has noted that individuals in competition are likely to develop a negative view of the competitor, have heightened anxiety, display a poor use of resources, exhibit lower productivity, act in hostile or aggressive ways toward the opponent, and exhibit a disruption of effective communication. He concluded from decades of research that competitive conflicts can be resolved by communication, coordination, shared goals, and control of threat.

Competition and Aggression

It's not news that a primary focus on winning and beating an opponent can produce hostility and aggression among teams. Fighting has often erupted in professional and college sports that encourage contact and collision between players, such as football, hockey, and basketball. It is not the competition per se that produces the aggressive behavior and hostility. Rather, the feelings and behavior stem from the focus on doing whatever it takes to win, even when this means unfair play or injuring an opponent. In his book *They Call Me Assassin,* former pro football player Jack Tatum (1980) describes premeditated, deliberate attempts at injuring opposing players to take them out of commission. In recent years, a couple of National Football League (NFL) coaches were said to have offered a bounty for any defensive player who could knock the opposing quarterback out of the game. Specifically, in 2012 coaches and players were suspended from the New Orleans Saints for offering and receiving rewards for knocking players out of games. In youth sports these feelings of hostility and aggression can spill over to parents. Unfortunately, in one such incident a parent actually beat another parent to death during an argument after a youth hockey game.

You can see in the next two examples how the focus on winning and on one's own glory can be a catalyst that produces negative behaviors in competition. First, two teammates competing for a starting position might develop hostility and try to undermine each other's play. Second, as suggested by figure skater Tonya Harding's involvement in the attack on Nancy Kerrigan in 1994 at the U.S. Figure Skating Championships in Detroit, competition for the same spot might lead to one competitor deliberately injuring another. As bizarre as it might seem, a mother planned to murder a young girl competing to be a high school cheerleader so that her own daughter could make the cheerleading team.

But certainly only a very small percentage of sport competition results in the type of aggressive behavior just noted. In fact, competitive sport can also help

athletes learn to work together to strive for mutual goals and reduce the overemphasis and pressure on winning. This can create a positive social environment and improve performance (Sherif & Sherif, 1969). For example, teammates might cooperate and try to help each other be the best player possible because this will help the team as a whole in the long run. To help their teams, veteran NFL quarterbacks typically mentor their younger quarterback teammates, even though the younger players may eventually take their jobs. Two rivals, however, might focus solely on beating each other and have no concern about how they play as long as they win. Or they might view each other as allies in the sense that each plays better because of the high performance level of the other. A great performance by one spurs the other to even greater heights. Thus, the way performers view competition determines whether its effect is positive or negative. A couple of examples of cooperation are provided in "Cooperation: Still Alive and Well."

Effect of Competition and Cooperation on Performance

We can see the potential negative effects of competition when we look at the relationship between competition and performance. Johnson and Johnson (1985) thoroughly analyzed 122 studies conducted between 1924 and 1981 for the effects of competitive and cooperative attitudes on performance. In 65 studies, cooperation was seen to produce higher achievement and performance than was competition; only 8 studies showed the opposite. Furthermore, in 108 studies, cooperation promoted higher achievement than did independent or individualistic work, whereas the opposite occurred in only 6 studies. The superiority of cooperation held across a variety of tasks involving memory and the quality, accuracy, and speed of performance. Johnson and Johnson concluded from their review that in no type of task are cooperative efforts less effective than competitive or individualistic efforts. Rather, on most tasks, cooperative efforts are more effective in promoting achievement.

However, the nature of the experimental tasks in many of these studies called for a cooperative strategy over a competitive strategy. That is, if participants had chosen to compete, their performances would have been poorer than when they cooperated. A study by Stuntz and Garwood (2012) provides a good example of the effects of different competitive or cooperative goals on performance where the competition

Cooperation: Still Alive and Well

With all the emphasis on competition, it is a breath of fresh air to see spontaneous cooperation and sportspersonship break out. A couple of recent examples are instructive.

First is the case of the 2008 high school track and field championships in the state of Washington. Nicole Cochran thought she had won the girls' title in the 3,200 meters but was disqualified for stepping outside her lane on one of the turns. Almost everyone, including her competition, agreed that the judge was in error (which was later confirmed by a video). Still, the title was awarded to runner-up Andrea Nelson. While on the platform during the medal ceremony with the top eight finishers, Nelson stepped off the podium and hung the first-place medal around the neck of the rightful winner. "It's your medal," she told Cochran. When Sarah Lord saw what Nelson had done, she took off her second-place medal and placed it around Nelson's neck. The other competitors followed suit, placing their medals on the runners who had finished ahead of them. Interestingly, Cochran finished eighth in the 800 meters and gave her medal to Lyndy Davis, who had given her eighth-place medal in the 3,200 to the girl who had finished in front of her and had subsequently been left without a medal.

Second is the case of a girls' softball game in which a player hit a home run and while circling the bases realized she had missed first base. When she turned to go back to first base to touch it, she hurt her knee so badly that all she could do was crawl. If a teammate touched her, she would be considered out. Therefore, two of the girls on the other team got together and carried her around the bases, touching each base as they crossed it, completing the home run. The girls simply said, "She hit a home run and she deserved to have it count on the scoreboard."

directions would not necessarily produce poorer performance when compared with the cooperative or individualistic instructions. Specifically, participants were given three types of instructions: cooperative, where the goal was for each group of two to score the most points; competitive, where the goal was for each person to score more points than his or her partner; or individualistic, where the goal was for each person to improve his or her performance over the series of trials. Results revealed that the cooperative instructions produced the best performance by far. This is interesting because some coaches and athletes believe that the path to optimal performance involves focusing on beating the opponent. However, research consistently demonstrates that working together with a cooperative mind-set enhances performance level above focusing on competition and individual improvement (Roseth, Johnson, & Johnson, 2008).

Although cooperative efforts appear to produce better performance than do competitive efforts when a performer has to work with another person to achieve a particular goal, individuals may perform better when competing against others than they would when simply performing the task alone. For example, Cooke, Kvussanu, McIntyre, and Ring (2011) had participants perform a hand dynamometer task (muscular endurance) either alone (with instructions to do their best) or against six other competitors. Results revealed that participants performed best in the competitive condition. To determine why performance was best in the competitive condition, the researchers took a variety of psychological and physiological measures. Results indicated that participants in the competitive condition exhibited greater effort, more enjoyment, increased muscle activity, and decreased heart rate variability compared with participants in the noncompetitive condition. In a follow-up study, Cooke, Kvussanu, McIntyre, and Ring (2013) investigated individual competition (one-on-one) versus team competition (two-on-two, four-on-four). Results revealed that performance was significantly better in the team competitions than in the individual competitions. Consistent with the previous study, enjoyment, effort, and anxiety were the primary mediators of this performance effect. It appears that participants felt the need to try harder because their partners depended on them, and their increased anxiety positively influenced their performance in this task.

It is important to remember that competition itself does not produce negative consequences; rather, it is the overemphasis on winning that is counterproductive. In fact, Johnson and Johnson (1999, 2005) note that they see a limited role for competition if properly constrained. Along these lines, appropriate competition has the following characteristics: It is voluntary, the importance of winning is not so high that it causes disabling stress, everyone must have a reasonable chance to win, the rules are clear and fair, and relative progress can be monitored.

Certainly, competitive orientations often lead to high levels of achievement in individual as well as team sports. For example, although Michael Jordan needed to cooperate with his teammates to form the unit that helped the Chicago Bulls dominate the National Basketball Association in the 1990s, it is generally recognized that his extremely competitive nature was what really drove him to reach the highest level of success and excellence. In essence, many situations in the world of sport and physical activity call for a blend of cooperative and competitive strategies and orientations. Finding the right mix for the specific situation is the real challenge. For example, many athletes have noted that playing against a really good opponent helped raise the level of their own games, which might be considered a form of cooperation. So when Roger Federer played Rafael Nadal, or when LeBron James played against Kobe Bryant, or when Greg Maddux pitched against Randy Johnson, they all relished this competition because they believed it raised the intensity and level of their own game. In essence, the competition served as positive motivation for these superstars to continually improve and refine their skills.

We know that cooperative teamwork benefits sport performance but also that sport can lead to cooperative teamwork. For example, Fraser-Thomas and Cote (2006) stated that "youth sport programs have long been considered important to youth's psychosocial development, providing opportunities to learn important life skills such as cooperation, discipline, leadership, and self-control" (p. 12). This idea is supported by Findlay and Coplan (2008), who found that children involved in sport were more likely to participate in cooperative behavior than were those not involved in sport.

DISCOVER Activity 5.2 helps you identify ways to design cooperative games.

Botterill (2005) highlighted the notion that competition and cooperation should be viewed as complementary. Let's consider the case of pickup games where kids simply meet at the playground or schoolyard, choose up sides, and play. If respect for and appreciation of one's competitors drop off, it is not long before the game breaks down and there is no one to compete against. Unfortunately, the dynamics of how competition and cooperation complement each other are often not taught. Rather than being polar opposites, competition and cooperation involve complementary skills and values, and both perspectives should be nourished to provide a healthy perspective on sport as well as life.

The melding of competitive and cooperative efforts can be seen in the Definite Dozen principles developed

Reducing Competition Through Cooperation

Sherif and Sherif (1969) conducted three field experiments with 11- and 12-year-old boys in isolated camps. First, two groups were formed, and each was provided the opportunity to develop a strong group identity. Sports and games were a large part of the groups' activities, and teamwork and group identity were emphasized. In the next phase of the study, Sherif and Sherif deliberately induced intergroup conflict, much of it through sport competitions that emphasized a winner and a loser. In addition, they put refreshments on a camp table for a party, and one group was invited up first. The first group ate almost all the food and left little for the second group, who naturally felt resentful.

The third phase consisted of an attempt to reduce or eliminate the hostility that the experimenters had helped build, but the boys maintained their dislike and ill will toward each other. Finally, the researchers contrived situations, such as the need to repair a leak in the camp's water pipe and fix a damaged food supply truck, that forced the two groups to cooperate for what the experimenters termed superordinate goals. These situations were set up so that neither group could achieve a highly desired outcome without the help of the other group. These cooperative efforts resulted in both a reduction of hostility and conflict between the groups and the development of friendships and communication between them. Thus, the studies underscore the critical roles that social context and emphasis on competition play in determining whether competition is beneficial and productive. Inherently, competition is neither good nor bad.

by Pat Summitt, arguably the most successful female collegiate basketball coach:

- *Respect yourself and others.* There is no such thing as self-respect without respect for others.
- *Take full responsibility.* Be accountable—there are no shortcuts to success.
- *Develop and demonstrate loyalty.* Loyalty is not unilateral. You have to give it to receive it.
- *Learn to be a great communicator.* This means being a great listener as well as speaker.
- *Discipline yourself so no one else has to.* Group discipline and self-discipline produce unified efforts.
- *Make hard work your passion.* Do the things that aren't fun first.
- *Don't just work hard, work smart.* Maximize strengths and minimize weaknesses of yourself and those around you.
- *Put the team before yourself.* Teamwork allows common people to achieve uncommon things.
- *Make winning an attitude.* Attitude is a choice.
- *Be a competitor.* Being competitive means being the best you can be.
- *Change is a must.* Change equals self-improvement.
- *Handle success like you handle failure.* You can't control what happens, but you can control how you react to it.

In a classic study, Kelley and Stahelski (1970) used the prisoner's dilemma to investigate how effective competitive responses were compared with cooperative ones. In this study, competitive players were paired with cooperative players. Over a series of games, the competitive players were able to draw their cooperative partners into competition. In essence, cooperators began by cooperating but were forced into competitive responses by their opponents. The cooperators knew they were being forced to change their style of play and compete, whereas the competitors perceived only the conflict of the game and were oblivious to the cooperative overtures being offered.

Let's take a look at a real-life example of this principle. Imagine you are playing in a pickup basketball game, and you're interested simply in getting some exercise and having fun (i.e., you're a cooperator). As you drive to the basket, another player pushes you in the back onto the floor. You're really angry and

confront the player, but all he says is, "That's how we play here. If you don't like it, leave" (i.e., he's a competitor). Now you have to decide whether to leave or stay. If you stay, you will most likely have to adopt the competitive style of the people playing the game. If you leave, you don't get the exercise you were hoping to get. In either case, the competitor has dictated the kind of action and behavior required of the cooperator.

Determining Whether Competition Is Good or Bad

As things now stand, the competitive ethic is a driving force in sport. You hear people say, "Competition brings out the best in us," "Without competition, even minimal productivity would disappear," and "To compete is to strive for goals and reach for success." Many Americans equate success with victory, doing well with beating somebody. They subscribe to an attitude attributed to former Green Bay Packers coach Vince Lombardi: Winning isn't everything—it's the only thing. Thus, whether they call it the competitive urge, competitive spirit, or competitive ethic, many people consider this type of thinking synonymous with the American way of life. For example, middle-distance runner Mary Decker Slaney, one-time holder of numerous world records, described her orientation toward competition:

" From the time I started running, I won . . . . To me, that was the only place to finish. I wasn't like some kids who would finish second and say, "I ran a good time." Good time, heck. I want to win. I'll do anything I have to to win. "

Likewise, a successful high school basketball coach had this to say about competition and winning:

" Through the years I've developed my own philosophy about high school basketball. Winning is all that matters. I don't care how many games you win. It's how many championships you win that counts. "

Finally, Olympic gymnastics coach Bela Karolyi has his own views on winning and having fun:

" Sometimes the preparation is so hard . . . the crying and the screaming . . . . We are not in the gym to have fun. The fun comes at the end, with the winning and the medals. "

This overemphasis on winning is seen in the scoring procedure in NFL games. Specifically, although a regular-season game can end in a tie (after one quarter of overtime), the Super Bowl is played out until one team finally wins. The assumption is that nobody would be satisfied with a Super Bowl that ended in a tie. We want a clear winner. Similarly, a coach's win–loss record is often the overriding criterion for his success. Although college presidents may claim that education is more important than athletics, a coach who graduates all his players but doesn't achieve a winning record is seldom retained, much less rewarded. At the home level, some parents hold their children back a grade in school so that with the extra year they can be bigger and stronger and thus more likely to achieve success in football.

The preoccupation with winning sometimes leads to cheating. One winner of the All-American Soap Box Derby was disqualified for cheating and forfeited his $7,500 scholarship when officials discovered that an electromagnet gave his car an unfair starting advantage. Similarly, charges were made regarding the actual ages of certain players in the 2001 Little League World Series (players were supposed to be less than 13 years of age). The abuse of steroids to improve performance is also a form of cheating. Although

Does Sport Competition Transfer to Life Skills and Achievement?

A persistent question that has been asked over the years is, To what extent does competitive sport participation help individuals prepare for life? The following is a summary of the results from studies investigating various aspects of this question (Coakley, 1997):

• *Sport participation and academic achievement.* Studies have shown in general that varsity athletes have higher grade point averages and higher educational aspirations than those who do not participate on varsity teams. This positive relationship is most likely to occur when sport participation somehow alters important relationships in a young person's life. Specifically, when participation leads parents, friends, coaches, counselors, or teachers to take young people more seriously as human beings and as students and to give them more academic support and encouragement, participation will be associated with positive academic outcomes. However, when participation occurs outside of school-sponsored sport, relationships do not seem to change in academically relevant ways. This is true also when athletes participate in minor sports or are low-status substitutes in major sports, are African American, or attend schools where academics are heavily emphasized and rewarded over and above performance.

• *Sport participation and social or occupational mobility.* Research has shown that former athletes, as a group, have no more and no less career success than others from comparable backgrounds. In addition, former athletes do not appear to have any systematic mobility advantage over their peers in similar jobs. That is, former athletes have a wide range of career successes and failures. Individual motivational or personality differences rather than sport experience itself seem to be better predictors of occupational success.

• *Sport participation and deviant behavior.* The question of whether participation in competitive sport may "keep young people off the street" and out of trouble has been hotly debated in recent years. Correlational analyses have not shown higher rates of deviance among athletes than among nonathletes, and this finding has been replicated across sports, societies, sexes, and socioeconomic status (Hanrahan & Gallois, 1993). However, research has also not consistently indicated that competitive sport participation actually reduces the prevalence of deviant behavior. The nature of the specific sport experience, differences among individuals, and the competitive environment all interact to determine the effect of sport participation on deviance.

Coakley (1997) argued that sport participation will have a positive effect on reducing athletes' deviant behavior *if* they play sports in connection with a clearly expressed emphasis on the following: philosophy of nonviolence, respect for self and others, the importance of fitness and the control of self, confidence in physical skills, and a sense of responsibility. In essence, simply getting kids off the streets to play sports is not enough to reduce deviance. If we emphasize hostility toward others—using aggression as a strategy and bodies as tools, dominating others, and winning at all costs—then we cannot expect rates of deviance to decrease.

many Olympic athletes probably have found ways to get around the standardized drug testing performed on elite and professional athletes, numerous others have been disqualified. Finally, in his book *No Contest: The Case Against Competition,* Kohn (1992) effectively argued against the following competition myths: that competition builds character (e.g., self-confidence, self-esteem), that competition motivates us to do our best, that competition is the best way to have a good time, and that competition is part of human nature. In fact, Kohn argues that competition has a number of negative consequences, including the following: creating stress, which interferes with optimal performance; focusing attention on beating others rather than on performing well; fostering insecurity and undermining self-esteem; fostering interpersonal hostility, prejudice, and aggression; and creating undue envy, humiliation, and shame.

DISCOVER Activity 5.3 helps you consider the factors that make competition good or bad.

Many elementary school physical education teachers complain that their students are overly competitive. Some adult exercisers have trouble working at their own pace because they want to keep up with their fitness-crazy friend. Some exercisers get caught up trying to do more than the other guy. More and more experts who note the overemphasis on winning have become proponents of cooperative sport and working together. In fact, new games have been developed that emphasize cooperation over competition (Coakley, 1994). The late tennis great Arthur Ashe (1981) said this about cultivating a cooperative frame of mind:

" I associate the killer instinct with a heightened emotional state, and I would not want to be known as somebody who had it . . . . I like harmony in everything. To me, there should be harmony among the crowd, court officials, and even the ball boys. (p. 176) "

The potential negative effects of competition do not mean, however, that competition or competitive sport is necessarily bad or that it causes these negative consequences. There have also been many instances in which competition has produced positive, healthy outcomes. For example, author James Michener (1976) stated,

" I am always on the side of healthy competition. I love it. I seek it out. I prosper under its lash. I have always lived in a fiercely competitive world and have never shied away. I live in such a world now and I would find life quite dull without the challenge. "

In addition, how we treat our opponents can influence our view of competition. Specifically, if we sustain a respectful and appreciative attitude toward opponents, we can view them as presenting opportunities. This can be seen in the comments of Mariah Burton Nelson (1998) in her book *Embracing Victory:*

" Opponents present you with a chance to learn who you are, to notice what you want. They give you a chance to rise to the occasion. This is what athletes learn; that opponents can make us swifter, wiser, more effective. We welcome them. (p. 277) "

Nelson goes on to point out that this view of opponents is not limited to the playing field. Gandhi, for example, viewed political opponents as teachers because they forced him to do his best. He learned from them about his own areas of weakness and grew through his efforts to address these areas. In fact, in sport, losing often brings more information and learning about your performance than does winning. True competitors want the best from their opponents so they can be pushed to play their best.

Especially with youth sports, the quality of adult leadership by parents, coaches, and others becomes crucial in determining whether competition affects young athletes positively or negatively. Anyone who has competed in sport knows that competition can be fun, exciting, challenging, and positive. Coaches and teachers should teach youngsters when it is appropriate to compete and when it is appropriate to cooperate. In fact, in most team sports, competition and cooperation occur simultaneously. Therefore, an integrated approach offers the greatest opportunities for personal development and satisfaction. Finally, to learn more about competition and cooperation, it has been suggested that enhanced technology (in the form of video games) would provide a unique opportunity to study a wide range of individuals in a wide range of situations (Murphy, 2009).

Competition: Is It Different for Boys and Girls?

With the increased participation of girls in competitive sport (both organized and unorganized), researchers have focused on the experiences of boys and girls in competitive sport. Coakley (1997) indicated that boys and girls often have these very different experiences while playing competitive sports and games:

- Boys play competitive games more frequently than girls do.
- Girls play in predominantly male groups more often than boys play games in predominantly female groups.
- When boys are with friends, they play in larger groups than girls do.
- Girls' games are more spontaneous, imaginative, and freer in structure than boys' games.
- Boys see themselves as more physically skilled than girls see themselves, even though sex differences in actual skill levels are small or nonexistent.
- Boys' games are more aggressive, involve taking greater risks, and reward individual achievement to a greater extent than girls' games do.
- Boys play games that are more complex than the games girls play: They have more rules, a greater number of different positions (roles), and more interdependence (teamwork).

Enhancing Cooperation

The positive outcomes produced by cooperative efforts are familiar to those in business, educational, and organizational settings. Yet most sport and game settings retain a competitive focus, and most sport psychology texts emphasize the various psychological factors that enhance performance in these competitive settings. Certainly, competitive sport offers positive benefits, including character development, discipline, and teamwork. With so much evidence from diverse fields attesting to the positive effects of *cooperation,* however, it's worthwhile to look at how cooperative games can complement traditional competitive sport and physical education.

Component Structure of Games

Canadian sport psychologist Terry Orlick (1978) originally argued that the design of a game largely influences the predominant behavioral response, be it competitive, individualistic, cooperative, or some combination of these. Competition and cooperation are complementary relationships that give people scope to realize their unique potential in sport and physical activity. Competition and cooperation have different potential interactions—ranging from purely cooperative to purely competitive—that a coach or exercise leader must understand in order to structure a good mix of physical activities and games. Most activities can be classified into the categories we discuss next, as defined by Orlick.

- *Competitive means—competitive ends.* The goal is to beat someone else or everyone else from the outset to the end. You might expect this goal, for example, in a 100-yard race or in the game King of the Mountain.

- *Cooperative means—competitive ends.* Participants cooperate in their group but compete outside their group, as you might find in soccer, basketball, football, and hockey when team members work together and try to coordinate their movements to defeat an opponent. However, not all team members are necessarily ensured cooperation (cooperative independent means) within teams. A basketball player, for example, can hog the ball and not pass to teammates. To ensure cooperative independent means with younger athletes, a rule can be introduced, such as requiring everyone to receive a pass before a shot at the basket can be taken.

- *Individual means—individual ends.* One or more players pursue an individual goal without cooperative or competitive interaction. Sport examples include cross-country skiing, calisthenics, and swimming.

- *Cooperative means—individual ends.* Individuals cooperate and help each other achieve their own goals. For example, two athletes can watch each other and provide feedback and cues so that both of them can improve their skills.

- *Cooperative means—cooperative ends.* Players cooperate with each other from the outset to the end.

Unstructured Sport: An Opportunity for Enhanced Cooperation and Growth

Most of today's sport for youths is structured and organized; there are coaches, officials, defined teams, schedules, strict rules, and parental involvement. But youngsters also play sport or games of another type, which has been termed unorganized, unstructured, or informal. Observational studies (including interviews of young athletes) have revealed tremendous differences in the philosophy and implementation of these two approaches to sport competition. Specifically, when youths get together and play on their own, they are predominantly interested in four things (Coakley, 1997):

1. *Action, especially leading to scoring.* Action is enhanced in numerous ways, including having fewer players playing the game, eliminating free throws in basketball, and eliminating halftimes or time-outs.

2. *Personal involvement in the action.* Youngsters typically maximize involvement through clever rule modifications and handicap systems that keep highly skilled players from dominating the action. Some examples are having no strikeouts in baseball (the batter is up until she hits a fair ball), giving everyone a chance to be a receiver and catch the ball in football, using "do-over" or "interference" calls to compensate for mistakes, and having a good hitter hit to only a certain part of the field.

3. *Closely matched teams.* Each team should have a good chance to win. Typically, teams are chosen by captains who each get one choice at a time. But deals are also arranged. For example, if one player is particularly good, the other captain may get two or three picks to offset the one pick of this particularly talented athlete.

4. *Opportunities to reaffirm friendships during the game.* There is time for players to talk informally with friends and "fool around" during small breaks in the action.

In summary, these informal and unorganized games are generally action centered, whereas organized sport is rule centered. The experience in unorganized sport revolves around the maintenance of action through decision making and managing relationships among players. The experience in organized sport revolves around learning and following the rules as well as obeying the adults who make and enforce the rules. However, many parents are concerned about the safety of their children and hesitate to let them play in an unsupervised environment. Therefore, another way to achieve the positive outcomes of unstructured sport is for coaches and parents to make organized sport more child centered, focusing on skill development, fun, and personal growth.

Everybody works toward a common goal and share the means as well as the ends. Modified volleyball is a good example. The objective is to keep the ball from hitting the floor for as long as possible. Each team is allowed only three hits before getting the ball over the net, but the goal is not to make your opponents miss; rather, it is to hit the ball over in such a way that ensures that they do not miss.

Philosophy of Cooperative Games

Although games that emphasize both cooperative means and cooperative ends are rare, some significant steps have been taken to develop alternatives to competitive games and sports (Orlick, 1978; Orlick, McNally, & O'Hara, 1978). Orlick argued that our competitive sports and games have become rigid, judgmental, highly organized, and excessively goal oriented. There is little relief from the pressure of evaluation and the psychological distress of disapproval. Many competitive sports for young athletes are designed by principles of elimination. In many sports there is only one winner and everyone else loses. This perceived failure is one reason for the large percentage of dropouts from competitive youth sports (see chapter 22). Even worse, many young athletes are taught to delight in others' failures that enhance their own chances of victory. Children become conditioned to the importance of winning so that it is more difficult to play simply for the fun of it, which is why most kids play sports in the first place. They don't learn how to help one another, be sensitive to another's feelings, or compete in a friendly, fun-filled way.

The beauty of cooperative games lies in part in their versatility and adaptability. Most cooperative games require little or no equipment or money. Anyone can play, and the rules of the game can be altered to fit the specific constraints of the situation. Furthermore, through cooperation children learn to share, empathize, and work to get along better. The players in the game must help one another by working together as a unit, leaving no one out of the action and merely waiting for a chance to play. Players have freedom to learn from mistakes rather than trying to hide them. (These attributes are similar to those of unorganized sport noted earlier in this chapter.) This is not to say that cooperative games are inherently better than competitive ones; rather, because some of the structure, goals, and outcomes differ between the two types of games, participants should have the opportunity to choose between cooperative and competitive games or to play both types.

Benefits of Blending Cooperation and Competition

Professionals in the physical education field play a crucial role in the development of the attitudes that young athletes and sport participants acquire. Coaches, for example, can convey a win-at-all-costs attitude that promotes overaggressive behavior, or they can emphasize and reward fair play and skill development. One junior high school basketball coach who wanted to emphasize good sporting behavior over winning gave rewards for good sporting behaviors, including the biggest trophy at the end-of-year awards dinner for the player who displayed the best sporting behavior. The good sporting behavior award became the most coveted prize, and players worked hard during the season to earn or win it.

Cooperation enhances enjoyment of the activity, communication, and sharing of information. Often it produces superior performance compared with competition. Consequently, focusing on cooperation as well as encouraging healthy competition in sport and physical activity appears to have many possible positive outcomes.

One way to enhance both competition and cooperation is through the use of team-building activities

Cooperative games teach children that there is more to playing than winning.

(discussed more in chapter 8). One activity in particular simply asks each team member "What do you need from the team to have a great year?" and "What can you bring to the team?" This exercise quickly demonstrates vulnerability (and need for one another) and identifies important roles that members can play. These types of activities help athletes develop cooperative and competitive skills and demonstrate how interrelated and complementary competition and cooperation are. In essence, we need ourselves as well as others to pursue excellence and compete at the highest level.

Another example of how competition and cooperation can work together was provided by Veach and May (2005), who promoted cooperative competition where athletes train and share their ideas with fellow teammates and competitors to facilitate mastery and teamwork at the highest level. Specifically, two U.S. sailing teams (same boat class) spent 2 years training and competing against one another and sharing ideas, techniques, and encouragement. At the Olympic trials, only one team could win, and they knew the winner would be a contender for a medal at the Olympics. They finished in first and second places at the Olympic trials and the winner went on to medal at the Olympics. The members of the second-place team were disappointed but had gained new confidence in their ability to compete at a world-class level. In fact, one of the second-place athletes went on to win a berth in the next Olympic sailing trials.

However, cooperation need not replace competition. We are advocating a blend of competition and cooperation in sport and physical activity. The focus on winning at all costs is an imbalance reflecting the values of one large segment of American society. Sport experiences should instead emphasize a blending of competition and cooperation. Along these lines, we provide some guidelines for teachers and coaches on the use of competition and cooperation in sport and games:

- Individualize instruction to meet each person's needs.
- Structure games for children to include both competitive and cooperative elements.
- When competition leads to fierce rivalry, use superordinate goals to get the groups together.
- Provide positive feedback and encouragement to students and athletes regardless of the competition's outcome.

- Stress cooperation to produce trust and open communication.
- Provide opportunities for both the learning of sport skills and the practice of these skills in competition.

The Special Olympics is a specific example of blending competition with cooperation to produce an optimal learning environment. Specifically, the Special Olympics is a carefully controlled competition where, in addition to outcome, the focus is on fellowship and pride in one's own physical accomplishments. Participants receive unconditional support from spectators, coaches, and peers as well as from fellow competitors. The competitive outcome is important to the athletes, but it takes a backseat to the sheer pleasure and camaraderie of personal involvement. The parents of the participants judge their children on the basis of effort and personal progress—not on the basis of wins and losses, medals, trophies, or championships. In essence, the overall social and psychological development of the athletes is paramount (Coakley, 1994).

Cooperative Games in the Gymnasium and on the Playing Field

Now that we have discussed the benefits of blending cooperation and competition for young participants, we can turn to the need to foster cooperative learning in physical education classes and on sport teams. Therefore, here we suggest specific ways to implement cooperative games and activities in your programs. First, coaches and physical educators should determine what they want to accomplish in their classes or on the athletic field. If they consider having fun, learning skills, reducing stress, providing maximum participation, and enhancing social relationships to be important outcomes, then integrating some cooperative games into programs and curricula is appropriate. This is not to say that cooperative games should be the main or only type of games taught, but rather that they should be included to complement other activities and competitive events. Often, cooperative games can be created simply by modifying the rules in existing sports and games. To implement a cooperative approach to learning, you can follow these general principles:

- Maximize participation
- Maximize opportunities to learn sport and movement skills

- Do not keep score in games
- Give positive feedback
- Provide opportunities for youngsters to play different positions

The following are some specific examples of rule modifications that encourage cooperation:

- *Volleyball:* The goal is to keep the ball from hitting the ground; each team still gets only three hits.
- *Soccer:* The ball should be passed to at least five different players before a shot on goal can be attempted.
- *Baseball:* No strikeouts or walks are allowed; every batter must hit the ball into fair territory to complete an at bat.

In an empirical study of cooperative games (Orlick, McNally, & O'Hara, 1978), 4-year-olds were exposed to 14 weeks of cooperative games; they played 2 days per week and used 12 types of games. The children were asked to play together toward a common end rather than to compete against other teams or individuals. The games were designed to tie all participants into continuous action. Researchers compared the responses of children playing these cooperative games with the responses of children participating in regular physical education classes. They found that children exposed to cooperative games engaged in three times as much cooperative

behavior during free play in the gymnasium than did the control group of children. Responses to the cooperative games were characterized as sharing, concern for others, helping, and cooperation. Children in the control group tended to focus on their own desires, making sure that they got what they wanted. Only during the final 6 weeks did these positive changes occur; during the first 8 weeks of the program no differences were found between the two groups. This underscores the importance of systematically carrying out such programs over time.

Cooperative games and cooperative learning have recently been used in physical education classes to help foster the acceptance of students with learning disabilities (Andre, Deneuve, & Louvet, 2011). Five elements critical to cooperative learning were emphasized by the teacher:

1. Students were divided into teams (one student with a learning disability on each team).
2. Positive interdependence was facilitated (team results consisted of each team member's score).
3. Each team member was individually accountable and had a specific role to play.
4. The task required social skills (students had to help each other in order to successfully complete the task).
5. After the task was completed, students assessed how well their group functioned throughout the group processes.

Cooperation in Business and the Military

In business, cooperation is believed to be a collaborative behavior and is grouped with other constructs such as coordination and information exchange (Rousseau, Aubé, & Savoie, 2006). Unlike sport, in which cooperation is discussed as an alternative to competition, business focuses on cooperation as a means of carrying out tasks that are difficult to complete independently (Carron, Martin, & Loughead, 2012). Jones and George (1998) noted that organizations attempt to create an environment rich in cooperation by making teams fairly equal in status, thus creating a feeling of empowerment. Research supports the idea that giving individuals more responsibility creates a more cooperative environment.

In the military, cooperation does more than merely enhance performance and productivity—it affects individual and group safety because acting in an uncooperative manner may lead to injury or death. Even the military health care system emphasizes the importance of cooperation, as evidenced by the creation of the Observational Assessment for Teamwork in Surgery, which assesses cooperation as well as communication and coordination (Healey, Undre, & Vincent, 2004).

In addition to cooperating in one's own unit, Mendel and Bradford (1995) noted that "mastering interagency cooperation is fundamental to success in military operations" (p. 6). Furthermore, they argue that the military must cooperate with other nations for missions such as peacekeeping, counterterrorism and insurgency, and disaster relief because at times independent power is insufficient.

Results indicated that cooperative learning positively influenced the acceptance of the disabled mainstreamed students by their peers. No differences in acceptance were found in the more traditional, individual physical education classes. Thus, it appears that mainstreaming alone does not foster acceptance of students with disabilities. Rather, cooperative, group-oriented activities appear to be one way to facilitate acceptance and integration.

Finally, one study (Goudas & Magotsiou, 2009) emphasized cooperation in a physical education program with the aim of improving students' social skills. Sixth graders were placed in either an experimental group or a control group. Students in the experimental group participated in a 13-unit cooperative learning program that emphasized interacting with peers, solving problems cooperatively, helping peers and receiving help in accomplishing a goal, meeting goals through cooperative play, and following or leading a group, depending on the circumstances. The control group received the same material and subject matter but was taught in a typical command style, with the teacher doing most of the talking. Compared with the control group, the experimental group showed enhanced communication skills, which led to increased cooperative skills and empathy and decreased quick-temperedness and tendency to disrupt.

LEARNING AIDS

SUMMARY

1. **Understand the difference between competition and cooperation.**
   Competition has been defined as a social process that occurs when rewards are given to people based on their performance relative to that of other competitors. Furthermore, the social evaluation component of competition is seen as critical to this process because competition always involves a comparative judgment and performers are evaluated on how well they do. Cooperation is also seen as a social process through which performance is evaluated and rewarded in terms of the collective achievements of a group of people working together to reach a common goal.

2. **Describe the process of competition.**
   Competition, in Martens' view, is a four-stage process. It involves an objective competitive stage, a subjective competitive stage, a response, and consequences. Understanding this framework helps you appreciate what determines and results from competitiveness and competitive behavior.

3. **Detail the psychological studies of competition and cooperation.**
   Overwhelming evidence from psychological studies suggests that cooperative activities produce more open communication, sharing, trust, friendship, and even enhanced performance than competitive activities do. These differences were found in laboratory and field settings as well as in a variety of experimental games. People compete even when it is irrational to do so, and it's hard to stop competition once it breaks out. The ways in which people choose to compete and the reasons they do so, athletes' evaluation of competition, the various potential responses to competition, and the ways in which competition affects athletes psychologically are just some of the questions still to be explored in research.

4. **Discuss the social factors influencing competition and cooperation.**
   Our social environments in large part influence competitive and cooperative behaviors. For example, cross-cultural work has indicated that children's competitive and cooperative behaviors are shaped by the reinforcement patterns of adults as well as by the particular cultural and social expectations placed on the children. In essence, coaches, teachers, and parents can influence the development of young participants by the degree to which they emphasize either the competitive or cooperative aspects of sport.

5. **Explain why competition can be both good and bad.**
   Competition is not inherently good or bad. It can lead to positive outcomes (e.g., enhanced self-esteem, confidence, having fun) or to negative outcomes (e.g., cheating, preoccupation with winning, excessive aggression). Especially in youth sports, the quality of adult guidance is critical in determining whether competition positively or negatively affects the participants.

6. **Understand how to balance competitive and cooperative efforts.**
   Research has investigated the role of both competition and cooperation in sport and physical activity. Cooperative games are viable alternatives that can complement the more traditional competitive games

dominating American culture. In addition, participation in unorganized sport provides youngsters with opportunities for personal growth, decision making, responsibility, and social interactions. We can all learn a great deal through participation in competitive sport. However, an overemphasis on competition can undermine some of the values of competitive sport. Physical educators, coaches, and parents must work together to provide athletes the most enjoyable, meaningful, and educational sport experience.

KEY TERMS

competition
cooperation
decompetition
objective competitive situation

subjective competitive situation
Sport Orientation Questionnaire (SOQ)
competitiveness
win orientation

goal orientation
response
consequences

REVIEW QUESTIONS

1. Discuss some of the common themes emerging from the psychological studies on competition and cooperation and their implications for sport and physical education.

2. Describe the classic field experiments that Sherif and Sherif conducted at summer camps for boys. How were competition and hostility created and finally eliminated? What implications does this have for sport competition?

3. Describe the four stages of Martens' model of competition, including examples of each stage.

4. Discuss Orlick's basic philosophy of cooperative games. Make up three games that have cooperative means and cooperative ends and explain how they are cooperative.

5. Discuss the effects of competition on deviance, academic achievement, and social or occupational mobility.

6. How do boys and girls view competition differently? What are some of the causes of these differences?

7. Discuss the notion of decompetition versus competition as put forth by Shields and Bredemeier.

8. Johnson and Johnson favor cooperation over competition. However, they say there is a limited place for competition under certain conditions. Discuss these conditions, including your reasons for agreeing or disagreeing.

9. Discuss the value of cooperation in business and military settings.

10. How can cooperative games be used to help include individuals with learning disabilities.

CRITICAL THINKING QUESTIONS

1. Winning isn't everything—it's the only thing. Do you agree or disagree? Provide research and personal or anecdotal examples to support your point of view.

2. You are hired as the new physical education teacher for an elementary school. You believe that at this age level, competition and cooperation should be blended to enhance personal growth and development. Discuss the specific games, activities, and sports you would devise to achieve this goal.

3. You want to get your 7-year-old child involved in sport but are unsure whether she should play organized or unorganized sports. Discuss the pros and cons of organized versus unorganized sport competition. Which would you want your child to focus on and why?

6

Feedback, Reinforcement, and Intrinsic Motivation

After reading this chapter, you should be able to

1. explain how positive feedback and negative feedback influence behavior;
2. understand how to implement behavior modification programs;
3. discuss the different types of intrinsic and extrinsic motivation;
4. describe the relationship between intrinsic motivation and external rewards (controlling and informational aspects);
5. detail different ways to increase intrinsic motivation;
6. describe how such factors as scholarships, coaching behaviors, competition, and feedback influence intrinsic motivation; and
7. describe the flow state and how to achieve it.

People thirst for feedback. An exerciser feels like a klutz and hopes for a pat on the back, some telling instruction, and a camera to capture the moment she finally gets the steps right. Similarly, a youngster trying to learn how to hit a baseball after a series of missed swings feels great when he finally connects with the next pitch. To create an environment that fosters pleasure, growth, and mastery, professionals use motivational techniques based on the principles of reinforcement. **Reinforcement** is the use of rewards and punishments that increase or decrease the likelihood of a similar response occurring in the future. The principles of reinforcement are among the most widely researched and accepted in psychology. They are firmly rooted in the theories of behavior modification and operant conditioning. The late B.F. Skinner, the most widely known and outspoken behavior theorist,

argued that teaching rests entirely on the principles of reinforcement.

Skinner (1968) argued that teaching is the arrangement of reinforcers under which students learn. "Students learn without teaching in their natural environment, but teachers arrange special reinforcements that expedite learning, hastening the appearance of behavior that would otherwise be acquired slowly or making sure of the appearance of behavior that might otherwise never occur" (pp. 64–65). Providing students, athletes, and exercisers with constructive feedback requires an understanding of the principles of reinforcement.

Principles of Reinforcement

Although many principles are related to changing behavior, two basic premises underlie effective reinforcement: First, if doing something results in a good consequence (e.g., being rewarded), people will tend to try to repeat the behavior to receive additional positive consequences; second, if doing something results in an unpleasant consequence (e.g., being punished), people will tend to try not to repeat the behavior so they can avoid more negative consequences.

Imagine a physical education class on soccer skills in which a player makes a pass to a teammate that leads to a goal. The teacher says, "Way to pass the ball to the open man—keep up the good work!" The player will probably try to repeat that type of pass in the future to receive more praise from the coach. Now imagine a volleyball player going for a risky jump serve and hitting the ball into the net. The coach yells, "Use your head—stop trying low-percentage serves!" Most likely, this player will not try this type of serve again, wanting to avoid the criticism from the coach.

Reinforcement principles are more complex than you might think, however, in the real world. Often the *same reinforcer will affect two people differently.* For example, a reprimand in an exercise class might make one person feel she is being punished, whereas it might provide attention and recognition for another person. A second difficulty is that *people cannot always repeat the reinforced behavior.* For instance, a point guard in basketball scores 30 points, although his normal scoring average is 10 points a game. He receives praise and recognition from the fans and the media for his high scoring output and naturally wants to repeat this behavior. However, he is a much better passer than a shooter. When he tries hard to score more points, he actually hurts his team and lowers his shooting percentage because he attempts more low-percentage shots. You must also *consider all the reinforcements available to the individual* as well as how she values them. For example, someone in an exercise program receives great positive reinforcement for staying in shape and looking good; however, because of her participation in the program she spends less time with her spouse. This aversive consequence outweighs the positive reinforcer, so she drops out of the program. Unfortunately, coaches, teachers, and exercise leaders are often unaware of these competing motives and reinforcers.

KEY POINT The principles of reinforcement are complex because people react differently to the same reinforcement, may not be able to repeat a desired behavior, and receive different reinforcers in different situations.

Approaches to Influencing Behavior

There are positive and negative ways to teach and coach. The positive approach focuses on rewarding appropriate behavior (e.g., catching people doing something correctly), which increases the likelihood of desirable responses occurring in the future. Conversely, the negative approach focuses on punishing undesirable behaviors, which should reduce the inappropriate behaviors. The positive approach is designed to strengthen desired behaviors by motivating participants to perform those behaviors and by rewarding participants when those behaviors occur. The negative approach, however, focuses on errors and attempts to eliminate unwanted behaviors through punishment and criticism. For example, if an exerciser is late for class, the exercise leader might criticize the person with the hope of producing more on-time behavior in the future.

Most coaches combine the positive and negative approaches in attempting to motivate and teach their athletes. However, sport psychologists agree that the predominant approach with sport and physical activity participants should be positive (Smith, 2006). We see this in a quote by Louisville basketball coach Rick Pitino: "You can program yourself to be positive. Being positive is a discipline . . . . And the more adversity you face the more positive you have to be. Being positive helps build confidence and self-esteem, which is critical to succeeding" (Pitino, 1998, pp. 78–80). Phil Jackson, eleven-time National Basketball Association championship coach, uses a 2-to-1 ratio of positive to negative feedback, although the Positive Coaching Alliance, which trains youth sports coaches, recommends a 5-to-1 ratio. Jackson argues that it is hard to come up with five positives for every negative at the professional level, but he does understand that players won't listen or react positively if a coach simply attacks them with criticism. He firmly believes that any message will be more effective if you pump up players' egos before you bruise their egos (Jackson, 2004).

KEY POINT Although some coaches still use threats of punishment as their primary motivational tool, a positive approach is recommended for working with athletes.

Guidelines for Using Positive Reinforcement

Sport psychologists highly recommend a positive approach to motivation to avoid the potential nega-

Coaches can influence behavior using both positive and negative approaches.

tive side effects of using punishment as the primary approach. Research demonstrates that athletes who play for positive-oriented coaches like their teammates better, enjoy their athletic experience more, like their coaches more, and have greater team cohesion (Smith & Smoll, 1997). The following quote by Jimmy Johnson, former coach of the Miami Dolphins and Dallas Cowboys, sums up his emphasis on the positive: "I try never to plant a negative seed. I try to make every comment a positive comment. There's a lot of evidence to support positive management" (cited in Smith, 2006, p. 40). Reinforcement can take many forms, such as verbal compliments, smiles or other nonverbal behaviors that imply approval, increased privileges, and the use of rewards. Let's examine some of the principles underlying the effective use of positive reinforcement.

Choose Effective Reinforcers

Rewards should meet the needs of those receiving them. It is best to know the likes and dislikes of the people you work with and choose reinforcers accordingly. Reinforcers include the following.

- Social reinforcers: praise, smile, pat on the back, publicity

- Material reinforcers: trophies, medals, ribbons, T-shirts
- Activity reinforcers: playing a game rather than drilling, playing a different position, taking a trip to play another team, getting a rest
- Special outings: going to a professional game, throwing a team party, hearing a presentation from a professional athlete

A physical education teacher might have students complete a questionnaire to determine what type of rewards (e.g., social, material, activity) they most desire. This information could help a teacher pinpoint the type of reinforcer to use for each student. Similarly, athletic trainers might develop a list of the types of reinforcements athletes react most favorably to when recovering from difficult injuries. Sometimes you might want to reward the entire team or class rather than a particular individual or to vary the types of rewards (it can become monotonous to receive the same reinforcement repeatedly).

The kinds of rewards that people receive from others are called *extrinsic* because they come from external (outside the individual) sources, such as the coach or the teacher. Other rewards are called *intrinsic* because they reside within the participant.

Examples of intrinsic rewards include taking pride in accomplishment and feeling competent. Although coaches, teachers, and exercise leaders cannot directly offer **intrinsic rewards**, they can structure the environment to promote intrinsic motivation. It has been demonstrated that if an environment is more focused on learning, effort, and improvement as opposed to competition, outcome, and social comparison, then participants tend to be more intrinsically motivated (see "Creating a Positive Motivational Climate"). We further discuss the relationship between extrinsic rewards and intrinsic motivation later in this chapter.

DISCOVER Activity 6.1 helps you identify your preferred types of rewards.

Schedule Reinforcements Effectively

Appropriate timing and frequency can ensure that rewards are effective. During the initial stages of training or skill development, desirable responses should be reinforced often, perhaps on an almost continuous schedule. A continuous schedule requires rewarding after every correct response, whereas on a partial schedule, behavior is rewarded intermittently.

KEY POINT In the early stages of learning, continuous and immediate reinforcement is desirable; in the later stages of learning, however, intermittent reinforcement is more effective.

Research has indicated that continuous feedback not only acts as a motivator but also provides the learner with information about how he is doing. However, once a particular skill or behavior has been mastered or is occurring at the desired frequency, the schedule can be gradually reduced to intermittent (Martin & Pear, 2003). To underscore the effects of continuous and intermittent reinforcement, it is important to understand the difference between learning and performance. In a study by Schmidt and Wrisberg (2004), giving feedback after every attempt (continuous—100%) was far better for performance during practice than giving it after every other attempt (intermittent—50%). However, when taking tests of retention without any feedback the next day, partici-

Creating a Positive Motivational Climate

Research originally conducted in schools (Epstein, 1989) and then applied to sport and physical education (Treasure & Roberts, 1995) has argued that a mastery-oriented climate can foster intrinsic motivation and self-confidence. The acronym TARGET was developed to represent the manipulation of environmental conditions that foster a mastery-oriented environment.

1. *Tasks.* Focus on learning and task involvement (play down competitive and social comparison aspects and focus on simply learning new skills).

2. *Authority.* Allow students to participate in the decision-making process (e.g., ask athletes for input on new drills).

3. *Reward.* Reward for improvement, not social comparison (e.g., reward when athletes improve the number of push-ups they can do regardless of how they rate against others).

4. *Grouping.* Create cooperative learning climates within groups (have athletes work together to solve problems rather than compete against each other).

5. *Evaluation.* Focus evaluations on personal improvement (evaluate progress and learning, not just who is the best at a given task).

6. *Timing.* Use proper timing for all of these conditions (provide feedback as immediately as possible after the athlete performs the task).

Research in sport has focused on coach-created motivational climate (Duda & Balague, 2007; Smoll & Smith, 2009), parent-created motivational climate (White, 2007), and peer-created motivational climate (Ntoumanis, Vazou, & Duda, 2007). Although in all three cases the focus is on creating more of a mastery-oriented environment (e.g., the TARGET program), the details are specific to each group forming the motivational climate. But all three approaches focus on creating a motivational climate that fosters equal treatment, cooperation, autonomy, mastery of skills, social support, and effort.

pants with only 50% feedback performed better than those given 100% feedback. In essence, feedback after every trial was used as a kind of crutch, and the learner was unable to perform effectively when the crutch was removed. Besides reducing the amount of feedback given, coaches might ask athletes to generate their own feedback. For example, after a tennis player hits a couple of balls into the net, a coach might ask, "Why do you think the ball went into the net?" This forces players to evaluate their own internal feedback, as well as the outcome, instead of relying too heavily on coach feedback.

The sooner a reinforcement is provided after a response, the more powerful the effects on behavior. This is especially true when people are learning new skills, when it is easy to lose confidence if the skill isn't performed correctly. Once someone masters a skill it is less critical to reinforce immediately, although it is still essential that the correct behaviors be reinforced at some point.

Reward Appropriate Behaviors

Choosing the proper behaviors to reward is also critical. Obviously you cannot reward people every time they do something right. You have to decide on the most appropriate and important behaviors and concentrate on rewarding these. Many coaches and teachers tend to focus their rewards purely on the outcome of performance (e.g., winning), but other behaviors could and should be reinforced, which we now discuss.

Reward Successful Approximations

When individuals are acquiring a new skill, especially a complex one, they inevitably make mistakes. It may take days or weeks to master the skill, which can be disappointing and frustrating for the learner. It is helpful, therefore, to reward small improvements as the skill is learned. This technique, called **shaping**, allows people to continue to improve as they get closer and closer to the desired response (Martin & Thompson, 2011). Specifically, individuals are rewarded for performances that approximate the desired performance. This spurs their motivation and provides direction for what they should do next. For example, if players are learning the overhand volleyball serve, you might first reward the proper toss, then the proper motion, then good contact, and finally the execution that puts all the parts together successfully. Similarly, an aerobics instructor might reward participants for learning part of a routine until they have mastered the entire pro-

gram, or a physical therapist might reward a client for improving the range of motion in her shoulder after surgery through adhering to her stretching program, even though she still has room for improvement.

KEY POINT With difficult skills, shape the behavior of the learner by reinforcing close approximations of the desired behavior.

Reward Performance, Not Only Outcome

Coaches who emphasize winning tend to reward players based on outcome. A baseball player hits a hard line drive down the third base line, but the third baseman makes a spectacular diving catch. In his next at bat, the same batter tries to check his swing and hits the ball off the end of the bat, just over the outstretched arm of the second baseman, for a base hit. Rewarding the base hit but not the out would be sending the wrong message to the player. If an individual performs the skill correctly, that's all he can do. The outcome is sometimes out of the player's control, so the coach should focus on the athlete's performance instead of the performance outcome.

It is especially important to use an individual's previous level of performance as the standard for success. For example, if a young gymnast's best score on her floor routine was 7.5 and she received a 7.8 for her most recent effort, then this mark should be used as the measure of success and she should be rewarded for her performance.

Reward Effort

Coaches and teachers must recognize effort as part of performance. Not everyone can be successful in sport. When sport and exercise participants (especially youngsters) know that they will be recognized for trying new and difficult skills and not just criticized for performing incorrectly, they do not fear trying. Former UCLA basketball coach John Wooden captured this concept of focusing on effort instead of winning:

" You cannot find a player who ever played for me at UCLA that can tell you he ever heard me mention winning a basketball game. He might say I inferred a little here and there, but I never mentioned winning. Yet the last thing that I told my players, just prior to tip-off, before we would go out on the floor was, when the game is over, I want your head up—and I know of only one way for your head to be up—and that's for you to know you did your best . . . . **This means to do the best you can do. That's the best; no one can do more . . . . You made that effort."**

Interestingly, a study conducted with youths (Mueller & Dweck, 1998) showed that performers who received effort-oriented feedback ("Good try") displayed better performance than those provided ability-oriented feedback ("You're talented"), especially after failure. Specifically, after failure, children who were praised for effort displayed more task persistence, more task enjoyment, and better performance than did children who were praised for high ability. Thus, effort (which is under one's control) appears to be critical to producing persistence, which is one of the most highly valued attributes in sport and exercise environments.

Reward Emotional and Social Skills

With the pressure to win, it is easy to forget the importance of fair play and being a good sport. Athletes who demonstrate good sporting behavior, responsibility, judgment, and other signs of self-control and cooperation should be recognized and reinforced. Unfortunately, some high-visibility athletes and coaches have not been good role models and have been accused or convicted of such acts as physical or verbal abuse of officials and coaches, substance abuse, physical or sexual abuse, and murder. One of the reasons that basketball administrators were so dismayed over the 2005 fight between the Detroit Pistons and Indiana Pacers and the fans (which resulted in significant suspensions of several players) was that it sent a negative message to youngsters. Displaying restraint despite being "egged on" by fans is an important social skill that athletes need to learn because it relates to many life situations. As leaders of sport and physical activity, we have a tremendous opportunity and responsibility to encourage positive emotional and social skills. We should not overlook the chance to reward such positive behaviors, especially in younger participants.

Provide Performance Feedback

Help participants by giving them information and feedback about the accuracy and success of their movements. This type of feedback is typically provided after the completion of a response. For example, an athletic trainer working with an injured athlete on increasing flexibility while rehabilitating from a knee injury asks the athlete to bend his knee as far as possible. The trainer then tells the athlete that he has

improved his flexibility from 50° to 55° since the week before. Similarly, a fitness instructor might give participants specific feedback about proper positioning and technique when they are lifting weights.

KEY POINT Providing specific feedback regarding the correctness (or incorrectness) of a person's response improves the person's performance and enhances his or her motivation.

When you give feedback to athletes, students, and exercisers, the feedback should be sincere and contingent on some behavior. Whether it is praise or criticism, the feedback needs to be tied to (contingent on) a specific behavior or set of behaviors. It would be inappropriate, for example, to say "Way to go, keep up the good work!" to a physical education student who is having difficulty learning a new gymnastics skill. Rather, the feedback should be specific and linked to performance. Inform the athlete how to perform the skill correctly, perhaps saying, "Make sure you keep your chest tucked close to your body during the tumbling maneuver." Such feedback, when sincere, demonstrates that you care and are concerned with helping the learner.

Interest has surged in performance feedback as a technique for improving performance in business, industry, and sport (Huberman & O'Brien, 1999; Stokes, Luselli, & Reed, 2010; Stokes, Luselli, Reed, & Fleming, 2010). The evidence indicates that this type of feedback is effective in enhancing performance: Performance increased by 53% on average after performance feedback and indicators of performance excellence had been instituted.

Along these lines, a study by Mouratidis, Lens, and Vansteenkiste (2010) indicates that how one provides corrective feedback makes a difference in the performer's motivation, emotional regulation, and performance. Making mistakes and errors is inevitable in training and competition, and even corrective feedback may convey the message that the performer has low competence. However, providing corrective feedback in response to mistakes and poor performance in an autonomy-supportive manner (e.g., "You could improve your free-throws by either changing your routine or following through on your shots") rather than a controlling manner (e.g., "You won't make this team unless you work on your three-point shot") produces higher levels of intrinsic motivation, positive affect, and performance.

Benefits of Feedback

Feedback about performance can benefit participants in several ways, and two of the main functions are to motivate and to instruct. **Motivational feedback** attempts to facilitate performance by *enhancing confidence, inspiring greater effort and energy expenditure,* and creating a positive mood. Examples include "Hang in there," "You can do it," and "Get tough." A second way that feedback can be motivating is by serving as a valuable *reinforcement* to the performer, which would in turn stimulate positive or negative feelings. For example, individuals receiving specific feedback indicating poor performance might become dissatisfied with their current level of performance. This feedback can motivate them to improve, but they should also have feelings of satisfaction that function as positive feedback when subsequent feedback indicates improvement. A third motivational function of feedback relates to establishing *goal-setting* programs. Clear, objective knowledge of results is critical to productive goal setting (see chapter 15) because effective goals are specific and measurable. Thus, individuals benefit from getting specific feedback to help them set their goals.

Instructional feedback provides information about the specific behaviors that should be performed, the levels of proficiency that should be achieved, and the performer's current level of proficiency in the desired skills and activities. When skills are highly complex, knowledge of results can be particularly important. Breaking down complex skills into their parts creates a more effective learning environment and gives the learner specific information on how to perform each phase of the skill.

A recent development in feedback is represented in a technique called the method of amplification error (MAE). MAE is based on the assumption that participants can learn to correct their movements through their mistakes. In essence, participants are asked to amplify their principal error during a given performance. Through this instruction, they achieve a better understanding of what not to do and are more capable of readjusting the entire motion during subsequent attempts. Studies (e.g., Milanese, Facci, Cesari, & Zancanzro, 2008) have supported the effectiveness of MAE compared with other instructional techniques.

Types of Feedback

Verbal praise, facial expressions, and pats on the back are easy, effective ways to reinforce desirable behaviors. Phrases such as "Well done!" "Way to go!" "Keep up the good work!" and "That's a lot better!" can be powerful reinforcers. However, this reward becomes more effective when you identify the specific behaviors you are pleased with. For instance, a track coach might say to a sprinter, "Way to get out of the blocks—you really pushed off strongly with your legs." Or an aerobics instructor might say to a participant who is working hard, "I like the way you're pumping your arms while stepping in place." The coach and the instructor have identified exactly what the participants are doing well.

Guidelines for Using Punishment

Positive reinforcement should be the predominant way to change behavior; in fact, most researchers suggest that 80% to 90% of reinforcement should be positive. Despite this near consensus among sport psychologists about what fosters motivation in athletes, some coaches use punishment as the primary motivator (Smith, 2006). For example, school achievement in athletes is often prompted by a fear of punishment, such as having one's eligibility taken away because of poor grades. Based on empirical research, Seifried (2008) presents a view of the pros and cons of using punishment. (A reaction to this article is presented by Albrecht, 2009.) A summary of Seifried's arguments is presented next.

Support of Punishment

Although a number of educators argue against the use of punishment by coaches, others (e.g., Benatar, 1998) argue that punishment can serve a useful educational purpose (i.e., maintain stability, order, mastery) due to the closeness of coaches and athletes. Punishment certainly can control and change negative behavior (Smith, 2006), and it has advocates among coaches and teachers who use punishment to improve learning and performance. A number of other arguments support the use of punishment in athletic settings:

- A strong expectation of cooperation and a strong animosity toward wrongdoers exist, and thus the use of punishment to deter future cheating or wrongdoing is supported (Goodman, 2006).
- Individuals who cheat should be punished because they are not sharing, helping, and cooperating with others (Walsh, 2000).

- Cheaters, although benefiting in the short run, will receive a significantly lower reward in the future because of their wrongdoing (e.g., violators of Major League Baseball's substance abuse policy will likely never make it into the Hall of Fame).

- Assigning punishment to wrongdoers assures others (e.g., teammates) that all individuals are held accountable for their actions and their effect on others (Radzik, 2003).

- It appears acceptable for coaches to deter inappropriate or unacceptable behaviors through significant and timely punishment because this sends a signal to potential violators that they will suffer the consequences if they don't follow the rules established by their team.

- Findings from 157 studies showed that individuals experiencing corporal punishment are at a negligible risk for developing emotional and behavioral problems (Paolucci & Violato, 2004).

Criticisms of Punishment

Several arguments have been put forth to suggest that punishment severely lacks any base of support and is in fact related to negative (unproductive) behaviors. These arguments include the following:

- Punishment can be degrading or shame producing, especially when individuals perceive their image or standing to be lowered in the eyes of others. Shame and guilt appear to be closely linked to failure or weakness when connected to the attainment of a standard, expectation, belief, or value (Hareli & Weiner, 2002).

- Punishment usually arouses a fear of failure. Athletes who fear failure are not motivated by and do not enjoy the fruits of victory; rather, they only try to avoid the agony of defeat. Research has indicated that athletes with a high fear of failure perform more poorly in competition and are more likely to get injured, enjoy the sport experience less, and drop out (Smith & Smoll, 1990).

- Punishment can unwittingly reinforce the undesirable behavior by drawing attention to it. Singling out a student who disrupts the class provides the student with the attention he craves. The punishment reinforces and strengthens the very behavior it was intended to eliminate.

- Punishment can create an unpleasant, aversive learning environment, producing hostility and resentment between the coach and the athletes. Over time, students and athletes may lose motivation as they become discouraged by frequent criticism. Furthermore, the undesirable behaviors may not be eliminated; rather, they may be suppressed only while the threat of punishment is present. For example, an exerciser may work hard in an aerobics class when the leader is watching her but slack off when she is not being watched.

Making Punishment Effective

Some coaches assume that punishing athletes for making mistakes will eliminate these errors. These coaches assume that if players fear making mistakes, they will try harder not to make them. However, successful coaches who used punishment usually were also masters of strategy, teaching, or technical analysis. Often those—not their negative approach—were the attributes that made them successful. Although not recommended as the major source of motivation, punishment might occasionally be necessary to eliminate unwanted behaviors. Here are some guidelines for maximizing the effectiveness of punishment (Martens, Christina, Harvey, & Sharkey, 1981):

- Be consistent by giving everyone the same type of punishment for breaking similar rules.

- Punish the behavior, not the person. Convey to the individual that it's his behavior that needs to change.

- Allow athletes to have input in making up punishments for breaking rules.

- Do not use physical activity or conditioning as a punishment. (However, research by Bandealy and Kerr [2013] revealed a great deal of individual differences with regard to using physical conditioning as punishment: While most athletes reported negative emotional responses such as embarrassment and humiliation, a small percentage perceived it as an effective way to enhance motivation and team cohesion.)

- Make sure the punishment is not perceived as a reward or simply as attention.

- Impose punishment impersonally—do not berate people or yell. Simply inform them of their punishment.

- Do not punish athletes for making errors while they are playing.
- Do not embarrass individuals in front of teammates or classmates.
- Use punishment sparingly, and enforce it when you use it.
- Do not punish other teammates for an individual's mistake.
- Make sure punishment is age appropriate.
- Make certain that athletes understand the reason for punishment.

KEY POINT Potential drawbacks of punishment and criticism include arousing fear of failure, reinforcing the unwanted behavior, producing shame, and hindering the learning of skills.

Coaches also need to be aware of cultural differences when administering punishment. A study by Hagiwara and Wolfson (2013) found differences between Japanese and English soccer players in terms of their reactions to certain types of punishment. Specifically, English players rated their coaches higher if they used verbal rather than physical punishment. However, Japanese athletes did not differ in how they viewed their coaches regardless of whether the coaches gave verbal or physical punishment.

Guilt appears to play an important role in English culture, whereas shame appears to play an important role in Japanese culture, which may account for these differences. Japanese athletes might be more ashamed after failure and feel that any sort of punishment is deserved.

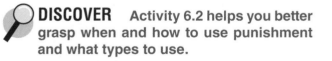 **DISCOVER** Activity 6.2 helps you better grasp when and how to use punishment and what types to use.

Behavior Modification in Sport

Systematic application of the principles of positive and negative reinforcement to help produce desirable behaviors and eliminate undesirable behaviors has been given various names in the sport psychology literature: **contingency management** (Siedentop, 1980), **behavioral coaching** (Martin & Lumsden, 1987), and **behavior modification** (Donahue, Gillis, & King, 1980). These terms all refer to attempts to structure the environment through the systematic

use of reinforcement, especially during practice. In general, behavioral techniques are used in sport and physical activity settings to help individuals stay task oriented and motivated throughout a training period. In what follows, we highlight a few studies that have used behavioral techniques in sport settings and then offer some guidelines for designing behavior programs.

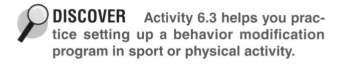 **DISCOVER** Activity 6.3 helps you practice setting up a behavior modification program in sport or physical activity.

Evaluating Behavioral Programs

The evidence to date suggests that systematic reinforcement techniques can effectively modify various behaviors, including specific performance skills and coaching and teaching behaviors, as well as reduce errors and increase exercising (see Cushing & Steele [2011] and Luiselli, Woods, & Reed [2011] for reviews). Behavioral techniques have successfully changed attendance at practice (Young, Medic, & Starkes, 2009); increased output by swimmers in practice (Koop & Martin, 1983); improved fitness activities (Leith & Taylor, 1992) and gymnastics performance (Wolko, Hrycaiko, & Martin, 1993); reduced errors in tennis, football, and gymnastics (Allison & Ayllon, 1980; Stokes et al., 2010a, 2010b); and improved golf performance (Simek, O'Brien, & Figlerski, 1994). Other programs have effectively used behavioral techniques to decrease off-task behaviors in figure skaters (Hume, Martin, Gonzalez, Cracklen, & Genthon, 1985), facilitate positive youth development (Camire, Forneris, Trudel, & Berhard, 2011), and develop healthier attitudes toward good sporting behavior and team support (Galvan & Ward, 1998). Let's look closely at a few examples of successful behavioral programs.

Feedback and Reinforcement in Football

In a classic study, Komaki and Barnett (1977) used feedback and praise to improve specific football performance skills. Barnett, who coached a Pop Warner football team, wanted to know whether his players were improving in the basic offensive plays. He and Komaki targeted three specific plays (plays A, B, and C) run from the wishbone offense (a formation that requires specific positioning of the running backs and quarterback) and the five players (center, quarterback, and running backs) responsible for the proper execution. For their study they broke each play into five stages. For instance, one play included (1) a quarterback–center exchange, (2) a quarterback–right halfback fake, (3) a fullback blocking the end, (4) a quarterback decision to pitch or keep, and (5) quarterback action.

After collecting data during an initial baseline period (10 practices or games), the coach systematically reinforced and provided feedback for play A, play B, and play C. This feedback included

- a demonstration of the correct behaviors at each stage,
- a checklist of parts that were successfully executed, and
- praise and recognition for performing each stage correctly.

To test the effectiveness of the behavioral program, the authors compared the percentage of stages performed correctly for each play during the baseline and reinforcement (about 2 weeks) periods. After 2 weeks, correct performances increased on play A from 62% at baseline to 82%, on play B from 54% to 82%, and on play C from 66% to 80%.

Behavioral Coaching in Golf

Another behavioral program targeted the performance of novice golfers (O'Brien & Simek, 1983). This study used a type of behavioral change program known as **backward chaining**. In this approach, the last step in a chain is established first. Then the last step is paired with the next-to-last step, and so forth, with the steps finally progressing back to the beginning of the chain. In the case of golf, the last step in the chain would be putting on the green into the hole. Putting the ball into the hole in the smallest number of strokes is the goal in golf, and the successful putt should therefore be reinforced. As the next step, chipping onto the green is the focus, and putts are made as reinforcement. Then comes the fairway shot, followed by a successful chip and an equally successful putt. The final step involves driving the ball off the tee box, followed in turn by successful completion of the previous three steps.

This behavioral approach using backward chaining was compared with traditional coaching methods used in training novice golfers. Results revealed that golfers receiving the backward chaining instruction scored some 17 strokes lower than golfers in the traditionally coached control group. In essence, the behavioral

coaching group scored almost 1 stroke per hole (18 holes) better than the traditional coaching group—an amazing improvement.

Recording and Shaping in Basketball

Another behavioral program targeted both performance and nonperformance behaviors (Siedentop, 1980). A junior high school basketball coach was distressed that his players criticized each other so often in practice and failed to concentrate on shooting skills. The coach decided to award points for daily practice in layups, jump shooting, and free-throw drills and for being a team player (which meant that players encouraged their teammates during play and practice). In this system, points were deducted if the coach saw an instance of a bad attitude. An "Eagle effort board" was posted in a conspicuous place in the main hall leading to the gymnasium, and outstanding students received an "Eagle effort" award at the postseason banquet.

The program produced some dramatic changes: After just a few weeks, jump shooting improved from 37% to 51%, layups increased from 68% to 80%, and foul shooting improved from 59% to 67%. But the most dramatic improvement was in the team player category. Before implementing the behavioral program, the coach had detected 4 to 6 instances of criticism during each practice session and 10 to 12 instances of encouragement among teammates. After only a few sessions, he recorded more than 80 encouraging statements during a practice session. At the end of the season the coach commented, "We were more together than I ever could have imagined." "Improving Attendance: A Behavioral Approach" provides an example of a behavioral program for increasing attendance and participation in an age-group swimming program.

Inappropriate Tennis Behaviors

In a case study by Galvan and Ward (1998), the aim was to reduce the amount of inappropriate on-court behavior in collegiate tennis players, including racket abuse, ball abuse, verbal abuse, and physical abuse of self. The number of inappropriate behaviors from each player was posted on the bulletin board in the players' locker room. To derive these numbers, the investigators observed all challenge matches (competitive matches between teammates) during practice and recorded the inappropriate behaviors. All players were told of their inappropriate behaviors during an initial meeting and were provided strategies for reducing

Improving Attendance: A Behavioral Approach

A swimming team was showing poor attendance and punctuality at practices. To solve the problem, sport psychologists recommended that the swim coach make an attendance board that listed each swimmer's name. She placed the board prominently on a wall by the swimming pool where everyone could see it. In the first phase of the program, swimmers who came to practice received a check on the board next to their names. In the second phase, swimmers had to show up on time to receive a check. In the final phase, swimmers had to show up on time and swim for the entire session to receive a check. Results indicated a dramatic increase in attendance at each phase of the study—45% for the first phase, 63% for the second phase, and 100% for the third phase (McKenzie & Rushall, 1974).

Then the sport psychologists who developed the program board had swimmers check off each lap of a programmed workout. The group increased its performance output by 27%—the equivalent of an additional 619 yards per swimmer during the practice session! The public nature of the attendance and program boards clearly served a motivational function: Every swimmer could see who was attending, who was late, who swam the entire period, and how many laps each swimmer completed. Coaches and swimmers commented that peer pressure, public recognition, and the attention, praise, and approval of the coaches helped make the program successful.

Finally, a study by Young, Medic, and Starkes (2009) found that self-monitoring logs improved attendance and punctuality of intercollegiate swimmers, but the effect lasted only about 2 to 3 weeks. Thus, additional motivation, possibly in the form of a public display, is needed for continued adherence.

these behaviors. All five players who were followed through a competitive tennis season had a significant reduction in inappropriate behaviors, especially the behaviors that they had initially exhibited most frequently. For example, one player had averaged more than 11 verbal abuses per match during the baseline period, and this number decreased to a little more than 2 per match by the end of the season. The behavior modification appeared to work well for this group of collegiate players.

Creating Effective Behavioral Programs

Although the examples demonstrate that behavioral change programs can alter behavior, actually changing behavior in sport and exercise settings can be a tricky proposition. Effective behavioral programs have certain major characteristics:

- They emphasize specific, detailed, and frequent measurement of performance and behavior and use these measures to evaluate the effectiveness of the program.
- They recognize the distinction between developing new behavior and maintaining existing behavior at acceptable levels, and they offer positive procedures for accomplishing both.
- They encourage participants to improve against their own previous level of performance. Thus,

a recreational athlete recovering from injury does not try to compare his performance against that of professional athletes but rather against what the physical therapist believes is optimal for the particular circumstance.

- They emphasize behavioral procedures that have been demonstrated by research to be effective. (This is more a science than an art.)
- They emphasize that the coach, teacher, or leader should carefully monitor behavior in a systematic fashion (e.g., film, behavioral checklist) so that ineffective behaviors can be eliminated.
- They encourage the leader to get feedback from participants regarding the effectiveness of various aspects of the behavioral intervention.

Clearly, behavioral techniques can produce positive changes in a variety of behaviors. As you apply behavioral techniques, the following guidelines can increase the effectiveness of your intervention programs.

• *Target the behaviors.* When you initiate a program, identify only a couple of behaviors to work with. If participants focus on changing just a couple of behaviors, they avoid being overwhelmed and confused by trying to do too much too fast. Furthermore, it is difficult to observe simultaneously what all the participants are doing. By tracking only one or two

Choosing and Monitoring Target Behaviors

Tkachuk, Leslie-Toogood, and Martin (2003) provide some guidelines and suggestions for selecting the behaviors to be changed and for observing and recording these behaviors. These include the following:

- *Direct observation of single behaviors.* Single behaviors should be observed by individuals who have been trained, which will ensure high reliability. Some behaviors that have been observed in previous research (see Martin & Pear, 2003, for a review) include swimming stroke errors, serving accuracy in volleyball, defensive skills of football players, skating speed of speed skaters, and skills performed correctly at gymnastics practices.

- *Behavioral checklists for recording multiple behaviors.* Researchers and consultants can develop checklists that enable observers to monitor multiple behaviors. Some examples include the Coaching Behavior Assessment System, the Self-Talk and Gestures Rating Scale, the teaching behaviors of an expert basketball coach, checklists of components of correct form of sprinters in track, and a checklist for evaluating freestyle and backstroke technique in swimming.

- *Athlete self-monitoring.* Sometimes self-monitoring can initiate the desired change of behavior. Some examples of skills that can be self-monitored include coaching skills, laps swum during swimming practices, and good shots in golf.

- *Filming practice, precompetition, and competition.* Filming behavior provides a permanent record of that behavior for observational analysis. The film can be used to assess strengths and weaknesses of opponents as well as components of effective or ineffective precompetition or preperformance routines.

- *Postperformance video reconstruction of verbal behavior.* Visual stimuli from the competitive environment captured on video may cue recall of verbal behavior and emotions experienced during the performance.

behaviors, you can more accurately record the targeted behaviors and reinforce them fairly. In addition to the typical performance behaviors, social and emotional behaviors are appropriate behaviors to target. Target the behaviors after you carefully assess the particular needs of the individuals in the program. To choose appropriate target behaviors, see "Choosing and Monitoring Target Behaviors."

- *Define targeted behaviors.* Try to define behaviors in a way that makes them readily observable and easy to record. Attendance, foul shooting percentage, the number of laps done, and correct execution of a skill are relatively objective, concrete behaviors. Such behaviors as hustle and effort are more difficult to pinpoint and measure. Individuals need to be told specifically what types of behaviors are expected so they can modify their behavior accordingly.

- *Record the behaviors.* Record observable behaviors on a checklist so you can give participants feedback. For maximum efficiency and effectiveness, checklists should be simple and straightforward. Head coaches, teachers, and exercise leaders are usually too busy to record behaviors, but often assistant coaches,

managers, trainers, or teacher aides can be enlisted to help. If you do ask others to help, you will need to teach them how to record the behaviors to ensure reliability.

- *Provide meaningful feedback.* Detailed feedback enhances motivation. A simple set of checkmarks on an easy-to-read graph that clearly displays someone's progress encourages self-praise, a teacher's or coach's praise, and knowledge of improvement, which all increase motivation. Public display of this feedback can stimulate peer interaction that might also reinforce increased output. At the same time, though, some people find this type of display embarrassing and aversive. The focus should always be on self-improvement; avoid creating unhealthy competition among teammates. It is a good idea to hold a team meeting to help determine the exact location and nature of the public display.

- *State the outcomes clearly.* Athletes and students want to be clear on what behaviors are required and what will be the result of performing or not performing these behaviors. If being eligible to start in the next game is the reward for certain practice behaviors, the coach should clarify this outcome along with the specific behaviors the athletes need to demonstrate.

Tailor the reward system. Many athletes and students are already fairly well motivated, but they need a systematic program to direct their motivation. The less motivated athletes and students are, the more they might initially need to rely on external rewards. But the strongest kind of motivation over the long haul is internal motivation, which should always be encouraged. The key point is to consider individual differences when you implement behavioral change programs.

Behavior Modification and Cognitive Behavior Therapy

Behavior modification and cognitive behavior therapy (which incorporate cognitive change methods such as self-talk and mental rehearsal) can be combined and integrated to produce even greater performance enhancements. Luiselli (2012) provides an example of how cognitive behavior therapy and behavior modification can be integrated into a figure skater's practice session.

- Before the skater takes the ice she refers to her practice checklist, which outlines her performance goals for the session.

- The skater then images reaching her goals by performing specific moves and jumps on the ice.
- The skater reviews the session with her coach before starting to skate.
- Throughout the session the coach provides positive feedback and reminds the skater of her objectives.
- The skater repeatedly practices specific difficult moves and jumps so the coach can provide targeted feedback.
- At the end of the session both the coach and skater complete identical rating forms for everything practiced in the session so they can compare ratings and prepare for the next practice session.

This list describes just a few of the methods that can be used in cognitive behavior therapy and behavior modification, including goal setting, self-monitoring, behavioral rehearsal, prompting, positive reinforcement, and cuing. Figure 6.1 provides an example of how cognitive behavior therapy and behavior modification principles can be combined in a coaching

Pregame	In-game	Postgame
Be sure all players are checked in and present 30 minutes preceding game time.	Designate bench coach assignments for forward and defense player positions.	Allow 5 minute cool-down period after players enter locker room.
• Give instructions to get dressed. • Allow 10 minutes dress time. • Announce "quiet and eye on coach" cue. • Using whiteboard, designate player positions and line assignments. • Review strategy and objectives: Puck control Passing puck Defensive play Shots on goal • Have players check gear and wait to exit locker room.	• Praise each player returning to bench on line changes: Hustle Position awareness Team play • Make corrections with players as warranted; tell them specifically what to do. • Between periods: Review preceding play Using whiteboard, highlight strategy points Remind players to hydrate Shots on goal	• Obtain game score sheet. • Assemble players with "quiet and eyes on coach" cue. • Review game successes. • Review areas that can be improved. • Ask a player to comment positively about team play—"what we did well." • Remind players of next practice or game (date and time).

FIGURE 6.1 Coaching checklist.

Reprinted from "Behavioral sport psychology consulting: A review of some practice concerns and recommendations." J. Luiselli, *Journal of Sport Psychology in Action* 3(1): 41-51, 2012, Taylor and Francis Ltd, reprinted by permission of publisher (Taylor & Francis Ltd, http://www.tandf.co.uk/journals).

checklist to help coaches work with youth hockey players. (See Gawande, 2010, for an in-depth discussion of the benefits of checklists.)

Intrinsic Motivation and Extrinsic Rewards

The world of sport and exercise uses **extrinsic rewards** extensively. Most leagues have postseason banquets in which participants receive such awards as medals, trophies, ribbons, money, and jackets. Elementary school teachers frequently give stickers and toys to reward good behavior in their students. Exercise participants frequently get T-shirts and other rewards for regular attendance and participation in classes. Advocates of extrinsic rewards argue that rewards increase motivation, enhance learning, and increase the desire to continue participation. As noted throughout this chapter, the systematic use of rewards can certainly produce some desired behavior changes in sport, physical education, and exercise settings. However, if rewards are used incorrectly, some negative consequences also can result.

We know that motivation has two sources: extrinsic and intrinsic. With extrinsic rewards, the motivation comes from other people through positive and negative reinforcements. But individuals also participate in sport and physical activity for intrinsic reasons. People who have **intrinsic motivation** strive inwardly to be competent and self-determining in their quest to master the task at hand. They enjoy competition, like the action and excitement, focus on having fun, and want to learn skills to the best of their ability. Individuals who participate for the love of sport and

exercise would be considered intrinsically motivated, as would those who play for pride. For example, when Steve Ovett, British elite middle-distance runner, was asked why he ran competitively, he answered, "I just did it because I wanted to . . . [get] the best out of myself for all the effort I'd put in" (Hemery, 1991, p. 142). Similarly, Tiger Woods observed that successful golfers "enjoy the serenity and the challenge of trying to beat their own personal records" (Scott, 1999, p. 47). A study investigating sustained motivation of elite athletes (Mallett & Hanrahan, 2004) found that athletes were driven mainly by personal goals and achievements rather than financial incentives. But competing against and defeating an opponent is still important for some, as noted by this quote from Sam Lynch, world rowing champion: "You don't go for a world record in a race like this. It may come, but winning the title comes first" (Jones, 2002, p. 15). Figure 6.2 presents the current view of intrinsic and extrinsic motivation, and "Types of Intrinsic and Extrinsic Motivation" explains the different types of motivation. We now turn our attention to what happens when we combine extrinsic rewards and intrinsic motivation.

Factors Affecting Intrinsic and Extrinsic Motivation

Both social and psychological factors can affect one's intrinsic and extrinsic motivation in sport and exercise. Some of the more prominent **social factors** include (a) success and failure (experiences that help define one's sense of competency), (b) focus of competition (competing against yourself and some standard of excellence where the focus is on improvement rather than competing against your opponent where the focus

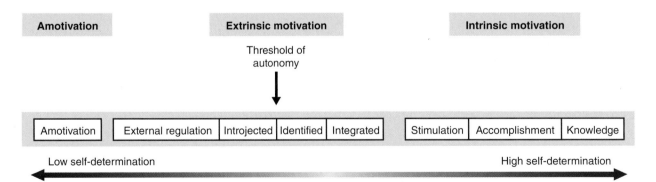

FIGURE 6.2 Continuum of intrinsic and extrinsic motivation. These concepts can be measured using the Sport Motivation Scale, developed by Pelletier and colleagues (1995).

Types of Intrinsic and Extrinsic Motivation

Current thinking views intrinsic and extrinsic motivation on a continuum and further elucidates different types of intrinsic and extrinsic motivation (i.e., these constructs are viewed as multidimensional).

Intrinsic Motivation

- *Knowledge*—The individual engages in an activity for the pleasure and satisfaction she has while learning, exploring, or trying to understand something new (e.g., learning a new defensive alignment).

- *Accomplishment*—The person engages in an activity for the pleasure and satisfaction he feels when creating something or mastering difficult skills (e.g., mastering a difficult dive he has been working on for a while).

- *Stimulation*—The person engages in an activity to experience pleasant sensations such as fun, excitement, and aesthetic pleasure (e.g., feeling the pleasure of climbing a mountain).

Extrinsic Motivation

- *Integrated regulation*—**Integrated regulation** is the most developmentally advanced form of extrinsic motivation. Activity is personally important because of a valued outcome rather than interest in the activity solely for itself. For example, a physical educator trains diligently for the valued outcome of completing a marathon. In essence, people can feel autonomous (act on their own free will) when there are external rewards for their actions (Standage, 2012).

- *Identified regulation*—The behavior is highly valued, accepted, and judged by the individual and thus is performed willingly, even if the activity is not pleasant in itself. For example, an athlete participates in a sport because she believes her involvement contributes to her growth and development. The three types of intrinsic motivation, as well as integrated regulation and **identified regulation**, all reflect the feeling of "want" rather than "ought" and thus have been found to positively relate to affective, cognitive, and behavioral outcomes (Vallerand, 1997; Vallerand & Rousseau, 2001). This is why the "threshold of autonomy" (where choice is more intrinsic in nature) as shown in figure 6.2 is placed right after identified regulation (which has some intrinsic aspects but is still more external than internal).

- *Introjected regulation*—The individual is motivated by internal prods and pressures; however, the behavior is still not considered self-determined because it is regulated by external contingencies. For example, an exerciser who stays in shape to impress the opposite sex is practicing **introjected regulation**.

- *External regulation*—The behavior is completely controlled by external sources such as rewards and constraints. For example, an athletic trainer who spends lots of time in the training room simply to get a raise in salary is externally motivated.

Amotivation

- In this case, individuals are neither intrinsically nor extrinsically motivated and thus have pervasive feelings of incompetence and lack of control. For instance, a physical education teacher who simply goes through the motions because he really doesn't care about teaching anymore is displaying **amotivation**.

is on winning), and (c) coaches' behaviors (positive vs. negative). Self-determination theory argues that competence, autonomy, and relatedness are the three basic human needs and that the degree to which they are satisfied go a long way in determining an individual's intrinsic motivation. Therefore, the **psychological factors** affecting motivation include (a) need for competence (to feel confident and self-efficacious), (b) need for autonomy (to have input into decisions or in some way "own" them), and (c) need for relatedness (to care for others and to have them care for you). Being aware of these factors and altering things when possible will enhance one's feelings of intrinsic motivation.

Passion: A Key to Sustained Motivation

Although the concept of passion has generated a lot of attention among philosophers, it has only recently received empirical attention in the sport and exercise psychology literature. Passion has been defined as a strong inclination and desire toward an activity one likes, finds important, and invests time and energy in (Vallerand, 2010). In line with self-determination theory (Ryan & Deci, 2002), it has been argued that when individuals like and engage in an activity on a regular basis, it will become part of their identity to the extent that it is highly valued (Vallerand et al., 2006). For example, having passion for playing basketball would mean that one is not merely playing basketball; rather, one is a basketball player.

Vallerand and colleagues (2011) identified two types of passion:

- *Harmonious passion (HP):* A strong desire to engage in an activity freely as it becomes part of one's identity. The activity occupies an important but not overwhelming space in one's identity. For example, collegiate athletes who have a **harmonious passion** toward their sport decide when to play and when to do other things such as study or see friends.

- *Obsessive passion (OP):* An uncontrollable desire to participate in an activity that does *not* become part of one's identity. The person becomes controlled by the activity (e.g., "I have to do it"), and thus it may conflict with other life activities (e.g., work, family). For example, collegiate athletes who have an **obsessive passion** toward their sport might sometimes end up playing their sport instead of doing something else such as studying.

The following are key findings regarding passion and sport (Donahue, Rip, & Vallerand, 2009; Lafreniere, Jowett, Vallerand, Donahue, & Lorimer, 2008; Vallerand et al., 2006, 2011):

- HP is related to positive affect, positive emotions, and flow.
- HP is associated with high-quality coach–athlete relationships.
- HP is related to higher levels of life satisfaction.
- HP is related to fewer long-term, chronic injuries.
- OP is related to negative emotions (especially shame).
- OP has no association with coach–athlete relationships.
- OP predicts rigid persistence in ill-advised activities (e.g., gambling).
- OP is related to higher levels of reactive aggression.
- OP is related to greater risk taking in choosing dangerous, unhealthy behaviors.
- An autonomous personality is related to HP, whereas a controlling personality is related to OP.

Do Extrinsic Rewards Undermine Intrinsic Motivation?

Intuitively, it seems that combining extrinsic and intrinsic motivation would produce more motivation. For instance, adding extrinsic rewards (e.g., trophies) to an activity that is intrinsically motivating (e.g., intramural volleyball) should increase motivation accordingly. Certainly you would not expect these extrinsic rewards to decrease intrinsic motivation. But let's look further at the effect of extrinsic rewards on intrinsic motivation.

Most early researchers and practitioners saw intrinsic and extrinsic motivation as additive: the more, the better. Some people, however, noted that extrinsic rewards could undermine intrinsic motivation. For example, Albert Einstein commented about exams, "This coercion had such a deterring effect that, after I passed the final examination, I found the consideration of any scientific problems distasteful to me for an entire year" (Bernstein, 1973, p. 88). When people see themselves as the cause of their behavior, they consider themselves intrinsically motivated. Conversely, when people perceive the cause of their behavior to be external to themselves (i.e., "I did it for the money"), they consider themselves extrinsically motivated. Often, the more an individual is extrinsically motivated, the less that person will be intrinsically motivated (deCharms, 1968).

What Research Says

In the late 1960s, researchers as well as theorists began to systematically test the relationship between extrinsic rewards and intrinsic motivation. Edward Deci (1971, 1972) found that participants who were rewarded with money for participating in an interesting activity subsequently spent less time at it than did people who were not paid. In his quite original and now classic study, Deci paid participants to play a Parker Brothers mechanical puzzle game called SOMA, which comprises many different-shaped blocks that can be arranged to form various patterns. Pilot testing had shown this game to be intrinsically motivating. In a later play period, the time these participants spent with the SOMA puzzles (as opposed to reading magazines) was significantly less (106 seconds) than the time spent by individuals who had not been rewarded for playing with the puzzles (206 seconds).

KEY POINT Being paid for working on an intrinsically interesting activity can decrease a person's intrinsic motivation for the activity.

In another early classic study called "Turning Play Into Work," Lepper and Greene (1975) used nursery school children as participants and selected an activity that was intrinsically motivating for these children—drawing with felt pens. Each child was asked to draw under one of three reward conditions. In the expected reward condition, the children agreed to draw a picture in order to receive a Good Player certificate. In the unexpected reward condition, the award was given to unsuspecting children after they completed the task. In the no reward condition, the children neither anticipated nor received an award. One week later, the children were unobtrusively observed for their interest in the same activity in a free-choice situation. The children who had drawn with the felt pen for expected rewards showed a decrease in intrinsic motivation, whereas the other two groups continued to use the felt pens just as much as they had before the experiment. When the expected reward was removed, the prime reason for the first group using the felt pen was also removed, although they had initially been intrinsically motivated to use the felt pen (Lepper, Greene, & Nisbett, 1973). This study demonstrates potential long-term effects of extrinsic rewards and the importance of studying how the reward is administered.

Not all studies have shown that extrinsic rewards decrease intrinsic motivation. To the contrary, *general* psychological studies of the relationship between extrinsic rewards and intrinsic motivation have concluded that external rewards undermine intrinsic motivation under certain select circumstances—for example, recognizing someone merely for participating without tying recognition to the quality of performance (Cameron & Pierce, 1994; Eisenberger & Cameron, 1996). However, Ryan and Deci (2000) debated this conclusion, arguing persuasively that the undermining effects of extrinsic rewards on intrinsic motivation are much broader and wider reaching. Similarly, research conducted specifically in the sport and exercise domains reveals a number of instances in which extrinsic rewards and other incentives do indeed undermine and reduce intrinsic motivation (Vallerand, Deci, & Ryan, 1987; Vallerand & Losier, 1999). Thus, we need to understand under what conditions extrinsic rewards can negatively affect intrinsic motivation.

Cognitive Evaluation Theory

To help explain the different potential effects of rewards on intrinsic motivation, Deci and colleagues (Deci, 1975; Deci & Ryan, 1985) developed a conceptual approach called **cognitive evaluation theory** (CET). CET is really a subtheory of the more general self-determination theory (SDT; Ryan & Deci, 2000). Self-determination theory (SDT) focuses on three basic psychological needs: effectance, relatedness, and autonomy. In essence, Deci and Ryan (1994) argued that "people are inherently motivated to feel connected to others within a social milieu (relatedness), to function effectively in that milieu (effectance), and to feel a sense of personal initiative in doing so (autonomy)" (p. 7). Therefore, intrinsic motivation, performance, and cognitive development are maximized in social contexts that provide people the opportunity to satisfy these basic needs.

Although SDT focuses on intrinsic motivation, it does not elaborate on what causes intrinsic motivation. Therefore, CET was developed to help explain the variability in intrinsic motivation. In essence, it focuses on the factors that facilitate or undermine the development of intrinsic motivation. Following the orientation of SDT, CET hypothesizes that any events that affect individuals' perceptions of competence and feelings of self-determination ultimately will also affect their levels of intrinsic motivation. These events (e.g., distribution of rewards, the quantity and quality of feedback and reinforcement, and the ways

Controlling aspect of a reward

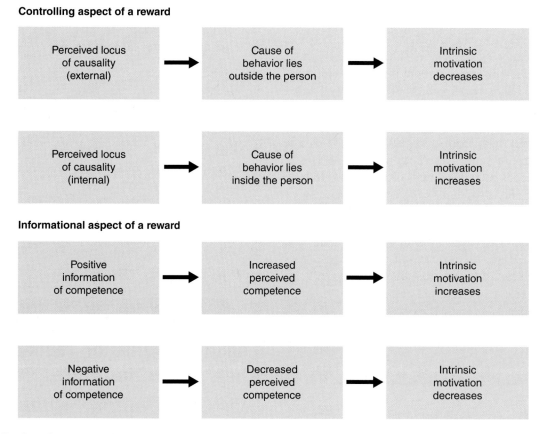

FIGURE 6.3 Cognitive evaluation theory.

in which situations are structured) have two functional components: a *controlling aspect* and an *informational aspect.* Both the informational and controlling aspects can increase or decrease intrinsic motivation depending on how they affect one's competence and self-determination (figure 6.3).

Controlling Aspect of Rewards

The controlling aspect of rewards relates to an individual's perceived **locus of causality** (i.e., what causes a person's behavior) in the situation. If a reward is seen as controlling one's behavior, then people believe that the cause of their behavior (an external locus of causality) resides outside themselves and thus intrinsic motivation decreases.

People often feel a direct conflict between being controlled by someone's use of rewards and their own needs for self-determination. That is, people who are intrinsically motivated feel that they do things because they *want to* rather than for external reward. When people feel controlled by a reward (e.g., "I'm only playing for the money"), the reason for their behavior resides outside of themselves. For example, many college athletes

feel controlled by the pressure to win, to compete for scholarships, and to conform to coaching demands and expectations. With the change to free agency in many professional sports, a number of athletes report feeling controlled by the large sums of money they earn. This in turn has led to them experiencing less enjoyment in the activity itself. Research has revealed six salient strategies that coaches use to control athletes' behaviors, thus undermining intrinsic motivation (Bartholomew, Ntoumanis, & Thogersen-Ntoumanis, 2009). These strategies include the following:

- Tangible rewards (e.g., a coach promises to reward athletes if they engage in certain training behaviors)
- Controlling feedback (e.g., a coach picks up on all the negative aspects of an athlete's behavior but says nothing positive and offers no suggestions for future improvement)
- Excessive personal control (e.g., a coach interacts with athletes in an authoritative manner and commands them to do things through the use of orders, directives, controlling questions, and deadlines)

- Intimidation behaviors (e.g., a coach uses the threat of punishment to push athletes to work harder or keep athletes in line during training)
- Promoting ego involvement (e.g., a coach evaluates an athlete's performance in front of their peers)
- Conditional regard (e.g., a coach says things to make athletes feel guilty, such as "You let me down" or "When you don't perform well . . . ")

In contrast, if a reward is seen as contributing to an internal locus of causality (i.e., the cause of one's behavior resides inside the person), intrinsic motivation will increase. In these situations individuals feel high levels of self-determination and perceive that their behaviors are determined by their own internal motivation. For example, sport and exercise programs in which individuals have the opportunity to provide input about the choice of activities, personal performance goals, and team or class objectives result in higher intrinsic motivation because they increase personal perceptions of control (Vallerand et al., 1987).

KEY POINT How recipients perceive a reward is critical in determining whether the reward will increase or decrease intrinsic motivation. Rewards that people perceive as controlling their behavior or as suggesting that they are not competent decrease intrinsic motivation. Rewards that emphasize the informational aspect and provide positive feedback about competence increase intrinsic motivation.

Informational Aspect of Rewards

The informational aspect affects intrinsic motivation by altering how competent someone feels. When a person receives a reward for achievement, such as the Most Valuable Player award, this provides positive information about competence and should increase intrinsic motivation. In essence, for rewards to enhance intrinsic motivation, they should be contingent on specific levels of performance or behavior.

Moreover, rewards or events that provide negative information about competence should decrease perceived competence and intrinsic motivation. For example, if a coach's style is predominantly critical, some participants may internalize it as negative information about their value and worth. This will decrease their enjoyment and intrinsic motivation. Similarly, striving for an award and *not* receiving it will decrease feelings of competence and lower intrinsic motivation.

Functional Significance of the Event

In addition to the controlling and informational aspects of rewards, a third major element in CET is the functional significance of the event (Ryan & Deci, 2002). In essence, every reward potentially has both controlling and informational aspects. How the reward will affect intrinsic motivation depends on whether the recipient perceives it to be more controlling or more informational. For example, on the surface it would seem positive to recognize individuals or teams with trophies. However, although the reward's message seems to be about the athletes' competence, the players may perceive that the coach is giving them rewards to control their behavior (i.e., make sure they don't join another team next year). It must be clear to participants that a reward provides positive information about their competence and is not meant to control their behavior. In general, perceived choice, competence, autonomy (self-determination), and positive feedback bring out the informational aspect, whereas rewards, deadlines, and surveillance make the controlling aspect salient.

Consider the example provided by Weiss and Chaumeton (1992) of a high school wrestler. According to the coach, the wrestler had a great deal of talent and potential, had won most of his matches, and had received positive feedback from the coach, teammates, and community. In addition, as a team captain, the wrestler had participated in developing team rules and practice regimens. Despite the amount of positive information conveyed about the student's wrestling competence, the coach was baffled by the wrestler's lack of positive affect, effort, persistence, and desire. Only later did the coach find out that the boy's father had exerted considerable pressure on him to join the wrestling team and was now living vicariously through his son's success—while still criticizing him when he believed his son's performance wasn't up to par. Thus, the wrestler perceived the controlling aspect, emanating from his overbearing father, as more important than the positive feedback and rewards he was getting through his wrestling performance. The result was a perceived external locus of causality with a subsequent decrease in intrinsic motivation.

How Extrinsic Rewards Affect Intrinsic Motivation in Sport

Magic Johnson was once asked if he received any outrageous offers while being recruited by various college basketball teams. He responded, "I received my share of offers for cars and money. It immediately turned me off. It was like they were trying to buy me, and I don't like anyone trying to buy me." Notice that what Magic Johnson was really referring to was the controlling aspect of rewards. He did not like anyone trying to control him through bribes and other extrinsic incentives. With the outrageous multimillion-dollar long-term contracts that are currently being offered to many professional athletes, the natural question is whether athletes will lose their motivation and drive to perform at the top level. Let's look at what some of the research has found.

Scholarships and Intrinsic Motivation

One of the first assessments of how extrinsic rewards affect intrinsic motivation in a sport setting was Dean Ryan's (1977, 1980) study of scholarship and non-scholarship collegiate football players. Players on scholarship reported that they were enjoying football less than their counterparts not on scholarship. Moreover, scholarship football players exhibited less intrinsic motivation every year they held their scholarship, so their lowest level of enjoyment occurred during their senior year. Ryan later surveyed male and female athletes from different schools in a variety of sports (1980). Again, scholarship football players reported less intrinsic motivation than nonscholarship football players. However, male wrestlers and female athletes from six sports who were on scholarship reported higher levels of intrinsic motivation than those who were not on scholarship.

These results can be explained by the distinction between the controlling and informational aspects of rewards. Scholarships can have an informational function—scholarships tell athletes that they are good. This would be especially informative to wrestlers and women, who receive far fewer scholarships than other athletes. Remember that in 1980, few athletic scholarships were available to wrestlers and women. In comparison, some 80 scholarships were awarded to Division I football teams, which would make the informational aspect of receiving a football scholarship a less positive confirmation of outstanding competence.

KEY POINT Athletic scholarships can either decrease or increase athletes' levels of intrinsic motivation depending on which is more emphasized—the controlling or the informational aspect.

Football is the prime revenue-producing sport for most universities. Consider how football scholarships, as well as scholarships in other revenue-producing sports, can be used. Some coaches may use scholarships as leverage to control the players' behavior. Players often believe that they have to perform well or lose their scholarships. Sometimes players who are not performing up to the coaches' expectations are made to participate in distasteful drills, are threatened with being dropped from the team, or are given no playing time. By holding scholarships over players' heads, coaches have sometimes turned what used to be play into work. Under these conditions, the controlling aspect of the scholarship is more important than the informational aspect, which evidently decreases intrinsic motivation among the scholarship players.

Given the changing trends in both men's and women's collegiate sport during the 1980s and 1990s, a study by Amorose, Horn, and Miller (1994) addressed the effect that scholarships have on intrinsic motivation. The investigation showed that among 440 male and female athletes in Division I, the players on scholarship had lower levels of intrinsic motivation, enjoyment, and perceived choice than their nonscholarship cohorts. This occurred with both the men and women, indicating that the growth of women's collegiate sport may have raised the pressure to win to the level experienced in men's collegiate athletics. Making more scholarships available to female athletes has reduced the informational aspect of these awards, and the concomitant pressure to win has enhanced the controlling aspect of scholarships, thus decreasing intrinsic motivation.

Along these lines, Amorose and Horn (2000) attempted to determine whether it was the scholarship itself or the actual coaching behaviors that produced changes in intrinsic motivation. In assessing how collegiate athletes perceived their coaches' behavior, the authors found that changes in feelings of intrinsic motivation were attributable primarily to coaching behaviors rather than to whether an athlete was on scholarship. Specifically, athletes who perceived that their coaches exhibited predominantly positive and instructional feedback as well as democratic and social support behaviors exhibited higher levels of intrinsic motivation than did athletes who perceived that their coaches displayed predominantly autocratic behaviors. Similarly, Hollembeak and Amorose (2005) found that democratic coaching behaviors produced higher levels of intrinsic motivation, whereas autocratic coaching behaviors produced lower levels of intrinsic motivation. Thus, regarding intrinsic motivation, it appears that the type of coach one plays for is more important than whether one is on scholarship.

Competition and Intrinsic Motivation

Competitive success and failure can also affect intrinsic motivation. Competitive events contain both controlling and informational components, and thus they can influence both the perceived locus of causality and perceived competence of the participants. By manipulating the success and failure that participants perceive on a motor task, several researchers have revealed that people have higher levels of intrinsic motivation after success than after failure (Vallerand, Gauvin, & Halliwell, 1986a; Weinberg & Jackson, 1979; Weinberg & Ragan, 1979). Further research (Vansteenkiste & Deci, 2003) investigated the effects of positive performance-based feedback on winning and losing. Results revealed that although losing was associated with reduced intrinsic motivation, positive feedback for meeting a specific standard (performance-contingent feedback) went a long way in reducing the undermining effect of losing on intrinsic motivation. Thus, focusing on performance goals (e.g., improvement) appears to help sustain motivation more than does focusing on outcome (e.g., winning and losing).

> **KEY POINT** Competitive success tends to increase intrinsic motivation, whereas competitive failure tends to decrease intrinsic motivation.

We tend to focus on who won or lost a competition, which represents the objective outcome. However, sometimes an athlete plays well but still loses to a superior opponent, whereas other times someone plays poorly but still wins over a weak opponent. These subjective outcomes also appear to determine an athlete's intrinsic motivation. People who perceive that they performed well show higher levels of intrinsic motivation than those with lower perceptions of success (McAuley & Tammen, 1989). Winning and losing are less important in determining intrinsic motivation than people's (subjective) perception of how well they performed. The adage "It's not whether you win or lose, but how you play the game" applies in determining how a performance affects intrinsic motivation.

In essence, the focus of one's performance appears to be more important than the actual outcome. For example, Vallerand, Gauvin, and Halliwell (1986b) found that youngsters who were asked to compete

against another child (interpersonal competition) on a motor task exhibited less intrinsic motivation than those who were instructed to simply compete against themselves (mastery). Similarly, other research (Kavussanu & Roberts, 1996; Koka & Hein, 2003) indicated that intrinsic motivation was higher when participants viewed the motivational climate of their classes to be more mastery oriented than ego oriented.

Feedback and Intrinsic Motivation

Feedback and intrinsic motivation involve how positive and negative information from significant others affects one's perceived competence and subsequent intrinsic motivation. Vallerand's (1983) first study investigated the effect of varying the amounts of positive feedback given to adolescent hockey players who were performing in simulated hockey situations. Players received 0, 6, 12, 18, or 24 positive statements from coaches while performing various hockey skills. The groups that received feedback scored higher in perceived competence and intrinsic motivation than did the group that received no feedback, although no differences existed among the various feedback groups. Therefore, the absolute quantity of positive feedback seems less important than the presence of at least some type of positive feedback.

A second study using a balance task also showed that positive feedback produced higher levels of intrinsic motivation than did negative feedback or no feedback (Vallerand & Reid, 1984). A study by Mouratidis, Vansteenkiste, Lens, and Sideridis (2008) showed that very positive feedback ("You're one of the best in the class") produced significantly more intrinsic motivation and a greater intent to participate in similar activities in the future compared with mild positive feedback ("You're about average"). These results underscore the importance of the quality of positive feedback and not just the amount.

Other Determinants of Intrinsic Motivation

Besides the factors already noted, researchers have found a variety of other factors related to intrinsic motivation (see Vallerand & Rousseau, 2001, for a review). Higher levels of intrinsic motivation appear to be related to

- playing for an autonomous (democratic) versus a controlling coach,

Principles for the Effective Use of External Rewards

- The best types of extrinsic rewards are novel, creative, and simple. In this era of exorbitant professional sport salaries, we often forget that the power of extrinsic rewards comes more from their meaning than from their monetary value. The true power of the reward often lies in what the reward represents. For example, in the movie (based on a true story) *A Beautiful Mind,* John Nash received the Nobel Prize for his work in economic theory although he suffered from mental illness. Despite the money and prestige surrounding the Nobel Prize, Nash received one of the most satisfying rewards at the end of the movie: In the Princeton University lunchroom, his colleagues walked up to his table and laid down their pens in acknowledgment of his brilliance. The pens had little monetary value but great symbolic value.

- Extrinsic rewards should be given to enable athletes, not control them. When giving individual honors, make sure athletes know that the reward is about their competence instead of a control issue. For example, scholarships should be seen as measures of competence and not something to be held over the heads of athletes.

- Extrinsic rewards can help when individuals are not motivated to participate in sport or exercise. For example, individuals may dislike the exercise bike, but external rewards can help them stay with it because they know in the end it will help them lose weight and tone muscle.

- External rewards should be contingent on behavior. To enhance motivation, rewards need to be earned. For example, getting a reward for merely participating (as in some youth sports leagues) is meaningless, but getting a reward for attending and working hard at all practices should fuel motivation.

- Use external rewards sparingly. Rather, build a motivational climate that fosters intrinsic motivation and in which athletes or exercisers motivate each other in the pursuit of excellence. The less a coach or exercise leader uses external rewards, the more likely the rewards will be seen as motivational rather than controlling, which will enhance feelings of self-determination.

- participation in a recreational versus competitive league,
- high versus low levels of perceived competence, and
- high versus low levels of perceived control.

Strategies for Increasing Intrinsic Motivation

Because rewards do not inherently undermine intrinsic motivation, coaches, physical educators, and exercise leaders do well to structure and use rewards and other strategies in ways that increase perceptions of success and competence and, by extension, the intrinsic motivation of participants. Read the following suggestions for increasing intrinsic motivation, and analyze how the use of rewards provides participants with information that will increase their intrinsic motivation and perception of competence.

• *Provide for successful experiences.* Perceived success strengthens feelings of personal competence.

For example, lowering the basket for young basketball players and structuring practice to provide successful experiences will enhance feelings of competence. Give positive feedback about what participants are doing right.

• *Give rewards contingent on performance.* Tie rewards to the performance of specific behaviors to increase their informational value. Give rewards based on proper execution of plays, good sporting behavior, helping other teammates, or mastering a new skill in order to provide information about the individual's competence. Make clear to the participants that the rewards are specifically for doing things well and that you are not trying to control them in any way. Emphasize the informational aspect of the rewards.

• *Use verbal and nonverbal praise.* Many people forget how powerful praise can be. Praise provides positive feedback and helps athletes continue to strive to improve. This is especially important for athletes who are second-string and who get little recognition as well as for students who are not particularly skilled in sport and physical activity. For example, overweight participants in an exercise class need plenty of positive feedback to stay motivated and feel good about themselves. A simple pat on the back or "Good job" can acknowledge each person's contribution to a team or achievement of a personal goal.

• *Vary content and sequence of practice drills.* Practices in sport and exercise can get boring. One way to break the monotony and maintain motivation levels is to vary the kinds of drills and the way they are sequenced. Such variety can also give young athletes an opportunity to try new positions or assignments. The youngsters have more fun and gain an awareness and appreciation of the demands of different positions and of their abilities to handle them. Similarly, exercise leaders should strive to vary the content and format of their classes to keep motivation high. (Dropout rates in exercise programs all too frequently reach more than 50%.)

• *Involve participants in decision making.* Allow participants more responsibility for making decisions and rules. Doing so will increase their perception of control and lead to feelings of personal accomplish-

ment. For example, participants might suggest how to organize a practice session, make up team or class rules, establish a dress code, or, if they are ready, proceed with game strategy. They might plan a new or innovative drill for practice. People perceive that they have greater competency when they are active in the learning process.

• *Set realistic performance goals.* Not all participants are highly skilled or apt to be winners in competition. However, people can learn to set realistic goals based on their individual abilities. These goals need not depend on objective performance outcomes; rather, they might include playing for a specified number of minutes, keeping emotional control, or simply improving over a previous performance. Base performance goals on a personal level of performance (e.g., to improve one's time in the mile run from 7:33 to 7:25), leaving participants in control of their performance (i.e., not depending on how well an opponent plays) and making success more likely. Reaching performance goals is a sign of competence that will increase motivation. Chapter 15 presents a more detailed discussion of how to set goals.

There are many strategies for increasing motivation, including setting realistic performance goals based on individual abilities.

Flow—A Special Case of Intrinsic Motivation

Some of the most innovative studies of enhancing intrinsic motivation come from the work of Mihaly Csikszentmihalyi (1990). Whereas many researchers have tried to determine which factors undermine intrinsic motivation, Csikszentmihalyi investigated exactly what makes a task intrinsically motivating. He examined rock climbing, dancing, chess, music, and amateur athletics—all activities that people do with great intensity but usually for little or no external reward. In sport, Sue Jackson has led the research in this area, studying flow experiences in athletes from a variety of sports. Jackson and Csikszentmihalyi have also collaborated on a book, *Flow in Sport: The Keys to Optimal Experiences and Performances* (Jackson & Csikszentmihalyi, 1999). Through their research, Jackson and Csikszentmihalyi identified a number of common elements that make sport activities intrinsically interesting. These elements of flow have been identified in a variety of performance settings, including the military, the performing arts, and business (Harmison & Casto, 2012; Jackson, 2011), and recreational performers can achieve flow just as well as elite performers can (Henning & Etnier, 2013). The essential elements of the flow state include the following:

• *Balance of challenge and skills.* The most important part of Csikszentmihalyi's definition of flow is the balance between one's perceived skill and challenge. An easy win or lopsided loss will rarely get one into flow. As one hockey player noted, "When I have a competitor to push me to my limits and provide a real challenge is when I can get into the zone." For flow to occur it is imperative that an athlete believe that he or she has the skills to successfully meet the physical, technical, and mental challenges faced.

• *Complete absorption in the activity.* The participant is so involved in the activity that nothing else seems to matter. A basketball player states, "The court—that's all that matters . . . . Sometimes I think of a problem, like fighting with my girlfriend, and I think that's nothing compared to the game. You can think about a problem all day but as soon as you get in the game, the hell with it . . . . When you're playing basketball, that's all that's on your mind."

• *Clear goals.* Goals are so clearly set that the athlete knows exactly what to do. This clarity of intention facilitates concentration and attention. As one swimmer said of the flow experience, "I knew exactly how I was going to swim the race."

• *Merging of action and awareness.* The athlete is aware of her actions but not of the awareness itself. This mental state is captured by a volleyball player who states, "The only thing that goes through my mind is performing well. I really don't have to think, though. When I'm playing [volleyball], it just comes to me. It's a good feeling. And when you're on a roll, you don't think about it at all. If you step back and think why you are so hot, all of a sudden you get creamed."

• *Total concentration on the task at hand.* Performers report that they feel like a beam of concentrated energy. Crowd noises, opponent reactions, and other distractions simply don't matter. The focus of attention is clearly on the task at hand. A tennis player demonstrates this total focus: "All that mattered was the tennis court and the ball. I was so into the zone and focused that the ball looked like a watermelon."

• *Loss of self-consciousness.* Performers report that their ego is completely lost in the activity itself. A rock climber captures this feeling well: "In rock climbing one tends to get immersed in what is going on around him—in the rock, in the moves that are involved . . . search[ing] for handholds . . . proper position[ing] of the body—so involved he might lose the consciousness of his own identity and melt into the rock."

• *A sense of control.* This element of flow refers to the fact that the athlete is not actively aware of control; rather, he is simply not worried by the possibility of lack of control. A racquetball player demonstrates this sense of control: "At times when I have super concentration in a [racquetball] game, nothing else exists—nothing except the act of participating and swinging at the ball. The other player must be there to play the game, but I'm not concerned with him. I'm not competing with him at that point. I'm attempting to place the ball in the perfect spot, and it has no bearing on winning and losing."

• *No goals or rewards external to the activity.* The athlete participates purely because of the activity itself, without seeking any other reward. A chess player makes this point by saying, "The most rewarding part of chess is the competition, the satisfaction of pitting your mental prowess against someone else . . . . I've won trophies and money, but considering expenses of entry fees, chess association, et cetera, I'm usually on the losing side financially."

• *Transformation of time.* Athletes in flow typically report that time seems to speed up, although for some it slows down. However, most individuals in flow report transformations in their perceptions of time. As one athlete said, "It was over before I knew it."

• *Effortless movement.* This element refers to the fact that the athlete is performing well yet is not really thinking about it and doesn't appear to be trying too hard. A figure skater captures this element well: "It was just one of those programs that clicked. It's just such a rush, like you feel it could go on and on and on, like you don't want it to stop because it's going so well. It's almost as though you don't have to think, it's like everything goes automatically without thinking. It's like you're in automatic pilot, so you don't have any thoughts."

These elements represent the essential features of optimal performances, which athletes have described as "hot," "in a groove," "on a roll," or "in the zone," a special state where everything is going well. Csikszentmihalyi calls this holistic sensation **flow**, in which people believe they are totally involved or on automatic pilot. He argued that the flow experience occurs when your skills are equal to your challenge. Intrinsic motivation is at its highest and maximum performance is achieved. However, if the task demands are greater than your capabilities, you become anxious and perform poorly. Conversely, if your skills are greater than the challenges of the task, you become bored and perform less well.

Figure 6.4 shows that flow is obtained when both capabilities (skills) and challenge are high. For example, if an athlete has a high skill level and the opponent is also highly skilled (e.g., high challenge), then the athlete may achieve flow. But if an athlete with less ability is matched against a strong opponent (high challenge), it will produce anxiety. Combining low skills and low challenge results in apathy or relaxation, whereas combining high skills and low challenge result in boredom. Stavrou, Jackson, Zervas, and Karterouliotis (2007) tested the notion of these four quadrants and the achievement of optimal experience. Results revealed that participants in the flow and relaxation quadrants exhibited the most optimal affective states (with flow being most optimal) and performance, whereas apathy produced the least optimal states; boredom was between apathy and flow. By structuring exercise classes, physical education, and competitive sport to be challenging and creative, you foster better performance, richer experiences, and longer involvement in physical activity.

How People Achieve Flow

If they knew how, coaches and teachers would likely want to help students and athletes achieve this narrow framework of flow. So the logical question is, How does one get into a flow state? Research studying

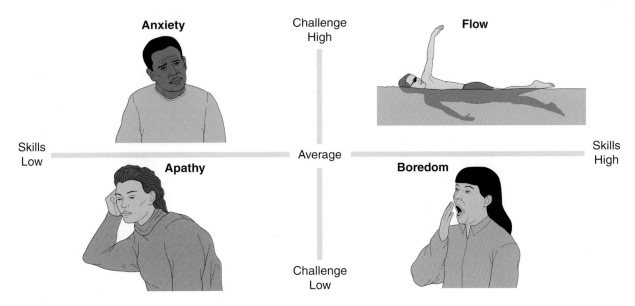

FIGURE 6.4 A flow model.

Reprinted from "Examining the flow experiences in sport contents: Conceptual issues and methodological concerns," J.S. Kimiecik and G. Stein, *Journal of Applied Sport Psychology* 4(2): 147, 1992, Taylor & Francis Ltd, reprinted by permission of the publisher (Taylor & Francis Ltd http://www.informaworld.com).

athletes from different sports (Jackson, 1992, 1995) found that the following factors were most important for getting into flow:

- *Motivation to perform.* Being motivated to perform—and to perform well—is important to getting into flow. When individuals lack such motivation, flow is much more difficult to achieve. The balance between challenge and skill may be the most relevant area to focus on to help ensure that the individual is optimally motivated.

- *Achieving optimal arousal level before performing.* Being relaxed, controlling anxiety, and enjoying the activity contribute to flow. Jackson found that some individuals clearly preferred to be more relaxed, whereas others wanted to be more energized. Several athletes spoke of finding a balance between calmness and arousal. As one skater said, "Relaxation and confidence—but you have to be on edge; you can't be too relaxed. You have to be concerned about something" (Jackson, 1992, p. 171).

- *Maintaining appropriate focus.* Keeping a narrow focus, staying in the present, focusing before the performance, and focusing on key points in one's activity are critical to maintaining proper focus. Csikszentmihalyi (1990) referred to concentration on the task at hand as one of the most frequently mentioned dimensions of the flow experience. One skater asserted the positive result of focusing fully on the upcoming performance this way: "The fact that you're so focused, you're able to concentrate easily" (Jackson, 1992, p. 172). In addition, research on mindfulness (the nonjudgmental focus of one's attention on the experience that occurs in the present moment) has revealed that, compared with athletes low on mindfulness, athletes higher on mindfulness score higher in skills–challenge balance, merging of action and awareness, concentration, and loss of self-consciousness (Kee & Wang, 2008).

- *Precompetitive and competitive plans and preparation.* Along with confidence and positive attitude, athletes mentioned planning most often in describing factors that influence achieving flow states. Following precompetitive routines, feeling totally ready, having a competitive plan, and anticipating potential unusual events are clearly important components of preparation. For example, a javelin thrower stated, "The fact that I've done everything possible on my mental and physical side makes me feel confident. Every facet is covered . . . . That reassures

my conscious mind that I've done everything—then I just have to let myself switch off and let it happen" (Jackson, 1995, p. 144).

- *Optimal physical preparation and readiness.* Having done the necessary training and preparation beforehand, working hard, and feeling that you are physically ready and able to have good practice sessions before competing are all critical to getting into and maintaining a flow state. In addition to rest and training, nutrition appears important for setting optimal conditions for the flow state to occur. In addition, athletes report that believing they were physically prepared helped boost their confidence and ability to stay in a flow state for a longer period of time.

- *Optimal environmental and situational conditions.* Although people can *set the tone* for achieving a flow state by altering their own internal climate, athletes also cited environmental and situational conditions that affected their ability to achieve a flow state. Such conditions as a good atmosphere, positive feedback from the coach, no outside pressures, and optimal playing conditions enhance the probability of flow occurring.

- *Confidence and mental attitude.* Confidence is a major help to achieving a flow state; conversely, self-doubt and putting pressure on one's self can disrupt flow. Believing you can win, thinking positively, blocking negatives, and enjoying what you're doing all help build confidence. But maybe most critical is believing that you can meet the challenge you face. As one athlete stated, "I think probably the most important thing for me is the feeling that I've got the ability to be in that situation" (Jackson, 1995, p. 144).

- *Team play and interaction.* In team sports, getting into flow sometimes depends on (or at least is influenced by) your teammates. Positive team interactions such as good passing, playing as a unit, and open communication are helpful in achieving flow. In addition, trusting your teammates and having a shared sense of purpose are important for cohesive team interactions.

- *Feeling good about performance.* The factor for getting into flow that athletes mentioned most often was feeling good about their performance and movements. In essence, receiving feedback from their movements and being in control of their bodies give athletes a sense of ease in moving. Anyone who has participated in sport knows that sometimes things just feel right, smooth, effortless, and in sync. These feelings are usually related to getting into a flow state.

Correlates of Flow

Jackson (2011) summarized the personal and situational correlates of flow as follows:

- *Length of sport involvement.* The longer an athlete participated in sport, the more flow-like experiences the athlete reported.
- *Sex.* No significant sex differences have been found in relation to flow states.
- *Self-concept.* Higher self-concept has been associated with a higher frequency of achieving flow states.
- *Autotelic personality.* Individuals with an autotelic personality (i.e., tendency to enjoy activity for its own sake) are more likely to experience flow states.
- *Hypnotic suggestibility.* Individuals higher in hypnotic suggestibility tend to achieve flow states more frequently.
- *Performance.* Although Csikszentmihalyi argues that flow is much more important as a phenomenon unto itself, studies have found that flow states are related to higher levels of performance.
- *Type of sport.* No significant differences in the frequency or quality of flow states have been found between individual-sport and team-sport athletes.

Controllability of Flow States

Can individuals control the thoughts and feelings connected with flow? The athletes interviewed by Jackson (1992, 1995) varied in their responses regarding the controllability of their flow states. Overall, 79% perceived flow to be controllable, whereas 21% believed it was out of their control. Athletes who believed that flow was controllable made comments such as this: "Yeah, I think you can increase it. It's not a conscious effort. If you try to do it, it's not going to work. I don't think it's something you can turn on and off like a light switch" (Jackson, 1992, p. 174). A triathlete noted, "I think I can set it up. You can set the scene for it, maybe with all that preparation. It should be something that you can ask of yourself and get into, I think, through your training and through your discipline" (Jackson, 1995, p. 158).

Some athletes, although considering flow to be controllable, placed qualifiers on whether flow would actually occur. A javelin thrower captured this perception in his remark, "Yeah, it's controllable, but it's the battle between your conscious and subconscious, and you've got to tell your conscious to shut up and let the subconscious take over, which it will because it's really powerful" (Jackson, 1995, p. 158). A rugby player believed that flow was not controllable in team sports: "It all comes back to the team—everybody, all the guys knotted in together and it just rolls along for 5, 10 minutes, half an hour, going very well, but then someone might lose concentration or go off beat or something and then you'd be out of that situation you were just in, and you can't have any control over that" (Jackson, 1995, p. 159).

Jackson's studies suggest that although athletes cannot control flow, they still can increase the probability of it occurring by following the guidelines stated here and focusing on things in their control, such as their mental preparation. In a study of 236 athletes, Jackson, Thomas, Marsh, and Smethurst (2001) also found that flow was related not only to performance but to the psychological skills athletes typically use. Particularly, keeping control of one's thoughts and emotions and maintaining an appropriate level of activation and relaxation were psychological skills related to flow. Most recently, Aherne, Moran, and Lonsdale (2011) found that a 6-week mindfulness training program produced higher levels of flow, especially in terms of clear goals and sense of control of their thoughts, feelings, and actions.

Factors That Prevent and Disrupt Flow

Although we need to understand how to enhance the likelihood that flow will occur, it is equally important to understand what factors may prevent or disrupt it (Jackson, 1995). These factors are identified in "Factors That Prevent and Disrupt Flow." Despite some consistency in what prevents and what disrupts the occurrence of flow, differences between these situations do exist. The factors athletes cited most often as *preventing* flow were less-than-optimal physical preparation, readiness, and environmental or situational conditions; the factors they cited most often as *disrupting* the flow state were environmental and situational influences.

DISCOVER Activity 6.4 helps you determine characteristics of flow and factors enhancing and disrupting the flow experience.

Professionals can try to structure the environment and provide feedback to maximize the possibility that athletes will reach and maintain a flow state. However, participants themselves must be aware of the factors that influence the occurrence of the flow state so that they can mentally and physically prepare for competition and physical activity accordingly. They should distinguish factors that are under their control and that they can change (e.g., physical or mental preparation, focus of attention, negative self-talk) from those they can't control (e.g., crowd responses, coach feedback, weather and field conditions, behavior of competitors). For example, an athlete can't control a hostile crowd, but she can control how she reacts both mentally and emotionally to the crowd. Similarly, a physical therapist can't control patients' attitudes or

Factors That Prevent and Disrupt Flow

Preventive Factors

- Nonoptimal physical preparation and readiness
  - Injury
  - Fatigue
  - Not feeling good physically
- Nonoptimal environmental or situational conditions
  - External stresses
  - Unwanted crowd response
  - Uncontrollable influences of the event
- Lacking confidence or a negative mental state
  - Negative thinking
  - Self-doubt
  - No control of mental state
- Inappropriate focus
  - Thinking too much
  - Worrying about what others are doing
  - Frustration with teammate's effort

- Problem with precompetitive preparation
  - Poor precompetitive preparation
  - Distraction before competition
  - Interruption of precompetitive preparation
- Lacking motivation to perform
  - No goals
  - Lack of challenge
  - Low arousal or motivation
- Nonoptimal arousal level before competition
  - Not being relaxed
  - Feeling too relaxed
- Negative team play and interactions
  - Team not performing well
  - Not feeling part of the team
  - Negative talk within the team
- Performance going poorly
  - Unforced errors
  - Poor technique
  - Things not going as planned

Disruptive Factors

- Nonoptimal environmental and situational influences
  - Stoppage in play
  - What opposition is doing
  - Negative referee decisions
  - Inappropriate, negative, or no feedback
- Problems with physical readiness or physical state
  - Lack of physical preparation
  - Injury during competition
  - Fatigue

- Problems with team performance or interactions
  - Negative talk on the field
  - Team not playing well
  - Lack of team interaction
- Inappropriate focus
  - Worrying about competitor's ability
  - Daydreaming
  - Loss of concentration
- Doubting or putting pressure on self
  - Self-doubt
  - Putting pressure on self

how crowded a clinic is, but he can strive to maintain a positive attitude in his interactions with clients. Finally, increasing psychological skills such as arousal regulation, emotion management, and thought control increases one's likelihood of experiencing flow.

Flow has thus far been presented as a very positive mental and emotional state associated with enhanced performance and positive affective states. However, recent research (Partington, Partington, & Oliver, 2009) has shown that the consequences of experiencing flow may not always be positive. The authors argue that one potential negative consequence might be the dependence on an activity once associated with a flow experience. In interviewing surfers, they found that some exhibited characteristics of dependence on surfing much like habitual drug users who need to continually increase their dosage to gain the appropriate sensations (i.e., they needed to increase the size and speed of the wave they were surfing to recapture the feelings they had previously). Surfers talked of being addicted to euphoric feelings and were willing to continue to surf to replicate these sensations despite family commitments, injury, or potential death. Some surfers admitted being unable to function normally in society because of their involvement in surfing. This research highlights the dark side of flow, although in most cases flow turns out to be a very positive and performance-enhancing feeling state.

LEARNING AIDS

SUMMARY

1. **Explain how positive feedback and negative feedback influence behavior.**
   In discussing two basic approaches to reinforcement—positive and negative control—we recommend a positive approach, although punishment is sometimes necessary to change behavior. Several factors can make reinforcements more effective, including the choice of effective reinforcers, the schedule of reinforcements, and the choice of appropriate behaviors (including performance and social and emotional skills) to reinforce. Punishment has potential negative effects, such as creating a fear of failure or creating an aversive learning environment.

2. **Understand how to implement behavior modification programs.**
   When we systematically use the principles of reinforcement to structure sport and exercise environments, the main goal is to help individuals stay task oriented and motivated throughout a training period.

3. **Discuss the different types of intrinsic and extrinsic motivation.**
   Contemporary thinking views intrinsic and extrinsic motivation on a continuum, from amotivation to various types of extrinsic motivation (introjected, identified, and integrated regulation) to different types of intrinsic motivation (knowledge, stimulation, accomplishment). Intrinsic motivation and extrinsic motivation are both viewed as multidimensional.

4. **Describe the relationship between intrinsic motivation and external rewards (controlling and informational aspects).**
   Extrinsic rewards have the potential to undermine intrinsic motivation. Cognitive evaluation theory has demonstrated that extrinsic rewards can either increase or decrease intrinsic motivation depending on whether the reward is more informational or controlling. Two examples of extrinsic incentives in sport are scholarships and winning and losing. If you want to enhance a participant's intrinsic motivation, the key is to make rewards more informational.

5. **Detail different ways to increase intrinsic motivation.**
   Coaches, teachers, and exercise leaders can enhance intrinsic motivation through several methods, such as using verbal and nonverbal praise, involving participants in decision making, setting realistic goals, making rewards contingent on performance, and varying the content and sequence of practice drills.

6. **Describe how such factors as scholarships, coaching behaviors, competition, and feedback influence intrinsic motivation.**
   Research has revealed a variety of factors related to intrinsic motivation. For example, higher levels of intrinsic motivation are found in nonscholarship athletes than in scholarship athletes, in athletes playing for democratic versus autocratic coaches, for recreational versus competitive environments, and for positive versus negative feedback.

7. **Describe the flow state and how to achieve it.**

A special state of flow epitomizes intrinsic motivation. This flow state contains many common elements of intrinsic motivation, but a key aspect is that a balance exists between an individual's perceived abilities and the challenge of the task. Several factors, such as confidence, optimal arousal, and focused attention, help us achieve a flow state; other factors, such as a self-critical attitude, distractions, and lack of preparation, can prevent or disrupt flow states. Psychological skills training has also been shown to facilitate flow.

KEY TERMS

reinforcement	behavior modification	harmonious passion
intrinsic rewards	backward chaining	obsessive passion
shaping	extrinsic rewards	social factors
feedback	intrinsic motivation	psychological factors
motivational feedback	integrated regulation	cognitive evaluation theory
instructional feedback	identified regulation	locus of causality
contingency management	introjected regulation	flow
behavioral coaching	amotivation	

REVIEW QUESTIONS

1. Discuss the two principles of reinforcement and explain why they are more complex than they first appear.

2. Discuss the differences between the positive and negative approaches to teaching and coaching. As evidenced by the research, which one is more beneficial and why?

3. Discuss the different types of reinforcers and the effectiveness of continuous and intermittent reinforcement schedules.

4. Discuss cognitive evaluation theory as a way to help explain the relationship between extrinsic rewards and intrinsic motivation. Compare the informational aspect with the controlling aspect of rewards.

5. Discuss the results of Ryan's studies on scholarships and intrinsic motivation. What are the implications of the findings? How did Horn and Amorose extend these studies?

6. Discuss the difference between harmonious passion and obsessive passion. Include three findings regarding passion and motivation.

7. Describe how motivation is conceptualized as varying on a continuum from amotivation to extrinsic motivation to intrinsic motivation. Describe the different types of intrinsic and extrinsic motivation.

8. Discuss the concept of flow. What are its major characteristics? In what sort of activity is flow most likely to occur?

9. Discuss three factors that help people get into flow and three barriers that inhibit it.

CRITICAL THINKING QUESTIONS

1. You are taking over as coach of a team that has a history of losing and that recently had a tyrannical coach. Intrinsic motivation is therefore low. What would you do to build intrinsic motivation with this team? What types of rewards and coaching behaviors would you use? Incorporate research findings and theory to support your methods.

2. You have learned about modifying behavior by using positive reinforcement and punishment. How would you use these two sources of motivation to help build motivation and confidence within your team?

PART IV

Focusing on Group Processes

How do group interaction, leadership, and communication affect performance in a physical activity setting?

This stop on our journey consists of four chapters, all focusing on group interaction. Group issues are especially important to professionals in our field because of the amount of time we spend working in or with groups, whether they be sport or exercise groups. In chapter 7 you'll learn how groups are formed and how they function. In addition, you will learn the relationship between individual and group performance, including why some people loaf in groups and how to reduce this social loafing phenomenon in sport and exercise settings. Chapter 8 examines whether a tightly knit (cohesive) group is necessary for optimal performance (based on the type of sport and cohesion involved) and addresses ways to develop cohesion.

The final two chapters of this part deal with leadership (chapter 9) and communication (chapter 10). Groups do not thrive unless someone exerts leadership, and effective leadership requires effective communication. You'll read about different styles of leadership, the importance of viewing leadership from a multidimensional perspective, as well as how

to be a transformational leader. In chapter 10 you'll learn the essentials of good communication and ways to build these skills in others, along with the most effective ways to deal with confrontation. With these skills in mind, coaches and exercise leaders can help participants reach their goals while also reaching the goals of the larger groups to which they belong.

VIEW   Dr. Dan Gould introduces part IV of the text in the Introduction activity.

 JOURNEY   This activity allows you to reflect on your preferences and expectations for working in group settings.

LISTEN   Go to part IV of the web study guide to meet the following experts in the field: Matthew S. Johnson, PhD and David Yukelson, PhD. In this activity, you'll hear or see the experts discussing communication.

7

Group and Team Dynamics

After reading this chapter, you should be able to

1. discuss how a group becomes a team,
2. understand how groups are structured,
3. explain how to create an effective team climate,
4. describe how to maximize individual performance in team sports,
5. understand the concept of social loafing, and
6. discuss the conditions under which social loafing is more likely to occur.

It isn't necessarily the talent on a team that makes it great, people have said, but how that talent is blended. Michael Jordan made just this point when he said, "Talent wins games, but teamwork wins championships" (Jordan, 1994, p. 24). We often see talented teams perform poorly, failing to use the resources of their individual members, whereas other teams with less talent and fewer resources succeed. Surely a team intends to take advantage of the various abilities, backgrounds, and interests of its members, but building effective teamwork requires considerable effort. Pat Riley, one of the most successful coaches in the National Basketball Association (NBA), highlighted this idea:

" Teamwork is the essence of life. If there's one thing on which I'm an authority, it's how to blend the talents and strengths of individuals into a force that becomes greater than the sum of its parts. My driving belief is this: great teamwork is the only way to reach our ultimate moments, to create the breakthroughs that define our careers, to fulfill our lives with a sense of lasting significance . . . .

However, teamwork isn't simple. In fact, it can be a frustrating, elusive commodity. That's why there are so many bad teams out there, stuck in neutral or going downhill. Teamwork doesn't appear magically just because someone mouths the words. It doesn't thrive just because of the presence of talent or ambition. It doesn't flourish simply because a team has tasted success. (Riley, 1993, pp. 15–16)"

Riley's comments make it obvious that teamwork, player–coach interactions, and group dynamics play an important role in the success of teams and groups. Team members must interact, work toward shared goals, adapt to environmental demands, and balance individual needs with those of other team members (Carron, Eys, & Burke, 2007). In fact, most sport activities, even so-called individual sports, require groups or teams, and competition almost always involves more than one person. Group physical activities include multiperson forums such as exercise groups, fitness clubs, and physical education classes. In addition, sports medicine and athletic training teams work together to help athletes prepare for competition and recover from injury. In short, almost any position in the sport and exercise field requires understanding the processes and dynamics of groups. A 2010 consensus conference that represented individuals from five countries who had practical and scientific expertise working with groups, teams, and organizations highlighted the importance of sport and physical activity groups. Most of the general findings from this conference are noted throughout chapters 7 and 8, and the special element titled "How Sport Psychologists Can Enhance Team Functioning" discusses how sport psychologists can contribute to enhanced group and team functioning.

Recognizing the Difference Between Groups and Teams

In a classic text, *Group Dynamics: Research and Theory*, Cartwright and Zander (1968) wrote,

" **Whether one wishes to understand or improve human behavior, it is necessary to know a great deal about the nature of groups. Neither a coherent view of people nor an advanced social technology is possible without dependable answers to a host of questions concerning the operation of groups, how individuals relate to groups, and how groups relate to larger society. (p. 4)** "

Although most researchers study the potential positive aspects of group formation and subsequent performance or productivity, some negative aspects to being part of a group exist. In his classic article titled "Humans Would Do Better Without Groups," Christian Buys (1978) argued that groups can have the following negative consequences: social loafing (discussed later in the chapter), self-deception ("we vs. they"), conformity, groupthink (suspension of critical thinking and overreliance on group opinion), and deindividuation (individuals' loss of a sense of their own identity). Of course groups have many positive functions, but we should keep in mind the potential drawbacks. As many researchers have asserted, to understand behavior in sport and physical activity we must understand the nature of sport and exercise groups. We begin by defining the terms *group* and *team*.

You may think it's easy to define a group or a team, but the differentiation can be quite complex. For example, social psychologists define a **group** as two or more people who interact with, and exert mutual influence on, each other (Aronson, Wilson, & Akert, 2002). A sense of mutual interaction or interdependence for a common purpose distinguishes a group from a mere collection of individuals. Along these lines, a volleyball team that trains together every morning before school shares a common objective (training) and interacts with each other in formal ways (warming up for competition) and thus is considered a group. Conversely, several people might decide to get together on Thursday nights to go to the volleyball game, which is not strictly a group because they do not interact with each other in a structured manner. In essence, a collection of individuals is not necessarily a group—and a group is not necessarily a team. So, how are groups and teams similar, and what distinguishes a group from a team?

For both groups and teams, members may like and be attracted to other members. Members of a group may have some common goals (e.g., all people in a fitness class may want to lose weight and tone muscle). Members of groups and members of teams, then, have some characteristics in common. But a sport team is really a special type of group. Apart from having the defining properties of mutual interaction and task interdependence, teams have four key characteristics:

- *Collective sense of identity*—"we-ness" rather than "I-ness"
- *Distinctive roles*—all members know their job
- *Structured modes of communication*—lines of communication
- *Norms*—social rules that guide members on what to do and not do

Identifying Three Theories of Group Development

As noted, a group of individuals does not necessarily form a team. Although all teams are groups, not all groups can be considered teams. A **team** is any group of people who must interact with each other to accomplish shared objectives (Carron & Hausenblas, 1998). Becoming a team, however, is really an evolutionary process. Teams are constantly developing and changing in their attempts to respond to both internal and external factors. Let's take a closer look at how a group becomes a team.

Teamwork Is Important for Individual and Team Success in Sport

The following quotes offer testimony to the importance of teamwork in successful groups:

Excellence has been defined for me in terms of a team's success. In high school it was whether our team from a very small school in a small town could defeat the bigger, city teams. In the pros, it was whether a team without a dominant star could be the best in the world. In the Senate, I finally realized that the passage of legislation, like teamwork, required getting people with different backgrounds, different interests, and different personal agendas to agree on a shared goal, and to work toward it.

—Bill Bradley, former professional basketball player and U.S. Senator (Bradley, 1976, p. iii)

The success of the Celtics is based on a philosophy wholly opposed to individualism. The basic Auerbach commandment is that to win, the individual must fit in; he must subordinate his desires and skills to those of the team. He must sacrifice himself, in his life on the court, to the working of the team.

—Red Auerbach, former coach and general manager of the Boston Celtics (cited in Greenfield, 1976, p. 205)

I wanted my players to adopt a shared perspective, rather than an individual one. Personal expectations, attitudes, and motives had to become team expectations, team attitudes, and team motives.

—Frank Selke, general manager of the Montreal Canadiens (cited in Goyens & Turowetz, 1986, p. 112)

In an effort to study team development, people have put forth different theories. These theories fall into three categories: **linear theory**, which holds that groups develop in stages or in a *linear* fashion; **cyclical theory**, which holds that groups follow a *cyclical* pattern; and **pendular theory**, which holds that groups develop in a *pendulum*-like manner.

Linear Perspective

In the linear perspective, the assumption is that groups move progressively through different stages. Critical issues arise in each stage, and when the issues are successfully dealt with, the group moves on. Probably the most popular example of a linear model was advanced by Bruce Tuckman (1965). Tuckman proposed that all groups go through four stages as they develop and prepare to carry out the group's tasks: forming, storming, norming, and performing. Although most groups go through all four stages, the duration of each stage and the sequence that the stages follow may vary from one group to another in the process of team development. For example, a coach's understanding of team formation in sport or a head athletic trainer's knowledge of her student trainers could lead to the use of different strategies that promote harmony among members of the respective teams.

In this first stage of team development, **forming**, team members familiarize themselves with other team members. Members of a team engage in social comparisons, assessing one another's strengths and weaknesses. For example, athletes might compare the amount of playing time they get with other athletes' playing time. Individuals also try to determine whether they belong in the group and, if so, in what role.

The second stage of team formation, **storming**, is characterized by resistance to the leader, resistance to control by the group, and interpersonal conflict. Great emotional resistance emerges, and infighting can occur as individuals and the leader establish their roles and status in the group. In this stage, sport or exercise leaders need to communicate with participants objectively and openly.

During **norming**, the third stage, hostility is replaced by solidarity and cooperation. Conflicts are resolved, and a sense of unity forms. Instead of watching out for their individual well-being, the athletes work together to reach common goals. Instead of competing for status or recognition, players strive for economy of effort and task effectiveness.

In the final stage, **performing**, team members band together to channel their energies for team success. The team focuses on problem solving, using group processes and relationships to work on tasks and test new ideas. Structural issues are resolved, interpersonal relationships stabilize, and roles are well defined.

DISCOVER Activity 7.1 helps you grasp the stages of the linear perspective.

Cyclical (Life Cycle) Perspective

Life cycle models have in common the assumption that groups develop in a manner similar to the life cycle of individuals—experiencing birth, growth, and death. Life cycle models are distinguished from linear models in their emphasis on the terminal phase before group dissolution. The main element in the cyclical approach to group development is the assumption that as the group develops, it psychologically prepares for its own breakup. This model has relevance for groups in physical activity in that exercise groups, for example, last approximately 10 to 15 weeks. Similarly, recreational teams typically play for a season (e.g., fall, winter, spring, or summer) and then break up.

Pendular Perspective

The majority of the earlier linear and life cycle models were based on the underlying assumption that groups possess an inherent static development that is unresponsive to the demands of the environment (Gersick, 1988). The pendular models emphasize the shifts that occur in interpersonal relationships during the growth and development of groups. The assumption is that a group does not move progressively through stages in a linear fashion from the instant it forms. A good example of a pendular model in operation, presented in table 7.1, comes from the book *A Season on the Brink,* which follows the Indiana University men's basketball team throughout a season (Feinstein, 1987).

TABLE 7.1 Pendular Model

Stage	Definition	Indiana Hoosiers
Stage 1	Orientation: Cohesion and feelings of unity are high; the athletes share many common feelings, anxieties, and aspirations.	Practices start: "In college basketball, no date means more than October 15. On that day, basketball teams all around the country begin formal preparations for the upcoming season" (p. 27).
Stage 2	Differentiation and conflict: The group physically or psychologically subdivides into smaller units; conflicts often arise as athletes compete for positions on the team.	Preseason practices continue: "November is the toughest for any college basketball team. The excitement of starting practice . . . has worn off and practice has become drudgery . . . . There is just day after day of practices—the same faces, the same coaches, the same drills, the same teammates" (p. 59).
Stage 3	Resolution and cohesion: Cohesion increases as group members share common concerns and feelings in preparing to face a common threat.	The first game: "The tension in the locker room was genuine. All the reminders about Miami, all the memories of last season, not to mention the memories of forty-eight practices that had led to this afternoon combined to create a sense of dread" (p. 96).
Stage 4	Differentiation and conflict: Team unity is weakened as various individuals are rewarded or punished, setting them off from the group.	During the season: "The locker room would not have been much quieter if Kent State had won the game . . . . Mentally, Knight had decided he needed Hillman and Smith in place of Robinson and Brooks. They were deep in the doghouse . . . . After (the team) showered, he blistered them one more time. Only three players had pleased him" (p. 102).
Stage 5	Termination: If the season was successful, feelings of cohesion are high. If the season was unsuccessful, feelings of cohesion are low.	Termination: "They jumped on each other, pummeled each other and cried . . . . Finally, they went back to the locker room. When it was quiet Knight spoke briefly. 'What you did,' he told them, 'was refuse to lose. You've been that kind of team all year'" (p. 348).

The preceding is an example of the pendular model of group development in a basketball setting (Indiana University as described by John Feinstein, 1987).

Although Feinstein's project wasn't undertaken as a scientific endeavor, *A Season on the Brink* is an excellent example of quality field research with an intact sport group.

Understanding Group Structure

Every group develops its own structure, which begins to emerge even at the group's first meeting. A group's structure depends largely on the interactions of its members—how they perceive one another and what they expect of themselves and each other. For a group of individuals to become an effective team, certain structural characteristics must develop. Two of the most important are group roles and group norms.

Group Roles

A **role** consists of the set of behaviors required or expected of the person occupying a certain position in a group. Teachers, parents, athletic trainers, corporate executives, and health professionals, for example, all have specific roles in their professions and in society.

Coaches, for instance, are expected to perform such behaviors as teaching, organizing practices, and interacting with other school officials and to be good role models. Similarly, head athletic trainers are expected to perform such behaviors as assigning and evaluating student trainers and to provide clinical evaluations for serious injuries.

Formal Versus Informal Roles

Two types of roles exist in any group or team: formal roles and informal roles. Formal roles are dictated by the nature and structure of the organization. Athletic director, coach, team captain, exercise leader, and the like are examples of specific formal roles in a sport or an exercise organization. Point guard in basketball, setter in volleyball, goalie in hockey, and other formal positions all have specific performance roles in a team. Each of these roles carries specific associated expectations. Usually, individuals are either trained or recruited to fill specific roles.

Informal roles evolve from interactions among group members. For example, the power and social

Juan DeLeon/Icon SMI

Coaches, athletes, and officials all have different roles in their respective groups. Knowing what one's role is in a group and how to perform that role makes for a stronger group.

structure of gangs evolve through informal means (see William Whyte's classic 1943 book on the social structure of street gangs). Using a content analysis of 448 *Sports Illustrated* articles and input from expert sport psychologists in group dynamics, Cope, Eys, Beauchamp, and Schinke (2011) identified 12 informal roles:

- *Comedian:* An athlete who entertains others through the use of comical situations, humorous dialogue, and practical jokes.
- *Spark plug:* An athlete who ignites, inspires, or animates a group toward a common goal.
- *Cancer:* An athlete who expresses negative emotions that spread destructively throughout a team.
- *Distracter:* An athlete who diverts the attention of other teammates, decreasing their focus.
- *Enforcer:* An athlete who is physically intimidating or willingly belligerent and who is counted on to retaliate when rough tactics are used by the opposing team.
- *Mentor:* An athlete who acts as a trusted counselor or teacher for another athlete on the team.
- *Informal leader (nonverbal):* An athlete who leads the team by example, hard work, and dedication.
- *Informal leader (verbal):* An athlete who leads the team both on and off the court through verbal commands. This role is assumed through social interactions.
- *Team player:* An athlete who gives exceptional effort and is willing to sacrifice his or her own interests for the good of the team.
- *Star player:* An athlete who is distinguished or celebrated because of his or her personality, performance, or showmanship.
- *Malingerer:* An athlete who prolongs psychological or physical symptoms of injury for some type of external gain (e.g., sympathy, attention).
- *Social convener:* An athlete who is involved in the planning and organization of social gatherings for a team to increase group harmony and integration.

The informal roles of cancer, distracter, and malingerer were perceived as having a detrimental effect on team functioning, whereas the others were perceived as having a positive effect. The degree to which these roles manifested on teams varied based on the type of team, the team's win–loss record, and other situational variables.

Role Clarity

You can improve a team's effectiveness by making sure players understand (role clarity) and accept (role acceptance) their roles. For example, role ambiguity has been found to have an effect on coach–athlete relationships. Athletes who perceived greater ambiguity in their offensive or defensive roles were more critical of their coach's ability to lead the team during competition (Bosselut et al., 2012). In addition, research has indicated that understanding one's role is critical to being effective in that role (Beauchamp, Bray, Fielding, & Eys, 2005). Research has revealed that role clarity mediates the relationship between **role ambiguity** and athlete satisfaction. Specifically, only when an athlete is high in need for role clarity will ambiguity about one's role lead to decreased satisfaction (Bray, Beauchamp, Eys, & Carron, 2005). Along these lines, one of the probable reasons for the long-term outstanding success of the Chicago Bulls in the 1990s was that players accepted their particular roles. Although Michael Jordan and Scottie Pippen were the leaders and the most talented players, they had significant ability (as did Coach Phil Jackson) to get the other players to believe in and fulfill roles, such as rebounder (Dennis Rodman), defensive specialist (Ron Harper), and shooter (Steve Kerr). Similarly, the Boston Celtics had "the big three" (Paul Pierce, Kevin Garnett, and Ray Allen), but the rest of the players knew their roles on the team and were able to turn that into the NBA championship in 2008. Finally, the Miami Heat had LeBron James and Dwyane Wade, but the role players—for example, Shane Battier, Ray Allen, Chris Anderson, and Mike Miller—made critical contributions to the team's success.

People in a specific role usually have a different perspective on the role's requirements than do other members of the group. Unclear roles hurt a team's performance. If two players on the same basketball team both think their role is to direct the team's offense, conflict will likely result over who brings the ball up court. Similarly, an athletic trainer and team doctor must agree on their roles so that athletes and coaches know whom to see for injury evaluation and whom to see for decisions on playing availability. Sometimes individuals' performances can blur their roles on a team. A National Hockey League coach once observed that the worst thing that could happen to a team is to have its enforcer score a few goals in consecutive games. The enforcer would then begin to think of his role as a scorer, to the detriment of the team as a whole.

An effective goal-setting program (see chapter 15) can clarify roles. Helping players set goals in specific areas gives the players direction and focus. If a football coach wanted a defensive lineman to focus on stopping the run instead of on sacking the quarterback, setting a specific goal would clarify the lineman's role. See "Role Clarity and Ambiguity in Teams" for more information.

Role Acceptance

Role acceptance is also important for enhancing a group's structure. A study by Benson, Eys, Surya, Dawson, and Schneider (2013) found that role acceptance is a salient perception among intercollegiate athletes and reaffirmed its distinctiveness from other related role concepts (e.g., role satisfaction).

Although role acceptance is generally related to role performance, this is not always the case. For example, athletes may accept a role even though the assigned responsibilities may exceed their capabilities, leading to subpar performance. Therefore, coaches need to be able to determine whether athletes are failing to accept their role responsibilities or whether the athletes are being asked to perform role responsibilities that exceed their level of ability.

Players who don't start or don't get significant playing time can easily feel left out and confused about their contribution to the team. Coaches can help players accept their roles by minimizing the status differences among roles and emphasizing that the success of the team depends on each individual's contribution. Role acceptance appears to depend on four conditions: opportunity to use specialized skills or competencies, feedback and role recognition, role significance, and autonomy (the opportunity to work independently).

For example, players are more willing to accept and carry out their roles when they perceive that their

Role Clarity and Ambiguity in Teams

Researchers have attempted to investigate role clarity and ambiguity in sport teams (Beauchamp, Bray, Eys, & Carron, 2003; Eys, Carron, Beauchamp, & Bray, 2003; Eys, Carron, Bray, & Beauchamp, 2005; Hølgaard, Fuglestad, Peters, De Cuyper, De Backer, & Boen, 2010). Some of the key findings include the following.

- Role clarity and ambiguity comprise a multidimensional concept including several facets:
  - *Scope of responsibility*—information about the extent of an individual's responsibilities
  - *Behavioral responsibilities*—information about which behaviors are necessary to fulfill an individual's role responsibilities
  - *Evaluation of performance*—information about how an individual's performance of required role responsibilities will be evaluated
  - *Consequences of not fulfilling responsibilities*—information about the consequences of failing to fulfill requisite role responsibilities
- Veterans displayed less role ambiguity than first-year players at the beginning of the season but not at the end.
- Role ambiguity decreased across a season.
- Role ambiguity on offense (scope of responsibility) was related to cognitive state anxiety.
- Role ambiguity on offense (consequences of not fulfilling responsibilities) was related to somatic state anxiety.
- Role ambiguity on defense was not related to cognitive or somatic anxiety.
- Players with higher role ambiguity stated they were less likely (lower intentions) to return to the team next year. However, this role ambiguity did not affect their intention to continue playing the sport.

The more clearly roles were defined, the more satisfied players were with their roles and the less likely they were to socially loaf, which is discussed later in this chapter.

responsibilities contribute to team success. For many years, Dean Smith, former basketball coach at the University of North Carolina, fostered the acceptance of the role of his reserves by playing them as a second unit in actual games for a short period of time. The reserves knew they were going to play in the game (even if for a short period), and they developed pride in trying to keep or extend a lead or reduce a deficit while giving the starters a rest. Mark Messier aptly summarizes the notion of accepting one's role on the team:

" I never felt I was playing in Wayne Gretzky's shadow . . . . I had a responsibility on the team that was different from Wayne's. Everyone had his role and I felt great about mine. So did many others about theirs. If we won, and won often, we knew everyone would get respect. (quoted in Swift, 1996, p. 60) "

Role Conflict

Role conflict exists when the role occupant doesn't have sufficient ability, motivation, time, or understanding to achieve that goal despite the presence of consensus on a desired goal or outcome. There are many types of role conflict, but a typical one is the conflict of "wearing too many hats" and having different people expect different things (i.e., roles) from you. The following quote from a 36-year-old nontraditional college athlete and mother of two children illustrates this type of role conflict.

" The whole week my son was sick. I hardly trained at all . . . . I would have to wait until my husband came home from work, but sometimes he would work a double shift so I would get no running in. So not only was my training hurt but I missed several classes because I had to stay home with my son. (Jambor & Weeks, 1996, p. 150) "

Group Norms

A **norm** is a level of performance, pattern of behavior, or belief. Norms can be either formally established or informally developed by a group. Individuals usually receive pressure to adhere to their group's norms, whether the norm is seen as relevant or irrelevant. For example, rookies (especially with professional teams) are often expected to carry the bags for the veterans. For males who play sports such as football and hockey, there is a strong social norm to be tough, aggressive,

and competitive, and negative consequences (e.g., cut from the team or ostracized) can occur if a player does not embrace these norms (Steinfeldt & Steinfeldt, 2012). Although this tough behavior may not appear functional, it is often the norm to indoctrinate new players onto the team. "Pressure of Social Norms" presents a famous research example.

On a sport team, the norm might involve practice behaviors, dress and hairstyle, the interactions between rookies and veterans, or who takes control in critical situations. Deviation from the expected behaviors might result in informal or formal sanctions. For example, in the movie *Chariots of Fire,* the British sprinter Harold Abrahams was chided by his Cambridge colleagues for hiring a professional trainer because this meant he was too serious about his running and not really an amateur any longer. In essence, he did not adhere to the social norms of his day. Because the pressure to conform to social norms in sport can be very powerful, a social norms workshop has been developed to help players effectively cope with these social pressures (Waldron, 2012).

Norm for Productivity

The standard for effort and performance accepted by the team is called the norm for productivity. For example, in a corporate fitness program, members of a fitness club may all exercise at lunch for 30 minutes; this then becomes an expectation for new members. In a sport setting, the captain or top performer on a team is often a role model who sets the norm of productivity. For example, when Olympic gold medalist Dan Gable was wrestling at Iowa State, he put in unbelievable hours of practice time. Because Gable was considered the best wrestler in his weight classification in the country, his teammates adopted his standards. A coach can also create a norm for productivity as evidenced by Tara VanDerveer, who inherited the 1996 women's U.S. Olympic basketball team. This team had lost in several international competitions in prior years and she felt the need to reestablish a strong productivity norm. She created an expectancy of success (including a mock medal ceremony that simulated a real ceremony) in which each player received a gold medal in the Georgia Dome, where the competition would actually happen. In addition, she demanded high levels of effort as noted by star center Lisa Leslie, who said, "With Tara giving us such hard workouts, we had to pick each other up. We became so close" (Wolff, 1996, p. 97).

Pressure of Social Norms

Norms can have an enormous influence on individual members of a group, as demonstrated by the classic experiment conducted by Solomon Asch (1956). Seven students were asked to judge which of three lines was like the standard line (figure 7.1). The standard line was 5 inches in length, whereas the comparison lines were 5 inches, 4 inches, and 6.25 inches. All but one of the participants (the naive participant) were told beforehand by the experimenter to give incorrect responses. Subjects answered aloud, one at a time, and the naive participant answered next to last. Although it was clear that the comparison line of 5 inches was the correct answer, one-third of the naive participants conformed to the group norm, even with as few as three other participants. Thus, even when people know the correct response, they feel pressure to conform to the norms of the group by choosing a response they know to be incorrect.

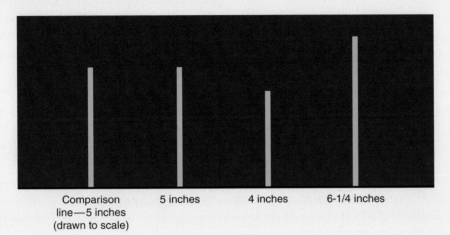

FIGURE 7.1 Typical comparison lines used in Asch's study of group effects on individual judgments.

This norm for productivity is sometimes associated with being part of a special team, as noted by University of North Carolina soccer player Angela Kelly: "No one would have dared to give any less than 100% when that Carolina shirt was on her back" (Dorrance & Averbuch, 2002). In a study by Munroe, Estabrooks, Dennis, and Carron (1999), the norm for productivity was the norm most frequently cited for competitions, practice, and the off-season. In fact, many other frequently cited norms indirectly reflected on productivity, such as the norms for punctuality, attendance, and preparedness for both practices and competitions.

Positive Norms

Because norms can have powerful effects on behavior, it is imperative for a coach, teacher, or exercise leader to establish positive group norms or standards. One good method for creating positive norms is to enlist the formal and informal leaders of a team to set positive examples. Dan Gable took the initiative and set the norm himself. But often the coach or teacher needs to encourage leaders to set high standards of achievement. Whenever possible, include all team members in decision making about norms adopted by the team.

Modification of Team Norms

When team norms need to be modified, there are two main things to consider: the source of the communication to change the norms and the nature of the communication. The individuals in a group who possess the greatest powers of persuasion are those who are more credible, are better liked, are similar to other group members, are attractive, have high status, or are perceived as powerful (Penrod, 1986). In addition, the style of speech one uses is important; asking rhetorical questions and speaking in a relatively rapid manner increase the effectiveness of persuasive arguments. The nature of the communication is also important. The process of changing group norms is more effective when people on both sides of the argument are present, there are multiple communications, a communication is novel, and conclusions are stated explicitly.

Creating an Effective Team Climate

Team climate develops from how players perceive the interrelationships among the group members. The players' perceptions and evaluations set the team's climate. Still, the coach has the final say on establishing team climate (although players do not necessarily have to buy into the coach's approach). Some factors of team climate are more easily changed than others, but all can influence the effective functioning of a group (Zander, 1982).

Social Support

Social support refers to "an exchange of resources between at least two individuals perceived by the provider or the recipient to be intended to enhance the well-being of the recipient" (Shumaker & Brownell, 1984, p. 13). Research has revealed that social support can have a positive effect on a variety of behaviors and feelings such as recovery from injury, coping with stress, burnout, youth physical activity, and performance (Duncan, Duncan, & Strycker, 2005; Freeman, Rees, & Hardy, 2009; Gould, Tuffey, Udry, & Loehr, 1996a,b; Rees, 2007). In addition, social support has been linked to increases in feelings of team cohesion and team climate. Along these lines, Mike Krzyzewski, men's basketball coach at Duke University, says the first thing he does at the beginning of the season is make sure all his players fit into the team concept and support each other. "Building an Effective Team

Building an Effective Team Climate Through Social Support

Social support is a multidimensional concept, and researchers (Rees, 2007; Rosenfeld & Richman, 1997) have outlined seven types of social support. The following are the types of social support and suggestions for enhancing each to help in team building.

1. Listening Support

Listening support is the perception that someone else is listening without giving advice or being judgmental. Some guidelines for enhancing listening support include the following:

- Provide group social events for staff, athletes, and assistant coaches to allow them to step out of their typical roles.
- Emphasize the value of regular, informal contact between athletes, coaches, trainers, and other support personnel.

2. Emotional Support

Emotional support is the perception that another person is providing comfort and caring and is indicating that he is on the support recipient's side. Guidelines for enhancing emotional support include the following:

- Stress the importance of emotional support to emergent and prescribed leaders.
- Encourage the team to give emotional support to injured players by visiting them.

3. Emotional-Challenge Support

Emotional-challenge support is the perception that another person is challenging the support recipient to evaluate her attitudes, values, and feelings. Guidelines for enhancing emotional-challenge support include the following:

- Encourage emotionally challenging verbal exchanges between players during practice and competitions (e.g., "You've been practicing that technique for the past several weeks; relax and let it happen").
- Challenge team members to do their best through individual and team meetings focusing on achieving team and individual goals.

4. Reality-Confirmation Support

Reality-confirmation support is the perception that another person, who is similar to the support recipient and who sees things the same way, is helping confirm the support recipient's perspective. Guidelines for enhancing reality-confirmation support include the following:

Climate Through Social Support" lists the different types of social support and ways to enhance them.

> **KEY POINT** Social support provides appraisal, information, reassurance, and companionship; reduces uncertainty during times of stress; aids in mental and physical recovery; and improves communication skills.

Proximity

People are more likely to bond when they are near each other. Although physical proximity alone does not usually develop a team concept, close contact with teammates promotes interaction, which in turn can hasten the group's development. Locker rooms, team training tables, and road trips ensure close proximity.

Some college coaches promote team unity by having athletes live together in a residence hall. In youth sports, car or bus trips and fund-raisers such as car washes often help build a positive team climate by providing opportunities for players to get to know one another better. These interactions, combined with a similarity of attitudes, can help establish team identity.

 VIEW Activity 7.2 allows you to apply your understanding of social support.

Distinctiveness

When a group feels distinct, its feelings of unity and oneness increase. Street gangs use distinctive dress

- Arrange small-group meetings in which athletes discuss dealing with pressure, preparing for competition, adjusting to college life, and other such issues.
- Create shared opportunities between experienced and inexperienced athletic trainers, such as a buddy or mentor system pairing older and younger student trainers.
- Use value-clarification exercises to promote sharing by asking different athletes to share an important value and why it is important.

5. Task-Appreciation Support

Task-appreciation support is the perception that another person is acknowledging the support recipient's efforts and expressing appreciation for the work that person does. Guidelines for enhancing task-appreciation support include the following:

- Recognize preseason and daily goal attainment of specific skill improvements.
- Provide award ceremonies for both sport and academic performances.

6. Task-Challenge Support

Task-challenge support is the perception that another is challenging the support recipient's way of thinking about a task or activity in order to stretch, motivate, and lead the support recipient to greater creativity, excitement, and involvement. Guidelines for enhancing task-challenge support include the following:

- Encourage team members to provide task-challenge support for one another as a team responsibility and norm. For example, asks questions such as why it is so important to work out hard in the off-season instead of just resting the body.
- Videotape fitness participants to allow them to review their level of activity and receive positive feedback from the fitness staff.

7. Personal-Assistance Support

Personal-assistance support is the perception that another is providing services or help, such as running an errand or driving the support recipient somewhere. Guidelines for lending personal-assistance support include the following:

- Encourage teammates to help each other with non-sport-related needs.
- Encourage each team member to get to know as many other team members on a personal level as possible and to demonstrate interest and caring about teammates.

and special initiation rites to set themselves apart from other gangs. In sport, distinctiveness is traditionally achieved through team uniforms and mottoes, special initiation rites, or special privileges. Some men's teams, such as the Boston Celtics, the New York Yankees, Notre Dame's football team, UCLA's basketball team, and Iowa's wrestling team, as well as women's teams, such as the University of Tennessee's basketball team and the University of North Carolina's soccer team, overtly foster distinctiveness (e.g., the Celtics are known for their kelly green uniforms, which are distinct from all other team uniforms). By making team members feel unique and distinct from other teams, a coach helps develop and mold a team concept. In exercise classes, Carron and Spink (1993) increased group distinctiveness and built group cohesion in part by providing group T-shirts and creating special slogans for participants. Similarly, personal trainers might develop special logo shirts for people training at the same workout facility.

Fairness

An important component of team climate is trust, and at the core of trust is athletes' perceptions that they are being treated fairly. Athletes should believe that their play, effort, and contributions to the team's success are evaluated objectively and evenly. The fairness with which a coach treats athletes influences their level of commitment, motivation, and satisfaction. Athletes interpret fairness on three central issues (Anshel, 2003):

- The degree of compatibility between the coach's and the players' assessments of the players' skills and contributions to the team
- How the coach communicates his views to the athletes
- The athletes' perceptions that the coach is trying to help them improve and be happy

Fairness, or lack of it, can bring a team close together or tear it apart. Coaches should deal with athletes honestly, openly, and fairly. Athletes need to believe they are treated fairly, even if they are not entirely happy with certain decisions. Some coaches do not pay much attention to their athletes' feelings of fairness. This is unfortunate given the degree to which these feelings can transfer into negative actions, such as disruptive behavior or even quitting the team.

Similarity

Similarity among team members in commitments, attitudes, aspirations, and goals is important to developing a positive team climate. As also noted in chapter 8, team members usually differ in ethnicity, race, socioeconomic background, personality, and ability. But research has shown that factors such as socioeconomic background and playing experience are not necessarily important in building a team concept (Widmeyer & Williams, 1991). However, it is up to the coach to get a diverse bunch of athletes working together for common and shared purposes. Specifically, the coach must develop similarity in attitudes, such as shared group performance goals, expectations for individual behavior, and clarity about various team roles. The more group members are aware of similarities among each other, the greater the probability they will develop a strong team concept.

Task Interdependence

A final way to improve team climate as well as increase performance is through outcome interdependence (Cunningham & Waltmeyer, 2007). In essence, outcome interdependence refers to the fact that all group members benefit (or suffer) from the group's performance. As coaches might say, *the team wins together and the team loses together.* Interdependence has been shown to be a way to help manage a team's conflict. Task conflict can turn out to be positive but "only when conflict is managed constructively and teams have high levels of openness, psychological safety, and within team trust" (DeDreu & Weingart, 2003, p. 748). One way to promote task interdependence is to provide team-level appraisals to reinforce a common fate among team members. This promotes a feeling of interdependence because all teammates are responsible to each other and everyone shares in the successes and failures.

DISCOVER Activity 7.3 enhances your understanding of developing an effective team climate.

Assessment of Team Climate

Coaches find it useful to know how their athletes are feeling. The "Team Climate Questionnaire" shows sample questions from a checklist for measuring athletes' feelings about being on the team and their perceptions of the coach's behavior and attitudes.

Athletes' responses give the coach valuable information about the team climate and possible ways to enhance cohesion. Because it is valuable to look at changes occurring over the course of a season, athletes should respond to the checklist at preseason, and then coaches should periodically monitor changes throughout the season. Players should be told that this is not a test and that there are no right or wrong answers. Keep the responses anonymous so that athletes are more likely to respond honestly.

Maximizing Individual Performance in Team Sports

Coaches are responsible for getting individual players to play together as a team, and they must understand how interactions among team members affect performance on the athletic field or court. Most coaches and sport psychologists agree that a group of the best individuals usually does not make the best team. Take the 1997 National Collegiate Athletic Association men's basketball tournament, for example. The two finalists, Kentucky and Utah, had lost their top players, all-Americans Keith Van Horn and Ron Mercer (both of whom were selected very high in the first round of the NBA draft). Yet, with less talent, the teams were able to reach the pinnacle of college basketball because of the teamwork and individual sacrifice of the returning players. Simply stated, a good team is more than the sum of its parts. How well a team works together is a key factor in the equation.

Steiner's Model of Actual Productivity

Ivan Steiner (1972) developed a model to show the relationship between individual abilities or resources on a team and how team members interact. Steiner's model is shown by this equation:

Actual productivity = potential productivity − losses attributable to faulty group processes

Potential productivity refers to a team's possible best performance, given each player's ability, knowledge, and skill (both mental and physical) as well as the demands of the task. According to Steiner's model, individual ability is probably the most important resource for sport teams—thus, the team made up of the best individuals will usually achieve the most success.

KEY POINT The abilities of individual team members do not always serve as good predictors of how a team will perform.

However, Steiner's model implies that a team's actual productivity does not usually match its potential productivity. Only when a team effectively uses its available resources to match the demands of the task will its actual productivity or performance approach its potential performance. Eccles (2010) explained how a group often coordinates these resources. However, a group's actual performance usually falls short of its potential productivity because of faulty group processes.

According to Steiner's model, it is predicted that team A will perform better than team B under the following circumstances:

- Team A possesses more ability (resources) than team B while experiencing equal process losses (loses due to not putting forth maximum effort).

- Team A possesses ability equal to that of team B but has fewer losses attributable to faulty group processes.

Team Climate Questionnaire

Read each statement and indicate how often it occurs, using the numbers on the following scale:

1 = Never occurs   **2** = Sometimes occurs   **3** = Usually occurs   **4** = Always occurs

_____ 1. I can make many of the decisions that affect the way I play.

_____ 2. I can count on the coach to keep things I say confidential.

_____ 3. Members of the coaching staff pitch in to help each other out.

_____ 4. I have enough time to do the things the coach asks me to learn and perform.

_____ 5. I can count on my coach to help me when I need it.

- Team A possesses more ability and has fewer process losses than team B.

This prediction suggests that the role of any coach is to increase relevant resources (through training, instruction, and recruiting) while at the same time reducing process losses (by enhancing cohesion and emphasizing individuals' contributions to the team concept).

Two kinds of losses are attributable to faulty group processes: motivation losses and coordination losses. **Motivation losses** occur when team members do not give 100% effort. Perhaps players believe that one or two stars can carry the load; thus, the other players slacken their efforts. **Coordination losses** occur when the timing between teammates is off or when ineffective strategies are used. For example, in a doubles match in tennis, if the ball is hit right down the middle of the court and neither player goes for it because each thinks the other will take it, that is a coordination loss.

Sports that require complex interaction or cooperation (e.g., basketball, soccer, football, or volleyball) are more susceptible to coordination losses than are sports requiring fewer interactions and less coordination (e.g., swimming or track and field). Basketball, soccer, and volleyball coaches typically spend much time and effort on fine-tuning coordination, timing, and team movement patterns. Swimming coaches, in contrast, spend most of their time developing individual swimming technique; they allot less time to integrative skills, such as the transitions between relay team members.

Different terms have been developed to distinguish between tasks that require coordination among team members and those that do not. Knowledge required to perform a task is known as taskwork knowledge, and knowledge required where coordination is needed to perform a task is known as teamwork knowledge (see Eccles & Tenenbaum, 2004, for a review). For example, a quarterback in football must acquire taskwork knowledge to be able to throw a pass accurately to a receiver. However, the successful completion of the pass also relies on teamwork knowledge of both the quarterback and receiver: They both must read the defense the same way and anticipate what the other is going to do. When Peyton Manning was traded to Denver in 2012, nobody knew how quickly he would develop teamwork knowledge in Denver—he certainly had it in Indianapolis—because he was throwing to a whole new set of receivers. However, to no surprise, he developed teamwork knowledge very quickly.

Effect of Individual Skills on Group Performance

Comrey and Deskin (1954) were two of the first researchers to investigate the relationship between individual and group performance to see how faulty group processes reduce productivity. These researchers found that no matter what level of motor skills individuals brought to the task, when two or more people tried to interact in precise ways, their ability to anticipate one another's movements and time their own actions accordingly was at least as important as their individual performance qualities. Other researchers have used laboratory tasks as well, finding that individual skills are only moderately good predictors of group performance.

Researchers in laboratories have studied the relationship between individual and group performance, but what about its application to real-world sports? Along these lines, Jones (1974) studied professional teams and players (tennis, basketball, football, and baseball), focusing on the statistics of individual players, such as their runs batted in and batting averages in baseball; points, assists, rebounds, and steals in basketball; singles rankings in tennis; and yards gained in football. Jones wanted to see how these statistics related to team success across a competitive season, and he found a positive relationship between a team's effectiveness and individual performance success for all four sports. This relationship was strongest in baseball, which has the lowest number of interactions, and weakest in basketball, which has the most complex interactions.

Thus, it appears that in sports in which more cooperation and interaction are necessary, the importance of individual ability decreases and the importance of group process increases. When teams of only two people play, they apparently work together best if they are close in ability. One investigation revealed that the best predictor of success was the averaged ability of the two players (i.e., summing the abilities of the two-person team); a large difference in ability between partners had a negative effect on performance (Gill, 1979). The closer teammates are in ability, the more likely they are to fully use their combined abilities (Gill, 2000). In tennis, when a superior player is paired with an inferior player, the better player will often try to do too much. Similarly, experienced teams quickly identify and target a weaker player and hit the majority of shots to that person. In short, all types of teams are usually as good as their weakest player. Usually, the top doubles teams are made up of two very good players (e.g., Bob and Mike Bryan of the United States) who complement each other rather than one star and another adequate player who have trouble combining their skills.

Finally, an interesting study by Cooke and colleagues (2013) compared individual competition with group competition (two-on-two and four-on-four). Results of an endurance task revealed that individual competitors exhibited higher levels of performance, effort, and enjoyment than did athletes competing as teams. These findings support the enjoyment-based and anxiety-based mechanisms that explain the effects of different types of competition on performance. Specifically, individuals supporting enjoyment-based mechanisms argue that changes in performance are due to increases in enjoyment which occur through increases in effort and intrinsic motivation. However, individuals supporting anxiety-based mechanisms argue that although increased performance is mediated by increased effort, increases in anxiety cause individuals to put forth increased effort.

Ringelmann Effect

Clearly, individual abilities do not neatly sum up to group or team performance. This is consistent with Steiner's model, which holds that faulty group processes can reduce potential productivity. But what causes these losses, and how much potential productivity is lost? The answers to these questions began to emerge from an obscure, unpublished study on individual and group performance (the **Ringelmann effect**) on a rope-pulling task conducted by Ringelmann nearly 100 years ago (cited by Ingham, Levinger, Graves, & Peckham, 1974). Ringelmann observed individuals and groups of two, three, and eight people pulling on a rope. If no losses attributable to faulty group processes occurred, then one

could assume that each individual pulled 100 pounds. Therefore, groups of two, three, and eight would be able to pull 200, 300, and 800 pounds, respectively. However, the relative performance of each individual progressively declined as the number of people in the group increased. That is, two-person groups pulled 93% of their individual potential, three-person groups 85%, and eight-person groups only 49%.

Because some of the early methodology and descriptions had been incomplete in Ringelmann's study, Ingham and colleagues (1974) attempted to replicate Ringelmann's findings while extending the work. Ingham and colleagues first had individuals and groups of two, three, four, five, and six persons perform the rope-pulling task. Results were similar to those in Ringelmann's study: Groups of two performed at 91% of their potential and groups of three at 82% of their potential. However, contrary to what Ringelmann found, increases in group size did not lead to corresponding decreases in efficiency. Rather, a general leveling-off occurred: Groups of six pulled at an average of 78% of their potential. Table 7.2 compares the Ringelmann and Ingham studies.

> **KEY POINT**   The phenomenon by which individual performance decreases as the number of people in the group increases is known as the Ringelmann effect.

In a second study, Ingham and colleagues wanted to determine whether the losses resulting from increased group size were attributable to poor coordination or reduced motivation. In an attempt to separate these two factors, the investigators reduced coordination losses by testing only one participant at a time, blindfolding the participant, and having trained helpers pretend to pull on the rope (participants thought the other members of the group were pulling on the rope, although they were not). Any decrease in performance was then primarily attributed to a loss in motivation

TABLE 7.2   Progressive Decline in Individual Rope-Pulling Performance Expressed as a Percentage of Individual Performance

Study	Group size							
	1	2	3	4	5	6	7	8
Ringelmann	100	93	85	n/a	n/a	n/a	n/a	49
Ingham (1)	100	91	82	78	78	78	n/a	n/a
Ingham (2)	100	90	85	86	84	85	n/a	n/a

n/a = not applicable.

(a slight amount of coordination loss that could not be controlled for still occurred) rather than a loss in coordination because only the real participant was actually pulling the rope. The results were almost identical to those in the first study: Average performance decreased to 85% in the three-person groups, and no further decrease in individual performance occurred as group size increased (see table 7.2). The authors concluded that the differences between actual and potential performance were partially attributable to motivation losses but that coordination losses also added to the reduced performance. In essence, some of the decreases in performance that occurred as the group got larger were purely motivational.

Two other experiments used shouting and clapping as group tasks and found that the average sound that each person produced decreased from the solo performance to 71% in two-person groups, 51% in four-person groups, and 40% in six-person groups. When the scientists controlled for coordination, they found that two-person groups performed at 82% of their potential and six-person groups at 74% of their potential (Hardy & Latane, 1988; Latane, Williams, & Harkins, 1979).

Social Loafing and Ways to Reduce It

Social loafing is the term psychologists use for the phenomenon in which individuals in a group or team put forth less than 100% effort because of losses in motivation. Researchers have found social loafing effects in swimming, track, and cheerleading as well as in a wide variety of laboratory motor tasks (see Hanrahan & Gallois, 1993, for a review). Numerous conditions seem to enhance the probability of social loafing. In testing these causes of increased social loafing, research has shown that the losses in individual productivity attributable to social loafing are greatest when the contributions of individual group members are not identified, are dispensable, or are disproportionate to the contributions of other group members. For example, offensive linemen in football might not block so hard if the running play is going in the direction opposite to where they are blocking. However,

How Sport Psychologists Can Enhance Team Functioning

Chapters 7 and 8 highlight important group and team variables in sport and physical activity and note the influence of these variables on effective group functioning. Sport psychologists can do the following to contribute to enhanced group functioning (Klinert et al., 2012):

- *Teach foundational psychosocial skills.* Harwood's 5 Cs (2008)—commitment, communication, concentration, control, and confidence—are a good example of some of the psychosocial skills that are especially important to young athletes.

- *Facilitate an optimal coaching environment based on athlete needs.* This could be done through interviewing athletes, administering psychological tests that assess athlete preferences for certain coaching behaviors (e.g., Leadership Scale for Sports), and observing behavior.

- *Develop the coach–athlete relationship.* Ensure that coach and athlete have an accurate understanding of how the other views the relationship as well as the attributes that are critical for a successful relationship.

- *Enhance role perceptions.* Have coaches and athletes list the formal and informal roles of the members of the team to look for congruity between coaches and athletes.

- *Increase group cohesion.* Use the "Group Environment Questionnaire" (Carron, Widmeyer, & Brawley, 1985) to assess task and social cohesion and then develop strategies for enhancing the specific cohesion needs of the team.

- *Coping with organizational and environmental stressors.* Teach athletes skills for coping with environmental or organizational stressors, including the following: factors that are intrinsic to the sport (e.g., travel, training schedules), roles in the sport organization (e.g., role ambiguity, lack of role acceptance), sport relationships and interpersonal demands (e.g., communication with teammates, social cliques), athletic career and performance development issues (e.g., retirement, salaries), and organizational structure and climate of the sport (e.g., levels of autonomy, result [winning] versus developmental [improvement] focus).

if they know that coaches will be reviewing the film of the game on Monday morning and that their lack of effort could be identified, they may block harder on each play regardless of the play's direction. Thus, if individual contributions to the group product are monitored directly, social loafing should be reduced. In addition, when individuals perceive that their contributions are essential to the group's productivity, social loafing should be reduced.

Reviews of the literature (Heuze & Brunel, 2003; Karau & Williams, 1993) have revealed that social loafing occurs across a wide variety of tasks, including those that are physical (e.g., rope pulling, swimming), cognitive (e.g., generating ideas), perceptual (e.g., maze performance), and evaluative (e.g., quality of output). In addition, social loafing generalizes across many populations and cultures and across sexes. Finally, social loafing is increased under the following conditions:

- The individual's output cannot be independently evaluated.
- The task is perceived to be low on meaningfulness.
- The individual's personal involvement in the task is low.
- A comparison against group standards is not possible.
- The individuals contributing to the collective effort are strangers.
- The individual's teammates or coworkers are seen as high in ability.
- The individual perceives that his contribution to the outcome is redundant.
- The individual is competing against what she believes to be a weaker opponent.

If athletes believe that social loafing is occurring on their team, even if it is not actually occurring, might they socially loaf as well? This notion of believing that social loafing is occurring has been termed perceived social loafing (Mulvey & Klein, 1998). A study by Hølgaard, Safvenboom, and Tonnessen (2006) examined the idea that perceived social loafing actually causes social loafing. The researchers found that when soccer players perceived social loafing among their

Recognizing the unique contribution of each player is vital in combating social loafing.

Lorne Collicutt/Icon SMI

teammates (i.e., they thought their teammates' poor performance was attributable to poor effort), they also exerted less effort. Enhancing social support among teammates can build trust, which may in turn help reduce perceived social loafing (Anshel, 2012). Using these findings, let's look at some specific examples, along with supporting research, of what sport and exercise leaders can do to reduce social loafing.

Emphasize the Importance of Individual Pride and Unique Contributions

When a coach stresses the team concept, some players may not recognize the importance of their own contributions to the team. All players should be challenged to examine their responsibility to the team and the ways in which they can improve for the team's benefit. Each individual's unique contribution to the team's success should be communicated and highlighted whenever possible. In addition, all athletes should take responsibility for their own efforts and not assume that a teammate will take care of things. For example, a basketball player may play great defense and set good screens that open up shots for his teammates. If the coach emphasizes to the player how important his contribution is to the success of the team, the player will likely put forth consistent effort and be more personally involved because he sees the importance of his contribution even though he scores only a few points.

Increase the Identifiability of Individual Performances

The most consistent finding across research studies points to identifiability as the most acceptable explanation for the social loafing phenomenon. As a result, social loafing may be eliminated when team members believe that their individual performances are identifiable (i.e., known to others) because players no longer feel anonymous (Evert, Smith, & Williams, 1992; Williams, Harkins, & Latane, 1981). Studies of swimmers showed that swimmers swam faster in relays than in individual events only when individual times in relays were announced (i.e., identifiability was high). However, swimmers swam slower in relays than in individual events when individual times in relays were not announced (i.e., identifiability was low). By evaluating the effort of participants as individuals, coaches, teachers, and exercise leaders make the participants aware of their concern and assure them that they are not lost in the crowd. For example, a fitness leader might call out the names of individuals doing a specific exercise or movement particularly well.

Filming or using observational checklists at team-sport practices or games can also provide increased identifiability. For example, at Ohio State University, the late Woody Hayes increased the identifiability of football linemen by filming and specifically grading each player on each play, providing "lineman of the week" honors, and awarding helmet decals to players who showed individual effort and performance. Include practices as well as games in the evaluation because many players don't get a lot of actual game time.

Determine Specific Situations in Which Loafing May Occur

Through filming or other observations, coaches can determine what situations seem to elicit loafing. However, social loafing is sometimes appropriate! For example, a basketball center gets a rebound and throws an outlet pass to the guard but does not follow the ball

Peer Relationships

When athletes reminisce about their sport careers, their relationships with teammates (and other competitors, to some extent) usually stand out as particularly important and meaningful. However, sport psychologists have only recently systematically studied these relationships in sport. Weiss and Stuntz (2004) and Smith (2007) offer suggestions for enhancing peer relationships:

- Generate cooperative goals in the sport setting.
- Encourage young athletes to engage in their own problem solving rather than expect adults to solve problems for them.
- Enable athletes to engage in shared decision making.
- Design sport settings for small-group activities and maximum participation.
- Select peer leaders based on criteria other than athletic ability (e.g., leadership skills).

down the floor. She is taking a rest on the offensive end, in effect, to make sure she is ready on the defensive end, which may be appropriate if she is tired. Bill Russell, MVP center for the champion Boston Celtics, popularized this exact strategy because he focused his efforts on the defensive end, letting his teammates run the fast break at the offensive end. This type of social loafing might be viewed as social engineering because it involves managing one's motivation and actions to match the task demands.

To better understand when social loafing might be appropriate, coaches should carefully analyze the dynamics and strategies involved in their sport. If changes need to be made, coaches should structure the practice sessions and competitions so that each player can economize efforts without interfering with team performance. For example, during a particularly tough part of the season, coaches might incorporate low-intensity practices into the schedule or complement high-intensity practices with fun activities. This will help keep players sharp and minimize their loafing.

Conduct Individual Meetings to Discuss Loafing

Coaches should discuss loafing with each player individually. A player may have reasons for motivational loss that are more complex than feeling lost in the crowd or assuming that someone else will get the job done. For example, athletes may have other commitments that place them under stress and require energy and time expenditure. Thus, the athlete may be economizing effort just to get through the day physically and mentally. Note that merely warning players about social loafing is not enough to prevent it from occurring (Huddleston, Doody, & Ruder, 1985). Rather, coaches must devise specific strategies for reducing the probability of social loafing.

Assign Players to Other Positions

Athletes should know not only their own role on the team but also the roles their teammates play. One of the best ways for players to gain an appreciation of their teammates and of how their own performance affects others on the team is to learn about teammates' positions. Talking about the unique challenges of other positions will help all players better understand the effect they have on other positions when they loaf. Coaches can help here by requiring athletes to spend a small period of time rotating to other positions to better understand their teammates' contributions and to experience the potential effects of these contributions on other positions.

Divide the Team Into Smaller Units

Forming subgroups in a team allows for greater recognition of the responsibility to others and helps develop a cohesive unit. Coaches should carefully monitor these subgroups and constantly reinforce the overall notion of team pride. Forming subgroups (e.g., defensive backs, offensive linemen, and receivers in football) can enhance feelings of group cohesion, which in turn leads to increased effort and commitment. Be careful, however, because placing too great an emphasis on subgroups at the expense of the larger group can result in the formation of destructive social cliques.

Attribute Failure to Internal Unstable Factors

After failure—especially consistent failure—teams often tend to give up and socially loaf because they start to attribute their failure to lack of ability, which is stable and internal. If a team feels they are not as good as the other team, they can start to put forth less than optimal effort because they start to ask, "What is the point in trying if the other team is better and we'll lose anyway?" Based on a meta-analysis, Martin and Carron (2012) recommend that teams attribute failure to internal, controllable, unstable factors such as effort and poor strategy because these can be changed. This will encourage teams to give full effort and not loaf because they attribute previous losses to things that are under their control.

LEARNING AIDS

SUMMARY

1. **Discuss how a group becomes a team.**
   Three major theories attempt to explain group development: linear theories, cyclical theories, and pendular theories. The most contemporary are the pendular theories, which argue that groups go through ups and downs throughout a season because of shifts in interpersonal relationships. A leader's knowledge

of these approaches can help the leader structure the environment to support individuals in the group through each stage.

2. **Understand how groups are structured.**
A group's structure depends largely on the interactions of its members. Two of the most important structural characteristics of groups are group roles and group norms. Roles consist of the set of behaviors required or expected of the person occupying a certain position in a group. Norms are levels of performance, patterns of behaviors, or beliefs characteristic of the group.

3. **Explain how to create an effective team climate.**
Team climate develops from how players perceive the interrelationships among the group members. Some of the critical factors affecting team climate are social support, proximity, distinctiveness, fairness, and similarity.

4. **Describe how to maximize individual performance in team sports.**
Individual skills are only moderately related to ultimate team success. Thus, getting greater contributions from each player is critical for high-level team performance. Through filming performances, helping players understand their roles, and increasing identifiability, you can maximize an individual's sense of contributing to the team effort.

5. **Understand the concept of social loafing.**
Social loafing is the phenomenon whereby individuals in a group put forth less than 100% effort because of losses in motivation. In essence, a diffusion of responsibility occurs and individuals believe that others in the group will pick up the slack.

6. **Discuss the conditions under which social loafing is more likely to occur.**
Social loafing appears to occur more often when an individual's output cannot be independently evaluated, the task is perceived to be low in meaningfulness, the individual's personal involvement in the task is low, a comparison against group standards is not possible, other individuals contributing to the collective effort are strangers, the individual's teammates are seen as high in ability, and individuals perceive that their contribution to the outcome is redundant.

KEY TERMS

group	storming	social support
team	norming	potential productivity
linear theory	performing	motivation losses
cyclical theory	role	coordination losses
pendular theory	role ambiguity	Ringelmann effect
forming	norm	social loafing

REVIEW QUESTIONS

1. Discuss why most definitions of a group agree that a collection of individuals is not necessarily a group.

2. Describe the four stages of team development and the key events that characterize each stage.

3. What might happen to a team when the roles are clearly defined yet only partially accepted (i.e., only some of the players are willing to accept their roles)?

4. Discuss an experience you have had in which Steiner's model of productivity was applicable and actual productivity was less than potential productivity. Was the loss attributable to a lack of coordination or motivation?

5. Describe the Ringelmann effect. What implications do Ringelmann's findings have for a coach, physical educator, or exercise leader?

6. Discuss three potential explanations for social loafing. How would you identify social loafing?

7. Compare and contrast the linear, cyclical, and pendular models of group development.

8. Role ambiguity has been shown to be a multidimensional concept. Discuss and give examples of the four aspects of roles.

9. Discuss the concept of the desire for group success, including at least three ways to promote this concept in a team.

10. Discuss three ways that principles from work teams can be applied to sport teams.

CRITICAL THINKING QUESTIONS

1. You are an exercise leader, and you want to build more unity in your class or group because you believe this will increase people's desire to attend class and participate. What kinds of things would you do (and why) to help build this sense of group or team unity?

2. You are a coach of a team sport, and you see that not everyone is hustling on every play. What would you say to your players to indicate that they are loafing and that the team needs them to stop loafing? What could you do to minimize or prevent loafing?

8

Group Cohesion

After reading this chapter, you should be able to

1. define task and social cohesion,
2. describe the conceptual model of cohesion,
3. discuss how cohesion is measured,
4. understand the cohesion–performance relationship,
5. better understand factors associated with cohesion, and
6. identify guidelines for building team cohesion.

In team sports, there have definitely been instances in which being a cohesive unit appeared to relate to success on the field. The great Babe Ruth, who was known predominantly for his individual achievement, had this to say about cohesion: "The way a team plays as a whole determines its success. You may have the greatest bunch of individual stars in the world, but if they don't play together, the club won't be worth a dime." When the Pittsburgh Pirates won the World Series in 1979, the team's motto was "We are family," suggesting that players owed their success to their ability to get along and work together toward a common goal. In 1994, superstar hockey player Mark Messier focused on the team goal of winning for the New York Rangers rather than on his personal statistics. In 2004, the Detroit Pistons won the National Basketball Association (NBA) championship without a superstar when players gave up individual glory for the sake of team success as championed by Coach Larry Brown. (Similarly, they reached the finals in 2005 but lost out to the San Antonio Spurs, also a close-knit team.) The Boston Red Sox ended the "curse" and won the World Series in 2004 by banding together as a cohesive unit. After winning the United European Football Association Euro soccer championship in 2008, Spanish soccer coach Vicente Del Bosque said, "We are enjoying one of the best moments in which Spanish football has ever lived. . . . I want to maintain the style which has allowed this team one of the best achievements in its history and the cohesion of the team." The notion of a cohesive unit is not reserved only for team sports. For example, Darren Clarke from the victorious 2004 European Ryder Cup golf team noted, "We played as a team, we dined as a team, we talked as a team, and we won as a team . . . . The team spirit this week was the best that I have experienced in this, my third Ryder Cup."

Although other sport and exercise professionals, such as exercise or aerobics leaders, receive less attention in the media, they also try to build cohesion in their classes. The purpose of fostering this spirit might be to enhance exercise adherence because the main goals of these types of programs are promoting adherence to an exercise program and promoting lifelong healthy lifestyles.

Yet we cannot always attribute success to team cohesion. Some teams win despite an apparent lack of cohesion. The Oakland Athletics in the early 1970s and the New York Yankees in the late 1970s won the World Series amid a lack of harmony in their ball clubs, which saw frequent battles among players and between players and coaches (Billy Martin and Reggie Jackson, for example). Similarly, Dennis Rodman of the Chicago Bulls was often at odds with his teammates because of his unusual and provocative antics, but on the court all he wanted to do was win, which allowed him to play within the team concept. Whenever Rodman was disruptive on the court, Coach Phil Jackson would bench him because he wasn't helping the team achieve its goal—winning an NBA championship.

Definition of Cohesion

In 1950, Festinger, Schacter, and Back defined **cohesion** as "the total field of forces which act on members to remain in the group" (p. 164). These authors believed that two distinct types of forces act on members in a group. The first class of forces, **attractiveness of the group**, refers to the individual's desire for interpersonal interactions with other group members and a desire to be involved in the group's activities. The second class of forces, **means control**, refers to the benefits that a member can derive by being associated with the group. For example, playing for a highly ranked college football team might increase an athlete's recognition and value in the draft.

Since 1950, several other definitions of group cohesion have been proposed, although the one suggested by Carron, Brawley, and Widmeyer (1998) and later refined by Carron and Eys (2012) appears to be the most comprehensive. Specifically, Carron and colleagues defined cohesion as "a dynamic process that is reflected in the tendency for a group to stick together and remain united in pursuit of its instrumental objectives and/or for the satisfaction of member affective needs" (p. 213). This underscores the notion that cohesion is multidimensional (many factors are related to why a group sticks together), dynamic (cohesion in a group can change over time), instrumental (groups are created for a purpose), and affective (members' social interactions produce feelings among group members). The definition of cohesion as multidimensional alludes to cohesion as a combination of task and social dimensions. **Task cohesion** reflects the degree

to which members of a group work together to achieve common goals. In sport, a common goal would be winning a championship, which in part depends on the team's coordinated effort or teamwork. **Social cohesion**, on the other hand, reflects the degree to which members of a team like each other and enjoy one another's company. Social cohesion is often equated with interpersonal attraction. In an exercise class, for example, a common goal would be enhanced fitness, and it has been shown that adherence to the exercise program increases as the social cohesion of the group increases (Spink & Carron, 1992).

> **KEY POINT** Task cohesion refers to the degree to which group members work together to achieve common goals and objectives, whereas social cohesion reflects the interpersonal attraction among group members.

Exercise professionals need to foster a sense of cohesion in order to help keep their clients motivated to continue with the exercise program.

The distinction between task and social cohesion helps explain how teams can overcome conflict to succeed. Take, for example, the New York Yankees and Oakland Athletics of the 1970s and 1980s and the Los Angeles Lakers in the early 2000s—teams that certainly appeared to be low in social cohesion (team members fought, formed cliques, and exchanged angry words). However, these teams clearly had a high degree of task cohesion—they wanted to win the World Series or NBA championship. It didn't matter if Reggie Jackson didn't get along with manager Billy Martin, or if Kobe Bryant got along with Shaquille O'Neal, because they shared the goal of winning. In terms of working together effectively, the baseball teams had excellent cohesion on the field and could turn double plays, hit cutoff players, and advance runners as well as or better than any other team. Similarly, the Lakers worked together on the court (e.g., switching defenses, setting screens, passing accurately) despite personality differences.

Conceptual Model of Cohesion

Carron and colleagues' (1998) definition of group cohesion is more useful for sport and exercise settings than the one suggested by Festinger and colleagues (1950) because it addresses both the task and social aspects of cohesion. Carron (1982) also developed a conceptual system as a framework for systematically studying cohesion in sport and exercise (figure 8.1). Carron's model outlines four major antecedents or factors affecting the development of cohesion in sport and exercise settings: environmental, personal, leadership, and team factors.

Environmental Factors

Environmental factors, which are the most general and remote, refer to the normative forces holding a group together. Environmental factors are present when, for example, players are under contract to the management, athletes hold scholarships, family members have expectations of athletes, geographical restrictions exist (e.g., having to play for a certain high school because of where you live), regulations specify the minimum playing time in a youth sport program, and exercisers pay an extra fee for their class. These influences can hold a group together, although other factors such as age, proximity, or eligibility requirements can also play an important role. For example,

having individuals in close proximity to each other with opportunities for interaction and communication fosters group development. In addition, the size of a group affects cohesion: Smaller groups are more cohesive than larger groups (Carron & Spink, 1995; Mullen & Cooper, 1994). Furthermore, level of competition seems to influence cohesion: High school teams are more cohesive than collegiate teams (Granito & Rainey, 1988).

Personal Factors

Personal factors refer to the individual characteristics of group members. Although situational factors are fairly constant and usually apply to all teams in a given league, a great deal of variation occurs in personal factors. For ease of investigation, Carron and Hausenblas (1998) classified these personal factors into three categories: demographic attributes (e.g., member similarity, sex), cognitions and motives (e.g., attributions for responsibility, anxiety), and behavior (e.g., adherence, social loafing).

Carron and Dennis (2001) suggested that the most important personal factor associated with the development of both task and social cohesion on sport teams is individual satisfaction. For example, Widmeyer and Williams (1991) found that member satisfaction was the best predictor of both social and task cohesion in the sport of golf. Another factor often cited as a correlate of cohesiveness is similarity (a demographic attribute)—similarity in attitudes, aspirations, commitments, and expectations. The importance of similarity is highlighted in the following quote about Jackie Robinson breaking the color (racial) barrier in baseball and the way Pee Wee Reese helped this transition:

" **Those early days were awfully tough on Jackie. I remembered times when on the train nobody would sit with him or talk to him. Pee Wee Reese always seemed to be the first to break the tension. He kidded Jackie before anyone else . . . . He started being friendly toward Jackie. In the beginning, Jackie was alone at the dining table. By the middle of the year you couldn't get a seat at the dining table. "**

—Bobby Bragen (cited in Allen, 1987, pp. 102–103)

Benefits found to be related to cohesion include passion, self-efficacy, high return rates (returning to the team), and decreased levels of anxiety and

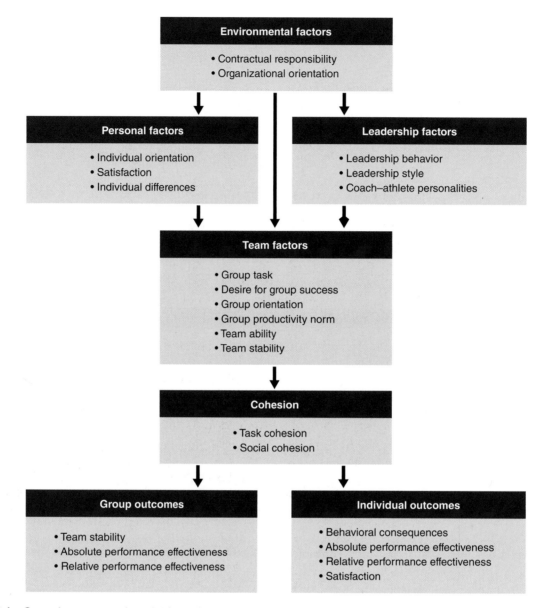

FIGURE 8.1 Carron's conceptual model for cohesion in sport teams.

Adapted, by permission, from A. Carron, 1982, "Cohesiveness in sports groups: Interpretations and considerations," *Journal of Sport Psychology* 4(2): 131.

depression (Paradis, Martin, & Carron, 2012). Many of these individual and group benefits have also been found in young athletes (see Martin, Paradis, Eys, & Evans, 2013, for a review).

Leadership Factors

Leadership factors include the leadership style and behaviors that professionals exhibit and the relationships they establish with their groups. (These factors are discussed more thoroughly in chapter 9.) Research has indicated that the role of leaders is vital to team cohesion. Specifically, clear, consistent communica-

tion from coaches and captains regarding team goals, team tasks, and team members' roles significantly influences cohesion (Brawley, Carron, & Widmeyer, 1993; Westre & Weiss, 1991). In addition, perceptions of compatibility between the leader and group members as evident in the coach–athlete relationship (commitment, closeness, complementarity) are important to enhancing feelings of cohesion (Jowett & Chaundy, 2004). Along these lines, Turman (2003) found that certain coaching behaviors or techniques such as inequity, embarrassment, and ridicule can decrease feelings of cohesion.

Team Factors

Team factors refer to group task characteristics (individual vs. team sports), group productivity norms, desire for group success, group roles, group position, and team stability. For example, Carron, Shapcott, and Burke (2011) argued that teams that stay together a long time and have a strong desire for group success also exhibit high levels of group cohesion. In addition, shared experiences, such as a series of successes or failures, are important in developing and maintaining cohesion because they unify a team to counter the threat of opposing teams (Brawley, 1990). Finally, some suggest that the relatively recent factor of collective efficacy is positively related to perceptions of team cohesion (Carron & Brawley, 2008; Paskevich, Estabrooks, Brawley, & Carron, 2001). The following quote by Michael Jordan (1994) illustrates the relationship between collective efficacy and cohesion:

" Naturally there are going to be ups and downs, particularly if you have individuals trying to achieve at a high level. But when we stepped between the lines, we knew what we were capable of doing. When a pressure situation presented itself, we were plugged into one another as a cohesive unit. That's why we were able to come back so often and win so many close games and beat more talented teams. (p. 23) "

Tools for Measuring Cohesion

To determine the relationship between cohesion and performance, we must be able to measure cohesion. Two types of measures have been developed: questionnaires and sociograms.

Questionnaires

Most early research on cohesion used the Sport Cohesiveness Questionnaire developed by Martens, Landers, and Loy (1972). This questionnaire has seven items that either measure interpersonal attraction or directly rate closeness or attraction to the group. Unfortunately, no reliability or validity measures were established on the Sport Cohesiveness Questionnaire, and most items address only social cohesion. To account for the multidimensional nature of cohesion, Yukelson, Weinberg, and Jackson (1984) developed a 22-item tool called the Multidimensional Sport Cohesion Instrument. It includes four broad dimensions of team cohesion: attraction to the group, unity of purpose, quality of teamwork, and valued roles.

The first factor, attraction to the group, reflects social cohesion. The other three factors relate to task cohesion because they all pertain to working together as a team in pursuit of common goals. Although the Multidimensional Sport Cohesion Instrument was designed for basketball teams, its versatility allows it to be used with other team sports.

Later, Widmeyer, Brawley, and Carron (1985) developed the Group Environment Questionnaire (GEQ), which distinguishes between the individual and the group and between task and social concerns. It is based on theory related to group processes and systematically developed to guarantee reliability and validity (Brawley, Carron, & Widmeyer, 1987; Carron et al., 1998).

The GEQ has been successfully used in numerous studies of group cohesion in sport as well as fitness settings (e.g., see Carron et al., 1998, for a review). For example, using the GEQ, researchers have shown level of cohesion to be related to team performance, increased adherence, group size, attributions for

Overcoming Low Social Cohesion With High Task Cohesion

The Los Angeles Lakers of the early 2000s were a classic example of a team on which the two top players—Shaquille O'Neal and Kobe Bryant—were constantly feuding but were able to win three consecutive NBA championships. These two superstars did not hang out together off the court and were critical of each other in public statements. However, they had one very important thing in common: They both wanted to win NBA championships. Thus, when they were on the court they worked together well, passed the ball to each other, and respected each other's abilities. They complemented each other on the court (high task cohesion) even though they didn't particularly like each other (low social cohesion). In fact, this dislike became so great that it led to Shaquille O'Neal being traded to the Miami Heat.

Group Environment Questionnaire (GEQ): Sample Items

	Strongly disagree					Strongly agree			
Attraction to group—task subscale									
I like this team's style of play.	1	2	3	4	5	6	7	8	9
Attraction to group—social subscale									
Some of my best friends are on this team.	1	2	3	4	5	6	7	8	9
Group integration—task subscale									
We all take responsibility for any loss or poor performance by our team.	1	2	3	4	5	6	7	8	9
Group integration—social subscale									
Our team would like to spend time together in the off-season.	1	2	3	4	5	6	7	8	9

Note: To score the GEQ, add up all answers for each subscale. The higher the score, the more strongly the individual feels about that particular aspect of group cohesion. (Scoring reverses for negatively worded items.) For example, scores in the category *attraction to group—task* can range from 4 to 36. Comparisons can be made among individuals or among groups.

Adapted, by permission, from A. Carron, W. Widmeyer, and L. Brawley, 1985, "The development of an instrument to assess cohesion in sports teams: The environment questionnaire," *Journal of Sport Psychology* 7(3): 244-267.

responsibility for performance outcomes, reduced absenteeism, member satisfaction, and intrateam communication.

> **KEY POINT** The Group Environment Questionnaire (GEQ) focuses on how attractive the group is to individual members and on how the members perceive the group. The GEQ is accepted as an assessment of team cohesion.

The model on which the development of the GEQ was based has two major categories: a member's perception of the group as a totality (group integra-tion) and a member's personal attraction to the group (individual attraction to the group). The members' perceptions of the group as a unit and their perceptions of the group's attraction for them can focus on task or social aspects. Thus, there are four constructs in the model, as noted in figure 8.2: group integration—task (e.g., our team is united in trying to reach its goals for performance), group integration—social (e.g., members of our team do not stick together outside of practices and games), individual attraction to group—task (e.g., I do not like the style of play on this team), and individual attraction to group—social (e.g., some of my best friends are on the team).

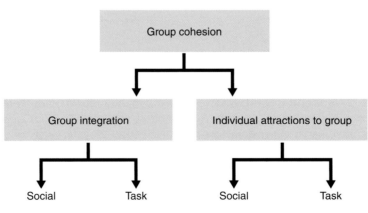

FIGURE 8.2 Conceptual model of group cohesion for the GEQ.

Adapted, by permission, from A. Carron, W. Widmeyer, and L. Brawley, 1985, "The development of an instrument to assess cohesion in sports teams: The environment questionnaire," *Journal of Sport Psychology* 7(3): 244-267.

DISCOVER Activity 8.1 gives you an opportunity to take and score the GEQ.

These beliefs and perceptions are thought to act together in creating a group's and an individual group member's sense of cohesion. In essence, both the group as a whole and the individuals in the group have both social and task aspects. The relationship of these four constructs is presented in figure 8.2. Recently, a group cohesion instrument developed for youth sports (Youth Sport Environment Questionnaire) revealed that young athletes discriminated mostly along the lines of task versus social cohesion and less along the individual–group dimension than adult athletes did (Eys, Loughead, Bray, & Carron, 2009).

Sociograms

Questionnaires have been the most popular way to measure group cohesion, but they do not show how particular individuals relate to each other, whether cliques are developing, or whether some group members are socially isolated. A **sociogram** is a tool for measuring social cohesion. It discloses affiliation and attraction among group members, including

- the presence or absence of cliques,
- members' perceptions of group closeness,
- friendship choices in the group,
- the degree to which athletes perceive interpersonal feelings similarly,
- social isolation of individual group members, and
- extent of group attraction.

To generate information for the sociogram, you ask individual group members specific questions such as "Name the three people in the group you would most like to invite to a party and the three people you would least like to invite," "Name the three people you would most like to room with on road trips and the three you would least like to room with," or "Name three people you would most like to practice with during the off-season and three you would least like to practice with." Confidentiality must be ensured, and honesty in responses should be encouraged.

Based on the responses to the questions, a sociogram is created (see an example in figure 8.3), which should reveal the pattern of interpersonal relationships in a group. As the sociogram is created, the most frequently chosen individuals are placed toward the center and less frequently chosen individuals are placed outside. Notice that the arrows in figure 8.3 indicate the direction of choice. Reciprocal choice is represented by arrows going in both directions between two individuals. In the baseball team represented in the figure, you can see that Tom is the person everyone seems to like. Larry is isolated from the team and is disliked by several members, so a problem exists that the coach should address. Jay and Bob form a closed unit and are not really involved with the rest of the team. Knowing about these relationships might

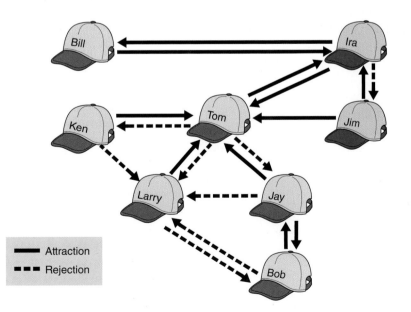

FIGURE 8.3 Sample sociogram for measuring cohesion on a baseball team.

help the coach deal with interpersonal problems before they become disruptive.

DISCOVER Activity 8.2 lets you develop and then discuss a sociogram.

Relationship Between Cohesion and Performance

Fans, coaches, and sport psychologists seem to have an enduring fascination with how team cohesion relates to performance success (see Paskevich et al., 2001, for a review). On an intuitive level, you might assume that the higher the level of a team's cohesion, the greater its success. Why else spend so much time trying to develop team cohesion? In fact, in a review of 30 studies, Widmeyer, Carron, and Brawley (1993) found that 83% of studies reported a positive relationship between cohesion and performance, with higher team cohesion linked to greater team success. Another review of 66 empirical studies assessing the cohesion–performance relationship in a variety of settings showed positive relationships in 92% of the studies; the strongest relationships were found in sport teams (Mullen & Cooper, 1994). Using just sport teams (46 studies including almost 10,000 athletes and more than 1,000 teams), Carron, Colman, Wheeler, and Stevens (2002) found moderate to large cohesion–performance effects and, similar to Mullen and Cooper, found that the strongest effects were in sport teams.

A clue to the way in which cohesion enhances performance comes from a study (Bray & Whaley, 2001) showing that higher levels of cohesion may increase performance by producing higher levels of effort. However, several studies show a negative cohesion–performance relationship. In fact, several reviews of the research literature have noted the somewhat contradictory nature of the results regarding cohesion and performance success (e.g., Carron, Spink, & Prapavessis, 1997). The best way to understand the inconsistencies is to consider the measurement of cohesion, characteristics of the task, and direction of causality with particular reference to the latest review of the cohesion–performance literature (Carron, Colman, Wheeler, & Stevens, 2002).

Type of Measurement

There has been a great deal of controversy over the years regarding the effects of task and social cohesion on performance. In a review of the literature, Carron and colleagues (2002) found that increases in both task and social cohesion were associated with increases in performance. Previous reviews had indicated that task cohesion was more important (as a predictor of performance) than social cohesion, but evidently this is not the case. These results have important implications for applied sport psychology and interventions undertaken with athletes and teams to enhance team cohesiveness. Specifically, these results suggest that both task and social cohesion interventions can be effective in enhancing cohesiveness and improving performance. Socially oriented techniques include team camp-outs (Cogan & Petrie, 1995), ropes and challenge courses (Meyer, 2000), social get-togethers outside of the sport context (Yukelson, 1997), and personal growth experiences (McClure & Foster, 1991). Some task-oriented interventions include team goal setting (Widmeyer & DuCharme, 1997), team communication (Yukelson, 1997), and understanding and conforming to team roles and norms (Prapavessis, Carron, & Spink, 1997).

Task Demands

A second explanation for the confusing cohesion–performance results involves the diversity of task demands that sport teams face. The explanation can be attributed to the original work of Landers and Lueschen (1974), who noted that one needs to consider task structure and demands when assessing the cohesion–performance relationship. Specifically, they characterized the nature of interactions among team members along a continuum, from interactive to coactive. **Interactive sports** require team members to work together and coordinate their actions. Players on a soccer team, for example, have to constantly pass the ball to each other, maintain certain positions, coordinate offensive attacks, and devise defensive strategies to stop opponents from scoring. **Coactive sports** require much less, if any, team interaction and coordination for the achievement of goals. For instance, members of a golf or bowling team have little to do with each other in terms of coordinated activity. Baseball is a good example of a sport that is both coactive and interactive: Batting or catching a fly ball is coactive, whereas making a double play or hitting the cutoff player (i.e., an outfielder throwing to an infielder who in turn throws the ball to home plate) is interactive.

Previous research argued that the cohesion–performance relationship was stronger in interactive sports than in coactive sports. However, the more recent review by Carron and colleagues (2002) revealed that task type is not a moderator for the cohesion–performance relationship. Specifically, more cohesiveness is related to better performance in both coactive and interactive sports. However, the absolute level of cohesiveness is typically higher in interactive sports than in coactive sports, which makes sense considering the close on-court or on-field interactions required in sports such as basketball, football, and ice hockey. As a result, in interactive sports, coaches inevitably and explicitly introduce many of the **team-building** strategies associated with increased cohesiveness, such as ensuring role clarity and acceptance, establishing team performance goals, and improving athlete–athlete and coach–athlete communication. Conversely, the nature of coactive sports means there are fewer natural or inevitable opportunities for group cohesion to develop. As a consequence, team-building interventions might have a greater effect on both team cohesion and team performance in that context.

> **KEY POINT** Cohesion increases performance in interactive sports (e.g., basketball) as well as coactive sports (e.g., golf).

Direction of Causality

The **direction of causality** refers to whether cohesion leads to performance success or performance success leads to cohesion. In other words, will a team that works together on and off the field be successful, or do players like each other more and work together well because they are successful? Researchers have investigated these questions from two perspectives:

- Cohesion leads to performance; that is, cohesion measures precede performance.
- Performance leads to cohesion; that is, performance measures precede cohesion.

Direction of causality or cause–effect relationships proved difficult to establish in past studies because there were too many uncontrolled factors, such as previous team success, coaching, or talent. The stronger effects of performance on cohesion were found in a study of intercollegiate female field hockey players (Williams & Hacker, 1982). In addition, research (Grieve, Whelan, & Meyers, 2000) has supported the idea that the effect of performance on cohesion is stronger than the effect of cohesion on performance. This is consistent with the

review by Mullen and Cooper (1994) using different types of teams: "Although cohesiveness may indeed lead the group to perform better, the tendency for the group to experience greater cohesiveness after successful performance may be even stronger" (p. 222). The most recent review using just sport teams, however, found no difference between the cohesion-to-performance and the performance-to-cohesion relationships. These findings appear to be consistent with research suggesting that the relationship between cohesion and performance is circular. Performance seems to affect later cohesion, and these changes in cohesion then affect subsequent performance (Landers, Wilkinson, Hatfield, & Barber, 1982).

In summary, then, the cohesion–performance relationship is complex. Considering the preponderance of evidence, we currently think that increased cohesion leads to greater performance and that better performances bring teams together and lead to increased cohesion. Hence, the relationship is circular. In this circular relationship, the effect of performance on cohesion appears to be stronger than that of cohesion on performance for teams in general (although not for sport teams).

> **KEY POINT** The relationship between cohesion and performance appears to be circular: Performance success leads to increased cohesion, which in turn leads to increased performance.

Other Factors Associated With Cohesion

Although researchers have focused predominantly on the relationship between cohesion and performance, other potentially important factors are also associated with cohesion. This section reviews some of the more traditional factors, and "Additional Correlates of Cohesion" highlights other factors.

Team Satisfaction

Satisfaction and cohesion are highly similar except that cohesion is about groups whereas satisfaction is an individual construct. Although researchers have found consistently strong relationships between cohesion and satisfaction (e.g., Widmeyer & Williams, 1991; Paradis & Loughead, 2012), two different models are used to explain the relationships among cohesion, satisfaction, and performance.

One model (A) hypothesizes a circular relationship in which team cohesion leads to performance success, which leads to feelings of satisfaction, which tend to strengthen and reinforce team cohesion. The other model (B) hypothesizes a circular relationship in which performance success leads to higher cohesion, which in turn leads to greater satisfaction. Thus, both the models suggest that relationships among satisfaction, cohesion, and performance do indeed exist. However, model A suggests that cohesion directly enhances performance, whereas model B argues that performance success leads to cohesion. In either case, leaders do well in building group cohesion because being in a cohesive group is satisfying and indirectly and directly enhances performance.

Conformity

Psychological research has shown that the more cohesive the group, the more influence the group has on its individual members. In a highly cohesive group, members might feel pressured about clothing style, hairstyle, practice habits, or game behavior. For example, when the Detroit Pistons won consecutive NBA titles in 1989 and 1990, they were known as the "bad boys," and the norm was to play rough, tough, aggressive, intimidating basketball. Rookies and new players had to adapt to this norm and style of basketball to fit in with the team. Similarly, people joining health clubs might feel pressured to purchase designer exercise clothing so they don't look out of place.

Highly cohesive groups demonstrate a greater conformity to the group's norm for productivity than do less cohesive groups. For example, the best performance occurs when the group norm for productivity is high and group cohesion is high, whereas the poorest performance occurs when the group norm is low and group cohesion is high. One of the reasons the Chicago Bulls were so successful in the 1990s is that Michael Jordan and Scottie Pippen set such a high group norm for productivity, which helped raise the level of their teammates' contributions to the team's success.

Adherence

A number of research studies have addressed the relationship between cohesion and adherence in a variety of exercise groups. A summary of these findings (Paskevich et al., 2001; Burke, Carron, & Shapcott, 2008) concluded that individuals in exercise classes who feel more cohesive (a) are likely to attend more classes, (b)

are more likely to arrive on time, (c) are less likely to drop out, (d) are more resistant to disruptions in the group, (e) are more likely to experience positive affect related to exercise, and (f) have stronger efficacy beliefs related to exercise. In addition, this positive relationship between cohesion and adherence appears to remain constant regardless of the exercise leader–participant ratio. In essence, cohesion positively influenced adherence in larger fitness centers (larger exercise leader–participant ratios) and in smaller, university-based classes (smaller exercise leader–participant ratios).

Social Support

Research on social support suggests a positive relationship between the social support an individual receives and her evaluations of group cohesion (Rees & Hardy, 2000). For example, social support provided by coaches has been positively related to athletes' perceptions of task cohesion in high school football teams (Westre & Weiss, 1991), cohesion and satisfaction in college basketball teams (Weiss & Friedrichs, 1986), and higher performance in collegiate football teams (Garland & Barry, 1990).

KEY POINT The more cohesive a group is, the greater an influence it has on individual members to conform to the group's norms. Teams higher in cohesion can better resist disruption than teams lower in cohesion. Teams that stay together longer tend to be more cohesive, which leads to improvements in performance. Exercise classes with high group cohesion have fewer dropouts and late arrivals than do classes low in cohesiveness. Exercise leaders can help increase a class's cohesiveness.

Although to many people social support simply means some sort of emotional support, researchers have identified seven distinguishable forms of social support (Rosenfeld & Richman, 1997). Rosenfeld and Richman (see chapter 7) provided numerous suggestions for enhancing these areas of social support. Coaches and leaders should understand the importance of social support and how and when to use the various types of social support to enhance group cohesion.

Stability

Stability refers to both the turnover rate for group membership and the length of time group members have been together. It seems logical that teams that remain relatively constant across a certain period of

Additional Correlates of Cohesion

In this text we have highlighted some of the traditional correlates of cohesion. Research (see Carron & Eys [2012] and Martin et al. [2013] for reviews) has indicated that the following factors are related to cohesion as well.

- *Group status.* The higher athletes' perceptions of task cohesion are, the less importance athletes place on rewards and on achieving status.
- *Role clarity and acceptance.* A circular relationship exists between role clarity and acceptance and task cohesion.
- *Collective efficacy.* High collective efficacy is related to higher levels of task cohesion, and higher task cohesion is related to higher levels of cohesion.
- *Group norms.* When normative expectations for certain behaviors are strong, cohesion is also strong.
- *Decision style.* Stronger perceptions of cohesion are related to a more participative decision style.
- *Self-presentation.* Self-presentation concerns decrease as group cohesion increases (Divine, Munroe-Chandler, & Loughead, 2013).
- *Sacrifice.* Players engage in sacrifices to the team to a greater extent when cohesion is high.
- *Self-handicapping.* Athletes engage in more self-handicapping behavior (strategies used to protect self-esteem such as externalizing failure and internalizing success) when task cohesion is viewed as high.
- *Skill level.* The relationship between cohesion and performance exists across a broad band of athletic skill and experience, from high school to professional sport.
- *Social loafing.* Athletes on teams higher in cohesion are less likely to think that their teammates may socially loaf and are less likely to socially loaf themselves.
- *Attributions for responsibility.* Successful, cohesive teams use team-enhancing attributional strategies such as distributing the credit for success and sharing the responsibility for failure.
- *Competitive state anxiety.* Athletes who perceived their cognitive or somatic anxiety to be facilitative have higher levels of task cohesion (Eys, Hardy, Carron, & Beauchamp, 2003).
- *Imagery.* Teams higher in cohesion are more likely to use certain types of imagery such as cognitive specific imagery (focus on a specific task or skill) and motivational general mastery (build confidence; Hardy, Hall, & Carron, 2003).
- *Motivational outcomes.* Group cohesion has been shown to be related to adaptive motivational outcomes such as increased effort, expectancies of success, and increased persistence (Gu, Solomon, Zhang, & Xiang, 2011).
- *Passion.* Passion increases as cohesion increases.

time will be more stable, cohesive, and ultimately successful. Carron and Hausenblas (1998) suggested that team cohesion and stability are related in a circular fashion. That is, the longer the team has been together, the more likely it is that cohesion will develop, and the more cohesive the team becomes, the less likely it is that members will choose to leave. Let's look at some research on this issue.

Studies of soccer and baseball teams across a single season showed that teams with few lineup changes were more successful than those that changed con-

stantly (Essing, 1970; Loy, 1970). Another study tried to determine whether there is an optimal time to keep a group of players together to maximize cohesion and subsequent success. This study showed that in Major League Baseball, teams with a half-life (defined as the time it took for the starting roster to reduce to half its original size) of 5 years were the most successful (Donnelly, Carron, & Chelladurai, 1978).

More recent studies examined the relationship between cohesion and a sport group's resistance to disruption (e.g., personnel changes or internal conflict)

Understanding Team Building: Expert Coaches' Perceptions

Bloom, Stevens, and Wickwire (2003) investigated team building as seen by a group of expert coaches. Results revealed several themes:

- *Fundamental elements of team building*—Coaches believed that team building was bringing a group of people together, establishing mutual goals, and unifying individuals to achieve those goals.

- *Team environment*—Coaches emphasized that organization and planning provided consistency and stability for the athletes, which contributed to a more positive environment in which team building could take place.

- *Coach's role and characteristics*—The coaches believed that their job was to facilitate, moderate, and supervise the team to keep it moving in the right direction. Coaches believed that their leadership style was central to team building, although they stressed the importance of player involvement and used analogies such as the team "steering its own ship."

- *Team-building activities*—These activities could be divided into those that were more social (e.g., team dinners), physical (e.g., 10K runs, ropes courses), and psychological (e.g., identifying and discussing the variables needed to achieve success, learning about teammates). However, no one simple formula for building team unity existed because it depended on the beliefs of the coach and his or her ability to gauge the atmosphere of the team.

- *Relationships among talent, cohesion, and performance*—Coaches believed that both cohesion and talent make important contributions to performance, but they disagreed about which had the greatest effect.

among elite sport athletes, recreational sport athletes, and fitness classes. Brawley, Carron, and Widmeyer (1988) compared the groups that exhibited either high or low cohesion on their perceived resistance to disruption. A reliable positive relationship existed between group cohesion and group resistance to disruption: The groups that were higher in cohesion exhibited a higher resistance to disruption than did teams that were lower in cohesion. Establishing positive group norms for productivity is one way to keep individuals working together as a unit over time.

Group Goals

Most people think that individuals set their own goals. But in group situations, such as with sport teams or exercise groups, goals are often set for the group as a whole. A group's goals are not merely the sum of the personal goals of group members; they are shared perceptions that refer to a desirable state for the group as a unit. The question is, What relationship exists among group goals, cohesion, and performance? One study of volleyball, hockey, basketball, and swimming teams revealed the following:

- Members who perceived that their team engaged in group goal setting for competition had higher levels of cohesion.

- The higher the level of satisfaction with team goals, the higher the level of team cohesion.

- Although individual group members' perceptions of cohesion changed across a season, cohesion was still related to team satisfaction and group goals throughout the season (Brawley et al., 1993).

Other studies (Widmeyer, Silva, & Hardy, 1992; Widmeyer & Williams, 1991) showed that a stated team goal—along with its acceptance—was the most important contributor to task cohesion and the second most important contributor to social cohesion. In addition, group cohesion increased as commitment to, clarity of, and importance of the goal increased for players. Having individuals participate in developing team or group goals also increased group cohesion.

On a practical note, athletes who perceive that a team goal encourages them to increase effort and who practice drills designed to achieve that goal (e.g., in volleyball, moving quickly from defensive to offensive sets) will likely feel satisfied with their team's practice goals. You might expect this to happen because team members receive feedback that drills were correctly completed (i.e., the goal was reached) and that the team's effort was high and its attention was focused. In this way, the group's goals can enhance its feelings of unity and cohesion.

Widmeyer and DuCharme (1997) suggested the following guidelines for instituting a team goal-setting program:

- Establish long-term goals first that are specific and challenging.
- Establish clear paths to the long-term goals through the use of short-term goals.
- Involve all team members in establishing goals.
- Carefully monitor progress toward team goals.
- Reward team progress toward team goals.
- Foster collective efficacy concerning team goal attainment.

Strategies for Enhancing Cohesion

Now that sport psychologists better understand the nature of group cohesion and the factors that help enhance cohesion and subsequent performance, some researchers have begun to focus on specific interventions for enhancing cohesion in sport and exercise groups.

Exercise Settings

With dropout rates from formal exercise programs at about 50%, researchers have been investigating ways to reduce this discouraging statistic. One innovative approach has focused on cohesion as a means to enhance attendance rates (see Paskevich et al., 2001, for a review). It has been found that dropouts from exercise programs have less regard for the task and social cohesion of their exercise class than do participants who stay with the program (Carron & Spink, 1993; Spink & Carron, 1992, 1993). In addition, exercisers with higher feelings of cohesion attend class more regularly and are more punctual than exercisers with lower cohesion.

In another innovative study, sport psychologists attempted to build cohesion in exercise classes through a team approach (Spink & Carron, 1993). Instructors were trained in team-building strategies to enhance adherence by improving group cohesion. They learned that distinctiveness contributes to a sense of group identity, unity, and cohesion. Some instructors emphasized distinctiveness by having a group name, making up a group T-shirt, or handing out neon headbands. Their classes showed higher levels of cohesion and

significantly fewer dropouts and late arrivals than did the classes not exposed to team building. This suggests that cohesion is an important ingredient in exercise settings as well as in traditional sport settings. Table 8.1 lists strategies for enhancing cohesion.

To further test the effects of team building on cohesion, Carron and Spink (1995) devised an intervention for small and large exercise classes. The team-building program actually offset the negative effect that increased size can have on perceptions of cohesion. Specifically, no differences existed in perceptions of cohesion for participants from small (fewer than 20 participants) and large (more than 40) exercise groups that had been exposed to a team-building intervention. In essence, it is possible to maintain a sense of cohesion even in relatively large groups with the implementation of an appropriate team-building program.

Sport Settings

Other research has focused on team building in sport settings (Prapavessis, Carron, & Spink, 1997). In this case, the intervention began with elite male soccer coaches attending a workshop during the off-season in which specific strategies for implementing a team-building program were established. The coaches then became active agents in the development of practical strategies to be used in the team-building program. Specifically, on the basis of the principles outlined in table 8.2, the coaches were asked to develop applied techniques and procedures that could be used for team building with their teams during the 6 weeks before the season. Although results did not show significant differences in cohesion between the team-building and control conditions, the authors believed that the coaches in the control conditions used many of the strategies from the cohesion intervention to enhance their own team's cohesion. Therefore, future research should continue to investigate how team-building interventions can complement what coaches already do to enhance cohesion.

Along these lines, Carron and Eys (2012) and Loughead and Bloom (2012) provided suggestions for practical exercises to help achieve the principles of team building (see table 8.2). These include the following:

- *Group norms.* Have team members work in small groups to describe how an ideal teammate would react to a list of hypothetical but realistic situations. The team as a whole then discusses and agrees on

TABLE 8.1 Specific Strategies for Enhancing Group Cohesiveness Suggested by Fitness Class Instructors

Factor	Examples of intervention strategies
Distinctiveness	Have a group name.
	Make up a group T-shirt.
	Hand out neon headbands or shoelaces.
	Make up posters and slogans for the class.
Individual positions	Divide the swimming pool into areas by fitness level.
	Make signs to label parts of the group.
	Use specific positions for low-, medium-, and high-impact exercisers.
	Let participants pick their own spot and encourage them to keep it throughout the year.
Group norms	Have members introduce each other.
	Encourage members to become fitness friends.
	Establish a goal to lose weight together.
	Promote a smart work ethic as a group characteristic.
Individual sacrifices	Ask two or three people for a goal for the day.
	Ask regulars to help new people.
	Ask people who aren't concerned with weight loss to make a sacrifice for the group on some days (more aerobics) and people who are concerned to make a sacrifice on other days (more mat work).
Interaction and communication	Use partner work and have partners introduce themselves.
	Introduce the person on your right and left.
	Work in groups of five and take turns showing a move.

Adapted, by permission, from A. Carron and K. Spink, 1993, "Team building in an exercise setting," *The Sport Psychologist* 7(1):13.

unacceptable (e.g., yelling at teammates, coming late to practice) and acceptable behaviors. By having a meeting and coming to a joint decision on acceptable team norms, players will better understand what is expected of them on and off the field.

• *Individual roles.* Each athlete anonymously writes "I want [player's name] on my team because . . ." for everyone on the team. The coach then collects and distributes the responses to the appropriate athletes. This helps each athlete understand the importance of their particular role on the team.

• *Distinctiveness.* Matching uniforms with team mottos is an easy way to bring the team together and create distinctiveness. Traveling to competitions together also increases interactions among athletes, bringing them closer together and making them more distinct from other groups.

• *Individual sacrifice.* Have an offensive player play a more defensive role, or ask a team captain or

veteran to make efforts to mentor a younger or new team member.

• *Communication and interaction.* Set out a small obstacle course using cones. Separate athletes into small groups and blindfold all but one member in each group. The athlete not wearing a blindfold directs teammates through the course using verbal instructions only.

A unique approach to improving the performance environment of competitive teams was developed and implemented in English soccer (Pain & Harwood, 2008, 2009; Pain, Harwood, & Mullen, 2012). The authors broadened the definition of cohesion to include the entire environment in which teams function, including coach–athlete interaction, organizational issues, team climate, communication, goal setting, and team socialization. Especially important was getting the coach and players involved in a reflective way so that they considered the game performance, which

TABLE 8.2   Principles Underlying the Team-Building Program in a Sport Setting

Category	Principle
Team structure	
Role clarity and acceptance	Cohesion is enhanced when group members clearly understand their roles in the group. Cohesion is enhanced when group members are satisfied and accept their roles in the group.
Leadership	The behavior of the team leaders influences task and social cohesion in the group. A participatory style of coaching leadership contributes to enhanced cohesion.
Conformity to standards	Conformity to group social and task norms contributes to enhanced cohesion. Group norms are highly resistant to change.
Team environment	
Togetherness	Feelings of cohesion increase when group members are repetitively put in close physical proximity.
Distinctiveness	The presence of group distinctiveness contributes to group cohesion.
Team processes	
Sacrifices	Cohesion is enhanced when high-status members make sacrifices for the group.
Goals and objectives	Group goals are more strongly associated with team success than are individual goals. Member participation in goal setting contributes to enhanced cohesion.
Cooperation	Cooperative behavior is superior to both individualistic and competitive behavior for individual and group performance. Cooperative behavior contributes to enhanced cohesion.

Adapted, by permission, from H. Prapavessis, A. Carron, and K. Spink, 1997, "Team building in sport groups," *International Journal of Sport Psychology* 27: 251-268.

led to valuable ideas regarding team functioning. This type of action research, conducted with athletes and coaches while carefully considering potential actual changes within the team, during a competitive season holds great promise for sport psychologists working with competitive teams. Along these lines, Rovio, Arviven-Barrow, Weigand, Eskola, and Lintunen (2012) used an action research model for team building in ice hockey. They used performance profiling, individual and group goal setting, role clarification, and group norms in this team-building effort. These studies indicate that team building requires a variety of methods because these methods interact with and complement each other.

In an ethnographic observational study, Holt and Sparkes (2001) investigated factors associated with building cohesion in a soccer team across a season. In-depth interviews and participant observations (one of the researchers was on the team) revealed factors associated with the development of cohesion at midseason and at the end of the season. At midseason, clear and meaningful roles, team goals, communication, and selfishness or personal sacrifice were most strongly related to cohesion. At the end of the season, the same four factors were still operative, although to varying degrees. This demonstrated the unstable nature of cohesion and the fact that it can significantly change over the course of a season. For example, in the soccer team considerable selfishness existed at midseason, but by the end of the season players were routinely sacrificing their own best interests for the better good of the team. Finally, a recent study using a collegiate soccer team found that open team discussions, sharing of information, open communication lines, and honesty led to enhanced feelings of cohesion as well as improved confidence in teammates and better overall performance (Pain & Harwood, 2009).

Taking some of this research, Veach and May (2005) developed a model (MAPS) to help guide the building of various sport teams.

- *Mission:* The mission helps guide the individuals on the team toward higher team-oriented goals. In essence, it is the philosophy driving these goals, which may focus on performance improvement, winning, moral development, intrinsic motivation, or enjoyment.

- *Assessment:* Identifying team strengths and areas of improvement can help coaches develop resources, changes, and processes that will improve the team's potential to achieve its goals.

- *Plan:* Action plans for each person and for the team as a whole can improve effort and commitment. These steps should have a clear consensus with concrete behaviors, targeted actions, and specific timelines.

- *Systematic evaluation:* Periodically reviewing the entire "road map" and looking at how plans were implemented and goals were reached provides a time for reflection, review, and revision.

Shared Team Values: A Prerequisite for Team Building

Team building has become a common technique in sport, business, and the military. Team building usually involves identifying team goals and a team mission. But before team-building activities and goals are identified, team values need to be developed and understood because values clarify the path to achieving goals and are critical to building trust among players and coaches. Common team values might include morality, teamwork, honesty, cooperation, communication, winning, fairness, and accountability. Knowing that other team members share common values will lead to a commitment to act in accordance with these values both on and off the field (Kramer & Lewicki, 2010).

Shoenfelt (2010) outlined a five-step process for clarifying goals:

- *Identify team goals.* An abundance of empirical evidence shows that goal setting is effective in helping teams accomplish objectives. Coaches should elicit athlete input in identifying and then developing team goals, as this enhances commitment toward achieving these goals (Weinberg, 2010a).

- *Individual team members identify potential team values.* Ask athletes to define the term *values* and to list their team values. Athletes then discuss why they feel each value is important for the team. Coaches should present last; this allows athletes to share their true values for the team without being influenced by the coaches' values.

- *Team discussion of how values support team goals.* The team as a whole then discusses these values and tallies the number of times each value is mentioned. Values that are seen as similar might be combined in a single value. For example, accountability and responsibility may be combined into one value.

- *Gain consensus on top five to seven team values.* Through continued discussions, highlight the importance of different values and, via consensus, choose the five to seven most important values. Differences in opinion should be considered objectively so that all explanations for the importance of each value are aired.

- *Prioritize team values.* Each athlete then assigns points to each of the values so that the points for each individual add up to 100. Values that receive only a few points are dropped from the list, and the remaining values are considered core values. The team should discuss how to use these values to help guide behavior. As a final step, the coach should ask each athlete for a verbal commitment to these values; this public commitment to the team values increases the level of commitment. These core values can be posted in the locker room as a reminder.

Guidelines for Building Team Cohesion

Cohesion doesn't always enhance group performance, but it can certainly create a positive environment that elicits positive interactions among group members. Along these lines, building team cohesion involves understanding the experience of individual athletes on the team and uncovering the ways in which they can become personally invested in the team, feel satisfied with the contributions that they are making, and feel responsibility for the team's cohesiveness and success (Schmidt, McGuire, Humphrey, Williams, & Grawer,

2005). Sport psychologists (e.g., Anshel, 2012; Carron et al., 1997; Klinert et al., 2012; Yukelson, 1997) have created guidelines for developing group cohesion. Of special note is an issue of *Journal of Applied Sport Psychology* (Hardy & Crace, 1997) devoted to team building. These ideas are appropriate for competitive sport, teaching, and exercise settings.

What Coaches or Leaders Can Do

As long as communication is effective and open, coaches and leaders can foster group cohesion in several ways. We discuss here what leaders can do to help build cohesion and what participants themselves can do.

Communicate Effectively

An effective group or team leader needs to create an environment where everyone is comfortable expressing thoughts and feelings (see chapter 10 for more discussion of communication). Open lines of communication can alleviate many potential problems. Here, Terry Orlick (2000) describes the critical role of communication in group cohesion:

" Harmony grows when you really listen to others and they listen to you, when you are considerate of their feelings and they are considerate of yours, when you accept their differences and they accept yours, and when you help them and they help you. (p. 200) "

Team building requires a climate of openness, where airing problems and matters of concern is not just considered appropriate but is also encouraged. One technique that Yukelson (1997) suggested to help individuals communicate and express their feelings positively and assertively is known as the DESC formula. This technique consists of describing (the situation), expressing (feelings), specifying (changes you want to take place), and noting the consequences (what to expect if agreement is not reached).

Leaders should ensure that everyone pulls together and is committed to the group's goals, which include improved interpersonal relationships. This improvement is important because increased communication has a circular relationship with increased group cohesiveness (Carron & Hausenblas, 1998). As communication about task and social issues increases, cohesiveness develops. As a result, group members are more open with each other, volunteer more, talk more,

and listen better. The group leader plays a major role in integrating the group into a unit that communicates openly and performs with a sense of pride, excellence, and collective identity (Yukelson, 1993, 1997).

Explain Individual Roles in Team Success

Coaches should clearly outline individual roles to team members, stressing the importance of each player's role to the team's success. The more team members there are who perceive their roles as unimportant, the more apathetic the team will become. Coaches need to carefully explain to these athletes what their roles on the team are and give them opportunities to contribute. When players understand what is required of their teammates, they can begin to develop support and empathy. The coach can help this process by having players observe and record the efforts of their teammates in different positions. Also, during practice, the coach might assign a player to a position other than his usual one. For example, a spiker in volleyball who is upset at the setter's poor passes could be asked to set during practice. This way he can see how hard it is to set the ball in just the right spot for the spiker.

Develop Pride Within Subunits

In sports in which subunits naturally exist (e.g., football, hockey, track and field), coaches should foster pride within these groups. Players need the support of their teammates, especially those playing the same position. The offensive linemen for the Washington Redskins in the 1980s called themselves "the hogs" because they did all the dirty work. The linemen took pride in this name and in what they contributed to the team's overall success. And the running backs and quarterback really appreciated the linemen's contributions—after all, their success depended on how well those hogs blocked.

Set Challenging Group Goals

Setting specific, challenging goals has a positive effect on individual and group performance (see chapter 15). Goals set a high norm for productivity and keep the team focused on what it needs to accomplish. As players reach goals, they should be encouraged to take pride in their accomplishments and strive toward new goals. These goals need to be clearly defined for them in order to foster group cohesion in their pursuits. The goals should be performance based (relating to players' abilities) rather than outcome based (relating to winning).

Does Team Building Work?

In a *Sports Illustrated* article (McCallum, 2001) titled "The Gang's All Here," the message was that players in collegiate football programs believe that team building builds champions. Activities are designed to draw players together, get them thinking like a team, help them find their leaders, and lay a foundation that players can build on during the season. For example, Louisiana State University players all participated in shotokan (a form of karate) workouts to help build team unity and quickness. University of Illinois football players created a football players-only softball league to help build team unity during the summer. University of Oregon linemen squeezed into big innertubes and floated along the Willamette River to help build team unity. The point of all these examples is that both coaches and players are using team-building activities to create a more closely knit unit that will have enhanced success on the field of play. But does this type of team building work?

Martin, Carron, and Burke (2009) conducted a meta-analysis (statistical analysis) on 17 studies investigating the effectiveness of team-building activities. Results revealed that team-building interventions had an overall positive effect on performance. Encouragingly, both the coach and sport psychology consultant found the team-building interventions to be effective. The duration of these interventions appears to be important: Those lasting less than two weeks had a minimal effect whereas those lasting longer than two weeks had a moderate effect. Results also revealed that the interventions focused on (in order from most successful to least successful) team goal setting, interpersonal relationships, adventure experiences, and a broad set of task variables that might include development of group structure (e.g., roles), environment (e.g., developing distinctiveness), or processes (e.g., cooperation). Contrary to popular belief, team-building interventions had less effect on interactive-sport teams (e.g., basketball, soccer) and more effect on individual-sport teams (e.g., wrestling, swimming). Finally, team-building interventions had no effect on task cohesion, a small positive effect on social cohesion, and large positive effects on both performance and perceptions of individual satisfaction.

Encourage Group Identity

A coach or leader can encourage team identity by ordering team jackets and scheduling social functions, for example, but these jackets and events should not interfere with the development of subunit identity. The two should work hand in hand. Groups should be made to feel special and in some sense different from other groups.

Avoid Formation of Social Cliques

Compared with subunits, which are groups of athletes working at a similar position or task, social cliques usually benefit only a few athletes—at the expense of alienating most team members. Players often form cliques when the team is losing, when their needs are not being met, or when coaches treat athletes differently and set them apart from each other (e.g., starters vs. substitutes). Cliques tend to be disruptive to a team, and coaches should quickly determine why cliques are forming and take steps to break them up. Changing roommate assignments on trips and encouraging team functions are ways to battle the development of cliques.

Avoid Excessive Turnover

Excessive turnover decreases cohesion and makes it difficult for members to establish close rapport. Of course, high school and college teams lose players to graduation each year. In this case, veteran players should be asked to help integrate new players into the team. Veterans can share team expectations in a warm, sincere, open manner, making the new players feel at ease with their new team and teammates. Similarly, exercise groups often have turnover as people drop out, and it's important to make newcomers feel welcome and part of these groups.

Conduct Periodic Team Meetings

Throughout the season, coaches should conduct team meetings to allow team members to honestly, openly, and constructively express positive and negative feelings. A team can resolve its internal conflicts, mobilize its resources, and take intelligent action only if it has a means for assessing the effectiveness of these efforts through its own experience. Teams can talk about learning from mistakes, redefining goals, and maintaining good sporting behavior.

Team-Building Model

In an attempt to guide coaches, teachers, and instructors, Carron and colleagues (Carron & Spink, 1993; Prapavessis et al., 1997; Spink & Carron, 1993) developed a team-building model that has been successfully implemented in sport and exercise settings. This four-stage process model uses a sport psychologist in the first three stages in a workshop format; then, in stage 4, coaches or leaders apply the workshop strategies to their group members. This original work has been adapted and extended by Paradis and Martin (2012).

1. *Introductory stage.* A brief overview of the benefits of group cohesion is conveyed, emphasizing the relationship between cohesion and exercise adherence (exercise group) and perceptions of cohesion and enhanced team dynamics (sport teams).

2. *Conceptual stage.* A conceptual model is presented, with group cohesion as a product of conditions in three categories: the group's environment, the group's structure, and the group's processes. Specific factors in each category may differ across situations because the importance of fundamental group processes is different across groups. For example, role acceptance and role clarity are important factors in team sports but not in exercise groups. Table 8.2 highlights some of the key aspects of team building during the conceptual stage. Finally, coaches or leaders are presented with research-based generalizations that undergird the team-building intervention.

3. *Practical stage.* Coaches or leaders attempt to generate as many specific strategies as possible in an interactive brainstorming session to use for team building in their groups. Table 8.1 presents examples of some of the strategies generated by fitness instructors. Having coaches or leaders generate specific intervention strategies is desirable because these people differ in personality and preferences—and the nature of groups differs (Loughead & Bloom, 2012). An intervention strategy that might be effective for one group might be ineffective for another.

4. *Intervention stage.* Coaches introduce the specific team-building strategies to their respective teams or exercise groups. Trained assistants should monitor the team-building sessions weekly to ensure that these strategies are being implemented.

If no particular problems or issues exist and the goal is simply to enhance feelings of cohesion, a technique known as group disclosures may be appropriate (Yukelson, 1997). Participants discuss individuals and teams that they admire the most along with the characteristics that contribute to the success of these individuals and groups. Then participants are asked to share things they admire about each other and what they have learned from each other.

Enhance Team Efficacy

Recent research (Heuze, Bosselut, & Thomas, 2007) indicates that focusing on developing team efficacy early in the season can have a positive influence on the development of a type of cohesion (individual attraction to the group—task) later in the season. In essence, the development of collective competence (especially in teams requiring integration and coordination, such as football, volleyball, and basketball) can increase players' feelings about their personal involvement with their team's productivity and objectives. For

example, strategies designed to build or maintain athletes' beliefs about their team efficacy should be encouraged. These could take the form of team drilling and instruction, emphasizing players' contributions to the team's efforts, or helping players help each other and cooperate in a task-involving climate, focusing on self-improvement rather than simply winning.

Know the Team Climate

Inside any formal organization lies an informal, interpersonal network that can greatly affect the organization's functioning. A coach or leader should identify the group members who have high interpersonal prestige and status in the group. These people can be the links for communication between the coaching staff and players and help give coaches and athletes vehicles for expressing ideas, opinions, and feelings regarding what's happening on the team. For example, the Player Council, implemented at Penn State University (Yukelson, 1997), holds regularly scheduled breakfast or lunch meetings with team leaders and

Team-Building Exercises

Now that you know the model of team building and coaches' perspectives on team building, we present a few practical exercises (Vealey, 2005).

- *Hope and Fear.* At the beginning of the season, index cards are passed out and players (possibly coaches) write down on the two sides of their card one hope for the upcoming season and one fear for the upcoming season. The cards are collected and redistributed randomly, and players read the hope and the fear on their card to initiate discussion.

- *TEAM Food for Thought.* Captains and other team leaders develop questions that will generate discussion around team culture, cohesion, and values. Some examples of questions are "If you could change anything about our practices, what would it be?", "If the coach were speaking at the end-of-the-year banquet, what would you want to be said?", "What behaviors or attitudes displayed by other athletes impress you the most?", and "I would like to be known as the type of athlete who . . . ."

- *Do You Really Know Me?* The objective is to help players get to know one another. Players write down something unusual (or unknown) about themselves or make up something about themselves. Each player reads his statement about himself. Team members vote on whether the statement is true or false and then receive a point if they are correct or lose a point if they are wrong.

- *Commitment Egg Relay.* Team members are paired up. One member from each pair is told that the activity is a competition and that the goal is to beat all the other pairs. The other member from each pair is told that they are to complete the task with minimal commitment; they should not try hard and should make mistakes frequently but should not let their partner know they are trying to fail. Each partner is provided a spoon. The first partner runs up a hill carrying an egg in the spoon behind their back and then transfers the egg to the second partner, who continues on to the finish line. After the task, the "committed" partners are asked what it felt like when their partner was not putting much effort into the activity, and the "uncommitted" partners are asked what they felt like knowing they were letting their partners down. All team members are then asked about the communication between partners during the activity, ways they can prevent players on the team from becoming uncommitted, and ways they can intervene if teammates do begin to exhibit low levels of commitment.

representatives from each class (e.g., freshman, junior) or subgroup (e.g., offense, defense, specialty teams) to keep coaches informed of prevailing attitudes, wants, and feelings that exist in the group.

Get to Know Others—Enhance Personal Disclosure

One way to get to know more about participants is to survey their individual values (e.g., achievement, health and activity, creativity, family, concern for others, independence) because values are central determinants of behavior. Crace and Hardy (1997) presented a model to help leaders survey and understand individual values in their groups. This assessment, using the Life Values Inventory (Crace & Brown, 1996), allows coaches and leaders to increase their awareness of individual characteristics from a values perspective, understand the predominant values of the group, identify the factors that promote and interfere with group cohesion from a values

perspective, and develop interventions and strategies for improving mutual respect and subsequent cohesion.

Getting to know and understand other team members' roles, views, motives, and needs is a cornerstone of the team-building process. Dunn and Holt (2004) examined hockey players' subjective responses to a personal disclosure, mutual-sharing team-building activity. Before a national championship tournament, players met and were asked to disclose something personal about themselves that would help define their character, motives, and desires. Participants described these meetings as emotionally intense and, at times, a significant life experience. Some benefits perceived by participants from the meetings included enhanced understanding of self and others, increased cohesion, and improved confidence in self and teammates. Thus, personal disclosure and mutual sharing appear to offer a number of benefits in building trust, cohesion, and confidence in teammates.

Fostering a sense of team unity early in the season can lead to better group cohesion as the season progresses.

 VIEW Activity 8.3 aids your understanding of the factors that can help build group cohesion.

DISCOVER Activity 8.4 helps you identify the factors that can overcome barriers to cohesion.

What Group Members Can Do

So far our guidelines have targeted coaches and leaders. But team unity is not only the coach's responsibility—group members can also promote team cohesion.

Here are some ways group members can improve communication and build a strong, cohesive unit.

• *Get to know members of the group.* The better team members know each other, the easier it is to accept individual differences. Individuals should take time to get to know their teammates, especially the new members in the group.

• *Help group members whenever possible.* Being a team means that individuals are mutually interdependent. Helping each other out creates team spirit and brings teammates closer together. For example, if a teammate is having trouble with free-throw shooting

Barriers to Group Cohesion

• A clash of personalities in the group
• A conflict of task or social roles among group members
• A breakdown in communication among group members or between the group leader and members
• One or more members struggling for power
• Frequent turnover of group members
• Disagreement on group goals and objectives

in basketball, you might offer to help her, especially if you are proficient in this aspect of the game.

• *Give group members positive reinforcement.* Supporting teammates instead of being negative and critical goes a long way toward building trust and support. Team members should be especially sensitive, positive, and constructive when a teammate is going through adversity. The help and support given to this player also help the team.

• *Be responsible.* Group members should not habitually blame others for poor performances. Blaming serves no useful purpose. When things are not going well, players should try to make positive, constructive changes and get themselves back on track.

• *Communicate honestly and openly with the coach or leader.* Team members should make sure the

coach receives accurate information concerning what is happening within the team. The better everyone understands everyone else, the better the chances for team success and harmony.

• *Resolve conflicts immediately.* If a team member has a complaint or a conflict with the coach or a teammate, he should take the initiative to resolve the situation and clear the air. Players should not just complain and vent their feelings. Players and coaches should respond to the problem quickly so that negative feelings don't build up and explode later.

• *Give 100% effort at all times.* Working hard, especially in practice, helps bring the team together. Dedication and commitment are contagious. Setting a good example usually has a positive effect on a team's unity.

LEARNING AIDS

SUMMARY

1. **Define task and social cohesion.**
   In measuring cohesion, researchers have found that it is multidimensional and comprises both task and social cohesion. Team cohesion is a dynamic process reflected in the group's tendency to stick together while pursuing its goals and objectives. Task cohesion refers to working together as a team to achieve goals, whereas social cohesion refers to the interpersonal attraction among team members.

2. **Describe the conceptual model of cohesion.**
   Carron's model of cohesion indicates that four areas affect the development of cohesion: environmental (team size, scholarships), personal (motivation, social background), team (team norms, team stability), and leadership (leadership style, leader's goals) factors. These factors do not exist in isolation but rather interact to affect both task and social cohesion.

3. **Discuss how cohesion is measured.**
   Cohesion has traditionally been measured through simple questionnaires. However, newer instruments such as the Group Environment Questionnaire take into account the multidimensional nature of cohesion. In addition to questionnaires, sociograms can be used to focus specifically on the social aspects of cohesion in a team or group.

4. **Understand the cohesion–performance relationship.**
   Researchers have been examining the relationship between cohesion and performance in sport for more than 30 years. However, this relationship is complex, and studying it involves three factors: measurement of cohesion, type of task, and direction of causality. Both task and social cohesion and interactive and coactive tasks are associated with positive effects on performance. In addition, the cohesion–performance relationship appears to be circular: Team success enhances cohesion, which leads in turn to success.

5. **Better understand factors associated with cohesion.**
   Cohesion is positively related to other important constructs, such as satisfaction, conformity, social support, group goals, and stability. In addition, cohesion has been shown to be related to role acceptance, group status, decision-making style, sex, collective efficacy, group norms, ability and experience, imagery, and self-handicapping. This knowledge is important to consider when coaches, teachers, and exercise leaders want to enhance cohesion in their teams or groups.

6. **Identify guidelines for building team cohesion.**
   Researchers have recently developed and outlined interventions for enhancing task and social cohesion in both sport and exercise settings. However, group members, as well as coaches or leaders, must assume responsibility for developing group cohesion.

KEY TERMS

cohesion
attractiveness of the group
means control
task cohesion
social cohesion

environmental factors
personal factors
leadership factors
team factors
sociogram

interactive sports
coactive sports
team building
direction of causality
stability

REVIEW QUESTIONS

1. Discuss the definitions of cohesion, including the difference between task and social cohesion.

2. Discuss how measuring cohesion has developed via questionnaires.

3. Findings in the research literature on the cohesion–performance relationship have been inconsistent. Explain whether or how the types of instruments used to measure these two factors and the demands of the task have affected this relationship.

4. Does cohesion lead to winning, or does winning lead to cohesion? In light of the research literature, discuss this question and its implications for coaches.

5. Although researchers have focused on the cohesion–performance relationship, cohesion appears to be related to several other potentially important variables. Discuss the relationship of cohesion to four factors other than performance.

6. Discuss how cohesion is related to social support. Discuss three types of social support and how you would develop these to enhance group cohesion.

7. Although it is often considered the job of a coach to build team cohesion, athletes can also help in the process. If you were an athlete on a team lacking cohesion, what might you do to build your team's unity?

8. Describe the conceptual model used for setting up team-building interventions in sport and exercise settings, providing specific examples for each of the four stages.

9. How could you enhance group cohesion among participants in exercise classes?

10. Discuss the effectiveness of team-building exercises, including the variables that affect the effectiveness of these activities.

CRITICAL THINKING QUESTIONS

1. You are a new coach who has inherited a high school team that had a great deal of dissension and in-fighting last season. Using the guidelines provided in this chapter, discuss what you would do before and during the season to build both task and social cohesion and identify team values in your team. Support your plan with research where appropriate.

2. You are a new physical education teacher and you want to better understand the personal relationships among your students so you can maximize your teaching strategies. You believe that a sociogram might be a good way to achieve this goal. Explain how a sociogram can help you understand the interpersonal attraction and cohesion of your class. Draw a hypothetical sociogram of your class (limit it to 15 people) and explain what information this gives you regarding the development of cohesion.

3. You are asked to devise a program for a local YMCA to help its coaches develop greater cohesion among their players, which has proved problematic in the past. Use Carron's conceptual model of cohesion, which focuses on four major antecedents of cohesion, to explain what kind of program you would develop and what information you would impart to these coaches.

9

Leadership

After reading this chapter, you should be able to

1. define leadership and describe the differences between leaders and managers;
2. understand the trait, behavioral, situational, and interactional approaches to studying leadership;
3. explain the cognitive–mediational model of leadership;
4. explain the multidimensional model of sport leadership;
5. discuss research investigating leadership in sport settings; and
6. discuss the four components of effective leadership.

Who can forget the numerous fourth-quarter comebacks of the Chicago Bulls led by Michael Jordan that resulted in six National Basketball Association (NBA) championships? Or the final series of hockey's Stanley Cup in 1994 when the Rangers were led by their captain, Mark Messier, to their first title in 54 years? In the world of sport, coaches such as John Wooden, Tara VanDerveer, Pat Summitt, Bill Parcells, Mike Krzyzewski, and Joe Torre and players such as Rebecca Lobo, Kevin Garnett, Peyton Manning, and Lisa Fernandez have shown great leadership capacity. Although not so visible to the public, great leaders also emerge in physical education, fitness, and athletic training settings, often meeting professional practice objectives and increasing the efficiency of all who are involved. It is easy to think of people who are great leaders, but it is much more difficult to determine what makes them leaders. Thousands of studies on leadership have been published, and researchers are still investigating the factors associated with effective leadership. Let us begin by discussing what leadership is and what leaders actually do.

Definition of Leadership

Leadership is "the process whereby an individual influences a group of individuals to achieve a common goal" (Northouse, 2010, p. 3). The process of influence typically involves facilitating motivation in others, where the leader focuses on getting individuals to collaborate in the pursuit of a common goal (Vroom & Jago, 2007). Management and organization professor Warren Bennis (2007) contends that exemplary modern leaders create a sense of vision or mission for the group, motivate others to join them in pursuit of that mission, create social architecture for followers to operate, generate optimism and trust in followers, develop other leaders in the group, and achieve results. Today, emphasis is also placed on better understanding leadership as a complex social process by examining the interaction among the leader, followers, leader and follower dyads, and the context in which leadership occurs (Eberly, Johnson, Hernandez, & Avolio, 2013). In sport and exercise, dimensions of leadership also include making decisions, motivating participants, giving feedback, establishing interpersonal relationships, and directing the group or team confidently.

A leader knows where the group or team is going and provides the direction and resources to help it get there. Coaches who are good leaders provide a vision of what to strive for as well as day-to-day structure, motivation, and support to translate vision into reality. Coaches, teachers, and exercise specialists are leaders who seek to provide each participant with maximum opportunities to achieve success. Successful leaders also try to ensure that individual success helps achieve team success.

Differences Between Leaders and Managers

A manager is generally concerned with planning, organizing, scheduling, budgeting, staffing, and recruiting. Although leaders often perform these same functions (or delegate them to others), leaders act in some other critical ways. For example, leaders provide vision that helps determine the direction that the organization or team pursues, including its goals and objectives. Leaders try to provide the resources and support to get the job done. Many coaches become excellent managers as they tackle operations that keep things running smoothly, but this is different from providing the leadership needed for players and teams to grow and mature. As Martens (1987a) stated, "Too many teams are overmanaged and underled" (p. 33).

> **KEY POINT** A manager takes care of such things as scheduling, budgeting, and organizing, whereas a leader is concerned more with the direction of an organization, including its goals and objectives.

Two Methods for Choosing Leaders

Leaders and coaches are usually appointed by someone in authority. In such cases they are called **prescribed leaders**. For example, in health clubs, owners choose the managers, and in schools, the principal chooses the teachers. Similarly, in college sport, the athletic director commonly selects coaches. Sometimes, however, leaders simply emerge from the group and take charge, as with captains and coaches of intramural or club teams. These are called **emergent leaders**. Many leaders who emerge are more effective than appointed leaders because they have the respect and support of team or group members. They probably have special leadership skills, lots of experience, or high ability in the particular sport or exercise. In any case, leaders typically have two functions: to ensure that the demands of the organization are satisfied in that the group meets its goals and objectives, and to ensure that the needs of the group members are satisfied.

Researchers have tried to identify leadership skills in the hope of being able to predict and select those people likely to become leaders. Researchers have also studied whether certain factors in a situation produce effective leadership and whether an environment might be structured to better develop leadership abilities. In the next section we review early research into organizational leadership and the studies it stimulated in sport settings. We also discuss how sport psychologists have studied leadership effectiveness, including the trait, behavioral, situational, and interactional approaches.

Approaches to Studying Leadership

Throughout the years, researchers have taken different types of approaches to studying leadership. The trait approach, which focused on consistency in individuals, was the first to dominate the literature. This was followed by the behavioral approach, which focused on behaviors. A third approach argued that leadership depends on characteristics of the situation rather than the leader him- or herself. Finally, these three approaches were combined in the interactional perspective, which is the dominant perspective for studying leadership today.

Trait Approach

In the 1920s, researchers tried to determine what characteristics or personality traits were common to great leaders in business and industry. They considered **leadership traits** to be relatively stable personality dispositions, such as intelligence, assertiveness, independence, and self-confidence. Proponents of the trait theory argued that successful leaders have certain personality characteristics that make it likely they will be leaders no matter what situation they are in. This would mean, for example, that LeBron James would be a great leader not only on the basketball court but also in other sports and in other areas of life such as business and community affairs. Or that Winston Churchill, Gandhi, or Martin Luther King, Jr., had similar personality characteristics that helped make them effective leaders.

The trait approach lost favor after World War II, when Stogdill (1948) reviewed more than 100 trait theory studies of leadership and found only a couple consistent personality traits. Although certain traits might be helpful for a leader to have, they are cer-

Peer Leadership in Sport

A number of investigators have studied peer leaders in sport, focusing sometimes on emergent leaders and at other times on prescribed leaders such as team captains. These investigators have identified antecedents of peer leadership, roles and responsibilities of team captains, and consequences of such leadership. Key findings from this research include the following:

- When compared with their teammates, peer leaders are found to have higher perceived competence, are more liked by their teammates, exhibit positive social behaviors, and are intrinsically motivated (Price & Weiss, 2011). They are characterized by their positive attitudes, their ability to control their emotions, their work ethic, and strong communication skills (Dupuis, Bloom, & Loughead, 2006).

- Peer leadership is positively related to a number of important team outcomes such as increased task and social cohesion and collective efficacy (Price & Weiss, 2011, 2013).

- When looking within the same teams, peer leadership and coach leadership have been found to be associated with both similar and different outcomes. For example, coach leadership has been found to be a stronger predictor of individual athlete outcomes (e.g., enjoyment, perceived competence) whereas peer leadership is more strongly related to team cohesion (Price & Weiss, 2013).

- Coaches feel that peer leadership is not solely the responsibility of team captains. All members of the team are expected to lead on occasion (Bucci, Bloom, Loughead, & Caron, 2012).

- When peer leaders "frequently inspire, motivate, enhance creativity, solve problems, and use contingent rewards," teammates report enjoying playing more, are interested in learning new skills, and are motivated to pursue challenging tasks (Price & Weiss, 2013, p. 272).

- Although coaches desire to have their captains lead, they provide little training on how to do so (Voelker, Gould, & Crawford, 2011).

- Captains' duties most often include organizational activities, setting an example, motivating and encouraging teammates, boosting morale, facilitating relationships, providing support to and mentoring teammates, providing feedback, being vocal, enforcing team rules and confronting teammates who do not adhere to them, and helping teammates mentally prepare (Voelker et al., 2011).

- The most difficult aspects of being a captain include being responsible and held accountable, dealing with others, the expectations that come with being a captain, staying neutral when dealing with teammate issues, maintaining composure, not overstepping boundaries, feeling isolated, and balancing roles (Voelker et al., 2011).

- Coaches who are effective at developing captains' leadership skills were proactive in their approaches and did such things as conduct formal leadership training (e.g., conferences, workshops, and courses), help captains develop good communication skills, provide feedback to captains about their leadership, and provide readings on leadership (Gould, Voelker, & Griffes, 2013).

- Mistakes coaches made in developing captains include giving too much or too little responsibility, using poor practices for selecting captains, not communicating enough with their captains, failing to reinforce and educate captains, having ineffective relationships with captains, and making assumptions about what captains know about leadership (Gould et al., 2013).

tainly not essential for successful leadership. Because common leadership traits among coaches, exercise leaders, and performers have not been found, little sport research today uses the trait approach to leadership theory. However, this does not mean that leader traits and attributes are unimportant in determining leader effectiveness. The latest research shows that enduring characteristics are important (especially in combination with each other) but are not universal and must be considered in light of the situation (Zaccaro, 2007).

KEY POINT Leaders have a variety of personality traits. No specific traits make all leaders successful.

Behavioral Approach

Researchers next focused on discovering universal behaviors of effective leaders (i.e., what leaders do). These *behaviorists* argued that anyone could become a leader by simply learning the behaviors of other effective leaders. Thus, unlike trait theory, the

Leading by Example

It was the fifth game of the 1997 NBA finals between the Chicago Bulls and Utah Jazz, and the series was even at 2-2. Utah had won the last two home games and was playing at home again, where the team was undefeated in the play-offs. Michael Jordan, who many consider the greatest ever to have played the game, was sick with an intestinal virus and had stayed in bed all day because he was so weak. He looked sick out on the court and his every movement appeared strained. But somehow he managed to conserve his energy and focus on what he had to do to win. Miraculously, he not only scored 38 points but also hit the key 3-point shot to win the game, and Chicago went on to win the championship in six games on its home floor. Jordan was voted most valuable player of the play-offs. Teammate Scottie Pippen commented on Jordan's performance: "What you saw out here tonight was an unbelievable display of courage and leadership. Michael is the leader of the team and he brought everyone along with him. He led by example, and his desire to win and be the best rubbed off on all of us."

behavioral approach argues that leaders are made, not born.

Leadership Behaviors in Nonsport Settings

To describe how leaders in nonsport (business, military, educational, and government) organizations behave or do their jobs, researchers at The Ohio State University developed the Leader Behavior Description Questionnaire. Using the questionnaire, the researchers found that most of what leaders do falls into two categories: **consideration** and **initiating structure**. Consideration refers to friendship, mutual trust, respect, and warmth between the leader and subordinates. Initiating structure refers to setting up rules and regulations, channels of communications, procedural methods, and well-defined patterns of organization to achieve goals and objectives. These two categories are distinct but compatible. For instance, successful leaders tend to score high on both consideration and initiating structure (Blake & Moulton, 1994). Some researchers argue that it is difficult for one person to exhibit a strong concern for both people and productivity at the same time. We see an example of this approach in sport when a head coach who is strong in initiating structure hires an assistant coach who is strong in consideration (usually a younger coach who can relate to players better).

KEY POINT Successful leaders tend to score high on both initiating structure and consideration.

Leadership Behaviors in Sport

One approach to studying leadership in sport and exercise settings is to focus on specific behavior in these situations. Former UCLA coach John Wooden, a coaching legend in basketball, won an unprecedented 10 National Collegiate Athletic Association (NCAA) basketball championships. He coached, among other greats, Kareem Abdul-Jabbar and Bill Walton. What was John Wooden's secret?

Tharp and Gallimore (1976) sought to identify coach Wooden's leadership behaviors using the event-recording technique. In event recording, an investigator lists several typical coaching behaviors and then records when and how often these behaviors occur. Using this technique for 30 hours of observation, Tharp and Gallimore identified 10 categories of behavior that Wooden exhibited. Most of his behaviors involved giving instructions (what to do and how to do it); Wooden also often encouraged intensity and effort. In communicating, for example, he spent about 50% of his time in verbal instruction, 12.7% in hustling players to intensify instruction, 8% in scolding and reinstructing with a combination statement, 6.9% in praising and encouraging, and 6.6% in simple statements of displeasure (i.e., scolding). This focus on instruction and conveying information over praising good performance and scolding errors is consistent with contemporary coaching research (Gilbert, 2002; Gilbert & Trudel, 2004).

Studying Wooden, the researchers noted that his demonstrations rarely lasted longer than 5 seconds, but they were so clear that they left an image in memory, much like a textbook sketch. Finally, although extremely successful, Wooden emphasized effort over winning and noted that the most important thing is doing the best that you can because that's all that you can do.

KEY POINT Coach Wooden focused his coaching on telling players what to do and how to do it. He accomplished this through short demonstrations that modeled the correct behavior.

In reflecting on this classic study, Gallimore and Tharp (2004) reanalyzed their data and conducted some additional interviews. Some of their key findings and interpretations were as follows:

- Exquisite and diligent planning lay behind the heavy information load, economy of talk, and practice organization.
- Wooden considered providing instruction via information as a positive approach to coaching.
- Reserves received more praise than starters.
- The seven laws of learning according to Wooden were explanation, demonstration, imitation, repetition, repetition, repetition, and repetition.
- Being an exemplary role model was a goal of Wooden's teaching philosophy.

Bloom, Crumpton, and Anderson (1999) replicated this classic study through observing the coaching behaviors of basketball coach Jerry Tarkanian, who was very successful but who does not enjoy the same teaching reputation as John Wooden. Researchers found similar results. Instruction (which was broken down into tactical, technical, and general instruction) accounted for approximately 55% of coaching behaviors. Praise and encouragement (13%) and hustles (16%) were the other coaching behaviors most often displayed, pointing to a definite focus on positive coaching behavior.

Taking a different approach, Côté, Salmela, and Russell (1995) investigated 17 elite gymnastics coaches using the qualitative interview. The behaviors these elite coaches most often exhibited were (a) providing a supportive environment through positive feedback, (b) giving technical instruction regarding gymnasts' progressions, (c) teaching mental skills such as dealing with stress, (d) providing opportunities that simulated the mental and technical demands of competition, (e) providing manual training to ensure safety, and (f) stressing conditioning to ensure physical readiness.

Both the observational studies of John Wooden and Jerry Tarkanian and the interviews of elite gymnastics coaches consistently showed a reliance on positive, supportive feedback and technical, corrective feed-

back in helping athletes improve. From a behavioral perspective, the key to providing effective sport leadership is to focus on the positive while providing clear feedback and technical instruction.

Finally, Loughead and Hardy (2005) compared leadership behaviors of coaches with leadership behaviors of peers (e.g., formal captains, informal leaders). Assessing a wide range of athletes in 15 teams revealed that coaches and peer leaders tended to exhibit different types of leadership behaviors. The athletes studied perceived that coaches exhibited more training, instruction, and autocratic behaviors than peer leaders, whereas peer leaders were seen as displaying more social support, positive feedback, and democratic behaviors than coaches. Athletes believed that approximately 25% of teammates served as peer leaders, so they saw others in addition to formal captains as serving in leadership roles.

Situational Approach

In the 1970s a third approach to leadership evolved. In reaction to the trait and behavioral approaches to leadership, Perrow (1970) argued that leader characteristics are not as important as commonly thought. Effective leadership depends much more on the characteristics of the situation than on the traits and behaviors of the leaders in those situations. This argument was based on evidence that organizational leaders often have less power than people think, that differences between candidates who become leaders are reduced through selection, and that differences between leaders are negated by situational demands (Vroom & Jago, 2007).

Although few contemporary leadership researchers endorse the situational approach in and of itself, it was important in facilitating our understanding of leadership because it showed that situational features have a major influence on leader success. Too often people fall into the heroic champion notion of leadership and assume that leader effectiveness is totally driven by leader traits and behaviors. Not recognizing situational influences on leadership is a grave mistake.

Interactional Approach

Trait and behavioral approaches emphasize personal factors at the expense of considering the interaction between people and their situational constraints (see chapter 2). Many researchers in industry and general psychology have proposed interactional models of leadership (see Horn [1993, 2002] and Hackman &

Leadership Development Through Sport

Many people argue that sport can build leaders, but nobody has investigated exactly how this might occur. An interesting article by Wright and Côté (2003) focused on the various activities of leader athletes as well as the influences of others on their leadership development. Four central components were the cornerstone of leadership development through sport:

- Development of high skill
- A strong work ethic
- Good rapport with people
- Enriched tactical knowledge

These tenets were primarily developed through feedback and interactions with parents, coaches, and peers. Some of these more important influences include the following:

- New players became involved with older peers through increasingly challenging competition.
- Parents mentored players on complex cognitive sport issues and decision making.
- Coaches appointed athletes to leadership positions (in part because of high skill level).
- Players maintained good relationships with peers and gained their trust.
- Parents supported sport involvement and activities (through monetary support, encouragement, and moral support).
- Coaches provided an excellent training environment to help develop skill.

Wageman [2007] for reviews of the literature). After reviewing the leadership research, Vroom and Jago (2007) concluded that "most social scientists interested in leadership have now abandoned the debate between person or situation in favor of a search for a set of concepts that are capable of dealing both with differences in situations and with differences in leaders" (p. 20). These interactional theories have important implications for effective leadership in sport and exercise settings.

- As we have seen, no one set of characteristics ensures successful leadership. Investigators believe that great leaders have had in common personality traits appropriate to leadership roles and distinct from nonleadership roles. However, leaders have not been predicted solely by their personality traits. The latest research also shows that some traits are open to change and interact in complex ways with situational factors (Zaccaro, 2007).

- Effective leadership styles or behaviors fit the specific situation and the athletes involved in the situation. For example, Horn, Bloom, Berglund, and Packard (2011) found that collegiate athletes who were high in somatic trait anxiety and high in self-determined motivation preferred coaches who were more democratic in their leadership style and who provided high amounts of training, social support, and

both positive and informational feedback. In contrast, athletes who were more amotivated preferred coaches who were more autocratic in their leadership style and who provided greater amounts of punishment-oriented feedback. Clearly, then, different athletes want different types of leadership from their coaches.

- Leadership styles can be changed. If you hear someone say, "Some people just have what it takes," don't believe it. Coaches and other leaders can alter their styles and behaviors to match the demands of a situation. As an example, we discuss two leadership styles and how they might change to fit a situation. **Relationship-oriented leaders** develop interpersonal relationships, keep lines of communication open, maintain positive social interactions, and ensure that everyone is involved and feeling good. Their style is analogous to the consideration function described earlier. On the other hand, **task-oriented leaders** primarily work to get the task done and meet their objectives. Their style is analogous to the initiating structure function described earlier.

KEY POINT A relationship-oriented leader focuses on developing and maintaining good interpersonal relationships; a task-oriented leader focuses on setting goals and getting the job done.

Zuma Press/Icon SMI

What traits made David Stern, commissioner of the NBA for three decades (1984-2014), an effective leader?

People can change from a relationship-oriented style to a task-oriented style and vice versa, depending on the situation. According to Fiedler's (1967) research as he developed his **contingency model** of leadership, the effectiveness of leadership depends equally on the leader's style of interacting with the group and on the favorableness of the situation. Specifically, Fiedler argued that a task-oriented leader is more effective in either very favorable or unfavorable situations; a relationship-oriented leader is more effective in moderately favorable situations. A physical education teacher in an inner-city school that lacks facilities, leadership, and community support might have to be very task oriented because her situation might be seen as very unfavorable. Getting things done and setting goals would override developing positive interpersonal relations. In contrast, a physical education teacher in a lower-middle-class school where the facilities are poor but the community support is good (moderately favorable situation) might be more effective as a relationship-oriented leader. Thus, sport and exercise professionals need to be flexible in leadership styles, tailoring them to meet the demands of the situation. If a coach feels more comfortable with one type of leadership style than another, she should seek out situations in which this style would be more effective.

Highly skilled players are typically already task oriented, and coaches who have a more relationship-oriented style appear to be more effective with these players. Conversely, less skilled players need more continuous instruction and feedback, and a task-oriented coach would be more appropriate for them. This does not mean that less skilled individuals do not need or want a caring, empathetic coach or that more highly skilled participants do not need specific feedback and instruction. It is a matter of what the coach should emphasize.

KEY POINT The effectiveness of an individual's leadership style stems from matching the style to the situation.

Gerry Faust was one of the most successful high school football coaches in the country when he became head coach at the University of Notre Dame. Faust could not maintain Notre Dame's standard of winning and was fired after several seasons. After coaching high school players, he may not have altered his coaching behavior to fit the maturity level of college athletes. Specifically, as a coach of high school students, he may have needed a relationship-oriented approach to bring out their best performance, personal growth, and development. However, traditional sport practices emphasize autocratic behaviors as one reaches college, and this might have been the downfall of Coach Faust.

Finally, a study assessing expert coaches who built a successful college program found that both personal and situational factors were critical as these coaches built a successful program (Vallee & Bloom, 2005). The common themes that emerged included coaches' attributes (e.g., commitment to learning, knowledge), individual growth (e.g., establishing a safe and positive environment to teach life skills and empower athletes), organizational skills (e.g., planning, administrative tasks), and visions (e.g., goals and direction of the program). In addition, it was emphasized that coaches had to consider the situation to determine which behavior or leadership style might be most effective.

Sport-Oriented Interactional Approaches to Leadership

From the preceding comments, it is apparent that it is necessary to consider both people and environmental or situational factors in developing models of leadership. Along these lines, two sport-specific interactional approaches have been developed to provide guidance and direction to the study of leadership in sport.

Cognitive–Mediational Model of Leadership

Smoll and Smith (1989) proposed a theoretical model of leadership behavior that emphasizes relationships among situational, cognitive, behavioral, and individual difference variables. They incorporated a situational approach to leadership behavior, arguing that coaching behaviors vary as a function of situational factors in the athletic context (e.g., level of competition, type of sport). However, these authors also argued that "a truly comprehensive model of leadership requires that consideration be given not only to situational factors and overt behaviors, but also the cognitive processes and individual (personality) differences which mediate relationships between antecedents, leader behaviors, and outcomes" (Smoll & Smith, 1989, p. 1532). In their model, they argue that the effects of coaches' behaviors are a function of the coaches' personal characteristics, which are mediated by both situational factors and the meaning that athletes attribute to those coaching behaviors. In essence, players' attitudes toward their coaches and sport experience are affected by their perception and recall of the coaches' behaviors. Figure 9.1 displays this mediational model, in which player perceptions of coach behaviors mediate the effect of coach behaviors on player responses. However, this entire process is affected by situational factors and coach and player individual differences. To objectively assess the actual behavior of coaches in natural field settings, the Coaching Behavior Assessment System was developed. With this system, several carefully trained observers record the behaviors of the coaches, noting on audio recorders the situations in which the behaviors occurred. These behaviors turn out to be either reactive or spontaneous (see "Categories of Coaching Behavior From the Coaching Behavior Assessment System"). **Reactive behaviors** are responses to a specific player behavior, as when a coach instructs after an error. **Spontaneous behaviors**, on the other hand, are initiated by the coach. For example, a coach might yell encouragement to his players as they go onto the field.

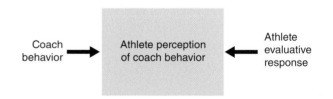

FIGURE 9.1 Cognitive–mediational model of leadership.

Other studies have used the Coaching Behavior Assessment System to assess specific coaching behaviors and the ways in which they affect young athletes. These behaviors relate in general to a leadership style that emphasizes a positive approach to coaching. About two-thirds of all observed coaching behaviors were found to be positive and fell into the following categories:

• Positive reinforcement ("You really got down on that ground ball. Keep up the good work.")

- General technical instruction ("Keep your head down when you complete your golf swing.")
- General encouragement ("Keep up the good work!")

In addition, players demonstrate greater self-esteem at the end of a season when they have played for coaches who frequently use mistake-contingent encouragement and reinforcement. Players rate their teammates and their sport more positively when they have played for coaches who use high amounts of general technical instruction. In one study, players with low self-esteem (personal factor) who had supportive and instructive coaches (situational factor) expressed the highest level of attraction toward the coaches, whereas players with low self-esteem who had less supportive and instructive coaches expressed the least amount of attraction to the coaches. Conversely, players with high self-esteem were not affected to the same extent by variations in the level of their coaches' support and instruction. In essence, it's particularly important for coaches to be supportive of youngsters with low self-esteem to maximize the potential positive experiences of competitive sport (Barnett, Smoll, & Smith, 1992).

Some coaches learned this positive approach to coaching young athletes by attending a workshop focusing on how to communicate positively with young athletes (Smith, Smoll, & Curtis, 1979). The aim of the workshop was to teach coaches to increase their positive behaviors and decrease their negative behaviors by 25%. As evidenced by results at the end of the season, the youngsters who played for these coaches reported that they liked their teammates

Categories of Coaching Behavior From the Coaching Behavior Assessment System

CLASS I. REACTIVE BEHAVIORS

Responses to desirable performance

- *Reinforcement*—A positive, rewarding reaction (verbal or nonverbal) to a good play or good effort
- *Nonreinforcement*—Failure to respond to a good performance

Responses to mistakes

- *Mistake-contingent encouragement*—Encouragement after a mistake
- *Mistake-contingent technical instruction*—Instruction or demonstration on how to correct a mistake the player has made
- *Punishment*—A negative reaction (verbal or nonverbal) after a mistake
- *Punitive technical instruction*—Technical instruction given in a punitive or hostile manner after a mistake
- *Ignoring mistakes*—Failure to respond to a player mistake

Response to misbehavior

- *Keeping control*—Reactions intended to restore or to maintain order among team members

CLASS II. SPONTANEOUS BEHAVIORS

Game related

- *General technical instruction*—Spontaneous instruction in the techniques and strategies of the sport that does not follow a mistake
- *General encouragement*—Spontaneous encouragement that does not follow a mistake
- *Organization*—Administrative behavior that sets the stage for play by assigning duties or responsibilities

Game irrelevant

- *General communication*—Interactions with players unrelated to the game

Adapted from F. Smoll and R. Smith, 1980, Psychologically-oriented coach training programs. Design, implementation and assessment. In *Psychology of motor behavior and sport—1979*, edited by C. Nadeau et al. (Champaign, IL: Human Kinetics), 115. By permission of R. Smith.

more, believed that their coaches were more knowledgeable, rated their coaches better as teachers, had a greater desire to play again the next year, and had higher levels of enjoyment compared with other young players whose coaches did not attend the workshop. In essence, this study established a direct relationship between coaching behaviors and players' evaluative reactions. Smith and colleagues concluded that "training programs designed to assist coaches, teachers, and other adults occupying leadership roles in creating a positive and supportive environment can influence children's personality development in a positive manner" (p. 74).

According to the results of another study (Barnett et al., 1992), Little League players whose coaches attended a workshop aimed at facilitating positive coach–athlete interaction had a dropout rate of 5% during the next season, whereas a control group of players had a dropout rate of 29%. Not surprisingly, facilitating positive interactions between coaches and young athletes ensures that the athletes enjoy the experience more and develop positive self-esteem and keeps them involved and participating in the sport. Drawing on their extensive research, Smith and Smoll (1996, 1997) developed leadership guidelines for coaching athletes in youth sports (see "Behavioral Guidelines for Coaches").

Multidimensional Model of Sport Leadership

Another interactional model developed specifically for sport or physical activity is the **multidimensional model of sport leadership** (Chelladurai, 1978, 1990, 2007). Similar to the Smith and Smoll model discussed previously, Chelladurai's model posits that leader effectiveness in sport will vary depending on the characteristics of the athletes and constraints of the situation (figure 9.2).

According to Chelladurai, an athlete's satisfaction and performance (box 7 in the figure) depend on three types of leader behavior: required (box 4), actual (box 5), and preferred (box 6). The situation (box 1), leader (box 2), and members (box 3) lead to these three kinds of behavior, so they are called antecedents.

If we put this model in interactional terms, leader characteristics (e.g., age, experience, coaching style, personality) are the personal factors, whereas situational characteristics and member characteristics (e.g., age, ability, sex) are the situational factors. Horn (2002) proposed that the sociocultural context (e.g., norms of the group) and organizational climate (e.g., competitive level, process vs. outcome oriented) are two key situational factors influencing leader expectancies and values, which then affect leader behavior. Whereas Chelladurai argued that a direct link exists

Behavioral Guidelines for Coaches

Drawing on 25 years of research, Smoll and Smith (2001) provided some guidelines for coaching young athletes:

- Provide reinforcement immediately after positive behaviors and reinforce effort as much as results.
- Give encouragement and corrective instruction immediately after mistakes. Emphasize what the athlete did well, not what he did poorly.
- Don't punish athletes after they make a mistake. Fear of failure is reduced if you work to reduce fear of punishment.
- Don't give corrective feedback in a hostile, demeaning, or harsh manner because this is likely to increase frustration and resentment.
- Maintain order by establishing clear expectations. Use positive reinforcement to strengthen the correct behaviors rather than punish incorrect behaviors.
- Don't nag or threaten athletes to prevent chaos.
- Use encouragement selectively so that it is meaningful.
- Encourage effort but don't demand results.
- Provide technical instruction in a clear, concise manner and demonstrate how to perform the skill whenever possible.

between these antecedent conditions and leader behavior, Horn argued that these antecedent conditions affect leader expectancies and values, which then affect leader behaviors.

Chelladurai hypothesized that a positive outcome is most likely if the three aspects of leader behavior agree. If the leader behaves appropriately for the particular situation and these behaviors match the preferences of the group members, the group members will achieve their best performance and feel satisfied. However, if the prescribed and actual behaviors are different from the preferred behavior, optimal performance without optimal satisfaction is predicted. Conversely, if the actual and preferred behaviors are different from the prescribed behavior, optimal satisfaction without optimal performance is predicted. For example, athletes might prefer a relationship-oriented style but the situation dictates a more task-oriented style. If the coach adheres to a task-oriented style (actual behavior), then optimal performance, but not satisfaction, is predicted. We now take a closer look at the three types of leader behavior and the ways in which the antecedent conditions affect these types of behavior.

Required Leader Behavior

In many situations, the organizational system itself dictates behaviors and people are expected to conform to the established norms. For example, physical education teachers are expected to behave in certain ways in front of their students, fellow teachers, and parents (e.g., high school physical education teachers shouldn't attend the same parties as their students). Similarly, coaches are expected to behave in specific ways with reporters, other coaches, and spectators.

Actual Leader Behavior

Actual leader behavior is simply the behavior that the leader exhibits, such as initiating structure or being considerate. According to Chelladurai (1993), the leader's characteristics, such as personality, ability, and experience (box 2 in figure 9.2), affect these behaviors directly. Actual behavior is believed to be indirectly affected by group preferences and what the situation dictates. A professional sport team, for example, usually has winning as a goal, and its coach would likely adopt performance-oriented behaviors. Although winning is among a high school team's goals, the experience itself is also valued, and a coach would likely adopt consideration-oriented behaviors.

Preferred Leader Behavior

Group members have preferences for specific leader behaviors. Personality variables as well as age, sex, and experience influence a member's preference for coaching and guidance, social support, and feedback. An adult in rehabilitation after a knee reconstruction, for example, probably expects to have more input

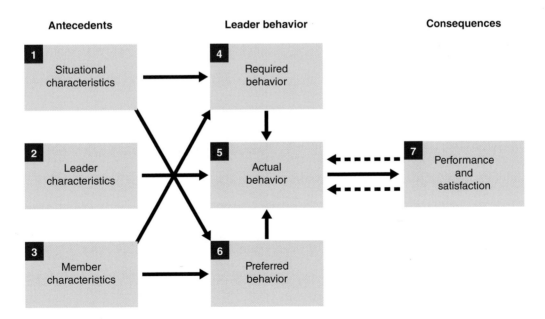

FIGURE 9.2 The multidimensional model of sport leadership.

Adapted, by permission, from P. Chelladurai, 1980, "Leadership in sport organization," *Canadian Journal of Applied Sport Sciences* 5: 266. © P. Chelladurai.

Meshing Leadership Style and Situation

Doug Collins had an up-and-down career as an NBA coach. After a wonderful career as a player, Collins was hired as the coach of the Chicago Bulls. A fiery, emotional leader, he also tended to be autocratic, taking just the right approach for the relatively young team. His volatile personality in fact helped motivate the somewhat immature and unpredictable group. However, these same personality characteristics and Collins' autocratic approach became a liability as the Bulls matured as a team; they began to tune him out (McCallum, 1991). Several years later, Collins emerged as the coach of the Detroit Pistons, another young team in need of direction and a strong hand. Collins provided this sense of direction and purpose, bringing with him an emotional volatility. Once again, this was the right approach—it helped the Pistons turn around after several seasons of losing records and start to contend for the division title. However, after a couple of successful seasons, Collins' fiery style was at odds with a maturing team, and he was fired. Optimal performance and satisfaction are achieved when a leader's required, preferred, and actual behaviors are consistent.

into program planning than a young athlete does. Situational characteristics can also affect a member's preferences. If an organization or school has an expectation that coaches conduct themselves in a certain manner, this expectation is typically shared by both coaches and players.

Leadership in the Pursuit of Excellence

Leadership is often associated with the pursuit of excellence, whether that excellence is in sport, business, the arts, or government. Chelladurai (2007) addressed this issue by identifying leadership factors that are best suited to facilitating the pursuit of excellence in sport. His suggestions emanate not only from his multidimensional model of sport leadership and the supporting research but from a revision of the model that addressed the popular business topic of transformational leadership. **Transformational leadership** occurs when the leader takes a visionary position and inspires people to follow that vision and supportively work with each other to excel. It involves having the ability to motivate and inspire followers to achieve new heights and accomplish more than they originally believed they could. These are Chelladurai's (2007) leadership guidelines for the pursuit of excellence:

- Creating a compelling vision for people to follow (as in the popular sport movies *We Are Marshall* and *Remember the Titans*)
- Inspirational communication (instilling pride, enhancing morale)
- Intellectual stimulation (followers understand the big picture behind what they are doing)
- Individualized attention and supportive behavior

- Personal recognition
- Demanding and directing behaviors
- Promoting self-efficacy and self-esteem
- Emphasizing the importance of winning but not winning at any cost
- Fostering competitiveness in the team
- Instilling task and ego orientations and climates (balancing a strong emphasis on task goals while integrating ego goals in an appropriate fashion)
- Providing cognitive, emotional, and technical training
- Facilitating flow

In summary, Chelladurai (2007) contends that leaders who help individuals and teams pursue excellence "transform" the person by facilitating attributes such as self-efficacy and competitiveness and at the same time create a situation or environment that supports a compelling vision, key goals, and productive motivational climates. Leading the pursuit of excellence involves the interaction of key personal and situational factors.

Schroeder (2010) interviewed 10 NCAA Division I coaches who had turned around losing programs and guided them to championships in their respective sports. Results revealed that the program turnarounds were characterized by changes in team culture driven by the coach leaders. The coaches changed the team culture by teaching core values, recruiting athletes who embraced the values, distributing punishment and rewards for behaviors that aligned with the core values, and considering the unique environment their

The Psychology of High-Performance Sport Administrative or Management Leadership

Historically, researchers interested in sport leadership have focused the majority of their attention on coaches and, more recently, peer leaders. However, little attention has been paid to athletic administrators despite the tremendous growth in the field of sport management. This is surprising because it is not uncommon to hear successful athletes and coaches thank their organizations for providing support when they win championships or lament the lack of organizational support when things don't go well. Moreover, in the business world, the field of executive coaching has grown tremendously in recent years. Because the position of an athletic administrator is similar to that of an executive in the business world, it is logical to assume that executive coaching would also be useful in the sport world. High-powered chief operating officers of major corporations now work on their mental game with private coaches. Wouldn't athletic administrators profit from the same kind of support?

Sport psychology researchers David Fletcher and Rachel Arnold (2011) broke new ground in the examination of high-performance sport administrators when they studied 13 British national performance directors of Olympic sports. This group of executives represented highly successful sport organizations whose athletes won a total of 24 medals at the London Olympic Games. Fletcher and Arnold conducted a series of interviews, and results revealed that four major themes characterized the performance leadership and best practices of these leaders and managers. First, these leaders developed a compelling vision for their organizations. They made sure that this vision of success was shared and evolved over time and, at the same time, monitored factors that influenced it. Second, they extensively discussed the management of logistics such as finances, worked with their staff to strategically plan and schedule competitions and training programs for the team, developed athlete selection processes, and upheld rules and regulations that were the underpinnings of elite performance. Third, these individuals were characterized by excellent people management practices such as effectively managing their staff, establishing and maintaining effective lines of communication, and making sure feedback mechanisms regarding external assessments of effectiveness were in place. Finally, they focused on developing the organization's culture by establishing role awareness and creating effective organization and team atmospheres.

In order to effectively lead and mange elite sport organizations, then, sport executives must understand how to create and disseminate an overarching vision for the organization, optimize resources, communicate with and manage their staff by finding a balance between supporting behaviors while at the same time pushing their direct reports (those individuals reporting to the leader) to pursue higher challenges, facilitate the development of group cohesion, and influence the attitudes of those who report to them. The authors concluded that organizations must pay more attention to the psychology of elite sport performance leadership.

program was situated in. Increases in resources were not always necessary for changing the culture of a program. Through their transformational leadership, the coaches helped their athletes learn to embrace the core values that led to the desired changes in team culture.

Research on the Multidimensional Model of Sport Leadership

Researchers have tested both the accuracy and the usefulness of Chelladurai's multidimensional model, applying the model in interesting ways. We briefly discuss several of these applications. For a more

detailed analysis of the multidimensional model of sport leadership, see Chelladurai (1993) and Horn (1993, 2002).

Sometimes group members become used to certain behaviors and grow to prefer them. For instance, Al Davis, the owner of the Los Angeles Raiders football team, has traditionally advocated a loose leadership style, allowing players individualism off the field as long as they perform well on the field. Players on his team have grown to prefer this style of leadership. Conversely, Pat Riley, the highly successful professional basketball coach, was demanding and intense, but players tended to adapt to his style because he had shown it to be successful.

Leadership Scale for Sports

The **Leadership Scale for Sports (LSS)** was developed to measure leadership behaviors, including athletes' preferences for specific behaviors, athletes' perceptions of their coaches' behaviors, and coaches' perceptions of their own behavior (e.g., Chelladurai & Riemer, 1998; Chelladurai & Saleh, 1978, 1980). The scale has been translated into several languages and has received extensive testing and psychometric support in recent years. The LSS has five dimensions:

- *Training (instructional behaviors).* A coach who is oriented toward training and instruction scores high in trying to improve the athletes' performances by giving technical instruction on skills, techniques, and strategies; by emphasizing and facilitating rigorous training; and by coordinating the activities of team members. Sullivan and Kent (2003) found that motivation and teaching efficacy of coaches appeared to lead to training and instruction leadership behaviors.

- *Democratic behavior (decision-making style).* A coach with a democratic style allows athletes to participate in decisions about the group's goals, practice methods, and game tactics and strategies.

- *Autocratic behavior (decision-making style).* A coach with an autocratic style makes decisions independently and stresses personal authority in working with the decisions. Input from athletes is generally not invited.

- *Social support (motivational tendencies).* A coach who scores high in social support shows concern for the welfare of individual athletes and attempts to establish warm relationships with them. Unlike the behaviors of a coach who stresses positive feedback during performance, social support-oriented coaching behaviors are independent of (not contingent on) the athletes' performance, and they typically extend beyond the athletic arena.

- *Positive feedback (motivational tendencies).* A coach who scores high in positive feedback consistently praises or rewards athletes for good performance. Positive feedback is contingent on the performance and is limited to the athletic context.

Zhang, Jensen, and Mann (1997) developed a revised leadership scale for sport that included two additional dimensions (group maintenance behavior and situational consideration behavior). However, Chelladurai (2007) has recommended using the original scale until more data are collected on the revised version.

Antecedents of Leadership

Some studies have concentrated on the conditions, or antecedents, that affect leader behavior, whereas others have focused on the consequences of leader behavior—that is, how it affects member performance (see Chelladurai, 1993, and Horn, 2002, for detailed discussions). The study of personal and situational factors that affect leader behavior has produced the following insights:

- *Age and maturity.* As people get older and mature athletically (reach college age), they increasingly prefer coaches who are more autocratic and socially supportive. More mature athletes are typically more serious about their sport and see sport as an autocratic enterprise. They want a coach who gets things done and is highly organized but who also is supportive of the players. However, other research suggests that younger (ages 10–13 years) and older (ages 14–17 years) adolescents prefer coaches who are less autocratic, allow athlete participation in decision making, give positive feedback, and give lots of tactical and technical instruction (Martin, Jackson, Richardson, & Weiller, 1999).

- *Sex.* Males prefer training and instructive behaviors and an autocratic coaching style more than females do. Hence, coaches should be more directive with males and provide plenty of instructional feedback. Females prefer more democratic coaching behaviors and a participatory coaching style that allows them to help make the decisions. Coaches and other group leaders should allow females opportunities for input. However, there are more similarities than differences between male and female preferences for specific coaching behaviors, as both want a high frequency of training and instructive behaviors and feedback from their coaches (Horn, 2002).

- *Nationality.* Cultural background may influence leadership preferences. Athletes from the United States, Great Britain, and Canada do not differ notably in the coaching styles they prefer. However, Japanese university athletes prefer more social support and autocratic behaviors than do Canadian athletes and perceive their coaches to be more autocratic. Canadian athletes prefer more training and instruction behaviors than Japanese athletes do.

- *Type of sport.* Athletes who play highly interactive team sports, such as basketball, volleyball, and soccer, prefer an autocratic coaching style more than do athletes in coacting sports, such as bowling, swimming, or tennis. Thus, a volleyball team would typically prefer an autocratic coach more than a track team would. In addition, Riemer and Chelladurai (1995) found that athletes performing different tasks in a sport prefer different coaching behaviors. Defensive players preferred greater amounts of democratic, autocratic, and social support behaviors than did offensive players.

• *Psychological characteristics.* Research has revealed that athletes' personalities also need to be considered when one is investigating preferences for coaching behaviors (see Chelladurai, 1990, 1993). For example, it was found that athletes with an internal locus of control showed a strong preference for training and instruction behaviors, whereas athletes with an external locus of control preferred autocratic coaching behaviors. In addition, females high in trait anxiety

preferred more positive and social support behaviors than did their counterparts low in trait anxiety. More research on the individual differences in personality related to coaching behavior preferences is needed.

Consequences of Leadership

According to Chelladurai (1990, 1993), optimal performance and satisfaction result when a coach leads in a style that matches the group members' preferences. Using Chelladurai's model to investigate the consequences of how a sport leader behaves, researchers have proposed several guidelines:

• *Satisfaction.* When coaches report having developed the same decision style that their athletes prefer, coaching effectiveness will be rated highly. Similarly, athletes' satisfaction will clearly be affected

Antecedents of Coaches' Expectancies, Values, Beliefs, and Behaviors

We know that coaches' expectancies can influence their behavior toward athletes. But what influences coaches' expectancies, values, beliefs, and behaviors? Three potential factors have been investigated:

• *Sociocultural context.* Research (e.g., Hayashi & Weiss, 1994; Kim & Gill, 1997) has revealed cross-cultural variations in achievement goals as well as differential expectations for coaching behaviors. In addition, it has been shown that notions of femininity and masculinity affect coaches' expectations. In fact, some sociologists have argued that teams may constitute a subculture with their own normative expectations, values, and beliefs. Thus, we need to understand the sociocultural context in which coaches work to better understand the expectations placed on them to exhibit certain coaching behaviors.

• *Organizational climate.* Although organizational climate can vary in many ways, researchers (e.g., Amorose & Horn, 2000; Chaumeton & Duda, 1988) have predominantly investigated this aspect as a function of sport level. For example, research has revealed that compared with collegiate athletes in Division III, collegiate athletes in Division I (where the expectation of and focus on winning is greater) perceived that their coaches exhibited a more autocratic leadership style that was less socially supportive and used lower frequencies of positive and information-based feedback. Among Division I coaches, those whose teams had more scholarships (maybe indicating a higher level of competition) were perceived by their athletes as being more autocratic and less socially supportive and as giving higher frequencies of punishment-oriented feedback. Thus, organizational climate (in this case, the level of competition) appears to be related to coaching expectations and subsequent behavior.

• *Personal characteristics of coaches or teachers.* The effects of a number of personal attributes on coaches' expectations and behaviors have been investigated. For example, Strean, Senecal, Howlett, and Burgess (1997) argued that individual differences such as self-reflectiveness, critical thinking aptitude, decision-making abilities, and knowledge bases can influence coaches' expectations and behaviors. It has also been found that coaches high in intrinsic motivation tend to be more autonomous in their **decision-making styles** (Fredrick & Morrison, 1999). Other research (Feltz, Chase, Moritz, & Sullivan, 1999) showed that coaches high in "coaching efficacy" (the extent coaches believe they have the capacity to affect the learning and performance of their athletes) gave more positive feedback and that teachers high in self-confidence displayed more persistence in the face of failure and were more committed to their profession than teachers who were low in confidence.

when they do not get the coaching style they prefer. The greater the discrepancy, the lower the satisfaction, especially with behavior related to training and instruction, social support, and positive feedback. Generous social support, rewarding of behavior, and democratic decision making are generally associated with high satisfaction among athletes. Research has also shown that such coach characteristics as younger age, better previous win–loss percentages, and less playing experience elicited higher satisfaction scores from athletes. Finally, the relationship between coaching behaviors and satisfaction is mediated by sport type: Team-sport athletes find positive coaching behaviors more important than do individual-sport athletes (Baker, Yardley, & Côté, 2003).

• *Cohesion.* Various studies (Gardner, Shields, Bredemeier, & Bostrom, 1996; Pease & Kozub, 1994; Westre & Weiss, 1991) have shown that coaches perceived as high in training and instruction, positive feedback behaviors, and democratic social support and low in autocratic behavior had teams that were more cohesive. These results have been obtained for athletes varying in age, sport type, and sex, so they can be generalized to a variety of situations and populations. In addition, exercise leaders who exhibited more task-related behaviors and provided task-specific reinforcement were associated with more cohesive exercise groups (Loughead & Carron, 2004).

• *Performance.* Most research supports the notion that specific coaching behaviors are related to increases in performance, especially when the actual and preferred coaching behaviors are congruent. One study indicated that frequent social support behaviors were related to poorer team performance (i.e., win–loss record). The increased social support did not cause the team to lose more; more likely, the results suggest that losing teams need more social support from leaders to sustain motivation (Weiss & Friedrichs, 1986).

• *Intrinsic motivation.* The literature linking various coaching behaviors or styles with changes in intrinsic motivation is growing (Horn, 2002). For example, one study (Vallerand & Losier, 1999) showed that coaches who exhibited a more autocratic style had athletes with lower levels of intrinsic motivation and perceived competence than did coaches who exhibited a more democratic leadership style. It has also been shown that the effect of coaching style on intrinsic motivation and competency in turn influences athletes' degree of persistence in the sport.

 DISCOVER   Activity 9.1 tests your comprehension of the leadership material presented in this chapter.

Leadership Training Interventions

Several individuals have begun to develop interventions for enhancing the leadership of those involved in sport and exercise settings. Gould (2011) developed a leadership training program for the National Wrestling Coaches Association in the United States. This program consists of a series of online course modules on topics such as leadership, communication, developing student-athletes, fund-raising, coaching ethics, and marketing and promotions; 360° feedback surveys where coaches receive valuable information about their leadership from their supervisors, peers, and athletes; an in-person leadership workshop that focuses on applying and discussing the content conveyed online; and peer mentoring from an experienced coach. Gould developed the program because he felt that the role of collegiate coaches has changed from primarily working with athletes on skills, tactics, and techniques to include a variety of managerial skills such as fund-raising, community relations, helping athletes develop off the field, and communicating with a variety of external constituents.

Voight (2012) reported a case study of a leadership development intervention in team captains of two elite collegiate volleyball teams. The intervention focused on four goals: helping the teams return to their respective NCAA championship finals, improving communication and team functioning, assisting in the daily team organization and communication, and enhancing the personal leadership development of the captains. Based on the business and organizational psychology literature, a 15-stage leadership development program was established. It included such topics as the captains' roles and duties, leaders' strengths and weaknesses, assessing team needs, team feedback for the captains, the best ways to fulfill responsibilities, and dealing with problems that arise. The program was judged as effective based on interviews conducted with the captains and because the two teams reached their performance goals of making it back to the championships.

Finally, Gould and Voelker (2010) described a leadership training program for high school sport captains that resulted from a partnership between the Institute for the Study of Youth Sports at Michigan State University and the Michigan High School Athletic Association. The program consisted of a series of 1-day leadership clinics where 100 to 200 current or potential high school sport captains took part in a variety of experiential activities in order to increase their awareness, knowledge, and leadership skills. Topics discussed include what captains need to know, common problems that captains confront and how to handle them, and specific issues the student-athletes may experience as captains. The student-athletes also receive a self-study captain's guide (Gould, 2007). Based on their experiences conducting these programs, the authors emphasized the need to be proactive in developing leadership skills in student-athletes, the importance of experiential learning, and the need for coaches to allow student-athletes in leadership roles to have meaningful responsibilities.

Four Components of Effective Leadership

We have emphasized that personal traits alone do not account for effective leadership, although some common components of effective leaders have been identified. Research has also identified general strategies for producing more effective leadership in physical education, sport, and exercise settings, including manipulating situational factors and promoting certain group member characteristics. Four general components that we discuss in this section are a leader's qualities, leadership styles, situational factors, and the followers' qualities.

The four components of effective leadership (figure 9.3) are really a composite of many different approaches to the study of leadership. No one approach is best—they all make some contribution to understanding what makes leadership effective. Consistent with the interactional model, the four components together show that behavior is best understood as an interaction between personal and situational factors.

Leaders' Qualities

Although there isn't one distinct set of essential core personality traits that will ensure that a person will become a leader, successful leaders appear to have many qualities in common. In *Finding a Way to Win* (Parcells & Coplon, 1995), Bill Parcells, successful football coach and winner of two Super Bowls, discussed what he believes to be the keys to successful leadership:

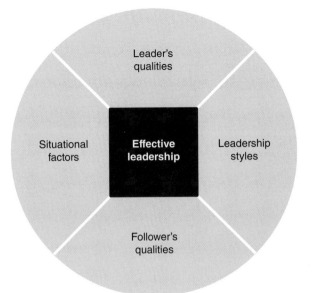

FIGURE 9.3 The four components of effective leadership.

Reprinted, by permission, from R. Martens, 1987, *Coaches guide to sport psychology* (Champaign, IL: Human Kinetics), 35.

- *Integrity.* A leader's philosophy must have a sound structure, be rooted in the leader's basic values, be communicated and accepted throughout the organization, be resistant to outside pressure, and remain in place long enough to allow for success.

- *Flexibility.* Traditions are made to be broken. If you're doing something just because it's always been done that way, then you may be missing an opportunity to do better.

- *Loyalty.* The first task of leadership is to promote and enforce collective loyalty, also known as teamwork.

- *Confidence.* If you want to build confidence in your players and coaching staff, give them responsibility and decision-making capabilities and support them in their attempts.

- *Accountability.* Accountability starts at the top. You can't build an accountable organization without leaders who take full responsibility.

- *Candor.* When sending a message, it's not enough to be honest and accurate. The effect of the message will hinge on who's receiving it—and what the recipients are willing to take in at that time.

- *Preparedness.* Well-prepared leaders plan ahead for all contingencies, including the ones they consider unlikely or distasteful.

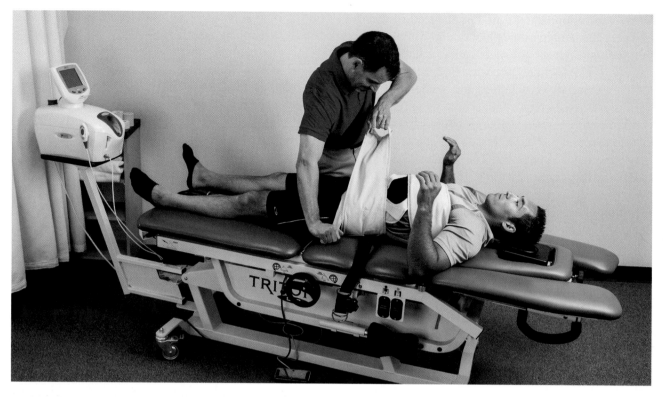

Leading a sports medicine team is no different than being a coach—both careers require effective leader qualities and styles along with the consideration of situational influences (e.g., who the medical staff reports to in the health care system) and follower characteristics (e.g., the cohesion level of the team).

- *Resourcefulness.* At its most basic level, resourcefulness is simply resilience—a refusal to quit or give in even when all seems bleak.

- *Self-discipline.* There is always a way to compete, even against superior forces, but strict adherence to a calculated plan is required.

- *Patience.* Patience is rarest—and most valuable—when an organization is performing poorly. It's not enough to know what changes must be made; it's equally important to decide when to make them.

Researchers have identified several other characteristics of successful leaders, including intelligence, optimism, intrinsic motivation, and empathy. These are requisite qualities that someone needs to become a leader, but still they are not sufficient—that is, the presence of all these qualities doesn't guarantee a leader. And these qualities will be needed in greater or lesser amounts depending on the preferences of group members and the specific situation.

Leadership Styles

We have talked about democratic and autocratic coaching styles. As you might expect, the coach with a democratic style is typically athlete centered, cooperative, and relationship oriented. Conversely, the coach with the autocratic style is usually win oriented, tightly structured, and task oriented. A coach need not act entirely one way or the other. Coaches can effectively integrate and blend democratic and autocratic leadership styles (Blake & Moulton, 1969). Different leadership behaviors are more optimal in various situations, as you have seen through the multidimensional model of sport leadership and the LSS. The challenge is determining what style best suits the circumstances and whether individuals are flexible enough to adapt their dominant style to a particular leadership situation. The appropriate coaching style depends most on situational factors and member characteristics.

One aspect of style that has been researched is how coaches make decisions. Coaching effectiveness largely depends on making good decisions and the degree to which athletes accept those decisions. Chelladurai and others (Chelladurai & Haggerty, 1978; Chelladurai, Haggerty, & Baxter, 1989; Chelladurai & Trail, 2001) have developed a model of decision making that applies in sport. Five primary styles of decision making are used in sport:

- *Autocratic style.* The coach solves the problem herself using the information available at the time.
- *Autocratic–consultative style.* The coach obtains the necessary information from relevant players and then comes to a decision.
- *Consultative–individual style.* The coach consults the players individually and then makes a decision. The decision may or may not reflect the players' input.
- *Consultative–group style.* The coach consults the players as a group and then makes a decision. The decision may or may not reflect the players' input.
- *Group style.* The coach shares the problem with the players; then the players jointly make the decision without any influence from the coach.

Although most coaches prefer the autocratic and consultative–group decision styles, the choice of the most effective decision style depends on the coach and her particular situation.

Situational Factors

A leader should be sensitive to the specific situation and environment. Leaders need to consider several situational factors that are relevant to planning for effective leadership in sport (Martens, 2004):

- Is the sport a team sport or an individual sport? Team-sport athletes typically prefer more autocratic leaders than do individual-sport athletes.
- Is it an interactive (e.g., basketball) or coactive (e.g., bowling) sport? Interactive-team athletes prefer more task-oriented leaders than do coactive-team athletes.
- What is the size of the team? As group size increases, it becomes more difficult to effectively use a democratic leadership style.
- How much time is available? When little time is available, a task-oriented leader is more desirable.
- Does the group have a particular leadership tradition? A group that has a tradition with one style of leadership will typically have difficulty changing to another style of leadership.

Followers' Qualities

The characteristics of the followers (athletes in sport settings) are also important in determining the effec-

tiveness of a leader. The need for the characteristics and styles of leaders and participants to mesh shows how important the interactional process is to effective leadership. For example, older and more experienced athletes usually prefer an autocratic coaching style, and female athletes prefer a democratic coach. Earlier we discussed specific characteristics (i.e., sex, age or maturity, nationality, ability, and personality) of participants that interact with leadership to determine leadership effectiveness in sport and exercise.

 DISCOVER Activity 9.2 explains how to use material from this chapter to select an effective team captain.

The Art of Leadership

One thing is clear: Leaders make a difference in general and in sport and exercise settings in particular. Research has shown that a variety of personal and situational factors interact to influence leader effectiveness.

Many of you reading this book are preparing for careers as certified athletic trainers, coaches, fitness specialists, athletic administrators, strength coaches, physical educators, or sport science scholars. Most of you will be leading people. For this reason you need to make a commitment to understand your strengths and weaknesses as a leader.

VIEW Activity 9.3 helps you see how coaches assess their performance to become more effective.

VIEW Activity 9.4 lets you match coaching behaviors to video examples.

After reviewing the literature in the area, Hackman and Wageman (2007) indicated that "leadership training must both bring to the surface the trainee's own preferred leadership strategies and then explore the conditions under which those strategies are and are not appropriate" (p. 46). Are you doing this? In an interesting study of leaders in the field of recreation (e.g., coaches, recreation leaders, fitness specialists), Little and Watkins (2004) found that factors such as years of experience, age, and qualifications were not sufficient predictors of leader performance. Effectiveness was determined by the leader's capacity to experience more complex ways of leading. Becoming an effective leader

Principles of Energy Management for Leaders

Jim Loehr (2005) has worked with leaders in a variety of high-performance situations such as sport, law enforcement, medicine, and business. He has developed a model of effective leadership based on the management of physical, mental, emotional, and spiritual energy. He considers energy to be the most critical resource required for accomplishing any team objective. Effective leaders are experts in mobilizing and focusing the energy resources of themselves and team members toward the team objective. Fundamentally, leadership is about managing energy. Following are 12 principles of energy management.

- Growth follows energy investment. Great leaders help team members make the right energy investments at the right time.

- Growth ceases when energy investment ceases. Great leaders ensure that an adequate energy supply goes to actions, beliefs, and feelings that are vital to the success of the mission.

- The best energy produces the most growth. It is not the amount of time team members invest that drives team success but rather the energy they bring to the time they have. Effective leaders help team members fully engage in anything that is significant to the team.

- Whatever receives energy gains strength. Just as investments in positive emotions stimulate positive growth, investments in negative or toxic emotions stimulate defensive growth.

- There are four energy sources. The power of full engagement is the power of properly aligned and skillfully managed human energy (physical, emotional, mental, and spiritual).

- Energy investments must be balanced with energy deposits. Both overtraining (too much energy expenditure relative to recovery) and undertraining (too much recovery relative to energy expenditure) threaten the success of a mission. During competition, examples of opportunities for renewing energy include the between-point time in tennis, shift changes in hockey, inning changes in baseball, and time-outs in basketball. Deep breathing, muscle relaxation, positive self-talk, mental routines, and imagery can all help renew energy and prepare for the next dose of stress.

- People must push beyond the comfort zone. Any form of energy expenditure that prompts discomfort has the potential to expand capacity. Great leaders know that discomfort is a prerequisite for growth and that every crisis can be used to expand team and individual capacity when managed properly.

- Positive rituals should be used to manage energy. Energy management is best achieved not through willpower and self-discipline but through habits. Examples of positive rituals include precompetition, preperformance, sleep, and hydration routines.

- Energy is highly contagious. Great leaders are quick to recognize individuals who have the potential to carry and transmit negative or positive energy to the team and to discourage or encourage this type of behavior.

- Negative energy should be kept outside the comfort zone. Great leaders help team members create boundaries (e.g., team rules) to contain their negative energy so that it does not contaminate the team.

- Self-esteem deficiencies require energy. Great leaders recognize that those with low self-esteem can create a powerful drain on the team, and they work to ensure that energy investments in these individuals do not compromise the team's mission.

- Repeated energy investment makes a difference. When positive and negative energy collide, the one with the greatest force dominates. Great leaders understand that a positive individual can be contaminated by too much negative energy, so this negative energy must be contained.

takes hard work, continued efforts to improve one's self, and the ability to learn from leadership experiences.

Finally, although there is a great deal of science behind effective leadership, top researchers (Bennis, 2007) indicate that effective leadership is also an art that is influenced by factors such as wisdom, intelligence (intellectual and practical), and creativity (Sternberg, 2007). Hence, make a commitment to read about and observe effective leaders. Focus not only on attributes and characteristics that make a leader effective but also on how those attributes work together and interact with situational factors to influence leader effectiveness.

LEARNING AIDS

SUMMARY

1. **Define leadership and describe the differences between leaders and managers.**
   Leaders influence individuals and groups toward set goals. They affect participants by establishing interpersonal relationships, providing feedback, influencing the decision-making process, and providing motivation. A leader knows where the group needs to go and provides the direction and resources to help it get there. Managers are more concerned with planning, organizing, scheduling, budgeting, staffing, and recruiting activities.

2. **Understand the trait, behavioral, situational, and interactional approaches to studying leadership.**
   The trait approach assumes that great leaders possess a set of universal personality traits that are essential for effective leadership. The behavioral approach assumes that a relatively universal set of behaviors characterizes successful leaders. The situational approach argues that effective leadership is much more dependent on the characteristics of the situation than on the traits and behaviors of the leaders in those situations. The interactional approach posits that the interaction of the situation and a leader's behaviors determines effective leadership. This approach assumes that there is not one best type of leader but rather that leadership style and effectiveness depend on fitting the situation and qualities of the group's members.

3. **Explain the cognitive–mediational model of leadership.**
   According to this model, athletes' perceptions of coach behaviors primarily determine players' reactions and responses to these behaviors. However, in the interactional model tradition, player and coach behaviors are influenced by situational factors as well as individual-difference characteristics of both the coaches and the players.

4. **Explain the multidimensional model of sport leadership.**
   According to the multidimensional model of sport leadership, group performance and member satisfaction depend on how well three types of leader behavior—required, preferred, and actual—mesh with the antecedent characteristics of the situation, the leader, and the members. Positive outcomes, better performance, and group satisfaction typically occur if the three types of leader behavior are congruent. That is, optimal performance and member satisfaction will result if a coach or other leader uses behaviors prescribed for the particular situation that are consistent with the preferences of the members.

5. **Discuss research investigating leadership in sport settings.**
   Research has found that several personal and situational factors affect leader behavior in sport and exercise. These antecedents include such specifics as age and maturity, sex, nationality, and type of sport. The consequences of the leader's behavior can be seen in terms of the satisfaction, performance, and cohesion of the group. For example, satisfaction of athletes is high when there is a good match between their preferred coaching style and the coach's actual coaching style.

6. **Discuss the four components of effective leadership.**
   Effective leadership in sport depends on the qualities of the leader, leadership style, situational factors, and characteristics of the followers. How these four interact is what really determines what makes a leader effective.

KEY TERMS

leadership	initiating structure	spontaneous behaviors
prescribed leaders	relationship-oriented leaders	multidimensional model of sport leadership
emergent leaders	task-oriented leaders	transformational leadership
leadership traits	contingency model	Leadership Scale for Sports (LSS)
consideration structure	reactive behaviors	decision-making styles

REVIEW QUESTIONS

1. Compare and contrast the trait, behavioral, situational, and interactional approaches to leadership.

2. Discuss three practical implications and principles that can be drawn from the psychological literature on leadership.

3. Discuss event recording as a technique for studying leadership behaviors in sport, along with the findings regarding Coach John Wooden.

4. Describe the major tenets of Chelladurai's multidimensional model of sport leadership, including the three antecedents and three types of leader behaviors.

5. Discuss the four components of effective leadership. What implications do these have for leaders in coaching, teaching, or exercise settings?

6. Describe five decision styles used by coaches and three factors that influence their effectiveness.

7. Discuss how organizational climate, sociocultural context, and leader personality can influence a coach's expectations, values, and behaviors.

8. Describe the critical components in the development of leadership through sport as well as the influence of parents, coaches, and peers on these components.

9. Discuss five leadership guidelines in the pursuit of excellence.

CRITICAL THINKING QUESTIONS

1. You have taken your first coaching and teaching position with a local high school. Describe how you might apply some of the principles and findings derived from Chelladurai's and Smith and Smoll's models to your coaching and teaching. Be specific about how you might alter your approach to your athletes and students in classes, practices, and competitions.

2. You are hired as the director of a Little League program in your city. You want to make sure that your volunteer coaches are effective leaders for the young athletes. You decide to hold a coaching clinic that all the volunteer coaches must attend. Describe what principles and information you would include in your clinic to help ensure that these novice coaches will be effective leaders.

10

Communication

After reading this chapter, you should be able to

1. describe the communication process,
2. describe how to send messages more effectively,
3. describe how to receive messages more effectively,
4. identify what causes breakdowns in communication,
5. explain the process of using confrontation, and
6. discuss how to offer constructive criticism.

" You can communicate without motivating but it is impossible to motivate without communicating. "

—John Thompson, former Georgetown University men's basketball coach

" People learn how to think by communicating. So in our program, we not only employ an offensive system and a defensive system—we employ a communication system. "

—Mike Krzyzewski, Duke University men's basketball coach

Communication, integral to our

daily lives, certainly is a critical element in sport and physical activity settings. Exercise leaders must convince sedentary individuals to engage in exercise. No matter how brilliant a coach is in planning strategy and in the technical aspects of the game, success still depends on being able to communicate effectively not only with athletes but also with parents, officials, assistant coaches, the media, and other coaches. Physical education teachers and certified athletic trainers also have to communicate in varied arenas. In essence, it's

not what you know but how well you can communicate information to others.

Good communication skills are among the most important ingredients contributing to performance enhancement and the personal growth of sport and exercise participants. In fact, the importance of good interpersonal relationships in sport and exercise settings led to a special issue of *Psychology of Sport and Exercise* edited by Jowett and Wylleman (2006). Studies have shown that Olympic swimmers look to their coaches' social competence relative to communication even before their coaches' technical skills (Phillippe & Seiler, 2006), that athletes prefer different amounts of information and emotions from their coaches' pregame talks (Vargas-Tonsing & Guan, 2007), that differences exist in the communication patterns of more versus less successful doubles tennis teams (Lausic, Tennebaum, Eccles, Jeong, & Johnson, 2009), and that the nonverbal behaviors of and clothing worn by athletes influence what we expect from them and ratings of their performance capabilities (Buscombe, Greenless, Holder, Thelwell, & Rimmer, 2006). To be a successful sport and exercise professional, you must develop strong communication skills.

Although much has been written about communication in general (e.g., Beebe, Beebe, & Redmond, 1996; Infante, Rancer, & Womack, 1997; von Gunten, Ferris, & Emanuel, 2000), sport psychologists have begun to study communication only in the past decade. Therefore, we often have to apply general communication findings to sport and exercise settings. But regardless of the setting, one of the biggest problems in communication is that we often expect others to be mind-readers. Frequently, coaches, athletes, teachers, and parents communicate in "shorthand," assuming that a simple gesture will be enough to convey their feelings and unique perspective.

It should not be surprising that breakdowns in communication often are at the root of problems as coaches talk to athletes or teachers talk to students. Ineffective communication may lead individuals to dislike each other, lose confidence in each other, refuse to listen to each other, and disagree with each other and may cause a host of other interpersonal problems (Whetten & Cameron, 1991). This can lead to remarks such as "I just can't talk to him," "If I've told her once, I've told her a thousand times," or "When I talk to him, it goes in one ear and out the other." On the other side, athletes and students often have these kinds of things to say about coaches and teachers: "She never explains why she does things," "He's so hard to approach," and "She's always shouting and yelling." Clearly, problems exist on both sides of communication. Repairing these communication gaps is essential in the learning and coaching environment. Following is a quote from an Olympic soccer player on a breakdown in communication between coach and athlete.

" Some time ago the coach decided not to include me in the start-up team for several matches. This was something I had never experienced before, and it was difficult to cope with. I was a regular member of the national team at the time and did not notice that my performance had declined in any way. If he had talked with me and told me his reasons, the problem could have been solved immediately and a lot of frustration could have been avoided. Regular talks between the coach and the player can make all the difference and should be high on the coach's priority list. (Jowett, Paull, Pensgaard, Hoegmo, & Riise, 2005, p. 166) "

Understanding the Communication Process

All one-way communication follows the same basic process. As the first step, one person decides to send a message to another. Then the sender translates (**encodes**) thoughts into a message. As the third step, the message is channeled (usually through spoken words but sometimes through nonverbal means, such as sign language) to the receiver. Next, the receiver interprets (**decodes**) the message. Finally, the receiver thinks about the message and responds internally (e.g., by becoming interested, getting mad, or feeling relieved). Figure 10.1 outlines this process.

Purposes of Communication

Although the same process occurs in all communications, the purposes of the communication can vary. You might communicate to persuade a person in an aerobics class that he can lose weight by exercising regularly, to evaluate how well a gymnast performs her routine on the balance beam, to inform students how to perform a new volleyball skill, to psych up your team for a tough opponent, or to deal with a conflict between two players on your team. However, all communication contains some content as well as relational (how we feel about someone) messages.

Communication may incorporate several purposes at once. For example, let's say an aerobic dance instructor wants to include harder and more vigorous movements in the class' exercise regimen. He would try motivating and persuading (to convince) the class regarding the benefits of this added exercise and then inform them how to perform the new skill.

Types of Communication

Communication occurs in two basic ways: interpersonally and intrapersonally. Usually when we talk about communicating, we mean **interpersonal communication**, which involves at least two people and a meaningful exchange. The sender intends to affect the response of a particular person or persons. The message or content may be received by the person for whom it was intended, by persons for whom it was not intended, or both. Sometimes that message gets distorted so that the sender's intended message does not get transmitted.

An important part of interpersonal communication involves **nonverbal communication**, or nonverbal cues. Research has indicated that this type of com-

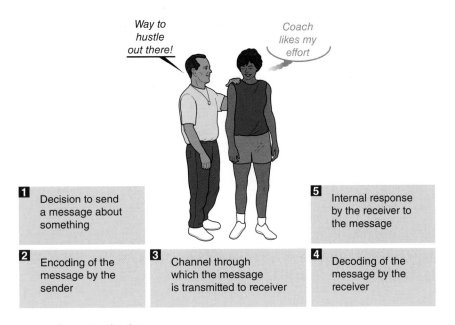

Way to hustle out there!

Coach likes my effort

1 Decision to send a message about something

2 Encoding of the message by the sender

3 Channel through which the message is transmitted to receiver

4 Decoding of the message by the receiver

5 Internal response by the receiver to the message

FIGURE 10.1 The process of communication.

Reprinted, by permission, from R. Martens, 1987, *Coaches guide to sport psychology* (Champaign, IL: Human Kinetics), 48.

munication is also critical to imparting and receiving information. In one study, participants watching a tennis match saw the players only between points—they never saw a player actually hit a ball or play a point. Still, about 75% of the time they could pick out who was winning the match. The nonverbal cues that players exhibited between points were strong enough to communicate who was ahead or behind. In another study, the opponents' prematch nonverbal behaviors and their clothing were found to influence ratings of performance and the outcome expectations of observers (Buscombe et al., 2006). Jowett and Frost (2007) found that black soccer players viewed their coaches' ethnic background as a meaningful factor influencing their relationships. Even though their coaches did not say anything that would influence their personal relationship with the players, the players made certain assumptions based on how the coach looked (not what he said).

Intrapersonal communication (self-talk) is the communication we have with ourselves. We talk a lot to ourselves, and this inner dialogue is important. What we say to ourselves usually helps shape and predict how we act and perform. For instance, perhaps a youngster in a physical education class is afraid of performing a new skill, the tennis serve, and tells herself that she can't do it and will look foolish if she tries. This intrapersonal communication increases the chances that she will not execute the skill properly. Self-talk can also affect motivation. If someone is trying to lose weight and tells himself that he's looking slimmer and feeling good, he is improving his motivation with his self-talk. (See chapter 16 for more on self-talk.)

KEY POINT Internal dialogue, or intrapersonal communication, affects motivation and behavior.

It is also important to recognize that the communications of exercise leaders, teachers, and coaches influence the self-talk of their athletes. Researchers (Zourbanos, Hatzigeorgiadis, & Theodorakis, 2007; Zourbanos, Hatzigeorgiadis, Tsiakaras, Chroni, & Theodorakis, 2010) found that both positive and negative statements made by coaches influenced their athletes' self-talk. In particular, positive and negative feedback by coaches produced more positive and negative self-talk, respectively, in their athletes. Thus, interpersonal communication influences intrapersonal communication.

Sending Messages Effectively

Effective communication often makes the difference between success and failure for teachers, coaches, and exercise leaders. Thus, they need to understand how to send effective messages, both verbally and nonverbally. Fortunately, research has indicated that effective communication skills can be taught to sport and exercise leaders, teachers, and coaches.

Communication Self-Evaluation Assessment

Think about how you communicate with others. How often do you find yourself engaging in the following behaviors? In the space provided, indicate whether you engage in the behavior.

1 = Almost always   **2** = Usually   **3** = Sometimes   **4** = Seldom   **5** = Almost never

_____ 1. I pay attention primarily to what an individual is saying and give little attention to what he or she is doing.

_____ 2. I let an individual's lack of organization get in the way of my listening.

_____ 3. I interrupt if I have something I want to say.

_____ 4. I stop listening when I think I understand the idea whether or not the reporter has finished.

_____ 5. I fail to repeat back what has been said before I react.

_____ 6. I give little verbal or nonverbal feedback to people I'm listening to.

_____ 7. I pay attention to only the words being used rather than the words, tone, and pitch.

_____ 8. I let emotion-laden words make me angry.

_____ 9. If I consider the subject boring I stop paying attention.

_____ 10. I find myself unable to limit my criticism to a friend's performance.

_____ 11. I find that getting in the face of a communicator gets my point across.

_____ 12. I allow distractions to interfere with my concentration.

_____ 13. I do not recognize when I am too upset or tired to speak or listen.

_____ 14. I raise my voice when I want someone to pay attention to what I am saying.

_____ 15. I try to give advice when someone is telling me his or her problems.

Add up your responses to the 15 items. The higher your score (highest score is 75), the more effective are your communication skills. Your total score is less important than your responses to specific items. Scores of 1 and 2 typically mean that you can improve on those aspects of your communication. Get feedback from others you typically communicate with to verify the information from this questionnaire.

John Madden, longtime successful coach of the Los Angeles Raiders and then a football commentator, summarized the nature of successful communication in the sport context:

" **Communication between a coach and his players was being able to say good things, bad things, and average things. Conversely, it's being able to listen to good, bad, and average things . . . . I tried to talk to each player. Sometimes it was merely a quick "How ya' doin'?" Sometimes it was a conversation. But by [my] talking to them every day, they didn't feel something was up when I would stop to talk to them. (Syer, 1986, pp. 99–110)** "

Along these lines, Hardy, Burke, and Crace (2005) noted that individuals (coaches in particular) need to feel good about their communication style. What are your strengths and areas of improvement regarding communication? To help increase your self-awareness about your communication style, we have adapted and provided a self-assessment scale (refer to the "Communication Self-Evaluation Assessment") developed by communication expert Lawrence Rosenfeld (Rosenfeld & Wilder, 1990). A study by Millar, Oldhan, and Donovan (2011) that investigated coaches' awareness of their verbal communications with athletes showed that self-awareness is extremely important. The researchers monitored the verbal instructions rowing coaches provided to rowers, and coaches completed a questionnaire about their perceived verbal behavior. Results revealed that coaches were inaccurate when recalling what they said to athletes. Coaches were observed giving predominantly concurrent (while athletes were rowing) and prescriptive (what to do) instructions but gave little evaluative (was it any good?) or affective (how did it feel?) feedback. These inaccurate perceptions by coaches can be problematic. Although coaches may think they verbalized instructions or information to athletes (like providing evaluative feedback), this may have never really happened. This highlights the need to develop methods for increasing coaches' self-awareness of communication.

In the following sections we briefly discuss interpersonal and intrapersonal communication, but our focus is on nonverbal communication—a subtle process that is critical to imparting and receiving information.

Verbal Messages

Verbal messages should be sent clearly and received and interpreted correctly. Bill Parcells, successful football coach of the New York Giants, New England Patriots, and New York Jets and general manager of the Miami Dolphins, understands the importance of both the effective sending and receiving of a message: "When sending a message, it's not enough to be honest and accurate. The impact of the message will hinge on who's receiving it and what they're willing to take in at that time" (Parcells & Coplon, 1995, p. 117). In essence, we have to pick the right time and place to deliver our communication. Unfortunately, coaches and parents often pick the most inappropriate time (e.g., right after a game or in front of the team) to deliver their communication.

Breakdowns occur because messages are sent ineffectively, are not received, or are misinterpreted. Sometimes the problem is simply the lack of trust between coach and athlete or teacher and student (Burke, 1997). More often, the problem is with the transmission of the message. Some people talk too much, rambling on about things that bore or distract others, whereas others talk too little, not communicating enough information.

Nonverbal Messages

People are often unaware of the many nonverbal cues they use in communicating. In fact, estimations from

---

Tips for Improving Communication

Here are some ways to improve coach–athlete and teacher–student communications:

- Convey rationales. Explain why you expect (or why you don't expect) certain behaviors from participants.

- Express empathy, not sympathy. Sympathy is the concern that a coach might show for a player. However, empathy involves being sensitive to another individual's feelings and connecting emotionally to the other person. The focus is on understanding the emotional experience of the athlete and then responding in a manner that conveys understanding.

- Use a communication style that is comfortable for you. Don't try to copy the communication style of another coach or teacher just because that individual's style happens to be successful for that person. Rather, communicate consistently according to your own personality and teaching style.

- Learn how to become more empathetic by placing yourself in the shoes of your athletes. Show genuine concern for them as people and work with them to find appropriate solutions.

- Use the positive approach when communicating, which includes the liberal use of praise, encouragement, support, and positive reinforcement.

- Always acknowledge the greetings of others—a hello and a smile are easy ways to communicate positive feelings.

- If you have an open-door policy for your students and athletes, show that you are sincere about it.

- Be consistent in administering discipline.

From "Principles of effective team building interventions in sport: A direct services approach at Penn State University," D. Yukelson, *Journal of Applied Sport Psychology,* 73-96, Taylor & Francis Ltd, adapted by permission of publisher (Taylor & Francis Ltd, http://www.tandf.co.uk/journals).

various researchers indicate that approximately 50% to 70% of the information conveyed in a communication is nonverbal (Burke, 2005). A study of track and field coaches and athletes found that communication was approximately 50% verbal and 50% nonverbal for both coaches and athletes during practice and training. During competition, nonverbal communication increased to approximately 75% for coaches and 66% for athletes (Rata, Rata, Rata, Mares, & Melinte, 2012). Therefore, it is critical that coaches, athletes, and exercise leaders be extremely observant of their nonverbal cues (as well as those of others) as a rich source of information. Understanding the various kinds of nonverbal communication improves both the sending and receiving of messages (see Yukelson, 1998, for an in-depth discussion of nonverbal communication).

> **KEY POINT** As much as 70% of human communication is nonverbal.

Nonverbal messages are less likely to be under conscious control, and therefore they are harder to hide than verbal messages. They can give away our unconscious feelings and attitudes. For example, just before starting an aerobics class, an exercise leader asks a young woman how she is feeling. The young woman shrugs, looks down, frowns, and mutters, "Oh, fine." Although her words say everything is okay, the leader knows otherwise from the nonverbal messages being conveyed. Although nonverbal messages can be powerful, they are often difficult to interpret accurately. Thus, we have to be cautious in giving them meaning, and we have to try to correctly judge the context.

Physical Appearance

Our first impression of a person often comes from physical appearance. We might think of someone as fat, skinny, handsome, sloppy, attractive, or homely. A detail can pack a large message. For example, 20 years ago a male athlete who walked into a coach's office wearing an earring would likely have been quickly escorted out. Now it is more accepted for males to wear earrings, and a different message is conveyed. Dress can convey powerful information. For example, a study by Greenlees, Bradley, Holder, and Thelwell (2005) found that athletes reported lower confidence when their opponent was wearing sport-specific sportswear (as opposed to general sportswear). Ath-

Nonverbal communication can convey as much—if not more—of what a person is really thinking and feeling as verbal communication can.

letes need to be careful about imparting information—whether positive or negative—through dress.

Posture

How we carry ourselves—our gait and posture—also sends a message. Someone who shuffles along with his head down and his hands in his pockets conveys sadness, whereas a bouncy step suggests a sense of control and confidence. Athletes often recognize frustrated or discouraged opponents by how they move. When they see an opposing player hanging his head, they know it's time to "go in for the kill." Tennis greats Pete Sampras and Steffi Graf knew the importance of posture and never let their opponents know how they were feeling: Whether they made a great shot or blew an easy one, they looked and acted the same. This made Graf and Sampras tougher to beat because opponents could not tell when they were down. Relatedly, Furley, Dicks, and Memmert (2012) investigated the influence of nonverbal behavior in taking a penalty kick. They found that penalty kickers with dominant body language (erect posture, head held up, chin parallel to the ground) were perceived more positively by soccer goalkeepers and players and were expected to perform better than players who displayed submissive body language (slouched posture, head and chin pointing down, shoulders hanging to the front). Body language certainly influences athletes' perceptions of their competitors; however, how that perception actually affects performance needs further investigation.

Gestures

People's gestures often convey messages, whether or not they want them to. For instance, folding your arms across your chest usually expresses that you're not open to others, whereas locking your hands behind your head connotes superiority. Coaches often express themselves through gestures—sometimes if they verbalize their thoughts to officials, they risk getting thrown out of the game!

Body Position

Body position refers to the personal space between you and others and to the position of your body with respect to others. Body position is really an aspect of **proxemics**, which is the study of how people communicate by the way they use space. An example of body position language is the coach surrounding herself with starting players rather than with reserves. Many coaches stand next to starting players, connoting favoritism. John Thompson, ex-basketball coach for Georgetown University, made it a habit to instead sit among the reserves to make them feel like valued members of the team.

Touching

Touching is a powerful form of nonverbal communication that can be used to calm someone or to express affection or other feelings, depending on the situation. We have become freer in recent years with the use of touching in sport, including more embracing between males, than was socially acceptable years ago. However, with the increased sensitivity regarding the issue of sexual harassment, coaches and teachers have to be especially careful in their use of touching. You must make sure that the touching is appropriate and is welcomed by the athlete or student. Touching should be restricted to public places to minimize any misinterpretation of the meaning of your touching.

Facial Expression

Your face is the most expressive part of your body. Eye contact is particularly important in communicating feelings. Getting eye contact usually means that your listener is interested in your message. When people feel uncomfortable or embarrassed, they tend to avoid direct eye contact and to look away. The smile is the universal bridge across language barriers and one of the most efficient ways of communicating. Smiles and other facial expressions can both invite verbal communication and elicit feedback about how effective your communication has been.

Voice Characteristics

The sound of a voice can powerfully reinforce or undercut verbal communication. As the adage goes, "It's not what you say but how you say it." The voice's quality often betrays true feelings, moods, and attitudes, revealing what we might never state verbally. Voice characteristics include pitch (high or low), tempo (speed), volume (loud or soft), rhythm (cadence), and articulation (enunciation).

Guidelines for Sending Messages

The following are guidelines for sending effective verbal and nonverbal messages (Martens, 1987a):

• *Be direct.* People who avoid straightforward communication assume that others know what they want or feel. Rather than expressing their message directly, they hint at what they have in mind—or they tell a third person, hoping the message will get to the intended recipient indirectly.

• *Own your message.* Use "I" and "my," not "we" or "the team," when referencing your messages. You disown your messages when you say, "The team feels . . ." or "Most people think you are . . . ." What you're saying is what *you* believe, and using others to bolster what you have to say implies cowardice in expressing your own messages.

• *Be complete and specific.* Provide the person to whom you are speaking with all the information he needs to fully understand your message.

• *Be clear and consistent.* Avoid double messages. "I really want to play you, Mary, but I don't think this is a good game for you. I think you're a fine athlete, but you'll just have to be patient." This is an example of a double message—acceptance and rejection—and it probably leaves Mary confused and hurt.

Double messages send contradictory meanings, and usually the person sending them is afraid to be direct.

• *State your needs and feelings clearly.* Because some societies (e.g., American) frown on those who wear their emotions on their sleeves, we tend not to reveal our feelings and needs to others. Yet to develop close relationships, you must share your feelings.

• *Separate fact from opinion.* State what you see, hear, and know, and then clearly identify any opinions or conclusions you have about these facts. You say to your son when he returns home late one night, "I see you've been out with the Williamson kid again." In the context in which you say it, your son will receive the message but not be certain of what exactly your concern is about the Williamson boy. A better way to send this message would be to say, "That was the Williamson kid, wasn't it?" (verifying a fact) and then, "I'm concerned that you spend time with him. I'm afraid he'll get you into trouble" (stating your opinion). Although your son may not be pleased with your opinion, at least he'll understand it.

• *Focus on one thing at a time.* Have you ever begun discussing how to execute a particular skill and abruptly switched to complaining about how the team hasn't been practicing well? Organize your thoughts before speaking.

• *Deliver messages immediately.* When you observe something that upsets you or that needs to be changed, don't delay sending a message. Sometimes holding back can result in your exploding later about a little thing. Responding immediately also makes for more effective feedback than a delayed response does.

• *Make sure your message does not contain a hidden agenda, which means that the stated purpose of the message is not the same as the real purpose.* To determine if your message contains a hidden agenda, ask yourself these two questions: Why am I saying this to this person? Do I really want the person to hear this, or is something else involved?

• *Be supportive.* If you want another person to listen to your messages, don't deliver them with threats, sarcasm, negative comparisons, or judgments. Eventually the person will avoid communicating with you or simply tune you out whenever you speak.

• *Be consistent with your nonverbal messages.* Perhaps you tell a player it is okay to make an error, but your body gestures and facial expressions contradict your words. Conflicting messages confuse people and hinder future communication.

• *Reinforce with repetition.* Repeat key points to reinforce what you are saying. However, don't repeat too often, because this causes the other person to stop listening. You can also reinforce messages by using additional channels of communication—show a picture or video along with explaining a skill, for example.

• *Make your message appropriate to the receiver's frame of reference.* Messages can be much better understood if you tailor them to the experiences of the person with whom you are communicating. It is inappropriate, for example, to use complex language when speaking to young athletes. They do not have the vocabulary to understand what you're saying.

• *Look for feedback that your message was accurately interpreted.* Watch for verbal and nonverbal signals that the person to whom you are speaking is receiving the message you intended. If no signal is given, ask questions to solicit the feedback: "Do you understand what I am telling you, Susan?" or "Are you clear about what you should do?"

Along these lines, a quick way to remember many of the main points in communication is noted by Glory, Kirubakar, and Kumutha (2010) as the six Cs:

• Clear
• Concise
• Courteous
• Correct
• Complete
• Constructive

DISCOVER Activity 10.1 helps you comprehend the guidelines for sending effective verbal messages.

Electronic Communication

Communication has traditionally been seen as verbal conversations between two or more people. However, technology has changed significantly in the past several years, and now coaches and athletes (i.e., coach–athlete, coach–coach, and athlete–athlete pairs) often communicate through electronic means such as e-mail, instant and text messaging, cell phones, Facebook, Twitter, and blogs. Social media is a rising force in marketing and appears to be fully embraced by the sport industry. Teams, leagues, coaches, athletes, and managers have all established social media presences, primarily on Twitter (a microblogging site that allows users to post their personal thoughts in 140 or fewer characters). Athletes in particular have engaged in tweeting at a fast pace, which raises the question "What are they saying?" Pegoraro (2010) followed athletes' tweets for 7 days and found that the athletes predominantly tweeted about their personal lives and responded to fans' queries. Thus, Twitter appears to be a powerful tool for increasing fan–athlete interaction. However, Browning and Sanderson (2012) interviewed 20 National Collegiate Athletic Association student-athletes and found that Twitter also presents challenges given the ease with which fans can write negative things about athletes. Accordingly, athletic departments must be proactive in helping student-athletes use Twitter strategically, particularly in responding to detractors. Athletes need to be careful when posting on social media or when sending texts, e-mails, or photos because these can quickly become known to the world via the Internet.

Sport psychology consultants also are communicating more and more with their athlete clients through electronic means. Today's generation Y is the first generation to grow up with all of these electronic means of communication (Burke, 2013). These young athletes feel more comfortable communicating in this fashion because they are familiar with electronic communication devices. Thus, it has become necessary for coaches and sport psychology consultants to familiarize themselves with electronic forms of communication in order to facilitate interactions with athletes.

Receiving Messages Effectively

" It's not what you tell them—it's what they hear. "

—Red Auerbach, former Boston Celtics championship coach

So far we've focused on the sender side of communication. However, people spend 40% of their communication time listening (Sathre, Olson, & Whitney, 1973). In addition, research with 88 organizations has shown that listening is consistently rated as one of the most important communication skills (Crocker, 1978). Although students learn writing and speaking skills, they seldom receive any formal training in listening. Before you read about how to improve your listening skills, complete the short "Listening Skills Test" that follows to learn what specific skills you need to improve.

Teacher and Coach Behaviors That Enhance Communication

Research has revealed that a number of teacher and coach behaviors can facilitate communication. This is especially true for **confirmation behaviors**, which refer to communication indicating that individuals are endorsed, recognized, and acknowledged as valuable and significant, resulting in increased motivation and affective learning (Ellis, 2000). Also important are **clarity behaviors**, which refer to how clear individuals perceive the teacher or coach as being, because clarity facilitates both cognitive and affective learning (Simonds, 1997). These behaviors include the following:

Confirmation Behaviors

- Communication indicates an appreciation of student or player questions or comments.
- Communication indicates that the coach or teacher believes that the student or player can do well.
- Teacher or coach checks on understanding before going on to the next point.
- Communication indicates an interest in whether students or players are learning.
- Feedback is provided on student or player performance.

Clarity Behaviors

- Teacher or coach uses clear and relevant examples.
- Teacher or coach relates examples back to the concept or rule.
- Teacher or coach uses concrete rather than abstract language.
- Teacher or coach stays on task and does not stray from the main points.
- Teacher or coach clearly explains the objectives for each assignment or drill.

Active Listening

The best way to listen better is to listen actively. **Active listening** involves attending to main and supporting ideas, acknowledging and responding, giving appropriate feedback, and paying attention to the speaker's total communication. Active listening also involves nonverbal communication, such as making direct eye contact and nodding to confirm that you understand the speaker. In essence, the listener shows concern for the content and the intent of the message and for the feelings of the sender.

Of all the things that can make an individual feel accepted, significant, and worthwhile, none is more

---

Listening Skills Test

Item	Rating scale			
	Never	Seldom	Sometimes	Often
1. You find listening to others uninteresting.	1	2	3	4
2. You tend to focus attention on the speaker's delivery or appearance instead of the message.	1	2	3	4
3. You listen more for facts and details, often missing the main points that give the facts meaning.	1	2	3	4
4. You are easily distracted by other people talking, chewing gum, rattling paper, and so on.	1	2	3	4
5. You fake attention, looking at the speaker but thinking of other things.	1	2	3	4
6. You listen only to what is easy to understand.	1	2	3	4
7. Certain emotion-laden words interfere with your listening.	1	2	3	4
8. You hear a few sentences of another person's problems and immediately start thinking about all the advice you can give.	1	2	3	4
9. Your attention span is very short, so it is hard for you to listen for more than a few minutes.	1	2	3	4
10. You are quick to find things to disagree with, so you stop listening as you prepare your argument.	1	2	3	4
11. You try to placate the speaker by being supportive through head-nodding and uttering agreement, but you're really not involved.	1	2	3	4
12. You change the subject when you get bored or uncomfortable with it.	1	2	3	4
13. As soon as someone says anything that you think reflects negatively on you, you defend yourself.	1	2	3	4
14. You second-guess the speaker, trying to figure out what he or she really means.	1	2	3	4

Add up your score. The following subjective scale will give you some help in determining how well you listen.

14–24 Excellent   25–34 Good   35–44 Fair   45–56 Weak

Adapted, by permission, from R. Martens, 1987, *Coaches guide to sport psychology* (Champaign, IL: Human Kinetics), 56.

vital than being listened to. If you really want people to confide in you, you should make a concerted effort to listen to them. Sometimes people think they are showing that they are available to others when they really are not. A coach may say of her policy, "Sure, my athletes can come to see me any time they want. I have an open-door policy," but her athletes may think, "The coach doesn't really listen to us. All she's interested in is telling us what to do." Good listening shows sensitivity and encourages an open exchange of ideas and feelings.

An active listener often paraphrases what the speaker has said. These are some typical lead-ins for a paraphrase:

- What I hear you saying is . . .
- Let me see if I've got this right. You said . . .
- What you're telling me is . . .

Asking specific questions to allow the person to express his feelings is also part of active listening, as is paraphrasing. Here are some examples:

Statement: "I am thinking about increasing my exercise times from 3 days a week to 5 days a week, but I'm not sure this is the best thing to do right now."

Question: "What do you gain or lose by increasing your exercise times?"

Paraphrase: "It sounds as though you're struggling with trying to balance getting fit with other demands in your life."

By paraphrasing a person's thoughts and feelings, you let the speaker know that you're listening and that you care. Often this leads to more open communication and exchange, as the speaker senses that you're interested. When you ask questions, avoid using the interrogative *why?*—this can seem judgmental. Rosenfeld and Wilder (1990) offered some additional information about active listening skills:

- Hearing should not be mistaken for listening.
- Hearing is simply receiving sounds, whereas listening is an active process.
- Hearing someone does not mean you're listening to the meaning of the message.
- It is frustrating to the speaker when a receiver hears but doesn't listen.
- Someone who finds herself not listening should practice focusing her concentration on the speaker.

Listening sometimes requires mental preparation. For example, before having an important discussion with your coach, develop a mental game plan for the exchange. That is, rehearse in your mind attending very carefully to the meaning of the coach's messages.

KEY POINT Active listening enhances communication because the speaker feels that she is being heard, acknowledged, and provided with appropriate feedback.

Supportive Listening

Being a supportive listener communicates that you are "with" the speaker and value the person's message. Here are some tips for **supportive listening**:

- *Use supportive behaviors as you listen.* These communicate the message that the other person is acknowledged, understood, and accepted. You are using supportive listening behaviors when you
  - describe the other's behavior instead of trying to evaluate or attack it;
  - focus on immediate thoughts and feelings;
  - are not calculating or manipulative;
  - ask open-ended questions to encourage the person to share his or her feelings;
  - are empathetic, not indifferent; and
  - remain open to new ideas, perspectives, and the possibility of change.

Along with these behaviors, use active attending behaviors, such as nodding your head and making clear, direct eye contact.

- *Use confirming behaviors as you listen.* Part of effective communication is letting people know that you are with them in the conversation and that you understand their message, even if you do not agree with it. Use confirming behaviors (such as rephrasing what the person is saying) along with supportive behaviors to show you are paying attention, accepting, and understanding. This is especially important for coaches and teachers and other sport and exercise leaders. Participants usually look up to the leader, and a lack of attention on the leader's part can be particularly disappointing to them.

- *Use both verbal and nonverbal listening behaviors.* Nonverbal behaviors that communicate interest and attention include
  - standing no more than a few feet from the person,
  - maintaining eye contact,

- making appropriate facial gestures,
- facing the speaker, and
- maintaining an open posture.

Verbal behaviors should communicate an understanding and acknowledgment of what the speaker is saying and feeling.

Aware Listening

Be aware that people react differently to the way you communicate. Here are tips for **aware listening**:

• *Be flexible.* There is no one best listening strategy. Different situations require different strategies. People prefer or feel more comfortable with one style of listening compared with another. Some people simply like to talk, and they may appear unconcerned about your understanding. Others will give you time to think about what they've said and will provide opportunities for feedback.

• *Be alert for barriers and breakdowns in communication. Barriers* involve noise, such as other people talking while you are trying to listen to a particular person. For example, coaches and athletes often have to listen above the roar of a crowd. It is useful to develop strategies for dealing with noise, such as using nonverbal signals. *Breakdowns* occur when messages are misinterpreted or misdirected. Often, we do not know a breakdown has occurred until something bad happens that can be traced back to the breakdown. We later discuss breakdowns at greater length.

Importance of Empathy and Caring

Empathy is the ability of a person to perceive, recognize, and understand the feelings, behaviors, intentions, and attitudes of others (Losoya & Eisenberg, 2003) and has been long viewed as an important prerequisite to effective communication. Jowett and colleagues (Jowett & Clark-Carter, 2006; Lorimer & Jowett, 2009a,b) have begun to uncover how empathy functions in coach–athlete relationships. They found in one study that athletes were more capable than their coaches of inferring feelings of closeness (Jowett & Clark-Carter, 2006). Looking only at coaches, they observed that individual-sport coaches were more accurate in predicting athlete feelings about the relationship than were team-sport coaches (Lorimer & Jowett, 2009a). The most likely explanation, the authors felt, was that individual-sport coaches had more time to spend with each athlete and more often

developed a shared common focus with athletes. Most encouraging was the finding that coaches' empathic accuracy improves with continued exposure to each athlete and when they receive feedback about what their athletes think and feel (Lorimer & Jowett, 2009b).

In a similar study, Lorimer and Jowett (2011) found that sharing similar ideas (e.g., determining game strategy) helps athletes and coaches understand each other and empathize with each other's thoughts and feelings. The authors recommend that both coaches and athletes should concentrate on the topic being discussed or task undertaken and make frequent checks to establish that they understand what is going on rather than simply make assumptions. These discussions should not be limited to the technical aspects of the sport but rather should encourage the athlete to discuss his or her thoughts and feelings about ongoing events.

These findings suggest that athletes and coaches are not always focused on similar issues and that coaches may be less skilled at reading their athletes' feelings and emotions than they think. Coaches, teachers, certified athletic trainers, and fitness instructors must, therefore, make concerted efforts to get to know their athletes, view them in social situations, and seek feedback from them about what they are thinking and feeling.

Lorimer (2013) suggests four ways to improve the accuracy of coaches' empathy:

1. *Gather information.* This information can be about athletes or sport in general ("I know when athletes raise their voices they are generally angry"), knowledge about a particular type of athlete ("I know when athletes stay after practice, they generally are interested in improving their skills"), or knowledge about a specific situation or athlete ("I know when John raises his voice in training he is usually upset or worried").

2. *Avoid biases.* Be aware of possible biases and stereotypes and seek additional feedback before making an assumption about an athlete.

3. *Maintain appropriate levels of empathy.* Make sure that you are aware of your own emotions and remain separate from your athletes emotionally. For example, while it might be appropriate to demonstrate empathy for an athlete whose father has just died, it might not be appropriate to demonstrate empathy simply because they made a couple of errors.

4. *Be reflexive.* Constantly reflect on your interactions with athletes so you can better understand why you and your athletes act in certain ways in certain situations.

Related to the topic of empathy is caring. It is generally believed that the more an athlete, exerciser, or student feels that the individuals who teach and mentor them care, the better the communication will be. Newton and colleagues (2007) define a caring climate as one perceived by individuals as "interpersonally inviting, safe, supportive, and capable of providing the experience of being valued and respected" (p. 67). Hence, a leader who structures a caring climate respects participants and treats them with respect; listens to them; and makes them feel safe, comfortable, and welcomed. Using the recently developed Caring Climate Questionnaire (Newton et al., 2007), Gano-Overway and colleagues (2009) found a significant relationship between perceptions of a caring climate in underserved youths in a summer sports camp and their increased prosocial and decreased antisocial behaviors. This suggests that creating a caring climate enhances the coach–athlete relationship and

leads to a number of desirable outcomes in youths. As the adage goes, they don't care what you know until they know you care!

DISCOVER Activity 10.2 gives you an opportunity to assess your listening skills.

Recognizing Breakdowns in Communication

Communicating effectively requires skill and effort on the part of both of the people involved. The process can be complicated and often breaks down (figure 10.2). Although technology (e.g., e-mail) has improved the efficiency and speed of some types of communication, comparable progress has not been achieved in the interpersonal aspects of communication (Burke, 2001). One of the main reasons communicating is sometimes problematic is that many people believe that it is others, rather than themselves, who are ineffective, and therefore they do not see the need to improve their own communication skills. Another

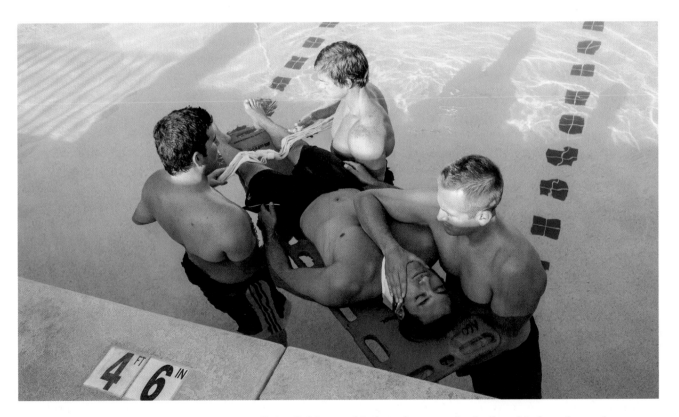

If a caring rapport has been established off the field, an athletic trainer may be better able to calm and reassure an athlete when an injury occurs.

Receiver's not paying attention to the sender

Receiver's tendency to evaluate and judge communication

Lack of trust between the individuals attempting to communicate

Socialization and hereditary differences, causing misinterpretations between the sender and receiver

Differences in the mental set or perception between people

Embarrassment (creates interference)

Tendency to tell people what they want to hear

Difficulties in expression or reluctance to communicate

Belief that silence is safer

Inconsistency between actions and words

Screening of messages by assistants for efficiency

FIGURE 10.2 Barriers to effective communication.

general issue leading to communication breakdowns is a lack of trust among people (e.g., teammates, coaches, exercise leaders, and exercisers). Good rapport and honesty need to be developed between individuals before effective communication can occur. When breakdowns occur, they usually result from either sender or receiver failures.

Sender Failures

Senders may transmit a message poorly. Ambiguous messages, for example, are ineffective communications. Say a coach tells an athlete that if he continues to do well in practice, he will be in the starting lineup when the season opens. Over the next few weeks, the coach compliments the athlete regularly and says nothing about him not starting. Two days before the start of the season, the athlete is taken aback when he is listed as a reserve. In this case, the coach should have been more specific about the criteria for starting and should have given the athlete ongoing feedback.

Inconsistent messages also cause communication breakdowns. Nothing is more frustrating than hearing one thing today and the opposite tomorrow. For example, if a coach is always supportive during practice but is harsh and critical during games, athletes get confused and may even fall apart during competitions. Often inconsistency results when verbal and nonverbal channels conflict. A physical education teacher might offer encouraging words to a student attempting a new skill while her body language and facial expression

convey disappointment and impatience. Physical educators want to establish credibility in their communications, and consistency is a good route toward this goal. And it's necessary to be consistent not only with each participant but also among participants. For example, say a coach tells the team that anyone who is late to practice will not play in the next game. If the coach then enforces this policy when a couple of reserves are late for practice, he must also enforce it if the star player is late.

Receiver Failures

Ineffective communication is a double-edged sword. Receivers as well as senders can contribute to miscommunication. As an illustration, let's look at Mary, an exercise leader. She is talking to Cindy, a member of her aerobics class who has missed several classes. "Cindy, I've missed you the past several weeks," says Mary. "If you don't keep up your regular exercise, you'll get fat again. In fact, I already see those love handles." Mary's intent is to motivate Cindy to stop missing exercise classes, but Cindy hears only the "getting fat" and "love handles" parts. She has been overweight for many years and is sensitive to comments about her weight. What she hears Mary saying is that she is getting fat, and she starts feeling depressed because she has worked so hard to lose weight. Had Mary been more aware of Cindy's tendency toward sensitivity, however, she could have simply told Cindy that she missed her in class and was glad to see her back and exercising. Thus, in this case there was a problem in both the sending and the receiving.

Apart from misinterpreting the message, receivers cause problems when they fail to listen. For example, a teacher may convey information very well, but if her students are looking out the window or thinking about an upcoming party, communication will break down. The receiver shares responsibility with the sender and should make every effort to listen.

Rosenfeld and Wilder (1990) identified three levels of listening. Level one is active listening (discussed previously), which is the desired way of listening. Level two refers to hearing only the content of the message when listening; this type of listening often makes the speaker feel that the listener is uninterested or preoccupied. In level three, the listener hears only part of the message and thus true understanding is not possible. In today's rushed society, people are often thinking about what they want to say rather than closely paying attention to what the sender is saying before formulating a response. Poor listening can often lead to interpersonal conflict and confrontation (discussed later in the chapter) as well as frustration and a breakdown in communication.

Improving Communication

Although definite barriers to effective communication exist, we can improve communication through active exercises and attention. DiBerardinis, Barwind, Flaningam, and Jenkins (1983) found that exercises designed to improve interpersonal relations in team sports did just that and that performance itself improved. In a more comprehensive study (Sullivan, 1993), a communication-skills training program that included seven interpersonal-communication exercises was developed for interactive-sport teams. Athletes indicated that the communication exercises raised awareness levels of communication skills and competencies and provided valuable opportunities for practicing communication skills (see "Impact of Interpersonal Training"). Therefore, carefully designed interpersonal-communication training can improve team morale and cohesion and open up lines of communication.

Another way to improve communication (especially in a group or team) is to set up team meetings. These meetings should be regularly scheduled (don't wait for a problem to appear before you meet), focus on team difficulties, and provide constructive assessment of the situation. Team meetings can be problematic if the coach or leader does not set parameters or rules for the meeting. Suggested rules include the following:

- Everyone on the team must be receptive to the opinions of others (i.e., don't be defensive or resistant).
- Be constructive, not destructive (e.g., criticize behaviors, not the person).
- Whatever is discussed in the meeting stays there (i.e., information is confidential).
- Everyone will have a chance to speak.
- Each team member should have at least one positive thing to say about everybody else.

Beauchamp, Maclachlan, and Lothian (2005) used a Jungian approach to help improve communication. One important point was that athletes need to approach interactions from the other person's point of view. To achieve this empathy, the authors recommended role playing in practices, whereby athletes are asked to act out different scenarios and seek to connect with other team members using preferences that are very different from their own. For example, placing players in situations in which their performance is critical (i.e., they don't want to let teammates down) or where they feel pressure from the coach (i.e., they may be benched if they don't perform well) may help athletes better appreciate what their other teammates are going through. This facilitates better communication and understanding of what the other person is experiencing and can enhance empathy.

Communication for Improving Team Coordination

Typically, coaches develop game plans that emphasize the coordination of all players on the team so that everyone is on the same page. For example, in soccer, all players must be in the right position and know their roles for the team to be effective. Eccles and Tran (2012) offer some suggestions for how coaches can communicate these plans to athletes:

- *Use multiple sensory modes.* Plans should be presented using different senses such as talking a game plan through, drawing it up on a whiteboard, demonstrating it with moveable magnets, showing a video, or providing a written playbook.
- *Use redundancy.* A concept called optimal redundancy underscores the need to repeat things

from time to time so that others learn and remember them. Constant reminders, talking through the game plan, and providing players with a playbook can all increase redundancy.

• *Use an enduring representation.* When athletes are simply told to do something (e.g., how to move during a full-court press in basketball), the information is gone when the coach finishes the explanation. Supplement verbal instructions with tangible items such as handouts, recordings, or videos so that players can access play information at all times.

• *Explain why.* Players who learn the rationale behind a certain strategy are more likely to be flexi-

ble during performance and be able to react better to changing circumstances than are players who simply learn how to execute the strategy. If a play breaks down, players with a deeper understanding are more likely to be able to think on their feet and figure out an alternative strategy.

In addition to enhancing how plans are communicated to team members, coaches need to increase the chances that the players actually listen to and understand the plans. Here are a few suggestions:

• *Enhance team members' listening skills.* Encourage team members to follow the HEAR prin-

Impact of Interpersonal Training

Sullivan (1993) assessed the effectiveness of his interpersonal communication exercises. Athletes increased their awareness and learned a great deal as evidenced by the following comments in reaction to the exercises:

• I should listen more before I react to what has been said.
• I see myself differently than others see me. It is scary to open up, but this makes it easier.
• It helps to understand what others expect of me.
• It helps to know the goals of my teammates.
• I have a heightened sense of awareness of my personal goals and communication skills.
• Laughing and sharing critical emotions ease tensions.

Athletes also stated that they would focus on or practice the following communication skills:

• I will not interrupt when others are speaking.
• I will confront issues right away—they only get worse over time.
• I will try not to make assumptions about what others are thinking.
• I should ask for help from my teammates.
• I will give my opinion more to people with whom I feel intimidated.
• I will have more eye contact with the person speaking.

In another approach to improving communication skills, Jones, Lavallee, and Tod (2011) employed the Enhancement of Leadership Interpersonal Teamwork and Excellence (ELITE) 8-week intervention using reflective practice to enhance self-awareness of communication skills (verbal and listening). Using a case study approach, five athletes were asked to

• describe the communication skills they used in in their last training session,
• describe a competition in which communication helped their performance,
• think about how communication skills can be used in future competitions as well as outside of sport, and
• practice the skills they had discussed with their teammates

Athletes also participated in interactive games and activities that gave them a chance to use their communication skills. Results of a communication questionnaire revealed that the athletes in the ELITE intervention improved their communication skills across the intervention and that these communication skills helped improve their sport performance.

ciples: **h**ead up, **e**yes front, **a**ttend fully, and **r**emain silent.

• *Encourage questions.* Athletes are often reluctant to ask questions because they don't want to appear "dumb." In addition to encouraging questions in meetings, provide time for athletes to ask questions in private to avoid the social pressure of potentially looking foolish in front of the team.

• *Check that plans are received.* Make sure players understand the game plans by asking players to describe plans verbally or demonstrate on the field.

DISCOVER   Activity 10.3 allows you to practice communicating with empathy.

One of the main reasons for wanting to improve communication skills is so athletes and coaches can maintain better interpersonal relationships. Rhind

and Jowett (2010) conducted one of the only studies that investigated the maintenance of coach–athlete relationships. After interviewing six athletes and six coaches, the researchers concluded that the following strategies (which they labeled the COMPASS method) were used to maintain coach–athlete relationships:

• *Conflict management.* This consisted of proactive strategies (e.g., taking steps to clarify expectations and avoid conflict) and reactive strategies (e.g., cooperating during discussion of disagreements).

• *Openness.* This involved talking about non-sport and personal issues and sharing feelings.

• *Motivation.* This involved coaches and athletes demonstrating effort, motivating each other, demonstrating ability, and making interactions enjoyable.

• *Positivity.* This refers to a coach's adaptability (e.g., changing one's behavior to suit the preferences of the coach/athlete), fairness (e.g., showing

Enhancing Communication Among Coaches, Athletes, and Parents

In today's world, the ability and desire to communicate instantaneously with people in any country have increased dramatically. Taking advantage of new technology, Mental Training Incorporated (the central mission of which is to help 1 million athletes build mental toughness by the 2016 Olympics) developed an application called MentalApp.

MentalApp helps athletes learn and practice 15 key mental skills and track performance improvements. Short videos teach the fundamentals of each mental skill as well as how and when to practice. Then, using an innovative monitoring chart, athletes can easily set goals and track how committed they are to their training. Because MentalApp is compatible with all smartphone, tablet, and computer devices, athletes everywhere and in any sport are able to gain access.

The app also enhances communication among coaches, parents, and athletes. One of the most challenging parts of being an effective coach or supportive parent is overseeing athlete progress. Coaches and parents might wonder what's happening with sleep, nutrition, and hydration or whether athletes are following through with their commitments when parents and coaches aren't present. A dashboard shows a real-time summary of all athletes as well as a more detailed view of any specific athlete. Parents can see how their children are preparing and performing, right from their device.

To see a video of MentalApp in action, go to www.mentaltraininginc.com/mentalapp.php. In addition, one screen shot from MentalApp highlights the enhanced communication possibilities.

The screen shot shows a specific athlete's monitoring chart, called an mChart, of made (green dot) and missed (red dot) goals. Coaches can quickly see whether each athlete is following through with commitments (e.g., eating properly, staying hydrated) and which athletes are struggling to understand or follow through on directions and thus might need additional motivation or clarification.

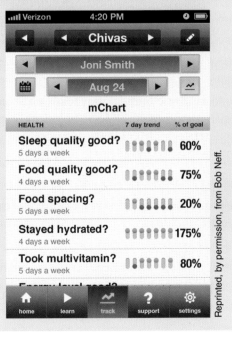

good sportsmanship), and external pressures (e.g., positively dealing with events outside of the coach/athlete's sporting life).

• *Advice.* This included giving and receiving feedback in a positive and open way and praising each other when appropriate.

• *Support.* This involved showing that one was committed to the coach–athlete relationship and available for the other person in terms of both sport-related and personal issues.

• *Social networks.* This involved spending time with each other, especially away from the track, field, or court.

Dealing With Confrontation

Many times, the nature of the communication is inherently difficult. For example, when coaches have to inform players that they are being cut from the team, removed from the starting lineup, or punished for a rule violation or for having made a critical performance error, athletes can get angry, upset, and defensive. Interpersonal conflict, which can lead to confrontation, has the dimensions of content and emotion (LaVoi, 2007). If an athlete has just a moderate amount of content conflict with the coach (e.g., disagreeing about how best to train anaerobically and aerobically), this can lead to a positive interaction as long as they both express their points of view unemotionally. However, emotional conflict (both coach and player are angry) can be debilitative to performance and interpersonal relationships. The inability to differentiate between content and emotional forms of communication causes most interpersonal conflicts and eventual confrontations (Mallett, 2013).

Along these lines, a study focusing on interpersonal conflict in female athletes noted that interpersonal conflict (which can turn into confrontation) was prevalent with teammates in their sports and was more destructive than performance conflict (Holt, Knight, & Zukiwski, 2012). Strategies that athletes felt would help alleviate, or at least manage, the interpersonal conflict included

- engaging in team building early in the season,
- addressing conflicts early,
- engaging mediators in the resolution of conflict, and

- holding structured (rather than unstructured) team meetings.

The authors also noted that athletes need to be taught conflict resolution skills because the resolution of conflict is critical to the effectiveness of teams. These skills might include enabling team members to identify the type and source of conflict, recognizing desirable conflict, and implementing appropriate conflict resolution using cooperative (win–win) negotiation strategies rather than competitive (win–lose) strategies (Deutsch, 2006).

If these types of conflicts and communications are not handled carefully, then communication breakdowns can occur, often leading to confrontations. A **confrontation** is usually a face-to-face discussion among people in conflict. Despite its negative connotations, confrontation when properly used can help both parties understand the issues more clearly without feeling undue stress, guilt, or inadequacy. Confrontations are useful not only in major conflicts but also to help clear the air in minor conflicts.

KEY POINT Use active and supportive listening techniques to avoid breakdowns that prevent effective communication.

When to Avoid or to Use Confrontation

Avoid confrontations when you are angry. It has been said that someone who speaks when she is angry will make the best speech she will forever regret. Many people feel uncomfortable with confrontations because they anticipate a negative, stressful encounter. When athletes and coaches or students and teachers have a confrontation, there is, in addition, a difference in power, which can be problematic. Thus, participants frequently avoid the meeting and let things fester. Other people jump to arguments and escalate feelings of hostility. Neither approach resolves the problem.

In what situations should you use confrontation? Decide by considering the purposes a confrontation might serve. The confrontation should not be meant to put other people "in their place" but rather to carefully examine the behavior and its consequences. For example, if a fitness instructor believes that his supervisor was wrong in reprimanding him in front of a client "just because" he used a different lifting technique than usual, then the instructor should meet with the supervisor to resolve their differences rather than let the situation fester and turn into a full-blown incident.

Individual Communication Styles and Managing Conflict

People typically find conflict difficult and develop different styles for coping with these situations. Thomas (2003) highlighted these styles in a model termed the Thomas-Kilmann model, and Mallett (2010, 2013) elaborated on the model regarding sport competition. The five styles are as follows:

- *Competing* (dominating) involves assertive but uncooperative behaviors between two parties who are concerned about themselves and their own goals rather than others. This style is best used when decisive action is necessary and the best outcome is sought for the person making the decision. For example, a coach who needs to choose the final runner for a relay chooses the fastest person even though he likes another runner better.

- *Collaborating* (integrating) involves assertive and cooperative behaviors between parties where high concern exists for both the self and others. Collaborating is especially effective when both parties have positive contributions to make to solve a problem. For example, coaches and athletes can both have input into setting up consequences for individuals who fail to meet team expectations of behavior.

- *Compromising* involves a balance between unassertive and assertive or between cooperative and uncooperative behaviors where moderate concern exists for both the self and others. Compromising works well when time is short and one needs a quick solution or an interim step toward resolving a more complex issue. For example, coaches may allow players to attend practices late because they know they are preparing for midterm exams.

- *Accommodating* (obliging) involves cooperative and unassertive behaviors where low concern exists for the self and high concern exists for others. In this approach to conflict, people view relationships with others as more important than satisfying their own needs. For example, although a coach feels that a star player missing a practice should result in missing the next game (which happens to be for the league title), the other players on the team encourage the coach to find another consequence because the team needs the player. Thus, for team harmony and cohesion, the coach accommodates their wishes.

- *Avoiding* involves uncooperative and unassertive behaviors where low concern exists for the self and others. Avoidance can be used either to ignore the conflict and hope it goes away or as a deliberate strategy for controlling the situation. Although it should be used sparingly, avoidance may be appropriate, such as when a coach deliberately avoids a player's issue in order to let the player calm down before addressing the issue.

Assumptions for Approaching a Confrontation

Once you decide that confrontation can be useful and appropriate, you need to know how to confront. Gerstein and Reagan (1986) discuss seven cooperating assumptions for approaching conflict:

- *All needs are legitimate and important and must be attended to.* When all needs are considered to be of equal importance, the focus becomes meeting these needs instead of meeting your own need. For example, if a coach believes an athlete is not working hard, then both the athlete's and coach's needs should be considered (especially the reasons underlying each point of view) in trying to resolve this conflict.

- *There are enough resources to meet all needs.* The human potential to create new ideas and resources has no limit. All of us collectively know more than any one of us.

- *In every individual lie untapped power and capacity, and people in conflict know what they need.* Coaches and exercise leaders should not impose solutions based on their own ideas of what the problem is with the athlete or participant. Imposing solutions without recognizing individual needs will create unhappy athletes and participants. Therefore, participants should be encouraged to offer solutions to problems.

- *Process is as important as content because it provides direction and focus.* Process is the flow of feelings, thoughts, and events. Many times the listener gets caught up in the specifics of the content (and oftentimes thus rehearses an attack) while missing important clues and information about what is going on with the person communicating.

Dos and Don'ts When Initiating Confrontation

Do

- Convey that you value your relationship with the person.
- Go slowly and think about what you want to communicate.
- Try to understand the other person's position.
- Listen carefully to what the other person is trying to communicate.

Don't

- Don't communicate the solution. Rather, focus on the problem. We are often overly eager to tell others what they must do instead of letting them figure it out.
- Don't stop communicating. Even if the confrontation isn't going as you planned, keep communicating about the problem in a constructive manner.
- Don't use "put-downs." Sarcasm and attacks usually alienate people. A confrontation is not a competition, and the idea is not to win it. The idea is to solve a problem together.
- Don't rely on nonverbal hints to communicate your thoughts. You need to be direct and forthright in communicating. Now is not the time for subtle nonverbal cues.

Adapted, by permission, from R. Martens, 1987, *Coaches guide to sport psychology* (Champaign, IL: Human Kinetics), 56.

• *Improving situations is different from solving problems.* Dealing with situations helps one focus on the underlying causes rather than just eliminate the problem or symptom. For example, punishing someone for being constantly late may alleviate the problem, but the causes of why she is constantly late still remain.

• *Everyone is right from his or her own perspective.* It is important to see the situation from the other person's perspective. In confrontations, people spend an inordinate amount of time defending their point of view, which simply solidifies that they are right. There are always two sides to every story, and we must be willing to listen to the other side.

• *Solutions and resolutions are temporary states of balance and are not absolute or timeless.* Circumstances can change and thus solutions may need to be altered and renegotiated to keep up with changing times. Many times a relationship is a balancing act, so we must be flexible and change as necessary.

Delivering Constructive Criticism

Although we generally want to be positive, there are times when criticism is necessary. Unfortunately, many people take criticism as a threat to self-esteem. They concentrate on defending themselves instead of on listening to the message. Some exemplary research and application of the research indicate that the **sandwich approach** is the most effective way to give criticism (Smith & Smoll, 1996; Smoll & Smith, 1996). The sandwich approach is a technique for offering constructive feedback in a sensitive yet effective manner. It consists of three sequential elements:

1. A positive statement
2. Future-oriented instructions
3. A compliment

Let's take a closer look. A participant who has made a mistake typically anticipates a negative remark from the coach or teacher. Often the person tunes out the anticipated unpleasant message and never hears it. To ensure that the individual attends to the first comment, make it positive. Appropriate positive phrases might be "Nice try, Janet," "Good effort, Marty," or "What a tough pitch to hit!" Once the person has become receptive through hearing the opening (positive) comment, he will also pay attention to the second part, the instructional feedback. However, for the sandwich approach to be effective, the recipient of the communication must perceive the positive statements as sincere and not just as efforts to make him feel better. When implementing this technique, be careful not to impart hollow praise.

The key aspect of the sandwich approach is the future-oriented instruction. After gaining the person's attention, provide the critical instructional feedback—behaviors or strategies for the person to use next time he or she performs the skill. Keeping the instruction future oriented keeps the person from thinking about the error immediately (thinking about an error will often result in repeating it). The message should be about what to do next time, not a comment that ridicules, embarrasses, or criticizes. The following are examples of future-oriented instructions:

- After a ground ball goes through a player's legs, say, "Next time you get a hard grounder, just get down on one knee and block the ball with your body."
- After a student who is trying a new skill on the balance beam falls off, say, "You really need to concentrate on keeping your eyes looking forward to help maintain your balance."

The final part of the sandwich is a compliment. After giving the instructional feedback, make sure the individual still feels good about the performance. Ending the interaction on a positive note makes it more likely that the instruction will be remembered. It also helps build trust and rapport; the individual realizes that making a mistake isn't the end of the world and that people can learn from their errors. See figure 10.3 for an example of the complete sandwich delivered by an instructor to a student who keeps getting out of step during aerobics dance class.

DISCOVER Activity 10.4 helps you practice providing constructive criticism.

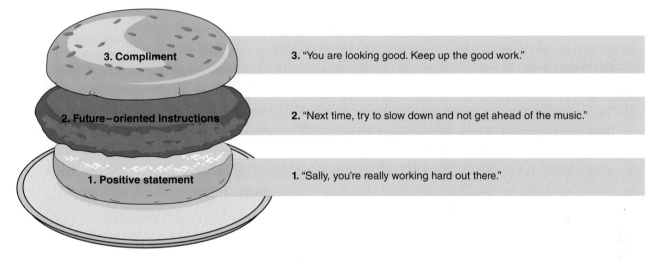

FIGURE 10.3 The sandwich approach to delivering constructive criticism.

Coach–Athlete Relationship

The coach–athlete relationship is one of the most important relationships in sport because it has been shown to likely determine the athlete's satisfaction, self-esteem, and performance accomplishments. Because previous models proved inadequate, Jowett and colleagues (Jowett, 2003; Jowett & Cockerill, 2003) proposed an alternative model of the coach–athlete relationship. Three interpersonal constructs were selected to form the basis of the new model of the coach–athlete relationship.

- *Closeness* reflects the emotional tone that coaches and athletes experience and express in describing their relationship. Terms such as *liking, trust,* and *respect* indicate the level of closeness.
- *Co-orientation* occurs when relationship members have established a common frame of reference, namely shared goals, values, and expectations. Open communication facilitates the development of co-orientation.
- *Complementarity* refers to the type of interactions in which the coach and athlete are engaged. This reflects coaches' and athletes' acts of cooperation.

(continued)

Coach-Athlete Relationship *(continued)*

A summary of findings from several studies is presented next:

- At the elite level, coach–athlete relationships are underlined by mutual respect, care, trust, concern, support, open communication, shared knowledge and understanding, and clear roles.
- There is typically a honeymoon period at the start of a coach–athlete relationship, but negative aspects (e.g., lack of trust, emotional closeness, or commitment) can emerge as the relationship continues.
- Negative closeness (distrust), disorientation (incongruent goals), and noncomplementary transactions (power struggles) together can compromise the quality of the relationship and its effectiveness.
- Because of the importance of the coach–athlete relationship, social skills should be incorporated into coach education programs.
- The quality of coach–athlete relationships (especially with younger athletes) is influenced a great deal by parents, who generally provide a range of information, opportunities, and extensive emotional support (Jowett & Timson-Katchis, 2005).

LEARNING AIDS

SUMMARY

1. **Describe the communication process.**
   Effective communication takes work and effort. Communication is a process. Basically, we communicate in two ways: interpersonally and intrapersonally. Interpersonal communication involves both verbal and nonverbal communication, whereas intrapersonal communication is communicating with oneself via self-talk.

2. **Describe how to send messages more effectively.**
   Effective communication, both verbal and nonverbal, is essential for positive interactions. In nonverbal communication, such factors as physical appearance, posture, gestures, body positioning, and touching are critical. Effective verbal communication includes such characteristics as being clear and consistent, being direct, and delivering messages immediately.

3. **Describe how to receive messages more effectively.**
   Active listening is the most useful way to become more effective at receiving messages. It involves attending to main and supporting ideas, acknowledging and responding, and giving appropriate feedback as well as using nonverbal cues such as eye contact and nodding one's head to show understanding.

4. **Identify what causes breakdowns in communication.**
   Effective communication is complex, and breakdowns often occur either in sending or in receiving a message. Senders who convey messages that are ambiguous or inconsistent can cause communication breakdowns. Similarly, receivers who do not pay close attention to a message can also cause ineffective communication.

5. **Explain the process of using confrontation.**
   Confrontation is a way of communicating, and although most people view confrontation as negative, it can lead to a mutual solution. Part of successfully resolving a problem is recognizing when and why a confrontation may be appropriate. The critical component is to express your feelings in a constructive manner.

6. **Discuss how to offer constructive criticism.**
   Constructive criticism can be provided through what is known as the sandwich approach. This involves a positive statement, future-oriented instructions, and a compliment. This type of criticism avoids the negativism that usually accompanies critical remarks and allows people to focus on the positive aspects of their behavior.

KEY TERMS

encodes
decodes
interpersonal communication
nonverbal communication
intrapersonal communication

proxemics
confirmation behaviors
clarity behaviors
active listening
supportive listening

aware listening
empathy
confrontation
sandwich approach

REVIEW QUESTIONS

1. Discuss the five steps of the communication process.
2. Describe three types of nonverbal communication, giving examples from applied settings.
3. Define active listening. How can practitioners enhance their listening skills?
4. Discuss three types of breakdowns in communication, including examples of each type.
5. Describe the process you would use when confronting someone.
6. Describe how you would help athletes become more assertive in their communication.
7. Three concepts have been shown to provide a good theoretical basis for understanding the coach–athlete relationship. Discuss and provide examples of closeness, co-orientation, and complementarity.
8. Describe five of the principles for approaching a confrontation.
9. Discuss three strategies that female athletes noted to help deal with interpersonal conflict.
10. Coaches generally have plans or strategies that they want their athletes to execute in an upcoming competition. Discuss three techniques for enhancing the probability that the athletes receive these plans and that coordination occurs among teammates.
11. Discuss how electronic communication has changed the way we communicate in sport and some of the effects of this relatively new way of communication.

CRITICAL THINKING QUESTIONS

1. As a paid consultant, you are asked to devise a guide for teachers and coaches at a local high school to help them communicate more effectively with their students and athletes. What are the most important guidelines you would include in your guide? What barriers are most likely to undermine effective communication?
2. As a coach, you have just had a brief confrontation with an athlete about breaking some team rules. He has stormed out of practice mad and upset. Soon you are to meet with the athlete and likely will have to confront him about his behavior—and possibly punish him for his actions. How would you prepare for this meeting, and what principles would you use to make this confrontation a positive meeting? How might the athlete best prepare for this encounter? How might you have prevented this confrontation in the first place?

PART V

Improving Performance

One of the main questions asked by sport and exercise psychologists is "How can we use psychological techniques to help people perform more effectively?" Besides performance in the specific areas of sport and exercise, learning these mental skills can transfer to other areas of your life such as business, academic, and personal. Performance enhancement has been a major focus of sport psychology since the field's early days, whereas the transfer to other life skills has become a focus as the field has evolved. In this part we convey what progress has been made toward answering this question.

Chapter 11 introduces you to psychological skills training. Here you'll discover that psychological skills are like physical skills and that they can be taught, learned, and practiced. You'll learn how to enhance performance in your students, athletes, and exercisers by teaching mental skills. This chapter ends with a discussion of ways to achieve peak performance through psychological preparation. You can use this in your personal life as well as in your professional life to help others achieve peak performance.

Chapters 12 through 16 focus on specific topics in developing psychological skills training for performance enhancement. In chapter 12 we examine arousal regulation and reduction; this will equip you to help athletes psych up rather than psych out. You'll become familiar with a variety of health-related stress-management techniques as well. Chapter 13 discusses imagery (or visualization). You will learn about the theories and data underlying imagery effectiveness as well as how to implement an imagery training pro-

gram. Chapter 14, which focuses on self-confidence, emphasizes the relationship between confidence and performance as well as confidence-building methods you can use. One of the best ways to build confidence is by effectively setting goals. Thus, in chapter 15 you'll learn about effective goals and goal-setting skills for enhancing confidence, other psychological skills, and performance. Part V ends with chapter 16, a discussion of the all-important topics of attention and concentration. Here we cover attentional problems and ways in which you can improve performance through enhanced concentration and attentional skills.

VIEW   Dr. Dan Gould introduces part V of the text in the Introduction activity.

 JOURNEY   This activity asks you to consider the balance between investing time in mental preparation versus physical preparation when participating in sport, including how to communicate with athletes and coaches about it.

LISTEN   Go to part V of the web study guide to meet the following experts in the field: Kirsten Peterson, PhD; Peter Giacobbi, Jr., PhD; Robin Vealey, PhD; Robert Weinberg, PhD; Craig Wrisberg, PhD; and Judy L. Van Raalte, PhD. In this activity, you'll hear or see the experts discussing psychological skills training.

11

Introduction to Psychological Skills Training

After reading this chapter, you should be able to

1. define psychological skills training and describe the myths surrounding it,
2. identify the knowledge base for psychological skills training,
3. discuss three phases of psychological skills training programs,
4. examine the process of psychological self-regulation,
5. develop a psychological skills training program, and
6. understand the problems of implementing a psychological skills training program.

How many times have you seen athletes attribute their poor performances to such factors as losing concentration or tightening up under pressure—the mental side of their game? Yet a mistake coaches and athletes alike commonly make is to attempt to correct poor performance simply through more practice time. Often, however, a lack of physical **skills** is not the real problem—rather, a lack of mental skills is the cause. Let's take a look at a scenario that makes this point.

Jim's high school basketball team is behind 66 to 67 with 1 second left on the clock when Jim is fouled in the act of shooting and awarded two shots. The opposing coach calls a time-out to try to ice Jim and let the pressure build. Jim's coach tells him to just relax and shoot the foul shots as he does in practice. But Jim knows how important the game is to his teammates, his coach, the school, his friends, and his family in the audience. He starts to think about how awful he

would feel if he let everybody down, and this worrying starts to affect him physically. As he approaches the free-throw line, the muscles in his shoulders and arms tighten up. As a result, he rushes his shots, lacks rhythm in his release, and misses both free throws, and his team loses the game.

The next day in practice, Jim's coach tells him to work more on his free-throw shooting, recommending that he stay after every practice to shoot 100 free throws. The coach believes that the extra practice will help Jim perfect his free-throw technique so that he won't choke at the next big game.

However, Jim's problem did not have to do with the mechanics of shooting a free throw. The real problem was that he got too tense and couldn't stay relaxed to shoot his free throws smoothly and rhythmically, just the way he does in practice. Having Jim rehearse free throws will not help him overcome the pressures of shooting when the game is on the line.

Jim needs to develop skills to relax physically and mentally when under great pressure. These skills (as well as others) can be developed through psychological skills training. So let's start by taking a closer look at what psychological skills training is all about.

What Psychological Skills Training Entails

Psychological skills training (PST) refers to systematic and consistent practice of mental or psychological skills for the purpose of enhancing performance, increasing enjoyment, or achieving greater sport and physical activity self-satisfaction. The **methods** and techniques that are standard elements of PST originally came from a wide range of sources, mostly in mainstream psychology. These areas included behavior modification, cognitive theory and therapy, rational emotive therapy, goal setting, attentional control, progressive muscle relaxation, and systematic desensitization. It appears that in the 1950s the first country to systematically engage in mental skills with athletes and coaches was the Soviet Union (Ryba, Stambulova, & Wrisberg, 2005). Avksenty Puni was the key leader in Soviet sport psychology and formalized perhaps the earliest mental training model, which included self-regulation of arousal, confidence, attentional focusing, distraction control, and goal setting (see chapter 1). This emphasis on mental training was systematically applied to other Eastern Bloc countries for the preparation of Olympic athletes during the 1970s and 1980s (Williams & Straub, 2006).

Coaches and athletes all know that physical skills need to be regularly practiced and refined through thousands and thousands of repetitions. Similar to physical skills, psychological skills such as maintaining and focusing concentration, regulating arousal levels, enhancing confidence, and maintaining motivation also need to be systematically practiced. In the example, Jim needed to practice the psychological skill of relaxation so he could deal with the pressure of shooting free throws under intense game pressure. Just telling an athlete to relax won't produce the desired response unless the player already knows how to relax through prior practice and training. Thus, guidelines have been developed to make mental training more effective.

Why PST Is Important

All sport and exercise participants fall victim to mental letdowns and mistakes. Which of the following sport and exercise experiences have you had or known others to have?

- You walked off a playing field in disgust after losing a game you believed you should have won.
- You choked at a critical point in a competition.
- You felt depressed because you weren't recovering quickly enough from an injury.
- You lacked the desire or motivation to exercise.
- Your mind wandered during a competition.
- You became angry and frustrated with your performance and put yourself down.

Chances are you have had at least one of the experiences on this list. Conversely, most sport performers also know what it feels like to be "in the zone," where everything seems to come together effortlessly and performance is exceptional. Mental and emotional components often overshadow and transcend the purely physical and technical aspects of performance.

The importance of mental skills is seen in the highly valued attribute of **mental toughness**. Olympic gold medalists perceived mental toughness as a crucial prerequisite of athletic success (Gould, Dieffenbach, & Moffett, 2002). Although mental toughness is defined in different ways, it usually has to do with an athlete's ability to focus, ability to rebound from failure, ability to cope with pressure, determination to persist in the face of adversity, and mental resilience (Bull, Shambrook, James, & Brooks, 2005; Crust & Clough, 2012; Gucciardi, Gordon, & Dimmock, 2008; Jones, Hanton, & Connaughton, 2002; Thelwell, Weston, & Greenlees, 2005). PST targets building and developing these mental skills, which are perceived to be critical for athletic success. For another view of mental toughness, see "Defining and Building Mental Toughness."

Most coaches consider sport to be at least 50% mental when competing against an opponent of similar ability, and certain sports (e.g., golf, tennis, and figure skating) are consistently viewed as 80% to 90% mental. Thus, as one coach noted, psychological testing can help identify each individual's psychological strengths and weaknesses, and then coaches can act on that knowledge by implementing an appropriate

Defining and Building Mental Toughness

Defining Mental Toughness

Studies have produced several different definitions of mental toughness, which has produced some conflict in the literature (e.g., Clough, Earle, Perry, & Crust, 2012; Gucciardi, Hanton, & Mallett, 2012). Jones and colleagues (2002), taking a qualitative approach, provided the first empirical data on what makes up mental toughness. These included the constructs of motivation, dealing with pressure, confidence, and concentration. Jones, Hanton, and Connaughton (2007) found that these attributes of mental toughness were employed before (e.g., goal setting), during (e.g., coping with pressure), and after (e.g., handling failure) competition.

Taking a more quantitative approach, Clough, Earle, and Sewell (2002) hypothesized four critical constructs in their 4C model defining mental toughness:

- *Control*—Handling many things at once; remaining influential rather than controlled
- *Commitment*—Being deeply involved with pursuing goals despite difficulties
- *Challenge*—Perceiving potential threats as opportunities for personal growth and thriving in constantly changing environments
- *Confidence*—Maintaining belief in the self despite setbacks

Gucciardi, Gordon, and Dimmock (2008, 2009) developed a scale for measuring mental toughness and focused on the situations requiring mental toughness (e.g., injury and rehabilitation, social pressure, environmental conditions, preparation for competition, internal pressures). In addition, Sheard, Golby, and van Wersch (2009) developed the Sport Mental Toughness Questionnaire, which includes the three subscales of confidence, constancy, and control. But controversy still exists about the measurement of mental toughness.

Harmison (2011) provided preliminary evidence of measuring mental toughness using a social-cognitive framework. This has a great deal of intuitive appeal and promise because mental toughness is seen as an interaction between the person and the environment. In essence, the individual and their perception of the situation will determine whether the individual acts in a mentally tough manner. For example, one athlete might perceive an upcoming championship game as a stressor, and another athlete might perceive it as a great opportunity. Their reactions, from a mental toughness perspective, would most likely be very different. Based on the athlete's perceptions of the situation, an athlete might be mentally tough in one competition but not in another or might even differ within a competition. Tiger Woods is a great example of an athlete who was seen as extremely mentally tough but whose mental toughness seems to have decreased after his personal hardships.

Building Mental Toughness

Researchers and practitioners have focused on how to build mental toughness. Some researchers (Connaughton, Thelwell, & Hanton, 2011; Connaughton, Wadey, Hanton, & Jones, 2008; Connaughton, Hanton, & Jones, 2010; MacNamara, Button, & Collins, 2010a,b) have found that athletes attribute their mental toughness to factors that are generally "caught" (i.e., not done deliberately to build mental toughness). These factors included sibling rivalries, supportive parents, coach expectations, a motivational training environment, teammate encouragement, tough practices, and coping with failure. Other researchers (Mallett & Coulter, 2011; Weinberg & Butt, 2011; Weinberg, Butt, & Culp, 2011) focused on what coaches actually do to enhance mental toughness (i.e., mental toughness is deliberately taught). The techniques included creating a positive motivational practice environment and intense competitive practices, creating simulations (pressure), setting specific goals, providing instructional and supportive feedback, building confidence through rigorous physical preparation and conditioning, enhancing attentional control through self-statements, and making appropriate attributions for success and failure.

training program (Leffingwell, Durand-Bush, Wurzberger, & Cada, 2005). Jimmy Connors, known for his mental tenacity and toughness, has often stated that professional tennis is 95% mental. Tiger Woods started his amazing run at winning the Masters by 18 strokes with a very poor first 9 holes. He said that after the disastrous first 9 holes, he knew he just needed to remain focused and get his mental game back together because it would be the key to his success. Still, many serious athletes allot 10 to 20 hours (or more) weekly to physical practice and little, if any, time to mental practice. This proportion doesn't make sense.

> **KEY POINT** Psychological factors account primarily for day-to-day fluctuations in performance.

A B tennis player usually plays against other B players who are similar in ability. Likewise, a nationally ranked swimmer probably competes against other high-caliber swimmers. Of course, athletes who compete against each other sometimes are clearly mismatched. In these cases, the outcome probably results from differences in physical skills and abilities. In most competitions, however, players win or lose depending on how they (and their opponents) perform that particular day. Physical ability being fairly equal, the winner is usually the athlete who has better mental skills.

The Summer and Winter Olympic Games demonstrate that minute differences result in gold, silver, and bronze medals or no medals at all. Swimmers "touch" another swimmer at the wall or runners simply hit the tape fractions of a second ahead of their opponent (as seen in Michael Phelps, who won a race by 1/100th of a second in the 2008 Olympics and lost another race by 1/100th of a second in the 2012 Olympics), gymnasts win or lose competitions by fractions of a point

Superior Performance Intelligence

Howard Gardner's (1983) classic work on **multiple intelligences** and Daniel Goleman's (1995) research on **emotional intelligence** have demonstrated the idea that different types of intelligences—not just one intelligence, traditionally measured by an intelligence quotient test—exist. Along these lines, Jones (2012) introduced the concept of **superior performance intelligence** to help explain sustained success in different performance domains (e.g., sport, military, business, or performing arts). Elite individuals in different domains were interviewed, and some common threads that make up superior performance intelligence were identified:

Knowing How to Maximize Your Potential

- Knowing yourself (knowing who you really are and what you are capable of doing)
- Stretching yourself (wanting to be the best, having a personal vision of success, belief in one's abilities to achieve success)
- Sustaining yourself (achieving good life balance, beginning with the end in mind, recovering from failure, celebrating success)

Knowing How to Work With Your Environment

- Knowing your environment (having a deep knowledge and awareness of the performance environment, especially which aspects are controllable and which are uncontrollable)
- Shaping your environment (ensuring that the people around you are committed to working together toward a common vision to deliver success)
- Being in tune with your environment (reacting quickly to changing circumstances, maintaining supportive relationships by staying humble)

Knowing How to Deliver High Performance

- Planning and preparing (being clear about what constitutes success, planning for every what-if situation, knowing and achieving your optimal emotional state)
- Delivering (performing under pressure, trusting your intuition, controlling the controllables, making crystal-clear decisions, knowing when to change the plan)
- Evaluating (comparing against measurement criteria, recognizing the positives as well as the negatives, identifying what needs work)

(maybe they took a step on a landing, for example), and downhill skiers often beat a competitor by less than a second to earn a medal. These very small differences in actual performance result in big differences in outcome (and medal counts). Most athletes and coaches would argue that these small differences are primarily "between the ears," yet little time is usually spent on this aspect of training. "Superior Performance Intelligence" highlights the importance of what goes on in an athlete's mind.

Why Sport and Exercise Participants Neglect PST

If psychological skills are so important for success, why do people spend so little time developing psychological skills in order to enhance performance? PST is neglected by many coaches and participants for three basic reasons: lack of knowledge, misunderstandings about psychological skills, and lack of time.

Lack of Knowledge

Many people don't really understand how to teach or practice psychological skills. For example, some coaches teach concentration by shouting, "Concentrate out there!" or "Will you get your mind on what you're supposed to be doing?" The implicit assumption is that the player knows how to concentrate but is just not doing it. Another common practice (remember Jim's errant free throws?) is telling a player to "just relax" as he goes into an important performance. But this is not easy to do unless one has had training in relaxation skills. A track and field coach would not expect a 100-meter runner to perform well in the 440 if she hadn't been running that distance in practice. Similarly, relaxation and concentration must be practiced to become effective tools one can use in competition. Coaches and teaching pros have told us that they simply do not feel comfortable teaching mental skills. They know about skill execution and technique (or "Xs and Os") but not about how to teach specific mental skills.

According to a survey, junior tennis coaches believed that they were fairly knowledgeable in sport psychology, although their knowledge of mental skills training did not come from books or formal courses. Rather, they were influenced by actual experience in working with players or attending clinics (Gould, Medbery, Damarjian, & Lauer, 1999a). Because researchers have not always conveyed their knowledge to practitioners, however, coaches have suggested that mental training information could be made more user friendly in several ways. The coaches suggested (a) developing "hands-on," concrete examples and exercises; (b) developing more mental skills training resources, particularly in audio and video formats; and

Sport Psychology at the Collegiate Level: Coach and Administrator Views

Two studies by Wrisberg and colleagues (Wrisberg, Loberg, Simpson, Withycombe, & Reed, 2010; Wrisberg, Withycombe, Simpson, Loberg, & Reed, 2012) examined coach and administrator views of using sport psychology consultants (SPC) at the NCAA Division I level and implementing PST with college athletes. Coaches were generally supportive of having their athletes seek mental training services from a qualified SPC for performance issues (e.g., anxiety, confidence, concentration) but less so for more personal issues (e.g., relationship problems, burnout, depression, homesickness). Administrators (e.g., athletic directors, presidents) also were more positive about using SPCs for help with performance issues compared with personal issues and saw many benefits of SPCs.

A qualitative study by Zakrajsek, Steinfeldt, Bodey, Martin, and Zizzi (2013) investigated what NCAA coaches felt were important for success as well as some of their concerns about using SPCs. Coaches defined a successful SPC as someone who is available and can fit into their schedule, can provide multiple contacts throughout the season, is active yet in the background (i.e., an observer in a supportive role), and is embedded in the team. Conversely, coaches' concerns included whether they would get enough time from the SPC, how they would pay the SPC, whether they would give up control to the SPC, and whether the SPC would put too many ideas into the athletes' heads (e.g., overthink).

Coaches were hesitant to hire full-time SPCs, citing finances as the major issue even though most universities generally have several full-time athletic trainers and strength and conditioning coaches, and studies in different countries have cited numerous barriers in hiring SPCs (Johnson, Andersson, & Falby, 2011; Pain & Harwood, 2004). Thus, it appears that the role that an SPC can play in both team and individual sports is not really understood or perceived as important.

(c) actively involving coaches in mental skills coach education programs (Gould, Medbery, Damarjian, & Lauer, 1999b). A study using imagery as the primary psychological skill (Callow, Roberts, Bringer, & Langan, 2010) revealed that coaches felt confident in delivering an imagery training session on their own after meeting individually with a sport psychology consultant (SPC) to learn about imagery and having an opportunity to devise and deliver an imagery session with feedback from the SPC.

The days of simply telling players, "Don't choke," "Get psyched up," "Be confident," "Stay loose," "Be mentally tough," or "Concentrate" are on their way out. We are learning that such advice requires action-oriented approaches and plans for improving mental skills.

Misunderstandings About Psychological Skills

People don't enter the world equipped with mental skills—it is a misconception that champions are born rather than made. Despite common assumptions that Serena Williams, Tiger Woods, Derek Jeter, Michael Phelps, Peyton Manning, and other such athletes were blessed with a congenital mental toughness and competitive drive as part of their personality, it doesn't quite work that way. Yes, we are all born with certain physical and psychological predispositions, but skills can be learned and developed, depending on the experiences we encounter. No great athlete ever achieved stardom without endless hours of practice, honing and refining physical skills and techniques. Although some athletes do possess exceptional physical skills, they had to work hard to develop their talents to become champions. For example, as physically talented and gifted as Michael Jordan was, his competitors said his most impressive trait was his competitiveness.

Lack of Time

A third reason that coaches and athletes cite for not practicing psychological skills is too little time. The study of junior tennis coaches noted earlier showed that the coaches saw lack of time as the most important roadblock to teaching mental skills to their players (Gould et al., 1999). Yet people reason that they lost a particular game or competition because "I wasn't up for the game today," "I just couldn't seem to concentrate," or "I got too tight and choked." You would think that if coaches thought their teams lost because of poor concentration, they would make time

to practice concentration skills. Instead they typically add time to physical practice.

Having noted the reasons that athletes cite for not practicing mental skills, research indicates that this is starting to change, although it depends somewhat on individual and task differences. Wrisberg and colleagues (2009, 2010) found an overall increase in athletes' openness to seeking out mental training. In particular, team-sport athletes were more interested in mental training that focused on group cohesion and team dynamics, whereas individual-sport athletes were interested in mental skills that would improve performance in practice and competition.

> **KEY POINT** Psychological skills training is often neglected because of a lack of knowledge, perceived lack of time, or a belief that psychological skills are innate and can't be taught.

Myths About PST

Several myths still circulate about the use of psychological techniques in optimizing performance. Research by Martin (2005) revealed that male athletes, younger athletes, and athletes who have been socialized in sports that involve physical contact still assign a particular stigma to sport psychology consulting. Unfortunately, many of these myths only confuse the issue of what SPC can and cannot do to help athletes maximize their performance.

Myth 1: PST Is for "Problem" Athletes Only

Many people wrongly think that all sport psychologists work with athletes who have psychological or clinical problems. This is simply not the case (see chapter 1). Rather, most athletes' psychological needs can be addressed by educational sport psychology specialists who focus on helping develop mental skills in athletes with a normal range of functioning. The following are some examples of the various PST needs addressed by educational and clinical sport psychology specialists.

Educational Sport Psychologists

- Goal setting
- Imagery
- Arousal regulation
- Concentration
- Mental preparation

Clinical Sport Psychologists

- Eating disorders
- Substance abuse
- Personality disorders
- Severe depression or anxiety
- Psychopathology

Myth 2: PST Is for Elite Training Only

PST is not only for the elite. It is appropriate for all athletes, including young, developing athletes (Chase, 2013) and special populations such as people who are mentally disabled or intellectually challenged (Gregg, 2013), physically challenged (Martin, 2013),

Conducting PST With Athletes With Intellectual or Physical Disabilities

Most research on PST has focused on the able-bodied athletic population. However, recent research has drawn attention to athletes with disabilities because these athletes are performing more and more in competition. Dieffenbach and Statler (2012) and Dieffenbach, Statler, and Moffett (2009) note that Paralympic athletes and coaches perceived high value in using mental skills, working with a sport psychologist, and simply learning more about how to apply mental skills effectively. They consistently rated concentration and confidence as the two most important mental skills. Overall, Paralympic athletes were seen as much more similar than dissimilar to Olympic athletes in terms of psychological factors affecting performance. The following are some suggestions for working with athletes with disabilities (Hanrahan, 2007):

Intellectual Disabilities

- The development of trust and rapport is critical.
- The sport psychologist must work at the individual's level of understanding.
- Soliciting help from relatives, case managers, or residential staff is important.
- Because an athlete with an intellectual disability may have certain cognitive deficits such as poor short-term memory and limited literacy or numerical skills, instructions should be kept simple, skills should be broken down into smaller teaching components, and sessions should be fun and enjoyable.

Physical Disabilities

- Ensure that venues are accessible.
- If working with a group of athletes in wheelchairs, improve communication by being at their level (e.g., in a chair).
- If the physical disability affects the control of muscles required for speech, be patient with verbal communication. Speak directly to the athlete even if a parent or other caretaker is present.
- Be careful of the temperature of the room because certain disabilities (e.g., spinal lesions) are negatively affected by certain temperatures.

Turnnidge, Vierimaa, and Cote (2012) used a model swim program to help teach positive values to young athletes with physical disabilities. Results revealed four distinct themes:

- *Refined capabilities.* Athletes learned new skills and refined their techniques.
- *Affirmed sense of self.* Athletes developed a stronger self-concept and enhanced sense of confidence.
- *Strengthened social connection.* Athletes made new friends and felt like part of a team.
- *Enhanced acceptance.* Athletes became more accepting of their own and others' disabilities.

One quote captures some of these themes:

Before I was a little tight cystic fibrosis kid. I could barely even move. I couldn't really fit in playing with other people . . . . Now, as I'm getting older and I've swam more, my right side basically isn't noticeable. Most people at school don't even know I have a disability. (p. 1134)

These positive outcomes were made possible due to three specific processes: positive peer interactions, positive coach–athlete relationships, and a welcoming team environment.

or hearing impaired (Vose, Clark, & Sachs, 2013). (See "Conducting PST With Athletes With Intellectual or Physical Disabilities.") Dedicated professionals work to help improve performance and personal growth. Popular magazines and news media tend to focus on Olympic and professional athletes who work with SPCs, but many other groups receive sport psychology consultation as well.

Myth 3: PST Provides "Quick Fix" Solutions

Many people mistakenly think that sport psychology offers a quick fix to psychological problems. Sometimes athletes and coaches expect to learn how to concentrate or to stay calm under pressure in one or two lessons. Actually, psychological skills take time and practice to develop. And PST is not magical—it won't turn an average player into a superstar. However, it will help athletes reach their potential and maximize their abilities.

Myth 4: PST Is Not Useful

Some people still think that sport psychology has nothing positive to offer. This is highlighted by the comment of former Wimbledon champion Goran Ivanisevic, who stated, "You lie on a couch, they take your money, and you walk out more bananas than when you walk in" (LeUnes & Nation, 2002, p. 18). However, substantial scholarly research, as well as anecdotal reports from athletes and coaches, indicates that psychological skills do in fact enhance performance (e.g., Greenspan & Feltz, 1989; Morris & Thomas, 2004; Weinberg & Comar, 1994). At the same time, the research also shows that effective PST efforts must be carried out in a systematic but individualized fashion, over time, using a variety of psychological techniques (Karageorghis & Terry, 2011; Meyers, Whelan, & Murphy, 1996). Sport psychology is neither a magical elixir nor useless bunk, and people should have realistic expectations of what PST can do.

KEY POINT Psychological skills can be learned, but they must be practiced over time and integrated into a person's daily training regimen.

PST Knowledge Base

PST has developed a knowledge base primarily from two sources: original research studies conducted with elite athletes, and the experience of coaches and athletes. Let's look at each of these sources.

Research on Elite Athletes

A number of studies have compared successful and less successful athletes in terms of their psychological skills and characteristics. Summarizing this research, Krane and Williams (2010) concluded that more successful athletes were characterized by higher confidence, greater self-regulation of arousal, better concentration and focus, an "in control but not forcing it" attitude, positive thoughts and imagery, and more determination and commitment. A conclusion was that successful athletes also achieved peak performance by using the mental skills of goal setting, imagery, arousal control and management, thought control, competitive plans, coping strategies, and mental preparation routines.

KEY POINT More successful players differ from less successful ones in how developed their psychological skills are.

Experiences of Athletes and Coaches

Increasingly, researchers are asking coaches and athletes about the content and core sport psychology topics to be included in PST programs. For example, Gould, Tammen, Murphy, and May (1991) surveyed elite coaches and athletes from the U.S. Olympic Committee's National Governing Body sport programs. The coaches and athletes rated relaxation training, concentration, imagery, team cohesion, concentration and attention training, and self-talk strategies as very important topics.

Studies with Olympic athletes (Gould, Guinan, Greenleaf, Medbery, & Peterson, 1999; Greenleaf, Gould, & Dieffenbach, 2001; Hodge, 2013) who performed up to potential (vs. those who did not) revealed that these athletes had developed plans for competition, performance evaluation, and dealing with disruptions. These athletes could overcome adversity and performance blocks by sticking to their plans and could channel performance anxiety and arousal positively. These Olympians who achieved peak performance demonstrated a total commitment to pursuing excellence by setting daily training goals, using simulations in practice to replicate competitive environments, and employing imagery to help focus attention and visualize successful outcomes. Finally,

Picture Alliance/Photoshot

The most successful athletes have plans for competition, performance evaluation, and dealing with disruptions.

13 of 15 Olympians interviewed by Greenleaf and colleagues (2001) indicated that they used PST. One athlete said, "I prepared mentally each and every day" (Greenleaf et al., 2001).

Interestingly, coaches also use psychological skills to help them perform their jobs more effectively. Elite coaches especially used the mental skills of imagery and self-talk (Thelwell, Weston, Greenlees, & Hutchings, 2008), both in training and during competition. Coaches used self-talk to overcome concerns in performance (to control emotions), to help plan sessions and pre- and postcompetition talks, to back up their judgments or give themselves confidence (reinforcement), and to get themselves in an appropriate frame of mind (instructions). Similarly, they used imagery to control emotions, to re-create experiences, to develop confidence, and to verbalize coaching points.

In summary, although individual program differences would exist, coaches and athletes would find these topics most useful in PST programs:

- Arousal regulation
- Imagery (mental preparation)
- Confidence building
- Increasing motivation and commitment (goal setting)
- Attention or concentration skills (self-talk, mental plans)
- Coping with injury

PST Effectiveness

Learning how effective PST programs can be in improving sport performance requires well-controlled, outcome-based intervention studies conducted in competitive environments. Greenspan and Feltz (1989) reviewed 23 published studies of the effectiveness of various psychological interventions (e.g., stress inoculation, imagery, relaxation, reinforcement, systematic desensitization) in many competitive settings. They concluded that, in general, educationally based psychological interventions improve competitive performance in collegiate and adult athletes. As a follow-up, Weinberg and Comar (1994) examined 45 studies using psychological interventions in competitive sport settings. Positive performance effects were apparent in 38 (85%) of the studies, although cause–effect relationships could be inferred in only 20 of them. A greater percentage of the more recent studies showed positive effects of psychological interventions (e.g., Fournier, Calmels, Durand-Bush, & Salmela, 2005); this is likely attributable to the more in-depth, multimodal approach taken in recent years, which combines different types of psychological skills (e.g., imagery, relaxation, self-talk, goal setting) in a packaged approach.

KEY POINT Psychological skills training that is educationally based enhances sport performance.

Compared with national-level athletes, international-caliber athletes use mental training more often and employ more elaborate and complex mental strategies and techniques (Calmels, d'Arripe-Longueville, Fournier, & Soulard, 2003). Applied sport psychologists have begun to understand that to be effective, a psychological intervention must be carried out in an individualized, systematic manner over time, often using a variety of psychological techniques to form an integrated program. For example, one's personality has been shown to affect the effectiveness of PST programs. Roberts and colleagues (2013) found that the personality trait of narcissism moderated the relationship between psychological skills and performance. Specifically, the use of emotional control strategies helped only those athletes low in narcissism, whereas self-talk and relaxation strategies did not help athletes low in narcissism.

Along these lines, research has investigated implementing PST programs from an SPC perspective (Sharp & Hodge, 2011) so that individual differences are taken into consideration. Although knowledge of mental skills training was seen as an important attribute for an effective consultant, many other things made SPCs effective:

- *Building a connection with athletes*—Developing connections with athletes enables the SPC to educate athletes and lead them toward positive changes in behavior.

- *Building a professional consulting relationship*—Effective SPCs are empathetic, accepting, open, approachable, and maintain professionalism at all times.

- *Meeting athletes' needs*—Effective SPCs balance professional knowledge and relationship skills in order to meet the needs of the athletes.

Although the focus was on the SPC, it was emphasized that athletes need to be active participants in the process. In essence, they need to demonstrate commitment and openness to building a relationship with the SPC.

Three Phases of PST Programs

Although PST programs take many forms to match participants' individual needs, they generally follow a set structure with three distinct phases: education, acquisition, and practice. We now discuss what each of these phases involves.

Education Phase

Because many sport participants are unfamiliar with how mental skills can enhance performance, the first phase of any PST program is educational. In the **education phase**, participants quickly recognize how important it is to acquire psychological skills and how the skills affect performance. The usual way to accomplish this is simply by asking participants how important they think the mental side of sport performance is. Most will say that it is very important. The next question to ask is "How often do you practice developing mental skills compared with practicing physical skills?" Usually the answer is "Hardly ever." The next step is to explain how psychological skills can be learned, just like physical skills.

The education phase may last for as little as an hour or for as long as several hours over the course of a few days. This might depend in part on individual differences in actually using PST. Research has revealed that, for example, individuals higher on task orientation integrate more mental skills into their training than do those higher in ego orientation (Harwood, Cumming, & Fletcher, 2004). Explain the importance of developing psychological skills. For example, in teaching the skill of regulating arousal states, you would explain the causes of anxiety and the relationship between arousal and performance. You would tell athletes to learn to find their own optimal level of arousal (see chapter 4). Some arousal is desirable, but skilled athletes have learned how to turn this tension or anxiety into positive energy instead of living with debilitating tension that can deter performance. Give players you work with examples of well-known athletes in the particular sport to reinforce the importance of developing mental skills.

Finally, top mental training consultant Ken Ravizza (2001) emphasizes that an important part of the education phase involves increasing athlete awareness of the role that mental skills play in performance. Ravizza does this in a highly innovative way by having athletes regularly use a traffic light analogy to think about their performance in three ways: green light, yellow light, and red light situations. In green light situations, the athlete is performing well and, as when driving a car, functions without a lot of awareness (automatic pilot). In yellow light performance situations, the athlete is struggling and needs to beware of destructive thoughts and the ways they can interfere with performance. In these situations, the athlete needs to use refocusing strategies to get back on track. Finally, in red light situations, the athlete is in real trouble and performing very poorly. Major coping strategies are needed in such cases, or, if a performance catastrophe (see chapter 4) has occurred, the athlete may need to come out of the contest, get totally relaxed, and then reactivate. By becoming aware of green, yellow, and red light situations, athletes learn how to monitor their mental states.

Acquisition Phase

The **acquisition phase** focuses on strategies and techniques for learning the various psychological skills. For the development of arousal regulation skills, for example, formal meetings might focus on replacing negative self-statements that surface under stressful competitive conditions with positive coping statements. You would follow these formal sessions with individual sessions to teach athletes how to use positive coping in actual competitive settings. Here you would tailor specific strategies to an athlete's unique needs and abilities (Seabourne, Weinberg, Jackson, & Suinn, 1985). For example, anxiety reduction strategies should be matched to the specific problem the individual is experiencing (Maynard, Smith, & Warwick-Evans, 1995). One athlete might worry too much about failure (cognitive anxiety): For this athlete, a cognitively based strategy for changing thought patterns might be most appropriate (Meichenbaum, 1977). Another athlete might suffer from increased muscle tension (somatic anxiety): In this case, a physically based relaxation technique, such as progressive relaxation (Jacobson, 1938), could be the best choice.

KEY POINT Psychological skills should be learned—and practiced. People should expect improvement as they develop these skills and refine them over time.

Practice Phase

The **practice phase** has three primary objectives: to automate skills through overlearning, to teach people to systematically integrate psychological skills into their performance situations, and to simulate skills people will want to apply in actual competition.

To develop skills in arousal regulation, for example, an athlete would begin the practice phase after becoming proficient in relaxation and cognitive coping skills. You could guide the athlete through an imagined competitive situation requiring relaxation and coping skills. During the practice phase, a performer might progress from guided imagery practice to self-directed imagery to the use of imagery in a practice session, as if it were a real competition. Finally, the athlete would incorporate arousal control strategies into preparing for and participating in actual competitions.

During the practice phase, it is helpful for athletes to keep a logbook in which they record the frequency and perceived effectiveness of the arousal control strategies used in practice and competition. A log helps to systematically chart progress and provides feedback for areas of improvement. For example, after every practice, athletes record how tense they felt, what relaxation procedure they used, and whether their relaxation techniques helped.

Self-Regulation: The Ultimate Goal of PST

The ultimate goal of PST is to have athletes effectively function on their own without needing constant direction from a coach or sport psychologist. Thus, after PST an athlete should be able to self-regulate her internal functioning in the desired manner and successfully adapt to changes in the world around her. The ability to work toward one's short- and long-term goals by effectively monitoring and managing one's thoughts, feelings, and behaviors has been termed **self-regulation**.

Figure 11.1 depicts a five-stage model of athlete self-regulation developed by Kirschenbaum (1984). This model begins with *problem identification*—that is, the ability to identify a problem, determine that change is possible and desirable, and take responsibility for its solution. In the example given at the opening of this chapter, Jim must recognize and accept his inability to hit shots in critical game situations because he becomes too nervous and lacks confidence.

Mental Skills Training: From Sport to Business and Life

More and more SPCs are transferring their skills to a variety of business and work environments, working with different professionals such as astronauts, physicians, police officers, firefighters, financial consultants, and dancers (Hays, 2012; Weinberg, 2010b). In fact, a special issue of *Journal of Applied Sport Psychology* (2001) was devoted to applying sport psychology principles to other arenas. Furthermore, a few companies have begun with professionals with sport psychology knowledge and background (working with teams and athletes) and then transferred these skills to focus on the business sector. Along these lines, many corporations have hired successful coaches and athletes to talk to their employees about becoming more mentally tough and staying motivated. For example, coaches and athletes such as Rick Pitino, Lou Holtz, Pat Riley, Pat Summitt, Michael Phelps, and Phil Jackson have been hired as motivational speakers in the corporate sector. Most speakers bring in their own particular philosophy, which usually has a catchy acronym. For example, Pat Riley uses the acronym TEAM (*t*ogetherness, *e*steem, *a*ttitude, and *m*ental toughness). The implicit assumption is that these qualities would transfer appropriately from the athletic field to the corporate setting. Fletcher (2012) provides many references for those interested in pursuing the link between sport and business.

Gould and colleagues (Gould & Carson, 2010, 2011; Gould, Collins, Lauer, & Chung, 2007; Gould, Flett, & Lauer, 2012; Gould & Wright, 2012) conducted several studies investigating how coaches teach to enhance life skills in addition to sport skills. These life skills include personal skills (e.g., organization, goal setting, coping with pressure) as well as social skills (e.g., respect, communication, leadership). It was clear that these coaches did not view the coaching of life skills as separate from their general coaching strategies for performance enhancement. Athletes appear to develop transferable life skills when their coaches have a philosophy that places primary importance on life skills and development, create positive coach–athlete relationships, and create mastery-oriented and caring climates. However, these findings should be tempered by the fact that although most coaches believe that life skills are developed via sport participation, few make intentional efforts to specifically teach these skills.

Sport and performance psychology have been tremendously applied in the military. As Janelle and Hatfield (2008) note, although the magnitude of stressors present in military situations is often greater than that in sport, issues surrounding preperformance preparation and training, decision making, attitudes, motivation, sustained concentration, stress regulation, teamwork, leadership, and situational awareness are critical to both arenas. The Army Center for Enhanced Performance was established to develop educational programs that help soldiers learn mental tools and skills and apply them to a variety of tasks in realistic training environments (DeWiggins, Hite, & Alston, 2010). A number of sport psychology graduate students have found employment in the military, teaching the mental skills they learned in sport psychology academic programs. SPCs are also being hired by military special forces units (e.g., Navy Seals) to help improve the members of special forces' mental preparation.

Andersen (2000) noted that psychological skills can also be used for a variety of purposes outside of performance concerns, such as coping with injuries, transitions out of sport, and personal issues. The following are some examples of using PST techniques and principles in aspects of sport besides performance:

- A physical educator might use relaxation training to teach a hyperactive child to learn to calm down.

- An athletic trainer might use mental imagery to help rebuild confidence in an athlete rehabilitating from a knee injury.

- A physical therapist might use goal setting to help maintain motivation for an individual with a prolonged, serious injury.

- A fitness instructor might use positive self-statements to enhance self-esteem in a client who is overweight.

Recognizing the problem, however, is not sufficient. Jim must make a *commitment* to change (stage 2) and deal with obstacles, such as slowness of progress and the need for regular practice of mental skills, that will arise during the change process. The primary stage of self-regulation is *execution* (stage 3). In this stage Jim will need to self-evaluate, self-monitor, develop appropriate expectancies, and self-reinforce as he learns to cope effectively with stress and to shoot more accurately under pressure. Thus, he might log or film his games and then, when watching the video, rate his anxiety levels while taking key shots and reward himself for improvements. In this stage it is especially important to sustain efforts when setbacks occur. *Environmental management*—planning and deriving strategies for managing the social and physical environment (e.g., coaches, spectators, teammates) that affects the athlete—is the fourth stage of self-regulation. Here Jim might plan on regularly seeing the SPC who is helping him (maximize social support) and making sure he has a quiet place in the dorm to practice his relaxation exercises. Finally, the *generalization* stage involves sustaining efforts over time and extending behaviors to new conditions and settings. Jim, for example, might use the same psychological skills that he successfully learned in basketball to help him deal with the anxiety he has while taking academic tests.

The majority of researchers who have examined whether various self-regulation strategies improve performance have found that these strategies do indeed help performance and facilitate positive thoughts and feeling states (Crews, Lochbaum, & Karoly, 2000). One interesting study was conducted by Kirschenbaum, Owens, and O'Connor (1998), who examined the effectiveness of Smart Golf, a self-regulation training program based on Kirschenbaum's (1984) model, on the performance of five experienced golfers. Specifically, in an 8-hour seminar the golfers learned principles of mental preparation, positive focusing (self-monitoring), and self-regulation. Very practical means were used to implement these principles, such as an expanded golf scorecard that included spaces to assess not only normal performance scores but also critical self-regulation information such as planning and positive self-focusing. Similarly, participants were taught the acronym PAR (**p**lan, **a**pply, **r**eact) for remembering three critical self-regulation components. As predicted, all five golfers improved their emotional control and positive self-talk as well as their golf performance relative to average score and handicap.

Who Should Conduct PST Programs

Ideally, a PST program should be planned, implemented, and supervised by a qualified SPC. However, except at the highest level of competition, it is often not feasible to have a consultant administer the program. Usually an SPC sets up the program and then either monitors it periodically or trains the coaching staff to implement it.

The selection of a qualified SPC is critical. In 1991, the Association for Applied Sport Psychology (AASP) adopted certification criteria for applied sport psychologists. Certification requires a person to have extensive backgrounds in both the sport and psychological sciences and some practical, supervised experience in implementing PST with athletes and teams. Certification by AASP ensures a certain level of experience, background, and competence in applied sport psychology. The U.S. Olympic Committee now requires sport psychologists to have AASP certification to practice applied sport psychology with Olympic athletes. However, also important is the fit between the skills, abilities, and orientations of the SPC and the needs and goals of the sport coaches and athletes.

Coaches, of course, see athletes daily, whereas a sport psychologist does not. Thus coaches are in a position to

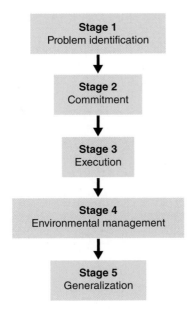

FIGURE 11.1 Kirschenbaum's five-stage model of self-regulation.

Stage 1
Problem identification

Stage 2
Commitment

Stage 3
Execution

Stage 4
Environmental management

Stage 5
Generalization

administer psychological interventions over the course of a season. However, the dual role of a coach–sport psychologist can present an ethical dilemma. Specifically, an athlete might have difficulty revealing very personal information that the sport psychologist–coach might perceive negatively (i.e., the coach is in a position to determine the playing time of the athlete). Therefore, the coaching and sport psychologist roles should be separated whenever possible (Burke & Johnson, 1992).

Many athletes either have no access to a mental training specialist or cannot afford one. To help athletes get around these barriers, Weinberg, Neff, and Jurica (2012) developed a method for providing online mental training that (a) is affordable, (b) is Internet based, (c) is fully automated, (d) generates individualized mental training programs, (e) is taught by sport psychology experts, (f) follows best practices in mental training, and (g) provides useful tools that enhance individual program success (e.g., PowerPoint presentations with voiceovers, interviews with sport psychology professionals, whiteboard presentations of mental skills, and simulations of different scenarios) along with innovative coach and parent education programs. In addition, a smartphone app has been developed that allows athletes to download mental training programs onto their phones.

When to Implement a PST Program

It is best to initiate a PST program during the off-season or preseason, when there is more time to learn new skills and athletes are not so pressured about winning. Some athletes report that it can take several months to a year to fully understand new psychological skills and integrate them into actual competitions. Mental training is an ongoing process that needs to be integrated with physical practice over time. Many coaches and athletes want to start a PST program in the middle of the season, usually because of some precipitating situation, such as a batter in a hitting slump. They become desperate to find a solution. However, mental training in such a situation is rarely effective. Thomas, Maynard, and Hanton (2007) did demonstrate that elite athletes who integrated mental skills into their training regimens 1 week before a match showed enhanced performance and self-confidence, decreased anxiety, and more positive interpretation of anxiety symptoms. However, in this situation, the athletes engaged in intensive mental skills training 5 to 7 days before competition, 1 or 2 days before competition, and on the day of competition, for a total of almost 20 hours of mental practice. Such training, although possible in dedicated, high-level athletes, is likely not feasible in most situations.

As already noted, the time needed for practicing mental skills varies according to what is being practiced and how well it is to be learned. If a new psychological skill is being learned, special 10- to 15-minute training sessions 3 to 5 days a week may be necessary. The first or last 10 to 15 minutes of practice is often a good time for training. As athletes become more proficient, they may be able to integrate the mental training more with physical training and may need fewer special training sessions. Once athletes have effectively integrated a skill into physical practice, they should try using it during simulated competition before using it during actual competition.

PST for Adolescent Athletes

Most PST programs are developed for and implemented with collegiate and elite athletes. However, a program called UNIFORM (**u**se goal setting, **n**o mistakes, **i**magery, **f**ully focused, **o**vertly positive, **r**elaxation and stress control, **m**ake routines) was developed for younger, less skilled athletes in high school and community college. The UNIFORM program is delivered via the Game Plan format (Gilbert et al., 2006) whereby student-athletes are divided into teams and are given conditioning (discussion about the mental skill and applied activities), practice (homework), games (quizzes), statistics (individual and team quiz scores), films (short movie clips demonstrating skill use), and playbooks (journal entries about using the skill). This approach helps athletes make connections between sport and using sport psychology skills.

Empirical research revealed that the UNIFORM approach enabled these younger athletes to learn psychological skills and apply them during practice, competition, and everyday life. Results also indicated that athletes enjoyed the intervention and significantly increased their application of goal setting and relaxation during practice and their use of relaxation, imagery, and self-talk during competition (Gilbert, 2011; Horn, Gilbert, Gilbert, & Lewis, 2011).

If an SPC (who is typically not present daily) implements the training, some scheduling adjustments may be necessary. Under such circumstances, it is usual to hold fewer and longer mental training sessions. SPCs typically start with some group sessions to explain general principles and their philosophy. They then follow up by meeting athletes individually (Vealey, 2007). It is critical that athletes be assigned training exercises to practice between meetings with the SPC. The coach can help ensure compliance and feedback by conducting the training exercises—or at least providing time for athletes to practice.

Ideally, PST continues as long as athletes participate in their sport. Rory McIlroy, Sue Bird, Lorena Ochoa, Roger Federer, Greg Maddux, and Peyton Manning—all highly skilled and physically talented athletes—have all been known for continually integrating the mental aspects of their sports into physical practice.

Although PST is an ongoing process, an athlete's first exposure to PST in a formal program should last 3 to 6 months. Learning, practicing, and integrating new mental skills require this much time. The specific sport, time available, existing mental skills, and commitment of the participants also are factors in determining how much time to allot to the formal program.

PST Program Development

You have learned why PST is important, who should conduct the program, when to implement it during the season, and how much time to spend on it. We now outline some key aspects of developing and implementing PST programs.

Discussing Your Approach

Describe to participants exactly what kind of PST services can be provided. Explain the distinction between educational and clinical SPCs. PST is an educational approach to mental training. Explain that if more serious mental problems occur (e.g., substance abuse, eating disorders), the SPC will make a referral to a qualified therapist or counseling center.

Emphasizing the educational approach also helps dispel the idea that seeing an SPC means something must be "wrong" with a person. You can explain that most people applaud the extra effort of an athlete who stays after practice to work with the coach on a particular move or to improve technique. Similarly, an athlete recognizing the need to work on concentration skills should also be applauded.

Characteristics of Effective and Ineffective SPCs

By interviewing athletes, researchers (Gould, Tammen, Murphy, & May, 1991; Orlick & Partington, 1987; Partington & Orlick, 1987) found consistent characteristics of effective and ineffective SPCs.

Effective consultants
- were accessible and could establish rapport with athletes,
- were flexible and knowledgeable enough to meet the needs of individual athletes,
- were likable and had something very concrete or practical to offer,
- conducted several follow-up sessions with athletes throughout the season, and
- were trustworthy and fit in with the team.

Ineffective consultants
- had poor interpersonal skills,
- lacked sensitivity to the needs of individual athletes,
- lacked specific psychology knowledge to apply to the sport setting,
- demonstrated inappropriate application of consulting skills at competitions, and
- relied on a "canned" approach when implementing psychological skills.

In discussing your approach, you need to establish trust and begin to build a quality relationship with athletes. The effectiveness of PST is closely tied to the quality of the relationship between the athlete and the sport psychologist (Andersen & Speed, 2013; Petitpas, Giges, & Danish, 1999). Use the communication guidelines discussed in chapter 10 to enhance your relationships with the athletes and exercisers with whom you work.

◉ **VIEW** Activity 11.1 helps you consider what PST skills you think are most important to athletic performance.

Assessing Athletes' Mental Skills

In first evaluating athletes' psychological strengths and weaknesses, bear in mind that not only psychological factors influence performance. A baseball player, for example, may attribute his slump to being overly anxious when in reality his problem is biomechanical, relating to a hitch in his swing. Thus, input from coaches, biomechanists, physiologists, and teachers is often useful. Two clues that an athlete might benefit from mental training are that the athlete performs better in practice than in competition or performs more poorly in important competitions than in unimportant ones.

An oral interview and written psychological inventories can provide useful subjective and objective information. Taylor (1995) summarized the strengths and limitations of both subjective and objective assessments in evaluating athletes' mental skills (table 11.1). In addition, Beckman and Kellmann (2003) discussed the factors that sport psychologists should consider before administering questionnaires and other formal assessments to athletes. These include the reliability

TABLE 11.1 Assessing Athletes' Needs

Type	Strengths	Limitations
Subjective assessment		
Interviewing (client)	• Establishes trust and rapport • Reveals self-perceptions, beliefs, and attitudes • Provides in-depth knowledge about sport participation and life issues	• Includes self-presentational bias • Is affected by lack of self-awareness • Is affected by poor insight
Interviewing (others)	• Provides new perspective of athlete • Establishes consensus	• Involves subjectivity bias • Is affected by alternative agenda
Observation	• Provides unambiguous behavioral data • Enables comparison of behavioral with expressed perceptions • Reveals patterns of behavior • Reveals relationship between practice and competitive performance • Provides cross-situational consistency	• Includes observer bias • Depends on representativeness of observed behaviors • Is affected by observational time limitations
Objective assessment		
Sport specific	• Provides impartial evaluation	• Is affected by resistance from athlete
General	• Confirms subjective assessment	• Is hampered by self-presentational bias • Uses non-sport-specific inventories
Trait versus state	• Assesses sport-specific issues • Uncovers new issues • Uses time efficiently • Provides ease of administration	• Uses nondiagnostic inventories • Lacks a relationship with performance • Measures only traits • Has restricted test usage

Adapted, by permission, from J. Taylor, 1995, "A conceptual model for integrating athletes' needs and sport demands in the development of competitive mental preparation strategies," *The Sport Psychologist* 9(3): 342.

and validity of the questionnaire, the usefulness of the questionnaire as seen by the athletes, and the honesty that athletes show in completing the questionnaire. Furthermore, Singer and Anshel (2006) provided some guidelines and ethical concerns regarding using psychological tests in a mental skills training program. The exact format and integration of objective and subjective assessments depend on the expertise of the sport psychologist as well as the rapport and trust between the athlete and the sport psychologist. However, in general, we recommend the semistructured interview, which includes general questions and opportunities to use the athlete's responses to form follow-up questions (Orlick, 2000). The interview is a good time to determine the areas in which the athlete needs help and to start building the trust critical to any therapeutic relationship. The following are sample interview items:

- Tell me about your involvement in your sport, summarizing what you consider important events, both positive and negative. (This is a good starting point because it lets athletes talk about themselves and become comfortable.)

- Describe in detail the thoughts and feelings surrounding your best and worst performances. What do you believe is your greatest psychological strength? Your biggest weakness?

- Try to describe any psychological problems you are having now. What is your relationship with your coach? Do you feel comfortable talking to your coach?

In addition, as noted by Simons (2013), an SPC should ask who, what, when, how, and where questions on the initial interview, but not why questions. The client may not know the answer to why questions and thus be embarrassed and confused, or the answer to a why question might cause emotional conflict and cause the client to withdraw. It is important to build a strong relationship and rapport with the client at the outset.

You may also try using some psychological inventories to assess various skills. Woodcock, Duda, Cumming, Sharp, and Holland (2012) provided recommendations for effective psychometric assessments that help practitioners more accurately assess athletes' mental skills. These are some of the most popular assessments with SPCs:

- Test of Attentional and Interpersonal Style (Nideffer, 1976b; Nideffer, Segal, Lowry, & Bond, 2001)

- Sport Anxiety Scale (Smith, Smoll, & Schutz, 1990)
- Test of Performance Strategies (Thomas, Murphy, & Hardy, 1999)
- Trait–State Confidence Inventory (Vealey, 1986)

Some sport- and situation-specific inventories have also been developed, such as the Baseball Test of Attentional and Interpersonal Style (Albrecht & Feltz, 1987), the Officials Stress Test (Goldsmith & Williams, 1992), and the Gymnastics Efficacy Measure (McAuley, 1985). Along these lines, Dosil (2006) provided specific information for implementing mental skills training programs for different sports. Although there are certain similarities in mental skills training programs for specific sports, programs can differ somewhat depending on the exact nature of the sport. For example, golf is a closed sport that is very predictable and not time stressed, whereas soccer is an open sport with lots of uncontrolled factors and is time stressed. Thus, you can have golfers work on their thinking process between shots because there is lots of time, whereas soccer players need to react quickly to changing conditions and cannot do as much thinking while on the playing field. In addition to evaluating the athlete's mental skills, you should consider the unique physical, technical, and logistical demands of the sport itself in order to maximize the effectiveness of the psychological intervention (Taylor, 1995). For example, sports that involve explosiveness and anaerobic output (e.g., the 100-meter dash) differ greatly from those that require endurance and aerobic output (e.g., marathon running). Sports that rely on fine motor skills (e.g., archery) differ from ones involving gross motor skills (e.g., powerlifting).

Along these lines, throughout the consultation process it is important to observe athletes during both practice and competition. These observations provide the consultant with important information regarding how the athlete reacts in different situations and demonstrates the consultant's commitment to the athlete, thus building the relationship between consultant and athlete. Watson and Shannon (2013) provide excellent guidelines for conducting systematic observations, including when, where, and what to observe for both individual- and team-sport athletes.

DISCOVER Activity 11.2 gives you experience in assessing psychological skills.

VIEW Activity 11.3 lets you complete your own performance profile.

Performance Profiling: Individualizing Psychological Interventions

The technique of performance profiling has been developed to both identify important PST objectives and help maximize the motivation of athletes to implement and adhere to a PST program (Butler & Hardy, 1992; Jones, 1993). A recent comprehensive review of performance profiling found that although the strategy does have some limitations, the literature clearly supports its usefulness for coaches, athletes, and sport psychologists (Weston, Greenlees, & Thelwell, 2010, 2011). Areas of change (e.g., improving concentration and coping with pressure) are identified by the athlete, so this approach provides a degree of self-determination not always evident in some other approaches to PST. For example, a female volleyball player might be asked to identify the characteristics or qualities of elite female volleyball players. The volleyball player would list all the qualities on paper (this could also be done with teams; one would ask athletes to generate qualities of elite athletes through brainstorming in small groups). The player would then rate herself on all the qualities she identified, and her responses would be translated into a performance profile (figure 11.2), providing a visual representation of the player's strengths and potential areas of improvement.

Empirical research has investigated the benefits of performance profiling from the perspectives of both athletes and sport psychologists (Weston, Greenlees, & Thelwell, 2011). From the SPC perspective, performance profiling

- provides a basis for goal setting;
- identifies athletes' mental strengths and weaknesses;
- raises athlete awareness;
- evaluates and monitors athlete performance; and
- facilitates discussion, communication, and interaction in teams.

From an athlete perspective, performance profiling

- raises athletes' self-awareness,
- helps athletes decide what to work on,
- motivates athletes to improve,
- helps athletes set goals for themselves,
- monitors and evaluates athletes' performance, and
- helps athletes take more responsibility for their own development.

Once the interview and psychological inventories have been completed, the evaluator should give feedback to each athlete to highlight her specific psychological strengths and weaknesses in sport performance. This assessment should conclude with a section identifying the types of psychological skills appropriate for each athlete. Athletes should have the opportunity to react to the consultants' evaluations and to agree on how to proceed. If an SPC works with an entire team, the coach, who is more likely to know the team's mental strengths and weaknesses, also should be involved in the assessment.

KEY POINT Tailor training programs to meet individual needs. You can provide general information to the group or team, but you should be specific when developing an individual's PST program.

Determining Which Psychological Skills to Include

After the assessment comes the decision about which psychological skills to emphasize during the program. This decision should be based on the coaches' and athletes' answers to these questions:

- How many weeks of practice or preseason are available?

- How much practice time will be devoted weekly to PST?

- How interested are the athletes in receiving PST?

- Will there still be time to practice mental skills after the competitive season begins?

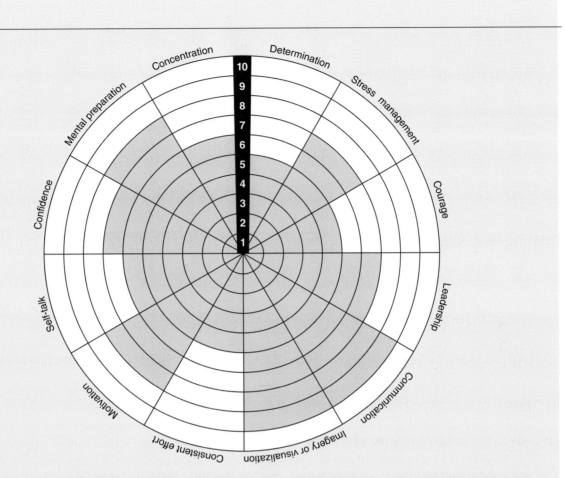

FIGURE 11.2 A performance profile. Darkened sections indicate the degree to which an athlete believes he or she has the mental skills of top performers in the sport.

Adapted, by permission, from R. Butler and L. Hardy, 1992, "The performance profile: Theory and application," *The Sport Psychologist* 6(3): 257.

When sufficient time and commitment are not available for a comprehensive training program, it is best to prioritize objectives and emphasize a few skills initially rather than superficially working on all the needed skills. A model proposed by Vealey (2007), developed from research over the past 25 to 30 years, emphasizes the development of mental skills to achieve performance success as well as personal well-being. This model emphasizes that multiple types of mental skills are important for success and well-being in coaches and athletes, including foundation, performance, personal development, and team skills.

- *Foundation skills* are intrapersonal resources that are the basic mental skills necessary to achieve success. These skills include the following:

  o Achievement drive
  o Self-awareness
  o Productive thinking
  o Self-confidence

- *Performance skills* are mental abilities critical to the execution of skills during sport performance. These skills include the following:

  o Energy management
  o Attentional focus
  o Perceptual-motor skill

- *Personal development skills* are mental skills that represent significant maturational markers of personal development allowing for high-level psychological functioning through clarity of self-concept, feelings of well-being, and

a sense of relatedness to others. These skills include the following:
- o Identity achievement
- o Interpersonal competence
- *Team skills* are collective qualities of the team that are instrumental to an effective team climate and overall team success. These skills include the following:
  - o Leadership
  - o Cohesion
  - o Team confidence

Based on R. Vealey, 1988, "Future directions in psychological skills training," *The Sport Psychologist* 2(4): 326.

Designing a Schedule

Needs have been assessed, psychological skill objectives have been identified, and specific strategies for achieving the objectives have been delineated. Now

comes the training schedule. Before or after practice 1 or 2 days a week might serve as a formal meeting time for educating participants on various other psychological skills. In general, it is better to hold frequent, short meetings rather than less frequent, long meetings. Informal meetings can occur during social events, on bus or plane rides to competitions, at the hotel, at meals, or at any other time and place. These informal meetings complement the structured meetings and individualize content to each athlete.

KEY POINT Formal and informal meetings with coaches and athletes are opportunities for the PST consultant to enhance communication and build rapport.

A critical point in setting up a training schedule is determining when to start and how long the training should last. As we noted earlier, it is best to develop

Olympic Sport Psychologists' Top Ten Guiding Principles for Mental Training

1. *Mental training can't replace physical training.* An athlete needs to be talented and well prepared physically for competition.

2. *Physical training and physical ability are not enough to succeed consistently.* Mental training needs to supplement physical training for consistent success.

3. *A strong mind may not win an Olympic medal, but a weak mind will lose you one.* Although mentally strong athletes do not always win medals due to a variety of conditions (e.g., health, training), athletes with a weak mental game virtually never win at the biggest competitions.

4. *Coaches frequently don't know what their athletes are thinking.* Although most coaches know athletes' behavior and know that psychological factors are important for competition success, few are aware of an athlete's mental state before and during competition.

5. *Thoughts affect behavior. Consistency of thinking = consistency of behavior.* Understanding and controlling the thinking process help athletes control their behavior.

6. *Coaches have a different view of changing technical mistakes versus mental mistakes.* Coaches work with athletes for years trying to fix technical errors but don't spend nearly as much time helping with mental errors.

7. *Coaches must be involved in the mental training process.* Although they don't have to be the prime provider of mental training, coaches need to be involved and support mental training for their athletes.

8. *Sometimes it is OK to force athletes to take the time to do mental training.* Just as coaches "force" athletes to work on certain technical skills, at times it is appropriate to "force" athletes to work on certain mental skills.

9. *Like any other skill, mental skills need to be measured in order to maximize performance of these skills.* "What gets measured gets done." This saying applies to training mental skills just as much as it applies to training physical skills.

10. *Coaches need to think about their own mental skills.* Coaches can benefit from the same mental skills that help their athletes because they too need to deal with pressure, maintain confidence, and keep their attention focused.

Adapted from McCann 2008.

psychological skills just before the season begins or during the off-season, but the key is to systematically schedule PST as part of the daily practice regimen. Holliday and colleagues (2008) have proposed a systematic periodization approach to the development of mental skills, similar to the periodization model used to train physical skills for many sports. Periodization refers to planned variation in key training variables, particularly volume and intensity, over predetermined training cycles. The aim is to maximize long-term development and peak performance for targeted competitions while minimizing training problems such as burnout, overtraining, and injury. Periodization has been proposed as a method for training mental skills through the preparatory, competitive, and peaking phases. This is an example for a golfer:

• *Preparatory phase:* The golfer performs high-volume, low-intensity imagery exercises every day, focusing on improving imagery vividness and controllability or making small swing adjustments in his mind.

• *Competitive phase:* The golfer performs imagery less frequently (i.e., decreased volume). He now images himself on the tee box, fairway, and green instead of imaging himself playing away from the golf course (e.g., at the driving range). In addition, golf-related imagery predominates (e.g., the golfer focuses on developing effective course management strategies) (increased intensity).

• *Peaking phase:* The golfer imagines himself performing the actual holes he will play in specific tournaments against key opponents (i.e., high intensity).

Evaluating the Program

Evaluating psychological skills development and change is an important but often overlooked element of PST programs. There are ethical obligations in evaluating the effectiveness of the program (Smith, 1989) but practical considerations as well:

• An evaluation provides feedback for gauging the program's effectiveness and for then modifying the program as necessary.

• An evaluation allows participants to suggest changes in how the program is conducted.

• An evaluation is the only way to objectively judge whether the program has achieved its goals.

Ideally, the evaluation should include interviews and written rating scales to supply both qualitative and quantitative feedback. Also useful to coaches and athletes are objective performance data. For example, if one of the program goals was to help a basketball player relax while shooting free throws under pressure, then free-throw percentage in critical situations (e.g., last 5 minutes of a game when there is less than a 5-point difference in the score) would be a good statistic for evaluation. The following questions are useful for evaluating the effectiveness of a PST program:

• What techniques appeared to work best?

• Was enough time allotted to practice the psychological skills?

• Was the consultant available?

• Was the consultant knowledgeable, informative, and easy to talk with?

• Should anything be added to or deleted from the program?

• What were the major strengths and weaknesses of the program?

Common Problems in Implementing PST Programs

By attending to some common problems that athletes, coaches, and consultants have encountered in implementing PST programs, you can enhance your program's effectiveness. We've already touched on some of these problems in various contexts. Here are some specific examples.

• *Lack of conviction.* Consultants often have to convince coaches and athletes that developing psychological skills will facilitate success. One good selling point is the example of highly visible athletes known for their psychological skills. For example, Tiger Woods has often remarked about the importance of imagery and mental training in his approach to golf.

• *Lack of time.* Coaches frequently claim there isn't enough time in their situation to practice mental skills. However, it is usually possible to find time if mental skills training is a priority. Get a commitment to set specific times during or after practice to devote to PST. If you value acquiring mental skills, it makes sense to set time aside to practice them.

• *Lack of sport knowledge.* Having some playing or coaching experience can help the consultant

Developing and Displaying Expertise

Increasing attention has been paid to the development of expertise as well as to how experts differ from nonexperts (Ericsson, 2007; Mann, Williams, Ward, & Janelle, 2007), culminating in a special edition of *Journal of Sport and Exercise Psychology* titled "How Do Experts Learn?" (Williams & Ericsson, 2008). Psychological, perceptual, and physical skills are involved in this training and in these differences. The following are some key principles regarding these two different but related areas:

Experts Versus Nonexperts

- Experts, compared with nonexperts, anticipated their opponents' intentions significantly more quickly.
- The experts were more accurate in their decision making.
- Experts had fewer fixations of the eyes but for longer durations.
- Experts extracted more task-relevant information from each eye fixation.
- Experts had longer "quiet eye" periods (time when task-relevant information cues were processed and motor plans were coordinated).
- Experts picked up information from opponents' movements more quickly.

Development of Expertise (Elite Performance)

- At a minimum, development of expertise requires a consistent amount of deliberate practice (typically designed by teachers or coaches with full concentration on improving some aspect of performance) approaching 10,000 hours.
- Many recreational performers practice (often less than 50 hours) to reach an acceptable level of performance at which some level of automation is reached, but further experience will not be associated with any marked improvement in performance.
- Even the most talented performers cannot reach an international level in less than around a decade of continuous deliberate practice.
- It is unclear how much of a role genetics plays in the development of expertise, although Ericsson argues that deliberate practice (environment) is the key determinant of the development of expertise.

understand the specific problems that athletes have and enables the consultant to talk to athletes using the sport's jargon. But even though having sport-specific experience is advantageous, it is not absolutely essential as long as consultants acquaint themselves with the nature of the sport and its competitive environment.

• *Lack of follow-up.* Some coaches and consultants implement a PST program enthusiastically but provide little follow-up once the program is under way. Psychological skills, like any skills, must be practiced in order to be learned well enough to use under pressure. Follow up throughout the season by making time for PST and skills.

DISCOVER Activity 11.4 helps you learn to solve common problems of PST implementation.

An SPC should be aware of these potential problems and be ready to deal with them if necessary. Many consultants make mistakes in their first years of consulting because they aren't aware of the nuances of setting up and implementing PST programs. Homework and planning should be prerequisites for any SPC working with athletes and teams.

A couple of developments relating to the acquisition of expertise are worth noting. First, in an ongoing experiment, Dan McLaughlin took up golf at the age of 30 years. About 3 years later he had logged about 4,000 hours of deliberate practice and became a 7 handicap (which is better than about 85% of the male American golfing public; Gregory, 2013). In going about his practice, he focuses more on variability than on blocked practice. Instead of simply hitting 50 drives off the tee or 50 putts from about the same place, he putts from all over the green, changes up targets, and switches clubs when hitting from the tee. The idea is that although golf requires repetition (especially in the early stages of learning), a player has to be ready for myriad situations and gets just one chance to get a shot right. Thus far, all research has been conducted on athletes in their teens or younger who are starting to accumulate 10,000 hours of practice. Time will tell whether someone starting at age 30 can log in close to 10,000 hours and what that does to his performance.

Developing expertise in one's specialty requires putting in around 10,000 hours of deliberate practice. Although, there is considerable variability in these numbers, with some athletes needing far less practice and others much more practice. For example, for great hitters such as Albert Pujols, that expertise would involve hitting a baseball thrown at them at more than 90 miles (145 km) per hour from a distance of about 60 feet (18 m). In an article in *Sports Illustrated*, Epstein (2013) argued and demonstrated that these great baseball hitters could not hit a softball pitched underhand at 65 miles (105 km) per hour from a distance of 43 feet (13 m)—the distance from the mound to the plate in women's softball—by Jennie Finch, pitcher on the 2004 women's gold medal softball team.

Why? Although these great hitters have developed the specific skills needed to hit a baseball thrown at more than 90 miles per hour, they have not developed the anticipatory skills necessary to hit a softball thrown at 65 miles per hour. In essence, despite thousands of hours of deliberate practice in baseball, they have not developed automatic processing for a skill that requires quick, softball-specific movements. These movements need to occur so quickly that they have to be done automatically, and this automatic control simply comes from thousands of hours of deliberate practice in hitting a softball—not a baseball.

LEARNING AIDS

SUMMARY

1. **Define psychological skills training and the myths surrounding it.**

   Psychological skills training refers to learning to systematically and consistently practice mental or psychological skills for the purpose of enhancing performance, increasing enjoyment, or achieving greater sport and physical activity self-satisfaction. As with physical skills, psychological skills, such as maintaining and focusing concentration, regulating arousal levels, enhancing confidence, and maintaining motivation, require systematic practice and refinement. A number of myths (not grounded in fact or empirical data) have developed regarding the use of PST. Some of these myths are that (a) PST is only for problem athletes, (b) PST is only for elite athletes, (c) PST provides "quick fix" solutions to complex problems, and (d) PST does not really work.

2. **Identify the knowledge base for psychological skills training.**

   The knowledge base for PST has developed from two principal sources: research studies and practical experience. Original research studies have been conducted with athletes who demonstrate superior psychological skills (compared with athletes who perform less successfully). The second source relates to coaches and athletes whose sport experience has convinced them of the importance of psychological skills in maximizing performance and has convinced them that these skills should be integrated into athletes' daily training regimens.

3. **Discuss three phases of psychological skills training programs.**

   Although PST programs take many forms to fit participant needs, programs generally follow a set structure with three distinct phases: education (learning the importance of PST), acquisition (learning the mental skills), and practice (using the mental skills during training—before using them in competition).

4. **Examine the process of psychological self-regulation.**

   The ability to work toward one's short- and long-term goals by effectively monitoring and managing one's thoughts, feelings, and behaviors is termed self-regulation and is the ultimate goal of PST. The process of self-regulation consists of five stages: problem identification, commitment, execution, environmental management, and generalization. This model should be used to guide PST efforts.

5. **Develop a psychological skills training program.**

   A first step is psychological needs assessment to determine the specific components of a PST program. The program should be tailored to an individual's specific personality, situation, and needs. The initial PST program should probably last 3 to 6 months and should start during the preseason or off-season. There are advantages to having a sport psychology consultant implement a PST program, but it's also possible for a coach or other trained personnel to conduct the program.

6. **Understand the problems of implementing a psychological skills training program.**

   There are a number of potential problems to be aware of when you are implementing PST programs. These include an athlete's lack of conviction, perceived lack of time for the training program, lack of sport-specific knowledge (when a program is administered by a sport psychology consultant), and lack of follow-up and evaluation.

KEY TERMS

skills	multiple intelligences	acquisition phase
psychological skills training (PST)	emotional intelligence	practice phase
methods	superior performance intelligence	self-regulation
mental toughness	education phase	

REVIEW QUESTIONS

1. Discuss three reasons why coaches and athletes often neglect PST and discuss why the myths concerning PST training are false.

2. Provide specific examples of the derivation of the PST knowledge base from research with elite athletes and athlete–coach experiences.

3. Describe the three phases of PST: education, acquisition, and practice.

4. What empirical evidence is there that PST enhances sport performance?

5. How would you assess an individual's psychological strengths and weaknesses in an interview and through written psychological inventories?

6. Describe how Vealey broke down PST programs into psychological methods and psychological skills. Give examples of each.

7. Discuss the term *mental toughness.* How does the research define this concept, how would you define it, and how would you develop it? Give specific examples. Discuss some special considerations for using PST with athletes who have physical or intellectual disabilities.

8. Discuss the differences between expert and nonexpert performers. How would you go about developing expertise in an athlete?

9. Discuss five things you would do to start an applied sport psychology practice.

10. Discuss the reasons why elite baseball players can hit a baseball thrown at more than 90 miles per hour but cannot hit a softball thrown at 65 miles per hour.

CRITICAL THINKING QUESTIONS

1. You are a coach, and you decide that you want to implement a PST program starting in the off-season. How will you do it? What are some of the potential pitfalls you should be aware of, and what would you do to overcome them?

2. You want to start a PST program with your team, and you decide to hire a sport psychologist to help administer the program. Discuss how you, the coach, would interact with the sport psychologist. What would be your role in the PST program? Discuss the limitations and advantages of this approach.

12

Arousal Regulation

After reading this chapter, you should be able to

1. understand how to increase self-awareness of arousal states;
2. use somatic, cognitive, and multimodal anxiety reduction techniques;
3. identify coping strategies for dealing with competitive stress;
4. describe on-site relaxation tips for reducing anxiety;
5. understand the matching hypothesis; and
6. identify techniques for raising arousal for competition.

We live in a world where stress has become part of our daily lives. Certainly the pressure to perform at high levels in competitive sport has increased in recent years with all the media attention and money available through sport. In essence, our society values winning and success at all levels of competition, and coaches and athletes feel pressure to be successful. People who don't cope effectively with the pressure of competitive sport, however, may have decreases in performance, mental distress, and even physical illness. Continued pressure sometimes causes burnout in sport and exercise (see chapter 21), and it can lead to ulcers, migraine headaches, and hypertension. Depending on the person and the situation, however, various ways of coping with the pressure of competitive sport exist. The following quotes show how a few athletes have approached the pressure of competition.

" The thing that always worked best for me whenever I felt I was getting too tense to play good tennis was to simply remind myself that the worst thing—the very worst thing that could happen to me—was that I'd lose a bloody tennis match. That's all! "

—Rod Laver, former top professional tennis player (Tarshis, 1977, p. 87)

" I love the pressure. I just look forward to it. "

—Daly Thompson, Olympic decathlon gold medalist

" I would calm my nerves with a playlist ready with the hottest rap songs out there and bob my head, think about the game, and relax. Then the game would start and I'd put my angry face on. "

—Shaquille O'Neal, Hall of Fame National Basketball Association player

Not only do athletes respond differently to pressure, but the type of sport or task they perform is also a critical factor in how they react. For example, opposing coaches calling a time-out before crucial field goal attempts in professional football results in a decrement in performance (80% to 64%), but doing the same in collegiate basketball does not undermine performance (Goldschmied, Nankin, & Cafri, 2010). A golfer preparing to knock in a 20-foot putt would probably control arousal differently than would a wrestler taking the mat. Similarly, one specific relaxation procedure might work better for controlling cognitive (mental) anxiety, whereas another might be more effective for coping with somatic (perceived physiological) anxiety. The relationship between arousal and performance can be complicated (see chapter 4), and athletes in competitive sport need to learn to control their arousal. They should be able to increase it—to psych up—when they're feeling lethargic and decrease it when the pressure to win causes them anxiety and nervousness. The key is for individuals to find their optimal levels of arousal without losing intensity and focus. In this chapter we discuss in detail a variety of arousal regulation techniques that should help individuals in sport and exercise settings reach their optimal levels of arousal. The first step in this process is to learn how to recognize or become aware of anxiety and arousal states.

Increasing Self-Awareness of Arousal

The first step toward controlling arousal levels is to be more aware of them during practices and competitions. This typically involves self-monitoring and recognizing how emotional states affect performance. As an athlete you can probably identify certain feelings associated with top performances and other feelings associated with poor performances. To increase awareness of your arousal states, we recommend the following process.

First, think back to your best performance. Try to visualize the actual competition as clearly as possible, focusing on what you felt and thought at that time. Take at least 5 minutes to relive the experience. Now complete the items in "Checklist of Performance States." Because you are reconstructing your best performance, for "played extremely well," you would circle the number 1. For the second item, if you felt moderately anxious, you might circle number 4. After completing the checklist for your best performance, repeat the process for your worst performance.

Now compare your responses between the two performances you brought to mind. Most people find that their thoughts and feelings are distinctly different when playing well compared with playing poorly. This is the beginning of awareness training. If you want to better understand the relationship between your thoughts, feelings, and performance, monitor yourself by completing the checklist immediately after each practice or competitive session over the next few weeks. Of course, your psychological state will vary during a given session. If you feel one way during the first half of a basketball game, for example, and another way during the second half, simply complete two checklists.

KEY POINT You must increase your awareness of your psychological states before you can control your thoughts and feelings. How individuals cope with anxiety is more important than how much anxiety they have.

Checklist of Performance States

Played extremely well	1	2	3	4	5	6	Played extremely poorly
Felt extremely relaxed	1	2	3	4	5	6	Felt extremely anxious
Felt extremely confident	1	2	3	4	5	6	Felt extremely unconfident
Felt in complete control	1	2	3	4	5	6	Had no control at all
Muscles were relaxed	1	2	3	4	5	6	Muscles were tense
Felt extremely energetic	1	2	3	4	5	6	Felt extremely fatigued
Self-talk was positive	1	2	3	4	5	6	Self-talk was negative
Felt extremely focused	1	2	3	4	5	6	Felt extremely unfocused
Felt effortless	1	2	3	4	5	6	Felt great effort
Had high energy	1	2	3	4	5	6	Had low energy

The study of the self-awareness of arousal states has started to focus on whether these states are felt as facilitative or debilitative. Olympic basketball coach Jack Donohue noted that "it's not a case of getting rid of the butterflies, it's a question of getting them to fly in formation" (Orlick, 1986, p. 112). Along these lines, it has been found that elite athletes generally interpret their anxiety as more facilitative than nonelite athletes do (Hanton & Jones, 1999a; Smith, Smoll, & O'Rourke, 2011). Sport psychologists can help athletes become more aware of their arousal states and interpret them in a positive manner. This is seen in the following quote by an Olympic swimmer:

" I mean you have to get nervous to swim well . . . . If you're not bothered about it, you are not going to swim well . . . . I think the nerves bring out the best in you and I soon realized that I wanted to feel this way. (Hanton & Jones, 1999b, p. 9) "

DISCOVER Activity 12.1 helps you to reflect on previous competitions and become aware of your feelings and thoughts at those times.

In addition, Eubank and Collins (2000) found that individuals who see their anxiety as facilitative are more likely to use both problem-focused and emotion-focused coping. Conversely, individuals who view their anxiety as debilitative appeared limited in their use of any coping strategies. Therefore, people who perceive their anxiety as facilitative typically perform better and cope more effectively with the anxiety. Let's now turn to some of the more popular anxiety reduction techniques in sport and exercise settings.

Using Anxiety Reduction Techniques

Excess anxiety can produce inappropriate muscle tension, which in turn can diminish performance. And it is all too easy to develop excess muscle tension. The common thinking is "The harder you try, the better you will perform." This reasoning, however, is incorrect.

As a quick, practical exercise, rest your dominant forearm and hand palm down on a desktop or table. Tense all the muscles in your hand and wrist and then try to tap your index and middle fingers quickly back and forth. Do this for about 30 seconds. Now relax the muscles in your hands and fingers and repeat the exercise. You will probably discover that muscular tension slows your movements and makes them less coordinated than they are when your muscles are relaxed.

Besides sometimes producing inappropriate muscle tension, excess anxiety can produce inappropriate thoughts and cognitions, such as "I hope I don't blow this shot" or "I hope I don't fail in front of all these people." A quote by baseball player B.J. Surhoff makes this point: "The power has always been there; I just had to find a way to tap it . . . . Mostly, it's a matter of learning to relax at the plate. You don't worry about striking out and looking bad as much as before."

In addition to simply reducing anxiety, as noted earlier, it is important to interpret anxiety in a facilitative rather than a debilitative manner. Research (Thomas, Hanton, & Maynard, 2007) revealed that three time periods were critical in the interpretation of anxiety: after performance (reviewing previous performance), 1 or 2 days before competition, and the day of competition. In each of these time frames, facilitators utilized a refined repertoire of psychological skills (e.g., imagery, reframing self-talk) to internally control and reinterpret the cognitive and somatic anxiety experienced. Conversely, debilitators did not possess these refined psychological skills and therefore lacked internal control to alter their anxiety states.

Kudlackova, Eccles, and Dieffenbach (2013) investigated which anxiety reduction techniques were used most often and which were most popular. The authors surveyed competitive athletes from collegiate, recreational, and professional levels. The results revealed that, as expected, professional athletes engaged in more relaxation in a typical week than collegiate or recreational athletes did. Athletes across competitive levels used anxiety reduction techniques to cope with both competitive anxiety and everyday anxieties associated with being an athlete. Interestingly, the athletes used more physical (e.g., muscle relaxation) than mental relaxation techniques in relation to coping with competitive anxiety and used more mental (e.g., imagery) than physical relaxation techniques in relation to coping with everyday anxiety.

We now present some relaxation procedures commonly used in sport and physical activity settings. Some of these techniques focus on reducing somatic anxiety, some on cognitive anxiety. Still others are multimodal in nature and use a variety of techniques to cope with both somatic and cognitive anxiety.

Somatic Anxiety Reduction Techniques

The first group of techniques works primarily to reduce physiological arousal associated with increased somatic anxiety.

Progressive Relaxation

Edmund Jacobson's **progressive relaxation** technique (1938) forms the cornerstone for many modern relaxation procedures. This technique involves tensing and relaxing specific muscles. Jacobson named the technique *progressive relaxation* because the tensing and relaxing progress from one major muscle group to the next until all muscle groups are completely relaxed. Progressive relaxation rests on a few assumptions: (a) It is possible to learn the difference between tension and relaxation; (b) tension and relaxation are mutually exclusive—it is not possible to be relaxed and tense at the same time; and (c) relaxation of the body through decreased muscle tension will, in turn, decrease mental tension. Jacobson's technique has been modified considerably over the years, but its purpose remains that of helping people learn to feel tension in their muscles and then let go of this tension.

The tension–relaxation cycles develop an athlete's awareness of the difference between tension and lack of tension. Each cycle involves maximally contracting one specific muscle group and then attempting to fully relax that same muscle group, all while focusing on the different sensations of tension and relaxation. With skill, an athlete can detect tension in a specific muscle or area of the body, like the neck, and then relax that muscle. Some people even learn to use the technique during breaks in an activity, such as a time-out. The first few sessions of progressive relaxation take an athlete up to 30 minutes, and less time is necessary with practice. The goal is to develop the ability to relax on site during competition.

Based on progressive relaxation, Ost (1988) developed an applied variant to teach an individual to relax within 20 to 30 seconds. The first phase of training involves a 15-minute progressive relaxation session, practiced twice a day, in which muscle groups are tensed and relaxed. The individual then moves on to a release-only phase that takes 5 to 7 minutes to complete. The individual then moves on to a 2- to 3-minute version with the use of a self-instructional cue, "Relax." This time is further reduced until only a few seconds are required, and then the technique is practiced in specific situations. For example, a golfer who becomes tight and anxious when faced with important putts could use this technique in between shots to prepare for difficult putts.

Breath Control

Proper breathing is often considered key to achieving relaxation, and **breath control** is another physically oriented relaxation technique. Breath control is one of the easiest, most effective ways to control anxiety and muscle tension. When you are calm, confident, and in control, your breathing is likely to be smooth,

Learning proper breath control can help an athlete regain and maintain control during high-anxiety situations.

deep, and rhythmic. When you're under pressure and tense, your breathing is more likely to be short, shallow, and irregular.

Unfortunately, many athletes have not learned proper breathing. Performing under pressure, they often fail to coordinate their breathing with the performance of the skill. Research has demonstrated that breathing in and holding your breath increases muscle tension, whereas breathing out decreases muscle tension. For example, most discus throwers, shot-putters, and baseball pitchers learn to breathe out during release. As pressure builds in a competition, the natural tendency is to hold one's breath, which increases muscle tension and interferes with the coordinated movement necessary for maximum performance. Taking a deep, slow, complete breath usually triggers a relaxation response.

To practice breath control, take a deep, complete breath and imagine that the lungs are divided into three levels. Focus on filling the lower level of the lungs with air, first by pushing the diaphragm down and forcing the abdomen out. Then fill the middle portion of the lungs by expanding the chest cavity and raising the rib cage. Finally, fill the upper level of the lungs by raising the chest and shoulders slightly. Hold this breath for several seconds and then exhale slowly by pulling the abdomen in and lowering the shoulders and chest. By focusing on the lowering (inhalation) and raising (exhalation) of the diaphragm, you'll have an increased sense of stability, centeredness, and relaxation. To help enhance the importance and awareness of the exhalation phase, people can learn to inhale to a count of four and exhale to a count of eight. This 1:2 ratio of inhalation to exhalation helps slow breathing and deepens the relaxation by focusing on the exhalation phase.

The best time to use breath control during competition is during a time-out or break in the action (e.g., before serving in tennis, just before putting a golf ball, preparing for a free throw in basketball). The slow and deliberate inhalation–exhalation sequence will help you maintain composure and control over your anxiety during particularly stressful times. Focusing on your breathing relaxes your shoulder and neck muscles and makes it less likely you will be bothered by irrelevant cues or distractions. Finally, deep breathing provides a short mental break from the pressure of competition and can renew your energy.

Biofeedback

Biofeedback is a physically oriented technique that teaches people to control physiological or autonomic responses. It usually involves an electronic monitoring device that can detect and amplify internal responses not ordinarily known to us. These electronic instruments provide visual or auditory feedback of physiological responses such as muscle activity, skin temperature, brain waves, or heart rate, although most studies have used muscle activity as measured by electromyography (Pop-Jordanova & Demerdzieva, 2010; Zaichkowsky & Takenaka, 1993).

KEY POINT Biofeedback training can help people become more aware of their autonomic nervous system and subsequently control their reactions.

For example, a tennis player might feel muscle tension in her neck and shoulders before serving on important points in a match. Electrodes could be attached to specific muscles in her neck and shoulder region, and she would be asked to relax these specific muscles. Excess tension in the muscles would then cause the biofeedback instrument to make a loud and constant clicking noise. The tennis player's goal would be to quiet the machine by attempting to relax her shoulder and neck muscles. She could accomplish relaxation through any relaxation technique, such as visualizing a positive scene or using positive self-talk. The key point is that the lower the noise level, the more relaxed the muscles are. Such feedback attunes the player to her tension levels and whether they are decreasing or increasing.

Once the tennis player learns to recognize and reduce muscle tension in her shoulders and neck, she needs to be able to transfer this knowledge to the tennis court. She can do this by interspersing sessions of nonfeedback (time away from the biofeedback device) in the training regimen. Gradually, the duration of these nonfeedback sessions is increased, and the tennis player depends less on the biofeedback signal while maintaining an awareness of physiological changes. With sufficient practice and experience, the tennis player can learn to identify the onset of muscle tension and control it so that her serve remains effective in clutch situations.

Research has indicated that rifle shooters can improve their performance by training themselves, using biofeedback, to fire between heartbeats (Daniels & Landers, 1981; Wilkinson, Landers, & Daniels, 1981). In addition, biofeedback has been effective for improving performance among recreational, collegiate, and professional athletes in a variety of sports (Crews, 1993; Hatfield & Hillman, 2001; Zaichkowsky

Instructions for Progressive Relaxation

In each step you'll first tense a muscle group and then relax it. Pay close attention to how it feels to be relaxed as opposed to tense. Each phase should take about 5 to 7 seconds. For each muscle group, perform each exercise twice before progressing to the next group. As you gain skill, you can omit the tension phase and focus just on relaxation. Because the exercise is quite long and might be difficult to memorize, you may wish to record the following instructions in an audio file or invest a few dollars in a progressive relaxation recording.

1. Find a quiet place, dim the lights, and lie down in a comfortable position with your legs uncrossed. Loosen tight clothing. Take a deep breath, let it out slowly, and relax.

2. Raise your arms, extend them in front of you, and make a tight fist with each hand. Notice the uncomfortable tension in your hands and fingers. Hold that tension for 5 seconds; then let go halfway and hold for an additional 5 seconds. Let your hands relax completely. Notice how the tension and discomfort drain from your hands, replaced by comfort and relaxation. Focus on the contrast between the tension you felt and the relaxation you now feel. Concentrate on relaxing your hands completely for 10 to 15 seconds.

3. Tense your upper arms tightly for 5 seconds and focus on the tension. Let the tension out halfway and hold for an additional 5 seconds, again focusing on the tension. Now relax your upper arms completely for 10 to 15 seconds and focus on the developing relaxation. Let your arms rest limply at your sides.

4. Curl your toes as tight as you can. After 5 seconds, relax the toes halfway and hold for an additional 5 seconds. Now relax your toes completely and focus on the spreading relaxation. Continue relaxing your toes for 10 to 15 seconds.

5. Point your toes away from you and tense your feet and calves. Hold the tension hard for 5 seconds; then let it out halfway for another 5 seconds. Relax your feet and calves completely for 10 to 15 seconds.

6. Extend your legs, raising them about 6 inches off the floor, and tense your thigh muscles. Hold the tension for 5 seconds, let it out halfway, and hold for another 5 seconds before relaxing your thighs completely. Concentrate on your feet, calves, and thighs for 30 seconds.

& Fuchs, 1988). Although not all studies of biofeedback have demonstrated enhanced performance, the technique has been shown to consistently reduce anxiety and muscle tension.

Cognitive Anxiety Reduction Techniques

Some relaxation procedures focus more directly on relaxing the mind than do progressive relaxation and deep breathing. The argument is that relaxing the mind will in turn relax the body. Both physical and mental techniques can produce a relaxed state, although they work through different paths. We next discuss some of the techniques for relaxing the mind.

Relaxation Response

Herbert Benson, a physician at Harvard Medical School, popularized a scientifically sound way of relaxing that he called the **relaxation response**

(Benson, 2000; Benson & Proctor, 1984). Benson's method applies the basic elements of meditation but eliminates any spiritual or religious significance. Many athletes use meditation to mentally prepare for competition, asserting that it improves their ability to relax, concentrate, and become energized. However, few controlled studies have addressed the effectiveness of the relaxation response in enhancing performance. The state of mind produced by meditation is characterized by keen awareness, effortlessness, relaxation, spontaneity, and focused attention—many of the same elements that characterize peak performance. The relaxation response requires four elements:

1. A quiet place, which ensures that distractions and external stimulation are minimized.

2. A comfortable position that can be maintained for a while. Sit in a comfortable chair, for

7. Tense your stomach muscles as tight as you can for 5 seconds, concentrating on the tension. Let the tension out halfway and hold for an additional 5 seconds before relaxing your stomach muscles completely. Focus on the spreading relaxation until your stomach muscles are completely relaxed.

8. To tighten your chest and shoulder muscles, press the palms of your hands together and push. Hold for 5 seconds; then let go halfway and hold for another 5 seconds. Now relax the muscles and concentrate on the relaxation until your muscles are completely loose and relaxed. Concentrate also on the muscle groups that have been previously relaxed.

9. Push your back to the floor as hard as you can and tense your back muscles. Let the tension out halfway after 5 seconds, hold the reduced tension, and focus on it for another 5 seconds. Relax your back and shoulder muscles completely, focusing on the relaxation spreading over the area.

10. Keeping your torso, arms, and legs relaxed, tense your neck muscles by bringing your head forward until your chin digs into your chest. Hold for 5 seconds, release the tension halfway and hold for another 5 seconds, and then relax your neck completely. Allow your head to hang comfortably while you focus on the relaxation developing in your neck muscles.

11. Clench your teeth and feel the tension in the muscles of your jaw. After 5 seconds, let the tension out halfway and hold for 5 seconds before relaxing. Let your mouth and facial muscles relax completely, with your lips slightly parted. Concentrate on totally relaxing these muscles for 10 to 15 seconds.

12. Wrinkle your forehead and scalp as tightly as you can, hold for 5 seconds, and then release halfway and hold for another 5 seconds. Relax your scalp and forehead completely, focusing on the feeling of relaxation and contrasting it with the earlier tension. Concentrate for about a minute on relaxing all of the muscles of your body.

13. Cue-controlled relaxation is the final goal of progressive relaxation. Breathing can serve as the impetus and cue for effective relaxation. Take a series of short inhalations, about one per second, until your chest is filled. Hold for 5 seconds; then exhale slowly for 10 seconds while thinking to yourself the word *relax* or *calm*. Repeat the process at least five times, each time striving to deepen the state of relaxation that you're experiencing.

example, but do not lie down in bed—you do not want to fall asleep.

3. A mental device, which is the critical element in the relaxation response, that involves focusing your attention on a single thought or word and repeating it over and over. Select a word, such as *relax, calm,* or *ease,* that does not stimulate your thoughts, and repeat the word while breathing out. Every time you exhale, repeat your word.

4. A passive attitude, which is important but can be difficult to achieve. You have to learn to let it happen, allowing the thoughts and images that enter your mind to move through as they will, making no attempt to attend to them. If something comes to mind, let it go and refocus on your word. Don't worry about how many times your mind wanders; continue to refocus your attention on your word.

KEY POINT The relaxation response teaches you to quiet the mind, concentrate, and reduce muscle tension.

Learning the relaxation response takes time. You should practice it about 20 minutes a day. You will discover how difficult it is to control your mind and focus on one thought or object. But staying focused on the task at hand is important to many sports. The relaxation response teaches you to quiet the mind, which will help you concentrate and reduce muscle tension. However, it is not an appropriate technique to use right before an event or competition because athletes could potentially become too relaxed and lethargic. Studies using meditation (which is related to the relaxation response in that focusing on the repetition of a sound is a key component) have demonstrated lower lactate levels, less self-reported tension, and increases in performance compared with control conditions (Solberg, Berglund, Engen, Ekeberg, & Loeb, 1996; Solberg et al., 2000).

Autogenic Training

Autogenic training consists of a series of exercises that produce sensations, specifically of warmth and heaviness. Used extensively in Europe but less in North America, the training was developed in Germany in the early 1930s by Johannes Schultz and later refined by Schultz and Luthe (1969). Attention is focused on the sensations you are trying to produce. As in the relaxation response, feeling should be allowed to happen without interference. The autogenic training program is based on six hierarchical stages, which should be learned in order:

1. Heaviness in the extremities
2. Warmth in the extremities
3. Regulation of cardiac activity
4. Regulation of breathing
5. Abdominal warmth
6. Cooling of the forehead

The statements "My right arm is heavy," "My right arm is warm and relaxed," "My heartbeat is regular and calm," "My breathing rate is slow, calm, and relaxed," and "My forehead is cool" are all examples of verbal stimuli commonly used in autogenic training. It usually takes several months of regular practice, 10 to 40 minutes a day, to become proficient, to experience heaviness and warmth in the limbs, and to produce the sensation of a relaxed, calm heartbeat and respiratory rate accompanied by warmth in the abdomen and coolness in the forehead.

Systematic Desensitization

This cognitive relaxation technique was developed by Wolpe (1958), who stated:

> **If a response antagonistic to anxiety can be made to occur in the presence of anxiety-provoking stimuli so that it is accompanied by a complete or partial suppression of the anxiety responses, the bond between these stimuli and the anxiety responses will be lessened.** (p. 18)

According to Wolpe, anxious people have learned through a process of classical (think Pavlovian) con-ditioning to have excessively high levels of anxiety, manifested through increased autonomic nervous system activity (e.g., increases in heart rate, blood pressure, breathing, and galvanic skin response), in the presence of certain stimuli. The goal of the treatment is to replace this nervous activity with a competing behavior.

Smith, Smoll, and O'Rourke (2011) provided an excellent example of using systematic desensitization. The client is first trained in deep muscle relaxation (see the section on progressive relaxation earlier in this chapter), and then an anxiety hierarchy is constructed that consists of 5 to 10 scenes ranging from least to most anxiety producing. The following list was created for a basketball player who developed excessive anxiety when shooting free throws after missing several critical free throws at the end of games, resulting in losses for his team.

- Thinking about the fact that the next game will be played in two days
- Waking in the morning and thinking of the game that evening
- Walking toward the arena where the game will be played
- Sitting in the locker room before the game as your coach tells you how important this game is
- Listening to the coach's final instructions in the huddle just before tip-off
- Preparing to shoot a free throw in the first half
- Preparing to shoot a free throw in the fourth quarter of a close game
- Preparing to shoot a free throw with 1 second left in a championship game when your team trails by 1 point

After learning progressive relaxation, the client is asked to imagine the first (least anxiety-producing) scene in the anxiety hierarchy. The client continues imaging this scene until he has no anxiety. He then images the next situation on the list until he has no anxiety. He does this until he can image the most anxiety-producing scene without producing any anxiety. In essence, the relaxation is paired with the anxiety-producing scene until it inhibits any anxiety from occurring. This can take weeks or even months if the anxiety reaction is very severe, such as in people who have extreme phobias (e.g., open spaces, closed spaces, heights).

Multimodal Anxiety Reduction Packages

The anxiety reduction techniques just presented focus on either the cognitive or the somatic aspects of anxiety. Multimodal stress management packages, however, can alleviate both cognitive and somatic anxiety and provide systematic strategies for rehearsing coping procedures under simulated stressful conditions. The two most popular multimodal techniques are cognitive–affective stress management training, developed by Ronald Smith (1980), and stress inoculation training, developed by Donald Meichenbaum (1985). A key feature of these techniques is that they help athletes develop a number of coping skills for managing a wide variety of problems emanating from different stressful situations. Thus, these coping skills training programs help athletes control dysfunctional emotions by producing more adaptive appraisals, improving coping responses, and increasing confidence in using their coping skills to manage numerous sources of athletic stress.

Cognitive–Affective Stress Management Training

Cognitive–affective stress management training (SMT) is one of the most comprehensive stress management approaches. SMT is a skills program that teaches a person a specific integrated coping response that uses relaxation and cognitive components to control emotional arousal. Bankers, business executives, social workers, and college administrators have all applied SMT, and athletes have found this technique to be effective (Crocker, Alderman, Murray, & Smith, 1988; Smith, Smoll, & O'Rourke, 2011). Athletes have proved to be an ideal target population: They acquire the coping skills (e.g., muscular relaxation) somewhat more quickly than other groups, face stressful athletic situations frequently enough to permit careful monitoring of their progress, and perform in ways that can be readily assessed.

The theoretical model of stress underlying SMT (figure 12.1) includes both cognitively based and physiologically based intervention strategies (derived from the work of Ellis, 1962; Lazarus, 1966; and Schachter, 1966). This model accounts for the situation, the person's mental appraisal of the situation, the physiological response, and the actual behavior. The program offers specific intervention strategies, such as relaxation skills, cognitive restructuring, and self-instructional training, for dealing with the physical and mental reactions to stress. Combining mental and physical coping strategies eventually leads to an integrated coping response.

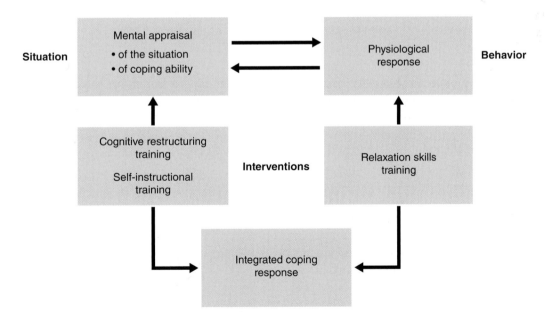

FIGURE 12.1 Mediational model of stress underlying the cognitive–affective stress management training program, together with the major intervention strategies used in developing the integrated coping response.

Adapted from F. Smoll and R. Smith, 1980, A cognitive-affective approach to stress management training for athletes. In *Psychology of motor behavior and sport—1979*, edited by C. Nadeau et al. (Champaign, IL: Human Kinetics), 56. By permission of R. Smith.

Smith's cognitive–affective SMT program has five phases and is briefly described here. A full description is available in a trainer's manual (Smith & Rohsenow, 2011).

1. *Pretreatment assessment.* During this phase, the consultant conducts personal interviews to assess the kinds of circumstances that produce stress, the player's responses to stress, and the ways in which stress affects performance and other behaviors. The consultant also assesses the player's cognitive and behavioral skills and deficits and administers written questionnaires to supplement the interview. This information is used to tailor the program to the player.

2. *Treatment rationale.* During the treatment rationale phase, the idea is to help the player understand his stress response by analyzing personal stress reactions and experiences. The consultant should emphasize that the program is educational, not psychotherapeutic, and participants should understand that the program is intended to increase their self-control.

3. *Skill acquisition.* The major objective of the SMT program is to develop an integrated coping response (see figure 12.1) by acquiring both relaxation and cognitive intervention skills. In the skill acquisition phase, participants receive training in muscular relaxation, cognitive restructuring, and self-instruction. The muscular relaxation comes from progressive relaxation. Cognitive restructuring is the attempt to identify irrational or stress-inducing self-statements, which are typically related to the fear of failure and disapproval (e.g., "I know I'll mess up," "I couldn't stand to let my teammates and coaches down"). These statements are then restructured into more positive thoughts (e.g., "I'll still be a good person whether I win or lose," "Don't worry about losing—just play one point at a time"). (Chapter 16 discusses changing negative self-statements into positive self-statements in more detail.) Self-instructional training teaches people to provide themselves with specific instructions to improve concentration and problem solving. This training teaches specific, useful self-commands that are especially helpful in stressful situations. Examples of such commands are "Don't think about fear; just think about what you have to do," "Take a deep breath and relax," and "Take things one step at a time, just like in practice."

4. *Skill rehearsal.* To facilitate the rehearsal process, the consultant intentionally induces different levels of stress (typically by using films, imaginary rehearsals of stressful events, and other physical and psychological stressors), even high levels of emotional arousal that exceed those in actual competitions (Smith, 1980). These arousal responses are then reduced through the use of coping skills that the participant has acquired. The procedure of induced affect can produce high levels of arousal, so only trained clinicians should use this component of the technique.

5. *Posttraining evaluation.* A variety of measures are used by the consultant to assess the effectiveness of the program. These include self-monitoring of emotional states and cognitive events by the athlete, performance measures that might be expected to improve with stress reduction, and standardized trait and state anxiety inventories. Comprehensive evaluation of the results of the program can be extremely valuable from a scientific perspective so that appropriate changes can be made if necessary, as well as for planning subsequent programs.

Stress Inoculation Training

One of the most popular multifaceted stress management techniques used both in and out of the sport environment is **stress inoculation training (SIT)** (Meichenbaum, 1985). Research has found SIT to be effective in reducing anxiety and enhancing performance in sport settings (Kerr & Leith, 1993) as well as in helping athletes cope with the stress of injury (Kerr & Goss, 1996). The approach for SIT has a number of similarities to that of SMT, so we provide only a brief outline of SIT.

In SIT, the individual is exposed to and learns to cope with stress in increasing amounts, thereby enhancing her immunity to stress. SIT teaches skills for coping with psychological stressors and for enhancing performance by developing productive thoughts, mental images, and self-statements. One application of SIT has athletes break down stressful situations using a four-stage approach: (1) preparing for the stressor (e.g., "It is going to be rough; keep your cool"), (2) controlling and handling the stressor (e.g., "Keep your cool; just stay focused on the task"), (3) coping with feelings of being overwhelmed (e.g., "Keep focused: What do you have to do next?"), and (4) evaluating coping efforts (e.g., "You handled yourself well"). SIT gives athletes opportunities to practice their coping skills starting with small, manageable doses of stress and progressing to greater amounts of stress. Thus, athletes develop a sense of learned resourcefulness by successfully coping with stressors through a variety of techniques, including imagery, role playing, and homework assignments. The use of a stage approach and the strategies of self-talk, cognitive restructuring, and relaxation make both SIT and SMT effective multimodal approaches for reducing anxiety.

Hypnosis

A somewhat controversial and often misunderstood technique for reducing anxiety (both cognitive and somatic), as well as enhancing other mental skills, is hypnosis. Although many definitions have been put forth, **hypnosis** is defined here as an altered state of consciousness that can be induced by a procedure in which a person is in an unusually relaxed state and responds to suggestions for making alterations in perceptions, feelings, thoughts, or actions (Kirsch, 1994). Originally used by clinical psychologists and psychiatrists outside of sport to enhance performance, focus attention, increase confidence, and reduce anxiety, hypnosis has been increasingly used in sport contexts. Although hypnotic procedures include components used in other applied sport psychology interventions such as relaxation and imagery, they differ from other techniques because they require participants to enter a hypnotic state before other techniques (e.g., relaxation, imagery) are applied.

Earlier research by Unesthal (1986) used hypnotic techniques, but little attention was given to this work. However, more recently an upsurge has occurred in the use of hypnosis as an arousal regulation technique. For example, research (Lindsay, Maynard, & Thomas, 2005; Pates, Oliver, & Maynard, 2001) revealed that hypnosis was related to feelings of peak performance states (see chapter 11) that resulted in improvements in basketball, cycling, and golf performance. Participants particularly noted greater feelings of relaxation. In addition, Barker and Jones (2008) found that hypnosis increased positive affect and decreased negative affect in soccer players. So, what are the specific stages of a hypnosis intervention?

- *Induction phase.* First, participants need to trust the hypnotist and must want to be hypnotized because suggestibility is critical for success. Although many induction techniques exist, these techniques are typically aimed at directing the participant's thoughts and feelings to being relaxed and peaceful. After achieving a relaxed state, participants are put in a hypnotic trance using imagery or attentional focusing techniques. Participants typically become very lethargic, have the relaxation response, and become very susceptible to suggestions. At this point, when participants are in a very relaxed state, suggestions can be made regarding future thoughts, feelings, and actions.

- *Hypnotic phase.* In this phase, the participant's physiological responses are virtually identical to those in the relaxation response. Participants are usually asked to respond to specific suggestions, which are carried out after they are fully awake. These are referred to as posthypnotic suggestions.

- *Waking phase.* In the next phase, the participant comes out of the trance. The hypnotist generally brings participants out of the trance by simply suggesting that they wake up on a given signal such as counting to three.

Facts About Hypnosis

Although researchers and practitioners don't always agree on the definition of hypnosis, they agree generally about the following aspects of hypnosis:

- The more open individuals are to receiving suggestions, the more likely they are to benefit from suggestions given under hypnosis.
- The deeper the trance, the more likely it is that suggestions given under hypnosis will be effective.
- General arousal techniques are more useful than hypnotic suggestions in enhancing muscular strength and endurance.
- Positive suggestions are effective in facilitating performance regardless of whether the athlete is hypnotized.
- Negative suggestions almost always are a detriment to performance.
- Hypnotic responsiveness depends more on the efforts and abilities of the individual being hypnotized than on the skill of the therapist.
- The ability to experience hypnotic phenomena does not indicate gullibility or personality weakness.

- *Posthypnotic phase.* Suggestions given to participants during hypnosis are often designed to influence them during the posthypnotic phase, or after they have come out of the hypnotic trance. Posthypnotic suggestions to athletes and exercisers typically focus on the way they should feel in competition or during exercise. For example, a basketball player might be told, "When you shoot the ball, you will feel relaxed and confident."

Sport psychologists who wish to use these techniques should acquire specialized training and education from mentors with appropriate clinical qualifications and experience. "Facts About Hypnosis" highlights some facts about hypnosis and its effects on performance.

Effectiveness of Anxiety Reduction Techniques

Are these stress management techniques indeed effective for reducing anxiety and increasing performance? Rumbold, Fletcher, and Daniels (2012) reviewed 64 intervention studies investigating techniques meant to reduce anxiety and increase performance. Of the 64 studies reviewed, 52 (81%) showed that stress components were optimized in at least one of the following ways: stressors were reduced, cognitive appraisals were modified, negative affect states were reduced and positive affect states were increased, and effective coping behaviors were facilitated.

When looking at overall effectiveness of interventions that measured both stress and performance outcomes, 30 of 39 studies (77%) found positive effects for performance, although only 22 of 39 (56%) found positive effects for both stress reduction and performance improvement. In essence, reducing athletes' anxiety states may not result in performance improvement; this underscores the complexity of sport performance. Of the different types of stress management interventions, multimodal approaches seem to be the most effective in terms of performance enhancement. Finally, a number of variables moderated the relationship between stress management and performance, including the competitive level and age of the athlete, the length of the intervention, as well as how performance was measured.

Exploring the Matching Hypothesis

You now have learned about a variety of relaxation techniques, and it is logical to ask when these techniques should be used to achieve maximum effective-

ness. In attempting to answer this question, researchers have explored what is known as the **matching hypothesis**. This hypothesis states that an anxiety management technique should be matched to a particular anxiety problem. That is, cognitive anxiety should be treated with mental relaxation, and somatic anxiety should be treated with physical relaxation. This individualized approach is similar to the stress model developed by McGrath (see chapter 4). A series of studies (Maynard & Cotton, 1993; Maynard, Hemmings, & Warwick-Evans, 1995; Maynard, Smith, & Warwick-Evans, 1995) have provided support for the matching hypothesis.

The studies by Maynard and colleagues showed a somatic relaxation technique (progressive relaxation) to be more effective than a cognitive one (positive thought control) in reducing somatic anxiety. Similarly, the cognitive relaxation technique was more effective than the somatic one in reducing cognitive anxiety. The reductions in somatic and cognitive anxiety were associated with some subsequent (but not quite consistent) increases in performance. More recent research (Rees & Hardy, 2004) found this same matching hypothesis appropriate for the use of social support as a way to cope with anxiety. More specifically, certain types of social support were found to be more effective in reducing anxiety among performers. The specific social support (e.g., informational emotional) should be matched to the specific anxiety problem of the athlete (e.g., competition pressure, technical problems in training) to produce maximum effectiveness in reducing anxiety.

However, crossover effects (whereby somatic relaxation techniques produce decreases in cognitive anxiety and cognitive relaxation techniques produce decreases in somatic anxiety) also occurred in these studies. In one study using a cognitive relaxation technique, the intensity of cognitive anxiety decreased by 30%; the intensity of somatic anxiety also decreased, although by only 15%. Similarly, when a somatic relaxation procedure was used, the intensity of somatic anxiety decreased by 31% and the intensity of cognitive anxiety decreased as well, although by 16%. In other words, somatic relaxation techniques had some benefits for reducing cognitive anxiety, and cognitive relaxation techniques had some benefits for reducing somatic anxiety. These crossover effects have led some researchers to argue that SMT and SIT are the more appropriate programs to use because these multimodal anxiety reduction techniques can work on both cognitive and somatic anxiety.

Given the current state of knowledge, we recommend that if an individual's anxiety is primarily cognitive, a cognitive relaxation technique should be used. If somatic anxiety is the primary concern, focus on somatic relaxation techniques. Finally, if you are not sure what type of anxiety is most problematic, use a multimodal technique.

Coping With Adversity

Athletes should learn a broad spectrum of coping strategies to use in different situations and for different sources of stress (Nicholls & Polman, 2007). Although athletes sometimes use similar coping strategies from situation to situation, in a more traitlike manner (Giacobbi & Weinberg, 2000), athletes also change strategies across situations (Jordet & Elferink-Gemser, 2012; Nicholls, Hemmings, & Clough, 2010). Successful athletes vary in their coping strategies, but all have skills that work when they need them most. Consider the strategies of two athletes:

" I started to prepare, talking to myself, and decide, clearly, what I would do. Above all I thought how to take it. "

—International-level soccer player in the World Cup (cited in Jordet & Elferink-Gemser, 2012, p. 75)

" If I get butterflies, I visualize putting them into a tumble drier in my stomach. I pretend these butterflies are going round . . . then I try and turn it back the other way. So I slow them down, and turn them the other way. "

—Professional golfer (cited in Hill, Hanton, Matthews, & Fleming, 2010a, p. 228)

Although the relaxation techniques we have discussed help individuals reduce anxiety in sport and exercise settings, the soccer player and the golfer demonstrate how athletes also use more specific coping strategies to help deal with potential adversity and stress in competitions. The stressors particular to competitions include the fear of injury, performance slumps, the expectations of others, crowd noises, external distractions, failure, and critical points in the competition. Let's first take a look at how coping is defined before discussing specific coping strategies used in sport.

Definition of Coping

Although many definitions of **coping** have been put forth in the psychological literature, the most popular definition is "a process of constantly changing cognitive and behavioral efforts to manage specific external and/or internal demands or conflicts appraised as taxing or exceeding one's resources" (Lazarus & Folkman, 1984, p. 141). This view considers coping as a dynamic process involving both cognitive and behavioral efforts to manage stress—a definition that is consistent with McGrath's (1970) model of stress (presented in chapter 4). In addition, it emphasizes an interactional perspective, in which both personal and situational factors combine to influence the coping responses. Although individuals appear to exhibit similar coping styles across situations, the particular coping strategies they use depend on both personal and situational factors (Nicholls & Polman, 2007).

Categories of Coping

The two most widely accepted coping categories are **problem-focused coping** and **emotion-focused coping**. Problem-focused coping involves efforts to alter or manage the problem that is causing the stress for the individual concerned. It includes such specific behaviors as information gathering, making precompetition and competition plans, goal setting, time management, problem solving, increasing effort, self-talk, and adhering to an injury rehabilitation program. Emotion-focused coping entails regulating the emotional responses to the problem that causes stress for the individual. It includes such specific behaviors as meditation, relaxation, wishful thinking, reappraisal, self-blame, mental and behavioral withdrawal, and cognitive efforts to change the meaning of the situation (but not the actual problem or environment). Lazarus (2000) suggested that problem-focused coping is used more often when situations are amenable to change, and emotion-focused coping is used more often when situations are not amenable to change. A third category of coping is known as social support coping (Smith, Smoll, & O'Rourke, 2011). Although not as popular as emotion-focused and problem-focused coping, social support coping occurs when one turns to others for assistance and emotional support in times of stress. For example, an athlete might seek a coach's or teammate's help in mastering a skill or dealing with a particularly difficult loss.

Given multiple stressors (e.g., interpersonal relationships, injury, expectation of others, financial matters), no single type of coping strategy is effective in all athletic settings. It is recommended, therefore, that athletes learn a diverse set of problem- and emotion-focused

Coping With the Yips

I was 18 years old when I won my first tournament on the European tour. That's where I developed "the yips." This is a jerky, uncontrolled putting stroke that sends scores soaring. All of my career I've struggled to control the yips. At one point I was yipping so badly that I four-putted from three feet and actually hit the ball twice. Those were extremely difficult times. I often thought about quitting

—Bernhard Langer, World Golf
Hall of Famer

Research examining "the yips" (most commonly associated with golf putting) has suggested that the yips are a psychoneuromuscular condition that lies on a continuum anchored by focal dystonia (type I) and choking (type II). Focal dystonia is characterized by involuntary tremors, freezing, or jerking of the hands. Choking is the result of attentional disturbances caused by self-focus or distraction (Beilock & Gray, 2007; Philippen & Lobinger, 2012). Whatever the type, it appears that perfectionism—especially the aspects of personal standards, organization, and concern over mistakes—is associated with a greater likelihood of suffering from the yips (Roberts, Rotherman, Maynard, Thomas, & Woodman, 2013). This condition can be devastating and can ruin the career of an elite or professional athlete. The yips are usually due to anxiety, nerves, or choking in high-pressure situations (type II). Golfers with the yips tend to have higher heart rates, a tighter grip on the putter, and increased forearm and muscle activity. In one of the few empirical studies of the attention and emotions associated with the yips (type II), Philippen and Lobinger (2012) interviewed tournament golfers who self-identified as having the yips. The yips made them lose confidence in their putting, feel out of control, worry about making mistakes, and fear having to putt. In addition, right before putting they tended focus on technical changes, the negative outcome of the yips, the alignment and follow-through, and keeping the head down. This focus on negative emotions and the technical aspects of the movement usually results in suboptimal performance (Beilock & Gray, 2007; Hill, Hanton, Matthews, & Fleming, 2010a). Sometimes a change in technique (e.g., changing the putting grip) or equipment (e.g., using a different putter) might help. But how can athletes cope with the yips from a psychological perspective?

- Relaxation training (either mental or physical)
- Positive thinking (tied to a multimodal relaxation procedure such as cognitive–affective stress management)
- Visualization (see chapter 13 for specific instructions)

In one of the few studies that have focused on the type I yips, Rotheram, Maynard, Thomas, Bawden, and Francis (2012) used a technique called the emotional freedom technique, which involves stimulating various acupuncture points on the body. The appropriate acupuncture points were tapped while the golfer was tuned in to the perceived psychological causes (significant life events or trauma) associated with his yips experience. This technique has also been used in individuals experiencing debilitating effects of traumatic events, such as soldiers suffering from posttraumatic stress disorder or victims of automobile accidents. Results revealed improvements in movement patterns associated with putting as measured through kinematic analysis as well as improved putting in actual competitive situations. This approach is promising, but more research is necessary to test its application in different people and different situations.

coping strategies and engage others in social support in order to prepare to manage emotions effectively in numerous stress situations.

Studies of Coping in Sport

Compared with what we see in the general psychology literature, there is a paucity of research in sport psychology on coping, although such studies have been increasing in the past 20 years (e.g., Anshel & Weinberg, 1995a; Jordet & Elfernink-Gemser, 2012; Nicholls, Hemmings, & Clough, 2010; Pensgaard & Duda, 2003; Tamminen & Holt, 2010). One of the top researchers in the world on stress and coping (Lazarus, 2000) has argued that sport provides a classic situation in which the effectiveness of different coping strategies can be tested. Along these

Resiliency: Bouncing Back From Adversity

Most of us probably know survivors of horrific circumstances and events such as cancer, the Holocaust, HIV/AIDS, war, school shootings, and the terrorist attacks of 9/11. Studies (e.g., Butler et al., 2005) have shown that many individuals not only survive but gain positive attributes because of adversity. It has been argued that experiences of adversity strengthen resilient qualities such as self-esteem and self-efficacy. In a thorough review of the literature, Fletcher and Sarkar (2013) noted that most definitions of resiliency revolve around the core concepts of adversity and adaptation. It appears that resilience is required in response to different adversities, ranging from daily hassles to major life events, and that positive adaptation must be appropriate to the type of adversity. The notion of resiliency seems appropriate for the study of sport because one needs to effectively bounce back from adversity in the form of injury, poor performance, being cut from a team, firing (coaches), lack of crowd or community support, and team conflicts (to name a few). Galli and Vealey (2008) interviewed athletes who described their experiences with resiliency in sport. Key points included the following:

- The heart of the resilience process was the use of a variety of coping strategies to deal with unpleasant emotions such as feeling sad, frustrated, hurt, embarrassed, angry, and confused.

- The adversity they had to overcome and their eventual resiliency in coping with the adversity extended over a considerable period of time (usually months).

- Mental toughness and personal resources such as determination, competitiveness, commitment, persistence, maturity, and optimism were keys to successfully coping with adversity.

- Sociocultural influences such as social support (or lack of it) were seen as critical to being resilient.

- Although coping with adversity was often unpleasant, many positive outcomes resulted from these coping efforts, including gaining perspective, gaining motivation to help others, learning, and generally being strengthened because of the adversity.

Morgan, Fletcher, and Sarkar (2013) expanded the notion of resiliency by investigating it in five elite sport teams. They defined team resilience as a "dynamic psychosocial process which protects a group of individuals from the potential negative effect of the stressors they collectively encounter" (p. 549). Results reveled four main resilience characteristics of elite sport teams:

- *Group structure.* Consisting of facilitating formal structure (e.g., coaches, captains, managers), positive group norms and values, and clearly defined communication channels

- *Mastery approaches.* Consisting of effective behavioral responses, effectively managing change, and having a learning orientation

- *Social capital.* Including social support, positive interpersonal interactions, and a strong group identity

- *Collective efficacy.* Including mastery experiences, group cohesion, and positive communications after failure

lines, several in-depth qualitative interviews (e.g., Dale, 2000; Gould, Eklund, & Jackson, 1992a,b; Hill, Hanton, Matthews, & Fleming, 2010b, 2011) assessed the coping strategies that elite athletes use. At least 40% of the athletes reported using the following:

- Thought control (blocking distractions, using coping thoughts such as "I can do it")

- Task focus (narrowing focus)

- Rational thinking and self-talk (taking a rational approach to one's self and the situation)

- Positive focus and orientation (focusing on belief in one's ability)

- Social support (encouragement from coach, family, and friends)

- Precompetitive mental preparation and anxiety management (mental practice, precompetition routines, relaxation strategies)

- Time management (making time for personal growth and daily goals)

- Training hard and smart (applying work ethic, taking responsibility for one's training)

Furthermore, research by Gould and colleagues (e.g., Gould, Guinan, Greenleaf, Medbery, & Peterson, 1999; Greenleaf, Gould, & Dieffenbach, 2001) on Olympic athletes revealed the following consistent findings:

- Athletes who prepared for unexpected events (e.g., bad call by an official, loud roommates) were more successful than athletes who did not prepare for these events.

- Psychological skills (e.g., mental preparation, mental skills, use of routines) are important for effectively coping with psychological (e.g., anxiety, loss of concentration, lack of confidence) and nonpsychological (e.g., poor housing, injury) stressors.

- A delicate balance existed between training and overtraining, which was seen as critical to success.

- All athletes reported on the importance of some aspect of mental preparation and stated that mental preparation had a positive effect on performance.

- Negative factors that were perceived to undermine Olympic performance included departures from the normal routine, media distractions, coach issues, injury, and overtraining.

Research (Giacobbi, Foore, & Weinberg, 2004) has found that nonelite athletes use avoidance coping techniques more than elite athletes do, so the use of these techniques could be a big problem with recreational athletes. Furthermore, research (Nicholls, Polman, Morley, & Taylor, 2009) has found that factors such as sex, age, and pubertal status can influence both the type of coping strategy employed and its perceived effectiveness. For example, mental distraction strategies were significantly more effective for female athletes, whereas venting emotions was significantly more effective for male athletes. Furthermore, research (Nicholas & Jebrane, 2009) on coping strategies within individuals has shown inconsistency in coping within athletes between competition and practice as well as inconsistency across and within different competitive settings. In essence, coping appears to be situation specific. Finally, a study by Balk, Adriaase, de Ridder, and Evers (2013) found that the coping strategies of distraction and reappraisal were effective in helping athletes cope, instead of choke, under pressure.

Research by Jordet and Elferink-Gemser (2012) highlighted the dynamic nature of coping in elite soccer players participating in the World Cup. They found that the athletes used coping strategies even in the four different phases of the penalty kick:

- break after extra time (from the end of the game to when the players are gathered in the midcircle—about 2 minutes 30 seconds),

- the midcircle (from entering the midcircle to leaving the midcircle—between 40 seconds and 8 minutes 30 seconds, depending on when the player took the shot),

- the walk (from leaving the midcircle to arriving at the penalty mark—about 20 to 30 seconds), and

- at the penalty mark (from arriving at the penalty mark to when the shot was taken—about 10 to 35 seconds).

Specifically, both problem-focused and emotion-focused coping was used at all phases, although the specific coping strategies used were different and included such strategies as concentrating only on the shot, positive affirmations, letting one's body take over, shooting in one's favorite corner, focusing on one's routine, breath control, social support, and confidence in one's ability. Nicholls, Perry, Jones, Morley, and Carson (2013) also found that coping strategies changed in the form of increased conscientiousness as athletes matured cognitively. Athletes became more task oriented and less disengagement oriented as they increased in conscientiousness from 11 to 18 years of age.

Nicholls and colleagues (Nicholls, Holt, & Polman, 2005; Nicholls, Holt, Polman, & Bloomfield, 2008) investigated the stressors most frequently cited and the effectiveness of coping strategies in golfers and rugby players. Although many stressors and coping strategies were noted (some specific to the sport), the stressors most frequently cited were physical and mental errors, and the most effective coping strategies were focusing on the task, positive reappraisal, thought stopping, and increased effort. Three other studies (Hoar, Crocker, Holt, & Tamminen, 2010; Reeves, Nicholls, & McKenna, 2011; Tamminen & Holt, 2010) focused on coping in adolescent athletes. One study (Hoar et al., 2010) revealed that coping effectiveness training enhanced athletes' self-efficacy, coping effectiveness, and performance. The second study (Reeves et al., 2011) found sex differences in adolescent coping; however, these differences depended on the interpersonal stress source with which the adolescent was coping. The third study (Tamminen & Holt, 2010) took a longitudinal approach to coping across a season and found that coping strategies changed as stressors changed across a season. In addition although most young athletes were reactive in terms of their coping, a few were proactive and actively planned to use certain coping strategies in specific situations. Given these results, coaches should be sensitive to the different coping strategies male and female adolescent athletes might use based on the interpersonal stressor involved. Finally, Anshel (2010) found that coping styles can often differ based on culture and race because different cultures and races have different cultural norms and customs. Sport psychology consultants should be sensitive to these differences in coping when counseling athletes from different cultures and races.

Anecdotal Tips for Coping With Stress

Other on-site procedures can help athletes cope with competitive stress. These techniques are not backed with scientific, empirical research but rather come from applied experience with athletes (Kirschenbaum, 1997; Weinberg, 1988, 2002). Choose the strategies that work best for your situation.

• *Smile when you feel tension coming on.* A simple and effective cue is to smile in the face of tension. It is difficult, if not impossible, to be mad or upset when you are smiling. By smiling you take the edge off an anxiety-producing situation. This keeps things in perspective so you can forget about the pressure and enjoy the competition.

• *Have fun—enjoy the situation.* Athletes who are highly skilled in their sport convey a sense of enjoyment and fun. Most of them look forward to and even relish pressure situations. For example, Al Oerter, four-time Olympic gold medalist in the discus, said, "I love competing in the Olympics. That's what training is all about." Similarly, tennis great Billie Jean King said, "I like the pressure, the challenge—it's exciting; I choose to be here!" Enjoying the game also helps keep young players from burning out. Try to keep winning and losing in perspective and focus on enjoying the experience without undue concern about the outcome.

• *Set up stressful situations in practice.* Practicing under simulated pressure can be good preparation for actual pressure situations. As athletes become more accustomed to playing under pressure, they will not be as negatively affected by it. You can create pressure during practice in many ways. Some college basketball coaches invite other students to practices, asking them to scream and boo so that the players know how it is to play on an opponent's home floor with the crowd against them. Football coaches sometimes set the stage for a 2-minute drill by telling the team there are 2 minutes left in the game, they are down by 2 points on their own 20-yard line, and there are two time-outs left: The offense must then move the ball into field-goal range. The effectiveness of setting up these situations in practice received empirical support from the research of Oudejans and colleagues (Nieuwenbuys & Oudejans, 2010; Oudejans & Pijpers, 2009, 2010), who found that practicing and training in the presence of anxiety led to improved performance in future stressful situations.

• *Slow down and take your time.* Many athletes report that when they are feeling frustrated and mad, they start to perform too quickly. It is as if the easiest way to cope with all the anger and pressure is to hurry up and finish. For example, tennis players and golfers tend to rush their shots when they get anxious. Conversely, some athletes take too much time between shots, and their thinking disrupts performance. You can find the middle ground if you develop highly consistent preshot routines and perform them regularly before each golf shot or tennis serve regardless of the situation and pressure (see chapter 16).

• *Stay focused on the present.* Thinking about what just happened or what might happen usually only increases anxiety. You can be sure that worrying about a fly ball you just dropped will not help you catch the next one that comes your way. In fact, worry makes you more anxious and increases your chances of missing. Similarly, thinking about what might happen on the next point or shot only increases pressure and anxiety (see chapter 16 for methods of focusing on the present).

• *Come prepared with a good game plan.* Indecisiveness produces anxiety. Making decisions can be stressful, and athletes and coaches have to make hundreds of decisions during the course of a game or match. Think of the decisions that point guards in basketball, football quarterbacks, golfers, baseball pitchers, tennis players, or soccer players have to make. But if they come prepared with a specific game plan or strategy, decision making is easier. For example, deciding what pitch to throw from behind in the count is often stressful for baseball pitchers. Some pregame scouting, however, can give pitchers a good idea of the best pitches to use if they fall behind to certain batters.

🔍 **DISCOVER** Activity 12.2 allows you to evaluate a relaxation training script.

Using Arousal-Inducing Techniques

So far we have focused on anxiety management techniques for reducing excess levels of anxiety. At times, however, you need to pump yourself up because you are feeling lethargic and underenergized. Perhaps you have taken an opponent too lightly and he has surprised you. Or you're feeling tired in the fourth quarter. Or you're feeling lackluster about your rehabilitation exercises. Unfortunately, coaches often inappropriately use various psyching-up or energizing strategies to pump athletes up for a competition. The key is to get athletes at an optimal level of arousal, and things such as pep talks and motivational speeches can often overarouse athletes. If arousal is to be raised, it should be done in a deliberate fashion with awareness of optimal arousal states. Certain behaviors, feelings, and attitudes signal that you are underactivated:

- Moving slowly, not getting set
- Mind wandering, becoming easily distracted
- Lack of concern about how well you perform
- Lack of anticipation or enthusiasm
- Heavy feeling in the legs, no bounce

You don't have to experience all these signs to be underactivated. The more you notice, however, the more likely it is that you need to increase arousal. Although these feelings can appear at any time, they usually indicate you are not physically or mentally ready to play. Maybe you didn't get enough rest, played too much (i.e., overtrained), or are playing against a significantly weaker opponent. The quicker you can detect these feelings, the quicker you can start to get yourself back on track. Here we provide suggestions for generating more energy and activating your system. Note that these are mostly individual strategies (although some could be altered for teams) rather than team energizing strategies such as team goal setting, bulletin boards, media coverage or reports, and pep talks.

KEY POINT To take the steps to increase or decrease your arousal level, first become aware of how activated or aroused you feel.

- *Increase breathing rate.* Breath control and focus can produce energy and reduce tension. Short,

Coping Strategies Used by World-Class Coaches

Most studies of coping have focused on athletes, but coaches often have to cope with high levels of stress too, especially at the elite level. Olusoga, Butt, Maynard, and Hays (2010) investigated the coping techniques of elite coaches and found that the major coping strategies could be categorized as follows:

- *Structuring and planning*—Planning ahead; communicating with athletes, coaches, and sometimes parents; managing time effectively; and taking time off to recharge
- *Psychological skills*—Putting things into perspective, practicing positive self-talk, controlling the controllables, and using relaxation techniques
- *Support*—Surrounding one's self with supportive people, seeking advice from trusted others, and spending quality time with friends and family
- *Distraction*—Taking time off to do things one enjoys, exercising
- *Experience and learning*—Continually educating one's self, using experiences as an athlete to help make decisions, and drawing on previous experience as a coach
- *Maintaining positive coach–athlete relationships*—Always making time for the athletes, taking the viewpoint of the athletes, and getting to know each athlete

See Fletcher and Scott (2010) for a more complete review of the sources of stress on coaches' appraisals and responses to stress, and the effects of stress on personal well-being and job performance.

deep breaths tend to activate and speed up the nervous system. You also may want to say "Energy in" with each inhalation and "Fatigue out" with each exhalation.

• *Act energized.* At times when you feel lethargic and slow, acting energetic can help recapture your energy. For example, to energize themselves, tennis players often jump up and down prior to serving or receiving serve. Many athletes like to jump rope or take a short jog just before starting a competition to "get the butterflies out."

• *Use mood words and positive statements.* The mind can certainly affect the body. Saying or thinking mood words (e.g., *strong, forward, tough, aggressive, move, quick, fast, hard*) can be energizing and activating. Positive self-statements can also energize you. Some examples are "Hang in there," "I can do it," "Get going," and "Get tough."

• *Yelling and shouting.* When performing an effortful, forceful activity such as lifting weights, many individuals yell, shout, or grunt. A study by Welch and Tschampl (2012) explored this notion using the martial arts procedure known as the kiap. The kiap starts low in the abdomen and rises throughout the chest and out of the mouth. It is more of a loud guttural yell from deep within the body rather than a scream or shout produced from just the vocal chords and the throat. Results revealed that the group using the kiap technique (which included both expert and novice performers) exhibited significantly better performance on a grip strength task.

• *Listen to music.* Energetic music can be a source of energy just before a competition, and many athletes use MP3 players with headphones before a game. A study by Bishop, Karageorghis, and Loizou (2007) found that athletes consciously selected music before competition to elicit various emotional states, including improved mood and increased arousal. The British Association for Sport and Exercise Sciences expert statement (Karageorghis, Terry, Lane, Bishop, & Priest, 2012), as well as a review of the literature (Karageorghis & Priest, 2012) regarding music and exercise found the following trends:

  o Music reduces perceptions of effort (ratings of perceived exertion) at low to moderate exercise intensities by about 10%.

Pep Talks: An Applied Perspective

For a team sport coach, giving a pregame or halftime speech is an art form as delicate as drawing up Xs and Os or structuring a game plan. Sometimes less is more and sometimes it's not.

Knute Rockne probably invented the modern-day pep talk with his reference to All-American George Gipp, who had died several years earlier from an infection. Notre Dame was about to play heavily favored Army, and Rockne told his team, "The day before he died, George Gipp asked me to wait until the situation seemed hopeless, and then ask a Notre Dame team to go out and beat Army for him. This is the day and you are the team." Notre Dame won 12-6 and thus "won one for the Gipper."

Now pep talks take all forms. For example, legendary coach Vince Lombardi came into the locker room at halftime with Green Bay losing to Detroit 21-3. The players feared an emotional outburst, but all Lombardi said was, "Men, we're the Green Bay Packers." Green Bay won 31-21. Urban Meyer, then coach for the University of Florida, felt his team was flat going against Kentucky and had his assistant coaches throw things around the room to get the players excited and activated. Years ago, John Unitas, Hall of Fame quarterback for the Baltimore Colts, would have this to say to his team before starting a game: "Talk is cheap." Then he'd just walk out of the locker room.

Finally, Lou Holtz, who has coached successfully at several major colleges, provides some guidelines for a successful pregame talk.

- Give them a plan. It's not enough to tell your players you want to win. You need to give them a blueprint for winning.

- Make them believe they can win. Players need confidence just like everyone else.

- Do not lie. The moment a coach lies to his players, he loses their respect.

- Be yourself. Players can spot a phony.

- Use humor. You can learn about a team's attitude by how they laugh. Don't make it life and death, as this can cause players to tighten up.

○ It doesn't seem to matter whether the music is selected by the self or by the experimenter.

○ Music appears to enhance affect regardless of exercise intensity.

• *Use energizing imagery.* Imagery is another way to generate positive feelings and energy (see chapter 13). Imagery involves visualizing something that is energizing to you. A sprinter, for example, might imagine a cheetah running swiftly over the plains. A swimmer might imagine moving through the water like a shark.

• *Complete a precompetitive workout.* When athletes are feeling a little sluggish, they sometimes practice and stretch before a performance to help activate themselves. A precompetitive workout typically occurs 4 to 10 hours before the athletic performance.

Thus far we have discussed individual strategies for becoming more energized, but at times a coach might have to energize an entire team. This might especially be the case if the team is playing a much weaker opponent and believes that winning is guaranteed. Two of the more typical strategies for energizing a team are setting team or individual performance (not focusing solely on winning) goals (discussed in more detail in chapter 15) and giving a pep talk. Setting goals can help keep team energy high. For example, a heavily favored football team might set some team goals (e.g., to keep the opposition under 70 yards rushing, to average 5 yards per carry, and to have no quarterback sacks) to maintain intensity regardless of the score. Pep talks have been used extensively throughout the years, the most famous probably being Knute Rockne's "Win one for the Gipper" speech at halftime of a Notre Dame football game. Many coaches have tried to emulate this pep talk, but contemporary thinking argues against such an approach because such a talk suggests that all athletes need to be more energized, which is most often not the case. However, coaches still give pep talks. "Pep Talks: An Applied Perspective" provides some guidelines for giving a successful pregame talk.

LEARNING AIDS

SUMMARY

1. **Understand how to increase self-awareness of arousal states.**
   The first step toward controlling arousal levels is for athletes to become aware of the situations in competitive sport that cause them anxiety and of how they respond to these events. To do this, athletes can be asked to think back to their best and worst performances and then recall their feelings at these times. In addition, it is helpful to use a checklist to monitor feelings during practices and competitions.

2. **Identify somatic, cognitive, and multimodal anxiety reduction techniques.**
   A number of techniques have been developed to reduce anxiety in sport and exercise settings. The ones used most often to cope with somatic anxiety are progressive relaxation, breath control, and biofeedback. The most prevalent cognitive anxiety reduction techniques include the relaxation response and autogenic training. Two multimodal anxiety management packages that use a variety of techniques are cognitive–affective stress management and stress inoculation training. Finally, hypnosis has received more recent attention as an anxiety reduction technique as well as a method of improving other mental skills.

3. **Identify coping strategies for dealing with competitive stress.**
   The two major categories of coping are problem-focused coping and emotion-focused coping. Problem-focused coping strategies, such as goal setting or time management, involve efforts to alter or manage the problem that is causing stress. Emotion-focused coping involves regulating the emotional responses to the problem causing the stress. Having an array of coping strategies allows athletes to effectively cope with unforeseen events in a competition.

4. **Describe on-site relaxation tips for reducing anxiety.**
   In addition to several well-developed and carefully structured techniques, on-site techniques can help sport and exercise participants cope with feelings of anxiety. These on-site techniques usually involve having participants remember that they are out there to have fun and enjoy the experience.

5. **Understand the matching hypothesis.**
   The matching hypothesis states that anxiety management techniques should be matched to the particular anxiety problem. That is, cognitive anxiety should be treated with mental relaxation, and somatic anxiety should be treated with physical relaxation.

6. **Identify techniques for raising arousal for competition.**

Sometimes energy levels need to be raised. Increased breathing, imagery, music, positive self-statements, and simply acting energized can all help increase arousal. The ability to regulate your arousal level is indeed a skill. To perfect that skill you need to systematically practice arousal regulation techniques, integrating them into your regular physical practice sessions whenever possible.

KEY TERMS

progressive relaxation	autogenic training	matching hypothesis
breath control	cognitive–affective stress management training (SMT)	coping
biofeedback	stress inoculation training (SIT)	problem-focused coping
relaxation response	hypnosis	emotion-focused coping

REVIEW QUESTIONS

1. Discuss the three basic tenets of progressive relaxation and give some general instructions for using this technique.

2. Describe the four elements of the relaxation response and how to use it.

3. How does biofeedback work? Provide an example of its use in working with athletes.

4. Discuss the four phases of cognitive–affective stress management, comparing and contrasting cognitive structuring and self-instructional training.

5. Describe and give contrasting examples of emotion-focused and problem-focused coping. Under what circumstances is each type of coping used in general?

6. Describe five coping strategies that elite Olympic athletes used in the studies by Gould and colleagues.

7. Discuss three strategies for on-site reductions in anxiety and tension.

8. Discuss the current state of knowledge regarding the effects of hypnosis on athletic performance.

9. Describe three strategies for coping with different emotions in sport.

10. Discuss how the relaxation procedure of systematic desensitization works and provide a practical example.

CRITICAL THINKING QUESTIONS

1. You are getting ready to play the championship game to end your volleyball season in two weeks. You know that some of your players will be tense and anxious, especially because it's the first time your team has reached the final game. But you have a few players who are always slow starters and seem lethargic at the beginning of competitions. What kinds of techniques and strategies would you use to get your players ready for this championship game?

2. Think back to a time when you were really anxious before a competition and when your anxiety had a negative effect on your performance. Now you know all about relaxation and stress management techniques as well as several specific coping strategies. If you were in this same situation again, what would you do (and why) to prepare yourself to cope more effectively with your excess anxiety?

Imagery

After reading this chapter, you should be able to

1. define imagery;
2. discuss the effectiveness of imagery in enhancing sport performance;
3. discuss the where, when, why, and what of imagery use by athletes;
4. discuss the factors influencing imagery effectiveness;
5. describe how imagery works;
6. discuss the uses of imagery;
7. explain how to develop a program of imagery training; and
8. explain when to use imagery.

For many years athletes have been mentally practicing their motor skills. In fact, mental practice—so named to distinguish it from physical practice—has a long tradition in sport and exercise psychology, and the large body of literature on the topic has been thoroughly reviewed on numerous occasions (e.g., Cumming & Williams, 2012; Richardson, 1967a,b; Weinberg, 1981, 2008). In the past two decades, this general focus on mental practice has given way to systematically studying the potential uses and effectiveness of imagery in sport and exercise settings. The following quote by all-time golf great Jack Nicklaus (1974, p.19) demonstrates his use of imagery:

" Before every shot I go to the movies inside my head. Here is what I see. First, I see the ball where I want it to finish, nice and white and sitting up high on the bright green grass. Then, I see the ball going there; its path and trajectory and even its behavior on landing. The next scene shows me making the kind of swing that will turn the previous image into reality. These home movies are a key to my concentration and to my positive approach to every shot. "

Nicklaus obviously believes that rehearsing shots in his mind before actually swinging is critical to his success. He has said that hitting a good golf shot is 10% swing, 40% stance and setup, and 50% mental picture of how the swing should occur. In the 1980s and 1990s, multiple gold medalist Greg Louganis repeatedly told of his use of imagery before performing any of his dives. Picturing the perfect dive helped build his confidence and prepared him to make minute physical changes based on his body positioning during various phases of the dive. The following quote by Michael Phelps, 18-time gold medalist and 22-time Olympic medalist, also underscores the importance of imagery:

" Before the Olympic trials I was doing a lot of visualization. And I think that helped me to get a feel of what it was going to be like when I got there. "

Nicklaus, Louganis, and Phelps are just a few of the many athletes who, for quite some time, have used imagery to enhance performance. Although athletes obviously use imagery on their own, there are times when coaches have also understood the importance of imagery in enhancing performance. This is seen in the quote by famous soccer (football) coach Sir Alex Ferguson, the former manager of Manchester United:

" I was always trying to add imagination to my coaching, emphasizing the need for players to have a picture in their minds, to visualize how they could have a creative impact on the shifting pattern of a game. (Ferguson & McIlvaney, 2000, p. 151) "

As scientific evidence accumulates supporting the effectiveness of imagery in sport and exercise settings, many more athletes and exercisers have begun using imagery to help their performances and make their experiences in sport and exercise settings more enjoyable. In this chapter we discuss the many uses of imagery in sport and exercise settings as well as the factors that make it more effective. Many people misunderstand the term, so let's start by defining imagery.

Defining Imagery

You probably have heard several terms that refer to an athlete's mental preparation for competition, including *visualization, mental rehearsal, symbolic rehearsal, covert practice, imagery,* and *mental practice.* These terms all refer to creating or re-creating an experience in the mind. The process involves recalling from memory pieces of information stored from experience and shaping these pieces into meaningful images. These pieces are essentially a product of your memory, experienced internally through the recall and reconstruction of previous events. **Imagery** is actually a form of simulation. It is similar to a real sensory experience (e.g., seeing, feeling, or hearing), but the entire experience occurs in the mind.

KEY POINT Through imagery you can re-create positive experiences or picture new events to prepare yourself mentally for performance.

All of us use imagery to re-create experiences. Have you ever watched the swing of a great golfer and tried to copy the swing? Have you ever mentally reviewed the steps and music of an aerobic dance workout before going to the class? We are able to accomplish these things because we can remember events and re-create pictures and feelings of them. We can also imagine (or "image") events that have not yet occurred. For example, an athlete rehabilitating from a shoulder separation could see herself lifting her arm over her head even though she has not yet been able to do this. Many soccer players picture themselves on the pitch and image themselves making certain moves or passes or shots on goal. Similarly, many football quarterbacks view films of the defense they will be facing and then, through imagery, see themselves using certain offensive sets and strategies to offset the specific defensive alignments. Tennis great Chris Evert would carefully rehearse every detail of a match, including her opponent's style, strategy, and shot selection. Here is how Evert described using imagery to prepare for a tennis match:

" Before I play a match, I try to carefully rehearse what is likely to happen and how I will react in certain situations. I visualize myself playing typical points based on my opponent's style of play. I see myself hitting crisp, deep shots from the baseline and coming to the net if I get a weak return. This helps me mentally prepare for a match, and I feel like I've already played the match before I even walk on the court. (Tarshis, 1977) "

Imagery can, and should, involve as many senses as possible. Even when imagery is referred to as "visualization," the kinesthetic, auditory, tactile, and olfactory senses are all potentially important. The **kinesthetic sense** is particularly useful in enhancing athletic performance (MacIntyre & Moran, 2010; Moran & MacIntyre, 1998) because it involves the feeling of the body as it moves in different positions. Using more than one sense helps create more vivid images, thus making the experience more real. As Tiger Woods said, "You have to see the shots and feel them through your hands."

Let's look at how you might use a variety of senses as a baseball batter. First, you use **visual sense** to watch the ball as the pitcher releases it and it comes toward the plate. You use kinesthetic sense to know where your bat is and to transfer your weight at the proper time to maximize power. You use **auditory sense** to hear the sound of the bat hitting the ball. You can also use your **tactile sense** to note how the bat feels

Imagery can help athletes prepare for difficult situations so that they are prepared to deal with a variety of circumstances during competition.

in your hands. Finally, you might use your **olfactory sense** to smell the freshly mowed grass.

Besides using your senses, learning to attach various emotional states or moods to your imagined experiences is also important. Re-creating emotions (e.g., anxiety, anger, joy, or pain) or thoughts (e.g., confidence and concentration) through imagery can help control emotional states. In one case study, a hockey player had difficulty dealing with officiating calls that went against him. He would get angry, lose his cool, and then not concentrate on his assignment. The player was instructed to visualize himself getting what he perceived to be a bad call and then to use the cue words "stick to ice" to remain focused on the puck. Similarly, an aerobic exerciser might think negatively and lose her confidence if she has trouble remembering a specific routine. But via imagery, she could mentally rehearse the routine and provide positive instructional comments to herself if she did in fact make a mistake.

In a thorough review of the literature, Cumming and Williams (2012) identified five key characteristics of the imagery process:

- *Modality.* The senses used in imagery—auditory, visual, tactile, olfactory, and kinesthetic
- *Perspective.* The visual perspective taken—first person (internal) or third person (external)
- *Angle.* The viewing angle when imaging from an external perspective—above, behind, front, or side
- *Agency.* The author or agent of the behavior being imagined—one's self or another person
- *Deliberation.* The degree to which imagery is deliberate or spontaneous (i.e., triggered)

Evidence of Imagery's Effectiveness

To determine whether imagery does indeed enhance performance, sport psychologists have looked at three kinds of evidence: anecdotal reports, case studies, and scientific experiments. **Anecdotal reports**, or people's reports of isolated occurrences, are numerous; the remarks by Jack Nicklaus, Michael Phelps, and Chris Evert are examples. Many of our best athletes and national coaches include imagery in their daily training regimens, and even more athletes report using imagery to help recover from injury. A study conducted at the United States Olympic Training Center (Murphy, Jowdy, & Durtschi, 1990) indicated that 100% of sport psychology consultants and 90% of Olympic athletes used some form of imagery and that 97% of these athletes believe that imagery helped their performance. In addition, 94% of the coaches of Olympic athletes used imagery during their training sessions, and 20% used it at every practice session. Orlick and Partington (1988) reported that 99% of Canadian Olympians used imagery. These percentages have remained fairly consistent over the years.

Although anecdotal reports might be the most interesting evidence supporting the effectiveness of imagery, they are also the least scientific. A more scientific approach is the use of **case studies**, in which the researcher closely observes, monitors, and records an individual's behavior over a period of time. Some case studies demonstrated the effectiveness of imagery, such as one using a field-goal kicker (Jordet, 2005; Titley, 1976). A study by Wakefield and Smith (2011) examined the effect of imagery on strength performance. More recently researchers have used **multiple-baseline case studies** (i.e., studies of just a few people over a long period of time, with multiple assessments documenting changes in behavior and performance) and have found positive effects of imagery on performance enhancement and other psychological variables such as confidence and coping with anxiety (e.g., Evans, Jones, & Mullen, 2004; Post, Muncie, & Simpson, 2012). Many other studies have focused on **psychological intervention packages**—approaches that use a variety of psychological interventions (e.g., self-talk, relaxation, concentration training) along with imagery. For example, Suinn (1993) used a technique known as visuomotor behavior rehearsal (VMBR), which combines relaxation with imagery. Research with skiers using VMBR showed increases in the neuromuscular activity of the muscles used for skiing; similar performance increases occurred in karate performers who used VMBR (Seabourne, Weinberg, Jackson, & Suinn,

1985). Other studies using imagery as part of a psychological intervention package have shown positive performance results with golfers, basketball players, triathletes, figure skaters, swimmers, and tennis players, although the improvements could not be attributed to imagery alone (Thelwell, Greenlees, & Weston, 2010; Weinberg & Williams, 2001). Finally, qualitative investigations (e.g., Hanton & Jones, 1999b; MacIntyre & Moran, 2007; Munroe, Giacobbi, Hall, & Weinberg, 2000; Thelwell & Greenlees, 2001) have also revealed the positive relationship between imagery and performance.

Evidence from **scientific experiments** in support of imagery is impressive and clearly demonstrates the value of imagery in learning and performing motor skills (Feltz & Landers, 1983; Martin, Moritz, & Hall, 1999; Morris, Spittle, & Perry, 2004; Murphy, Nordin, & Cumming, 2008; Weinberg, 2008). These studies have been conducted across different levels of ability and in many sports, including basketball, football, kayaking, track and field, swimming, karate, downhill and cross-country skiing, volleyball, tennis, and golf.

Imagery in Sport: Where, When, Why, and What

We now know from research that imagery can positively enhance performance. More recent findings, especially with the Sport Imagery Questionnaire (Hall, Mack, Pavio, & Hausenblas, 1998), have revealed some details of imagery use that should help practitioners design imagery training programs (discussed later in the chapter).

Where Do Athletes Image?

The majority of imagery use occurs in practice and competition; athletes consistently use imagery more frequently in competition than in training (Munroe et al., 2000; Salmon, Hall, & Haslam, 1994). Interestingly, although the majority of imagery research has focused on practice situations (e.g., using imagery to facilitate learning), athletes appear to use imagery more for performance enhancement (i.e., competing effectively), especially during precompetition. Therefore, coaches might want to focus more on teaching athletes proper imagery use during practice so that the athletes can transfer it over to competition as well as practice the correct use of imagery on their own.

When Do Athletes Image?

Research has revealed (see Hall, 2001, for a review) that athletes use imagery before, during, and after practice; outside of practice (home, school, work); and before, during, or after competition. Some studies have indicated that athletes use imagery even more frequently outside of practice than during practices. Interestingly, athletes report using more imagery before competition than during or after competition, whereas imagery use is more frequent during practices than before or after practices. Imagery appears to be underused after practices and competitions. This is unfortunate because vivid images of performance should be fresh in athletes' minds after practice, which should facilitate the efficacy of imagery right after practicing or performing.

It has also been suggested that athletes use imagery while they are injured. However, research has revealed that athletes use imagery more frequently during competition and practice than during injury rehabilitation. When imagery is used for rehabilitation purposes, the focus tends to be on motivation to recover and to rehearse rehabilitation exercises. More emphasis should be placed on imagery during recovery from injury because a variety of benefits (including faster healing) have been identified.

Why Do Athletes Image?

When attempting to determine why performers and exercisers use imagery, we should differentiate content from function. Content relates to what a person images (e.g., muscles feeling loose after a hard workout),

whereas function refers to why the person images (e.g., to feel relaxed). In discussing why individuals image, we focus on function. To help in this regard, Pavio (1985) distinguished between two functions of imagery: motivational and cognitive. He suggested that imagery plays both cognitive and motivational roles in mediating behavior and that each is capable of being oriented toward either general or specific behavioral goals (figure 13.1).

On the motivational-specific (MS) side, people can use imagery to visualize specific goals and goal-oriented behaviors, such as winning a particular contest or being congratulated for a good performance. In fact, imagery can help an individual set specific goals and then adhere to the training to reach these goals (Martin, Moritz, & Hall, 1999). Empirical testing has determined that motivational-general imagery should be classified into motivational general—mastery (MG-M) and motivational general—arousal (MG-A). Imaging performing well to maintain confidence is an example of MG-M, and achieving positivism and focus has been identified as a potential outcome of MG-M imagery. Mattie and Munroe-Chandler (2012) found that MG-M imagery was a strong and consistent predictor of mental toughness. Using imagery to "psych up and increase arousal" (Caudill, Weinberg, & Jackson, 1983; Munroe et al., 2000) is an example of MG-A, as is using imagery to help achieve relaxation and control (Page, Sime, & Nordell, 1999). Investigating the effectiveness of these different types of motivational imagery, Nordin and Cumming (2008) found that MS imagery was most

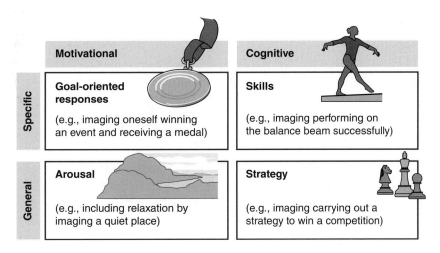

FIGURE 13.1 Cognitive and motivational functions of imagery.

Adapted, by permission, from A. Pavio, 1985, "Cognitive and motivational functions of imagery in human performance," *Canadian Journal of Applied Sport Sciences* 10: 222-228.

effective in helping athletes maintain confidence and stay focused. However, all three types of motivational imagery were effective in enhancing motivation, and MG-A and MG-M were both effective in regulating arousal (e.g., psyching up and calming down).

Cognitive-specific (CS) imagery focuses on the performance of specific motor skills, whereas cognitive-general (CG) imagery refers to rehearsing entire game plans, strategies of play, and routines inherent in competitions. Along these lines, research (Nordin & Cumming, 2008) has revealed that CS imagery was rated most effective for skill learning and development, skill execution, and performance enhancement. CG imagery was rated most effective for strategy learning and development and for strategy execution. It should be noted that such mental training should supplement and complement physical practice, not replace it.

An interesting study by Short and Short (2005) demonstrated that the function of imagery might be dependent on the individual athlete; that is, different athletes viewed the same image differently. Therefore, when developing an imagery script, make sure the athlete perceives the function as facilitative. For example, an athlete might perceive the image of an Olympic gold medalist as threatening rather than motivational because she feels pressure to win a medal.

What Do Athletes Image?

Various researchers (e.g., Munroe et al., 2000) have investigated exactly what and how individuals image. The findings relate to four aspects of imaging: images of the surroundings in which the athlete competes, the positive or negative character of images, the types of imagery (visual, kinesthetic, auditory, and olfactory), and the perspective (internal vs. external) the athlete takes in creating imagery.

Surroundings

It is not surprising that athletes have reported imagining competition surroundings (e.g., venue, spectators). They have most often done this when using imagery to prepare for an event because imagining competition surroundings can increase the vividness of the image and make it more realistic. A cross country runner illustrates this type of imagery well.

" I think about the whole course in the evening . . . before I go to sleep I lay there . . . and I'll just imagine from start to finish every part of the course and where the hills are. "

Nature of Imagery

Most studies classify imagery as positive or negative. Positive images are most often reported during practices and precompetition. For example, one athlete reported imaging this way:

" During practices I am thinking about nice places and nice things. It gets your mind off it. Then it's been a half-hour into practice. "

Negative images were most often reported during competitions, as in this example:

" I sometimes imagine hitting a bad shot in golf. And guess what—I usually do hit a bad shot. "

Although the focus of imagery research has been on generating positive images, sometimes imagery (especially negative images) can have an adverse effect on performance. When directly asked, 35% of athletes, 25% of coaches, and 87% of sport psychologists could point to examples where imagery inhibited performance. The following situations should be monitored carefully because they might contribute to adverse outcomes of imagery use (Murphy et al., 2008; Murphy & Martin, 2002):

- Imagery that creates too much anxiety
- Imagery that directs attention to irrelevant factors
- Imagery that is not controllable, leading participants to image failure or mistakes
- Imagery that makes the athlete overconfident and cocky

Oftentimes we tell ourselves not to do something. But does this have a positive or negative effect? Beilock, Afremow, Rabe, and Carr (2001) investigated the notion of suppressive imagery (trying to avoid a particular error; e.g., "Don't picture a double fault"). Results revealed that the accuracy of a group that used positive imagery improved regardless of imagery frequency. However, for the group that used imagery suppression (participants were told not to image undershooting the cup and then not to image overshooting the cup), accuracy improved when they imaged before every third putt but decreased when they imaged before each putt. Even replacing this negative image with a positive image did not help performance. These results are consistent with research by Ramsey, Cumming, and Edwards (2008), who found that suppressive imagery

© Actionplus/Photoshot

An athlete can use imagery to visualize competition surroundings before an event. Visualizing the surroundings can make the imagery more realistic.

(not thinking about hitting the ball into the sand bunker next to the green) produced significantly poorer putting performance than did facilitative imagery (seeing yourself making the putt). They argue that simply mentioning the sand bunker increased players' awareness of the bunker, which in turn negatively affected their concentration. This reinforces the notion that telling yourself not to image something that you don't want to do will in fact make it more likely that you will image it, thus hindering actual performance.

An investigation by Cumming, Nordin, Horton, and Reynolds (2006) looked at how positive or negative imagery combined with self-talk influenced performance. The researchers found that participants in the facilitative imagery and facilitative self-talk condition improved their performance, whereas participants in the debilitative imagery and debilitative self-talk condition decreased their performance. Future research needs to determine the exact combinations that produce the best performance.

Finally, Post and Wrisberg (2012) conducted a qualitative interview investigation of gymnasts' experiences with imagery. Several themes were consistent. Gymnasts talked about manipulating the speed of their imagery, how they corrected their inadvertent negative or failure imagery, the multisensory nature of their imagery, the use of response and stimulus propositions (explained later in the chapter), how imagery prepared them mentally before a competition, and how they incorporated body movements with their imagery. Interestingly, some gymnasts reporting using imagery during the actual movement describing the experience of "snapshot" imagery of a skill they were about to perform. Gymnasts also used imagery to prepare for a shift in focus to the next component of a routine.

Type of Imagery

Researchers have found that athletes describe four types of imagery (visual, kinesthetic, auditory, and olfactory) and that they use visual and kinesthetic imagery most often and to the same extent. However, this does not mean that the auditory and olfactory aspects of imagery are not important. For example, a professional tennis player remarked on the importance of auditory imagery:

" If you're really visualizing something, then you should be aware of the sounds because different balls have different sounds. Balls sound different when they are sliced than when they are hit with topspin. The sound can be really important because if you imagine what it sounds like to hit a sliced backhand, it will have a different sound than a topspin. It gets to you especially in your mind set. "

Farahat, Ille, and Thon (2004) compared the effectiveness of learning a new task using visual information (i.e., watching a video) with the effectiveness of learning via kinesthetic awareness (i.e., feeling where one's arm was in space as one performed the movement blindfolded). Results revealed that the visual imagery group performed significantly better than the kinesthetic imagery group, although both imagery groups performed better than the control group. The best way to proceed (if possible) is to combine both the visual and kinesthetic information in imaging skills to maximally enhance performance.

Imagery Perspective

Athletes usually take either an internal or external perspective for viewing their imagery (Mahoney & Avener, 1977). The perspective used depends on the athlete and the situation. We look briefly at each perspective.

In using **internal imagery**, you image the execution of a skill from your own vantage point. As if you had a camera on your head, you see only what you would see if you actually executed the particular skill. As a softball pitcher, for instance, you would see the batter at the plate, the umpire, the ball in your glove, and the catcher's target, but not the shortstop, second baseman, or anything else out of your normal range of vision. Because internal imagery comes from a first-person perspective, the images emphasize the feel of the movement. As a softball pitcher, you would feel your fingers gripping the ball, the stretch of your arm during the backswing, the shift of weight, and finally the extension of your arm upon release.

In using **external imagery**, you view yourself from the perspective of an outside observer. It is as if you

are watching yourself in a movie. For example, if a baseball pitcher imagined pitching from an external perspective, he would see not only the batter, catcher, and umpire but also all the other fielders. There is little emphasis on the kinesthetic feel of the movement because the pitcher is simply watching himself perform.

Initial studies suggested that elite athletes favored an internal perspective, but other research has failed to support this contention (see Hall, 2001, for a review). Regarding performance results, few reliable differences have been established between external and internal imagery. In addition, it was virtually impossible to characterize participants as strictly internal or external imagers because people's images varied considerably, both within and between images (Epstein, 1980; Mumford & Hall, 1985). In fact, most Olympic athletes surveyed by Murphy, Fleck, Dudley, and Callister (1990) indicated that they used both internal and external imagery.

Hardy and his colleagues (Hardy, 1997; Hardy & Callow, 1999; White & Hardy, 1995) argued that task differences may influence the use of each perspective. They proposed that external imagery has superior effects on the acquisition and performance of skills that depend heavily on form for successful execution, whereas the internal perspective is predicted to be superior for the acquisition and performance of tasks that depend heavily on perception and anticipation for successful execution. Hardy and colleagues provide some preliminary data to support their contentions on form-based tasks such as gymnastics, karate, and rock climbing (Hardy & Callow, 1999), although other data suggest that imagery perspective did not make a difference in relation to the type of task performed (Cumming & Ste-Marie, 2001).

On a final note, tasks varying along the continuum of open (time pressured, changing environment; e.g., basketball) and closed (not time stressed, stable environment; e.g., golf) sports may be affected by internal and external imagery (Munroe-Chandler & Morris, 2011). For example, research by Spittle and Morris (2007) indicated that internal imagery might be more beneficial for closed tasks and external imagery more beneficial for open tasks. More research is clearly necessary to untangle this thorny issue.

Even though the research is somewhat inconclusive, a review of this literature showed that internal imagery produced more electrical activity in the muscles involved in the imagined activity than did external imagery (Hale, 1994). Internal imagery appears to make it easier to bring in the kinesthetic sense, feel the movement, and approximate actual performance skills.

In summary, many people switch back and forth between internal and external imagery. As one Olympic rhythmic gymnast reported, "Sometimes you look at it from a camera view, but most of the time I look at it as what I see from within, because that's the way it's going to be in competition" (Orlick & Partington, 1988, p. 114). The important thing appears to be getting a clear, controllable image regardless of whether it is from an internal or an external perspective.

Factors Affecting the Effectiveness of Imagery

Several factors seem to determine the extent to which imagery can improve performance. Keep these in mind to maximize the effectiveness of imagery.

• *Nature of the task.* Years of research have indicated that tasks involving mostly cognitive components, such as decision making and perception, show the greatest positive benefits from imagery rehearsal (Feltz & Landers, 1983). The performer practicing mentally can think about what to do and how to overcome potential barriers and can rehearse the temporal and spatial regularities of a skill. For instance, to make the right decision to finish off a fast break, a basketball point guard might visualize running a break and note the changing positions of the offensive and defensive players. Note, however, that imagery has proved to be effective in a wide range of tasks, not just those comprising mostly cognitive and decision-making components. Research on both discrete or serial tasks (e.g., golf) and continuous tasks (e.g., swimming) shows positive effects of imagery.

• *Skill level of the performer.* Experimental evidence shows that imagery significantly helps performance for both novice and experienced athletes, although the effects are somewhat stronger for experienced players (Hall, 2001). In addition, experienced athletes appear to use imagery more frequently (Arvinen-Barrow, Weigand, & Thomas, 2007; Gregg & Hall, 2006). Imagery may help novice performers learn cognitive elements relevant to the successful performance of the skill. For example, after a physical education teacher demonstrates serving a volleyball, she might have the students picture themselves per-forming the serve. In experienced performers, imagery appears to help refine skills and prepare for making rapid decisions and perceptual adjustments.

KEY POINT The nature of the task and the skill level of the performer affect the extent to which imagery will enhance performance. Novice and highly skilled performers who use imagery on cognitive tasks show the most positive effects.

• *Imaging ability.* Probably the most powerful factor influencing the effectiveness of imagery is the person's ability in the use of imagery. Research has indicated that imagery is more effective when individuals have higher ability to imagine (Issac, 1992). For example, Robin and colleagues (2007) found that service returns in tennis (open skill) improved significantly more for players higher in image ability than for those lower in image ability. Good imaging ability has been defined mostly in terms of the vividness and controllability of images. In addition, Gregg, Hall, McGowan, and Hall (2011) argue that imagery should be assessed multiple ways because it has multiple uses and takes multiple forms. The better athletes are at a specific imagery ability, the more they will use this type of imagery. Using imagery is a skill; therefore, with practice one can improve the vividness and controllability of one's imagery (Rodgers, Hall, & Buckholtz, 1991; Wakefield & Smith, 2011) Finally, in the general psychology literature, imagery has often been investigated by focusing on the differences between clinical and normal populations. MacIntyre, Moran, Collet, and Guillot (2013) argued that motor imagery in sport should be studied by focusing on athletes with high imagery ability. This should more fully help our understanding of the imagery process.

• *Using imagery along with physical practice.* Imagery needs to be added to one's normal physical practice. However, imagery does not take the place of physical practice. A combination of physical and mental practice is not better than physical practice alone if the mental component takes time away from physical practice (Hird, Landers, Thomas, & Horan, 1991). However, mental practice does improve performance more than no practice at all. An individual who is injured, fatigued, or overtrained might use imagery as a substitute for physical practice. We might think of imagery as a vitamin supplement to physical practice—something that could give individuals an edge in improving performance (Vealey & Greenleaf, 2010).

• *Personality.* Personality characteristics have been considered fundamental to psychological preparation. Therefore, personality may influence the effectiveness of psychological skills used by athletes (Hardy, Roberts, Thomas, & Murphy, 2010). Although some studies have found a relationship between personality and other psychological skills (e.g., goal setting), the only study to date that has focused on personality and imagery used the personality variable of narcissism (Roberts, Callow, Hardy, Woodman, & Thomas, 2010). Narcissism is generally defined as "a pervasive pattern of grandiosity, need for admiration, and a lack of empathy" (American Psychiatric Association, 2000, p. 714). Results revealed that narcissists who used external imagery had greater increases in performance than those who used internal imagery. The researchers hypothesized that external imagery allowed narcissists to fuel their focus on themselves because an external perspective allowed them to actually see themselves performing. Clearly, more research is needed to investigate the influence of other personality traits on imagery effectiveness.

How Imagery Works

How can just thinking about jumping over the high bar, hitting a perfect tennis serve, healing an injured arm, or sinking a golf putt actually help athletes accomplish these things? We can generate information from memory that is essentially the same as an actual experience; consequently, imaging events can have an effect on our nervous system similar to that of the real, or actual, experience. According to Marks (1977), "Imagined stimuli and perceptual or 'real' stimuli have a qualitatively similar status in our conscious mental life" (p. 285). Sport psychologists have proposed five explanations of this phenomenon. As Munroe-Chandler and Morris (2011) noted, although no one theory can really explain all the different findings surrounding imagery research and practice, each theory can shed light on the mechanisms driving imagery and why it can enhance performance.

Psychoneuromuscular Theory

The **psychoneuromuscular theory** originated with Carpenter (1894), who proposed the **ideomotor principle** of imagery. According to this principle, imagery facilitates the learning of motor skills because of the nature of the neuromuscular activity patterns activated during imaging. That is, vividly imagined events innervate the muscles in somewhat the same way that physically practicing the movement does. These slight neuromuscular impulses are hypothesized to be identical to those produced during actual performance but reduced in magnitude (indeed, the impulses may be so minor that they do not actually produce movement).

The first scientific support of this phenomenon came from the work of Edmund Jacobson (1931), who reported that the imagined movement of bending the arm created small muscular contractions in the flexor muscles of the arm. In research with downhill skiers, Suinn (1972, 1976) monitored the electrical activity in the skiers' leg muscles as they imagined skiing the course; results showed that the muscular activity changed during the skiers' imaging. Muscle activity was highest when the skiers were imagining themselves skiing rough sections in the course, which would actually require greater muscle activity. Guillot and colleagues (2007) found that electromyographic activation in nine upper-arm muscles of participants who imaged lifting a dumbbell correlated with actual physical movement of lifting a dumbbell. Furthermore, more electromyographic activity occurred when participants imagined lifting a heavier weight than occurred when participants imagined lifting a lighter weight.

When you vividly imagine performing a movement, you use neural pathways similar to those you use when actually performing the movement. Let's take the example of trying to perfect your golf swing. The goal is to make your swing as fluid and natural as possible. To accomplish this, you imagine taking a bucket of balls to the driving range and practicing your swing, trying to automate it (i.e., groove your swing). In effect, you are strengthening the neural pathways that control the muscles related to your golf swing. Although some research supports this explanation of how imagery works, other research indicates that the electrical activity produced by the muscles does not mirror the pattern of activity that occurs when actually performing the movement (Slade, Landers, & Martin, 2002). More definitive research is necessary to empirically substantiate the idea that imagery actually works as predicted by the psychoneuromuscular theory.

Murphy (2005b) noted that with new imaging techniques such as positron emission tomography scanning and functional magnetic resonance imaging, we can compare pictures of the brain of a person who is resting quietly with pictures taken when that person is imaging, for example, a 400-meter race. These pictures show that certain areas of the cerebral cortex are much more active when a person uses imagery than when he or she is resting. Decety (1996) found that when someone imagines starting a movement, various areas of the brain become active, including the premotor cortex as the action is prepared, the prefrontal cortex as the action is initiated, and the cerebellum during the control of movement sequences that require a specific order. Even more fascinating is the discovery that many of the areas of the brain that are used during the process of visual perception are also used during visual imagery, which means that imagery shares some of the same brain processes and pathways with actual vision. These are exciting new developments, and more research is required to document how imagery actually changes our physiology and, in turn enhances performance.

Williams, Cumming, and Balanos (2010) found that the way individuals perceive imagery scripts affects their physiological responses. Specifically, if a stressor is perceived as a challenge or threat, then heart rate, stroke volume, and cardiac output increase. If a script is perceived as neutral, no change occurs. This demonstrates that what we image and the way in which we image can have an important influence on our physiological responses.

Symbolic Learning Theory

Sackett (1934) argued that imagery can help individuals understand their movements. His **symbolic learning theory** suggests that imagery may function as a coding system to help people understand and acquire movement patterns. That is, one way individuals learn skills is by becoming familiar with what needs to be done to successfully perform them. When an individual creates a motor program in the central nervous system, a mental blueprint is formed for successfully completing the movement. For example, in a doubles match in tennis, a player will be able to better plan her own course if she knows how her partner will move on a certain shot.

Thorough reviews of the literature (Driskell, Cooper, & Moran, 1994; Feltz & Landers, 1983; Feltz, Landers, & Becker, 1988) have shown that participants using imagery performed consistently better on tasks that were primarily cognitive (e.g., football quarterbacking) than on those that were more mostly motoric (e.g., weightlifting). Of course, most sport skills have both motor and cognitive components; imagery can be effective to an extent, therefore, in helping players with a variety of skills.

Bioinformational Theory

Probably the best-developed theoretical explanation for the effects of imagery is Lang's (1977, 1979) **bioinformational theory**. Based on the assumption that an image is a functionally organized set of propositions stored by the brain, the model holds that a description of an image consists of two main types of statements: response propositions and stimulus propositions. *Stimulus propositions* are statements that describe specific stimulus features of the scenario to be imagined. For example, a weightlifter at a major competition might imagine the crowd, the bar he is going to lift, and the people sitting or standing on the sidelines. *Response propositions,* on the other hand, are statements that describe the imager's response to the particular scenario. They are designed to produce physiological activity. For example, having a weightlifter feel the weight in his hands as he gets ready for his lift as well as feel a pounding heart and a little tension in his muscles is a response proposition.

The crucial point is that response propositions are a fundamental part of the image structure in Lang's theory. In essence, the image is not only a stimulus in the person's head to which the person responds. Imagery instructions (especially MG-A) that contain response propositions elicit greater physiological responses (i.e., increases in heart rate) than do imagery instructions that contain only stimulus propositions (Cumming, Olphin, & Law, 2007; Cumming & Williams, 2012). Imagery scripts should contain both stimulus and response propositions, which are more likely to create a vivid image than stimulus propositions alone.

Triple Code Model

The final model goes a step further in stating that the meaning the image has to the individual must also be incorporated into imagery models. Specifically, Ahsen's (1984) **triple code model** of imagery highlights understanding three effects that are essential parts of imagery; the effects are referred to as ISM. The first part is the image (I) itself. According to Ahsen (1984), "The image represents the outside world and its objects with a degree of sensory realism which enables us to interact with the image as if we were interacting with the real world" (p. 34). The second part is the somatic response (S): The act of imagination results in psychophysiological changes in the body (this contention is similar to Lang's bioinformational theory). The third aspect of imagery (mostly ignored by other models) is the meaning (M) of the image. According to Ahsen, every image imparts a definite significance, or meaning, to the individual imager. The same set of imagery instructions will never produce the same imagery experience for any two people.

Individual differences can be seen in Murphy's (1990) description of figure skaters who were asked to relax and concentrate on "seeing a bright ball of energy, which I inhale and take down to the center of my body." One skater imagined a glowing energy ball "exploding in my stomach [and] leaving a gaping hole in my body." Another skater said that the image of the ball of energy "blinded me so that when I began skating I could not see where I was going and crashed into the wall of the rink." In essence, Ahsen's triple code model recognizes the powerful reality of images for the individual and encourages us to seek the *meanings* of the images to the individuals.

Psychological Explanations

Although not full-blown theories, a number of **psychological explanations** have been put forth to explain the effects of imagery. For example, one notion is based on **attention–arousal set** theory and argues that imagery functions as a preparatory set that assists in achieving an optimal arousal level. This optimal level of arousal allows the performer to focus on task-relevant cues and screen out task-irrelevant cues.

A second area explaining imagery effectiveness from a psychological perspective argues that imagery helps build psychological skills that are critical to performance enhancement, such as increased confidence and concentration and decreased anxiety (Munroe-Chandler & Morris, 2011). For example, a golfer might have missed a crucial putt in the past and lost a tournament because he tightened up and got distracted by the crowd. Now, he sees himself taking a deep breath, going through his preshot routine, and feeling confident about making the putt. In his imagery he sees himself sinking the putt and winning the tournament.

Imagery can also serve a motivational function by helping the performer focus on positive outcomes, whether that be improving on previous performance or doing well against the competition. Therefore, an exerciser could image a great workout with her body getting leaner and stronger, or an athlete could image winning a competition and having a gold medal placed around his neck.

In summary, the five theories or explanations—psychoneuromuscular theory, symbolic learning theory, bioinformational theory, the triple code model, and psychological explanations—all assert that imagery can help program an athlete both physically and mentally. All these explanations have found some support from research, although they have also been closely scrutinized. You might regard imagery as a strong

---

Response Versus Stimulus Propositions: Lang's Bioinformational Theory

To be most effective, imagery scripts should contain both stimulus and response propositions, although with emphasis on response propositions. Here are examples of each:

Script Weighted With Stimulus Propositions

It is a beautiful autumn day and you are engaged in a training program, running down a street close to your home. You are wearing a bright red track suit, and as you run you watch the wind blow the leaves from the street onto a neighbor's lawn. A girl on a bicycle passes you as she delivers newspapers. You swerve to avoid a pothole in the road, and you smile at another runner passing you in the opposite direction.

Script Weighted With Response Propositions

It is a crisp autumn day and you are engaged in a training run, going down a street close to your home. You feel the cold bite of air in your nose and throat as you breathe in large gulps of air. You are running easily and smoothly, but you feel pleasantly tired and can feel your heart pounding in your chest. Your leg muscles are tired, especially the calf and thigh muscles, and you can feel your feet slapping against the pavement. As you run you can feel a warm sweat on your body.

mental blueprint of how to perform a skill, which should result in quick and accurate decision making, increased confidence, and improved concentration. In addition, the increased neuromuscular activity in the muscles helps players make movements more smooth and automatic. As Moran (2004) suggested, taken together, these approaches suggest that imagery might be best understood as a centrally mediated cognitive activity that mimics perceptual, motor, and emotional experiences in the brain. Thus, the cognitive, physiological, and psychological components of an activity can be captured through different modalities with the use of imagery.

Uses of Imagery

Athletes can use imagery in many ways to improve both physical and psychological skills. Uses include improving concentration, enhancing motivation, building confidence, controlling emotional responses, acquiring and practicing sport skills and strategies, preparing for competition, coping with pain or injury, and solving problems.

• *Improve concentration.* By visualizing what you want to do and how you want to react in certain situations, you can prevent your mind from wandering. You can imagine yourself in situations in which you often lose your concentration (e.g., after missing an easy shot in basketball, forgetting a step in an aerobic dance class, or dropping a pass in football) and then imagine yourself remaining composed and focused on the next play or step. In a study by Calmels, Berthoumieux, and d'Arripe-Longueville (2004), national softball players who were trained in the use of imagery had an enhanced ability to integrate external stimuli without being overloaded with them and to narrow attentional focus. Imagery can help facilitate perceptual processes and actually prime the visual system by helping an athlete more effectively and selectively attend to relevant stimuli (Michelson & Koenig, 2002). Furthermore, imagery can increase awareness of competitive cues that can contribute to faster decision making and improved execution of individual or team tactics (Hale, Seiser, McGuire, & Weinrich, 2005).

• *Enhance motivation.* Imagery can help build motivation to participate, especially in exercise

Rich Graessle/Icon SMI

Imagery can be used to build confidence in uncomfortable or highly stressful situations.

classes. For example, it has been found that regular participants in an aerobic dance class frequently used imagery to see themselves becoming healthier and improving physical appearance (Hausenblas, Hall, Rodgers, & Munroe, 1999). In addition, imagery has been shown to enhance motivation by adding purpose to repetitive and monotonous exercises. For example, elderly women performed more repetitions of a reaching-up exercise when they imagined themselves reaching up to pick apples compared with a condition in which no imagery was used. From a sport perspective, seeing one's self being successful, such as winning a gold medal (i.e., using MG-M imagery), has been shown to increase motivation to perform.

• *Build confidence.* If you have had trouble with serving in recent volleyball matches, for example, you might imagine hitting hard, accurate serves to build up your self-confidence. An official whose confidence is shaken when the crowd starts booing her calls against the home team could visualize herself taking control and maintaining confidence and impartiality on subsequent calls. One study showed that athletes who were high in confidence used more mastery imagery (e.g., "I imagine myself to be focused during a challenging situation") and arousal imagery (e.g., "I imagine the excitement associated with competing") and had better ability with kinesthetic and visual imagery than did athletes with low confidence (Moritz, Hall, Martin, & Vadocz, 1996). In addition, Nordin and Cumming (2005) found that debilitative imagery (imagery of negative performance) had a negative effect on self-confidence, whereas facilitative imagery did not have as strong a positive effect as expected. Generally, positive imagery has been shown to enhance confidence. In particular, Callow and Waters (2005) found that kinesthetic imagery (imagery emphasizing the feel of the movement, force, effort, and spatial sensations) improved sport confidence. Furthermore, different types of imagery are most effective for developing, maintaining, or regaining confidence, although MG-M imagery was generally used the most in all three conditions (Ross-Stewart & Short, 2009). The following statement by an elite swimmer describes using imagery to build confidence:

> Using imagery can enhance your confidence because if you imagine yourself having a good race and finishing a competition, and being excited about the time, you see that this gives you confidence before the next race . . . . Imagery can definitely give you confidence the next time you step up to the blocks.

Imagery can enhance a variety of skills to improve performance and can facilitate the learning of new techniques and strategies.

• *Control emotional responses.* Imagery can be used both to create higher levels of arousal (e.g., get "pumped up") if an athlete feels lethargic and to reduce anxiety if an athlete gets too "uptight." Along these lines, Pat Summitt, the retired, highly successful women's basketball coach at the University of Tennessee, used imagery for relaxation before important games when players tend to get too pumped and play out of control. However, research has also shown that competitive state anxiety can be both facilitative and debilitative. Therefore, an athlete who is having trouble getting up for a competition might want to use arousal imagery (anxiety seen as facilitative), whereas an athlete who finds anxiety a problem (anxiety seen as debilitative) may use imagery to control arousal and reduce anxiety (Mellalieu, Hanton, & Thomas, 2009; Vadocz, Hall, & Moritz, 1997). In addition, imagery can be used simply to increase positive affect and enjoyment of the competitive experience (McCarthy, 2009). A study by Williams and Cumming (2012) investigated the effect of imagery on stress appraisal in threat and challenging conditions. Two groups were given the same imagery scripts (using stimulus and response propositions) except that the challenge group viewed the task as a challenge (i.e., they had the resources needed to complete the task), whereas the threat group perceived the task as threatening (i.e., they did not have the resources needed to complete the task). Results revealed that those who imaged they didn't have the resources for the task perceived the task as more threatening, exhibited more cognitive anxiety, interpreted their anxiety to be more debilitating, felt less in control, and believed they would perform poorer than the challenge group. Thus, the implication of this study is that imagery can be used before performance to alter stress appraisal of the situation, which in turn can result in psychological responses that are associated with more successful performance outcomes.

• *Acquire, practice, and correct sport skills.* Probably the best-known use of imagery is for practicing a particular sport skill. Athletes practice putting a golf ball, executing a takedown in wrestling, throwing the javelin, doing a routine on the balance beam, or swimming the backstroke—all in their minds. You can practice skills to fine-tune them, or you can pinpoint weaknesses and visualize correcting them. A physical education teacher might have students imagine the proper execution of a backward roll as they wait in line for their turn. An aerobics instructor might have students imagine a sequence of movements as they listen to the music before physically attempting the steps (figure 13.2). This practice can take the form of a preview or a review. A participant can look forward to and visualize what to do in an upcoming competition or a player can review a past performance, focusing on specific aspects of the movement that were done particularly well. Finally, athletes can use imagery to detect and correct errors in their routine, motion, or movement pattern.

• *Acquire and practice strategy.* Imagery can be used to practice and learn new strategies or review alternative strategies for either team or individual sports. A quarterback, for example, might visualize different defenses and the plays that he would call to counteract them. A hockey goalie might imagine what he would do on a breakaway as three players converge on the goal. To prepare himself mentally to bat, Hank Aaron, the all-time leading home run hitter, used to visualize the various types of pitches a particular pitcher might throw him and the strategies he would use to counteract these pitches.

• *Prepare for competition.* Imagery is used most often right before competition to get athletes ready to perform their best. This preparation could take the form of imagining the arena where the athlete will perform. Or an athlete could image her preperformance routine (e.g., getting ready to go on the balance beam) to enhance focus and concentration. Similarly, a quarterback might review the different defenses he could face and the different decisions that he could make given a specific defensive alignment.

• *Cope with pain and injury.* Imagery is also useful for coping with pain and injury. It can help speed up recovery of the injured area and keep skills from deteriorating (Ievleva & Orlick, 1991). It is hard for athletes to go through an extended layoff. But instead of feeling sorry for themselves, they can imagine doing practice drills and thereby facilitate recovery. (We further discuss using imagery during injury rehabilitation later in the chapter.) In addition, Guillot, Tolleron, and Collet (2010) found that imagery can help improve flexibility, which in turn would allow a player to recover faster.

• *Solve problems.* People can use imagery to discover or solve problems in performance. A player who is not performing up to past or expected levels can use imagery to critically examine all aspects of the performance to find the potentially confounding factor. If a gymnast is experiencing trouble on a particular aspect of her floor routine, for example, she can visualize what she is doing now and compare this with what she did in the past when she was performing the moves successfully.

Keys to Effective Imagery

Like all psychological techniques, imagery skill is acquired through practice. Some participants are good at it, whereas others may not even be able to get an image in their minds. There are two keys to good images: **vividness** and **controllability**. We consider each of these in turn.

Vividness

Good imagers use all of their senses to make their images as vivid and detailed as possible. It is important

FIGURE 13.2 Imaging is a way to practice movement skills.

to create as closely as possible the actual experience in your mind. Pay particular attention to environmental detail, such as the layout of the facilities, type of surface, and closeness of spectators. Experience the emotions and thoughts of the actual competition. Try to feel the anxiety, concentration, frustration, exhilaration, or anger associated with your performance. All of this detail will make the imagined performance more real. If you have trouble getting clear, vivid images, first try to imagine things that are familiar to you, such as the furniture in your room. Then use the arena or playing field where you normally play and practice. You will be familiar with the playing surface, grandstands, background, colors, and other environmental details. Karageorghis and Terry (2011) recommend increasing the vividness of imagery by experiencing the image through the different senses; for example, the pungent smell of chlorine as you enter an indoor swimming pool, your favorite sport video game, a bright yellow tennis ball, the sound of a baseball hitting the bat squarely, the cold metal surface of a weight disc in a gym, and riding a bicycle on a bumpy path. You can practice getting vivid images with the three vividness exercises that follow. We also recommend trying the exercises in DeMille (1973).

• *Vividness exercise 1: Imagining home*—Imagine that you are in your living room. Look around and take in all the details. What do you see? Notice the shape and texture of the furniture. What sounds do you hear? What is the temperature like? Is there any movement in the air? What do you smell? Use all your

Using Imagery in Exercise

This chapter has focused predominantly on imagery in sport. However, imagery in exercise has begun to receive more attention (Gammage, Hall, & Rodgers, 2000; Hausenblas et al., 1999; Stanley, Cumming, Standage, & Duda, 2012). The following quote illustrates the use of imagery in exercise:

> For weeks before actually exercising, I visualized myself moving freely as I worked out. I enjoyed this image and it helped me to start working out.

Giacobbi, Hausenblas, Fallon, and Hall (2003) found a number of functions of exercise imagery, including the following:

- Exercise technique—images that help develop perfect exercise technique
- Aerobics routines—images that help develop routines
- Exercise context—images that create a particular scene or environment
- Appearance images—images of your body as you would like it to be
- Competitive outcomes—images of doing well in competition (e.g., winning a race, improving on past performance)
- Fitness and health outcomes—images related to improvements in fitness and health
- Emotions and feelings associated with imagery—images that increase arousal and excitement or reduce stress
- Exercise self-efficacy—images that provide confidence to sustain workouts

These functions suggest that **exercise imagery** helps sustain the motivation and self-efficacy beliefs of exercise participants, which may then lead to greater involvement in physical activity. Stanley and colleagues (Stanley & Cumming, 2010a,b; Stanley et al., 2012) found a new type of exercise imagery called enjoyment imagery, in which the participant focuses on exercise that has been very enjoyable in the past. This type of imagery increased the autonomous motivation of exercisers and produced increases in positive affect. Thus, exercise participants should be encouraged to use imagery—especially appearance, technique, and enjoyment imagery, which have been shown to be related to intrinsic motivation (Wilson, Rodgers, Hall, & Gammage, 2003)—to see themselves achieving their goals. In addition, individual differences need to be considered; for example, active individuals use more appearance or health imagery than do less active individuals, and younger males (aged 18–25 years) use more exercise technique imagery than do older males (aged 45–65 years) (Giacobbi, 2007).

senses and take it all in. You can also do this using the gym you usually work out in as a trigger.

• *Vividness exercise 2: Imagining a positive performance of a skill*—Select a particular skill in your sport and visualize yourself performing it perfectly. Perform the skill over and over in your mind, and imagine every feeling and movement in your muscles. For example, in serving a tennis ball, start by seeing yourself in the ready position, looking at your opponent and the service court. Then pick the spot where you want the serve to go. See and feel how you start the service motion and release the ball at the perfect height. Feel your back arch and your shoulder stretch as you take the racket back behind your head. Feel your weight start to transfer forward and your arm and racket reach high to contact the ball at just the right height and angle. Feel your wrist snap as you explode into the ball. Now see and feel the follow-through with your weight coming completely forward. The ball goes exactly where you want it to, forcing a high floating return from your opponent. Close in on the net and put the ball away with a firm cross-court volley.

• *Vividness exercise 3: Imagining a positive performance*—Recall as vividly as possible a time when you performed very well. If you can recall your "finest hour" in recent memory, use that. Your visualization will cover three specific areas of recall: visual, auditory, and kinesthetic.

  ○ First, visually recall how you looked when you were performing well. Notice that you look different when you're playing well compared with when you're playing poorly. Try to get as clear a picture as possible of what you look like when you are playing well. Review films of successful performances to help crystallize the image.

  ○ Now reproduce in your mind the sounds you hear when you are playing well, particularly the internal dialogue you have with yourself. What is your internal dialogue like? What are you saying to yourself, and how are you saying it? What is your internal response when you face adversity during play? Re-create all the sounds as vividly as you can.

  ○ Finally, re-create in your mind all the kinesthetic sensations you have when playing well. How do your feet and hands feel? Do you have a feeling of quickness, speed, or intensity? Do your muscles feel tight or relaxed?

Stay focused on the sensations associated with playing well.

KEY POINT When using imagery, involve as many senses as possible and re-create or create the emotions associated with the task or skill you're trying to execute.

DISCOVER Activity 13.1 helps you learn about developing imagery vividness.

Controllability

Another key to successful imagery is learning to manipulate your images so they do what you want them to. Many athletes have difficulty controlling their images and often find themselves repeating their mistakes as they visualize. A baseball batter might visualize his strikeouts; a tennis player, her double faults; or a gymnast, falling off the uneven parallel bars. Controlling your image helps you picture what you want to accomplish instead of seeing yourself make errors. The key to control is practice. The following description by an Olympic springboard diver shows how practice can help overcome an inability to control one's images:

" It took me a long time to control my images and perfect my imagery, maybe a year, doing it every day. At first I couldn't see myself; I always saw everyone else, or I would see my dives wrong all the time. I would get an image of hurting myself, or tripping on the board, or I would see something done really bad. As I continued to work on it, I got to the point where I could see myself doing a perfect dive and the crowd at the Olympics. But it took me a long time. (Orlick & Partington, 1988, p. 114) "

KEY POINT Whether a person uses an internal or an external image appears to be less important than choosing a comfortable style that produces clear, controllable images.

We suggest the following controllability exercises for practice.

• *Controllability exercise 1: Controlling performance*—Imagine working on a specific skill that has given you trouble in the past. Take careful notice of what you were doing wrong. Now imagine yourself performing that skill perfectly while seeing and feeling your movements. For example, a basketball player might see and feel herself shooting a free throw perfectly, getting nothing but net. Now, think about a competitive situation in which you have had trouble in the past. Taking the basketball example, you might see yourself shooting two free throws at the end of a game with your team down by one point. See yourself remaining calm as you sink both shots.

• *Controllability exercise 2: Controlling performance against a tough opponent*—Picture yourself playing a tough opponent who has given you trouble in the past. Try to execute a planned strategy against this person just as you would in a competition. Imagine situations in which you are getting the best of your opponent. For example, a quarterback might imagine different defenses and see himself calling the correct audible at the line of scrimmage to beat each defense. Make sure you control all aspects of your movements as well as the decisions you make.

• *Controllability exercise 3: Controlling emotions*—Picture yourself in a situation in which you tense up, become angry, lose concentration, or lose confidence (e.g., missing a field goal, blowing a breakaway layup). Re-create the situation, especially the feelings that accompany it. Feel the anxiety, for example, of playing in a championship game. Then use anxiety management strategies (see chapter 12) to feel the tension drain from your body and try to control what you see, hear, and feel in your imagery.

DISCOVER Activity 13.2 aids your understanding of developing controllability in imagery.

How to Develop an Imagery Training Program

Now that you know the principles underlying the effectiveness of imagery and are familiar with techniques for improving vividness and controllability, you have the basics you need to set up an imagery training program. To be effective, imagery should become part of the daily routine. Imagery programs should be tailored to the needs, abilities, and interests of each athlete or exerciser. When an intervention is personalized to the specific needs of the performer, it will carry greater weight and he or she will likely find it more enjoyable and easier to perform (Cumming

Imagery Training Programs

Morris, Spittle, and Watt (2005) and Morris (2013) outlined the following components that need to be considered when developing an imagery training program:

• *Prerequisites*—Personal factors, such as age, sex, skill level, imagery ability, and imagery use preferences

• *Environment*—Situational factors, such as training or competition setting, noise level, physical location, and open versus closed skills

These pre-existing factors should be considered first because they influence the three following components related to structure and content:

• *Content*—What is actually put in the imagery training program, including use of sense modalities, perspective selection (internal vs. external), timing (slow, fast, or real time), cognitive and motivational content

• *Rehearsal routines*—Characteristics associated with the delivery of the imagery training program (i.e., when and how it is rehearsed), including duration of imagery sessions, scheduling of sessions (how often and when they occur), and patterning of sessions (simple to complex)

• *Enhancements*—Ways in which imagery training programs can be improved, such as audio scripts, modeling, video or portable devices, biofeedback, and cues and triggers

After the imagery training program has been implemented for a while, it is important to conduct an evaluation to judge what is and is not working. These assessments include formative and summative testing, verbal discussions with athletes, reports written by athletes, self-evaluation ratings, and observation of athletes by sport psychologists and coaches.

& Ramsey, 2009). Simons (2000) has provided some practical tips for implementing an imagery training program in the field. In addition, Holmes and Collins (2001) offered some guidelines for making imagery more effective, which they call their PETTLEP program because it emphasizes the following:

- The *physical* nature of the movement
- The specifics of the *environment*
- The type of *task*
- The *timing* of the movement
- *Learning* the content of the movement
- The *emotion* (meaning to the individual) of the movement
- The *perspective* of the person (internal or external)

Wakefield and Smith (2012) have taken the key points of the model and provided some specific recommendations for practitioners. These are highlighted in "Implementing PETTLEP Imagery."

In testing this model, Smith, Wright, Allsopp, and Westhead (2007) found support for including the elements of the PETTLEP model in one's imagery. More specifically, they found that an athlete performing imagery while wearing the clothing she would usually wear when playing her sport, along with doing the imagery on the actual field (i.e., imaging while wearing her hockey uniform and standing on the team's hockey pitch), produced significantly better performance than simply doing imagery in a more traditional manner (imaging at home without sport-specific clothing). In a second study, Wright and Smith (2007) found that the PETTLEP group performed as well as a performance-only group and better than a traditional imagery group on a cognitive task. These results provide initial support for using PETTLEP principles to enhance the effectiveness of imagery.

Following up these initial studies, Wright and Smith (2009) and Ramsey, Cumming, Edwards, Williams, and Brunning (2010) provided further support for the PETTLEP approach to imagery. In a study by Ramsey and colleagues (2010), participants imagined performing a soccer penalty kick. One group focused on the environment and task aspects of PETTLEP imagery using only stimulus propositions (e.g., "Decide which corner of the goal you will aim at"), whereas the other group focused on PETTLEP emotion-based imagery using response propositions (e.g., "As you take the ball and walk toward the penalty spot, you feel ner-

vous tension build in your leg muscles and butterflies appear in your stomach"). Results revealed that both groups performed significantly better than a stretching (control) group. A study by Smith, Wright, and Cantwell (2008) even found that experienced golfers who replaced some physical practice with PETTLEP imagery for bunker shots improved their performance significantly more than golfers who continued performing a full quota of physical practice shots.

Wright and Smith (2009) compared two groups: a traditional imagery group, who relaxed before doing imagery (without any physical practice), and a PETTLEP imagery group, who performed a strength task on a biceps curl machine while doing imagery to ensure functional equivalence (i.e., making the imagery equivalent to what the performer is actually doing). Results indicated that the PETTLEP imagery group performed significantly better on the strength task than the traditional imagery group. It appears that maximizing functional equivalence via PETTLEP imagery maximizes the positive effects of imagery on performance. This is supported by the findings of Wakefield, Smith, Moran, and Holmes (2013), who reviewed 15 years of PETTLEP research and concluded that "most studies in this field appear to support the efficacy of PETTLEP imagery with a wide variety of tasks and populations" (p. 112).

Guillot and Collet (2008) proposed a model, called the motor imagery integrative model, to help guide imagery research and practice. The model posits four specific areas and some subareas in which imagery can affect various aspects of sport performance:

- Motor learning and performance: task characteristics, imagery ability, duration and number of trials, mental and physical practice, individual characteristics
- Strategies and problem solving: competitive routines, problem solving, tactical and game skills, athlete goals
- Motivation, self-confidence, and anxiety: anxiety regulation, enhancement of self-confidence and intrinsic motivation, mental warm-up
- Injury rehabilitation: pain management and healing imagery, strength gains, stretching gains, speeding-up of recovery

KEY POINT Tailor imagery programs to the exerciser's or athlete's individual needs, abilities, and interests.

Implementing PETTLEP Imagery

- *Physical*—The athlete should adopt the correct stance, wear the same clothing as (or clothing similar to) that worn in competition, and hold any implements that would be used in competition. For example, a tennis player could image hitting an ace in tennis clothing while holding a racket.

- *Environment*—The athlete should use imagery in the environment where the competition is held. When this is not possible, videos, photographs, or a similar environment can be used as a substitute. For example, a baseball player could imagine hitting while standing in or near the batter's box on the field.

- *Task*—The image of performing the task should be identical to the actual performance of the task. For example, a gymnast would mimic the exact elements of performing on the balance beam. A beginner's imagery would be different from the imagery of an elite athlete.

- *Timing*—Imagery should be completed in real time (i.e., the time it takes to actually perform the task). For example, if a figure skater's long routine lasts 3 minutes, then her imagery should last 3 minutes.

- *Learning*—Imagery should reflect the learning stage of the athlete, so changes in imagery should occur as the athlete becomes more proficient at the task. For example, a basketball player might first imagine dribbling the ball while watching the ball, but as he learns the skill he would image dribbling while keeping his eyes up on his opponent.

- *Emotion*—The emotions one normally feels when competing and performing the task should be included in the imagery. For example, a soccer player might feel anxious before taking a penalty kick that decides the winner of the competition.

- *Perspective*—The athlete should perform imagery using either an internal perspective (i.e., through the athlete's own eyes) or an external perspective (i.e., through the eyes of spectators) depending on the athlete's preference and type of skill. For example, a basketball player might see himself shoot a free throw from an internal perspective, whereas an athlete practicing form-based skills where proper form is scored (e.g., gymnastics, diving) might take an external perspective.

Evaluate Imagery Skill Level

The first step in setting up imagery training is to evaluate the athlete's or student's current level of imagery skill. Individuals differ in how well they can image. Measuring someone's ability in imaging is not easy, however, because imagery is a mental process and therefore not directly observable. As a result, sport psychologists use mostly questionnaires to try to discern the various aspects of imagery content. Tests of imagery date back to 1909 when the Betts Questionnaire on Mental Imagery was first devised. Later the Vividness of Movement Imagery Questionnaire (Issac, Marks, & Russell, 1986) was developed to measure visual imagery as well as kinesthetic imagery. The Movement Imagery Questionnaire–Revised (Gregg, Hall, & Butler, 2010) provides an updated measure of visual and kinesthetic movement imagery.

In addition, Hall and colleagues (1998) developed the Sport Imagery Questionnaire, which contains questions about the frequency with which individuals use various types of imagery (e.g., imaging sport skills, strategies of play, staying focused, or the arousal that may accompany performance). The frequency items in the Sport Imagery Questionnaire indicate that athletes found these particular imagery techniques and strategies effective (Weinberg, Butt, Knight, Burke, & Jackson, 2003). In further extending the Sport Imagery Questionnaire (Short, Monsma, & Short, 2004), researchers found that the function, not the content, of the image was the most critical. In essence, if an athlete uses imagery to enhance self-confidence, then it doesn't matter exactly what the image is as long as it enhances confidence. Gregg and Hall (2006) developed a measure for assessing motivational imagery ability, which focuses on the ability to generate emotional content in one's imagery. Finally, Williams and Cumming (2011) presented an initial development of the Sport Imagery Ability Questionnaire, which uses sport-specific images rather than general movement images to assess imaging ability. These imagery questionnaires can be used to evaluate various aspects of imagery ability and use; the practitioner chooses the most appropriate instrument for a specific situation.

 DISCOVER Activity 13.3 helps you assess your imagery skills.

Tips and Guidelines for Implementing a Successful Imagery Training Program

After compiling feedback from the questionnaire, players and coaches can determine which areas to incorporate into an athlete's daily training regimen. The imagery program need not be complex or cumbersome, and it should fit well into the individual's daily training routine. Following are tips and guidelines for implementing a successful program in imagery training (Vealey & Greenleaf, 2010).

Practice in Many Settings

Many people think that lying down on a couch or chair is the only way to do imagery. Although athletes might want to start to practice imaging in a quiet setting with few distractions, once they become proficient at imagery they should practice it in many different settings (e.g., in the locker room, on the field, during practice, at the pool). People who are highly skilled in the use of imagery can perform the technique almost anywhere. As skills develop, people learn to use imagery amid distractions and even in actual competition. Sometimes athletes' imagery practice might include holding a bat, club, or ball in their hands or moving into or being in the position called for in performance of the skill (e.g., sitting on your knees for kayaking or getting into a batting stance for baseball).

Aim for Relaxed Concentration

Imagery preceded by relaxation is more effective than the use of imagery alone (Weinberg, Seabourne, & Jackson, 1981). Before each imagery session, athletes should relax by using deep breathing, progressive relaxation, or some other relaxation procedure that works for them. Relaxation is important for two reasons: It lets the person forget everyday worries and concerns and concentrate on the task at hand, and it results in more powerful imagery because there is less competition with other stimuli.

Establish Realistic Expectations and Sufficient Motivation

Some athletes are quick to reject such nontraditional training as imagery, believing that the only way to improve is through hard physical practice. They are skeptical that visualizing a skill can help improve its performance. Such negative thinking and doubt undermine the effectiveness of imagery. Other athletes believe that imagery can help them become the next Tiger Woods or Serena Williams, as if imagery is magic that can transform them into the player of their dreams. The truth is simply that imagery can improve athletic skills if you work at it systematically. Excellent athletes are usually intrinsically motivated to practice their skills for months and even years. Similar dedication and motivation are needed to develop psychological skills. Yet many athletes do not commit to practicing imagery systematically.

Use Vivid and Controllable Images

When you use imagery relating to performance of a skill, try to use all your senses and feel the movements as if they were actually occurring. Many Olympic teams visit the actual competition site months in advance so they can visualize themselves performing in that exact setting, with its colors, layout, construction, and grandstands. Moving and positioning your body as if you were actually performing the skill can make the imagery and feeling of movement more vivid. For example, instead of lying down in bed to image kicking a soccer goal, stand up and kick your leg as if you were actually doing so. Imagery can be used during quick breaks in the action, so it is important to learn to image with your eyes open as well as closed. Work on controlling images to do what you want them to do and thus produce the desired outcome.

Apply Imagery to Specific Situations

Make sure to use imagery in specific situations, tailored to your individual needs. For example, if a softball pitcher has trouble staying calm with runners on base, she should simulate different situations with different counts, game scores, numbers of outs, and numbers of base runners to groove strong and consistent mental and physical responses to the pressure of these situations. Repeatedly imaging just pitching well would not be as effective as imaging pitching in these different difficult situations.

Maintain Positive Focus

Focus in general on positive outcomes, such as kicking a field goal, getting a base hit, completing a successful physical therapy session, or scoring a goal. Sometimes using imagery to recognize and analyze errors is beneficial (Mahoney & Avener, 1977) because nobody is perfect and we all make mistakes every time we play. It is also important, however, to be able to leave the mistake behind and focus on the present. Try using imagery to prepare for the eventuality of making a mistake and effectively coping with the error.

For trouble with a particular mistake or error, we suggest the following: First try to imagine the mistake and determine the correct response. Then immediately imagine performing the skill correctly. Repeat the image of the correct response several times, and follow this immediately with actual physical practice. This process will help you absorb what it looks like and how it feels to perform the skill well.

Errors and mistakes are part of competition, so athletes should be prepared to deal with them effectively. The importance of preparing for errors and unlikely events was chronicled by Gould and colleagues through interviews with Olympic coaches and athletes (e.g., Gould, Greenleaf, Lauer, & Chung, 1999; Gould, Guinan, et al., 1999). This focus on errors and a coping strategy is highlighted in the following quote by a three-time Olympian:

" **It's as if I carry around a set of tapes in my mind. I play them occasionally, rehearsing direct race strategies. Usually I imagine the**

Developing Imagery Scripts

Williams, Cooley, Newell, Weibull, and Cummings (2013) provided specific guidelines for developing an imagery script. They recommend that coaches and athletes consider the 5 Ws when planning an imagery script:

- *Who.* Characteristics such as age, sport, competitive level, motivational tendencies, and imagery ability
- *Where.* The training and competition environments or, away from training/performance environments (e.g., at home)
- *When.* Before, during, or after competition or training
- *Why.* The goal of the imagery (e.g., to cope with precompetitive anxiety, to enhance confidence, to focus attention, to increase motivation)
- *What.* The content of the image, which is tailored to the who, why, where, and when (e.g., thoughts and feelings immediately before competition, sensory modalities used, descriptions of the environment)

The following is an example of a short imagery script for tennis. You step out on the court to warm up, and your feet feel light and bouncy. Your ground strokes are fluid and easy, yet powerful. You feel the short backswing and nice follow-through on your shots. You are moving around the court freely and effortlessly, getting to all of your opponent's shots. You feel a nice stretch on the back of your arm and in your low back as you warm up your overhead. The overheads are hit clean and right in the middle of your racket. You warm up your serve, and your motion feels fluid; you're really stretching out and transferring your weight into the ball. The ball is hitting the spots in the service box you are aiming for with a variety of spins and speeds.

See yourself starting the match serving and getting right into the flow of the match. Visualize some strong serves where your opponent can only get the ball back in the midcourt and you decisively put the ball away with short, topspin, angled strokes. Your next point is a long rally from the baseline. See yourself keeping the ball deep and hitting it firmly but with a good margin for error. Finally your opponent hits a short ball and you come in on a slice down the line to the backhand side. Your opponent tries a down-the-line passing shot but you anticipate this and are right there to hit a short cross-court volley winner. You finish the game with a big serve ace down the middle. The game gets you off to a good start and gets your adrenaline flowing and concentration focused on the match. As you get ready to walk on the court you are feeling relaxed and confident. You can't wait to hit the ball.

race going the way I want—I set my pace and stick to it. But I have other tapes as well—situations where someone goes out real fast and I have to catch him, or imaging how I will cope if the weather gets really hot. I even have a "disaster" tape where everything goes wrong and I'm hurting badly, and I imagine myself gutting it out." (Murphy & Jowdy, 1992, p. 242)

Consider Use of Video and Audio

Many athletes can get good, clear images of their teammates or frequent opponents but have trouble imaging themselves. The reason is that it is difficult to visualize something you have never seen. Seeing yourself on videotape for the first time is quite eye-opening, and people typically ask, "Is that me?" A good procedure for filming athletes is to film them practicing, carefully edit the video (usually in consultation with the coach or athlete) to identify the perfect or near-perfect skills, and then duplicate the sequence repeatedly on the video. The athlete observes her skills in the same relaxed state prescribed for imagery training. After watching the film for several minutes, she closes her eyes and images the skill.

Another way to use video is to make highlight videos of individuals playing well in particular situations during a competition. People can use such videos with their own imagery to boost confidence and motivation or simply to enhance the clarity and vividness of their images. In addition, many athletes make their own audio recordings. Personal audio or video recordings should include specific verbal cues that are familiar and meaningful to the performer, including specific responses to various situations that may arise during a game. Performers can also modify a recording to fit their particular needs and help them feel comfortable using the recording. For example, on one professional baseball team, individual players selected specific scenes from movies (e.g., where the hero displayed courage and persistence), types of music, clips of themselves or other players, and quotes. The video staff then put together a video for each player based on these specific suggestions, and the player could watch it whenever he wanted.

Smith and Holmes (2004) reported that golfers in a video or audio group performed significantly better than golfers in a written script or control group. In addition, Wakefield and Smith (2011) found that the use of video-assisted imagery helped improve strength performance. This is significant because the great majority of imagery interventions in published studies have used written scripts, which now do not appear to be optimally effective. The modality in which the imagery is presented appears to be important and should provide the participant with the most accurate motor representation of the skill (Holmes & Collins, 2001).

Include Execution and Outcome

Imagery should include both the execution and end result of skills. Many athletes image the execution of the skill and not the outcome, or vice versa. Athletes need to be able to feel the movement and control the image so that they see the desired outcome. For instance, divers must first be able to feel their body in different positions throughout a dive. Then they should see themselves making a perfectly straight entry into the water. An interesting study (Caliari, 2008) found that focusing on the movement directly related to the movement technique (e.g., the trajectory of the racket when playing tennis) produced significantly better performance than focusing on a more distant effect (e.g., the trajectory of the ball after hitting it in tennis). Therefore, athletes in sports requiring the use of an implement (e.g., baseball, tennis, golf, hockey) should focus their imagery more on the movement itself than the direction of the ball, which is external to the movement itself. Athletes should still include the outcome of their performance in their imagery, but it is most important to focus on the process.

Image Timing

From a practical and intuitive perspective, it makes sense to image in real time. In other words, the time spent imaging a particular skill should be equal to the time it takes to execute the skill in actuality. If a golfer normally takes 20 seconds to perform a preshot routine before putting, then his imaging of this routine should also take 20 seconds. Imaging in real time makes the transfer from imagery to real life easier. Research reveals that overall, athletes voluntarily choose real-time imagery over fast or slow imagery (O & Hall, 2009). This is consistent with the model of Holmes and Collins (2001) mentioned earlier, which argues that "if motor preparation and execution and motor imagery access the same motor representation then the temporal characteristics should be the same" (p. 73).

The congruence between actual practice time and imagery practice can be influenced by many variables, such as the nature of the task, imagery ability, level of expertise, task difficulty, preperformance routines, and temporal constraints. For example, O & Munroe-Chandler (2008) did not find any differences in performance between participants who used slow-motion imagery and those who used regular-speed imagery. However, this might be because the task was novel, and slow motion might be more beneficial for a beginner trying to get the idea of the movement. In addition, research (Munzert, 2008) indicates that keeping real and imagined movements similar is more important for closed tasks (e.g., golf, figure skating, and gymnastics), where the timing is under the athlete's control and not affected by the opponent, than for open tasks (e.g., football, basketball), where actions of the opponent might affect the length and exact movement patterns of a play.

In a thorough review of the literature, Guillot, Hoyek, Louis, and Collet (2012) found that overall, the more congruence between actual and imagined practice times, the better the performance. However, athletes often have difficulty achieving temporal congruence between imagery and actual physical practice times. To alleviate this problem, the researchers suggest that one might measure intermediate times (some specific times throughout the performance of the skill) and not just total time to determine exactly when athletes might be speeding up or slowing down their imagery; have athletes combine imagery with video observation of their own performance because the visual feedback may provide some information about movement timing; and have athletes perform imagery in the same competitive environment in which they actually perform their skills, which helps integrate imagery practice into physical training sessions.

 DISCOVER Activity 13.4 helps you better grasp the timing of imagery.

When to Use Imagery

Imagery can be used virtually any time—before and after practice, before and after competition, during the off-season, during breaks in the action in both practice and competition, during personal time, and during recovery from injury. In the following sections we describe how imagery can be used during each of these times. A study by Wakefield and Smith (2012) found that the more athletes practice imagery, the stronger the positive effects on performance. In particular, they

found that imaging three times a week was better than two times a week, which was better than once a week.

Before and After Practice

One way to schedule imagery systematically is to include it before and after each practice session. Limit these sessions to about 10 minutes; most athletes have trouble concentrating on imagery any longer than this (Murphy, 1990). To focus concentration and get ready before practice, athletes should visualize the skills, routines, and plays they expect to perform. After each practice they should review the skills and strategies they worked on. Tony DiCicco, former coach of the U.S. Women's Soccer national team, used imagery with the following scenario after practice to help build confidence:

" Imagine in your mind when you do well. If you're a great header, visualize yourself winning headers. If you're a great defender, visualize yourself stripping the ball from an attacking player. If you're a great passer of the ball, visualize yourself playing balls in. If you've got great speed, visualize yourself running by players and receiving the ball. Visualize the special skills that separate you from the rest—the skills that make your team better because you possess them. " (DiCicco, Hacker, & Salzberg, 2002, p. 112)

 VIEW Activity 13.5 lets you develop an imagery script.

Before and After Competition

Imagery can help athletes focus on the upcoming competition if they review exactly what they want to do, including different strategies for different situations. Optimal timing of this precompetition imagery differs from one person to another: Some athletes like to visualize right before the start of a competition, whereas others prefer doing so an hour or two before. What's important is that the imaging fits comfortably into the pre-event routine. It should not be forced or rushed. After competition, athletes can replay the things they did successfully and get a vivid, controllable image.

Similarly, students in physical education classes can imagine themselves correcting an error in the execution of a skill they just learned and practiced. They can also replay unsuccessful events, imagining performing successfully or choosing a different strategy. Imagery can also be used to strengthen the blueprint and muscle memory of those skills already performed well. Hall of Famer Larry Bird was a great shooter, but he still practiced his shooting every day. Good performance of a particular skill does not preclude the use of imaging; the usefulness of imagery continues as long as one is performing one's skill.

During the Off-Season

The lines between season and off-season are often blurred. In many cases, there is no true off-season because athletes do cardiovascular conditioning, lift weights, and train sport-specific skills during time away from their sport. Using imagery during the off-season is a good opportunity to stay in practice with imaging, although recent research has revealed that athletes use imagery significantly less during this time than during the season (Vealey & Greenleaf, 2010).

During Breaks in the Action

Most sporting events have extended breaks in the action during which an athlete can use imagery to prepare for what's ahead. In many sports there is a certain amount of dead time after an athlete performs—this is an ideal opportunity to use imagery.

During Personal Time

Athletes can use imagery at home or in any other appropriate quiet place. It may be difficult to find a quiet spot before practicing, and there may be days when an athlete does not practice at all. In such cases athletes should try to set aside 10 minutes at home so that they do not break their imagery routine. Some people like to image before they go to sleep; others prefer doing it when they wake up in the morning.

When Recovering From Injury

Athletes have been trained to use imagery with relaxation exercises to reduce anxiety about an injury. They have used imagery to rehearse performance as well as the emotions they anticipate experiencing on return to competition, thereby staying sharp and ready for return. Positive images of healing or full recovery have been shown to enhance recovery. Ievleva and Orlick (1991) found that positive healing and performance imagery were related to faster recovery times. (Similarly, terminally ill cancer patients have used imagery to see themselves destroying and obliterating the cancerous cells. In a number of cases, the cancer has reportedly gone into remission; see Simonton, Matthews-Simonton, & Creighton, 1978.) Imagery can also help athletes, such as long-distance runners, fight through a pain threshold and focus on the race and technique instead of on their pain. Furthermore, different types of imagery have been shown to be effective at different parts of the rehabilitation process (Hare, Evans, & Callow, 2008).

> **KEY POINT** For imagery to be effective, it should be built into the daily routine.

How Various Professionals Use Imagery

As we have seen, imagery can be used in all sports and activities. The following are examples of how coaches and sport professionals in several activities can use imagery to enhance performance:

- *Physical education.* After finishing a period of vigorous physical activity, ask students to stretch, sit down, and imagine themselves feeling relaxed and calm. Have them practice while they wait in line to participate in an activity.

- *Volleyball.* Before matches, reserve a quiet, dark room where players can visualize themselves performing against a specific opponent.

- *Exercise class.* During a cool-down period, ask participants to visualize how they want their bodies to look and feel.

- *Basketball.* Before practice, have players imagine their specific assignments for different defenses and offensive sets.

- *Tennis.* During changeovers, instruct players to visualize what type of strategy and shots they want to use in the upcoming game.

- *Swimming.* After every practice, give swimmers 5 minutes to pick a certain stroke and imagine doing it perfectly, or have them visualize it during rest periods between intervals.

LEARNING AIDS

SUMMARY

1. **Define imagery.**

   Imaging refers to creating or re-creating an experience in the mind. A form of simulation, it involves recalling from memory pieces of information that are stored there regarding all types of experiences and shaping them into meaningful images. The image should optimally involve all the senses and not rely totally on the visual.

2. **Discuss the effectiveness of imagery in enhancing sport performance.**

   Using anecdotal, case study, and experimental methods, researchers have found that imagery can improve performance in a variety of sports and in different situations. Of course, the principles of the effective use of imagery need to be incorporated into imagery studies to maximize imagery effectiveness.

3. **Discuss the where, when, why, and what of imagery used by athletes.**

   Imagery is used at many different times but most typically before competition. Categories of imagery that athletes use include cognitive general (e.g., using strategy), cognitive specific (e.g., using skills), motivational specific (e.g., receiving a medal), motivational general—arousal (arousal or relaxation), and motivational general—mastery (building confidence). Athletes image internally and externally; image positive and negative events or their surroundings; and use the visual, kinesthetic, olfactory, and auditory senses.

4. **Discuss the factors influencing imagery effectiveness.**

   Consistent with the interactional theme that is prominent throughout this text, the effectiveness of imagery is influenced by both situational and personal factors. These include the nature of the task, the skill level of the performer, and the imaging ability of the person.

5. **Describe how imagery works.**

   A number of theories or explanations address how imagery works. These include the psychoneuromuscular theory, symbolic learning theory, bioinformational theory, triple code theory, and psychological explanations. All five explanations have some support from research findings, and they basically propose that physiological and psychological processes account for the effectiveness of imagery.

6. **Discuss the uses of imagery.**

   Imagery has many uses, including enhancing motivation, reducing anxiety, building confidence, enhancing concentration, recovering from injury, solving problems, and practicing specific skills and strategies.

7. **Explain how to develop a program of imagery training.**

   Motivation and realistic expectations are critical first steps in setting up a program of imagery training. In addition, evaluation using an instrument such as the Sport Imagery Questionnaire should occur before the training program begins. Basic training in imagery includes exercises in vividness and controllability. Athletes should initially practice imagery in a quiet setting and in a relaxed, attentive state. They should focus on developing positive images, although it is also useful occasionally to visualize failures in order to develop coping skills. Both the execution and outcome of the skill should be imaged, and imaging should occur in real time.

8. **Explain when to use imagery.**

   Imagery can be used before and after practice and competition, during the off-season, during breaks in action, and during personal time. Imagery can also benefit the injury rehabilitation process.

KEY TERMS

imagery	multiple-baseline case studies	bioinformational theory
kinesthetic sense	psychological intervention packages	triple code model
visual sense	scientific experiments	psychological explanations
auditory sense	internal imagery	attention–arousal set
tactile sense	external imagery	vividness
olfactory sense	psychoneuromuscular theory	controllability
anecdotal reports	ideomotor principle	exercise imagery
case studies	symbolic learning theory	

REVIEW QUESTIONS

1. What is imagery? Discuss re-creating experiences that involve all the senses.

2. What are three uses of imagery? Provide practical examples for each.

3. Compare and contrast the psychoneuromuscular and symbolic learning theories as they pertain to imagery.

4. Describe some anecdotal and some experimental evidence supporting the effectiveness of imagery in improving performance, including evidence relating to the nature of the task and ability level.

5. Compare and contrast internal imagery and external imagery and their effectiveness.

6. Discuss three of the basic elements of a successful imagery program, including why they are important.

7. Compare and contrast the different types of imagery including cognitive general, cognitive specific, motivational specific, motivational general—arousal, and motivational general—mastery.

8. Discuss the important factors that have been shown to influence the effectiveness of imagery.

9. List five functions of exercise imagery.

10. Describe the elements of PETTLEP imagery, including how you would include these in an imagery training program.

11. Describe five components that need to be considered when implementing an imagery training program.

CRITICAL THINKING QUESTIONS

1. Think of a sport or physical activity you enjoy (or used to enjoy). If you were to use imagery to help improve your performance as well as enhance your participation experience, how would you put together an imagery training program for yourself? What would be the major goals of this program? What factors would you have to consider in order to enhance the effectiveness of your imagery?

2. As an exercise leader you want to use imagery with a class, but the students are skeptical of its effectiveness. Using anecdotal, case study, and experimental evidence, convince the students that imagery would be a great way to make the class experiences more positive.

3. As a coach, how might you use the five types of imagery discussed in this chapter to enhance the performance, affect, and thoughts of your athletes in different situations?

14

Self-Confidence

After reading this chapter, you should be able to

1. define and understand the benefits of self-confidence,
2. discuss the sources of sport confidence,
3. understand how expectations affect performance and behavior,
4. explain the theory of self-efficacy,
5. explain how you would assess self-confidence,
6. explain the various aspects of coaching efficacy, and
7. describe strategies for building self-confidence.

During interviews after competitions, athletes and coaches inevitably discuss the critical role that self-confidence (or a lack of self-confidence) played in their mental success (or failure). For example, Trevor Hoffman, who was one of the top "closers" pitching in the major leagues, has stated, "Confidence is everything; if you start second guessing yourself, you're bound to run into more bad outings." Or, as Tiger Woods has noted, "The biggest thing is to have the belief that you can win every tournament going in. A lot of guys don't have that. Jack Nicklaus did." Great athletes also keep their confidence high despite poor recent performance. For example, former New York Yankee star shortstop Derek Jeter stated that even in the midst of a slump (which he had in the 2004 season and recovered from to have an excellent year), "I never lose my confidence. It doesn't mean I'm going to get hits, but I have my confidence all the time" (McCallum & Verducci, 2004). Finally, sometimes confidence is felt not only by athletes but by their competitors. At the end of 2004, Andy Roddick said about Roger Federer (winner of the most Grand Slam

singles titles in men's tennis), "He's got an aura about him in the locker room. Mentally, he's so confident right now. A lot of his success right now is between the ears." These comments by Roddick are echoed by Federer himself, who has said, "I believe strongly in my capabilities. There's a lot of confidence as well, with my record over the past few years. I've built up this feeling on big points that I can do it over and over again. Things are now just coming automatically." (This is bad news for other men's professional tennis players, because Federer won 22 consecutive finals in which he played, until he finally lost a 5 setter to David Nalbandian. Federer has gone on to make the semifinals of 23 consecutive Grand Slam tournaments and the quarterfinals of 35 Grand Slam tournaments.)

Research, too, indicates that the factor most consistently distinguishing highly successful from less successful athletes is confidence (Jones & Hardy, 1990; Vealey, 2005). Gould, Greenleaf, Lauer, and Chung (1999) found that confidence (efficacy) was among the chief factors influencing performance at the Nagano Olympic Games. Along these lines, in interviews with 63 of the highest achievers from a wide variety of sports, nearly 90% stated that they had a very high level of self-confidence. Top athletes, regardless of the sport, consistently display a strong belief in themselves and their abilities. Let's look at how Olympic decathlon gold medalist Daley Thompson and all-time tennis great Jimmy Connors view confidence.

" **I've always been confident of doing well. I know whether or not I'm going to win. I have doubts, but come a week or ten days before the event, they're all gone. I've never gone into competition with any doubts. I've always had confidence of putting 100% in and at the end of the day, I think regardless of where you come out, you can't do any more than try your best.** "

—Daley Thompson (cited in Hemery, 1986, p. 156)

" **The whole thing is never to get negative about yourself. Sure, it's possible that the other guy you're playing is tough and that he may have beaten you the last time you played, and okay, maybe you haven't been playing all that well yourself. But the minute you start thinking about these things you're dead. I go out to every match convinced that I'm going to win. That's all there is to it.** "

—Jimmy Connors (cited in Weinberg, 1988, p. 127)

Even elite athletes sometimes have self-doubts, however, although they still seem to hold the belief that they can perform at high levels. Former world-class middle-distance runner Herb Elliott stated, "I think one of my big strengths has been my doubts of myself; if you're very aware of the weaknesses and are full of your own self-doubts, in a sense, that's quite a motivation." Similarly, former elite middle-distance runner Steve Ovett stated, "There's always a worry that I'd never live up to the expectations of my friends" (Hemery, 1986, p. 155). Finally, even basketball legend Michael Jordan speaks of gaining confidence through failure:

" **I've missed more than 9,000 shots in my career. I've lost almost 300 games. Twenty-six times I've been trusted to take the game-winning shot and missed. I've failed over and over and over again in my life—and that is why I succeed.** "

So sometimes there is a struggle between feeling self-confident and recognizing your weaknesses. Let's begin by defining what we mean by self-confidence.

Defining Self-Confidence

Although we hear athletes and exercisers talk about confidence all the time, the term is not easy to define. Sport psychologists define **self-confidence** as the belief that you can successfully perform a desired behavior. The desired behavior might be kicking a soccer goal, staying in an exercise regimen, recovering from a knee injury, serving an ace, or hitting a home run. But the common factor is that you believe you will get the job done.

Although Vealey (1986) originally viewed self-confidence as both a disposition and a state, the latest thinking (Vealey, 2001; Vealey & Chase, 2008) is that sport self-confidence is a social cognitive construct that can be more traitlike or more statelike, depending on the temporal frame of reference used. For example, confidence could differ if we look at confidence about today's competition versus confidence about the upcoming season versus one's typical level of confidence. In essence, confidence might be something you feel today and therefore it might be unstable (**state self-confidence**), or it might be part of your personality and thus be very stable (**trait self-confidence**). Another recent development is the view that confidence is affected by the specific organizational culture as well as the general sociocultural forces surrounding sport and exercise. For instance, an exerciser may get lots of positive feedback from the instructor, which helps to build his confidence, in contrast to no feedback (or even negative comments), which might undermine confidence. In sport, participation in certain activities is seen as more appropriate for males (e.g., wrestling) or females (e.g., figure skating), and this would certainly affect an athlete's feelings of confidence. Here is how a college basketball player described self-confidence and its sometimes transient nature:

" **The whole thing is to have a positive mental approach. As a shooter, you know that you will probably miss at least 50% of your shots. So you can't get down on yourself just because you miss a few in a row. Still, I know it's easy for me to lose my confidence fast. Therefore, when I do miss several shots in a row I try to think that I am more likely to make the next one since I'm a 50% shooter. If I feel confident in myself and my abilities, then everything else seems to fall into place.** "

When you expect something to go wrong, you are creating what is called a **self-fulfilling prophecy,** which means that expecting something to happen actually helps cause it to happen. Unfortunately, this phenomenon is common in both competitive sport and exercise programs. Negative self-fulfilling prophecies are psychological barriers that lead to a vicious cycle: The expectation of failure leads to actual failure, which lowers self-image and increases expectations of future failure. For example, a baseball batter in a slump begins to expect to strike out, which leads to increased anxiety and decreased concentration, which in turn usually result in lowered expectancies and poorer performance.

A great example of someone overcoming a negative self-fulfilling prophecy is the story of how Roger Bannister broke the 4-minute mile. Before 1954, most people claimed there was no way to run a mile in less than 4 minutes. Many runners were timed at 4:03, 4:02, and 4:01, but most runners agreed that to get below 4 minutes was physiologically impossible. Roger Bannister, however, did not. Bannister believed that he could break the 4-minute barrier under the right conditions—and he did. Bannister's feat was impressive, but what's really interesting is that in the next year more than a dozen runners broke the 4-minute mile. Why? Did everyone suddenly get faster or start training harder? Of course not. What happened was that runners finally believed it could be done. Until Roger Bannister broke the barrier, runners had been placing psychological limits on themselves because they believed it just wasn't possible to break the 4-minute mile.

Research (Vealey & Knight, 2002) has revealed that like many other personality constructs, self-confidence is multidimensional. Specifically, there appear to be several types of self-confidence in sport, including the following:

© Mary Evans Picture Library Ltd/age fotostock

When Roger Bannister broke the 4-minute mile, the idea that it couldn't be done was also broken. He paved the way for the self-fulfilling prophecy that others could run the mile that fast.

- Confidence about one's ability to execute physical skills
- Confidence about one's ability to use psychological skills (e.g., imagery, self-talk)
- Confidence about one's ability to use perceptual skills (e.g., decision making, adaptability)
- Confidence in one's level of physical fitness and training status
- Confidence in one's learning potential or ability to improve one's skill

Hays, Maynard, Thomas, and Bawden (2007) assessed types of self-confidence in elite performers and found additional types, such as belief in one's ability to achieve (both winning and improved performance) and belief in one's superiority over the opposition. This underscores the notion that elite athletes have strong beliefs in their abilities and is consistent with the importance of self-belief as seen in the mental toughness literature.

Benefits of Self-Confidence

Self-confidence is characterized by a high expectancy of success. It can help individuals arouse positive emotions, facilitate concentration, set goals, increase effort, focus their game strategies, and maintain momentum. In essence, confidence can influence *a*ffect, *b*ehavior, and *c*ognitions (the ABCs of sport psychology). We discuss each of these briefly.

- *Confidence arouses positive emotions.* When you feel confident, you are more likely to remain calm and relaxed under pressure. This state of mind and body allows you to be aggressive and assertive when the outcome of the competition lies in the balance. In addition, research (Jones & Swain, 1995) has revealed that athletes with high confidence interpret their anxiety levels more positively than do those with less confidence. This provides a more productive belief system in which one can reframe emotions as facilitative to performance.

Robust Sport Confidence

Although most researchers and practitioners understand the importance of self-confidence in enhancing performance, there has still been some controversy over how to define self-confidence. A concept called robust sport confidence has recently emerged in the literature. It has been defined as "a set of enduring yet malleable positive beliefs that protect against the ongoing psychological and environmental challenges associated with competitive sport" (Thomas, Lane, & Kingston, 2011, p. 202). In essence, robust sport confidence comprises a set of beliefs (rather than one belief) that includes multiple types of sport confidence (e.g., confidence associated with achievement, preparation, and skill execution) that are intense and generally stable over time. This set of beliefs is seen in the following quote from a male judoka:

> Robust confidence is about everything. It's about being confident in lots of areas, confident in winning, confident in preparing, believing in yourself no matter what . . . believing you have done everything you possibly could have done and believing that you can cope with the challenge. (Thomas et al., 2011, p. 195)

The characteristics of robust sport confidence include the following:

- *Multidimensional.* Robust sport confidence consists of several types of sport confidence, such as belief in your abilities, performance outcomes, coping skills, and physical and mental preparation.
- *Malleable.* Being responsive and reacting to confidence-debilitating factors; having the ability to bounce back quickly after any setback or dip in confidence
- *Durable.* Confidence that is long lasting, resistant to change, and solid
- *Developed.* Robust sport confidence can be developed over time and grow stronger.
- *Protective.* Robust sport confidence can act as a buffer against debilitating factors such as losing, injury, pressures, and expectations.
- *Strong set of beliefs.* An underlying belief that you can do it and that you are the best (borderline arrogance rather than outright arrogance)

• *Confidence facilitates concentration.* When you feel confident, your mind is free to focus on the task at hand. When you lack confidence, you tend to worry about how well you are doing or how well others think you are doing. In essence, confident individuals are more skillful and efficient in using cognitive processes and have more productive attentional skills, attributional patterns, and coping strategies.

• *Confidence affects goals.* Confident people tend to set challenging goals and pursue them actively. Confidence allows you to reach for the stars and realize your potential. People who are not confident tend to set easy goals and never push themselves to the limits (see chapter 15).

• *Confidence increases effort.* How much effort someone expends and how long the individual will persist in pursuit of a goal depend largely on confidence (Hutchinson, Sherman, Martinovic, & Tenenbaum, 2008; Weinberg, Yukelson, & Jackson, 1980). When ability is equal, the winners of competitions are usually the athletes who believe in themselves and their abilities. This is especially true in situations that necessitate persistence (e.g., running a marathon or playing a 3-hour tennis match) or in the face of obstacles such as painful rehabilitation sessions (Maddux & Lewis, 1995).

• *Confidence affects game strategies.* People in sport commonly refer to "playing to win" or, conversely, "playing not to lose." Confident athletes tend to play to win: They are usually not afraid to take chances, and so they take control of the competition to their advantage. When athletes are not confident, they often play not to lose: They are tentative and try to avoid making mistakes. For example, a confident basketball player who comes off the bench will try to make things happen by scoring, stealing a pass, or getting an important rebound. A less confident player will try to avoid making a mistake, such as turning over the ball. Players with less confidence are content not to mess up and are less concerned with making something positive happen.

• *Confidence affects psychological momentum.* Athletes and coaches refer to momentum shifts as critical determinants of winning and losing (Miller & Weinberg, 1991). Being able to produce positive momentum or reverse negative momentum is an important asset. Confidence appears to be a critical ingredient in this process. People who are confident in themselves and their abilities never give up. They view situations in which things are going against them as challenges and react with increased determination. For example, Wayne Gretzky, LeBron James, Serena Williams, and Rory McIlroy have exuded confidence to reverse momentum when the outlook looked bleak.

• *Confidence affects performance.* Probably the most important relationship for practitioners is the one between confidence and performance. Although we know from past research that a positive relationship exists between confidence and performance (Feltz, 1984b; Vealey, 2001), the factors affecting this relationship are less well known. However, such factors as organizational culture (e.g., high school vs. collegiate expectations), personality characteristics (e.g., competitive orientation), demographic characteristics (e.g., sex, age), affect (e.g., arousal, anxiety), and cognitions (e.g., attributions for success or failure) have been suggested to be important. All these factors affect whether confidence is too low, too high, or just right, as we briefly discuss in the following sections.

Optimal Self-Confidence

Although confidence is a critical determinant of performance, it will not overcome incompetence. Confidence can take an athlete only so far. The relationship between confidence and performance can be represented by the form of an inverted U with the highest point skewed to the right (figure 14.1). Performance improves as the level of confidence increases—up to an optimal point, whereupon further increases in confidence produce corresponding decrements in performance. Optimal self-confidence means being so convinced that you can achieve your goals that you will strive hard to do so. It does not necessarily mean

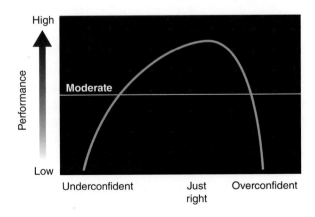

FIGURE 14.1 The inverted U illustrating the confidence–performance relationship.

that you will always perform well, but it is essential to reaching your potential. A strong belief in yourself will help you deal with errors and mistakes effectively and keep you striving toward success. Each person has an optimal level of self-confidence, and performance problems can arise with either too little or too much confidence.

> **KEY POINT** People strive for an individual, optimal confidence level but sometimes become either overconfident or underconfident.

Lack of Confidence

Many people have the physical skills to be successful but lack confidence in their ability to perform these skills under pressure—when the game or match is on the line. For example, a volleyball player consistently hits strong and accurate spikes during practice. In the match, however, her first spike is blocked back in her face. She starts to doubt herself and becomes tentative and conservative in subsequent spikes, thus losing her effectiveness.

Self-doubts undermine performance: They create anxiety, break concentration, and cause indecisiveness. Individuals lacking confidence focus on their shortcomings rather than on their strengths, distracting themselves from the task at hand. As one athlete noted, "Once you start to doubt yourself and your abilities, you are through." Sometimes athletes in the training room doubt their ability to fully recover from injury. Exercisers often have self-doubts about the way they look or about their ability to stay with a regular exercise program. But, as noted earlier, for some individuals a little self-doubt helps maintain motivation and prevents complacency or overconfidence.

Overconfidence

Overconfident people are actually falsely confident. That is, their confidence is greater than their abilities warrant. Their performance declines because they believe that they don't have to prepare themselves or exert effort to get the job done. This occurs when a top-rated team takes another team for granted, its members thinking that all they have to do is show up to win. You cannot be overconfident, however, if your confidence is based on actual skill and ability. As a general rule, overconfidence is much less a problem than underconfidence. When overconfidence does occur, however, the results can be just as disastrous.

In the mid-1970s, Bobby Riggs lost a famous "battle of the sexes" tennis match against Billie Jean King. Riggs explained the loss this way:

" **It was mainly a case of overconfidence on my part. I overestimated myself. I underestimated Billie Jean's ability to meet the pressure. I let her pick the surface and the ball because I figured it wouldn't make a difference, that she would beat herself. Even when she won the first set, I wasn't worried. In fact, I tried to bet more money on myself. I miscalculated. I ran out of gas. She started playing better and better. I started playing worse. I tried to slow up the game to keep her back but she kept the pressure on. (Tarshis, 1977, p. 48) "**

More common is the situation in which two athletes or teams of different abilities play each other. The better player or team often approaches the competition overconfidently. The superior players slight preparation and perform haphazardly, which may well cause them to fall behind early in the competition. The opponent, meanwhile, starts to gain confidence, making it even harder for the overconfident players to come back and win. Another situation that most of us have seen is that of an athlete who is faking overconfidence. Often athletes do this in an attempt to please others and to hide actual feelings of self-doubt. It would be more constructive for athletes to express such feelings to the coach so the coach can then devise programs to help athletes remove their doubts and gain back their self-confidence.

Bandura (1997) argued that overconfidence is simply a post hoc explanation for failure and that it doesn't truly exist. In essence, after athletes lose to an inferior opponent, they often note that they took the opponent too lightly (i.e., they were overconfident) and simply didn't prepare well enough, resulting in failure. But if athletes win, they almost never say that they were overconfident but still won. The empirical question of whether overconfidence exists still needs to be answered.

Sport Confidence Model

Now that we've discussed different aspects of sport self-confidence, it is time to put things together in a model of sport confidence (figure 14.2) described by Vealey and colleagues (Vealey 1986, 2001; Vealey & Chase, 2008). The sport confidence model has four components:

Psychological Momentum: Illusion or Reality?

Most coaches and athletes speak about the concept of psychological momentum and how it is often elusive—one minute you have it and the next minute you don't. Some researchers have found that this feeling of momentum might be more an illusion than a reality. For example, one study addressed the **hot hand** phenomenon in basketball, which traditionally has meant that a player who hits a few shots in a row is likely to continue making baskets. Using records from professional basketball teams, researchers discovered that a player was just as likely to miss the next basket as to make the next basket after making several successful shots in a row (Gillovich, Vallone, & Tversky, 1985; Koehler & Conley, 2003).

Other researchers also found that having momentum did not affect subsequent performance in baseball (Albright, 1993) and volleyball (Miller & Weinberg, 1991). However, additional research has shown a relationship between psychological momentum and performance in sports such as tennis, basketball, and cycling (Jackson & Mosurki, 1997; Perreault, Vallerand, Montgomery, & Provencher, 1998). It has been hypothesized that psychological momentum affects performance through cognitive (increased attention and confidence), affective (changes in perceptions of anxiety), and physiological (increased arousal) mechanisms (Taylor & Demick, 1994). Although some support for these notions exists (Kerick, Iso-Ahola, & Hatfield, 2000), further research is necessary to more clearly elucidate these intervening mechanisms. Along these lines, a study by Briki, Hartigh, Hauw, and Gernigon (2012) found that an unexpected event that was inconsistent with established performance expectations triggered momentum. For example, a team that is behind 2-0 and being thoroughly outplayed in a soccer game could reverse momentum if they score a goal—even a lucky goal—because the performance goes against what was happening before the goal.

The jury is still out on whether psychological momentum is real or simply an illusion. In a thorough review of 20 years of "hot hand" research, Bar-Eli, Avugos, and Raab (2006) found 12 studies in support of psychological momentum and 16 studies that did not support psychological momentum. The authors conclude that although there is evidence against the existence of psychological momentum in basketball and a few other sports, simulations do lend some support to the presence of psychological momentum. However, Gula and Raab (2004) as well as Avugos, Bar-Eli, Ritov, and Sher (2013) offered a sort of compromise position. Specifically, they argued that it would be best for a coach to select the player with the hot hand to shoot the last shot, but only if this player has a high base rate of success (e.g., is a good shooter to begin with). Thus, they perceive the hot hand as neither myth nor reality but rather as information to use when selecting a shooter for a critical situation.

Researchers have also studied the effect of athletes' perceptions of momentum on their decision making (Koppen & Raab, 2012). They found that both individual- and team-sport athletes, regardless of level of expertise, were influenced by their perception of psychological momentum. The athletes were shown a video where a volleyball player was hot (made several successful spikes in a row) or cold (missed several spikes in a row). The athletes in the study indicated that they would pass the ball (given that they weren't actually playing) significantly more to the player with the hot hand, who they perceived as more likely to be successful, than to the player with the cold hand. This occurred even though, in reality, neither player was more or less likely to be successful on the next trial.

A study by Moesch and Apitzsch (2012) investigated coaches' perceptions of positive and negative momentum. Strategies for increasing the chances that positive momentum will occur include coach strategies such as time-outs, successful substitution, clear instructions to players, and appropriate tactical changes and player strategies such as going back to basics, creating optimal arousal level, doing what works, and being task oriented. Strategies that increase the risk that negative momentum will occur include coach strategies such as unsuccessful substitutions, poor tactical decisions, and wrong perception of the match and player strategies such as focusing on results, poor attention control, having no clear match plan, and having no strategy if things go wrong.

• *Constructs of sport confidence.* As noted earlier in the chapter, sport confidence is seen as varying on a continuum from more traitlike to more statelike, as opposed to either purely trait or state self-confidence. Self-confidence is defined as the belief or degree of certainty that individuals possess about their ability to be successful in sport. Furthermore, sport confidence is conceptualized as multidimensional, including confidence about physical ability, psychological and perceptual skills, adaptability, fitness and training level, learning potential, and decision making.

• *Sources of sport confidence.* As described in "Sources of Sport Self-Confidence" later in this chapter, a number of sources are hypothesized to underlie and affect sport self-confidence. These can be further categorized as focusing on achievement, self-regulation, and social climate.

• *Consequences of sport confidence.* These consequences refer to athletes' affect (A), behavior (B), and cognitions (C), which Vealey (2001) labeled the ABC triangle. It is hypothesized that athletes' level of sport confidence would continuously interplay with these three elements. In general, high levels of confidence arouse positive emotions, are linked to productive achievement behaviors such as effort and persistence, and produce more skilled and efficient use of cognitive resources such as attributional patterns, attentional skills, and coping strategies.

• *Factors influencing sport confidence.* It is hypothesized that *organizational culture* as well as *demographic and personality characteristics* influence sport confidence. Organizational culture represents the structural and cultural aspects of the sport subculture, which can include such things as level of competition, motivational climate, coaching behaviors, and expectations of different sport programs. In addition, personality characteristics (e.g., goal orientation, optimism) and demographic characteristics (e.g., sex, race) affect sport confidence.

Understanding How Expectations Influence Performance

Because self-confidence is the belief that one can successfully perform a desired behavior, one's expectations play a critical role in the behavior change process. Research has shown that giving people a sugar pill for extreme pain (and telling them that it's morphine) can produce as much relief as a painkiller. In essence, the powerful effect of expectations on

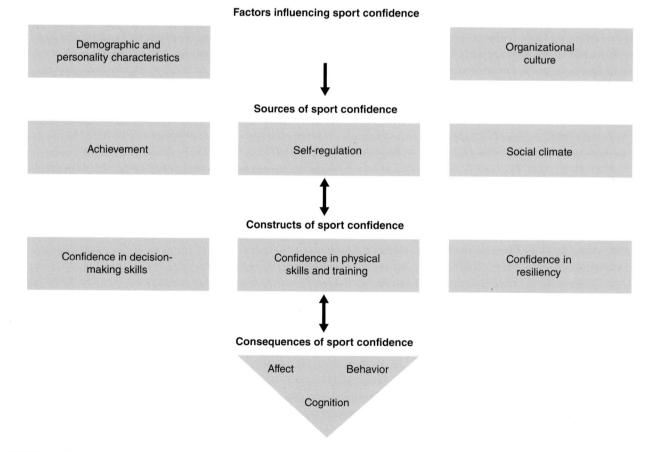

FIGURE 14.2   Model of sport confidence.

performance is evident in many aspects of daily life, including sport and exercise. Keeping expectations high and maintaining confidence under adversity are important not only for athletes and exercisers but also for officials. Here is what a professional tennis umpire has said on the subject:

" The chair umpire in tennis is a job that requires individuals who have confidence in themselves and are not easily shaken. The players hit the ball so hard and fast and close to the lines that it is virtually impossible to be absolutely certain of all the calls. But . . . you can't start to doubt yourself, because once you do, you start to lose control of the match. In the end the players will respect you and your calls more if you show them that you are confident in your judgment and your abilities. "

Self-Expectations and Performance

Some interesting studies have demonstrated the relationship between expectations and performance. In one study, subjects were each paired with someone they thought (incorrectly) was clearly superior in arm strength and then instructed to arm wrestle (Nelson & Furst, 1972). Remarkably, in 10 of the 12 contests, the objectively weaker subject (who both subjects believed was stronger) won the competition. Clearly, the most important factor was not actual physical strength but who the competitors expected to win.

KEY POINTS
- Positive expectations for success have been shown to produce positive effects in many realms of life, including sport.
- Expecting to beat a tough opponent or successfully perform a difficult skill can produce exceptional performance as psychological barriers are overcome.

In other studies, two groups of participants were told that they were lifting either more weight or less weight than they actually were (Ness & Patton, 1979; Wells, Collins, & Hale, 1993). For example, someone who had already lifted 130 pounds was told he had been given 130 pounds again, when in fact he had been given 150 pounds, or vice versa. Participants lifted the most weight when they thought they were lifting less—that is, when they believed and expected they could lift the weight.

Recent studies, as well as more classic studies (Mahoney & Avener, 1977), also showed that self-confidence was a critical factor in discriminating between successful and less successful performers (Gould, Guinan, et al., 1999; Jones et al., 1994; Mahoney, Gabriel, & Perkins, 1987). In addition, Maganaris, Collins, and Sharp (2000) reported that weightlifters who were told that they had been given anabolic steroids (but who had actually been given a placebo, saccharine) increased their performance, whereas performance decreased when lifters were told the true nature of the substance administered. Finally, Greenlees, Bradley, Holder, and Thelwell (2005) found that other athletes' behavior could influence expectations. Specifically, table tennis players who viewed other players exhibiting positive body language had more favorable impressions of the

Confidence has a profound effect on a person's belief about whether he can complete a given task.

opponent and hence lower levels of outcome expectations (i.e., they believed they were going to lose) than when the opponent displayed negative body language. These studies demonstrate the critical role that self-expectations play in an athlete's performance.

Coaching Expectations and Athletes' Performance

The idea that a coach's expectations could affect athletes' performances evolved from a classic study. Rosenthal and Jacobson (1968) informed teachers that a standardized test of academic ability had identified certain children in each of their classes as "late bloomers" who could be expected to show big gains in academic achievement and IQ over the course of the school year. In fact, these children had been selected at random, so there was no reason to expect they would show greater academic progress than their classmates. But at the end of the school year, these so-called late bloomers did in fact achieve greater gains in IQ scores than the other children did. Rosenthal and Jacobson suggested that the false test information made the teachers expect higher performance from the targeted students, which led them to give these students more attention, reinforcement, and instruction (as demonstrated by a video of the teachers giving feedback to the students). The students' performance and behavior thus conformed to the teachers' expectations that they were gifted students.

> **KEY POINT** Your expectations of others affect not only your own behavior but also the feelings and behaviors of others.

Studies in physical education classrooms (Martinek, 1988) and competitive sport environments (Chase, Lirgg, & Feltz, 1997; Solomon, Striegel, Eliot, Heon, & Maas, 1996) also indicate that teachers' and coaches' expectations can alter their students' and athletes' performances. These studies showed that head coaches provided more of all types of feedback to athletes for whom they had high expectations and that these athletes viewed their coaches more positively than did other athletes. In addition, the coaches' expectations were a significant predictor of their athletes' performances. A study by Becker and Solomon (2005) found that National Collegiate Athletic Association head basketball coaches used athletes' hard work, receptivity to coaching, willingness to learn, love of the sport, and willingness to listen as the most

important items in determining an athlete's ability. These are all psychological attributes. Interestingly, physical attributes such as athleticism, coordination, and agility were not in the top 10 items for judging athletes' ability. This process does not occur in all situations because some teachers and coaches let their expectations affect their interaction with students and athletes but others do not. A sequence of events that occurs in athletic settings seems to explain the expectation–performance relationship (Horn, Lox, & Labrador, 2001).

Step 1: Coaches Form Expectations

Coaches usually form expectations of their athletes and teams. Sometimes these expectations come from an individual's race, physical size, sex, or socioeconomic status. These expectations are called **person cues**. The exclusive use of person cues to form judgments about an athlete's competence could certainly lead to inaccurate expectations. Interestingly enough, research (Becker & Solomon, 2005) indicates that psychological characteristics were the most salient factors that coaches relied on to judge athletic ability. This might be because coaches believe that athletes at this level of competition are more likely to possess comparable levels of physical ability and thus it is psychological factors that really distinguish one athlete from another. However, coaches also use **performance information**, such as past accomplishments, skill tests, practice behaviors, and other coaches' evaluations.

Assessing more than 200 coaches, Solomon (2008a, 2010) found that these person and performance factors fall under four categories: coachability, physical ability, being a team player, and maturity. When these sources of information lead to an accurate assessment of the athlete's ability and potential, there's no problem. However, inaccurate expectations (either too high or too low), especially when they are inflexible, typically lead to inappropriate behaviors on the part of the coach. Unfortunately, research has found that coaches tended to not change their initial expectations of athletes (Solomon, Golden, Ciaponni, & Martin, 1998). This brings us to the second step in the sequence of events—coaches' expectations influencing their behaviors.

Step 2: Coaches' Expectations Influence Their Behaviors

Among teachers and coaches who behave differently if they have high or low expectancies of a given student or athlete, behaviors usually fit into one of the following categories (Solomon, 2008b; Solomon, DiMarco, Ohlson, & Reese, 1998):

Frequency and Quality of Coach–Athlete Interaction

- Coach spends more time with high-expectation athletes because he expects more of them.
- Coach shows more warmth and positive affect toward high-expectation athletes.

Quantity and Quality of Instruction

- Coach lowers his expectations of what skills some athletes will learn, thus establishing a lower standard of performance.
- Coach allows the athletes whom he expects less of correspondingly less time in practice drills.
- Coach is less persistent in teaching difficult skills to low-expectation athletes.

Type and Frequency of Feedback

- Coach provides more reinforcement and praise for high-expectation athletes after a successful performance.
- Coach provides quantitatively less beneficial feedback to low-expectation athletes, such as praise after a mediocre performance.
- Coach gives high-expectation athletes more instructional and informational feedback.

In addition to the type, quantity, and quality of feedback provided, teachers can exhibit their expectancies through the kind of environment they create. When coaches create a more task- or learning-oriented environment, students do not perceive any differential treatment of high and low achievers. However, when teachers create an outcome-oriented environment focused on performance, then students perceive that their teachers favor high achievers as opposed to low achievers (Papaioannou, 1995).

Here is an example of how a coach's expectations might affect her behavior. During the course of a volleyball game, Kira (whose coach has high expectations of her) attempts to spike the ball even though the setup was poor, pulling her away from the net. The spike goes into the net, but the coach says, "Good try, Kira, just try to get more elevation on your jump so you can contact the ball above the level of the net." When Janet (whom the coach expects less of) does the same thing, the coach says, "Don't try to spike the

ball when you're not in position, Janet. You'll never make a point like that."

Step 3: Coaches' Behaviors Affect Athletes' Performances

In this step, the coaches' expectation-biased treatment of athletes affects performance both physically and psychologically. It is easy to understand that athletes who consistently receive more positive and instructional feedback from coaches will show more improvement in their performance and enjoy the competitive experience more. Look at these ways in which athletes are affected by the negatively biased expectations of their coaches:

- Low-expectation athletes exhibit poorer performances because they receive less effective reinforcement and get less playing time.
- Low-expectation athletes exhibit lower levels of self-confidence and perceived competence over the course of a season.
- Low-expectation athletes attribute their failures to lack of ability, thus substantiating the notion that they aren't any good and have little chance of future success.

Step 4: Athletes' Performances Confirm the Coaches' Expectations

Step 4, of course, communicates to coaches that they were correct in their initial assessment of the athletes' ability and potential. Few coaches observe that their own behaviors and attitudes helped produce this result. Not all athletes allow a coach's behavior or expectations to affect their performance or psychological reactions. Some athletes look to other sources, such as parents, peers, or other adults, to form perceptions of their competency and abilities. The support and information from these other people can often help athletes resist the biases communicated by a coach.

Clearly, sport and exercise professionals, including trainers and rehabilitation specialists, need to be aware of how they form expectations and how their behavior is affected. Early on, teachers and coaches should determine how they form expectations and whether their sources of information are reliable indicators of an individual's ability. Coaches and teachers should also monitor the quantity and quality of reinforcement and instructional feedback they give so that they make sure all participants get their fair share. Such actions help ensure that all participants have a fair chance to

Expectations and Behavior Guidelines for Coaches

The following recommendations are based on the literature regarding expectations of coaches (Horn, 2002; Horn et al., 2001; Solomon, 2010):

- Coaches should determine what sources of information they use to form preseason or early-season expectations for each athlete.
- Coaches should realize that their initial assessment of an athlete's competence may be inaccurate and thus needs to be revised continuously as the season progresses.
- During practices, coaches need to keep a running count of the amount of time each athlete spends in non-skill-related activities (e.g., waiting in line).
- Coaches should design instructional activities or drills that provide all athletes with an opportunity to improve their skills.
- Coaches should generally respond to skill errors with corrective instructions about how to perform the skill correctly.
- Coaches should emphasize skill improvement as a means of evaluating and reinforcing individual athletes rather than using absolute performance or levels of skill achievement.
- Coaches should interact frequently with all athletes on their team to solicit information concerning athletes' perceptions, opinions, and attitudes regarding team rules and organization.
- Coaches should try to create a mastery-oriented environment in team practices, focused on improvement and team play.
- Coaches should communicate their expectations to athletes so that athletes are aware of how they are being evaluated.
- Coaches should use concrete measures to evaluate athlete improvement in psychological factors, which are often difficult to objectively measure. For example, coaches could assess anxiety levels before critical moments to determine if they were related to the amount of attention and feedback given to the athlete.

reach their potential and enjoy the athletic experience. Based on research regarding the effects of coaching expectancy, "Expectations and Behavior Guidelines for Coaches" provides some behavioral recommendations for coaches.

Expectations and Judges' Evaluation

There has been a lot of speculation regarding the effect of previous information and reputation on judges' rating of performance (Baltes & Parker, 2000). In essence, are performers graded more leniently if they have had performance success in the past and possibly there are higher expectations of these performers? In one study (Findlay & Ste-Marie, 2004), figure skaters were evaluated by judges to whom the athletes were either known or unknown. Ordinal rankings were found to be higher when skaters were known by the judges compared with when they were unknown. Furthermore, skaters received higher technical merit marks when known, although artistic marks did not

differ. Judges should be made aware of this potential bias, and skaters need to simply skate their best and not be affected by any potential bias because it is not under their control.

Examining Self-Efficacy Theory

Self-efficacy, the perception of one's ability to perform a task successfully, is really a situation-specific form of self-confidence. For our purposes, we use the terms *self-efficacy* and *self-confidence* interchangeably. Psychologist Albert Bandura (1977a, 1986, 1997) brought together the concepts of confidence and expectations to formulate a clear and useful conceptual model of self-efficacy. Later, Bandura (1997) redefined self-efficacy to encompass those beliefs regarding individuals' capabilities to produce performances that will lead to anticipated outcomes. In this regard, the term *self-regulatory efficacy* is now used, which focuses more on one's abilities to overcome obstacles or challenges to successful performance (e.g., carrying out one's walking regimen when tired or during bad weather).

Researchers have discovered a number of other specific types of efficacy (Beauchamp, Jackson, & Morton, 2012; Donlop, Beatty, & Beauchamp, 2011). Additional efficacy constructs that play a role in shaping individual functioning in achievement pursuits include some of the following:

- *Learning efficacy*—Individuals' beliefs in their capability to learn a new skill
- *Decision-making efficacy*—Individuals' beliefs that they are competent decision makers
- *Coping efficacy*—Individuals' beliefs in their ability to cope in the face of perceived threats
- *Self-presentational efficacy*—Individuals' beliefs in conveying a desired impression to others (e.g., appearing strong, coordinated, fit, or physically attractive)
- *Other efficacy*—Individuals' beliefs in the ability of others (e.g., partner, teammates, coach)

Bandura's theory of self-efficacy has been adapted to explain behavior in several disciplines of psychology, and it has formed the theoretical basis adopted for most performance-oriented research in self-confidence and sport. The theory was originally developed in the framework of a social cognitive approach to behavior change that viewed self-efficacy as a common cognitive mechanism for mediating motivation and behavior. Consistent with the orientation of this textbook, self-efficacy theory takes an interactional approach whereby self-efficacy (a person factor) and environmental determinants interact to produce behavior change in a reciprocal manner.

> **KEY POINT** Self-efficacy theory provides a model for studying the effects of self-confidence on sport performance, persistence, and behavior.

Bandura's self-efficacy theory has several underlying premises, including the following:

- If someone has the requisite skills and sufficient motivation, then the major determinant of the individual's performance is self-efficacy. Self-efficacy alone cannot make a person successful—an athlete must also want to succeed and have the ability to succeed.
- Self-efficacy affects an athlete's choice of activities, level of effort, and persistence.

Athletes who believe in themselves tend to persevere, especially under adverse conditions (Hutchinson, Sherman, Martinovic, & Tenenbaum, 2008).

- Although self-efficacy is task specific, it can generalize, or transfer to other similar skills and situations.
- Self-efficacy is related to goal setting: Those who exhibit high self-efficacy are more likely to set challenging goals (Tolli & Schmidt, 2008).

Sources of Self-Efficacy

According to Bandura's theory, one's feelings of self-efficacy are derived from six principal sources of information: performance accomplishments, **vicarious experiences (modeling)**, verbal persuasion, imaginal experiences, physiological states, and emotional states. The fact that these six sources of efficacy are readily applicable in sport and exercise contexts is largely responsible for the theory's popularity among sport and exercise psychologists. These six categories are not mutually exclusive in terms of the information they provide, although some are more influential than others. Figure 14.3 diagrams the relationships between the major sources of efficacy information, efficacy expectations, and performance. We discuss each source in the sections that follow.

Performance Accomplishments

Performance accomplishments (particularly clear success or failure) provide the most dependable foundation for self-efficacy judgments because they are based on one's mastery experiences (Bandura, 1997), although contextual factors (e.g., the nature of an audience, situational barriers, resources available) can enhance or hinder the relationship (Feltz, Short, & Sullivan, 2008). If experiences are generally successful, they will raise the level of self-efficacy. However, repeated failures result in expectations of lower efficacy. For example, if a field-goal kicker has kicked the winning field goal as time was running out in several games, he will have a high degree of self-efficacy that he can do it again. Similarly, an athlete rehabilitating from a wrist injury will persist in exercise after seeing steady improvement in her range of motion and wrist strength.

Research on a variety of tasks and skills has clearly shown that performance accomplishments increase

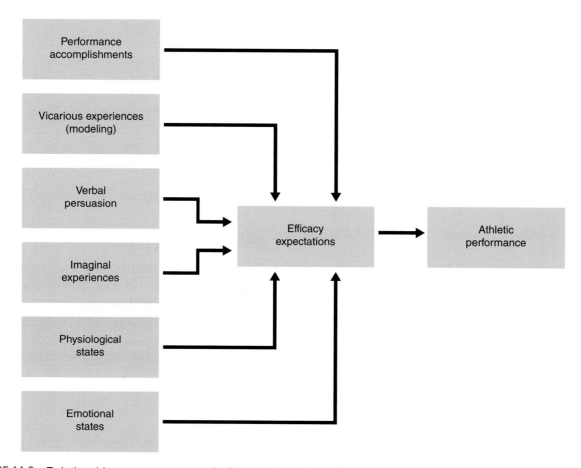

FIGURE 14.3 Relationships among sources of efficacy information, efficacy expectations, and athletic performance.

Adapted, by permission, from D. Feltz, 1984, Self-efficacy as a cognitive mediator of athletic performance. In *Cognitive sport psychology,* edited by W. Straub and J. Williams (Lansing, NY: Sport Science Associates), 192. By permission of D. Feltz.

self-efficacy, which in turn increases subsequent performance (Samson & Solomon, 2011) as well as exercise adherence (Hu, Motl, McAuley, & Konopack, 2007; McAuley, 1992, 1993a). However, the type of performance accomplishment information (e.g., coming from practice of skills or competition success) appears to differ based on skill level. In a study by Bruton, Mellalieu, Shearer, Roderique-Davis, and Hall (2013), golfers with high ability relied mostly on handicap (a representation of previous performance over time) for efficacy information, whereas golfers with lower ability relied on practice. In essence, golfers higher in skill relied more on their overall ability, whereas golfers lower in skill relied more on how they were playing at the moment. Similarly, Valiante and Morris (2013) found that even one great shot can enhance self-efficacy as much as a series of successes can. Coaches and teachers can help participants experience the feeling of successful performance by using such tactics as guiding a gymnast through a complicated move, letting young

baseball players play on a smaller field, providing progress charts and activity logs, or lowering the basket for young basketball players.

Vicarious Experiences

Physical educators, exercise leaders, athletic trainers, and coaches all often use vicarious experiences, also known as demonstration or modeling, to help students learn new skills. This can be a particularly important source of efficacy information for performers who lack experience with a task and rely on others to judge their own capabilities. For example, seeing a team member complete a difficult move on the uneven parallel bars can reduce anxiety and help convince other gymnasts that they, too, can accomplish this move. In addition, the fitness and exercise shows proliferating on television are compelling examples of attempts to enhance efficacy expectations and behavior through modeling.

How does modeling actually help us perform better? According to Bandura (1986; also see McCullagh,

Weiss, & Ross, 1989), it is best to understand modeling as a four-stage process: **attention, retention, motor reproduction**, and **motivation**. To learn through watching, people must first give careful attention to the model. Our ability to attend to a model depends on respect for the person observed, interest in the activity, and how well we can see and hear. The best teachers and coaches focus on a few key points, demonstrate several times, and let you know exactly what to look for.

For people to learn effectively from modeling, they must commit the observed act to memory. Methods of accomplishing retention include mental practice techniques, use of analogies (e.g., telling the athlete to liken the tennis serve motion to throwing a racket), and having learners verbally repeat the main points aloud. The key is to help the observer remember the modeled act.

Even if people attend to demonstrated physical skills and remember how to do them, they still may not be able to perform the skills if they have not learned motor reproduction (i.e., how to coordinate their muscle actions with their thoughts). For example, you could know exactly what a good approach and delivery in bowling look like and even be able to mimic the optimal physical action, but without physical practice to learn the timing, you will not roll strikes. When modeling sport and exercise skills, teachers and coaches must make sure they have taught lead-up skills, provided optimal practice time, and considered the progression to order related skills.

The final stage in the modeling process is motivation, which affects all the other stages. Without being motivated, an observer will not attend to the model, try to remember what was seen, and practice the skill. The key, then, is to motivate the observer by using praise, promising that the learner can earn rewards, communicating the importance of learning the modeled activity, or using models who will motivate the learner.

Verbal Persuasion

Coaches, teachers, and peers often use persuasive techniques to influence behavior. For example, a baseball

Modeling: A Key to Teaching, Learning, and Performance

Modeling (sometimes called observational learning) has been shown to influence confidence and lead to enhanced performance, depending on a number of factors:

- *Model similarity.* Studies have found that people watching skilled models who were similar to the observers themselves had enhanced self-efficacy and performance (Gould, Weiss, & Weinberg, 1981; McCullagh, Law, & Ste-Marie, 2012). In the 2004 Olympic Games, the nonfavored 4 × 100 meter British relay team attributed their victory to the mental boost in confidence they received in seeing their teammate, Kelly Holmes, win her second unexpected gold medal just before their relay race.

- *Coach models.* Coaches view their own modeling of self-confidence as an important source of confidence for their athletes (Gould, Hodge, Peterson, & Giannini, 1989; Weinberg, Grove, & Jackson, 1992).

- *Mastery versus coping models.* Models who progress through challenges and adversity in the task and gradually show positive improvements (coping models) have been shown to be superior to correct performance (mastery models) in enhancing self-efficacy of observers (Kitantas, Zimmerman, & Cleary, 2000; McCullagh & Weiss, 2001).

- *Self-modeling.* Although a great deal of anecdotal evidence attests to the positive effects of self-modeling (e.g., watching yourself perform well on video from a previous competition) on competitive performance, the results from empirical studies have been equivocal. More research is necessary to identify the conditions under which self-modeling is effective (McCullagh, Law, & St. Marie, 2012).

- *Multidimensional modeling.* Research has shown that modeling is multidimensional in nature and can influence efficacy beliefs in a variety of areas, such as learning and performance (Law & Hall, 2009).

- *Virtual models.* This new technology allows individuals to view themselves working out with a virtual partner using the Eye Toy camera and a modified PlayStation 2 game. In essence, an individual will be working out with a virtual partner to increase adherence rates. Individuals seem to stick with exercise more often if they exercise with a partner—a virtual partner, in this case.

coach may tell a player, "I know you're a good hitter, so just hang in there and take your swings. The base hits will eventually come." Similarly, an exercise leader may tell an exercise participant to "hang in there and don't get discouraged, even if you have to miss a couple of days." This type of encouragement is important to participants and can help improve self-efficacy (Weinberg, Gould, & Jackson, 1979) as well as enhance enjoyment, reduce perceived effort, and enhance affective responses (Hutchinson, Sherman, Martinovic, & Tenenbaum, 2008). Verbal persuasion for enhancing confidence can also take the form of self-persuasion. Janel Jorgensen, silver medalist in the 100-meter butterfly in the 1988 Olympic Games, explained:

" You have to believe it's going to happen. You can't doubt your abilities by saying, Oh I'm going to wake up tomorrow and I'm going to feel totally bad since I felt bad today and yesterday. You can't go about it like that. You have to say OK, tomorrow I'm going to feel good. I didn't feel good today. That's that. We will see what happens tomorrow. (Ripol, 1993, p. 36) "

Verbal persuasion coming from one's self—generally known as self-talk—has been shown to increase feelings of self-efficacy (Hatzigeorgiadis, Zourbanos, Goltsios, & Theodorakis, 2008). (Chapter 16 further discusses the notion of self-talk.) Finally, even athletes' belief that teammates are confident in them (regardless of whether this is true) will enhance their feelings of self-efficacy (Jackson, Beauchamp, & Knapp, 2007).

Imaginal Experiences

Individuals can generate beliefs about personal efficacy or lack of efficacy by imagining themselves or others behaving effectively or ineffectively in future situations. The key to using imagery as a source of confidence is to see one's self demonstrating mastery (Moritz et al., 1996; Munroe-Chandler & Morris, 2011). Chapter 13 provides a detailed discussion of the use of imagery in sport and exercise settings.

Physiological States

Physiological states influence self-efficacy when individuals associate aversive physiological arousal with poor performance, perceived incompetence, and perceived failure. Conversely, if physiological arousal is seen as facilitative, then self-efficacy is enhanced.

Thus, when people become aware of unpleasant physiological arousal (e.g., racing heartbeat), they are more likely to doubt their competence than if they were experiencing pleasant physiological arousal (e.g., smooth, rhythmic breathing). Negative physiological states have been negatively correlated with efficacy beliefs, meaning that higher levels of negative physiological states are related to lowered levels of self-efficacy (Hauck, Carpenter, & Frank, 2008). Some athletes may interpret increases in their physiological arousal or anxiety (e.g., fast heartbeat, shallow breathing) as a fear that they cannot perform the skill successfully (lowered self-efficacy), whereas others might perceive such increases as a sign that they are ready for the upcoming competition (enhanced self-efficacy).

Emotional States

Although physiological cues are important components of emotions, emotional experiences are not simply the product of physiological arousal. Thus, emotions or moods can be an additional source of information about self-efficacy. For example, research has revealed that an injured athlete who is feeling depressed and anxious about his rehabilitation and is fatigued and in pain reports lowered feelings of self-efficacy (Jackson, Knapp, & Beauchamp, 2008). Conversely, an athlete who feels energized and positive would probably have enhanced feelings of self-efficacy. Research has also shown that positive emotional states such as happiness, exhilaration, and tranquility are more likely to enhance efficacy judgments than are negative emotional states such as sadness, anxiety, and depression (Maddux & Meier, 1995; Martin & Gill, 2002).

Reciprocal Relationship Between Efficacy and Behavior Change

Research has clearly indicated both that efficacy can act as a determinant of performance and exercise behavior and that exercise or sport behavior acts as a source of efficacy information (for reviews, see Feltz, Short, & Sullivan, 2008; McAuley & Blissmer, 2002; Samson & Solomon, 2011). More specifically, a variety of studies including cross-sectional and longitudinal designs have demonstrated that changes in efficacy correspond to changes in performance and exercise behavior, including the following findings:

- Self-efficacy (among a host of social learning variables) was the best predictor of exercise in a 2-year, large community sample.

- Self-efficacy was particularly critical in predicting exercise behavior in older sedentary adults.
- Self-efficacy was a strong predictor of exercise in symptomatic populations.
- Self-efficacy was a good predictor of exercise 9 months after program termination.

Although the focus of research has been on efficacy as a determinant of exercise or sport behavior, research also indicates that exercise or sport behavior (both acute and chronic) can influence feelings of efficacy (e.g., McAuley et al., 2007). For example, keeping up one's level of self-efficacy (especially regarding exercise behavior) seems to be particularly important for older adults, who typically have some decrease in exercise function as they age. Therefore, if self-efficacy can be kept high via exercise, then the likelihood of continuing to exercise also increases; this underscores the reciprocal nature of the efficacy–behavior relationship (McAuley et al., 2006; Samson & Solomon, 2011). Researchers have documented individuals using exercise to enhance self-efficacy in a variety of populations, including adolescent girls, college students, older adults, people with chronic illness and disabilities, and depressed individuals (Koehn & Morris, 2011). This reciprocal relationship has also been shown in athletes (Hatzigeorgiadis et al., 2008). Tennis players who underwent a motivational self-talk intervention reported higher levels of self-efficacy and performance than did a control group. Furthermore, the type of exercise should be specific to the type of efficacy targeted. For example, task efficacy is more important in starting an exercise program, whereas barrier efficacy is more important in adhering to an exercise program (Higgins, Middleton, Winner, & Janelle, 2013).

Finally, a novel study assessed changes in self-efficacy in older adults (aged 60–80 years) across the duration of a 12-month exercise program (McAuley et al., 2011). Results revealed that before the exercise intervention program started, participants overestimated their adherence-related efficacy; this was followed by a decline in adherence-related efficacy after 3 weeks. In essence, participants needed to recalibrate their efficacy upon being exposed to the actual exercise experience because most of them had been inactive and their initial estimations of efficacy may have been hopeful overestimations. These 3-week efficacy assessments indicated that the participants' efficacy was either maintained or increased at 6 months. This was followed by a sharp decline in efficacy at the end of the 12-month program. This steep decline was likely due to the impending challenge of maintaining an exercise regimen after the termination of the structured intervention. This has important practical significance for individuals who are transitioning from organized, structured, group-based activity to home-based activity. Thus, the authors suggest including an "intervention within an intervention," woven into the last few weeks of a structured program, to help individuals overcome the challenges of maintaining exercise beyond the intervention.

Self-Efficacy and Sport Performance

A number of meta-analyses (e.g., Moritz, Feltz, Fahrbach, & Mack, 2000) and studies have indicated that higher levels of self-efficacy are associated with superior performance (for reviews, see Feltz, Short, & Sullivan, 2008; Koehn & Morris, 2011; Samson & Solomon, 2011). More specifically, analyses of 28 studies revealed that the correlations between self-efficacy and performance ranged from .19 to .73, with a median of .54. Thus, the perception of one's ability to perform a task successfully clearly has a consistent effect on actual performance. These findings have held for a variety of individual and team sports. Because performance accomplishments are the strongest source of self-efficacy, it stands to reason that these performance accomplishments enhance self-efficacy and that these increased feelings of self-efficacy then have a positive effect on subsequent performance. Hence, we see a reciprocal relationship between self-efficacy and performance. Interestingly, self-efficacy also allows individuals to overcome adverse experiences (e.g., suboptimal performance) without any lasting damage to their sense of self (Coffee & Rees, 2008).

Assessing Self-Confidence

Now that you understand the relationship between confidence or efficacy and performance and are aware that overconfidence or underconfidence can hamper effectiveness, the next step is to identify confidence levels in a variety of situations. Athletes might do this by answering the following questions:

- When am I overconfident?
- How do I recover from mistakes?
- When do I have self-doubts?

Sport Confidence Inventory

Read each question carefully and think about your confidence with regard to each item as you competed during the past year or season. For each item, indicate the percentage of the time you believe you had too little, too much, or just the right degree of confidence. An example question for a pole vaulter follows to give you some confidence in filling out the inventory correctly.

	Underconfident (%)	Confident (%)	Overconfident (%)
How confident are you each time you attempt to clear 17 feet?	20	70	10

The three answers in a row should always add up to 100%. You may distribute this 100% in any way you think is appropriate. You may assign all 100% to one category, split it between two categories, or, as in the example, divide it among all three categories.

	Underconfident (%)	Confident (%)	Overconfident (%)
How confident are you with respect to . . .			
1. your ability to execute the skills of your sport or exercise?	_____	_____	_____
2. your ability to make critical decisions during the contest?	_____	_____	_____
3. your ability to concentrate?	_____	_____	_____
4. your ability to perform under pressure?	_____	_____	_____
5. your ability to execute successful strategy?	_____	_____	_____
6. your ability to put forth the effort needed to succeed?	_____	_____	_____
7. your ability to control your emotions during competition?	_____	_____	_____
8. your physical conditioning or training?	_____	_____	_____
9. your ability to relate successfully to your coaches?	_____	_____	_____
10. your ability to come back when behind?	_____	_____	_____

Adapted, by permission, from ACEP, 1994, *ACEP psychology, level 2* (Champaign, IL: Human Kinetics), 251.

- Is my confidence consistent throughout an event?
- Am I tentative and indecisive in certain situations?
- Do I look forward to and enjoy tough, highly competitive games?

- How do I react to adversity?

"Sport Confidence Inventory" presents a more formal and detailed assessment of self-confidence levels. To score your overall confidence, add up the percentages in the three columns and then divide by 10. The higher your score in the "Confident" column, the more likely you are to be at your optimal level of confidence during competition. High scores in the "Underconfident" or "Overconfident" columns indicate some potential problem areas. To determine specific strengths and weaknesses, look at each item. The scale assesses confidence in both physical and mental terms. You can use this questionnaire to inform yourself or others of what to work on.

A relatively recent development in the measurement of sport confidence is known as sport confidence pro-filing (Hays, Thomas, Butt, & Maynard, 2010). This assessment technique stems from the work of Butler and Hardy (1992) on performance profiling (see chapter 11), which takes an idiographic (i.e., interview or individualized) approach to the measurement of sport confidence. This allows athletes to construct a picture of themselves rather than forcing them to respond to fixed measures in a questionnaire. Because it is athlete driven, performance profiling is in accordance with the empowering ideologies of many psychological

Sources of Sport Self-Confidence

Researchers have identified nine sources of self-confidence specific to sport. Many of these are similar to the six sources that Bandura earlier identified in his self-efficacy theory. The nine sources fall into the three general categories of achievement, self-regulation, and climate.

- *Mastery:* Developing and improving skills
- *Demonstration of ability:* Showing ability by winning and outperforming opponents
- *Physical and mental preparation:* Staying focused on goals and being prepared to give maximum effort
- *Physical self-presentation:* Feeling good about one's body and weight
- *Social support:* Getting encouragement from teammates, coaches, and family
- *Coaches' leadership:* Trusting coaches' decisions and believing in their abilities
- *Vicarious experience:* Seeing other athletes perform successfully
- *Environmental comfort:* Feeling comfortable in the environment where one will perform
- *Situational favorableness:* Seeing breaks going one's way and feeling that everything is going right

Researchers (Hays, Maynard, Thomas, & Bawden, 2007; Hays, Thomas, Maynard, & Bawden, 2009; Kingston, Lane, & Thomas, 2010) have investigated sources of confidence in elite, world-class performers. Although a number of sources similar to those on the preceding list were noted, some additional sources emerged from these elite athletes. These included experience (having been there before), innate factors (natural ability, innate competitiveness), and competitive advantage (having seen competitors perform poorly or crack under pressure before). In addition, Machida, Ward, and Vealey (2012) found that adaptive perfectionism (motivation to succeed and do your best), task goal orientation, and a task-oriented motivational climate all positively predicted both controllable (e.g., mastery, physical and mental preparation) and uncontrollable (e.g., situation favorableness, social support) self-confidence. For example, athletes who were high on task goal orientation (focus on achieving personal best) also tended to be higher on both controllable and uncontrollable sources of confidence. Thus, to build confidence, practitioners should encourage athletes to focus on task goals and on doing their best to succeed and should create a task-oriented environment where effort is valued.

It is interesting to note that although both males and females derived confidence from performance accomplishments, males gained most confidence by winning in competition, whereas females gained most confidence by performing well (mastery) and achieving personal goals and through physical self-presentation, social support, and the coach's leadership. In addition, it was found that elite athletes' levels of confidence are susceptible to periods of instability and can fluctuate over time. As time to competition neared, demonstration of ability (also ranked as the most important source of sport confidence as competition drew closer), physical and mental preparation, physical self-presentation, and situation favorableness (e.g., the supportiveness of the spectators) all increased in importance for elite athletes. In essence, these sources of confidence became more important as the start of competition came closer and closer (Hays, Maynard, Thomas, & Bawden, 2007; Hays, Thomas, Maynard, & Bawden, 2009).

skills training programs. Confidence profiling also uses motivational interviewing (see chapter 18), which emphasizes the athlete-centered approach. This approach can provide a strong foundation from which individualized, athlete-centered confidence-building interventions could be developed.

Building Self-Confidence

Many people believe that either you have confidence or you don't. Confidence can be built, however, through work, practice, and planning. Jimmy Connors is a good example. Throughout his junior playing days, Connors' mother taught him to always hit out and go for winners. Because of this playing style, he lost some matches he should have won. Yet Connors said he never could have made it without his mother and grandmother: "They were so sensational in their support, they never allowed me to lose confidence. They just kept telling me to play the same way, and they kept assuring me that it would eventually come together. And I believed them" (Tarshis, 1977, p. 102).

Confidence can be improved in a variety of ways: focusing on performance accomplishments, acting confident, responding with confidence, thinking confidently, using imagery, using goal mapping, optimizing physical conditioning and training, and preparing. Both athletes (Myers, Vargas-Tonsing, & Feltz, 2005) and coaches (Gould et al., 1989) generally agree on these confidence-building activities. We consider each of these in turn.

DISCOVER Activity 14.1 helps you assess your self-confidence.

Focusing on Performance Accomplishments

We have already discussed the influence of performance accomplishments on self-efficacy, but we elaborate on some of those points here. The concept is simple: Successful behavior increases confidence and leads to further successful behavior. The successful accomplishment might be beating a particular opponent, coming from behind to win, fully extending your knee during rehabilitation, or exercising continuously for 30 minutes. Of course, when a team loses eight games in a row, it will be hard-pressed to feel confident about winning the next game, especially against a good team. Confidence is crucial to success, but

how can you be confident without previous success? This appears to be a catch-22 situation: As one coach put it, "We're losing now because we're not feeling confident, but I think the reason the players don't feel confident is that they have been losing."

You are certainly more likely to feel confident about performing a certain skill if you can consistently execute it during practice. That's why good practices and preparing physically, technically, and tactically to play your best enhance confidence. Nothing elicits confidence like experiencing in practice what to accomplish in the competition. Similarly, an athlete rehabilitating a shoulder separation needs to experience some success in improving range of motion to keep up her confidence that she will eventually regain full range of motion. Short-term goals can help her believe she has made progress and can enhance her confidence (also see chapter 15). A coach should structure practices to simulate actual performance conditions. For example, if foul shooting under pressure has been a problem in the past, each player should sprint up and down the floor several times before shooting any free throw (because this is what happens during a game). Furthermore, to create pressure, a coach might require all players to make five free throws in a row or to continue this drill until they do so.

> **KEY POINT** Performance accomplishments are the most powerful way to build confidence. Manipulate or create situations that allow participants to succeed and have a sense of accomplishment.

Acting Confident

Thoughts, feelings, and behaviors are interrelated: The more confident an athlete acts, the more likely he is to feel confident. This is especially important when an athlete begins to lose confidence and the opponent, sensing this, begins to gain confidence. Acting confident is also important for sport and exercise professionals because this models behavior you'd like participants to have. An aerobics instructor should project confidence when leading her class if she wants to have a high-spirited workout. An athletic trainer should act confident when treating athletes so that they feel trust and confidence during the rehabilitation process. Athletes should try to display a confident image during competition. They can demonstrate their confidence by keeping their head up high—even after a critical error. Many people give themselves away through body language and movements that indicate they are lacking confidence. Acting confident can also lift spirits during difficult times. If someone walks around with slumped shoulders, head down, and a pained facial expression, he communicates to all observers that he is down, which pulls him even further down. It is best to keep your head up, shoulders back, and facial muscles loose to indicate that you are confident and will persevere. This keeps opponents guessing.

Responding With Confidence

Athletes should focus on responding to mistakes and errors with control and confidence rather than reacting

Self-Efficacy in Coaches

A relatively recent addition to the self-efficacy literature has been research on coaching efficacy. Feltz and colleagues (Feltz et al., 1999; Malete & Feltz, 2000) have developed the notion of coaching efficacy, defined as the extent to which coaches believe they have the capacity to affect the learning and performance of their athletes. Although coaching efficacy was originally conceptualized as comprising four areas, Myers, Feltz, Chase, Reckase, and Hancock (2008) added a fifth area. These areas include the following:

- *Game strategy:* Confidence that coaches have in their ability to coach during competition and lead their team to a successful performance
- *Motivation:* Confidence that coaches have in their ability to affect the psychological skills and states of their athletes
- *Technique:* Confidence that coaches have in their instructional and diagnostic skills
- *Character building:* Confidence that coaches have in their ability to influence a positive attitude toward sport in their athletes
- *Physical conditioning:* Confidence that coaches have in their ability to prepare their athletes physically for participation in their sport

Some findings regarding coaching efficacy include the following:

- The most important sources of coaching efficacy were years of experience and community support, although past winning percentage, perceived team ability, and parental support also were related to feelings of coaching efficacy.
- Coaches with higher efficacy had higher winning percentages, had players with higher levels of satisfaction, used more praise and encouragement, and used fewer instructional and organizational behaviors than did coaches with low efficacy.
- A coaching education program enhanced perceptions of coaching efficacy compared with a control condition.
- Male assistant coaches had higher levels of coaching efficacy and desire to become a head coach, whereas females had greater intentions to leave the profession (Cunningham, Sagas, & Ashley, 2003). Social support was a stronger source of efficacy for female coaches than for male coaches (Myers, Vargas-Tonsing, & Feltz, 2005).
- The most frequently cited source of coaching efficacy was player development (Chase, Feltz, Hayashi, & Hepler, 2005). This was seen in such things as getting players to play hard, teaching team roles, developing players' skills, and having confidence in the team.
- Athletes felt that coaches who were efficacious in the different aspects of coaching helped them enjoy their experience more and try harder (motivation efficacy), develop more confidence (technique efficacy), and improve prosocial behavior (character-building efficacy) (Boardley, Kavussanu, & Ring, 2008).
- Coaches who were higher on coaching efficacy felt they were better able to control their emotions and were generally higher on emotional intelligence (Thelwell, Lane, Weston, & Greenlees, 2008).
- Coaches had higher perceptions of their coaching efficacy than did their athletes (Kavussanu, Boardley, Jukiewicz, Vindent, & Ring, 2008).

with emotion or unproductive behaviors. Vealey and Vernau (2013) use the acronym ACT to represent accepting, centering, and thinking:

- *Accept.* Accept the bad feelings of a poor performance or mistake. Own your feelings rather than suppressing them.
- *Center.* Center yourself physically through a confident posture and deep breathing (exhale the tension and negative thoughts).

- *Think.* Use your prepared self-talk strategy (e.g., "Just take it one play at a time"). Focus your thoughts on controllable things and the process of performance.

Thinking Confidently

Confidence consists of thinking that you can and will achieve your goals. As a collegiate golfer noted, "If I think I can win, I'm awfully tough to beat." A

Collective Efficacy: A Special Case of Self-Efficacy

Another focus of research has been the concept of collective, or team, efficacy. Collective efficacy refers to a belief or perception shared by members of the team regarding the capabilities of their teammates (rather than merely the sum of individual perceptions of their own efficacy). In short, collective efficacy is each individual's perception of the efficacy of the team as a whole. Research (Lirgg & Feltz, 2001) demonstrated that athletes' belief in the team's collective efficacy was positively related to performance; the sum of the individuals' personal self-efficacy, however, was not related to team performance. This was substantiated in a comprehensive meta-analysis that found collective efficacy to be a strong predictor of team performance (Stajkoviv, Lee, & Nyberg, 2009). In addition, higher collective efficacy is predictive of reduced task anxiety, improved task engagement, and greater satisfaction (Beauchamp et al., 2012). Therefore, coaches should be more concerned with building the efficacy of the team as a whole than with building each individual player's self-efficacy. Along these lines, it appears that performance in practice is a more important source of collective efficacy than is performance in the previous game. In addition, events outside of the sport realm (e.g., personal life problems, relationships with friends, school demands) are less important for team efficacy than is self-efficacy (Chase, Feltz, & Lirgg, 2003).

Creating a belief in the team and the players' ability to be successful as a group appears to be critical to success. Many great teams (Chicago Bulls, Boston Celtics, New York Yankees, Montreal Canadiens, San Francisco 49ers) have had this sense of team efficacy during their winning years. Therefore, to enhance performance and productivity—whether you are a coach, teacher, exercise leader, or head athletic trainer—it seems crucial that you get your team, group, or class to believe in themselves as a unit (as opposed to simply believing in themselves individually). In addition, research has revealed that creating a mastery-oriented climate (focus on performance improvement instead of winning) enhances feelings of collective efficacy (Magyar, Feltz, & Simpson, 2004). In a large study using more than 2,000 Belgian volleyball players, Fransen and colleagues (2012) found that positive supportive communication (e.g., enthusiasm after making a point) was most predictive of positive beliefs about collective efficacy, whereas negative emotional reactions of players (e.g., discouraging body language) was most predictive of negative beliefs about collective efficacy. Finally, in a review of the literature in this area, Shearer, Holmes, and Mellalieu (2009) argue from a neuroscience perspective that imagery and observation-based interventions (e.g., video footage of successful team plays and interactions) are particularly effective in building collective efficacy, especially when an individual's perspective is directed toward his teammates' perspectives (e.g., "My team believes . . .").

A related concept that has recently appeared in the literature is known as relation-inferred self-efficacy (Beauchamp & Whinton, 2005; Jackson, Grove, & Beauchamp, 2010). This refers to the belief one has in another person (e.g., the belief a coach has in an athlete). Research has underscored the importance of developing a strong sense of relational efficacy in both coach–athlete and athlete–athlete dyads. For example, coaches' confidence in their athletes' capabilities not only predicted greater effort and commitment on behalf of the coaches, but it also appeared to transfer to the athletes, who were more committed and displayed greater effort.

positive attitude is essential to reaching potential. Athletic performers need to discard negative thoughts *(I'm so stupid; I can't believe I'm playing so badly; I just can't beat this person;* or *I'll never make it)* and replace them with positive thoughts *(I'll keep getting better if I just work at it; Just keep calm and focused; I can beat this guy;* or *Hang in there and things will get better)*. Thoughts and self-talk should be instructional and motivational rather than judgmental (see chapter 16). Positive self-talk can provide specific performance cues as well as keep motivation and energy high. Although it is sometimes difficult to do, positive self-talk results in a more enjoyable and successful athletic experience, making it well worth using. Thinking that you can achieve something realistic can actually help you achieve it, as the following quote demonstrates:

" **I know I am the greatest. I said that even before I knew I was.** "

—Muhammad Ali, three-time world heavyweight boxing champion

Associated with thinking positively is the idea of remembering your good performances, not simply your poor performances, mistakes, and errors (Houston & Newton, 2010). Athletes who are in a slump and who have a number of recent performance failures especially tend to focus only on these poor performances. Instead, athletes should focus more on their excellent performances and compare them with present performance in order to determine what needs to be changed.

Using Imagery

As you recall from chapter 13, one use of imagery is to help build confidence. You can see yourself doing things that you either have never been able to do or have had difficulty doing. For example, a golfer who consistently has been slicing the ball off the tee can imagine herself hitting the ball straight down the fairway. A football quarterback can visualize different defensive alignments and then try to counteract these with specific plays and formations. Similarly, trainers can help injured athletes build confidence by having them imagine getting back on the playing field and performing well. Selk (2009) suggests that athletes create a 1- to 2-minute mental film of their best performances to remind them of their capabilities and

help generate positive feelings and thoughts. The use of imagery to build confidence is seen in the following quote by an Olympic pistol shooter:

" **I would imagine to myself, "How would a champion act and feel . . . ." This helped me to find out about myself. Then as the actual roles I had imagined came along, and as I achieved them, that in turn helped me to believe that I would be the Olympic champion. (Orlick & Partington, 1988, p. 113)** "

Using Goal Mapping

Because the focused and persistent pursuit of goals serves as a basic regulator of human behavior, it is important to use **goal mapping** to enhance the confidence and performance of athletes. A goal map is a personalized plan for an athlete that contains various types of goals and goal strategies as well as a systematic evaluation procedure for assessing progress toward goals. (See chapter 15 for a detailed discussion of goal setting.) Research and interviews with both coaches and athletes indicate that the focus should be more on performance and process goals, as opposed to outcome goals, because the former provide more of a sense of control and enhanced attention to the task. Stable, resilient confidence is based on the pursuit and achievement of goals in personalized goal maps. Goal mapping, imagery, and self-talk are three primary self-regulatory tools that sport psychologists advocate to enhance confidence.

Optimizing Physical Conditioning and Training

Being in your best possible physical shape is another key to feeling confident. Athletes in most sports today train year-round to improve strength, endurance, and flexibility, and they rate physical preparation as one of their top sources of confidence. Tennis great Andre Agassi has repeatedly said that his rigorous physical conditioning regimen has allowed him to feel confident that he can outlast opponents and play long, arduous points throughout a match. In addition, world-class athletes have particularly emphasized the importance of quality training for building confidence. No mental training intervention can ever take the place of the physical skill and conditioning needed to perform in sport. Rather, rigorous training and practice should be integrated with solid mental training.

Building Coaching Efficacy

A unique program was developed and implemented to enhance coaching efficacy in a professional soccer academy with players ranging from 9 to 14 years old (Harwood, 2008). After a year of consultation with the players and coaches, an intervention program aimed specifically at enhancing coaches' efficacy in shaping positive psychological and interpersonal skills of the young players was implemented. Five areas were targeted:

- *Commitment* (e.g., encouraging persistence after mistakes, skill-specific feedback and reinforcement)
- *Communication* (e.g., teaching listening skills, reinforcement of players who send information and acknowledge feedback)
- *Concentration* (e.g., incorporating use of distractions, drills for practicing focusing on internal and external cues)
- *Control* (e.g., introducing players to routines in dead-ball situations, reinforcement for quick recovery and response to mistakes)
- *Confidence* (e.g., encouraging peer acknowledgment of skill achievement, setting challenging goals)

Vealey and Vernau (2013) suggest an exercise for optimizing confidence. First, during a team meeting, athletes are asked to grade (from 0% to 100%) their team's commitment to physical conditioning, physical skill execution, and mental skill development. Then, the scores are posted on a chalkboard for all to see. The coach then leads a discussion about the various grades for the three categories. Finally, in small groups and as a whole team, athletes generate ideas about how to raise the team's grade in each category.

Preparing

Jack Nicklaus has said in interviews, "As long as I'm prepared, I always expect to win." The flip side of this is that you can't expect to win if you're unprepared. Being prepared gives you confidence that you have done everything possible to ensure success. A plan gives you confidence because you know what you're going to do. Many athletes enter a competition without a strategy. But there should always be a plan of attack, which requires that you have at least a general idea of what you want to accomplish and how you will do it.

Most successful Olympic athletes have detailed plans and strategies for what they want to do. They also have alternative strategies (Gould, Eklund, & Jackson, 1992c; Gould, Guinan, et al., 1999). For example, a miler should go into every race with both a plan for how to run the race and an adjustment strategy if the pace of the race dictates such a move. A good plan considers your own abilities as well as your opponent's.

Good preparation also includes a set precompetition routine. Knowing exactly what will happen and when it will happen gives you confidence and puts your mind at ease. Being sure when you will eat, practice, stretch out, and arrive at the competition helps build confidence that extends to the competition itself. (See chapter 16 for more on precompetition routines.) Remember the well-known maxim of the 7 Ps: Proper planning and perspiration prevent pitifully poor performance.

Fostering Social Climate

Performance does not occur in a vacuum, and you need to consider the social climate when attempting to build confidence. Social climate factors that seem to influence confidence include leadership style; types of goals and their evaluation; social support networks; social feedback sources; and types, availability, and characteristics of models. Coaches who use autonomous coaching styles that facilitate athletes' perceptions of control are more likely to enhance the confidence of their athletes than are coaches who use more controlling leadership styles. Similarly, providing effective models not only for skill execution but also for achievement behaviors (e.g., effort and persistence) is recommended. Coaches can help structure the social climate to maximize athletes' feelings of confidence, although athletes should learn to base their confidence more on self-regulatory control of perceptions, emotions, and behaviors so that they are not subject to the inconsistent type of self-confidence that is dependent on social and environmental confidence builders.

Building Team (Collective) Efficacy

Research (Ronglan, 2007) using interviews from a women's handball team participating in the world championships and Olympics presents some ideas for building collective efficacy across a season. Building collective efficacy was broken down into three dimensions:

• *Before competition*—The *production process* focused on developing joint perceptions of capabilities and fitness to manage the upcoming competition in a successful manner. This involved perceptions of being well prepared mentally and physically, of having sufficient abilities (individually, collectively), of being a strong team unit, and of being ready to handle the upcoming tasks.

• *During competition*—The *activation process* focused on getting team members believing in one another right before and during the game. The team demonstrated confidence during the competition by showing enthusiasm, willpower, persistence, and team morale. Because the opponents tried to demonstrate similar confidence in their own team, it was important for the players to show the other team how confident they felt as a unit.

• *After competition*—The *evaluation process* was about developing intrateam interpretations of experiences and incidents during the game. After unsuccessful performances the evaluation was the starting point in regaining confidence, and after successful performances the evaluation was the starting point in enhancing confidence.

In addition to specific ways to build collective efficacy, research (Heuze, Bosselut, & Thomas, 2007) has indicated that collective efficacy is an antecedent of task cohesion. So building collective efficacy is not only important in and of itself, but it also enhances the development of players getting along on the court and having common goals.

VIEW Activity 14.2 helps you identify ways to enhance self-efficacy.

LEARNING AIDS

SUMMARY

1. **Define and understand the benefits of self-confidence.**
   Self-confidence has been defined as the belief that you can successfully perform a desired behavior. In addition, a recent view is that self-confidence is multidimensional, consisting of confidence about one's ability to execute physical skills, psychological skills, and perceptual skills; one's physical fitness and training status; and one's learning potential. High levels of self-confidence can enhance emotional state, concentration, goal setting, effort expended, and development of effective competitive strategies. Robust sport-confidence, which has been recently introduced, involves a set of beliefs indicating that sport confidence is multidimensional.

2. **Discuss the sources of sport confidence.**
   There are nine sources of sport confidence: mastery, demonstration of ability, physical and mental preparation, physical self-presentation, social support, vicarious experience, coach leadership, environmental comfort, and situation favorableness.

3. **Understand how expectations affect performance and behavior.**
   Expectations can have a critical effect on performance. Expecting to win or expecting to lose can greatly affect one's performance in a competition. Coaches' or teachers' expectations can also have a tremendous influence on the performance and behavior of students and athletes. Studies have shown that coaches and teachers act differently depending on whether they have high or low expectations of a player or student.

4. **Explain the theory of self-efficacy.**
   Self-efficacy is seen as a situationally specific form of self-confidence. Self-efficacy theory takes an interactional approach to the study of self-confidence, holding that self-efficacy interacts with environmental determinants to produce behavioral change. The theory views self-efficacy as the major determinant of performance as long as one has the requisite skills and is motivated to perform. According to the theory,

self-efficacy affects one's choice of activities, persistence, and level of effort. The sources of self-efficacy include performance accomplishments, vicarious experiences, verbal persuasion, imaginal experiences, physiological states, and emotional states.

5. **Explain how you would assess self-confidence.**

You can assess self-confidence by asking some key questions: How does one deal with adversity? How does one recover from a mistake? How easily does one lose confidence? Does the person get tentative in pressure situations? You can also measure self-confidence more formally through psychological confidence inventories. One such inventory asks you to rate yourself as being underconfident, overconfident, or confident about various aspects of your performance.

6. **Explain the various aspects of coaching efficacy.**

Coaching efficacy is a relatively new concept in the literature. It consists of efficacy in game strategy, motivation, technique, and character building. (A fifth concept called physical conditioning—the coach's ability to enhance the physical conditioning of athletes—has recently been added.) It appears that years of experience and community support are most predictive of feelings of coaching efficacy.

7. **Describe strategies for building self-confidence.**

A number of strategies can help build self-confidence in either the short term or the long term. These include focusing on performance instead of outcome, acting confident (body language), thinking confidently through the use of positive and instructional self-talk, responding confidently, goal mapping (setting appropriate goals), using imagery to visualize positive outcomes, and preparing both physically and mentally.

KEY TERMS

self-confidence	person cues	retention
state self-confidence	performance information	motor reproduction
trait self-confidence	self-efficacy	motivation
self-fulfilling prophecy	vicarious experiences (modeling)	goal mapping
hot hand	attention	

REVIEW QUESTIONS

1. What is self-confidence? How is it related to expectations?

2. Discuss the implications of Rosenthal and Jacobson's (1968) study of expectation effects for coaches and physical education teachers.

3. What is self-efficacy? How does it affect behavior? Why is it now called regulatory self-efficacy? Briefly discuss three other specific types of self-efficacy.

4. Discuss the six sources of self-efficacy. What evidence supports the idea that these various sources influence efficacy?

5. Describe the relationship between self-confidence and athletic performance, including the ideas of overconfidence and underconfidence. Is there such a thing as overconfidence?

6. Discuss three strategies for building self-efficacy, and describe how they affect sport performance.

7. Briefly discuss the model of self-confidence, including the sources of confidence, factors that affect confidence, and the consequences of confidence.

8. Describe the four components of coaching efficacy, including the best predictors of coaching efficacy.

9. Describe strategies for building self-confidence.

10. Describe the concept of robust sport confidence and two factors that help predict sport confidence.

CRITICAL THINKING QUESTIONS

1. You are a new coach for a high school basketball team. You have just selected your team after rigorous tryouts. You believe that you have a wide range of talent and ability on the team, and you want to be able to develop the younger talent. But you also know how easy it is to fall into the trap of creating differential expectations of the various athletes. Using the four-step process relating to how coaches' expectations might influence their own behavior and that of their athletes, explain what specific types of feedback or instruction you would use to keep the expectations of all your athletes high. How would you structure practices to help keep athlete expectations high?

2. Sometimes we create psychological barriers for ourselves by not believing that we can accomplish something. Discuss three situations in your life (or a close friend's or family member's) when a psychological barrier was created. How could you handle things differently to create a more positive expectation?

15

Goal Setting

After reading this chapter, you should be able to

1. define what goals are and identify major types of goals,
2. describe the latest research on and theory of goal setting,
3. describe goal-setting principles,
4. explain group goals and how to use them,
5. explain how to design a goal-setting system,
6. identify common problems in goal setting and how to overcome them, and
7. summarize the findings regarding coaches' goal-setting practices.

" **If you don't know where you are going, you might wind up someplace else.** "

—Hall of Fame baseball great Yogi Berra

" **What keeps me going is goals.** "

—Boxing great Muhammad Ali

" **You don't have to be a fantastic hero to do certain things—to compete. You can be just an ordinary chap, sufficiently motivated to reach challenging goals.** "

—Legendary mountaineer and first to reach the summit of Mount Everest, Sir Edmund Hillary

These quotes from outstanding athletes tell us a great deal about the importance and power of goal setting. Goals provide us direction, help us stay motivated, and allow us to accomplish feats that we may not have believed were possible. And it's not just great athletes who tap into the power of goals and goal setting. People often set **goals** like these in sport and exercise activities:

- I want to lose 10 pounds.
- I want to fully recover from my injury by August 15.
- I want to make the starting lineup.
- I want to be able to bench press my own weight.
- I intend to improve my golf game and win the club tournament.
- My objective is to become a high school varsity basketball coach.

You may be wondering, then, why devote an entire chapter to goal setting if people already set goals on their own? The problem is not getting people to identify goals. It is getting them to set the right kind of goals—ones that provide direction and enhance motivation—and helping them learn how to stick to and achieve their goals. As most of us have learned from the New Year's resolutions we've made, it is much easier to set a goal than to follow through on it. Seldom are goals to lose weight or to exercise set realistically in terms of commitment, difficulty, evaluation of progress, and specific strategies for achieving the goals. Most people do not need to be convinced that goals are important; they need instruction on setting effective goals and designing a program for achieving them.

Definition of Goals

People in sport and exercise have often looked at goals in terms of objective and subjective goals. **Objective goals** focus on "attaining a specific standard of proficiency on a task, usually within a specified time" (Locke & Latham, 2002, p. 705). Attempting to attain a specified level of weight loss within 3 months, aiming for a certain team win–loss record by the end of the season, and achieving a lower performance time by the next competition are all examples of objective goals. **Subjective goals**, on the other hand, are general statements of intent (e.g., "I want to do well"; "I want to have fun") that are not measurable or objective.

> **KEY POINT** An objective goal is the desire to attain a specific standard of proficiency on a task, usually within a specified time.

Types of Goals

In the sport and exercise psychology literature, goals have been viewed as focused on outcome, performance, or process (Burton, Naylor, & Holliday, 2001; Hardy et al., 1996). We briefly review these types of goals.

- **Outcome goals** typically focus on a competitive result of an event, such as winning a race, earning a medal, or scoring more points than an opponent. Thus, achieving these goals depends not only on your own efforts but also on the ability and play of your opponent. You could play the best tennis match of your life and still lose, and thus you would fail to achieve your outcome goal of winning the match.

- **Performance goals** focus on achieving standards or performance objectives independently of other competitors, usually on the basis of comparisons with one's own previous performances. For this reason, performance goals tend to be more flexible and in your control. Running a mile in 6 minutes 21 seconds and improving the percentage of successful slice-first serves from 70% to 80% are examples of performance goals.

- **Process goals** focus on the actions an individual must engage in during performance to execute or

perform well. For example, a swimmer may set a goal of maintaining a long, stretched-out arm pull in her freestyle stroke, or a basketball player may set a goal of squaring up to the basket and releasing the ball at the peak of his jump. Interestingly, research by Kingston and Hardy (1997) has shown that process goals are particularly effective in positively influencing golfers' self-efficacy, cognitive anxiety, and confidence.

> **KEY POINT** Outcome goals in sport focus on achieving a victory in a competitive contest, whereas performance goals focus on achieving standards based on one's own previous performances, not the performances of others.

Outcome, Performance, and Process Goals in Behavior Change

Athletes and exercisers should set outcome, performance, and process goals because all three play important roles in directing behavioral change (Burton et al., 2001). Outcome goals can facilitate short-term motivation away from the competition (e.g., thinking about how it felt to lose to an arch-rival may motivate one to train in the off-season). Focusing on outcome goals just before or during competition, however, often increases anxiety and irrelevant, distracting thoughts (e.g., worrying too much about the score of the game and not attending enough to the task at hand). Research by Mullen and Hardy (2010) showed that athletes who adopted holistic, process goals that helped them focus on the general feelings of the skills to be performed (e.g., *drive, spring,* or *smooth*) were most effective at helping highly capable but anxious athletes avoid the negative effects of anxiety on performance.

Performance and process goals are important because you usually can make much more precise adjustments to these goals (e.g., increase the goal from 80% to 82%) than you can to outcome goals, which often have fewer levels (i.e., you either win or lose a game). Achieving a performance or process goal also depends much less on your opponent's behavior. For these reasons, performance and process goals are particularly useful for athletes at the time of competition, although they should be used in practice as well.

Under special circumstances, too much emphasis on a specific performance goal (e.g., running a personal-best 5-minute mile) can create anxiety, although this is less likely to occur than with an outcome goal. In addition, it is often difficult to prioritize

⫸ Prioritizing General Subjective Goals

Most sport psychology research concerns objective goals, but the importance of subjective goals must not be overlooked. In the popular or commercial literature about personal productivity and business management, for example, considerable attention has been paid to identifying and clarifying one's personal values and priorities and then using these general, subjective goals to formulate more specific goals that guide day-to-day behavior (Smith, 1994). The following case makes this point.

Kim is an undergraduate student majoring in exercise and sport science. Her goals are to graduate with excellent grades, get into graduate school, and become a physical therapist. Already a good student, she runs on the cross country team, works in the training room, holds a part-time job, participates in several campus social groups, and tries to get home to visit her family whenever she can. Kim has struggled lately because she has not been achieving her goals. After talking to the sport psychologist in the athletic department, Kim realizes that the problem is not with the specific goals she sets (e.g., get an A in biomechanics, run a specified time on the home cross country course) but with her global priorities or subjective goals. She is trying to do too much and needs to prioritize her activities. After considerable reflection, Kim develops the following list of governing values and then prioritizes each subjective goal using ratings of A (most important), B (somewhat important), and C (less important). She subsequently uses this list of general priorities each week to formulate more specific weekly goals, making sure she devotes most of her attention to achieving goals in the high-priority areas. This ensures that Kim spends most of her time accomplishing her highest-priority goals, not the ones that *seem* critical on a particular day but that in actuality aren't of highest priority.

Goal	Priority
Do well in school	A
Run cross country	B
Volunteer in the training room	B
Participate in campus social activities	C
Visit home	C
Work a part-time job	C

specific performance and process goals unless one also considers long-term outcome goals. For example, you would design quite a different fitness program if someone's outcome goal was to bulk up and gain 20 pounds than you would if someone wanted to lose 20 pounds. All three types of goals, then, have a purpose. The key is knowing when to focus on each type of goal and not to fall into the trap of placing all your attention on outcome goals.

Along these lines, a study by Filby, Maynard, and Graydon (1999) showed that using a combination of goal strategies (outcome, performance, process) produced significantly better performance than simply relying on one type of goal. It was concluded that performers need to prioritize their goals and that different types of goals may be more effective at different times (e.g., competition vs. practice). The authors highlighted this point in stating, "The benefits of adopting an outcome goal are realized only when

the outcome goal is combined with the prioritization of a process orientation immediately before and during performance" (p. 242).

🔍 **DISCOVER** Activity 15.1 allows you to take a moment to examine your own goals.

Effectiveness of Goal Setting

Motivation depends on goal setting.

" **The coach must have goals. The team must have goals. Each tennis player must have goals; real vivid living goals . . . . Goals keep everyone on target. Goals commit me to the work, time, pain, and whatever else is part of the price of achieving success.** "

—Top collegiate tennis player (cited in Weinberg, 1988, p. 145)

Individuals in sport and exercise have been setting goals for a long time, and the tennis player captures some of the key ingredients in goal setting. Psychologists (especially business psychologists) have also studied goal setting as a motivational technique for a long time (longer than sport scientists), looking at whether setting specific, difficult goals improves performance more than setting no goals, setting easy goals, or setting the general goal of simply doing your best. Most of these studies were designed to test the propositions of Locke's (1968) theory of goal setting. The reviewers (Burton & Weiss, 2008; Locke & Latham, 1990; Locke, Shaw, Saari, & Latham, 1981; Mento, Steel, & Karren, 1987) concluded that goal setting works extremely well. In fact, more than 90% of the general psychology studies (more than 500 in all) show that goal setting has a consistent and powerful effect on behavior, whether it's used with elementary school children or professional scientists and whether for brainstorming or for loading logs onto trucks. Moreover, goal-setting effects have remained consistent with more than 40,000 participants using more than 90 tasks and across 10 countries. Goal setting is a behavioral technique that most definitely works!

A meta-analysis (a statistical review of the literature that combines the results of independent studies and indicates whether results were significant across all the studies) of 36 studies in sport and exercise psychology presented a similar conclusion (Kyllo & Landers, 1995). More recently, Burton and Weiss (2008) found that 70 of 88 studies (80%) in sport and exercise demonstrated moderate to strong effects and concluded that goal setting works well in sport, although not quite as well as in business. Over the years the strength and consistency of goal-setting effects in sport and exercise have also increased, leading to the conclusion that goal setting is a successful technique for improving performance in sport and exercise as well as in business.

Researchers on goal setting have found that the following factors most consistently enhance the effectiveness of goal setting in sport and exercise environments: goals of moderate difficulty, both short- and long-term goals, the presence of feedback on progress toward goal attainment, specificity of goals, public acknowledgment of goals, commitment to goal attainment, participants' input in the goal-setting process, and use of a combination of different goals.

Even recreational athletes can benefit from setting goals.

Goal-Setting Research

Researchers have examined the relationship between various types of goals (e.g., specific or general, long-term or short-term, difficult or easy) and physical fitness tasks (e.g., the number of sit-ups performed in 3 minutes, performance times in a swimming event, free-throw shooting in basketball) (see Burton & Weiss [2008], Weinberg [1994, 2000, 2004], and Weinberg & Butt [2005] for detailed reviews). Results generally indicated that specific goals that were of both short- and long-term duration and were moderately to very difficult were associated with the best performances. In one study, college students in an 8-week basketball course set either specific or general goals for fundamental basketball skill tasks (e.g., defensive footwork, free-throw shooting, dribbling). Setting specific rather than general goals enhanced performance, although not on all tasks. Specifically, goal setting appeared to enhance performance on low-complexity tasks better than on high-complexity tasks (Burton, 1989a). In addition, a number of intervention studies using goal setting to help change performance and behavior over time in sport or exercise settings have consistently demonstrated the positive effect that goals can have on improving performance in such sports as lacrosse (Weinberg, Stitcher, Richardson, & Jackson, 1994), basketball (Swain & Jones, 1995), football (Ward & Carnes, 2002), ice hockey (Anderson, Crowell, Doman, & Howard, 1988), soccer (Brobst & Ward, 2002), swimming (Burton, 1989b), tennis (Galvan & Ward, 1998), and golf (Kingston & Hardy, 1997). Researchers are also starting to apply goal setting to physical education and exercise situations, finding that goal setting influences intrinsic motivation and exercise adherence (Wilson & Brookfield, 2009) as well as persistence and effort in physical education students (Guan, Xiang, McBride, & Bruene, 2006).

KEY POINT Goal setting is an extremely powerful technique for enhancing performance, but it must be implemented correctly.

In addition to improving our understanding of what makes goals more effective, sport psychology researchers have learned a good deal about the *process* of goal setting, including how people set goals, what goals are most important to people, what barriers impede goal attainment, and how different types of individuals differ in their goal setting. Research using questionnaires and interviews with collegiate, Olym-

pic, and youth athletes (Weinberg, Burke, & Jackson, 1997; Weinberg, Burton, Yukelson, & Weigand, 1993, 2000) has revealed much about athletes' preferences and goal-setting strategies, including the following:

- Almost all athletes used some type of goal setting to enhance performance and found their goals to be moderately to highly effective.
- Improving performance (Olympic athletes), winning (collegiate athletes), and enjoyment (youth athletes) were the most important goals for athletes. These were the top three goals for each type of athlete, although the number one goal varied.
- Athletes commented that they preferred goals that were moderately difficult, difficult, and very difficult; these were, in order, the top three preferences for **goal difficulty**. However, great individual differences emerged concerning preference for goal difficulty.
- For collegiate athletes, major barriers to achieving goals included stress, fatigue, academic pressures, social relationships, and a lack of time. For Olympians, barriers were basically internal (e.g., lack of confidence, lack of goal feedback, too many goals or conflicting goals) or external (e.g., lack of time, work commitments, family and personal responsibilities).
- Females set goals more often and found them to be more effective than males did (except for outcome goals).
- Athletes did not systematically write down their goals, although they thought about them a great deal.
- The more experience athletes had with setting goals, the better they became in developing effective goal-setting strategies.
- The number one reason athletes gave for setting goals was to provide them direction and keep them focused on the task at hand.
- Athletes who used multiple goal strategies exhibited the best performance.
- Individual differences (e.g., goal orientation, locus of control) need to be considered when setting goals.

Although researchers in both general psychology and sport psychology have produced considerable evidence that goal setting is a powerful technique for enhancing performance, it is not a foolproof method. It must be implemented with thought, understanding of the process, and planning. Systematic approaches and monitoring of the process are necessary if one is to be able to determine when and where goal setting is most effective in a program.

Why Goal Setting Works

Researchers have explained why goal setting works in two ways. Outcome, performance, and process goals influence behavior indirectly by affecting important psychological factors such as confidence and anxiety. This has been labeled the **indirect thought-process view** because goals lead to changes in psychological factors, which then influence performance. For instance, in an empirical study by Burton (1989b), swimmers learned the strategy of setting performance goals. Swimmers who were high in goal-setting ability demonstrated less anxiety, higher confidence, and improved performance compared with those who were low in goal-setting ability. In essence, goals were found to influence performance indirectly through effects on psychological states.

In a more recent study, Gano-Overway (2008) assigned athletes to either a task- or ego-involving condition and then had them perform motor tasks on which they received negative feedback. Findings revealed that the athletes involved in task-oriented conditions demonstrated better self-regulation—they more effectively monitored and evaluated their current performance and more often used planning strategies for dealing with setbacks. Creating environments that emphasize self-referenced process and performance goals helped participants better deal with failure.

In contrast is the more thoroughly researched **direct mechanistic view**, which specifies that goals influence performance in one of four direct ways (Locke & Latham, 2002):

1. Goals direct attention to important elements of the skill being performed.
2. Goals mobilize performer efforts.
3. Goals prolong performer persistence.
4. Goals foster the development of new learning strategies.

Goal-Setting Practices of High School and Collegiate Coaches

Most goal-setting research in sport or exercise has centered on the performer. However, research by Weinberg and colleagues (Weinberg, Butt, & Knight, 2001; Weinberg, Butt, Knight, & Perritt, 2001) addressed the goal-setting practices of coaches. The following are highlights of the findings:

- Virtually all coaches set goals for competition and practice (individual and team) as well as personal coaching-related goals.
- There was a good deal of variability in coaches' understanding of the principles of goal setting as well as in the frequency with which they used goals.
- Coaches reevaluated their goals, although how systematically and how often they did so varied greatly across coaches.
- Coaches dictated some goals and got input from the players about others.
- Although coaches used performance, process, and outcome goals, they tended to favor performance and process goals.
- The main reason for setting goals was to provide purpose and direction, followed by player improvement and fostering team cohesion (team goals).
- Goal barriers were seen as physical (e.g., injury), psychological (e.g., lack of confidence), and external (e.g., parental overinvolvement).
- The most important aspect of goal commitment was personal enjoyment.
- The only disadvantage to goal setting was seen when goals were set too high and produced consistent failure.
- Coaches set both short- and long-term goals but focused more on short-term goals that provided feedback on the progression toward meeting the long-term goals.
- Coaches were inconsistent in writing down their goals.

First, goals direct performers' attention to important elements of the skill that the performer may not normally attend to. For example, when soccer players set specific goals to improve their games, they concentrate on the particular skills that need improving such as corner kicks, movement of the ball, and winning 50-50 balls. In fact, research with athletes (Weinberg et al., 1993, 2000) has confirmed that the primary reason performers set goals is to provide direction and focus to their actions. Goals also mobilize effort and persistence by providing incentives. For instance, a swimmer may not want to practice on a given day and find it difficult to muster her effort to do so. However, by dividing the distance she needs to swim into 10 equal parts, or goals, she has a series of incentives that seem reasonable. Similarly, safely losing 50 pounds may seem like an insurmountable goal that requires considerable persistence. But by setting a subgoal of losing 1 to 2 pounds weekly and charting subgoal accomplishment, you are much more likely to stay motivated and persist with the weight-loss program. Finally, goal setting has a hidden advantage in that it encourages new learning strategies. An exerciser wanting to lose 20 pounds might decide that he has to exercise in the early morning (new strategy) if he wants to make sure that he exercises regularly. Similarly, a basketball player with a goal of improving her free-throw percentage from 70% to 80% might refine her preshot routine, change the biomechanics of her shot, or practice more shots even when she feels tired.

Although the mechanistic explanation of goal setting appears straightforward, Locke and Latham (2002) note that the goal–performance relationship is not always simple. Rather, the relationship is influenced by factors such as self-efficacy, feedback, and task complexity.

 VIEW Activity 15.2 lets you prioritize your own subjective goals.

Principles of Goal Setting

A number of goal-setting principles can be identified from research and practice (Gould, 2005; Murphy, 1996). The correct application of these principles provides a strong foundation for designing a goal-setting program. However, although research can provide the "science" of setting goals, the "art" of setting goals (when and for whom goals should be set) can be practiced only by the coach or individual performer. In essence, the effectiveness of any goal-setting program is dependent on the interaction between individuals and the situation in which the individuals are placed. These are the principles of goal setting:

- Set specific goals.
- Set moderately difficult but realistic goals.
- Set long- and short-term goals.
- Set performance, process, and outcome goals.
- Set practice and competition goals.
- Record goals.
- Develop goal achievement strategies.
- Consider participants' personalities and motivations.
- Foster an individual's goal commitment.
- Provide goal support.
- Provide evaluation of and feedback about goals.

We discuss each of these principles in the following sections.

Set Specific Goals

Specific goals influence behavioral change more effectively than do general "do-your-best" goals or having no goals at all. However, many teachers, coaches, and exercise leaders still simply tell their students or clients to do their best. Goals should be stated in very specific, measurable terms that relate to behavior. For example, the goal of improving your golf game is too vague. A better goal would be to lower your golf handicap from 14 over par to 11 by improving the accuracy of your short-iron approach shots to the green. Similarly, the goal of lowering your cholesterol level is broad and imprecise compared with the goal of lowering your cholesterol level from 290 to 200 by eliminating an evening snack of high-fat potato chips and beginning an exercise program of walking 4 days a week. To be most effective, goals must be stated in specific terms.

KEY POINT Specific goals, compared with general "do-your-best" goals, are more effective for producing behavioral change.

Set Moderately Difficult but Realistic Goals

Effective goals are difficult enough to challenge a participant yet realistic enough that they can be achieved. A meta-analysis by Kyllo and Landers (1995) showed that moderately difficult goals lead to best performance, and a study by Bueno, Weinberg, Fernandez-Castro, & Capdevila (2008) showed that if goals are perceived as too difficult, not reaching them can be threatening and lead to learned helplessness. Goals are of little value if no effort is needed to achieve them, and participants soon lose interest in a program involving these types of goals. But goals that are too difficult to achieve can lead to frustration, reduced confidence, and poor performance. The secret is to strike a balance between goal challenge and achievability, which is no easy task. Professionals must know the capabilities and commitment of the individuals they are working with. As people gain professional experience, it becomes easier to judge capabilities and how long improvement will take to occur. If a coach or instructor does not have extensive experience with the activity or the individuals involved in the program, it is better to err on the side of setting goals that can be more easily achieved. That way, participants will not become frustrated. As soon as it becomes clear that participants are easily mastering the goals, however, it is time to set more challenging, moderately difficult goals.

Set Long- and Short-Term Goals

Major behavioral change does not occur overnight. Thus, both long- and short-term goals should be set, and research has demonstrated that both are important (Kane, Baltes, & Moss, 2001; Vidic & Burton, 2010), especially with complex tasks (Locke & Latham, 2002). Long-term goals provide direction while short-term goals serve as intermediate steps that lead to long-term objectives (Vidic & Burton, 2010). Focusing only on long-term goals does not improve performance (Kyllo & Landers, 1995). Think of a staircase with a long-term goal or dream at the top, the present level of ability at the lowest step, and a sequence of progressively linked, short-term goals connecting the top and bottom of the staircase. Figure 15.1 depicts a goal-setting staircase used with a group of 8- to 11-year-old figure skaters. The skaters had a long-term goal of achieving the next test level (performing a prescribed set of skills) but were not ready to test at the time. Thus, the coach charted a progression of skills, or short-term goals, that would prepare the young skaters to achieve the next test level. The goal-setting staircase was posted and a gold skate sticker was placed on the graph each time a skater mastered a particular skill until all the

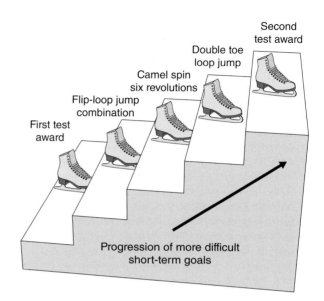

FIGURE 15.1 A goal-setting staircase for a group of 8- to 11-year-old figure skaters.

subgoals were accomplished and the long-term test goal was achieved.

The short- and long-term goal-setting staircase has been successfully adapted and used with elite athletes as well, including several world and Olympic champions. It also can be easily adapted for exercise programs. For example, figure 15.2 shows a goal-setting staircase (depicted in the form of climbing the mountain of behavioral change) for an individual beginning an exercise program designed to improve overall health and fitness. As was the case in the figure skating example, the key is to develop a progression of short-term goals that lead to a long-term objective.

Short- and long-term goals should be linked. A performer's long-term goals should be linked to a series of more immediate, short-term physical and psychological goals. This should create a progression of goals, starting with some that the person can achieve immediately and that lead to more difficult and distant objectives.

DISCOVER Activity 15.3 lets you analyze your personal goals and become aware of your goal-setting strengths and weaknesses.

Set Performance, Process, and Outcome Goals

It is difficult not to think about winning or how your performance compares with that of others. After all,

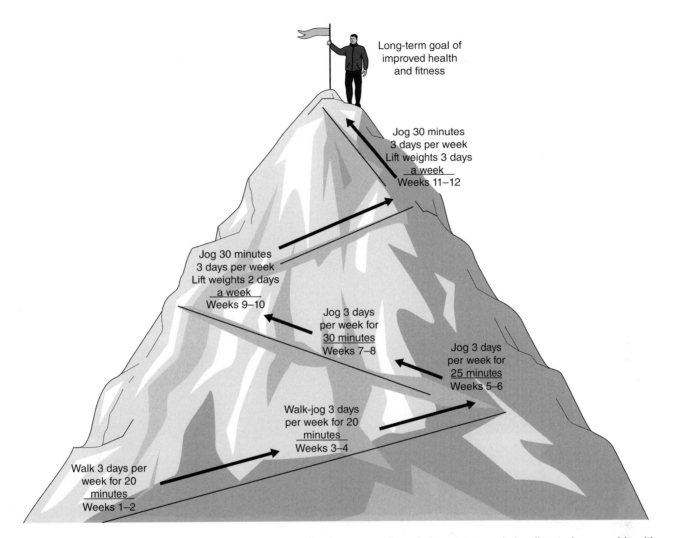

Long-term goal of improved health and fitness

Jog 30 minutes
3 days per week
Lift weights 3 days
a week
Weeks 11–12

Jog 30 minutes
3 days per week
Lift weights 2 days
a week
Weeks 9–10

Jog 3 days
per week for
30 minutes
Weeks 7–8

Jog 3 days
per week for
25 minutes
Weeks 5–6

Walk-jog 3 days
per week for 20
minutes
Weeks 3–4

Walk 3 days per
week for 20
minutes
Weeks 1–2

FIGURE 15.2 Climbing the mountain of behavior change—a progression of short-term goals leading to improved health and fitness.

winning and losing receive much more attention from others than do an individual's personal goal achievements. Not surprisingly, then, athletes often cite as their goals outcomes such as winning games, winning championships, or beating particular opponents. Ironically, the best way to win a championship or beat a particular opponent is to focus on performance or process goals. Placing too much emphasis on outcome goals creates anxiety during competition, and the athlete spends undue time worrying instead of focusing on the task at hand. It's not that outcome goals are bad; it's just that an overemphasis on them (especially during performance) can reduce, instead of enhance, performance. The key, then, is to continually emphasize performance and process goals. For every outcome goal an athlete sets, there should be several performance and process goals that would lead to that

outcome (Filby et al., 1999). For example, if you are working with the members of a junior high school softball team who want to win the city championship, you should emphasize the relevant performance goals of improving fielding percentage, the team's batting average, and stolen bases. In addition, you should emphasize process goals, such as players improving their sliding technique and pitchers improving their pickoffs in practice and then in games. Encourage efforts to achieve these goals and chart progress toward them throughout the season.

Set Practice and Competition Goals

Too often, athletes and coaches focus only on competition goals. Setting **practice goals** is important because of the large amount of time athletes spend practicing (especially compared with competing) and the potential that the long hours of practice can become boring to some individuals. Setting practice goals, then, is a good way to get a competitive edge by focusing on making improvements that one may not normally work on and by maintaining motivation. Interestingly, in studying successful Olympic athletes compared with less successful ones, Orlick and Partington (1988) found that the setting of practice goals for quality practice was one factor that differentiated the two groups. As examples of a practice goal, a downhill skier may aim to ski three flat sections of the course on a given day, or a tennis player may try to come more often to the net a certain number of times.

> **KEY POINT** For every outcome goal an athlete sets, the individual should set several performance and process goals that will lead to that outcome.

Record Goals

The adage "out of sight, out of mind" has relevance to goal-setting procedures. Several sport psychologists (Botterill, 1983; Gould, 2005; Ward & Carnes, 2002)

have recommended that once goals are set, they should be recorded and placed where they can be easily seen. Unfortunately, many athletes do not systematically record goals (Weinberg et al., 1993, 2000). There are many ways to record goals. Athletes or exercisers can simply write down their goals on index cards, or they can formulate complex behavioral contracts. No one strategy is optimal. However, the more efficient the method of recording, the more useful it is. For example, writing down goals on a card and posting the card in a locker or on the bedroom mirror at home are more effective and time efficient than composing an in-depth behavioral contract that is signed and placed in a drawer never to be looked at again. Athletes who use training logs often find it useful to include sections in which they record goals and their progress toward the goals.

Develop Goal Achievement Strategies

Vidic and Burton (2010) identified developing systematic **goal achievement strategies** as one of the most important goal-setting steps. Setting goals

Goals must be appropriate for the athlete. Setting a goal for this young athlete to compete in the 2016 FIFA Futsal World Cup is unrealistic and won't help her be successful.

without developing corresponding goal achievement strategies is like driving a car to a strange city without consulting a map or global positioning device. You must have strategies to accompany the goals you set. Chipping a bucket of golf balls onto a practice green 3 days a week is a strategy for achieving the goal of lowering your handicap by three shots. Participating in a walking program that burns 2,500 calories a week is a strategy for achieving a weight-loss goal of 20 pounds in 5 months. Strategies should be specific and should involve definite numbers (e.g., how much, how many, how often) so one knows how to achieve one's goal. Athletes and exercisers should build flexibility into their goal achievement strategies. Instead of saying they will lift weights on Monday, Wednesday, and Friday, it is better to say they will lift 3 days a week. That way, someone who cannot lift on one of the designated days can lift on another day and still achieve the goal.

Consider Participants' Personalities and Motivations

When you help athletes and exercisers set and achieve goals, consider their personalities and psychological orientations (Burton, Gillham, Weinberg, Yukelson, & Weigand, 2013; Evans & Hardy, 2002; Lambert, Moore, & Dixon, 1999). An individual's personality, motivation and goal orientations influence the goals the person adopts and how well the goal-setting process functions. Stoeber, Uphill, and Hotham (2009) found that being high in the personal standards component of perfectionism was associated with setting goals that enabled triathletes to achieve best performances. Burton and colleagues (2013) found that performance-oriented athletes who judge success relative to their ability to learn new skills and master performance are best at using goal setting and that failure-oriented athletes who judge success by comparing themselves with others are least skilled in using goal setting. High achievers (see chapter 3 on achievement motivation), then, whose personalities are characterized by high levels of the motive to achieve success and low levels of the motive to avoid failure, readily seek out and adopt challenging but realistic goals. In contrast, low achievers (with high levels of the motive to avoid failure and low levels of the motive to achieve success) avoid challenging goals and adopt either very easy or very difficult goals. Furthermore, a motivational climate that is created by

the teacher, coach, or exercise leader should help foster maximum participation by individuals with different personalities and needs (Ntoumanis & Biddle, 1999). Similarly, children in the social-comparison stage of achievement tend to focus on competitive and outcome goals. Competitive people also focus on outcome goals, whereas task-oriented athletes and exercisers are much more open to performance and process goals. Finally, as "Dispositional Hope and the 4W System for Developing It" shows, researchers have found that people high in dispositional **hope** approach goal setting differently than do those low in hope.

Understanding and recognizing these personality differences will help you know what to expect from the people you help set goals for. High achievers, those high on the personal standards component of perfectionism, people high in hope, and task- or performance-oriented athletes and exercisers should respond well to your goal-setting efforts. For low achievers, those high on the concern for mistakes component of perfectionism, people low in hope, and outcome- or failure-oriented participants, you will need to repeatedly emphasize the importance of setting realistic performance and process goals. You will also need to monitor participants in this category to ensure that they do not gravitate back to more familiar outcome goals. Extra efforts to focus on performance and process goals are also necessary with young children. Goal setting should be easier once youngsters reach the integrated stage and feel comfortable focusing on personal improvement.

Foster an Individual's Goal Commitment

A person will not achieve a goal without commitment to achieving it. Instructors should promote **goal commitment** by encouraging progress and providing consistent feedback. Teachers or coaches should not set their students' or athletes' goals for them, either directly or indirectly. Rather, they should make participants part of the goal-setting process by soliciting their input and letting them set their own goals. This does not imply that exercise and sport science professionals are not involved in the goal-setting process. For example, Shilts, Horowitz, and Townsend (2004) developed a computer-based guided goal-setting program aimed at improving the dietary and physical activity behaviors of middle school students. The strategy provided the youths with enough guidance to make scientifically based goal selections and allowed self-choice, which facilitated their commitment.

Dispositional Hope and the 4W System for Developing It

Why do some people go after and achieve their goals, but others seem to be much less effective at doing so? Psychologist Charles Snyder (1994) addressed this issue in his research on hope. For Snyder and his colleagues, hope is not wishing for something to happen without working for it. Instead, it involves the thinking process whereby people have an overall perception that goals can be met and the skills to go about achieving those goals. Specifically, people high in hope have a sense of goal-directed determination or agency and plan ways to meet goals or labeled pathways. Consistent with the person-by-situation interaction model of personality, trait and state measures of hope have been developed and found to correlate to psychological adjustment, achievement, problem solving, and health.

Building on the research on hope and as part of a coaching life skills program for athletes, Gould and colleagues (2000) developed the Power 4W goal-setting system for helping young people learn to set goals and develop high levels of hope. It is based on the finding that people who are successful in sport and life are positive, optimistic go-getters. Successful people on and off the field set goals, develop strategies for achieving goals, work hard to accomplish those goals, and view difficulties and challenges as opportunities rather than insurmountable obstacles (Snyder, 1994).

When using the Power 4W system, an athlete develops the following four program components:

- *Wish power:* Identifying his or her dream goals (e.g., Dan wants to earn a starting spot on his high school football team)

- *Want power:* Setting realistic short- and long-term goals that, when accomplished, lead to one's dream goal (e.g., Dan will need to play intelligently, become physically stronger, and get in great physical condition)

- *Way power:* Developing multiple plans, paths, and strategies for achieving one's goals (e.g., Dan lifts weights 4 days per week, runs 3 miles a day to increase endurance, and studies films from last year's games)

- *Will power:* Finding the determination, commitment, and discipline needed to consistently work toward one's goals and overcome obstacles that arise (e.g., Dan talks to his friend Bob, who agrees to work out with him and encourage him; he writes out and memorizes five motivational phrases to say during the tough parts of his run; and he places the team's photo on his bedroom mirror to remind him of his dream)

Similarly, O'Brien, Mellalieu, and Hanton (2009) reported that having boxers identify their strengths and areas needing improvement using the performance profiling technique was especially effective for increasing goal acceptance.

Provide Goal Support

Other people also can support athletes, students, and exercisers in their goal setting. Too often this **goal support** is not present. For example, a high school lacrosse coach whose team is competing for the district championship may have the athletes set a series of performance goals. Meanwhile, the athletes' parents, teachers, and friends frequently ask the players about winning the championship. Letters to parents, staff meeting announcements, and stories in the school newspaper can help educate these significant others

about the importance of performance and process (rather than outcome) goals.

KEY POINT Enlist support from significant others to make goal setting effective.

Spousal support is a critical factor affecting exercise adherence (Dishman, 1988). Many corporate fitness specialists have found it useful to involve spouses in weight-loss and conditioning programs and invite them to support the achievement of the participants' goals. Fitness professionals also need to show a genuine interest in the people with whom they work. They should review their participants' goals, ask about their progress, empathize with their struggles, and foster a caring, upbeat, and encouraging atmosphere.

Finally, Maitland and Gervis (2010) emphasized that goal support should not be taken for granted because goal setting is more than remembering facts and principles—it is a complex process. They found that elite English youth soccer coaches failed to become engaged or involved in the goal-setting process, were not responsive enough to player needs, and did not give the feedback and reassurance that players desired as they worked to achieve their goals. As a result, the effectiveness of the goal setting process was lessened.

Provide Evaluation of and Feedback About Goals

Feedback about performance progress is absolutely essential if goals are going to effectively change performance and behavior. Yet too often coaches and exercise leaders fail to provide evaluation and feedback concerning a participant's goals.

> **KEY POINT** Goal evaluation and feedback are essential parts of facilitating behavior change.

Goal evaluation strategies should be initiated at the start of the goal-setting program and continually implemented as the program progresses. Evaluation can take many forms (see table 15.1 for some examples). The key is to be consistent. Too often, people spend considerable time defining and setting goals only to have their work wasted because they don't follow through with essential evaluation and feedback. Thus, coaches should provide specific feedback to athletes on how they are progressing toward their goals, and athletes should write down their goals and record their progress.

Development of Group Goals

To date, sport and exercise psychologists have placed most emphasis on the individual goals of exercisers and athletes and the ways in which these goals influence behavioral change. However, research by Brawley, Carron, & Widmeyer (1992) revealed the widespread use of group or team goals both in practice and in competition. The type of goal varied considerably between practice and competition. In practice, approximately 90% of goals were process oriented and most focused on effort. However, in competition, goals were split between outcome and process and emphasized implementation of skills or strategies. Other than this initial study, group and team goal setting received little attention until the research of Widmeyer and DuCharme (1997). These authors underscored the notion that to understand the effects of goals on groups, you must know more than the individual goals of the group members. This point was further verified in a study by Dawson, Bray, and Widmeyer (2002), who found four types of goals evident in sport teams: a team member's goal for himself or herself, an individual member's goal for the team, the team's or group's goal, and the group's goal for the individual team member. Hence, group as well as individual goals must be considered.

The definition of a group's or team's goal is "the future state of affairs desired by enough members of a group to work towards its achievement" (Johnson & Johnson, 1987, p. 132). More specifically, **group goals** refer to the attainment of specific standards of group (not individual) proficiency, usually within a specified time. Hence, common group goals might

TABLE 15.1 Forms of Goal Evaluation

Goal	Goal evaluation strategy
Lose 20 pounds in 6 months	Client informs fitness instructor of weight each week.
Increase free-throw shooting percentage from 65% to 72% by the end of the season	Team manager charts free-throw percentage statistics after each game and calculates year-to-date free-throw average.
Attend injury rehabilitation clinic 3 days a week until recovery	Attendance is posted weekly at rehabilitation center, and coach is notified of attendance.
Improve concentration levels during practice	Coach gives player weekly report card rating practice concentration on a 0 (low) to 10 (high) scale.
Improve class cooperation in elementary school physical education class	Teacher tallies cooperative acts on behavioral checklist during week and charts the improvement of various classes on gym bulletin board.

include winning the state high school basketball league championship, having the lowest dropout rate of any cardiac rehabilitation program in the state, or improving school scores on a standardized physical fitness test.

Burke, Shapcott, Carron, Bradshaw, and Easterbrook (2010) demonstrated the power of group goals in a large-scale walking-group study designed to examine the relationship between group goals and the total miles walked by the participants in each group. More than 6,000 participants comprised 1,225 walking groups; each group consisted of 3 to 6 people. Results revealed that the more groups set goals, the farther they walked. Although goal setting facilitated the performance of all groups, it was especially effective for groups highly confident in their ability to schedule walking into their lives and who had more experience exercising. Group goals, then, have a powerful application for those working with exercise groups.

Having a team or group meeting to develop a list of shared group goals is not enough to bring about behavioral change, however. Setting group goals is only the first step in the process (Widmeyer & DuCharme, 1997). After identifying group goals, it is critical to identify the task that the group must perform in order to accomplish its goals as well as the process through which the group will interact to achieve the goals. Not surprisingly, group or team goals are linked to change in behavior via increases in motivation and cohesion. For example, Senecal, Loughead, and Bloom (2008) found that a season-long intervention of team building and goal setting facilitated team cohesion in high school basketball teams.

Widmeyer and DuCharme (1997) outlined six principles of effective team goal setting. Following these principles will allow you to effectively set and achieve goals with the groups you help:

- Establish long-term goals first.
- Establish clear paths of short-term goals en route to long-term goals.
- Involve all members of the team in establishing team goals.
- Monitor progress toward team goals.
- Reward progress made toward team goals.
- Foster collective team confidence or efficacy concerning team goals.

Design of a Goal-Setting System

Just as a basketball coach develops a game plan from individual plays, the fitness professional should develop a goal-setting system or plan from the 11 principles of goal setting discussed earlier. Although many goal-setting systems exist, most include three stages: preparation and planning, education and acquisition, and implementation and goal follow-up and evaluation. Next we discuss each of these stages separately.

First Stage: Preparation and Planning

An effective instructor, trainer, or coach does not want to enter a physical activity setting unprepared. Thought and preparation must precede effective goal setting. The time spent preparing for the goal-setting process saves hours of work once the program is implemented.

Assess Abilities and Needs

The first step is to assess the participant's abilities and needs. Based on his knowledge of the individual, the fitness professional should identify the areas he thinks most need improvement. When little is known about

SMARTS Goals

A good tip for helping athletes or exercisers remember characteristics of effective goals is to think of the acronym *SMARTS* and remember the following principles (Smith, 1994):

Specific. Goals should indicate precisely what is to be accomplished or achieved.

Measurable. Goals should be quantifiable.

Action oriented. Goals should indicate something that needs to be done, specific actions to achieve the stated goal.

Realistic. Goals should be achievable given various constraints.

Timely. Goals should be achievable in a reasonable amount of time.

Self-determined. Goals should be set by, or with input from, the participant.

the individual's background, it can also be useful to develop a list of all the skills that are needed in the activity. Then the individual is asked to rate her ability relative to each of the skills identified.

Set Goals in Diverse Areas

As we have emphasized, people too often consider only performance-related goals. Goals can and should be set in a variety of areas including individual skills, team skills, fitness levels, playing time, enjoyment, and psychological skills. Goals should be set in a variety of areas because students, athletes, and exercisers participate in physical activity for diverse reasons (e.g., skill improvement, fun, achievement). In addition, goals must be closely tied to the needs assessment so that the needs determine the goals. Many factors influence individual and team performance in physical activity settings, so goals should be set not only for skill improvement and performance but in other areas as well. Table 15.2 lists sample goals for a number of diverse areas in physical activity.

Identify Influences on Goal-Setting Systems

Goals can't be set in a vacuum. The athlete's potential, commitment, and opportunities for practice must be assessed before goals can be set. For instance, it does little good to establish after-hours practice goals for an athlete who is not committed or disciplined enough to do them on his own. It would be more effective for this person to have goals that he can achieve during regular practice times or, better yet, to set a goal of

becoming more independent and disciplined enough to practice on his own.

> **KEY POINT** Goals will not be effective unless they are tied to specific and realistic strategies for achieving them.

Plan Goal Achievement Strategies

Strategies that participants can use to achieve their goals must be planned. Goals are not effective unless they are tied to specific and realistic strategies. When goal setting fails, it is often because individuals focus all their time on identifying their goals but fail to derive specific strategies for achieving them.

Second Stage: Education and Acquisition

Once the preparation and planning stage has been completed, the coach, teacher, or exercise leader can begin educating the athlete directly on the most effective ways to set goals. This involves imparting goal-setting information and principles.

Schedule Meetings

A formal meeting or a series of brief, less formal meetings should be scheduled before practices or classes. In these meetings, the coach and athlete can identify examples of effective and ineffective goals. Participants should not be expected to list goals right on the spot. Instead, they can be introduced to goal

TABLE 15.2 Areas in Which Goals Can Be Set

Goal area	Goal
Individual skills	I will decrease my time by 0.4 seconds in the 400-meter dash by increasing my speed in the initial 100 meters through a more explosive start.
Team skills	Our high school wrestling team will increase the percentage of successful takedowns achieved from 54% to 62% by midseason.
Fitness	An executive will lower her resting heart rate from 71 beats per minute to 61 beats per minute by participating in a 50-minute aerobic dance class at least 3 days per week for the next 5 months.
Playing time	A junior in high school will earn a varsity football letter by participating in at least 16 game quarters during the season.
Enjoyment	A veteran professional tennis player will get more pleasure from touring by identifying and visiting one restaurant and historic site in each tour city.
Psychological skills	A diver will attempt to regain his confidence on an inward 2 1/2 dive by visualizing a successful dive before each practice attempt and repeating at least one positive self-statement.

setting and given time to think about their goals and the process. The coach or instructor can schedule a follow-up meeting or subsequent practice to discuss specific goals as well as strategies for meeting these goals. If goals are being set in an athletic environment, both team and individual goals should be included.

Focus on One Goal at a Time

Unless an athlete has had considerable experience in setting goals, it is better to set only one goal at a time. The coach can help each individual select one goal from her list. The athlete then focuses on correctly defining that particular goal and outlining realistic strategies for achieving it. After participants have learned to set and achieve a single goal, they might be ready to try multiple goals.

Third Stage: Implementation and Goal Follow-Up and Evaluation

Once participants have learned to set goals, the next step is to list the goals that have been identified as appropriate. The coach or instructor will need to assist in the goal evaluation and follow-up process.

Identify Appropriate Goal Evaluation Procedures

The stage that likely is most neglected is the evaluation stage because professionals become so busy with other things that they just don't make the time to evaluate the goals that were set. Coaches, teachers, and fitness instructors should avoid designing a goal-setting system that is impossible to keep up with. For example, they should anticipate their busiest time of the year and estimate how much time they will have available for goal evaluation and follow-up. Moreover, they should identify the most effective system for managing goal evaluation and follow-up. Many coaches streamline the evaluation process by having managers keep and post practice and game statistics related to player goals. Similarly, some physical educators schedule periodic skill tests during class, when students receive feedback about their performance progress toward their goals. In these cases, the feedback process costs the instructor or coach little time.

Provide Support and Encouragement

Throughout the season, the coach or exercise leader should ask participants about their goals and publicly encourage their goal progress. Showing enthusiasm about the goal-setting process supports the athletes and exercise participants and helps keep them motivated to fulfill their goals.

Plan for Goal Reevaluation

Goal setting is not a perfect science, and sometimes the goals that have been set don't work out. For example, a tennis player sets a goal to hit 40% of his first serves in, but he discovers that with practice he has little trouble hitting 50% of his first serves in. In such a case, his goal must be modified in order to challenge him. Other athletes set initial goals that are too difficult and that need to be made easier. Injuries and illness may also require an athlete to modify goals. It is necessary to reevaluate goals intermittently. Modifying and reestablishing goals are a normal part of the process.

> **KEY POINT** Goal setting is not a perfect science. Plan for specific re-evaluation of goals.

Common Problems in Goal Setting

Goal setting is not a difficult psychological technique to understand, but this doesn't mean that problems will not arise in implementing a goal-setting program (Gould, 2005; Murphy, 1996). Some common problems include convincing students, athletes, and exercisers to set goals; failing to set specific goals; setting too many goals too soon; failing to adjust goals when they are not being achieved; failing to set performance and process goals; and not initiating goal-setting evaluation and follow-up procedures. By understanding and anticipating these problems, you can reduce their effects and even circumvent some problems altogether. Anticipating problems and understanding how to avoid them are major components of effective goal setting.

Convincing Students, Athletes, and Exercisers to Set Goals

Drawing on years of experience as a sport psychologist working at the U.S. Olympic Training Center, Shane Murphy identified several common obstacles to formal goal setting in individuals (Murphy, 1996). These include the notion that goal setting takes too much time, people's previous negative (failure) experiences setting goals, the perception that people will become a public failure if they do not reach certain goals, and the feeling that goal setting is too structured and will not work with "spontaneous" people. Murphy pointed out that goal setting actually saves time because with goals, one becomes much better organized. He argued that goal failure typically results from an overemphasis on setting goals outside of one's control (i.e., choosing outcome goals rather than performance goals), and he reassured athletes that writing out and working toward specific goals does not mean losing spontaneity or becoming rigid. Anticipating these reactions and being able to effectively disarm them will help you convince those whom you work with to set goals.

Failing to Set Specific Goals

The most frequent problem that people in sport and exercise settings have is failing to set specific goals. Even when activity participants are told how important it is to state goals in specific, behavioral terms, they often identify goals in a general, vague way. For example, the stated goal might be "improving my tennis serve" instead of "improving the accuracy of good serves from 60% to 70% by developing a more consistent ball toss."

The physical fitness professional should monitor initial goals and give feedback about their **goal specificity**. Additionally, we need to teach people to form numerical goals that include numbers for assessing behaviors (e.g., an improved percentage). Finally, when establishing sport skill goals, people should include specific characteristics of improved technique in their goal statements (e.g., "improve downhill running by shortening stride length" or "improve the percentage of strikes thrown by bending my back more").

Setting Too Many Goals Too Soon

Novices at setting goals tend to take on too many goals at once. Their desire to improve leads them to become overzealous and unrealistic. On the practical side, monitoring, tracking, and providing individualized feedback across time become virtually impossible for the fitness leader when participants have too many goals. Plus, when too many goals are set at once, they are all almost invariably abandoned. Inexperienced goal setters should set only one or two goals at a time. Making the goals short term (e.g., to be achieved within 2 weeks rather than 5 months) keeps them in the foreground and maximizes the performer's enthusiasm. Tracking the goals and providing feedback are also easier over a shorter time period. Once the individual has gained experience, however, she can set multiple or simultaneous goals.

> **KEY POINT** Initially set only one or two goals. Participants can set more goals once they have gained experience in the process.

Failing to Adjust Goals

Adjusting goals, especially lowering them once they have been set, can be difficult. For example, swimmers who had no difficulty adjusting goals upward found that adjusting goals downward after an injury or illness was extremely difficult from a psychological perspective (Burton, 1989b). There are two ways to alleviate this problem. First, at the start of the goal-setting program, discuss the need to adjust goals upward and downward. That way, participants can view adjustments as a normal part of the process rather than as an indication of a problem on their part. Second, if goals must be lowered because of illness or injury, make the adjustment part of a new staircase of goals (figure 15.3) that ultimately surpasses the original goal. In that way, the person can view the lowered goal as a temporary setback to ultimately overcome.

Failing to Recognize Individual Differences

Not all performers are excited about setting goals, and some may even have negative attitudes about doing so. Forcing individuals to set goals is ineffective because individual commitment is needed. Instructors or leaders should introduce goal setting and work with those who show an interest in hope that their success will motivate the less committed individuals. An investigation by Lambert and colleagues (1999) demonstrated the importance of recognizing individual differences. Specifically, results showed that the most effective type of goal setting for gymnasts depended on their locus of control. For gymnasts who had an internal locus of control, setting their own goals was most effective, whereas for gymnasts with an external locus of control, coach-set goals were most effective. Goal perspective (see chapter 3) is another important individual-difference factor to take into consideration when setting goals because being more task oriented or ego oriented will affect the type of goals (i.e., process, performance, outcome) to be used.

Not Providing Follow-Up and Evaluation

A problem that teachers, coaches, and exercise leaders have too frequently is setting goals at the

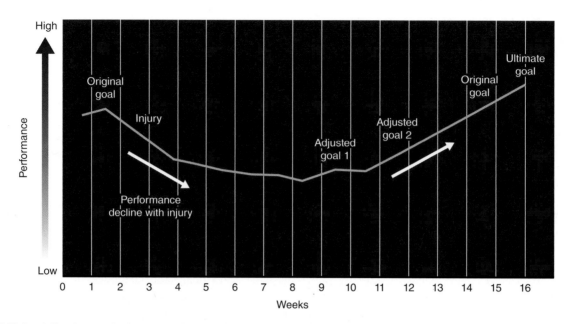

FIGURE 15.3 Adjusting goals downward: Maintaining a positive perspective through a stepwise approach.

start of a season and then not using them effectively throughout the season or year. A lack of follow-up and evaluation is one of the major factors in the failure of goal-setting programs. It is imperative to develop a follow-up and evaluation plan for goals and to examine it critically for ease and efficiency. It must be simple to implement. Goal setting without follow-up and evaluation is simply a waste of time and effort!

VIEW Activity 15.4 helps you become better prepared to overcome problems you may encounter in setting goals for behavioral change.

LEARNING AIDS

SUMMARY

1. **Define what goals are and identify major types of goals.**
   Goals are objectives or aims of actions. They may be subjective or objective and may be directed toward performance (self-comparisons for improvement), process (actions that lead to improved performance), or outcome (beating or surpassing others). All these types of goals can be useful. The key is knowing when to focus on each goal type and not devoting all one's attention to outcome goals.

2. **Describe the latest research on and theory of goal setting.**
   The research on goal setting demonstrates that goals are a powerful means for effecting behavior changes, either directly or indirectly. Goals influence behavior directly by bringing a performer's attention to important elements of the skill or task. Goals also can increase motivation and persistence and can facilitate the development of new learning strategies. Goals influence behavior indirectly by causing changes in important psychological factors such as self-confidence, anxiety, and satisfaction.

3. **Describe goal-setting principles.**
   Goal-setting principles include developing helpful kinds of goals: specific, moderately difficult but realistic, both short and long term, both practice and competition, and both performance and process. Some other principles of effective goal setting are recording the goals, developing concomitant goal achievement strategies, considering a participant's personality and motivation, fostering commitment to goals, providing support to the goal setter, and providing evaluation and feedback of performance toward goals.

4. **Explain group goals and how to use them.**
   Group goals focus on attaining specific standards of group proficiency, usually within a specified time. Setting group goals is important because having goals has been linked to increases in a group's motivation and cohesion. When establishing group goals you should (a) establish long-term goals first; (b) establish clear, short-term goals as paths to long-term goals; (c) involve all members of the group in establishing its goals as a team; (d) monitor progress toward team goals; (e) reward progress toward team goals; and (f) foster collective team confidence or efficacy.

5. **Explain how to design a goal-setting system.**
   A significant number of goal-setting principles form the foundation of a three-stage system (preparation and planning, education and acquisition, and implementation and follow-up). The preparation and planning stage entails assessing individual abilities and needs, setting goals in diverse areas, identifying influences on goal-setting systems, and planning goal achievement strategies. The education and acquisition stage involves scheduling meetings and limiting the number of goals one initially focuses on. Finally, the implementation and follow-up stage involves the use of appropriate goal evaluation procedures, goal support and encouragement, and goal re-evaluation.

6. **Identify common problems in goal setting and how to overcome them.**
   Common goal-setting problems that a good program must address include failing to convince students, athletes, and exercisers to set goals; failing to set specific goals; setting too many goals too soon; failing to adjust goals flexibly as the situation requires; failing to set performance and process goals; and not initiating goal-setting follow-up and evaluation.

7. **Summarize the findings regarding coaches' goal-setting practices.**
   Interviews with coaches about their goal-setting practices showed that (a) goals were set predominantly to focus attention and provide direction; (b) the most important aspect of goal commitment was personal enjoyment; (c) coaches were variable in writing down their goals and their understanding of goal-setting principles; (d) goal barriers were seen as physical, psychological, and external; (e) coaches used performance, process, and outcome goals although they favored process and performance goals; and (f) coaches used both short- and long-term goals but focused more on short-term goals.

KEY TERMS

goals	goal difficulty	hope
objective goals	indirect thought-process view	goal commitment
subjective goals	direct mechanistic view	goal support
outcome goals	practice goals	group goals
performance goals	goal achievement strategies	goal specificity
process goals		

REVIEW QUESTIONS

1. What is the difference between a subjective and an objective goal? Between a performance, a process, and an outcome goal?

2. Describe the four major processes that affect goal setting (why it works) as explained by the direct mechanistic view of goal setting.

3. Identify a goal-setting principle or guideline that relates to each of the following areas: goal specificity, goal difficulty, short- and long-term goals, performance and process compared with outcome goals, written goals, strategies for achieving goals, participant personality, individual commitment, goal support, and goal evaluation.

4. What are the different advantages of outcome, performance, and process goals?

5. What is a goal-setting staircase and why is it important?

6. What are the three stages to consider in designing a goal-setting system? What should happen during each stage?

7. Identify six common problems with goal setting.

8. Why is it important to adjust goals periodically?

CRITICAL THINKING QUESTIONS

1. Using what you have learned in this chapter, design a goal-setting program for a fellow student who wants to begin an exercise program to lose 25 pounds.

2. The chapter discusses the importance of prioritizing general subjective goals. Identify, list, and prioritize your most important subjective goals. How can you use these goals to guide your day-to-day actions?

Concentration

After reading this chapter, you should be able to

1. define concentration and explain how it is related to performance,

2. explain the main theories of concentration effects,

3. identify different types of attentional focus,

4. describe some attentional problems,

5. explain how self-talk works,

6. explain how to assess attentional ability, and

7. discuss how to improve attentional focus.

Abernethy, Maxwell, Masters,

Van der Kamp, and Jackson (2007) stated that "it is difficult to conceive of any aspect of psychology that may be more central to the enhancement of skill learning and expert performance than attention" (p. 245). We hear the word *focus* more and more when athletes and coaches discuss getting ready to play and when they evaluate actual performance. Staying focused for an entire game or competition is often the key to victory (and losing that focus is the ticket to failure). Even in competitions lasting hours or days (such as golf), a brief loss of concentration can mar total performance and affect outcome. It is critical to concentrate during a competition, even through adverse crowd noise, weather conditions, and irrelevant thoughts. Top-level athletes are known to focus their attention and maintain that focus throughout a competition. This intense focus throughout an event is evident in the recollections of Olympic swimming gold medalist Michelle Smith: "I was never more focused in a race. No looking about, tunnel vision all the way . . . my concentration was so intense that I

almost forgot to look up to see my time after touching the finishing pads" (cited in Roche, 1995, p. 1). A similar single-minded focus is seen in the following quote by gold medalist and world record holder in the 400 meters, Michael Johnson:

> **" I have learned to cut all unnecessary thoughts on the track. I simply concentrate. I concentrate on the tangible—on the track, on the race, on the blocks, on the things I have to do. The crowd fades away and other athletes disappear and now it's just me and this one lane. "**

On the other hand, we have all heard stories of athletes who have performed poorly because they lost concentration, such as the 100-meter sprinter who "missed" the gun; the basketball player distracted by the fans when shooting free throws; the tennis player whose thoughts fixated on a bad line call; and the baseball player mired in a slump, simply thinking that he would probably strike out again. In essence, the temporary loss of focus can spell defeat, as George

Foreman commented after defeating Michael Moorer in the World Boxing Association championship: "They urged me to pile up some points, but I knew I could only win the fight by a knock-out. I waited and waited, until Moorer briefly lost his concentration and gave me an opening" (cited in Jones, 1994, p. 1). Or, as Shaquille O'Neal noted when he missed three dunks and went 0 for 5 from the foul line: "I wasn't even concentrating, I was so upset. I simply lost my cool."

Many athletes mistakenly believe that concentrating is important only during actual competition. All-time tennis great Rod Laver—the only male player to win all four Grand Slams in the same year, twice—in effect says that the adage "practice makes perfect" is apt when it comes to developing concentration skills:

" If your mind is going to wander during practice, it's going to do the same thing in a match. When we were all growing up in Australia, we had to work as hard mentally as we did physically in practice. If you weren't alert, you could get a ball hit off the side of your head. What I used to do was force myself to concentrate more as soon as I'd find myself getting tired, because that's usually when your concentration starts to fail you. If I'd find myself getting tired in practice, I'd force myself to work much harder for an extra ten or fifteen minutes, and I always felt as though I got more out of those extra minutes than I did out of the entire practice. (Tarshis, 1977, p. 31) "

In this chapter we explain how to effectively cope with the pressures of competition and maintain concentration despite momentary setbacks, errors, and mistakes. We start by describing what concentration is and how it is related to performance. The terms *concentration* and *attention* are used interchangeably throughout the chapter because researchers tend to use the term *attention* and practitioners seem to prefer the term *concentration*.

Defining Concentration

Attention and its role in human performance have been subjects of debate and examination for more than a century, beginning with the following classic description by William James (1890):

" Everyone knows what attention is. It is taking possession by the mind, in clear and vivid form, of one out of what seems several simultaneously possible objects or trains of thought. Focalization, concentration of consciousness are the essence. It implies withdrawal from some things in order to deal effectively with others. (pp. 403–404) "

James' definition focuses on one particular aspect of concentration (selective attention), although a more contemporary definition views attention more broadly as the concentration of mental effort on sensory or mental events (Moran, 2013). Moran (2004) stated that "concentration refers to a person's ability to exert deliberate mental effort on what is most important in any given situation" (p. 103). You also hear popular metaphors for concentration, such as "spotlight" or "zoom lens." But a useful definition of **concentration** in sport and exercise settings typically contains four parts: (a) focusing on the relevant cues in the environment (**selective attention**), (b) maintaining that **attentional focus** over time, (c) having awareness of the situation and performance errors, and (d) shifting attentional focus when necessary.

Focusing on Relevant Environmental Cues

Part of concentration refers to focusing on the relevant environmental cues, or selective attention. Irrelevant cues are either eliminated or disregarded. For example, a football quarterback with less than 2 minutes to play needs to pay attention to the clock, distance for a first down, and field position. But after the play is called, his focus needs to be on the defense, his receivers, and executing the play to the best of his ability. The crowd, noise, and other distracters should simply fade into the background. Or as Donovan Bailey, Olympic champion in the 100-meter dash, noted:

" I was not thinking about the world record. When I go into a race thinking about times, I always screw up so I was thinking about my start and trying to relax. Just focus on doing the job at hand. "

KEY POINT Concentration is the ability to maintain focus on relevant environmental cues. When the environment changes rapidly, attentional focus must also change rapidly. Thinking of the past or the future raises irrelevant cues that often lead to performance errors.

Similarly, learning and practice can help build selective attention—a performer does not have to attend to all aspects of the skill because some of these become automated via extended practice. For example, when learning to dribble a basketball or kick a soccer ball, a player typically needs to place all of her attention on the task, which means watching the ball constantly. However, when the player becomes more proficient, she can take her eyes off the ball (because this aspect of the skill has become automated and does not require consistent attentional focus); now she can be concerned with the other players on the court or field, who become relevant cues for the execution of a successful play.

A study by Bell and Hardy (2009) provides information regarding exactly what to focus on. Specifically, they found that an external focus (outside the body) was better than an internal focus (on the body). Moreover, a distal external focus produced better performance than a proximal external focus. For example, a golfer should focus more on the flight of the ball (distal external) than on the club face (proximal external) throughout the swing. Similarly, in a study by McKay and Wulf (2012) using dart throwing, focusing on the target (distal external) produced significantly better performance than did focusing on the flight of the dart (proximal external). Evidently, the more you focus on yourself or things near you (e.g., the club in golf), the poorer the performance. Finally, Schucker, Hagemann, Strauss, and Volker (2009) found that an external focus can also help the economy of movement (running in this case) by increasing the efficiency of oxygen consumption.

An extensive review by Wulf (2013) of the literature highlighted the importance of focusing externally instead of internally. He found that an external focus of attention was more beneficial to performance in a variety of tasks, such as those that focus on balance, accuracy, speed and endurance, and maximum force production. An external focus results in increases in performance outcomes, movement efficiency, and movement kinematics. These performance and biomechanical results also apply to a variety of populations, both learning and performance situations, and individuals with differing levels of skill expertise. Thus, because the effectiveness of an external focus generalizes across many situations and skill levels, teacher and coach should definitely teach athletes skills for focusing externally.

Maintaining Attentional Focus

Maintaining attentional focus for the duration of the competition is also part of concentration. This can be difficult because thought-sampling studies have revealed that the median length of time during which thought content remains on target is approximately 5 seconds. So, on average, people engage in about 4,000 distinct thoughts in a 16-hour day. Thus, reigning in the thought process is not an easy task. Many athletes have instances of greatness, yet few can sustain a high level of play for an entire competition. Chris Evert was never the most physically talented player on the women's tour, but nobody could match her ability to stay focused throughout a match. She was virtually unaffected by irrelevant cues such as bad line calls, missing easy shots, crowd noise, and her opponent's antics. Concentration helped make her a champion. Similarly, anyone who saw the 2012 Australian Open men's tennis final between Rafael Nadal and Novak Djokovic witnessed one of the reasons why these are two of the best tennis players in the world: their ability to maintain attentional focus for a match lasting nearly 6 hours.

Maintaining focus over long time periods is no easy task. Tournament golf, for example, is usually played over 72 holes. Say that after playing great for 70 holes, you have 2 holes left in the tournament and lead by a stroke. On the 71st, just as you prepare to hit your drive off the tee, an image of the championship trophy flashes in your mind. This momentary distraction causes you to lose your focus on the ball and hook your drive badly into the trees. It takes you three more strokes to get on the green, and you wind up with a double bogey. You lose your lead and wind up in second place. Thus, one lapse in concentration over the course of 72 holes costs you the championship. Tiger Woods has repeatedly noted that one of his great attributes is his ability to maintain his concentration throughout the 3 to 4 days of a golf tournament. Bjorn Borg, tennis great and former number one player in the world, has said that he was more mentally tired than physically tired after a match due to his total concentration on each and every point. The problem with having many breaks in the action, like in golf, is the risk of having trouble regaining concentration after the breaks. Ian Botham, former cricketer, switched his concentration on and off as necessary to keep his appropriate attentional focus:

" I switch off the moment the ball is dead—then I relax completely and have a chat and joke . . . . But as soon as the bowler reaches his mark, I switch back on to the game. I think anybody who can concentrate totally all the time is inhuman. I certainly can't. "

Maintaining Situation Awareness

One of the least understood but most interesting and important aspects of attentional focus in sport is an athlete's ability to understand what is going on around him. Known as **situation awareness**, this ability allows players to size up game situations, opponents, and competitions to make appropriate decisions based on the situation, often under acute pressure and time demands. For example, Boston Celtics announcer Johnny Most gave one of the most famous commentary lines in basketball when, in the seventh game of the 1965 NBA play-offs between the Boston Celtics and Philadelphia 76ers and with 5 seconds left, he screamed repeatedly, "and Havlicek stole the ball!" The Celtics' John Havlicek later described how his situation awareness helped him make this critical play. The 76ers were down by a point and were taking the ball in from out-of-bounds. Havlicek was guarding his man, with his back to the passer, when the referee handed the ball to the player in-bounding the ball. A team has 5 seconds to put the ball into play when throwing it in from out of bounds, and Havlicek started counting to himself *1,001, 1,002, 1,003*. When nothing had happened, he knew that the passer was in trouble. He turned halfway to see the passer out of the corner of his eye, still focusing on his own man. A second later he saw a poor pass being made and reacted quickly enough to deflect the ball to one of his own players, who ran out the clock. The Celtics won the game—and went on to win the NBA championship. Had Havlicek not counted, he would not have had a clear sense of the most important focus at that instant (Hemery, 1986).

Along these lines, we all know of athletes who seem to be able to do just the right thing at the right time.

Association or Dissociation: What Do We Know?

More than 35 years ago, studies of the cognitive strategies of marathon runners showed that the most successful marathoners tended to use an **associative attentional strategy** (monitoring bodily functions and feelings, such as heart rate, muscle tension, and breathing rate), whereas nonelite runners tended to use a **dissociative attentional strategy** (distraction and tuning out) during the race (Morgan & Pollock, 1977). Since then, many studies have been published in this area, including some that are more recent (e.g., Hutchinson & Tenenbaum, 2007; Stanley, Pargman, & Tenenbaum, 2007; Tenenbaum & Connolly, 2008). Recent research as well as a review of the past 20 years of research (Masters & Ogles, 1998) has found the following consistencies and yielded several recommendations regarding the use of associative and dissociative strategies in sport and exercise:

- Association and dissociation should be seen more along a continuum than as a dichotomy, especially when used in longer events (e.g., marathon running).

- Use of associative strategies is generally correlated with faster running performance compared with use of dissociative strategies.

- Runners in competition prefer association (focusing on monitoring bodily processes and forms as well as information management strategies related to race tactics), whereas runners in practice prefer dissociation, although both strategies are used in both situations. In essence, runners flip between these two strategies.

- Dissociation is inversely related to physiological awareness and feelings of perceived exertion, especially in laboratory studies, although not as consistently as in the field.

- Dissociation does not increase the probability of injury, but it can decrease the fatigue and monotony of training or recreational runs.

- Association appears to allow runners to continue performing despite painful sensory input because they can prepare for and be aware of such physical discomfort.

- Dissociation should be used as a training technique for individuals who want to increase adherence to exercise regimens because it makes the exercise bout more pleasant while not increasing the probability of injury or sacrificing safety.

- As workload increases, a shift from dissociation to association tends to focus needed mental attention to the task at hand.

Some who come to mind are LeBron James, Rafael Nadal, Misty May-Treanor, and Teresa Edwards. Their awareness of the court and competitive situation always makes it seem as if they are a step ahead of everyone else. In fact, research has indicated that experts and nonexperts differ in their attentional processing (see "Expert–Novice Differences in Attentional Processing").

Shifting Attentional Focus

Often it is necessary to shift attentional focus during an event, and this attentional flexibility is known as the ability to alter the scope and focus of attention as demanded by the situation. Let's take a golf example. As a golfer prepares to step up to the ball before teeing off, she needs to assess the external environment: the direction of the wind; the length of the fairway; and the positioning of water hazards, trees, and sand traps. This requires a broad–external focus. After appraising this information, she might recall experience with similar shots, note current playing conditions, and analyze the information she's gathered to select a particular club and determine how to hit the ball. These considerations require a broad–internal focus.

Once she has formulated a plan, she might monitor her tension, image a perfect shot, or take a deep, relaxing breath as part of a preshot routine. She has moved into a narrow–internal focus. Finally, shifting to a narrow–external focus, she addresses the ball. At this time her focus is directly on the ball. This is not the time for other internal cues and thoughts, which would probably interfere with the execution of the shot. Golfers have ample time to shift attentional focus because they themselves set the pace. However, it is important to be able to relax and lower the intensity of concentration at times between shots because concentrating for extended periods of time is very energy consuming.

A qualitative study by Bernier, Codron, Thienot, and Fournier (2011) investigated the change in attentional focus that many athletes and coaches have hypothesized. Using professional golfers, research revealed that golfers were more internally process oriented when training but were more externally result oriented during competition. Focus of attention also

Expert–Novice Differences in Attentional Processing

We all know that being able to size up a situation to know what to do—and possibly what your opponent is about to do—is a key attentional skill. Researchers (e.g., Abernethy, 2001) have studied how expert and novice performers differ in their attentional processes across a variety of sports even though they do not differ in eyesight (visual hardware) or perceptual–motor characteristics. Along these lines, a growing body of evidence suggests that "knowledge-based" factors, such as where an athlete directs her attention, can account for performance differences between expert and novice athletes in a variety of sports (Moran, 1996, 2004). Research has also revealed that the attentional skills of experts can be learned by novices (Williams, Ward, & Smeeton, 2004), although there appear to be some innate differences. Some of the consistent differences that have emerged from research (see Mann, Williams, Ward, & Janelle, 2007, for a review) include the following:

- Expert players attend more to advance information (e.g., arm and racket cues) than do novices and thus can make faster decisions and can better anticipate future actions.
- Expert players attend more to movement patterns of their opponents than do novices.
- Expert players search more systematically for cues than do novices.
- Expert players selectively attend to the structure inherent in their particular sport more than do novices (e.g., they can pick up structured offensive and defensive styles of play).
- Expert players are more successful in predicting the flight pattern of a ball than novices are.

Besides these attentional differences, recent research revealed that experts set more specific goals, selected more technique-oriented strategies to achieve these goals, made more strategy attributions, and displayed higher levels of self-efficacy than nonexperts (Cleary & Zimmerman, 2001). These attentional and psychological differences have important implications for the teaching and learning of motor skills. What implications might these be?

changed rapidly, as shown by the following quote from one of the golfers:

" So here were are on the ninth tee. I start to take in information: the distance, the wind. I place my tee, and just after that I focus on the target I have chosen. Here it was the tree shadow on the left. I take my practice swings and at the same time I focus on letting go, and try to feel the rhythm well. There. And here I walk to the ball. I visualize the trajectory, only the ball at the start. I address the ball and I look at my target one last time . . . . And bang. (Bernier et al., 2011, pp. 334–335) "

Explaining Attentional Focus: Three Processes

It is beyond the scope of this chapter to thoroughly discuss the various theories that have been proposed to help explain the attention–performance relationship. Thus, we provide a very brief description of the theories and refer interested readers to other work (Abernethy, 2001; Boutcher, 2008; Moran, 2003) for more complete reviews.

The major theories attempting to explain the role of attention in performance have used an **information-processing approach**. Early approaches favored either a *single-channel* (fixed capacity) approach, where information is processed through a single channel, or a *variable* (flexible) approach, where individuals can choose where to focus their attention, allocating it to more than one task at a time. However, neither of these approaches proved fruitful, and current thinking now favors a *multiple pools theory* approach, which views attention like multiprocessors, with each processor having its own unique relationship with the performer. In essence, **attentional capacity** is seen not as centralized but rather as distributed throughout the nervous system. A possible application is that extensive practice could lead to the development of automaticity, where less actual processing time is needed because of overlearning of skills.

Within the information-processing approach, three processes have received the most focus in trying to explain the attention–performance relationship.

Attentional Selectivity

Selective attention refers to letting some information into the information-processing system while screening out or ignoring other information. Drawing on the work of Abernethy (2001), Perry (2005) proposed that a useful metaphor for understanding selective attention is a person who uses a "spotlight" to focus only on what is important. According to the spotlight metaphor, selective attention resembles a mental beam that illuminates a circumscribed part of the visual field, and information lying outside the illuminated region is ignored (Moran, 2012). A review by Memmert (2009) found that it is not how long athletes focus but rather what they focus on that helps produce top performance. Three common errors are made when this searchlight is focused inappropriately:

- Failure to focus all the attention on the essential or relevant elements of the task (i.e., searchlight beam is too broad)

Ray Carlin/Icon SMI

This athlete's proficiency at basketball allows him to use automatic control. This means he can focus on aspects of the game other than just dribbling the ball.

- Being distracted from relevant information by irrelevant information (i.e., searchlight is pointing in the wrong direction)
- Inability to divide attention among all the relevant cues that need to be processed concurrently (i.e., searchlight beam is too narrow, or the person is unable to shift it rapidly enough from one spot to the next)

As performers become more proficient in a given skill, they can move from more conscious control to more automatic control. In essence, when one is learning a skill, attention has to be targeted to all aspects of performing the skill itself (e.g., dribbling a basketball). But as one becomes more proficient, attention can be focused on watching other players (keeping one's head up) because dribbling the ball has become more automatic. Most sport skills involve some conscious control, which can be cumbersome, and some automatic processing, which is more typical of skilled performance. The notion of selective attention is highlighted by Scotty Bowman's comments (the U.S. Golf Association scorer) when referring to Tiger Woods at the U.S. Open in 2000 (which Woods won by an amazing 15 strokes):

" His eye contact is right with his caddie and nowhere else when he's preparing to hit a shot. He's oblivious to everyone else. (Garrity, 2000, p. 61) "

Attentional Capacity

Attentional capacity refers to the fact that attention is limited in that one can process only so much information at one time. But athletes seem to be able to pay attention to many things when performing. This is because they can change from controlled processing to automatic processing as they become more proficient. *Controlled processing* is mental processing that involves conscious attention and awareness of what you are doing when you perform a sport skill. For example, when learning to hit a golf swing, athletes need to think about how to grip the club, address the ball, and perform the backswing and downswing. *Automatic processing* is mental processing without conscious attention. For example, as gymnasts become more proficient at performing their routine on the floor, they don't need to attend to all the details of the jumps, dance moves, and sequences, as these should be virtually automatic after much practice. So

as performers become more proficient and attentional capacity becomes more automatic, attention is freed up to focus on different aspects of the playing situation. That is why a skilled soccer player, for example, can focus on his teammates, opposition, playing style, and formations; he doesn't have to pay much attention to dribbling the ball because this is basically on automatic processing. Boston Celtics basketball great Bill Russell referred to this limited channel capacity in a slightly different way:

" Remember, each of us has a finite amount of energy, and things you do well don't require as much. Things you don't do well take more concentration. And if you're fatigued by that, then the things you do best are going to be affected. (Deford, 1999, p. 110) "

Attentional Alertness

Attentional alertness is related to the notion that increases in emotional arousal narrow the attentional field because of a systematic reduction in the range of cues that a performer considers in executing a skill. Numerous studies have indicated that in stressful situations, performance on a central visual task decreases the ability to respond to peripheral stimuli (Land & Tenenbaum, 2012). Thus, it appears that arousal can bring about sensitivity loss to cues that are in the peripheral visual field. A point guard in basketball, for instance, can miss some important cues in the periphery (players on her team) if she is overaroused and as a result starts to narrow her attentional focus and field.

Connecting Concentration to Optimal Performance

As noted at the outset of the chapter, athletes and coaches certainly recognize the importance of proper attentional focus in achieving high levels of performance. Research from several sources substantiates their experience. Jackson and Csikszentmihalyi (1999) investigated the components of exceptional performance and found eight physical and mental capacities that elite athletes associate with peak performance. Three of these eight are associated with high levels of concentration. Specifically, athletes describe themselves as (a) being absorbed in the present and having no thoughts about the past or future, (b) being mentally relaxed and having a high degree of concentration and control, and (c) being in a state of extraordinary awareness of both their own bodies and the external environment. In addition, in Orlick and Partington's (1988) landmark study of Canadian Olympic athletes, concentration was a central component of performance that was repeatedly reinforced whether referring to quality training, mental preparation, distraction control, competition focus plans, or competition evaluation. For example, one athlete said this about quality training:

" When I'm training I'm focused . . . . By focusing all the time on what you're doing when you're training, focusing in a race becomes a by-product. (p. 111) "

Researchers comparing successful and less successful athletes have consistently found that attentional control is an important discriminating factor. In general, the studies reveal that successful athletes are less likely to become distracted by irrelevant stimuli; they maintain a more task-oriented attentional focus rather than worrying or focusing on the outcome. Some researchers have argued that peak performers have developed exceptional concentration abilities appropriate to their sport. These observations led Gould and colleagues (1992c) to conclude that opti-

mal performance states have a characteristic that is variously referred to as concentration, the ability to focus, a special state of involvement, or awareness of and absorption in the task at hand. This complete focus on the task is seen in Pete Sampras' comment during his 1999 Wimbledon championship run when serving on match point (where he hit a second serve ace): "There was absolutely nothing going on in my mind at that time."

KEY POINT Athletes need to focus on only the relevant cues in the athletic environment and to eliminate distractions.

Eye movement patterns also confirm that expert players have a different focus of attention than novice performers. Researchers have found this phenomenon in a variety of individual and team sports such as basketball, volleyball, tennis, soccer, baseball, and karate (Moran, 1996; Wilson, 2012). Think about the no-look passes that Magic Johnson was famous for making. Most good point guards in basketball, such as Dawn Staley and Chris Paul, now throw these kinds of passes. In reality, these point guards "see the floor" and use advance cues to anticipate where players will go (this skill gets better the more you play with teammates and become familiar with their movement patterns).

To Watch or Not Watch the Ball: That is the Question

Anyone who has played a sport involving a ball has probably often heard the admonishment, "Keep your eye on the ball." Tennis players learn, "Watch the ball right onto the racket," and baseball players, "Never take your eyes off the ball if you want to catch it." However, researchers indicate that these long-held beliefs are not necessarily correct. Researchers have found that the eyes can be removed from the flight of the ball at some stage without causing a performance decrement (Savelsbergh, Whiting, & Pijpers, 1992). In addition, contrary to popular belief, top professional tennis players do not watch the ball approaching them as they prepare to return serve because it is virtually impossible for someone to track a ball traveling at speeds of 130 to 140 miles per hour (Abernethy, 2001). The same is true for baseball hitters trying to hit fastballs thrown at more than 90 miles per hour. Instead, these expert players use advance cues—such as the server's racket and toss or the pitcher's motion—to make informed judgments on where the ball will be going and what type of serve or pitch is coming toward them. This is not to say that watching the ball is unimportant. Rather, optimal performance is inevitably enhanced by an athlete's ability to predict the flight of a ball from cues.

A related study (Castaneda & Gray, 2007) showed that batting performance of skilled baseball players was best when their attention was directed away from skill execution itself (internal) and focused on the effect of their body movements (external), which in this case was on the ball leaving the bat. In essence, the authors argue that the optimal focus for highly skilled batters is one that does not disrupt knowledge of skill execution (external focus) and permits attention to the perceptual effect of the action. Thus, after picking up the cues from the pitcher's motion, players should stay externally focused instead of refocusing on body mechanics and skill execution.

Identifying Types of Attentional Focus

Most people think concentration is an all-or-none phenomenon—you either concentrate or you don't. However, researchers have discovered that various types of attentional focus are appropriate for specific sports and activities. The most intuitively appealing work on the role of attentional style in sport (although we should note that this research has been questioned by some other researchers) has developed from the theoretical framework and practical work of Nideffer and colleagues (Nideffer, 1976a,b, 1981; Nideffer & Segal, 2001), who view attentional focus along two dimensions: width (broad or narrow) and direction (external or internal).

• A **broad attentional focus** allows a person to perceive several occurrences simultaneously. This is particularly important in sports in which athletes have to be aware of and sensitive to a rapidly chang-ing environment (i.e., they must respond to multiple cues). Two examples are a basketball point guard leading a fast break and a soccer player dribbling the ball upfield.

• A **narrow attentional focus** occurs when you respond to only one or two cues, as when a baseball batter prepares to swing at a pitch or a golfer lines up a putt.

• An **external attentional focus** directs attention outward to an object, such as a ball in baseball or a puck in hockey, or to an opponent's movements, such as in a doubles match in tennis.

• An **internal attentional focus** is directed inward to thoughts and feelings, as when a coach analyzes plays without having to physically perform, a high jumper prepares to start her run-up, or a bowler readies his approach.

Through combinations of width and direction of attentional focus, four categories emerge, appropriate to various situations and sports (figure 16.1).

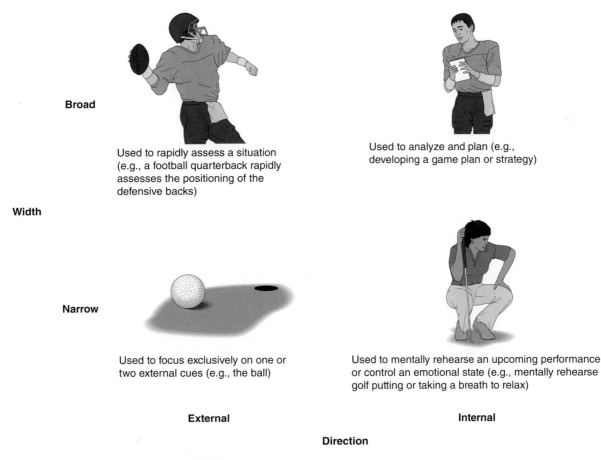

Broad

Used to rapidly assess a situation (e.g., a football quarterback rapidly assesses the positioning of the defensive backs)

Used to analyze and plan (e.g., developing a game plan or strategy)

Width

Narrow

Used to focus exclusively on one or two external cues (e.g., the ball)

Used to mentally rehearse an upcoming performance or control an emotional state (e.g., mentally rehearse golf putting or taking a breath to relax)

External

Internal

Direction

FIGURE 16.1 Four types of attentional focus.

Recognizing Attentional Problems

Many athletes recognize that they have problems concentrating for the duration of a competition. Usually, their concentration problems are caused by inappropriate attentional focus. As seen through interviews with elite athletes (Jackson, 1995; Jones, 2012), worries and irrelevant thoughts can cause individuals to move their concentration "beam" from what they are doing to what they hope will not happen. They are not focusing on the proper cues; rather, they become distracted by thoughts, other events, and emotions. They haven't as much lost concentration as they have focused their concentration on inappropriate cues. We now discuss some of the typical problems that athletes have in controlling and maintaining attentional focus and divide these problems into distractions that are internal and those that are external.

Internal Distracters

Some distractions come from within ourselves—our thoughts, worries, and concerns. Jackson (1995) showed through interviews with elite athletes that worries and irrelevant thoughts can cause performers to lose concentration and develop an inappropriate focus of attention. Let us look at some of these **internal distracters** that present attentional problems.

Attending to Past Events

Some people cannot forget about what has just happened—especially a bad mistake. Focusing on past events has been the downfall of many talented athletes because looking backward prevents them from focusing on the present. For example, archers who are preoccupied with past mistakes tend to produce poorer performances than those whose minds are focused on the present (Landers, Boutcher, & Wang, 1986). Interestingly, one of the mental challenges of individual sports is that they provide ample opportunity for rueful reflections about past mistakes and errors. But note how Lori Fung, the 1994 gold medalist in rhythmic gymnastics, positively deals with mistakes:

> " If you have a bad routine just go out and do the next one, and pretend the next one is the first routine of the day. You can't do anything about it. You can't do anything about the score you are getting; it's over and done with. Sometimes it's hard to make yourself forget it, but the more you try, the better you're going to get at it in the future. (Orlick, 2000, p. 139) "

Can You Identify the Proper Attentional Focus?

See if you can identify the proper attentional focus of a football quarterback under time duress. Fill in the term for the proper focus in the blank spaces. The answers, which correspond to the numbers in the blanks, are given afterward.

As the quarterback calls the play, he needs a (1) _____ focus to analyze the game situation, including the score, what yard line the ball is on, the down, and time left in the game. He also considers the scouting reports and the game plan that the coach wants him to execute in calling the play. As the quarterback comes up to the line of scrimmage, his focus of attention should be (2) _____ while he looks over the entire defense and tries to determine whether the originally called play will be effective. If he believes that another play might work better, he may change the play by calling an "audible" at the line of scrimmage. Next the quarterback's attention shifts to a (3) _____ focus to receive the ball from the center. Mistakes sometimes occur in the center–quarterback exchange because the quarterback is still thinking about the defense or what he has to do next (instead of making sure he receives the snap without fumbling). If a pass play is called, the quarterback drops back into the pocket to look downfield for his receivers. This requires a (4) _____ perspective so the quarterback can evaluate the defense and find the open receiver while still avoiding onrushing linemen. Finally, after he spots a specific receiver, his focus becomes (5) _____ as he concentrates on throwing a good pass.

Within a few seconds, the quarterback shifts attentional focus several times to effectively understand the defense and pick out the correct receiver. Examples of different types of attentional focus are shown in figure 16.1.

Answers

1. broad–internal; 2. broad–external; 3. narrow–external; 4. broad–external; 5. narrow–external

Attending to Future Events

Concentration problems can also involve attending to future events. In essence, individuals engage in a form of "fortune telling," worrying or thinking about the outcome of the event rather than what they need to do now to be successful. Such thinking often takes the form of "what if" questions, such as "What if I lose the game?", "What if I make another error?", or "What if I let my teammates down?"

This kind of future-oriented thinking and worry negatively affects concentration, making mistakes and poor performance more likely. For example, Pete Sampras was leading 7-6, 6-4, and serving at 5-2 in the 1994 Australian Open finals. He double-faulted and lost two more games before holding out by 6-4 in the third set. Interviewed afterward, Sampras explained that his lapse in concentration was caused by speculating about the future: "I was thinking about winning the Australian Open and what a great achievement [it would be] looking ahead and just kind of taking it for granted, instead of taking it point by point."

Sometimes future-oriented thinking has nothing at all to do with the situation. Your mind wanders without much excuse. For example, athletes report thinking during the heat of competition about such things as what they need to do at school the next day, what they have planned for that evening, or their girlfriend or boyfriend. These irrelevant thoughts are often involuntary—suddenly the players just find themselves thinking about things that have nothing to do with the present exercise or competition.

Choking Under Pressure

Emotional factors such as the pressure of competition often play a critical role in creating internal sources of distraction, and we often hear the word **choking** to describe an athlete's poor performance under pressure. Tennis great John McEnroe underscores the point that choking is part of competition:

" When it comes to choking, the bottom line is that everyone does it. The question isn't whether you choke or not, but how—when you choke—you are going to handle it. Choking is a big part of every sport, and a part of being a champion is being able to cope with it better than everyone else. (cited in Goffi, 1984, pp. 61–62) "

Although most players and coaches have their own ideas about what choking is, providing an objective definition is not easy. For example, read the three scenarios that follow and determine whether the athlete choked.

- A basketball game is tightly fought, the lead shifting after each basket. Finally with 2 seconds left and her team down by two points, steady guard Julie Lancaster gets fouled in the act of shooting and is awarded two foul shots. Julie is a 90% free-throw shooter. She steps up to the line and makes her first shot but misses her second. Her team loses. Did Julie choke?

- Jane is involved in a close tennis match. After splitting the first two sets with her opponent, she is now serving for the match at 5-4; the score is 30-30. On the next two points, Jane double-faults to lose the game and even the set at 5-5. However, Jane then comes back to break serve and hold her own serve to close out the set and match. Did Jane choke?

- Bill is a baseball player with a batting average of .355. His team is in a one-game play-off to decide who will win the league championship and advance to the district finals. Bill goes 0 for 4 in the game, striking out twice with runners in scoring position. In addition, in the bottom of the ninth he comes up with the bases loaded and one out, and all he needs to do is hit the ball out of the infield to tie the game. Instead he grounds into a game-ending—and game-losing—double play. Did Bill choke?

When people think of choking, they tend to focus on the bad performance at a critical time of the game or competition, such as a missed shot or dropped pass. However, choking is much more than the actual behavior—it is a process that leads to impaired performance. The fact that you missed a free throw to lose a game does not necessarily mean you choked. The more important questions to answer are why and how you missed the free throw.

Let's take a closer look at the process that is characteristic of what we have come to call choking. Behaviorally, we infer that athletes are choking when their performance progressively deteriorates and they cannot regain control over performance. An example is the gymnast who allows an early mistake of falling off the balance beam to upset her and cause additional errors once she's back on the beam. Choking usually occurs in a situation of emotional importance to the athlete. For example, Jana Novotna was serving at 4-1 in the third set of the 1993 Wimbledon finals against Steffi Graf and was one point away from a seemingly insurmountable 5-1 lead. But she proceeded to miss an easy volley, later served three consecutive double faults, and hit some wild shots, allowing Graf to come back to win 6-4. Many consider Wimbledon the most prestigious tournament to win, and thus the pressure for Novotna was extremely high.

The choking process is shown in figure 16.2. Sensing pressure causes your muscles to tighten. Your heart rate and breathing increase, your mouth gets dry, and your palms get damp. But the key breakdown occurs at the attentional level: Instead of focusing externally on the relevant cues in your environment (e.g., the ball, the opponent's movements), you focus on your own worries and fears of losing and failing, as your attention becomes narrow and internal. At the same time, the increased pressure reduces your flexibility to shift your attentional focus—you have problems changing your focus as the situation dictates. Impaired timing and coordination, fatigue, muscle tension, and poor decision making soon follow.

A study by Wilson, Vine, and Wood (2009) found that increased anxiety affected basketball free-throw shooters by reducing the duration of the "quiet eye" (QE) period (the time of the final fixation on the target before the initiation of the movement). The QE period is a time where task-relevant cues are processed and motor plans are developed. Thus, a longer duration minimizes distractions and allows focusing on rele-vant cues. In essence, the process of choking might, in part, result in shorter periods of focus on the task itself, leading to performance decrements.

Following up on their study, Vine and Wilson (2010) provided athletes with QE training to help them better cope with learning and performing under pressure. Because the task was golf putting, the QE training focused on preparation, aiming, putter–ball alignment, swing, and follow-through and included specific instructions on where and for how long athletes should keep their gaze. Results revealed that the QE-trained group maintained more effective attentional focus and performed significantly better under pressure compared with the control group.

A qualitative study by Hill and colleagues (2010a) interviewed athletes who self-identified as chokers and focused on the antecedents, mechanisms, and consequences of choking.

Antecedents of Choking

- Event importance (focusing on outcome; e.g., winning the tournament)
- High expectations (putting expectations on themselves)
- Evaluation apprehension (meeting the expectations of others)
- Unfamiliarity (feeling like they had not been through the situation before)
- Overload (the accumulation of demands placed on them)

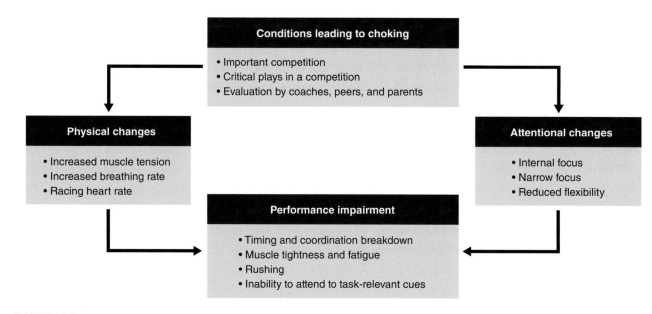

FIGURE 16.2 The choking process.

Mechanisms of Choking

- Distraction (fear of negative evaluation, fear of failure, negative thoughts)
- Anxiety (high levels of cognitive and somatic anxiety)
- Perceived control (inability to control themselves during pressure situations)
- Inadequate coping (inability to cope with the demands of the situation)
- Self-focus (monitoring their technique)

Consequences of Choking

- Significant decrease in performance (feeling like nothing is going right)
- Highly self-critical (beating themselves up for not performing up to standards)
- Lowered self-confidence (expecting to fail under pressure)

Another look at choking analyzed situations in which athletes were more likely to choke. Jordet and Hartman (2008) found that soccer players were more likely to choke (i.e., miss the shot) in a shootout (i.e., score tied) when a miss meant they would lose the game as opposed to a miss where the game would remain tied. In essence, when faced with needing a goal to keep from losing, players were more likely to miss than when faced with needing a goal to win the game. It appeared that players took more time before shots that might result in a loss, and this loss of automaticity was hypothesized to produce these performance differences. In addition, Hill, Hanton, Fleming, and Matthews (2009) found that individual differences moderated the choking process and its consequences. Specifically, low self-confidence accompanied by dysfunctional thinking (e.g., I can't believe I hit such a stupid shot), low mental toughness, and lack of a balanced sport–life perspective (keeping winning and losing in perspective) helped predict choking.

Finally, Mesagno, Harvey, and Janelle (2011) provided evidence that self-presentation is an essential part of choking. The authors argue that athletes who have public self-awareness are likely to become aware of being observed, will be concerned with the audience's judgments, and may feel they are the object of others' attention. During high-pressure situations, public awareness is elevated because the performer perceives that the audience's attention is focused solely on him. Results revealed that the high-pressure self-presentation groups (performing in front of an audience) exhibited higher cognitive state anxiety and lower levels of performance than did the control or low-pressure groups (performing with no audience). In essence, a direct relationship was found between increased cognitive anxiety and performance decrements in high-stress situations (i.e., self-presentation concerns were high). This increased attention to self (which other researchers have called self-consciousness) seems to be particularly detrimental to the performance of well-learned tasks, during which the performer should be on automatic pilot (Beilock & McConnell, 2004).

Overanalyzing Body Mechanics

Another type of inappropriate attention is focusing too much on body mechanics and movements. When you're learning a new skill, you should focus internally to get the kinesthetic feel of the movement. If you're learning to ski downhill, for instance, you might focus on the transfer of weight, the positioning of your skis and poles, and simply avoiding a fall or running into other people. As you attempt to integrate this new movement pattern, your performance is likely to be uneven. That is what practice is all about—focusing on improving your technique by getting a better feel of the movement.

The problem arises when narrow–internal thinking continues after you have learned the skill. At this point the skill should be virtually automatic, and your attention should be primarily on what you're doing with a minimum of thinking. If you are skiing in a competition for the fastest time, you should not be focusing on body mechanics. Rather, you should be externally focused on where you're going, skiing basically on automatic pilot.

> **KEY POINT** Once a skill is learned well, an overemphasis on body mechanics is detrimental to performance.

This doesn't mean that no thinking occurs once a skill is well learned. But an emphasis on technique and body mechanics during competition is usually detrimental to performance because the mind gets in the way of the body. Or, to use attentional terminology, a performer using conscious control processing (which is slow, requires effort, and is important in learning a skill) would have difficulty performing a skill in competition because he would be spending too much time focusing on what to do rather than using automatic processing (which requires little attention and effort).

Some interesting research (Beilock & Carr, 2001; Beilock, Carr, MacMahon, & Starkes, 2002) demonstrates the important role that attention plays in the choking process and the overanalysis of the movement itself. Specifically, focusing attention on the task to be performed (attention to step-by-step execution) appeared to be helpful to performers learning the skill, and thus teachers and coaches should draw learners' attention to task-relevant, kinesthetic, and perceptual cues. However, skilled performers exhibited decreases in performance under conditions designed to prompt attention to step-by-step execution. Thus, what often happens when athletes choke is that they focus too much on the specifics of performing the task, and this added attention breaks down the movement pattern that has been automated and practiced over and over. In essence, what was once automatic is now being performed through conscious thought processes, but the skill is best performed without (or with minimum) conscious thought processes (Nieuwenhuys, Pijpers, Oudejans, & Bakker, 2008). Thus, added attention might be beneficial as performers learn a task, but it becomes counterproductive and detrimental in competition, when skills need to be performed quickly and automatically. Along these lines, Otten (2009) found that athletes who developed a greater sense of control and confidence through practice performed better in pressure situations than did athletes who merely focused more attention on the task.

A study by Gucciardi and Dimmock (2008) highlights exactly what happens when someone chokes. The authors investigated two theoretical hypotheses for why athletes choke. The first is called the *conscious processing hypothesis,* which states that choking occurs when skilled performers focus too much of their conscious attention on the task, much as they would do if they were a novice at the task. In essence, they no longer perform on automatic pilot; rather, their conscious attention reverts back to the task when they are put in a pressure situation. The *attention threshold hypothesis* states that the increased pressure along with the attention needed to perform the task simply overloads the system and attentional capacity is exceeded. Performance deteriorates because there is not enough attentional capacity left in the system.

Results supported the conscious processing hypothesis because performance decreased only with increased focus on task-relevant cues (see also Toner & Moran, 2012). The authors argue that one global cue word (as opposed to several cues related to the task) would still focus the performer on the task (i.e., avoid irrelevant anxiety thoughts) while avoiding the increased attention seen when the focus is on several cues. For example, Curtis Granderson (currently with the New York Mets) tends to think too much and gets analytical at the plate, which causes him problems. So he tries to set an overall cue to focus on, which is "Don't think; have fun." For him, this means going up and hitting while trusting his instincts. Similarly, Novak Djokovic said the following about Andy Murray after beating him in the Australian Open finals: "It is likely a mental issue, not winning a Grand Slam after three tries and wanting it so bad. You start thinking too much. You're worrying too much in your head. It's a mental battle." (Evidently, Murray has now won the mental battle because he has gone on to win two Grand Slams.) Wilson (2008, 2012) and Hill and colleagues (2010b) provide thorough reviews of the relationship between anxiety and attention, exploring attentional theories as well as moderators of choking.

Fatigue

Given our definition of attention, which involves mental effort, it is not surprising that concentration can be lost simply through fatigue. A high school football coach makes this point by saying, "When you get tired, your concentration goes. This results in impaired decision making, lack of focus and intensity, and other mental breakdowns. This is why conditioning and fitness are so important." In essence, fatigue reduces the amount of processing resources available to the athlete to meet the demands of the situation.

Inadequate Motivation

If an individual is not motivated, it is difficult to maintain concentration, as the mind is likely to wander. As Jack Nicklaus (1974) stated:

> **Whenever I am up for golf—when either the tournament or course, or best of all both, excite and challenge me—I have little trouble concentrating . . . . But whenever the occasion doesn't stimulate or challenge me, or I'm just simply jaded with golf, then is the time I have to bear down on myself with a vengeance and concentrate. (p. 95)**

Irrelevant thoughts can occur simply because one is not focused, because a performer may believe it is

Alleviating Choking Under Pressure

Why athletes choke has been a major concern of both researchers and practitioners. From a practical point of view, the next step is to somehow eliminate or at least reduce the probability of athletes choking. Fortunately, several studies have used a variety of techniques or interventions for reducing choking (e.g., Hill et al., 2011; Land & Tenenbaum, 2012; Mesagno, Marchant, & Morris, 2008). The process of the intervention often included individual face-to-face meetings between athletes and sport psychology consultants, telephone calls and e-mails, a reflective diary, and observations. Actual interventions for alleviating choking have included some combination of the following:

- *Imagery.* This technique has been employed primarily to build athletes' feelings of confidence. Athletes prone to choking typically note a decrease in confidence due to their focus on failure. Thus, imagery may strengthen athletes' belief in themselves.

- *Preshot routines.* Athletes who choke typically either focus on irrelevant, anxiety-producing thoughts (e.g., "I hope I don't choke again") or focus too much on the task (e.g., too many thoughts). Thus, a consistent preshot routine helps keep athletes task focused and relaxed.

- *Secondary task focus.* Similar to the preshot routine, this intervention helps skilled athletes focus on one task-relevant cue (although not the primary focus) instead of having all the thoughts (many negative) typically associated with poor performance. For example, in golf, a secondary task such as saying the word *hit* (out loud or internally) when the club strikes the ball helps keep the focus away from irrelevant thoughts.

- *Exposure to stressful situations.* Having athletes practice under stressful situations allows them to start to feel more comfortable under pressure and use their strategies to help alleviate choking.

not really necessary to focus when the competition is relatively weak. This extra mental space is quickly filled by thoughts of irrelevant cues.

External Distracters

External distracters may be defined as stimuli from the environment that divert people's attention from the cues relevant to their performance. Unfortunately for performers, a variety of potential distractions exist.

Visual Distracters

One of the difficult aspects of remaining focused throughout an exercise bout or competition is that so many **visual distracters** in the environment are competing for your attention. One Olympic diver described it this way:

" I started to shift away from the scoreboard a year and a half before the Olympics because I knew that every time that I looked at the scoreboard my heart went crazy . . . . At the Olympics, I really focused on my dives rather than on other divers . . . . Before that I used to just watch the event and watch the Chinese and think, "Oh, how can she do that? She's a great diver." I thought, "I'm as good as anyone else, let's stop thinking about them and focus on your own dives." That was an important step in my career. "

—Sylvie Bernier, 1984 Canadian Olympic diving champion (cited in Orlick, 2000, p. 91)

Spectators can cause a visual distraction and may affect some people's concentration and subsequent performance by making them try too hard. We all want to look good when playing in front of people we know and care for, so we often start to press, tighten up, and try too hard. This usually results in poorer play instead of better, which embarrasses us and causes us to tighten up even more. In fact, in his research on "the championship choke," Baumeister (1984) argued that increased self-consciousness elicited by home crowds can cause athletes to focus too much on the process of movement (i.e., control processing), causing a decrement in performance. Of course, some people actually play better in front of audiences they know. For many others, though, knowing people in the audience is a powerful distraction. Other visual distracters reported by athletes include the leader board in professional golf tournaments, the scoreboard that has scores of other games, and the television camera crews at courtside. The Turkish football (soccer) club Galatasaray is infamous for using flares, drums, smoke, and incessant shouting to intimidate and distract opposing teams at their home field, which is known as "Hell" (Moran, 2013). Not surprisingly, some of the world's leading soccer teams (e.g., Manchester United, Barcelona, Real Madrid, AC Milan) have been defeated in this hostile environment, where maintaining attentional focus on relevant cues is extremely difficult.

Auditory Distracters

Most sport competitions take place in environments where various types of noise may distract from one's focus. Common **auditory distracters** include crowd noise, airplanes flying overhead (typically noted at the U.S. Open tennis championships in New York), announcements on the public address system, mobile telephones, and loud conversations among spectators. An Olympic weightlifter competing in a major international competition missed out on a gold medal because a train rattled past the rear of the stadium as he prepared for his final lift. Similarly, earlier in her career, several top players complained that tennis great

Monica Seles' grunting hurt their concentration. As Seles tried to eliminate her grunting, she noted that the effort to do so impaired her own concentration because she was now not hitting the ball automatically; rather, she was thinking about not grunting! A good example of an external distracter comes from Olympic archer Grace Gaughan:

" **I was distracted by a low-flying helicopter that was taking people up to see a big mountain behind where we were shooting in Atlanta. For just a second, I lost concentration. It was a head to head competition with only 12 arrows so there was no margin for error—that was a short, sharp, swift end to my chances.** "

Accordingly, athletic success may hinge on an athlete's ability to ignore such distracters while focusing on the most relevant cues to complete the task at hand. Noise and sounds are part of most team sports (e.g., basketball, soccer, hockey), although very quiet environments are expected for most individual sports (e.g., golf, tennis). Thus, a loud sound from the crowd

Courtesy of Casey A. Gentis

Many external distractions can make it difficult for athletes to focus. What external distracters can you identify here?

is typically more disturbing to a golfer, who expects near silence, than to a hockey player, who probably expects the sound.

Using Self-Talk to Enhance Concentration

The previous section covered a variety of internal and external distractions typically present in the competitive environment. Although it can be used to deal with distractions, **self-talk** is another potential internal distracter. Anytime you think about something, you are in a sense talking to yourself. Self-talk has many potential uses besides enhancing concentration, including breaking bad habits, initiating action, sustaining effort, and acquiring skill. Figure 16.3 shows the process of self-talk in which self-talk functions as a mediator between an event and a response. As the relationship shows, self-talk plays a key role in reactions to situations, and these reactions affect future actions and feelings.

Self-talk can take many forms, but for convenience we categorize it into three types: positive (motivational), instructional, and negative. Positive self-talk typically focuses on increasing energy, effort, and positive attitude but does not carry any specific task-related cue (e.g., "I can do it" or "Just hang in there a little longer"). For example, gold medalist swimmer Nelson Diebel has used the word *now* to motivate him to kick extra hard at certain points in a race. Instructional self-talk usually helps the individual focus on the technical or task-related aspects of the performance in order to improve execution (e.g., "Keep your eyes on the ball" or "Bend your knees"). For instance, many volleyball spikers use the word *extend* to cue them to extend their arm when spiking a ball. Similarly, a beginner in tennis might be instructed to think of the cue "sweep the dishes off the table" to get a sense of how to perform the tennis forehand (Cutton & Hearon, 2013).

Negative self-talk is critical and self-demeaning, gets in the way of a person reaching his or her goals, and is counterproductive and anxiety producing. Saying things such as "That was a stupid shot," "You stink," or "How can you play so bad?" does not enhance performance or create positive emotions. Rather, it creates anxiety and fosters self-doubt. The performers who think positively about these negative events are usually the most successful. A study by Hardy, Roberts, and Hardy (2009) found that athletes using a logbook to monitor self-talk became more aware of the content of their negative self-talk as well as the consequences of using negative self-talk. This could have important applied applications because, for most athletes, negative self-talk is detrimental to performance.

Zourbanos, Hatzigeorgiadis, Chroni, Theodorakis, and Papaioannou (2009) developed a scale for assessing self-talk and found eight types (factors) of self-talk. This added some specificity to simply classifying

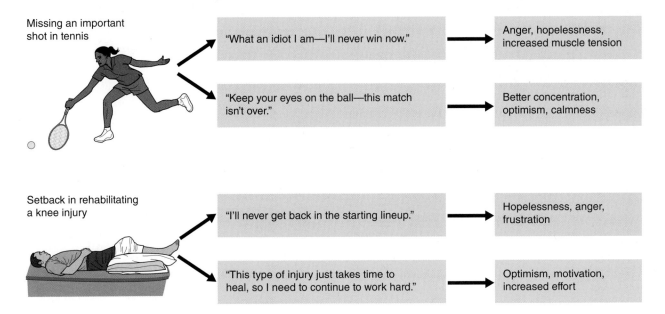

FIGURE 16.3 Two examples of the self-talk process.

self-talk as positive (motivational), instructional, or negative. The eight types were broken down into four positive categories including psych-up ("Power"), confidence ("I can make it"), instruction ("Focus on your technique"), and anxiety control ("Calm down"); three negative categories including worry ("I'm wrong again"), disengagement ("I can't keep going"), and somatic fatigue ("I am tired"); and one neutral category termed irrelevant thoughts ("What will I do later tonight?").

Research conducted under the term *ironic processes in sport* has shown that trying not to perform a specific action can inadvertently trigger its occurrence (Janelle, 1999; Wegner, 1997; Wegner, Ansfield, & Piloff, 1998). In the laboratory, empirical evidence demonstrates that what's accessible in our minds can exert an influence on judgment and behavior simply because it is there. So, people trying to banish a thought from their minds—of a white bear, for example—find that the thought keeps returning about once a minute. Likewise, people trying not to think about a specific word continually blurt it out during rapid-fire word-association tests.

These same "ironic errors" are just as easy to evoke in the real world. Therefore, instructions such as "Whatever you do, don't double-fault now," "Don't drive the ball into the bunker or lake," and "Don't choke" will typically produce the unwanted behavior. This is especially the case under pressure. For example, soccer players told to shoot a penalty kick anywhere but a certain spot of the net, such as the lower right corner, look at that spot more often than any other. Similarly, golfers instructed to avoid a specific mistake, such as overshooting, do it more often under pressure. In essence, to comply with these instructions to suppress a certain thought or image, we have to remember the instructions that include the forbidden thought—so we end up thinking it. A study (Woodman & Davis, 2008) demonstrated that "repressors" were particularly vulnerable to ironic processing errors. The reason is that repressors' cognitive strategy is to inhibit the subjective distress related to anxiety, which simply increases their cognitive load, making them even more prone to ironic errors. In essence, by trying to reduce or get rid of their anxiety, they spend more time thinking about it, which just overloads the system and results in reduced performance. Therefore, we should focus on what to do instead of what not to do.

Self-talk has many uses in addition to enhancing concentration, including increasing confidence, enhancing motivation, regulating arousal levels, improving mental preparation, breaking bad habits, acquiring new skills, and sustaining effort. These uses of self-talk are typically motivational or instructional, depending on the needs of the athlete. Interestingly, some research (Hanin & Stambulova, 2002) has shown that athletes make extensive use of metaphors in their self-talk (e.g., quick like a cheetah; strong like a bull) and that these metaphors, when generated by the performers themselves, are particularly helpful for changing behavior and performance.

Furthermore, other qualitative and quantitative research (Hardy, Gammage, & Hall, 2001; Hardy, Hall, & Hardy, 2004) has suggested that the content of self-talk can be divided into the following categories: (a) nature (positive or negative; internal or external), (b) structure (single cue words like *breathe* and *concentrate* vs. phrases like "Park it" and "Come on" vs. full sentences like "Don't worry about mistakes that occur"), (c) person (one talks to one's self in the first person, using *I* and *me,* or in the second person, using *you*), and (d) task instruction (skill-specific phrases like "Tackle low" and "Keep your head up" vs. general instructions like "Get there faster" and "Stay tough throughout the race"). The researchers found two major functions of self-talk: cognitive (e.g., relating to skill development and skill execution) and motivational (e.g., relating to self-confidence, regulation of arousal, mental readiness, coping with difficult situations, and motivation).

What factors affect the specific types of self-talk reported by athletes? A study by Zourbanos and colleagues (2011) investigated how coaching behaviors might influence self-talk. In a series of three studies they found that supportive coaching behaviors help produce more positive self-talk and less negative self-talk. In addition, negative or punishing coaching behaviors produced more negative self-talk and less positive self-talk. Definite empirical links—not just anecdotal reports of links—between coaching behaviors and athletes' self-talk indicate that coaches have an effect on athletes' thoughts.

Self-Talk and Performance Enhancement

Although practitioners and researchers have argued the potentially important benefits of positive self-talk in enhancing task performance, only relatively recently has empirical research corroborated this assumption. In addition, although the focus here is on performance enhancement, some research has shown self-talk to be effective in enhancing exercise adherence (Cousins & Gillis, 2005).

Research using a variety of other athletic samples has shown that different types of positive self-talk (i.e., instructional, motivational, mood related, self-affirmative) can enhance performance. These studies have been conducted, for example, with cross-country skiers (Rushall, Hall, & Rushall, 1988), beginning and skilled tennis players (Landin & Hebert, 1999; Mamassis & Doganis, 2004; Van Raalte, Brewer, Rivera, & Petitpas, 1994), sprinters (Mallett & Hanrahan, 1997), soccer players (Johnson, Hrycaiko, Johnson, & Halas, 2004), and figure skaters (Ming & Martin, 1996). The study with figure skaters is particularly impressive because self-report follow-ups a year after the intervention indicated that the participants continued to use the self-talk during practices and believed that it enhanced their competitive performance.

Furthermore, several investigations (Hatzigeorgiadis, Theodorakis, & Zourbanos, 2004; Hatzigeorgiadis, Zourbanos, Goltsios, & Theodorakis, 2008; Perkos, Theodorakis, & Chroni, 2002) have found both instructional and motivational self-talk effective for tasks varying in strength, accuracy, endurance, and fine motor coordination. This works by reducing the frequency of interfering thoughts while increasing the frequency of task-related thoughts. In addition, instructional self-talk can even help performance when knowledge of performance feedback is eliminated. In essence, even though subjects never received any feedback about their movement patterns, self-talk instructional cues were enough to produce performance increases during the learning of a skill (Cutton & Landin, 2007). Zourbanos, Hatzigeorgiadis, Bardas, and Theodorakis (2013) found that instructional self-talk in the form of externally focused cues was more beneficial for performance in the early stage of learning than was motivational self-talk. Furthermore, research by Hamilton, Scott, and MacDougall (2007) revealed that both positive and negative self-talk may lead to enhanced performance. The authors hypothesize that the nature, content, and delivery of self-talk may not be as important as the individual interpretation of that self-talk. This underscores the importance of individual differences in relation to the effectiveness of different types of self-talk (Hatzigeorgiadis, Zourbanos, & Theodorakis, 2007).

Finally, results of a meta-analytic review of 32 studies on self-talk revealed that self-talk was consistently positively related to performance improvements (Hatzigeorgiadis, Zourbanos, Galanis, & Theodorakis, 2011). In addition, results indicated that self-talk interventions were more effective for relatively fine motor tasks compared with gross motor tasks, for novel tasks compared with well-learned tasks, for instructional self-talk compared with motivational self-talk, and training compared with no training. Similarly, in a systematic review by Tod, Hardy, and Oliver (2011), agreement was found regarding the beneficial effects of positive, motivational, and instructional self-talk on performance. The authors also found that negative self-talk was not necessarily detrimental to performance, although only a few studies showed this finding.

Peters and Williams (2006) demonstrated the need to consider culture when looking at the effects of positive and negative self-talk on performance. Specifically, the authors compared the self-talk of European Americans and East Asians and found that East Asians had a significantly larger proportion of negative versus positive self-talk than European Americans. Although negative self-talk was related to poorer performance for the European Americans, it was related to better performance for the East Asians. It has been argued that there are fewer negative consequences of self-criticism for individuals from collectivist cultural backgrounds (e.g., East Asians) than for those from individualistic cultural backgrounds (e.g., European Americans). In any case, this has important implications for sport psychology consultants working with different populations and highlights the need to be sensitive to cultural differences.

Another situational factor affecting self-talk in athletes is coaching behaviors. Zourbanos and colleagues (2010, 2011) found that supportive coaching behaviors were related to more positive self-talk and less negative self-talk in athletes. However, negative coaching behaviors (e.g., punishment, autocratic behaviors) were related to more negative self-talk and less positive self-talk in athletes. Thus, coaches have an influence not just on how athletes perform but also on how they think. Finally, personality appears to be related to self-talk: Mastery-oriented individuals appear to have more positive self-talk compared with failure-oriented individuals (Burton, Gillham, & Glenn, 2011).

In one of the only self-talk interventions conducted in a field setting, Weinberg, Miller, and Horn (2012) investigated different types of self-talk as well as whether differences in performance occur when the self-talk is assigned versus when it is chosen. Collegiate runners were matched on baseline 1-mile times and then randomly assigned to a self-talk strategy (motivational, instructional, or combined) and practiced that strategy through the use of personalized compact discs. The self-talk statements on the disc were either chosen by the runner or assigned to the runner. Each runner in the chosen group selected 1 of 12 individualized statements (e.g., "Get tough"), and the corresponding runner in the assigned group received the same 12 statements. Results showed that the combined chosen and motivational chosen groups displayed the greatest decreases in time in the 1-mile run. However, all self-talk groups demonstrated increases in performance. Coaches agreed that such significant increases in performance would not have ordinarily occurred without such an intervention. In conclusion, self-talk worked in a real-life setting.

An interesting line of research related to self-talk is known as counterfactual thinking. Counterfactual thinking involves thoughts that are contrary to the actual results and has been defined as "mental representations of alternatives to past occurrences, features, and states" (Roese, Sanna, & Galinsky, 2005, p. 138). Counterfactual thoughts occur very frequently (88% of athletes) and are typically elicited after outcomes that are close. For example, a soccer player might say after a 1-0 defeat, "If I just would have run a little harder to get the pass I could have had a great chance for a goal." Research (Dray & Uphill, 2009) found that counterfactual thinking usually focuses on how things could have been better as opposed to worse. In addition, it was found that counterfactual thinking influences athletes' affect, motivation, confidence, decision making, attributions, and behavioral responses. Whether these counterfactual thoughts produce positive or negative psychological or behavioral effects appears to depend on athletes' interpretation of these thoughts. More research is necessary to explore the specific conditions under which these counterfactual thoughts are associated with positive or negative outcomes.

Techniques for Improving Self-Talk

Mikes (1987) suggested six rules for creating self-talk for performance execution: (a) Keep your phrases short and specific, (b) use the first person and present tense, (c) construct positive phrases, (d) say your phrases with meaning and attention, (e) speak kindly to yourself,

and (f) repeat phrases often. Various techniques or strategies for improving self-talk have also been found. Two of the most successful involve thought stopping and changing negative self-talk to positive self-talk.

Thought Stopping

One way to cope with negative thoughts is to stop them before they harm performance. **Thought stopping** involves concentrating on the undesired thought briefly and then using a cue or trigger to stop the thought and clear your mind. The trigger can be a simple word like *stop* or a trigger like snapping your fingers or hitting your hand against your thigh. What makes the most effective cue depends on the person.

Initially, it's best to restrict thought stopping to practice situations. Whenever you start thinking a negative thought, just say "Stop" (or whatever cue you have chosen) aloud and then focus on a task-related cue. Once you have mastered this, try saying "*Stop*" quietly to yourself. If a particular situation (e.g., falling during a figure skating jump) produces negative self-talk, you might want to focus on that one performance aspect to stay more focused and aware of the particular problem. Old habits die hard, so you should practice thought stopping continuously.

VIEW Activity 16.1 helps you apply the skill of thought stopping.

Changing Negative Self-Talk to Positive Self-Talk

It would be nice to eliminate all negative self-talk, but in fact almost everyone has negative thoughts from time to time. When negative thoughts come, one way to cope with them is to change them into positive self-talk, which redirects attentional focus to provide encouragement and motivation. First, list all the types of self-talk that hurt your performance or that produce other undesirable behaviors. The goal here is to recognize what situations produce negative thoughts and why. Then try to substitute a positive statement for the negative one. When you've done this, create a chart with negative self-talk in one column and your corresponding positive self-talk in another (figure 16.4).

To work on changing self-talk from negative to positive, use the same guidelines that you used for thought stopping. That is, do it in practice before trying it in competition. Because most negative thoughts occur under stress, first try to halt the negative thought and then

Negative self-talk	Positive self-talk
"You idiot—how could you miss such an easy shot?"	"Everyone makes mistakes—just concentrate on the next point."
"I'll never recover from this injury."	"Healing takes time. Just continue to exercise every day."
"He robbed me on the line call—that ball was definitely in."	"There's nothing I can do about it. If I play well, I'll win anyway."
"I'll take it easy today and work out hard tomorrow."	"If I work hard today, then the next work out will be easier tomorrow."
"That was a terrible serve."	"Just slow down and keep your rhythm and timing."
"I'll never stay with this exercise program."	"Just take one day at a time and make exercise fun."
"I never play well in the wind."	"It's windy on both sides of the court. This just requires extra concentration."

FIGURE 16.4 Changing negative to positive self-talk.

take a deep breath. As you exhale, relax and repeat the positive statement. Let's now look at some other skills connected with attention or concentration—specifically, how to assess attentional strengths and weaknesses.

Combine Self-Talk With Self-Feedback

Most researchers and practitioners simply try to change or eliminate negative self-talk. However, research has found that adding self-feedback to instructional self-talk can enhance both concentration and perfor-

mance. Latinjak, Torregrosa, and Renom (2011) had participants use instructional self-talk (e.g., "Bend your knees") that the participants had developed for themselves. Participants then gave themselves feedback: When they performed the skill correctly they simply told themselves *yes, good,* or *okay,* and when they performed the skill incorrectly they simply told themselves *no* or *bad.* The addition of this self-feedback improved performance above and beyond simply using a specific cue word (i.e., self-talk). This might help performers get more involved in the learning process, give themselves adequate technical feedback, and positively solve problems when the coach is not available.

🔍 **DISCOVER** Activity 16.2 lets you practice changing negative self-talk to positive self-talk.

Assessing Attentional Skills

Before trying to improve concentration, you should be able to pinpoint problem areas, such as undeveloped attentional skills. Nideffer's distinctions concerning attentional focus—that is, external versus internal and broad versus narrow—are useful in this regard. Nideffer argued that people have different attentional styles that contribute to differences in the quality of performance.

Test of Attentional and Interpersonal Style

Nideffer (1976b) devised the Test of Attentional and Interpersonal Style (TAIS) to measure a person's attentional style, or disposition. The TAIS has 17 subscales; 6 of them measure attentional style, and the others measure interpersonal style and cognitive control. Notice in table 16.1 that three of the scales indicate aspects of effective focusing (broad–external, broad–internal, and narrow focus) and three assess aspects of ineffective focusing (external overload, internal overload, and reduced focus).

Effective and Ineffective Attentional Styles

People who concentrate well (**effective attenders**) deal well with simultaneous stimuli from external and internal sources (figure 16.5). They have high scores on broad–external and broad–internal focusing and can effectively switch their attention from a broad to a narrow focus as necessary. Effective attenders are also low on the three measures of ineffective attention mentioned in the preceding paragraph, which means that they can attend to many stimuli without becoming overloaded with information. They also can narrow their attentional focus when necessary without omitting or missing any important information.

> **KEY POINT** Effective attenders can concentrate on several stimuli without getting overloaded and can narrow attentional focus without leaving out important information. Ineffective attenders are easily confused by multiple stimuli.

In contrast, people who don't concentrate well (**ineffective attenders**) tend to become confused and overloaded by multiple stimuli, both internal and external. When they assume either a broad–internal or a broad–external focus, they have trouble narrowing their attentional width. For example, they may have trouble blocking out crowd noises or movement in the stands. Furthermore, the high score on the reduced-focus scale indicates that when they assume a narrow focus, it is so narrow that important information is left out. A soccer player, for example, might narrow his attentional focus to the ball and fail to see an opposing player alongside him who steals the ball! For ineffective attenders to perform better in sport competition, they must learn to switch their direction of attention at will and to narrow or broaden attention as the situation demands.

Test of Attentional and Interpersonal Style as a Trait Measure

Nideffer's TAIS is a trait measure of a person's generalized way of attending to the environment.

TABLE 16.1 Attentional Scales of the Test of Attentional and Interpersonal Style

Scale	Description
Broad–external	High scores indicate an ability to integrate many external stimuli simultaneously.
External overload	High scores indicate a tendency to become confused and overloaded with external stimuli.
Broad–internal	High scores indicate an ability to integrate several ideas at one time.
Narrow focus	High scores indicate an ability to narrow attention when appropriate.
Reduced focus	High scores indicate chronically narrowed attention.
Internal overload	High scores indicate a tendency to become overloaded with internal stimuli.

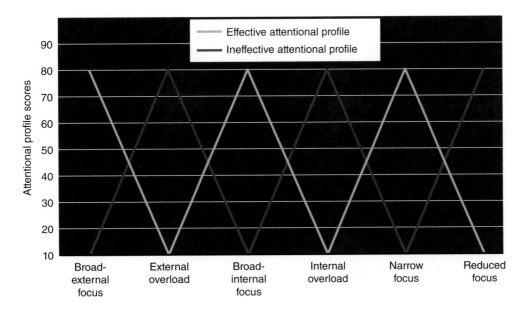

FIGURE 16.5 Effective and ineffective attentional profiles.

It does not consider situational factors. Recall the interactional paradigm from chapter 3, a model that presents a fuller description of human behavior than the more traditional trait approach does. If a soccer coach used the TAIS to measure the attentional style of players without considering that different positions require different types of attentional focus, the coach would gain little pertinent information for enhancing performance.

The TAIS would be more useful if it had sport-specific measures of attentional styles because questions assessing attentional abilities would be directed at the specific skills used in a particular sport. Sport-specific attentional style measures have been developed for tennis (Van Schoyck & Grasha, 1981) and pistol shooting (Etzel, 1979). Using sport-specific measures of attentional focus can help identify particular attentional weaknesses for athletes and coaches to work on. Despite the usefulness of the TAIS for practitioners in assessing attentional style, the test has been criticized by researchers in terms of its validity and some of its underlying assumptions. Researchers argue that other measures should be used for assessing attentional capacities. We next discuss a couple of these alternatives.

Psychophysiological Measures

Although practitioners have relied mostly on questionnaire measures of attentional style, such as the TAIS, researchers have also used psychophysiological assessments to help measure attentional processes (Abernethy, Summers, & Ford, 1998; Wilson, 2012). The psychophysiological indicators of attention they have used most often in sport and exercise environments are brain waves, as measured by an electroencephalogram (EEG), and heart rate measures. Functional magnetic resonance imaging has also been employed to learn more about brain functioning and attentional demands (Bishop, 2009). In general, physiological measures of attention have been administered most frequently to performers of "closed" skills (i.e., those that are self-paced, repetitive, and performed in a relatively unchanging environment), such as golf, bowling, pistol shooting, and archery.

EEG Measures

In the studies using EEG, brain activity patterns of pistol and rifle shooters and archers have typically been assessed preshot. One consistent finding is that the accuracy of shooting performance tends to be associated with alpha frequencies (usually linked to relaxed wakefulness) in the left cerebral hemisphere. In particular, alpha activity increases in the left hemisphere in the few seconds before the performer releases the arrow or pulls the pistol's trigger. This increase in alpha activity suggests that elite shooters have gained such control over their attentional processes that they can voluntarily reduce cognitive activity in their left hemisphere. This, in turn, can lead to lower task-irrelevant cognitive distractions that might otherwise disrupt shooting performance (Summers & Ford, 1995).

Neurological Measures

One neurological approach to studying attention is the use of heart rate. This originated from work in the 1960s, when Lacey (1967) explained that the deceleration in heart rate during the preparatory period in shooting was caused by the shooters directing their attention outward at that time—focusing not only on the visual target but also on the best way to stabilize and align the gun. These observations have been supported by more recent research (see Hatfield & Hillman, 2001, for a review), which indicates that cardiac deceleration tends to occur just before performance among elite performers in self-paced activities (e.g., archery, pistol shooting, rifle shooting). These results can be explained by the shooters focusing their attention on external cues that prime them to respond.

A second neurological approach to assessing attention is the measurement of brain-wave technology, including EEG techniques. Research suggests that just before expert archers and pistol shooters execute their shots, their EEG records tend to display a distinctive shift from left-hemisphere to right-hemisphere activation. It appears that executive control is being moved from the verbally based left hemisphere to the visuospatially focused right hemisphere. Verbal processes such as self-talk (which can get in the way of skilled performance) are dramatically reduced so that the right hemisphere can let the athlete perform on automatic pilot.

We have thus far discussed some of the background and findings regarding attentional processes. In the next section we suggest specific methods for improving attentional focus and shifting between types of attention.

Improving Concentration

Being able to maintain a focus on relevant environmental cues is critical for effective performance. In describing ways to improve concentration, we focus first on things that can be done on the field of play. Then we suggest exercises that athletes can practice at other times and in other places. Note, though, that in this chapter we do not discuss some of the important things performers can do to enhance their concentration because other chapters cover these in detail. For example, using imagery (chapter 13), controlling arousal levels (chapter 12), and setting performance and process goals (chapter 15) have been shown to be effective ways to enhance concentration.

On-Site Techniques

Competitive athletes can use one of the following six techniques to improve concentration on the field. Note that different techniques work better for different athletes (MacPherson, Collins, & Morriss, 2008).

Use Simulations in Practice

Anyone who has played a competitive sport understands that the competitive environment includes numerous factors that are not present to the same degree in the training environment. Such environmental factors as a noisy and antagonistic crowd, the presence of officials, and the behavior of the opposition undoubtedly make the competitive environment very different from the practice setting. In addition, psychological factors, such as competitive anxiety, motivation, and confidence, are all likely to vary between practice and competition. All these factors represent potential distractions to the athletes and may impair performance.

You can prepare yourself to cope with distractions and the environmental conditions by systematically practicing in this situation (Schmid, Peper, & Wilson, 2001). For example, Glencross (1993) prepared the Australian women's Olympic field hockey team for the Barcelona Olympics by mirroring the potential conditions of the competition, including climatic conditions, tournament rules, umpire rulings, crowd bias, competition schedule, opponent styles of play, accommodation and meals, transport conditions, and media exposure. This type of practice is known as **simulation training** because the coaches are trying to simulate an actual competitive environment.

In working with Canadian Olympic athletes (Orlick & Partington, 1988) and with American Olympic athletes (Habert & McCann, 2012), it was found that these successful athletes emphasized the importance of simulation training as part of their preparation: "The best athletes made extensive use of simulation training. They approached training runs, routines, plays, scrimmages in practice as if they were at the competition, often wearing what they would wear and preparing like they would prepare" (Orlick & Partington, 1988, p. 114).

Elite athletes also reported using simulations to prepare mentally. For example, British Olympic javelin thrower Steve Backley stated that he sometimes structured his training to put himself under the same sort of pressure that he expected to encounter on the qualifying day of a major competition: "I'd have three throws to get over 75 to 76 meters, and I'd mark out the distance and actually go through the process of trying to simulate the pressure" (Jones & Hardy, 1990, p. 270). Similarly, former world champion trampolinist Sue Challis simulated conditions during training as follows: "I actually do the routines in training and imagine that I've got one chance . . . . I often get quite uptight if I don't get it right, but if it's good, it really boosts my confidence" (Jones & Hardy, 1990, p. 271).

Use Cue Words

Cue words are used to trigger a particular response and are really a form of self-talk. They can be instructional (e.g., "Follow through," "Shoulders back," "Stretch," "Watch the ball") or motivational or emotional (e.g., "Strong," "Move," "Relax," "Hang in there," "Get tough"). The key is to keep the cue words simple and let them automatically trigger the desired response. For example, a gymnast performing a floor routine might use the cue word *forward* to make sure that she pushes ahead at a certain point during her performance. Similarly, a sprinter might say "Explode" to make sure that he gets off the starting blocks well. It would seem important to use these cue words in practice so that they become familiar and well learned before being used in competition. However, research (Miller & Donohue, 2003) indicates that providing runners with motivational and technique-oriented statements (chosen by the runners) on headphones immediately before competition (even without practice) was effective in enhancing running performance. Perhaps practicing would have made these statements even more effective, or maybe simply giving runners the choice of statements improved their motivation and enjoyment.

> **KEY POINT** Cue words should be either instructional or motivational to help focus on the task at hand.

Cue words are particularly useful when you are trying to vary or change a movement pattern—whether it is changing your golf swing, batting stance, aerobic dance routine, or service motion. In the training room, athletes could use cue words like *relax* or *easy* when stretching injured muscles and joints. In addition, attentional cues are helpful for trying to break a bad habit. For instance, if a miler tends to tighten up in the last lap of a race and his stride becomes shorter, thus spoiling his rhythm, a cue such as *smooth, stretch,* or *relax* might help him keep focused on relaxing and lengthening his stride.

Use Nonjudgmental Thinking

One of the biggest obstacles athletes face in maintaining concentration is the tendency to evaluate performance and classify it as good or bad. Such judgments tend to elicit personal, ego-involved reactions. The process of evaluating and judging what you do on the athletic field or in exercise class usually hinders performance. After you become judgmental about a portion of your performance or behavior, it is common to start generalizing. For example, a soccer player who misses a couple of opportunities to score a goal might think, "I always miss the easy ones," "I'm just a choke artist," or "I just can't kick one when I need to." Such thoughts and judgments make you lose your fluidity, timing, and rhythm. Your brain starts to override your body, causing excess muscle tension, excess effort, concentration lapses, and impaired decision making. Suppose someone in an exercise class misses a few workouts and thinks, "I just don't have what it takes to stay with the program." Such thinking undermines her motivation to adhere to an exercise program (more about this in chapter 18).

Instead of judging the worth of a performance and categorizing it as either good or bad, learn to look at your actions nonjudgmentally. For instance, a baseball pitcher realizes he doesn't have good control today—he has walked five batters in the first three innings. This observation could lead him to generalize that he's a bad pitcher and doesn't have control over his pitches. This thinking could lead to anger, frustration, and discouragement. Instead, this pitcher might evaluate how he is pitching and simply notice that most of his pitches out of the strike zone have been high. This would tell him, for example, that he is not following through properly. In response, he could focus on getting a good wrist snap and following through to keep the ball from rising on him, which should translate into better performance and a more enjoyable experience.

Recently, a form of nonjudgmental thinking called mindfulness has become popular in training attentional focus. Kabat-Zinn (2005) defines mindfulness as "an openhearted, moment-to-moment, nonjudgmental awareness of oneself and of the world" (p. 24). In essence, instead of trying to eliminate negative thoughts, mindfulness involves acceptance of thoughts and focusing on the present moment (Moran, 2012). Recent studies found that athletes receiving mindfulness training experienced flow (see chapter 6) significantly more often than those not receiving training (Aherne, Moran, & Lonsdale, 2011) and that mindfulness can lead to enhanced attentional focus (Kee, Chatzisarantis, Kong, Chow, & Chen, 2012).

Establish Routines

Routines can focus concentration and can be extremely helpful in mental preparation for an upcoming performance. The generally accepted definition of preperformance routines was put forth by Moran (1996), who defined such a routine as "a sequence of task-relevant thoughts and actions which an athlete engages in systematically prior to his or her performance of a specific sports skill" (p. 177). Research investigating routines of Olympic swimmers found that routines were divided into two parts: the plan itself and the enactment of the plan in the performance setting (Grant & Schempp, 2013). Researchers have argued that preperformance routines work by helping athletes transfer their attention from task-irrelevant thoughts to task-relevant thoughts. Routines increase the likelihood that individuals will not be distracted internally or externally before and during performance and often allow the performance to stay automatic without the interference of conscious awareness.

The effectiveness of routines has substantial support (see Cotterill, Sanders, & Collins [2010] on golf; Feltz & Landers [1983] on mental rehearsal; Gould, Eklund, & Jackson [1992c] on wrestling; Hill & Borden [1993] on bowling; Mack [2001] on basketball; Mesagno, Marchant, & Morris [2008] on alleviating choking; and Moore & Stevenson [1994] on tennis). Although the focus of routines has been right before the start of performance or between performances, they should be used systematically during practice so they are learned and can then be transferred from practice to competition (Schack, Whitmarsh, Pike, & Redden, 2005). Finally, a study by Cotterill, Sanders, and Collins (2010) found that personality, coping resources, and situational demands of individual performers need to be considered when developing preperformance routines. This approach would recognize the individuality of the performer, avoiding a "one size fits all" mentality.

> **KEY POINT** Routines can be used before or during an event to focus attention, reduce anxiety, eliminate distractions, and enhance confidence.

The mind often starts to wander during breaks in the action. Such times are ideal for routines. For example, a tennis player during changeovers might sit in a chair, take a deep breath, and image what she wants to do in the next game. Then she might repeat two or three cue words to help her focus attention before taking the court. Routines can help structure the time before performance and between performances so that an athlete can be mentally focused when it's time to perform.

Athletes have routines varying from short and simple to complex and lengthy. However, research

---

A Five-Step Approach to Developing Preperformance Routines

Cotterill (2011) discussed a five-step approach to developing effective preperformance routines. This approach includes the following elements:

- *Videotaping performance.* To determine the player's current routine, the player's competition and practice routines are videotaped.

- *Clarifying behavior meaning.* The player watches the videos and determines his awareness of the routines.

- *Developing focus and function for each behavioral component.* The player executes his existing preperformance behaviors and then discusses with the consultant the meaning and function of each discrete behavior.

- *Routine construction and agreement.* The sport psychology consultant explores what the player is seeking to achieve in the preparation period (e.g., relaxation, focused attention, engaging in imagery). Then a relevant trigger word (e.g., *relax* or *focus*) is negotiated that fits with the meaning and time period associated with the behavior.

- *Practice.* After the behavioral and mental routines are developed, they are integrated into regular practices. At first this includes a think-aloud approach in which the player vocalizes the thoughts that had been developed to go with the specific preperformance behaviors. The player practices this way until the trigger is fully integrated into the routine and saying it aloud is no longer necessary.

has revealed that, in general, the shorter the time of the routine (regardless of the number of behaviors in the routine), the more successful the performance (Farrow & Kemp, 2003). Some routines border on superstition, such as wearing a lucky pair of socks, tying one's shoelaces a certain way, or walking to the pitcher's mound without stepping on the foul lines. The routine needs to feel comfortable to the individual and help sharpen focus as the time of performance nears. Velentzas, Heinen, and Schack (2011) found that a good way to integrate routines into performance is to have athletes image the routine consistently. Specifically, when using the routine to perform the volleyball serve, athletes from the imagery group performed significantly better than all other groups.

Preperformance routines structure the athlete's thought processes and emotional states, keeping the focus of attention in the present and on task-related cues. Although more empirical research is necessary, Cotterill (2010) notes that routines have been hypothesized to reduce the effect of distractions, focus attention on relevant cues, act as a trigger for well-learned movement patterns, enhance the recall of psychological and physiological states, help performers achieve behavioral and temporal consistency, and improve performance under pressure. (See figure 16.6 for examples of preperformance routines for tennis and golf.) Several models or approaches for creating preperformance routines have been developed, including Singer's (2002) five-step approach, Murphy's (1995) four-point model, and Lidor and Singer's (2000) model for learning new skills.

DISCOVER Activity 16.3 helps you learn to develop routines.

Develop Competition Plans

In-depth interviews with elite athletes in a variety of sports clearly indicate the importance to these individuals of establishing precompetition and competition plans to help maintain attentional focus (Gould, Eklund, & Jackson, 1992a; Greenleaf, Gould, & Dieffenbach, 2001; Orlick & Partington, 1988). These

Golf shot

1. Take a deep breath.
2. Look at the fairway's lie and assess weather conditions and possible hazards.
3. Look at the target and decide on the shot required.
4. Picture your target and the shot you want to hit. Imagine not only your swing but also the trajectory of the ball and its final resting place.
5. Address the ball, adjusting and readjusting your position until you feel comfortable.
6. Feel the shot with your whole body.
7. Again, picture the desired shot and while feeling the shot, think target.
8. Think target and swing.

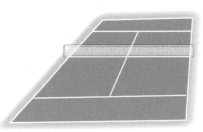

Tennis serve

1. Determine positioning and foot placement.
2. Decide on service type and placement.
3. Adjust racket grip and ball.
4. Take deep breath.
5. Bounce the ball for rhythm.
6. See and feel the perfect serve.
7. Focus on ball toss and serve to programmed spot.

FIGURE 16.6 Sport-specific examples of preperformance routines.

plans help athletes not only prepare for their events but also prepare for what they would do in different circumstances. In most cases, athletes design these detailed plans of action to facilitate attentional focus on the process of performance (as opposed to factors over which they have no direct control, such as other competitors and final outcome). These remarks by an Olympic kayaker highlight this emphasis on a detailed plan:

" My focus was very concentrated throughout the race. We have a start plan, and in it I concentrate only on the first few strokes . . . . Then I concentrate on the next little bit of the race . . . . Then it's getting to the end, [and] we have to really push. Almost every 3 seconds or so toward the end I'd have to say "Relax" and let my shoulders and my head relax, and I'd think about putting on the power and then I'd feel the tension creeping up again so I'd think about relaxing again, then power, then relax. (Orlick & Partington, 1988, p. 116) "

One way to develop competition plans is to use a "what if" approach so that athletes can prepare a plan for different scenarios that might be likely or unlikely but possible. For example, the Australian netball team prepared for an important match with the Jamaican team (on their field) by planning for what to do in case the lights in the stadium went out. Surprisingly, this "what if" situation actually occurred but the Australians coped with it very well, in part because of their extensive preparation for just such a situation.

Inherent in competition plans is a focus on process goals. In other words, the plans stress what is under the control of the athlete rather than the outcome of the competition. For example, the kayaker's process goals related to maintaining relaxed muscles in his shoulders and neck and concentrating on his stroke. A soccer player may focus instead on his positioning and footwork and a volleyball player on the position of her arms when striking the ball. In any case, detailed, specific plans can help an athlete focus and maintain attention throughout the competition.

Overlearn Skills

To perform at high levels, athletes report that overlearning the skills involved in their sport helps concentration in the competitive situation (Hardy et al., 1996). Overlearning helps make the performance of a skill automatic. This in turn frees up one's attention to

concentrate on other aspects of the performance environment. Research, too, has shown that overlearning facilitates the concurrent performance of more than one task by enabling athletes to establish automatic attentional processes. For example, a basketball point guard doesn't have to focus much attention on dribbling the ball once that has become automatic; he can then focus on the movement and positioning of the other players on the court, which allows him to throw the most effective pass.

Exercises for Improving Concentration

In addition to the six techniques we presented to improve concentration on the field, people can do exercises to increase concentration skills. These exercises can be adapted to any sport.

Exercise 1: Learning to Shift Attention

This exercise can be practiced in its entirety or broken down into separate exercises (Gauron, 1984). Before starting the exercise, sit or lie down in a comfortable position and take a few deep breaths from the diaphragm.

1. Pay attention to what you hear. Take each separate sound and label it—is it voices, footsteps, the radio? Next, listen to all the sounds around you without attempting to label or classify them. Simply dismiss your thoughts and listen to the blend of sounds as if you were listening to music.

2. Now become aware of body sensations, such as the feeling of the chair, bed, or floor supporting you. Mentally label each sensation as you notice it. Before moving on to another sensation, let each sensation linger for a moment while you examine it closely, considering its quality and source.

3. Turn your attention to your thoughts and emotions. Let each emotion or thought simply arise; do not try to specifically think about anything. Remain relaxed and at ease no matter what you are thinking or feeling. Now try to experience each of your feelings and thoughts one at a time. Finally, see if you can just let go of all these thoughts and emotions and relax.

Exercise 2: "Parking" Thoughts

This exercise concerns effectively eliminating negative, intruding thoughts by "parking" them in a safe and nondistracting place until after the performance. Parking is typically accomplished through some form of self-talk instruction or visualization. After identifying these unwanted thoughts in their minds, athletes are instructed to write them down on paper and then place the paper in another location (this is the parking component). After the performance, the athlete can go back and deal with the issue by "unparking" it.

Exercise 3: Learning to Maintain Focus

Find a quiet place with no distractions. Choose an object to focus on (you might choose something related to the sport that you play, such as a hockey puck, soccer ball, baseball, or volleyball). Hold the object in your hands. Get a good sense of how it feels and its texture, color, and any other distinguishing characteristics. Now put the object down and focus your attention on it, examining it in great detail. If your thoughts wander, bring your attention back to the object. Record how long you can maintain your focus on the object. It isn't easy to stay focused on one object. Once you are able to maintain focus for at least 5 minutes, start practicing with distractions present. Chart how long you can maintain your attention under these conditions.

Exercise 4: Searching for Relevant Cues

The grid exercise has been used extensively in Eastern Europe as a precompetition screening device. It can give you a sense of what it means to be totally focused. The exercise requires a block grid containing two-digit numbers ranging from 00 to 99 (figure 16.7). The object is to scan the grid within a set period of time (usually 1 or 2 minutes) and make a slash mark through as many sequential numbers as possible (00, 01, 02, 03, etc.). You can use the same grid several times by just starting with a higher number (e.g., 33, 41, 51) than before. You can make new grids using any combination of numbers. People who concentrate intensely, scan, and store relevant cues reportedly score in the upper 20s and into the 30s (in terms of how many numbers they find within 1 minute).

This exercise helps you learn to focus your attention and scan the environment for relevant cues (which is especially important in fast-moving sports such as basketball, hockey, and soccer), and you can modify it for different situations. For instance, you can scan the grid amid different types of distractions, such as conversation or loud music. As your concentration improves, you will be better able to block out such distractions and focus exclusively on the task. Isn't this what most athletes want to accomplish in terms of concentration—complete absorption and the elimination of all distractions?

DISCOVER Activity 16.4 helps you practice the concentration grid exercise.

Future Developments in Concentration Training

Karageorghis and Terry (2011) provide a brief list of cutting-edge technologies that aim to enhance athletes' concentration skills. These include the following:

- *Eye scanners.* These track eye movements in response to a variety of sport scenarios, such as a quarterback passing, tennis serves, and soccer penalty kicks. Tracking athletes' visual focus helps train them to focus on relevant cues.

32	42	39	34	99	19	84	44	03	77
37	97	92	18	90	53	04	72	51	65
95	40	33	86	45	81	67	13	59	58
69	78	57	68	87	05	79	15	28	36
09	26	62	89	91	47	52	61	64	29
00	60	75	02	22	08	74	17	16	12
76	25	48	71	70	83	06	49	41	07
10	31	98	96	11	63	56	66	50	24
20	01	54	46	82	14	38	23	73	94
43	88	85	30	21	27	80	93	35	55

FIGURE 16.7 Concentration grid exercise.

- *Virtual reality.* In a virtual environment, athletes are placed in a situation with the exact same sights, noise, and feel of the actual event. This allows athletes practice in the exact situation in which they will compete.

- *Eye training equipment.* Companies are manufacturing sporting equipment that makes the athlete's task more challenging. For example, a basketball that is not exactly round would bounce unevenly, thus making it more difficult to dribble. This would require the athlete to focus greater attention on her dribbling skills.

- *Video games.* Companies have developed three-dimensional games to simulate some of the attentional and perceptual demands of the skills required in different sports. This can help improve reaction times and hand–eye coordination, which are critical for success in many sports.

- *Eye training and concentration software.* These train athletes to recognize advanced relevant cues in their sport in order to improve their anticipation times in different situations (e.g., a penalty kick in soccer).

LEARNING AIDS

SUMMARY

1. **Define concentration and explain how it is related to performance.**

   Concentration in sport and exercise settings usually involves focusing on the relevant cues in the environment, maintaining that focus over time, being aware of the changing situation, and shifting focus as necessary. Athletes who describe their best performances inevitably mention that they are completely absorbed in the present, focused on the task at hand, and acutely aware of their own bodies and the external environment. Research, too, has shown that a key component of optimal performance is the performer's ability to focus attention and become fully absorbed in the game. Expert performers use various attentional cues, picking these cues up more quickly than do novices, to help themselves perform their skills more quickly and more effectively.

2. **Explain the main theories of concentration effects.**

   The three main approaches to studying attentional processes are single-channel (fixed capacity) theories, variable (flexible)-allocation theories, and multiple resource pools theories. The current thinking endorses the multiple resource pools approach, which views attention as a series of resource pools or multiprocessors, each with its own unique capabilities and resource–performer relationships.

3. **Identify different types of attentional focus.**

   Nideffer identified four types of attentional focus: broad–external, narrow–external, broad–internal, and narrow–internal. Different sports or tasks within sports require these different types of attention for effective performance.

4. **Describe some attentional problems.**

   Attentional problems can be categorized as coming from internal or external distracters. Internal distracters include attending to past events, attending to future events, choking under pressure, feeling fatigue, feeling a lack of motivation, and overanalyzing body mechanics. External distracters include visual factors, such as the audience, and auditory ones, such as crowd noise, as well as the opponent's gamesmanship.

5. **Explain how self-talk works.**

   Self-talk takes many forms, but it can be categorized simply as motivational, instructional, and negative. Motivational self-talk and instructional self-talk are typically assets that can enhance self-esteem, motivation, and attentional focus. These types of self-talk have been shown to enhance performance, although the type of self-talk needs to be matched to the type of task for maximum benefits. Negative self-talk is critical and self-demeaning, and it tends to produce anxiety, which undermines concentration.

6. **Explain how to assess attentional ability.**

   Attentional style can be measured by the Test of Attentional and Interpersonal Style, and strengths and weaknesses can then be assessed for developing programs to improve an individual's focus. Attentional processes can also be measured by brain wave activity and heart rate.

7. **Discuss how to improve attentional focus.**

   Practicing simple techniques and exercises both on and off the court or field will help improve concentration skills. These techniques include such activities as using simulations, using cue words, using nonjudgmental thinking, self-monitoring, developing competitive plans, and establishing routines.

KEY TERMS

attention
concentration
selective attention
attentional focus
situation awareness
associative attentional strategy
dissociative attentional strategy
information-processing approach
attentional capacity

attentional alertness
broad attentional focus
narrow attentional focus
external attentional focus
internal attentional focus
internal distracters
choking
external distracters

visual distracters
auditory distracters
self-talk
thought stopping
effective attenders
ineffective attenders
simulation training
cue words

REVIEW QUESTIONS

1. How did William James originally define concentration more than 100 years ago? How has its definition evolved since then? Why is the ability to focus on relevant cues in the environment and maintain that focus essential to the definition of a proper attentional focus?

2. When is this type of focus inappropriate? What effect does physical and psychological skill development have on an appropriate attentional focus during competition?

3. Nideffer's TAIS is a trait measure of a person's generalized way of attending to the environment. What are the limitations inherent in a trait measure of an athlete's perceptions? What could be done to make the TAIS a better assessment tool? What steps would you take in setting up an athletic practice using concentration-enhancing techniques? Explain why each technique is likely to get participants to focus on the relevant stimuli.

4. Discuss why routines work as preparation for performance (i.e., different functions of routines) and when is the best time to perform a routine. How would you develop a new routine for an athlete?

5. Describe the different types and uses of self-talk. Give a practical example of thought stopping to enhance performance.

6. Briefly describe the three main theories of attention. Which approach is most current?

7. Discuss how culture, personality, and coaching behaviors could be important when explaining self-talk effects.

8. Discuss three new technologies that might help improve attentional focus.

9. Discuss three strategies for alleviating the effects of choking.

CRITICAL THINKING QUESTIONS

1. You are asked to write an article about choking for an applied journal in your sport. The editors want you to define what choking is (and isn't), when it occurs, why it occurs, and how you could help athletes avoid it. Write the article.

2. You are coaching a high school team (pick your sport), and the team has a habit of losing concentration at critical times during the competition. You want to work with the athletes to enhance their concentration skills and keep their attention focused throughout the competition. Describe the drills, exercises, and strategies you would use with the team to help the members build concentration skills.

PART VI

Enhancing Health and Well-Being

In the past 30 years we have witnessed an increased interest in health, exercise, and wellness, including exercise and health psychology. With greater attention has come better understanding of the roles that psychological factors play in health and exercise. More and more career paths include the psychology of health and exercise as a major component, such as working in a rehabilitation or physical therapy center helping clients recover from injury. In addition, today's professionals need to be able to help others who are coping with the emotions of being injured or dealing with an eating disorder or gambling problem.

This sixth part begins with two chapters that specifically address exercise. In chapter 17 we examine the psychological benefits of exercise, such as reduced depression and anxiety, and tell you how to maximize these benefits. In addition, exercise and changes in personality and cognitive functioning are discussed along with the use of exercise as an adjunct to therapy. Chapter 18 discusses exercise motivation and ways to keep people exercising regularly. New models, determinants of exercise behavior, and approaches to improving exercise adherence are presented, along with practical tips for improving health and well-being through consistent exercise.

The next three chapters deal with more general health-related concerns. Chapter 19 focuses on the psychological antecedents and consequences of athletic and exercise-induced injuries and the role of psychological factors in injury rehabilitation. Psychological theories of injury are presented, and the stress–injury relationship is discussed. In chapter 20, we examine three of today's most critical concerns: substance abuse, eating disorders, and gambling. We prepare you to recognize the signs of such problems and to help people with these problems receive the specialized assistance they require. Finally, chapter 21 examines the potential negative effects of athletic and exercise participation, including burnout and overtraining. The chapter deals with the prevalence, causes, treatment, and prevention of burnout and overtraining.

VIEW Dr. Dan Gould introduces part VI of the text in the Introduction activity.

JOURNEY This activity asks you to define well-being in the context of your anticipated career.

LISTEN Go to part VI of the web study guide to meet the following experts in the field: Bonnie Berger, EdD; Jean M. Williams, PhD; Britton Brewer, PhD; and Dan Gould, PhD. In this activity, you'll hear or see the experts discussing sport, exercise, and well-being.

Exercise and Psychological Well-Being

After reading this chapter, you should be able to

1. explain the effects of exercise on anxiety and depression;
2. describe the relationship between exercise and mood states;
3. discuss the effects of exercise on psychological well-being;
4. describe the relationships among exercise, personality changes, and cognitive functioning;
5. discuss the runner's high; and
6. discuss the use of exercise as an adjunct to therapy.

Much of technology was meant to make our lives easier. However, the advent of cell phones, instant messaging, the Internet, and other communication devices has made our world increasingly complex and pressured. Ever more demands seem to be built into our daily existence, and noise, smog, inflation, unemployment, racism, sexism, drug abuse, gambling, and random violence add still more stress to our lives. These demands have affected the mental health and psychological well-being of society.

The most common disorders in the United States are anxiety disorders and depression. These affect 17% and 11%, respectively, of people aged 15 to 54 years, and each costs the public about $45 billion a year. Lifetime prevalence rates are approximately 25% for anxiety disorders and 20% for depression (Dishman, Washburn, & Heath, 2004). In addition, the World Health Organization projected that depression will be second only to cardiovascular disease as the world's leading cause of death and disability by the year 2020 (Murray & Lopez, 1997). Although people typically deal with these mood disturbances through psychological counseling, drug therapy, or both, more and more individuals are looking to exercise to promote their psychological well-being. Many researchers, clinicians, and laypeople have observed that physical activity enhances feelings of well-being, in particular by reducing anxiety and depression and increasing vigor. In addition, in the past 10 to 15 years, reviews of the literature have concluded that exercise is related to decreases in anxiety and depression as well as to increases in feelings of general well-being (Berger & Tobar, 2011; Biddle, 2011b; Landers & Arent, 2001).

Recent epidemiological data add credibility to these observations of the beneficial influences of exercise. These epidemiological data refer to statistics and information about the distribution and determinants of health problems or health-related events in populations as they apply to the control of health problems. For example, Stephens (1988) analyzed data from 56,000 participants and concluded that "the level of physical activity is positively associated with good mental health in the household population of the United States and Canada, when mental health is defined as positive mood, general well-being, and relatively infrequent symptoms of anxiety and depression" (p. 41). The positive effects of exercise on physical well-being are well documented and include changing the course of such illnesses as osteoporosis, hypertension, coronary heart disease, and cancer as well as improving feelings of psychological well-being (Blair, 1995).

In this chapter we look at the psychological benefits of exercise in four broad areas: reduction of anxiety and depression, enhancement of mood, improvement in self-concept, and improvement in quality of life. It is important to note that terms such as *subjective well-being, psychological well-being, emotional well-being,* and simply *well-being* have all been used in the literature and often have been defined somewhat differently (Lundquist, 2011). Because defining these terms is beyond the scope of this chapter, we use these terms interchangeably to refer to the six dimensions that make up well-being:

- Self-acceptance (positive views of one's self)
- Positive relations with others (trusting, caring, and empathetic relationships)
- Autonomy (self-determined with intrinsic motivation and self-referenced standards)
- Environmental mastery (effective mastery of the environment to fulfill personal values)
- Personal growth (sense of development and self-fulfillment over time)
- Purpose in life (directed toward purposeful goals for living)

Reducing Anxiety and Depression With Exercise

Mental health problems account for some 30% of the total days of hospitalization in the United States and about 10% of total medical costs. The mental health problems that have received the most attention are anxiety and depression. Although millions of Americans have anxiety disorders and depression, not all of them have psychopathological states; many simply have subjective distress, a broader category of unpleasant emotions. For these people, regular exercise appears to have some therapeutic value in

reducing feelings of anxiety and depression. Participating in regular exercise for psychological well-being is more than an American phenomenon. For example, in a survey conducted in England, Londoners also found exercise to be one of the most effective things to do when feeling depressed.

So far, most studies of the relationship between exercise and reductions in anxiety and depression have been correlational, so we cannot conclusively state that it was exercise that caused or produced the change in mood state. Rather, exercise appears to be *associated with* positive changes in mood states and reductions in anxiety and depression.

The effects of exercise on anxiety and depression can be classified as acute or chronic. **Acute effects** refer to immediate and possibly, but not necessarily, temporary effects arising from a single bout of exercise. Sport psychologists have also studied the long-term or **chronic effects** of exercise, investigating the validity of the old motto "A sound mind in a sound body." Research on the chronic effects of exercise has focused on changes over time in both anxiety and depression. The vast majority of research on the relationship between exercise and psychological well-being has used aerobic exercise. Although it was once believed that exercise needed to be of a certain or sufficient duration and intensity to produce positive psychological effects, research has indicated that high-intensity aerobic activity is not absolutely necessary to produce these positive benefits (e.g., Berger & Motl, 2001; Landers & Arent, 2001). In fact, activities such as weight or strength training, yoga, and other nonaerobic exercises have produced positive effects on psychological well-being. "Chronic Exercise and Mental Health" presents the conditions most associated with reductions in anxiety and depression and positive changes in mood.

KEY POINT Although a cause–effect relationship has not been established, regular exercise is associated with reductions in anxiety and depression.

Exercise in the Reduction of Anxiety

Studies of how exercise influences the reduction of anxiety have typically investigated either acute (short-term) or chronic (long-term) effects; studies have tended to focus more on the short-term effects. Investigations on the chronic effects of exercise have involved programs that typically last about 2 to 4 months, with two to four exercise sessions per

Exercise has been shown to reduce anxiety, depression, and chronic diseases and increase feelings of well-being, relaxation, and overall good health.

week. For example, two studies (Long, 1984; Long & Haney, 1988) compared different anxiety reduction techniques, such as stress inoculation and progressive relaxation, with jogging as stress management interventions. In both studies the jogging groups and stress management groups exhibited significant decreases in state anxiety over the course of the intervention period compared with the waiting-list control participants. But, more important, these reductions in state anxiety were maintained in follow-ups of up to 15 weeks (figure 17.1). Other studies (see O'Connor & Puetz, 2005, for a review) have also found chronic effects of exercise in reducing anxiety.

Most research on the acute effects of exercise has focused on the reduction of state anxiety. Similar to earlier studies (see Landers & Arent [2001] and Taylor [2001] for reviews), more recent studies showed that aerobic exercise resulted in lowered state anxiety and higher tranquility scores. In addition, research has revealed that moderate-intensity exercise produced the greatest positive effects in affective responses (Arent, Landers, Matt, & Etnier, 2005). Markowitz

and Arent (2010) showed that exercise at or 5% below lactate threshold (the point at which lactate begins to accumulate in the bloodstream faster than it is removed) produces the maximal affective benefit during the task and for 30 minutes after the task. Conversely, exercise above the lactate threshold produces comparable affective improvements only 30 minutes after completing the task and worsens affect while performing the task. Knowledge of what psychological changes to expect for given exercise intensity levels can help individuals choose the most appropriate level of exercise for their continued adherence.

How long does the tranquilizing effect of exercise last? Raglin and Morgan (1987) found that state anxiety was reduced for up to 24 hours (although more typically 2–4 hours) after the exercise bout, whereas participants in a control rest condition returned to baseline levels within 30 minutes. Although acute exercise is no more effective in decreasing state anxiety than quiet rest or distraction, the effects last longer. Specifically, Breus and O'Connor (1998) found that the decreases in state anxiety after exercise lasted

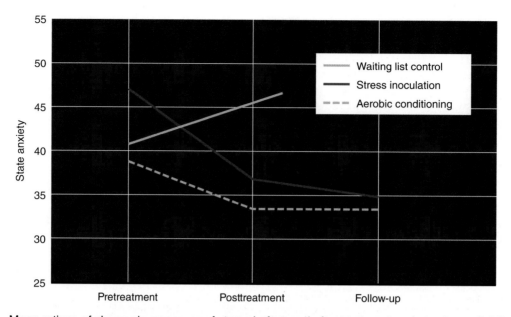

FIGURE 17.1 Mean ratings of change in measures of stress before and after treatment and at a 3-month follow-up.

Adapted, by permission, from B.C. Long, 1984, "Aerobic conditioning and stress inoculation: A comparison of stress-management interventions," *Cognitive Therapy and Research* 8(5): 529.

several hours, which was more than in the distraction and quiet rest groups.

Some literature reviews using the statistical technique called meta-analysis (e.g., Landers & Petruzzello, 1994; Long & Stavel, 1995), as well as narrative reviews (Martinsen & Stephens, 1994; Mutrie & Biddle, 1995), were conducted to determine the relationship between exercise and anxiety reduction. For example,

according to a comprehensive examination of 27 narrative reviews (Landers & Petruzzello, 1994), 81% of studies conducted between 1960 and 1992 concluded that physical activity was related to anxiety reduction after exercise (and the other 19% showed partial support for this conclusion). Reed and Ones (2006), examining 158 studies between 1979 and 2005, found strong results for the ability of even low-intensity exercise to

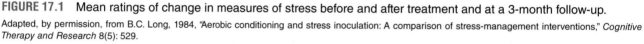

Chronic Exercise and Mental Health

The National Institute of Mental Health convened a panel to discuss the possibilities and limitations of physical activity for coping with stress and depression (Morgan & Goldston, 1987). Although the recommendations regarding the relationship between chronic exercise and mental health have been updated over the years, the basic conclusions remain the same:

- Physical fitness is positively associated with mental health and well-being.
- Exercise is associated with the reduction of stress emotions such as state anxiety.
- Anxiety and depression are common symptoms of failure to cope with mental stress, and exercise has been associated with a decreased level of mild to moderate depression and anxiety.
- Long-term exercise is usually associated with reductions in traits such as neuroticism and anxiety.
- Severe depression usually requires professional treatment, which may include medication, electroconvulsive therapy, psychotherapy, or a combination of these, with exercise as an adjunct.
- Appropriate exercise results in reductions in various stress indicators, such as neuromuscular tension, resting heart rate, and some stress hormones. Current clinical opinion holds that exercise has beneficial emotional effects across ages and sexes.
- Physically healthy people who require psychotropic (mood-altering) medication may safely exercise under close medical supervision.

improve affect. In addition, Wipfli, Rethorst, and Landers (2008) reviewed 49 studies that used randomized control trials (the highest level of scientific evidence). Results revealed greater reductions in anxiety for exercise groups than for groups that received other forms of anxiety-reducing treatment. These reviews (based on hundreds of studies involving thousands of participants) show general consensus about the positive effects (generally moderate) of exercise in reducing both acute and chronic anxiety (not simply attributable to a time-out or rest), including the following additional findings:

- Longer training programs (sessions conducted over weeks rather than hours or days) are more effective than shorter ones in producing positive changes in well-being.

- Reductions in state anxiety and depression after aerobic exercise may be achieved with exercise intensities between 30% and 70% of maximal heart rate (as opposed to earlier research suggesting that one needs to exercise at 70% of the maximal heart rate to achieve psychological benefits). For anaerobic exercise (e.g., weightlifting), mood-enhancing effects appear evident at a lower range (30%–50%) of maximal heart rate.

- Exercise training is particularly effective for individuals who have elevated levels of anxiety, but it reduces anxiety even for people with low levels of anxiety.

- All durations of exercise significantly reduced anxiety, although larger effects were found for periods up to 30 minutes (especially under moderate intensity conditions).

- State anxiety returns to pre-exercise anxiety levels within 24 hours (maybe as quickly as 4–6 hours).

- Exercise is associated with reductions in muscle tension.

- Reductions in anxiety are not necessarily tied to the physiological gains resulting from the exercise bout.

- The anxiety reduction after exercise occurs regardless of the intensity, duration, or type of exercise (although greater effects occurred for aerobic vs. anaerobic activities).

- Aerobic exercise can produce anxiety reductions similar in magnitude to those produced by other commonly used anxiety treatments.

- Anxiety reduction after exercise occurs for all types of participants (e.g., male or female, fit or unfit, active or inactive, anxious or nonanxious, healthy or nonhealthy, younger or older, with or without anxiety disorders).

Exercise in the Reduction of Depression

Depression is a well-documented source of human suffering, and about one in four Americans suffers from clinical depression at any given time. The prevalence of major depression has increased steadily during the past 50 years (Kessler et al., 2003). Depression is especially prevalent in girls and women, who have two (under 25 years old) to six (25–54 years old) times the rate of depression of boys and men (Regier et al., 1988). Finally, depressive disorders are estimated to affect approximately 6% of adolescents. Although most of the time depression is treated through prescription drugs or therapy, a recent Gallup poll identified exercise as a close second behind religion as an effective alternative means of relieving depression. In addition, physical inactivity has been shown to be related to higher levels of depression.

In a study by Blumenthal and colleagues (1999), participants (who were diagnosed as clinically depressed) were randomly assigned to a supervised aerobic exercise program three times per week, a medication treatment (Zoloft), or a combined treatment of medication and exercise. Results revealed that after 16 weeks of intervention, all three groups significantly reduced depressive symptoms; the exercise was as effective as the other two treatments. In another study, exercise was shown to reduce clinical depression; this reduction was attributable predominantly to successful coping self-efficacy (Craft, 2005). A study by Desha, Ziviani, Nixholson, Martin, and Darnell (2007) showed that adolescent males who were not involved in extracurricular organized sporting activities exhibited greater severity of depressive symptoms than males involved in sporting activities, underscoring the importance of sport participation for young males.

In addition, Legrand and Heuze (2007) found that the frequency of exercise might be important in relieving depressive symptoms. Specifically, they found that exercising three to five times per week produced significant reductions in depression compared with exercising once per week. Furthermore, adding a group-based intervention for the group that exercised three to five times per week did not significantly reduce depressive symptoms, underscoring the importance of exercise per se in reducing depression. Finally, a series of studies revealed that physical activity interventions were successful in reducing depression among adolescent boys and girls. These results demonstrate, from a sequencing perspective, that exercise precedes changes in depression.

Consistent agreement about the moderate relationship between exercise and depression is also seen in other studies; these include several narrative (e.g., Martinsen & Stephens, 1994; Mutrie, 2001; Mutrie & Biddle, 1995) and statistical (Craft & Landers, 1998; North, McCullagh, & Tran, 1990) reviews as well as empirical studies (e.g., Dunn, Trivedi, Kampert, Clark, & Chambliss, 2005). Note that the relationships between exercise and depression are correlational: Exercise is associated with, but may not cause, changes in depression. Some of the consistent findings from these reviews of the literature regarding the relationship between exercise and depression are as follows:

- The positive effects are seen across age groups, health status, race, socioeconomic status, and sex.

- Exercise is as effective as psychotherapy in reducing depression.

- Exercise produces larger antidepressant effects when the training program is at least 9 weeks long.

- Both aerobic and anaerobic exercise are associated with reductions in depression.

- Reductions in depression after exercise do not depend on fitness levels.

Although people report feeling better after exercise, approximately 50% of individuals drop out of exercise programs and many more do not exercise at all. So, does exercise actually make us feel better? An article by Backhouse, Ekkekakis, Biddle, Foskett, and Williams (2007) offers some thoughtful alternatives to the well-known "feel better" phenomenon based on empirical data:

- Occasional findings of negative affective changes tend to be discounted.

- Potentially relevant affective states (e.g., unpleasant high activation) are not always measured.

- Examining changes pre- to postexercise could miss negative changes that occur during exercise (i.e., require more measurement points).

- Analyzing changes only at the group level might conceal divergent patterns at the level of individuals or subgroups (i.e., individual differences).

The authors conclude that they were not trying to undermine the "feel better" phenomenon regarding exercise and psychological well-being. Rather, they suggest that the focus should be on the exercise–affect relationship as it bears on the public health problem of exercise adherence rather than on exercise related to mental health.

> **KEY POINT** Mood is generally defined as a state of emotional or affective arousal of varying, impermanent duration.

Mood changes have been studied in a variety of settings, and considerable experiential and anecdotal evidence supports the existence of changes in positive mood states related to exercise (Berger & Tobar, 2011; Biddle, 2000). For example, psychologists and psychiatrists rate exercise as the most effective technique for changing a bad mood; they are more likely to use exercise than other techniques to energize themselves (Thayer, Newman, & McClain, 1994). In addition, various studies have concluded that physical activity is positively related to positive mood, general well-being, and relatively infrequent symptoms of anxiety and depression. Other findings have revealed that exercise is related to decreases in fatigue and anger as well as increases in vigor, clear thinking, energy, and alertness and an increased sense of well-being. Hansen, Stevens, and Coast (2001) showed increases in positive mood states with as little as 10 minutes of moderate exercise, highlighting the notion that short bouts of exercise can produce positive psychological benefits. Frith, Kerr, and Wilson (2011) found that a variety of types of exercise, including weight training aerobics and tai chi, helped improve anger, sullenness, resentment, tension, and anxiety. Furthermore, exercise improved positive mood regardless of the number of negative and positive events in a given day (Giacobbi, Hausenblas, & Frye, 2005). Finally, Daley and Maynard (2003) found that increasing the choice of exercise mode was related to exercisers scoring lower on negative affect. A quote from Sarah Ban Breatnach (1998) makes the point that exercise is related to changes in mood:

" A half hour of walking every other day increases your vitality and energy level and you find yourself less depressed. Suddenly, you become more relaxed and fun to be around. You smile, maybe even laugh. You catch a reflection of yourself in a mirror and you're pleasantly surprised. " (p. 86)

Researchers (Thayer et al., 1994) identified various techniques for altering mood and categorized and evaluated the effectiveness of these methods used by men and women (ranging in age from 16 to 89 years). Mood regulating, they say, has three interrelated components: changing a bad mood, raising one's energy level, and reducing tension. The researchers conclude, "Of all the separate behavioral categories described to self-regulate mood, a case can be made that exercise is the most effective. This behavior was self-rated as the most successful in changing a bad mood, fourth most successful in raising energy, and third most

successful at tension reduction" (p. 921). Although we know that exercise is related to positive changes in mood states (Gauvin, Rejeski, & Reboussin, 2000), little evidence suggests that exercise itself causes the benefits. Perhaps, for example, those who have more desirable ("better") moods simply exercise more often. Along these lines, Carels, Colt, Young, and Berger (2007) found that a positive morning mood was associated with an increased likelihood of exercising and that as positive mood increased throughout the day, exercise initiation and intensity both were increased. So, how you feel also is related to your propensity to exercise, apart from the effect of exercise itself on improving mood. Finally, positive mood changes do not come automatically with exercise. Rather, as noted in "Guidelines for Using Exercise to Enhance Mood," certain types of exercises with certain levels of intensity, duration, and frequency are most likely to produce these positive mood changes.

Guidelines for Using Exercise to Enhance Mood

For an exerciser who wants to achieve positive mood changes (including reduced anxiety and depression), researchers recommend the following procedures and guidelines (Berger & Tobar, 2011; Berger & Motl, 2001).

• *Rhythmic abdominal breathing.* Many investigators have studied the role of aerobic versus anaerobic exercise in producing mood alteration. Although the original research suggested that exercise needs to be aerobic to produce positive psychological benefits, more recent research has shown that either aerobic or anaerobic exercise can be effective. What seems more important is that rhythmic abdominal breathing be generated, as in activities such as hatha yoga, tai chi, walking, running, riding a bicycle ergometer at light workloads, and swimming.

• *Relative absence of interpersonal competition.* Although some people find competition enjoyable, the vast majority of research has found that the absence of competition enhances psychological well-being. Competition can produce overtraining, pressure to win, and social evaluation, whereas in a noncompetitive environment the participants can focus on enjoying the activity itself.

• *Closed and predictable activities.* Closed environments (e.g., golf, swimming) allow participants to plan their movements, and unexpected events are unlikely. These self-paced activities enable participants to tune out the environment and engage in free association while they are exercising.

• *Rhythmic and repetitive movements.* The rhythmicity of repetitive movements such as walking or running encourages introspective or creative thinking, or both, during participation. This focus of attention can free the mind to attend to more important issues.

• *Duration, intensity, frequency.* Research has indicated that exercise should be at least 20 to 30 minutes in duration and of moderate intensity, and that it should be done regularly (two to three times per week).

• *Enjoyment.* Although the characteristics of the exercise are important (as just outlined), probably the most critical component is that the exercise is enjoyable (Berger & Tobar, 2011). Recent research in naturalistic settings (Raedeke, 2007) found that enjoyment was related to increases in positive affect. Thus, unless an activity is enjoyable, it is not likely that individuals will keep exercising over a long period of time (see chapter 18).

Jones and Sheffield (2007) investigated the effects of the outcome of a competition on psychological well-being. University and club sport athletes were assessed 4 to 6 days after a regular-season contest. Results revealed that winners, compared with losers, exhibited lower levels of depression and anger as well as higher levels of vigor. In addition, winners reported fewer somatic symptoms, fewer social dysfunction symptoms, and less anxiety than losers. Evidently, winning or losing (even for regular-season games) stays with athletes for at least several days, and losing could have an adverse effect on motivation levels for subsequent training and competition. Accordingly, coaches and athletes should be aware of affective control strategies for help in controlling negative affect after a loss.

Understanding the Effect of Exercise on Psychological Well-Being

The evidence we've reviewed so far suggests a positive relationship between exercise and psychological well-being (figure 17.2 summarizes the psychological benefits of exercise for adults). The psychological benefits of exercise for children and adolescents are often forgotten, although Biddle (2011b) summarizes these findings. In general, increased exercise is correlated with higher levels of self-efficacy and perceived competence, increased achievement motivation and intention to exercise, higher levels of task goal orientation (self-referenced goals), and lower levels of depression. In addition, the amount of exercise is related to perceived body attractiveness, importance of appearance, and physical self-worth in adolescent girls.

Several hypotheses, both psychological and physiological, have been proposed to explain how exercise enhances well-being. However, no one hypothesis has support as the sole or primary mechanism producing these positive changes. In fact, it is likely that the positive changes in psychological well-being are attributable to an interaction of physiological and psychological mechanisms. Therefore, we simply list the potential physiological and psychological mechanisms that researchers propose may account for the positive effect of exercise on psychological well-being.

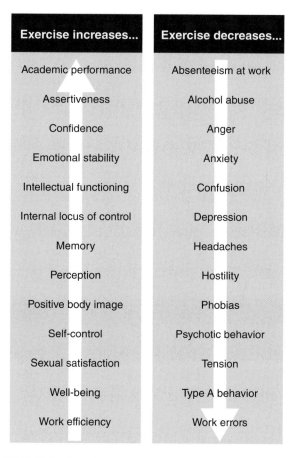

Exercise increases...	Exercise decreases...
Academic performance	Absenteeism at work
Assertiveness	Alcohol abuse
Confidence	Anger
Emotional stability	Anxiety
Intellectual functioning	Confusion
Internal locus of control	Depression
Memory	Headaches
Perception	Hostility
Positive body image	Phobias
Self-control	Psychotic behavior
Sexual satisfaction	Tension
Well-being	Type A behavior
Work efficiency	Work errors

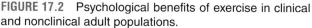

FIGURE 17.2 Psychological benefits of exercise in clinical and nonclinical adult populations.

Adapted from C. Taylor, J. Sallis, and R. Needle, 1985, "The relation of physical activity and exercise to mental health," *Public Health Reports* 100: 195-202.

Physiological Explanations

- Increases in cerebral blood flow
- Changes in brain neurotransmitters (e.g., norepinephrine, endorphins, serotonin)
- Increases in maximal oxygen consumption and delivery of oxygen to cerebral tissues
- Reductions in muscle tension
- Structural changes in the brain
- Increase in serum concentrations of endocannabinoid receptors

Psychological Explanations

- Enhanced feeling of control
- Feeling of competency and self-efficacy
- Positive social interactions
- Improved self-concept and self-esteem
- Opportunities for fun and enjoyment

Changing Personality and Cognitive Functioning With Exercise

In addition to examining the relationships among exercise and anxiety, depression, and mood, researchers have asked whether exercise can change personality and mental (cognitive) functioning. We briefly review the research in these areas and offer some suggestions to practitioners.

Personality

A classic study to determine the effects of a fitness program on middle-aged men led to some information on how exercise might change personality (Ismail & Young, 1973). Over the course of the program, the men improved their fitness levels and reported feeling dramatic psychological effects. They reported higher levels of self-confidence, greater feelings of control, improved imagination, and a greater sense of self-sufficiency. Other studies have since been conducted to investigate the relationship of exercise to various personality factors. In a review of these studies, McDonald and Hodgdon (1991) found that aerobic fitness training increased scores on self-sufficiency and intelligence and decreased scores on insecurity. In addition, studies using clinical populations showed positive changes in various aspects of personality adjustment.

Exercise and Development of the Self

Exercise and physical activity can be related to a participant's self-concept, self-esteem, and self-efficacy (Fox, 1997). These concepts of the self are interrelated yet distinct, although they all refer to how we feel about ourselves and our capabilities. Self-concept incorporates all aspects of what we think we are: It is central to our conscious lives. Thus, many people consider self-concept the most important measure of psychological well-being.

KEY POINT Regular exercise has been shown to be related to increased self-esteem.

It is commonly believed that bodily changes that result from physical fitness training can alter one's body image and thus enhance self-concept and self-esteem. In reviewing the research literature, Sonstroem and Morgan (1989) found that exercise programs are associated with significant increases in self-esteem and that increases are especially pronounced among individuals who were initially lower in self-esteem. Sonstroem (1997a,b) qualified his earlier observations, saying that the increases in self-esteem seen after exercise may result from perceptions of improvement or other program factors (either biological or psychological) rather than from fitness improvement itself. In addition, positive changes in self-esteem have been found more recently in normal populations such as adult females, college students, obese teenage males, seventh-grade males, elementary school children, sedentary adolescent females, and adult male rehabilitation clients as well as in individuals who initially had low self-esteem—although individuals lower in fitness or ability also demonstrated significant positive changes in self-esteem.

According to the latest studies, changes in self-esteem have been maintained over a period of at least 1 year. For example, a study of middle-aged and older women (Hardcastle & Taylor, 2005) found that exercise over time was related to changes in self-identity as participants noted changes in feelings of achievement, sense of belonging, and social interactions as well as changes in actual self-cognitions. In addition, a longitudinal study of older adults (at least 60 years old) found that both a traditional exercise program and a lifestyle physical activity program (incorporating physical activity into daily living and working out at home) improved self-esteem as well as feelings of competence and physical self-worth (Opdenacker, Delecluse, & Boen, 2009).

Another study testing Sonstroem's self-esteem model found that for women, physical acceptance (how the women regarded their own bodies) was an important predictor of self-esteem (Levy & Ebbeck, 2005). In another study, Elavsky (2010) longitudinally followed middle-aged women (aged 42–58 years) for a 2-year period. (Few studies have followed the same group of exercisers this long.) This age group of women is especially significant because the North American Menopause Society advocates lifestyle changes such as physical activity as the first line of defense against the adverse symptoms of menopause. Healthy self-esteem is an essential component of mental health, and women who report low self-esteem also report more menopausal distress and poorer quality of life (Elavsky, 2009). Along these lines, results indicated that the effects of physical activity on changes in physical self-worth and global

Exercise for Enhancing Well-Being in Special Cases

Research has begun to study the relationship between exercise and different chronic diseases. The goal has been to determine whether some form of exercise will help reduce symptoms of different diseases and thus enhance quality of life for these individuals. The following is a sample of some of the diseases that have been investigated in relation to the effects of exercise.

Human Immunodeficiency Virus

One of the deadliest diseases that has recently appeared on the scene is acquired immunodeficiency syndrome (AIDS), which is usually preceded by human immunodeficiency virus (HIV-1). Since the first reported cases of HIV-1 infection in 1981, the number of individuals contracting the disease has grown exponentially, as has the number of deaths. Enhancing perceptions of well-being is particularly relevant for persons with HIV-1 and AIDS because perceived control over physical health is a primary concern for these groups. If individuals with HIV-1 and AIDS feel some sense of control over their psychological health and well-being, this may profoundly affect how they cope with the disease.

In one study (Lox, McAuley, & Tucker, 1995), individuals with HIV-1 were randomly assigned to an aerobic training group, a resistance weight-training group, or a stretching flexibility control group. Results revealed that both the aerobic and weight-training exercise groups (compared with the control group) had enhanced physical self-efficacy, improved moods, and higher satisfaction in life. In a more recent 16-week intervention study, Rojas, Schlicht, and Hautinger (2003) found that the exercise group had significant improvements in cardiopulmonary fitness and health-related quality of life compared with the control group. The authors suggest that moderate exercise may enhance health-related quality of life in individuals with HIV-1 and should therefore be considered a complementary therapy for these individuals.

Multiple Sclerosis

Multiple sclerosis (MS) is another disease for which no known cure exists. It is characterized pathologically by inflammatory lesions that disseminate in separate parts of the white matter of the brain and spinal cord. Although new drug therapies have become available recently, no pharmacological therapies clearly arrest the progression of the primary neurological deficits in the long term (Johnson, 1996). Thus, individuals' quality of life is often compromised by the symptoms of MS.

Because one of the main symptoms of MS is chronic fatigue, many people with MS avoid regular exercise. But given the many positive benefits of exercise, some believe that leading a relatively sedentary life may in fact exacerbate the debilitating effects of MS. Thus, Sutherland, Andersen, and Stoove (2001) investigated whether regular physical activity (in this case, water aerobics) could enhance the quality of life of people with MS. After a 10-week program, results revealed that the exercise group (compared with the control group) exhibited higher levels of energy and vigor and had better social and sexual functioning and less pain and fatigue. More recently, Motl and McAuley (2009) found that changes in physical activity levels were related to positive changes in quality of life over 6 months. These changes included less pain and fatigue along with higher levels of social supports and self-efficacy. Motl, Gappmaeir, Nelson, and Benedict (2011) found that physical activity was positively related to cognitive processing speed in people with MS. Finally, in a review of the literature, Stork, Stapelton, and Martin-Ginis (2013) found that social support increases the likelihood that people with MS actually exercise. This is important because physical activity is related to positive changes in people with MS.

Cancer

A review of 47 studies investigated the effects of exercise on quality of life of survivors of breast cancer and other cancers (Courneya, 2003, 2005). Results revealed that exercise was beneficial

self-esteem were mediated by changes in self-perceptions related to physical condition and body attractiveness. Thus, women can enhance their self-esteem and how they perceive their physical condition and body attractiveness through continued participation in physical activity.

A thorough review of literature involving 113 studies found that regular exercise brought a consis-

in both breast cancer and nonbreast cancer groups as well as during and after cancer treatment. It is also becoming more common for people to survive cancer. In fact, the 5-year survival rate for all cancers is 62%; this increases to 90% for some of the more common cancers (e.g., prostate, breast, and colon) if they are detected early. Thus, exercise appears to offer a viable mechanism for enhancing quality of life in this population (Culos-Reed, Robinson, Lau, O'Connor, & Keats, 2007; Rabin, Pinto, & Frierson, 2006). In addition, a recent study suggests that physical activity in breast cancer survivors can be predicted by increased autonomy and competence within self-determination theory (Milne, Wallman, Guilfoyle, Gordon, & Courneya, 2008). Mutrie, Kirk, and Hughes (2011) and Ferrer, Huedo-Medina, Johnson, Ryan, and Pescatello (2011) provide meta-analysis and review of studies linking exercise to the quality of life in cancer survivors.

Parkinson's Disease

Although no empirical studies have been conducted to date, there have been increasing anecdotal reports regarding the effect of Pilates (a popular exercise program that focuses on increasing core strength and improving flexibility and balance) on improving Parkinson's disease (a degenerative disease that inhibits a person's ability to control movement, as seen in tremors, slowness of movement, rigidity, and balance problems). Special Pilates classes for people with Parkinson's disease have started to spring up around the country. Although empirical testing is needed, many positive quotes have been heard, such as this one by a person diagnosed with Parkinson's disease 17 years earlier: "Now I realized how stiff and boxed up I was."

Diabetes

The psychological effects of facing a lifetime of dealing with diabetes and its effect on emotional and social adjustments, including lower quality of life and well-being, are well documented by health psychologists (Mutrie, Kirk, & Hughes, 2011). Regular physical activity has been recommended for individuals suffering from diabetes, and specific guidelines have been provided (Diabetes Prevention Program Research Group, 2002; Kirk, Barnett, & Mutrie, 2007). Several studies have shown that regular supervised physical activity (both individual and group) is associated with higher quality of life and overall better psychological functioning for individuals with either type 1 (insulin-resistant) or type 2 (non-insulin-resistant) diabetes (Kirk et al., 2007). Unfortunately, about 55% of adults with diabetes do not exercise at all. This underscores the importance of educating those with diabetes about the importance of exercise and strategies for starting and adhering to exercise programs (Durstine, Gordon, Wang, & Luo, 2013).

Coronary Heart Disease

Cardiac rehabilitation is an essential component in the treatment of individuals with coronary heart disease. Although meta-analyses of cardiac rehabilitation studies conducted on people with coronary heart disease have shown significant reductions (22%–31%) in total and cardiac mortality (Durstine et al., 2013; Taylor et al., 2004), psychological benefits have also been found. For example, several systematic reviews have shown that cardiac rehabilitation results in reductions in symptoms of anxiety and depression and increases in quality of life (McGhee, Hevey, & Horghan, 1999; Milani & Lavie, 2007). Individuals who are depressed (15%–45% of people are depressed after a cardiac event occurs) report poorer quality of life and more cardiac symptoms and are less likely to adhere to medical treatment and lifestyle changes than are people who are not depressed (Turner, Bethell, Evane, Goddard, & Mullee, 2002). Therefore, cardiac rehabilitation through exercise has very positive benefits on the psychological states of patients with coronary heart disease.

tent (although small) positive change in individuals' self-esteem. This relationship was enhanced for individuals displaying large increases in physical fitness (Schneider, Dunton, & Cooper, 2008) and those involved in exercise programs as compared with skills training (Spence, McGannon, & Poon, 2005). Another review of the literature involving 57 interventions found that the exercise interventions improved

Regular exercise can help increase children's self-esteem, which may lead to better grades in school.

participants' body image (Campbell & Hausenblas, 2009). In summary, exercise has clearly and consistently been linked to positive psychological changes in self-esteem, self-concept, and body image, which are critical for effective psychological functioning.

In a review of children's programs, Gruber (1986) discovered that positive changes in self-concept and self-esteem were associated with participation in directed play and physical education programs. Physical fitness activities were also found to be superior to other components of elementary school physical education programs in developing self-concept. In an interesting study with elementary and middle school children in Sweden, Ericsson and Karlsson (2011) found that increasing physical activity and motor skill training (especially for children with deficits in motor skills) increased motor skills as well as several aspects of self-esteem.

Despite these positive findings, other research studies have *not* found positive relationships between exercise and self-concept. Perhaps this relationship varies according to exercise mode or a host of environmental conditions. In essence, self-concept is multidimensional, and certain aspects of self-concept (e.g., physical) might be more affected by exercise than others (e.g., social; Fox, 1997; Marsh, 1997). For example, physical self-concept has been shown to include a variety of factors such as sport competence, physical condition, body attractiveness, and physical strength, and the factor of physical condition is particularly influenced by physical activity (Fox, 1997).

A strong self-concept is critical to the healthy psychological development and adjustment of children, and exercise can be an important ingredient in helping children and adults feel good about themselves. In fact, Taylor and Fox (2005) found positive effects of exercise on physical self-perceptions and self-worth up to 40 weeks after the exercise program (10 weeks) had finished. Another study found that even though participants had no change in body shape or weight, they displayed an increase in body image after six 40-minute exercise bouts (Appleton, 2013). Berger (1996) proposed that exercise programs designed to enhance self-esteem and self-concept should emphasize experiences of success, feelings of increased physical competence, and attainment of goals. Whaley and Shrider (2005) found that enhancing positive self-perceptions in older adults focusing on hoped-for selves (e.g., remaining healthy and independent) as opposed to feared selves (e.g., avoiding dependence and negative health outcomes) produced higher levels of exercise and adherence.

Exercise and Hardiness

Hardiness is a personality style that enables a person to withstand or cope with stressful situations. Stress produces minimal debilitating effects in a hardy personality. You are hardy if you have these three traits (Gentry & Kosaba, 1979):

- A sense of personal control over external events
- A sense of involvement, commitment, and purpose in daily life
- The flexibility to adapt to unexpected changes by perceiving them as challenges or opportunities for further growth

KEY POINT Exercise can help protect against stress-related illness, especially for hardy people.

Some research has focused on how exercise in combination with hardiness can reduce some of the negative effects of stress. One study showed that business executives who scored high in both hardiness and exercise remained healthier than those who scored high in only one or the other component. Another study indicated that exercise combined with social support resulted in the least amount of illness in individuals with hardy personalities (Kosaba, Maddi, Puccetti, & Zola, 1985). In essence, a hardy personality and exercise in combination are more effective in preserving health than either one alone.

Cognitive Functioning

For a long time we have assumed that motor development is important to the development of intelligence in children (Piaget, 1936) and that learning potential (cognitive capacity) varies with a person's physical fitness level. Since the 1970s, researchers have looked for evidence that would validate these two assumptions. Neuroscientists, psychologists, and physicians rarely agree unequivocally on anything, but they do seem to agree that exercising is the best thing you can do for your brain. The latest research shows that cognitive decline is not inevitable. Yes, brain volume shrinks slightly, but the brain continues to make new neurons and fine-tune neural connections throughout the life span. Aerobic exercise appears to jump-start this process and thus reduces the level of brain loss and keeps cognitive abilities sharp. This is seen in the fact that regular aerobic exercise slashes one's lifetime risk of Alzheimer's in half and one's risk of general dementia by 60%.

The research findings have become more and more consistent, demonstrating that a strong relationship exists between exercise and cognitive functioning. Narrative reviews, for example, have generally demonstrated the beneficial effect of exercise on cognitive functioning (Chodzko-Zajko & Moore, 1994). Statistical reviews of more than 100 studies (Etnier et al., 1997; Thomas, Landers, Salazar, & Etnier, 1994) showed that exercise had a modest positive relationship with improved cognitive functioning. Chang and colleagues (2011) found that acute aerobic exercise was related to increased executive cognitive functioning in the areas of planning and problem solving, and

Alves and colleagues (2012) found positive effects for both aerobic and strength activities. Similarly, a multidisciplinary review of the literature found that aerobic physical activity has a positive effect on cognition and brain function (Hillman, Erickson, & Kramer, 2008). Specifically, it appears that executive central command, which includes working memory, planning, scheduling, multitasking, and dealing with ambiguity (e.g., doubt and uncertainty), are most affected by aerobic exercise. Furthermore, chronic exercise, in comparison with acute exercise, showed greater effects on cognitive performance; that is, exercise programs conducted over longer periods of time are associated with gains in cognitive functioning.

Sibley and Beilock (2007) found that acute exercise increased cognitive functioning in the form of working memory (short-term memory involved in the attentional control, regulation, and active maintenance of a limited amount of information with immediate relevance to the task at hand) only for individuals low in working memory. This underscores the individual-difference nature of the effects of exercise on cognitive functioning. The same can be said about executive control (higher-level functions that manage other more basic cognitive processes where individual differences again appear important) (Etnier & Chang, 2009). For example, the planning aspect of executive functioning seemed to be positively influenced by physical activity (Davis et al., 2007).

Moderate to vigorous physical activity has been shown to enhance executive functioning even in children with attention deficit/hyperactivity disorder (Gapin & Etnier, 2010). In addition, in a study by Vazou and colleagues (2012), 10 minutes of physical activity was integrated into six consecutive traditional lessons over a 2-week period. This integration produced increases in children's intrinsic motivation, perceived competence, and effort without enhancing perceptions of pressure or negatively affecting the value of the academic lesson being taught. Furthermore, the effects of exercise on cognitive functioning appear to be mediated by task type. Specifically, moderate-intensity exercise is related to increased performance of executive functioning (e.g., working memory, attentional flexibility), whereas high-intensity exercise improves speed of information processing (Chang & Etnier, 2009). The notion that exercise can improve cognitive functioning has been extended to children (especially those who are overweight). In a study by Davis and colleagues (2011), 3 months of aerobic exercise improved cognitive functioning as well as math achievement. A dose–response relationship was also observed, meaning that more physical activity led to greater improvements in cognitive functioning. To support this increased cognitive functioning, increased prefrontal cortex activity and reduced posterior parietal cortex activity in the brain were also found.

Finally, reviews of the literature on the relationship between cardiovascular fitness and cognitive functioning in older adults (Colcombe & Kramer, 2002; McAuley, Kramer, & Colcombe, 2004) have revealed some interesting findings, including the following:

- Fitness training had beneficial effects on the cognitive functioning of older adults. These effects were largest for tasks involving executive control (e.g., planning, scheduling, working memory, task coordination).

- Fitness training combined with strength and flexibility programs had a greater positive effect on cognition than did fitness training with only an aerobic component. These effects appear to occur more in females than in males.

- Exercise effects on cognition were largest when exercise training exceeded 30 minutes per session.

- Cardiovascular exercise appears to protect the brain against the normal effects of aging and help repair or restore the aged brain.

Enhancing Quality of Life With Exercise

Researchers have also been investigating the more global question of how regular exercise affects our

---

Transitions Out of Sport: Relationship to Psychological Well-Being

Although this chapter focuses on the influence of exercise on psychological well-being, many highly competitive athletes confront psychological issues when they transition out of sport. Much has been written and many models have been developed regarding the psychological issues that occur when transitioning out of competitive sport (Alferman & Stambulova, 2007; Lavalle, Park, & Tod, 2013; Stambulova, Alfermann, Statler, & Cote, 2009). When athletes freely choose to retire and plan for it, leaving sport can add to their psychological well-being because they spend more time with their families, don't have the stresses of winning or losing, and have more time to pursue their hobbies.

However, leaving competitive sport is often not under an athlete's control. The two most prevalent reasons for forced retirement are being deselected (cut) from a team due to a decrease in performance or being injured and unable to perform at the normal level. Other reasons for involuntary retirement include drug use, gambling or other infractions of league policy, lockouts, financial issues, family problems, or boycotts. Retirement under these conditions often produces strong emotional reactions (e.g., anxiety, depression) and high levels of life dissatisfaction, which are seen in about 20% of athletes who retire. Petitpas, Tinsley, and Walker (2012) note a number reasons for these negative reactions, including the following:

- Bitterness of being forced to retire
- Loss of camaraderie with teammates and relationships with coaches
- Loss of self-identity because their identities have been closely tied to their sport
- Lack of confidence in their abilities to cope effectively with everyday life situations
- Loss of adulation from fans
- Inability to replace the excitement of the sport experience with anything else

Traditional stress management and cognitive–behavioral interventions have been used to help athletes with these negative reactions to retirement. Additionally, a program called the Life Development Intervention has been shown to help athletes cope with career transitions (Danish, Petitpas, & Hale, 1995; Lavalle, 2005). The Life Development Intervention provides useful strategies to use before an event (e.g., retirement), supportive strategies to use during an event, and counseling strategies to use after an event. Athletes are taught life skills to help them make decisions about retirement, coping skills, and goal-setting skills that can transfer to other areas of life.

quality of life (Berger & Tobar, 2011; Berger & Motl, 2001; Shepard, 1996). The nebulous phrase **quality of life** has been defined as "individuals' perception of their position in life in the context of the culture and value systems in which they live and in relation to their goals, expectations, standards, and concerns" (World Health Organization Group, 1995, p. 1405). Quality of life emphasizes the spirit, rather than objective conditions of life and affluence (Mroczek & Kolarz, 1998), and has been seen as the perceived degree to which individuals are able to satisfy psychophysiological needs. Quality of life has been investigated in the workplace, and it has been found that a regular exercise program can enhance employees' feelings of life satisfaction, job satisfaction, and self-worth (Thogersen-Ntoumani, Fox, & Ntoumanis, 2005). Quality of sleep has also been shown to be important in quality of life (Brassington & Goode, 2013; Sadeh, Keinan, & Daon, 2004). In general, the positive effects of physical activity on quality of life can be grouped into four categories (Berger, 2009): enhanced physical functioning; subjective well-being, as indicated by personal enjoyment and mood alteration; experiencing peak moments such as peak experiences; and personal meaning.

This is what research can already tell us about the relationship between exercise and quality of life (see Berger & Tobar [2011] and Diener & Suh [1999] for a complete discussion):

- Physically active individuals tend to be in better health, report more stamina, have more positive attitudes toward work, and report a greater ability to cope with stress and tension than people who are not physically active.
- Exercise produces small increases in total sleep time, although it has no effect on how long it takes to fall asleep.
- College students participating in an endurance conditioning program reported significantly higher quality of life than did nonexercisers.
- Older adults who are physically active report greater life satisfaction—attributable to less dependence on others—and better overall physical health than those who are not physically active.
- Sociodemographic variables such as income, education, marital status, and age are not significantly related to perceptions of quality of life.

- Exercise programs contribute to a person's quality of life by influencing affect, perceived stress, physical health, and life satisfaction.

Although exercise can have negative effects (e.g., fatigue, overuse injuries, decreased energy) on the quality of life if the individual habitually overtrains, exercise for the most part is linked to a variety of indexes that all relate to quality of life. These include the following:

- Increased levels of self-esteem and self-concept
- Increased feelings of enjoyment
- Decreased feelings of physiological and psychological stress
- Increased feelings of self-confidence
- Elevated mood states
- Decreased levels of anxiety and depression

Examining the Runner's High

Many regular exercisers report feeling better psychologically, emotionally, and spiritually after exercising. This phenomenon is so pervasive among runners (in fact, among runners who have previously experienced the phenomenon, up to 30% experience it on their daily runs) that it has been termed the runner's high. The **runner's high** includes a sense of mental alertness and awareness; a feeling of liberation; a lift in the legs; suppressed pain or discomfort; and the sense of ease, perfect rhythm, and exhilaration.

Definition of the Runner's High

Sachs (1984) and Berger (1996) found 27 words or phrases used in the literature to characterize the runner's high, including *euphoria, spirituality, power, gracefulness, effortless movement, a glimpse of perfection,* and *spinning out.* Sachs and Berger consolidated these to define the runner's high as a euphoric sensation felt during running, usually unexpected, in which the runner feels a heightened sense of well-being, an enhanced appreciation of nature, and a transcendence of time and space. This definition recalls aspects of peak performance and especially of flow (Jackson & Csikszentmihalyi, 1999; see chapter 6) in that the runner's high requires rhythmic, long-lasting, and uninterrupted activity, which is similar to tasks where flow is achieved.

To See or Not to See: Questioning the Effect of Mirrors

With increasingly fast-paced lifestyles, concomitant stress, and a rise in obesity, there has been an increased emphasis on creating more positive feelings and mood during exercise. Along these lines, the American College of Sports Medicine has suggested that all exercise classrooms should have mirrors on at least two of their four walls (American College of Sports Medicine, 1997). Although these guidelines may aid exercisers in improving their form and maximizing the physical benefits of workouts, it appears that the presence of mirrors may have some negative consequences, including less positive and more negative affect.

To test this proposition, Martin Ginis, Jung, and Gauvin (2003) had college-aged sedentary women exercise moderately on a stationary bicycle in front of either a mirror or a nonmirrored wall for a 20-minute period. Results after just one bout of exercise revealed that regardless of body image, women in the mirrored condition felt worse after exercising than women in the unmirrored condition. However, another recent study (Lamarche, Gammage, & Strong, 2009) found that mirrors did not have a negative effect on social physique anxiety, although these women were generally more active and confident in their ability to exercise than were women in the previous study.

What does this all mean from a practical point of view? Specifically, a review of the literature (Fejfar & Hoyle, 2000) found that women, in particular, have an increased sensitivity and self-awareness when looking into a mirror because this heightens focus on the self and the potential discrepancy between the actual and the ideal self. Thus, in an exercise class with mirrors, women tend to focus more often on their own physique and this appears to increase negative affect because it heightens the perceived discrepancy between the actual and the ideal physique. But this seems to occur only if women are generally sedentary and have poor perceptions of self. Therefore, the recommended practice of placing mirrors in exercise centers might be dependent on the particular women who are exercising, which emphasizes an individual-difference approach.

KEY POINT The runner's high is a euphoric sensation, usually unexpected, of heightened well-being, an enhanced appreciation of nature, and the transcendence of time and space.

Characteristics of the Runner's High

In a qualitative study, Sachs (1980) interviewed 60 runners to discover what conditions (internal to the runner and external in the environment) facilitate the runner's high. Although there were individual differences in how often runners achieved this high, the participants told him that the runner's high cannot be reliably predicted but is facilitated by the presence of few distractions and cool, calm weather with low humidity. It requires long distances (6 or more miles) and at least 30 minutes of running at a comfortable pace—although there must be no concern with pace or time. The runners described the mood as a very positive psychological state with feelings of well-being, euphoria, relaxation, and effortlessness.

Here's a personal example of the runner's high:

" [With] my first step I felt lighter and looser than ever before. My shirt clung to me, and I felt like a skeleton flying down a wind tunnel. My times at the mile were so fast that I almost felt like I was cheating. It was like getting a new body that no one else had heard about. My mind was so crystal clear that I could have held a conversation. The only sensation was the rhythm and the beat, all perfectly natural, all and everything part of everything else . . . . Distance, time, motion were all one. There were myself, the cement, a vague feeling of legs, and the coming dusk. I tore on. I could have run and run. Perhaps I had experienced a physiological change, but whatever, it was magic. I came to the side of the road and cried tears of joy and sorrow. Joy for being alive; sorrow for a vague feeling of temporalness, and a knowledge of the impossibility of giving this experience to anyone. "

—Mike Spino, 1971 (p. 222)

 VIEW Activity 17.1 assesses how exercise affects you psychologically.

Some preliminary results out of Germany provide initial evidence that a chemical change in the brain is related to the runner's high. Specifically, long-distance runners took a positron emission tomography scan before and after a 2-hour run. Data revealed that endorphins (the brain's naturally occurring opiates) were produced during running and that they attached themselves to areas of the brain associated with endorphins—in particular, the limbic and prefrontal areas. These areas are activated when people are involved in romantic love or are listening to music that gives them a sense of euphoria. The greater the euphoria reported by runners, the higher the levels of endorphins found in the brain. Thus, after many years of speculation, there now appears to be initial evidence of a biochemical explanation for the feeling of euphoria reported by many long-distance runners.

Using Exercise as an Adjunct to Therapy

As noted earlier, millions of Americans have some sort of depression or anxiety disorder every year. Research has demonstrated that exercise can help reduce such negative psychological states and that aerobic exercise is related to enhanced self-esteem, improved mood, and higher levels of work productivity. Not surprisingly, the use of physical interventions, including some form of exercise, has received increased attention since the late 1970s (Folkins & Sime, 1981; Griest, Klein, Eischens, & Faris, 1978), and some physicians and mental health professionals now routinely recommend exercise for their patients (Hays, 2002, 2009). It's interesting that more psychologists don't use exercise as part of their interventions given the wealth of data on the immediate "feel good" effects of exercise. It usually takes time to show physical benefits of exercise (e.g., weight loss, lower cholesterol), but the positive effects of exercise on mood can be felt immediately. It would take more time for exercise to alleviate mood disorders such as anxiety and depression, of course, but people can at least begin to feel better right away, which may encourage them to exercise in the long run (Weir, 2011).

Exercise therapy has long been known to produce physiological benefits in a broad variety of rehabilitation settings, but its benefits for mental health and psychological well-being are only more recently being discovered. For example, because depression has been shown to be a predictor of future heart attacks in cardiac patients, exercise that reduces depression would be extremely beneficial in this population. Researchers (Tennant et al., 1994) have shown that exercise

in cardiac rehabilitation in fact decreased anger and hostility, depression, anxiety, and emotional disturbances. Large-scale epidemiological studies have also indicated that regular exercise programs are related to positive mental health, especially for more at-risk populations (e.g., Weyerer, 1992), and experimental studies using exercise with institutionalized patients have shown improvements in mood and affect and decreases in depression (Martinsen, 1993). Therefore, there appears to be ample evidence supporting the use of exercise to improve psychological well-being in clinical and other special populations.

Of all the aerobic activities shown to enhance psychological well-being, running has received the most attention in both the professional and popular literature. Running provides a natural, practical, inexpensive, and time-efficient adjunct to traditional psychotherapies (Long & Stavel, 1995). For example, one classic study demonstrated that running was four times more cost effective than more traditional verbal-oriented psychotherapies for treating depression (Griest et al., 1978). Running as an adjunct to therapy takes on added importance because of the high cost of health care and the trend toward cost-effective counseling. Running therapies add health benefits such as increased respiratory efficiency and cardiovascular endurance, and they improve muscle tone, weight control, and blood volume. Running as part of therapy can encourage a positive approach to health promotion as clients learn a healthier style of living through exercise.

> **KEY POINT** Running can be an inexpensive, time-efficient adjunct to traditional psychotherapies, and it offers added health benefits such as increased cardiovascular efficiency and weight control.

Despite its psychological benefits, exercise should not be used in all cases of depression, stress, or other emotional disorders. For example, aerobic exercise therapy should not be prescribed for people who are obese (40% or more over ideal body weight), those with severe heart disease, or those with high blood pressure that cannot be controlled by medication. Exercise may also be contraindicated for people who are severely depressed and for those who have tenuous contact with reality or suicidal tendencies. Another caution is that for exercise to be effective, people must adhere to the program; dropout rates from regular exercise programs are approximately 50% (see chapter 18). Therefore, special care must be taken to support individuals who incorporate exercise as part of therapy.

Guidelines for Using Exercise as Therapy

- Explore the client's exercise history (good and bad experiences).
- Provide a precise diagnosis of the psychological problem.
- Use an individualized exercise prescription for duration, intensity, and frequency of exercise.
- Evaluate the influence of family and friends (to facilitate support).
- Develop a plan for any lack of adherence and irregular patterns of exercise.
- Make exercise practical and functional (e.g., bicycling to work, doing hard physical work).
- Encourage exercise as an *adjunct* to other forms of therapy. A multimodal therapeutic approach is more effective than the use of a single intervention.
- Include a variety of activities, which enhances adherence to the exercise regimen.
- Ensure that exercise therapy is done only by qualified professionals. Although no exact criteria have been established, it is suggested that formal training and practical experience in both the psychological and sport sciences are necessary because exercise therapy takes a multidisciplinary approach to treatment.

LEARNING AIDS

SUMMARY

1. **Explain the effects of exercise on anxiety and depression.**

   Many people have problems attributable to depression and anxiety, and exercise has been shown to be related to reductions in these negative emotional states. Both the acute and chronic effects of exercise have been studied, and reductions in anxiety and depression are maximized with regular exercise of moderate intensity that is 20 to 30 minutes in duration, aerobic in nature, and enjoyable. However, the relationship between exercise and psychological well-being is correlational rather than causal.

2. **Describe the relationship between exercise and mood states.**

   Regular exercise has been shown to be related to changes in mood states, such as decreases in fatigue and anger and increases in vigor, alertness, and energy. These positive changes are maximized with low-intensity exercise, which can be either aerobic or anaerobic.

3. **Discuss the effects of exercise on psychological well-being.**

   Research has revealed a positive relationship between exercise and psychological well-being. These positive effects have been explained by both psychological (e.g., feelings of competency and a sense of control) and physiological (e.g., reductions in muscle tension, increases in cerebral blood flow) mechanisms.

4. **Describe the relationship among exercise, personality changes, and cognitive functioning.**

   Physical activity has been shown to be positively related to changes in personality and cognitive functioning. Changes in personality (e.g., increased self-confidence) and intelligence, as well as changes in cognitive functioning (e.g., attentional control), have been linked to increases in exercise.

5. **Discuss the runner's high.**

   Many exercisers report feeling psychologically, emotionally, and spiritually better after exercise. This phenomenon is particularly pervasive among runners; thus it has been termed the runner's high. The feelings associated with the runner's high include a sense of mental alertness, liberation, a lift in the legs, suppressed pain or discomfort, ease, and exhilaration. These feelings occur only after the person has run a considerable distance (usually at least 6 miles) at a comfortable pace.

6. **Discuss the use of exercise as an adjunct to therapy.**

   Exercise has been demonstrated to be a useful adjunct to traditional psychotherapy, but does not replace therapy (especially in patients who have a clinical disorder). Running therapies have been particularly popular because they provide a natural, practical, inexpensive, and time-efficient adjunct to traditional psychotherapies. It should be noted that exercise therapy should not be used for people who are obese, those with severe heart disease, or those with high blood pressure that cannot be controlled by medication.

KEY TERMS

acute effects	depression	quality of life
chronic effects	hardiness	runner's high

REVIEW QUESTIONS

1. Discuss the research findings concerning the acute and chronic effects of exercise on anxiety and depression.

2. Discuss the research findings regarding the relationship between exercise and changes in mood, personality, and cognitive functioning.

3. List three plausible physiological and three plausible psychological explanations for the ability of exercise to enhance psychological well-being.

4. What guidelines should you remember in using exercise as an adjunct to other types of therapy?

5. Discuss how exercise might be related to the quality of life in patients with HIV-1, multiple sclerosis, cancer, diabetes, chronic heart disease, or Parkinson's disease.

6. How does having a mirror in an exercise room affect one's mood (especially females)? What implications does this have for practice?

7. Does running produce changes in the brain due to the release of endorphins? Discuss this issue and provide evidence to support your argument.

8. Discuss the question, "If people feel good after exercising, why do so many people not exercise at all?"

9. Discuss the studies investigating the cognitive effects of exercise on children with attention deficit/hyperactivity disorder as well as those who are overweight.

10. Describe the psychological issues many athletes cope with when they transition out of sport.

CRITICAL THINKING QUESTIONS

1. You have been asked to contribute to the surgeon general's report on the relationship between exercise and psychological well-being. What key points would you include based on the empirical research in this area? What guidelines would you suggest for maximizing the effectiveness of exercise in enhancing psychological well-being?

2. You are an administrator in a YMCA program or fitness club and have learned that many participants are dropping out of your exercise programs. You believe that one way to get people to return is through emphasizing the positive feelings that are often associated with exercise. What would you advise your exercise leaders to do to adjust the structure of their programs so they might maximize the effects of exercise on psychological well-being?

18

Exercise Behavior and Adherence

After reading this chapter, you should be able to

1. discuss why people do or do not exercise,
2. explain the different models of exercise behavior,
3. describe the determinants of exercise adherence,
4. identify strategies for increasing exercise adherence, and
5. give guidelines for improving exercise adherence.

Lots of people appear to be exercising in an attempt to stay young and to improve the quality of their life. In addition, judging from the looks of store windows, we're in the midst of a fitness craze. Most department stores carry a wide variety of athletic sportswear, not only for physical activity but also for leisure and even work. More and more fitness clubs appear to be opening up as people try to get or stay in shape. However, the fact is that most Americans do not regularly participate in physical activity (U.S. Department of Health and Human Services, 1996, 1999).

Let's look at some statistics to get a better idea of the level of exercise participation. These data are drawn from a variety of sources representing extensive surveys in many of the industrialized countries (e.g., Canadian Fitness and Lifestyle Research Institute, 1996; Centers for Disease Control and Prevention, 2011; Gauvin, Levesque, & Richard, 2001; Health Survey for England, 2009; Higgins, 2004; King et al., 2000; Sallis & Owen, 1999; U.S. Department of

Health and Human Services, 1999, 2000; Vainio & Biachini, 2002; Weir, 2012):

- Physical activity rates in the United States are similar to those in other industrialized nations. Only 10% to 25% of American adults are active enough to maintain or increase cardiorespiratory and muscular fitness levels.

- Among American adults, 19.8% (40 million) were considered obese in 2000 compared with 12% in 1991.

- Among Americans, 66% were seen as overweight or obese in 2005. From 2000 to 2005, obesity increased by 24% and the percentage of super obese increased by 75%.

- In 2013, two thirds of all U.S. adults were overweight and one third was obese.

- In 1990, no state had an obesity rate greater than 19%. By 2010, no state had an obesity rate less than 20%.

- Severe obesity is increasing at a much faster rate than moderate obesity, quadrupling from 1986 to 2000.
- The propensity to be overweight increases with age, as 44% of people aged 18 to 29 and 77% of people aged 46 to 64 were overweight in 2005.
- Among youths aged 12 to 21 years, 50% do not participate in physical activity regularly.
- Among adults, only 10% to 15% participate in vigorous exercise regularly (three times a week for at least 20 minutes).
- Of sedentary adults, only 10% are likely to begin a program of regular exercise within a year.
- Among both boys and girls, physical activity declines steadily through adolescence from about 70% at age 12 to 30% to 40% by age 21.
- In England, only approximately 32% of boys and 24% of girls aged 2 to 15 achieve the recommended levels of physical activity.
- Of people who start an exercise program, 50% will drop out within 6 months.

The Centers for Disease Control and Prevention (2010) has provided information on physical activity patterns using revised definitions for minimum levels of physical activity. Some findings for 2008 include the following:

- Approximately 72% of adults did not engage in a minimum of 20 minutes of vigorous physical activity for at least 3 days per week (little change from 2000).
- Approximately 50% of adults did not engage in a minimum of 20 minutes of vigorous physical activity for at least 3 days per week or moderate physical activity for at least 30 minutes at least 5 days per week.
- Approximately 47% of high school graduates and 15% of college graduates reported no leisure time physical activity.
- Approximately 25% of adults reported no leisure time physical activity—down from 30% throughout the 1990s.
- Approximately 19% of individuals aged 18 to 24 reported no leisure time physical activity compared with 27% of individuals aged 45 to 64 and 33% of individuals over 65 years of age.

- Approximately 26% of females and 22% of males reported no leisure time physical activity.
- Blacks and Hispanics reported significantly more leisure time physical activity (33%) than did whites (22%).

Thus, it is clear that as a society we are not exercising enough and that this lack of physical activity is exacerbated by certain individual differences. This occurs despite the physiological and psychological benefits of exercise, including reduced tension and depression, increased self-esteem, lowered risk of cardiovascular disease, better weight control, and enhanced functioning of systems (metabolic, endocrine, and immune systems). Only a relatively small percentage of children and adults participate in regular physical activity. This prompted a special issue of papers from the Academy of Kinesiology and Physical Education (Morgan & Dishman, 2001) targeted at exercise adherence. So let's start by looking at why people exercise—as well as the reasons they give for not exercising.

Reasons to Exercise

With much of the adult population either sedentary or not exercising enough to gain health benefits, the first problem that exercise leaders and other health and fitness professionals face is how to get these people to start exercising. People are motivated for different reasons (see chapter 3), but a good place to start is to emphasize the diverse benefits of exercise (President's Council on Physical Fitness and Sport, 1996). Note that the issue of maintenance of physical activity is critical because individuals must continue to be physically active to sustain the full health benefits of regular exercise (Marcus et al., 2000). Let's look at some of the more typical reasons for people to start an exercise program.

Weight Control

American society values fitness, good looks, and thinness, so staying in shape and keeping trim concern many people. However, an estimated 70 to 80 million American adults and 15 to 20 million American teenagers are overweight, and these numbers have been increasing over the past 10 years. In fact, focus has increased on teenage obesity and obesity in general as a national epidemic. The first thing most people think to do when facing the fact that they are overweight is diet. Although dieting certainly helps people lose weight, exercise plays an important and often underrated role (and although dieting is never fun, exercise certainly can be fun). For example, some people assume that exercise does not burn enough calories to make a significant difference in weight loss; however, this is contrary to fact. Specifically, running 3 miles (4.8 km) five times a week can produce a weight loss of 20 to 25 pounds (9–11.3 kg) in a year if caloric intake remains the same. Weight loss can have important health consequences beyond looking and feeling good. Obesity and physical inactivity are primary risk factors for coronary heart disease. Thus, regular exercise not only improves weight control and appearance but also eliminates physical inactivity as a risk factor.

Exercising to lose weight can be seen as a self-presentational reason for exercising because this typically will result in enhancing physical appearance and improving muscularity (Hausenblas, Brewer, & Van Raalte, 2004). It is not surprising that some people are motivated to exercise for self-presentational reasons considering that positive self-presentation is strongly influenced by the aesthetic-ideal physique. Regardless of the current ideal physique (which has changed over time), people are influenced by it because of a concern to look good and be popular.

KEY POINT Exercise combined with proper eating habits can help people lose weight. But weight loss should be slow and steady, occurring as people change their exercise and eating patterns.

Reduced Risk of Cardiovascular Disease

Research has produced evidence that regular physical activity (although we do not know the exact dose–response relationship) or cardiorespiratory fitness decreases the risk of mortality from cardiovascular disease in general and from coronary heart disease in particular. In fact, the decreased risk for coronary heart disease that is attributable to regular physical activity is similar in level to that for other lifestyle factors, such as refraining from cigarette smoking. In addition, regular exercise has been shown to prevent or delay the development of high blood pressure, and exercise reduces blood pressure in people with hypertension. Like obesity, hypertension is a prime risk factor in coronary heart disease, but research has indicated that it can be reduced through regular physical activity. So it is not surprising that a summary of studies identified improvement in people's physical and psychological health as the most salient behavioral advantage of exercise (Downs & Hausenblas, 2005).

Reduction in Stress and Depression

As discussed in chapter 17, regular exercise is associated with an improved sense of well-being and mental health. Our society has recently seen a tremendous increase in the number of people who have anxiety disorders and depression. Exercise is one way to cope more effectively with the society we live in and with everyday life. This notion is supported by a review of 49 studies (Wipfli, Rethorst, & Landers, 2008) that revealed greater reductions in anxiety for exercise groups than for groups that received other forms of anxiety reducing treatments.

Fighting teenage obesity is one of the most pressing reasons to encourage daily exercise in young populations. Creating healthy habits now can lead to continued exercise commitment as an adult.

Enjoyment

Although many people start exercise programs to improve their health and lose weight, it is rare for people to continue these programs unless they find the experience enjoyable. In general, people continue an exercise program because of the fun, happiness, and satisfaction it brings (Kimiecik, 2002; Titze, Stonegger, & Owen, 2005). Along these lines, Williams and colleagues (2006) found that individually tailored physical activity programs were more effective for individuals reporting greater enjoyment of physical activity at baseline. In essence, special attention needs to be paid to individuals who do not enjoy physical activity to start with, and exercise should be intrinsically motivating if a person is to adhere over a long period of time. (This is discussed in more detail later in the chapter.)

> **KEY POINT** Both the physiological and psychological benefits of exercising can be cited to help persuade sedentary people to initiate an exercise program.

Enhancement of Self-Esteem

Exercise is associated with increased feelings of self-esteem and self-confidence (Buckworth & Dishman, 2002), as many people get a sense of satisfaction from accomplishing something they couldn't do before. Research (Whaley & Schrider, 2005) has revealed that the hoped-for self of older adults (staying healthy and independent) was related to increases in exercise behavior. Something as simple as walking around the block or jogging a mile makes people feel good about moving toward their goals. In addition, people who exercise regularly feel more confident about the way they look. Finally, Huberty and colleagues (2008) found self-worth to be the best predictor of longer-term (i.e., more than 6 months) adherence.

Opportunities to Socialize

Often people start an exercise program for the chance to socialize and be with others. They can meet people, fight loneliness, and shed social isolation. Many people who lead busy lives find that the only time they have to spend with friends is when exercising together. In fact, almost 90% of exercise program participants prefer to exercise with a partner or group rather than alone. Exercising together gives people a sense of personal commitment to continue the activity

and to derive social support from each other (Carron, Hausenblas, & Estabrooks, 1999). Interestingly, a study of a senior walking group found that conversing with other walkers and the camaraderie of walking with others were more motivating than the use of pedometers (Copelton, 2010).

DISCOVER Activity 18.1 helps you understand why people exercise.

Reasons for Not Exercising

Despite the social, health, and personal benefits of exercising, many people still choose not to exercise, usually citing lack of time, lack of energy, and lack of motivation as their primary reasons for inactivity (Canadian Fitness and Lifestyle Research Institute, 1996). These are all factors that individuals can control, as opposed to environmental factors, which are often out of their control. ("Barriers to Physical Activity" shows that virtually all barriers to exercise are in the control of the individual.) This is consistent with research (McAuley, Poag, & Gleason, 1990) showing that the major reasons for attrition in an exercise program were internal and personally controllable causes (e.g., lack of motivation, time management), which are amenable to change.

A recent population-based study of more than 2,200 individuals between the ages of 18 and 78 found important age and sex differences regarding reasons for not exercising (Netz, Zeev, Arnon, & Tenenbaum, 2008). Older adults (aged 60–78 years) cited more health-related reasons (e.g., bad health, injury or disability, potential damage to health) for not exercising than their younger counterparts. In addition, older adults selected more internal barriers (e.g., "I'm not the sporty type") than situational barriers (e.g., "I don't have the energy") than younger adults. Furthermore, compared with men, women selected more internal barriers (e.g., lack of self-discipline). Because internal barriers are not easily amenable, this poses a difficult problem regarding adherence to exercise programs for these women. These findings underscore the notion that age and sex need to be considered in any discussion of reasons for not exercising.

For adolescents, some of the major barriers to participation in physical activity involve other factors such as lack of parental support, previous physical inactivity, siblings' nonparticipation in physical activity, and being female (Sallis, Prochaska, & Taylor, 2000). In an analysis of 47 studies investigating

Barriers to Physical Activity

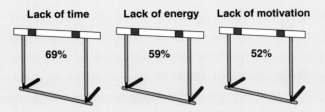

Lack of time 69% **Lack of energy** 59% **Lack of motivation** 52%

Almost 70% of nonexercisers cited lack of time as a major barrier to physical activity

In addition to the major barriers—lack of time, lack of energy, and lack of motivation—nonexercisers identified moderate and minor barriers to physical activity.

Barrier	Individuals who cite this as a barrier to participation (%)	Type of barrier
Moderate barriers		
Excessive cost	37	Individual
Illness or injury	36	Individual
Lack of facilities nearby	30	Environmental
Feeling uncomfortable	29	Individual
Lack of skill	29	Individual
Fear of injury	26	Individual
Minor barriers		
Lack of safe place	24	Environmental
Lack of child care	23	Environmental
Lack of a partner	21	Environmental
Insufficient programs	19	Environmental
Lack of support	18	Environmental
Lack of transportation	17	Environmental

Data from Canadian Fitness and Lifestyle Research Institute 1995.

exercise behavior that included special populations (Downs & Hausenblas, 2005), the main reasons for not exercising were (a) health issues (physical limitations, injury, poor health, pain or soreness, psychological problems), (b) inconvenience (lack of access to facilities, facility too crowded, lack of transportation, other commitments), (c) lacking motivation and energy (feeling lazy, feeling unmotivated, believing that exercise requires too much effort), (d) lacking social support (no exercise partner, no support from spouse), (e) insufficient time, and (f) lacking money (finding exercise programs too expensive).

A study by Ruby, Dunn, Perrino, Gillis, and Viel (2011) points to a slightly different reason for why many people do not exercise. Results from three experiments revealed that participants enjoyed exercising more than they predicted they would, demonstrating that people may systematically underestimate their enjoyment of exercise. This forecasting bias emerged across diverse forms of exercise, from aerobics to weight training to Pilates to yoga. Furthermore, results showed that people place disproportionate weight on the beginning of an exercise experience, which negatively colors their judgments regarding how much they might enjoy exercising. The authors devised an intervention whereby participants viewed their upcoming exercise as more enjoyable, which led to an increased intention to exercise.

Although most researchers have focused on increasing physical activity, a few have focused on reducing sedentary behavior (Biddle, 2011a). One might think that increasing physical activity and decreasing sedentary behaviors are the same, but they are actually different. Sedentary behavior has been defined as primarily sitting or lying behaviors, such as watching TV, using the computer, socializing (sitting and talking), riding in a car or public transportation, reading, or sitting at school. Thus, if the focus is on reducing sedentary behaviors, one aspect of behavior change is to help people sit less. This means that in addition to promoting moderate to vigorous physical activity, we need to encourage light exercise, such as standing and light moving. This light exercise is not meant to replace more vigorous exercise; rather, it is meant to replace some of the time spent sitting and being sedentary.

> **KEY POINT** People often cite time constraints as a reason for not exercising, but such constraints are more perceived than real and often reveal a person's priorities.

Perceived Lack of Time

The reason most frequently given for inactivity is a lack of time. In fact, 69% of truant exercisers cited lack of time as a major barrier to physical activity (Canadian Fitness and Lifestyle Research Institute, 1996). However, a closer look at schedules usually reveals that this so-called lack of time is more a perception than a reality. The problem lies in priorities—after all, people seem to find time to watch TV, hang out, or read the newspaper. When fitness professionals make programs enjoyable, satisfying, meaningful, and convenient, exercising can compete well against other leisure activities.

Lack of Energy

Many people keep such busy schedules that fatigue becomes an excuse for not exercising. In fact, 59% of nonexercisers said that lack of energy was a major barrier to physical activity. Fatigue is typically more mental than physical and often is stress related. Fitness professionals should emphasize that a brisk walk, bicycle ride, or tennis game can relieve tension and

stress and be energizing. If these activities are structured to be fun, a person will look forward to them after a day that may be filled with hassles.

Lack of Motivation

Related to a lack of energy is a lack of sufficient motivation to sustain physical activity over a long period. It takes commitment and dedication to maintain regular physical activity when one's life is busy with work, family, and friends. Because it is easy to let other aspects of life take up all your time and energy, keeping in mind the positive benefits of physical activity becomes even more important to maintaining your motivation.

Problem of Exercise Adherence

Once sedentary people have overcome inertia and started exercising, the next barrier they face has to do with continuing their exercising program. Many people find it easier to start an exercise program than to stick with it: About 50% of participants drop out of exercise programs within the first 6 months. Figure 18.1 illustrates this steep decrease in exercise participation during the first 6 months of an exercise program, which then essentially levels off until 18 months. Exercisers often have lapses in adhering to exercise programs. A few reasons have been put forth for why people have a problem with exercise adherence even though it is both physiologically and psychologically beneficial. These include the following:

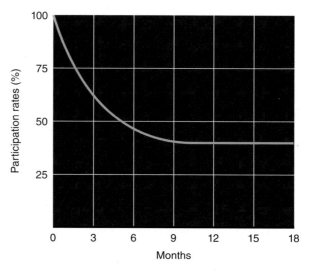

FIGURE 18.1 Change in rate of exercise program participation over time.

- The prescriptions are often based solely on fitness data, ignoring people's psychological readiness to exercise.
- Most exercise prescriptions are overly restrictive and are not optimal for enhancing motivation for regular exercise.
- Rigid exercise prescriptions based on principles of intensity, duration, and frequency are too challenging for many people, especially beginners.
- Traditional exercise prescription does not promote self-responsibility or empower people to make long-term behavior change.

However, Dishman and Buckworth (1997) noted that potential relapses may have a more limited effect if the individual plans and anticipates them, recognizes them as temporary impediments, and develops self-regulatory skills for preventing them (see "Preventing a Relapse"). Finally, a study by Emery, Hauck, Shermer, Hsiao, and MacIntyre (2003) showed the importance of maintaining exercise over time (i.e., not relapsing). Participants (individuals with chronic obstructive pulmonary disease) who adhered to an exercise program for a year had gains in cognitive functioning, functional capacity, and psychological well-being compared with individuals who did not maintain an exercise program.

Given that exercise programs have a high relapse rate, they are like dieting, smoking cessation, or cutting down on drinking alcohol (Prochaska & Velicer, 1997). People intend to change a habit that negatively affects their health and well-being. New enrollments in fitness clubs are typically highest in January and February, when sedentary individuals feel charged by New Year's resolutions to turn over a new leaf and get in shape. The marketing of exercise by sportswear companies has accelerated in North America in a campaign of mass persuasion. So why do some people who start an exercise program fail to stick with it, whereas others continue to make it part of their lifestyle?

KEY POINT Exercise professionals should consistently provide sound, scientific information about exercise and physical activity to increase the likelihood that clients will adhere to a fitness program.

Theories and Models of Exercise Behavior

One way to start answering this question is through the development of theoretical models that help us understand the process of exercise adoption and adherence (Culos-Reed, Gyurcsik, & Brawley, 2001). In this section we discuss some of the major models and theories.

Health Belief Model

The **health belief model** is one of the most enduring theoretical models associated with preventive health behaviors (Hayslip, Weigand, Weinberg, Richardson, & Jackson, 1996). It stipulates that the likelihood of

Preventing a Relapse

Unfortunately, when people start to exercise they often relapse into no exercise at all, or they exercise less frequently. Here are some tips for preventing a relapse:

- Expect and plan for lapses (e.g., schedule alternative activities while on vacation).
- Develop coping strategies for dealing with high-risk situations (e.g., relaxation training, time management, imagery).
- Replace "shoulds" with "wants" to provide more balance in your life. "Shoulds" put pressure and expectations on you.
- Use positive self-talk and imagery to avoid self-dialogues focusing on relapse.
- Identify situations that put you at risk and attempt to avoid or plan for these settings.
- Do not view a temporary relapse as catastrophic because this undermines confidence and willpower (e.g., you are not a total failure if you didn't exercise for a week; just start again next week).

an individual engaging in preventive health behaviors (e.g., exercise) depends on the person's perception of the severity of the potential illness as well as his appraisal of the costs and benefits of taking action (Becker & Maiman, 1975). An individual who believes that the potential illness is serious, that he is at risk, and that the pros of taking action outweigh the cons is likely to adopt the target health behavior. Although there has been some success in using the health belief model to predict exercise behavior, the results have been inconsistent because the model was originally developed to focus on disease, not exercise (Berger, Pargman, & Weinberg, 2007).

Theory of Planned Behavior

The **theory of planned behavior** (Ajzen & Madden, 1986) is an extension of the theory of reasoned action (Ajzen & Fishbein, 1980). The theory of reasoned action states that intentions are the best predictors of actual behavior. Specifically, intentions are the product of an individual's attitude toward a particular behavior and what is normative regarding the behavior (**subjective norm**). This subjective norm is the product of beliefs about others' opinions and the individual's motivation to comply with others' opinions. For example, if you are a nonexerciser and believe that other significant people in your life (e.g., spouse, children, friends) think you should exercise, then you may wish to do what these others want you to do.

Planned behavior theory extends the theory of reasoned action by arguing that intentions cannot be the sole predictors of behavior, especially in situations in which people might lack some control over the behavior. So in addition to the notions of subjective norms and attitudes, planned behavior theory states that perceived behavioral control—that is, people's perceptions of their *ability* to perform the behavior—will also affect behavioral outcomes. A meta-analysis by Hagger, Chatzisarantis, and Biddle (2002) supported the effectiveness of the different constructs in the theory of planned behavior in predicting exercise.

Behavioral intentions to increase exercise behavior have been distinguished from intentions to maintain exercise (Milne, Rodgers, Hall, & Wilson, 2008). Thus, when developing exercise interventions, the notion that exercise might unfold in phases (see the transtheoretical model later in this chapter) needs to be considered. In a study by Parrott, Tennant, Olejnik, and Poudevigne (2008) using the theory of planned behavior, e-mail messages reminding participants to

exercise as well as highlighting the benefits of exercise were effective in increasing both intentions to exercise and actual exercise behavior compared with a control condition. Hamilton and White (2008) extended the theory of planned behavior by adding self-identity and group norms to the existing theory variables to help predict exercise behavior in adolescents. Finally, Dimmock and Banting (2009) argue that intentions, as the theory predicts, don't necessarily influence behavior; rather, the quality and strength of intentions are more important.

A study by Motl and colleagues (2005) found that behavioral control was a good predictor of physical activity in more than 1,000 black and white female adolescents across a 1-year period. Martin and colleagues (2005) were able to predict moderate physical activity and cardiorespiratory fitness in African American children using the variables in the theory of planned behavior. Furthermore, studies focused on predicting exercise behaviors and adherence (Rhodes & Courneya, 2005) found that an individual may need to meet a certain threshold regarding perceived behavioral control and subjective norms. Finally, the effectiveness of using the theory of planned behavior was demonstrated in predicting exercise intentions in non-Hodgkin's lymphoma survivors (Courneya, Vallance, Jones, & Reiman, 2005) as well as in substance users in recovery (Savvidou, Lazaras, & Tsorbatzoudia, 2012).

Social Cognitive Theory

Social cognitive theory (Bandura, 1986, 1997, 2005) proposes that personal, behavioral, and environmental factors operate as reciprocally interacting determinants of each other. In essence, the environment affects behaviors and behaviors affect the environment. Such personal factors as thoughts, emotions, and physiology are also important. Despite this interaction among different factors, probably the most critical piece to this approach is an individual's belief that he can successfully perform a behavior (self-efficacy). Self-efficacy has been shown to be a good predictor of behavior in a variety of health situations, such as smoking cessation, weight management, and recovery from heart attacks. In relation to exercise, self-efficacy theory has produced some of the most consistent findings, revealing an increase in exercise participation as self-efficacy increases (e.g., Buckworth & Dishman, 2007; Maddison & Prapavessis, 2004) as well as increases in self-efficacy as exercise participation increases (McAuley & Blissmer, 2002). Self-efficacy is strongly related to exercise participation throughout the life span but especially in middle-aged and older adults (Avotte, Margrett, & Hicks-Patrick, 2010).

Self-efficacy is especially important when exercise is most challenging, such as in the initial stages of exercise adoption or for persons with chronic diseases. For example, self-efficacy theory has predicted exercise behavior, which has been especially helpful for individuals with type 1 or type 2 diabetes as well as those with cardiovascular disease (Luszczynska & Tryburcy, 2008; Plotnikoff, Lippke, Courneya, Birkett, & Sigal, 2008). In addition, when individuals relapse in their exercise behavior, the best predictor of whether they will resume exercise is recovery self-efficacy (Luszczynska, Mazurkiewicz, Ziegelmann, & Schwarzer, 2007). Martin and McCaughtry (2008) investigated physical activity in inner-city African American children. Somewhat contrary to previous findings, results revealed that time spent outside and social support, as opposed to self-efficacy, were the best predictors of physical activity levels. This population has rarely been studied from a social cognitive perspective, and thus other factors besides self-efficacy may be the primary determinants of exercise behavior. In summary, research has consistently supported social cognitive theory and the role that self-efficacy plays in enhancing exercise behavior (Biddle, Hagger, Chatzisarantis, & Lippke, 2007).

Self-Determination Theory

Self-determination theory (SDT) is discussed in chapter 6 in relation to its influence on sport motivation and performance. Basically, the theory proposes that people are inherently motivated to feel connected to others in a social milieu (relatedness), to function effectively in that milieu (effectance), and to feel a sense of personal initiative in doing so (autonomy). Hagger and Chatzisarantis (2007, 2008) summarized the research that has employed SDT to predict exercise behavior. The studies generally indicate that participants who display autonomy in their exercise behavior (Standage, Sebire, & Loney, 2008) and have strong social support systems exhibit stronger motivation and enhanced exercise adherence. SDT was also able to predict adherence in overweight and obese participants (Edmunds, Ntoumanis, & Duda, 2007).

Further support for SDT was found in the fact that physical activity participants were able to distinguish between intrinsic and extrinsic goals in a physical activity context (McLachlan & Hagger, 2011). Along

these lines, Fortier and colleagues (2012) found that individuals who progressed through the stages of change exhibited more self-determined forms of behavior regarding exercise. Finally, two studies (Duncan, Hall, Wilson, & O, 2010; Lewis & Sutton, 2011) found that exercise that was affected by more autonomous regulations (e.g., doing something by one's own choice) produced higher levels of adherence than exercise affected by controlled regulations (doing something because one is supposed to do it). These studies all underscore the relationship between self-determined forms of motivation and stages of change in predicting exercise behavior.

SDT has emerged as an important theoretical approach in exercise psychology in general and exercise adherence in particular. It has helped researchers view intrinsic and extrinsic motivation on a continuum rather than as a dichotomy. This has implications for exercise adherence because exercise is not intrinsically motivating for many individuals, especially those starting an exercise program. The challenge for practitioners remains how to create an autonomous-supportive climate in which self-determined forms of motivation are promoted in the physical activity context but still allow for some less self-directed extrinsic motivation (e.g., social support, rewards).

Transtheoretical Model

Although the models just discussed are useful as we try to grasp why people do or do not exercise, these constructs tend to focus on a given moment in time. However, the **transtheoretical model** (Prochaska, DiClemente, & Norcross, 1992) argues that individuals progress through stages of change and that movement across the stages is cyclic (figure 18.2) rather than linear because many people do not succeed in their efforts at establishing and maintaining lifestyle changes This model argues that interventions and information need to be tailored to match the particular stage an individual is in at the time (see "Matching the Exercise Intervention to the Individual"). There are six stages in the transtheoretical model.

1. *Precontemplation stage.* In this stage, individuals do not intend to start exercising in the next 6 months. They are couch potatoes. People in this first stage may be demoralized about their ability to change, may be defensive because of social pressures, or may be uninformed about the long-term consequences of their behavior.

Evaluation Criteria for Theories of Health Behavior

A consensus exists that unhealthy behaviors are major causes of disease, premature death, and increased health care costs. Certainly lack of exercise has been related to many negative health outcomes (e.g., coronary heart disease, obesity). As a result, many theories (noted in this chapter) have been applied to exercise behavior. Recently, Prochaska, Wright, and Velicer (2008) provided guidelines for evaluating the effectiveness of these different theories in predicting exercise behavior. In the following list, these are ordered from least to most important in terms of usefulness in practice and value of enhancing health.

- *Clarity:* The theory has well-defined terms that are operationalized and explicit.
- *Consistency:* The components do not contradict each other.
- *Parsimony:* The theory explains the phenomenon in the least complex manner possible.
- *Testability:* The propositions can be tested.
- *Empirical adequacy:* The theory predicts when a behavior change will and will not occur.
- *Productivity:* The theory generates new questions and ideas and adds to the knowledge base.
- *Generalizability:* The theory generalizes to other situations, places, and times.
- *Integration:* Constructs are combined in a meaningful and systematic pattern.
- *Utility:* The theory provides health-related service and is usable.
- *Practicality:* A theory-based intervention produces greater behavior change than a placebo or a control.
- *Impact:* Impact equals reach (the percentage of the target population participating) times the number of behaviors changed times efficacy (amount of change).

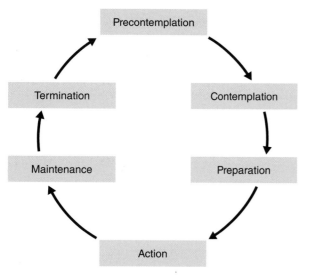

FIGURE 18.2 Cyclic pattern of stages of change.

3. *Preparation stage.* People in this stage are exercising some, perhaps fewer than three times a week, but not regularly. Hence, though our couch potato now exercises a bit, the activity is not regular enough to produce major benefits. In the preparation stage, individuals typically have a plan of action and have indeed taken action to make behavioral changes, such as exercising a little.

4. *Action stage.* Individuals in this stage exercise regularly (three or more times a week for 20 minutes or longer) but have been doing so for fewer than 6 months. This is the least stable stage; it tends to correspond with the highest risk for relapse. It is also the busiest stage, in which the most processes for change are being used. So our couch potato is now an active potato who could easily fall back into her old ways.

5. *Maintenance stage.* Individuals in this stage have been exercising regularly for more than 6 months. Although they are likely to maintain regular exercise throughout the life span (except for time-outs because of injury or other health-related problems), boredom and loss of focus can become a problem. Sometimes the vigilance initially required to establish a habit is tiring and difficult to maintain. Ideally, to

2. *Contemplation stage.* In this stage people seriously intend to exercise within the next 6 months. Despite their intentions, individuals usually remain in this second stage, according to research, for about 2 years. So the couch potato has a fleeting thought about starting to exercise but is unlikely to act on that thought.

help prevent a relapse, the exerciser works to reinforce the gains made through the various stages. Although most studies testing the transtheoretical model have focused on the earlier stages, Fallon, Hausenblas, and Nigg (2005) focused on the maintenance stage. Results revealed that increasing self-efficacy in order to overcome barriers to exercise was a critical factor in continuing to exercise for both males and females. In addition, people in the maintenance phase were found to be more intrinsically than extrinsically motivated (Buckworth, Lee, Regan, Schneider, & DiClemente, 2007).

6. *Termination stage.* Once an exerciser has stayed in the termination stage for 5 years, the individual is considered to have exited from the cycle of change, and relapse simply does not occur. At this stage one is truly an active potato—for a lifetime. In an interesting study of more than 550 participants (Cardinal, 1997), approximately 16% indicated that they were in the termination stage (criteria of 5 or more years of continuous involvement in physical activity and 100% self-efficacy in an ability to remain physically active for life). Cardinal concluded that individuals in the termination stage are resistant to relapse despite common barriers to exercise such as lack of time, no energy, low motivation, and bad weather.

In making decisions about exercise, people go through a kind of cost–benefit analysis called *decisional balance.* Specifically, when people are considering a change in lifestyle, they weigh the pros and cons of a given behavior (e.g., "Should I begin exercising?"). In a meta-analysis, Marshall and Biddle (2001) found that pros increase for every forward stage and that the largest change occurs between the precontemplative and contemplative stages. Similarly, the cons decreased for every forward stage. This is consistent with research (Landry & Solmon, 2004) using African American women, which found that motives for exercise became more internal as participants progressed through stages. Thus, approaches that focus on a sense of guilt or obligation rather than fostering self-motivation may actually have a negative effect on adherence. Therefore, exercise specialists need to help individuals who are contemplating exercise realize all of the benefits of exercise (i.e., become more intrinsically motivated) to help them move from precontemplation to contemplation to preparation.

Physical Activity Maintenance Model

The models previously mentioned were not designed specifically for exercise adherence. To help better understand the long-term maintenance of physical activity, the **physical activity maintenance model** was developed (Nigg, Borrelli, Maddock, & Dishman, 2008). The key aspects of the model predicting the maintenance of physical activity include

- goal setting (commitment attainment, satisfaction),
- self-motivation (persistence in the pursuit of behavioral goals independent of any situational constraints),
- self-efficacy (confidence to overcome barriers and avoid relapse),
- physical activity environment (access, aesthetics or attractiveness, enjoyable scenery, social support), and
- life stress (recent life changes, everyday hassles).

Interestingly, although the goal of exercise programs is for participants to maintain exercise behavior over a lifetime (or at least for a long period of time), few exercise intervention studies even measure maintenance behavior. In a comprehensive and systematic review of behavior change after physical activity, Fjeldsoe, Neuhaus, Winkler, and Eakin (2011) found that only 35% of the 157 studies reviewed presented maintenance data (defined as at least 3 months past completion of the intervention). Even if exercise was helpful throughout the course of the intervention, the efficacy of interventions is limited if exercise is not continued after the intervention. Therefore, maintenance data need to be collected for longer periods of time (i.e., in longitudinal studies) if we are to evaluate the effectiveness of different physical activity interventions.

Ecological Models

One class of models that has recently gained support in the study of exercise behavior is the **ecological model**. The term *ecological* refers to models, frameworks, or perspectives rather than a specific set of variables (Dishman et al., 2004). The primary focus of these models is to explain how environments and behaviors affect each other, bringing into consideration

Matching the Exercise Intervention to the Individual

A central theme in the transtheoretical model is that different intervention techniques are more effective for people in different stages of change. This idea was tested by Marcus, Rossi, Selby, Niaura, and Abrams (1992), who developed the following stage-matched self-help materials and other resources using the exercise adherence literature and the transtheoretical model:

- "What's in It for You," for people in the contemplation stage, focused on the benefits of and barriers to physical activity.

- "Ready for Action," developed for people in the preparation stage, focused on getting people to exercise three times a week by using such strategies as setting short-term goals, using time management skills, and rewarding one's self for activity.

- "Keeping It Going," for participants in the action stage who exercise only occasionally and are at great risk of falling back to the preparation stage, focused on troublesome situations that may lead to a relapse (e.g., injury) and provided suggestions for dealing with these situations (e.g., gaining social support).

Results revealed that between 30% and 60% of participants in the exercise program progressed to either the preparation or action stage, and only 4% in preparation and 9% in action regressed. Therefore, matching the intervention to the stage of exercise appears to be an effective way to enhance exercise.

Furthermore, things outside one's control may at times influence the maintenance of exercise. For example, a recent study showed that individuals who had more major life events during maintenance exercised significantly less than those who had fewer major life events (Oman & King, 2000). Being prepared for these high-risk situations that can lead to missed exercise sessions or to program attrition is important. In addition, it appears that in a worksite setting a diversified intervention can increase energy expenditure of participants as well as move them from a lower (less active) stage of change to a higher (more active) stage of change (Titze, Martin, Seiler, Stronegger, & Marti, 2001). Research with a walking program (Jo, Song, Yoo, & Lee, 2010) supported the stages of change model in Korea, although the researchers noted that it is still difficult to get people in the precontemplation and contemplation stages to undertake consistent physical activity. Finally, a thorough review of the literature assessing the effect of the transtheoretical model (TTM) on exercise behavior found that in 25 of 31 studies, a stage-matched intervention demonstrated success in motivating participants toward higher stages and amounts of exercise (Spencer, Adams, Malone, Roy, & Yost, 2006).

A stage of change model that is more parsimonious than the transtheoretical model is known as the health action process approach (Schwarzer, 1992). It consists of three phases: (1) the nonintentional stage, in which a behavioral intention is being developed (similar to the contemplation stage in the transtheoretical model); (2) the intentional stage, in which the person has formed an intention but still remains inactive while the exercise behavior is being planned and prepared; and (3) the action phase, in which plans are translated into physical action. Results revealed findings similar to those with the transtheoretical model in that individuals in different stages had different levels of self-efficacy, risk perception, attrition rates, and planning cognitions as related to exercise (Lippke,

intrapersonal (e.g., biological), interpersonal (e.g., family), institutional (e.g., schools), and policy (e.g., laws at all levels) influences. In a review of 129 studies from 1979 to 2003, the strongest evidence for influencing physical activity was for prompts to increase stair use, access to fitness centers, health clubs, and opportunities for physical activity, school-based physical education, and comprehensive worksite approaches (Matson-Koffman, Brownstein,

Neiner, & Greaney, 2005). Although all of these environments are important, it is argued (Sallis & Owen, 1999) that physical environments are really the hallmark of these ecological models. The most provocative claim is that ecological models can have a direct effect on exercise above that provided by social cognitive models. Zhang, Solomon, Gao, and Kosma (2012) used an ecological perspective to help promote physical activity in middle school students.

Ziegelmann, & Schwarzer, 2005). Thus, this approach might augment the transtheoretical model as a way to study changes in exercise thoughts, feelings, and behaviors.

The stages of change characterize when people change, but the processes of change have to do with *how* people change. People use a range of strategies and techniques to change behaviors, and these strategies are their processes of change. We can divide processes into two categories: cognitive and behavioral. These processes are listed in table 18.1. Some interesting research (Rosen, 2000a,b) showed that the processes of change used by individuals in relation to exercise differ from those used in programs involving smoking cessation, substance abuse, and diet change. Specifically, people who are exercising use cognitive–affective processes more frequently during action and maintenance phases than during other phases because it is hypothesized that exercise is a positive behavior that might be increased if people continually think about it.

TABLE 18.1 Processes of Change for Exercise

Processes	Examples
Cognitive processes	
Consciousness raising	I recall information that people have personally given me on the benefits of exercise.
Dramatic relief	Warnings about health hazards of inactivity move me emotionally.
Environmental reevaluation	I believe I would be a better role model for others if I exercised regularly.
Self-reevaluation	I am considering the idea that regular exercise would make me a healthier, happier person.
Social liberation	I find society changing in ways that make it easier for the exerciser.
Behavioral processes	
Counterconditioning	Instead of remaining inactive, I engage in some physical activity.
Helping relationships	I have someone on whom I can depend when I am having problems with exercising.
Reinforcement management	I reward myself when I exercise.
Self-liberation	I tell myself I am able to keep exercising if I want to.
Stimulus control	I put things around my home to remind me of exercising.

Adapted from Marcus et al. 1992.

Social environmental variables (e.g., support from parents, friends, and physical education teachers) and physical environmental variables (e.g., equipment accessibility, neighborhood safety) along with barrier self-efficacy (i.e., belief you can overcome barriers to exercise) were found to predict physical activity. In addition, the environmental variables (social and physical) predicted physical activity beyond individual factors such as barrier self-efficacy.

Integration of Models

Thus far we have presented different models that attempt to predict exercise behavior. However, in reality, a combination of models might provide the best prediction. Zhang and Solmon (2013) describe the possibility of combining the ecological model with SDT to promote exercise behavior. Specifically, the basic principle of the social ecological model is that each behavior setting has environmental characteristics that are relevant to specific types and purposes of physical activity. In addition, it has been demonstrated that psychological need satisfaction (i.e., SDT) is an important mediator between different environmental factors and individuals' autonomous motivation and subsequent physical activity.

Integrating these two approaches could help enhance physical activity levels. For instance, an active-friendly school physical environment (includes places where students can walk, play, or participate in some physical activity) might foster students' sense of autonomy (e.g., by providing enough equipment and spaces to increase choices), competence (e.g., by providing the physical activity resources that enable students to feel competent, such as different types of motor skill equipment to help develop skills requiring perceptual-motor ability and hand-eye coordination), and relatedness (e.g., by creating a setting where children can interact with each other). Satisfying these needs through the physical and social environment should promote engagement in physical activity.

Determinants of Exercise Adherence

Theories help us understand the process of adopting, and later maintaining, exercise habits and give us a way to study this process. Another way researchers have attempted to study adherence to exercise programs is through investigating the specific determinants of exercise behavior. In a broad sense, the determinants fall into two categories: personal factors and environmental factors.

We examine each category, highlighting the most consistent specific factors related to adherence and dropout rates. Table 18.2 summarizes the positive and negative influences on adherence, along with the variables that have no influence on exercise adherence (Dishman & Buckworth, 1998, 2001). However, it should be noted that the determinants of physical activity are not isolated variables; rather, they influence and are influenced by each other as they contribute to behavioral outcomes (King, Oman, Brassington, Bliwise, & Haskell, 1997). For example, someone who values physical fitness and is self-motivated may be less influenced by the weather and thus more likely to exercise when it is cold than someone for whom fitness is less important and who needs more external support and motivation.

Biddle, Atkin, Cavill, and Foster (2011) conducted an extensive review to investigate correlates of physical activity in youths. Many of the findings are similar to those for adults. The major correlates of physical activity for youths are as follows:

- *Demographic*—Age, sex
- *Psychological*—Positive motivation, positive body image
- *Behavioral*—Previous physical activity, sport participation, smoking, sedentary behavior
- *Sociocultural*—Parental influences, social support
- *Environmental*—Access to facilities, distance from home to school, time spent outside, local crime

Biddle and colleagues (2011) note that the factors of sex and age appear to have the most consistent and strongest effects on physical activity. In addition, they suggest that most of the other correlates of physical activity are most likely to have only small or small to moderate effects in isolation and may work best in interaction with other influences.

Personal Factors

We can distinguish three types of personal characteristics that may influence exercise adherence: demographic variables, cognitive variables, and behaviors. We discuss these in order.

Demographic Variables

Demographic variables traditionally have had a strong association with physical activity. Education, income, and socioeconomic status have all been consistently and *positively* related to physical activity. Specifically, people with higher incomes, more education, and higher occupational status are more likely to be physically active. Of individuals earning less than $15,000 annually, 65% are inactive compared with 48% of those earning more than $50,000. In addition, among people with less than a high school education, 72% are sedentary compared with 50% of college-educated individuals (U.S. Centers for Disease Control and Prevention, 1993). Conversely, people who smoke and are blue-collar workers (e.g., construction or factory workers) are less likely to be as physically active as their nonsmoking and white-collar (e.g., money managers, banking) counterparts. Many blue-collar workers may have the attitude that their job requires

TABLE 18.2 Factors That Influence Overall Physical Activity

Personal factors

Determinant	Positive	Negative	Neutral
Demographics			
Age		✓	
Blue-collar occupation		✓	
Education	✓		
Sex (male)	✓		
High risk for heart disease		✓	
Income and socioeconomic status	✓		
Overweight and obesity		✓	
Cognitive and personality variables			
Attitudes			✓
Barriers to exercise		✓	
Enjoyment of exercise	✓		
Expectation of health and other benefits	✓		
Intention to exercise	✓		
Knowledge of health and exercise			✓
Lack of time		✓	
Mood disturbance		✓	
Perceived health or fitness	✓		
Self-efficacy for exercise	✓		
Self-motivation	✓		
Behaviors			
Diet	✓		
Past unstructured physical activity during childhood			✓
Past unstructured physical activity during adulthood	✓		
Past program participation	✓		
School sports			✓
Smoking		✓	
Type A behavior pattern		✓	
Social environment			
Class size			✓
Group cohesion	✓		
Physician influence	✓		

(continued)

TABLE 18.2 *(continued)*

Determinant	Positive	Negative	Neutral
Personal factors			
Past family influence	✓		
Social support from friends and peers	✓		
Social support from spouse and family	✓		
Social support from staff and instructor	✓		
Physical environment			
Climate and season		✓	
Cost			✓
Disruption in routine			✓
Access to facilities: actual	✓		
Access to facilities: perceived	✓		
Home equipment	✓		
Physical activity characteristics			
Intensity		✓	
Perceived effort		✓	
Group program	✓		
Leader qualities	✓		

enough physical activity for health and fitness, but with the use of technology in industry today, most workers do not expend as much energy as workers did 50 years ago.

Although males have a higher level of participation in physical activity than females, there are no differences in intensity of exercise. Furthermore, physical activity typically decreases with age. A particularly large decrease in physical activity occurs during adolescence (ages 12–19 years) and is maintained throughout most of adulthood (Buckworth & Dishman, 2007). Finally, as might be expected, overweight and obesity are negatively associated with physical activity (Janssen, Katzmarzyk, Boyce, King, & Pickett, 2004).

Some studies have used nonwhite participants because groups who are nonwhite have been virtually absent from the literature and have been shown to be at higher risk for low levels of physical activity (Grunbaum et al., 2004). Along these lines, in one study (Kimm et al., 2002), black females decreased their physical activity by 100% from ages 10 to 19,

whereas white females decreased physical activity by 64%. However, results have shown that barriers to exercise were similar between white and nonwhite individuals, although the populations differed in other determinants of exercise (King et al., 2000). Clearly this is an area that needs more research. Finally, culture and ethnicity have also been shown to be important factors in determining exercise adherence (Pan & Nigg, 2011; Rovinak et al., 2010).

KEY POINT Blue-collar workers typically have lower exercise adherence rates than white-collar workers. However, increased choices can increase their adherence rates.

Cognitive and Personality Variables

Many cognitive variables have been tested over the years to determine whether they help predict patterns of physical activity. Of all the variables tested, self-efficacy and self-motivation have been found to be the most consistent predictors of physical activity. Self-efficacy is simply an individual's belief that he can successfully perform a desired behavior. Getting started in an exercise program, for example, is likely affected by the confidence one has in being able to perform the desired behavior (e.g., walking, running, aerobic dance) and keep the behavior up. Therefore, exercise specialists need to help people feel confident about their bodies through social support, encouragement, and tailoring of activities to meet their needs and abilities. Specialists also should provide beginning exercisers with a sense of success and competence in their exercise programs to enhance their desire to continue participation. Rovniak and colleagues (2010) found self-efficacy to be the strongest predictor of physical activity across sex, ethnicity, and body mass index, supporting the generalized positive effects of self-efficacy on physical activity.

Self-motivation has also been consistently related to exercise adherence and has been found to distinguish adherents from dropouts across many settings, including adult fitness centers, preventive medicine clinics, cardiac rehabilitation units, and corporate fitness gyms (Dishman & Sallis, 1994). Evidence suggests that self-motivation may reflect self-regulatory skills, such as effective goal setting, **self-monitoring** of progress, and self-reinforcement, which are believed to be important in maintaining physical activity. Combined with other measures, self-motivation can predict adherence even more accurately. For example, Polman, Pieter, Bercades, and Ntoumanis (2004) found that the best predictor of adherence to physical activity was the combination of self-motivation and body fat percentage.

The cumulative body of evidence also supports the conclusion that beliefs about and expectations of benefits from exercise are associated with increased physical activity levels and adherence to structured physical activity programs among adults (e.g., Marcus, Pinto, Simkin, Audrain, & Taylor, 1994; Marcus et al., 2000). Population-based educational campaigns can modify knowledge, attitudes, values, and beliefs regarding physical activity; these changes then can influence individuals' intentions to be active and finally their actual level of activity. Therefore, specialists need to inform people of the benefits of regular physical activity and give them ways to overcome perceived barriers. A way to provide this type of information (see Marcus, Rossi, et al., 1992), for example, is to distribute exercise-specific manuals to participants based on their current stage of physical activity.

Behaviors

Among studies of the many behaviors that might predict physical activity patterns in adulthood, research on a person's previous physical activity and sport participation has produced some of the most interesting findings. In supervised programs in which activity can be directly observed, past participation in an exercise program is the *most reliable predictor* of current participation (Trost, Owenm, Bauman, Sallis, & Brown, 2002). That is, someone who has remained active in an organized program for 6 months is likely to be active a year or two later.

KEY POINT Early involvement in sport and physical activity should be encouraged because a positive relationship exists between childhood exercise and adult physical activity patterns.

There is little evidence that mere participation in school sports, as opposed to a formal exercise program, in and of itself will predict adult physical activity. Similarly, there is little support for the notion that activity patterns in childhood or early adulthood are predictive of later physical activity. Evidently, the key element in predicting later physical activity is that an individual has developed a fairly recent habit of being physically active during the adult years regardless of the particular types and frequency of physical activity. However, active children who receive parental encouragement for physical activity will be more active as adults than will children who are sedentary and do not receive parental support. Along these lines, an extensive survey of some 40,000 schoolchildren in 10 European countries revealed that children whose parents, best friends, and siblings took part in sport and physical activity were much more likely themselves to take part and continue to exercise into adulthood (Wold & Anderssen, 1992). In addition, just the most active 10% of children did not have declines in physical activity from ages 12 to 18. These results underscore the importance of adults encouraging youngsters, getting them involved in regular physical activity and sport participation early in life, and serving as positive role models.

Environmental Factors

Environmental factors can help or hinder regular participation in physical activity. These factors include the social environment (e.g., family and peers), the physical environment (e.g., weather, time pressures, and distance from facilities), and characteristics of the physical activity (e.g., intensity and duration of the exercise bout). Environments (i.e., communities) that promote increased activity—offering easily accessible facilities and removing real and perceived barriers to an exercise routine—are probably necessary for the successful maintenance of changes in exercise behavior. For example, adherence to physical activity is higher when individuals live or work closer to a fitness club, receive support from their spouse for the activity, and can manage their time effectively. Although most of the determinants studied in the past have been demographic, personal, behavioral, psychological, and programmatic factors, more attention is now being given to environmental variables (Sallis & Owen, 1999).

Social Environment

Social support is a key aspect of one's social environment, and such support from family and friends has consistently been linked to physical activity and adherence to structured exercise programs among adults (U.S. Department of Health and Human Services, 1996). A spouse has great influence on exercise adherence, and a spouse's attitude can exert even more influence than one's own attitude (Dishman, 1994). Along these lines, Raglin (2001a) found a dropout rate for married singles (only one person from a married couple exercising) of 43%, whereas for married pairs (both people in the exercise program) the dropout rate was only 6.3%. Thus, actually taking part in an exercise program provides a great deal of support for a spouse. Social support was also found to be effective in injury rehabilitation settings (Levy, Remco, Polman, Nicholls, & Marchant, 2009). Specifically, athletes felt that social support helped them cope with the stress of being injured and not being able to participate in their sport. Friends, family, and the physiotherapist were seen as offering different types of social support (e.g., task support, emotional support). Finally, a review by Carron, Hausenblas, and Mack (1996) found that for social variables, the strongest predictor of adherence was the influence of support from family and important others on attitudes about exercise.

KEY POINT Spousal support is critical to enhancing adherence rates for people in exercise programs. Spouses should be involved in orientation sessions or in parallel exercise programs.

Physical Environment

A convenient location is important for regular participation in community-based exercise programs. Both the perceived convenience and the actual proximity to home or work are factors that consistently affect whether someone chooses to exercise and adheres to a supervised exercise program (Buckworth & Dishman, 2007). The closer to a person's home or work the exercise setting is, the greater the likelihood that the individual will begin and stay with a program. Such locations as schools and recreation centers offer potentially effective venues for community-based physical activity programs (Smith & Biddle, 1995). Along these lines, King and colleagues (2000) found that approximately two thirds of the women in their study expressed a preference for undertaking physical activity on their own in their neighborhood rather than going to a fitness facility. In addition, Sallis

Incorporating short bouts of exercise during the day is one way to counter the argument that there isn't enough time to fit in a complete workout.

(2000) argued that one of the major reasons for the current epidemic of inactive lifestyles is the modern built environment, which includes formidable barriers to physical activity such as a lack of biking and walking trails, parks, and other open places where physical activity could occur. Crust, Henderson, and Middleton (2013) found that exercisers who walked in the countryside exhibited higher levels of enjoyment and self-esteem than did exercisers who walked in urban green environments (e.g., urban parks). Because enjoyment is related to exercise adherence, exercising in the countryside should facilitate exercise adherence.

The climate or season can also influence one's participation in physical activity. Activity levels are lowest in winter and highest in summer. In addition, observational studies have found that time spent outdoors is one of the best correlates of physical activity in preschool children (Kohl & Hobbs, 1998).

Still, the most prevalent reason people give for dropping out of supervised clinical and community exercise programs is a perceived lack of time (Buckworth & Dishman, 2007; Dishman & Buckworth, 1997). When time seems short, people typically drop exercise. How many times have you heard someone say, "I'd like to exercise but I just don't have the time"? For many people, however, this perceived lack of time reflects a more basic lack of interest or commitment. Regular exercisers are at least as likely as sedentary people to view time as a barrier to exercise. For example, women who work outside the home are more likely to exercise regularly than those who do not, and single parents are more physically active than parents in two-parent families. So it is not clear that time constraints truly predict or determine exercise participation. Rather, physical inactivity may have to do more with poor time management skills than with too little time. Helping new exercisers deal more effectively with the decision of when to exercise might be especially beneficial.

Although lack of time has been cited as a major reason for physical inactivity, home exercise equipment has not solved the inactivity problem. Americans spent nearly three times as much on home exercise equipment in 1996 as in 1986 ($1.2 billion to 3 billion, and the amount spent on home exercise equipment has been rising each year). However, during that period, moderate to vigorous physical activity increased only 2%, and a lot of that equipment ended up in people's garages and closets.

Physical Activity Characteristics

The success or failure of exercise programs can depend on several structural factors. Some of the more important factors are the intensity, frequency, and duration of the exercise; whether the exercise is done in a group or alone; and qualities of the exercise leader.

Exercise Intensity, Frequency, and Duration

Discomfort during exercise can certainly affect adherence to a program. High-intensity exercise is more stressful on the system than low-intensity exercise, especially for people who have been sedentary. People in walking programs, for example, continue their regimens longer than do people in running programs. One study showed that dropout rates (25%–35%) with a moderate-level activity are only about half what is seen (50%) for vigorous exercise (Sallis et al., 1986). Furthermore, research indicated that adherence rates in exercise programs were best when individuals were exercising at 50% or less of their aerobic capacity (Dishman & Buckworth, 1997; U.S. Department of Health and Human Services, 1996). Williams (2007, 2008) provided evidence that individuals (especially those who were inactive, obese, or both) who chose self-paced intensities that produced positive affect exhibited higher levels of adherence. Interestingly, even a 10% increase in desired intensity has a negative effect on mood; over time, this would probably undermine adherence (Lind, Ekkekakis, & Vazou, 2008). This is contrary to many recommendations that individuals should exercise at a certain intensity level. Williams concludes that allowing participants to select intensity levels related to pleasant feelings while avoiding exercise that elicits unpleasant feelings can be particularly helpful in terms of adherence for obese and sedentary individuals, who often exhibit discomfort when exercising and subsequently drop out.

Finally, research has revealed that the level of past activity may moderate the effects of exercise intensity on adherence (Anton et al., 2005). Specifically, it was found that participants with higher levels of past physical activity exhibited better adherence to higher-intensity exercise but tended to have poorer adherence to moderate-intensity exercise. Thus, an individual's exercise experience should be considered when prescribing an exercise regimen.

Different scholarly organizations have made different recommendations regarding the frequency and duration of exercise. The American College of Sports Medicine and the Centers for Disease Control and Prevention recommend that people accumulate 30 minutes or more of moderate-intensity physical activity most days of the week to encourage sedentary people (who usually do very little physical activity) to perform activities such as gardening, walking, and household chores in short doses (e.g., 5–10 minutes). Other groups such as the Food and Nutrition Board of the Institute of Medicine recommend at least 1 hour per day of moderate-intensity physical activity (Couzin, 2002). However, research has revealed that multiple short bouts of exercise led to similar long-term increases in physical activity and weight loss compared with traditional sessions of 30 minutes or longer (Jakicic, Winters, Lang, & Wing, 1999). In addition, Bartlett and colleagues (2011) found that people exercising at high intensity intervals had higher levels of enjoyment than people doing continuous exercise at moderate levels, which may have implications for adherence. Thus, the key point is that people need to get regular physical activity, and there appears to be no best way to accomplish this goal.

More vigorous physical activity carries a greater risk for injury. In fact, injury is the most common reason given for the most recent relapse from exercise, and participants who report temporary injuries are less likely than healthy individuals to report vigorous exercise (Dishman & Buckworth, 1997). In starting an exercise program, many people try to do too much the first couple of times out and wind up with sore muscles, injuries to soft tissues, or orthopedic problems. Of course, they find such injury just the excuse they need to quit exercising. The message to give them is that it is much better to do some moderate exercise than try to shape up in a few weeks by doing too much too soon.

Comparing Group With Individual Programs

An initial review found that group exercising leads to better adherence than does exercising alone (Dishman & Buckworth, 1996). More recently, two reviews of the literature (Burke, Carron, Eys, Ntoumanis, & Estabrooks, 2006; Hong, Hughes, & Prochaska, 2008) compared physical activity interventions that targeted individuals with interventions that used principles of group dynamics (i.e., group structure, group environment, group processes; see chapters 7 and 8) to increase cohesiveness. Results revealed that physical activity interventions based on group dynamics were more effective than were individually targeted interventions. A study by Estabrooks and colleagues (2011) applied principles of group dynamics to a physical activity intervention, called the

"Move More" program, in a large corporate setting. Because this was a real exercise program in a corporate setting, only group dynamic principles that would fit this natural setting were implemented. Compared with a traditional physical activity program, results still revealed increased physical activity along with positive changes in self-efficacy, satisfaction, goals, and social support.

Group programs offer enjoyment, social support, an increased sense of personal commitment to continue, and an opportunity to compare progress and fitness levels with others. One reason people exercise is for affiliation. Being part of a group fulfills this need and provides other psychological and physiological benefits. There tends to be a greater commitment to exercise when others are counting on you. For example, if you and a friend agree to meet at 7 a.m. four times a week to run for 30 minutes, you are likely to keep each appointment so that you don't disappoint your friend. Although group programs are more effective in general than individual programs, certain people prefer to exercise alone for convenience. In fact, about 25% of regular exercisers almost always exercise alone. Therefore, it is important for exercise leaders to understand the desires of participants to exercise in a group or alone.

KEY POINT Although exercising with a group generally produces higher levels of adherence than does exercising alone, tailoring programs to fit individuals and the constraints they feel can help them adhere to the program.

Leader Qualities

Although little empirical research has been conducted in the area, anecdotal reports suggest that program leadership is important in determining the success of an exercise program. A good leader can compensate to some extent for other program deficiencies, such as a lack of space or equipment. By the same token, weak leadership can result in a breakdown in the program, regardless of how elaborate the facility is. This underscores the importance of evaluating not only a program's activities and facilities but also the expertise and personality of the program leaders. Good leaders are knowledgeable, are likeable, and show concern for safety and psychological comfort.

Bray, Millen, Eidsness, and Leuzinger (2005) found that a leadership style that emphasized being interactive, encouraging, and energetic as well as providing face-to-face feedback and encouragement produced the most enjoyment in novice exercisers. A study by Puente and Anshel (2010) indicated that exercise leaders who have a democratic leadership style enhance the self-determination (i.e., increased feelings of competence and autonomy) of participants, which in turn leads to increased adherence rates and heightened levels of enjoyment. In addition, Loughead, Patterson, and Carron (2008) found that exercise leaders who promoted task cohesion (i.e., everyone in the group should be focused on improving fitness in one way or another) enhanced feelings of group cohesion and positive affect in individual members of the group. Thus, an interaction of leadership style and characteristics of the program produced the greatest enjoyment, which has been shown to affect exercise adherence.

An exercise leader may not be equally effective in all situations. Take the examples of Jillian Michaels, Richard Simmons, and Arnold Schwarzenegger, all of whom have had a large effect on fitness programs. Although they are all successful leaders, they appeal to different types of people. Thus, an individual trying to start an exercise program should find a good match in style with a leader who is appealing and motivating to that person. Finally, Smith and Biddle (1995) and Biddle (2011b) have noted that programs in Europe have been developed to train and empower leaders to promote physical activity. These have focused on behavioral change strategies rather than teaching a repertoire of physical movement skills.

Settings for Exercise Interventions

In their in-depth review of the literature, Dishman and Buckworth (1996) were among the first to systematically investigate the role of the exercise setting in relation to the effectiveness of exercise interventions. They found that school-based interventions had modest success, whereas the typical interventions conducted in worksites, health care facilities, and homes have been virtually ineffective. However, interventions applied in community settings have been the most successful. After reviewing the literature, the Task Force on Community Preventive Services recommended the following as the most effective types of community interventions (Kahn et al., 2002):

- Informational interventions that used "point-of-decision" prompts to encourage stair use or community-wide campaigns
- Behavioral or social interventions that used school-based physical education, social support in community settings, or individually tailored health behavior change
- Environmental and policy interventions that created or enhanced access to places for physical activity combined with informational outreach activity

An example of a successful community-based program is the Community Health Assessment and Promotion Project (CHAPP), sponsored by the Centers for Disease Control and Prevention. Designed to modify dietary and exercise behaviors in some 400 obese women from a predominantly black Atlanta community, CHAPP features a working coalition of various community organizations (e.g., churches, YMCAs). The program has seen participation rates of 60% to 70%, which is significantly higher than was

Adherence to Mental Training Programs

Intervention research has traditionally focused on adherence to exercise programs. However, more recent research has focused on adherence to psychological training programs (Shambrook & Bull, 1999). The following summarizes how to promote adherence to sport psychology training programs:

- Integrate psychological skills into existing routines and practice.
- Reduce perceived costs (not enough time) that are associated with using a mental training program.
- Reinforce athletes' feelings of enjoyment gained from using mental training strategies.
- Show the relationship between mental training and achievement of personal goals.
- Individualize mental training programs as much as possible.
- Promote mental training as much as possible before the individual starts to work on specific mental training exercises.

typical in this community previously (Lasco et al., 1989). These findings underscore the notion, discussed earlier, that the environment can have an important influence on physical activity levels.

KEY POINT Exercise intensities should be kept at moderate levels to enhance the probability of long-term adherence to exercise programs.

Strategies for Enhancing Adherence to Exercise

In this chapter we have presented reasons people participate (or don't participate) in physical activity, models of exercise behavior, and determinants of exercise adherence. Unfortunately, these reasons and factors are correlational, telling us little about the cause–effect relationship between specific strategies and actual behavior. Therefore, sport psychologists have used information about the determinants of physical activity, along with the theories of behavior change discussed earlier, to develop and test the effectiveness of various strategies that may enhance exercise adherence. As you'll recall, the transtheoretical model argues that the most effective interventions appear to match the stage of change the person is in, and therefore its proponents recommend that programs be individualized as much as possible. In making these individualized changes to enhance adherence to exercise, exercise leaders can use six categories

Promoting Physical Activity in School and Community Programs

Schools and communities have the potential to improve the health of young people by providing instruction, programs, and services that promote enjoyable, lifelong physical activity. To realize this potential, the following recommendations have been made (U.S. Department of Health and Human Services et al., 1997).

- *Policy.* Establish policies that promote enjoyable, lifelong physical activity among young people (e.g., require comprehensive, daily physical education for students in kindergarten through grade 12).

- *Environment.* Provide physical and social environments that encourage and enable safe and enjoyable physical activity (e.g., provide time during the school day for unstructured physical activity).

- *Physical education.* Implement physical education curricula and instruction that emphasize enjoyable participation in physical activity and that help students develop the knowledge, attitudes, motor skills, behavioral skills, and confidence needed to adopt and maintain physically active lifestyles.

- *Health education.* Implement health education curricula and instruction that help students develop the knowledge, attitudes, behavioral skills, and confidence needed to adopt and maintain physically active lifestyles.

- *Extracurricular activities.* Provide extracurricular activities that meet the needs of all students (e.g., provide a diversity of developmentally appropriate competitive and noncompetitive physical activity programs for all students).

- *Parental involvement.* Include parents and guardians in physical activity instruction and in extracurricular and community physical activity programs; encourage them to support their children's participation in enjoyable physical activities.

- *Personnel training.* Provide training for education, coaching, recreation, health care, and other school and community personnel that imparts the knowledge and skills needed to effectively promote enjoyable, lifelong physical activity among young people.

- *Health services.* Assess physical activity patterns among young people, counsel them about physical activity, refer them to appropriate programs, and advocate for physical activity instruction and programs for young people.

- *Community programs.* Provide a range of developmentally appropriate community sport and recreation programs that are attractive to all people.

- *Evaluation.* Regularly (every 3 weeks) evaluate school and community physical activity instruction, programs, and facilities (Lombard, Lombard, & Winett, 1995).

of strategies: behavior modification approaches, reinforcement approaches, cognitive–behavioral approaches, decision-making approaches, social support approaches, and intrinsic approaches. We discuss each of these approaches in some detail. Note that interventions often use a variety of these approaches to enhance adherence. In addition, researchers (Biddle & Gorley, 2012) discuss guidelines for implementing effective physical activity interventions. So conducting exercise adherence intervention studies is difficult and take lots of planning, knowledge of the literature, and the transition from theory to practice.

> **KEY POINT** Exercise leaders influence the success of an exercise program, so they should be knowledgeable, give lots of feedback and praise, help participants set flexible goals, and show concern for safety and psychological comfort.

Behavior Modification Approaches

Behavior modification is the planned, systematic application of learning principles to the modification of behavior. An exhaustive review by Dishman and Buckworth (1996) showed that behavior modification approaches to improving exercise adherence consistently produced extremely positive results and are usually associated with a 10% to 25% increase in the frequency of physical activity when compared with control groups (Buckworth & Dishman, 2007).

Behavior modification approaches may have an effect on something in the physical environment that acts as a cue for habits of behavior. The sight and smell of food are cues to eat; the sight of a television after work is a cue to sit down and relax. If you want to promote exercise until the exercise becomes more intrinsically motivating, one technique is to provide cues that will eventually become associated with exercise. There are interventions that attempt to do just that.

Prompts

A **prompt** is a cue that initiates a behavior. Prompts can be verbal (e.g., "You can hang in there"), physical (e.g., getting over a "sticking point" in weightlifting), or symbolic (e.g., workout gear in the car). The goal is to increase cues for the desired behavior and decrease cues for competing behaviors. Examples of cues for increasing exercise behavior include posters, slogans, notes, placing exercise equipment in visible locations, recruiting social support, and performing exercise at the same time and place every day. In one study, cartoon posters (symbolic prompts) were placed near elevators in a public building to encourage stair climbing (Brownell, Stunkard, & Albaum, 1980). In that study, the percentage of people using the stairs rather than the escalators increased from 6% to 14% within 1 month after the posters were put in place. The posters were removed, and after 3 more months stair use returned to 6%.

Motivational Interviewing

Motivational interviewing (MI) has been defined as "a collaborative, person-centered form of guiding to elicit and strengthen motivation for change (Miller & Rollnick, 2009, p. 137). More specifically, it is a brief psychotherapeutic intervention for increasing the likelihood that a client will consider, initiate, and maintain specific strategies for reducing harmful behavior. Although it was developed to enhance motivation in a variety of health contexts, it has been applied to adherence to exercise behavior. Breckon (2002) provides an overview of motivational interviewing, but the spirit of MI can be captured in the following principles.

- It is the client's task, not the counselor's, to articulate and resolve the client's ambivalence (e.g., exercise vs. not exercising).
- Motivation to change is elicited from the client rather than the counselor.
- The style of the counselor is more client centered (as opposed to confrontational or aggressive), letting the client figure out his ambivalence regarding exercise.
- Readiness to change is not a client trait but rather a fluctuating product of interpersonal interaction (i.e., the counselor might be assuming a greater readiness for change than is the case).
- The client–counselor relationship is more of a partnership, with the counselor respecting the autonomy and decision making of the client.

In an experiment by Vallerand, Vanden Auweele, Boen, Schapendonk, and Dornez (2005), a health sign linking stair use to health and fitness was placed at a junction between the staircase and elevator, increasing stair use significantly from baseline (69%) to intervention (77%). A second intervention involved an additional e-mail sent a week later by the worksite's doctor, pointing out the health benefits of regular stair use. Results revealed an increase in stair use from 77% to 85%. Once the sign was removed, however, stair use declined to around baseline levels of 67%. Finally, it has been shown that sending text messages regarding one's exercise goals produced significantly more brisk walking and greater weight loss compared with a control condition (Prestwich, Perugini, & Hurling, 2009).

Thus, removing a prompt can have an adverse effect on adherence behavior. Signs, posters, and other materials should be kept in clear view of exercisers to encourage adherence. Eventually, prompts can be gradually eliminated through a process called **fading**. Using a prompt less and less over time allows an individual to gain increasing independence without the sudden withdrawal of support, which occurred in the stair-climbing study. Finally, prompts can be combined with other techniques. For example, frequent (once a week) calls or prompts resulted in three times the number of physical activity bouts than did infrequent (every 3 weeks) calls (Lombard et al., 1995).

Contracting

Another way to change exercise behavior is to have participants enter into a contract with the exercise practitioner. The contract typically specifies expectations, responsibilities, and contingencies for behavioral change. Contracts should include realistic goals, dates by which goals should be reached, and consequences for not meeting goals (Willis & Campbell, 1992). A different type of contract, in which participants sign a statement of intent to comply with the exercise regimen, has also been used effectively (Oldridge & Jones, 1983). Research has shown that people who sign such a statement have significantly better attendance than those who refuse to sign. Thus, people's choosing not to sign a statement of intent to comply can be a signal that they need special measures to enhance their motivation. Furthermore, when contracting is used, the focus should be on helping the person take action, establishing criteria for meeting goals, and providing a means for clarifying consequences (Kanfer & Gaelick, 1986).

Reinforcement Approaches

Reinforcement, either positive or negative, is a powerful determinant of future action. To increase exercise adherence, incentives or rewards (e.g., T-shirts) can be given for staying with the program. We discuss a few reinforcement interventions in detail.

Charting Attendance and Participation

Public reporting of attendance and performance is another way to increase the motivation of participants in exercise programs. Performance feedback can be made even more effective if the information is converted to a graph or chart (e.g., Franklin, 1984). The chart is helpful and motivational in that it can tell people at a glance what changes are taking place (even small changes) and whether they are on target for the behavior involved. This may be important for maintaining interest, especially later in a program when people reach the point where improvements are often small and occur less frequently.

In addition, recording and charting keep individuals constantly informed, and often the increased cognitive awareness is all that is necessary to bring about changes in the target behavior. Furthermore, if people know that their workout record is available for everyone to see, they are much more likely to strive to keep up the positive behavior. (This information also tells exercise leaders, as well as other program participants, when is the right time to offer praise and encouragement.) An example of public charting focusing on increasing physical activity, but also offering some rewards for goal attainment, is a program called the Miles Club (Henning, 1987) in which runners and walkers recorded their weekly mileage on a public chart.

Besides public charting, a recent summary of the literature (Miche, Abraham, Whittington, McAteer, & Gupta, 2009) found that simply self-monitoring behaviors has shown to be one of the most effective ways to increase exercise adherence. Arrigo, Brunner-LaRocca, Lefkovits, Pfisterer, and Hoffmann (2008) demonstrated that just keeping a personal diary could enhance adherence. Results revealed that 73% of cardiac rehabilitation participants who kept a diary remained active a year later, whereas only 40% of participants in the control group remained physically active. Furthermore, Anshel and Seipel (2009) found that simply monitoring exercise-related behaviors via a checklist improved participants' strength and aerobic fitness and their adherence significantly more compared with a control group.

Furthermore, as participants reached certain designated intervals, they were rewarded with engraved paperweights and gift certificates, which enhanced the desired behavior. In addition, a competition was set up among different teams of people in the program. A team challenge board posted in a prominent location generated interest and enthusiasm for the contest. This competition also improved overall participation and group morale.

Although not classically a charting approach (but a participation approach), including top managers in corporate fitness programs has also been a successful strategy. Involvement of top managers greatly helped the success of one fitness program (Hobson, Hoffman, Corso, & Freismuth, 1987). When employees see the company president exercising in the gymnasium or fitness facility, they often see that person in a different light and may be challenged to match the commitment. Certainly, if top managers, CEOs, and the like have the time for fitness activities, then these activities must be important to the company. However, not all managers feel comfortable exercising with their employees, and programmers must take their needs into consideration when devising corporate physical activity programs.

Rewarding Attendance and Participation

Besides simply charting attendance and participation records, some studies have used rewards to enhance exercise adherence. In one study, two rewards were given for attendance during a 5-week jogging program: a $1 weekly deposit return, contingent on participation, and an attendance lottery coupon to win a prize, which was awarded for each class attended. The two interventions resulted in 64% attendance, whereas participants in a control group attended only 40% of the classes (Epstein, Wing, Thompson, & Griffiths, 1980).

An approach that has proved effective in corporate programs is for the company to pay most (but not all) of the cost of the exercise program. Researchers compared four methods of payment and found that program attendance was better when participants either received reimbursement based on attendance or split the fee with their employer. Interestingly, the lowest attendance occurred when the company paid the entire fee (Pollock, Foster, Salisbury, & Smith, 1982). Following this research, Campbell Soup Company required employees to pay $50 for the first year

of participation in a program. If they exercised three times a week or more during the second year, they paid only $25. If employees continued to exercise at this rate, they paid nothing the third year (Legwold, 1987). In general, the results have been encouraging for initial attendance or adherence but less so for long-term improvement. Additional incentives or reinforcement must be provided throughout the program to encourage adherence over longer time periods. In a case study of adolescents with cystic fibrosis, rewards were effective in improving adherence, but the adherence rates went down to baseline levels when the rewards were removed (Bernard, Cohen, & Moffett, 2009).

Feedback

Providing feedback to participants on their progress can have motivational benefits. For example, Scherf and Franklin (1987) developed a data documentation system for use in a cardiac rehabilitation setting in which the participants' body weight, resting heart rate, exercise heart rate, laps walked, laps run, and total laps after each session were recorded on individual forms. Staff members reviewed these records monthly with the participants and then returned record cards to the participants with appropriate comments. Individuals who met certain performance goals were then recognized in a monthly awards ceremony. This program resulted in improved exercise participation and adherence as well as in higher levels of motivation and enthusiasm than before the program was implemented. Otis and colleagues (2007) found that the more specific the feedback regarding exercise patterns, the higher the levels of adherence and intrinsic motivation. Finally, in a study by Marcus and colleagues (2007), participants who received printed feedback about exercises levels displayed higher levels of exercise and adherence than did participants who received feedback via telephone. Perhaps being able to see the printed feedback at all times reminded those in the print group to exercise.

KEY POINT The more individualized feedback is, the more likely it is to succeed.

Cognitive–Behavioral Approaches

Cognitive–behavioral approaches assume that internal events (i.e., thinking) have an important role in behavior change. Two techniques that we consider here are goal setting and a technique that involves association versus dissociation.

Goal Setting

Goal setting can be a useful motivational technique for improving exercise behavior and adherence. In one study, 99% of participants who were enrolled in an intermediate fitness class set multiple, personally motivating goals for their exercise participation (Poag-DuCharme & Brawley, 1994). The exercise goals that were most often reported included increasing cardiovascular fitness (28%), toning or strengthening muscles (18%), and losing weight (13%). Along with these goals were multiple action plans for reaching the goals, such as bringing fitness clothes to school or work (25%), attending fitness classes regularly (16%), and organizing time or work around fitness (9%).

Martin and colleagues (1984) found that flexible goals that participants set themselves resulted in better attendance and maintenance of exercise behavior (for a 3-month span) than did fixed, instructor-set goals. Specifically, attendance rates were 83% when participants set their own goals compared with 67% when instructors set the goals. Furthermore, 47% of those who set their own goals were still exercising 3 months after the program ended (compared with 28% of the people for whom the instructor set goals). Time-based goals resulted in better attendance (69%) than did distance-based goals (47%).

Several studies investigated the influence of goals that were intrinsic in content versus those that were extrinsic (Sebire, Standage, Gillison, & Vanteenkiste, 2013; Sebire, Standage, & Vansteenkiste, 2009, 2012). Using SDT as a guiding approach, the authors compared exercisers who set intrinsic goals (focusing on developing personal interests, values, and potential such as improving health) with those who set extrinsic goals (focusing outward, with pursuits directed toward external indicators of worth such as fame, wealth, and appealing image). Exercisers who set intrinsic goals reported higher levels of self-esteem, psychological well-being, psychological need satisfaction, and moderate to vigorous physical activity and lower levels of anxiety than did exercisers who set extrinsic goals. In addition, in extensive qualitative interviews, exercisers with intrinsic motives reported more satisfaction in achieving relatedness, autonomy, and competence. The authors argue that setting intrinsic goals influences physical activity behavior because such goals are associated with more autonomous forms of exercise motivation (Sebire, Standage, & Vansteenkiste, 2009, 2012).

Karoly and colleagues (2005) investigated the role of goal setting in regular and irregular exercisers. Results revealed that irregular exercisers tended to place greater motivational significance on their interfering goals (e.g., academic, relationships, family) than did regular exercisers, who were better able to balance their goals. In essence, regular exercisers have evidently acquired the capacity to elevate the self-regulatory significance of their relatively infrequent bouts of exercise to the same level as their academic and interpersonal goals. The authors suggest that irregular exercisers should reorganize their goal systems so that exercise goals receive just as much attention as do other important goals in their lives. Finally, Wilson and Brookfield (2009) compared the effects of process goals (e.g., maintain a minimum heart rate for 30 minutes of exercise) with those of outcome goals (e.g., lose 10 pounds in 5 weeks). Results revealed that the process goal group had higher adherence rates 6 months later (66%) than did the outcome goal group (44%). In addition, the process goal group exhibited higher intrinsic motivation than did the outcome goal group. These results demonstrate the importance of process goals in exercise adherence.

> **KEY POINT** Exercise-related goals should be self-set rather than instructor set, flexible rather than fixed, and time based rather than distance based.

Association and Dissociation

Thoughts or cognitions—what people focus their attention on—during exercising are also important to adherence to the exercise program. When the focus is on internal body feedback (e.g., how the muscles feel, or breathing), it is called **association**; when the focus is on the external environment (e.g., how pretty the scenery is), it is called **dissociation** (a distraction). In a study of a 12-week exercise program, the dissociative participants were superior in long-term maintenance of exercise after 3 months (87% vs. 37%) and 6 months (67% vs. 43%) compared with associative participants (Martin et al., 1984). Focusing on the environment instead of on how one feels may improve exercise adherence rates because thinking about other things reduces a person's boredom and fatigue. In individuals beginning to exercise, the use of dissociative strategies helped focus their attention away from the pain and discomfort of exercise (Lind, Welch, & Ekkekakis, 2009).

Decision-Making Approaches

Whether to start an exercise program can often be a difficult decision. To help people in this decision-making process, psychologists developed a technique known as a **decision balance sheet** (Hoyt & Janis, 1975; Wankel, 1984; see figure 18.3). This technique can make people more aware of potential benefits and costs of an exercise program. In devising a decision balance sheet, individuals write down the anticipated consequences of exercise participation in terms of gains to self, losses to self, gains to important others, losses to important others, approval of others, disapproval of others, self-approval, and self-disapproval.

In one study, participants who completed a decision balance sheet attended 84% of the classes during a 7-week period, whereas controls attended only 40% of the classes (Hoyt & Janis, 1975). In a variant of this study, Wankel (1984) compared the use of a full balance sheet with the use of a positive-only balance

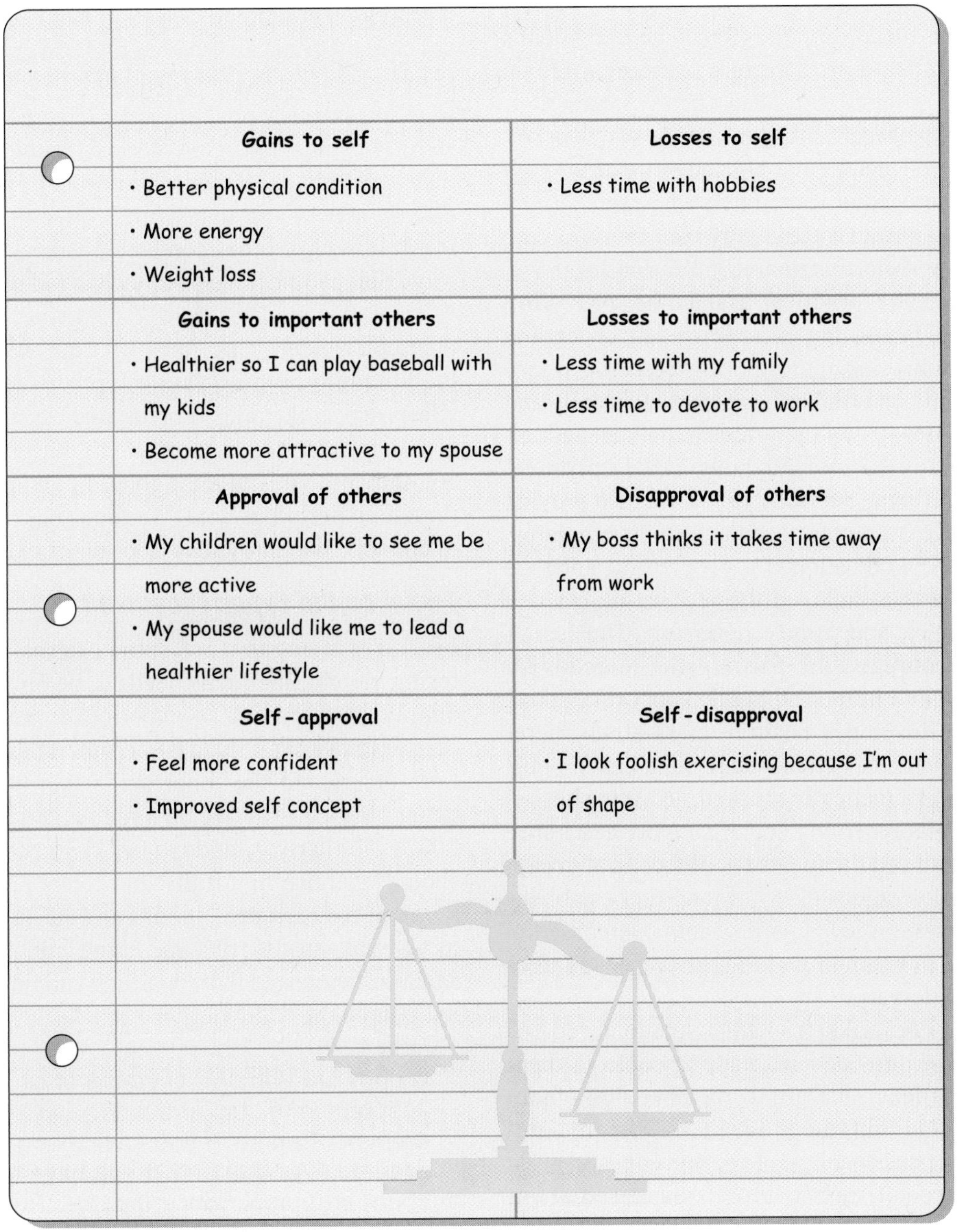

Gains to self	Losses to self
• Better physical condition	• Less time with hobbies
• More energy	
• Weight loss	
Gains to important others	**Losses to important others**
• Healthier so I can play baseball with my kids	• Less time with my family
	• Less time to devote to work
• Become more attractive to my spouse	
Approval of others	**Disapproval of others**
• My children would like to see me be more active	• My boss thinks it takes time away from work
• My spouse would like me to lead a healthier lifestyle	
Self-approval	**Self-disapproval**
• Feel more confident	• I look foolish exercising because I'm out of shape
• Improved self concept	

FIGURE 18.3 A decision balance sheet.

sheet, which deleted reference to any anticipated negative outcomes. Both types of balance sheets produced higher attendance rates than a control condition. Collectively, the available evidence demonstrates the effectiveness of involving participants in decisions before initiating an exercise program.

DISCOVER Activity 18.2 aids you in developing a decision balance sheet.

Social Support Approaches

In our context, social support refers to an individual's favorable attitude toward someone else's involvement in an exercise program. Social and family interactions may influence physical activity in many ways. Spouses, family members, and friends can cue exercise through verbal reminders. Significant others who exercise may model and cue physical activity by their behavior and reinforce it by their companionship during exercise. Often people give practical assistance, providing transportation, measuring exercise routes, or lending exercise clothing or equipment. In any case, social support from family and friends has been consistently and positively related to adult physical activity and adherence to structured exercise programs (U.S. Department of Health and Human Services, 1996). We next provide several specific examples of social support programs.

Wankel (1984) developed a program to enhance social support that included the leader, the class, a buddy (partner), and family members. The leader regularly encouraged the participants to establish and maintain their home and buddy support systems, attempted to develop a positive class atmosphere, and ensured that class attendance and social support charts were systematically marked. Results showed that participants receiving social support had better attendance than did the members of a control group. Hobson and colleagues (1987) found that establishing a buddy system helps participants overcome the initial anxiety of beginning a program and encourages continued participation.

King and Frederiksen (1984) set up three- or four-member groups and instructed people in them to jog with at least one group member throughout the study. In addition, the groups took part in team-building exercises to promote group cohesiveness. These small social support groups increased attendance and improved exercise behavior. The fact that exercise adherence improves when a leader gives per-

sonalized, immediate feedback and praises attendance and maintenance of exercise (Martin et al., 1984) also shows the importance of social support.

Intrinsic Approaches

Most of the approaches discussed so far rely on some sort of gimmick, knowledge, feedback, or reward system to enhance exercise behavior. Although these cues and rewards can certainly help improve exercise adherence, we all know that the most lasting motivation comes from within. We have learned from research on attempted cessation from smoking, alcohol, and other negative behaviors that most people do not change their exercise behavior over the long term based on extrinsic rewards or consequences. People do start an exercise program for extrinsic reasons (e.g., losing weight, decreasing the probability of certain disease states) and many times have initial success. But follow-up studies conducted years later typically show that people never really changed their lifestyles in a way that made exercise fun and enjoyable so that they could keep it up for a lifetime. In a review of the literature on the relationship between affect and adherence, Ekkekakis, Parfitt, and Petruzello (2011) concluded that if individuals don't find exercise pleasant, they probably are not going to maintain exercise for a long period of time. We focus next on two ways to enhance the enjoyment and fun of exercising.

Focus on the Experience Itself

Instead of trying to reach some external goal such as losing weight, the focus needs to be on changing the quality of the exercise experience. Although most people understand the desired outcomes of exercise, few understand the inner skills that are critical to being physically active on a regular basis (Kimiecik, 2002). Similarly, Maddux (1997) argued that people should exercise mindfully and focus on the present moment—in essence, should engage in exercise for its own sake instead of some future gain. For example, Maddux suggested that regarding running, we should tell people the following:

" Do not run thinking anything at all. Just run. Just take one step at a time. Just be in the present moment. If you have discomfort or even pain, notice that. If you have thoughts about stopping, notice that too. The focus on the present and the activity itself will make the activity enjoyable over the long haul. (p. 343) "

Focus on the Process

One way to make physical activity more enjoyable is to focus on the process instead of the product of the movement activities. In essence, we must move from an extrinsic orientation to an intrinsic one. Without this transformation, many people will drop out of an exercise program or bounce from one exercise program to the next (Kimiecik, 1998). Research has revealed that the focus on process, as opposed to outcome, is related to long-term maintenance of exercise (Field & Steinhart, 1992). People who focus on outcome usually run into the various societal and physical barriers discussed earlier. So to become lifelong exercisers, individuals need to make the shift from being more outcome oriented to being more process oriented.

Engage in Purposeful and Meaningful Physical Activity

In an interesting approach, Morgan (2001) argued that one of the key reasons that exercise adherence has hovered around 50% for more than 30 years is that activities prescribed for individuals often lack meaning and purpose for participants. Morgan persuasively argued that many activities such as stair climbing, treadmill walking or running, weightlifting, biking, and rowing tend to be regarded as nonpurposeful activities, yet they are just the type of activities that are prescribed in exercise programs. Several authors (e.g., Fahlberg & Fahlberg, 1990; Kretchmar, 2001) have noted that meaning is the key aspect of continued exercise. Kretchmar provided case studies of 10 exercisers (mostly walkers) who had maintained an exercise regimen for anywhere from 5 to 79 years. In addition, Kasch (2001) reported a 33-year longitudinal study of 15 individuals who had an adherence rate of 100% after this long time period. Although some alternative explanations can be put forth, these authors argue that the consistent factor among these longtime exercisers is that the physical activity was purposeful and meaningful to them. Thus, when we are designing exercise programs, we need to consider the interests of the particular people involved if we are to overcome the 50% dropout rate that has plagued us for more than 30 years.

Guidelines for Improving Exercise Adherence

Several elements have emerged as keys to enhancing adherence to exercise. We consolidate these elements now into guidelines for the aspiring fitness professional.

- Match the intervention to the stage of change of the participant.
- Provide cues for exercises (signs, posters, cartoons).
- Make the exercises enjoyable.
- Tailor the intensity, duration, and frequency of the exercises.
- Promote exercising with a group or friend.
- Have participants sign a contract or statement of intent to comply with the exercise program.
- Offer a choice of activities.
- Provide rewards for attendance and participation.
- Give individualized feedback.
- Find a convenient place for exercising.
- Have participants reward themselves for achieving certain goals.
- Encourage goals to be self-set, flexible, and time based (rather than distance based).
- Remind participants to focus on environmental cues (not bodily cues) when exercising.
- Use small-group discussions.
- Have participants complete a decision balance sheet before starting the exercise program.
- Obtain social support from the participant's spouse, family members, and peers.
- Suggest keeping daily exercise logs.
- Practice time management skills.
- Help participants choose a purposeful physical activity.

Brown and Fry (2011) suggest that fitness center staff—including front desk and membership staff, group fitness instructors, personal trainers, supervisors, and support staff (e.g., maintenance, child care)—can help members commit to physical activity and enjoy their fitness journey by creating a caring and task-involving environment. Relatedly, Huddleston, Fry, and Brown (2012) found that members' perception of a task-involving climate (i.e., climates that emphasized best effort, improvement, and cooperation and where everyone felt valued and welcomed) in corporate fitness centers were positively related to members' intrinsic motivation. (As discussed in chapter 6, intrinsic motivation is related to higher positive affect, greater physical self-worth, and increased exercise commitment.) Finally, Walsh (2012) provided practical guidelines to individual fitness professionals for enhancing exercise adherence. Specifically, he discussed the importance of active listening, intrinsic motivation, affect, and goals in promoting maximum exercise adherence.

DISCOVER   Activity 18.3 helps you develop ways to enhance exercise adherence.

VIEW   Activity 18.4 helps you assess motivational interviewing.

Treatment of Childhood and Adolescent Obesity: Seven-Step Model

The obesity epidemic has been well documented, as have the tremendous negative health implications and financial drain associated with it. Kirschenbaum's (2010) seven steps to success model, which takes a multidisciplinary approach to treating obesity, has received empirical support and produced some encouraging results. The seven steps are as follows:

- *Medical management.* Primary care pediatricians need to evaluate obese children for potential health problems caused by excess weight and offer feedback.

- *Education.* Parents should learn about the best ways to eat, stay active, and solve problems relating to weight.

- *Environmental changes.* Families making changes in the environments in which they live (e.g., taking televisions and computers out of bedrooms, eliminating high-fat foods in the house) can facilitate effective weight control among obese children.

- *Support groups.* Sustained contact can promote improved maintenance of weight loss. Take Off Pounds Sensibly is one such support group.

- *Cognitive–behavioral therapy: Clinics or short-term immersion.* Professionally conducted cognitive–behavioral programs for overweight children are available at local hospitals and clinics. Immersion programs (24-hour stays for at least 10 days) can focus on cognitive–behavioral therapy.

- *Cognitive–behavioral therapy: Long-term immersion.* Longer immersion programs generally lead to better outcomes.

- *Bariatric surgery.* For some seriously overweight teenagers who have tried the first six steps, specialized surgeries performed in surgical centers that have experience with and understanding of this problem are important options.

LEARNING AIDS

SUMMARY

1. **Discuss why people do or do not exercise.**
   Although the notion of a fitness boom has been sold to the public, most adults still do not exercise regularly, and only a small percentage of those who do exercise actually work out enough to receive health benefits. Thus, the first problem is getting people started in an exercise program. People usually follow a program to derive the many benefits of exercise, including weight control, reduced risk of cardiovascular disease, reduction of stress and depression, enhanced self-esteem, and increased enjoyment. The major reasons why people drop out include a perceived lack of time, lack of energy, and lack of motivation.

2. **Explain the different models of exercise behavior.**
   Theoretical models provide an introduction to the process of exercise adoption and adherence to an exercise regimen, and the major models that have been developed in this area include the health belief

model, the theory of planned behavior, social cognitive theory, the physical activity maintenance model, self-determination theory, the ecological model, and the transtheoretical model. The transtheoretical model offers the advantage of accounting for the process by which individuals move through different stages of exercise adoption, exercise behavior, and exercise maintenance.

3. **Describe the determinants of exercise adherence.**

The determinants of exercise behavior fall into two categories: personal factors and environmental factors. Personal factors include demographic variables (e.g., sex, socioeconomic status), cognitive and personality variables (e.g., self-efficacy, knowledge of health and exercise), and behaviors (e.g., smoking, diet). Environmental factors include the social environment (e.g., social support, past family influences), the physical environment (e.g., access to facilities, weather), and the characteristics of the physical activity itself (e.g., intensity, group or individual program). Recently, the setting the intervention takes place in has also been shown to be important, with community settings producing the most adherence.

4. **Identify strategies for increasing exercise adherence.**

Six types of approaches are useful for increasing exercise adherence: (a) behavior modification (e.g., prompts, contracting), (b) reinforcements (e.g., charting and rewarding attendance, feedback), (c) cognitive–behavioral approach (e.g., goal setting, association or dissociation), (d) decision making (e.g., decision balance sheet), (e) social support (e.g., classmates, family), and (f) intrinsic approaches.

5. **Give guidelines for improving exercise adherence.**

To implement exercise programs that maximize participant adherence, a group leader should make the exercise enjoyable and convenient, provide social support, encourage exercising with a friend, provide rewards for attendance and participation, and offer participants a range of activities from which to choose.

KEY TERMS

health belief model	transtheoretical model	prompt
theory of planned behavior	physical activity maintenance model	fading
subjective norm	ecological model	association
social cognitive theory	self-monitoring	dissociation
self-determination theory (SDT)	motivational interviewing	decision balance sheet

REVIEW QUESTIONS

1. Why is it important to understand the reasons people start and adhere to exercise programs (as well as drop out of exercise programs)? Use data from the Department of Health and Human Services to discuss your answer.

2. Your friend is sedentary and should start a regular exercise program but doesn't consider it important. What are three reasons you would cite to convince your friend?

3. Discuss the major points regarding the health belief model, the theory of planned behavior, and social cognitive theory as they relate to exercise behavior.

4. Discuss the transtheoretical model of behavioral change for an exerciser, including the different stages of change.

5. Discuss three personal factors and the ways in which they affect and predict adherence rates.

6. Discuss three environmental (physical and social) factors as they relate to exercise adherence and the structuring of exercise programs.

7. Discuss three behavior modification approaches to exercise adherence, and describe studies that have found these approaches effective.

8. How is a decision balance sheet used to help people stick with an exercise program? What research studies demonstrate its effectiveness?

9. Discuss three principles of motivational interviewing.

10. Discuss how self-determination theory could be used to predict exercise adherence.

CRITICAL THINKING QUESTIONS

1. You are hired as the new director of fitness by your local health and fitness club. The dropout rate has been large in the past. You know that adherence to exercise is difficult, but your boss wants you to increase participation and adherence rates. How would you go about designing a program that would maximize adherence rates? Be specific about the principles you would use and programs you would implement.

2. A big company is getting ready to build a new physical fitness facility. The company hires you as a consultant to discuss what to include in the building, where to build it, what equipment to purchase, and other factors to maximize participation by the public. Given what you know from research on the determinants of exercise adherence, what specific recommendations would you give the company?

19

Athletic Injuries and Psychology

After reading this chapter, you should be able to

1. discuss the role of psychological factors in athletic and exercise injuries,
2. identify psychological antecedents that may predispose people to athletic injuries,
3. compare and contrast explanations for the stress–injury relationship,
4. describe typical psychological reactions to injuries,
5. identify signs of poor adjustment to injury, and
6. explain how to implement psychological skills and strategies that can speed the rehabilitation process.

Ask anyone who has had a sport-related injury, and he will say that his injury experience involved a physical dysfunction as well as a number of psychological issues. It is not uncommon for injured athletes to feel isolated, frustrated, anxious, and depressed. And it is not just the psychological reactions to being injured that are issues. Sport and exercise participants who have major life stress or changes and who do not have good strategies for dealing with these stresses are more likely to be injured. Finally, anyone who has rehabilitated from a major athletic injury knows that issues such as motivation and goal setting are involved in a successful recovery and return to play.

Being injured is a significant life event, and it is one that happens quite often. It is estimated that more than 25 million people in the United States are injured each year in sport, exercise, and recreational settings (Williams & Andersen, 2007). Approximately 3.5 million U.S. children aged 14 and under are injured each year playing sports or participating in recreational activities (National Safe Kids Campaign, 2004). It is also estimated that 3.7 million people in the United States visit the emergency room each year for recreation- and sport-related injuries (Burt & Overbeck, 2001). Finally, data from Sweden show that 75% of elite soccer players will suffer an injury sometime during a season (Luthje, Nurmi, Kataga, Belt, Helenius, & Kaukonen, 1996). It is clear that injury is a potential outcome of regular and rigorous physical exercise. But what exactly is injury?

What Is Injury?

For the purposes of this text, the term *injury* means trauma to the body that results in at least temporary (but sometimes permanent) physical disability and inhibition of motor function. Injury is perceived to be multifaceted and is operationalized as participating while feeling pain so that (a) the pain or injury needs mental attention during participation; (b) the pain or injury involves some sort of loss of, or change in, function that directly affects performance capabilities; and (c) the injured person must decide whether to initiate and continue participation while experiencing the pain or injury.

A fine line separates injury from discomfort, which is a feeling associated with injury, but discomfort alone does not necessarily result in impaired movement. Acute discomfort or pain is typically—though not always—indicative of injury. Also, it is not necessarily true that pain or discomfort immediately accompany injury. An individual may be stiff and sore after a fall or after exercising excessively but may not be injured or have to withdraw from activity. Authorities may suggest abstaining from physical activity for 1, 2, or 3 days after an exercise injury occurs.

Causes of Injury

Most people think of injuries as being physical in nature, and generally that is true. However, outside of the physical, there are other factors that influence not only why performers get injured but also how well and how quickly they recover. Specifically, physical, social, psychological, and personality factors influence injuries, while stress also plays a role.

Physical Factors

Physical factors, such as muscle imbalances, high-speed collisions, overtraining, and physical fatigue, are the primary causes of exercise and sport injuries. However, psychological factors have also been found to play a role. In one study, psychosocial factors explained up to 18% of the time lost due to injury (Smith, Ptacek, & Patterson, 2000). Evidence also shows that psychological factors play a key role in injury rehabilitation. Thus, fitness professionals should understand both psychological reactions to injuries and ways in which mental strategies can facilitate recovery. In a survey of more than 800 sports medicine physicians, 80% indicated that they often or sometimes discussed emotional and behavioral problems related to injury with patient-athletes (Mann, Grana, Indelicato, O'Neil, & George, 2007). These physicians most often discussed the psychological issues of stress or pressure, anxiety, and burnout.

Social Factors

Social reasons have also been cited as a potential cause of athletic injury. One such factor is athletes' perception that playing with pain and injury is highly valued in American society (Malcom, 2006). Many studies illustrate that playing with injury is seen as a

A Biopsychosocial View of Injury

To better understand issues surrounding injury, some researchers recommend taking a biopsychosocial view, which examines the influence of sociocultural, ethical, and biomedical issues on the psychological aspects of sport injury (Brewer, Andersen, & Van Raalte, 2001; Wiese-Bjornstahl, 2010). In this view, which considers how psychology can help prevent and manage sport injury, outcomes related to both athlete health and performance excellence are of equal importance. This view is especially relevant in high-intensity sports that require explosive physical speed and strength, mental fortitude to push physical limits, and maximum effort and commitment to highly challenging goals associated with achieving high-level performance. Proponents of this view strongly believe that continued efforts in psychological research and professional practice are needed to protect the physical and mental health of athletes and that such efforts contribute to athletes' performance excellence and career longevity.

Along the lines of the biopsychosocial model, a model put forth by Brewer and colleagues (2001) considers seven key components: injury characteristics (e.g., severity, location), sociodemographic factors (e.g., age, sex), biological factors (e.g., neurochemistry, circulation), psychological factors (e.g., personality, affect), social or contextual factors (e.g., social support, life stress), intermediate biopsychological outcomes (e.g., range of motion, pain), and outcomes of sport injury rehabilitation (e.g., quality of life, readiness to return to sport).

desired characteristic by others such as friends, family, parents, teammates, and coaches. Albert (1999) found that cyclists describe injuries as one of the potential dangers and risks that one takes when cycling. In addition, individuals appear to endure pain and injury to reach their goals, such as running a marathon or making the starting team. In the past, this notion of playing with pain and injury was typically a masculine phenomenon because sport and exercise participation was traditionally seen as a masculine activity (Liston, Reacher, Smith, & Waddington, 2006). However, with the growth of female sport and exercise participation, females have adopted the value of minimizing injury and continuing to play with pain. For example, Malcom (2006) found that although girls playing softball did not start with the intention of playing through pain and injury, it did not take long for them to minimize injury, make fun of others who showed their pain, and play after occurrences that were later described as painful.

Psychological Factors

Sport psychologists Jean Williams and Mark Andersen (Andersen & Williams, 1988; Williams & Andersen, 1998, 2007) have helped clarify the role that psychological factors play in athletic injuries. Figure 19.1 shows a simplified version of their model. In this model, the relationship between athletic injuries and

psychological factors centers on stress. In particular, a potentially stressful athletic situation (e.g., competition, important practice, poor performance) can contribute to injury, depending on the athlete and how threatening he perceives the situation to be (see chapter 4). A situation perceived as threatening increases state anxiety, which causes a variety of changes in focus or attention and muscle tension (e.g., distraction and tightening up). This in turn leads to an increased chance of injury.

Stress isn't the only psychological factor that influences athletic injuries, however. As you also see in figure 19.1, personality factors, a history of stressors, and coping resources all influence the stress process and, in turn, the probability of injury. Furthermore, after someone sustains an injury, these same factors influence how much stress the injury causes and the individual's subsequent rehabilitation and recovery. Moreover, people who develop psychological skills (e.g., goal setting, imagery, and relaxation) deal better with stress, reducing both their chances of being injured and the stress of injury should it occur. It has also been suggested that the stress–athletic injury model can be extended to explain not only physical injuries but also physical illnesses that may result from the combination of intense physical training and psychosocial variables (Petrie & Perna, 2004). Thus, the model may also be useful in explaining why

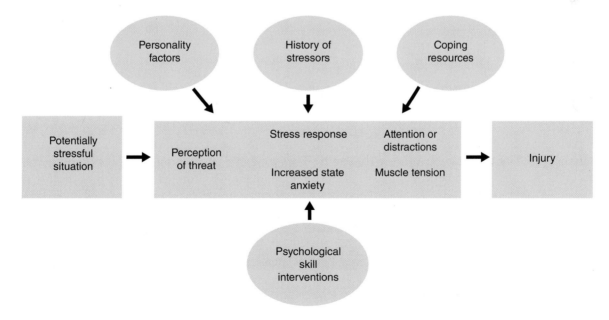

FIGURE 19.1 A model of stress and athletic injury.

Adapted, by permission, from M. Anderson and J. Williams, 1988, "A model of stress and athletic injury: Prediction and prevention," *Journal of Sport and Exercise Psychology* 10(3): 297.

athletes develop infections, poor adaption to training, and physical complaints when highly stressed. With this overview of the roles that psychological factors can play in athletic and exercise-related injuries, we now examine in more depth the pieces of the Anderson and Williams (1988) model, starting with personality factors.

Personality Factors

Personality traits were among the first psychological factors to be associated with athletic injuries. Investigators wanted to understand whether such traits as self-concept, introversion–extroversion, and tough-mindedness were related to injury. For example, would athletes with low self-concepts have higher injury rates than their counterparts with high self-concepts? Unfortunately, most of the research on personality and injury has suffered from inconsistency and the problems that have plagued sport personality research in general (Feltz, 1984a; also see chapter 2). Of course, this does not mean that personality is not related to injury rates; it means that to date we have not successfully identified and measured the particular personality characteristics associated with athletic injuries. In fact, recent evidence (Ford, Eklund, & Gordan, 2000; Smith et al., 2000) shows that personality factors such as optimism, self-esteem, hardiness, and trait anxiety do play a role in athletic injuries. However, this role is more complex than first thought because personality factors tend to moderate the stress–injury relationship. That is, if a person is characterized by high trait anxiety, the life stress–injury relationship may be stronger than in a person who has low trait anxiety.

Stress Levels

Stress levels, on the other hand, have been identified as important antecedents of athletic injuries. Research has examined the relationship between life stress and injury rates (Andersen & Williams, 1988; Johnson, 2007; Williams & Andersen, 1998, 2007). Measures of these stresses focus on major life changes, such as losing a loved one, moving to a different town, getting married, or experiencing a change in economic status. Such minor stressors and daily hassles as driving in traffic have also been studied. Overall, the evidence suggests that athletes with higher levels of life stress have more injuries than do those with lower levels of life stress: 85% of the studies verify that this rela-

tionship exists (Williams & Andersen, 2007). Thus, fitness and sport professionals should ask about major changes and stressors in athletes' lives and, when such changes occur, carefully monitor and adjust training regimens as well as provide psychological support.

Stress and injuries are related in complex ways. A study of 452 male and female high school athletes (in basketball, wrestling, and gymnastics) addressed the relationship between stressful life events; social and emotional support from family, friends, and coaches; coping skills; and the number of days athletes could not participate in their sport because of injury (Smith, Smoll, & Ptacek, 1990). No relationship was found among these factors across a school season. However, life stress was associated with athletic injuries in the specific subgroup of athletes who had both low levels of **social support** and low coping skills. These results suggest that when an athlete with few coping skills and little social support has major life changes, he or she is at a greater risk of athletic injury. Similarly, individuals who have low self-esteem, are pessimistic and low in hardiness (Ford et al., 2000), or have higher levels of trait anxiety (Smith et al., 2000) have more athletic injuries or lose more time as a result of their injuries. Certified athletic trainers and coaches should be on the lookout for these at-risk individuals. This finding supports the Andersen and Williams model, emphasizing the importance of looking at the multiple psychological factors in the stress–injury relationship.

According to recent studies, athletes at high risk of being injured had fewer injuries after stress management training interventions than their high-risk counterparts who did not take part in such training (Johnson, Ekengren, & Andersen, 2005; Maddison & Prapavessis, 2005). For example, Maddison and Prapavessis (2005) randomly assigned 48 rugby players at risk of injury (low in social support and high in avoidance coping) to either a stress management training or a no-training control condition. The stress management training involved progressive muscle relaxation, imagery thought management, goal setting, and planning. Results revealed that those in stress management training missed less time due to injuries and had an increase in coping resources and decreased worry after completing the program.

Research has also identified the specific stress sources for athletes when injured and when rehabilitating from injury (Gould, Udry, Bridges, & Beck, 1997b; Podlog & Eklund, 2006). Interestingly, the greatest sources of stress were not the result of the physical aspects of the injuries. Rather, psychological reactions (e.g., fear of reinjury, feeling that hopes and dreams were shattered, watching others get to perform) and social concerns (e.g., lack of attention, isolation, negative relationships) were mentioned more often as stressors (Gould et al., 1997b). For example, one elite skier commented,

" I felt shut up, cut off from the ski team. That was one of the problems I had. I didn't feel like I was being cared for, basically. Once I got home, it was like they (the ski team) dropped me off at home, threw all my luggage in the house, and were [saying] like 'See you when you get done.' I had a real hard time with that. "

Another injured athlete said,

" I [have a fear of reinjury] because I had a few recurrences and I hurt it a few times. So when I'm training now I'm always thinking about it and if it feels uncomfortable I think maybe something is going to happen. " (Podlog & Eklund, 2006, p. 55)

Other stresses that athletes experienced involved physical problems (e.g., pain, physical inactivity), medical treatment (e.g., medical uncertainty, seriousness of diagnosis), rehabilitation difficulties (e.g., dealing with slow progress, rehabbing on their own), financial difficulties, career worries, and their sense of missed opportunities (Gould et al., 1997b). Being familiar with these stress sources is important for the people working with injured athletes.

Teaching stress management techniques (see chapter 12) may help athletes and exercisers perform more effectively and may reduce their risk of injury and illness. In a well-designed clinical trials study, collegiate rowers who were randomly assigned to cognitive behavioral stress management training versus a control condition (those who received only the conceptual elements of the program but not the actual skills training) had fewer days lost to injury or illness across a season (Perna, Antoni, Baum, Gordon, & Schneiderman, 2003), verifying in a more controlled study earlier results found with competitive gymnasts (Kerr & Goss, 1996). Several other studies (Johnson et al., 2005; Maddison & Prapavessis, 2005) have also verified the effectiveness of stress management training in reducing injuries in athletes.

There are many factors that can lead to injury; physical, social, psychological, personality, and stress factors all contribute.

Relationship Between Stress and Injury

Understanding why athletes who have high stress in life are more prone to injury can significantly help you in designing effective sports medicine programs that deal with stress reactions and injury prevention. Two major theories have been advanced to explain the stress–injury relationship.

Attentional Disruption

One promising view is that stress disrupts an athlete's attention by reducing peripheral attention (Williams, Tonyman, & Andersen, 1991). Thus, a football quarterback under great stress might be prone to injury because he does not see a charging defender rushing in from his off side. When his stress levels are lower, the quarterback has a wider field of peripheral attention and is able to see the defender in time to avoid a sack and subsequent injury. It has also been suggested that increased state anxiety causes distraction and irrelevant thoughts. For instance, an executive who jogs at lunch after an argument with a colleague might be inattentive to the running path and step into a hole, twisting her ankle.

Increased Muscle Tension

High stress can be accompanied by considerable muscle tension that interferes with normal coordination and increases the chance of injury (Smith et al., 2000). For example, a highly stressed gymnast might have more muscle tension than is desirable and fall from the balance beam, injuring himself. Increased stress may also lead to generalized fatigue, muscle inefficiency, reduced flexibility, and motor coordination problems (Williams & Andersen, 2007). Teachers and coaches who work with an athlete undergoing major life changes (e.g., a high school student whose parents are in the midst of a divorce) should watch the athlete's behavior closely. If she shows signs of increased muscle tension or abnormal attentional difficulties when performing, it would be wise to ease training and initiate stress management strategies.

Other Psychologically Based Explanations for Injury

In addition to stress, sport psychologists working with injured athletes have identified certain attitudes that predispose players to injury. Rotella and Heyman (1986) observed that attitudes held by some coaches—such as "Act tough and always give 110%" or "If you're injured, you're worthless"—can increase the probability of athlete injury.

Act Tough and Give 110%

Slogans such as "Go hard or go home," "No pain, no gain," and "Go for the burn" typify the 110%-effort orientation many coaches promote. By rewarding such effort without also emphasizing the need to recognize and accept injuries, coaches encourage their athletes to play hurt or take undue risks (Rotella & Heyman, 1986). A college football player, for instance, may be repeatedly rewarded for sacrificing his body on special teams. He becomes ever more daring, running down to cover kickoffs, until one day he throws his body into another player and sustains a serious injury.

KEY POINT Teach athletes and exercisers to distinguish the normal discomfort accompanying overload and increased training volumes from the pain accompanying the onset of injuries.

This is not to say that athletes should not play assertively and hit hard in football, wrestling, and rugby. But giving 110% should not be emphasized so much that athletes take undue risks—such as spearing or tackling with the head down in football—and increase their chances of severe injuries.

The act-tough orientation is not limited to contact sports. Many athletes and exercisers are socialized into believing that they must train through pain and that "more is always better." They consequently overstrain and are stricken with tennis elbow, shin splints, swimmer's shoulder, or other injuries. Some sports medicine professionals believe that these types of overuse injuries are on the rise, especially in young athletes (DiFiori, 2002; Hutchinson & Ireland, 2003). Hard physical training does involve discomfort, but athletes and exercisers must be taught to distinguish the normal discomfort that accompanies overloading and increased training volumes from the pain that accompanies the onset of injuries.

If You're Injured, You're Worthless

Some people learn to feel worthless if they are hurt, an attitude that develops in several ways. Coaches may convey, consciously or otherwise, that winning is more important than the athlete's well-being. When a player is hurt, that player no longer contributes toward winning. Thus, the coach has no use for the player—and the player quickly picks up on this. Athletes want to feel worthy (like winners), so they play while hurt and sustain even worse injuries. A less direct way of conveying this attitude that injury means worthlessness is to say the "correct" thing (e.g., "Tell me when you're hurting! Your health is more important than winning") but then act very differently when a player is hurt. The player is ignored, which tells him that to be hurt is to be less worthy. Athletes quickly adopt the attitude that they should play even when they are hurt. The "Injury Pain and Training Discomfort" case study shows how athletes should be encouraged to train hard without risking injury.

Sport Ethic

Over the past 20 years, a growing body of sociological research has contributed to a greater understanding of the sport norms, values, and environments that are linked to the occurrence of injury (see Heil & Podlog, 2012, for a review). Much of this research examines the personal experiences of injured athletes, the ways in which athletes internalize "macho" and gendered beliefs about playing with pain and injury, and the normalization of pain and injury. From a sociological perspective, injury risk increases the more a culture narrowly defines success according to win–loss records, values external forms of success (e.g., scholarships, prize money) over intrinsic achievement, and promotes an unquestioning adoption of or overconformity to the norms of a sport ethic that cultivates a culture of risk.

The statement "Winners never quit and quitters never win" seems accurate at first glance, but the message is really that athletes should play through pain and injury because winning is more important than losing. Athletes who do play with injury and pain are valued more by coaches and teammates, which increases the pressure to play when hurt, even when it may risk the athlete's career. Long-term health is often jeopardized by the short-term goal of winning. Many athletes who play with injury and pain years later walk with crutches, take an hour to get out of bed, or suffer from brain injury (usually caused by multiple concussions). Deciding whether an athlete should play or sit out is not easy. However, the long-term health and well-being of athletes must be paramount for the coaches, athletic trainers, and medical personnel making these types of decisions.

This sport ethic is especially evident in football, where bravado and machismo lead to a denial of pain and injury (Gregory, 2010). The negative effects of this culture are seen in the recent highlighting of concussions, which revealed that many football players suffered multiple concussions during their careers but still went back in and continued playing. Some of these players exhibited disturbing psychological reactions (e.g., suicide, cognitive deficits, severe depression, cumulative deterioration of brain functioning) after retiring from football. Mounting evidence is starting to indicate that concussions caused these psychological issues after retirement. As a result, new procedures of monitoring concussions much more closely and taking precautions with players who have more than one concussion are being put in place.

◉ VIEW Activity 19.1 helps you gain insight into the stress–injury relationship.

Psychological Reactions to Exercise and Athletic Injuries

Despite taking physical and psychological precautions, many people engaged in vigorous physical

Injury Pain and Training Discomfort

Sharon Taylor coaches a swimming team that has been plagued over the years by overuse injuries. Yet her team is proud of its hard-work ethic. Incorporating swimming psychologist Keith Bell's (1980) guidelines, Sharon taught the team to view the normal discomfort of training (pain) as a sign of growth and progress rather than something awful or intolerable. For her team, normal training discomfort is not a signal to stop but a challenge to do more.

Along the way, Sharon's swimmers took their training philosophy too far and misinterpreted Bell's point. Therefore, Sharon set a goal of having her swimmers distinguish between the discomfort of training and the pain of injury. At the start of the season she discussed her concerns and asked swimmers who had sustained overuse injuries during the preceding season to talk about the differences between pushing through workouts (overcoming discomfort) and ignoring injury (e.g., not stopping or telling the coach when a shoulder ached). She changed the team slogan from "No pain, no gain" to "Train hard and smart." She also revamped the training cycle to include more days off and initiated a team rule that no one could swim or lift weights on the days off. Sharon periodically discussed injury in contrast to discomfort with her swimmers during the season, and she reinforced correct behavior with praise and occasional rewards. Sharon informed the parents of her swimmers about the need to monitor their children's chronic pains.

As the season progressed, the swimmers began to understand the difference between injury pain and the normal discomfort of hard training. At the end of the season, most of the swimmers had remained healthy and were excited about the state meet.

activity sustain injuries. Even in the best-staffed, best-equipped, and best-supervised programs, injury is inherently a risk. Therefore, it is important to understand psychological reactions to activity injuries. Sport psychology specialists and athletic trainers have identified varied psychological reactions to injuries. Some people view an injury as a disaster. Others may view their injury as a relief—a way to get a break from tedious practices, save face if they are not playing well, or even have an acceptable excuse for quitting. Although many different reactions can occur, some are more common than others. Sport and fitness professionals must observe these responses.

Emotional Responses

As they began to examine the psychology of injury in athletes, sport psychologists first speculated that people's reaction to athletic or exercise-related injury was similar to the response of people facing imminent death. According to this view, exercisers and athletes who have become injured often follow a five-stage **grief response** process (Hardy & Crace, 1990). These stages are

1. denial,
2. anger,
3. bargaining,
4. depression, and
5. acceptance and reorganization.

This grief reaction has been widely cited in articles about the psychology of injury, but evidence shows that although individuals may exhibit many of these emotions in response to being injured, they do not follow a set, stereotypical pattern or necessarily feel each emotion in these five stages (Brewer, 1994; Evans & Hardy, 1995; Quinn & Fallon, 1999; Udry, Gould, Bridges, & Beck, 1997). Sport psychologists now recommend that we view typical responses to injury in a more flexible and general way—people do not move neatly through set stages in a predetermined order. Rather, many have more than one of these emotions and thoughts simultaneously or revert back to stages that they have experienced previously. Nevertheless, although emotional responses to being injured have not proved to be as fixed or orderly as sport psychologists once thought, you can expect injured individuals to exhibit three general categories of responses (Udry et al., 1997):

1. *Injury-relevant information processing.* The injured athlete focuses on information related to the pain of the injury, awareness of the extent of injury, and questions about how the injury happened, and the individual recognizes the negative consequences or inconvenience.

2. *Emotional upheaval and reactive behavior.* Once the athlete realizes that she is injured, she may become emotionally agitated; have vacillating emotions; feel emotionally depleted; feel isolated and disconnected; and feel shock, disbelief, denial, or self-pity.

3. *Positive outlook and coping.* The athlete accepts the injury and deals with it, initiates positive coping efforts, exhibits a good attitude and is optimistic, and is relieved to sense progress.

Most athletes move through these general patterns in reaction to injury, but the speed and ease with which they progress vary widely. One person may move through the process in a day or two; others may take weeks or even months to do so. One long-term study of 136 severely injured Australian athletes showed that the period immediately after the injury was characterized by the greatest negative emotions (Quinn & Fallon, 1999).

Other Reactions

Athletes have additional psychological reactions to injury (Petitpas & Danish, 1995). Some of these other reactions may include the following:

1. *Identity loss.* Some athletes who can no longer participate because of an injury have a loss of personal identity; that is, an important part of themselves is lost, seriously affecting self-concept. Research has found that athletes had higher levels of intrinsic motivation when coaches provided a supportive environment during the rehabilitation process, which, in turn, helped them maintain an important part of their self-identity as athletes (Horn, Brinza, & Massie, 2013).

2. *Fear and anxiety.* When injured, many athletes have high levels of fear and anxiety. They worry about whether they will recover, whether reinjury will occur, and whether someone will replace them permanently in the lineup. Because the athlete cannot practice and compete, there's plenty of time for worry.

3. *Lack of confidence.* Given the inability to practice and compete and their deteriorated physical status,

athletes may lose confidence after an injury. Lowered confidence can result in decreased motivation, inferior performance, or even additional injury if the athlete overcompensates.

4. *Performance decrements.* Because of lowered confidence and missed practice time, athletes may have postinjury declines in performance. Many athletes have difficulty lowering their expectations after an injury and may expect to return to a preinjury level of performance.

5. *Group processes.* Injury to an athlete can affect group processes in a team either negatively or positively. For example, an injured basketball player who can't play for two months might disrupt the smooth flow and teamwork that was developed through working together with the other four players. Conversely, sometimes when a high scorer gets injured, the other players rally around each other and contribute more effort, actually bringing the team closer together (see Benson et al., 2013).

The loss of personal identity is especially significant to athletes who define themselves solely through sport. People who sustain a career- or activity-ending injury may require special, often long-term, psychological care.

Signs of Poor Adjustment to Injury

Most people work through their responses to injury, showing some negative emotions but not great difficulty in coping. One national survey of athletic trainers revealed that they refer 8% of their injured clients to psychological counseling (Larson, Starkey, & Zaichkowsky, 1996). How can you tell whether an athlete or exerciser exhibits a normal injury response or is having serious difficulties that require special attention? The following are warning signs of poor adjustment to athletic injury (Petitpas & Danish, 1995):

- Feelings of anger and confusion
- Obsession with the question of when one can return to play

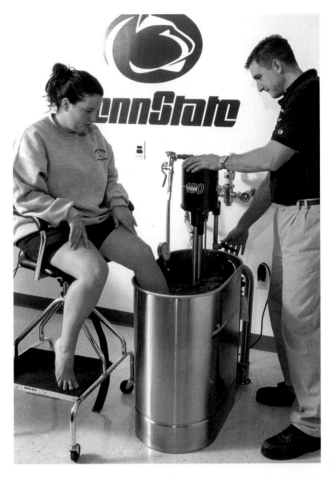

Sport psychology can be used to aid in an athlete's rehabilitation. Athletes who use goal setting, self-talk, and healing imagery tend to recover more quickly from injuries than do athletes who don't use these strategies.

Physiological Components of Injury Recovery

One of the most interesting research developments in medicine deals with how psychological stress and emotions influence the physiology of injury recovery. Cramer Roh and Perna (2000), for example, indicated that high levels of depression and stress can disrupt the body's natural healing process. These authors contended that psychological stress increases catecholamines and glucocorticoids, which impair the movement of healing immune cells to the site of the injury and interfere with the removal of damaged tissue. Prolonged stress may also decrease the actions of insulin-like growth hormones that are critical during the rebuilding process. Finally, stress is also believed to cause sleep disturbance, another factor identified to interfere with physiological recovery (Perna et al., 2003).

- Denial (e.g., "The injury is no big deal")
- Repeatedly coming back too soon and becoming reinjured
- Exaggerated bragging about accomplishments
- Dwelling on minor physical complaints
- Guilt about letting the team down
- Withdrawal from significant others
- Rapid mood swings
- Statements indicating that recovery will not occur no matter what is done

A fitness instructor or coach who observes someone with these symptoms should discuss the situation with a sports medicine specialist and suggest the specialized help of a sport psychologist or counselor. Similarly, a certified athletic trainer who notices these abnormal emotional reactions to injuries should make a referral to a sport psychologist or another qualified mental health provider just as she should if an uninjured athlete exhibits general life issues (e.g., depression, severe generalized anxiety) of a clinical nature.

KEY POINT Most people have a typical reaction to injury, but the speed and ease with which they progress through the stages can vary widely.

Role of Sport Psychology in Injury Rehabilitation

Tremendous gains have been made in recent years in the rehabilitation of athletic and exercise-related injuries. An active recovery, less invasive surgical techniques, and weight training are among these advances in rehabilitation. New psychological techniques also facilitate the injury recovery process, and professionals increasingly use a holistic approach to healing both the mind and body. Understanding the psychology of injury recovery is important for everyone involved in sport and exercise.

Psychology of Recovery

In one study of how psychological strategies help injury rehabilitation, Ievleva and Orlick (1991) examined whether athletes with fast-healing (fewer than 5 weeks) knee and ankle injuries demonstrated greater use of psychological strategies and skills than those with slow-healing (more than 16 weeks) injuries. The researchers conducted interviews and assessed attitude and outlook, stress and stress control, social support, positive self-talk, healing imagery, goal setting, and beliefs. They found that fast-healing athletes used more goal-setting and positive self-talk strategies and, to a lesser degree, more healing imagery than did slow-healing athletes. Additional studies have shown that psychological interventions positively influenced athletic injury recovery (Cupal & Brewer, 2001), mood during recovery (Johnson, 2000), coping (Evans, Hardy, & Fleming, 2000), and confidence (Magyar & Duda, 2000).

Increasing recognition that physical healing does not necessarily coincide with psychological readiness to return has spawned research on the transition to the return to play (Podlog & Eklund, 2006, 2009, 2010). Challenges involved in the return to sport include anxiety over reinjury, heightened performance anxiety, uncertainty about meeting the expectations of others, diminished physical self-efficacy, and concerns about performing at preinjury levels. The type of motivation to return to play also appears to be important. For example, athletes who exhibited higher levels of intrinsic motivation to return to play displayed a greater appreciation of the sport, enhanced mental toughness, and heightened motivation for success, whereas ath-

How Athletes Use Imagery When Recovering from Injury

Driediger, Hall, and Galloway (2006) studied imagery use in injured athletes taking part in sport rehabilitation. They discovered that the athletes most often used imagery while observing practices, while driving, and at home in bed. These athletes mainly used imagery during their rehabilitation sessions, as opposed to before or after. They used imagery to rehearse rehabilitation exercises, improve performance of certain exercises, facilitate goal setting, facilitate relaxation, control anxiety, motivate themselves to engage in their rehabilitation exercises, maintain a positive attitude, and maintain concentration. Most interesting was the use of healing imagery to aid in injury recovery and for controlling pain. The findings clearly show that athletes use imagery during their rehabilitation from athletic injuries.

letes with extrinsic motivation displayed diminished confidence, unsatisfying performances, and heightened competitive anxiety (Podlog & Eklund, 2010).

Psychological training and psychological factors affect adherence to treatment protocols as well (Brewer et al., 2000; Scherzer et al., 2001). Brewer and colleagues (2000) found that self-motivation was a significant predictor of home exercise compliance, and Scherzer and colleagues (2001) discovered that goal setting and positive self-talk were positively related to home rehabilitation exercise completion and program adherence. These findings are important because failure to adhere to medical advice (e.g., doing rehabilitation exercises, icing) is a major problem in injury rehabilitation.

Surveys of athletic trainers also support these conclusions (Gordon, Milios, & Grove, 1991; Larson et al., 1996; Ninedek & Kolt, 2000; Wiese, Weiss, & Yukelson, 1991). Larson and colleagues, for example, asked 482 athletic trainers to identify the primary characteristics of athletes who most or least successfully coped with their injuries. The trainers observed that athletes who more successfully coped with their injuries differed from their less successful counterparts in several ways: They complied better with their rehabilitation and treatment programs; they demonstrated a more positive attitude about their injury status and life in general; they were more motivated, dedicated, and determined; and they asked more questions and became more knowledgeable about their injuries. Some 90% of these trainers also reported that it is important or very important to treat the psychological aspects of injuries. This research makes it clear that psychological factors play an important role in injury recovery. Thus, injury treatment should include psychological techniques for enhancing healing and recovery.

Implications for Injury Treatment and Recovery

Research on the psychology of athletic injury clearly shows that a holistic approach—one that supplements physical therapy with psychological strategies to facilitate recovery from injury—is to be recommended. The first step in providing such a holistic approach to recovery is to understand the process of psychological rehabilitation and recovery. Figure 19.2 depicts the three phases of injury and injury recovery that Bianco, Malo, and Orlick (1999) identified in their study of seriously injured and ill elite skiers. Each stage poses specific challenges to the athlete and thus often dictates different approaches to the psychology of recovery.

In the initial phase of injury or illness, for example, it is best to focus on helping the athlete deal with the emotional upheaval that accompanies the onset of injury. A major source of stress at this initial stage is the uncertainty that accompanies the undiagnosed condition and the implications of any diagnosis, so the clinician should focus on helping the athlete understand the injury. During the rehabilitation and recovery stage, the clinician should focus on helping the athlete sustain motivation and adherence to rehabilitation protocols. Goal setting and maintaining a positive attitude, especially during setbacks, are very important in this regard. Last is the return to full activity; even though an athlete is physically cleared for participation, his recovery is not complete until he can return to normal functioning in his sport. Moreover, evidence reveals

Predicting and Enhancing Adherence to Sport Injury Rehabilitation

Brewer (2013) highlighted some of the key predictors of adherence to injury rehabilitation as well as some ways to enhance adherence. These are listed as follows:

- *Personal attributes*—Pain tolerance, tough-mindedness, self-motivation, athletic identity
- *Environmental characteristics*—Social support, practitioner expectations of adherence, comfortable clinical settings, convenient scheduling of appointments
- *Effective adherence interventions*—Reinforcement, goal setting, education, multimodal interventions
- *Predictors of adherence*—Rehabilitation self-efficacy, personal control over injury recovery, perceptions of injury severity, emotional distress, treatment efficacy

Sport psychology professionals can play a role in helping sport injury practitioners learn and implement interventions for enhancing adherence.

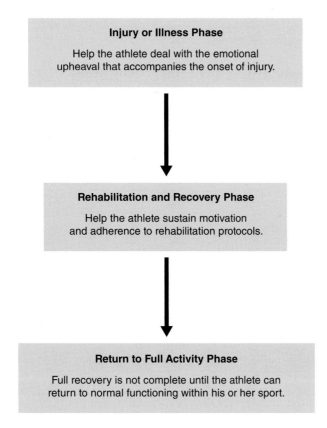

Injury or Illness Phase

Help the athlete deal with the emotional upheaval that accompanies the onset of injury.

Rehabilitation and Recovery Phase

Help the athlete sustain motivation and adherence to rehabilitation protocols.

Return to Full Activity Phase

Full recovery is not complete until the athlete can return to normal functioning within his or her sport.

FIGURE 19.2 Three phases of injury recovery.

that after severe injury, return to normal competitive functioning is much harder than often thought and often takes considerable time—from 6 weeks to a year (Bianco et al., 1999; Evans et al., 2000).

Understanding the psychological aspects of injury rehabilitation derives from understanding responses to injury. However, understanding the process of injury response is not enough. Several psychological procedures and techniques facilitate the rehabilitation process, including building rapport with the injured athlete, educating the athlete about the injury and recovery process, teaching specific psychological coping skills, preparing the athlete to cope with setbacks, fostering social support, and learning (and encouraging the athlete to learn) from other injured athletes. We discuss these in more detail in the following section. It is the sport psychologist's or trainer's responsibility to learn and administer these procedures as appropriate.

Identify Athletes and Exercisers Who Are at Risk for Injury

Several studies (Johnson et al., 2005; Maddison & Prapavessis, 2005) have shown that athletes at higher

risk of sustaining athletic injuries can be identified. These athletes have been characterized by combinations of high trait anxiety, high life stress, low psychological and coping skills, low social support, and high avoidance coping. Especially promising were the findings that when these athletes at risk of injury took part in stress management training, they lost less time due to injuries and had fewer injuries than at-risk athletes who did not receive such training. Coaches, certified athletic trainers, and fitness personnel should therefore work to identify athletes at high risk for injury.

Build Rapport With the Injured Person

When athletes and exercisers are injured, they often feel disbelief, frustration, anger, confusion, and vulnerability. Such emotions can make it difficult for helpers to establish rapport with the injured person. Empathy—trying to understand how the injured person feels—is helpful. Showing emotional support and striving to be there for the injured party also help. Visit, phone, and show your concern for the person. This is especially important after the novelty of the injury has worn off and the exerciser or athlete feels forgotten. In building rapport, do not be overly optimistic about a quick recovery. Instead, be positive and stress a team approach to recovery: "This is a tough break, Mary, and you'll have to work hard to get through this injury. But I'm in this with you, and together we'll get you back."

Educate the Injured Person About the Injury and Recovery Process

Especially when someone is working through a first injury, tell him what to expect during the recovery process. Help him understand the injury in practical terms. For example, if a high school wrestler sustains a clavicular fracture (broken collarbone), you might bring in a green stick and show him what his partial "green stick" break looks like. Explain that he will be out of competition for about 3 months. Equally important, tell him that in 1 month his shoulder will feel much better. Tell him he will likely be tempted to try to resume some normal activities too soon, which might cause a setback.

Outline the specific recovery process. For instance, the certified athletic trainer may indicate that a wrestler can ride an exercise cycle in 2 to 3 weeks, begin range-of-movement exercises in 2 months, and follow this with a weight program until he regains his preinjury strength levels in the affected area. Then and only then may he return to wrestling, first in drill situations and then slowly progressing back to full contact. (For a comprehensive discussion of the progressive rehabilitation process, see Tippett & Voight, 1995.)

Teach Specific Psychological Coping Skills

The most important psychological skills to learn for rehabilitation are goal setting, positive self-talk, imagery or visualization, and relaxation training (Hardy & Crace, 1990; Petitpas & Danish, 1995; Wiese & Weiss, 1987).

> **KEY POINT** For complete recovery, both physical and psychological aspects of injury rehabilitation must be considered.

Goal setting can be especially useful for athletes rehabilitating from injury. For example, Theodorakis, Malliou, Papaioannou, Beneca, and Filactakidou (1996) found that setting personal performance goals with knee-injured participants facilitated performance, just as it did with uninjured individuals. They concluded that, combined with strategies for enhancing self-efficacy, personal performance goals can be especially helpful in decreasing an athlete's recovery time. Some goal-setting strategies to use with injured athletes and exercisers include setting a date to return to competition; determining the number of times per week to come to the training room for therapy; and deciding the number of range-of-motion, strength, and endurance exercises to do during recovery sessions. Highly motivated athletes tend to do more than is required during therapy, and they can reinjure themselves by overdoing it. Emphasize the need to stick to goal plans and not do more when they feel better on a given day.

> **KEY POINTS**
>
> Build rapport with the injured athlete by
>
> - taking his perspective (thinking about how he must feel),
> - providing emotional support, and
> - being realistic but positive and optimistic.

Self-talk strategies help counteract the lowered confidence that can follow injury. Athletes should learn to stop their negative thoughts ("I am never going to get better") and replace them with realistic, positive ones ("I'm feeling down today, but I'm still on target with my rehabilitation plan—I just need to be patient and I'll make it back").

Visualization is useful in several ways during rehabilitation. An injured player can visualize herself in game conditions to maintain her playing skills and facilitate her return to competition. Or someone might use imagery to quicken recovery, visualizing the removal of injured tissue and the growth of new healthy tissue and muscle. This may sound far-fetched, but the use of healing imagery often characterizes fast-healing patients (see Ievleva & Orlick, 1991, for a study on healing from knee injury). Finally, Sordoni, Hall, and Forwell (2000) found that athletes who use imagery in sport do not automatically use it to the same degree when they are injured. Thus, those assisting in injury rehabilitation need to encourage athletes to use imagery during rehabilitation just as they do when participating in their sport.

Relaxation training can be useful for relieving pain and stress, which usually accompany severe injury and the injury recovery process. Athletes can also use relaxation techniques to facilitate sleep and reduce general levels of tension. For example, Walsh (2011) describes how the relaxation response can be used to help injured athletes reduce stress and recover from injury.

> **KEY POINT** Highly motivated people tend to overdo. Recovering athletes should not exceed their program just because they feel better on a given day.

Teach How to Cope With Setbacks

Injury rehabilitation is not a precise science. People recover at different rates, and setbacks are not uncommon. Thus, an injured person must learn to cope with setbacks. Inform the athlete during the rapport stage that setbacks will likely occur. At the same time, encourage the person to maintain a positive attitude toward recovery. Setbacks are normal and not a cause for panic, so there's no reason to be discouraged. Similarly, rehabilitation goals need to be evaluated and periodically redefined. To help teach people coping skills, encourage them to inform significant others when they have setbacks. By discussing their feelings, they can receive the necessary social support.

> **KEY POINT** Prepare the injured person for coping with setbacks during the recovery process.

Foster Social Support

Social support of injured athletes can take many forms, including emotional support from friends and loved ones; informational support from a coach in the form of statements such as "You're on the right track"; and even tangible support, such as money from parents (Hardy & Crace, 1991). Research (Bianco, 2001; Green & Weinberg, 2001) has shown that social support is critical for injured athletes. They need to know that their coaches and teammates care, to feel confident that people will listen to their concerns without judging them, and to learn how others have recovered from similar injuries.

It is a mistake to assume that adequate social support occurs automatically. As previously noted, social support tends to be more available immediately after an injury and to become less available during the later stages of recovery. Remember that injured people benefit from receiving adequate social support throughout the recovery process. In providing social support, consider these guidelines and recommendations:

• Social support serves as a resource that facilitates coping. It can help reduce stress, enhance mood, increase motivation for rehabilitation, and improve treatment adherence. Thus, efforts must be made to provide social support to injured athletes. Medical personnel should receive training in the provision of social support, and efforts should be made to involve and inform coaches and significant others about how they might socially support the injured athlete.

• In general, athletes turn to coaches and medical professionals for informational support and to family and friends for emotional support. Athletes are less likely to seek support from persons who have not been helpful in the past or who do not seem committed to their relationship. Finally, people with low self-esteem are less likely than others to seek social support (Bianco & Eklund, 2001).

• Recognize that the type of social support an athlete needs varies across rehabilitation phases and support sources (Bianco, 2001). For example, in the injury or illness phase, informational social support is critical so that the athlete clearly understands the nature of the injury. Knowledgeable sports medicine personnel who are able to explain injuries in terms that athletes understand are critical in this regard. However, in the recovery stage, athletes may need a coach to help challenge them and motivate them to adhere to their rehabilitation plan.

• The need for social support is greatest when the rehabilitation process is slow, when setbacks occur, or when other life demands place additional stress on athletes (Evans et al., 2000).

• Although generally helpful, social support can have negative effects on injured athletes. This occurs in cases in which the support provider does not have a good relationship with the athlete, lacks credibility in the athlete's eyes, or forces support on the athlete. Athletes view social support as beneficial when the type of social support matches their needs and conveys positive information toward them (Bianco, 2001).

Learn From Injured Athletes

Another good way to help injured athletes and exercisers cope with injury is to heed recommendations that injured athletes have made. Members of a U.S. ski team who sustained season-ending injuries made several suggestions for injured athletes, the coaches working with them, and sports medicine providers (Gould, Udry, Bridges, & Beck, 1996, 1997a). These recommendations, summarized in "Elite Skiers' Recommendations for Coping With Season-Ending Injuries and Facilitating Rehabilitation," should be considered by both injured athletes and those assisting them.

DISCOVER Activity 19.2 explains how to design a sport psychology injury rehabilitation program.

Elite Skiers' Recommendations for Coping With Season-Ending Injuries and Facilitating Rehabilitation

Members of a U.S. ski team who sustained season-ending injuries offered the following recommendations for other injured athletes, coaches, and sports medicine personnel.

Recommendations for Other Injured Athletes

- Read your body and pace yourself accordingly.
- Accept and positively deal with the situation.
- Focus on quality training.
- Find and use medical resources.
- Use social resources wisely.
- Set goals.
- Feel confident with medical staff coaches.
- Work on mental skills training.
- Use imagery and visualization.
- Initiate and maintain a competitive atmosphere and involvement.

Recommendations for Coaches

- Foster coach–athlete contact and involvement.
- Demonstrate positive empathy and support.
- Understand individual variations in injuries and injury emotions.
- Motivate by optimally pushing.
- Engineer the training environment for high-quality, individualized training.
- Have patience and realistic expectations.
- Don't repeatedly mention injury in training.

Recommendations for Sports Medicine Personnel

- Educate and inform the athlete about the injury and rehabilitation.
- Use appropriate motivation and optimally push.
- Demonstrate empathy and support.
- Have a supportive personality (e.g., be warm, open, and not overly confident).
- Foster positive interaction and customize training.
- Demonstrate competence and confidence.
- Encourage the athlete's confidence.

LEARNING AIDS

SUMMARY

1. **Discuss the role of psychological factors in athletic and exercise injuries.**
   Psychological factors influence the incidence of injury, responses to injury, and injury recovery. Professionals in the field must be prepared to initiate teaching and coaching practices that help prevent injuries, assist in the process of coping with injury, and provide supportive psychological environments that facilitate injury recovery.

2. **Identify psychological antecedents that may predispose people to athletic injuries.**
   Psychological factors, including stress and certain attitudes, can predispose athletes and exercisers to injuries. Professional sport and exercise science personnel must recognize antecedent conditions, especially major life stressors, in individuals who have poor coping skills and little social support.

3. **Compare and contrast explanations for the stress–injury relationship.**

When high levels of stress are identified, stress management procedures should be implemented and training regimens adjusted. Athletes must learn to distinguish between the normal discomfort of training and the pain of injury. They should understand that a "no pain, no gain" attitude can predispose them to injury.

4. **Describe typical psychological reactions to injuries.**

Injured athletes and exercisers exhibit various psychological reactions that typically fall into three categories: injury-relevant information processing, emotional upheaval and reactive behavior, and positive outlook and coping. Increased fear and anxiety, lowered confidence, and performance decrements also commonly occur in injured athletes.

5. **Identify signs of poor adjustment to injury.**

If you work with an injured athlete or exerciser, be vigilant in monitoring warning signs of poor adjustment to an injury. These include feelings of anger and confusion, obsession with the question of when one can return to play, denial (e.g., "The injury is no big deal"), repeatedly coming back too soon and becoming reinjured, exaggerated bragging about accomplishments, dwelling on minor physical complaints, guilt about letting the team down, withdrawal from significant others, rapid mood swings, and statements indicating that recovery will not occur no matter what is done.

6. **Explain how to implement psychological skills and strategies that can speed the rehabilitation process.**

Psychological skills training has been shown to facilitate the rehabilitation process. Psychological foundations of injury rehabilitation include identifying athletes who are at high risk of injury; building rapport with the injured individual; educating the athlete about the nature of the injury and the injury recovery process; teaching specific psychological coping skills, such as goal setting, relaxation techniques, and imagery; preparing the person to cope with setbacks in rehabilitation; and fostering social support. Athletes themselves have also made specific recommendations for coping with injury that are useful for other injured athletes, coaches, and sports medicine providers.

KEY TERMS

social support   grief response

REVIEW QUESTIONS

1. What is the Andersen and Williams (1988) stress–injury relationship model? Why is it important?
2. Discuss in detail the physical, social, and psychological causes of injury.
3. Identify two explanations for the stress–injury relationship.
4. Describe three general categories of emotional reactions to athletic injuries.
5. Describe the role of social support in athletic injury rehabilitation.
6. Give six implications for working with exercisers and athletes during injury treatment and recovery, briefly identifying and describing each.
7. Discuss how stress management could be used for the prevention of injury.
8. Define injury in terms of its three components. Also discuss the notion of injury versus pain.
9. Discuss the biopsychosocial model of injury, including how it differs from other models.
10. Describe some of the predictors and antecedents of adherence to sport injury rehabilitation.

CRITICAL THINKING QUESTIONS

1. A close friend sustains a major knee injury and needs surgery. What have you learned that can help you prepare your friend for surgery and recovery?
2. Design a persuasive speech to convince a sports medicine center to hire a sport psychology specialist. How would you convince the center's directors that patients or clients would benefit?

20

Addictive and Unhealthy Behaviors

After reading this chapter, you should be able to

1. define and discuss the prevalence of eating disorders and disordered eating in sport,
2. identify predisposing factors for developing eating disorders,
3. describe how to recognize disordered eating,
4. define and discuss the prevalence of substance abuse in sport,
5. explain why some athletes and exercisers take drugs,
6. discuss how to detect and prevent substance abuse,
7. discuss the concepts of positive and negative addiction to exercise, and
8. discuss the problem of compulsive sports gambling.

In 2004, the Bay Area Laboratory Co-Operative scandal hit front-page news, implicating a number of high-visibility athletes such as Olympic champion Marion Jones but especially baseball players such as Barry Bonds, Roger Clemens, Mark McGwire, Rafael Palmeiro, Sammy Sosa, Alex Rodriguez, and Jason Giambi. Many of these baseball players were also named in the famous Mitchell Report, former senator George Mitchell's in-depth report of steroid use in baseball, which identified many players—including some bigger names such as Roger Clemens, Barry Bonds, Ken Caminiti, Miguel Tejada, Andy Pettitte, Gary Sheffield, Jose Canseco, Kevin Brown, and Jason Giambi—who had allegedly taken steroids to enhance performance.

Questions continued to arise about steroids in baseball. Despite juries finding some athletes not guilty (i.e., Roger Clemens) or guilty only on one count of obstruction of justice (i.e., Barry Bonds), general public opinion is that these athletes took steroids to enhance performance. No team picked Barry Bonds up for the 2008 season despite his availability, presumably because of the cloud of steroid use revolving around him. When several of these players were eligible for the Hall of Fame in 2013, none of them received close to the 75% of the votes needed to be inducted despite having the statistics that would normally get a player voted into Cooperstown. More recently, Alex Rodriguez again was implicated in taking steroids after he said he stopped taking them in 2002. Only time will tell if any of these players will make it into the Hall of Fame, although if they do it will probably be a number of years before they get voted in.

Melky Cabrera and Bartolo Colon were both suspended for 50 games in 2012 due to failing a drug test. In 2013, Ryan Braun, National League MVP, was suspended for 65 games because of his association with a Biogenesis clinic in Miami, Florida. Alex Rodriquez, who was linked with this same clinic, received a 211-game suspension that lasted until the end of 2014. About a dozen other players were also associated with the Biogenesis clinic, and all agreed to take the 50-game suspensions they were given.

In 2006, Tour de France winner Floyd Landis and 100-meter Olympic gold medalist Justin Gatlin both tested positive for steroids. They both denied knowingly taking steroids as they appealed their respective cases, which they eventually lost. In 2013, sprinter Tyson Gay, triple gold medalist at the world championships and silver Olympic medalist, tested positive for steroids, as did Asafa Powell, former record holder in the 100-meter dash.

The athlete with the highest visibility who vehemently denied taking performance-enhancing drugs is Lance Armstrong, seven-time winner of the Tour de France. Not only did Armstrong deny using drugs, he sued and attacked people and organizations who went after him and threatened riders who might testify against him. Finally, after years of denials and overwhelming evidence from other riders who testified against him, he admitted to using drugs and was stripped of all seven of his titles. He was banished from taking part in any organized competition pending a complete admission of his drug-taking activities.

University of Maryland basketball star Len Bias did not use steroids. He tried cocaine only once—and died of cocaine-induced heart failure just before he was to have embarked on his National Basketball Association (NBA) career. He died not because he was a drug addict but because he decided to celebrate his success with a recreational drug.

Many athletes have had alcohol problems. For example, Mickey Mantle, the legendary center fielder for the New York Yankees, suffered from alcoholism over much of his career and eventually died of liver problems resulting from this abuse. Pitcher Steve Howe of the Los Angeles Dodgers was in and out of rehabilitation for alcohol numerous times during his professional career.

Elite gymnast Christy Henrich not only suffered from anorexia, she died from it. The mortality rate associated with anorexia nervosa is 5%, the highest mortality rate of any psychiatric condition. In addition, the suicide risk among people with this disorder is 50% higher than that of the general population. Even with such troubling outcomes the research in this area has been relatively sparse, resulting in a special issue of *The American Psychologist* dedicated to better understanding, predicting, and treating eating disorders (Park, 2007).

Art Schlichter, former professional football quarterback who was touted while an all-American at Ohio State, progressed from being an occasional visitor at the racetrack to betting with a bookie on pro sports and later to being a full-fledged gambler. His addiction to gambling and the actions he took to secure the money to pay his losses landed him in prison. In 2007, NBA referee Tim Donaghy admitted to betting on games, some of which he officiated, creating a crisis in confidence. Even hockey great Wayne Gretzky was associated with a gambling ring. Two Italian professional tennis players were also suspended for making bets on tennis matches involving other players.

Addictive and unhealthy behaviors certainly are not limited to elite athletes. Even high school and youth sport participants abuse drugs, steroids, alcohol, and smokeless tobacco; people also are known to start gambling at a young age. In addition, cheerleaders are typically seen as supporting other athletes. However, anecdotal reports have revealed that cheerleaders feel the pressure to look good, perform, and recover from injury, leading to the use of steroids. Physical education, sport, and exercise professionals must be prepared to deal with these issues.

Substance abuse, eating disorders, and compulsive gambling are clinical problems that require treatment by specialists. Still, nonspecialists must learn to detect signs of these conditions and refer affected students, exercisers, and athletes to specialists for the treatment they need. Let's begin with a discussion of eating disorders.

Eating Disorders

Anorexia nervosa and bulimia are the two most common eating disorders. Before we discuss the prevalence and potential treatment of these conditions, here are some relevant definitions. According to *Diagnostic and Statistical Manual of Mental Disorders* (American Psychiatric Association, 2013) **anorexia nervosa** includes the following characteristics:

- Refusal to maintain a minimal body weight normal for a particular age and height (this is typically defined as weight 15% below average)
- Intense fear of gaining weight or becoming fat despite being underweight
- Disturbance in how one experiences one's body weight, size, or shape (e.g., feeling fat even when one is clearly underweight)

- In females, the absence of at least three consecutive menstrual cycles otherwise expected to occur (i.e., primary or secondary amenorrhea)

Anorexia is potentially fatal: It can lead to starvation and other medical complications, such as heart disease. In addition, this severe condition is made worse because affected individuals often don't see themselves as abnormal. Finally, anorexia is a multidimensional disorder in which psychological, cognitive,

Physical and Psychological–Behavioral Signs of Eating Disorders

Physical Signs
- Weight too low
- Considerable weight loss
- Extreme weight fluctuations
- Bloating
- Swollen salivary glands
- Amenorrhea
- Carotenemia (yellowish palms or soles of feet)
- Sores or calluses on knuckles or back of hand from self-inducing vomiting
- Hypoglycemia (low blood sugar)
- Muscle cramps
- Stomach complaints
- Headaches, dizziness, or weakness from electrolyte disturbances
- Numbness and tingling in limbs attributable to electrolyte disturbances
- Stress fractures

Psychological–Behavioral Signs
- Excessive dieting
- Excessive eating without weight gain
- Excessive exercise that is not part of normal training program
- Guilt about eating
- Claims of feeling fat at normal weight despite reassurance from others
- Preoccupation with food
- Avoidance of eating in public and denial of hunger
- Hoarding food
- Disappearing after meals
- Frequent weighing
- Binge eating
- Evidence of self-induced vomiting
- Use of drugs such as diet pills, laxatives, or diuretics to control weight

Adapted, by permission, from D. Garner and L. Rosen, 1991, "Eating disorders among athletes: Research and recommendations," *Journal of Applied Sport Science Research* 5(2): 100-107.

perceptual, and biological factors interact in varying combinations to produce slightly different types of disorders (Bordo, 1993).

The diagnostic criteria for **bulimia** include the following (American Psychiatric Association, 2013):

- Recurrent episodes of binge eating (rapid consumption of large quantities of food in a discrete period of time)
- A feeling of lacking control over eating behavior during the eating binges
- Engaging in regular, self-induced vomiting, use of laxatives or diuretics, strict dieting or fasting, or vigorous exercise to prevent weight gain
- An average minimum of two binge-eating episodes a week for at least 3 months
- Persistent overconcern with body shape and weight

KEY POINT Anorexia nervosa is a psychological disease characterized by an intense fear of becoming obese, a disturbed body image, significant weight loss, the refusal to maintain normal body weight, and amenorrhea.

A person with bulimia often becomes depressed because of low self-esteem, eats excessively in an effort to feel better (bingeing), feels guilty about eating, and then induces vomiting or takes laxatives to purge the food. Although it is a severe problem, bulimia is usually less severe than anorexia. People with bulimia are aware that they have a problem, whereas people with anorexia are not. Bulimia can lead to anorexia, and some individuals are characterized as bulimarexic (see "Physical and Psychological–Behavioral Signs of Eating Disorders").

KEY POINT Bulimia is an episodic eating pattern of uncontrollable food bingeing followed by purging. It is characterized by an awareness that the pattern is abnormal, fear of being unable to voluntarily stop eating, depressed mood, and self-deprecation.

Disordered Eating

Although anorexia and bulimia most certainly occur in sport, the notion of disordered eating, referring to an entire spectrum of exaggerated eating patterns involving increased health risks, has recently gained favor. At the extremes of disordered eating are anorexia and bulimia. However, a great deal of middle ground

(in fact, this might be the largest category of eating disorders) is occupied by eating problems that are not quite severe enough to meet the criteria of *Diagnostic and Statistical Manual of Mental Disorders* for either anorexia or bulimia. Therefore, we must understand the variety of disordered eating patterns that might fit along this continuum. Research has revealed that it is often difficult to distinguish athletes with an eating disorder from those that have many of the psychological symptoms of an eating disorder but no official diagnosis of an eating disorder (Petrie, Greenleaf, Reel, & Carter, 2009). It should be noted that this discussion of eating disorders and disordered eating takes an objectivist perspective, which is grounded in the prevailing literature. However, for readers who are interested in an alternative view to the relationship between eating, exercise, and the body, Busanich and McGannon (2010) discuss eating disorders from a feminist perspective.

Hudson, Hiripi, Pope, and Kessler (2007) surveyed more than 9,000 adults. Their findings are as follows:

- Lifetime prevalence of bulimia nervosa is 1.5% in women and 0.5% in men.
- Lifetime prevalence of binge-eating disorder is 3.5% in women and 2% in men.
- Binge eating is more common than anorexia or bulimia and is commonly associated with severe obesity.
- Eating disorders display substantial comorbidity with other mental health disorders.
- Eating disorders have more than doubled since the 1960s.
- Forty to sixty percent of high school girls diet.
- Thirteen percent of high school girls purge.
- Thirty to forty percent of junior high school girls worry about weight.
- Forty percent of 9-year-old girls have dieted.
- Five-year-old girls are concerned about diet.

Prevalence of Eating Disorders and Disordered Eating in Sport

For a variety of reasons, it has traditionally been difficult to accurately assess eating disorders in any population. For example, in the competitive sport environment, an athlete risks being dropped from a program or team if his eating problem is discovered. Therefore, athletes with these types of disorders are often very secretive and are not willing to share information until the problem becomes almost catastrophic and professional help is necessary. The underreporting of eating disorders and disordered eating was highlighted in a study by Kerr, Berman, and De Souza (2006), who found that gymnasts still active in their careers reported having far fewer eating disorders (3%) and less disordered eating (18%) than retired gymnasts (20% and 73%, respectively). The accuracy of studies assessing eating disorders in sport is also questionable because there are doubts about the validity of many of the questionnaires used to measure eating problems (O'Connor, Lewis, & Kirchner, 1995). Because of these assessment problems, you should view even the data we present here with caution.

Various researchers (e.g., Arthur-Cameselle & Quatromoni, 2010; Byrne & McClean, 2001; Goss, Cooper, Croxon, & Dryden, 2005; Krentz & Warschburger, 2011; Sanford-Martens et al., 2005; Petrie & Greenleaf, 2012) have summarized the prevalence of eating disorders in sport. Although there is some inconsistency in the findings, some of their general conclusions include the following:

- Frequency rates of eating disorders in athletic populations ranged from as low as 1% to as high as 62% across a variety of sports.

- Female athletes, in general, reported higher frequencies of eating disorders than male athletes, which is similar to the general population. Male athletes with eating disorders are less prevalent and thus have not been studied as extensively as female athletes.

- Although some studies have revealed that athletes appear to have a greater occurrence of eating-related problems than does the general population, prevalence rates tend to approximate those found in the general population. However, athletes (compared with nonathletes) may have higher frequencies of disordered eating patterns rather than eating disorders per se.

- Athletes and nonathletes have similar psychopathologies and eating-related symptoms. In essence, if an athlete develops an eating disorder, her psychological profile is probably no different from that of nonathletes with the same disorder.

- A significant percentage of athletes engage in disordered eating or weight loss behaviors (e.g., binge eating, rigorous dieting, fasting, vomiting, use of diuretics), and these behaviors

are important to examine even though they are subclinical in intensity.

- Eating disorders and the use of pathogenic weight loss techniques among athletes tend to have a sport-specific prevalence (e.g., they occur more among gymnasts and wrestlers than among archers or basketball players).

- Up to 66% of female athletes may be amenorrheic compared with approximately 2% to 5% of nonathletes. These data (along with higher levels of disordered eating by female athletes) suggest that female athletes may eventually develop osteoporosis, which can result in increased bone fractures, increased skeletal fragility, and permanent bone loss.

- Compared with nonathletes, athletes in sports that emphasize leanness (e.g., gymnastics, diving) are at greater risk of developing eating disorders.

KEY POINT Approximately 63% of all female athletes develop symptoms of an eating disorder between the 9th and 12th grades.

Although anorexia and bulimia are of special concern in sports emphasizing form (e.g., gymnastics, diving, figure skating) or weight (e.g., wrestling), athletes with eating disorders have been found in a wide array of sports.

Predisposing Factors

Practitioners need to understand the factors that might predispose an athlete to develop an eating disorder or disordered eating. Knowing these factors might help you prevent or reduce the probability that an eating disorder (or disordered eating) will occur in someone—or yourself. Swoap and Murphy (1995), Thompson and Sherman (1999), Petrie and Greenleaf (2012), and Anderson, Petrie, and Neumann (2011) outlined the factors we now describe.

Weight Restrictions and Standards

Sports such as weightlifting, wrestling, and boxing commonly use weight classifications to subdivide competitor groups. Often athletes try to "make weight" so they can compete at a lower weight classification, which presumably would give them an advantage against a lighter opponent. This can result in an athlete trying to drop 10 or even 15 pounds immediately before weigh-ins, usually resulting primarily in rapid dehydration. Techniques for achieving this rapid weight loss include fasting, fluid restriction, the use of diuretics or laxatives, and purging. But weight loss and dieting are not limited to athletes; these behaviors are a common problem among young people. Researchers (Hudson, Hiripi, Pope, & Kessler, 2007; Sedula, Collins, & Williamson, 1993) who investigated more than 11,000 high school students found that between 40% and 60% of the females were attempting to lose weight through some type of diet. Coaches, trainers, and parents should discourage these weight loss methods, even those that are embedded in the sport culture.

Coach and Peer Pressure

Coaches and peers can play an important role in shaping the attitude and behaviors of athletes. Unfor-

Evidence of eating disorders among male athletes has been found in recent years, especially in sports that require weight classifications for athletes.

tunately, coaches sometimes knowingly or unknowingly exert pressure on athletes to lose weight, even when they have information about safe and effective weight management procedures. In one study, retired gymnasts who received disparaging comments from coaches about their bodies or instructions to lose weight had significantly more disordered eating patterns than did those who did not receive such comments (Kerr, Berman, & De Souza, 2006). Some coaches tend to decide about the need for weight control based on appearance rather than objective indicators (e.g., body fat assessments). The following account from the newspaper *Austin American Statesman* describes a coach who promoted unhealthy attitudes toward weight and weight reduction:

> " The coach emphasized weight in training and competition and insisted that his swimmers remain under maximum weight limits. According to current and former swimmers, the pressure to meet those guidelines was so intense that many routinely fasted, induced vomiting, used laxatives and diuretics, or exercised in addition to workouts. They did not want to be relegated to the group they called 'The Fat Club.' Primarily, the pressure came from the coach, until you started to internalize it. Then it became self-inflicted torture, almost to where some people would weigh themselves three or four times a day. " (Halliburton & Sanford, 1989, pp. D1, D7)

In a study of more than 400 athletes, Shanmugam, Jowett, and Meyer (2012) investigated the relationships between athletes and their coaches, parents, and closest teammate. Results revealed that parental and coach–athlete relationships characterized by increased conflict and decreased support were related to lower levels of self-esteem and increased self-critical perfectionism and depression, which in turn was related to increased eating psychopathology. Teammate relationships were not predictive of disordered eating.

Sociocultural Factors

Although genetics can certainly influence disordered eating, the current thinking is that the condition has more to do with the cultural emphasis on thinness, which can lead to widespread body dissatisfaction (especially in women). For example, the American Society for Aesthetic Plastic Surgery reported that more than 200,000 cosmetic surgeries were done on children under 18 years of age in 2007 (Marcus,

2009). Research reveals that eating disorders are on the rise, especially in sports in which leanness confers a competitive advantage such as swimming and long-distance running (Glazer, 2008). American culture values thinness. According to some figures, up to 95% of women estimate their body size as 25% larger on average than it actually is. The media constantly tell us that we should look thin and beautiful like the models we see on billboards and television. McGannon and Busanich (2010) offered women some suggestions for combating the societal pressures to conform to the idealized body type. These suggestions included pushing their bodies to the limits in the weight room, taking pride in a muscular or larger physique, and participating in more aggressive sports that challenge femininity.

Although men report less body image disturbance than women do, most studies report that about 50% of men desire to change their physique (Cohane & Pope, 2001). Interestingly, boys obsess over unattainable bodies, just like girls have long been known to do. Researchers argue that boys who are too eager to bulk up are prone to risky behaviors such as illegal steroid use. It is recommended that boys emphasize moderation in behaviors and focus on skill development, fitness, and general health rather than development of a muscular appearance. However, some well-developed males never think they are big enough. When they look in the mirror, they see a skinny person—a phenomenon often called bigorexia.

Petrie and Greenleaf (2007) proposed a model that identified a number of psychosocial variables that were hypothesized to increase female athletes' risk of developing an eating disorder. A central factor in body dissatisfaction was the internalization of societal body and appearance ideals (i.e., thin, attractive). In testing the model with bulimic athletes, it was found that body dissatisfaction, feelings of guilt, and a focus on dietary restraint were related to bulimic symptomatology (Greenleaf, Petrie, Reel, & Carter, 2010). This focus on body image, especially for women, is particularly important in predicting disordered eating when the dissatisfaction with their body image is related to their specific sport, more than just a general dissatisfaction with body image (Francisco, Narciso, & Alarcao, 2012).

Performance Demands

The past 25 years have seen an increased focus on the relationship between body weight or body fat and performance. Research has indicated that a correlation exists between a low percentage of body fat and high levels of performance in a number of sports (Wilmore, 1992). This has led many coaches and athletes to focus on weight control for the purpose of reaching optimal weight. However, lower body fat does not always mean better performance. Individual differences are critical here, and strict weight standards are therefore inappropriate. As Petrie and Greenleaf (2012) have suggested, there is typically a range of values for body fat related to optimal performance, and ideal levels vary between males and females.

Judging Criteria

In sports in which physical attractiveness, especially for females, is considered important to success (gymnastics, figure skating, diving), coaches and athletes may perceive that judges tend to be biased toward certain body types. When athletes do not conform to these images, they may stand out among their teammates and feel incredible pressure to achieve unrealistic and unhealthy body weights and shapes. For example, very slender body builds are often seen as desirable, and this is typically communicated to the athletes in informal ways. The following quote by a national champion figure skater suggests how appearances are perceived to be tied to judging criteria:

" Skating is such an appearance sport. You have to go up there with barely anything on . . . . I'm definitely aware of [my weight]. I mean I have dreams about it sometimes. So it's hard having people look at my thigh and saying 'Oops, she's an eighth of an inch bigger' or something. It's hard . . . . Weight is continually on my mind. I am never, never allowed to be on vacation." (Gould, Jackson, & Finch, 1993, p. 364)

KEY POINT Fitness professionals must be able to recognize the physical and psychological signs of eating disorders.

Critical Comments About Body Shape and Weight

Although there has long been anecdotal evidence that critical comments about body shape and weight (e.g., "fat cow," "Pillsbury dough boy," "tubby") particularly negatively affect female athletes, little empirical research was conducted until the first decade of the 20th century. In 2008, Muscat and Long found that athletes who recalled more critical comments and more

Factors Contributing to the Onset of Eating Disorder Symptoms

Arthur-Cameselle and Quatromoni (2010) conducted an interview study of athletes and listed the following factors, both internal and external, that precipitated the onset of eating disorder symptoms. Accompanying quotes highlight these factors.

Internal Factors

- *Negative mood.* "My grandfather died . . . I think I started to get depressed."
- *Low self-esteem.* "I definitely would look in the mirror and be like, 'That's ugly.' I would always be scrutinizing myself . . . . I hated myself."
- *Perfectionism and achievement.* "I was obsessed with how I looked and perfection. I won't stop short of supermodel looks even though that's completely unreasonable."
- *Desire for control.* "It was absolutely just a way to have control over something because I didn't have control over my own emotions."

External Factors

- *Negative influences on self-esteem.* "My mom was like, 'Oh, you are getting kind of chunky.' My dad would make comments when I was in bathing suits."
- *Hurtful relationships.* "I wasn't really getting along with some people on my floor anymore. I liked this guy on my floor and so I think that had an issue with it because he liked this other girl."
- *Hurtful role models.* "I was noticing another tennis player's eating patterns and she clearly had a problem, but I didn't realize it at the time . . . . I started doing what she was doing and working out excessively."
- *Sport performance.* "I had started running more intensely, was following the media knowledge about fat-free foods and what was healthy . . . . I just wanted to be a good runner."

severely critical comments than others reported greater disordered eating as well as more intense negative emotions (e.g., shame, anxiety). In addition, females at the highest level of competition (i.e., international) were more likely to remember critical comments than athletes performing at lower competitive levels. Furthermore, these critical comments (coming mostly from family members) were very prevalent, cited by approximately 45% of the athletes.

Genetic and Biological Factors

All of the predisposing factors already noted regarding the development of an eating disorder relate in some manner to the environment. However, with the pervasiveness of these environmental factors, a persistent question might be, "Why do only a small fraction of individuals (mostly females) go on to develop an eating disorder?" In an excellent review article, Striegel-Moore and Bulik (2007) discuss a number of studies investigating biological as well as sociocultural predictors of eating disorders. There seems to be ample evidence from the findings of twin studies and molecular-genetic studies that biology plays a role in the development of eating disorders. However, Streigel-Moore and Bulik note that, to date, studies of biological (genetic and early developmental trauma) and cultural factors have progressed largely along parallel tracks. Therefore, the authors argue that researchers should investigate the interaction of biological and sociocultural factors in the prediction of eating disorders because this would provide a fuller understanding of their development. So, although the environmental and sociocultural factors already discussed are important, it may be that certain genetic factors interact with the environment to increase the probability of an eating disorder developing. Coaches, parents, and significant others should be very cognizant of this potential interaction.

Mediating Factors

Although several factors (noted previously) are directly related to the development of eating disorders in sport, this relationship is mediated by several factors. For example, the personality factors of asceticism, submissiveness, and conformity were all related to eating pathology among athletes. Thus, if a coach has an athlete with any of these personality factors, extra attention should be given to the possible development of an eating disorder. In addition, higher levels of exercise were associated with higher levels of eating pathology in nonathletes but not in varsity or casual athletes (i.e., those who practice but do not compete in sport). Thus, exercise appears to carry a different meaning for athletes and nonathletes in the eating disorder population (Sherman & Thompson, 2001).

Prevention of exercise is often considered a treatment for people with an eating disorder, but this should not be the case for athletes. Furthermore, Hulley, Currie, Njenga, and Hill (2007) found that nationality may be an important factor mediating the propensity to develop an eating disorder. Specifically, elite female distance runners from Kenya were less likely to have an eating disorder (8.2%) than runners from the United Kingdom (19.5%). Thus, culture and ethnicity should be considered when investigating the potential problems of long-distance running for females. Finally, researchers (de Bruin, Bakker, & Oudejans, 2009) have found that athletes who are ego-oriented tend to display more disordered eating. Thus, they recommend that coaches emphasize a mastery-oriented climate focusing on improvement.

Recognition and Referral of an Eating Problem

Practitioners are in an excellent position to spot individuals with eating disorders (Thompson, 1987). Thus, they must be able to recognize the physical and psychological signs and symptoms of these conditions (see "Physical and Psychological–Behavioral Signs of Eating Disorders"). Often, unusual eating patterns are among the best indicators of problems. People with anorexia often pick at their food, push it around on their plate, lie about their eating, and frequently engage in compulsive or ritualistic eating patterns such as cutting food into tiny morsels or eating only a very limited number of bland, low-calorie foods. People with bulimia often hide food and disappear after eating (so they can purge the food just eaten) or simply eat alone. Whenever possible, fitness educators should observe the eating patterns of students and athletes, looking for abnormalities. In addition, it is commonly assumed that the frequency and duration of exercise are related to eating disorders. However, research (Lipsey, Barton, Hulley, & Hill, 2006) has shown that the presence of eating disorders cannot be inferred from exercise behavior alone. Rather, commitment to exercise as well as weight and mood regulation, not just exercise per se, predicted an eating

Are You a Dysfunctional Eater?

Answering yes to more than three of the following questions can indicate a pattern of dysfunctional eating (Berg, 2000):

1. Do you regularly restrict your food intake?
2. Do you skip meals regularly?
3. Do you often go on diets?
4. Do you count calories or fat grams or weigh or measure your food?
5. Are you afraid of certain foods?
6. Do you turn to food to reduce stress or anxiety?
7. Do you deny being hungry or claim to feel full after eating very little?
8. Do you avoid eating with others?
9. Do you feel worse (e.g., anxious, guilty) after eating?
10. Do you think about food, eating, and weight more than you'd like?

Dysfunctional eating typically comprises three general categories. *Chaotic eating* refers to irregular eating such as fasting, bingeing, and skipping meals. *Consistent undereating* usually means not paying attention to hunger signals and regularly eating less food than meets one's daily needs. *Consistent overeating* means that a person is overriding normal satiety signals and eating more on a daily basis than the body wants or needs.

disorder. Standardized self-report inventories can also be used to diagnose eating disorders, but these should be administered and interpreted only by trained professionals (e.g., a licensed psychologist). Finally, Selby and Reel (2011) offer a couple other signs to watch for, such as changes in mood and personality, atypical behaviors, a strong need for control, and an extreme emphasis on body image.

DISCOVER Activity 20.1 helps you further understand what to do when confronting an individual who may have an eating disorder.

As a practitioner, if you identify someone who demonstrates symptoms, you'll need to solicit help from a specialist familiar with eating disorders. But this is a difficult judgment because some people exhibit some of these signs without having a disor-

der, whereas others do have a disorder and do need a referral. If you or a colleague suspects an eating disorder, the person who has the best rapport with the individual should schedule a private meeting to discuss his concerns (Petrie & Greenleaf, 2007). The emphasis here should be on feelings rather than on eating behaviors. Be supportive in such instances and keep all information confidential. Make a referral then to a specific clinic or person rather than giving a vague recommendation, such as "You should seek some help." If an athlete is still hesitant, suggest that he see the clinic or the individual professional simply for an assessment to determine whether a problem exists. Selby and Reel (2011) offer similar suggestions for referring an athlete believed to have an eating disorder, such as avoiding use of the term *eating disorder*, consistently showing concern for the athlete as a person, having a list of potential referrals ready, and supporting the treatment recommendations

Preventing Eating Disorders in Athletes and Exercisers

Although professionals must be able to recognize and effectively deal with eating disorders among participants in sport and exercise settings, an even greater contribution would be to help prevent these disorders in the first place or at least reduce the probability that they will occur. Petrie and Greenleaf (2012) offer some excellent suggestions and interventions for preventing eating disorders. Coaches, parents, teammates, and significant others can use the following suggestions to be proactive in reducing eating disorders in athletes and exercisers.

• *Promote proper nutritional practices.* Research indicates that many sport participants have limited information or have incorrect views about proper sport nutrition. Because many individuals turn to coaches, trainers, and peers for nutritional advice, these exercisers and athletic personnel should become educated about good nutrition and methods of weight control. *Coaches' Guide to Nutrition and Weight Control* (Eisenman, Johnson, & Benson, 1990) is one good source of information about nutrition.

• *Focus on fitness, not body weight.* We must move away from obsessing about weight to focusing on health and fitness itself. There is no ideal body composition or weight for an athlete or exerciser because weight and body composition fluctuate greatly depending on the type of sport, body build, and metabolic rate. Rather, an ideal *range* might better be targeted, with input from professionals such as nutritionists and exercise physiologists.

• *Be sensitive to weight issues.* Athletic personnel should be made aware of the issues athletes contend with regarding weight control and diet, and they should act with sensitivity in these areas. Coaches and fitness leaders often exert powerful influence on individuals, and they should exercise care when making remarks about weight control. Practices such as repeating weigh-ins, associating weight loss with enhanced performance, setting arbitrary weight goals, and making unfeeling remarks must be avoided at all costs.

• *Promote healthy management of weight.* As the incidence of and focus on disordered eating practices in sport and exercise have increased, so too has the availability of educational material. For example, the National Collegiate Athletic Association (NCAA; 1989) produced a set of three informative videos along with supportive educational material on eating disorders in sport. Sport

from the trained mental health professional. "Dealing With Eating Disorders" presents several suggestions regarding eating disorders. (For comprehensive discussion of the many issues and variables in this complex subject, see Thompson & Sherman, 1993.)

Substance Abuse

It is no secret that performance-enhancing drugs have been used by world-class athletes and Olympians for decades or that some athletes will do almost anything to gain a competitive advantage. The disqualification of athletes for using performance-enhancing drugs in recent Olympics and Tour de France competitions bears witness to the potential negative sport-related consequences of substance abuse. What is especially surprising is that despite dire warnings about the negative psychological and physiological effects of steroids and other performance-enhancing drugs, their

use appears to be on the upswing. Even the threat of death is evidently not a deterrent as long as victory is guaranteed. Consider the results from a 1995 poll of 195 sprinters, swimmers, powerlifters, and other athletes, most of them U.S. Olympians or aspiring Olympians, who were given the following scenarios:

- You are offered a banned performance-enhancing substance with two guarantees: (a) You will not be caught and (b) you will win. Would you take the substance?
- You are offered a banned performance-enhancing substance that comes with two guarantees: (a) You will not be caught and (b) you will win every competition you enter for the next 5 years and then die from the side effects of the substance. Would you take the substance?

In answering the first question, 192 athletes—a stunning 98%—said yes; 3 said no. Even more shocking,

and exercise science professionals need to keep up with the latest information regarding weight loss and eating disorders.

• *Teach mental skills*. A study by Estanol, Shepperd, and MacDonald (2013) found that the development of mental skills can help mediate the relationship between negative affect and the risk of eating disorders. Dancers who coped better with adversity, exhibited freedom from worry, and had high levels of confidence and achievement motivation had lower levels of eating disorders. In essence, teaching athletes mental skills appears to help them deal more positively with the negative affect that typically precedes the onset of an eating disorder.

Most recommendations for dealing with athletes with eating disorders are directed at coaches. Arthur-Cameselle and Baltzell (2012) asked athletes who had recovered from eating disorders for recommendations for athletes who currently have an eating disorder and their parents. Recommendations for parents and athletes are as follows:

Parents of Athletes With Eating Disorders

- Provide emotional support.
- Encourage use of professional treatment.
- Become educated about eating.

Athletes With Eating Disorders

- Keep hope that recovery is possible.
- Determine the underlying cause and triggers for the disorder.
- Seek professional treatment.
- Reach out to important others in your life for emotional support.
- Focus on the benefits of recovery.
- Put your life and eating disorder behaviors into perspective.

Dealing With Eating Disorders

Do

- Get help and advice from a specialist.
- Be supportive and empathetic.
- Express concern about general feelings, not specifically about weight.
- Make referrals to a specific person and, when possible, make appointments for the individual.
- Emphasize the importance of long-term good nutrition.
- Provide information about eating disorders.

Don't

- Do not ask the athlete to leave the team or curtail participation, unless so instructed by a specialist.
- Do not recommend weight loss or gain.
- Do not hold team weigh-ins.
- Do not single out or treat the individual unlike other participants.
- Do not talk about the problem with nonprofessionals who are not directly involved.
- Do not demand that the problem be stopped immediately.
- Do not make insensitive remarks or tease individuals regarding their weight.

Adapted, by permission, from D. Garner and L. Rosen, 1991, "Eating disorders among athletes: Research and recommendations," *Journal of Applied Sport Science Research* 5(2): 100-107.

in answering the second question, 120 athletes—approximately 60%—said yes; 75 said no. A study by Connor and Mazanov (2009) asking the same question to nonathletes found that only 2 in 250 would take the drug. Thus, athletes appear to prioritize performance outcomes over health concerns; they would exchange longevity for Olympic success. This says a lot about the psyche of elite athletes and the importance of sport and winning in their lives.

Fortunately, not all drugs are bad or even out of place in sport or physical activity settings. Imagine undergoing surgery without painkilling drugs or treating a serious infection without antibiotics. Drugs per se are not the problem as long as the drugs that are being used are legal, are prescribed by appropriate medical personnel, and are not among the substances banned in the world of competitive sport. But this latter issue can get confusing because some drugs are seen as legal in some sports (e.g., Mark McGwire's use of androstenedione was not considered illegal in baseball even though research has shown that androstenedione increased testosterone concentrations by more than 300% in males and 600% in females and maintained elevated testosterones levels for about a week) but illegal in other sports or sporting bodies such as the NCAA, National Football League, and International

Olympic Committee (IOC). The misuse of drugs (whether performance enhancing or recreational) and the use of illegal and harmful drugs are the real problems in sport and exercise.

People abuse drugs for different reasons but with the same negative consequences. Substance abuse can lead to long-term—sometimes fatal—health and psychological problems, including addiction. *Diagnostic and Statistical Manual of Mental Disorders* (American Psychiatric Association, 2013) lists the following criteria as indicating psychoactive **substance abuse**:

a. A maladaptive pattern of psychoactive substance use, indicated by at least one of the following:

1. Continued use despite knowledge of having a persistent or recurring social, occupational, psychological, or physical problem that is caused or exacerbated by use of the psychoactive substance

2. Recurrent use in situations in which the use is physically hazardous (e.g., driving while intoxicated)

b. Persistence of some symptoms of the disturbance for at least 1 month, or repeated occurrence over a longer period of time

These diagnostic criteria apply to people using any psychoactive substance, including alcohol, marijuana, cocaine, amphetamines, and hallucinogens. Later in the chapter we discuss the identification of signs and symptoms of substance use and abuse.

KEY POINT Drug addiction is a state in which either discontinuing or continuing the use of a drug creates an overwhelming desire, need, and craving for more of the substance.

An in-depth examination of how substance abuse affects athletes is beyond our scope here. For more detailed information, we recommend several excellent books or chapters on the subject (Anshel, 2010; Bacon, Lerner, Trembley, & Seestedt, 2005; Hildebrandt, Varangis, & Lai, 2012; Mazanov, 2013, Swoap & Murphy, 1995). Here we concentrate on four issues: prevalence of substance abuse, the reasons athletes and exercises take and abuse drugs, major drug categories and their effects, and the fitness or sport professional's role in detecting and preventing substance abuse.

Prevalence of Substance Abuse in Sport

Similar to the situation with eating disorders, it is inherently difficult to get an accurate picture of **substance use** and abuse because of the sensitive and

---

Drug Testing in Different Sports: Different Approaches

Different sport organizations have enacted different drug-testing programs. Here are a few:

- *Major League Baseball*—Players submit to at least one random test during the season, and they might be tested off-season (usually only 3%–6% of drug tests are administered off-season). In 2005 a new agreement was passed, according to which players are suspended for 50 games for a first positive drug or steroid test, for 100 games for a second positive test, and permanently for a third positive test. In addition, they are tested for amphetamines, and a first positive test leads to mandatory additional testing. A second offense draws a 25-game suspension, and a third offense an 80-game suspension. As a side note, J.C. Romero, relief pitcher for the 2008 World Champion Philadelphia Phillies, tested positive for steroids in September, but because players can appeal findings he was allowed to pitch in the play-offs and World Series. He won two games in the World Series and in the play-offs had a 0.00 earned run average. His appeal was eventually denied, and he served a 50-game suspension at the start of the 2009 season. Is it fair that he was able to pitch very successfully in the play-offs and World Series even though he had a positive drug test? In 2012, MVP Ryan Braun of the Milwaukee Brewers tested positive for steroids but got off on a technicality. (However, he later received a 65-game suspension for his association with the Biogenesis clinic noted earlier.)

- *National Basketball Association*—Rookies are tested up to four times a season, and veterans and rookies are subject to random tests during training camp. Penalties range from 5- to 25-game suspensions (along with counseling or attending the league's antidoping program) for the first three offenses and a 2-year ban for a fourth offense. Athletes are not tested in the off-season.

- *National Football League*—All players are tested at least once every season. Players also are randomly tested throughout the year. The first positive test results in a 4-game suspension without pay, a second positive test results in an 8-game suspension without pay, and a third positive test results in a 1-year suspension.

- *National Hockey League.* Players are subject to up to two random tests every year; at least one such test is conducted on a team-wide basis. Athletes are not tested in the off-season. The first offense results in a 20-game suspension without pay (along with referral to the league's substance abuse and behavioral program for evaluation, education, and possible treatment), the second offense results in a 60-game suspension without pay, and the third offense results in a lifetime ban (although players can apply for reinstatement after 2 years).

- *Olympics.* Elite Olympic athletes must essentially let drug-testing officials know their whereabouts from 6 a.m. to 11 p.m. 365 days a year. Testers can knock on doors or appear at training sites without notice and demand a urine sample. The United States Anti-Doping Agency administers 65% of its tests out of competition. The first positive test results in a 2-year ban, and a second positive test results in a lifetime ban.

personal nature of the issue. Data are usually based on self-reports, which may help explain why usage estimates vary from 10% to 90% (National Center on Addiction and Substance Abuse, 2000). Thus, you should view the data with caution. There is much anecdotal evidence going back to the third century BC in Greece (Chappel, 1987; Hildebrandt, Varangis, & Lai, 2012) regarding substance use and abuse. However, it wasn't until the 20th century that substances such as amphetamines, stimulants, and testosterone extract reached the athletic world and became a significant impediment to fair competition.

Tommy Chaikin, football player for the University of South Carolina, provided a poignant report on drug use in *Sports Illustrated* (Chaikin & Tealander, 1988). Chaikin's report offers significant insight into the numerous social and psychological pressures that foster drug use (in this case anabolic steroids) in sport, including the encouragement of coaches and the pressures to succeed. Consistent with research, from his abuse of steroids Chaikin developed chronic aggression, depression, testicular shrinkage, hair loss, insomnia, poor vision, chronic anxiety, hypertension, a heart murmur, and benign tumors—and almost died. A variety of athletes taking high doses of steroids have since made similar reports. Finally, using a needle to inject drugs (especially anabolic steroids) may increase the probability of one getting infected with human immunodeficiency virus (HIV) or hepatitis C.

Kanayama, Brower, Wood, Hudson, and Pope (2010) documented the many potential side effects of steroid use (noted anecdotally by Tommy Chaikin and others), such as acne, testicular shrinkage, loss or increase of libido, water retention, impaired liver function, hypertension, clotting abnormalities, and increased aggression as well as a deepening voice, clitoral enlargement, and hair growth in females. Furthermore, another study indicated that individuals who take drugs for performance enhancement or physical appearance are most at risk (of developing a pathology or from a health perspective) if they take several distinct substances, have rigid practices and preoccupation with diet and exercise, and have significant body image disturbance (Hildebrandt et al., 2011).

As alluded to by Chaikin, coaches often are knowingly involved—implicitly or explicitly—in their athletes' use of drugs (Swift, 1999). For example, after having his gold medal taken away, sprinter Ben Johnson asserted that his coach knowingly gave him a banned substance. "Charlie Francis was my coach

. . . . If Charlie gave me something to take, I took it" (*Time,* June 26, 1989, p. 57). Barry Bonds said that he used a clear substance and a cream given to him by his trainer, Greg Anderson, but that he didn't know they were steroids. Then there is a list of high-profile professional athletes who have admitted (sometimes after denying it for a long time) to or been caught using illegal drugs or have abused alcohol, such as John Daly, Darryl Strawberry, Lance Armstrong, Josh Hamilton, and Lawrence Taylor. In some cases, their careers have been terminated and they have served prison sentences for repeated drug use and violations of league policy. Unfortunately, athletes have also died from drug use and abuse in sport, as in the case of consistent steroid use by football player Lyle Alzado and one-time cocaine use by Len Bias, mentioned earlier.

As for the scientific evidence, most studies have focused on alcohol and steroid use, sometimes showing a good deal of variability. One study indicated that 55% of high school athletes reported using alcohol in the previous year (Green, Burke, Nix, Lambrecht, & Mason, 1996), whereas in another study the figure was 92% (Carr, Kennedy, & Dimick, 1990). In college samples, alcohol intake was consistent across studies, with reported uses of 88% (College of Human Medicine, 1985), 87% (Evans, Weinberg, & Jackson, 1992), and 85% (Nelson & Wechsler, 2001). These numbers are similar to those of nonathletes; however, college athletes appear to engage in significantly heavier episodic drinking than do nonathletes.

Most studies show the use of alcohol by male athletes to be higher than that by nonathletes but no significant differences between the use of alcohol by female athletes and nonathletes. Relative to the general college population, student-athletes have been identified as a high-risk group for heavy drinking. Furthermore, Martens, Dams-O'Connor, and Duffy-Paiement (2006) found that alcohol use and negative alcohol-related consequences decreased during the competitive season. Although this may outwardly seem like a positive finding, increased drinking in the off-season could cause other academic, social, or health-related problems and possibly affect off-season training and performance. Individuals who work with athletes should recognize this problem and help educate athletes about the many potential drawbacks of this pattern of behavior.

A study by Grossbard, Hummer, Labrie, Pederson, and Neighbors (2009) revealed that attraction to the team was a good predictor of substance use. Specifically, alcohol use was higher but marijuana use was lower as attraction to the team increased; this was especially the case in males. Another study linked the increased use of sport (energy) drinks to alcohol use (Woolsey, Waigandt, & Beck, 2010). Specifically, it found that athletes who use energy drinks are more likely to drink more alcohol as well as engage in risky alcohol behavior such as binge drinking. Because most energy drinks are stimulants, the combination with increased alcohol use can have serious health implications and should be monitored closely by athletes, coaches, and parents.

Regarding the use of performance-enhancing drugs, especially anabolic steroids, several large-scale studies conducted in the United States, Canada, Australia, and Europe showed in general that only a small percentage (usually less than 5%) of athletes and high school or college students reported using performance-enhancing drugs (see Anshel, 2010). However, a survey by the Centers for Disease Control and Prevention (2010) found that steroid use was up from 1 in 27 high school students in 1999 to 1 in 16 students in 2003. In a 2003 anonymous survey of high school baseball players, 5% to 10% admitted using performance-enhancing drugs. During U.S. Congressional hearings in 2005 regarding steroid use among baseball players, a topic of discussion was the effect that drug use by well-known players has on youths, who might be tempted to take steroids to either enhance athletic performance or simply look better to the opposite sex. The possible use of steroids, a topic usually avoided, was brought into the spotlight in the tell-all book by former baseball player Jose Canseco, who admitted taking steroids and openly accused others of taking them.

With respect to sex differences, males appear to use anabolic steroids three to five times more frequently than females (Gaa, Griffith, Cahill, & Tuttle, 1994). Interestingly, many of the nonathletes in that study (mostly males again) took steroids to improve physical appearance and self-esteem and to increase peer approval. A study by Miller, Barner, Sabo, Melnick, and Farrell (2002) focusing on adolescent athletes and steroid use revealed that 71% of steroid users were male and 29% were female. Rates of steroid use in elite Olympic-level athletes have sometimes been estimated to approach 50% for both males and females. When athletes are asked about their teammates' use of performance-enhancing drugs, estimates again rise to between 40% and 60%. This is clearly an area in which usage estimates must be viewed with extreme caution. Finally, regarding recreational drug use by college athletes, approximately 25% to 33% use marijuana and less than 10% use any other kind of recreational drug (e.g., cocaine, psychedelics; NCAA, 2001).

From a spectator point of view, the use of performance-enhancing drugs has certainly called into question whether it is the natural ability and training of a player or the addition of drugs that has led to outstanding performance. For example, Mark McGwire hit 70 home runs and had a career total of more than 580 home runs, which ordinarily would automatically get him into the Hall of Fame. However, the baseball

Girls and Steroid Use

Traditionally, the use of performance-enhancing drugs such as steroids has been seen as predominantly a male domain. However, research has revealed that young girls (some as young as 9 years old) are using bodybuilding steroids—not necessarily to get an edge on the playing field but to get the toned, sculptured look of models and movie stars.

Girls are getting their hands on the same dangerous testosterone pills, shots, and creams that created a scandal in Major League Baseball and other sports. Often these are the same girls who have eating disorders. Overall, up to about 5% of high school girls and 7% of middle school girls admit trying anabolic steroids at least once. The use of the drug has risen steadily since 1991.

Researchers say most girls are using steroids to get bigger and stronger on the playing field, and they attribute some of the increase in steroid use to girls' increasing participation in sport. But plenty of other girls are using steroids to give themselves a slightly muscular look. With young women, steroid use is typically tied to weight control and body fat reduction.

In teenage girls, the side effects from taking male sex hormones can include severe acne, smaller breasts, deeper voice, excess facial and body hair, irregular periods, depression, paranoia, and fits of anger dubbed "roid rage." Steroids also carry higher risks of heart attack, stroke, and some forms of cancer.

writers' association that votes on the Hall of Fame gave him only 27% of the vote on the first ballot (in 2014 he received only 11% of the vote), whereas a 75% vote is needed to get into the Hall of Fame (Verducci, 2006). As one sports editor wrote regarding voting for McGwire, "He is a no. I will not vote for him ever. I think he was artificially pumped up. He was not a Hall of Famer until he hit the juice" (Strupp, 2006, p. 46).

Still, the use of illegal drugs is minimal compared with the widespread use of legal drugs, such as alcohol and tobacco, the two most abused drugs in America. Sustained use of these substances has been linked to a host of negative health effects (figure 20.1).

Why Athletes and Exercisers Take Drugs

Athletes and exercisers do not start out abusing drugs. Rather, they take drugs for what they perceive to be good reasons. Although the reasons for using performance-enhancing drugs might differ from those for taking recreational substances, we group the reasons together into three general categories: physical, psychological, and social (see Anshel, 2010, for an extensive review of the causes of drug use).

Physical Reasons

The most common physical reasons for taking drugs are to enhance performance, to look more attractive to others, to cope with pain and injury rehabilitation,

and to control weight. Although all these reasons are valid, athletes take drugs primarily to improve performance with the expectation that they might increase their strength, endurance, alertness, and aggression or decrease their fatigue, reaction time, and anxiety. Winning is paramount, and doing anything to improve performance is critical. However, performance-enhancing drugs have clearly documented health risks. In addition, taking drugs to enhance performance is clearly cheating. If caught, athletes will be subjected to considerable public scorn. Even if they are not caught, they'll always know the victory was not their own.

Rehabilitation from injury is another physical reason athletes take drugs. They sometimes take drugs without a prescription from a doctor in an attempt to attenuate pain or cope psychologically with the physical discomfort of the injury. Fear of losing a starting position is a reason athletes often give: They want to rush back from an injury and sometimes think drugs can speed that recovery process. This was the reason that star pitcher Andy Pettitte gave for using steroids; he just wanted to heal quicker so he could get back on the mound.

Many exercisers take drugs (especially steroids) simply to look better and be more attractive to others. These individuals are not necessarily interested in performing better; rather, they are concerned with simply having their bodies look good, strong, and firm. In one study of almost 4,000 male high school students (Whitehead, Chilla, & Elliott, 1992), the most common

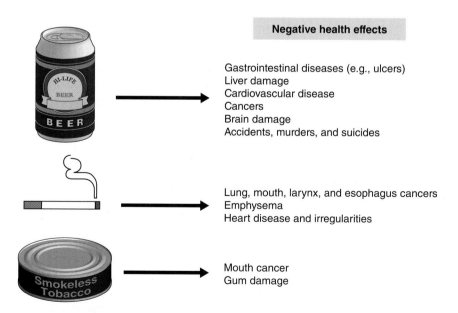

Negative health effects

Gastrointestinal diseases (e.g., ulcers)
Liver damage
Cardiovascular disease
Cancers
Brain damage
Accidents, murders, and suicides

Lung, mouth, larynx, and esophagus cancers
Emphysema
Heart disease and irregularities

Mouth cancer
Gum damage

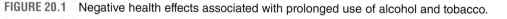

FIGURE 20.1 Negative health effects associated with prolonged use of alcohol and tobacco.

Adapted from L. Bump, 1988, Drugs and sport performance. In *Successful coaching*, edited by R. Martens (Champaign, IL: Human Kinetics), 135-147.

reason for using steroids was to improve physical appearance (48%). Subsequent research (Martens, Dams-O'Connor, & Kilmer, 2007) has supported the finding that improving physical appearance is the reason adolescents most often give for taking steroids.

Finally, athletes take drugs, especially amphetamines and diuretics, to control appetite and reduce fluid weight as well as boost energy for workouts. Large-scale studies indicate that up to 80% of drug users (across ages) use some form of these drugs (Hildebrandt, Langenbucher, Carr, & Sanjuan, 2007). These drugs can reduce weight quickly, allowing athletes to compete in a lower weight classification, as noted earlier. Some exercisers also consider taking diuretics to keep slim and trim. One such diet-controlling drug known as ephedra has received attention because of the unfortunate deaths of Minnesota Vikings football player Korey Stringer and Baltimore Orioles pitcher Steve Belcher. Belcher took ephedra to control weight and died of heatstroke during spring training, whereas Stringer took ephedra and died during team workouts. Although no research proves that ephedra can keep weight off or enhance athletic performance, this has not stopped athletes from taking it to control weight in an effort to increase performance.

Psychological Reasons

By far the most common rationale for using recreational drugs among athletes is psychological or emotional. These drugs seem to offer a convenient escape from unpleasant emotions in the course of dealing with competitive experiences. In addition, some individuals take drugs to offset the stress caused by trying to balance academic pursuits, training schedules, and personal relationships. Michael Phelps, 18-time Olympic gold medalist, was caught smoking marijuana at a party. Although this did not occur right before a major competition, it did create a furor because it is illegal and because of the effect it might have on aspiring athletes. The incident underscores some of the potential negative side effects of recreational drug use above and beyond any performance effects.

Still other athletes and exercisers use drugs to build self-confidence. Doubts about their ability often haunt participants, and certain drugs can help make them feel better about their abilities and feel more competitive. Friends, parents, and coaches often set expectations of success that are too high, and in this case athletes may view drugs as a resource for combating this source of stress and protecting their self-esteem.

Finally, a study by Donahue and colleagues (2006) investigated a motivational model of performance-enhancing substance use in elite athletes. Approximately 1,300 national-level athletes in Canada were tested regarding the relationships between intrinsic and extrinsic motivation, sportspersonship, and use of performance-enhancing drugs. Results revealed that athletes who were predominantly intrinsically motivated were more likely to endorse sportspersonship orientations and consequently less likely to

Viagra: Performance Enhancement From the Bedroom to the Ball Field

Viagra was originally devised to treat pulmonary hypertension or high blood pressure in arteries or the lungs. The drug works by suppressing an enzyme that controls blood flow, allowing the vessels to relax and widen. The mechanism also facilitates blood flow into the penis of impotent men. Additionally, this same mechanism can increase cardiac output and more efficient transport of oxygenated fuel to the muscles and thus can enhance endurance. One study has shown that Viagra improved performance of some participants by nearly 40% in a 10-kilometer cycling time trial conducted at a simulated altitude of 12,700 feet—a height far above general elite athlete competition. Viagra did not increase performance at sea level where blood vessels are fully dilated in healthy athletes (Hsu et al., 2006).

Currently, little evidence shows that use of Viagra is widespread in elite athletes. However, because the drug is not prohibited and thus not screened, there is no way to know precisely how popular it is. Even if Viagra increases stamina by a small amount, it could have a significant effect on results in sports such as distance running, cycling, and Nordic skiing, where events can be held at altitudes of 6,000 feet or above. For example, the difference between first and fourth place in the 15-kilometer cross-country ski race at the 2006 Olympics was less than 1%. Researchers suspect that Viagra will be put on the banned substance list in the future because it is easily detected and appears to provide an unfair advantage, at least at altitude.

use performance-enhancing substances. Conversely, extrinsically motivated athletes were more likely to use performance-enhancing substances in sport, in part because of the unsportspersonship orientations they hold. Thus, it appears that *why* one plays the game (i.e., motivation) predicts *how* one plays the game (i.e., sportspersonship orientations), which then predicts the use (or not) of performance-enhancing substances.

Finally, research by Hodge, Hargreaves, Gerrard, and Lonsdale (2013) found that moral disengagement was a strong predictor of positive attitudes toward the use of performance-enhancing drugs. The researchers used Bandura's (2005) social cognitive theory of moral thought and action to explain why moral disengagement can lead to positive attitudes toward (and possibly actual use of) performance-enhancing drugs. This theory argues that moral disengagement allows individuals to transgress moral standards without feeling negative affect or guilt, thereby decreasing constraint on future immoral behavior. For example, immoral behavior such as using performance-enhancing drugs could be justified as a way of maintaining a team's winning legacy and rationalized as just another way to maximize one's potential. In addition, athletes may invoke their opponent's use of performance-enhancing drugs (i.e., "Everyone else is doing it") or displace responsibility to an authority figure such as the coach. In essence, there are many ways that athletes can justify using performance-enhancing drugs without feeling guilt or negative affect.

Social Reasons

Social pressures are also important causes of drug use. Pressure from peers and the need to gain group acceptance are especially apparent among adolescents who want to fit in. They may drink, smoke, or take performance-enhancing drugs not so much because they want to but rather to be accepted by their peers. Studies of adolescents (Hildebrandt et al., 2012; Newman & Newman, 1991) found that the lure of steroids is often too strong for many adolescents to resist because of the extreme demands regarding conformity in this age group. This is especially problematic for males, who seem to be more prone to "macho behavior" in the desire to fit in with the group. Thus, practitioners must repeatedly communicate the importance of being one's self and not giving in to pressure from so-called friends.

Athletes have become highly visible on television and through other media, and for many youngsters these professional, Olympic, and college athletes are role models. For some youngsters, making enormous amounts of money and becoming a national celebrity have become part of the culture to which they aspire. This combination seemingly provides easy access to drugs. Unfortunately, perceptions that these highly skilled athletes ingest drugs and the mind-set that "it doesn't hurt them so much so it won't hurt me" provide an attractive rationale for aspiring young athletes to take drugs (Anshel, 2010; Martens, Dams-O'Connor, & Kilmer, 2007). In fact, several sports writers have argued that the biggest danger with someone as famous as Barry Bonds taking steroids is that many young athletes might get the idea that you have to take drugs to be really successful in sport. Despite his negative publicity, lots of kids still want to be like Barry Bonds (in terms of home runs). Drugs can be obtained in various ways, including online, at gymnasiums, and through muscle magazines. Oftentimes, it is teenagers who seek out these drugs, and their bodies and minds are not even fully developed yet. These drugs often cause damage that is not seen until years later. However, many times the allure of stardom and heightened success is just too appealing to pass up.

Drug use seems implicitly sanctioned to young athletes for whom professionals are role models. This modeling effect is particularly influential during adolescence, when many youngsters are exploring their identities and often experimenting with drugs. In addition, the notion of using drugs for fun and experimentation promotes the idea that drugs (especially alcohol) are not really harmful and helps contribute to an individual's comfort level with the behavior. To counter all this, practitioners should provide alternative models for youngsters that focus on personal responsibility.

Finally, in one of the few studies using a theoretical approach to study drug use in athletes, Lazarus, Barkoukis, Rodafinos, and Tzorbatzoudis (2010) investigated predictors of drug use using the theory of planned behavior (see chapter 18). Results from this study of more than 1,100 athletes revealed that situational temptation (i.e., how tempted you would be to use performance-enhancing drugs if your coach suggests you do so, if you believe most of your competitors are using prohibited substances, or when you prepare for an important competition) and attitudes toward drug use were the strongest predictors of past and current drug use. Changing favorable attitudes toward doping into unfavorable ones and teaching athletes how to resist pressure to engage in doping

Common Recreational Drugs and Their Side Effects

Alcohol

- Mood swings
- Euphoria
- False confidence
- Slowed reaction time
- Distorted depth perception
- Difficulty staying alert
- Reduced strength
- Reduced speed

- Emotional outbursts
- Lost inhibitions
- Muscular weakness
- Dizziness
- Liver damage
- Reduced power
- Reduced endurance

Marijuana

- Drowsiness
- Decreased hand–eye coordination
- Increased blood pressure
- Distorted vision
- Decreased physical performance
- Decreased alertness
- Increased heart rate
- Memory loss
- Slowed reaction time
- Decreased mental performance

Cocaine

- Physical and psychological addiction
- Increased strength
- Dizziness
- Rapid blood pressure fluctuations
- Anxiety
- Death from circulatory problems
- Violent mood swings
- Decreased reaction time
- Vomiting
- Distorted depth perception
- Hallucination

Adapted from L. Bump, 1988, Drugs and sport performance. In *Successful coaching*, edited by R. Martens (Champaign, IL: Human Kinetics), 135-147.

under risk-conducive circumstances may lead to weaker intentions to engage in doping, even among athletes with a history of drug use.

> **KEY POINT** Reasons athletes and exercisers take drugs include peer pressure, thrill seeking and curiosity, the need to achieve success, and the desire to increase self-esteem.

Major Drug Categories and Their Effects

In the sport and exercise realm, drugs are classified by their purpose: (a) performance-enhancing drugs and (b) recreational, social, or street drugs. **Performance-enhancing drugs** include anabolic steroids, beta-blockers, and stimulants used by athletes or exercisers to increase strength, calm nerves, or block pain. Table 20.1 lists six general categories of performance-enhancing drugs, their potential performance-enhancing effects, and psychological and medical side effects associated with their use.

Recreational drugs (also known as street drugs) are substances that people seek out and use for personal pleasure. They may be trying to escape pressures, fit in with friends who use drugs, or find thrills and excitement that seem to escape them in everyday life. "Common Recreational Drugs and Their Side Effects" lists the side effects of alcohol, marijuana, and cocaine. Tobacco is another widely used recreational drug associated with negative health effects. Most people know the negative effects of cigarettes and cigars, but smokeless tobacco is significant as well because its use has recently increased in teenage athletic populations. Snuff and chewing tobacco are associated with lip, gum, and other oral cancers.

> **KEY POINT** Snuff and chewing tobacco are associated with lip, gum, and other oral cancers; nevertheless, the use of smokeless tobacco is on the rise in some populations.

TABLE 20.1   Major Categories of Performance-Enhancing Drugs in Sport

Drug category	Definition and use	Performance-enhancing effect	Side effects
Stimulants	Various types of drugs that increase alertness, reduce fatigue, and may increase competitiveness and hostility	Reduced fatigue; increased alertness, endurance, and aggression	Anxiety, insomnia, increased heart rate and blood pressure, dehydration, stroke, heart irregularities, psychological problems, death
Narcotic analgesics	Various types of drugs that kill pain through psychological stimulation	Reduced pain	Constricted pupil size, dry mouth, heaviness of limbs, skin itchiness, suppression of hunger, constipation, inability to concentrate, drowsiness, fear and anxiety, physical and psychological dependence
Anabolic steroids	Derivatives of the male hormone testosterone	Increased strength and endurance, improved mental attitude, increased training and recovery rates	Increased risk of liver disease and premature heart disease, increased aggression, loss of coordination, a variety of sex-related effects (e.g., infertility in males, development of male sex characteristics in females)
Beta-blockers	Drugs used to lower blood pressure, decrease heart rate, and block stimulatory responses	Steadied nerves in sports such as shooting	Excessively slowed heart rate, heart failure, low blood pressure, light-headedness, depression, insomnia, weakness, nausea, vomiting, cramps, diarrhea, bronchial spasm, tingling, numbness
Diuretics	Drugs used to help eliminate fluids from the tissues (increase secretion of urine)	Temporary weight loss	Increased cholesterol levels, stomach distress, dizziness, blood disorders, muscle spasms, weakness, impaired cardiovascular functioning, decreased aerobic endurance
Peptide hormones and analogs (e.g., human growth hormone)	Chemically produced drugs that are chemically similar to or have effects similar to those of already-existing drugs	Increased strength and endurance, muscle growth	Increased growth of organs, heart disease, thyroid disease, menstrual disorders, decreased sexual drive, shortened life span

Adapted from L. Bump, 1988, Drugs and sport performance. In *Successful coaching,* edited by R. Martens (Champaign, IL: Human Kinetics), 135-147.

Detection of Substance Abuse

Substance use and abuse are detected by formal procedures (e.g., drug testing) and informal procedures (e.g., observation and listening). Unfortunately, properly conducted drug testing is very expensive.

KEY POINT   Only specifically trained professionals work in drug treatment programs. However, sport and fitness personnel play a major role in drug prevention and detection.

Several signs and symptoms characterize people who are substance abusers:

- Changes in behavior (e.g., lack of motivation, tardiness, absenteeism)
- Changes in peer group
- Major changes in personality
- Major changes in athletic or academic performance
- Apathetic or listless behaviors

- Impaired judgment
- Poor coordination
- Poor hygiene and grooming
- Profuse sweating
- Muscular twitches or tremors

If you observe these symptoms in athletes and exercisers, it is not necessarily the case that they are substance users or abusers; these symptoms can also reflect other emotional problems. Thus, a fitness professional who observes particular symptoms should first talk to the person involved to validate her suspicions. Hard-core substance abusers are notorious for lying and denying the problem, however. Hildebrandt and colleagues (2012) discuss how athletes may increase and taper the use of steroids (a practice known as pyramiding) or cycle their drug use to evade scheduled drug tests (e.g., in-season vs. off-season). So, if doubts remain after the initial talk with the individual, you should solicit confidential advice from a substance abuse specialist. When you deal with an individual who has substance abuse problems, follow a referral process similar to the one described earlier for eating disorders.

Sport Deterrence Model of Drug Abuse

One recent model put forth to help detect substance abuse (and eventually deter drug use) uses **deterrence** theory to help understand the process individuals go through when deciding whether to use drugs (Strelan & Boeckmann, 2003). The drugs in sport decision model (DSDM) consists of three major components: the costs of a decision to use, the benefits associated with using, and specific situational factors that may in some way affect the cost–benefit analysis of using. The DSDM is therefore consistent with the rational choice perspective, which states that individuals conduct a cost–benefit analysis of the consequences of lawbreaking behavior before deciding to break a law.

Costs

- Legal sanctions (fines, suspensions, jail time)
- Social sanctions (disapproval, criticism by important others, material loss)
- Self-imposed sanctions (guilt, reduced self-esteem)
- Health concerns (negative side effects)

The most consistent deterrent reported in the literature is self-imposed sanctions, especially when the action of taking drugs goes against one's moral values. In contrast, the least effective deterrent is legal sanctions. This was found in 25 studies between 1969 and 1986 (Paternoster, 1987) and another 24 studies from 1987 to 2002 (Strelan & Boeckmann, 2003). However, this result is most likely because the majority of behaviors studied are misdemeanors, and individuals have therefore tended to perceive the likelihood of arrest and punishment to be low.

The use of drug testing as a deterrent at the high school level was investigated in a study based on questionnaires given to student-athletes at 11 high schools in Oregon (Goldberg & Elliot, 2005). Results did not reveal any evidence that drug testing was a deterrent to further drug use. Similarly, the SATURN (Student Athlete Testing Using Random Notification) study used six high schools with no drug testing and five with random drug and alcohol testing. Results found that the presence of a drug-testing program was a minimal deterrent to drug use. Researchers from both studies found that although drug testing often produced few (if any) positive results, the questionnaires revealed widespread drug use among high school athletes. So administrators are happy they have a testing program, but in reality they are probably not catching or deterring many athletes from using drugs. The researchers call for more education and doing a better job of actually detecting drug use. Some perceived benefits of drug use, as well as situational variables affecting the decision to use or not use drugs, are presented below.

Benefits

- Material (prize money, sponsorship, endorsements, contracts)
- Social (prestige, glory, acknowledgment by important others)
- Internalized (satisfaction of high achievement)

Depending on the athlete's orientation, any one of the three benefits might be perceived as most important and motivating. Thus coaches must know their athletes to better understand the lure of drugs to different athletes.

Situational Variables

- Prevalence perceptions (how frequently others use this drug)

- Experience with punishment and punishment avoidance
- Professional status (how much money and status might be lost)
- Perception of authority legitimacy (the ability of the agency to enforce the law)
- Type of drug (its effects and side effects)

This is not meant to be an exhaustive list of potential mediating situational variables but instead includes some of the most common variables affecting the perceived cost and benefit analysis of drug use. Thus, once again, an interactional model should be used, suggesting that an individual's perceived cost–benefit analysis is affected by several situational factors to produce a decision to use or not use drugs.

The DSDM is predicated on the assumption that drug-free sport is desirable, as is specifying the factors that may affect drug-use decisions. The literature suggests that an individual's sense of morality is a powerful deterrent. Morality research further suggests that the more ingrained a particular belief, and the earlier in life it is ingrained, the more likely an individual will adhere to that belief. This implies that efforts to convince promising young athletes that performance-enhancing drug use is unfair are likely to have a greater effect than is investing more in legal deterrence.

KEY POINT Hard-core substance abusers are notorious for lying and denying their substance abuse.

Setting up policies and procedures for detecting substance use and abuse under the umbrella of a formal drug education program has also proved to be effective. For example, the NCAA Drug Education Committee originally developed a set of minimum guidelines for policy consideration by its member institutions (Carr & Murphy, 1995); these might be successful for athletes at other levels as well. This model provides drug education for athletes and athletic officials; treatment support; and training sessions for coaches, athletic trainers, and team physicians to help detect and handle drug- and alcohol-related problems. These educational and drug testing guidelines are updated regularly and can be found at www.NCAA.org/drugtesting.

Prevention and Control of Substance Abuse

Because substance abuse is a clinical matter, sport and fitness personnel are unlikely to be involved in drug treatment programs. We can play major roles in drug prevention by providing resources to our athletes, but keep in mind that education, although important, has typically deterred only 5% of sport or exercise participants from experimenting with drugs (Tricker, Cook, & McGuire, 1989). As stated by Nicholson (1989) in a thorough review of the literature, "While distribution of information plays an important consciousness-raising function, it should not be considered a critical strategy to reduce the drug use of athletes and exercisers" (pp. 50–51). Conversely, an NCAA survey of athletes conducted from 2010 to 2011 found that more

Coaches and Substance Abuse

With so much news coverage of athletes and substance abuse, we sometimes forget that some coaches also have alcohol problems. For example, police made public the drunken rampage that Gary Moeller, ex-Michigan football coach, embarked on inside and outside of a restaurant. The accounts depicted a 54-year-old man out of control, smashing drink glasses on his table, singing loudly, and attempting to dance with other women after his wife left the restaurant. He sustained alcohol poisoning and was incoherent, abusive, and relentlessly vulgar. When police arrived, Moeller punched an officer before being arrested and charged with disorderly conduct and assault and battery. These actions forced him to resign the next day.

Dennis Erickson, ex-coach of the Seattle Seahawks, was ordered to enter an alcohol rehabilitation program after being arrested for driving while intoxicated and having an alcohol-induced car accident. Erickson's drinking problems had surfaced earlier and were known from his coaching at the University of Miami. Unfortunately, problems among coaches demonstrating a lack of self-control, such as excessive drinking and even spousal abuse, have been reported with alarming frequency in recent years. Perhaps the high stress associated with coaching is contributing to these out-of-control episodes (see chapter 21). Coaches, like their players, aren't icons but only imperfect humans.

than 50% of athletes believed that mandatory drug testing has reduced NCAA athletes' use of drugs. The following are some suggestions for helping prevent or at least reduce the probability of drug use:

1. Provide a supportive environment that addresses the reasons individuals take drugs. Empower participants through increased self-esteem and self-confidence, because people who feel good about themselves are less likely to take drugs. Keep winning in perspective and reduce the pressure to win at all costs. Be attuned to the symptoms of substance abuse.

2. Educate participants about the effects of drug use. The key here is to be informative and accurate regarding both the negative and positive (performance-enhancing) effects of various drugs. Using examples of well-known athletes (or actually bringing in high-visibility athletes) can be effective. You could cite the example of Green Bay quarterback Brett Favre: Addicted to painkilling drugs, Favre had to undergo therapy at a treatment center to deal with the problem. There is also the uplifting story of tennis champion Jennifer Capriati's return to the tour from a bout with drugs and working her way back to winning Grand Slam tournaments. You might also convey information through peer athlete leaders and use role playing and group-facilitation techniques.

3. Early on, expose athletes to the notion that using performance-enhancing drugs amounts to cheating and unfair competition. As noted earlier, enhancing athletes' morality appears to have the largest effect on inhibiting drug use. Start programs early and continue to expose young athletes to the notion that it is unfair and simply wrong to win via drugs.

4. Set a good example. Actions speak louder than words, so coaches and exercise leaders should monitor their own actions and not smoke, chew tobacco, or drink excessively. This in itself sends a powerful message against the use of drugs. Professionals are not immune to drug abuse. Coaches who have personal concerns should themselves get help. An excellent example of this type of effort is the United States Anti-Doping Agency's True Sport program, a community outreach and education program for parents, coaches, and athletes, that seeks to ensure a positive youth sport experience by emphasizing "clean" competition, sportsmanship, and drug-free strategies to achieve peak performance (visit www.truesport.org).

5. Teach coping skills. As noted earlier, increased anxiety and stress along with decreased levels of self-confidence can contribute to drug use. Therefore, coping strategies such as changing negative to positive self-talk, managing stress, reframing, and thought

ATLAS and ATHENA: Drug Prevention for High School Athletes

ATLAS (Athletes Training and Learning to Avoid Steroids) for boys and **ATHENA** (Athletes Targeting Healthy Exercise and Nutrition Alternatives) for girls are two sex-specific, evidence-based drug prevention and health promotion programs for high school sport teams. The program, developed by Goldberg and Elliot (2005), consists of a network of high schools across the country where coaches, athletic directors, and student-athlete leaders are trained to teach such things as eating better before and after workouts and how to get stronger with various strength training techniques. Rather than stressing the long-term effects of anabolic steroids, diet pills, marijuana, and alcohol, the program focuses on the immediate effects on athletic potential—informing students, for example, that alcohol is a muscle toxin; that marijuana can reduce muscle coordination; and that anabolic steroids can cause acne, shrink testicles (males), and cause facial hair (females). Participants also learn to be cautious with supplements because of the lack of government oversight in ensuring product purity and safety.

As noted earlier, drug testing does not seem to be especially effective as a deterrent, and thus the program takes a more educationally based approach. Although still in the early stages, some research and anecdotal reports suggest that the program is effective. In a summary of the findings to date, Hildebrandt and colleagues (2011) argue that the ATLAS and ATHENA programs have been shown to be effective for reducing intentions to engage in unhealthy body shaping behaviors, although their effect on reducing actual behaviors has not yet been empirically supported. Members of these programs also reported not intending to partake in unhealthy weight loss practices and being more aware of the negative consequences of using drugs. Although further controlled studies are needed, the ATLAS and ATHENA programs are off to a good start.

stopping can be used to cope with stress and enhance self-confidence.

6. A web-based personalized feedback program (Martens, Dams-O'Connor, & Beck, 2006) was shown to significantly reduce drinking in high-risk drinking athletes. Athletes received personalized feedback (e.g., comparing their own drinking with national peer norms); a summary of their drinking frequency over the past year; and information on the financial cost of drinking, calories associated with drinking, and their risk status for negative consequences associated with drinking. Thus, the Internet appears to be a way to deliver a personalized program for reducing drinking to large numbers of student-athletes.

Addiction to Exercise

Another type of addiction (although not everyone sees it as an addiction) is addiction to exercise. For example, some people develop exceptionally strong feelings about their exercise, as you can sense in the following quote by Waldemar Cierpinski, the two-time gold medalist from East Germany:

" I have run since infancy . . . . It's the passion of my life. Running as long as possible—I've made that into a sport. I have no other secrets. Without running I wouldn't be able to live. (Cierpinski, 1980, p. 27) "

The intense involvement with exercise, particularly running, has been described in such terms as *compulsion* (Abell, 1975), *dependence* (Sachs & Pargman, 1984), *obsession* (Waters, 1981), *exercise fix* (Benyo, 1990), and *addiction* (Glasser, 1976). In the exercise psychology literature, most writers use the term *addiction* to refer to an intense involvement in exercise.

What Is Exercise Addiction?

Exercise addiction is a psychological or physiological (or psychological *and* physiological) dependence on a regular regimen of exercise that is characterized by withdrawal symptoms after 24 to 36 hours without exercise (Sachs, 1981). Note, in addition, that exercise addiction typically incorporates both psychological and physiological factors. Some withdrawal symptoms commonly associated with the cessation of exercising include anxiety, irritability, guilt, muscle twitching, a bloated feeling, and nervousness. But these occur only if an individual is prevented from exercising for some

reason (e.g., injury, work, or family commitments), as opposed to purposefully taking a day or two off.

Positive Addiction to Exercise

The concept of beneficial addiction to exercise, running in particular, was popularized by William Glasser in his book *Positive Addiction* (1976). Glasser argued that positive addictions such as running and meditation promote psychological strength and increase life satisfaction. This is in sharp contrast to negative addictions, such as addiction to heroin or cocaine (noted earlier), that inevitably undermine psychological and physiological functioning. Glasser saw exercise as a compulsion (rather than an addiction) that increases an individual's psychological and physical strength, thereby enhancing the person's state of well-being and functioning. Rather than using standard quantitative assessments and analyses, Glasser included qualitative data from clinical and psychiatric assessments.

In **positive addiction to exercise**, the variety of psychological and physiological benefits just referred to typically occur as a person continues to participate in regular physical activity. With a positive addiction to exercise, exercisers view their involvement in regular physical activity as important to their lives, and they can successfully integrate this activity with other aspects of their lives, including work, family, and friends. Exercise becomes a habit of daily activity, and this level of involvement represents a "healthy habit."

Negative Addiction to Exercise

Although many exercisers develop a positive addiction to their exercise, for a small percentage of people, exercise can control their lives (Benyo, 1990; Berger & Tobar, 2011; Morgan, 1979a). When this occurs, the person has a **negative addiction to exercise** that eliminates other choices in life. Lives become structured around exercise to such an extent that home and work responsibilities suffer and relationships take a backseat. This condition apparently reflects personal or social maladjustment and parallels other addictive processes characterized by increasing dose dependence and withdrawal symptoms under deprivation. Chan (1986) described how people typically become addicted to exercise:

" The typical addict is . . . female or male, and began exercising in adulthood as a way to lose weight and become more physically fit. As these individuals improve their heart rate,

Some addictions can be positive. When someone successfully integrates a balanced exercise routine into his or her daily lifestyle, a positive addiction to exercise can occur.

lose weight, and feel better physically, they also begin to feel better about themselves. They develop a sense of control over their bodies—something they had been unable to do through dieting—and this feeling of control generalizes to a sense of control over their lives. In other words, they feel more powerful and more self-confident. (p. 430)

Many addicted exercisers recognize their own symptoms of negative addiction. However, they often feel that although exercise may control their lives, it enhances their existence. Runner and physician George Sheehan (1979) demonstrated this perspective when he wrote:

The world will wait. Job, family, friends will wait; in fact, they must wait on the outcome . . . . Can anything have a higher priority than running? It defines me, adds to me, and makes me whole. I have a job and family and friends that can attest to that. (p. 49)

Along these lines, it is instructive to differentiate between primary and secondary exercise dependence (Kerr, Linder, & Blaydon, 2007). In primary exercise dependence, exercise is an end in itself, although it may include altering eating behaviors for the purpose of enhancing performance. In secondary exercise dependence, the exercise is a symptom of another primary pathological condition, such as an eating disorder. Kerr and colleagues (2007) recommend that the criteria for diagnosing those who are hooked on exercise include three or more symptoms in a 12-month period. Symptoms include the following:

- Tolerance or need for increased amounts of exercise
- Withdrawal symptoms (e.g., anxiety, fatigue)
- Loss of control
- Conflict as exercise takes precedence over other activities
- Devoting more and more time to exercise

- Exercising in larger amounts than was intended
- Continuing to exercise despite knowledge of problems

McNamara and McCabe (2012) attempted to develop a biopsychosocial model to help explain the development and maintenance of exercise dependence among elite athletes. Results revealed that athletes classified as exercise dependent had a higher body mass index, had more extreme and maladaptive exercise dependence, and reported higher pressure from coaches and teammates and lower social support compared with athletes who were not exercise dependent. This initial study supports the utility of using a biopsychosocial model of exercise dependence to understand the etiology of exercise dependence among elite athletes.

Addiction to Exercise and Self-Esteem

A study by Martin, Martens, Serrao, and Rocha (2008) revealed that a person can become exercise depen-

dent when they attempt to use exercise as a means to enhance self-esteem. In addition, exercise dependence was found to be related to alcohol-related problems in college students (Hall, Hill, Appelton, & Kozub, 2009). It appears that exercise dependence can be related to (although not causative of) inappropriate behaviors. Finally, a review of the literature indicates that athletes and exercisers who were addicted to their sport or exercise tend to have higher levels of alcoholism and other chemical addictions later in life (Krivoschekov & Lushnikov, 2011). Therefore, these people need to be extremely careful that a sport or exercise addiction does not turn into a chemical addiction later in life.

When an Addicted Exerciser Can't Exercise

What happens when an addicted exerciser is injured and cannot exercise? The exerciser will probably

Sexual Harassment and Abuse in Sport

Unfortunately, mirroring society, documented **sexual harassment and abuse** in sport have increased. This is highlighted in a special issue of *International Journal of Sport and Exercise Psychology* (Leahy, 2008). The severity of the problem has prompted the International Olympic Committee (2008) to issue a consensus statement regarding sexual harassment and abuse in sport. The IOC has stated that its aim is to improve the health and protection of all athletes through the promotion of effective preventive policy and to increase awareness of these problems among the athlete's entourage.

Sexual harassment refers to behavior toward an individual that involves sexualized verbal, nonverbal, or physical behavior, whether intended or unintended, that is based on an abuse of power and trust and is considered by the victim to be unwanted or coerced. Data collected over a 16-year period showed that the commonalities of intimacy, opportunity, and coercion or power most frequently characterized sexual abuse of athletes by coaches (or other authority figures). Specifically, building trust and friendship, developing isolation and control, building loyalty, securing secrecy, and targeting a potential victim were aspects of what has been termed the grooming process leading to sexual abuse. Specific situational risk factors included going to the coach's house, getting massages from the coach, and being driven home by the coach. In addition, athletes' low self-esteem, distant parent–athlete relationships, and devotion to the coach were personal risk factors.

The IOC recommends that all sport organizations develop specific policies for the prevention of sexual harassment and abuse, monitor the implementation of these policies and procedures, foster strong partnerships with parents and caregivers, and develop an education and training program on sexual harassment and abuse in their sport.

National League Cy Young award winner R.A. Dickey and Olympic judo gold medalist Kayla Harrison were two of the first world-class athletes to tell their stories about years of sexual abuse at the hands of a coach and a babysitter. The years were filled with shame, guilt, fear, suicidal thoughts, and gut-wrenching depression. The stories of how these courageous athletes have achieved greatness while fighting demons should give hope to others and help them break away or recover from any sexual abuse they have experienced. For a full account of these athletes' stories, see Smith (2012).

The most visible sexual abuse case in sport is likely the child sex abuse scandal that broke in 2011 at Pennsylvania State University, involving longtime football coach Jerry Sandusky's sexual

suffer withdrawal symptoms including tension, restlessness, irritability, depression, interpersonal problems, and feelings of guilt. In one study (Chan & Grossman, 1988), injured runners who were prevented from running suffered greater overall tension, anxiety, depression, confusion, anger, and hostility—along with lower self-esteem and vigor—than their still-running counterparts. The authors concluded that these withdrawal symptoms were similar to those commonly noted in withdrawal from other addictions. One way to cope with an injury is to try other activities. A runner who injures her lower leg might still swim and possibly ride a bicycle. However, the substitution will likely not satisfy the true addict.

An exerciser can do a number of things to help guard against falling into the trap of negative addiction, including the following:

- Schedule rest days or take them when necessary.
- Work out regularly with a slower partner.
- If you're injured, stop exercising until you are rehabilitated and healed.
- Train hard–easy: Mix in low intensity and less distance with days of harder training.
- If you're interested in health benefits, exercise three or four times a week for 30 minutes.
- Set realistic short- and long-term goals.

Compulsive Gambling: An Odds-On Favorite for Trouble

The focus of this chapter has thus far been on three problems prevalent in today's sport and exercise environments. We turn now to a problem that, despite its long history in competitive sport, is only now getting the attention of the media and the public: compulsive gambling. Bookies have been taking and placing bets (legally and illegally) for a long time in and on sports.

assault of at least nine underage boys on or near university property and the alleged actions by some university officials to cover up the incidents. Based on an extensive grand jury investigation, Sandusky was indicted and found guilty on 45 counts of sexual abuse, resulting in a minimum of 30 years in prison. In addition, based on findings of the grand jury and an independent investigation commissioned by the Penn State board and conducted by former FBI director Louis Freeh, several high-level school officials were charged with perjury, suspended, or dismissed for covering up the incidents or failing to notify authorities. Most notably, school president Graham Spanier was forced to resign, and head football coach Joe Paterno (who reportedly did tell his boss about the abuse but did nothing further when his boss did not report the abuse to the proper authorities) and athletic director Tim Curley were fired. In his report, Freeh stated that the most senior leaders at Penn State showed "a total disregard for the safety and welfare of Sandusky's child victims for 14 years and empowered Jerry Sandusky to continue his abuse." This incident was particularly troubling because Penn State had a reputation for running a clean program in which athletes' academic and personal growth was paramount. Steps are being taken around the country to protect young boys and girls from being the target of sexual abuse by coaches or other adults in positions of power.

Although sexual harassment and abuse are totally unacceptable in and out of sport, an interesting study by Kerr and Stirling (2013) noted that completely eliminating any touching between coach and athlete via "no touch" policies could be overreacting. Results of the study, in which both young athletes and coaches were interviewed, revealed that both athletes and coaches felt that touch was important for teaching and learning purposes, praise and recognition, consolation, and ensuring athlete welfare. However, the acceptability of touch was affected by such factors as the interpersonal qualities of the coach and athlete, the nature of the interpersonal relationship between the coach and athlete, and the context in which the touch occurs. The findings suggest that rather than supporting a "no touch" culture, safe and healthy ways for negotiating the use of touch should be understood and promoted. A diving coach, for example, made it a practice to always ask his female divers for permission to touch them when he needed to physically spot their dives.

The Black Sox baseball scandal in the 1920s was one of the first large-scale documented scandals in which players were betting on their own games and sometimes performing poorly to ensure that the proper bets were covered. Basketball scandals received publicity in the 1950s and early 1960s when 37 basketball players from 22 schools were documented to have participated in point shaving and illegal betting. The point shaving done by collegiate basketball players from the City University of New York especially shook the sporting world. Back then, the players didn't see anything wrong with winning by 6 points instead of 12. They weren't being asked to lose the game but to control the point spread.

You might wonder why these athletes and others after them got involved with gamblers and started shaving points. Interviews with gamblers (oftentimes mobsters turned straight) note that they try one of three things. First, gamblers might help an athlete run up a gambling tab he can't pay. That leaves the athlete with a choice: Cough up the cash or "provide a service" (usually shaving points). Second, gamblers seduce athletes with fancy dinners, booze, and drugs and set up opportunities for sex. Third, a bribe of a certain amount of money (usually $10,000) will often persuade a reluctant athlete to cross over to the dark side.

Gambling in and on sports has become increasingly visible in high-profile cases involving, for example, quarterback Art Schlichter; Pete Rose (banned from the Hall of Fame in 2004 for betting on baseball, he admitted to betting on baseball after 13 years of denying it); and Boston College, Northwestern, and Tulane University basketball and football players betting on their games. Even Michael Jordan has been known to wager large amounts of money (usually on his golf game—not on basketball). But the high-profile cases are evidently only the tip of the iceberg, and gambling on sporting events is evidently widespread. Furthermore, the seriousness of betting on sport is underscored by the number of cases of athletes and college students who have committed suicide due to escalating gambling debts.

Prevalence of Sports Gambling

Betting on sports is almost a national pastime, as an ESPN survey found that about 118 million Americans gambled on sports in some manner in 2008. Sports betting, illegal in almost all locales, is clearly thriving across the country. For example, the vast majority (72%) of athletes in Division I NCAA football and basketball programs engage in some form of gambling (e.g., betting on sports, playing slot machines, casino gambling, playing cards for money) while in college (Cross & Vollano, 1999). In addition, it has been estimated that gambling has reached problematic or pathological levels for 12% of males and 3% of females participating in intercollegiate athletics (Weinstock, Whelan, & Meyers, 2000). This illegal gambling is often fostered by the publication of betting odds and lines for upcoming events in daily newspapers. People interested in gambling can simply choose from a growing number of websites. With this easy access to gambling, experts on compulsive gambling agree that college students are especially vulnerable. According to national statistics, about 1.5% of the population are compulsive gamblers and another 4% are problem gamblers (i.e., not addicted to but overindulging in gambling). It is estimated that 6% to 8% of college students are compulsive gamblers—those believed to be so addicted that they are out of control. This is more than in any other demographic group.

The fact that these gambling figures are estimated to be significantly higher for college students than for others in the populace is one reason *Sports Illustrated* in 1995 ran a three-part series detailing the vast gambling activity on campuses throughout the country (Layden, 1995). Extensive student bookmaking operations were documented, and the report revealed how easy it is for students to bet with a bookie, who is usually a fellow college student consumed with wagering and in over his head. For example, a student from the University of Nevada at Las Vegas stole a total of $89,000 from eight Las Vegas banks, and a University of Texas student stole more than $12,000 from a bank, both of them trying to pay off gambling debts. The students received prison sentences of about 10 years.

An NCAA (2004) study of 21,000 athletes focused on gambling by college students on college sports. Results revealed that 35% of male athletes and 10% of female athletes bet on college sports in the past year and that Division III athletes were most likely to gamble. The study also revealed that 2.3% of football players were asked to influence the outcome of games because of gambling debts, and 1.4% admitted to actually altering their performance to change the outcome. Interestingly enough, approximately 60% of Division

I athletes and 40% of Division III athletes said they did not know the NCAA rules about sports gambling, which call for penalties that could include a loss of scholarship. Due to the high numbers of athletes participating in gambling activities, the NCAA initiated several educational programs. Thus, the NCAA (2009) conducted a follow-up study to test the effectiveness of these programs. Results, in general, revealed some decrease in gambling activity (partly because athletes were more familiar with the rules regarding gambling behavior), although it was still a problem. For example, 30% of male athletes still gambled, compared with 35% in 2004. Efforts to reduce gambling behavior in NCAA athletes remain ongoing.

Ellenbogen, Jacobs, Derevensky, Gupta, and Paskus (2008) surveyed more than 20,000 NCAA student-athletes regarding their gambling behaviors. Results revealed that 62% and 43% of male and female college athletes, respectively, reported gambling, although only 4% and 0.4% of male and female athletes, respectively, reported having a gambling problem; these percentages are similar to those for nonathlete college students. However, 13% of male athletes and 3% of female athletes reported gambling weekly; these percentages are three times greater than those for nonathlete college students. In addition, male athletes in high-profile sports (e.g., baseball, football) were more likely to report a gambling problem than those in other sports (e.g., track and field, volleyball). Interestingly, almost half of the athletes in the sample were either unsure or unaware of the NCAA rules concerning college gambling. As a result of these problems and confusion, the NCAA has appointed a task force to make recommendations regarding gambling among college athletes.

Gambling doesn't start in college. Experts agree that gambling by high school students is "incredibly extensive." In surveys conducted in 2007 by *USA Today* and 2009 by ESPN, 26% of male athletes reported that they started gambling before high school and 66% reported starting in high school. Police arrested four men in New Jersey for running a sports betting and loan sharking operation that had at least 50 high school students as clients. The problem in investigating these types of cases is that parents tend to have one of three reactions: They are afraid to say anything because they think organized crime is involved; they think they can handle the issue themselves at home; or—most commonly—they say, "Thank God it's not drugs." In essence, parents often don't think of teenage gambling as a serious problem, and they are often wrong in this assessment (Layden, 1995).

Gambling and Officiating: A Threat to the Integrity of the Game

In 2007 NBA official Tim Donaghy, a 13-year veteran referee, admitted to gambling on NBA games (some of which he officiated) as well as alerting gamblers to such things as the health status of players, relationships among players, and which referees were working specific games—information that is not supposed to be public until shortly before tip-off. He also picked games based on the referee crews working the games and got paid for every pick that was correct. He was sentenced to 15 months in jail, although the bigger problem is his betrayal of the confidence the public and players have in the integrity of the officials.

Although Donaghy probably did not help determine the outcome of games, he most assuredly behaved in a way that could alter the final score and thus influence the many people betting on the game (based on the "line," which determines the number of points by which a team is favored or seen as underdog). A basketball referee can influence the point spread in several ways, including the following:

- Take a key player out of the game with early foul trouble (as one scout said, "If a referee puts a big man in foul trouble early we are in BIG trouble")
- Blow the whistle on a "ticky tack" foul (referees have plenty of leeway in determining what fouls to call)
- Enforce minor infractions (palming the ball, offensive 3 seconds, illegal defenses, and lane violations on free throws are often committed but rarely called)
- Create a free-throw discrepancy (calling fouls predominantly on one team can easily lead to changes in strategy and final score)

Signs of Compulsive Gambling

Compulsive gamblers exhibit certain characteristics such as boastfulness, arrogance, unbounded optimism, and extreme competitiveness and are often quite intelligent. But picking a compulsive gambler out of a crowd, experts say, is next to impossible because they are experts at denial. Because gambling is something lots of people do, it falls into the same realm as alcohol consumption—it's not noticed until there are negative consequences, as in the case of Art Schlichter. One expert noted, "Sports gambling on campus is a dirty little secret of college life in America, and it's rampant and thriving" (Layden, 1995). Therefore, as professionals, we must be cognizant of this problem and not put our collective heads in the sand. Referrals to such programs as Gamblers Anonymous or the National Council on Problem Gambling are appropriate if you identify a compulsive gambling problem.

In a series on college gambling, *USA Today* (2007) offered a number of signs of a gambling problem to college students and their parents:

College Students

- Missing classes because of gambling
- Having trouble focusing in class because they are thinking about gambling
- Buying a book or otherwise educating themselves on becoming a more skillful bettor
- Facing more financial debts than they can handle

Parents

- An unexplained need for money
- A sudden increase in credit card debt
- Displays of unexplained wealth
- Money and valuables missing from home
- Sudden dip in grades

Gamblers Anonymous 20 Questions

Gamblers Anonymous has 20 questions that it asks new members. Compulsive gamblers usually answer yes to at least 7 of the 20 questions.

1. Did you ever lose time from work or school because of gambling?
2. Has gambling ever made your home life unhappy?
3. Did gambling affect your reputation?
4. Have you ever felt remorse after gambling?
5. Did you ever gamble to get money with which to pay debts or otherwise solve financial difficulties?
6. Did gambling cause a decrease in your ambition or efficiency?
7. After losing did you feel you must return as soon as possible and win back your losses?
8. After a win did you have a strong urge to return and win more?
9. Did you often gamble until your last dollar was gone?
10. Did you ever borrow to finance your gambling?
11. Have you ever sold anything to finance gambling?
12. Were you reluctant to use "gambling money" for normal expenditures?
13. Did gambling make you careless of the welfare of yourself or your family?
14. Did you ever gamble longer than you had planned?
15. Have you ever gambled to escape worry or trouble?
16. Have you ever committed, or considered committing, an illegal act to finance gambling?
17. Did gambling cause you to have difficulty in sleeping?
18. Do arguments, disappointments, or frustrations create within you an urge to gamble?
19. Did you ever have an urge to celebrate any good fortune by a few hours of gambling?
20. Have you ever considered self-destruction or suicide as a result of your gambling?

Reprinted with permission from Gambler's Anonymous 2002.

- Poor attendance in class
- Depression and anxiety
- Withdrawal from family, friends, and outside interests
- Watching more televised sports
- Calls to betting lines and 900 numbers for sports results

- Getting excessively emotional over sporting events

DISCOVER Activity 20.2 helps you better grasp the extent of gambling on college campuses.

LEARNING AIDS

SUMMARY

1. **Define and discuss the prevalence of eating disorders and disordered eating in sport.**

   Anorexia nervosa and bulimia are the two most common eating disorders. Both of these eating disorders are defined in *Diagnostic and Statistical Manual of Mental Disorders.* Although a variety of symptoms are associated with each of these disorders, anorexia nervosa is characterized by an intense fear of gaining weight and a distorted body image, whereas bulimia is characterized by recurrent episodes of binge eating and regular, self-induced vomiting. Athletes (particularly in sports in which weight is a concern, such as wrestling, gymnastics, and track) appear to have higher rates of eating-related problems than does the general population. But disordered eating does not necessarily mean an eating disorder.

2. **Identify predisposing factors for developing eating disorders.**

   Many factors predispose individuals to developing an eating disorder. Some are more biological and genetic and others are more environmental (e.g., weight restrictions and standards) or sociological (coach and peer pressure).

3. **Describe how to recognize disordered eating.**

   The signs and symptoms of bulimia and anorexia nervosa are both physical (e.g., weight too low, bloating, swollen salivary glands) and psychological or behavioral (e.g., excessive dieting, binge eating, preoccupation with food). We must help individuals get appropriate specialized assistance. A referral system should be set up confidentially and professionally to help individuals deal with eating-related problems.

4. **Define and discuss the prevalence of substance abuse in sport.**

   Substance abuse is one of the most severe problems facing many societies. It is typically related to the continued and recurrent use of psychoactive substances in situations that are physically hazardous or in which one's personal or professional life suffers. Although it is difficult to get exact figures regarding the use of certain drugs, we do know that many athletes and exercisers take both performance-enhancing drugs and recreational drugs; both types of drugs have dangerous side effects. Evidence from baseball and other professional sports underscores that use of performance-enhancing drugs is widespread.

5. **Explain why some athletes and exercisers take drugs.**

   Athletes and exercisers usually take drugs for physical (e.g., to enhance performance), psychological (e.g., to relieve stress), or social (e.g., to satisfy peer pressure) reasons.

6. **Discuss how to detect and prevent substance abuse.**

   Substance use and abuse are detected by both formal procedures (e.g., drug testing) and informal procedures (e.g., observation and listening). Because drug testing is expensive and often difficult to implement, we must be able to recognize the signs and symptoms of substance use and abuse. Sport and exercise professionals can help prevent substance abuse by setting a good example; educating participants about the effects of substance use and abuse; and, most important, providing a supportive environment that addresses the reasons individuals take drugs. Programs such as ATLAS and ATHENA have demonstrated some preliminary positive results in combating drug use in high school athletes.

7. **Discuss the concepts of positive and negative addiction to exercise.**

   The term *positive addiction to exercise* was popularized because running and other forms of exercise have been shown to be associated with positive psychological outcomes and increases in life satisfaction. However, for a small percentage of people, this "healthy" habit of exercise can turn into a negative addiction in which the exercise starts to control their lives. This is typically associated with negative outcomes at home and at work.

8. **Discuss the problem of compulsive sports gambling.**
   Gambling in and on sports has a long history, although it appears to have increased in recent years. Estimates in national statistics suggest that 6% to 8% of college students are compulsive gamblers, and extensive bookmaking can be found on many college campuses. Gambling is often not thought of as a serious problem, but, like drugs and alcohol, it can be an addiction. Usually compulsive gamblers are boastful and arrogant, have unbounded optimism, and are extremely competitive.

KEY TERMS

anorexia nervosa	performance-enhancing drugs	exercise addiction
bulimia	recreational drugs	positive addiction to exercise
substance abuse	deterrence	negative addiction to exercise
substance use	ATLAS	sexual harassment and abuse
Viagra	ATHENA	

REVIEW QUESTIONS

1. Define, compare, and contrast anorexia nervosa, bulimia, and disordered eating.

2. Discuss three predisposing factors that might increase the likelihood that an eating disorder could occur.

3. Identify the major categories of performance-enhancing and recreational drugs and their reported side effects.

4. Compare and contrast the characteristics of positive and negative addictions. What are some steps for avoiding a negative addiction to exercise?

5. Discuss the deterrence model of drug use, including its three major components (along with specific examples of these components).

6. Discuss the ATLAS and ATHENA programs in terms of prevention of drug use and other high-risk behaviors.

7. Discuss the reasons behind sexual harassment and abuse of athletes by coaches. Include the International Olympic Committee's recommendations for dealing with this problem.

8. Discuss why Viagra has been mentioned as a possible performance-enhancing drug in athletics.

9. Briefly describe the anecdotal and empirical reports on the negative side effects of steroids.

10. What is your conclusion about the anecdotal evidence (and some empirical findings) regarding why athletes use performance-enhancing drugs?

CRITICAL THINKING QUESTIONS

1. You are hired as a consultant for a collegiate athletic department. Your main job is to devise a program that will reduce drug and alcohol use by athletes on the campus. Discuss in detail what type of program you would implement, showing how it relates to the reasons for substance use.

2. You are coaching a women's gymnastics team at the high school level. You know that eating disorders tend to be high with this population. How would you structure your practices and competitions to minimize the possibility of eating disorders occurring in your athletes? What would you do if you found out that one of your athletes had an eating disorder?

21

Burnout and Overtraining

After reading this chapter, you should be able to

1. define overtraining, staleness, and burnout;
2. discuss different models of burnout;
3. describe the causes of overtraining and burnout;
4. identify the symptoms of overtraining and burnout;
5. explain the research evidence of burnout in sport; and
6. describe the treatment and prevention of burnout.

The pressure to win and train year-round with vigor and intensity has increased dramatically in recent years, in large part because of the tremendous financial rewards, publicity, and status achieved by successful coaches and athletes. There used to be separate seasons and off-seasons for various sports, whereas now one season tends to run into the next, leaving little time for an extended rest. Even in the off-season, athletes lift weights and do other physical fitness activities to keep in shape and get bigger and stronger for the upcoming season. In addition, many sports now have specialized training camps or academies where youngsters attend school and train (usually away from parents) with the hope of later obtaining a college scholarship, professional career, or Olympic medal. The theory is that more training is better, you have to start training early, and you must train year-round if you are to compete at a high level.

But the price of this unrelenting focus on training and winning can be overtraining and subsequent burn-out. And it is not only competitive athletes and coaches who overdo it and burn out. Exercisers, in their quest to feel and look better, sometimes go too far, overtrain, and burn out. Support personnel, too, such as officials and certified athletic trainers, get caught up in the pressures to win, which can lead to increased stress and potential burnout. And with budget problems plaguing many schools, physical educators are asked to do more with less and to work longer hours, which makes them susceptible to burnout. Several quotes describe overtraining and the pressures that can lead to burnout:

" **It's a long, long grind. It's either preseason practice, the season itself, postseason weight training, or recruiting. The demands to win can also be very stressful. When we were successful, there was pressure and high expectations to stay successful. When we were losing, there was pressure to start winning real soon. This schedule and pressure**

> *can wear you down and make you just want to leave everything behind for awhile.* **"**
>
> —College football coach

> **"** *I didn't have an option to choose not to do that event after making the team . . . . The timing was very poor and that contributed to overtraining and my performance was probably 80% at the Games due to fatigue and lack of recovery.* **"**
>
> —Olympic athlete

Overtraining and burnout have become significant problems in the world of sport and physical activity, short-circuiting many promising careers. Therefore, coaches, exercise leaders, health care providers, and other administrative personnel need to better understand the symptoms and causes of burnout and learn strategies that help reduce the possibility that burnout will occur. Let's start by specifying what we mean by overtraining and burnout.

Definitions of Overtraining, Staleness, and Burnout

Some confusion still arises with respect to common definitions for the related terms *overtraining, burnout,* and *staleness.* We provide a set of definitions that represent our viewpoint, although we recognize that not all sport and exercise psychologists would define these terms exactly the same way.

Overtraining

Periodized training is the deliberate strategy of exposing athletes to high-volume and high-intensity training loads that are followed by a lower training load, known as the *rest* or *taper* stage (McCann, 1995). The goal in periodized training is to condition athletes so that their performance peaks at a specific date or in a particular time frame (usually before major competitions or championships). Coaches purposefully overload and taper athletes. Thus, the scientific and artistic challenge for athletes and coaches is to slowly increase the training load so that optimal adaptations accrue and negative side effects, such as injury and staleness, do not (O'Connor, 1997).

Overtraining refers to a short cycle of training (lasting a few days to a few weeks) during which athletes expose themselves to excessive training loads that are near or at maximal capacity. Overload-

ing athletes is a normal part of the physical training process. That is, in accordance with principles of exercise physiology, one intentionally overloads athletes by having them experience higher training volumes (e.g., they swim or run more meters or lift more weight than normal). After rest and recovery, the body adapts to the overload and becomes stronger or more fit, and these changes result in improved performance. Unfortunately, the overload process is far from perfect and is highly individualistic, and attempts to purposefully overload athletes can sometimes result in negative consequences. If the training volume is too great or if the athlete is affected by a lack of rest or other physical or psychological stressors, maladaptations occur and overtraining results in deteriorated performance. This negative overtraining syndrome is defined as excessive, usually physical overload on an athlete without adequate rest, resulting in decreased performance and the inability to train at normal levels (U.S. Olympic Committee, 1998). Hence, the process of overloading one's body can result in positive adaptation and improved performance or maladaptation and decreased performance.

> **KEY POINT** One athlete's overtraining might be another athlete's optimal training regimen.

Using the work of Kentta (2001) and Kentta and Hassmen (1998), we can view overtraining as a process that unfolds over time (figure 21.1). As you can see, this process is begun by overloading the athlete (demanding training designed to improve performance) through overtraining. This results in short-term (from 72 hours to 2 weeks) impaired performance, labeled an overreached state. When overtraining optimally taxes the performer and after proper rest, the body adapts and supercomposition or positive overtraining and improved performance result (box A). However, if the overtraining demand and overreached state are excessive and the body does not properly adapt, maladaptations or negative overtraining and poor performance result (box C). Negative overtraining leads first to staleness and, if continued over time without adequate rest and recovery, to a more severe state of burnout. It is also possible that the overtraining will not improve or decrease performance—only maintain it (box B).

The difference between overtraining and periodized training depends largely on individual differences and capabilities. What is overtraining (detrimental) for one athlete can be positive or optimal training for another. For example, Olympic great Mark Spitz, who broke

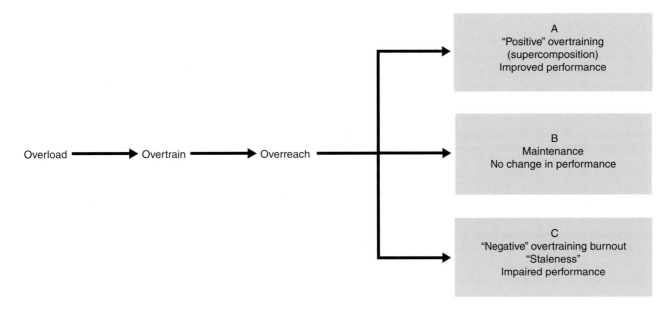

FIGURE 21.1 The overtraining process.
Based on Kentta et al. 2001.

seven world records in swimming and won seven gold medals, never trained more than 10,000 yards a day. On the other hand, Vladimir Salnikov, a Soviet Olympic swimming champion, trained at 2-week schedules called "attack mesocycles," which involved swimming up to 20,000 meters (21,880 yards) a day. His distances would be excessive for many elite swimmers, but they apparently facilitated Salnikov's performance (Raglin, 1993). Evidence also shows that overtraining is not just about the physical training volumes and intensities athletes experience: Psychological and social stresses and the amount and type of rest athletes experience greatly influence the overtraining and periodization process (Gustafsson, Kentta, & Hassmen, 2011).

The exercises prescribed for athletes vary substantially, and the most talented performers are not necessarily the ones with the greatest capacity to endure periods of overtraining. Furthermore, it has been demonstrated that athletes of similar capacity respond differently to standard training regimens: Some resist the negative effects of intensive training, whereas others are quite vulnerable. Thus, a particular training schedule may improve the performance of one athlete, be insufficient for another, and be downright damaging for a third.

Staleness

The American Medical Association (1966) has defined **staleness** as "a physiological state of overtraining which manifests as deteriorated athletic readiness" (p. 126). Thus, staleness is seen as the end result or outcome of overtraining when the athlete has difficulty maintaining standard training regimens and can no longer achieve previous performance results. The truly stale athlete has a significant reduction (5% or greater) in performance for an extended period of time (2 weeks or longer) that occurs during or after a period of overtraining and fails to improve in response to short-term reductions in training (O'Connor, 1997). The principal behavioral sign of staleness is impaired performance, whereas the principal psychological symptoms are mood disturbance and increases in perceptual effort during exercise. It has been reported that about 80% of stale athletes are clinically depressed.

KEY POINT A stale athlete has difficulty maintaining standard training regimens and can no longer achieve previous performance results.

Burnout

Burnout has received more attention than overtraining or staleness in many anecdotal reports as well as research investigations focusing on burnout (e.g., Black & Smith, 2007; Dale & Weinberg, 1990; Gould, Tuffey, Udry, & Loehr, 1996a,b; Gustafsson, Kentta, Hassmen, & Lindquist, 2007; Isoard-Gautheur, Guillet-Descas, & Duda, 2012; Raedeke & Smith, 2004; Vealey, Udry, Zimmerman, & Soliday, 1992).

Still, no one universally accepted definition of burnout exists. After reviewing the literature, Gould and Whitley (2009) defined burnout as

" a physical, emotional, and social withdrawal from a formerly enjoyable sport activity. This withdrawal is characterized by emotional and physical exhaustion, reduced sense of accomplishments, and sport devaluation. Moreover, burnout occurs as a result of chronic stress (a perceived or actual imbalance between what is expected of an athlete physically, psychologically, and socially and his or her response capabilities) and motivational orientations and changes in the athlete. (p. 3) "

The following are characteristics of burnout:

• *Exhaustion, both physical and emotional.* The exhaustion takes the form of lost energy, interest, and trust.

• *Feelings of low personal accomplishment, low self-esteem, failure, and depression.* This is often visible in low job productivity or a decreased performance level.

• *Depersonalization and devaluation.* Depersonalization is seen as the individual being impersonal and unfeeling. This negative response to others is in large part attributable to mental and physical exhaustion. Whereas depersonalization characterizes burnout in helping professionals such as counselors, coaches, and teachers, Raedeke and Smith (2001) found that depersonalization in athletes takes the form of devaluation of the activity—the athletes stop caring about their sport and what is important to them in it.

Unlike what happens in other phases of the training stress syndrome, once a person is burned out, withdrawal from the stress environment is often inevitable. In sport, burnout differs from simply dropping out because it involves such characteristics as psychological and emotional exhaustion, negative responses to others, low self-esteem, and depression.

Athletes drop out of sport participation for many reasons, and burnout is just one of them. In fact, it appears that few athletes and coaches completely drop out of sport solely because of burnout, although they often exhibit many of the characteristics of burnout. For example, despite feeling burned out, athletes often remain in their sport for such reasons as financial

Burnout can manifest in many ways, including exhaustion, depression, staleness, and withdrawal.

rewards (e.g., scholarships) and parental or coach pressures and expectations. Individuals typically discontinue sport involvement only when the costs outweigh benefits relative to alternative activities. Athletes and coaches who discontinue sport involvement as a consequence of the high cost of excessive long-term stress are typically viewed as being burned out.

Frequency of Overtraining, Staleness, and Burnout

Although no large-scale, systematic studies have been conducted on the epidemiology of overtraining, staleness, and burnout, what we know from research suggests that these are not trivial problems. For example, a survey revealed that 66% of college varsity athletes from the Atlantic Coast Conference believed they had been overtrained (the average was two experiences during their collegiate careers); almost 50% of all respondents indicated that it was a bad experience. In addition, 72% of the athletes reported some staleness during their sport seasons, and 47% reported feeling burned out at some point during their collegiate career (Silva, 1990). Gould, Greenleaf, Chung, and Guinan (2002) reported that as many as 18% of U.S. Olympians overtrained in preparation for their Olympic performance. In an interview study (Cohn, 1990) of 10 high school golfers, all said they had burned out of golf at some time during their careers, resulting in 5 to 14 days of discontinued participation. Gustafsson, Kentta, Hassmen, and Lindquist (2007) studied 980 elite adolescent athletes and discovered that 1% to 9% of females and 2% to 6% of males had symptoms of high-level burnout. When the most stringent criteria for severe burnout were used, 1% to 2% of these young athletes fell into this category.

Other research showed that 60% of female and 64% of male elite distance runners had at least one episode of staleness in their running careers, whereas staleness was reported in 30% of subelite highly trained distance runners (Morgan, O'Connor, Ellickson, & Bradley, 1988; Morgan, O'Connor, Sparling, & Pate, 1987). Additional research (Raglin, Sawamura, Alexiou, Hassmen, & Kentta, 2000) has shown that staleness is a problem for 34% of adolescent swimmers from different cultures. Moreover, Kentta, Hassmen, and Raglin (2001) found that 37% of 272 adolescent Swedish athletes training at sport high schools experienced staleness; individual-sport athletes (48%) had higher levels than team-sport athletes (30%).

Although more common in elite athletes, staleness is not confined to these athletes, as has been commonly assumed. Staleness is a problem for athletes in all sports and for athletes from various cultures. Raglin and Morgan (1989) showed that of swimmers who developed staleness during their freshman year, 91% became stale in one or more subsequent seasons. Yet only 30% of the swimmers who did not become stale as freshmen developed the disorder in a subsequent season. Apparently, once an athlete has staleness, subsequent bouts become more probable.

Studies on the frequency of burnout in teachers, coaches, certified athletic trainers, and other fitness professionals are sparse. In one of the few studies conducted in the area, Raedeke (2004) found that 49% of swimming coaches surveyed had moderate or high levels of emotional exhaustion. This certainly suggests that exercise and sport science professionals, like coaches, are at risk for burnout.

Models of Burnout

Six sport-specific models of burnout have been developed to help explain the burnout phenomenon. Each model contains some interesting and useful information concerning the various factors affecting burnout as well as individuals' responses to burnout. All have received some scientific support and should be considered when attempting to understand the complex process of burnout.

Cognitive–Affective Stress Model

Smith (1986) developed a four-stage, stress-based model of burnout in sport (figure 21.2). In Smith's model, burnout is a process involving physiological, psychological, and behavioral components that progress in predictable stages. In turn, each of these components is influenced by level of motivation and personality.

In the first stage, termed **situational demands**, high demands are placed on the athlete, such as high volumes of physical practice or excessive pressure to win. Typically, when the demands of a situation outweigh potential resources, stress occurs, which over time can lead to burnout. In the second stage, which Smith labeled **cognitive appraisal**, individuals interpret and appraise the situation. Some individuals will view the situation as more threatening than others will. For example, a football coach whose team loses three games in a row may get uptight and fear that he

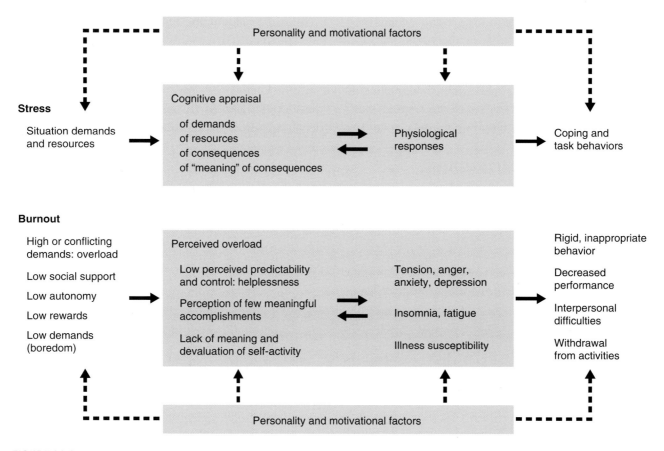

FIGURE 21.2 Smith's cognitive–affective model of athletic burnout.

Adapted, by permission, from R. Smith, 1986, "Toward a cognitive-affective model of athletic burnout," *Journal of Sport Psychology* 8(1): 40.

will lose his job, whereas another coach in the same situation may see the losing streak as a challenge and an opportunity to show that the team can come back from adversity. The third stage focuses on **physiological responses**. If you appraise a situation as harmful or threatening, then over time, as your perception becomes chronic, stress can produce physiological changes such as increases in tension, irritability, and fatigue. Typically, those who have athletic burnout feel emotionally depleted and, having little positive emotion, develop a susceptibility to illness and lethargy. In the fourth stage, **behavioral responses**, the physiological response leads to certain types of coping and task behaviors, such as decreased performance, interpersonal difficulties, and eventual withdrawal from the activity. Finally, Smith argued that reaction to stress in sport is moderated by personality and motivation and that an individual's unique personality and motivational orientations often determine whether the person will burn out or cope. Research has generally supported Smith's cognitive–affective stress model. In a study of junior tennis burnout, Gould,

Tuffey, Udry, and Loehr (1996b, 1997) concluded that Smith's model provided a good explanation for the cases of burnout examined. Gustafsson, Kentta, Hassmen, Lindquist, and Durand-Bush (2007) and Cresswell and Eklund (2007) found further support for the cognitive–affective stress model.

KEY POINT The concept of cognitive appraisal reflects the idea that nothing is either good or bad, but thinking makes it so. People differ in how they respond to prolonged stress in sport and exercise settings.

Negative-Training Stress Response Model

Silva's (1990) model for explaining burnout focuses more on responses to physical training, although it recognizes the importance of psychological factors. Specifically, Silva suggested that physical training stresses the athlete physically and psychologically and that it can have both positive and negative effects.

Positive adaptation is a desirable outcome of training, as when an athlete overloads the body by doing lots of sprint work in order to become faster. Too much training, however, can result in negative adaptation. This negative adaptation is hypothesized to lead to negative training responses, such as overtraining and staleness, which eventually will result in burnout. The research has revealed that physical training is certainly involved in the burnout process (Kentta & Hassmen, 1998; Kentta et al., 2001), supporting the general predictions of the negative-training stress response model. However, the intensity of training, along with a variety of psychological and social stressors and recovery factors, must be considered. In addition, researchers have identified some cases of athlete burnout that were not driven by physical overtraining (Gould et al., 1997).

Unidimensional Identity Development and External Control Model

The models by Smith (1986) and Silva (1990) focus primarily on stress, whereas Coakley's (1992) model is more sociological. Although Coakley agreed that stress is involved in burnout, he argued that it is simply a symptom. He believes that the real cause of burnout, especially in young athletes, is related to the social organization of high-performance sport and its effects on identity and control issues. In particular, Coakley contended that burnout occurs because the structure of highly competitive sport does not allow youngsters to develop a normal identity: They don't get to spend enough time with their peers outside of the sporting environment. Thus, young athletes focus on and identify almost exclusively with success in sport, and when they have an injury or lack of success, the associated stress can ultimately lead to burnout. Coakley also contended that the social worlds of competitive young athletes are organized in such a way that their control and decision making are inhibited. In essence, coaches and parents make most of the decisions and exert wide-ranging control in most organized competitive youth sport settings, leaving young athletes powerless to control events and make decisions about the nature of their experiences and the direction of their own development. Once again, this leads to stress and potentially burnout. Coakley (1992) based his original model on informal interviews with young athletes from a number of sports. Black and Smith (2007) directly tested Coakley's predictions in

182 swimmers and provided some support for Coakley's contentions. Gould and colleagues (1997) also provided some support for the model's predictions in qualitative interviews with junior tennis players.

Commitment and Entrapment Theory

Although most researchers have conceptualized burnout to be closely related to stress, another viewpoint explains burnout in the context of sport commitment. Specifically, drawing on the sport commitment work of Schmidt and Stein (1991), Raedeke (1997) argued that athletes commit to sport for three reasons: because they want to participate, because they believe they have to participate, or both. He argued that athletes who are prone to burnout feel "entrapped" by sport when they do not really want to participate in it but believe they must maintain their involvement. They maintain their involvement even though they would rather not, for a number of reasons—because their self-identity is so tied to being an athlete that they would feel personally lost without sport, because they lack attractive alternatives to sport, or because they believe they have invested too much time and energy in sport to stop participating. According to this view, then, burnout occurs when athletes become entrapped in sport and lose motivation but continue to participate.

Using this approach, Raedeke (1998) studied more than 200 competitive swimmers. He showed that some swimmers who were no longer attracted to swimming—feeling little enjoyment or benefit but high costs—still believed they had to participate because of social pressure from others and their perceived lack of control over the situation. Compared with swimmers who did not feel entrapped, these swimmers were most likely to burn out and experience a decreased commitment to swimming. These findings support the **entrapment theory** and suggest that coaches and parents should ensure that athletes enjoy their participation and that it remains fun, encourage and support the athletes but not pressure them, and make sure the athletes are involved in or have input into decision making regarding practice and competition.

Self-Determination Theory

Sport psychologists have also applied self-determination theory as an explanation of sport burnout (e.g., Cresswell & Eklund, 2006; Lemyre, Treasure, & Roberts, 2006; Perreault, Gaudreau, Lapointe, & Lacrois, 2007). In fact, this has been the most prevalent approach to studying burnout in recent years. Recall from chapter 6 that according to self-determination theory, people have three basic psychological needs: autonomy, competence, and relatedness. When these needs are met, a person's motivation and psychological well-being are maximized (Deci & Ryan, 1985) and the person is less likely to burn out. Individuals who do not have these basic needs met will be more prone to burnout.

Perreault and colleagues (2007) found support for the self-determination theory explanation of sport burnout using 259 student-athletes from a Canadian sports school. As predicted, they found that satisfaction of the basic needs (autonomy, competence, and relatedness) was associated with lower levels of athlete burnout. Studies conducted with elite rugby players (Cresswell & Eklund, 2005a,b; Lemyre, Hall, & Roberts, 2008; Lemyre, Roberts, & Stray-Gundersen, 2007) also showed that self-determined forms of motivation were negatively related to athlete burnout. Quested and Duda (2011) conducted a longitudinal study that examined antecedents of burnout in elite dancers and found that burnout was predicted by satisfaction of basic needs, supporting the predictions of self-determination theory. A statistical review by Li, Wang, Pyun, and Kee (2013) of the literature showed that key components of self-determination theory (e.g., basic psychological needs, intrinsic motivation, extrinsic autonomous regulation, and amotivation) were all significant predictors of overall burnout and its three dimensions: reduced sense of accomplishments, physical and emotional exhaustion, and sport devaluation. Although these findings are very encouraging, the athletes tested were typically characterized by low levels of burnout. Additional research is needed to further verify the findings in athletes with high levels of burnout.

Integrated Model of Athlete Burnout

After reviewing the existing literature and the previously discussed theories on burnout in athletes, Gustafsson, Kentta, and Hassmen (2011) developed an integrated model of athlete burnout. As the name suggests, this model integrates the previous models for the purpose of creating a more complete conceptual understanding of the burnout research and theory. Depicted in figure 21.3, this model shows that the burnout process can best be understood by examining its antecedents, such as excessive training and school and work demands (the box on the left); its early signs,

such as mood disturbances and diminished motivation, which can turn into full-fledged burnout manifested in physical and emotional exhaustion, feelings of reduced accomplishment, or sport devaluation (the large box in the middle); and ultimately the maladaptive consequences of burnout, such as partial or complete withdrawal from sport or impaired immune function (the box on the right). The model also shows that entrapment has a major influence and provides an excellent explanation for burnout in many athletes (the box on the top). Finally, the model depicts that certain personality, coping, and social environment factors (e.g., perfectionistic personality characteristics, trait anxiety, low autonomy, ego-oriented motivational climates) have been shown to influence the burnout process in athletes (the box on the bottom).

Factors Leading to Athlete Overtraining and Burnout

We now discuss specific factors that lead to or cause overtraining and burnout. Before turning to the research evidence, we consider some anecdotal reports.

Anecdotal Reports

Anecdotal evidence regarding why some athletes overtrain and even burn out at a relatively young age is plentiful. Some players start as early as 5 years of age, and others are pressured to turn pro when they are barely teenagers. Tennis phenomenon Jennifer Capriati turned pro at age 13 and, as a result of a clothing contract, was a millionaire before she even hit a ball as a professional. Her early fame and fortune might have been partly to blame for her dropping out of tennis and experimenting with drugs. She later made a successful comeback, which she attributed to reduced stress and more parental support versus parental and sponsor pressure. The names Vince Cartier, Curtis Beck, and Eric Hulst (all elite junior runners) are probably less familiar. These athletes were national champions as teenagers, only to become burned out and discontinue their participation in competitive sport a few years after setting national records or winning junior division titles. In these highly competitive environments, young athletes practice 25 to 30 hours a week and have little time off for vacation. In fact, one study found that young athletes who specialized in one sport exhibited higher levels of emotional exhaustion

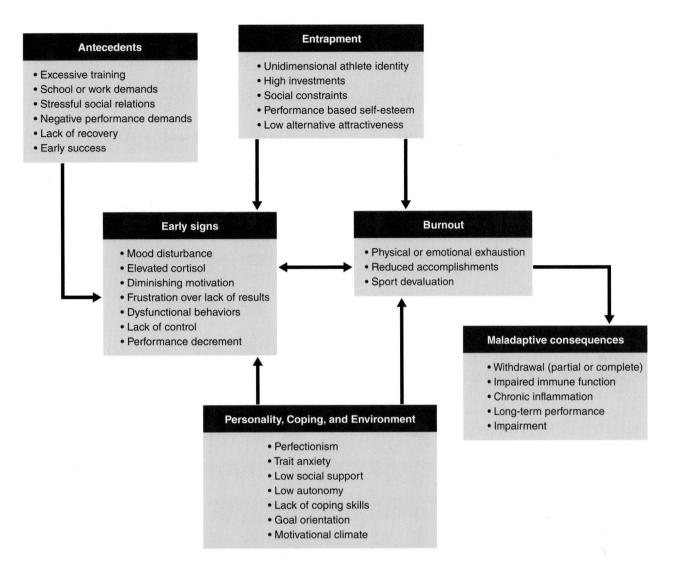

Antecedents
- Excessive training
- School or work demands
- Stressful social relations
- Negative performance demands
- Lack of recovery
- Early success

Entrapment
- Unidimensional athlete identity
- High investments
- Social constraints
- Performance based self-esteem
- Low alternative attractiveness

Early signs
- Mood disturbance
- Elevated cortisol
- Diminishing motivation
- Frustration over lack of results
- Dysfunctional behaviors
- Lack of control
- Performance decrement

Burnout
- Physical or emotional exhaustion
- Reduced accomplishments
- Sport devaluation

Maladaptive consequences
- Withdrawal (partial or complete)
- Impaired immune function
- Chronic inflammation
- Long-term performance
- Impairment

Personality, Coping, and Environment
- Perfectionism
- Trait anxiety
- Low social support
- Low autonomy
- Lack of coping skills
- Goal orientation
- Motivational climate

FIGURE 21.3 An integrated model of athletic burnout.

Reprinted from "Athlete burnout: An integrated model and future research directions," H. Gustafsson, G. Kentta, and P. Hassmen, *International Review of Sport & Exercise Psychology*, 4(1): 10, 2011, reprinted by permission of publisher (Taylor & Francis Ltd, http://www.tandf.co.uk/journals).

than those who sampled and played multiple sports (Stracchan, Côté, & Deakin, 2009).

KEY POINT Athletes are starting to train at younger ages, which can negatively affect their home and family life.

Besides so early a start and the pressures and expectations placed on young athletes, training in most sports now involves year-round workouts, and off-seasons become ever shorter. In sports such as tennis, gymnastics, and swimming, there really is no off-season. For ice skating, tennis, golf, and gymnastics, specialized training camps and academies have been developed where young athletes live, attend

school, and train. This extended time away from home can put great strains on youngsters, who typically cannot maintain a normal home and family life. Given these excessive psychological and physical demands, it is no wonder that some athletes burn out.

KEY POINT In many sports athletes train virtually year-round, and the intensity of training loads makes it almost impossible to compete successfully in more than one sport.

Overtraining Research Evidence

Later in this chapter we discuss the research on overtraining and changes in athlete mood states. However, at this point we note that a number of investigators have found a link between the volume of an athlete's physical training and overtraining responses. That is, overtraining symptoms increase as the volume of physical training increases, and overtraining symptoms decrease when physical training volume decreases.

Although physical training volume is certainly related to overtraining, other investigators have linked nonsport stress to the onset of overtraining, For example, Meehan, Bull, Wood, and James (2004) studied the overtraining syndrome in five competitive endurance athletes. The athletes were diagnosed as overtrained when a consistent decrease in performance was observed in the absence of any medically diagnosed disease. Each specific case was explored using a medical examination, questionnaires assessing life stress and coping responses, and in-depth individual interviews. Results revealed that although these overtrained athletes all reported high motivation toward training and competition and demanding training and competition schedules, all had considerable nonsport stress resulting from such things as occupational and educational demands, finances, and living arrangements. The authors concluded that "nonsport stress appears to make an important contribution to the experience of those athletes diagnosed with the overtraining syndrome" (p. 154). Tobar (2012) also found that overtraining was related to mood disturbances in both male and female swimmers, but these effects were dependent on the athletes' levels of trait anxiety. Thus, the psychological effects of overtraining vary depending on the individual's psychological make-up.

The research on sport science overtraining, then, demonstrates that sources of physical and psychological stress in an out-of-sport venue contribute to overtraining. Monitoring these stress sources and how they influence specific athletes has important implications for preventing overtraining in athletes.

Burnout Research Evidence

Although a wide variety of factors have been hypothesized to lead to burnout, until recently few empirical data substantiated these contentions. However, a number of studies (Cresswell & Eklund, 2004; Gustafsson, Kentta, Hassmen, Lindquist, & Durand-Bush, 2007; Harlick & McKenzie, 2000; Kjormo & Halvari, 2002; Lai & Wiggins, 2003; Raedeke & Smith, 2004) have examined factors leading to burnout in athletes, and several reviews of the research have been published (Cresswell & Eklund, 2006; Goodger, Gorley,

Lavallee, & Harwood, 2007; Gould & Whitley, 2009; Raedeke, Smith, Kenttta, Arce, & de Francisco, 2014). Raedeke and Smith (2004) found significant relationships between burnout, the amount of stress athletes feel, and their social support and coping. Lai and Wiggins (2003) found that burnout increases across the season in soccer players, whereas Kjormo and Halvari (2002) found that a lack of free time to spend with significant others and role conflict influenced the burnout levels of Norwegian Olympians. Harlick and McKenzie (2000) showed that parental pressure was related to burnout in New Zealand tennis players, whereas Cresswell and Eklund (2005a,b) linked athlete autonomy, competence, social support, and money hassles to burnout in New Zealand rugby players. Gustafsson, Kentta, Hassmen, Lindquist, and Durand-Bush (2007) found that burnout was related to early sport success and resulted in high expectations for athletes to live up to as well as a chronic lack of mental and physical recovery. Other factors found to be related to burnout include harmonious and obsessive passion (Curran, Appleton, Hill, & Hall, 2011), a lack of hope (Gustafsson, Skoog, Podlog, Lundqvist, & Wagnsson, 2013), and peer-related motivational climate (Smith, Gustafsson, & Hassmen, 2010). Although this research shows that a wide variety of factors are associated with burnout in athletes, these studies should be viewed with some caution. Most of the studies suffer from the fact that the athletes studied had low to moderate (vs. high) levels of burnout. We cannot be sure whether athletes exhibiting high levels of burnout would have had the same types of antecedent factors.

Gould and colleagues (1996a,b, 1997) conducted one of the few studies that examined potential causes of high levels of burnout in athletes. This series of studies conducted on competitive youth tennis players revealed that an interaction of personal and situational factors, including these categories, causes burnout:

- *Physical concerns.* These include injury, overtraining, feeling tired all the time, lack of physical development, erratic performance, losing, and getting beat by people you used to beat.

- *Logistical concerns.* These include the travel grind as well as the demands on time that tennis players believed could dominate their lives, leaving them little or no time with friends or at school.

- *Social or interpersonal concerns.* These include dissatisfaction with social life, negative parental influences (e.g., being "suffocated" by one's father or mother), and competing with a sibling for a parent's attention. Other dissatisfactions were identified in the tennis world, such as a negative team atmosphere, cheating by competitors, and unhelpful coaches.

• *Psychological concerns.* By far the most frequently noted factor, accounting for more than 50% of the reasons given for burnout, psychological concerns include unfulfilled or inappropriate expectations such as an overemphasis on rankings, a realization that a professional career was unlikely, and feeling a lack of improvement or talent. Lack of enjoyment, another theme, was characterized by coach and parental pressure to practice and win, pressure to win or maintain scholarships, self-pressure to win and play well, and being uncertain of parental support. Motivational concerns included wanting to try other sport and nonsport activities as well as simply being "sick" of tennis and lacking motivation.

In summary, Gould and colleagues (1996b) suggested that two "strains" of burnout exist. The dominant strain is social–psychological and is further divided into substrains of athlete perfectionism and situational pressure. Specifically, some young athletes are such perfectionists that this eventually predisposes them to or puts them at risk for burnout (even in situations that are not considered unusually demanding by most tennis professionals). In other cases athletes are placed in situations in which others, particularly parents, generate tremendous psychological pressure. Stress results from having expectations to win in an effort to please others and feel worthy. A strain of burnout that surfaces much less frequently is physically driven. In these cases athletes cannot meet the demands for physical training placed on them, which results in considerable physical and psychological stress and then burnout.

Individual Differences

Although there are common factors related to burnout, burnout is a unique personal experience. People attempting to help athletes cope with feelings of burnout must recognize and appreciate these variations. Figure 21.4 provides what Gould and colleagues (1997) called a "motivational map" depicting the varying reasons three athletes gave for discontinuing or curtailing their involvement in tennis. This figure shows that the players did not burn out for only one reason; rather, there were multiple causes. For example, the three players shared such reasons as overtraining, not having fun, having social concerns, and pressure from others. Other reasons, such as injury, erratic play, and disliking travel, were specific to a particular athlete.

Symptoms of Overtraining and Burnout

Overtraining and burnout are physical and psychological in nature. Some common symptoms of overtraining include physical fatigue, mental exhaustion, grouchiness, depression, apathy, and sleep disturbances. Symptoms of burnout include a loss of interest, lack of desire to play, physical and mental exhaustion, lack of caring, depression, and increased anxiety. "Signs and Symptoms of Overtraining and Burnout" presents research summarizing the characteristics of overtraining and burnout (Gould et al., 1996b; Hackney, Perlman, & Nowacki, 1990).

DISCOVER Activity 21.1 helps you learn more about athletic overtraining and burnout.

Overtraining and Mood States

It is assumed that overtraining affects athletic performance and mental health; a few researchers have asked how. For example, Morgan, Brown, Raglin, O'Connor, and Ellickson (1987) investigated the relationship between overtraining and psychological mood states. To measure mood, they administered the Profile of Mood States (POMS; McNair et al., 1971) to 400 competitive swimmers during different parts of the training and competitive season. The POMS measures six transitory emotional states: tension, depression, anger, vigor, fatigue, and confusion. After analyzing the data from studies done over a 10-year period, the researchers concluded that mood state disturbances increase as the training stimulus increases in a dose-responsive manner. The heavier the training (in this case, the swimming distance each week), the greater the mood disturbance. This mood disturbance included increased depression, anger, and fatigue and decreased vigor. Conversely, reductions in training load are associated with improvements in mood (Raglin, Eksten, & Garl, 1995; Raglin, Stager, Koceja, & Harms, 1996).

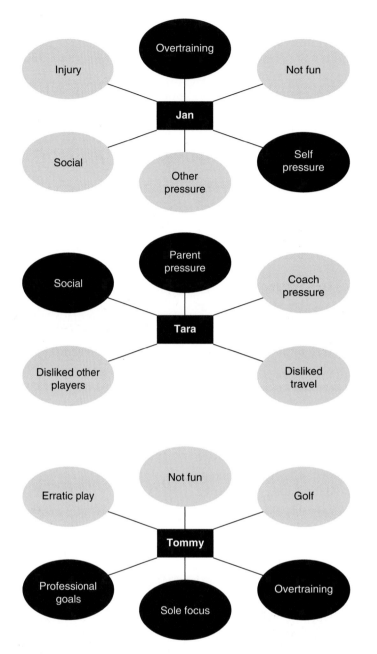

FIGURE 21.4 Individual differences in athlete burnout.

KEY POINT Athletes have increased mood disturbance under especially heavy training workloads, especially over time. The heavier the workload, the greater the mood disturbance.

The psychological mood profile of successful athletes also differed from that of unsuccessful athletes. Specifically, top-level athletic performers had what Morgan called an iceberg profile (see chapter 2). The iceberg profile shows that, compared with the population average, more successful athletes tend to score higher on vigor and lower on anxiety, depression, fatigue, and confusion (figure 21.5). Interestingly, when athletes are overtrained and become stale because of the increased training demands, they display an inverted iceberg profile; that is, the negative states of depression, anger, fatigue, confusion, and tension become elevated and vigor is decreased. A stepwise increase in the swimmers' mood disturbances coincided directly with increases in swimming training. Subsequent decreases in the training regimen (i.e., tapering off) were associated with improvements in mood state.

Signs and Symptoms of Overtraining and Burnout

Overtraining	Burnout
Poor performance	Low motivation or energy
Apathy	Concentration problems
Lethargy	Loss of desire to play
Sleep disturbance	Lack of caring
Weight loss	Sleep disturbance
Elevated resting heart rate	Physical and mental exhaustion
Muscle pain or soreness	Lowered self-esteem
Mood changes	Negative affect
Elevated resting blood pressure	Mood changes
Gastrointestinal disturbances	Substance abuse
Retarded recovery from exertion	Changes in values and beliefs
Appetite loss	Emotional isolation
Overuse injuries	Increased anxiety
Immune system deficiency	Highs and lows
Concentration loss	

From "Physiological profiles of overtrained and stale athletes," A. Hackney, S. Perlman, and J. Nowacki, *Journal of Applied Sport Psychology,* 21(1): 21-33, 1990, adapted by permission of the publisher (Taylor & Francis Group, Ltd http://www.tandf.co.uk/journals).

KEY POINT Successful athletes exhibit high levels of vigor and low levels of negative mood states—an optimal combination. Overtrained athletes show an inverted iceberg profile, with pronounced negative states.

Overtraining and Performance

One well-controlled study addressed the effects of increased training loads on mood states and performance of Olympic judoists (Murphy, Fleck, Dudley, & Callister, 1990). The conditioning-training volume

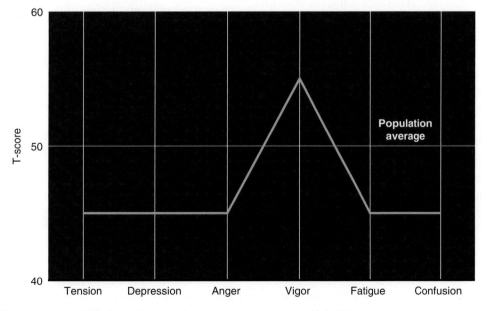

FIGURE 21.5 The iceberg profile of psychological mood states in successful athletes.

was increased for 4 weeks and then the sport-specific training volume was increased for 2 weeks. The increased volume of conditioning training did not increase negative mood state, whereas the increased volume of sport-specific training increased levels of anger and anxiety. (No signs of clinical distress, such as depression or irrational thinking, were evident.) However, decreases in the physical performance measures of strength and anaerobic endurance occurred during both the conditioning and sport-specific training sessions. This study shows that overtrained and stale athletes are at risk of developing mood disturbances, which can result in decreased performance levels and dropout. In another study, Kellman and Gunther (2000) examined changes in stress and recovery in elite German rowers preparing for the Olympic Games. Results revealed that physical components of stress (e.g., lack of energy, soreness, and injury) as well as recovery factors (e.g., being in shape) were correlated with the length of daily training sessions. Most interesting was the finding that interpersonal processes in the team (e.g., conflicts) were reflected in training stress and recovery. These studies, then, show that sport and exercise professionals should carefully monitor how much training athletes require. The old strategy "more is better" may backfire in the long run.

Ways to Measure Burnout

Probably the best way to study burnout would be to find people who are leaving sport because they feel burned out and compare them with athletes who are currently participating in sport and exercise but are not feeling burned out (as was done by Gould et al., 1996b). However, it is difficult to locate these people, and many burned-out players remain in sport for reasons such as money, prestige, or pressure from a coach or parent. Therefore, researchers have developed a paper-and-pencil method for measuring burnout. The most widely used and accepted instrument in general psychology is the Maslach Burnout Inventory (Maslach & Jackson, 1981), which measures both the perceived frequency and intensity of the feelings of burnout. The inventory measures three components of burnout:

- *Emotional exhaustion.* This includes feelings of emotional overextension and exhaustion.
- *Depersonalization.* This appears as an unfeeling and impersonal response to other people

in one's environment. Feelings toward people are detached, and there is a sense of just going through the motions.

- *Low sense of personal accomplishment.* This refers to a decreased feeling of competence and achievement in one's work with people. Low feelings of achievement often result in perceived lack of ability to control situations.

KEY POINT The Maslach Burnout Inventory has been used with professionals in a variety of potentially stressful occupations, including nurses, lawyers, social workers, physicians, psychologists, police officers, counselors, and probation officers. It has been especially useful in studying teachers, whose work environment typically includes long hours, excessive expenditure of mental and emotional energy, and high expectations from principals and parents.

Coaches and athletes face similar stressors in competitive sport: long hours of practice, great expenditure of physical and mental energy, and performance pressures on game days. However, only recently has empirical research focused on burnout in competitive sport. Some of this research has adapted Maslach's Burnout Inventory to sport (Weinberg & Richardson, 1990). In an especially encouraging development, Raedeke and Smith (2001) constructed the Athlete Burnout Questionnaire, a 15-item instrument that provides three burnout subscale measures: emotional and physical exhaustion, reduced sense of accomplishment, and sport devaluation. The scale has been shown to have good reliability and validity and allows researchers to study athlete burnout with a strong assessment tool. It is the most widely used burnout instrument in sport settings today.

Burnout in Sport Professionals

We now turn to some of the major findings regarding burnout in competitive sport. Studies have examined burnout not only in athletes but also in certified athletic trainers, officials, and coaches.

Burnout in Certified Athletic Trainers

Few people are aware of the long hours that athletic trainers put in before and after games and during practice. Certified athletic trainers at the high school or college level are often responsible for several teams and work in the training room or on the field most of the day. Coaches pressure trainers to prepare athletes for game day, which adds stress. Gieck, Brown, and Shank (1982), who were the first to study how burnout affects athletic trainers, demonstrated that trainers indeed have great job stress. Many trainers reported that being at the beck and call of several teams made it difficult to devote enough quality time to individuals. Trainers with type A personalities (i.e., excessive anxiety about time urgency) were especially prone to burnout.

> **KEY POINT** Trainers with type A personalities (individuals who are prone to experience excessive anxiety about time urgency) are more likely to burn out than are their type B counterparts (who generally live at lower stress levels and have a more laid back approach).

Some trainers believe that they are more likely to feel burned out when their several roles become blurred (i.e., *role ambiguity*) (Capel, 1986). For example, trainers often play the role of counselor and friend, which can conflict with their official role. Also, athletic trainers who feel more in control of their situations (i.e., *internal locus of control*) have less burnout than do colleagues with little sense of control (i.e., *external locus of control*).

> **KEY POINT** Role conflict and role ambiguity are related to burnout in both trainers and sport officials.

Seasoned professional certified athletic trainers are not the only ones who become burned out. A study of more than 200 graduate assistant certified athletic trainers found that this student population is at risk for burnout as a result of the time needed to fulfill their academic and clinical duties (Mazerolle, Monsma, Colin, & James, 2012).

Burnout in Officials

Officials also face great stress, and they receive little compensation for the stress other than the satisfaction of a job well done. This leads to high turnover rates and a shortage of officials. Evidently, the fear of failure is the strongest predictor of burnout in sport officials (Taylor, Daniel, Leith, & Burke, 1990). In a study focusing on sources of stress, officials reported that making bad calls is a major stressor related to perceived burnout and that players, coaches, and spectators are more likely to evaluate officials nega-

tively than positively (Anshel & Weinberg, 1995b). It is hypothesized that this increased stress can lead to higher levels of burnout in officials. In addition, like athletic trainers, officials who have role conflicts also have higher levels of perceived burnout.

Burnout in Coaches

Coaches are prime candidates for burnout. The wide variety of stressors that coaches report include the pressure to win, administrative and parental interference or indifference, disciplinary problems, need to fulfill multiple roles, extensive travel commitments, and intense personal involvement. Research also revealed that burned-out coaches were viewed by their athletes as providing less instruction, training, and social support (Price & Weiss, 2000). Another study revealed that burnout in coaches stems from issues generated from both work and home and that coaches who had difficulties handling the high performance demands of elite sport and who lacked the tools to facilitate recovery were particularly prone to burnout (Lundkvist, Gustafsson, Hjalm, & Hassmen, 2012). Thus, burnout affects the on-the-field actions of coaches and results from both personal and situational factors. Let's look at some of the research examining the specific factors related to burnout in coaches.

Sex Differences

Most studies (Caccese & Mayerberg, 1984; Kelley, 1994; Kelley, Eklund, & Ritter-Taylor, 1999; Kelley & Gill, 1993; Vealey et al., 1992) have shown that females have higher levels of perceived burnout than males do, although some studies (e.g., Dale & Weinberg, 1990) do report higher levels of burnout in males. It has been suggested that female coaches perceive increased levels of stress and burnout because they are expected not only to fulfill coaching responsibilities but also to nurture their athletes. Athletic administrators may need to re-examine the differential demands placed on female coaches and possibly make some changes to ensure that roles and responsibilities are equitable with those placed on male coaches.

Looking at coaches of men's and women's sports (not the sex of the coach per se), Hjalm, Kentta, and Gustafsson (2007) found that 71% of coaches of elite women's soccer teams had moderate to high levels of emotional exhaustion compared with 23% of coaches of men's teams. The authors suggested that this difference may be the result of smaller support staffs and different leadership demands. They further suggested

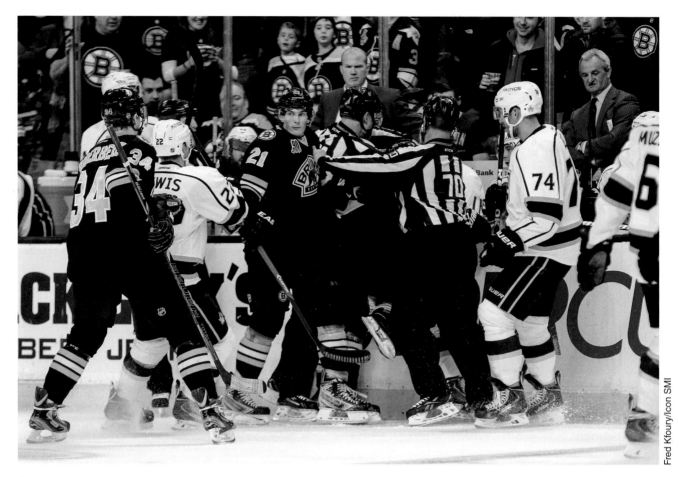

Stressful jobs, long hours, and low compensation can all lead to burnout in officials.

that coaches of women's teams were at higher risk of burnout.

Differences in Age and Experience

Studies have indicated that younger and less experienced coaches tend to have higher levels of perceived burnout than do older coaches (Dale & Weinberg, 1990; Kelley & Gill, 1993; Taylor et al., 1990). Of course, coaches who feel extremely high levels of stress and burnout have probably already quit coaching. Thus, the older coaches who remain likely have good coping skills for handling stressors in their environment. Researchers thus face the problem that coaches who have truly burned out (i.e., are out of the profession) are unavailable for study.

Coaching Style

In an investigation of high school and college coaches, Dale and Weinberg (1990) found that those with a consideration style of leadership (i.e., caring and people oriented) had higher levels of perceived burn-

out than did those with an initiating structure style of leadership (i.e., goal oriented and authoritarian). It may well be that coaches who develop closer personal ties with their athletes suffer greater burnout because they care more. This is not to say that coaches should care less—rather, they should be aware that this style requires a lot of energy, emotion, and time, which can take a toll in the long term.

> **KEY POINT** Young coaches appear to have higher levels of perceived burnout than older coaches, partly because some older coaches have already burned out of the profession.

Entrapped Coaches

In tests of the entrapment theory of burnout, coaches feeling higher levels of entrapment have been found to report significantly higher levels of emotional exhaustion (Raedeke, Granzyk, & Warren, 2000). Entrapped coaches were also found to show decreased commitment and interest in coaching (Raedeke, 2004).

Thus, coaches who do not really want to coach but believe they must maintain their involvement for some reason are at higher risk of burnout.

Social Support

Coaches who report higher levels of satisfaction with social support have lower levels of perceived stress and burnout (Goodger et al., 2007; Kelley, 1994; Kelley & Gill, 1993). Some coaches need reminders to seek out satisfying social support during times of high stress and to become more aware of the importance of social support in their personal and professional lives.

> **KEY POINT** Coaches who are more caring and more oriented toward people appear to be more vulnerable to perceived burnout than goal-oriented, authoritarian coaches.

Burnout in Fitness Instructors, Administrators, and Physical Education Teachers

There is no reason to believe that fitness instructors, administrators, and physical educators are less susceptible to stress and burnout than other sport and exercise professionals are. Research in nonsport settings with teachers and others in the helping professions has shown significant levels of burnout. After all, these professionals are often asked to do more with less, help others, and cope with hectic schedules. Although sport psychologists have not extensively studied fitness instructors, administrators, and physical educators, people in these positions should also take steps to prevent burnout.

Treatment and Prevention of Burnout

The goal in studying overtraining, staleness, and burnout is to learn how to develop programs and strategies that help sport personnel prevent these conditions or at least treat them effectively. We offer the following suggestions.

- *Monitor critical states in athletes.* Factors such as stress levels, stress sources (on and off the field), training volumes, and recovery activities have all been shown to be involved in overtraining and burnout. Although more research is certainly needed

Reducing Burnout in Young Tennis Players

In interviewing burned-out tennis players, Gould and colleagues (1996b) asked what advice the players would give parents, coaches, and other players to help prevent burnout. Some of the players' suggestions include the following:

Advice for Other Players

Play for your own reasons.

Try to make it fun.

Balance tennis and other things.

Take time off and relax.

Advice for Parents

Recognize what is an optimal amount of "pushing."

Give support, show empathy, and reduce the importance of outcome.

Involve players in decision making.

Lessen involvement.

Advice for Coaches

Have two-way communication with players.

Use player input.

Cultivate personal involvement with players.

Understand players' feelings.

to determine exactly how these factors are involved, it is clear that they can be important signs that athletes are becoming overtrained or burned out. Personal trainers, coaches, sports medicine specialists, and athletes themselves must monitor such states so that athletes in the early stages of overtraining and burnout can be identified and helped.

• *Communicate.* When professionals constructively analyze their feelings and communicate them to others, burnout is less likely and is less severe if it does occur. Coaches, athletes, officials, certified athletic trainers, and physical education teachers should be encouraged to express their feelings of frustration, anxiety, and disappointment and to seek out social support from colleagues and friends. In fact, social support networks should be developed so they can be tapped when necessary. Self-awareness and preparation early on might prevent burnout later.

• *Foster an autonomy-supportive coaching style.* Evidence has shown that type of coaching style is related to athlete burnout. Specifically, the use of controlling coaching styles has been shown to more likely to lead to burnout whereas the use of autonomy-supportive coaching styles has been shown to less likely lead to burnout (Isoard-Gautheur, Guillet-Descas, & Lemyre, 2013). Paying attention to the coaching style athletes experience, then, can help us predict who might be more likely to burn out.

• *Set short-term goals for competition and practice.* Setting short-term goals and incentives for reaching them provides feedback that the athlete is on the right course and enhances long-term motivation. Meeting short-term goals is a success, which can enhance self-concept. Toward the end of the season it is particularly important to include fun goals. Most of an athlete's time is taken up by practice rather than competition, so fun goals should be incorporated there. For example, if a team has been working really hard, the coach could say that the goal of practice is to simply have fun. She might let a soccer team play basketball or relax the game so that there are no rules. These activities provide a break and reduce monotony. Similarly, exercisers trying to maintain a regular program of physical activity need short-term goals to keep them motivated and provide them with feedback concerning their progress in meeting their long-term goals.

• *Take relaxation breaks.* It is essential for mental and physical well-being to take some time off from jobs and other stresses. The business world has vacations, holidays, and weekends away from work. But in competitive sport and the fitness industry, many people work under continuous pressure almost year-round. The myth that more is better is still afloat when it comes to practice and workouts. Time off is seen as falling behind your opposition. Yet the weekly grind of practice and competitions produces mental and physical fatigue. In truth, cutting back on training loads and intensities as a way to treat or prevent burnout is associated with increases in positive mental health. The key here is to develop balance in life.

• *Learn self-regulation skills.* Developing psychological skills such as relaxation, imagery, goal setting, and positive self-talk can ward off much of the stress that leads to burnout. For example, setting realistic goals can help athletes manage time for balancing professional and personal lives. People who overtrain in sport or exercise usually do so at the expense of their family and personal lives. By setting realistic goals, you have time for both sport and exercise and other responsibilities, which will help you avoid the burnout syndrome.

Time-Out

An Olympic athlete used to live and train in southern California, where the weather is typically good year-round. In that sunny, warm environment, she said she always felt guilty for missing a practice or taking a day off, but with her year-round training regimen she found herself getting injured often and feeling stressed and somewhat burned out. She moved to the middle of the United States, where the weather was more variable—often extremely hot in the summer and extremely cold in the winter. When the weather was very bad, she either took the day off or shortened her workout. To her surprise, the days off did not hurt her performance; her performance actually improved because she avoided injury and started to regain her enthusiasm. This led her to schedule relaxation or "off" days into her training.

• *Keep a positive outlook.* It is easy for officials to let news or social media commentary and criticism from coaches, spectators, and players get them down. Even when they officiate a great game, the losing coach may be upset and blame them. The antidote for officials is to focus on what they do well. A positive focus means working on the things you can control in order to get better and not dwelling on unwarranted criticism. One way to accomplish this is to seek people who provide social support (e.g., other colleagues).

• *Manage postcompetition emotions.* Although many coaches and athletes know to control pregame anxiety and tension, few consider what happens after competition. The final buzzer does not necessarily stop the intense psychological feelings aroused by the competition. Emotions often intensify and erupt

It's Not Just How Hard You Train, It's How You Recover!

Early research on overtraining in athletes focused primary attention on the training loads involved. However, more recent efforts have addressed not only how hard, long, and frequently the athlete trains but also how he goes about recovering after training bouts. To avoid overtraining or staleness and burnout and to optimize performance, training recovery should be systematically planned and implemented (Kellmann & Gunther, 2000). Another suggestion is that the recovery method used should match the source of overload stress (Kentta & Hassmen, 1998). So if an athlete is primarily overtrained as a result of the physical load (meters run, weight lifted), physical strategies such as nutrition, hydration, and massage might be best. However, if the overload results from psychological and social factors, methods such as visualization and dissociation through watching a favorite movie might be best. Of course, overtraining often results from a combination of physical, psychological, and social stressors, so it is often best to use several methods. The model that follows can help guide individuals' efforts by matching the recovery strategy to the type of overload source.

OVERLOAD SOURCE: PHYSICAL STRESSOR

Recovery strategy—nutrition and hydration

Eat more carbohydrate

Stay hydrated

Recovery strategy—active rest

Low-intensity training in a different sport

Stretching

Recovery strategy—rest

No physical activity

Passive rest

Sufficient sleep

OVERLOAD SOURCE: PSYCHOLOGICAL OR SOCIAL STRESSOR

Recovery strategy—relaxation and emotional support

Flotation tanks, massage, sauna

Visualization

Time-out

Minimize nontraining stressors (e.g., limit work hours)

Progressive muscle relaxation

Recovery strategy—thought management methods

Dissociation (e.g., watch movie)

Negative thought replacement

into postgame quarrels, fights, drinking binges, and other destructive behaviors. On the other hand, some athletes become depressed, despondent, and withdrawn after losing or performing poorly. Henschen (1998) suggested some ways for coaches to handle postcompetition stress in athletes:

- Provide a supportive atmosphere immediately after the contest.
- Concentrate on your players' emotions, not your own.
- Try to be with your team (not on the radio or television) after a contest.
- Provide an unemotional, realistic assessment of each athlete's performance.
- Talk to all team members, even those who did not play.
- Once athletes have dressed, have a group activity for the team (e.g., postgame meal, swimming, bowling, movie).

- Keep athletes away from well-meaning but demanding peers and parents.
- Do not allow team members to gloat over success or be depressed over a loss.
- Begin preparation for the next opponent at the very next practice.

- *Stay in good physical condition.* Your body and mind have a reciprocal relationship: Each affects the other. Chronic stress usually takes a toll on your body, so it's critical that you take good care of yourself through diet and exercise. Eating improperly, gaining weight, or losing too much weight only contributes to low self-esteem and self-worth and feeds into the burnout syndrome. When you feel particularly stressed, make a special attempt to stay in good physical condition to help your mental state stay strong.

LEARNING AIDS

SUMMARY

1. **Define overtraining, staleness, and burnout.**

   Overtraining refers to a short cycle of training (lasting a few days to a few weeks) during which athletes expose themselves to excessive training loads that are near or at maximal capacity. Staleness is the end result of overtraining, a state in which athletes have difficulty maintaining their standard training regimens and performance results. Burnout is another, more exhaustive psychophysiological response of withdrawal from excessive training and competitive demands.

2. **Discuss different models of burnout.**

   Six sport-specific models of burnout have been developed to help explain the burnout phenomenon. The cognitive–affective stress model presents a four-stage process of burnout involving situational demands, cognitive appraisal of the situation, physiological responses, and coping behaviors. The negative-training stress response model focuses more attention on responses to physical training, although psychological factors are also seen as important. The unidimensional identity development and external control model is more sociological, viewing stress as a symptom of social and societal factors. The commitment and entrapment theory contends that athletes and coaches who are prone to burnout feel "entrapped" by sport when they do not really want to participate in it but believe they must maintain their involvement for such reasons as maintaining their identity or because they have so much invested in their involvement. Self-determination theory holds that people have three basic psychological needs (autonomy, competence, and relatedness) and that individuals are more likely to burn out when these needs are not met. Finally, the integrated model builds from the five previous frameworks and offers a comprehensive understanding of what is known about antecedents, signs and symptoms, consequences, and factors related to burnout such as entrapment, the environment, personality, and coping resources.

3. **Describe the causes of overtraining and burnout.**

   The causes of burnout and overtraining fall into four general categories: physical concerns (e.g., injury, a high frequency and intensity of training), logistical concerns (e.g., travel grind, time demands), social–interpersonal concerns (e.g., dissatisfaction with social life, negative parental influences), and psychological concerns (e.g., inappropriate expectations, lack of enjoyment).

4. **Identify the symptoms of overtraining and burnout.**
   Some common symptoms of overtraining include apathy, mood changes, muscle pain, and appetite loss. Some common symptoms of burnout include a lack of caring, emotional isolation, and increased anxiety.

5. **Explain the research evidence of burnout in sport.**
   Although the interest in burnout originally focused on athletes, recent research has examined burnout in other sport professionals such as coaches, officials, and athletic trainers. In general, these people share much in terms of the causes of burnout and their reactions to it.

6. **Describe the treatment and prevention of burnout.**
   Several strategies have been developed to help prevent or reduce the probability of burnout in sport and exercise settings. These include setting short-term goals for practices and competitions, taking relaxation breaks, keeping a positive outlook, and learning self-regulation skills.

KEY TERMS

periodized training	burnout	physiological responses
overtraining	situational demands	behavioral responses
staleness	cognitive appraisal	entrapment theory

REVIEW QUESTIONS

1. Discuss the research regarding the frequency of overtraining, staleness, and burnout in athletes.

2. Define the terms *overtraining, staleness,* and *burnout,* pointing out similarities and differences.

3. Using research by Gould and colleagues, discuss five causes of burnout in athletes, including the importance of individual differences.

4. Use Morgan's iceberg profile to discuss the relationship between psychological mood and performance.

5. Describe Raedeke's entrapment theory of sport burnout.

6. Discuss the findings of research on burnout among athletic trainers and officials.

7. Discuss the effect of sex, age, experience, and social support on the susceptibility and reactions to burnout that coaches have.

8. Describe three antidotes, or treatments, for burnout and overtraining in sport.

CRITICAL THINKING QUESTIONS

1. This chapter presents six models of burnout in sport: the cognitive–affective stress model, the negative-training stress model, the unidimensional identity development and external control model, the commitment and entrapment theory, self-determination theory, and the integrated model. Describe the similarities and differences among these models. Use these models to determine three things you would do if you were a coach to prevent burnout in your athletes.

2. Gould and colleagues conducted in-depth interviews with young tennis players who had left the game early because they felt burned out. Drawing on the findings from that study, discuss five pieces of advice that you might give coaches, parents, and athletes for avoiding burnout.

PART VII

Facilitating Psychological Growth and Development

Can participation in sport and physical activity lead to psychological growth and character development?

Unfortunately, this subject has become big news over the past several years as many athletes (young and old) are getting noticed for their poor on- and off-the-field behaviors. Dealing with these attitudes effectively as a coach and as an athlete is critical to both improving performance and, more importantly, enhancing personal growth and well-being. Hopefully, learning some of the mental skills discussed throughout this text will help you improve this situation and provide athletes, exercisers, and coaches with tools for creating a more positive environment while highlighting the positive aspects of sport and exercise participation. This effort will make the sport and physical activity experience more positive for participants. In addition, a number of researchers suggest that if sport is done right, the lessons learned transfer to other life situations as well.

As we have learned, one focus of sport and exercise psychology is helping people enhance performance through the use of mental skills. But this represents only part of the field. Sport and exercise psychology also deals with how psychological development and well-being occur as consequences of participation in sport and physical activity. The chapters in this part deal with three main topics of psychological development and well-being that are important to both society and sport and exercise psychology.

Chapter 22 examines children's psychological development through sport participation, looking at such important issues as the levels of stress that youngsters experience, the development of their self-esteem, and effective coaching practices for helping kids. Chapter 23 focuses on the important topic of aggression in sport. Unfortunately, the number of incidents of aggression has grown recently, with athletes (and sometimes coaches) losing control of their emotions both on and off the playing field and displaying a variety of aggressive and abusive behaviors. In this chapter you'll read about the causes underlying aggression among athletes and spectators as well as some recommendations that might lessen unwanted aggression. In chapter 24, after defining character and good sporting behavior, we discuss issues of moral development and sporting behavior in sport and physical activity contexts. Finally, we describe new programs in physical education targeted at enhancing moral development.

VIEW Dr. Dan Gould introduces part VII of the text in the Introduction activity.

JOURNEY This activity allows you to reflect on whether exercise has been a positive force in your personal development, and why.

22

Children and Sport Psychology

After reading this chapter, you should be able to

1. discuss the importance of studying the psychology of the young athlete,
2. explain the major reasons children participate in and drop out of sport,
3. discuss the importance of peer relationships in youth sport,
4. describe stress and burnout effects in young athletes,
5. identify and explain how to apply effective coaching practices with youngsters, and
6. discuss the role of parental involvement in youth sport.

As many as 45 million children participate in sport in the United States. What motivates them? Is competitive sport too stressful for them? Why do so many youngsters drop out of sport after the age of 12? Is there something wrong with how they're being coached? These are among the important questions we try to answer in this chapter.

Most people think of sport psychology as something that applies principally to elite athletes. In fact, youngsters compose the greatest population of sport participants, and since the mid-1970s a growing number of highly committed sport psychologists have devoted their careers to examining the important psychological issues in children's sport participation. Their work has major implications for creating safe and psychologically healthful sport programs for children.

Importance of Studying the Psychology of Young Athletes

In the United States alone, an estimated 45 million children under the age of 18 years are involved in school and extracurricular physical activity programs, ranging from youth basketball and baseball to cross-country skiing and rodeo (Ewing & Seefeldt, 2002). Sport participation has been found to represent 66% of all out-of-school activities for youths (Duffett & Johnson, 2004). Some of sport psychology's most important contributions, therefore, are potentially to children's sport.

Many children are intensely involved in organized sport. On average, they participate in their specific sport 11 hours weekly for an 18-week season (Gould & Martens, 1979). Sport is one of the few areas in children's lives in which they can participate intensively in an activity that has meaningful consequences for themselves, their peers and family, and the community alike (Coleman, 1974; Larson, 2000). For most children, sport participation peaks near the age of 12 years (State of Michigan, 1976). We know from research in developmental psychology that this age and the time leading up to it are critical periods for children and have important consequences on their self-esteem and social development. Thus, the youth sport experience can have important lifelong effects on the personality and psychological development of children.

One reason youth sports are so popular is that people feel youths receive psychological and social values from participation. Sport parents, for example, list the development of personal and social values as highly important when they are asked what they hope their children develop from playing sports (U.S. Anti-Doping Agency, 2011). Contrary to popular belief (and as shown in chapters 23 and 24), participation in organized sport is not always automatically beneficial for the child (Gould & Bean, 2011; Martens, 1978). Character development, leadership, good sporting behavior, and achievement orientations do not magically occur through mere participation. These benefits usually follow competent adult supervision from leaders who understand children and know how to structure programs that provide positive learning experiences. In one national survey by the U.S. Anti-Doping Agency (2011), coaches were ranked as the most important positive influence on young athletes. At the same time, the adult respondents highlighted their concerns about too much emphasis on winning in youth sport today. An important first step to becoming a qualified youth sport leader is understanding the psychology of youth sport and physical activity participation.

> **KEY POINT** Some of the most important implications of sport psychology are in children's sport. For most children, sport participation peaks at around 12 years of age.

Children's Reasons for Participation and Nonparticipation

A good place to start is to look at children's motives for both participation and nonparticipation in sport.

Why Children Participate in Sport

Some 8,000 youths (49% male, 51% female) involved in sponsored sports throughout the United States,

both in school and after school, were asked to rank in importance a number of possible reasons for their participation (Ewing & Seefeldt, 1996). Boys and girls in both school and nonschool athletic programs had similar responses (see "Motives for Participation in Youth Sport"), and their comments were consistent with findings from previous research into the motivation for participation (Gould & Horn, 1984). Most children participate in sport to have fun. Other reasons most of them cite are to do something they are good at, improve their skills, get exercise and become fit, be with their friends and make new friends, and compete.

Sex (Sirard, Pfeiffer, & Pate, 2006) and cultural differences (Yan & McCullagh, 2004) have been found in youth motives for participation. For example, in a study of 1,602 middle school students, Sirard and colleagues (2006) found that boys were more motivated by the competitive aspects of sports and girls were more attracted by social opportunities. However, more differences exist within these groups than between them, making it very important for practitioners to strive to understand the unique motivations of each young person they work with.

Why Children Discontinue Participation in Sport

Children's sport participation peaks between the ages of 10 and 13 years and then consistently declines to the age of 18, when a relatively small percentage of youths remain involved in organized sport (Ewing & Seefeldt, 1989; State of Michigan, 1976). Moreover, dropout rates for organized youth sport programs average 35% in any given year (Gould & Petlichkoff, 1988). So, of every 10 children who begin a sport season, 3 to 4 will drop out by the start of the next season.

An in-depth study of 50 swimming dropouts, ranging in age from 10 to 18 years, indicated that "other things to do" and "a change in interest" were the major reasons the vast majority of children gave for discontinued involvement (Gould, Feltz, Horn, & Weiss, 1982). Other reasons that the sample rated as important (but less important than other interests and change of interests) were "not as good as I wanted to be," "not enough fun," "wanted to play another sport," "didn't like the pressure," "boredom," "didn't like the coach," "training was too hard," and "not exciting enough." So, although most young swimmers who quit did so because of interest in other activities, up to 28% cited negative factors such as excessive pressure, dislike of the coach, failure, a lack of fun, and an overemphasis on winning as important influences on their decision to withdraw.

In a more recent study of more than 500 youth sport dropouts in soccer, ice hockey, and basketball, "other things to do" and a "decline in excitement" were the two items rated as the most important reasons for withdrawal (Rottensteiner, Laakso, Pihlaja, & Knottinen, 2013). Rounding out the top five reasons for dropping out were "not able to be with my friends," "not enough team spirit," and "wanted to play another sport." The results also showed that coaches and teammates were the two most influential groups affecting the young athletes' decision to discontinue. Most interesting was the finding that a lack of teamwork, team affiliation issues, and concerns about a lack of ability were more important reasons for discontinuing in females than in males. Coaches and other youth sport leaders should be particularly sensitive to these issues when working with young female athletes.

KEY POINT   For every 10 children who begin a sport season, 3 to 4 discontinue before the start of the next season.

Deeper Motives: Perceived Competence, Goal Orientations, and Intrinsic Motivation

The reasons youths give for participation and dropping out are their surface-level responses, not the deeper, underlying motives some sport psychologists have sought (figure 22.1). For example, children who discontinue often have low perceived competence, tend

Motives for Participation in Youth Sport

REASONS FOR PARTICIPATING IN NONSCHOOL SPORTS

Boys
1. To have fun
2. To do something I'm good at
3. To improve my skills
4. For the excitement of competition
5. To stay in shape
6. For the challenge of competition
7. To get exercise
8. To learn new skills
9. To play as part of a team
10. To go to a higher level of competition

Girls
1. To have fun
2. To stay in shape
3. To get exercise
4. To improve my skills
5. To do something I'm good at
6. To learn new skills
7. For the excitement of competition
8. To play as part of a team
9. To make new friends
10. For the challenge of competition

REASONS FOR PARTICIPATING IN SCHOOL SPORTS

Boys
1. To have fun
2. To improve my skills
3. For the excitement of competition
4. To do something I'm good at
5. To stay in shape
6. For the challenge of competition
7. To be part of a team
8. To win
9. To go to a higher level of competition
10. To get exercise

Girls
1. To have fun
2. To stay in shape
3. To get exercise
4. To improve my skills
5. To do something I'm good at
6. To be part of a team
7. For the excitement of competition
8. To learn new skills
9. For team spirit
10. For the challenge of competition

Adapted, by permission, from M. Ewing and V. Seefeldt, 1989, *Participation and attrition patterns in American agency-sponsored and interscholastic sports: An executive summary.* Final Report Sporting Goods Manufacturer's Association (North Palm Beach, FL: Sporting Goods Manufacturer's Association).

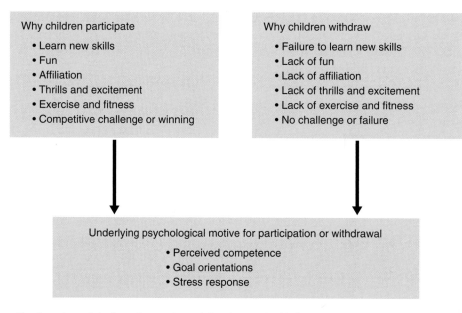

FIGURE 22.1 A motivational model of youth sport participation and withdrawal.

Adapted from Gould and Petlichkoff 1988.

to focus on outcome goals, exhibit less self-determined forms of motivation, and experience considerable stress.

Maureen Weiss, a leading researcher in this area, concluded that youth sport participants differ from nonparticipants and those who drop out in their level of **perceived competence** (Weiss & Ferrer-Caja, 2002). That is, children with low perceptions of their abilities to learn and perform sport skills do not participate (or they drop out), whereas children who persist have higher levels of perceived competence. In addition, youths who focus on outcome goals (especially if they have low perceptions of ability), are more extrinsically than intrinsically motivated, and have greater levels of stress are more likely to discontinue. From this information, you can infer that one crucial task of youth sport leaders and coaches is to discover ways to enhance children's self-perceived ability. One way is to teach children to evaluate their performances by their own standards of improvement rather than by competitive outcomes (winning or losing). Leaders must also create task-oriented motivational climates, foster self-determined behavior through the use of autonomous competent coaching strategies, and reduce stress placed on young athletes.

KEY POINT Children with low perceptions of their athletic abilities do not participate in sport, or they drop out, whereas children with high perceptions of their competence participate and persist.

Sport-Specific and Sport-General Dropouts

Youth sport leaders usually want to know whether children are withdrawing from their programs and entering other sports (**sport-specific dropouts**) or are withdrawing from sport participation altogether (**sport-general dropouts**). For example, in the swimming study cited earlier, 68% of the youngsters who discontinued competitive swimming were active in other sports (Gould et al., 1982). Similarly, in a study of former competitive gymnasts, 95% were participating in another sport or were still in gymnastics but at a less intense level (Klint & Weiss, 1986). Thus, we need to distinguish between sport-specific dropouts or sport transfers and those children who discontinue involvement in all of sport (Gould & Petlichkoff, 1988).

KEY POINT It is useful to learn whether children are withdrawing from a particular sport or program or from sport participation altogether.

Youth Sport Participation: Implications for Practice

The research on why children participate or withdraw from sport leads to a number of general conclusions:

• Most of the motivations children have for participating in sport (i.e., having fun, learning new skills, doing something one is good at, being with friends, making new friends, maintaining fitness, exercising, and experiencing success) are intrinsic in nature. Winning clearly is neither the only nor the most common reason for participation.

• Most young athletes have multiple reasons for participation, not a single motive. Although most children withdraw because of interest in other activities, a significant minority discontinue for negative reasons such as a lack of fun, too much pressure, or dislike of the coach.

• Underlying the descriptive reasons for sport withdrawal (e.g., no fun) is the child's need to feel worthy and competent. When young athletes feel worthy and competent about the activity, they tend to participate. If they don't feel confident about performing the skills, they tend to withdraw. Recent research also shows that young people are more likely to be involved in sport if their relatedness needs are met in the youth sport environment.

Think about the interactional model of motivation—how a person interacts with a situation (see chapter 3). If you understand the reasons children participate in sport, you can enhance their motivation by structuring environments that better meet their needs. Study "Strategies for Structuring Sport Situations to Meet the Needs of Young Athletes" for suggestions.

> **KEY POINT** Teach young athletes that success means exceeding their own goals, not merely winning contests.

Emphasizing individual goal setting, in which children compare their athletic performances with

---

Strategies for Structuring Sport Situations to Meet the Needs of Young Athletes

Coaches who understand children's motives for participating in sport can use a number of strategies to structure the environment for skill development, fun, affiliation, excitement, fitness, and success.

Strategies for Meeting the Need for Skill Development
• Implement effective instructional practices (e.g., effective demonstrations, contingent feedback).
• Foster a positive approach to instruction, emphasizing what the child does correctly.
• Know the technical and strategic aspects of the sport.

Strategies for Meeting the Need for Fun
• Form realistic expectations to avoid negative coaching results and athlete frustration.
• Keep practices active—avoid lines and standing around.
• Joke and kid around freely with the children.

Strategies for Meeting the Need for Affiliation or Relatedness
• Provide time for children to make friends.
• Schedule social events (e.g., pizza party) outside practice.
• Incorporate periods of free time before and during practices.

Strategies for Meeting the Need for Excitement
• Do not overemphasize time spent on drills; incorporate variety into practices.
• Incorporate change-of-pace activities (e.g., water polo for swimmers) into practices.
• Focus on short, crisp practices.

Strategies for Meeting the Need for Fitness
• Teach young athletes how to monitor their own fitness.
• Organize planned, purposeful practices specifically designed to enhance fitness.

Strategies for Meeting the Need for Success
• Allow children to compete.
• Help children define winning not only as beating others but as achieving one's own goals and standards.

their own standards (self-referenced standards), helps children avoid focusing solely on the outcomes of competitions (Martens, 2004), and they will more likely feel competent. At least 50% of young athletes will lose, so when self-evaluation depends on winning and losing, 50% of young athletes can develop low self-worth and thus become less likely to continue sport participation. Youth sport leaders can keep and analyze participation statistics and conduct "exit interviews" with children who drop out. In this way leaders can track how many children begin, continue, and complete seasons and—if children discontinue—whether they chose to participate in another sport or to discontinue involvement in sport altogether. The leader can ask whether young athletes discontinued because of conflicts with other interests (something adult leaders may not have control over) or because of poor coaching, competitive pressure, or a lack of fun (which adult leaders can better control).

For example, a high school football coach was concerned about the low number of players coming out for his squad. He examined previous participation records at all levels of play and saw that many youngsters had participated in elementary and middle school programs but that few had participated in the ninth grade. The coach spoke with some of the players who had discontinued during middle school and discovered that some very negative coaching had occurred at the seventh- and eighth-grade levels. He discussed with these coaches the advantages of a positive approach to coaching (explained later in this chapter) and found in subsequent years that more players were coming out for his high school team.

Petlichkoff (1996) suggested that when children discontinue sport involvement, a coach should ask the following questions:

- Has the child developed an interest in another sport or activity?
- Does the child's withdrawal appear to be permanent or temporary?
- Did the child have a part or choice in the decision to withdraw, or was she cut from a team or injured?
- What effect does the withdrawal have on the child's well-being?

On the basis of the responses to these questions, the coach can determine whether the child's withdrawal is appropriate (a child selects soccer participation over

basketball) or inappropriate (a child discontinues all sport and physical activity participation because of low perceived competence). We should be particularly concerned when children permanently withdraw, especially today when so many children who could benefit from sport are inactive; when children have no choice in the decision; or when the withdrawal has negative effects on their well-being.

KEY POINT Rigorously analyze why young athletes withdraw from sport.

Role of Friends in Youth Sport

Affiliation motive is a major motive that children have for sport participation. Thus, children enjoy sport because of the opportunities it provides to be with friends and make new friends. Although affiliation is certainly important in its own right, sport psychology researchers have discovered that friends and the peer group have other important effects on young athletes.

Peer Relationships and Children's Psychological Development

Developmental psychologists have long known that friends and peers play a major role in the psychological development of children. Peer relations are linked to a child's sense of acceptance, self-esteem, and motivation, so it is natural that sport psychology researchers have turned their attention to this important area. Leading developmental sport psychologist Maureen Weiss and her colleagues have studied friendship and peer relationships in sport. For example, they conducted in-depth interviews with 38 sport participants, 8 to 16 years of age, to learn how children view the component of friendship in sport (Weiss, Smith, & Theeboom, 1996). They identified both positive and negative dimensions in this facet of sport participation. These were some positive dimensions that the researchers heard about:

- Companionship (spending time or "hanging out" together)
- Pleasant play association (enjoying being around one's friend)
- Enhancement of self-esteem (friends saying things or taking actions that boost one's self-esteem)

Maximizing Sport Involvement in Underserved Youths

Millions of children live in poverty today, and research indicates that these children are less often involved in sport and physical activity. They also have high obesity rates relative to same-aged peers who are of middle and upper socioeconomic status. Recognizing this state of affairs, sport and exercise psychologists began to examine both the benefits of involvement in and factors influencing poor children's participation in sport and physical activity. Riley and Anderson-Butcher (2012) interviewed low-income parents whose children participated in a summer sport-based youth development program at Ohio State University. The parents reported that their children received a variety of benefits from participation, including facilitated biopsychosocial development (e.g., increased peer interactions, enhanced personal and social skills); broadened opportunities (e.g., exposure to college opportunities, interaction and exposure to different peers, constructive use of discretionary time); and enhanced cognition, affect, and behaviors (e.g., enhanced thoughts about self, increased positive behaviors). Similarly, Holt, Kingsley, Tink, and Scherer (2011) interviewed low-income parents and youths in Canada and found that a variety of personal (e.g., emotional control, confidence, discipline, and academic performance) and social (e.g., relationships with coaches, making new friends, teamwork, and social skills) attributes were identified as benefits of participation. Thus, low-income youths can gain a variety of benefits from sport and physical activity participation.

Examining factors influencing participation, Dollman and Lewis (2010) found that children of higher socioeconomic status participated in sport more often than their less well-off peers and that these discrepant participation rates—especially among girls—could be explained by the fact that girls of high socioeconomic status received more tangible (e.g., more access to equipment), transportation, and emotional (e.g., permission to play, encouragement and play time with parents) support. In another study, low-income parents reported challenges associated with sports participation (Holt, Kingsley, Tink, & Scherer, 2011). They found that parental time and scheduling demands limited their children's participation (parents often worked multiple jobs), as did financial barriers resulting from the costs required to have children initially participate in sport or to maintain participation as the child progresses. In other studies, safety has been cited as barrier to participation (Humbert et al., 2006). These results suggest that those parties interested in enhancing sport participation in low-income children and youths need to make special efforts to overcome these barriers and facilitate sport and physical activity participation.

- Help and guidance (friends providing assistance relative to learning sport skills as well as general assistance in other domains, such as school)
- Prosocial behavior (saying and doing things that conform to social convention, such as not saying negative things, sharing)
- Intimacy (mutual feelings of close, personal bonds)
- Loyalty (a sense of commitment to one another)
- Things in common (shared interests)
- Attractive personal qualities (friends have positive characteristics such as personality or physical features)
- Emotional support (expressions and feelings of concern for one another)
- Absence of conflicts (some friends do not argue, fight, or disagree)
- Conflict resolution (other friends are able to resolve conflicts)

The young athletes identified fewer negative dimensions of friendship, but those they commented on included the following:

- Conflict (verbal insults, arguments, and disagreements)
- Unattractive personal qualities (friends have undesirable behavioral or personality characteristics, such as being self-centered)
- Betrayal (disloyalty or insensitivity on the part of a friend)
- Inaccessibility (lack of opportunity to interact with one another)

Girls were more apt than boys to identify emotional support as a positive feature of friendship in sport. The older children among these participants saw intimacy as more important, whereas children under 13 years mentioned prosocial behavior and loyalty more often. Respondents older than 10 years also cited attractive personal qualities more frequently.

Using this initial research, Weiss and Smith (1999) developed the Sport Friendship Quality Scale to measure six aspects of sport friendships. These include self-esteem enhancement and supportiveness, loyalty and intimacy, things in common, companionship and pleasant play, conflict resolution, and conflict. With the development of this measure of friendship, researchers can begin to study peer relations in sport more extensively.

Conducting additional peer relationship research is especially important. Smith (1997, 1999) found that children who perceived more positive relationships with peers in physical activity also reported more positive feelings toward physical activity, higher physical activity motivation, and higher physical self-worth. Positive peer relationships have also been found to be related to lower stress, higher self-determined motivation, and continued participation in youth soccer players (Ullrich-French & Smith, 2006, 2009). Hence, peer relations had a great deal to do with the child's motivation for physical activity, which suggests that promoting positive peer relationships can enhance participation in physical activity.

Although research in this area is relatively new, Weiss and Stuntz (2004) have identified implications for practitioners. Most notably, practitioners should enhance peer relationships by creating motivational climates that enhance task goals and foster cooperation versus competition (see chapter 3). Practitioners can also conduct drills that require small groups of players to interact, which will maximize athlete or student involvement. Last, reducing displays of social status (e.g., public picking of teams) will enhance peer relationships.

Friendship in Sport: Implications for Practice

The research on peer relationships and friendship has a number of implications for practice (Weiss et al., 1996). First, time should be provided for children to be with their friends and for making new friends. The adage that all work and no play makes Jack (or Jill) a dull boy (or girl) seems to ring true. Fraser-Thomas, Cote, and Deakin (2008) found that peer support and peer relations were associated with prolonged engagement in competitive junior swimmers. Second, in an effort to enhance self-esteem among youngsters participating in physical activity, coaches and parents should encourage positive peer reinforcement. Positive statements to teammates should be reinforced, whereas derogatory remarks, teasing, and negative comments should not be tolerated. Children must be taught to respect others, refrain from verbal aggression and bullying, and learn how to resolve conflicts with peers. In chapter 23 we discuss a number of techniques for doing this. Third, the importance of teamwork and the pursuit of group goals should be emphasized. Techniques for fostering group cohesion (see chapter 8) and goal setting (see chapter 15) should be frequently used in the youth sport setting.

Stress and Burnout in Children's Competitive Sport

Stress and burnout are among the most controversial concerns in children's competitive sport. Critics argue that competitive sport places excessive levels of stress on youngsters, who often burn out as a result. Proponents contend that young athletes do not experience excessive competition and that competition teaches children coping strategies, which transfer to other aspects of their lives.

Stress Levels in Young Athletes

Levels of stress in young athletes have been assessed through the use of state anxiety measures administered in competitive game situations (where stress is predicted to be maximal). Most young athletes do not have excessive levels of state anxiety in competition. For example, 13- and 14-year-old wrestlers took the Competitive State Anxiety Inventory for Children just before competition (figure 22.2, showing the distribution of anxiety scores of the 112 wrestlers). Their prematch state anxiety level averaged 18.9 out of a possible 30. Only 9% of the wrestlers had scores in the upper 25% of the scale, which could be considered extremely high. Thus, 91% of the wrestlers did not have excessive stress (Gould, Eklund, Petlichkoff, Peterson, & Bump, 1991).

Simon and Martens (1979) measured state anxiety levels of boys aged 9 to 14 in both practice and socially evaluative settings. State anxiety levels in this study were compared among participants in band (both soloists with the band and band ensemble members);

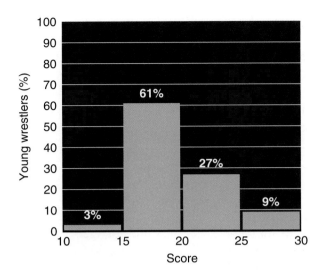

FIGURE 22.2 Prematch state anxiety levels in youth wrestlers as measured with the Competitive State Anxiety Inventory for Children.

students taking academic tests; students in competitive physical education classes; and participants in competitive baseball, basketball, tackle football, gymnastics, ice hockey, swimming, and wrestling. Levels exhibited in sport competition were not significantly greater than those exhibited in the other activities tested. State anxiety was elevated more in competition than in practices, but this change was not dramatic. In fact, band soloists reported the greatest mean state anxiety levels ($M = 21.5$ of 30).

> **KEY POINT** State anxiety levels in children during sport competitions are not usually significantly higher than those during other childhood evaluative activities.

These studies didn't answer the question of whether long-term stress effects might be apparent in the children's trait anxiety levels. Later investigators examined the influence of sport participation on children's trait anxiety (i.e., their predisposition to perceive competition as threatening and respond with heightened nervousness). This research indicated that young athletes have at most only slightly elevated trait anxiety levels. Moreover, in half the studies, no differences were found (see Gould, 1993, for a detailed review).

An interesting study conducted by Dimech and Seiler (2011) examined whether sport participation could buffer the effects of social anxiety, or fear that social or performance situations will result in embarrassment, on children aged 7 and 8 years. Results

revealed that children participating in team sports had reduced social anxiety symptoms over the course of a year. Although more research is needed on this topic, the results show that team sport participation might be valuable for helping children overcome social anxiety.

Factors Associated With Heightened State Anxiety in Young Athletes

Although most children who participate in sport do not have excessive levels of state or trait anxiety, stress can be a problem for certain children in specific situations. And although this may be true of only 1 of 10 children who participate in the United States, among 45 million young participants that could mean 4.5 million children with heightened stress. For this reason, sport psychologists also look at what personal and situational factors are associated with heightened state anxiety by administering various background and personality measures away from the competitive setting (e.g., trait anxiety, self-esteem, team and individual performance expectancies, ratings of parental pressure to participate) as well as state anxiety assessments in practice, immediately before competition, and immediately after competition. Links are then made between heightened levels of state anxiety and factors related to these changes (see Scanlan, 1986, for a detailed review).

- High stress levels resulting from youth sport participation are relatively rare yet can affect more than 4.5 million children in specific situations.

- Excessive trait anxiety does not appear to be associated with youth sport participation.

Using the findings from these studies, researchers have developed a profile of the young athlete at risk for having unhealthy levels of competitive state anxiety (see "Characteristics of Children at Risk for Heightened Competitive State Anxiety"). A thorough knowledge of these characteristics will help you detect a child at risk.

Most of the research has involved youngsters under 14 years of age, usually in local competitions. However, some studies have looked at elite junior athletes of high school age. For instance, elite high school distance runners had stress in performing up to their ability, improving on their last performance, participating in championship meets, not performing well, and not being mentally ready (Feltz & Albrecht,

1986). Elite junior wrestlers cited similar stressors (Gould, Horn, & Spreemann, 1983). Thus, elite junior competitors seem stressed primarily by a fear of failure and feelings of inadequacy.

Situational Sources of Stress

Situations, too, can increase stress, particularly these types of factors:

- *Defeat.* Children have more state anxiety after losing than after winning.
- *Event importance.* The more importance placed on a contest, the more state anxiety felt by the participants.
- *Sport type.* Children in individual sports have more state anxiety than children in team sports.

Consequently, youth sport leaders must understand both the personalities of children who are at risk of having high levels of competitive stress and the situations most likely to produce heightened state anxiety. We cannot help children deal with excessive stress until we identify the particular stresses that specific situations elicit in them.

> **KEY POINT** Stress in elite junior competitors is caused by a fear of failure and feelings of inadequacy.

Stress-Induced Burnout

We discuss burnout at length in chapter 21, including its implications for children. Here we only elaborate on earlier points, focusing on burnout as a stress-induced

Young athletes are not immune to the pressures of their sport and are prone to stress, anxiety, and burnout.

Characteristics of Children at Risk for Heightened Competitive State Anxiety

- High trait anxiety
- Low self-esteem
- Maladaptive perfectionism (a disposition to set high standards and at the same time be very concerned about making mistakes and parental evaluation)
- Low performance expectancies relative to the team
- Low self-performance expectations
- Frequent worries about failure
- Frequent worries about adult expectations and social evaluation by others
- Less perceived fun
- Less satisfaction with their performance, regardless of winning or losing
- Perceiving that it is important to their parents that they participate in sport
- Outcome goal orientation and low perceived ability

phenomenon in young athletes. Burnout, which is a growing concern with children's competitive sport, is thought to occur when children lose interest as a result of specializing in a particular sport at a very early age and practicing for long hours under intense pressure for several years. Children as young as age 4 begin participating in sports such as gymnastics, swimming, and tennis, and some attain world-class levels by their early teens. When careers end early or performance declines prematurely, burnout is suspected. We can understand burnout as a special case of sport withdrawal when a young athlete discontinues or curtails sport involvement in response to chronic or long-term stress or motivational concerns (Gustafsson et al., 2011; Smith, 1986). A previously enjoyable activity is no longer pleasurable because of the stress it causes and shifts in children's motivation. Children withdraw from sport, of course, for reasons other than burnout.

> **KEY POINT** Burnout is a special case of sport withdrawal in which a young athlete discontinues sport involvement in response to chronic stress.

As mentioned in chapter 21, Coakley (1992) found that adolescents who burned out of sport typically had one-dimensional self-definitions, seeing themselves only as athletes and not in other possible roles, such as students, musicians, or school activity leaders. Also, young athletes who burned out had seriously restricted control of their own destinies, both in and out of sport. Their parents and coaches made the important decisions regarding their sporting lives with little or no input from them. As discussed in the section on feedback and reinforcement in chapter 6, control of

one's destiny by someone else almost always results in decreased intrinsic motivation.

Some prominent factors associated with burnout have been reported that also result in increased state anxiety (see "Factors Associated With Burnout in Young Athletes"; Gould, 1993). Unlike the usual state anxiety felt before a contest, however, for a child en route to burnout the stress does not abate but instead builds constantly. Thus, burnout is best viewed as the end result of long-term stress.

> **DISCOVER** Activity 22.1 helps you determine your youth sport motives and stress sources.

Dealing With Stressed Children: Implications for Practice

Once children with stress, or at high risk of experiencing stress, have been identified, what can adult leaders do to help them learn to cope? Adults should make concerted efforts, first, to create a positive environment and a constructive attitude toward mistakes, which will help children develop confidence. Stress can be alleviated by reducing social evaluation and the importance of winning (e.g., no more fiery pep talks). Adult anxiety reduction techniques (progressive muscle relaxation, breath control, mental training, autogenic training, systematic desensitization, biofeedback, and cognitive–affective stress management strategies) can be adapted for use with children. For instance, Terry Orlick (1992) adapted progressive muscle relaxation for children by creating a "spaghetti toes"

Factors Associated With Burnout in Young Athletes

- Very high self- and other-imposed expectations
- Win-at-all-costs attitude
- Parental pressure
- Long repetitive practices with little variety
- Inconsistent coaching practices
- Overuse injuries from excessive practice
- Excessive time demands
- High travel demands
- Love from others displayed on the basis of winning and losing
- Maladaptive perfectionism

exercise (see "Orlick's Spaghetti Toes Relaxation Exercise"). Orlick and McCaffrey (1991) also have these suggestions for modifying arousal regulation and stress management strategies for children:

- Use concrete and physical strategies (e.g., a little "stress bag" for children to put their worries in).
- Use fun strategies (e.g., have children release muscle tension by making their bellies turn to gelatin).
- Use simple strategies (e.g., imagine changing television channels to change one's mind focus).
- Vary approaches to the same exercise.
- Individualize approaches in relation to the children's interests.
- Remain positive and optimistic.
- Use role models (e.g., tell them Peyton Manning uses positive self-talk).

General directions (e.g., "Just relax" or "You can do it") are not enough to help children manage stress. You'll need to develop strategies for making the directions fun and relevant to the children.

Effective Coaching Practices for Young Athletes

You may have heard about or seen Little League coaches who emulate big-time college or professional coaches to try to achieve success and impress people. For example, former vice president Dan Quayle once boasted that he modeled his coaching of his 12-year-old son's basketball team after then Indiana University basketball coach Bobby Knight. But is Knight's style (especially his use of punishment, severe criticism, and emotional outbursts) appropriate to use with 12-year-olds? Probably not. Coaching practices designed for adult elite athletes are often inappropriate for young athletes who are developing. Sport psychologists have found many coaching practices that are more effective with youngsters; in fact, an organization called the Positive Coaching Alliance (www.positivecoaching.org) has been developed to emphasize the need for youth coaches to be more positive with young athletes. Let's look at what the research says about coaching children.

What the Research Says About Coaching Children

The classic research about coaching children was conducted at the University of Washington by Ron Smith, Frank Smoll, and their colleagues. These investigators examined the relationship between coaching behaviors (e.g., reinforcement, mistake-contingent technical instruction) and self-esteem in young baseball players and looked at whether coaches could learn effective coaching practices (Smith, Smoll, & Curtis, 1979). Their study had two phases. In the first phase, 52 male youth baseball coaches were observed while they were coaching and were assessed using a specially developed instrument, the Coaching Behavior Assessment System (CBAS) (chapter 9). The researchers also interviewed 542 players about their Little League baseball experiences and found that coaches who gave technical instruction were rated more positively than those who used general communication and encouragement. The coaches who used more reinforcement and mistake-contingent technical instruction (gave instruction after errors) were also highly rated, and these results held even when the team's win–loss records were considered. Positive reinforcement and mistake-contingent encouragement (encouraging a player after a mistake) positively affected postseason self-esteem measures, liking of teammates, and liking of baseball.

KEY POINT Children have special coaching needs that are much different from the needs of adults.

Unfortunately, the first phase did not show that the coaching behaviors actually changed the athletes' perceptions, only that these factors were correlated. In a second phase, the investigators assigned 32 baseball coaches either to a control condition, in which they coached as they had always done, or to an experimental coaching education program, in which they received training based on results of the first phase. The experimental group received guidelines on desirable coaching behaviors, saw these behaviors modeled, and were monitored until they had increased the frequency of their encouraging remarks by 25%. The control group did not receive any special training (their coaching, however, was not excessively negative). As you might expect, the experimental group coached differently from the control group: They were more encouraging, gave more reinforcement, and were less

Orlick's Spaghetti Toes Relaxation Exercise

There are lots of games you can play with your body. We'll start with one called Spaghetti Toes. I wonder how good you are at talking to your toes. I'll bet you're pretty good. Let's find out.

Tell the toes on one of your feet to wiggle. Are they wiggling? On just one foot? Good! Now tell these toes to stop wiggling. Tell the toes on your other foot to wiggle. Tell them to wiggle real slow . . . and faster . . . and real slow again . . . slower . . . stop! Did your toes listen to you? Good. If you talk to different parts of your body, as you just did with your toes, your body will listen to you . . . especially if you talk to them a lot. I'm going to show you how you can be the boss of your body by talking to it.

First, I want to tell you something about spaghetti. I like spaghetti. I bet you do, too. But did you ever see spaghetti before it's cooked? It's kind of cold and hard and stiff, and it's easy to break. When it's cooked, it's warm and soft and kinda lies down and curls up on your plate.

I want to see if you can talk to your toes to get them to go soft and warm and sleepy like cooked spaghetti lying on your plate. You might have to talk to them quite a bit to make them know what you want them to do, but I know they can do it.

Wiggle your toes on one foot. Now tell these toes to stop wiggling. Tell them to go soft and sleepy like warm spaghetti lying on your plate. Now wiggle the toes on your other foot. Stop wiggling. Turn those toes into soft spaghetti. Good.

Now wiggle one leg. Stop wiggling. Tell the leg to go soft and sleepy like warm spaghetti. Now wiggle the other leg. Stop. Tell it to go soft and sleepy. Wiggle your behind. Let it go soft and sleepy.

Wiggle your fingers on one hand. Tell your fingers to stop wiggling. See if you can make those fingers feel warm and soft and sleepy like spaghetti lying on your plate. Now wiggle your fingers on your other hand. Slowly. Stop. Make those fingers feel warm. Tell them to go soft and sleepy. Now wiggle one arm. Stop. Tell your arm to go soft and sleepy. Now wiggle the other arm and tell it to go soft and sleepy. Good.

Try to let your whole you go soft and warm and sleepy, like soft spaghetti lying on your plate. [Pause] That's really good. Your body is listening well. Let your body stay like spaghetti and just listen to me. I want to tell you about when spaghetti toes can help you.

When you are worried or scared of something, or when something hurts, your toes and your hands and muscles get kinda hard and stiff—like hard spaghetti before it's cooked. If you are worried, scared, or something hurts you, you feel a lot better and it doesn't hurt so much if your hands and toes and muscles are like warm, soft spaghetti lying on a plate. If you practice doing your spaghetti toes, you'll get really good at it. Then you can tell your hands and toes and muscles to help you by going warm and soft and sleepy, even if you are scared or something hurts.

Before you go, let's try talking to your mouth. Wiggle your mouth. Let it go soft and sleepy. Wiggle your tongue. Let it go soft and sleepy. Wiggle your eyebrows. Let them go soft and sleepy. Let your whole you go warm and soft and sleepy. Let your whole you feel good. (Orlick, 1992, p. 325)

Reprinted from T. Orlick, 2004, *Feeling great: Teaching children to excel at living* (Carp, Ontario, Canada: Creative Bound). By permission of T. Orlick.

punitive. Compared with the players in the control group, the players in the experimental group rated their coaches as better teachers, liked their teammates more, liked their coaches more, and showed greater positive changes in self-esteem.

These findings clearly identified coaching behaviors associated with positive psychological development in children and have been further verified in recent research with youth swimmers (Coatsworth & Conroy, 2006). Moreover, the research shows that coaches can learn these positive behaviors. Other studies have shown that remarks from coaches must be not only positive but also sincere to be effective (Horn, 1985); giving information frequently after good performances and giving encouragement combined with information after poorer performances are associated with effectiveness, competence, and enjoyment (Black & Weiss, 1992). Also, learning a positive approach to coaching results in lower (5%, compared with 26% with untrained coaches) player dropout rates (Barnett, Smoll, & Smith, 1992). Finally, players taught by coaches who used a positive, mastery-oriented approach to coaching reported decreased anxiety over the course of a playing season, whereas athletes taught by control coaches reported increases in anxiety (Smith, Smoll, & Cumming, 2007).

Relative to this line of research, Langan, Blake, and Longsdale (2013) reviewed all of the studies conducted on the effectiveness of interpersonal coach education programs. They concluded that these programs enhance the interpersonal effectiveness of coaches as well as selected personal and social outcomes in young athletes. However, the findings were sometimes mixed: Self-esteem showed effects in some studies but not others, whereas anxiety and attrition effects were more consistent. Most important, the reviewers found no evidence that these interventions have any harmful effects.

KEY POINT A coach's technical instruction, reinforcement, and mistake-contingent encouragement correlate with a player's self-esteem, motivation, and positive attitudes.

Coaching Young Athletes: Implications for Practice

Some ready observations for practical work follow from these studies. The following 12 coaching guidelines are drawn from Smoll and Smith (1980), Weiss (1991), and Conroy and Coatsworth (2006).

1. Affirming, instructional, supportive, and autonomy-supportive behaviors are highly desirable to use when coaching young athletes. You should avoid punitive, hostile, and controlling coaching behaviors.

2. Focus on catching kids doing things right and give them plenty of praise and encouragement. Praise young children frequently. Add such rewards as a pat on the back and a friendly smile. The best way to give encouragement is to focus on what youngsters do correctly rather than on the errors they make.

3. Give praise sincerely. Praise and encouragement are ineffective unless they are sincere. Telling a young athlete he did a good job when he knows he did not conveys that you are trying only to make him feel better. Insincerity destroys your credibility as a leader or coach. Recognize poor performance in a nonpunitive, specific way (put your arm around the child and say, "It can be really tough out there"), but also offer some encouragement ("Stick with it; it will come").

4. Develop realistic expectations. Realistic expectations appropriate to the child's age and ability level make it much easier for a coach to offer sincere praise. You can't expect of an 11-year-old what you might of a 16-year-old.

5. Reward effort as much as outcome. It's easy to be positive when everything is going well. Unfortunately, things don't always go well—teams lose and sometimes perform poorly. However, if a youngster gives 100% effort, what more can you ask? Reward efforts of young athletes as much as—or even more than—game outcomes.

6. Focus on teaching and practicing skills. All the positive coaching techniques in the world will do little good unless youngsters see improvement in their physical skills. Design practice sessions that maximize participation and include plenty of activity and drill variety. Keep instructions short and simple. Give plenty of demonstrations from multiple angles. Maximize equipment and facility use.

7. Modify skills and activities. One of our goals is for children to have successes in performance. Modifying activities so they are developmentally appropriate is an excellent way to ensure success. For example, make sure that baskets are lowered, batting tees are used, and field distances are modified. "Match the activity to the child, not the child to the activity" (Weiss, 1991, p. 347). Use appropriate skill progressions. An excellent example of this comes from the U.S. Tennis Association, which has reformatted tennis for children under 10 years of age, changing from adult equipment, courts, and scoring to equipment scaled to the size of the child, smaller courts, and age-appropriate instruction and play formats. (For more details see www.10andundertennis.com.)

8. Modify rules to maximize action and participation. Rules can also be modified to ensure success and enhance motivation. You might modify the traditional baseball or softball rules so that coaches pitch to their own teams, which greatly increases the probability of hits. In basketball, instruct referees to call only the most obvious fouls until the child becomes more skilled. Children can rotate positions to give everyone a chance to be in the action. Modify rules to increase scoring and action. This will keep scores close and games exciting.

9. Reward correct technique, not just outcome. A common mistake in coaching youngsters is to reward the outcome of a skill (e.g., getting a base hit in baseball or softball) even when the skill is executed incorrectly (e.g., poor swing). In the long run,

this isn't helpful: Proper form is usually needed to achieve desirable outcomes consistently. Encourage and reward correct technique regardless of outcome.

10. Use a positive "sandwich" approach, as discussed in chapter 10, when you correct errors. How can you give frequent praise when young athletes are learning and making many mistakes? When a child makes a mistake, first mention something she did correctly ("Good try; you didn't give up on the dive"). This will help reduce her frustration in making the error. Second, provide information to correct the error made (e.g., "Tuck earlier and tighter"). Then end positively with an encouraging remark ("Stick with it—it's a tough dive, but you'll get it"). Of course, the sandwich approach is much more likely to work if you are sincere in your remarks.

11. Create an environment that reduces the fear of trying new skills. Mistakes are a natural part of the learning process and what UCLA basketball coach John Wooden called the "building blocks of success." Provide an encouraging atmosphere in which ridicule is not tolerated.

12. Be enthusiastic! Children respond well to positive, stimulating environments. Breed enthusiasm in the pool, in the gym, or on the playing field. As Maureen Weiss says, enthusiasm is contagious! Smile, interact, and listen.

Finally, coaches have been found to have limited awareness of their actual coaching behaviors (Cushion, Ford, & Williams, 2012). It is very important that youth sport coaches understand the ways they are behaving, perhaps through the use of techniques such as video analysis, and take the time to reflect on their coaching actions.

Role of Parents

In recent years considerable attention has been given to better understanding and identifying the role that parents play in youth sport and physical activity participation. Much of this increased interest has been stirred by accounts in the popular press of the negative side effects that children's participation in sport can cause. For example, Joan Ryan's (1995) bestselling

Parents can have a positive effect on their children's sporting experiences when they use appropriate practices and guard against the creation of a negative environment.

book *Little Girls in Pretty Boxes* presented heartbreaking stories of young girls whose dreams of becoming Olympic gymnasts and figure skaters were shattered by unhealthy and abusive training environments, often fueled by overly involved, pushy parents. Parental concerns are not limited to elite youth sport: Accounts of overzealous "Little League" parents pushing their children on the playing field or in the gym are all too common in every community. One national survey of junior tennis coaches, for example, found that 3 of 10 parents do things that interfere with their child's development (Gould, Lauer, Rolo, Jannes, & Pennisi, 2006).

Parenting Research in Youth Sport

Responding to these concerns, sport psychologists have begun to examine the role of parents in children's sport. Krane, Greenleaf, and Snow (1997), for example, conducted a case study of a former elite youth gymnast. The researchers found that this athlete participated in an overly competitive, ego goal-oriented environment (e.g., an environment created by coaches and parents who emphasized winning, perfect performance, and performing with or despite pain), which led to an overreliance on social comparison, a need to demonstrate her superiority, and an emphasis on external rewards and feedback. Another result was unhealthy behaviors, such as practicing when seriously injured, disordered eating, overtraining, and refusing to listen to medical advice.

On a more positive note, Fredricks and Eccles (2004) found that parents play a critical role as socializers, role models, providers, and interpreters of their children's sport experience. Brustad (1993), for example, studied male and female youth basketball participants and their parents and found that parental enjoyment of physical activity was related to parents encouraging their children's involvement and, in turn, that the encouragement influenced the child's perceived competence and actual participation. In a study of adolescent elite soccer players, VanYperen (1995) found that parental support buffered the youngsters who might otherwise have suffered adverse, stress-related effects after their below-average soccer performances. Duda and Hom (1993) demonstrated that children's goal orientations were significantly related to those adopted by their parents. Finally, Wuerth, Lee, and Alfermann (2004) found that pressure perceived by young athletes was related to directing and controlling parental behaviors. These studies all showed

ways in which the climate provided by the parents influenced (positively or negatively) the child's sport experience.

One final example of parental influence appears in an interview study of youth sport coaches. Strean (1995) identified instances of parents interfering with or facilitating children's involvement in a sport program. Negative interference included parents coaching their child from the sidelines in ways that contradicted what the child was told by the official coach, encouraging their child to fight, or saying vicious things to opposing players. Facilitating actions included parents positively affecting the motivation of their children and disciplining their child for misbehaving in practices.

Although research has documented increasing issues with youth sport parents, this does not explain why parents are behaving the way they are. Coakley (2006) suggests that family life expectations have changed dramatically over the past several decades and that today's parents are held increasingly responsible for the actions of their children. This standard, then, forms a basis of what society views as good parenting; parents' success is tied to the achievements and success of their children. Because sport provides objective measures of success, parents invest tremendous amounts of time and money in their child athletes. This causes the parents to become overly involved and do things that interfere with healthy development. Thus, Coakley contends that because their child's success reflects their worth as parents, parents are becoming overinvolved in their children's sport experiences.

Sport parenting research has flourished in recent years: A recent review of the literature shows that more than 100 studies have been conducted on the topic (Gould, Cowburn, & Pierce, 2013). Key conclusions include the following:

1. Sport parenting matters and has important influences on young athletes' attitudes, dispositions, motivation, affective responses, and behavior at all stages of the athletic talent development process.

2. Factors influencing sport parenting include parents' personality dispositions, parenting styles, expectations, attitudes, and behaviors and the climates they help create.

3. Sport parenting is a complex process that changes as the child matures physically, psychologically, and socially and depends on what type of

program the child enters and his or her stage of athlete talent development.

4. Although it is clear that the actions of parents have a number of important consequences on child athletes and that certain types of sport parenting practices are correlated with positive and negative developmental outcomes, there is no one correct way to sport parent. Effective sport parenting depends on the child, his or her stage of development, the parent, and the context. Because these variables constantly change, effective parenting practices are likely to change as well.

5. The majority of young athletes believe that their parents have a positive influence on their sporting experience. However, some parents are overbearing, and they often damage the relationship they have with their child or cause problems related to longer term athletic and personal development.

6. The more aligned parent and child perceptions, attitudes, and belief are, the more likely the child will have a positive youth sport experience.

7. Parents have stereotypes about youths and sport; for example, football is appropriate for boys but not girls. These stereotypes influence the parents' own perceptions, attitudes, and behaviors and then those of their child.

8. Parents have a strong influence in creating and altering the motivational climate for youths in sport. A mastery, task-oriented climate is most often found to create the most beneficial experience for youths in sport, whereas ego-oriented climates are most often associated with less positive behaviors and affect.

9. Parental pressure is a major issue in youth sport. Some pressure may be beneficial for young athletes. For example, highly supportive parents of many elite athletes were found to challenge their child to push themselves and do their best (e.g., high support/high challenge). Yet too much pressure is consistently reported to have negative effects on young athletes. Unfortunately, although the idea of optimal parental push has been identified, no complete or definitive understanding of what this entails exists.

10. Sport parenting behaviors, attitudes, and expectations that help youths enjoy the athletic experience and enhance their learning and performance include providing financial, logistical, and socioemotional support and sport opportunities; exhibiting unconditional love; making sacrifices for the player; and emphasizing hard work and maintaining a positive attitude.

11. Competitive success can be achieved with both developmentally appropriate and inappropriate sport parenting. However, developmentally inappropriate sport parenting often is associated with some type of negative consequence, such as damaged parent–child relationships or fluctuations in player motivation and burnout.

Researchers, then, have found that parents can play a highly positive or a highly negative role in the youth sport experience. The challenge for people involved in youth sport is to identify the precise ways in which parents can positively affect the experience for youngsters and to encourage parents to use these practices. Simultaneously, we must identify negative actions and facilitate efforts to eliminate them.

Educating Parents

Although negative parental behaviors will never be completely eliminated from youth sport, much can be accomplished by educating parents and improving the lines of communication among parents, coaches, and league organizers. The American Sport Education Program (1994), for instance, has developed a sport parent program that offers excellent suggestions concerning parental responsibilities and practices (see "Sport Parent Responsibilities and Code of Conduct"). Additionally, parent orientation meetings should take place at the start of the season to inform parents and to discuss such things as the coach's qualifications; program philosophy; the roles played by coach, parent, and athlete; good sporting behavior; and team rules. Having an assistant coach or parent as a liaison is also an excellent way to maintain good lines of communication (Strean, 1995).

VIEW Activity 22.2 helps you determine what to include in a youth sport parent orientation program.

The Professionalization of Children's Sports

Although sport certainly has a number of benefits for youths, concern is growing on the part of athletic administrators (e.g., Roberts, 2001), sport psychologists (e.g., Gould, 2009), and journalists (e.g., Farrey, 2008) that youth sport is becoming increasing professionalized in the sense that the focus is shifting from physical, social, and psychological development to more extrinsic goals such as winning, rankings, renown, and earning college athletic scholarships. A professionalized approach to youth sport is also characterized by **early sport specialization**, year-round intense training, and private coaching. In his provocative book *Game On: The All-American Race to Make Champions of Our Children,* journalist Tom Farrey (2008) provides evidence of professionalization by discussing the world golf championships for children aged 6 years and under, examples of parents going to sperm banks and buying elite athlete sperm in the hopes of producing more athletic offspring, and coaches recruiting children to build powerhouse teams to compete in the Little League World Series of baseball.

Most sport scientists are opposed to taking a professionalized approach to youth sport because this focuses the majority of resources on only the most talented children and ignores the majority of young people who can physically, psychologically, and socially develop through sport but won't become elite athletes. The professionalized approach is typically based on folklore and not on a scientific understanding of athletic talent development and may actually impede the long-term development of athletic talent (see "Stages of Athletic Talent Development" and "Sport Specialization Guidelines"). Gould and Carson (2004) identified a number

Sport Parent Responsibilities and Code of Conduct

Responsibilities

1. Encourage your children to play sports, but don't pressure them. Let your child choose to play and to quit if he or she wants to.
2. Understand what your child wants from sport, and provide a supportive atmosphere for achieving those goals.
3. Set limits on your child's participation in sport. Determine when your child is physically and emotionally ready to play and ensure that the conditions for playing are safe.
4. Make sure that the coach is qualified to guide your child through the sport experience.
5. Keep winning in perspective, and help your child do the same.
6. Help your child set realistic performance goals.
7. Help your child understand the valuable lessons sports can teach.
8. Help your child meet his or her responsibilities to the team and the coach.
9. Discipline your child appropriately when necessary.
10. Turn your child over to the coach at practices and games; don't meddle or coach from the stands.
11. Supply the coach with information regarding any allergies or special health conditions your child has. Make sure your child takes any necessary medications to games and practices.

Code of Conduct

1. Remain in the spectator area during games.
2. Don't advise the coach on how to coach.
3. Don't make derogatory comments to coaches, officials, or parents of either team.
4. Don't try to coach your child during the contest.
5. Don't drink alcohol at contests or come to a contest having drunk too much.
6. Cheer for your child's team.
7. Show interest, enthusiasm, and support for your child.
8. Be in control of your emotions.
9. Help when asked to do so by coaches or officials.
10. Thank coaches, officials, and other volunteers who conduct the event.

Adapted, by permission, from American Sports Education Program, 1994, *SportParent* (Champaign, IL: Human Kinetics), 29, 30.

of myths associated with the professionalized approach to athletic talent development in youths. Those interested in working with talented young athletes should keep these myths in mind.

• *Myth 1: Athletic talent can be accurately predicted at a young age.* Because of variations in children's maturational, motivational, and learning rates, it is very difficult to accurately predict before puberty which children will become the most talented adult athletes. Children should be encouraged to try multiple sports and develop a wide array of fundamental motor skills.

• *Myth 2: More is always better!* Although research shows it takes thousands of hours of deliberate practice and play to become an expert athlete, amounts of practice must be developmentally appropriate in order to prevent injury and burnout. Adult dosages of practices and competitions are inappropriate for children and youths.

• *Myth 3: Stages of talent development can be skipped.* To tolerate the high dosages of intense training and competition at elite levels of sport, athletes must first develop fundamentals and a love of the game. They must progress through the stages of athletic talent development in developmentally appropriate ways.

• *Myth 4: Intense training will lead to a college athletic scholarship.* Well under 5% of young athletes will earn college scholarships, and even fewer will play at the professional levels. Having the goal of earning a college athletic scholarship as the sole focus of youth sport participation is simply a bad bet!

• *Myth 5: Early single-sport specialization is essential.* Although most elite athletes begin playing their primary sport at a young age, they typically play a number of sports and in doing so stay motivated and develop fundamental physical proficiencies that underlie elite athletic development.

• *Myth 6: A child cannot have fun if he is going to be an elite athlete.* Although elite sport requires tremendous effort and focus, enjoyment, fun, and love of the game are essential to sustaining motivation and controlling anxiety. Finding ways to make sport fun is essential at all levels of athletic talent development.

• *Myth 7: Talented children need different entry programs and coaching approaches than their less talented counterparts.* All children need to develop fundamental skills in an enjoyable atmosphere at the entry levels of sport. Only later are special programs and coaching needed.

Sport psychologists are not suggesting that opportunities for athletic talent development should not be provided for young people but rather that programs must be carried out in developmentally appropriate ways, guided by scientific evidence, and not pushed on children at younger and younger ages.

An excellent example of how talent can be appropriately developed comes from women's tennis today, though we would not have seen it in the past. In the 1990s, female tennis players were turning professional at very young ages, and major concerns were being voiced about stress, injuries, exploitation, and burnout. To ensure the safety of the players, the Women's Tennis Association Tour consulted with experts and instituted an age-eligibility rule that restricted the amount of play for the youngest participants and increased the amounts of tournament play allowed as the players aged.

In 2004, the WTA Professional Development Advisory Panel evaluated the success of the rule in ensuring the psychological and physical health of players over its 10 years of existence (Otis et al., 2006). Surveys were administered, experts were interviewed, and data on players' careers were statistically analyzed. The findings supported the effectiveness of the rule: More than 75% of the more than 600 survey respondents supported the principles of the rule, and 90% indicated a need for it. The survey also showed that stress was reduced, players had longer careers (career length increased by 43%), and premature retirement declined (7% of players left the tour before age 21 before the rule was implemented and less than 1% after). Using a sport science approach to talent development, then, was shown to counteract negative effects of youth sport participation, protect the health of players, and strengthen the game at the professional ranks.

Understanding the Tricky Business of Parental Support

Finally, as professionals we must appreciate how difficult the job of successful sport parenting really is. It is easy to blame parents for inappropriate actions and problems in our programs. Unfortunately, however, when children are born they do not come with a sport involvement instruction manual, and most parents have had scant training in sport parenting. Moreover, as the child grows and develops, the role of the sport parent changes. For instance, research has shown that before age 10, youngsters feel a much greater effect from parental feedback, whereas after age 10, peer feedback becomes much more important to them (Horn & Weiss, 1991).

An excellent example of the tricky business of parental support comes from the youth sport burnout research discussed in chapter 21. Junior tennis players who had burned out from tennis indicated that an optimal amount of parental push exists. That is, these young athletes indicated that at times they needed their parents to push them—for example, getting them out of bed to practice when they were being lazy. However, the players also mentioned that such pushing was appropriate only up to a point and that parents who became overly involved in tennis created a great deal of stress and contributed to burnout. A critical role for the exercise and sport science professional, then, is to educate parents about how they can help optimize their child's sport experience.

Sport Specialization Guidelines

The International Society of Sport Psychology published a position stand on sport specialization (Côté, Lidor, & Hackfort, 2009) that advances seven postulates. These postulates, based on existing research in the area, are as follows:

1. Early diversification (sampling a number of different sports) does not hinder elite sport participation in sports in which peak performance is reached after maturation.

2. Early diversification (sampling) is linked to a longer sport career and has positive implications for long-term sport involvement.

3. Early diversification (sampling) allows participation in a range of contexts that most favorably affects positive youth development.

4. High amounts of deliberate play during the sampling years build a solid foundation of intrinsic motivation through involvement in activities that are enjoyable and promote intrinsic regulation.

5. A high amount of deliberate play during the sampling years establishes a range of motor and cognitive experiences that children can ultimately bring to their principal sport interest.

6. Around the end of primary school (about age 13), children should have the opportunity to either choose to specialize in their favorite sport or to continue in sport at a recreational level.

7. Late adolescents (around age 16) have developed the physical, cognitive, social, emotional, and motor skills needed to invest their effort into highly specialized training in one sport.

Postulates reprinted from Côté, Lidor, and Hackfort, 2009.

Stages of Athletic Talent Development

Extending the classic research of Bloom (1985), several investigators (Côté, 1999; Durand-Bush & Salmela, 2002; Gould, Dieffenbach, & Moffett, 2002) examined the history of talent development in elite athletes and found that champion athletes go through various phases of involvement, as follows.

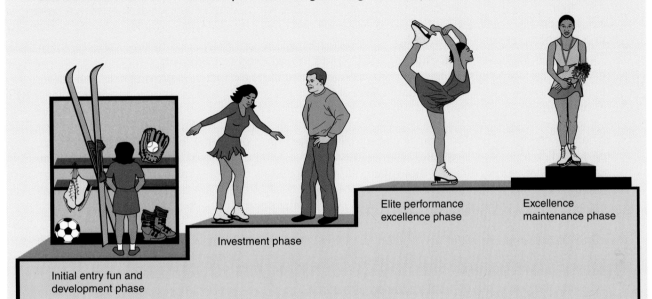

Initial entry fun and development phase

Investment phase

Elite performance excellence phase

Excellence maintenance phase

1. *Entry or initial phase*—The child tries various sports and develops a love of the sport that she ends up specializing in later. The focus of participation is on fun and development, and the child receives encouragement from significant others, is free to explore the activity, and achieves a good deal of success. Parents instill the value of hard work and doing things well but typically do not emphasize winning as the primary goal of participation.

2. *Investment phase*—Talent is recognized, and the child begins to specialize in one sport. An expert coach or teacher promotes long-term systematic talent development in the individual. The focus is on technical mastery, tactical development, and excellence in skill development. Parents provide extensive logistical, time, emotional, and financial support.

3. *Elite performance excellence phase*—The athlete is recognized as truly elite and practices many hours a day under the supervision of a master coach. The goal is to turn training and technical skills into personalized performance excellence. Everyone involved realizes that the activity is very significant in the athlete's life. Parents are less involved but are an important source of social support.

4. *Excellence maintenance phase*—The athlete is recognized as exceptional and focuses on maintaining the excellence he has achieved. Considerable demands are placed on the athlete.

Most interesting in this research is the finding that most champion athletes did not start out their sport careers with aspirations to be elite champions (nor did the parents have these aspirations for the child). Instead, these individuals were exposed to active lifestyles and numerous sports and were encouraged to participate for fun and development. They participated in many sports and then found the right sport for their body type and mental makeup. Only later, after they fell in love with the activity and showed talent, did they develop elite sport aspirations. Moreover, once these athletes developed elite competitor dreams, parents and coaches provided them with the support they needed to turn dreams into reality. This research, then, emphasizes the importance of children *not* specializing in sports too early, of focusing on fun and development early, and of having highly supportive but not overbearing parents.

LEARNING AIDS

SUMMARY

1. **Discuss the importance of studying the psychology of the young athlete.**

   Applying strategies from sport psychology is vital in youth sport settings because children are at such critical points in their developmental cycles. Qualified adult leadership is crucial to ensure a beneficial experience. Moreover, the youth sport experience can have important lifelong effects on the personality and psychological development of children.

2. **Explain the major reasons children participate in and drop out of sport.**

   Children cite many reasons for sport participation, including having fun, improving skills, and being with friends. They also have various reasons for dropping out of sport, including new or additional interests in other activities. Underlying these motives is the young athlete's need to feel worthy and competent. Children who perceive themselves as competent seek out participation and stay involved in sport, whereas children who see themselves as failing often drop out. Adult leaders can facilitate children's participation in sport activity and deter withdrawal in a number of ways: structuring the environment to encourage the young athletes' motivation, enhancing self-worth by focusing on individual performance goals and downplaying social comparison or outcome goals, tracking participation and dropout statistics, and conducting exit interviews to determine why youngsters discontinue program involvement.

3. **Discuss the importance of peer relationships in youth sport.**

   Peer relationships in youth sport affect a child's sense of acceptance, level of motivation, and self-esteem. Adult leaders should provide time for children to be with friends and make new friends, encourage positive peer reinforcement, emphasize teamwork and the pursuit of group goals, and teach children to respect others and refrain from verbal aggression.

4. **Describe stress and burnout effects in young athletes.**

   Most young athletes do not have excessive levels of competitive stress in sport, but a significant minority do. High trait anxiety, low self-esteem, low self-performance expectations, frequent worry about evaluation, less fun and satisfaction, and parental pressure combine to put children at risk for excessive state anxiety. Losing a competition, attaching great importance to an event, and individual events are situational factors that add to stress. Stress-induced burnout is a specialized withdrawal in which a young athlete discontinues or curtails involvement in response to long-term stress. Knowing potential causes of burnout helps adults teach children to cope with stress. Arousal management techniques can be adapted for use with children.

5. **Identify and explain how to apply effective coaching practices with youngsters.**

   Research findings in sport psychology have clearly shown that certain coaching behaviors are associated with positive psychological development in children. Effective coaching behaviors include having realistic expectations; using techniques that provide youngsters with positive, encouraging, and sincere feedback; rewarding effort and correct technique as much as outcomes; modifying skill requirements and rules; and using a positive approach to error correction. Following the 12 guidelines in this chapter can create a good sport environment for children.

6. **Discuss the role of parental involvement in youth sport.**

   Parents play a particularly important role in the youth sport experience. Parental attitudes and behaviors have major effects, both positive and negative, on young athletes' sport involvement, motivation, self-esteem, and mental health. Educating parents and maintaining open lines of coach–parent communication are important ways to ensure beneficial parental influence in children's sport. Successful parenting for youth sport can be difficult but is worthwhile.

KEY TERMS

perceived competence   sport-general dropouts   early sport specialization
sport-specific dropouts   affiliation motive

REVIEW QUESTIONS

1. Why is it important for people who work with young athletes to know sport psychology?
2. What reasons do children cite for sport participation and withdrawal? How does a child's level of perceived athletic competence relate to participation and withdrawal?
3. Distinguish between sport-specific and sport-general withdrawal. Why is this distinction important?
4. What are the positive and negative components of peer relationships in young athletes? Why are these important?
5. Are young athletes placed under too much stress in sport? What children in what situations are at risk of experiencing the highest levels of stress?
6. What is burnout? What causes young athletes to burn out of sport?
7. What can be done to help young athletes cope with stress? What strategies can be used?
8. What were the major findings of the research by Smith, Smoll, and their colleagues?
9. Describe how parents influence the youth sport experience.
10. Discuss four myths surrounding young athletes, including how they might be used by a coach.

CRITICAL THINKING QUESTIONS

1. You are working as a youth sport director of a YMCA that sponsors numerous sport programs. Based on what you learned in this chapter, what policies and programs would you initiate to ensure positive psychological experiences for the children involved?
2. You are the coach of a middle school basketball program. Identify and outline topics that would be important to discuss in a parent orientation meeting for a team of 10- to 12-year-old athletes.
3. You are thinking about some early specialization training for your athletic child. Using the research and guidelines presented regarding early specialization in sport, discuss why you would or would not involve your child in early specialization.

23

Aggression
in Sport

After reading this chapter, you should be able to

1. define aggression,
2. identify the causes of aggression,
3. examine special considerations relative to aggression and sport,
4. explain the aggression–performance relationship, and
5. derive from research implications for helping to control aggression.

Who can forget the much-publicized NBA Detroit Pistons–Indiana Pacers brawl that involved a number of players and fans and resulted in the Pacers' Ron Artest receiving a 140-game suspension for going into the stands to fight unruly Pistons fans? Or when in ice hockey Todd Bertuzzi of the Vancouver Canucks blind-sided rookie Steve Moore with a punch to the head and a subsequent face-first push to the ice? Moore suffered broken neck vertebrae and a concussion in this violent act that ended his NHL career, whereas Bertuzzi was suspended from the league and convicted in the Canadian courts for his role in the assault. In another ice hockey incident, a firestorm of controversy arose when a local youth coach was caught conducting a drill in which his players paired up and practiced taking off their helmets and gloves and fist-fighting until one drew blood. Even more unbelievable than the drill was the reaction of some members of the ice hockey community who did not think the coach's actions were inappropriate!

Unfortunately, incidents of aggression like these are becoming all too common throughout the sport world. We see it in the bleachers, on the benches, and most commonly on the fields or courts of sport arenas: bench-clearing brawls, brushback pitches and retaliatory beanings, and ice hockey fights. Fan behavior at professional soccer matches has become so violent that it led to a decision to dig moats and construct electric fences. Still other examples of unbridled aggression are citywide rioting to "celebrate" championship wins, stalkers preying on star athletes, weapons uncovered at high school football games, an Australian sport psychologist held hostage at gunpoint by a disgruntled athlete, and a frenzied fan attacking a popular tennis star during a break between games. Even Little League coaches settle altercations with their fists, and one father murdered a coach in a dispute over his son's playing time. Numerous acts of aggression are aimed at officials. For instance, more than 90% of ice hockey referees have reported that they were recipients of verbal abuse and 46% have reported that referees in general are recipients of physical abuse (Ackery, Tator, & Snider, 2012).

We have all witnessed the increased violence in our schools. Fist-fighting by itself is bad enough, but more and more children are bringing knives and guns to school and using them to deal with conflicts that may arise. This has caused school administrators to hire security guards and use metal detectors, and it has created a climate of fear for students and teachers alike. Security guards and metal detectors, though necessary, are not enough. Children must be taught the skills of nonviolent conflict resolution. Sport has the potential to be a vehicle for controlling or curbing violence. Midnight inner-city basketball games have become popular because they are thought to keep gang members off the street; many people see boxing, wrestling, and, to a lesser extent, football as socially acceptable channels for aggression. Others see these very sports as primarily aggressive. Given these examples, it is clear that aggression is a major concern for those involved in sport. Before we can begin to examine these issues, however, we must understand what aggression is and is not.

Defining Aggression

The term **aggression** is used in several ways in sport and exercise. We speak of "good" aggression (e.g., going after a loose ball in volleyball or lowering your shoulder in a drive toward the basket) and "bad" aggression (e.g., taking a cheap shot in soccer or committing a flagrant foul in basketball). The term seems to draw automatic associations and produce positive or negative value judgments and emotional responses (Gill, 2000). However, most aggressive behavior in sport and physical activity settings appear not to be inherently desirable or undesirable; instead, whether it is good or bad seems to depend on interpretation. Two people watching a particularly hard but clean check in ice hockey might disagree on whether the hit was good or bad aggression. Aggression is easier to talk about if you avoid the good–bad dichotomy and instead view it neutrally—as a behavior you want to understand (Gill & Williams, 2008).

Criteria for Aggression

Psychologists define aggression as "any form of behavior directed toward the goal of harming or injuring another living being who is motivated to avoid

such treatment" (Baron & Richardson, 1994, p. 7). As we examine this and similar definitions, four criteria of aggression emerge (Gill & Williams, 2008):

- It is a behavior.
- It involves intent.
- It involves harm or injury.
- It is directed toward a living organism.

Aggression is physical or verbal behavior; it is not an attitude or emotion. Aggression involves harm or injury, which may be either physical or psychological (e.g., we would all agree that hitting someone with a baseball bat is an aggressive act, but so too is purposely embarrassing someone, saying something hurtful, purposefully making someone feel inadequate, or trying to intimidate someone). Aggression is directed toward another living thing. Punching someone is certainly aggressive, as is slapping a cat that scratches your new chair. But throwing your helmet in disgust after striking out in softball, although in bad taste, is not aggressive. Finally, aggression is also intentional. Accidental harm, even unintentionally shooting someone, is not aggressive when harm was not intended.

> **KEY POINT** Aggression is defined as any behavior directed toward intentionally harming or injuring another living being.

When sport psychologists discuss aggression in general, they are referring to what many people would call "bad" aggression. But not all "bad" aggression is aggressive according to the sport psychology definition. What many people call examples of good aggression in sport (e.g., charging the net in tennis) are labeled *assertive* behaviors by most sport psychologists (e.g., Widmeyer, Dorsch, Bray, & McGuire, 2002)—that is, playing within the rules with high intensity and emotion but without intention to do harm.

Now that you're getting comfortable with this new way of thinking about aggression, take the test in "Aggressive or Nonaggressive?" to check your understanding of the criteria that mark aggression.

Hostile and Instrumental Aggression

Psychologists distinguish two types of aggression (Husman & Silva, 1984): hostile (or reactive) aggression and instrumental aggression. With **hostile**

Whether aggression in sport is good or bad often depends on one's perception.

© Panoramic/Photoshot

aggression the primary goal is to inflict injury or psychological harm on someone else. **Instrumental aggression**, on the other hand, occurs in the quest of some nonaggressive goal. For instance, when a boxer lands a solid blow to an opponent's head, injury or harm is usually inflicted. However, such an action is usually an example of instrumental aggression: The boxer's primary goal is to win the bout, and he can do that by inflicting harm on his opponent (e.g., scoring points or knocking the opponent out). If a boxer pinned his opponent to the ropes and purposely tried to punish him with blows to the head and body while consciously trying not to end the match, this would qualify as hostile (reactive) aggression.

KEY POINT   In hostile aggression, the primary goal is to inflict injury or psychological harm on another, whereas instrumental aggression occurs in the quest of some nonaggressive goal.

Although the distinction between instrumental and hostile aggression has been stressed for many years, Anderson and Bushman (2002) argued that thinking of these two types of aggression as a simple dichotomy is too simplistic. Supporting this argument is an observation study of aggressive acts in sport, in which Kirker, Tenenbaum, and Mattson (2000) reported that the clear majority of instrumental aggressive acts occur in conjunction with some type of reactive process. Specifically, they cited an example from their study of an athlete who planned to attack an opposing player for strategic reasons (instrumental aggression) but did not do so until the opposing player frustrated and angered him (reactive aggression). Because of findings such as this, Anderson and Bushman (2002) argued that we should think of hostile and instrumental aggression as anchoring the opposite ends of a continuum and recognize that at times aggression might involve elements of both types.

The previous argument notwithstanding, most aggression in sport is much more instrumental than reactive, such as these examples:

- A wrestler squeezes an opponent's ribs to create discomfort and turn him over.
- A cornerback delivers a particularly hard hit to a receiver to deter him from running a pass route across the middle of the field.
- A basketball coach calls a time-out when an opposing player is on the foul line, trying to cause psychological discomfort (heightened state anxiety) and poor performance.

Aggressive or Nonaggressive?

Using Gill's four criteria, circle A or N to indicate whether you consider the behavior in each of these situations to be aggressive (A) or nonaggressive (N).

A N 1. A football safety delivers an extremely vicious but legal hit to a wide receiver and later indicates he wanted to punish the receiver and make him think twice about coming across the middle again.

A N 2. A football safety delivers an extremely vicious and illegal hit to a wide receiver.

A N 3. A basketball coach breaks a chair in protesting a disputed call.

A N 4. Marcia, a field hockey midfielder, uses her stick to purposely hit her opponent in the shin in retaliation for her opponent doing the same thing to her.

A N 5. A race car driver kills a fellow competitor by running into the competitor's stalled car coming out of a turn.

A N 6. Trying to make a field-goal kicker on the opposing team worry and think about the negative ramifications of a game-winning field goal, Coach Sullivan calls a time-out.

A N 7. Barry knows that John is sensitive and self-conscious about his ability to putt under pressure, so he falsely tells John that Coach Hall said he will be replaced in the lineup if he does not putt better.

A N 8. Jane beans Fran with a fastball that got away from her.

Answers

1. Aggressive. (Although the hit was legal, the intent was to inflict harm.)
2. Nonaggressive. (There was no intent to inflict harm.)
3. Nonaggressive. (The action was not directed at another living being.)
4. Aggressive. (Although the athlete believed she had been hit first, her intent was to inflict harm.)
5. Nonaggressive. (Although the other driver was killed, there was no intent to do harm.)
6. Aggressive. (Although many would consider this a tactically smart move, the intent was to inflict psychological harm on another in the form of fear and anxiety.)
7. Aggressive. (As in question 6, the intent was to inflict psychological harm.)
8. Nonaggressive. (Although harm resulted, there was no intent to harm.)

Adapted from R. Martens, 1982, Kids sports: A den of iniquity or land of promise. In *Children in sport*, edited by R.A. Magill, M.J. Ash, and F.L. Smoll (Champaign, IL: Human Kinetics), 204-218.

KEY POINT Professionals in sport and exercise science must have well-thought-out philosophies that distinguish between acceptable assertive behavior, unacceptable instrumental aggressive behavior, and unacceptable antisocial behavior.

Of course, hostile and instrumental aggression both involve the intent to injure and harm and often cannot be clearly distinguished. Although most sporting aggression is primarily instrumental, that does not make it acceptable.

Finally, some researchers have examined antisocial behavior that includes actions such as vandalism, unwanted sexual advances, humiliating someone, or yelling insults (O'Brien, Kolt, Martens, Ruffman, Miller, & Lynott, 2012). These may or may not involve aggression but certainly have important consequences for both participants and society.

Regardless of whether one is studying aggression or antisocial behavior, one thing is clear: Professionals in sport and exercise science must have a well-thought-out philosophy regarding what is acceptable assertive behavior, what is unacceptable instrumental aggressive behavior, and what is unacceptable antisocial behavior. Let's now examine causes of aggression. Understanding the causes of aggression might help us reduce the occurrence of aggressive acts.

Understanding the Causes of Aggression

Why are some children more aggressive than others? What causes some athletes to lose control? Are aggressive individuals born, or are they a product of their environment? Psychologists have historically advanced four important theories regarding causes of aggression: instinct theory, frustration–aggression theory, social learning theory, and revised frustration–aggression theory. Moreover, Anderson and Bushman (2002) offered a unifying framework that cuts across the various theories and ties together much of the current thinking on aggression. We next discuss each of these theories.

Instinct Theory

According to the **instinct theory** (Gill, 2000), people have an innate instinct to be aggressive that builds up until it must inevitably be expressed. This instinct can either be expressed directly through an attack on another living being or be displaced through **catharsis**, in which aggression is released or "blown off" through socially acceptable means such as sport. Thus, for an instinct theorist, sport and exercise play an extremely important function in society in that they allow people to channel their aggressive instincts in socially acceptable ways. Unfortunately, no biologically innate aggressive instinct has ever been identified, although research does show that variants of the serotonin transporter gene influence aggression (Sysoeva, Kulikova, Malyuchenko, Tonevitskii, & Ivanitskii, 2010). There is also no support for the notion of catharsis. Therefore, we cannot cite the instinct theory in claiming that physical education and sport programs provide a socially acceptable means of channeling natural aggressive urges.

KEY POINT Little support exists for the instinct theory of aggression or its tangential notion of catharsis.

Frustration–Aggression Theory

The **frustration–aggression theory**, sometimes called the drive theory, states simply that aggression is the direct result of a frustration that occurs because of goal blockage or failure (Dollard, Doob, Miller, Mowrer, & Sears, 1939). The hypothesis at first made intuitive sense to psychologists because most aggressive acts are committed when people are frustrated. For example, when a soccer player believes she has been illegally held by her opponent, she becomes frustrated and takes a swing at the defender. However, this view has little support today because of its insistence that frustration must always cause aggression. Research and experience repeatedly show that people often cope with their frustration or express it in nonaggressive ways.

- Little evidence shows that frustrated athletes lower their levels of aggression by participating in contact sports.
- The frustration–aggression theory, which maintains that frustration always causes aggression, is generally dismissed today.

According to the frustration–aggression theorists' counterargument, aggressive responses that occur are not always obvious: They may get channeled through socially acceptable outlets such as competitive contact sports. Thus, like instinct theorists, frustration–aggression proponents view catharsis as playing a major role. As we've mentioned, little evidence exists of catharsis in sport. Consequently, there's also little evidence that participation in contact sports lowers the aggression levels of frustrated, aggressive participants (Gill & Williams, 2008). In fact, in some instances these participants become more aggressive (Arms, Russell, & Sandilands, 1979). Despite its shortcomings, the frustration–aggression hypothesis has contributed a valuable awareness of the role of frustration in the aggression process.

Social Learning Theory

Social learning theory explains aggression as behavior that people learn through observing others who model particular behaviors and by receiving reinforcement for exhibiting similar actions. Psychologist Albert Bandura (1973) found that children who watched adult models commit violent acts (beat up "bobo dolls") repeated those acts more than children not exposed to such aggressive models. These modeling effects were especially powerful when the children were reinforced for copying the actions of the adult models.

KEY POINT The social learning theory, which explains aggression as behavior learned through observing others and then having similar behavior reinforced, has considerable scientific support.

Consistent with the tenets of social learning theory, researchers also convincingly demonstrated that the observation of media violence is positively related to aggression, with correlations exceeding those of homework and academic achievement, passive smoking and lung cancer, and condom use and sexually transmitted human immunodeficiency virus (Bushman & Anderson, 2001). Specifically, this research suggests that all individuals (especially children) are exposed to countless incidents of violence in the media and learn many ways to be aggressive. Thus, many individuals socially learn that such actions are appropriate ways to handle disagreements and confrontations. Although sport violence was not the specific focus of these studies, we have all witnessed the frequency with which the media portray violence in sport, and there is no reason to believe that young athletes are affected any less by media violence than are children in general.

Sport psychologists and sport sociologists have studied ice hockey because of the pervasiveness of illegal aggressive actions, such as fighting, in the sport. Smith (1988) found that the violence prevalent in the professional game is modeled by young amateur players. In fact, aggression is valued in ice hockey, and players quickly learn that being aggressive is a way to gain personal recognition. Many coaches, parents, and teammates accept and reinforce these aggressive acts. Young hockey players watch their heroes on television modeling aggressive behavior and later receive reinforcement for exhibiting similar behavior. Even the type of league can convey signals about aggression. Emery, McKay, Campbell, and Peters (2009) found that youth ice hockey players who played in leagues that allowed checking had more positive attitudes about checking and scored higher on an aggression measure than did players who played in nonchecking leagues.

Gee and Leith (2007) also found support for social learning theory in a study of aggressive behavior in professional ice hockey. Examining penalty records in 200 NHL games, they found that North American-born players committed significantly more aggressive acts than did European-born players. This is an important finding because for years many in hockey have argued that North American players are socialized to be more aggressive than European players. Interestingly, results also showed that European players who join the NHL are significantly less aggressive than the North Americans when they are rookies but do not differ from the North American players by the time they become veterans. This suggests that European players

adopt the more aggressive North American orientation as they spend more time in the league. These results refute the notion that aggressive behaviors result naturally from the frustration inherent in hockey. In contrast, they are socially learned.

Social learning research in sport shows that most athletes are not taught to be blatantly violent. However, aggression can and does occur in every sport. Recent evidence also indicates that athletes intend to be aggressive during competitions (Widmeyer, Dorsch, Bray, & McGuire, 2002). A figure skater, for example, may attempt to psych out an opponent and make upsetting remarks, such as, "I heard that the judges said a costume like that is illegal this year." This is a subtler example of aggression, but the intent still is to harm another. Most parents and coaches do not condone unprovoked attacks on others, yet aggression is often sanctioned in response to another person's aggressive act. For example, a young basketball player is instructed not to violate rules and hit others, but she is taught to retaliate in kind in a particularly rough game with shoving and elbowing under the boards. Finally, sport psychological research has also shown that illegal aggressive acts in sport (e.g., slashing or hooking in ice hockey) are often not penalized. Therefore, athletes are reinforced by athletic success for such acts (Sheldon & Aimar, 2001).

Social learning theory has considerable scientific support (Bandura, 1977b; Thirer, 1993). It emphasizes the important role that significant others have in the development or control of aggression because modeling and reinforcement are the key ways in which people learn aggressive behavior.

Revised Frustration–Aggression Theory

A **revised frustration–aggression theory**, also referred to as cognitive neoassociation theory by contemporary theorists, combines elements of the original frustration–aggression hypothesis with social learning theory. According to this widely held view, although frustration does not always lead to aggression, it increases the likelihood of aggression by increasing arousal, anger, and other thoughts and emotions (Baron & Richardson, 1994; Berkowitz, 1965, 1969, 1993). However, increased arousal and anger result in aggression only when socially learned cues signal the appropriateness of aggression in the particular situation. If the socially learned cues signal that aggression is inappropriate, it will not result. For example, a football safety who is frustrated after being badly

A Case of Learned Behavior: Aggressive Billy

Seven-year-old Billy, a goalie with the midget hockey league's Buffalo Bombers, gets entangled with teammates and opponents in a skirmish around his net. Billy is hit and dazed but uncertain about who or what hit him. Angry, he retaliates by punching the nearest opponent. The referee throws Billy out of the game. Billy's coach tells him he shouldn't throw a punch because the team needs him and he is of no help sitting on the bench. However, Billy later overhears his coach boast to an assistant, "What a tough competitor that Billy is," which makes Billy feel good.

At home, Billy's dad seems proud of Billy's performance. He tells Billy never to start a fight and just hit anybody out there on the ice, but that he's got to be a man and defend himself: "Hockey is a dog-eat-dog game, and you can't let anybody push you around out there—after all, you don't see the NHL goalies take any guff."

Lately, Billy has become a goalie his opponents fear—anybody in the crease is liable to get extra-rough treatment from him. Billy now watches the pros to learn how to be rough and tough without getting kicked out of the game.

Adapted from R. Martens, 1982. Kids sports: A den of iniquity or land of promise. In *Children in sport,* edited by R.A. Magill, M.J. Ash, and F.L. Smoll (Champaign, IL: Human Kinetics), 204-218.

beaten on a deep pass pattern for a touchdown might lash out at his opponent if his coaches previously tolerated this behavior. However, if he has learned that he will be benched for the next game for lashing out, the aggressive behavior is much less likely to occur.

General Aggression Model

Although the social learning and revised frustration–aggression theories have increased our understanding of aggression in sport, contemporary researchers are finding that aggression is much more complicated than originally thought (Anderson & Bushman, 2002; Widmeyer, Dorsch, Bray, & McGuire, 2002). For example, although it has been found that frustration certainly increases the likelihood of aggression, it is only one situational cause. A variety of personal factors (e.g., beliefs, attitudes) and situational factors (e.g., provocation, hot and crowded venues, incentives for being aggressive) influence aggressive behavior. To help guide those interested in studying and reducing aggression, Anderson and Bushman (2002) have developed a unifying framework (the general aggression model) for understanding aggression.

Figure 23.1 depicts the aggression process, based on Anderson and Bushman's model. First, some

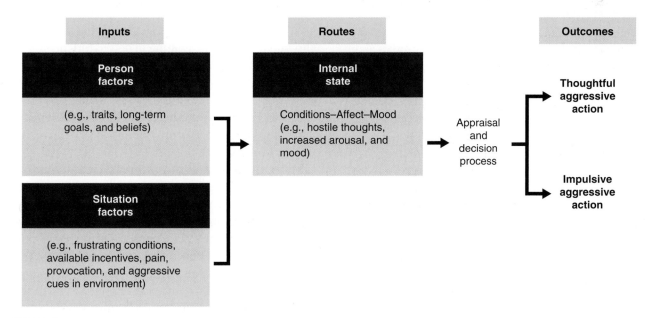

FIGURE 23.1 The general aggression model.

sort of aggressive input exists. Consistent with the person-by-situation interaction view of behavior highlighted throughout this text, for example, both personal and situational factors and their unique interaction determine one's propensity to behave aggressively. That is, personality (e.g., ego-oriented athletes have been found to be more aggressive than task-oriented athletes) and situation (e.g., intense rivalries are associated with increased aggression) will determine the likelihood that someone will be aggressive. As these aggressive inputs are experienced, one's internal state is altered. For instance, an athlete will undergo a change in internal state when he becomes frustrated in some way, perhaps by losing the game or playing poorly, and he may believe that aggression is an appropriate way to settle disputes. The athlete's change in internal state is characterized by increased arousal, mood changes, and hostile thought sequences or schema, which all feed off one another and lead to certain outcomes: a thought-out versus an impulsive aggressive action, depending on how he appraises the input and resulting internal state. Thus, aggression occurs as a result of a complex process mediated by one's thoughts and emotions and caused by the interaction of numerous personal and situational factors.

DISCOVER Activity 23.1 helps you determine when aggression is most likely to occur.

Examining Aggression in Sport: Special Considerations

In addition to testing theories of aggression in the sport setting, sport psychologists have examined other important issues, including spectators and aggression, game reasoning and aggression, moral disengagement and aggression, athletic injuries and aggression, athletic performance and aggression, team moral atmosphere and aggression, sport-specific aggression determinants, sex and cultural differences, and alcohol-related aggression and sport. We discuss each of these in the following sections.

Spectators and Aggression

Competitive sport differs from many activities in that it is usually conducted in the presence of fans and spectators. Fans at games and matches are not usually passive observers—they actively identify with their teams. Their involvement is usually well mannered and supportive, but instances of fan violence appear to be on the rise. In response to concerns about fan violence, sport psychologists have studied spectator aggression.

Psychologists first tested the catharsis theory to determine whether fans become more or less aggressive after watching sporting events. In general, researchers found that observing a sporting event does not lower the level of the spectator's aggression. Moreover, watching some violent contact sports actually increases a spectator's readiness to be aggressive (Wann, Schrader, & Carlson, 2000). However, aggression usually does not occur unless other environmental or game-related factors are present. For instance, studies of hockey spectators have shown that fan aggression is more likely to occur with younger, disadvantaged male spectators in crowded conditions and under the influence of alcohol (Cavanaugh & Silva, 1980; Russell & Arms, 1995). Wann, Culver, Akanda, Daglar, De Divitiis, and Smith (2005) found that losing was associated with a greater propensity toward fan violence, especially when the fans had high team identification. Rivalries are also associated with fan violence. In addition, Smith (1983) found that small-scale aggressive acts on the field (e.g., a brief shoving match between players or a heated argument over a call) were associated with subsequent spectator aggression. Finally, one study showed that aggression (e.g., penalty minutes) in intercollegiate ice hockey was related to fan enjoyment (DeNeui & Sachau, 1996), and another study concluded that some fans who find pleasure in engaging in derogatory behaviors do so because it helps them affirm a positive social or group identity (Amiot, Sansfacon, & Louis, 2013). Thus, fans may be looking for more than good, clean action in games—they may be looking for violent behavior as a source of enjoyment and an affirmation of their social identity.

Sport managers and administrators should be apprised of these findings to help them decrease the probability of violence (e.g., by eliminating sales of alcohol and enforcing strict seating capacities that minimize crowd density). Coaches and players should maintain emotional control on the field to ensure that they are not triggers for fan aggression. Parents should also educate their children about the purposes of sport and the inappropriateness of witnessing aggressive acts as a source of enjoyment.

Game Reasoning and Aggression

An alarming research finding is that many athletes view some aggressive acts as inappropriate in general but appropriate in the sport environment (Bredemeier & Shields, 1984, 1986). For example, fighting is deemed appropriate in certain sport situations (e.g., if a pitcher intentionally beans you), whereas no form of fighting would be tolerated in the school band. This double standard is called **game reasoning** (or *bracketed morality*).

Unfortunately, people are learning and believing that it is okay to be more aggressive in sport than in other life contexts. This presents a problem. First, aggression carries the risk of injury and harm. Also, sport can and should teach children how to behave appropriately inside and outside of sport. Allowing (or applauding) aggressive behavior in sport sends the wrong message to children. Sport professionals must specifically define appropriate behavior and make clear that any form of aggression not sanctioned in society is also inappropriate in sport.

Interestingly, on banning Latrell Sprewell for attacking his coach, NBA commissioner David Stern said, "A sports league does not have to accept or con-

Can aggressive behavior by one teammate lead to increased team performance and team morale? Is that increase in aggressive behavior worth it?

Doug Murray/Icon SMI

done behavior that would not be tolerated in any other segment of society" (Mihoces, 1997), clearly showing that bracketed morality would not be tolerated. Fan reaction supported the action taken by Stern and the league, which we hope signals a change in a previously accepting attitude toward bracketed morality in sport.

Moral Disengagement and Aggression

A growing body of research on aggression in sport focuses on moral disengagement, or how athletes self-regulate and justify their aggressive actions (Boardley & Kavussanu, 2011; Traclet, Romand, Moret, & Kavussanu, 2011). This work has been guided by Bandura's (1999) social cognitive theory of moral thought and action, which identifies eight psychosocial mechanisms for justifying one's aggressive action. These mechanisms include displacing responsibility to others (e.g., officials) or cognitively restructuring the violent action so that it is not viewed as immoral. To determine the types of moral disengagement used in sport, Traclet and colleagues (2011) interviewed 30 soccer players after they had viewed video clips of aggressive and antisocial behaviors that occurred in games. Findings revealed that moral disengagement was relevant as the players gave two or more justifications for each clip they saw; displacement of responsibility to others (e.g., "Pro players do it, so we do it as well") and moral justification (e.g., "My job is to prevent my opponent from scoring no matter what it takes") occurred most often. Studying moral disengagement helps us better understand why people commit aggressive acts even when they know they are wrong.

Athletic Injuries and Aggression

In addition to the ethical issues regarding the appropriateness of aggression in sport, amassing evidence shows that aggressive play is related to athletic injuries. Katorji and Cahoon (1992), for example, reported results from interviews with players and trainers who indicated that 59% of injuries in junior B hockey players resulted from opponents' aggressive acts. Similarly, studying university hockey in North America, Hayes (1975) found that 15% of all injuries that occurred were penalty related and that many of these were for acts such as tripping. Finally, 40% of spinal cord injuries in Canadian hockey players aged 16 to 20 years were the result of checking from behind, a form of aggression. Although not all penalties involve the intent to harm, Widmeyer, Dorsch, Bray, and McGuire (2002) found that players sometimes intend to harm. Although the precise number of intentional injuries cannot be determined, it is clear that aggression is related to increased athletic injuries.

Athletic Performance and Aggression

Some coaches and athletes believe that aggressiveness enhances athletic performance at either the team or the individual level. For instance, basketball player Kermit Washington said that being mean helped keep him from being pushed around on the court. Football safety Jack Tatum said his team had a greater likelihood of succeeding if he punished his opponent on every play (Papanek, 1977). Certainly, the relationship between aggression and performance is complex, and there have been many cases in which aggressive acts have "paid off" regarding outcome. Consider, for example, the strategy of having a less skilled player commit aggressive acts against an opponent with higher skill levels to distract the superior player or draw him into a fight.

Some sport psychologists agree that aggression facilitates performance outcome (Widmeyer, 1984), whereas others believe it does not (Gill, 2000). The research is difficult to interpret because clear distinctions have not been drawn between aggression and assertive behaviors. Silva (1980) argued that aggression would not facilitate performance because it elevates a person's arousal level and shifts attention to nonperformance issues (e.g., hurting the opponent). In the end, the relation of aggression to performance may be of secondary importance. More central issues are whether sport and exercise science professionals value performance at any cost, their concern about sport participants, and their willingness to ensure that aggression does not pay—but that those who act aggressively do (Widmeyer, 1984).

> **KEY POINT** Sport and exercise science professionals must decide whether they value enhanced performance at the cost of increased aggression or whether they are more concerned about how sport affects its participants.

Team Moral Atmosphere and Aggression

Researchers have uncovered a strong link between the moral atmosphere of teams and aggressive acts of athletes (Stephens, 2004; Stephens & Bredemeier,

1996; Stephens & Kavanagh, 2003). For example, Stephens (2004) found that the primary predictors of aggressive tendencies in young basketball players included perceptions of their teammates' aggressive behavior in the same situation and their willingness to injure others at their coach's request. Stephens and Bredemeier (1996) showed that athlete aggressiveness is influenced by team norms and perceptions of aggressiveness as well as coach support for such norms, and Chow, Murray, and Feltz (2009) found that team norms for aggression predicted the likelihood that youth soccer players would be aggressive. Thus, coaches and teammates play an especially important role in creating a team moral atmosphere that influences aggression in athletes.

Sport-Specific Aggression Determinants

In addition to the general theories of aggression discussed previously, researchers have made a number of sport-specific explanations for aggression (Widmeyer, Bray, Dorsch, & McGuire, 2001). Specifically, athletes behave aggressively because

- someone has committed aggression against them,
- the opposition has annoyed them,
- they are highly ego oriented and have a low level of moral development (see chapter 24),
- they want to show how tough they are,
- they believe it is part of their role, and
- they feel group pressures to be aggressive.

Another finding has been that the more frequently teams compete with each other, the more likely they are to be aggressive (Widmeyer & McGuire, 1997).

Sex and Cultural Differences

Sport psychologists have studied sex and cultural differences in aggression. The research shows that males exhibit high frequencies of aggression when compared with females (VaezMousavi, 2005). Several investigators have also begun to compare aggression across cultures (Maxwell, Moores, & Chow, 2007; Maxwell, Visek, & Moores, 2009). Maxwell and colleagues (2007) found that experiences of aggression in Chinese athletes were similar to those in Western populations in many ways. However, Chinese athletes ruminated more about the aggression, suggesting that members of a collectivist culture are less likely to accept aggression as a means of goal achievement. Although it is too early to draw firm conclusions, this research suggests that practitioners should make efforts to understand the experience of those from other cultures and not blindly assume that all athletes and exercisers will understand and manifest aggression in the same manner.

Alcohol-Related Aggression and Sport

A consistent finding in the literature is that college athletes report higher rates of alcohol-related aggression and antisocial behavior than their nonathlete counterparts do (e.g., Nelson & Wechsler, 2001; O'Brien et al., 2012). This is especially the case for male athletes. Athletes have also been found to more heavily engage in binge drinking and extreme alcohol consumption because they spend more time socializing, have close friends who drink, and report more peer pressure to drink. Thus, in addition to the major health-related consequences of the misuse of alcohol (see chapter 20), the aggression that often results can have dire effects on both property and individuals. It is important to address alcohol-related aggression, and research suggests that discussing the negative effects of excessive drinking on athletic performance and working to modify the social environment of athletes maybe the best ways of doing so (Nelson & Wechsler, 2001).

Applying Knowledge to Professional Practice

Let's now consolidate what we know of aggression and discuss how we might develop strategies for controlling aggression in sport and physical activity settings. First, we examine situations in which aggression is most likely to occur. Next, we discuss strategies for modifying aggressive actions and teaching appropriate behavior.

Understand When Aggression Is Most Likely to Occur

Expect certain situations to provoke aggressive behavior. Aggression is likely when athletes are frustrated. Participants typically feel frustrated when they are losing, perceive unfair officiating, are embarrassed, are physically in pain, or are playing below their capabilities. Losing by a large margin, losing to an oppo-

nent one is outplaying, and playing poorly have been found to be especially important situations related to aggression (Widmeyer, Dorsch, Bray, & McGuire, 2002). Athletes who are passionate about their sport and who perceive failure as a threat to their identity are more likely to be aggressive (Donahue, Rip, & Vallerand, 2009), as are athletes who focus on outcome goals. Teachers and coaches, therefore, should be particularly sensitive to detecting and controlling aggression in these frustrating situations.

Modify Aggressive Reactions

Unfortunately, we cannot always control situations that cause frustration. But we can observe participants more closely and remove them from the situation at the first signs of aggression. Or, better yet, we can teach athletes skills for controlling their emotions and their reactions to frustration. For example, an ice hockey player who often became frustrated during games, responded aggressively, and spent increasingly more time in the penalty box was able to learn stress management skills (Silva, 1982). Through training, the player reduced his aggressive responses and remained in the game instead of in the box. On the basis of a study of more than 400 athletes, Maxwell and colleagues (2009) found that individuals who can control their anger tend to be less aggressive and do not feel that aggression is as legitimate. Finally, in a recent intervention study, youth hockey players were taught cognitive and emotional skills as well as on-ice routines designed to decrease aggressive acts (Lauer & Paiement, 2009). A single-subject design with three participants was used to evaluate the effect of the intervention on the players' aggressive behaviors. Results revealed that all the young athletes showed decreased aggression, although some differences were slight. The greatest reductions were found in retaliatory and major aggressive acts, which is important because these more serious aggressive actions often lead to injuries and suspensions. Because of findings like these, sport psychologists (e.g., Widmeyer, 2002) have recommended that coaches teach emotion control strategies to athletes and simulate frustrating conditions so their players have an opportunity to practice emotion control strategies under pressure.

KEY POINT Stress management training can help students and athletes deal with frustrating situations.

Playing Tough and Clean: Hockey Aggression Intervention

Sport psychologists Larry Lauer and Craig Paiement (2009) developed an intervention for helping youth ice hockey players better control their emotions and lower aggressive acts. The program was implemented over several months in the following way:

- *Session 1:* A distinction between aggressive (dirty) and assertive (clean) play was made, and what constituted each was discussed. The notion of aggression as macho or cool was de-emphasized, and empathy and compassion for opponents were emphasized.

- *Session 2:* Players were made aware of the role emotions play in hockey and how one's emotions are related to aggression. Emphasis was placed on the importance of controlling emotions via deep breathing.

- *Session 3:* A four-step plan for controlling emotions while playing tough but clean hockey was conveyed. The steps included (1) respond positively to emotions, (2) identify one's emotional "hot" buttons, (3) develop a new response to emotional hot buttons, and (4) develop a strategy for practicing on-ice emotional control. A 3-R (respond, relax, refocus) emotional management routine was taught to the players.

- *Sessions 4, 5, and 6:* Arousal and stress management techniques such as goal setting and imagery were taught, practiced, and self-monitored by players.

- *Sessions 7, 8, and 9:* Players practiced skills and used them in games. Self-regulation was emphasized, goals were set, and emotions were self-monitored. Game video was reviewed and discussed.

An overemphasis on winning is at the root of much frustration. Trying to win isn't wrong, but winning should not be emphasized to the point that aggression results after a loss. This level of frustration is a sign that winning needs to be put into perspective. Sport and exercise science professionals have a moral responsibility to delineate aggression from intensity and assertiveness (good aggression) and instruct participants accordingly.

KEY POINT Sport and exercise professionals have a moral responsibility to clearly distinguish between assertive behavior and aggression with the intent to harm.

Teach Appropriate Behavior

Once you know what constitutes aggression and what is appropriate, intense, or assertive play, you can use social learning strategies (modeling and reinforcement; see chapter 6) to teach participants the appropriate behaviors and explain why particular behaviors are appropriate or inappropriate. (Chapter 24 discusses this topic in more detail.)

Establish Team Norms

One strategy for decreasing sport aggression is to help establish appropriate team norms. This involves talking to athletes, and especially team leaders, about the difference between aggression and assertive behavior. Having captains monitor team members' actions is also important so that athletes' actions can be discussed at the first sign of aggression. Physical activity participants should also know how to resolve conflicts and disputes in a nonviolent fashion. A middle school in Maryland instituted a program to provide this training, which improved the school climate (Miller, 1993). In the school's peer conflict resolution program, students with good leadership and communication skills were identified to serve as peer mediators in resolving conflicts among other students. These peer leaders were then taught to implement the following steps in nonviolent conflict resolution:

1. Agree to meet. Have disputants agree to meet with the student mediator (but not sit next to one another at the meeting).

2. Record the facts. Each disputant is given an opportunity to tell her account of the event. The student mediator listens but does not take sides.

3. Express feelings. Each disputant expresses her feelings regarding the event, and the mediator repeats what is said to ensure clarity of meaning.

4. Aim to resolve. Each disputant expresses the desirable consequences of resolving the conflict. The

Good or Bad Aggression?

Tom Martinez is the new head football coach at Aurora High School. He takes over a program with a losing tradition and a reputation for overly aggressive players who commit flagrant fouls and take cheap shots. A former major college player himself, Tom knows it takes intensity to be successful, but he is committed to his philosophy that taking cheap shots and playing to physically hurt opponents are inappropriate. He believes that the first step toward remedying the situation at Aurora is to differentiate for the players between appropriate and inappropriate aggression. He remembers how confusing and frustrating it was for him when one coach rewarded him for aggressive play and others reprimanded him for the same actions.

Tom meets with his coaching staff, and they all agree to be consistent in distinguishing between assertive play and aggression. They adopt the following guidelines, explain them to the team, and consistently reward the demonstration of good, clean, intense play while immediately punishing aggression.

AURORA HIGH SCHOOL GUIDELINES

Appropriate Actions

Hard hits within the rules and within the field of play

Helping opponents off the turf after hard hits

Acknowledging good plays by the opponents

Inappropriate Actions

Out-of-bounds tackles and hits

Legal acts aimed at physically punishing opponents (e.g., forearm shivers to the head of receivers)

Head hunting (tackles aimed at the head) or blind-side blocks aimed at the knees

Pushing and shoving opponents after the whistle has blown

Intimidating remarks (e.g., "If you think that was a hard shot, wait for the next one")

Off-the-field trash talk about hurting or getting opponents

mediator emphasizes areas of agreement relative to the benefits of resolving the conflict.

5. Outline necessary changes. The disputants list what they each could do to resolve the conflict.

6. Develop an action plan. A plan of action is developed and each disputant signs it, indicating her commitment to the action plan and to resolving the conflict cooperatively.

7. Follow up on the plan. After a short time, the disputants are asked whether the problem still exists.

Although this is not the only conflict resolution model and would not necessarily work in all settings, it clearly demonstrates the value and importance of teaching children how to resolve conflicts nonviolently.

Given the increasing levels of violence in society, it is unlikely that school violence will abate on its own. Physical educators and coaches must teach children nonviolent techniques for resolving disputes.

Control Spectator Aggression

In addition to working with athletes to control aggression, athletic and school administrators can use the following strategies to control aggression in spectators:

1. Develop strict alcohol-control policies or ban alcohol for spectators at athletic competitions. Increased alcohol use is associated with increased aggression in the stands as well as increased postgame crime such as assaults, vandalism, and disorderly conduct (Rees & Schnepel, 2009).

2. Penalize spectators (e.g., kick them out) immediately for aggressive acts. Stop aggression as soon as it starts and inform other spectators that it will not be tolerated.

3. When hiring officials, request people who you know won't tolerate aggression on the field.

4. Inform coaches that aggressive displays on their part will not be tolerated.

Recommendations for Controlling Aggression and Violence in Sport

The International Society of Sport Psychology has adopted the following stand on aggression and violence in sport:

- *Recommendation 1:* Management should make fundamental penalty revisions so that rule-violating behavior results in punishments that have greater punitive value than potential reinforcement.

- *Recommendation 2:* Management must ensure proper coaching of teams, particularly at junior levels, which emphasizes a fair-play code of conduct among participants.

- *Recommendation 3:* Management should ban the use of alcoholic beverages at sporting events.

- *Recommendation 4:* Management must make sure facilities are adequate regarding catering and spacing needs and the provision of modern amenities.

- *Recommendation 5:* The media must place in proper perspective the isolated incidents of aggression that occur in sport rather than making them "highlights."

- *Recommendation 6:* The media should promote a campaign to decrease violence and hostile aggression in sport, which should also involve the participation and commitment of athletes, coaches, management, officials, and spectators.

- *Recommendation 7:* Coaches, managers, athletes, media, officials, and authority figures (i.e., police) should take part in workshops on aggression and violence to ensure they understand the topic of aggression, why it occurs, the cost of aggressive acts, and how aggressive behavior can be controlled.

- *Recommendation 8:* Coaches, managers, officials, and the media should encourage athletes to engage in prosocial behavior and punish those who perform acts of hostility.

- *Recommendation 9:* Athletes should take part in programs aimed at helping them reduce behavioral tendencies toward aggression. The tightening of rules, imposing of harsher penalties, and changing of reinforcement patterns are only parts of the answer to inhibiting aggression in sport. Ultimately, the athlete must assume responsibility.

Reprinted, by permission, from G. Tenenbaum et al., 1997, "Aggression and violence in sport: An ISSP position stand," *ISSP Newsletter* 1: 14-17. © Gershon Tenenbaum, ISSP.

5. Work with the media to convey the importance of not glorifying aggressive acts in sport coverage.

The International Society of Sport Psychology has developed a position statement on aggression in sport (see "Recommendations for Controlling Aggression and Violence in Sport"). It includes recommendations for all personnel involved in sport: managers, coaches, media representatives, and athletes (Tenenbaum, Stewart, Singer, & Duda, 1997).

LEARNING AIDS

SUMMARY

1. **Define aggression.**
   Aggression is behavior directed toward the goal of harming or injuring another living being. For an act to be considered aggression it must meet four criteria: It must be an actual behavior, must involve harm or injury, must be directed toward another living thing, and must involve intent. Aggression is distinct from assertive behavior in sport.

2. **Identify the causes of aggression.**
   Four theories explain why aggression occurs: the instinct, frustration–aggression, social learning, and revised frustration–aggression theories. Little support has been found for the instinct theory or the original frustration–aggression hypothesis, and no support exists for the notion that catharsis (releasing pent-up aggression through socially acceptable sport and physical activity) abates aggression. Strong support has

been found for the revised frustration–aggression and social learning theories. Frustration predisposes individuals to aggressiveness, and aggression occurs if people have learned that it is an appropriate reaction to frustration. Modeling and reinforcement can be powerful determinants of aggressive behavior. Spectators also use aggression, and they as well as sport participants sometimes condone behaviors that would not be considered appropriate in society (game reasoning). Today, the general model of aggression is used to tie these theories together.

3. **Examine special considerations relative to aggression and sport.**
   It has been found that observing a sporting event does not lower levels of spectator aggression. Fan violence is more likely to occur under certain conditions (e.g., crowded conditions) with certain individuals (e.g., younger disadvantaged males). Athletes have been found to view some aggressive acts as inappropriate in general but appropriate in the sport environment. This double standard is called bracketed morality, or game reasoning.

4. **Explain the aggression–performance relationship.**
   Aggression has been found to facilitate athletic performance in some cases but not in others. In the end, the relation of aggression to performance may be less important than whether coaches believe that performance is worth any cost or are more concerned with whether participants learn that aggression is not appropriate or useful. Finally, a strong link has been found between the moral atmosphere of play and aggressive acts of athletes.

5. **Derive implications from research for helping to control aggression.**
   Some research findings yield important implications for guiding practice. These include recognizing when aggression is most likely to occur, teaching athletes how to handle these situations, teaching appropriate behaviors, and modifying inappropriate aggressive actions.

KEY TERMS

aggression	instinct theory	social learning theory
hostile aggression	catharsis	revised frustration–aggression theory
instrumental aggression	frustration–aggression theory	game reasoning

REVIEW QUESTIONS

1. What is aggression? How does it differ from assertive behavior?
2. Describe the four criteria for considering an act aggression.
3. What are four theories of aggression? Describe the major contentions of each. Which have the strongest support and why?
4. What is catharsis? What implications does it have for guiding practice?
5. What factors are associated with spectator aggression?
6. What is sport-specific game reasoning, or bracketed morality? What are its implications for professionals?
7. Explain the relationship between athlete aggression and performance.
8. In what situations is aggression most likely to occur?

CRITICAL THINKING QUESTIONS

1. You have learned that aggression can involve both physical and psychological harm to others. It is fairly easy to come up with examples of physical aggression in sport and physical activity settings, but psychological aggression may be subtler and harder to identify. Identify forms of psychological aggression that you have experienced or witnessed in sport and physical activity settings.

2. You have been named commissioner of the National Hockey League. Because of increasing concerns over fighting and aggressive play, the government has threatened to intervene in the league's administration unless the situation improves within a year. Discuss what you will do to curb fighting and aggression.

24

Character Development and Good Sporting Behavior

After reading this chapter, you should be able to

1. define character development and good sporting behavior,
2. explain how character and good sporting behavior develop,
3. identify the important link between moral reasoning and moral behavior,
4. discuss how character and good sporting behavior can be influenced, and
5. describe the effects of winning on character development and good sporting behavior.

For years we have heard that sport and physical activity build character and develop moral values. There are dozens of shining examples. Soccer legend Mia Hamm started a foundation that raises money and increases awareness for families needing bone marrow transplants. Football great Warrick Dunn began a program that assists struggling single parents with owning their own homes. Olympic champion Joey Cheek donated the $25,000 he received for winning a gold medal to Right to Play, an international organization that provides physical play opportunities for children living in poverty. Yet some of the most popular role models have been the "bad boys and girls" of sport—John McEnroe in tennis and Jack Tatum (nicknamed The Assassin) in football. And it is not just elite athletes who behave badly. The Internet is filled with examples of poor sporting behavior, such as the University of North Dakota ice hockey player who sucker punched his opponent during the postgame handshake or the University of New Mexico soccer player who physically attacked her Brigham Young

University opponent by pulling her to the ground by her hair. In the face of such occurrences, can we really say that sport participation builds character? Not really. Evidence shows that 13% of youths report trying to hurt an opponent, 31% argue with officials, and 27% act like bad sports after losing (Shields, LaVoi, Bredemeier, & Power, 2005). High school athletes also feel that gamesmanship is just part of their sport and report that they at times put morals aside in order to win (Camire & Trudel, 2010). College student basketball fans reported that it is legitimate to distract opponents or engage in abusive cheering to win (Rudd & Gordon, 2009). In this chapter we focus on the role sport and exercise science professionals play in character development. Let's first delineate what we mean by character and good sporting behavior.

DISCOVER Activity 24.1 helps you understand what good sporting behavior involves.

Defining Character, Fair Play, and Good Sporting Behavior

Defining character and good sporting behavior is difficult. We all generally know what these terms mean, but we seldom define them precisely (Martens, 1982) or agree exactly on their meaning. Tennis great Chris Evert, for example, says that sportspersonship (or what we refer to as good sporting behavior) is acting in a classy, dignified way (Ross, 1992). Basketball great David Robinson defines it as playing with all your heart and intensity, yet still showing respect for your opponents (Ross, 1992). These are two very different definitions. And what exactly does acting respectfully or in a classy and dignified manner mean? A golfer might say it means you don't talk to your opponent during play, but a baseball player might think it's fine to talk to the opposing pitcher. Similarly, sliding hard into second base to break up a double play is expected and not inappropriate in college baseball, yet most of us would discourage it in tee ball with 6- and 7-year-olds.

In their book *Character Development and Physical Activity,* Shields and Bredemeier (1995) indicated that although character and good sporting behavior are difficult to define, they fall in the general area of morality in the context of sport. That is, they have to do with our beliefs, judgments, and actions concerning what is right and ethical and what is wrong and unethical in sport. Specifically, Shields and Bredemeier contended that morality in sport comprises three related concepts: fair play, good sporting behavior, and character.

KEY POINT No universally accepted definition of good sporting behavior exists.

Fair Play

Fair play is necessary if all participants are to have an equitable chance to pursue victory in competitive sport. Fair play requires that all contestants understand and adhere not only to the formal rules of the game but also to the spirit of cooperation and unwritten rules of play necessary to ensure that a contest is fair (Shields & Bredemeier, 1995). For example, a youth

Dan Rowley/Colorsport/Icon SMI

Helping up a fallen athlete is an example of good sporting behavior.

football program that maximizes participation of all the children may require that each player take part in each quarter of the contest. However, a coach may violate the spirit of the rule by having substitutes enter the game to play only one play per quarter or to bring in plays and then leave before the play is actually executed. It is essential that parents, coaches, and officials espouse the virtue of fair play early, often, and throughout the athletic careers of the participants.

Good Sporting Behavior

Good sporting behavior is the second component of morality in sport. Shields and Bredemeier (1995) contended that good sporting behavior "involves an intense striving to succeed, tempered by commitment to the play spirit such that ethical standards will take precedence over strategic gain when the two conflict" (p. 194). In other words, you adhere to fair play even when it may mean losing. For example, U.S. Open tennis champion Patrick Rafter demonstrated good sporting behavior when he informed an official that a line call was incorrect—even though doing so meant that he lost the match. Tennis great Andy Roddick demonstrated the same type of good sporting behavior during a match in Italy.

Whereas Shields and Bredemeier defined good sporting behavior based on their conceptual understanding of the literature, Canadian sport psychologist Robert Vallerand and colleagues (Vallerand, Briere, Blanchard, & Provencher, 1997; Vallerand, Deshaies, Cuerrier, Briere, & Pelletier, 1996) conducted an extensive study to understand how athletes themselves define the term. The researchers constructed a sporting behavior survey and administered it to 1,056 French-Canadian athletes between the ages of 10 and 18 years who represented seven sports. Factor analysis (a statistical technique that groups like response patterns in data) revealed that good sporting behavior consists of these five factors:

1. Full commitment toward participation (showing up and working hard during all practices and games; acknowledging one's mistakes and trying to improve)

2. Respect and concern for rules and officials (even when the official appears incompetent)

3. Respect and concern for social conventions (shaking hands after the contest; recognizing the good performance of one's opponent; being a good loser)

4. Respect and concern for the opponent (lending one's equipment to the opponent; agreeing to play even if the opponent is late; refusing to take advantage of injured opponents)

5. Avoiding poor attitudes toward participation (avoiding a win-at-all-costs approach; not showing temper after a mistake; not competing only for individual trophies and prizes)

Hence, this research suggests that athletes define good sporting behavior as "concern and respect for the rules and officials, social conventions, the opponent, as well as one's full commitment to one's sport, and the relative absence of a negative approach toward sport participation" (Vallerand et al., 1997, p. 198).

Although these attempts to define good sporting behavior are helping to guide research in the area, from a practical perspective Martens' (1982) conclusion still holds true—no one universally accepted definition of good sporting behavior exists. Rather, good sporting behaviors must be specifically identified: They are tied to the type of sport, level of play, and age of the participant. So although there is no universal definition of the term, it is still important that we each identify good sporting behavior and try to develop situation-specific definitions of it as we work professionally in sport, physical education, and exercise settings.

Finally, in discussing morality, psychologist Albert Bandura (1999) indicated that two important aspects of these behaviors need to be considered: engaging in positive social behaviors and refraining from engaging in negative social behaviors. Thus, in sport and physical activity settings we should be concerned with people exhibiting good sporting behavior while simultaneously refraining from bad sporting behaviors.

Character

Character, the third concept in morality, refers to an array of characteristics (usually connoting a positive moral overtone—we all want participants to develop good character in sport) that can be developed in sport. Those who espouse the character-developing benefits of sport contend that participants learn to overcome obstacles, cooperate with teammates, develop self-control, and persist in the face of defeat (Ewing, Seefeldt, & Brown, 1996). Shields and Bredemeier (1995) view character as an overarching concept that integrates fair play and good sporting behavior with two other important virtues, compassion and integrity. Hence, character in sport comprises four interrelated

Kids Take on Moral Issues in Sports

Sport psychologist Moria Stuart (2003) was interested in identifying what moral issues children aged 10 to 12 years experienced in sport. The children said such things as these:

"A big problem with my coach is that his daughter is on the team and he (coach) lets her play most of the game and some of the players who are better don't get to play as much as his (coach) daughter . . . he should not play favorites because then we all can't play as much as her and that's not fair to the rest of us." (p. 451)

"They know that they are supposed to shake hands, so when we went to shake their hand after the game, the other team spit on their hands before they would shake our hands . . . that isn't right . . . that's not how you act after a game." (p. 451)

These and the many other statements the children made were classified into three general categories of moral issues. These included concerns about

- the fairness of adult actions (e.g., unfair decisions by officials, coaches playing favorites, parents pressuring them to play or win),
- negative game behaviors (e.g., verbal intimidation by opponents, intentional fouls, violations of the spirit of the game), and
- negative team behaviors (e.g., selfish teammates, dishonesty, teammate misbehavior).

In another study, Long, Pantaleon, Bruant, and d'Arripe-Longueville (2006) interviewed 10 young elite athletes and found that both respect for and transgression of competitive rules depended on the athletes' individual characteristics (e.g., the desire to win), the social environment (e.g., team norms and pressure from the coach), sport values and virtues (e.g., fair play), and sport rewards (e.g., media recognition). Most interesting were the findings of moral disengagement: These young athletes justified rule breaking in the name of defending sport values such as team spirit or playing smart.

Although these findings confirm and extend adult perspectives on moral issues in sport, they also show that issues of rightness and wrongness occur in practices, before and after games, and at home, not just during the game. These findings also highlight the importance of obtaining children's perspectives when studying moral issues in sport.

virtues: compassion, fairness, good sporting behavior, and integrity.

We have already defined fair play and good sporting behavior, but not compassion and integrity. **Compassion** is related to empathy and is the ability to take on and appreciate the feelings of others. Hence, when we have compassion, we feel for our competitors and seek to understand their feelings and perspectives. **Integrity** is the ability to maintain one's morality and fairness coupled with the belief that one can (and will) fulfill one's moral intentions. In essence, integrity is an athlete's or a coach's moral self-efficacy—the belief that she will do the right thing when faced with a moral dilemma. In summary, when we discuss character in sport we are referring to knowing the rules and standards of behavior expected of participants (good sporting behavior); adhering to the rules and the spirit of the rules while competing (fairness); being compassionate, or being able to take on the feelings

of others; and having integrity, or being confident that we know what is right and will exhibit behaviors in line with what is right even when alternative choices make doing so difficult.

One thing is clear, societies are becoming increasingly more diverse and it is important that professionals in sport and exercise psychology and related fields recognize this diversity and create inclusive environments that are open and welcoming, regardless of an athlete's race, gender, or sexual orientation.

Developing Character and Good Sporting Behavior: Three Approaches

Although people have differing views about how character and good sporting attitudes and behaviors develop, three particular approaches are the

Sexual Orientation in Sport

For many years, being anything but heterosexual was simply taboo in sport. Of course, some high-visibility (and not so high-visibility) athletes were found to be gay or openly came out, such as Billie Jean King (tennis), Martina Navratilova (tennis), Greg Louganis (diving), Brendan Burke (hockey), John Amaechi (English basketball), Scott Norton (bowling), Glenn Burke (baseball), Justin Fashanu (English football), and Robbie Rogers (soccer). But the first athlete currently playing a major sport in the United States to announce that he is gay was Jason Collins. In a story appearing in *Sports Illustrated* (Collins & Lidz, 2013), Collins stated, "I'm a 34-year-old NBA center. I'm black and I'm gay. I didn't set out to be the first openly gay athlete playing in a major American team sport. But since I am, I'm happy to start the conversation" (p. 34).

Although Collins did not receive universal support, he did appear to have the support of most players as well as the public in general. It is the hope of many that this type of announcement will not be newsworthy in the future because gay athletes will simply be accepted as they are. This acceptance seemed to be the case in 2014 for Michael Sam, All-American football player from the University of Missouri. Sam announced he was gay before the NFL draft, which did not appear to affect his position in the draft. Although not exactly the same situation, people may remember all the racial slurs that were thrown at Jackie Robinson, the first black baseball player. Now black athletes are integral players in all major U.S. sports.

most widely accepted today: the social learning, structural–developmental, and social–psychological approaches.

Social Learning Approach

Aggression and character development are linked in many ways, and they are explained by similar theories. According to the social learning approach to character development, best summarized in the work of Albert Bandura (1977b), specific positive sporting attitudes and behaviors deemed appropriate by society are learned through modeling or observational learning, reinforcement, and social comparison (figure 24.1) and then internalized and used to guide behavior. This approach, then, contends that people's social learning history determines their level of good sporting behavior (Shields & Bredemeier, 2001), although more recent versions also emphasize that behavior is determined by an interaction of personal and situational factors (Bandura, 1991).

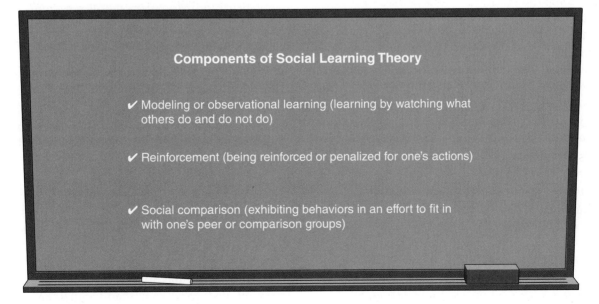

Components of Social Learning Theory

✔ Modeling or observational learning (learning by watching what others do and do not do)

✔ Reinforcement (being reinforced or penalized for one's actions)

✔ Social comparison (exhibiting behaviors in an effort to fit in with one's peer or comparison groups)

FIGURE 24.1 Components of social learning theory.

For example, by observing that other children are being praised for reporting false sit-up scores to the instructor, Zoe learns in physical education class that it is acceptable to cheat on a fitness test. Wanting praise and attention from the teacher, she copies or models the behavior of the other students whom she compares herself with and begins to report more sit-ups than she has really done. The physical educator notes the reported improvement in the number of sit-ups executed and praises her. Thus, Zoe learns from observing the other children and through her own experience that if she lies about the number of sit-ups, she receives reinforcement. Conversely, a selfish child may learn to share and be more caring by observing that classmates receive attention and praise for helping. And, over time, when the child models these helping actions and is praised, the prosocial behavior is reinforced. Thus, the social learning process affects both positive and negative attitudes and behaviors. In one study of social learning theory, fifth-grade boys who acted in unsportspersonlike ways saw the appropriate behaviors modeled and took part in a reinforcement system (they could earn points leading to desired prizes for exhibiting good sporting behaviors). Over time the reinforcement system was effective, although more so in eliminating undesirable behaviors than in getting the boys to exhibit desirable behaviors (Geibenk & McKenzie, 1985).

Tennis great Bjorn Borg was known for his good sporting behavior, but he hadn't always behaved that way. When he was 12, Borg threw his racket in disgust, exhibiting a temper tantrum on the court. Such actions were quickly curtailed because his mother would not tolerate them. Borg had his racket taken away and was not allowed to play for 6 months.

The latest research on social learning suggests that learned self-regulatory mechanisms such as negative affective efficacy (the ability to regulate one's negative emotions) or resistive self-efficacy (the ability to resist reacting to negative emotions) operate together to influence the acceptability and likelihood of cheating in athletes. The higher one's negative affective efficacy, the less likely the individual would cheat or engage in moral disengagement (the disengagement of moral self-sanctions), whereas the lower one's resistive self-efficacy, the more likely the individual will engage in moral disengagement and view cheating as acceptable (d'Arripe-Longueville, Corrion, Scoffier, Roussel, & Chalabaev, 2010).

Structural–Developmental Approach

Instead of focusing on modeling, reinforcement, and social comparison, the structural–developmental approach focuses on how psychological growth and developmental changes in a child's thoughts and judgments underlying behavior interact with environmental experiences to shape moral reasoning (Weiss & Bredemeier, 1991). Moreover, sport psychologists have derived specific definitions of moral reasoning, moral development, and moral behavior. Note that when we use the term *moral,* we do not mean to imply religious values.

Moral reasoning is defined as the decision process in which a person determines the rightness or wrongness of a course of action. Thus, moral reasoning pertains to how one decides whether some course of action (e.g., if a coach violates National Collegiate Athletic Association rules by paying to fly a player home to see his dying mother) is right or wrong. In contrast, **moral development** is the process of experience and growth through which a person develops the capacity to reason morally. For example, in planning a system-wide physical education curriculum, a district coordinator would want to understand what experiences and cognitive developmental changes are most likely to enhance the children's abilities to determine the rightness or wrongness of an action. Last, **moral behavior** is actually carrying out an act that is deemed right or wrong. So, moral reasoning results from individual experiences, as well as the psychological growth and development of the child, and is thought to guide moral behavior. Moreover, moral reasoning is seen as a series of general ethical principles that underlie situationally specific acts of good sporting behavior.

> **KEY POINT** Moral reasoning is the decision process through which one determines the rightness or wrongness of a course of action. Moral development is the process of experience and growth through which a person develops the capacity to reason morally. Moral behavior is the execution of an act that is deemed right or wrong.

Structural developmentalists contend that the ability to reason morally depends on a person's level of cognitive or mental development (e.g., a child's ability to think in concrete or abstract terms). Thus, if a 4-year-old boy, able to think in only very concrete terms, is inadvertently pushed in line at preschool, he responds by hitting the child who was pushed into him. This child, not able to judge intent, knows only that the other child pushed him. However, given the process of normal growth and cognitive development, an 11-year-old child who is inadvertently pushed in line will not necessarily push back because she can judge intent and realizes the other child didn't bump her on purpose. Thus, structural developmentalists view moral reasoning and behavior as dependent, in large part, on cognitive development.

KEY POINT Moral reasoning and behavior depend on an individual's level of cognitive development.

Developmental psychologists have identified sequential stages of moral development in children. Figure 24.2 depicts the five levels, or stages, of moral development first identified by Norma Haan (Haan, Aeerts, & Cooper, 1985) and later explained in more practical sport psychological terms by Maureen Weiss (1987; Weiss & Bredemeier, 1991). As a child matures, she progresses in moral reasoning from level 1 through level 5. Not everyone reaches level 5, however, and we don't always use the highest level of moral thinking that we're capable of. In fact, we may use several different levels at once.

• Level 1 reasoning is at the external control stage—the "It's okay as long as I don't get caught" stage. At this level a child determines what is right or wrong based on self-interest and, in particular, the out-come of her actions. Thus, Kim would decide whether kicking an opponent in soccer (illegally playing the person, not the ball) is right or wrong depending on whether she got away with it. If she did get away with it, she would think it was an acceptable course of action. But if she was penalized for it, she would view playing the person as inappropriate behavior.

• Level 2 still focuses on maximizing self-interests, but the child now doesn't see only the action's outcome. Instead, this is an "eye-for-an-eye" stage in which the individual can compromise and make tradeoffs to maximize self-interest. For instance, Kim decides that it is acceptable to illegally kick another player because Lee has been doing just that to her for most of the first half. Or an elite track and field athlete takes illegal performance-enhancing drugs and defends the action on the premise that "everybody does it."

• In level 3, the person treats others as he or she would like to be treated. Unlike in the first two levels, self-interest is not the sole focus. The person adopts a helping or altruistic view. Kim now views illegally kicking another player as inappropriate because she would not want to be treated that way.

• Level 4 of moral reasoning focuses on following external rules. The person has learned that not all people can be trusted to do the right thing and recognizes that official rules were developed for the common good. At this stage, Kim views illegally kicking an opponent as inappropriate because it is against

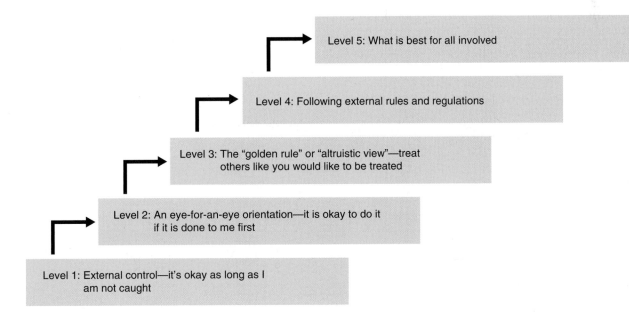

Level 5: What is best for all involved

Level 4: Following external rules and regulations

Level 3: The "golden rule" or "altruistic view"—treat others like you would like to be treated

Level 2: An eye-for-an-eye orientation—it is okay to do it if it is done to me first

Level 1: External control—it's okay as long as I am not caught

FIGURE 24.2 Levels of moral reasoning.

Adapted from Weiss 1987.

the rules and believes that one must play by the rules because they promote everyone's self-interest.

• Moral reasoning at level 5 focuses on what is best for everyone involved, whether or not it is in accordance with official rules and regulations. This reasoning is considered the most mature because the individual seeks to maximize the interests of the group through mutual agreements or "moral balances." Kim reasons that it is inappropriate to kick another player not only because it is against the rules but because it violates the fundamental rights of both parties—the right to play in a safe and healthy environment.

In summary, in moral development, reasoning progresses from decisions based on self-centered interests to a concern with mutual interests of all the people involved. This development depends on the person's ability to think abstractly.

Social–Psychological Approach

Vallerand and colleagues (1996, 1997) offered a third approach to studying morality in physical activity: a broader social–psychological approach. That is, in looking at morality and character you would consider the personal elements in the structural–developmental approach (e.g., the individual's level of moral development) plus a wide range of social factors (e.g., type of sport, competitive level of athletes, pressure from the coach) that go beyond the reinforcement, modeling, and social comparison elements of the social learning approach. An important feature of this view is the notion that social agents (e.g., parents and coaches) label or define good sporting behavior. Vallerand's

team proposed taking a more complex, person-by-situation perspective that considers a variety of both personal and situational factors in determining good sporting behavior.

KEY POINT Character development progresses from basing one's decisions about the rightness or wrongness of actions on self-centered interests to being concerned with the mutual interests of all involved.

Evidence supporting the social–psychological approach has been found in studies such as one conducted by Shields, LaVoi, Bredemeier, and Power (2007). Studying more than 600 youth soccer players from different geographic regions of the United States, they found that poor sporting behaviors were predicted by coach and spectator actions, team norms, participant attitudes toward sportspersonship, and perceptions of parental and coach norms. Thus, it is necessary to consider cultural attitudes, values, and norms of particular individuals and groups as well as the stages of moral reasoning to understand how to enhance character development and good sporting behavior. Consequently, it seems best to take advantage of what has been learned through both the social learning and structural–developmental approaches and to adopt the social–psychological approach.

Examining Moral Development Research

In comprehensive reviews of the literature (Kavussanu, 2008; Shields & Bredemeier, 2001, 2007), it has

Measuring Good Sporting Behavior

Bolter and Weiss (2013) developed the Sportsmanship Coaching Behavior Scale, (SCBS) which allows athletes to assess in their coaches behaviors that have been shown to affect athletes' sportspersonship outcomes. The scale comprises six subscales:

• Teaching,

• modeling,

• reinforcement,

• prioritizing winning over sportspersonship,

• punishing poor sportspersonship, and

• setting expectations for good sporting behavior.

Scale validation results showed that the SCBS subscales were, for the most part, related to athletes' prosocial and antisocial actions in the expected ways and that the SCBS was a valid and reliable measure of sportspersonship coaching behaviors.

been concluded that although much more needs to be known about moral development in sport, the research to date leads to a number of general conclusions. These include the following:

- Moral behavior is best understood from an interactive perspective that considers the characteristics of the individual and the social environment.
- Professionalization of attitude occurs in athletes. Winning becomes the dominant value the longer one stays involved in sport and the higher the competitive level attained.
- Game reasoning occurs. Many athletes use a pattern of moral reasoning in sport that differs from their pattern in everyday life.
- Athletes in some sports (e.g., contact sports) have lower levels of moral reasoning than nonathletes.
- Athletes characterized by lower levels of moral reasoning are more likely to sanction and use aggression.
- Females tend to use higher levels of moral reasoning than males do.
- Moral variables are related to motivational orientations. Higher levels of ego orientation are associated with lower levels of moral development and action, and higher levels of task orientation are associated with higher levels of moral development and action.
- Social factors such as team norms and ego-oriented motivational climates created by parents, spectators, and coaches influence sport morality in negative ways.

Understanding the Connection Between Moral Reasoning and Moral Behavior

As Shields and Bredemeier (2001) found, a consistent relationship exists between aggression and people with less mature moral reasoning: People whose moral reasoning is less mature behave more aggressively. (Not surprisingly, the link between moral reasoning and behavior is not perfect. Nor would you expect it to be—all of us, at one time or another, have known that something was probably wrong but did it anyway.)

KEY POINT Although aggression is linked with immature moral reasoning, the connection between reasoning and behavior is not perfectly understood.

One reason the link between moral reasoning and behavior is not absolute is that several steps must take place to translate moral reasoning into moral action. Basing their work on that of Rest (1984), Miller, Bredemeier, and Shields (1997) identified four stages of moral action in the moral reasoning–behavior link:

1. Interpreting the situation as one that involves some sort of moral judgment
2. Deciding on the best course of moral action
3. Making a choice to act morally
4. Implementing a moral response

For instance, Brian, the captain of the tennis team, must judge whether his opponent's serve at match point is in or out (Brian believes that it is in). If he says it is out, he and his team win the sectional tournament. If he says it is in, he and his team may lose. Following the four stages of moral action, Brian must first interpret the situation and see it as involving a moral choice. His compassion and his ability to see the perspective of others are critical here. Brian remembers how he felt when an opponent cheated on line calls against him. If Brian interprets the situation as involving a moral choice, he must then weigh various competing moral choices (make the correct call, lie, or say he couldn't tell whether the serve was in or out). That is, he must use his moral reasoning to define a moral course of action. Brian then engages in a process to decide whether to give priority to moral values or to self-gain. Will he do the honest thing by making the correct call and potentially losing the match? Will he say the ball was out and receive the rewards associated with the victory? He may be influenced in this stage by such factors as his coach's leadership style and the team's norms about right and wrong. Finally, Brian must marshal his physical and psychological resources to translate his moral decision into action. For example, Brian must be confident that he will be able to deal with what his teammates might say if he makes the correct call and loses the match. His integrity would be important here. Only after working through these stages will Brian act.

Hazing in Sport

- Girls are forced to run naked across a football field.
- In the back of the bus on the ride home, older team members hold freshmen down and shove testicles in their faces.
- Players are forced to drink a keg of beer as a part of team initiation.
- Athletes are forced to cross dress and eat gross combinations of foods and are physically beaten as a part of a team ritual.

These are just a few examples of sport **hazing** incidents that have been reported in recent years. Hazing is "any activity expected of someone joining a group that humiliates, degrades, abuses, or endangers [that person], regardless of a person's willingness to participate. This does not include activities such as rookies carrying the balls, team parties with community games, or going out with . . . teammates, unless an atmosphere of humiliation, degradation, abuse, or danger exists" (Hoover, 1999, p. 8). Since it was first identified as a problem in the 1980s, reports of sport hazing have steadily increased. Many states have even passed legislation making hazing illegal. Hazing does not appear to be specific to the United States; professionals in the United Kingdom have also become more concerned with these practices (Goves, Griggs, & Leflay, 2012). Hazing is clearly a moral issue in contemporary sport.

Given the increased concern about sport hazing, researchers have begun to study the topic. Waldron and Kowalski (2009) interviewed 21 athletes about their experiences related to hazing in sport and found that three types of hazing were evident: physical, psychological, and alcohol related. Motives for hazing identified in the study included having fun, carrying out part of an initiation, and intimidation and jealousy. Hazing was reported to occur more often in contact, team, and competitive sports. It was also influenced by the athlete's physical ability, physical size, personal leadership, and the presence of an older sibling on the team. The authors concluded that athletes engaged in risky hazing practices in a desire to adhere to sport values and to be accepted by teammates.

The fact that hazing is viewed as a rite of passage and as part of team tradition does not make it acceptable. If such activities degrade, abuse, or endanger participants, even if the recipient is willing to participate, they are inappropriate. Scholars are concerned that many athletes do not view hazing practices as risky and negative and really are unknowingly practicing a form of deviant overconformity—that is, doing things that would not be acceptable outside of sport under the justification that the activities are part of the sport's tradition and history. The athletes are motivated to be part of the team, and hazing is part of the process.

Sport psychologists contend that steps must be taken to ensure that sport environments do not condone any form of hazing (Waldron & Kowalski, 2009). Waldron (2012) called for coaches to conduct hazing prevention workshops and outlined a five-step approach for empowering athletes to prevent hazing:

1. Notice the hazing event.
2. Interpret the hazing event as a problem.
3. Take responsibility for the solution.
4. Acquire or have the skills to react.
5. Intervene to prevent the hazing.

Coaches must challenge athletes to think critically about the consequences of hazing. Positive traditions and rituals that promote team unity and cooperation among teammates should be substituted for hazing traditions that promote rivalry and hostility because hazing may do more to harm team chemistry than to contribute to it. Sport leaders and educators have a moral obligation to stop hazing practices and teach athletes how to team build in positive ways.

Knowing how individuals morally reason and how they translate the reasoning into action is important for understanding the people we work with and for guiding our practical interventions. Miller and colleagues (1997) designed a sociomoral educational program for at-risk physical education students based on these moral action processes. They identified specific psychological objectives related to those processes and then designed and developed intervention strategies, such as cooperative learning, for achieving these goals and influencing the moral action processes (see table 24.1).

Studying the Connection Between Character Development and Physical Activity

Most of us like to believe that participation in physical activity programs automatically builds character, enhances moral reasoning, and teaches good sporting behavior, but little evidence supports the belief that it builds character (Hodge, 1989). Participation in sport and physical education settings does not automatically produce better or worse people. Character is not caught, but taught, in sport and physical activity settings. Teaching moral reasoning and good sporting behavior involves the systematic use of certain strategies.

KEY POINT Character is not caught, but taught, in sport, exercise, and physical activity settings.

Let's look at an example of such a strategy. Gibbons, Ebbeck, and Weiss (1995) investigated moral judgment, reason, intention, and prosocial behavior changes in fourth-, fifth-, and sixth-grade children.

The children were randomly assigned to one of three groups: control, Fair Play for Kids activities during physical education only, and Fair Play for Kids activities during all school subjects. The Fair Play for Kids (1990) program that the treatment conditions were based on included activities from the teacher resource manual developed by the Commission for Fair Play in Canada. Activities in the manual are based on both the structural–developmental and social learning theories and are aimed at increasing respect for rules, officials, and opponents; providing all individuals with an equal chance to participate; and maintaining self-control (see "Fair Play for Kids Sample Activities"). The intervention lasted for 7 months of the academic year, and moral development measures were taken before and after the intervention.

Results revealed that children who participated in the treatment groups had significantly higher posttest scores on all measures, whereas no changes were evident in the control participants, validating the Fair Play for Kids curriculum for effecting change in moral development in children. In addition, because no differences existed between the two treatment groups, the results showed that addressing fair play in physical education alone or in conjunction with academic classes was equally effective.

These results are consistent with those of Bredemeier, Weiss, Shields, and Shewchuk (1986) and Romance, Weiss, and Bockoven (1986), and they show that the systematic and organized delivery of moral development information can change children's character. In fact, after reviewing the moral development intervention research in physical activity, leading developmental sport psychologists Maureen Weiss and Al Smith (2002) concluded that "there is much cause for optimism that physical activity offers an attractive vehicle for effective moral and social development

TABLE 24.1 Moral Action Processes, Sociomoral Education Goals, and Program Intervention Strategies

	Stage 1	Stage 2	Stage 3	Stage 4
Moral action process	Perception and interpretation	Judgment and deciding	Choice	Implementation
Program goal	Empathy	Moral reasoning	Task orientation	Self-responsibility
Intervention	Cooperative learning	Moral community	Mastery climate	Power transfer

Reprinted, by permission, from S. Miller, B. Bredemeier, and D. Shields, 1997, "Sociomoral education through physical education with at-risk children," *Quest* 49(1): 119.

Fair Play for Kids Sample Activities

- *The problem-solving running shoe.* This is a problem-solving activity in which children learn to resolve moral conflicts. A drawing of a giant running shoe with separate areas labeled *problem, alternative, consequences,* and *solution* is posted. When children have conflict, they are instructed to go to a special area ("the listening bench") and complete a running shoe form or use the running shoe steps to resolve peer conflicts.

- *Improv.* Fair play dilemmas (e.g., a player argues with the umpire after a perceived bad call in softball) are written on "improvisation cards." Children then make up skits that address how to deal with the situation outlined on the card.

- *Relay games.* Children take part in relay games in which they share ideas with teammates, discuss strategy, learn to work within the rules, and show self-control. A "Let's Talk" time is built in at the end of each game to discuss specific questions, such as "What conflicts did you have to resolve?"

Adapted from Gibbons, Ebbeck, and Weiss 1995.

change in children and adolescents" (p. 273). Under the right conditions, then, moral reasoning can be taught through physical education and sport.

Youth Sports as a Deterrent to Negative Behavior

It is not only physical educators who claim that participation enhances character development and positive behaviors. Sport administrators, coaches, and community leaders often claim that taking part in sport keeps youths off the street, out of trouble, and out of gangs. Youth development expert Reed Larson (2000), for example, indicates that extracurricular activities such as sport have tremendous potential to lead to positive youth development for several reasons. First, sport is intrinsically motivating for many adolescents. Second, it involves sustained efforts on the part of the participant directed toward reaching a goal over time. Third, it requires a youth to experience setbacks, make adjustments, and learn to overcome challenges. The potential of sport as a vehicle for positive youth development has led sport psychologists and sociologists to study two specific questions: Does sport participation deter delinquency? Does participation in sport decrease gang violence?

Sport Participation and Delinquency

Research has supported the claim that participants in organized sport are less likely than nonparticipants to engage in delinquent behavior (Seefeldt & Ewing, 1997; Shields & Bredemeier, 1995). Moreover, the negative relationship between sport participation and delinquency seems especially strong for youths in

poorer neighborhoods and athletes in minor sports. What is not clear, however, is why this relationship exists. We look at four possible explanations for findings that sport participants are less likely to engage in delinquent behavior: differential association, social bonding, labeling, and economic strain.

- Those who explain the negative relationship between sport participation and delinquency by a **differential association** propose that athletes have less frequent, shorter, and less intense interactions with delinquent others. In other words, participation in sport keeps kids off the streets and out of trouble.

- The **social bonding** view contends that kids who participate in sport develop attachments with significant others who represent dominant, prosocial values. A young athlete identifies with his coach and team and, in so doing, learns such values as teamwork, hard work, and achievement.

- The **labeling hypothesis** takes a different tack, contending that sport participation does not facilitate youth values. Rather, because many people in society value sport, being labeled an "athlete" often leads to special treatment. That is, because of their athletic status, some youngsters receive preferential treatment and get away with more delinquent behaviors than their nonathletic counterparts. At the same time, other youngsters get labeled as "delinquents" and then fall into a self-fulfilling prophecy of escalating trouble, meanwhile getting no breaks in the legal system.

- The **economic strain** explanation for the sport–delinquency relationship holds that delinquency occurs because many youths are impoverished but still desire the high standard of living they see others enjoying. Sport participation, however, allows impoverished youngsters to gain prestige and status and, in turn, reduces the strain between their dreams of a better life and beliefs about attainable goals.

Although these explanations may help us better understand why sport participation is associated with decreases in delinquency, they do not give us definitive conclusions (Shields & Bredemeier, 1995). Most likely the sport participation–delinquency relationship is best explained by some combination of these views, and in any case, requires further research.

Sport Participation and Gang Behavior

Gangs and the negative behaviors associated with them (e.g., crime, fights, murder) are of critical concern in both suburban and rural communities as well as many inner-city neighborhoods. Benedict and Keteyian (2011) estimate that there are more than 1 million gang members in the United States—and more than 40,000 in Los Angeles alone. Not only do gangs negatively influence their members and lead to increased crime, but they also affect physical activity involvement by making neighborhoods so unsafe that parents are afraid to let their children play outside or walk to physical activity settings such as gyms, pools, and parks (Stodolska, Acevedo, & Shinew, 2009).

Sport participation is proposed as an alternative to gang behavior for several reasons (Buckle & Walsh, 2013; Seefeldt & Ewing, 1997; Weintraub, 2009). First, some of the reasons that youths join gangs are alienation from family and peers, low self-esteem, and a lack of positive role models—all things that sport can alleviate. Second, kids maintain their gang membership because the gang fills their needs in some way. That is, the gang provides an identity for its members and serves many functions that a family might. Again, these are things that membership in a sport team can provide. Finally, gang members often live in communities where they have little access to healthy alternatives such as sport programs. An interview study of gangs in Scotland showed, however, that many gang members resist or move out of gangs if attractive alternatives such as sport are offered (Deuchar, 2009).

Sport participation can serve as an important substitute for gang membership. Specifically, sport participation can fill the gap for underserved youths (e.g., children who are economically deprived or who have little or no parental supervision) by facilitating increased self-esteem, providing an important source of identity, lending social support, and giving partici-

pants positive role models. Some contend that putting youths from different neighborhoods on the same teams helps prevent gang violence, which often results from territorial disputes between groups that have little contact with each other and do not see themselves as similar (Taylor, 2012). In fact, Ewing and Seefeldt (1996) observed that selling sport participation as an alternative to gang activity has become an important recruitment strategy for youth sport leaders.

Sport will serve as an alternative to negative behavior only if programs are properly run, organized, and implemented. Sport does nothing by itself. As repeatedly emphasized in this book, high-quality experiences in sport give rise to psychological benefits.

Nowhere is this principle better demonstrated than in Trulson's (1986) study of delinquent teenagers where boys were matched in background and important personality characteristics (e.g., aggression) and assigned to one of three groups that met three times a week for 1 hour. One group participated in a modern taekwondo program emphasizing fighting and self-defense techniques. The second group took part in traditional taekwondo, which emphasized philosophical reflection, meditation, and physical practice. The third group served as a control and played football and basketball. After 6 months, members of the modern taekwondo group were less well adjusted and scored higher on delinquency and aggression measures than when the study had begun! Members of the traditional taekwondo group, however, exhibited below-normal aggression, less anxiety, more social skills, and enhanced self-esteem. Children in the control football and basketball group showed little change in personality or delinquency but improved in self-esteem and social skills.

Buckle and Walsh (2013) described an inner-city soccer program that was guided by Hellison's (2011) model of teaching personal and social responsibility. Gang members took part in a 28-week soccer program in which program providers used relational time (planned times where adult leaders had opportunities to individually interact with program participants), sport lessons, large-group meetings, awareness talks, and routines to teach personal and social responsibility. After completing the program, one participant noted:

" **I learned five words that I always have with me wherever I go, and they are respect, self-control, leadership, participation, and effort. Those five words helped me in so many ways that I don't have the words to express how these words have changed my life. (Buckle & Walsh, 2013, p. 57)"**

Most important, these findings reveal that sport participation alone was not enough to positively influence negative behaviors—the program had to blend the physical activities with social and psychological teachings to accomplish this.

> **KEY POINT** People do not know what constitutes acceptable and unacceptable behavior if it is not defined.

Strategies for Enhancing Character Development

The social learning, structural–developmental, and social–psychological approaches have facilitated our understanding of good sporting behavior and enhanced character development. Nine strategies have been derived from these approaches. We discuss each of these strategies to suggest how it can enhance character development.

Define Good Sporting Behavior in Your Program

As you have learned, there is no universal definition of good sporting behavior. And without a specific definition, people in your program will not know what you mean by appropriate and acceptable behavior or inappropriate and unacceptable behavior. Camire and Trudel (2010) found that it was not enough for coaches to make simple references to broad concepts such as character or good morals—athletes did not understand general definitions. The authors concluded that coaches must define specific moral values and their meanings. Table 24.2 presents an example of such a written code that specifically identifies positive and negative sporting behaviors for a children's sport program.

Reinforce and Encourage Good Sporting Behaviors

Reinforce and encourage those behaviors and attitudes that you define in your program as good sporting behavior. Conversely, penalize and discourage inappropriate behaviors. Consistency in reinforcing and penalizing these behaviors and actions is essential. Follow the behavior modification guidelines in chapter 6.

Model Appropriate Behaviors

Many people look up to professionals in our field, identifying with them and modeling their actions. Because actions speak louder than words, exercise

TABLE 24.2 A Written Code of Good Sporting Behavior for a Youth Sports Program

Areas of concern	Positive sporting behaviors	Negative sporting behaviors
Behavior toward officials	Questioning officials in the appropriate manner (e.g., lodging an official protest; having only designated individuals, such as a captain, address officials)	Arguing with officials Swearing at officials
Behavior toward opponents	Treating all opponents with respect and dignity at all times	Arguing with opponents Making sarcastic remarks about opponents Making aggressive actions toward opponents
Behavior toward teammates	Giving only constructive criticism and positive encouragement	Making negative comments or sarcastic remarks Swearing at or arguing with teammates
Behavior toward spectators	Making only positive comments to spectators	Arguing with spectators Making negative remarks and swearing at spectators
Rule acceptance and infractions	Obeying all league rules	Taking advantage of loopholes in rules (e.g., every child must play, so coach tells unskilled players to be sick on day of important game)

Adapted, by permission, from D. Gould, 1981, Sportsmanship: Build character or characters. In *A winning philosophy for youth sports programs,* edited by Youth Sports Institute (Lansing, MI: Institute for The Study of Youth Sports).

and sport professionals must provide a good model of positive sporting behavior. Easier said than done, you say? Indeed, professionals may make mistakes (e.g., they may lose control and be charged with a technical foul for arguing with the officials). When they lose control, they should admit their error and apologize to the players or students. Some coaches with strict guidelines for good sporting behavior for their players believe it is their job to argue with officials and stick up for their team. Their efforts may be well intended, but coaches should realize that by demonstrating poor sporting behavior they send mixed messages that undermine their efforts to enhance positive behaviors.

Explain Why Certain Behaviors Are Appropriate

Only when people have internalized a guiding moral principle for determining right or wrong can we expect them to consistently behave well in various situations. Thus, you should include a rationale for the various components of your positive behavior code. Rationales provide explanations based on the key elements underlying the levels of moral reasoning: altruism, impartial rules, and moral balances based on mutually determined agreements (Weiss, 1987). Most important, you should regularly convey rationales to participants. For example, if several youngsters are excluding a less skilled classmate in a physical education game, you need to ensure that the less skilled child is included and emphasize the reason behind the decision (e.g., "It is important to treat others as you want them to treat you instead of just doing what you want").

KEY POINT Frequently explain your rationales for the rightness or wrongness of actions.

Intention is important in regard to actions. The ability to judge intent starts developing at about the age of 7 or 8 years (Martens, 1982). With children who are about 10 years old, you can emphasize **role taking** (i.e., seeing one's self in someone else's role). Then you can add higher levels of empathy—the ability of two people to take each other's perspectives into account when deciding how to act (Newman & Newman, 1991). Many coaches like to have players officiate practice scrimmages of their teammates. The players can then better understand the rules of the game and see things from an official's perspective. With the addition of a brief postscrimmage discussion, this role taking can be a valuable tool for helping players learn to empathize.

KEY POINT Fitness and sport professionals must be models of good sporting behavior.

Discuss Moral Dilemmas and Choices

For effective moral education to occur, participants should engage in self-dialogue and group discussions about choices and moral dilemmas. A **moral dilemma** requires participants to decide what is morally correct or incorrect (see "When to Shoot Toward an Opponent's Injured Leg"). Rule violations, when and why injured participants should play, and who should play are excellent topics for discussion (Bredemeier & Shields, 1987). Discuss various gray areas of right and wrong that may or may not be against the rules. For example, is it okay to intentionally say something upsetting to an opponent at the start of a contest (Weiss, 1987)?

Build Moral Dilemmas and Choices Into Practices

Some dilemmas you might pose to young athletes during practice include the following (Weiss, 1987, p. 148):

When to Shoot Toward an Opponent's Injured Leg

Rodd and Kevin are two evenly matched 150-pound wrestlers involved in a close match. Rodd injures his left knee, takes an injury time-out for treatment, and then returns to the mat. He is in obvious pain, his movement is greatly constrained, and he cannot place weight on his injured leg. Imagine that you are Kevin and respond to the following questions:

- Should you execute moves to the side of the injured leg because it will be easier to score points?
- Once you are in contact with your injured opponent, should you put extra pressure on his injured leg to cause him pain and allow you to turn him to his back and pin him?
- Should you avoid executing moves toward his injured leg unless the match is close in score?
- Should you avoid executing moves toward his injured leg entirely and try to beat him at his best?

- Not putting out enough of the "best" equipment for all athletes
- Devising a drill with unequal opportunities for practice—for example, one person is always on defense
- Devising a drill in which players might be tempted to hurt with words (laughing, yelling), such as having someone demonstrate weak skills or having unfair relay teams
- Devising a drill that provides possible opportunities for rough play—for example, the hamburger rebound drill, in which two individuals block out one person simultaneously and go for the ball

After the players try to solve the dilemmas, follow up with discussion about the underlying moral reasoning. Implementing these strategies for enhancing character development and good sporting behavior requires time, planning, and effort. For optimal effect they should be repeated consistently across time, not just once or twice at the start of the season or when a child is causing a problem.

Teach Cooperative Learning Strategies

Competition and cooperation are defined and discussed in chapter 5. Although both competition and cooperation are necessary for the optimal development of achievement motivation, children in Western society are much more often exposed to competition than to cooperation. For this reason, physical activity participants should be taught cooperative learning strategies. Researchers into moral development also have shown that learning how to cooperate is critical to character development (Miller et al., 1997). This learning might involve using superordinate goals (e.g., make the most possible passes in 3 minutes) rather than competitive goals (e.g., score more points than your opponents) in games or focusing on cooperative games.

Create a Task-Oriented Motivational Climate and Employ Autonomy-Supportive Coaching

A task-oriented motivational climate stresses having participants adopt task, rather than ego, goals (see chapter 3) so they can judge their ability by their own performance rather than through socially compared improvements. Athletes who perceive an ego-oriented motivational environment are characterized by lower moral judgments as well as a higher sense of the legitimacy of using physical intimidation (Kavussanu

& Ntoumanis, 2003; Miller, Roberts, & Ommundsen, 2005). Ntoumanis and Standage (2009) also found that athletes who perceived that their coaches supported their autonomy and better met their autonomy, relatedness, and competence needs were more autonomy motivated. Autonomous motivation, in turn, was found to positively predict good sporting behavior and negatively predict antisocial attitudes. Controlling motivation, however, was positively related to antisocial attitudes and negatively related to good sporting behavior. It is easier to teach good sporting behavior and develop character, then, when social comparison and competition are de-emphasized and individual improvement, learning, autonomy, and relatedness are emphasized (Miller et al., 1997; Ntoumanis and Standage, 2009). However, this does not mean that character cannot be developed in a competitive climate—only that there are major benefits to initiating the efforts toward character development in a task-oriented and autonomy-supportive motivational climate. Once participants have developed good character, competition might indeed provide good tests of what values they have developed.

Transfer Power From Leaders to Participants

Character development is best fostered in environments that progressively transfer power from leaders to participants. Hellison and Templin (1991), for example, developed a physical education curriculum designed to help students grow in their sense of personal and social responsibility. This realistic program first focuses on children who are acting irresponsibly, helping them regain their self-control by removing them from class so that they do not disrupt others. Self-control is then developed, followed by later steps toward involvement, self-direction, and caring (see "Hellison's Levels of Responsibility").

Guiding Practice in Character Development

To guide your practice, you should consider several philosophically oriented issues that cover a broad range. These include the physical educator's and coach's roles in moral development and making character development a mind-set versus an isolated activity. In addition, you should look at the role of winning and the ways in which the moral behavior you teach can be transferred beyond the playing field as well as recognize the imperfect nature of character development.

Educator's Role in Character Development

Some people believe that teachers and coaches have no business teaching morals and values to youths. Character and morals are the domain of parents and the church, they argue, not the school—especially not the public schools. We certainly agree that it is not sound practice to mix religious values into the public school curriculum. However, avoiding character education in basic values such as honesty, empathy, and methods of solving disputes is a grave mistake. And we contend that physical educators, coaches, and exercise leaders do influence many values, intentionally or not. As Shields and Bredemeier (1995) stated, "Despite the problems associated with competitive sport, sport is replete with opportunities to encounter, learn, transform, and enact moral values" (p. 3). For example, coaches recommend whether to argue with officials, physical educators take positions on teaching competitive or cooperative games, and athletic trainers recommend when to play an injured athlete. Such decisions often affect the participants' attitudes, so it is important to develop a philosophical stance on these issues. It is much better to recognize the moral values you're fostering and discouraging than to affect someone else's values haphazardly. It is also important that you carefully study the contents of this chapter because recent findings reveal that although coaches are strong proponents of sport's potential to develop character, most have little training in how to teach values that lead to the development of character (Trudel, Lemyre, Werthner, & Camire, 2007).

Character Development as Mind-Set Versus an Isolated Activity

As we just argued, it is critical that sport and physical activity leaders make a strong commitment to moral

Hellison's Levels of Responsibility

Hellison and Templin (1991) developed a physical education program that focuses on helping children grow in their sense of responsibility.

- *Level 0—Irresponsibility.* This level characterizes students who are unmotivated and whose behavior is disruptive. The goal of the physical educator is to help them get their behavior under control (thereby advancing them to level 1) or to remove them from the setting so they do not interfere with others' rights.

- *Level 1—Self-control.* Students at this level may not participate in the day's activities, but they control their behavior enough to not need to be removed from the setting. The goal of the physical educator is to help these students become involved in the activities (thereby advancing them to level 2) or, minimally, to learn to respect the rights and feelings of others enough that their behaviors and attitudes do not interfere with teaching and learning.

- *Level 2—Involvement.* Students at level 2 participate in the physical education activities. Involvement may take many forms, from going through the motions to setting and pursuing objectives. The goal of the physical educator is to encourage students to take increasing responsibility for their own development and definitions of success. For example, students may come to define success as effort, improvement, goal setting, achievement of a norm or standard, or being socially responsible as a player or leader.

- *Level 3—Self-direction.* This level characterizes students who can work effectively and independently on self-improvement in areas of personally identified need or aspiration. The goal of the physical educator is to enable students to acquire the skills needed to work independently and set realistic goals. A relevant knowledge base is also critical, and students should be gradually confronted with broader philosophical issues that connect with their self-defined objectives: "Who do I want to be? Why do I want to . . . ?"

- *Level 4—Caring.* Up to this point, the only necessary regard for others is a respect for their fundamental rights. At level 4, students move beyond the focus on self and are motivated by a prosocial orientation. The goal of the physical educator is to provide opportunities to cooperate, give support, show concern, and help others.

Reprinted, by permission, from D. Shields and B. Bredemeier, 1995, *Character development and physical activity* (Champaign, IL: Human Kinetics), 208.

and character development education. However, just having a character education goal, or from time to time implementing several character development strategies, is not enough. Moral development and good sporting behavior must become part of a leader's mind-set whereby he or she is constantly looking for opportunities to develop and enhance these positive qualities in participants. Too often physical educators and coaches assume that, because they believe in the character-enhancing virtues of sport and physical activity involvement, desirable characteristics will automatically result from participation or by simply imparting one or two strategies from time to time. Drawing on the moral education literature, however, Arnold (2001) indicated that to effectively develop morals and character in young people, teachers and coaches must teach these values, become an enlightened leader of moral discussions, be an exemplar of the values embodied in sport, and provide individual mentoring to participants who have difficulty with moral issues. Clearly, developing morals and positive sporting behavior takes forethought and consistent

efforts on the part of physical educators and coaches. It must be a mind-set that runs constantly versus an isolated activity that occurs from time to time.

VIEW Activity 24.2 helps you learn how to enhance character development and good sporting behavior.

Reducing Youth Risk by Fostering Resiliency

Despite the strategies that physical educators and coaches can use to teach character and good sporting behavior to children and youths, we must recognize that many children live in environments that place them at risk for negative behavioral development (e.g., drug addiction, teenage pregnancy, and gang activity). Moreover, it is unlikely that physical activity specialists can eliminate such major risk factors as poverty, an absence of parental involvement in someone's life, abuse, and undesirable role models. Nevertheless, Martinek and Hellison (1997), two physical educators

Young athletes who develop strong social networks may be better able to overcome less-than-ideal environmental influences.

who have spent countless hours working with underserved youths, contend that psychological resiliency is one of the most important life skills that we can foster in these children. **Resiliency** is the ability to bounce back successfully after exposure to severe risk or distress; in essence, it is righting oneself in conditions in which one is thwarted (Martinek & Hellison, 1997). Moreover, educators and social scientists have studied resilient youths and found that they possess three primary attributes: social competence, autonomy, and optimism and hope.

Social Competence

Social competence is the ability to interact socially with others and in so doing create strong networks of social support. Flexibility and empathy are seen as critical to the development of this important attribute. Especially important is learning how to negotiate, confront, and handle challenges from others (e.g., learning nonviolent peer conflict resolution skills; see chapter 23).

Autonomy

Resilient youths also have a clear sense of who they are, believe they can exert control over their environments, and believe they can act independently. In essence, they feel a sense of **autonomy**—that they can function as individuals on their own.

Optimism and Hope

In chapter 3 we discuss learned helplessness, a condition in which an individual feels that little change will take place despite putting forth effort. Resilient youths are at the other end of the spectrum: They haven't learned helplessness. Rather, they have a sense of **optimism and hope** and believe that their efforts will be rewarded. Martinek and Hellison (1997) contended that one of the best ways to enhance resiliency in underserved youths is through the development of physical activity programs. Moreover, these authors outlined specific strategies for doing so (see "Strategies for Developing Resiliency in Youths").

Double-Sided Role of Winning

Winning plays a dual role in character development (Martens, 1982). On one hand, an emphasis on winning pressures some individuals to cheat, break rules, and behave in ways they would consider inappropriate off the field. On the other hand, when a player resists temptations to cheat or commit other immoral acts despite the high value placed on winning, integrity develops and moral lessons become more meaningful. Winning itself is neutral to moral development. The key is finding the right emphasis to place on winning.

Strategies for Developing Resiliency in Youths

- Focus on athletes' strengths rather than weaknesses. Build their self-confidence.
- Don't focus only on the sport or physical activity. Focus on the whole child and her emotional, social, economic, and educational needs.
- Be sensitive to the youngster's individuality and his cultural differences. Get to know him as a person.
- Encourage independence and control over one's life by providing the athlete with input about the program and leadership responsibilities.
- Incorporate a strong set of values and clear expectations into the program. Make sure the athlete knows what you expect and value.
- Help youths see possible future occupations for themselves.
- Provide a physically and psychologically safe environment.
- Keep program numbers small and emphasize long-term involvement.
- Provide leadership that makes the program work despite obstacles.
- Make sure the program links with the community and neighborhood.
- Provide quality contact with adult models who care and offer support.

Adapted from Martinek and Hellison 1997.

Transferring Values to Nonsport Environments

It is a myth that the lessons and values learned in the gym or pool or on the athletic field transfer automatically to other environments. For such a transfer to occur, the lesson must be drawn out or extended (Danish & Nellen, 1997; Danish, Nellen, & Owens, 1996; Danish, Petitpas, & Hale, 1992). If you want to teach values through sport and physical activity, you must discuss how the values transfer to the nonsport environment. For instance, a coach who wants to teach young athletes an attitude of cooperation to carry over to nonsport situations can discuss how and when teamwork is useful in other contexts (e.g., working on a school project). This is one advantage of a structural–developmental approach. Social learning principles, which enhance specific good sporting attitudes and behaviors, tend to be highly situation specific; that is, teaching a child to be honest in gym class will not transfer to math class. However, if you can help raise someone's underlying moral reasoning, the person's behavior tends to be affected across a variety of situations.

> **KEY POINT** If your goal is to teach values through sport and physical activities, learn to discuss how these values transfer to nonsport environments.

Having Realistic Expectations

Unfortunately, enhancing good sporting behavior and developing character through sport and physical activity are imperfect processes (Martens, 1982). We cannot reach all individuals at all times. More likely, we'll have some tremendous successes along with disappointing failures. Recognizing the imperfect nature of character development and having realistic expectations enable us to remain optimistic despite having some setbacks.

LEARNING AIDS

SUMMARY

1. **Define character development and good sporting behavior.**
   Character development and good sporting behavior concern morality in sport and physical activity; that is, they have to do with our views and actions about what is right or ethical and what is wrong or unethical in sport and physical activity settings. Character comprises four interrelated virtues: compassion, fairness, good sporting behavior, and integrity. These virtues are also closely related to moral development, moral reasoning, and moral behavior.

2. **Explain how character and good sporting behavior develop.**
   There are three views about how character and good sporting behavior develop in athletes. The social learning approach emphasizes modeling, reinforcement, and social comparison. The structural–developmental approach contends that moral reasoning is related to a person's level of cognitive development. The analysis of five levels in moral reasoning reflects a progression from judging an action's rightness or wrongness according to self-centered interests to having concern for the mutual interests of all involved. Third, the social–psychological approach combines the first two approaches and suggests that a complex person-by-situation interplay determines character development and good sporting behavior.

3. **Identify the important link between moral reasoning and moral behavior.**
   One's moral reasoning and moral behavior are linked by a moral action process that includes four stages: interpreting the situation as one that involves some sort of moral judgment, deciding on the best course of action, making a choice to act morally, and implementing a moral response. Although a consistent relationship exists between moral reasoning and moral behavior, the relationship is not perfect.

4. **Discuss how character and good sporting behavior can be influenced.**
   Research shows that physical education and youth sports participation can deter negative behaviors such as delinquency and gang violence and can enhance positive character development. For this positive development to occur, it is necessary to use well-thought-out, well-designed, and well-implemented strategies for character development. Nine strategies for developing character and positive sporting behavior can be delineated based on the social learning, structural–developmental, and social–psychological

approaches. These strategies are as follows: defining in precise terms what you consider good sporting behavior; reinforcing and encouraging good sporting behaviors and penalizing and discouraging bad sporting behaviors; modeling appropriate behaviors; conveying rationales, emphasizing why actions are appropriate or inappropriate considering the intent of actions, role taking, compassion, and empathy; discussing moral dilemmas; building moral dilemmas and choices into practice and class contexts; teaching cooperative learning strategies; engineering task-oriented motivational climates; and transferring power from leaders to participants.

5. **Describe the effects of winning on character development and good sporting behavior.**
   Some philosophically oriented issues to consider in facilitating character development are the educator's role in character development, the double-sided role of winning, transferring values to nonsport environments, and maintaining realistic expectations of the character development process. Physical activity specialists also play an important role in fostering resiliency in underserved youths.

KEY TERMS

fair play
good sporting behavior
character
compassion
integrity
moral reasoning
moral development

moral behavior
hazing
differential association
social bonding
labeling hypothesis
economic strain

role taking
moral dilemma
resiliency
social competence
autonomy
optimism and hope

REVIEW QUESTIONS

1. Define character and its components.

2. Describe the social learning, structural–developmental, and social–psychological approaches to moral reasoning and development.

3. What are Haan's five stages of moral reasoning? Why are these important?

4. What is the relationship between athletic participation and delinquency or gang behaviors?

5. Describe the relationship between moral reasoning and moral behavior. What implication does this have for guiding practice?

6. Explain each of the following strategies for enhancing character development and good sporting behavior:
   - Defining good sporting behavior in your particular context
   - Reinforcing and encouraging positive sporting behaviors; penalizing and discouraging negative sporting behaviors
   - Modeling appropriate behaviors
   - Explaining your thinking about appropriate behaviors
   - Discussing moral dilemmas
   - Building moral dilemmas and choices into practices and classes
   - Teaching cooperative learning strategies
   - Engineering a task-oriented motivational climate
   - Transferring power from leaders to participants

7. How can winning both enhance and deter the development of good sporting behavior and moral reasoning?

8. Why is it important to teach how to transfer character lessons learned in sport to nonsport settings?

9. Why is it important to think of developing character as a mind-set versus the use of specific isolated activities?

10. Discuss the notion of hazing, including why it occurs and how it may be reduced.

CRITICAL THINKING QUESTIONS

1. What should be the role of the physical educator in enhancing character development and teaching good sporting behavior?

2. Design a moral dilemma for the following situations:
   - Physical education class
   - Youth sports team practice
   - Varsity high school contest

Continuing
Your Journey

How can you put your knowledge into practice?

This section signals the end of your journey to developing an understanding of sport and exercise psychology. We began your journey by introducing you to the field and defining what it involves as well as ways we acquire knowledge and then use that knowledge to help individuals achieve their personal development and performance-enhancement goals in practical settings. The second stop on your journey focused on learning about participants—what makes them tick, their personalities, and motivational orientations. The third stop turned our attention to understanding sport and exercise environments and addressed important topics such as competition and cooperation and feedback and reinforcement. The fourth stop on our journey helped us learn about group processes and discussed important issues such as how groups function, ways to build group cohesion, effective leadership strategies, and the best ways to communicate. Improving performance was the focus of the fifth stop. In this section you learned how to design psychological skills training programs, the keys to regulating arousal, how to use imagery to improve performance and help recover from injury, ways to become confident, the most effective ways to set and monitor goals, and how to improve concentration. With many countries facing a crisis of obesity and lack of physical activity, the sixth stop discussed ways to enhance health and well-being, the role physical activity plays in improving cognitive functioning, and strategies for helping people adhere to their exercise programs. At this stop you also learned about the psychology of athletic injuries, how to prevent and effectively deal with addictive and unhealthy behaviors that can occur in sport and exercise contexts, and burnout and overtraining. Finally, at the seventh and final stop we discussed ways to facilitate psychological growth and development through physical education and participation in sport and exercise. Critical psychological issues in sport and exercise for children were emphasized. We also discussed aggression in sport and whether sport and physical activity involvement can be used to develop character and good sporting behavior in participants.

This journey has provided you with a good grasp of strategies that can be used to foster performance improvement, psychological change, and develop-ment. This knowledge will help you choose the most appropriate ways to achieve the objectives of your psychological skills program. However, unless you put this knowledge into practice, it will be of little use. In other words, even though your journey through the field of sport and exercise psychology is now finished in this text, your journey in the field is just beginning. You will continue to learn a great deal more from your efforts to employ that knowledge or may study the field even further—some of you may even desire to become sport psychologists.

As a professional in sport and exercise science, you will be responsible for implementing what you have learned. You now know that a knowledge of sport and exercise psychology can have tremendous payoffs when applied in professional practice settings. So adopt the active approach to professional practice that we discussed in the beginning of this text, implement the ideas conveyed here, and consistently evaluate your strategies in light of your professional experience. Be aware of current research. Use the gym, pool, and athletic field as your laboratory to continue your growth and professional development. Don't make the mistake of simply taking your final exam, finishing the course, and then never again thinking about the material. Refer to the text when you are faced with practical problems. Use what you have learned and try to improve on it. Take it from us: Seeing someone achieve his or her goals through developing psychological skills is one of the most rewarding professional experiences you can have.

VIEW Dr. Dan Gould recaps your journey through *Foundations of Sport and Exercise Psychology* in this Introduction activity.

JOURNEY In the first Journey activity you completed in the web study guide, you were asked to record your expectations as you began your semester studies. This final summary activity gives you a chance to revisit those questions so that you can see how your answers may have changed and how much you've grown on your journey.

Abell, R. (1975). Confessions of a compulsive. *Runner's World, 10,* 30–31.

Abernethy, B. (2001). Attention. In R. Singer, H. Hausenblas, & C. Janelle (Eds.), *Handbook of sport psychology* (2nd ed., pp. 53–85). New York: Wiley.

Abernethy, B., Maxwell, J., Masters, R., Van der Kamp, J., & Jackson, R. (2007). Attentional processes in skill learning and expert performance. In G. Tenenbaum & R. Eklund (Eds.), *Handbook of sport psychology* (3rd edition, pp. 245–263). New York: Wiley.

Abernethy, B., Summers, J., & Ford, S. (1998). Issues in the measurement of attention. In J. Duda (Ed.), *Advances in sport and exercise psychology measurement* (pp. 173–193). Morgantown, WV: Fitness Information Technology.

Ackery, A.D., Tator, C.H., & Snider, C. (2012). Violence in Canadian amateur hockey: The experience of referees in Ontario. *Clinical Journal of Sports Medicine, 22*(2), 86–90.

Aherne, C., Moran, A., & Lonsdale, C. (2011). The effects of mindfulness training on athletes' flow: An initial investigation. *The Sport Psychologist, 25,* 177–189.

Ahsen, A. (1984). The triple code model for imagery and psychophysiology. *Journal of Mental Imagery, 8,* 15–42.

Ajzen, I., & Fishbein, M. (1980). *Understanding attitudes and predicting social behavior.* Englewood Cliffs, NJ: Prentice Hall.

Ajzen, I., & Madden, T.J. (1986). Prediction of goal-directed behavior: Attitudes intentions, and perceived behavioral control. *Journal of Experimental Social Psychology, 22,* 453–474.

Albert, E. (1999). Dealing with danger: The normalization of risk in cycling. *International Review for the Sociology of Sport, 42,* 202–210.

Albrecht, R. (2009). Drop and give us 20, Siefried; A practical response to "defending the use of punishment by coaches." *Quest, 61,* 470–475.

Albrecht, R.R., & Feltz, D.L. (1987). Generality and specificity of attention related to competitive anxiety and sport performance. *Journal of Sport Psychology, 9,* 241–248.

Albright, S.C. (1993). A structural analysis of hitting streaks in baseball. *Journal of the American Statistical Association, 88,* 1175–1183.

Alfermann, D., & Stambulova, N. (2007). Career transition and career termination. In G. Tenenbaum & R. Eklund (Eds.), *Handbook of sport psychology* (3rd ed., pp. 712–733). New York: Wiley.

Allen, J.B. (2003). Social motivation in youth sports. *Journal of Sport and Exercise Psychology, 25,* 551–567.

Allen, M. (1987). *Jackie Robinson: A life remembered.* New York: Franklin Watts.

Allen, M.S., Coffee, P., & Greenlees, I. (2012). A theoretical framework and research agenda of studying team attributions in sport. *International Review of Sport and Exercise Psychology, 5*(2), 121–144.

Allen, M.S., Greenless, I., & Jones, M. (2013). Personality in sport: A comprehensive review. *International Review of Sport and Exercise Psychology, 6*(1), 184–208.

Allison, M.G., & Ayllon, T. (1980). Behavioral coaching in the development of skills in football, gymnastics, and tennis. *Journal of Applied Behavior Analysis, 13,* 297–314.

Alves, C., Gualano, B., Takao, P., Avakian, P., Fernandes, R., Morine, D., et al. (2012). Effects of acute physical exercise on executive functions: A comparison between aerobic and strength exercise. *Journal of Sport and Exercise Psychology, 34,* 539–549.

American Coaching Effectiveness Program (ACEP). (1994). *ACEP psychology, level 2.* Champaign, IL: Human Kinetics.

American College of Sports Medicine. (1997). *ACSM's health/fitness facility standards and guidelines* (2nd ed.). Champaign, IL: Human Kinetics.

American Medical Association. (1966). *Standard nomenclature of athletic injuries.* Chicago: American Medical Association.

American Psychiatric Association. (2013). *Diagnostic and statistical manual of mental disorders* (5th ed.). Washington, DC: American Psychiatric Association.

American Psychological Association and National Council on Measurement in Education. (1999). *Standards for educational and psychological testing.* Washington, DC: American Psychological Association.

American Psychological Association. (2002). Ethical principles for psychologists and the code of conduct. *American Psychologist, 57,* 1060–1073.

American Sport Education Program. (1994). *Sport parent.* Champaign, IL: Human Kinetics.

Ames, C. (1987). The enhancement of student motivation. In D.A. Klieber & M. Maehr (Eds.), *Advances in motivation and achievement* (pp. 123–148). Greenwich, CT: JAI Press.

Ames, C. (1992). Achievement goals, motivational climates, and motivational processes. In G.C. Roberts (Ed.), *Motivation in sport and exercise* (pp. 161–176). Champaign, IL: Human Kinetics.

Amiot, C.E., Sansfacon, S., & Louis, W.R. (2013). Uncovering hockey fans' motivations behind their derogatory behaviors and how these motives predict psychological well-being and quality of social identity. *Psychology of Sport and Exercise, 14,* 379–388.

Amorose, T., & Horn, T. (2000). Intrinsic motivation: Relationships with collegiate athletes' gender, scholarship status, and perceptions of their coaches' behavior. *Journal of Sport and Exercise Psychology, 22,* 63–84.

Amorose, T., Horn, T., & Miller, V. (1994). Intrinsic motivation in collegiate athletes: Relationships with athletes' scholarship status and coaching behaviors. *Journal of Sport and Exercise Psychology, 16,* S26.

Andersen, M. (2000). *Doing sport psychology.* Champaign, IL: Human Kinetics.

Andersen, M., & Speed, H. (2013). Therapeutic relationships in applied sport psychology. In S. Hanrahan & M. Andersen (Eds.), *Routledge handbook of applied sport psychology: A comprehensive guide for students and practitioners* (pp. 3–11). New York: Routledge.

Andersen, M.B., & Williams, J.M. (1988). A model of stress and athletic injury: Prediction and prevention. *Journal of Sport and Exercise Psychology, 10,* 294–306.

Anderson, C., Petrie, T., & Neumann, C. (2011). Psychosocial correlates of bulimic symptoms among NCAA Division-1 female collegiate gymnasts and swimmers/divers. *Journal of Sport and Exercise Psychology, 33,* 483–505.

Anderson, C.A., & Bushman, B.J. (2002). Human aggression. *Annual Review of Psychology, 53,* 27–52.

Anderson, D., Crowell, C., Doman, M., & Howard, G. (1988). Performance positing, goal-setting and activity-contingent praise as applied to a university hockey team. *Journal of Applied Sport Psychology, 73,* 87–95.

Andre, A., Deneuve, P., & Louvet, B. (2011). Cooperative learning in physical education and acceptance of students with learning disabilities. *Journal of Applied Sport Psychology, 23,* 474–485.

Anshel, M. (2003). *Sport psychology: From theory to practice.* San Francisco, CA: Benjamin Cummings.

Anshel, M. (2010). Drug abuse in sport: Causes and cures. In J. Williams (Ed.), *Applied sport psychology: Personal growth to peak performance* (pp. 463–491). New York: McGraw-Hill.

Anshel, M. (2012). *Sport psychology: From theory to practice* (5th ed.). San Francisco: Benjamin Cummings.

Anshel, M.H., & Seipel, S.J. (2009). Self-monitoring and selected measures of aerobic and strength fitness and short-term exercise attendance. *Journal of Sport Behavior, 32,* 125–151.

Anshel, M.H., & Weinberg, R.S. (1995a). Coping with acute stress among American and Australian basketball referees. *Journal of Sport Behavior, 19,* 180–203.

Anshel, M.H., & Weinberg, R.S. (1995b). Sources of acute stress in American and Australian basketball referees. *Journal of Applied Sport Psychology, 7,* 11–22.

Anton, S., Perri, M., Riley, J., Kanasky, W., Rodrigue, J., Sears, S., et al. (2005). Differential predictors of adherence in exercise programs with moderate versus higher levels of intensity and frequency. *Journal of Sport and Exercise Psychology, 27,* 171–187.

Apitzsch, E. (1995). Psychodynamic theory of personality and sport performance. In S.J.H. Biddle (Ed.), *European perspectives on exercise and sport psychology* (pp. 111–127). Champaign, IL: Human Kinetics.

Appleton, K. (2013). 6 x 40 mins. exercise improves body image even though body weight and shape do not change. *Journal of Health Psychology, 18,* 110–120.

Appleton, P.R., Hall, H.K., & Hill, A.P. (2009). Relations between multidimensional perfectionism and burnout in junior-elite athletes. *Psychology of Sport and Exercise, 10,* 457–465.

Appleton, P.R., Hall, H.K., & Hill, A.P. (2010). Family patterns of perfectionism: An examination of elite junior athletes and their parents. *Psychology, Sport and Exercise, 11,* 363–371.

Arent, S.M., & Landers, D.M. (2003). Arousal, anxiety, and performance: A reexamination of the inverted-U hypothesis. *Research Quarterly for Exercise and Sport, 74*(4), 436–444.

Arent, S., Landers, D., Matt, K., & Etnier, J. (2005). Dose-response and mechanistic issues in the resistance training and affect relationship. *Journal of Sport and Exercise Psychology, 27,* 92–110.

Arms, R.L., Russell, G.W., & Sandilands, M.L. (1979). Effects of viewing aggressive sports on the hostility of spectators. *Social Psychology Quarterly, 42,* 275–279.

Arnold, P.J. (2001). Sport, moral development, and the role of the teacher: Implications for research and moral education. *Quest, 53,* 135–150.

Aronson, E., Wilson, T., & Akert, R. (2002). *Social psychology* (4th ed.). Upper Saddle River, NJ: Prentice Hall.

Arrigo, I., Brunner-LaRocca, H., Lefkovits, M., Pfisterer, M., & Hoffmann, A. (2008). Comparative outcome one year after formal cardiac rehabilitation: The effects of a randomized intervention to improve exercise adherence. *European Journal of Cardiovascular Prevention and Rehabilitation, 15,* 306–311.

Arthur-Cameselle, J., & Baltzell, A. (2012). Learning from collegiate athletes who have recovered from eating disorders: Advice to coaches, parents, and other athletes with eating disorders. *Journal of Applied Sport Psychology, 24,* 1–9.

Arthur-Cameselle, J., & Quatromoni, P. (2010). Factors related to the onset of eating disorders reported by female collegiate athletes. *The Sport Psychologist, 25,* 1–17.

Arvinen-Barrow, M., Weigand, D., & Thomas, S. (2007). Elite and novice athletes' imagery use in open and closed sports. *Journal of Applied Sport Psychology, 19,* 93–104.

Asch, S. (1956). Studies of independence and conformity: A minority of one against a unanimous majority. *Psychological Monographs, 70*(9, Whole No. 416).

Ashe, A. (1981). *Off the court.* New York: New American Library.

Atkinson, J.W. (1974). The mainstream of achievement-oriented activity. In J.W. Atkinson & J.O. Raynor (Ed s.), *Motivation and achievement* (pp. 13–41). New York: Halstead.

Auweele, Y.V., Cuyper, B.D., Van Mele, V., & Rzewnicki, R. (1993). Elite performance and personality: From description and prediction to diagnosis and intervention. In R.N. Singer, M. Murphey, & L.K. Tennant (Eds.), *Handbook of sport psychology* (pp. 257–289). New York: Macmillan.

Avotte, B., Margrett, J., & Hicks-Patrick, J. (2010). Physical activity in middle-aged and young-old adults: The roles of self-efficacy, barriers, outcome expectations, self-regulatory behaviors and social support. *Journal of Health Psychology, 15,* 173–185.

Avugos, S., Bar-Eli, M., Ritov, I., & Sher, E. (2013). The elusive reality of efficacy-performance cycles in basketball shooting: An analysis of players' performance under invariant conditions. *International Journal of Sport and Exercise Psychology, 11,* 184–202.

Backhouse, S., Ekkekakis, P., Biddle, S., Foskett, A., & Williams, C. (2007). Exercise makes people feel better but people are inactive: Paradox or artifact? *Journal of Sport and Exercise Psychology, 29,* 498–517.

Bacon, U., Lerner, B., Trembley, D., & Seestedt, M. (2005). Substance abuse. In J. Taylor & G. Wilson (Eds.), *Applying sport psychology: Four perspectives (pp. 229-248).* Champaign, IL: Human Kinetics.

Baker, J., Yardley, J., & Côté, J. (2003). Coach behaviors and athlete satisfaction in team and individual sports. *International Journal of Sport Psychology, 34,* 226–239.

Balk, Y., Adriaase, M., de Ridder, D., & Evers, C. (2013). Coping under pressure: Employing emption regulation strategies to enhance performance under pressure. *Journal of Sport and Exercise Psychology, 35,* 408–418.

Baltes, B., & Parker, C. (2000). Understanding and removing the effects of performance cues on behavioral ratings. *Journal of Business and Psychology, 15,* 229–246.

Bandealy, A., & Kerr, G. (2013). Physical conditioning as a form of punishment in inter-university football. *Journal of Sport and Exercise Psychology, 35,* s75.

Bandura, A. (1973). *Aggression: A social learning analysis.* Englewood Cliffs, NJ: Prentice Hall.

Bandura, A. (1977a). Self-efficacy: Toward a unifying theory of behavioral change. *Psychological Review, 84,* 191–215.

Bandura, A. (1977b). *Social learning theory.* Englewood Cliffs, NJ: Prentice Hall.

Bandura, A. (1986). *Social foundations of thought and actions: A social cognitive theory.* Englewood Cliffs, NJ: Prentice Hall.

Bandura, A. (1991). Social-cognitive theory of moral thought and action. In W.M. Kurtines & J.L. Gewirtz (Eds.), *Handbook of moral behavior and development: Vol. 1: Theory* (pp. 45–103). Hillsdale, NJ: Erlbaum.

Bandura, A. (1997). *Self-efficacy: The exercise of control.* New York: Freeman.

Bandura, A. (1999). Moral disengagement in the perpetration of inhumanities. *Personality and Social Psychology Review, 3,* 193–209.

Bandura, A. (2005). Health promotion by social cognitive means. *Health Education and Behavior, 32,* 143–162.

Bar-Eli, M., Avugos, S., & Raab, M. (2006). Twenty years of "hot hand" research: Review and critique. *Psychology of Sport and Exercise, 7,* 525–553.

Barker, J., & Jones, M. (2008). The effect of hypnosis on self-efficacy. Affect and soccer performance: A case study. *Journal of Clinical Sport Psychology, 2,* 127–147.

Barnett, N.P., Smoll, F.L., & Smith, R.E. (1992). Effects of enhancing coach-athlete relationships on youth sport attrition. *The Sport Psychologist, 6,* 111–127.

Baron, R.A., & Richardson, D.R. (1994). *Human aggression.* New York: Plenum Press.

Bartholomew, K., Ntoumanis, N., & Thogersen-Ntoumanis, C. (2009). A review of controlling motivational strategies from a self-determination theory perspective: Implications for sport coaches. *International Review of Sport and Exercise Psychology, 2,* 215–233.

Bartlett, J., Clodre, G., MacLaren, D., Gregson, W., Drust, B., & Morton, J. (2011). High-intensity interval running is perceived to be more enjoyable than moderate-intensity continuous exercise: Implications for exercise adherence. *Journal of Sport Sciences, 29,* 547–553.

Baumeister, R.F. (1984). Choking under pressure: Self-consciousness and the paradoxical effects of incentives on skillful performance. *Journal of Personality and Social Psychology, 46,* 610–620.

Baumeister, R.F., & Steinhilber, A. (1984). Paradoxical effects of supportive audiences on performance under pressure: The home field disadvantage in sports championships. *Journal of Personality and Social Psychology, 43,* 85–93.

Beauchamp, M., Bray, S., Eys, M., & Carron, A. (2003). The effect of role ambiguity on competitive state anxiety. *Journal of Sport and Exercise Psychology, 25,* 77–92.

Beauchamp, M., Bray, S., Fielding, A., & Eys, M. (2005). A multilevel investigation of the relationship between role ambiguity and role efficacy in sport. *Psychology of Sport and Exercise, 6,* 289–302.

Beauchamp, M., Jackson, B., & Morton, K. (2012). Efficacy beliefs and human performance: From independent action to interpersonal functioning. In S. Murphy (Ed.), *The Oxford handbook of sport and performance psychology* (pp. 273–293). New York: Oxford University Press.

Beauchamp, M., Maclachlan, A., & Lothian, A. (2005). Communication within sport teams: Jungian preferences and group dynamics. *The Sport Psychologist, 19,* 203–220.

Beauchamp, M., & Whinton, L. (2005). Self-efficacy and other-efficacy in dyadic performance: Riding as one in an equestrian event. *Journal of Sport and Exercise Psychology, 27,* 245–252.

Becker, A., & Solomon, G. (2005). Expectancy information and coach effectiveness in intercollegiate basketball. *The Sport Psychologist, 19,* 251–266.

Becker, M.H., & Maiman, L.A. (1975). Sociobehavioral determinants of compliance with health care and medical care recommendations. *Medical Care, 13,* 10–24.

Beckman, J., & Kellmann, M. (2003). Procedures and principles of sport psychological assessment. *Journal of Sport and Exercise Psychology, 17,* 338–350.

Beebe, S., Beebe, S., & Redmond, M. (1996). *Interpersonal communication: Relating to others.* Boston: Allyn & Bacon.

Beilock, S.L., Afremow, J.A., Rabe, A.L., & Carr, T.H. (2001). "Don't miss!" The debilitating effects of suppressive imagery on golf putting performance. *Journal of Sport and Exercise Psychology, 23,* 200–221.

Beilock, S.L., & Carr, T.H. (2001). On the fragility of skilled performance: What governs choking under pressure? *Journal of Experimental Psychology: General, 130,* 701–725.

Beilock, S.L., Carr, T.H., MacMahon, C., & Starkes, J.L. (2002). When paying attention becomes counterproductive: Impact of divided versus skill-focused attention on novice and experienced performance of sensorimotor skills. *Journal of Experimental Psychology: Applied, 8,* 6–16.

Beilock, S., & Gray, R. (2007). Why do athletes choke under pressure? In G. Tenenbaum & R. Eklund (Eds.), *Handbook of sport psychology* (3rd ed., pp. 425–444). Hoboken, NJ: Wiley.

Beilock, S., & McConnell, A. (2004). Stereotype threat and sport: Can athletic performance be threatened? *Journal of Sport and Exercise Psychology, 26,* 597–609.

Bell, J., & Hardy, J. (2009). Effects of attentional focus on skilled performance in golf. *Journal of Applied Sport Psychology, 21,* 163–177.

Bell, K. (1980). *The nuts and bolts of psychology for swimmers.* Austin, TX: Keel.

Benatar, D. (1998). Corporal punishment. *Social Theory and Practice, 24,* 237–260.

Benedict, J., & Keteyian, A. (2011). Straight out of Compton. *Sports Illustrated, 115*(22), 82–88.

Bennis, W. (2007). The challenge of leadership in the modern world: Introduction to the special issue. *American Psychologist, 62,* 2–5.

Benson, A., Eys, M., Surya, M., Dawson, K., & Schneider, M. (2013). Athletes' perceptions of role acceptance in interdependent sport teams. *The Sport Psychologist, 27,* 269–280.

Benson, A., Surya, M., Balish, S., & Eys, M. (2013). Exploring the influence of injury on group processes in sport teams. *Journal of Sport and Exercise Psychology, 35,* S77.

Benson, H. (2000). *The relaxation response.* New York: HarperCollins.

Benson, H., & Proctor, W. (1984). *Beyond the relaxation response.* New York: Berkley.

Benyo, R. (1990). *The exercise fix.* Champaign, IL: Human Kinetics.

Berg, F.M. (2000). *Women afraid to eat: Breaking free in today's weight-obsessed world.* Hettinger, ND: Healthy Weight Network.

Berger, B. (1996). Psychological benefits of an active lifestyle: what we know and what we need to know. *Quest, 48,* 330-353.

Berger, B. (2009). Roles of exercise in quality of life: Exploring integral relationships. *Sport and Exercise Psychology Review, 5,* 60–63.

Berger, B., & Motl, R. (2001). Physical activity and quality of life. In R. Singer, H. Hausenblas, & C. Janelle (Eds.), *Handbook of sport psychology* (2nd ed., pp. 636–670). New York: Wiley.

Berger, B., Pargman, D., & Weinberg, R. (2007). *Foundations of exercise psychology (2nd ed.).* Morgantown, WV: Fitness Institute Technology.

Berger, B., & Tobar, D. (2011). Exercise and quality of life. In T. Morris & P. Terry (Eds.), *The new sport and exercise psychology companion* (pp. 483–505). Morgantown, WV: Fitness Information Technology.

Berkowitz, L. (1965). The concept of aggressive drive: Some additional considerations. In L. Berkowitz (Ed.), *Advances in experimental social psychology* (Vol. 2, pp. 301–329). New York: Academic Press.

Berkowitz, L. (1969). *Roots of aggression.* New York: Atherton Press.

Berkowitz, L. (1993). *Aggression: Its causes, consequences and control.* Philadelphia: Temple University Press.

Bernard, R.S., Cohen, L.L., & Moffett, K. (2009). A token economy for exercise adherence in pediatric cystic fibrosis: A single-subject analysis. *Journal of Pediatric Psychology, 34*(4), 354–365.

Bernier, M., Codron, R., Thienot, E., & Fournier, J. (2011). The attentional focus of expert golfers in training and competition: A naturalistic investigation. *Journal of Applied Sport Psychology, 23,* 326–341.

Bernstein, F. (1973, March 16). *New Yorker,* pp. 87–88.

Betts, G.H. (1909). *The distributions and functions of mental imagery.* New York: Teachers College, Columbia University.

Bianco, T. (2001). Social support and recovery from sport injury: Elite skiers share their experiences. *Research Quarterly for Exercise and Sport, 72*(4), 376–388.

Bianco, T., & Eklund, R.C. (2001). Conceptual considerations for social support research in sport and exercise settings: The case of sport injury. *Journal of Sport and Exercise Psychology, 23,* 85–107.

Bianco, T., Malo, S., & Orlick, T. (1999). Sport injury and illness: Elite skiers describe their experiences. *Research Quarterly for Exercise and Sport, 70*(2), 157–169.

Biddle, S. (1995). Exercise and psychosocial health. *Research Quarterly for Exercise and Sport, 66,* 292–297.

Biddle, S. (2000). Exercise, emotions, and mental health. In Y.L. Hanin (Ed.), *Emotions in sport* (pp. 267–291). Champaign, IL: Human Kinetics.

Biddle, S. (2011a). Fit or sit? Is there a psychology of sedentary behavior. *Sport and Exercise Psychology Review, 7,* 5–10.

Biddle, S. (2011b). Overview of exercise psychology. In T. Morris & P. Terry (Eds.), *The new sport and exercise psychology companion* (pp. 443–460). Morgantown, WV: Fitness Information Technology.

Biddle, S., Atkin, A., Cavill, N., & Foster, C. (2011). Correlates of physical activity in youth: A review of quantitative systematic reviews. *International Review of Sport and Exercise Psychology, 4,* 25–49.

Biddle, S., & Gorley, T. (2012). Physical activity interventions. In S. Murphy (Ed.), *The Oxford handbook of sport and performance psychology* (pp. 660–675). New York: Oxford University Press.

Biddle, S., Hagger, M., Chatzisarantis, N., & Lippke, S. (2007). Theoretical frameworks in exercise psychology. In G. Tenenbaum & R. Eklund (Eds.), *Handbook of sport psychology* (3rd ed., pp. 537–559). New York: Wiley.

Biddle, S.J.H., Hanrahan, S.J., & Sellars, C.N. (2001). Attributions: Past, present, and future. In R. Singer, H. Hausenblas, & C. Janelle (Eds.), *Handbook of sport psychology* (2nd ed., pp. 444–471). New York: Wiley.

Bishop, D., Karageorghis, C., & Loizou, G. (2007). A grounded theory of young tennis players' use of music to manipulate emotional state. *Journal of Sport and Exercise Psychology, 29,* 584–607.

Bishop, S. (2009). Trait anxiety and impoverished prefrontal control of attention. *Nature Neuroscience, 12,* 92–98.

Black, J.B., & Smith, A.L. (2007). An examination of Coakley's perspectives on identity, control, and burnout among adolescent athletes. *International Journal of Sport Psychology, 38,* 417–436.

Black, S.J., & Weiss, M.R. (1992). The relationship among perceived coaching behaviors, perceptions of ability, and motivation in competitive age-group swimmers. *Journal of Sport and Exercise Psychology, 14,* 309–325.

Blair, S. (1995). Exercise prescription for health. *Quest, 47,* 338–353.

Blake, R., & Moulton, J. (1969). *Building a dynamic corporation through grid organization development.* Reading, MA: Addison-Wesley.

Blake, R., & Moulton, J. (1994). *The managerial grid.* Houston: Gulf.

Bloom, B.S. (1985). *Developing talent in young people.* New York: Ballantine.

Bloom, G.A., Crumpton, R., & Anderson, J. (1999). A systematic observation study of the teaching behaviors of an expert basketball coach. *The Sport Psychologist, 13,* 157–170.

Bloom, G.A., Stevens, D., & Wickwire, T. (2003). Expert coaches' perceptions of team building. *Journal of Applied Sport Psychology, 15,* 129–143.

Blumenthal, J., Babyak, M., Moore, K., Craighead, W., Herman, S., Kharti, P., et al. (1999). Effects of exercise training on older patients with major depression. *Archives of Internal Medicine, 159,* 2349–2356.

Blumenthal, J.A., Emery, C.F., Walsh, M.A., Cox, D.K., Kuh, C.M., Williams, R.B., et al. (1988). Exercise training in healthy type A middle-aged men: Effects on behavioral and cardiovascular responses. *Psychosomatic Medicine, 50,* 418–433.

Boardley, I.D., & Kavussanu, M. (2011). Moral disengagement in sport. *International Review of Sport and Exercise Psychology, 4*(2), 93–108.

Boardley, I., Kavussanu, M., & Ring, C. (2008). Athletes' perceptions of coaching effectiveness and athlete-related outcomes in rugby-union: An investigation based on the coaching efficacy model. *The Sport Psychologist, 22,* 269–287.

Bolter, N.D., & Weiss, M.R. (2013). Coaching behaviors and adolescent athletes' sportspersonship outcomes: Further validation of the Sportsmanship Coaching Behaviors Scale (SCBS). *Sport, Exercise and Performance Psychology, 2*(1), 32–47.

Bordo, S. (1993). *Unbearable weight: Feminism, western culture and the body.* Los Angeles: University of California Press.

Bosselut, G., Heuze, J., Eys, M., Fontayne, P., & Sarrazin, P. (2012). Athletes' perceptions of role ambiguity and coaching competency in sport teams: A multi-level analysis. *Journal of Sport and Exercise Psychology, 34,* 345–364.

Botterill, C. (1983). Goal setting for athletes with examples from hockey. In G.L. Martin & D. Hrycaiko (Eds.), *Behavior modification and coaching: Principles, procedures, and research (pp. 67–86).* Springfield, IL: Charles C Thomas.

Botterill, C. (2005). Competitive drive: Embracing positive rivalries. In S. Murphy (Ed.), *The sport psych handbook* (pp. 37–48). Champaign, IL: Human Kinetics.

Boutcher, S. (2008). Attentional processes and sport performance. In T. Horn (Ed.), *Advances in sport psychology* (3rd ed., pp. 325–338). Champaign, IL: Human Kinetics.

Bowers, K.S. (1973). Situationism in psychology: An analysis and a critique. *Psychological Review, 80,* 307–336.

Bradley, B. (1976). *Life on the run.* New York: Bantam.

Brassington, G., & Goode, C. (2013). Sleep. In S. Hanrahan & M. Andersen (Eds.), *Routledge handbook of applied sport psychology: A comprehensive guide for students and practitioners* (pp. 270–282). New York: Routledge.

Brawley, L. (1990). Group cohesion: Status, problems, and future directions. *International Journal of Sport Psychology, 21,* 355–379.

Brawley, L., Carron, A., & Widmeyer, W. (1987). Assessing the cohesion of teams: Validity of the Group Environment Questionnaire. *Journal of Sport Psychology, 9,* 275–294.

Brawley, L., Carron, A., & Widmeyer, W. (1988). Exploring the relationship between cohesion and group resistance to disruption. *Journal of Sport and Exercise Psychology, 10,* 199–213.

Brawley, L., Carron, A., & Widmeyer, W. (1992). The nature of group goals in team sports: A phenomenological analysis. *The Sport Psychologist, 6,* 323–333.

Brawley, L., Carron, A., & Widmeyer, W. (1993). The influence of the group and its cohesiveness on perception of group goal-related variables. *Journal of Sport and Exercise Psychology, 15,* 245–266.

Bray, C.D., & Whaley, D.E. (2001). Team cohesion, effort, and objective individual performance of high school basketball players. *Sport Psychologists, 15,* 260–275.

Bray, S., Beauchamp, M., Eys, M., & Carron, A. (2005). Does the need for role clarity moderate the relationship between role ambiguity and athlete satisfaction. *Journal of Applied Sport Psychology, 17,* 306–318.

Bray, S., Millen, J., Eidsness, J., & Leuzinger, C. (2005). The effects of leadership style and exercise program choreography on enjoyment and intentions to exercise. *Psychology of Sport and Exercise, 6,* 415–425.

Breatnach, S.B. (1998). *Something more: Excavating your authentic self.* New York: Warner Books.

Breckon, J. (2002). Motivational interviewing and exercise prescription. In D. Lavellee & I. Cockerill (Eds.), *Counseling in sport and exercise contexts* (pp. 48–60). Leicester, England: British Psychological Society.

Bredemeier, B.J., & Shields, D. (1984). Divergence in moral reasoning about sport and everyday life. *Sociology of Sport Journal, 1,* 234–257.

Bredemeier, B., & Shields, D. (1986). Athletic aggression: An issue of contextual morality. *Sociology of Sport Journal, 3,* 15–28.

Bredemeier, B.J., & Shields, D. (1987). Moral growth through physical activity: A structural developmental approach. In D. Gould & M.R. Weiss (Eds.), *Advances in pediatric sport sciences: Vol. 2. Behavioral issues* (pp. 143–165). Champaign, IL: Human Kinetics.

Bredemeier, B., Weiss, M.R., Shields, D.L., & Shewchuk, R.M. (1986). Promoting growth in a summer sports camp: The implementation of theoretically grounded instructional strategies. *Journal of Moral Education, 15,* 212–220.

Breus, M.J., & O'Connor, P.J. (1998). Exercise-induced anxiolysis: A test of the time-out hypothesis in high-anxious females. *Medicine and Science in Sports and Exercise, 30,* 1107–1112.

Brewer, B.W. (1994). Review and critique of models of psychological adjustment to athletic injury. *Journal of Applied Sport Psychology, 6,* 87–100.

Brewer, B. (2013). Adherence to sport injury rehabilitation. In S. Hanrahan & M. Andersen (Eds.), *Routledge handbook of applied sport psychology: A comprehensive guide for students and practitioners* (pp. 233–241). New York: Routledge.

Brewer, B., Andersen, M., & Van Raalte, J. (2001). Psychological aspects of sport injury rehabilitation: Toward a biopsychosocial approach. In D. Mostofsky & L. Zaichkowsky (Eds.), *Medical and psychological aspects of sport and exercise* (pp. 41–54). Morgantown, WV: Fitness Information Technology.

Brewer, B.W., & Petrie, T.A. (2014). Psychopathology in sport and exercise psychology. In J.L. Van Raalte & B.W. Brewer (Eds.), *Exploring sport and exercise psychology* (3rd ed., pp. 311–335). Washington, DC: American Psychological Association.

Brewer, B.W., Van Raalte, J.L., Cornelius, A.E., Petitpas, A.J., Sklar, J.H., Pohlman, M.H., et al. (2000). Psychological factors, rehabilitation adherence, and rehabilitation outcome after anterior cruciate ligament reconstruction. *Rehabilitation Psychology, 45*(1), 20–37.

Briki, W., Hartigh, R., Hauw, D., & Gernigon, C. (2012). A qualitative exploration of the psychological contents and dynamics of momentum in sport. *International Journal of Sport Psychology, 43,* 365–384.

Brobst, B., & Ward, P. (2002). Effects of public posting, goal setting, and oral feedback on the skills of female soccer players. *Journal of Applied Behavior Analysis, 35,* 247–257.

Brown, C., Gould, D., & Foster, S. (2005). A framework for developing contextual intelligence. *The Sport Psychologist, 19,* 51–62.

Brown, T., & Fry, M. (2011). Helping members' commit to exercise: Specific strategies to impact the climate at fitness centers. *Journal of Sport Psychology in Action, 2,* 70–80.

Brownell, K., Stunkard, A., & Albaum, J. (1980). Evaluation and modification of exercise patterns in the natural environment. *American Journal of Psychiatry, 137,* 1540–1545.

Browning, B., & Sanderson, J. (2012). The positives and negatives of Twitter: Exploring how student-athletes use Twitter and respond to critical tweets. *International Journal of Sport Communication, 5,* 503–522.

Brunet, J., & Sabiston, C.M. (2009). Social physique anxiety and physical activity: A self-determination theory perspective. *Psychology of Sport and Exercise, 10,* 329–335.

Brustad, R.J. (1993). Who will go out and play? Parental and psychological influences on children's attraction to physical activity. *Pediatric Exercise Science, 5,* 210–223.

Bruton, A., Mellalieu, S., Shearer, D., Roderique-Davis, G., & Hall, R. (2013). Performance accomplishment information as predictors of self-efficacy as a function of skill level in amateur golf. *Journal of Applied Sport Psychology, 25,* 197–208.

Bucci, J., Bloom, G.A., Loughead, T.M., & Caron, J.G. (2012). Ice hockey coaches' perceptions of athlete leadership. *Journal of Applied Sport Psychology, 24,* 243–259.

Buckle, M.E., & Walsh, D.S. (2013). Teaching responsibility to gang-affiliated youths. *Journal of Physical Education, Recreation and Dance, 84*(2), 53–58.

Buckworth, J., & Dishman, R.K. (2002). *Exercise psychology.* Champaign, IL: Human Kinetics.

Buckworth, J., & Dishman, R. (2007). Exercise adherence. In G. Tenenbaum & R. Eklund (Eds), *Handbook of sport psychology* (3rd ed., pp. 509–536). New York: Wiley.

Buckworth, J., Lee, R., Regan, G., Schneider, L., & DiClemente, C. (2007). Decomposing intrinsic and extrinsic motivation for exercise: Application to stages of motivational readiness. *Psychology of Sport and Exercise, 8,* 441–461.

Bueno, J., Weinberg, R.S., Fernandez-Castro, J., & Capdevila, L. (2008). Emotional and motivational mechanisms mediating the influence of goal setting on endurance athletes' performance. *Psychology of Sport and Exercise, 9,* 786–799.

Bull, S., Shambrook, C., James, W., & Brooks, J. (2005). Toward an understanding of mental toughness in elite English cricketers. *Journal of Applied Sport Psychology, 17,* 209–227.

Bump, L.A. (1988). Drugs and sport performance. In R. Martens (Ed.), *Successful coaching* (pp. 135–147). Champaign, IL: Human Kinetics.

Burke, K.L. (1997). Communication in sports: Research and practice. *Journal of Interdisciplinary Research in Physical Education, 2,* 39–52.

Burke, K.L. (2001). But coach don't understand: Dealing with coach and team communication quagmires. In M. Andersen (Ed.), *Sport psychology in practice* (pp. 45-60). Champaign, IL: Human Kinetics.

Burke, K.L. (2005). But coach doesn't understand: Dealing with team communication quagmires. In M. Andersen (Ed.), *Sport psychology in practice* (pp. 45–59). Champaign, IL: Human Kinetics.

Burke, K.L. (2013). Constructive communication. In S. Hanrahan & M. Andersen (Eds.), *Routledge handbook of applied sport psychology: A comprehensive guide for students and practitioners* (pp. 315–323). New York: Routledge.

Burke, K.L., & Johnson, J.J. (1992). The sport-psychologist-coach dual role position: A rebuttal to Ellickson and Brown (1990). *Journal of Applied Sport Psychology, 4,* 51–55.

Burke, S., Carron, A., Eys, M., Ntoumanis, N., & Estabrooks, P. (2006). Group versus individual approach? A meta-analysis of the effectiveness of interventions to promote physical activity. *Sport and Exercise Psychology Review, 2,* 13–29.

Burke, S., Carron, A., & Shapcott, K. (2008). Cohesion in exercise groups: An overview. *International Review of Sport and Exercise Psychology, 1,* 107–123.

Burke, S.M., Shapcott, K.M., Carron, A.V., Bradshaw, M.H., & Easterbrook, P.A. (2010). Group goal setting and group performance in a physical activity context. *International Journal of Sport and Exercise Psychology, 8,* 245–261.

Burt, C.W., & Overbeck, M.D. (2001). Emergency visits for sport-related injuries. *Annals of Emergency Medicine, 37,* 301–308.

Burton, D. (1989a). The impact of goal specificity and task complexity on basketball skill development. *The Sport Psychologist, 3,* 34–47.

Burton, D. (1989b). Winning isn't everything: Examining the impact of performance goals on collegiate swimmers' cognitions and performance. *The Sport Psychologist, 3,* 105–132.

Burton, D., Gillham, A., & Glenn, S. (2011). Motivational styles: Examining the impact of personality on self-talk patterns of adolescent female soccer players. *Journal of Applied Sport Psychology, 23,* 413–428.

Burton, D., Gillham, A., Weinberg, R., Yukelson, D., & Weigand, D. (2013). Goal setting styles: Examining the impact of personality factors on the goal setting practices of prospective Olympic athletes. *Journal of Sport Behavior, 36,* 23–44.

Burton, D., Naylor, S., & Holliday, B. (2001). Goal setting in sport: Investigating the goal effectiveness paradigm. In R. Singer, H. Hausenblas, & C. Janelle (Eds.), *Handbook of sport psychology* (2nd ed., pp. 497–528). New York: Wiley.

Burton, D., & Weiss, C. (2008). The fundamental goal concept: The path to process and performance success. In T. Horn (Ed.), *Advances in sport psychology* (3rd ed., pp. 339–375). Champaign, IL: Human Kinetics.

Busanich, R., & McGannon, K. (2010). Deconstructing disordered eating: A feminist psychological approach to the body, food, and exercise in female athletes. *Quest, 62,* 385–405.

Buscombe, R., Greenless, I., Holder, T., Thelwell, R., & Rimmer, M. (2006). Expectancy effects in tennis: The impact of opponents' pre-match non-verbal behaviour on male tennis players. *Journal of Sports Sciences, 24,* 1265–1272.

Bushman, B.J., & Anderson, C.A. (2001). Media violence and the American public: Scientific facts versus media misinformation. *American Psychologist, 56,* 477–489.

Butler, L., Blasey, C., Garlan, R., McCaslin, S., Azarow, J., Chen, X., et al. (2005). Posttraumatic growth following the terrorist attacks of September 11, 2001: Cognitive coping, and trauma symptom predictors in an internet convenience sample. *Traumatology, 11,* 247–267.

Butler, R.J., & Hardy, L. (1992). The performance profile: Theory and application. *The Sport Psychologist, 6,* 253–264.

Butt, J., Weinberg, R., & Horn, T. (2003). The intensity and directional interpretation of anxiety: Fluctuations throughout competition and relationship to performance. *The Sport Psychologist, 17,* 35–54.

Buys, C.J. (1978). Humans would do better without groups. *Personality and Social Psychology Bulletin, 4,* 123–125.

Byrne, S., & McClean, N. (2001). Eating disorders in athletes: A review of the literature. *Journal of Science and Medicine in Sport, 4,* 149–159.

Caccese, T.M., & Mayerberg, C.K. (1984). Gender differences in perceived burnout of college coaches. *Journal of Sport Psychology, 6,* 279–288.

Caliari, P. (2008). Enhancing forehand acquisition in table tennis: The role of mental practice. *Journal of Applied Sport Psychology, 20,* 88–96.

Callow, N., Roberts, R., Bringer, J., & Langan, E. (2010). Coach education related to the delivery of imagery: Two interventions. *The Sport Psychologist, 18,* 277–299.

Callow, N., & Waters, A. (2005). The effect of kinesthetic imagery on the sport confidence of flat-race horse jockeys. *Psychology of Sport and Exercise, 6,* 443–459.

Calmels, C., Berthoumieux, C., & d'Arripe-Longueville, F. (2004). Effects of an imagery training program on selective attention of national softball players. *The Sport Psychologist, 18,* 272–296.

Calmels, C., d'Arripe-Longueville, F., Fournier, J., & Soulard, A. (2003). Competitive strategies among elite female gymnasts: An exploration of the relative influence of psychological skills training and natural learning experiences. *International Journal of Sport and Exercise Psychology, 1,* 327–352.

Cameron, J., & Pierce, W.D. (1994). Reinforcement, reward and intrinsic motivation: A meta-analysis. *Review of Educational Research, 64,* 363–423.

Camire, M., Forneris, T., Trudel, P., & Berhard, D. (2011). Strategies for helping coaches facilitate positive youth development through sport. *Journal of Sport Psychology in Action, 2,* 92–99.

Camire, M., & Trudel, P. (2010). High school athletes' perspectives on character development through sport participation. *Physical Education and Sport Pedagogy, 15*(2), 193–197.

Campbell, A., & Hausenblas, H. (2009). Effects of exercise interventions on body image: A meta-analysis. *Journal of Health Psychology, 14,* 780–793.

Canadian Fitness and Lifestyle Research Institute. (1996). *Progress in prevention.* Ottawa: Partners for Physical Activity.

Capel, S.A. (1986). Psychological and organizational factors related to burnout in athletic trainers. *Research Quarterly for Exercise and Sport, 57,* 321–328.

Cardinal, B.J. (1997). Construct validity of stages of change for exercise behavior. *American Journal of Health Promotion, 12,* 68–74.

Carels, R., Colt, C., Young, K., & Berger, B. (2007). Exercise makes you feel good, but does feeling good make you exercise? An examination of obese dieters. *Journal of Sport and Exercise Psychology, 29,* 706–722.

Carpenter, W.B. (1894). *Principles of mental physiology.* New York: Appleton.

Carr, C.M., Kennedy, S.R., & Dimick, K.M. (1990). Alcohol use and abuse among high school athletes: A comparison of alcohol use and intoxication in male and female high school athletes and non-athletes. *Journal of Alcohol and Drug Education, 36,* 39–45.

Carr, C.M., & Murphy, S.M. (1995). Alcohol and drugs in sport. In S.M. Murphy (Ed.), *Sport psychology interventions* (pp. 283–306). Champaign, IL: Human Kinetics.

Carron, A. (1982).Cohesiveness in sport groups: Interpretations and considerations. *Journal of Sport Psychology, 4,* 123-138.

Carron, A., & Brawley, L. (2008). Group dynamics in sport and physical activity. In T. Horn (Ed.), *Advances in sport psychology* (3rd ed., pp. 213–237). Champaign, IL: Human Kinetics.

Carron, A.V., Brawley, L.R., & Widmeyer, W.N. (1998). The measurement of cohesion in sport groups. In J.L. Duda (Ed.), *Advances in sport and exercise psychology measurement* (pp. 213–226). Morgantown, WV: Fitness Information Technology.

Carron, A.V., Colman, M., Wheeler, J., & Stevens, D. (2002). Cohesion and performance in sport: A meta-analysis. *Journal of Sport and Exercise Psychology, 24,* 168–188.

Carron, A.V., & Dennis, P. (2001). The sport team as an effective group. In J.M. Williams (Ed.), *Applied sport psychology: Personal growth to peak performance* (4th ed., pp. 120–134). Mountain View, CA: Mayfield.

Carron, A.V., & Eys, M. (2012). *Group dynamics in sport* (4th ed.). Morgantown, WV: Fitness Information Technology.

Carron, A., Eys, M., & Burke, S. (2007). Team cohesion: Nature, correlates and development. In S. Jowett & D. Lavellee (Eds.), *Social psychology of sport* (pp. 91–102). Champaign, IL: Human Kinetics.

Carron, A.V., & Hausenblas, H.A. (1998). *Group dynamics in sport* (2nd ed.). Morgantown, WV: Fitness Information Technology.

Carron, A.V., Hausenblas, H., & Estabrooks, P. (1999). Social influence and exercise involvement. In S. Bull (Ed.), *Adherence issues in sport and exercise* (pp. 1–18). Sussex, UK: Wiley.

Carron, A., Hausenblas, H., & Eys, M. (2005). *Group dynamics in sport* (3rd ed.). Morgantown, WV: Fitness Information Technology.

Carron, A.V., Hausenblas, H., & Mack, D. (1996). Social influence and exercise: A meta-analysis. *Journal of Sport and Exercise Psychology, 18,* 1–16.

Carron, A., Martin L., & Loughead, T. (2012). Teamwork and performance. In S. Murphy (Ed.), *The Oxford handbook of sport and performance psychology* (pp. 309–327). New York: Oxford Press.

Carron, A., Shapcott, K., & Burke, S. (2011). Team dynamics. In T. Morris & P. Terry (Eds.), *The new sport and exercise psychology companion* (pp. 195–209). Morgantown, WV: Fitness Information Technology.

Carron, A.V., & Spink, K.S. (1993). Team building in an exercise setting. *The Sport Psychologist, 7,* 8–18.

Carron, A.V., & Spink, K.S. (1995). The group size-cohesion relationship in minimal groups. *Small Group Research, 26,* 86–105.

Carron, A.V., Spink, K.S., & Prapavessis, H. (1997). Team building and cohesiveness in the sport and exercise setting: Use of indirect interventions. *Journal of Applied Sport Psychology, 9,* 61–72.

Carron, A., Widmeyer, W., & Brawley, L. (1985). The development of an instrument to assess cohesion in sport teams: The Group Environment Questionnaire. *Journal of Sport Psychology, 7*, 244–267.

Cartwright, D., & Zander, A. (1968). *Group dynamics: Research and theory* (3rd ed.). New York: Harper & Row.

Castaneda, B., & Gray, R. (2007). Effects of focus of attention on baseball batting performance in players of differing skill levels. *Journal of Sport and Exercise Psychology, 29*, 60–77.

Cattell, R.B. (1965). *The scientific analysis of personality.* Baltimore: Penguin.

Caudill, D., Weinberg, R., & Jackson, A. (1983). Psyching-up and track athletes: A preliminary investigation. *Journal of Sport Psychology, 5*, 231–235.

Cavanaugh, B.M., & Silva, J.M. (1980). Spectator perceptions of fan misbehavior: An attitudinal inquiry. In C.H. Nadeau, W.R. Halliwell, K.M. Newell, & G.C. Roberts (Eds.), *Psychology of motor behavior and sport—1979 (pp. 189-198).* Champaign, IL: Human Kinetics.

Centers for Disease Control and Prevention. (2010). *Behavioral Risk Factor Surveillance System survey data.* Atlanta: U.S. Department of Health and Human Services, Centers for Disease Control and Prevention.

Centers for Disease Control and Prevention. (2011). *Summary health statistics for U.S. adults: National health interview survey, 2011.* Atlanta: U.S. Department of Health and Human Services, Centers for Disease Control and Prevention.

Chaikin, T., & Tealander, R. (1988, October 24). The nightmare of steroids. *Sports Illustrated*, pp. 84–93, 97–98, 100–102.

Chan, C. (1986). Addicted to exercise. In *Encyclopedia Britannica medical and health annual* (pp. 429–432). UK: Encyclopedia Britannica.

Chan, C., & Grossman, H. (1988). Psychological effects of running loss on consistent runners. *Perceptual and Motor Skills, 66*, 875–883.

Chang, Y., & Etnier, J. (2009). Exploring the dose-response relationship between resistance exercise intensity and cognitive functioning. *Journal of Sport and Exercise Psychology, 31*, 640–656.

Chang, Y., Tsai, C., Hung, T., So, E., Chen, F., & Etnier, J. (2011). Effects of acute exercise on executive function: A study with a Tower of London task. *Journal of Sport and Exercise Psychology, 33*, 847–865.

Chappel, J.N. (1987). Drug use and abuse in the athlete. In J.R. May & M.J. Asken (Eds.), *Sport psychology: The psychological health of the athlete* (pp. 187–212). New York: PMA.

Chase, M. (2013). Children. In S. Hanrahan & M. Andersen (Eds.), *Routledge handbook of applied sport psychology: A comprehensive guide for students and practitioners* (pp. 377–386). New York: Routledge.

Chase, M., Feltz, D., Hayashi, S., & Hepler, T. (2005). Sources of coaching efficacy: The coaches' perspective. *International Journal of Sport and Exercise Psychology, 3*, 27–40.

Chase, M., Feltz, D., & Lirgg, C. (2003). Sources of collective and individual efficacy of collegiate athletes. *International Journal of Sport Psychology, 1*, 180–191.

Chase, M., Lirgg, C., & Feltz, D. (1997). Do coaches' efficacy expectations for their teams predict team performance? *The Sport Psychologist, 11*, 8–23.

Chaumeton, N., & Duda, J. (1988). Is it how you play the game or whether you win or lose? The effect of competitive level and situation on coaching behaviors. *Journal of Sport Behavior, 11*, 157–174.

Chelladurai, P. (1978). *A contingency model of leadership in athletics.* (Unpublished doctoral dissertation). Ontario: Department of Management Sciences, University of Waterloo.

Chelladurai, P. (1980). Leadership in sport organization. *Canadian Journal of Applied Sport Sciences, 5*, 266.

Chelladurai, P. (1990). Leadership in sports: A review. *International Journal of Sport Psychology, 21*, 328–354.

Chelladurai, P. (1993). Leadership. In R.N. Singer, M. Murphey, & L.K. Tennant (Eds.), *Handbook of sport psychology* (pp. 647–671). New York: Macmillan.

Chelladurai, P. (2007). Leadership in sports. In G. Tenenbaum & R.C. Eklund (Eds.), *Handbook of sport psychology* (3rd ed., pp. 113–135). Hoboken, NJ: Wiley.

Chelladurai, P., & Haggerty, T.R. (1978). A normative model of decision styles in coaching. *Athletic Administrator, 13*, 6–9.

Chelladurai, P., Haggerty, T.R., & Baxter, P.R. (1989). Decision style choices of university basketball coaches and players. *Journal of Sport and Exercise Psychology, 11*, 201–215.

Chelladurai, P., & Riemer, H. (1998). Measurement of leadership in sport. In J. Duda (Ed.), *Advances in sport and exercise psychology measurement* (pp. 227–256). Morgantown, WV: Fitness Information Technology.

Chelladurai, P., & Saleh, S.D. (1978). Preferred leadership in sports. *Canadian Journal of Applied Sport Sciences, 3*, 85–92.

Chelladurai, P., & Saleh, S.D. (1980). Dimensions of leader behaviors in sports: Development of a leadership scale. *Journal of Sport Psychology, 2*, 34–45.

Chelladurai, P., & Trail, G. (2001). Styles of decision-making in coaching. In J.M. Williams (Ed.), *Applied sport psychology: Personal growth to peak performance* (4th ed., pp. 107–119). Mountain View, CA: Mayfield.

Cheng, W.K., Hardy, L., & Markland, D. (2009). Toward a three-dimensional conceptualization of performance anxiety: Rationale and initial measurement development. *Psychology of Sport and Exercise, 10*, 271–278.

Chodzko-Zajko, W.J., & Moore, K.A. (1994). Physical fitness and cognitive functioning in aging. *Exercise and Sport Sciences Reviews, 22*, 195–220.

Chow, G.M., Murray, K.E., & Feltz, D.L. (2009). Individual, team, and coach predictors of players' likelihood to aggress in youth soccer. *Journal of Sport and Exercise Psychology, 31*, 425–443.

Cierpinski, W. (1980). Athletics in the 1980 Olympics. *Track and Field News*, p. 27.

Cleary, T., & Zimmerman, B. (2001). Self-regulation differences during athletic practice by experts, non-experts and novices. *Journal of Applied Sport Psychology, 13*, 185–206.

Clough, P., Earle, K., Perry, J., & Crust, L. (2012). Comment on "Progressing measurement in mental toughness: A case example of the mental toughness questionnaire 48" by Gucciardi, Hanton, and Mallett (2012). *Sport, Exercise, and Performance Psychology, 1*, 283–287.

Clough, P., Earle, K., & Sewell, D. (2002). Mental toughness: The concept and its measurement. In I. Cockerill (Ed.), *Solutions in sport psychology* (pp. 32–45). London: Thompson.

Coakley, J. (1992). Burnout among adolescent athletes: A personal failure or social problem? *Sociology of Sport Journal, 9*, 271–285.

Coakley, J. (1994). *Sport in society: Issues and controversies* (4th ed.). St. Louis: Times Mirror/Mosby College.

Coakley, J. (1997). *Sport in society: Issues and controversies* (5th ed.). St. Louis: Times Mirror/Mosby College.

Coakley, J. (2006). The good father: Parental expectations in youth sports. *Leisure Studies, 25*, 153–163.

Coatsworth, J.D., & Conroy, D.E. (2006). Enhancing the self-esteem of youth swimmers through coach training: Gender and age effects. *Psychology of Sport and Exercise, 7*, 173–192.

Coffee, P., & Rees, T. (2008). The CSGU: A measure of controllability, stability, globality and universality attributions. *Journal of Sport and Exercise Psychology, 30*, 611–641.

Cogan, K., & Petrie, T. (1995). Sport consultation: An evaluation of a season-long intervention with female collegiate gymnasts. *The Sport Psychologist, 9,* 282–296.

Cohane, G., & Pope, H. (2001). Body image in boys: A review of the literature. *International Journal of Eating Disorders, 29,* 373–379.

Cohn, P. (1990). An exploratory study on sources of stress and acute athlete burnout in youth golf. *The Sport Psychologist, 4,* 95–106.

Colcombe, S.J., & Kramer, A.F. (2002). Fitness effects on the cognitive function of older adults: A meta-analytic review. *Psychological Science, 14,* 125–130.

Coleman, J.S. (1974). *Youth: Transition to adulthood.* Chicago: University of Chicago Press.

College of Human Medicine, Michigan State University. (1985, June). *The substance use and abuse habits of college student-athletes.* Report presented to NCAA Drug Education Committee, Michigan State University, East Lansing.

Collins, J., & Lidz, F. (2013, May 6). The gay athlete. *Sports Illustrated,* pp. 33–41.

Comrey, A., & Deskin, G. (1954). Group manual dexterity in women. *Journal of Applied Psychology, 38,* 178.

Connaughton, D., Hanton, S., & Jones, G. (2010). The development and maintenance of mental toughness in the world's best performers. *The Sport Psychologist, 24,* 168–193.

Connaughton, D., Thelwell, R., & Hanton, S. (2011). Mental toughness development: Issues, practical implications and future directions. In D. Gucciardi & S. Gordon (Eds.), *Mental toughness in sport: Developments in theory and research* (pp. 135–162). New York: Routledge.

Connaughton, D., Wadey, R., Hanton, S., & Jones, G. (2008). The development and maintenance of mental toughness: Perceptions of elite performers. *Journal of Sport Sciences, 26,* 83–95.

Connor, J., & Mazanov, J. (2009). Would you dope? A general population test of the Goldman Dilemma. *British Journal of Sports Medicine, 43,* 871–872.

Conroy, D.E., & Benjamin, L.S. (2001). Psychodynamics in sport performance enhancement consultation: Application of an interpersonal theory. *The Sport Psychologist, 15,* 103–117.

Conroy, D.E., & Coatsworth, J.D. (2006). Coaching training as a strategy for promoting youth social development. *The Sport Psychologist, 20,* 128–144.

Cooke, A., Kvussanu, M., McIntyre, D., & Ring, C. (2011). Effects of competition on endurance performance and the underlying psychological and physiological mechanisms. *Biological Psychology, 86,* 370–378.

Cooke, A., Kvussanu, M., McIntyre, D., & Ring, C. (2013). The effects of individual and team competitions on performance, emotions, and effort. *Journal of Sport and Exercise Psychology, 35,* 132–143.

Cope, C., Eys, M., Beauchamp, M., & Schinke, R. (2011). Informal roles on sport teams. *International Journal of Sport and Exercise Psychology, 9,* 19–30.

Copelton, D. (2010). Output that counts: Pedometers sociability and the contested terrain of older adult fitness walking. *Sociology of Health and Illness, 32,* 304–318.

Côté, J. (1999). The influence of the family in the development of talent in sport. *The Sport Psychologist, 13,* 395–417.

Côté, J., Lidor, R., & Hackfort, D. (2009). ISSP position stand: To sample or to specialize? Seven postulates about youth sport activities that lead to continued participation and elite performance. *International Journal of Sport and Exercise Psychology, 9,* 7–17.

Côté, J., Salmela, J.H., & Russell, S. (1995). The knowledge of high-performance gymnastic coaches: Competition and training considerations. *The Sport Psychologist, 9,* 76–95.

Cotterill, S. (2010). Pre-performance routines in sport: Current understanding and future directions. *International Review of Sport and Exercise Psychology, 3,* 132–153.

Cotterill, S. (2011). Experiences of developing pre-performance routines with elite cricket players. *Journal of Sport Psychology in Action, 2,* 81–91.

Cotterill, S., Sanders, R., & Collins, D. (2010). Developing effective pre-performance routines in golf: Why don't we ask the golfer. *Journal of Applied Sport Psychology, 22,* 51–64.

Courneya, K. (2003). Exercise in cancer survivors: An overview of research. *Medicine and Science in Sports and Exercise, 35,* 1846–1852.

Courneya, K. (2005). Exercise and quality of life in cancer survivors. In G. Faulkner & A. Taylor (Eds.), *Exercise, health, and mental health: Emerging relationships* (pp. 114–134). London: Routledge.

Courneya, K., Vallance, J., Jones, L., & Reiman, T. (2005). Correlates of exercise intentions in non-Hodgkin's lymphoma survivors: An application of the theory of planned behavior. *Journal of Sport and Exercise Psychology, 27,* 335–349.

Cousins, S., & Gillis, M. (2005). "Just do it . . . before you talk yourself out of it": The self-talk of adults thinking about physical activity. *Psychology of Sport and Exercise, 6,* 313–334.

Couzin, J. (2002). Nutrition research. IOM panel weighs in on diet and health. *Science, 297,* 1788–1789.

Cox, R.H. (1998). *Sport psychology: Concepts and applications* (4th ed.). Boston: WCB/McGraw-Hill.

Cox, R.H., Qui, Y., & Liu, Z. (1993). Overview of sport psychology. In R.N. Singer, M. Murphey, & L.K. Tennant (Eds.), *Handbook of sport psychology* (pp. 3–31). New York: Macmillan.

Crace, R.K., & Brown, D. (1996). *Life values inventory.* Chapel Hill, NC: Life Values Resources.

Crace, R.K., & Hardy, C.J. (1997). Individual values and the team building process. *Journal of Applied Sport Psychology, 9,* 41–60.

Craft, L. (2005). Exercise and clinical depression: Examining two psychological mechanisms. *Psychology of Sport and Exercise, 6,* 151–171.

Craft, L., & Landers, D. (1998). The effects of exercise on clinical depression and depression resulting from mental illness. *Journal of Sport and Exercise Psychology, 20,* 339–357.

Cramer Roh, J.L., & Perna, F.M. (2000). Psychology/counseling: A universal competency in athletic training. *Journal of Athletic Training, 35*(4), 458–465.

Crawford, S., & Eklund, R.C. (1994). Social physique anxiety, reasons for exercise, and attitudes toward exercise settings. *Journal of Sport and Exercise Psychology, 16,* 70–82.

Cresswell, S.L., & Eklund, R.C. (2004). The athlete burnout syndrome: Possible early signs. *Journal of Science and Medicine, 7*(4), 481–487.

Cresswell, S., & Eklund, R.C. (2005a). Changes in athlete burnout and motivation over a 12-week league tournament. *Medicine and Science in Sports and Exercise, 37,* 1957–1966.

Cresswell, S., & Eklund, R.C. (2005b). Motivation and burnout among top amateur rugby players. *Medicine and Science in Sports and Exercise, 37,* 469–477.

Cresswell, S.L., & Eklund, R.C. (2006). Athlete burnout: Conceptual confusion, current research and future directions. In S. Hanton & S.D. Mellalieu (Eds.), *Literature reviews in sport psychology* (pp. 91–126). New York: Nova.

Cresswell, S.L., & Eklund, R.C. (2007). Athlete burnout: A longitudinal study. *The Sport Psychologist, 21*(1), 1–20.

Crews, D. (1993). Self-regulation strategies in sport and exercise. In R. Singer, M. Murphey, & K. Tennant (Eds.), *Handbook of research in sport psychology* (pp. 557–568). New York: Macmillan.

Crews, D.J., Lochbaum, M.R., & Karoly, P. (2000). Self-regulation: Concepts, methods and strategies in sport and exercise. In R. Singer, H. Hausenblas, & C. Janelle (Eds.), *Handbook of sport psychology* (2nd ed., pp. 566–581). New York: Wiley.

Crocker, P.R.E. (1978). *Speech communication instruction based on employers' perceptions of selective communication skills for employees on the job.* Paper presented at the meeting of the Speech Communication Association, Minneapolis.

Crocker, P.R.E., Alderman, R., Murray, F., & Smith, R. (1988). Cognitive-affective stress-management training with high performance youth volleyball players: Effects on affect, cognition, and performance. *Journal of Sport and Exercise Psychology, 10,* 448–460.

Cross, M.E., & Vollano, A.G. (1999). *The extent and nature of gambling among college student athletes.* Ann Arbor: University of Michigan, Department of Athletics.

Crust, L., & Clough, P. (2012). Developing mental toughness: From research to practice. *Journal of Sport Psychology in Action, 2,* 21–32.

Crust, L., Henderson, H., & Middleton, G. (2013). The acute effects of urban green and countryside walking on psychological health: A field-based study of green exercise. *International Journal of Sport Psychology, 44,* 160–167.

Csikszentmihalyi, M. (1990). *Flow: The psychology of optimal experience.* New York: Harper & Row.

Culos-Reed, S.N., Gyurcsik, C., & Brawley, L.R. (2001). Using theories of motivated behavior to understand physical activity. In R. Singer, H. Hausenblas, & C. Janelle (Eds.), *Handbook of sport psychology* (2nd ed., pp. 695–717). New York: Wiley.

Culos-Reed, S.N., Robinson, J., Lau, H., O'Connor, K., & Keats, M. (2007). Benefits of a physical activity intervention for men with prostate cancer. *Journal of Sport and Exercise Psychology, 29,* 118–127.

Cumming, J., Nordin, S., Horton, R., & Reynolds, S. (2006). Examining the direction of imagery and self-talk on dart-throwing performance and self-efficacy. *The Sport Psychologist, 20,* 257–274.

Cumming, J., Olphin, T., & Law, M. (2007). Self-reported psychological states and physiological responses to different types of motivational general imagery. *Journal of Sport and Exercise Psychology, 29,* 629–644.

Cumming, J., & Ramsey, R. (2009). Imagery intervention in sport. In S. Mellalieu & S. Hanton (Eds.), *Advances in applied sport psychology: A review* (pp. 5–36). London: Routledge.

Cumming, J.L., & Ste-Marie, D.M. (2001). The cognitive and motivational effects of imagery training: A matter of perspective. *The Sport Psychologist, 15,* 276–288.

Cumming, J., & Williams, S. (2012). The role of imagery in performance. In S. Murphy (Ed.), *The Oxford handbook of sport and performance psychology* (pp. 213–232). New York: Routledge.

Cunningham, G., Sagas, M., & Ashley, F. (2003). Coaching self-efficacy, desire to become a head coach and occupational turnover intent: Gender differences between NCAA assistant coaches of women's teams. *International Journal of Sport Psychology, 34,* 125–137.

Cunningham, G., & Waltmeyer, D. (2007). The moderating effect of outcome interdependence on the relationship between task conflict and group performance. *International Journal of Sport Psychology, 38,* 163–177.

Cupal, D.D., & Brewer, B.W. (2001). Effects of relaxation and guided imagery, reinjury anxiety, and pain following anterior cruciate ligament reconstruction. *Rehabilitation Psychology, 46*(1), 28–43.

Curran, T., Appleton, P.R., Hill, A.P., & Hall, H.K. (2011). Passion and burnout in elite junior soccer players: The mediating role of self-determined motivation. *Psychology of Sport and Exercise, 12,* 655–661.

Cushing, C., & Steele, R. (2011). Establishing and maintaining physical exercise. In J. Luiselli & D. Reed (Eds.), *Behavioral sport psychology: Evidence-based approaches to performance enhancement* (pp. 127–141). New York: Springer.

Cushion, C., Ford, P.R., & Williams, A.M. (2012). Coach behaviors and practice structures in youth soccer: Implications for talent development. *Journal of Sport Sciences, 30*(15), 1631–1641.

Cutton, D., & Hearon, C. (2013). Applied attention-related strategies for coaches. *Journal of Sport Psychology in Action, 4,* 5–13.

Cutton, D., & Landin, D. (2007). The effects of self-talk and augmented feedback on learning the tennis forehand. *Journal of Applied Sport Psychology, 19,* 288–303.

Dale, G. (2000). Distractions and coping strategies of elite decathletes during their most memorable performances. *The Sport Psychologist, 14,* 17–41.

Dale, J., & Weinberg, R.S. (1990). Burnout in sport: A review and critique. *Journal of Applied Sport Psychology, 2,* 67–83.

Daley, A., & Maynard, I. (2003). Preferred exercise mode and affective responses in physically active adults. *Psychology of Sport and Exercise, 4,* 347–356.

Daniels, F.S., & Landers, D.M. (1981). Biofeedback and shooting performance: A test of disregulation and systems theory. *Journal of Sport Psychology, 4,* 271–282.

Danish, S.J., & Nellen, V.C. (1997). New roles for sport psychologists: Teaching life skills through sport to at-risk youth. *Quest, 49*(1), 100–113.

Danish, S. J., Nellen, V. C., & Owens, S.S. (1996). Teaching life skills through sport: Community-based programs for adolescents. In J.L. Van Raalte & B.W. Brewer, (Eds.). *Exploring sport and exercise psychology* (pp. 205-225). Washington, DC: American Psychological Association.

Danish, S.J., Petitpas, A.S., & Hale, B.D. (1992). A developmental-educational intervention model of sport psychology. *The Sport Psychologist, 6,* 403–415.

Danish, S., Petitpas, A., & Hale, B. (1995). Psychological interventions: A life development model. In S. Murphy (Ed.), *Sport psychology interventions* (pp. 19–38). Champaign, IL: Human Kinetics.

d'Arripe-Longueville, F., Corrion, K., Scoffier, S., Roussel, P., & Chalabaev, A. (2010). Sociocognitve self-regulatory mechanisms governing the judgements of the acceptability and likelihood of sport cheating. *Journal of Sport and Exercise Psychology, 32,* 595–618.

Davis, C., Tomprowski, P., Boyle, C., Waller, J., Miller, P., & Naglieri, J. (2007). Effects of aerobic exercise on overweight children's cognitive functioning: A randomized controlled trial. *Research Quarterly for Exercise and Sport, 78,* 510–519.

Davis, L., Tomporowski, P., McDowell, J., Austin, J., Millerm P., Yanasak, N., et al. (2011). Exercise improves executive function and achievement and alters brain activity in overweight children: A randomized controlled trial. *Health Psychology, 30,* 91–98.

Dawson, K.A., Bray, S.R., & Widmeyer, W.N. (2002). Goal setting for intercollegiate sport teams and athletes. *Avante, 8*(2), 14–23.

de Bruin, P., Bakker, F., & Oudejans, R. (2009). Achievement goal theory and disordered eating with goal orientations and motivational climate in female gymnasts and dancers. *Psychology of Sport and Exercise, 10,* 72–79.

Decety, J. (1996). Neural representations for action. *Reviews in the Neurosciences, 7,* 285–297.

deCharms, R. (1968). *Personal causation.* New York: Academic Press.

Deci, E.L. (1971). Effects of externally mediated rewards on intrinsic motivation. *Journal of Personality and Social Psychology, 18,* 105–115.

Deci, E.L. (1972). The effects of contingent and noncontingent rewards and controls on intrinsic motivation. *Organizational Behavior and Human Performance, 8,* 217–229.

Deci, E.L. (1975). *Intrinsic motivation.* New York: Plenum Press.

Deci, E.L., & Ryan, R.M. (1985). *Intrinsic motivation and self-determination in human behavior.* New York: Plenum Press.

Deci, E.L., & Ryan, R.M. (1994). Promoting self-determined education. *Scandinavian Journal of Educational Research, 38,* 3–41.

Deci, E.L., & Ryan, R.M. (2000). The "what" and "why" of goal pursuits: Human needs and self-determination of behavior. *Psychology of Inquiry, 11,* 227–268.

DeDreu, C.K., & Weingart, L.R. (2003). Task versus relationship conflict, team performance, and team member satisfaction: A meta-analysis. *Journal of Applied Psychology, 88,* 741–749.

Deford, F. (1999, May 10). The ring leader. *Sports Illustrated, 90,* 96–114.

DeMille, R. (1973). *Put your mother on the ceiling: Children's imagination games.* New York: Viking Press.

Demulier, V., Le Scanff, C., & Stephan, Y. (2013). Psychological predictors of career planning among active elite athletes: An application of the social cognitive career theory. *Journal of Applied Sport Psychology, 25*(3), 341–353.

DeNeui, D.L., & Sachau, D.A. (1996). Spectator enjoyment of aggression in intercollegiate hockey games. *Journal of Sport and Social Issues, 20,* 69–77.

Desha, L., Ziviani, J., Nixholson, J., Martin, G., & Darnell, R. (2007). Physical activity and depressive symptoms in American adolescents. *Journal of Sport and Exercise Psychology, 29,* 534–543.

Deuchar, R. (2009). *Gangs, marginalized youth and social capital.* Stoke-on-Trent, Staffordshire: Trentham Books.

Deutsch, M. (1949). An experimental study of the effects of cooperation and competition upon group process. *Human Relations, 2,* 199–231.

Deutsch, M. (2000). Cooperation and competition, In M. Deutsch & P. Coleman (Eds.), *Handbook of conflict resolution: Theory and practice* (pp. 21–40). San Francisco: Jossey-Bass.

Deutsch, M. (2006). Cooperation and cooperation. In M. Deutsch, P. Coleman, & E. Marcus (Eds.), *The handbook of conflict resolution* (pp. 23–42). San Francisco: Jossey-Bass

DeWiggins, S., Hite, B., & Alston, V. (2010). Personal performance plan: Application of mental skills training to real-world military tasks. *Journal of Applied Sport Psychology, 22,* 458–473.

Diabetes Prevention Program Research Group. (2002). Reduction in the incidence of type 2 diabetes with lifestyle interventions. *New England Journal of Medicine, 346,* 396–403.

DiBerardinis, J., Barwind, J., Flaningam, R., & Jenkins, V. (1983). Enhanced interpersonal relations as a predictor of athletic performance. *International Journal of Sport Psychology, 14,* 243–251.

DiCicco, T., Hacker, C., & Salzberg, C. (2002). *Catch them being good.* New York: Penguin.

Dieffenbach, K., & Statler, T. (2012). More similar than different: The psychological environment of Paralympic sport. *Journal of Sport Psychology in Action, 3,* 109–118.

Dieffenbach, K., Statler, T., & Moffett, A. (2009). *Pre and post Games perceptions of factors influencing coach and athlete performance at the Beijing Paralympics.* Colorado Springs: USOC and Paralympic Program.

Diener, E., & Suh, E. (1999). National differences in subjective well-being. In D. Kahnmeman, E. Diener, & N. Schwartz (Eds.), *Well-being: The foundations of hedonistic psychology* (pp. 434–450). New York: Russell Sage Foundation.

DiFiori, J.P. (2002). Overuse injuries in young athletes: An overview. *Athletic Therapy Today, 7*(6), 25–29.

Dimech, A.S., & Seiler, R. (2011). Extra-curricular sport participation: A potential buffer against social anxiety in primary school children. *Psychology of Sport and Exercise, 12,* 347–354.

Dimmock, J., & Banting, L. (2009). The influence of implicit cognitive processes on physical activity: How the theory of planned behavior and self-determination theory can provide a platform for understanding. *International Review of Sport and Exercise Psychology, 2,* 3–22.

Dishman, R.K. (Ed.). (1988). *Exercise adherence: Its impact on public health.* Champaign, IL: Human Kinetics.

Dishman, R.K. (1994). *Advances in exercise adherence.* Champaign, IL: Human Kinetics.

Dishman, R.K., & Buckworth, J. (1996). Increasing physical activity: A quantitative synthesis. *Medicine and Science in Sports and Exercise, 28,* 706–719.

Dishman, R.K., & Buckworth, J. (1997). Adherence to physical activity. In W.P. Morgan (Ed.), *Physical activity and mental health* (pp. 63–80). Philadelphia: Taylor & Francis.

Dishman, R.K., & Buckworth, J. (1998). Exercise psychology. In J.M. Williams (Ed.), *Applied sport psychology: Personal growth to peak performance* (pp. 445–462). Mountain View, CA: Mayfield.

Dishman, R.K., & Buckworth, J. (2001). Exercise psychology. In J.M. Williams (Ed.), *Sport psychology: Personal growth to peak performance* (pp. 497–518). Mountain View, CA: Mayfield.

Dishman, R.K., & Sallis, J.F. (1994). Determinants and interventions for physical activity and exercise. In C. Bouchard, R.J. Shepard, & T. Stephens (Eds.). *Physical activity, fitness, and health* (pp. 214-238). Champaign, IL: Human Kinetics.

Dishman, R.K., Washburn, R.A., & Heath, G.W. (2004). *Physical activity epidemiology.* Champaign, IL: Human Kinetics.

Divine, A., Munroe-Chandler, K., & Loughead, T. (2013). Being part of a team: Cohesion and self-presentation in sport. *Journal of Sport and Exercise Psychology, 35,* S83.

Dollard, J., Doob, J., Miller, N., Mowrer, O., & Sears, R. (1939). *Frustration and aggression.* New Haven, CT: Yale University Press.

Dollman, J., & Lewis, N.R. (2010). The impact of socioeconomic position on sport participation among South Australian youth. *Journal of Science and Medicine in Sport, 13,* 318–322.

Donahue, E., Miquelon, P., Valois, P., Goulet, C., Buist, A., & Vallerand, R. (2006). A motivational model of performance-enhancing substance use in elite athletes. *Journal of Sport and Exercise Psychology, 28,* 511–520.

Donahue, E.G., Rip, B., & Vallerand, R.J. (2009). When winning is everything: On passion, identity, and aggression in sport. *Psychology of Sport and Exercise, 10,* 526–534.

Donahue, J.A., Gillis, J.H., & King, H. (1980). Behavior modification in sport and physical education: A review. *Journal of Sport Psychology, 2,* 311–328.

Donlop, W., Beatty, D., & Beauchamp, M. (2011). Examining the influence of other-efficacy and self-efficacy on personal performance. *Journal of Sport and Exercise Psychology, 33,* 586–593.

Donnelly, P., Carron, A.V., & Chelladurai, P. (1978). *Group cohesion and sport* (Sociology of Sport Monograph Series). Ottawa: Canadian Association for Health, Physical Education and Recreation.

Dorrance, A., & Averbuch, C. (2002). *The vision of a champion.* Ann Arbor, MI: Huron River Press.

Dorsch, K.D., & Paskevich, D.M. (2007). Stressful experiences among six certified levels of ice hockey officials. *Psychology of Sport and Exercise, 8,* 585–593.

Dosil, J. (2006). *The sport psychologist's handbook: A guide for sport-specific performance enhancement.* West Sussex, UK: Wiley.

Downs, D., & Hausenblas, H. (2005). Elicitation studies and the theory of planned behavior: A systematic review of exercise beliefs. *Psychology of Sport and Exercise, 6,* 1–31.

Dray, K., & Uphill, M. (2009). A survey of athletes' counterfactual thinking: Precursors, prevalence, and consequences. *Sport and Exercise Psychology Review, 5,* 16–26.

Driediger, M., Hall, C., & Galloway, N. (2006). Imagery used by injured athletes: A qualitative analysis. *Journal of Sport Sciences, 24,* 261–271.

Driskell, J.E., Cooper, C., & Moran, A. (1994). Does mental practice enhance performance? *Journal of Applied Psychology, 79,* 481–492.

Duda, J.L. (2005). Motivation in sport: The relevance of competence and achievement goals. In A.J. Elliot & C.S. Dweck (Eds.), *Handbook of competence and motivation* (pp. 318–335). New York: Guilford Press.

Duda, J., & Balague, G. (2007). Coach-created motivational climate. In S. Jowett & D. Lavelle (Eds.), *Social psychology of sport* (pp. 117–130). Champaign, IL: Human Kinetics.

Duda, J.L., & Hall, H. (2001). Achievement goal theory in sport: Recent extensions and future directions. In R. Singer, H. Hausenblas, & C. Janelle (Eds.), *Handbook of sport psychology* (2nd ed., pp. 417–443). New York: Wiley.

Duda, J.L., & Hom, H.L. (1993). Interdependence between the perceived and self-reported goal orientations of young athletes and their parents. *Pediatric Exercise Science, 5,* 234–241.

Duffett, A., & Johnson, J. (2004). *All work and no play? Listening to what kids and parents really want from out-of-school time.* New York: Public Agenda and the Wallace Foundation.

Duncan, L., Hall, C., Wilson, P., & O, J. (2010). Exercise motivation: A cross-sectional analysis examining its relationships with frequency, intensity, and duration of exercise. *International Journal of Behavioral Nutrition and Physical Activity, 7,* 1–10.

Duncan, S., Duncan, T., & Strycker, L. (2005). Sources and types of social support in youth physical activity. *Health Psychology, 24,* 3–10.

Dunn, A., Trivedi, M., Kampert, J., Clark, C., & Chambliss, H. (2005). Exercise treatment for depression: Efficacy and dose response. *American Journal of Preventive Medicine, 28,* 1–8.

Dunn, J.G.H., Craft, J.M., & Dunn, J.C. (2011). Comparing a domain-specific and global measure of perfectionism in competitive female figure skaters. *Journal of Sport Behavior, 34*(1), 25–46.

Dunn, J.G.H., Dunn, J.C., & McDonald, K. (2012). Domain-specific perfectionism in intercollegiate athletes: Relationships with perceived competence and perceived importance in sport and school. *Psychology, Sport, and Exercise, 13,* 747–755.

Dunn, J., & Holt, N. (2004). A qualitative investigation of a personal-disclosure mutual-sharing team building activity. *The Sport Psychologist, 18,* 363–380.

Dunn, J.G.H., & Syrotuik, D.G. (2003). An investigation of multidimensional worry dispositions in a high contact sport. *Psychology of Sport and Exercise, 4,* 265–282.

Dupuis, M., Bloom, G.A., & Loughead, T.M. (2006). Team captains' perceptions of athlete leadership. *Journal of Sport Behavior, 29,* 60–78.

Durand-Bush, N., & Salmela, J.H. (2002). The development and maintenance of expert athletic performance: Perceptions of world and Olympic champions. *Journal of Applied Sport Psychology, 14*(3), 159–176.

Durstine, L., Gordon, B., Wang, Z., & Luo, X. (2013). Chronic disease and the link to physical activity. *Journal of Sport and Health Science, 2,* 3–11.

Dweck, C.S. (1975). The role of expectations and attributions in the alleviation of learned helplessness. *Journal of Personality and Social Psychology, 31,* 674–685.

Dweck, C.S. (1980). Learned helplessness in sport. In C.M. Nadeau, W.R. Halliwell, K.M. Newell, & G.C. Roberts (Eds.), *Psychology of motor behavior and sport—1979* (pp. 1–11). Champaign, IL: Human Kinetics.

Dweck, C.S. (1986). Motivational processes affecting learning. *American Psychologist, 41,* 1040–1048.

Dweck, C.S. (1999). *Self-theories: Their role in motivation, personality and development.* Philadelphia: Taylor & Francis.

Dwyer, J.J.M. (1992). Informal structure of participation motivation questionnaire competed by undergraduates. *Psychological Reports, 70,* 283–290.

Eberly, M.B., Johnson, M.D., Hernandez, M., & Avolio, B.J. (2013). An integrative process model of leadership: Examining, loci, mechanisms, and event cycles. *American Psychologist, 68*(6), 427–443.

Eccles, D. (2010). The coordination of labour in sport teams. *International Review of Sport and Exercise Psychology, 3,* 154–170.

Eccles, D., & Tenenbaum, G. (2004). Why an expert team is more than a team of experts: A social-cognitive conceptualization of team coordination and communication in sport. *Journal of Sport and Exercise Psychology, 26,* 542–560.

Eccles, D., & Tran, K. (2012). Getting them on the same page: Strategies for enhancing coordination and communication in sports teams. *Journal of Sport Psychology in Action, 3,* 30–40.

Eccles, J.S., & Harold, R.D. (1991). Gender differences in sport involvement: Applying the Eccles expectancy-value model. *Journal of Applied Sport Psychology, 3,* 7–35.

Edmunds, J., Ntoumanis, N., & Duda, J. (2007). Adherence and well-being in overweight and obese patients referred to an exercise on prescription scheme: A self-determination theory perspective. *Psychology of Sport and Exercise, 8,* 722–740.

Eisenberger, R., & Cameron, J. (1996). Detrimental effects of reward: Myth or reality? *American Psychologist, 51,* 1153–1166.

Eisenman, P.A., Johnson, S.C., & Benson, J.E. (1990). *Coaches' guide to nutrition and weight control* (2nd ed.). Champaign, IL: Human Kinetics.

Egli, T., Bland, H.W., Melton, B.F., & Czech, D.R. (2011). Influence of age, sex, and race on students' exercise motivation for physical activity. *Journal of American College Health, 59*(5), 399–406.

Ekkekakis, P., Parfitt, G., & Petruzello, S. (2011). The pleasure and displeasure people feel when they exercise at different intensities: Decennial update and progress towards a tripartite rationale for exercise intensity prescription. *Sports Medicine, 41,* 641–671.

Eklund, R.C., Kelley, B., & Wilson, P. (1997). The social physique anxiety scale: Men, women, and the effects of modifying item 2. *Journal of Sport and Exercise Psychology, 19,* 188–196.

Elavsky, S. (2009). Physical activity, menopause, and quality of life: The role of affect and self-worth over time. *Menopause, 16,* 265–271.

Elavsky, S. (2010). Longitudinal examination of the exercise and self-esteem model in middle-aged women. *Journal of Sport and Exercise Psychology, 32,* 862–880.

Ellenbogen, S., Jacobs, D., Derevensky, J., Gupta, R., & Paskus, T. (2008). Gambling behavior among college student-athletes. *Journal of Applied Sport Psychology, 20,* 349–362.

Elliott, A.J. (1999). Approach and avoidance motivation and achievement goals. *Educational Psychologist, 34,* 169–189.

Elliott, E.S., & Dweck, C.S. (1988). Goals: An approach to motivation and achievement. *Journal of Personality and Social Psychology, 54,* 5–12.

Ellis, A. (1962). *Reason and emotion in psychotherapy.* New York: Lyle Stuart.

Ellis, K. (2000). Perceived teacher confirmation: The development and validation of an instrument and two studies of the relationship to cognitive and affective learning. *Human Communication Research, 26,* 264–291.

Emery, C., Hauck, E., Shermer, R., Hsiao, W.E., & MacIntyre, N. (2003). Cognitive and psychological outcomes of exercise in a 1 year follow-up study of patients with chronic obstructive pulmonary disease. *Health Psychology, 22,* 598–604.

Emery, C.A., McKay, C.D., Campbell, T.S., & Peters, A.N. (2009). Examining attitudes toward body checking, levels of emotional empathy, and levels of aggression in body checking and non-body checking youth hockey leagues. *Clinical Journal of Sports Medicine, 19*(3), 207–215.

Epstein, D. (2013, July). Why Pujols can't (and A-Rod wouldn't) touch this pitch. *Sports Illustrated,* pp. 55–62.

Epstein, J. (1989). Family structures and student motivation: A developmental perspective. In C. Ames & R. Ames (Eds.), *Research on motivation in education* (Vol. 3, pp. 259–295). New York: Academic Press.

Epstein, L.H., Wing, R.R., Thompson, J.K., & Griffiths, M. (1980). Attendance and fitness in aerobics exercise: The effects of contract and lottery procedures. *Behavior Modification, 4*, 465–479.

Epstein, M.L. (1980). The relationship of mental imagery and mental rehearsal in performance of a motor task. *Journal of Sport Psychology, 2*, 211–220.

Ericsson, A. (2007). Deliberate practice and the modifiability of body and mind: Toward a science of the structure and acquisition of expert and elite performance. *International Journal of Sport Psychology, 38*, 4–34.

Ericsson, I., & Karlsson, M. (2011). Effects of increased physical activity and motor training on motor skills and self-esteem: An intervention study in school years 1–9. *International Journal of Sport Psychology, 42*, 461–479.

Essing, W. (1970). Team line-up and team achievement in European football. In G.S. Kenyan (Ed.), *Contemporary psychology of sport* (pp. 349–354). Chicago: Athletic Institute.

Estabrooks, P., Smith-Ray, R., Almeida, F., Hill, J., Gonzales, M., Schreiner, P., et al. (2011). Move more: Translating an efficacious group dynamics physical activity intervention into effective clinical practice. *International Journal of Sport and Exercise Psychology, 9*, 4–18.

Estanol, E., Shepperd, C., & MacDonald, T. (2013). Mental skills as protective attributes against eating disorder risk in dancers. *Journal of Applied Sport Psychology, 25*, 209–222.

Etnier, J., & Chang, Y. (2009). The effect of physical activity on executive function: A brief commentary on definitions, measurement issues, and the current state of the literature. *Journal of Sport and Exercise Psychology, 31*, 469–483.

Etnier, J.L., Salazar, W., Landers, D.M., Petruzzello, S.J., Han, M., & Nowell, P. (1997). The influence of physical fitness and exercise upon cognitive functioning: A meta-analysis. *Journal of Sport and Exercise Psychology, 19*, 249–277.

Etzel, E. (1979). Validation of a conceptual model characterizing attention among international rifle shooters. *Journal of Sport Psychology, 1*, 281–290.

Eubank, M., & Collins, D. (2000). Coping with pre- and in-event fluctuations in competitive state anxiety: A longitudinal analysis. *Journal of Sports Sciences, 18*, 121–131.

Evans, L., & Hardy, L. (1995). Sport injury and grief responses: A review. *Journal of Sport and Exercise Psychology, 17*, 227–245.

Evans, L., & Hardy, L. (2002). Injury rehabilitation: A qualitative follow-up study. *Research Quarterly for Exercise and Sport, 73*(3), 320–329.

Evans, L., Hardy, L., & Fleming, S. (2000). Intervention strategies with injured athletes: An action research study. *The Sport Psychologist, 14*(2), 188–206.

Evans, L., Jones, L., & Mullen, R. (2004). An imagery intervention during the competitive season with an elite rugby union player. *The Sport Psychologist, 18*, 252–271.

Evans, M., Weinberg, R.S., & Jackson, A.W. (1992). Psychological factors related to drug use in college athletes. *The Sport Psychologist, 6*, 24–41.

Evert, J., Smith, R., & Williams, K. (1992). Effects of team cohesion and identifiability on social loafing in relay swimming performance. *International Journal of Sport Psychology, 23*, 311–324.

Ewing, M.E., & Seefeldt, V. (1989). *Participation and attrition patterns in American agency-sponsored and interscholastic sports: An executive summary.* North Palm Beach, FL: Sporting Goods Manufacturers Association.

Ewing, M.E., & Seefeldt, V. (1996). Patterns of sport participation and attrition in American agency-sponsored sports. In F.L. Smoll & R.E. Smith (Eds.), *Children and youth in sport: A biopsychosocial perspective* (pp. 31–45). Madison, WI: Brown & Benchmark.

Ewing, M.E., & Seefeldt, V. (2002). Patterns of participation in American agency-sponsored sports. In F.L. Smoll & R.E. Smith (Eds.), *Children and youth in sport: A biopsychosocial perspective* (2nd ed., pp. 39–56). Dubuque, IA: Kendall/Hunt.

Ewing, M.E., Seefeldt, V.D., & Brown, T.P. (1996). *Role of organized sport in the education and health of American children and youth.* New York: Carnegie Corporation of New York.

Eys, M., Carron, A., Beauchamp, M., & Bray, S. (2003). Role ambiguity in sport teams. *Journal of Sport and Exercise Psychology, 25*, 534–550.

Eys, M., Carron, A., Bray, S., & Beauchamp, M. (2005). The relationship between role ambiguity and intention to return the following season. *Journal of Applied Sport Psychology, 17*, 255–261.

Eys, M., Hardy, J., Carron, A., & Beauchamp, M. (2003). The relationship between task cohesion and competitive state anxiety. *Journal of Sport and Exercise Psychology, 25*, 66–76.

Eys, M., Loughead, T., Bray, S., & Carron, A. (2009). Development of a cohesion questionnaire for youth: The Youth Sport Environment Questionnaire. *Journal of Sport and Exercise Psychology, 31*, 390–408.

Eysenck, H.J., & Eysenck, S.B.G. (1968). *Eysenck personality inventory manual.* London: University of London Press.

Fahlberg, L.L., & Fahlberg, L.A. (1990). From treatment to health enhancement: Psychological considerations in the exercise components of health promotion programs. *The Sport Psychologist, 4*, 168–179.

Fair Play for Kids. (1990). *Fair play for kids.* Ottawa, ON: Commission for Fair Play.

Fallon, E., Hausenblas, H., & Nigg, C. (2005). The transtheoretical model and exercise adherence: Examining construct associations in later stages of change. *Sport and Exercise Psychology Journal, 6*, 629–641.

Farahat, E., Ille, A., & Thon, B. (2004). Effect of visual and kinesthetic imagery on the learning of a patterned movement. *International Journal of Sport Psychology, 35*, 119–132.

Farrey, T. (2008). *Game on: The All-American race to make champions of our children.* New York: ESPN Books.

Farrow, D., & Kemp, J. (2003). *Run like you stole something (the science behind the score line).* Sydney: Allen & Unwin.

Feinstein, J. (1987). *A season on the brink: A year with Bobby Knight and the Indiana Hoosiers.* New York: Simon & Schuster.

Fejfar, M.C., & Hoyle, R.H. (2000). Effect of private self-awareness on negative affect and self-referent attribution: A quantitative review. *Personality and Social Psychology Review, 4*, 131–142.

Feltz, D.L. (1984a). The psychology of sport injuries. In P.E. Vinger & E.F. Hoerner (Eds.), *Sport injuries: The unthwarted epidemic* (2nd ed., pp. 336–344). Boston: Wright, PSG.

Feltz, D.L. (1984b). Self-efficacy as a cognitive mediator of athletic performance. In W.F. Straub & J.M. Williams (Eds.), *Cognitive sport psychology* (pp. 191–198). Lansing, NY: Sport Science Associates.

Feltz, D.L., & Albrecht, R.R. (1986). Psychological implications of competitive running. In M.R. Weiss & D. Gould (Eds.), *Sport for children and youths* (pp. 225–230). Champaign, IL: Human Kinetics.

Feltz, D.L., Chase, M., Moritz, S., & Sullivan, P. (1999). Development of the multidimensional coaching efficacy scale. *Journal of Educational Psychology, 91*, 765–776.

Feltz, D.L., & Landers, D.M. (1983). The effects of mental practice on motor skill learning and performance: A meta-analysis. *Journal of Sport Psychology, 5*, 25–57.

Feltz, D., Landers, D., & Becker, B. (1988). A revised meta-analysis of the mental practice literature on motor skill learning. In D. Druckman & J. Swets (Eds.), *Enhancing human performance: Issues, theories, and techniques* (pp. 1–65). Washington, DC: National Academy Press.

Feltz, D., Short, S., & Sullivan, S. (2008). *Self-efficacy in sport: Research and strategies for working with athletes, teams, and coaches.* Champaign, IL: Human Kinetics.

Ferguson, A., & McIlvaney, H. (2000). *Managing my life: An autobiography.* London: Hodder and Stoughton.

Ferrer, R., Huedo-Medina, T., Johnson, B., Ryan, S., & Pescatello, L. (2011). Exercise interventions for cancer survivors: A meta-analysis of quality life outcomes. *Annuals of Behavioral Medicine, 41,* 32–47.

Festinger, L. (1954). A theory of social comparison processes. *Human Relations, 7,* 117–140.

Festinger, L., Schacter, S., & Back, K. (1950). *Social pressures in informed groups: A study of a housing project.* New York: Harare.

Fiedler, F. (1967). *A theory of leadership effectiveness.* New York: McGraw-Hill.

Field, L., & Steinhart, M. (1992). The relationship of internally directed behavior to self-reinforcement, self-esteem, and expectancy value for exercise. *American Journal of Health Promotion, 7,* 21–27.

Filby, W., Maynard, I., & Graydon, J. (1999). The effect of multiple-goal strategies on performance outcomes in training and competition. *Journal of Applied Sport Psychology, 11,* 230–246.

Findlay, L., & Coplan, R. (2008). Come out and play: Shyness in childhood and the benefits of organized sports participation. *Canadian Journal of Behavioral Sciences, 40,* 153–161.

Findlay, L., & Ste-Marie, D. (2004). A reputation bias in figure skating judging. *Journal of Sport and Exercise Psychology, 26,* 154–166.

Fisher, A.C., & Zwart, E.F. (1982). Psychological analysis of athletes' anxiety responses. *Journal of Sport Psychology, 4,* 139–158.

Fjeldsoe, B., Neuhaus, M., Winkler, E., & Eakin, M.E. (2011). Systematic review of maintenance of behavior change following physical activity and dietary interventions. *Health Psychology, 30,* 99–109.

Fletcher, D. (2012). Applying sport psychology in business: A narrative commentary and bibliography. *Journal of Sport Psychology in Action, 3,* 139–149.

Fletcher, D., & Arnold, R. (2011). A qualitative study of performance leadership and management in elite sport. *Journal of Applied Sport Psychology, 23,* 223–242.

Fletcher, D., & Sarkar, M. (2013). Psychological resilience. A review and critique of definitions, concepts, and theories. *European Psychologist, 18,* 12–23.

Fletcher, D., & Scott, M. (2010). Psychological stress in sports coaches: A review of concepts, research, and practice. *Journal of Sport Sciences, 28,* 291–298.

Flett, G.L., & Hewitt, P.L. (2005). The perils of perfectionism in sports and exercise. *Current Directions in Psychological Science, 14,* 14–18.

Flett, G.L., Pole-Langdon, L., & Hewitt, P.L. (2003). *Trait perfectionism and perfectionistic self-presentation in compulsive exercise.* (Unpublished manuscript). Toronto: York University.

Folkins, C.H., & Sime, W.E. (1981). Physical fitness training and mental health. *American Psychologist, 36,* 373–389.

Ford, I.W., Eklund, R.C., & Gordan, S. (2000). An examination of psychosocial variables moderating the relationship between life stress and injury time-loss among athletes of a high standard. *Journal of Sports Sciences, 18*(5), 301–312.

Fortier, M., Sweet, S., Tulloch, H., Blacchard, C., Sigal, R., Kenny, G., et al. (2012). Self-determination and exercise stages of change: Results from the diabetes, aerobic, and resistance exercise trial. *Journal of Health Psychology, 17,* 110–120.

Fournier, J., Calmels, C., Durand-Bush, N., & Salmela, J. (2005). Effects of a season-long PST program on gymnastic performance and on psychological skill development. *International Journal of Sport and Exercise Psychology, 3,* 59–78.

Fox, K.R. (1997). *The physical self: From motivation to well-being.* Champaign, IL: Human Kinetics.

Francisco, R., Narciso, I., & Alarcao, M. (2012). Specific predictors of disordered eating among elite and non-elite gymnasts and ballet dancers. *International Journal of Sport Psychology, 43,* 479–502.

Franklin, B.A. (1984). Exercise program compliance. In J. Storlie & H.A. Jordan (Eds.), *Behavioral management of obesity* (pp. 105–135). New York: Spectrum Press.

Fransen, K., Vanbeslaere, N., Exadaktylos, V., Broek, G., Cuyper, B., Berckmans, D., et al. (2012). "Yes we can": Perceptions of collective efficacy sources in volleyball. *Journal of Sport Sciences, 30,* 641–649.

Fraser-Thomas, J., & Cote, J. (2006). Youth sports: Implementing findings and moving forward with research. *Athletic Insight, 8,* 12–27.

Fraser-Thomas, J., Cote, J., & Deakin, J. (2008). Examining adolescent sport dropout and prolonged engagement from a developmental perspective. *Journal of Applied Sport Psychology, 20,* 318–333.

Fredrick, C., & Morrison, C. (1999). Collegiate athletes: An examination of motivational style and its relationship to decision making and personality. *Journal of Sport Behavior, 22,* 221–233.

Fredricks, J.A., & Eccles, J.S. (2004). Parental influences on youth involvement in sports. In M.R. Weiss (Ed.), *Developmental sport and exercise psychology: A lifespan perspective* (pp. 145–164). Morgantown, WV: Fitness Information Technology.

Freeman, P., Rees, T., & Hardy, L. (2009). An intervention to increase social support and improve performance. *Journal of Applied Sport Psychology, 21,* 186–200.

Frey, M. (2007). College coaches' experiences with stress—"Problem solvers" have problems too. *The Sport Psychologist, 21,* 38–57.

Frith, J., Kerr, J., & Wilson, G. (2011). Immediate improvements in emotion and stress following participation in aerobics, circuit training, and tai chi. *International Journal of Sport Psychology, 42,* 480–492.

Fuchs, A. (2009). Psychology and baseball: The testing of Babe Ruth. In C.D. Green & L.T. Benjamin, Jr. (Eds.), *Psychology gets in the game: Sport, mind, and behavior. 1880–1960* (pp. 144–167). Lincoln, NE: University of Nebraska Press.

Furley P., Dicks, M., & Memmert, D. (2012). Nonverbal behavior in soccer: The influence of dominant and submissive body language on the impression formation and expectancy of success of soccer players. *Journal of Sport and Exercise Psychology, 34,* 61–82.

Gaa, G.L., Griffith, E.H., Cahill, B.R., & Tuttle, L.D. (1994). Prevalence of anabolic steroid use among Illinois high school students. *Journal of Athletic Training, 29,* 216–222.

Galli, N., & Vealey, R. (2008). "Bouncing back" from adversity: Athletes' experiences of resilience. *The Sport Psychologist, 22,* 316–335.

Gallimore, R., & Tharp, R. (2004). What a coach can teach a teacher, 1975–2004: Reflection and reanalysis of John Wooden's teaching practices. *The Sport Psychologist, 18,* 119–137.

Galvan, Z., & Ward, P. (1998). Effects of public posting on inappropriate court behaviors by collegiate tennis players. *The Sport Psychologist, 12,* 419–426.

Gammage, K., Hall, C., & Rodgers, W. (2000). More about exercise imagery. *The Sport Psychologist, 14,* 348–359.

Gano-Overway, L.A. (2008). The effect of goal involvement on self-regulatory processes. *International Journal of Sport and Exercise Psychology, 6,* 132–156.

Gano-Overway, L.A., Newton, M., Magyar, T.M., Fry, M.D., Kim, M., & Guivernau, M.R. (2009). Influence of caring youth sport contexts on efficacy-related beliefs and social behaviors. *Developmental Psychology, 45,* 329–340.

Gapin, J., & Etnier, J. (2010). The relationship between physical activity and executive function performance in children with attention-deficit hyperactivity disorder. *Journal of Sport and Exercise Psychology, 32,* 753–763.

Gardner, D.E., Shields, D.L., Bredemeier, B.J., & Bostrom, A. (1996). The relationship between perceived coaching behaviors and team cohesion among baseball and softball players. *The Sport Psychologist, 10,* 367–381.

Gardner, H. (1983). *Frames of mind: The theory of multiple intelligences.* New York: Basic Books.

Garland, D.L., & Barry, J.R. (1990). Personality and leader behaviors in collegiate football: A multidimensional approach to performance. *Journal of Research in Personality, 24,* 355–370.

Garrity, J. (2000, June). Open and shut. *Sports Illustrated, 92,* pp. 58–64.

Gaskin, C.J., Andersen, M.B., & Morris, T. (2009). Physical activity in the life of a woman with severe cerebral palsy: Showing competence and being socially connected. *International Journal of Disability, Development and Education, 56,* 285–299.

Gaskin, C.J., Andersen, M.B., & Morris, T. (2010). Sport and physical activity in the life of a man with cerebral palsy: Compensation for disability with psychosocial benefits and costs. *Psychology, Sport and Exercise, 11,* 197–205.

Gauron, E. (1984). *Mental training for peak performance.* Lansing, NY: Sport Science Associates.

Gauvin, L., Rejeski, W.J., & Reboussin, B.A. (2000). Contributions of acute bouts of vigorous physical activity to explaining diurnal variations in feeling states in active middle-aged women. *Health Psychology, 19,* 265–375.

Gawande, A. (2010). *The checklist manifesto: How to get things right.* New York: Metropolitan Books.

Gee, C.J., & Leith, L.M. (2007). Aggressive behavior in professional ice hockey: A cross-cultural comparison of North American and European born NHL players. *Psychology of Sport and Exercise, 8,* 567–583.

Geibenk, M.P., & McKenzie, T.C. (1985). Teaching sportsmanship in physical education and recreation: An analysis of intervention and generalization efforts. *Journal of Teaching Physical Education, 4,* 167–177.

Gentry, W.D., & Kosaba, S.C. (1979). Social and psychological resources mediating stress illness relationships in humans. In R.B. Haynes, D.W. Taylor, & D. Sackett (Eds.), *Compliance in health care* (pp. 87–116). Baltimore: Johns Hopkins University Press.

Gershgoren, L., Tenenbaum, G., Gerhgoren, A., & Eklund, R.C. (2011). The effect of parental feedback on young athletes' perceived motivational climate, goal involvement, goal orientation, and performance. *Psychology of Sport and Exercise, 12,* 481–489.

Gersick, C.J.G. (1988). Time and transition in work teams: Toward a new model of group development. *Academy of Management Journal, 31,* 9–41.

Gerstein, A., & Reagan, J. (1986). *Win-win: Approaches to conflict resolution.* Salt Lake City: Smith.

Giacobbi, P. (2007). Age and activity differences in the use of exercise imagery. *Journal of Applied Sport Psychology, 19,* 487–493.

Giacobbbi, P., Foore, B., & Weinberg, R. (2004). Broken clubs and expletives: The sources of stress and coping responses of skilled and moderately skilled golfers. *Journal of Applied Sport Psychology, 16,* 166–182.

Giacobbi, P., Hausenblas, H., Fallon, E., & Hall, C. (2003). Even more about exercise imagery: A grounded theory of exercise imagery. *Journal of Applied Sport Psychology, 15,* 160–175.

Giacobbi, P., Hausenblas, H., & Frye, N. (2005). A naturalistic assessment of the relationship between personality, daily life events, leisure-time exercise, and mood. *Psychology of Sport and Exercise, 6,* 67–81.

Giacobbi, P., & Weinberg, R. (2000). An examination of coping in sport: Individual trait anxiety differences and situational consistency. *The Sport Psychologist, 14,* 42–62.

Gibbons, S.L., Ebbeck, V., & Weiss, M.R. (1995). Fair play for kids: Effects on the moral development of children in physical education. *Research Quarterly for Exercise and Sport, 66,* 247–255.

Gieck, J., Brown, R.S., & Shank, R.H. (1982, August). The burnout syndrome among athletic trainers. *Athletic Training,* pp. 36–41.

Giges, B. (1998). Psychodynamic concepts in sport psychology: Comments on Strean and Strean (1998). *The Sport Psychologist, 12,* 223–227.

Gilbert, J. (2011). Teaching sport psychology to high school student-athletes: The psychological UNIFORM and the game plan format. *Journal of Sport Psychology in Action, 2,* 1–9.

Gilbert, J., Gilbert, W., Loney, B., Wahl, M., & Michel, E. (2006). Sport psychology in an urban high school: Overview of a two-year collaboration. *Journal of Education, 187,* 67–95.

Gilbert, W. (2002, June). *An annotated bibliography and analysis of coaching science: 1970–2001.* Washington, DC: American Alliance for Health, Physical Education, Recreation and Dance.

Gilbert, W., & Trudel, P. (2004). Analysis of coaching science research published from 1970–2001. *Research Quarterly for Exercise and Sport, 75,* 388–399.

Gill, D.L. (1979). The prediction of group motor performance from individual member abilities. *Journal of Motor Behavior, 11,* 113–122.

Gill, D. (1993). Competitiveness and competitive orientation in sport. In R.A. Singer, M. Murphey, & K. Tennant (Eds.), *Handbook of research on sport psychology* (pp. 314–327). New York: Macmillan.

Gill, D. (2000). *Psychological dynamics of sport and exercise.* Champaign, IL: Human Kinetics.

Gill, D.L., & Deeter, T.E. (1988). Development of the Sport Orientation Questionnaire. *Research Quarterly for Exercise and Sport, 59,* 191–202.

Gill, D., & Williams, L. (2008). *Psychological dynamics of sport and exercise* (3rd ed.). Champaign, IL: Human Kinetics.

Gillovich, T., Vallone, R., & Tversky, A. (1985). The hot hand in basketball: On the misperceptions of random sequences. *Cognitive Psychology, 17,* 295–314.

Girdano, D.A., Everly, G.S., & Dusek, D.E. (1990). *Controlling stress and tension: A holistic approach* (3rd ed.). Englewood Cliffs, NJ: Prentice Hall.

Glasser, W. (1976). *Positive addiction.* New York: Harper & Row.

Glazer, J. (2008). Eating disorders among male athletes. *Current Sports Medicine Reports, 7,* 332–338.

Glencross, D. (1993). Simulation camp. *Sports Coach, 6,* 7–10.

Glory, M., Kirubakar, S.G., & Kumutha, N. (2010). Communication skills: A cognitive-behavioral approach to enhance relationship skills in young sport coaches. *British Journal of Sports Medicine, 44,* i49–i50.

Goffi, C. (1984). *Tournament tough.* London: Ebury Press.

Goldberg, L., & Elliot, D. (2005). Preventing drug abuse among high school athletes: The ATLAS and ATHENA programs. *Journal of Applied Social Psychology, 21,* 63–87.

Goldschmied, N., Nankin, M., & Cafri, G. (2010). Pressure kicks in the NFL: An archival exploration into the deployment of timeouts and other environmental correlates. *The Sport Psychologist, 18,* 300–312.

Goldsmith, P.A., & Williams, J.M. (1992). Perceived stressors for football and volleyball officials from three rating levels. *Journal of Sport Behavior, 15,* 106–118.

Goleman, D. (1995). *Emotional intelligence.* New York: Bantam.

Goodger, K., Gorely, T., Lavallee, D., & Harwood, C. (2007). Burnout in sport: A systematic review. *The Sport Psychologist, 21*(2), 125–149.

Goodman, J. (2006). School disciple in moral disarray. *Journal of Moral Education, 35,* 213–230.

Gordon, S., Milios, D., & Grove, R.J. (1991). Psychological aspects of the recovery process from sport injury: The perspective of sport physiotherapists. *Australian Journal of Science and Medicine in Sport, 23*(2), 53–60.

Goss, J., Cooper, S., Croxon, S., & Dryden, N. (2005). Eating disorders. In J. Taylor & G. Wilson (Eds.), *Applying sport psychology: Four perspectives* (pp. 207–228). Champaign, IL: Human Kinetics.

Goudas, M., & Magotsiou, E. (2009). The effects of a cooperative physical education program on students' social skills. *Journal of Applied Sport Psychology, 21*, 356-364.

Gould, D. (1981). Sportsmanship: Build character or characters. In Youth Sports Institute (Ed.), *A winning philosophy for youth sports programs*. Lansing, MI: Institute for the Study of Youth Sports.

Gould, D. (1993). Intensive sport participation and the prepubescent athlete: Competitive stress and burnout. In B.R. Cahill & A.J. Pearl (Eds.), *Intensive participation in children's sports* (pp. 19–38). Champaign, IL: Human Kinetics.

Gould, D. (2005). Goal setting for peak performance. In J. Williams (Ed.), *Applied sport psychology: Personal growth to peak performance* (5th ed., pp. 240–259). Palo Alto, CA: Mayfield.

Gould, D. (Ed.). (2007). *Becoming an effective team captain: Student-athlete guide*. East Lansing, MI: Michigan High School Athletic Association.

Gould, D. (2009). The professionalization of youth sports: It's time to act! *Clinical Journal of Sports Medicine, 19*, 81–82.

Gould, D. (2011, September). *Drawing from all AASP foci to educate America's college wrestling coaches*. Presented at the Association for Applied Sport Psychology Conference, Honolulu.

Gould, D., & Bean, E. (2011). Children in sport. In T. Morris & P. Terry (Eds.), *Sport psychology: Theory, applications, and issues* (3rd ed., pp. 509–529). Morgantown, WV: Fitness Information Technology.

Gould, D., & Carson, S. (2004). Myths surrounding the role of youth sports in developing Olympic champions. *Youth Studies Australia, 23*(1), 19–26.

Gould, D., & Carson, S. (2010). The relationship between perceived coaching behaviors and developmental benefits of high school sport participation. *The Hellenic Journal of Psychology, 7*, 298–314.

Gould, D., & Carson, S. (2011). Young athletes' perceptions of the relationship between coaching behaviors and developmental experience. *International Journal of Coaching Science, 5*, 3–29.

Gould, D., Collins, K., Lauer, L., & Chung, Y. (2007). Coaching life skills through football: A study of award winning high school coaches. *Journal of Applied Sport Psychology, 19*, 16–37.

Gould, D., Cowburn, I., & Pierce, S. (2013). *Sport parenting research: Current status, future directions and practical implications*. U.S. Tennis Association White Paper report. Boca Raton, FL: U.S. Tennis Association.

Gould, D., Danish, S., Fazio, R., Medbery, R., Collins, K., & Rolo, C. (2000). The power 4W success program. In D. Gould (Ed.), *Coaching academy playbook* (pp. 302–317). Morristown, NJ: National Football Foundation and College Hall of Fame.

Gould, D., Dieffenbach, K., & Moffett, A. (2002). Psychological talent and its development in Olympic champions. *Journal of Applied Sport Psychology, 14*, 177–210.

Gould, D., Eklund, R., & Jackson, S. (1992a). Coping strategies used by more versus less successful Olympic wrestlers. *Research Quarterly for Exercise and Sport, 64*, 83–93.

Gould, D., Eklund, R.C., & Jackson, S. (1992b). 1988 U.S. Olympic wrestling excellence: I. Mental preparation, precompetitive cognition, and affect. *The Sport Psychologist, 6*, 358–382.

Gould, D., Eklund, R.C., & Jackson, S. (1992c). 1988 U.S. Olympic wrestling excellence: II. Thoughts and affect occurring during competition. *The Sport Psychologist, 6*, 383–402.

Gould, D., Eklund, R., & Jackson, S. (1993). Coping strategies used by U.S. Olympic wrestlers. *Research Quarterly for Exercise and Sport, 64*, 83–93.

Gould, D., Eklund, R., Petlichkoff, L., Peterson, K., & Bump, L. (1991). Psychological predictors of state anxiety and performance in age-group wrestlers. *Pediatric Exercise Science, 3*, 198–208.

Gould, D., Feltz, D., Horn, T., & Weiss, M. (1982). Reasons for attrition in competitive youth swimming. *Journal of Sport Behavior, 5*, 155–165.

Gould, D., Flett, R., & Lauer, L. (2012). The relationship between psychosocial development and the sport climate experienced by underserved youth. *Psychology of Sport and Exercise, 13*, 80–87.

Gould, D., Greenleaf, C., Chung, Y., & Guinan, D. (2002). A survey of U.S. Atlanta and Nagano Olympians: Factors influencing performance. *Research Quarterly for Sport and Exercise, 73*(2), 175–186.

Gould, D., Greenleaf, C., & Krane, V. (2002). The arousal–athletic performance relationship: Current status and future directions. In T. Horn (Ed.), *Advances in sport psychology* (2nd ed.). Champaign, IL: Human Kinetics.

Gould, D., Greenleaf, C., Lauer, L., & Chung, Y. (1999). Lessons learned from Nagano. *Olympic Coach, 9*, 2–5.

Gould, D., Guinan, D., Greenleaf, C., Medbery, R., & Peterson, K. (1999). Factors affecting Olympic performance. Perceptions of athletes and coaches from more and less successful teams. *The Sport Psychologist, 13*, 371–394.

Gould, D., Hodge, K., Peterson, K., & Giannini, J. (1989). An exploratory examination of strategies used by elite coaches to enhance self-efficacy in athletes. *Journal of Sport and Exercise Psychology, 11*, 128–140.

Gould, D., & Horn, T. (1984). Participation motivation in young athletes. In J.M. Silva & R.S. Weinberg (Eds.), *Psychological foundations of sport* (pp. 359–370). Champaign, IL: Human Kinetics.

Gould, D., Horn, T., & Spreemann, J. (1983). Sources of stress in junior elite wrestlers. *Journal of Sport Psychology, 5*, 159–171.

Gould, D., Jackson, S., & Finch, L. (1993). Life at the top: The experience of U.S. national champion figure skaters. *The Sport Psychologist, 7*, 354–374.

Gould, D., Lauer, L., Rolo, C., Jannes, C., & Pennisi, N.S. (2006). Understanding the role parents play in tennis success: A national survey of junior tennis coaches. *British Journal of Sports Medicine, 40*, 632–636.

Gould, D., & Martens, R. (1979). Attitudes of volunteer coaches toward significant youth sport issues. *Research Quarterly, 50*(3), 369–380.

Gould, D., & Maynard, I. (2009). Psychological preparation for the Olympic Games. *Journal of Sport Sciences, 27*(13), 1393–1408.

Gould, D., Medbery, R., Damarjian, N., & Lauer, L. (1999a). A survey assessment of mental skills training knowledge, opinions, and practices of a national sample of junior tennis coaches. *Journal of Applied Sport Psychology, 11*, 28–50.

Gould, D., Medbery, R., Damarjian, N., & Lauer, L. (1999b). An examination of mental skills training in junior tennis coaches. *The Sport Psychologist, 13*, 371–395.

Gould, D., & Petlichkoff, L. (1988). Participation motivation and attrition in young athletes. In F. Smoll, R. Magill, & M. Ash (Eds.), *Children in sport* (3rd ed., pp. 161–178). Champaign, IL: Human Kinetics.

Gould, D., Tammen, V., Murphy, S., & May, J. (1991). An evaluation of U.S. Olympic sport psychology consultant effectiveness. *The Sport Psychologist, 5*, 111–127.

Gould, D., & Tuffey, S. (1996). Zones of optimal functioning research: A review and critique. *Anxiety, Stress, and Coping, 9*, 53–68.

Gould, D., Tuffey, S., Udry, E., & Loehr, J. (1996a). Burnout in competitive junior tennis players: I. A quantitative psychological assessment. *The Sport Psychologist, 10*, 322–340.

Gould, D., Tuffey, S., Udry, E., & Loehr, J. (1996b). Burnout in competitive junior tennis players: II. Qualitative content analysis and case studies. *The Sport Psychologist, 10*, 341–366.

Gould, D., Tuffey, S., Udry, E., & Loehr, J. (1997). Burnout in competitive junior tennis players: III. Individual differences in the burnout experience. *The Sport Psychologist, 11*, 257–276.

Gould, D., & Udry, E. (1994). Psychological skills for enhancing performance: Arousal regulation strategies. *Medicine and Science in Sports and Exercise, 26*(4), 478–485.

Gould, D., Udry, E., Bridges, D., & Beck, L. (1996). Helping skiers come back from season-ending injuries. *American Ski Coach, 18*, 10–12.

Gould, D., Udry, E., Bridges, D., & Beck, L. (1997a). Psychological strategies for helping elite athletes cope with season-ending injuries. *Athletic Therapy Today, 2*, 50–53.

Gould, D., Udry, E., Bridges, D., & Beck, L. (1997b). Stress sources encountered when rehabilitating from season-ending ski injuries. *The Sport Psychologist, 11*, 361–378.

Gould, D., & Voelker, D. (2010). Youth sport leadership development: Leveraging the sports captaincy experience. *Journal of Sport Psychology in Action, 1*, 1-13.

Gould, D., & Voelker, D.K. (2014). The history of sport psychology. In R. Eklund & G. Tennenbaum (Eds.), *Encyclopedia of sport psychology* (pp. 346-351). Thousand Oaks, CA: Sage.

Gould, D., Voelker, D.K., & Griffes, K. (2013). How coaches mentor team captains. *The Sport Psychologist, 27*, 13–26.

Gould, D., Weiss, M., & Weinberg, R. (1981). Psychological characteristics of successful and less successful Big Ten wrestlers. *Journal of Sport Psychology, 3*, 69–81.

Gould, D., & Whitley, M. (2009). Sources and consequences of athletic burnout among college athletes. *Journal of Intercollegiate Athletics, 2*, 16–30.

Gould, D., & Wright, M. (2012). The psychology of coaching. In S. Murphy (Ed.), *The Oxford handbook of sport and performance psychology* (pp. 343–363). Oxford, UK: Oxford University Press.

Goves, M., Griggs, G., & Leflay, K. (2012). Hazing and initiation ceremonies in university sport: Setting the scene for further research in the United Kingdom. *Sport and Society, 15*(1), 117–131.

Gowan, G.R., Botterill, C.B., & Blimkie, C.J.R. (1979). Bridging the gap between sport science and sport practice. In P. Klavora & J.V. Daniel (Eds.), *Coach, athlete, and the sport psychologist* (pp. 3–9). Ottawa, ON: Coaching Association of Canada.

Goyens, C., & Turowetz, A. (1986). *Lions in winter.* Scarborough, ON: Prentice Hall.

Granito, V., & Rainey, D. (1988). Differences in cohesion between high school and college football teams and starters and nonstarters. *Perceptual and Motor Skills, 66*, 471–477.

Grant, M., & Schempp, P. (2013). Analysis and description of Olympic gold medalists' competition-day routines. *The Sport Psychologist, 27*, 156–170.

Green, E.K., Burke, K.L., Nix, C.L., Lambrecht, K.W., & Mason, D.C. (1996). Psychological factors associated with alcohol use by high school athletes. *Journal of Sport Behavior, 18*, 195–208.

Green, S.L., & Weinberg, R.S. (2001). Relationships among athletic identity, coping skills, social support, and the psychological impact of injury in recreational participants. *Journal of Applied Sport Psychology, 13*(1), 40–59.

Greenfield, J. (1976). *The world's greatest team: A portrait of the Boston Celtics 1957–1969.* New York: Random House.

Greenleaf, C., Gould, D., & Dieffenbach, K. (2001). Factors influencing Olympic performance: Interviews with Atlanta and Nagano U.S. Olympians. *Journal of Applied Sport Psychology, 13*, 154–184.

Greenleaf, C., Petrie, T., Reel, J., & Carter, J. (2010). Psychosocial risk factors of bulimic symptomatology among female athletes. *Journal of Clinical Sport Psychology, 4*, 177–190.

Greenlees, I., Bradley, A., Holder, T., & Thelwell, R. (2005). The impact of opponents' non-verbal behavior on the first impressions and outcome expectations of table-tennis players. *Psychology of Sport and Exercise, 6*, 103–115.

Greenspan, M.J., & Feltz, D.F. (1989). Psychological interventions with athletes in competitive situations: A review. *The Sport Psychologist, 3*, 219–236.

Gregg, M. (2013). Working with athletes with intellectual disabilities. In S. Hanrahan & M. Andersen (Eds.), *Routledge handbook of applied sport psychology: A comprehensive guide for students and practitioners* (pp. 441–449). New York: Routledge.

Gregg, M., & Hall, C. (2006). The relationship of skill level and age to the use of imagery by golfers. *Journal of Applied Sport Psychology, 18*, 363–375.

Gregg, M., Hall., C., & Butler, A. (2010). The MIQ-RS: A suitable option for examining movement imagery ability. *Evidence Based Complementary and Alternative Medicine, 7*, 249–257.

Gregg, M., Hall, C., McGowan, E., & Hall, N. (2011). The relationship between imagery ability and imagery use among athletes. *Journal of Applied Sport Psychology, 23*, 129–141.

Gregory, S. (2010). The problem with football: How to make it safer. *Time, 175*, 36–43.

Gregory, S. (2013). Practice makes perfect? An amateur's golf quest sheds light on how we learn. *Time, 182*, 56.

Griest, J.H., Klein, M.H., Eischens, R.R., & Faris, J.T. (1978). Running out of depression. *The Physician and Sportsmedicine, 6*, 49–56.

Grieve, F., Whelan, J., & Meyers, A. (2000). An experimental examination of the cohesion-performance relationship in an interactive sport team. *Journal of Applied Sport Psychology, 12*, 219–235.

Grossbard, J., Hummer, J., Labrie, J., Pederson, E., & Neighbors, C. (2009). Is substance use a team sport? Attraction to team, perceived norms, and alcohol and marijuana use among male and female intercollegiate athletes. *Journal of Applied Sport Psychology, 21*, 247–261.

Gruber, J.J. (1986). Physical activity and self-esteem development in children: A meta-analysis. *American Academy of Physical Education Papers, 19*, 30–48.

Grunbaum, J., Kann, I., Kinchen, S., Ross, J., Hawkins, J., & Lowry, R. (2004). Youth risk behavior surveillance: United States, 2003. *Morbidity and Mortality Weekly Report, Surveillance Summary, 53*, 1–96.

Gu, X., Solomon, M., Zhang, T., & Xiang, P. (2011). Group cohesion, achievement motivation, and motivational outcomes among female college students. *Journal of Applied Sport Psychology, 23*, 175–188.

Guan, J., Xiang, P., McBride, R., & Bruene, A. (2006). Achievement goals, social goals, and students' reported persistence and effort in high school physical education. *Journal of Teaching Physical Education, 25*, 58–74.

Gucciardi, D., & Dimmock, J. (2008). Choking under pressure in sensorimotor skills: Conscious processing or depleted attentional resources. *Psychology of Sport and Exercise, 9*, 45–59.

Gucciardi, D., Gordon, S., & Dimmock, J. (2008). Towards an understanding of mental toughness in Australian football. *Journal of Applied Sport Psychology, 20*, 261–281.

Gucciardi, D., Gordon, S., & Dimmock, J. (2009). Development and preliminary validation of a mental toughness inventory for Australian football. *Psychology of Sport and Exercise, 10*, 201–209.

Gucciardi, D., Hanton, S., & Mallett, C. (2012). Progressing measurement in mental toughness: A case example of the mental toughness questionnaire 48. *Sport, Exercise and Performance Psychology, 1*, 194–214.

Guillot, A., & Collet, C. (2008). Construction of the motor imagery integrative model in sport: A review and theoretical investigation of motor imagery use. *International Review of Sport and Exercise Psychology, 1,* 31–44.

Guillot, A., Hoyek, N., Louis, M., & Collet, C. (2012). Understanding the timing of motor imagery: Recent findings and future directions. *International Review of Sport and Exercise Psychology, 3,* 3–22.

Guillot, A., Lebon, F., Rouffet, D., Champely, S., Doyon, J., & Collet, C. (2007). Muscular responses during motor imagery as a function of muscle contraction types. *International Journal of Psychophysiology, 66,* 18–27.

Guillot, A., Tolleron, C., & Collet, C. (2010). Does motor imagery enhance stretching and flexibility? *Journal of Sport Sciences, 28,* 291–298.

Gula, B., & Raab, M. (2004). Hot hand belief and hot hand behavior: A comment on Koehler and Conley. *Journal of Sport and Exercise Psychology, 26,* 167–170.

Gustafsson, H., Kentta, G., & Hassmen, P. (2011). Athlete burnout: An integrated model and future research directions. *International Review of Sport and Exercise Psychology, 4*(1), 3–24.

Gustafsson, H., Kentta, G., Hassmen, P., & Lindquist, C. (2007). Prevalence of burnout in adolescent competitive athletes. *The Sport Psychologist, 21*(1), 21–27.

Gustafsson, H., Kentta, G., Hassmen, P., Lindquist, C., & Durand-Bush, N. (2007). The process of burnout: A multiple case study of 3 elite endurance athletes. *International Journal of Sport Psychology, 38,* 388–416.

Gustafsson, H., Skoog, T., Podlog, L., Lundqvist, C., & Wagnsson, S. (2013). Hope and athlete burnout: Stress and affect mediators. *Psychology of Sport and Exercise, 14,* 640–649.

Haan, N., Aeerts, E., & Cooper, B. (1985). *On moral grounds.* New York: University Press.

Habert, P., & McCann, S. (2012). Evaluating USOC sport psychology consultant effectiveness: A philosophical and practical imperative at the Olympic Games. *Journal of Sport Psychology in Action, 3,* 65–76.

Hackman, J.R., & Wageman, R. (2007). Asking the right questions about leadership. *American Psychologist, 62,* 43–47.

Hackney, A.C., Perlman, S.N., & Nowacki, J.M. (1990). Psychological profiles of overtrained and stale athletes: A review. *Journal of Applied Sport Psychology, 2,* 21–33.

Hagger, M., & Chatzisarantis, N. (2007). Editorial: Advances in self-determination theory research in sport and exercise. *Psychology of Sport and Exercise, 8,* 597–599.

Hagger, M., & Chatzisarantis, N. (2008). Self-determination theory and the psychology of exercise. *International Review of Sport and Exercise Psychology, 1,* 79–103.

Hagger, M., Chatzisarantis, N., & Biddle, S. (2002). A meta-analytic review of the theories of reasoned action and planned behavior in physical activity: Predictive validity and the contribution of additional variables. *Journal of Sport and Exercise Psychology, 24,* 3–32.

Hagiwara, H., & Wolfson, S. (2013). Attitudes toward soccer coaches' use of punishment in Japan and England: A cross-cultural study. *International Journal of Sport and Exercise Psychology, 11,* 57–69.

Hale, B.D. (1994). Imagery perspectives and learning in sports performance. In A. Sheikh & E. Korn (Eds.), *Imagery in sports and physical performance* (pp. 75–96). Farmingdale, NY: Baywood.

Hale, B., Seiser, L., McGuire, E., & Weinrich, E. (2005). Mental imagery. In J. Taylor & G. Wilson (Eds.), *Applying sport psychology: Four perspectives* (pp. 117–135). Champaign, IL: Human Kinetics.

Hall, C.R. (2001). Imagery in sport and exercise. In R. Singer, H. Hausenblas, & C. Janelle (Eds.), *Handbook of sport psychology* (2nd ed., pp. 529–549). New York: Wiley.

Hall, C.R., Mack, D., Pavio, A., & Hausenblas, H.A. (1998). Imagery use by athletes: Development of the Sport Imagery Questionnaire. *International Journal of Sport Psychology, 28,* 1–17.

Hall, H., Hill, A., Appelton, P., & Kozub, S. (2009). The mediating influence of unconditional self-acceptance and labile self-esteem on the relationship between multidimensional perfectionism and exercise dependence. *Psychology of Sport and Exercise, 10,* 35–45.

Halliburton, S., & Sanford, S. (1989, July 31). Making weight becomes torture for UT swimmers. *Austin American Statesman,* pp. D1, D7.

Hamilton, K., & White, K. (2008). Extending the theory of planned behavior: The role of self and social influences in predicting adolescent regular moderate-to-vigorous physical activity. *Journal of Sport and Exercise Psychology, 30,* 56–74.

Hamilton, R., Scott, D., & MacDougall, M. (2007). Assessing the effectiveness of self-talk intervention on endurance performance. *Journal of Applied Sport Psychology, 19,* 226–239.

Hanin, Y.L. (1980). A study of anxiety in sports. In W.F. Straub (Ed.), *Sport psychology: An analysis of athlete behavior* (pp. 236–249). Ithaca, NY: Mouvement.

Hanin, Y.L. (1986). State and trait anxiety research on sports in the USSR. In C.D. Spielberger & R. Diaz-Guerreo (Eds.), *Cross-cultural anxiety* (Vol. 3, pp. 45–64). Washington, DC: Hemisphere.

Hanin, Y.L. (1997). Emotions and athletic performance: Individual zones of optimal functioning. *European Yearbook of Sport Psychology, 1,* 29–72.

Hanin, Y.L. (2000). *Emotions in sport.* Champaign, IL: Human Kinetics.

Hanin, Y.L. (2007). Emotions in sport: Current issues and perspectives. In G. Tenenbaum & R.C. Eklund (Eds.), *Handbook of sport psychology* (3rd ed., pp. 31–58). Hoboken, NJ: Wiley.

Hanin, Y.L., & Stambulova, N. (2002). Metaphoric description of performance states. *The Sport Psychologist, 16*(4), 396–415.

Hanin, Y., & Syrja, P. (1996). Predicted, actual and recalled affect in Olympic-level soccer players: Idiographic assessment on individualized scales. *Journal of Sport and Exercise Psychology, 18,* 325–335.

Hanrahan, S. (2007). Athletes with disabilities. In G. Tenenbaum & R. Eklund (Eds.), *Handbook of sport psychology* (pp. 845–858). Hoboken, NJ: Wiley.

Hanrahan, S., & Gallois, C. (1993). Social interactions. In R.N. Singer, M. Murphey, & L.K. Tennant (Eds.), *Handbook of sport psychology* (pp. 623–646). New York: Macmillan.

Hansen, C.J., Stevens, L.C., & Coast, J.R. (2001). Exercise duration and mood state: How much is enough to feel better? *Health Psychology, 20,* 267–275.

Hanson, T.W., & Gould, D. (1988). Factors affecting the ability of coaches to estimate their athletes' trait and state anxiety levels. *The Sport Psychologist, 2,* 298–313.

Hanton, S., & Jones, G. (1999a). The acquisition and development of cognitive skills and strategies: I. Making the butterflies fly in formation. *The Sport Psychologist, 13,* 1–21.

Hanton, S., & Jones, G. (1999b). The effects of multimodal intervention program on performers. II. Training the butterflies to fly in formation. *The Sport Psychologist, 13,* 22–41.

Hanton, S., Neil, R., & Mellalieu, S.D. (2008). Recent developments in competitive anxiety: Direction and competitive stress research. *International Review of Sport and Exercise Psychology, 1,* 45–57.

Hanton, S., Neil, R., & Mellalieu, S.D. (2011). Competitive anxiety and sporting performance. In T. Morris & P. Terry (Eds.), *The new sport and exercise psychology companion (pp. 89–104).* Morgantown, WV: Fitness Information Technology.

Hanton, S., Thomas, O., & Mellalieu, S. (2009). Management of competitive stress in elite sport. In B. Brewer (Ed.), *The Olympic handbook of sports medicine and science: Sport psychology* (pp. 30–42). Oxford, UK: Wiley-Blackwell.

Hardcastle, S., & Taylor, A. (2005). Finding an exercise identity in an older body: "It's redefining yourself and working out who you are." *Psychology of Sport and Exercise, 6,* 173–188.

Hardy, C.J., Burke, K.L., & Crace, R.K. (2005). Coaching: An effective communication system. In S. Murphy (Ed.), *The sport psych handbook* (pp. 191–214). Champaign, IL: Human Kinetics.

Hardy, C.J., & Crace, R.K. (1990). Dealing with injury. *Sport Psychology Training Bulletin, 1*(6), 1–8.

Hardy, C.J., & Crace, R.K. (1991). Social support within sport. *Sport Psychology Training Bulletin, 3*(1), 1–8.

Hardy, C.J., & Crace, R.K. (1997). Foundations of team building: Introduction to the team-building primer. *Journal of Applied Sport Psychology, 9,* 1–10.

Hardy, C.J., & Latane, B. (1988). Social loafing in cheerleaders: Effects of team membership and competition. *Journal of Sport and Exercise Psychology, 10,* 109–114.

Hardy, J., Gammage, K., & Hall, C. (2001). A descriptive study of athlete self-talk. *The Sport Psychologist, 15,* 306–318.

Hardy, J., Hall, C., & Carron, A. (2003). Perceptions of team cohesion and athlete imagery use. *International Journal of Sport Psychology, 34,* 151-167.

Hardy, J., Hall, C.R., & Hardy, L. (2004). A note on athletes' use of self-talk. *Journal of Applied Sport Psychology, 16,* 251–257.

Hardy, J., Roberts, R., & Hardy, L. (2009). Awareness and motivation to change negative self-talk. *The Sport Psychologist,* 23, 435–450.

Hardy, L. (1990). A catastrophe model of performance in sport. In G. Jones & L. Hardy (Eds.), *Stress and performance in sport* (pp. 81–106). Chichester, UK: Wiley.

Hardy, L. (1996). Testing the predictions of the cusp catastrophe model of anxiety and performance. *The Sport Psychologist, 10,* 140–156.

Hardy, L. (1997). Three myths about applied consultancy work. *Journal of Applied Sport Psychology, 9,* 277–294.

Hardy, L., & Callow, N. (1999). Efficacy of external and internal visual imagery perspectives for the enhancement of performance on tasks in which form is important. *Journal of Sport and Exercise Psychology, 21,* 95–112.

Hardy, L., Jones, G., & Gould, D. (1996). *Understanding psychological preparation for sport: Theory and practice for elite performers.* Chichester, UK: Wiley.

Hardy, L., Roberts, R., Thomas, P., & Murphy, S. (2010). Test of Performance Strategies (TOPS): Instrument refinement using confirmatory factor analysis. *Psychology of Sport and Exercise, 11,* 27–35.

Hare, R., Evans, L., & Callow, N. (2008). Imagery use during rehabilitation from injury: A case study of an elite athlete. *The Sport Psychologist, 22,* 405–422.

Hareli, S., & Weiner, B. (2002). Social emotions and personality inferences: A scaffold for a new research direction in the study of achievement motivation. *Educational Psychologist, 37,* 183–193.

Harlick, M., & McKenzie, A. (2000). Burnout in junior tennis: A research report. *The New Zealand Journal of Sports Medicine, 28*(2), 36–39.

Harmison, R. (2011). A social-cognitive framework for understanding and developing mental toughness in sport. In D. Gucciardi & S. Gordon (Eds.), *Mental toughness in sport: Developments in theory and research* (pp. 47–68). New York: Routledge.

Harmison, R., & Casto, K. (2012). Optimal performance: Elite level performance in "the zone." In S. Murphy (Ed.), *The Oxford handbook of sport and performance psychology* (pp. 707–724). New York: Oxford Press.

Hart, E., Leary, M.R., & Rejeski, W.J. (1989). The measurement of social physique anxiety. *Journal of Sport and Exercise Psychology, 11,* 94–104.

Harter, S. (1988). Causes, correlates, and functional role of global self-worth: A life-span perspective. In J. Kolligan & R. Sternberg (Eds.), *Perceptions of competence and incompetence across the life-span.* New Haven, CT: Yale University Press.

Harwood, C. (2008). Developmental consulting in a professional football academy: The 5Cs coaching efficacy program. *The Sport Psychologist, 22,* 109–133.

Harwood, C., Cumming, J., & Fletcher, D. (2004). Motivational profiles and psychological skill use within elite youth sport. *Journal of Applied Sport Psychology, 16,* 318–332.

Hatfield, B.D., & Hillman, C.H. (2001). The psychophysiology of sport: A mechanistic understanding of the psychology of superior performance. In R. Singer, H. Hausenblas, & C. Janelle (Eds.), *Handbook of sport psychology* (2nd ed., pp. 362–386). New York: Wiley.

Hatzigeorgiadis, A., & Biddle, S.J.H. (2001). Athletes' perceptions of cognitive interference during competition influence concentration and effort. *Anxiety, Stress, and Coping, 14,* 411–422.

Hatzigeorgiadis, A., Theodorakis, Y., & Zourbanos, N. (2004). Self-talk in the swimming pool: The effects of self-talk on thought content and performance on water-polo tasks. *Journal of Applied Sport Psychology, 16,* 138–150.

Hatzigeorgiadis, A., Zourbanos, N., Galanis, E., & Theodorakis, Y. (2011). Self-talk and sports performance: A meta-analysis. *Perspectives on Psychological Science, 6,* 348–356.

Hatzigeorgiadis, A., Zourbanos, N., Goltsios, C., & Theodorakis, Y. (2008). Investigating the functions of self-talk: The effects of motivational self-talk on self-efficacy and performance in young tennis players. *The Sport Psychologist, 22,* 458–472.

Hatzigeorgiadis, A., Zourbanos, N., & Theodorakis, Y. (2007). The moderating effect of self-talk content on self-talk function. *Journal of Applied Sport Psychology, 19,* 240–251.

Hauck, L., Carpenter, M., & Frank, J. (2008). Task-specific measures of balance efficacy, anxiety and stability and their relationship to clinical balance. *Gait and Posture, 27,* 676–682.

Hausenblas, H., Brewer, B., & Van Raalte, J. (2004). Self-presentation and exercise. *Journal of Applied Sport Psychology, 16,* 3–18.

Hausenblas, H., Hall, C., Rodgers, W., & Munroe, K. (1999). Exercise imagery: Its nature and measurement. *Journal of Applied Sport Psychology, 11,* 171–180.

Hayashi, C., & Weiss, M. (1994). A cross-cultural analysis of achievement motivation in Anglo and Japanese marathon runners. *International Journal of Sport Psychology, 25,* 187–202.

Hayes, D. (1975). Hockey injuries: How, why and when? *The Physician and Sportsmedicine, 3,* 61–65.

Hays, K.F. (2002). The enhancement of performance excellence among performance artists. *Journal of Applied Sport Psychology, 14*(4), 299–312.

Hays, K. (Ed.). (2009). *Performance psychology in action.* Washington, DC: American Psychological Association.

Hays, K. (2012). The psychology of performance in sport and other domains. In S. Murphy (Ed.), *The Oxford handbook of sport and performance psychology* (pp. 24–45). Oxford, UK: Oxford University Press.

Hays, K., Maynard, I., Thomas, O., & Bawden, M. (2007). Sources and types of confidence identified by world class performers. *Journal of Applied Sport Psychology, 19,* 434–456.

Hays, K., Thomas, O., Butt, J., & Maynard, I. (2010). The development of confidence profiling for sport. *The Sport Psychologist, 24,* 373–392.

Hays, K., Thomas, O., Maynard, I., & Bawden, M. (2009). The role of confidence in world-class sport performance. *Journal of Sport Sciences, 27,* 1185–1199.

Hayslip, B., Weigand, D., Weinberg, R., Richardson, P., & Jackson, A. (1996). The development of new scales for assessing health belief model constructs in adulthood. *Journal of Aging and Physical Activity, 4,* 307–324.

Healey, A., Undre, S., & Vincent, C. (2004). Developing observational measures of performance in surgical teams. *Quality and Safety in Health Care, 13,* 133–140.

Health Survey for England. (2009). *Volume 1. Physical activity and fitness. The Information Center for health and social care 2009.* London: The Stationary Office.

Heider, F. (1958). *The psychology of interpersonal relations.* New York: Wiley.

Heil, J., & Podlog, L. (2012). Injury and performance. In S. Murphy (Ed.), *The Oxford handbook of sport and performance psychology* (pp. 593–617). New York: Oxford University Press.

Hellison, D. (2011). *Teaching personal and social responsibility through physical activity (3rd ed.).* Champaign, IL: Human Kinetics.

Hellison, D., & Templin, T. (1991). *A reflective approach to teaching physical education.* Champaign, IL: Human Kinetics.

Hemery, D. (1986). *Sporting excellence: A study of sport's highest achievers.* Champaign, IL: Human Kinetics.

Hemery, D. (1991). *Sporting excellence: What makes a champion* (2nd ed.). New York: Wiley.

Henning, A.D. (1987). Exercise at work? I don't have time. *Fitness in Business, 2,* 68–69.

Henning, D., & Etnier, J. (2013). Predictors of flow in recreational participants at a large group event. *Journal of Sport and Exercise Psychology, 35,* S90.

Henschen, K. (1998). Athletic staleness and burnout: Diagnosis, prevention and treatment. In J.M. Williams (Ed.), *Applied sport psychology: Personal growth to peak performance* (pp. 398–408). Mountain View, CA: Mayfield.

Heuze, J.P., Bosselut, G., & Thomas, J.P. (2007). Should the coaches of elite female handball teams focus on collective efficacy or group cohesion? *The Sport Psychologist, 21,* 383–399.

Heuze, J.P., & Brunel, P. (2003). Social loafing in a competitive context. *International Journal of Sport and Exercise Psychology, 1,* 246–263.

Higgins, M. (2004, July). Obesity deemed an illness. *The Washington Times,* pp. 77–78.

Higgins, T., Middleton, K., Winner, L., & Janelle, C. (2013). Do physical activity interventions differentially affect exercise task and barrier self-efficacy? Findings from a systematic review and meta-Analysis. *Journal of Sport and Exercise Psychology, 35,* S91.

Hildebrandt, T., Lai, J., Langenbucher, J., Schneider, M., Yehuda, R., & Pfatt, D. (2011). The diagnostic dilemma of appearance and performance-enhancing drug misuse. *Drug and Alcohol Dependence, 114,* 1–11.

Hildebrandt, T., Langenbucher, J., Carr, S., & Sanjuan, P. (2007). Modeling population heterogeneity in appearance-and performance-enhancing drug (APED) use: Applications of mixture modeling in 400 regular APED users. *Journal of Abnormal Psychology, 116,* 717–733.

Hildebrandt, T., Varangis, E., & Lai, J. (2012). Appearance and performance-enhancing drugs. In S. Murphy (Ed.), *The Oxford handbook of sport and performance psychology* (pp. 545–561). New York: Oxford University Press.

Hill, A.P., Hall, H.K., & Appleton, P.R. (2010). A comparative examination of the correlates of self-oriented perfectionism and conscientious achievement striving in male cricket academy players. *Psychology of Sport and Exercise, 11,* 162–168.

Hill, D., Hanton, S., Fleming, S., & Matthews, N. (2009). A re-examination of choking in sport. *European Journal of Sport Sciences, 9,* 203–212.

Hill, D., Hanton, S., Matthews, N., & Fleming, S. (2010a). A qualitative exploration of choking in elite golf. *Journal of Clinical Sport Psychology, 4,* 221–240.

Hill, D., Hanton, S., Matthews, N., & Fleming, S. (2010b). Choking in sport: A review. *International Review of Sport and Exercise Psychology, 3,* 24–39.

Hill, D., Hanton, S., Matthews, N., & Fleming, S. (2011). Alleviation of choking under pressure in elite golf: An action research study. *The Sport Psychologist, 25,* 465–488.

Hill, D., Porter, C., & Quilliam, C. (2013). An investigation of choking in sport and the moderating influence of physiological stress. *International Journal of Sport Psychology, 44,* 310-330.

Hill, K., & Borden, F. (1993). The effect of attentional cueing on competitive bowling performance. *International Journal of Sport Psychology, 26,* 503–512.

Hillman, C.H., Erickson, K.I., & Kramer, A.F. (2008). Be smart, exercise your heart: Exercise effects of brain cognition. *Nature, 9,* 58–65.

Hird, J.S., Landers, D.M., Thomas, J.R., & Horan, J.J. (1991). Physical practice is superior to mental practice in enhancing cognitive and motor task performance. *Journal of Sport and Exercise Psychology, 8,* 281–293.

Hjalm, S., Kentta, G., & Gustafsson, H. (2007). Burnout among elite soccer coaches. *Journal of Sport Behavior, 30,* 415–427.

Hoar, S., Crocker, P., Holt, N., & Tamminen, A. (2010). Gender differences in adolescent athletes' coping with interpersonal stressors in sport: More similarities than differences. *Journal of Applied Sport Psychology, 22,* 134–149.

Hobson, C.J., Hoffman, J.J., Corso, L.M., & Freismuth, P.K. (1987). Corporate fitness: Understanding and motivating employee participation. *Fitness in Business, 2,* 80–85.

Hodge, K. (1989). Character-building in sport: Fact or fiction? *New Zealand Journal of Sports Medicine, 17*(2), 23–25.

Hodge, K. (2013). Working at the Olympics. In S. Hanrahan & M. Andersen (Eds.), *Routledge handbook of applied sport psychology: A comprehensive guide for students and practitioners* (pp. 405–413). New York: Routledge.

Hodge, K., Hargreaves, E., Gerrard, D., & Lonsdale, C. (2013). Psychological mechanisms underlying doping attitudes in sport: Motivation and moral disengagement. *Journal of Sport and Exercise Psychology, 35,* 419–432.

Hølgaard, R., Fuglestad, S., Peters, D., De Cuyper, B., De Backer, M., & Boen, F. (2010). Role satisfaction mediates the relation between role ambiguity and social loafing among elite women handball players. *Journal of Applied Sport Psychology, 22,* 408–410.

Hølgaard, R., Safvenboom, R., & Tonnessen, F. (2006). The relationship between group cohesion, group norms, and perceived social loafing in soccer teams. *Small Group Research, 37,* 217–232.

Hollander, E.P. (1967). *Principles and methods of social psychology.* New York: Holt, Rinehart & Winston.

Hollembeak, J., & Amorose, A. (2005). Perceived coaching behaviors and college athletes' intrinsic motivation: A test of self-determination theory. *Journal of Applied Sport Psychology, 17,* 20–36.

Holliday, B., Burton, D., Sun, G., Hammermeister, J., Naylor, S., & Freigang, D. (2008). Building the better mental training mouse trap: Is periodization a more systematic approach to promoting performance excellence? *Journal of Applied Sport Psychology, 29,* 199–219.

Holmes, P., & Collins, D. (2001). The PETTLEP approach to motor imagery: A functional equivalence model for sport psychologists. *Journal of Applied Sport Psychology, 13,* 60–83.

Holt, N.L., Kingsley, B.C., Tink, L.N., & Scherer, J. (2011). Benefits and challenges associated with sport participation by children and parents from low-income families. *Psychology of Sport and Exercise, 12,* 490–499.

Holt, N., Knight, C., & Zukiwski, P. (2012). Female athletes' perceptions of teammate conflict in sport: Implications for sport psychology consultants. *The Sport Psychologist, 26,* 135–154.

Holt, N.L., & Sparkes, A.C. (2001). An ethnographic study of cohesiveness in a college soccer team over a season. *The Sport Psychologist, 15,* 237–259.

Hong, S., Hughes, S., & Prochaska, T. (2008). Factors affecting exercise attendance and completion in sedentary older adults: A meta-analytic approach. *Journal of Physical Activity and Health, 5,* 385–397.

Hoover, N.C. (1999). National survey: Initiation rites and athletics for NCAA sports teams. Available: www.alfred.edu/sports_hazing/docs/hazing.pdf

Horn, C., Gilbert, J., Gilbert, W., & Lewis, D. (2011). Psychological skills training with community college athletes: The UNIFORM approach. *The Sport Psychologist, 25,* 321–340.

Horn, T.S. (1985). Coaches' feedback and children's perception of their physical competence. *Journal of Educational Psychology, 77,* 174–186.

Horn, T.S. (1987). The influence of teacher-coach behavior on the psychological development of children. In D. Gould & M.R. Weiss (Eds.), *Advances in pediatric sport sciences: Vol. 2. Behavioral issues* (pp. 121–142). Champaign, IL: Human Kinetics.

Horn, T.S. (1993). Leadership effectiveness in the sport domain. In T.S. Horn (Ed.), *Advances in sport psychology* (pp. 151–200). Champaign, IL: Human Kinetics.

Horn, T.S. (2002). Coaching effectiveness in the sport domain. In T. Horn (Ed.), *Advances in sport psychology* (2nd ed., pp. 309–365). Champaign, IL: Human Kinetics.

Horn, T.S., Bloom, P., Berglund, K.M., & Packard, S. (2011). Relationship between collegiate athletes' psychological characteristics and their preferences for different types of coaching behaviors. *The Sport Psychologist, 25,* 190–211.

Horn, T., Brinza, L., & Massie, B. (2013). Perceived injury climate in intercollegiate athletic programs: Links to athletes' self-determined motivation. *Journal of Sport and Exercise Psychology, 35,* S91.

Horn, T., Lox, C., & Labrador, F. (2001). The self-fulfilling prophesy: When coaches' expectations become reality. In J.M. Williams (Ed.), *Applied sport psychology: Personal growth to peak performance* (4th ed., pp. 63–81). Mountain View, CA: Mayfield.

Horn, T.S., & Weiss, M.R. (1991). A developmental analysis of children's self-ability judgments in the physical domain. *Pediatric Exercise Science, 3,* 310–326.

Houston, M., & Newton, M. (2010). Building confidence. In T. Morris & P. Terry (Eds.), *The new sport and exercise psychology companion.* Morgantown, WV: Fitness Information Technology.

Hoyt, M.F., & Janis, I.L. (1975). Increasing adherence to a stressful decision via a motivational balance-sheet procedure: A field experiment. *Journal of Personality and Social Psychology, 35,* 833–839.

Hsu, A., Barnholt, K., Grundmann, N., Lin, J., McCallum, S., & Friedlander, A. (2006). Sildenafil improves cardiac output and exercise performance during acute hypoxia, but not normoxia. *Journal of Applied Physiology, 100,* 2031-2040.

Hu, L., Motl, R., McAuley, E., & Konopack, J. (2007). Effects of self-efficacy on physical activity enjoyment in college-aged women. *International Journal of Behavioral Medicine, 14,* 92–96.

Huberman, W., & O'Brien, R. (1999). Improving therapist and patient performance in chronic psychiatric group homes through goal-setting, feedback and positive reinforcement. *Journal of Organizational Behavior Management, 19,* 16-36.

Huberty, J., Ransdell, L., Sidman, C., Flohr, J., Shultz, B., & Grosshans, O. (2008). Explaining long-term exercise adherence in women who complete a structured exercise program. *Research Quarterly for Exercise and Sport, 79,* 374–384.

Huddleston, S., Doody, S.G., & Ruder, M.K. (1985). The effect of prior knowledge of the social loafing phenomenon on performance in a group. *International Journal of Sport Psychology, 16,* 176-182.

Huddleston, H., Fry, M., & Brown, T. (2012). Corporate fitness members' perceptions of the environment and their intrinsic motivation. *Revista de Psicologia del Deporte, 21,* 15–23.

Hudson, J., Hiripi, E., Pope, H., & Kessler, R. (2007). The prevalence and correlates of eating disorders in the National Comorbidity Survey replication. *Biological Psychiatry, 61,* 348–358.

Hulley, A., Currie, A., Njenga, F., & Hill, A. (2007). Eating disorders in elite female distance runners: Effects of nationality and running environment. *Psychology of Sport and Exercise, 8,* 521–533.

Humbert, M.L., Chad, K.E., Spink, K.S., Muhajarine, N., Anderson, K.D., Bruner, M.W., et al. (2006). Factors that influence physical activity participation among high-versus low-SES youth. *Qualitative Health Research, 16*(4), 467–483.

Hume, K., Martin, G., Gonzalez, P., Cracklen, C., & Genthon, S. (1985). A self-monitoring feedback package for improving freestyle figure skating practice. *Journal of Sport Psychology, 7,* 333-345.

Husman, B.F., & Silva, J.M. (1984). Aggression in sport: Definitional and theoretical considerations. In J.M. Silva & R.S. Weinberg (Eds.), *Psychological foundations of sport* (pp. 246–260). Champaign, IL: Human Kinetics.

Hutchinson, J., Sherman, T., Martinovic, N., & Tenenbaum, G. (2008). The effect of manipulated self-efficacy on perceived sustained effort. *Journal of Applied Sport Psychology, 20,* 457–472.

Hutchinson, J., & Tenenbaum, G. (2007). Attention focus during physical effort: The mediating role of task intensity. *Psychology of Sport and Exercise, 8,* 233–245.

Hutchinson, M.R., & Ireland, M.L. (2003). Overuse and throwing injuries in the skeletally immature athlete. *Instruction Course Lecture, 52,* 25–36.

Ievleva, L., & Orlick, T. (1991). Mental links to enhanced healing. *The Sport Psychologist, 5*(1), 25–40.

Infante, D., Rancer, A., & Womack, D. (1997). *Building communication theory* (3rd ed.). Prospect Heights, IL: Waveland Press.

Ingham, A.G., Levinger, G., Graves, J., & Peckham, V. (1974). The Ringelmann effect: Studies of group size and group performance. *Journal of Experimental Social Psychology, 10,* 371–384.

International Olympic Committee. (2008). Consensus statement: Sexual harassment and abuse. *International Journal of Sport and Exercise Psychology, 6,* 442–449.

Ismail, A., II, & Young, R.J. (1973). The effect of chronic exercise on the personality of middle-aged men by univariate and multivariate approaches. *Journal of Human Ergology, 2,* 47–57.

Isoard-Gautheur, S., Guillet-Descas, E., & Duda, J. (2012). A prospective study of the influence of perceived coaching style on burnout propensity in high level young athletes: Using self-determination theory perspective. *The Sport Psychologist, 26,* 282–298.

Isoard-Gautheur, S., Guillet-Descas, E., & Lemyre, P.-N. (2013). How to achieve in elite training centers without burning out? An achievement goal theory perspective. *Psychology of Sport and Exercise, 14,* 72–83.

Issac, A. (1992). Mental practice—Does it work from the field? *The Sport Psychologist, 6,* 192–198.

Issac, A., Marks, D., & Russell, D. (1986). An instrument for assessing imagery of movement: The vividness of movement imagery questionnaire. *Journal of Mental Imagery, 10,* 23–30.

Jackson, B., Beauchamp, M., & Knapp, P. (2007). Relational efficacy beliefs in athlete dyads: An investigation using actor-partner interdependence models. *Journal of Sport and Exercise Psychology, 29,* 170–189.

Jackson, B., Grove, R., & Beauchamp, M. (2010). Relational efficacy beliefs and relationship quality within coach-athlete dyads. *Journal of Social and Personal Relationships, 27,* 1035–1050.

Jackson, B., Knapp, P., & Beauchamp, M. (2008). Origins and consequences of tripartite efficacy beliefs within elite athlete dyads. *Journal of Sport and Exercise Psychology, 30,* 512–540.

Jackson, D., & Mosurki, K. (1997). Heavy defeats in tennis: Psychological momentum or random effect. *Chance, 10,* 27–34.

Jackson, P. (2004). *The last season: A team in search of its soul.* New York: Penguin.

Jackson, S. (1992). Athletes in flow: A qualitative investigation of flow states in elite figure skaters. *Journal of Applied Sport Psychology, 4,* 161–180.

Jackson, S. (1995). Factors influencing the occurrence of flow state in elite athletes. *Journal of Applied Sport Psychology, 7,* 138–166.

Jackson, S. (2011). Flow. In T. Morris & P. Terry (Eds.), *The new sport and exercise psychology companion* (pp. 327–357). Morgantown: WV: Fitness Information Technology.

Jackson, S., & Csikszentmihalyi, M. (1999). *Flow in sport.* Champaign, IL: Human Kinetics.

Jackson, S.A., Thomas, P.R., Marsh, H.W., & Smethurst, C.J. (2001). Relationships between flow, self-concept, psychological skills, and performance. *Journal of Applied Sport Psychology, 13*(1), 129–153.

Jacobson, E. (1931). Electrical measurements of neuromuscular states during mental activities. *American Journal of Physiology, 96,* 115–121.

Jacobson, E. (1938). *Progressive relaxation.* Chicago: University of Chicago Press.

Jakicic, J.M., Winters, C., Lang, W., & Wing, R.R. (1999). Effects of intermittent exercise and use of home exercise equipment on adherence, weight loss, and fitness in overweight women. *Journal of the American Medical Association, 282,* 1554–1560.

Jambor, E.A., & Weeks, E.M. (1996). The non-traditional female athlete: A case study. *Journal of Applied Sport Psychology, 8,* 146–159.

James, W. (1890). *Principles of psychology.* New York: Holt, Rinehart & Winston.

Janelle, C. (1999). Ironic mental processes in sport: Implications for sport psychologists. *The Sport Psychologist, 13,* 201–220.

Janelle, C.M. (2002). Anxiety, arousal and visual attention: A mechanistic account of performance variability. *Journal of Sports Sciences, 20,* 237–251.

Janelle, C., & Hatfield, B. (2008). Visual attention and brain processes that underlie expert performance: Implications for sport and military psychology. *Military Psychology, 20,* S39–S69.

Janssen, I., Katzmarzyk, P., Boyce, W., King, M., & Pickett, W. (2004). Overweight and obesity in Canadian adolescents and their association with dietary habits and physical activity patterns. *Journal of Adolescent Health, 35,* 360–367.

Jo, H., Song, Y., Yoo, S., & Lee, H. (2010). Effectiveness of a province-wide walking campaign in Korea on the stages of change for physical activity. *International Journal of Sport and Exercise Psychology, 8,* 433–445.

Johnson, D.W., & Johnson, F.P. (1987). *Joining together: Group therapy and group skills* (3rd ed.). Englewood Cliffs, NJ: Prentice Hall.

Johnson, D.W., & Johnson, R.T. (1985). Motivational processes in cooperative, competitive, and individualistic learning situations. In C. Ames & R. Ames (Eds.), *Research on motivation in education* (Vol. 2, pp. 249–286). Orlando, FL: Academic Press.

Johnson, D.W., & Johnson, R.T. (1999). *Learning together and alone: Cooperative, competitive and individualistic learning* (5th ed.). Boston: Allyn & Bacon.

Johnson, D.W., & Johnson, R.T. (2005). New developments in social interdependence theory. *Genetic, Social, and General Psychology Monographs,* 131, 285–358.

Johnson, J.M., Hrycaiko, D., Johnson, G., & Halas, J. (2004). Self-talk and female youth soccer. *The Sport Psychologist, 18,* 44–59.

Johnson, K.B. (1996). Exercise, drug treatment, and optimal care of multiple sclerosis patients. *Annals of Neurology, 39,* 422–423.

Johnson, U. (2000). Short-term psychological interventions: A study of long-term injured athletes. *Journal of Sport Rehabilitation, 9,* 207–218.

Johnson, U. (2007). Psychosocial antecedents of sport injury, prevention, and intervention: An overview of theoretical approaches and empirical findings. *International Journal of Sport and Exercise Psychology, 5,* 352–369.

Johnson, U., Andersson, K., & Falby, J. (2011). Sport psychology consulting among Swedish premier soccer coaches. *International Journal of Sport and Exercise Psychology, 9,* 308–322.

Johnson, U., Ekengren, J., & Andersen, M.B. (2005). Injury prevention in Sweden: Helping soccer players at risk. *Journal of Sport and Exercise Psychology, 27,* 32-38.

Jones, G. (1993). The role of performance profiling in cognitive behavioral interventions in sport. *The Sport Psychologist, 7,* 160–172.

Jones, G. (1995). More than just a game: Research developments and issues in competitive anxiety in sport. *British Journal of Psychology, 86,* 449–478.

Jones, G. (2002). Performance excellence: A personal perspective on the link between sport and business. *Journal of Applied Sport Psychology, 14*(4), 268–281.

Jones, G. (2012). The role of superior performance intelligence in sustained success. In S. Murphy (Ed.), *The Oxford handbook of sport and performance psychology* (pp. 62–80). New York: Oxford University Press.

Jones, G., & George, J. (1998). The experience and evolution of trust: Implications for cooperation and teamwork. *Academy of Management Review, 23,* 531–546.

Jones, G., Hanton, S., & Connaughton, D. (2002). What is this thing called mental toughness? An investigation of elite sport performers. *Journal of Applied Sport Psychology, 14,* 205–218.

Jones, G., Hanton, S., & Connaughton, D. (2007). A framework of mental toughness in the world's best performers. *The Sport Psychologist, 21,* 243–264.

Jones, G., Hanton, S., & Swain, A. (1994). Intensity and interpretation of anxiety symptoms in elite and non-elite sports performers. *Personality and Individual Differences, 17*(5), 657–663.

Jones, G., & Hardy, L. (1990). Stress in sport: Experiences of some elite performers. In G. Jones & L. Hardy (Eds.), *Stress and performance in sport* (pp. 247–277). Chichester, UK: Wiley.

Jones, G., & Swain, A. (1992). Intensity and direction as dimensions of competitive state anxiety and relationships with competitiveness. *Perceptual and Motor Skills, 74,* 467–472.

Jones, G., & Swain, A. (1995). Predisposition to experience debilitative and facilitative anxiety in elite and nonelite performers. *The Sport Psychologist, 9,* 201–211.

Jones, G., Swain, A., & Hardy, L. (1993). Intensity and direction dimensions of competitive state anxiety and relationships with performance. *Journal of Sports Sciences, 11,* 525–532.

Jones, K. (1994, November). Foreman is again the man. *The Irish Times.*

Jones, M. (2012). Emotion regulation in sport. In S. Murphy (Ed.), *The Oxford handbook of sport and performance psychology* (pp. 154–172). New York: Oxford University Press.

Jones, M., Lavallee, D., & Tod, D. (2011). Developing communication and organization skills: The ELITE life skills reflective practice intervention. *The Sport Psychologist, 25,* 35–52.

Jones, M.B. (1974). Regressing group on individual effectiveness. *Organizational Behavior and Human Performance, 11,* 426–451.

Jones, M.V., & Sheffield, D. (2007). The impact of game outcome on the well-being of athletes. *International Journal of Sport and Exercise Psychology, 5,* 54–65.

Jones, R.T. (2002, September). Golden moment as Lynch storms to glory. *Irish Independent, 23,* 15.

Jordan, M. (1994). *I can't accept not trying.* New York: Harper Collins.

Jordet, G. (2005). Perceptual training in soccer: An imagery intervention study with elite athletes. *Journal of Applied Sport Psychology, 17,* 140–156.

Jordet, G., & Elferink-Gemser, M.T. (2012). Stress, coping, and emotions on the world stage: The experience of participating in a major soccer tournament penalty shootout. *Journal of Applied Sport Psychology, 24,* 73–91.

Jordet, G., & Hartman, E. (2008). Avoidance motivation and choking under pressure in soccer penalty shootouts. *Journal of Sport and Exercise Psychology, 30,* 450–457.

Jowett, N., & Spray, C.M. (2013). British Olympic hopefuls: The antecedents and consequences of implicit ability beliefs in elite track and field athletes. *Psychology of Sport and Exercise, 14,* 145–153.

Jowett, S. (2003). When the "honeymoon" is over: A case study of a coach-athlete dyad in crisis. *The Sport Psychologist, 17,* 444–460.

Jowett, S., & Chaundy, V. (2004). An investigation into the impact of coach leadership and coach-athlete relationship on group cohesion. *Group Dynamics: Theory, Research, and Practice, 8,* 302–311.

Jowett, S., & Clark-Carter, D. (2006). Perceptions of empathic accuracy and assumed similarity in the coach-athlete relationship. *British Journal of Social Psychology, 45,* 617–637.

Jowett, S., & Cockerill, I. (2003). Olympic medalists' perspective of the athlete-coach relationship. *Psychology of Sport and Exercise, 4,* 313–331.

Jowett, S., & Frost, T. (2007). Race/ethnicity in the all-male coach-athlete relationship: Black footballers' narratives. *International Journal of Sport and Exercise Psychology, 3,* 255–269.

Jowett, S., Paull, G., Pensgaard, M., Hoegmo, P., & Riise, H. (2005). Coach-athlete relationship. In J. Taylor & G. Wilson (Eds.), *Applying sport psychology: Four perspectives* (pp. 153–170). Champaign, IL: Human Kinetics.

Jowett, S., & Timson-Katchis, M. (2005). Social networks in sport: Parental influence on the coach-athlete relationship. *The Sport Psychologist, 19,* 267–287.

Jowett, S., & Wylleman, P. (2006). Interpersonal relationships in sport and exercise settings: Crossing the chasm. *Psychology of Sport and Exercise, 7,* 119–124.

Kabat-Zinn, J. (2005). *Coming to our senses: Healing ourselves and the world through mindfulness.* New York: Hyperion.

Kahn, E.R., Ramsey, L.T., Brownson, R.C., Heath, G.W., Howze, E.H., Powell, K.E., et al. (2002). The effectiveness of interventions to increase physical activity: A systematic review. *American Journal of Preventive Medicine, 22*(4 Suppl.), 73–107.

Kanayama, G., Brower, K., Wood, R., Hudson, J., & Pope, H. (2010). Treatment of anabolic- androgenic steroid dependence: Emerging evidence and its implications. *Drug and Alcohol Dependence, 109,* 6–13.

Kane, T., Baltes, T., & Moss, M. (2001). Causes and consequences of free-set goal: An investigation of athletic self-regulation. *Journal of Sport and Exercise Psychology, 23,* 55–75.

Kanfer, F.H., & Gaelick, L. (1986). Self-management methods. In F.H. Kanfer & A.P. Goldstein (Eds.), *Helping people change: A textbook of methods* (pp. 283–345). New York: Pergamon Press.

Karageorghis, C., & Priest, D. (2012). Music in the exercise domain: A review and synthesis (Part 1). *International Review of Sport and Exercise Psychology, 5,* 44–66.

Karageorghis, C., & Terry, P. (2011). *Inside sport psychology.* Champaign, IL: Human Kinetics.

Karageorghis, C., Terry, P., Lane, A., Bishop, D., & Priest, D. (2012). The BASES expert statement on use of music in exercise. *Journal of Sport Sciences, 30,* 953–956.

Karau, S.J., & Williams, K.D. (1993). Social loafing: A meta-analytic review and theoretical integration. *Journal of Personality and Social Psychology, 65,* 681–706.

Karoly, P., Ruehlman, L., Okun, M., Lutz, R., Newton, C., & Fairholme, C. (2005). Perceived self-regulation of exercise goals and interfering goals among regular and irregular exercisers: A lifespace analysis. *Psychology of Sport and Exercise, 6,* 427–442.

Kasch, F.W. (2001). Thirty-three years of aerobic exercise adherence. *Quest, 53,* 362–365.

Katorji, J., & Cahoon, M.A. (1992). The relationship between aggression and injury in junior "B" hockey (Unpublished master's thesis). Waterloo, ON: University of Waterloo.

Kavussanu, M. (2008). Moral behavior in sport: A critical review of the literature. *International Review of Sport and Exercise Psychology, 1,* 124–138.

Kavussanu, M., Boardley, I., Jukiewicz, N., Vindent, S., & Ring, C. (2008). Coaching efficacy and coaching effectiveness: Examining their predictors and comparing coaches' and athletes' reports. *The Sport Psychologist, 22,* 383–404.

Kavussanu, M., & Ntoumanis, N. (2003). Participation in sport and moral functioning: Does ego orientation mediate the relationship? *Journal of Sport and Exercise Psychology, 25,* 501–518.

Kavussanu, M., & Roberts, G.C. (1996). Motivation in physical activity contexts: The relationship of perceived motivational climate to intrinsic motivation and self-efficacy. *Journal of Sport and Exercise Psychology, 18,* 254–280.

Kee, Y., Chatzisarantis, N., Kong, P., Chow, J., & Chen, L. (2012). Mindfulness, movement control, and attentional focus strategies: Effects of mindfulness on a postural balance task. *Journal of Sport and Exercise Psychology, 34,* 562–579.

Kee, Y., & Wang, C. (2008). Relationships between mindfulness, flow dispositions and mental skills adoption: A cluster analytic approach. *Psychology of Sport and Exercise, 9,* 393–411.

Kelley, B.C. (1994). A model of stress and burnout in collegiate coaches: Effects of gender and time of season. *Research Quarterly for Exercise and Sport, 65,* 48–58.

Kelley, B.C., Eklund, R.C., & Ritter-Taylor, M. (1999). Stress and burnout among collegiate tennis coaches. *Journal of Sport and Exercise Psychology, 21,* 113–130.

Kelley, B.C., & Gill, D.L. (1993). An examination of personal/situational variables, stress appraisal, and burnout in collegiate teacher-coaches. *Research Quarterly for Exercise and Sport, 64,* 94–102.

Kelley, H.H., & Stahelski, A.J. (1970). Social interaction basis of cooperators' and competitors' beliefs about others. *Journal of Personality and Social Psychology, 36,* 385–418.

Kellmann, M., & Gunther, K. (2000). Changes in stress and recovery in elite rowers during preparation for the Olympic Games. *Medicine and Science in Sports and Exercise, 35,* 676–683.

Kentta, G. (2001). Training practices and overtraining syndrome in Swedish age-group athletes. *International Journal of Sports Medicine, 22,* 1–6.

Kentta, G., & Hassmen, P. (1998). Overtraining and recovery: A conceptual model. *Sports Medicine, 1,* 1–16.

Kentta, G., Hassmen, P., & Raglin, J.S. (2001). Training practices and overtraining syndrome in Swedish age-group athletes. *International Journal of Sports Medicine, 22,* 1–6.

Kerick, S., Iso-Ahola, S., & Hatfield, B. (2000). Psychological momentum in target shooting: Cortical, cognitive-affective, and behavioral responses. *Journal of Sport and Exercise Psychology, 22,* 1–20.

Kerlinger, F.N. (1973). *Foundations of behavioral research* (2nd ed.). New York: Holt, Rinehart & Winston.

Kerr, G., Berman, E., & De Souza, M.J. (2006). Disordered eating in women's gymnastics: Perspectives of athletes, coaches, parents, and judges. *Journal of Applied Sport Psychology, 18,* 28–43.

Kerr, G., & Goss, J. (1996). The effects of a stress management program on injuries and stress levels. *Journal of Applied Sport Psychology, 8,* 109–117.

Kerr, G., & Leith, L. (1993). Stress management and athletic performance. *The Sport Psychologist, 7,* 221–231.

Kerr, G., & Stirling, A. (2013). Negotiating touch in the coach-athlete relationship. *Journal of Sport and Exercise Psychology, 35,* S94.

Kerr, J.H. (1985). The experience of arousal: A new basis for studying arousal effects in sport. *Journal of Sport Sciences, 3,* 169–179.

Kerr, J.H. (1997). *Motivation and emotion in sport: Reversal theory.* East Sussex, UK: Psychology Press.

Kerr, J., Linder, K., & Blaydon, M. (2007). *Exercise dependence.* London: Routledge.

Kessler, R.C., Berglund, P., Demler, O., Jin, R., Koretz, D., Merikanges, K.R., et al. (2003). The epidemiology of major depressive disorder: Results from the National Comorbidity Survey Replication (NCSR). *Journal of the American Medical Association, 289,* 3095–3105.

Kilpartrick, M., Hebert, E., & Bartholomew, J. (2005). College students' motivation for physical activity: Differentiating men's and women's motives for sport participation and exercise. *Journal of American College Health, 54,* 87–94.

Kim, B., & Gill, D. (1997). A cross-cultural extension of goal perspective theory to Korean youth sport. *Journal of Sport and Exercise Psychology, 19,* 142–155.

Kim, B.J., Williams, L., & Gill, D.L. (2003). A cross-cultural study of achievement orientation and intrinsic motivation in young USA and Korean athletes. *International Journal of Sport Psychology, 34,* 168–184.

Kimiecik, J. (1998, March). The path of the intrinsic exerciser. *IDEA Health and Fitness Source,* pp. 34–42.

Kimiecik, J. (2002). *The intrinsic exerciser: Discovering the joy of exercise.* Boston: Houghton Mifflin.

Kimiecik, J., & Gould, D. (1987). Coaching psychology: The case of James "Doc" Counsilman. *The Sport Psychologist, 1,* 350–358.

Kimm, S.Y., Glynn, N.W., Kriska, A.M., Barton, B.A., Kronsberg, S.S., Daniels, S.R., et al. (2002). Decline in physical activity in black girls and white girls during adolescence. *New England Journal of Medicine, 347,* 709–715.

King, A.C., Castro, C., Wilcox, S., Eyler, A.A., Sallis, J.F., & Brownson, R.C. (2000). Personal and environmental factors associated with physical inactivity among different racial-ethnic groups of middle-aged and older-aged women. *Health Psychology, 19,* 354–364.

King, A.C., & Frederiksen, L.W. (1984). Low-cost strategies for increasing exercise behavior: Relapse preparation training and social support. *Behavior Modification, 8,* 3–21.

King, A.C., Oman, R.F., Brassington, G.S., Bliwise, D., & Haskell, W.L. (1997). Moderate-intensity exercise and self-rated quality of sleep in older adults: A randomized controlled trial. *Journal of the American Medical Association, 277,* 32-37.

Kingston, K.M., & Hardy, L. (1997). Effects of different types of goals on processes that support performance. *The Sport Psychologist, 11,* 277–293.

Kingston, K., Lane, A., & Thomas, O. (2010). A temporal examination of elite performers sources of sport-confidence. *The Sport Psychologist, 18,* 313–332.

Kioumourtzoglou, E., Tzetzis, G., Derri, V., & Mihalopoulou, M. (1997). Psychological skills of elite athletes in different ball games. *Journal of Human Movement Studies, 32,* 79–93.

Kirk, A., Barnett, J., & Mutrie, N. (2007). Physical activity consultation for people with Type 2 diabetes: Evidence and guidelines. *Diabetic Medicine, 24,* 809–816.

Kirker, B., Tenenbaum, G., & Mattson, J. (2000). An investigation of the dynamics of aggression: Direct observation of ice hockey and basketball. *Research Quarterly for Exercise and Sport, 71*(4), 373–386.

Kirsch, I. (1994). Defining hypnosis for the public. *Contemporary Hypnosis, 11,* 142–143.

Kirschenbaum, D.S. (1984). Self-regulation and sport psychology: Nurturing and emerging symbiosis. *Journal of Sport Psychology, 6,* 159–183.

Kirschenbaum, D. (1997). *Kind matters: seven steps to smarter sport performance.* Carmel, IN: I.L. Cooper.

Kirschenbaum, D. (2010). Expert recommendations for the treatment of childhood and adolescent obesity: Advantaged of the Seven Step Model and immersion treatment. *Journal of Sport Psychology in Action, 1,* 66–75.

Kirschenbaum, D., Owens, D., & O'Connor, E. (1998). Smart golf: Preliminary evaluation of a simple, yet comprehensive approach to improving and scoring the mental game. *The Sport Psychologist, 12,* 271-282.

Kitantas, A., Zimmerman, B., & Cleary, T. (2000). The role of observation and emulation in the development of athletic self-regulation. *Journal of Educational Psychology, 92,* 811–817.

Kjormo, O., & Halvari, H. (2002). Relation of burnout with lack of time for being with significant others, role conflict, cohesion, and self-confidence among Norwegian Olympic athletes. *Perceptual and Motor Skills, 94,* 795–804.

Klinert, J., Ohlert, J., Carron, B., Eys, M., Frltz, D., Harwood, C., et al. (2012). Group dynamics in sports: An overview and recommendations on diagnostic and intervention. *The Sport Psychologist, 26,* 412–434.

Klint, K.A., & Weiss, M.R. (1986). Dropping in and dropping out: Participation motives of current and former youth gymnasts. *Canadian Journal of Applied Sport Sciences, 11,* 106–114.

Koehler, J., & Conley, C. (2003). The "hot hand" myth in professional basketball. *Journal of Sport and Exercise Psychology, 25,* 253–259.

Koehn, S., & Morris, T. (2011). Self-confidence. In T. Morris & P. Terry (Eds.), *The new sport and exercise psychology companion* (pp. 159-194). Morgantown, WV: Fitness Information Technology.

Kohl, H.W., & Hobbs, W. (1998). Development of physical activity behavior among children and adolescents. *Pediatrics, 101*(Suppl. 5), 549–554.

Kohn, A. (1992). *No contest: The case against competition (2nd ed.).* Boston: Houghton Mifflin.

Koka, A., & Hein, A. (2003). Perceptions of teacher's feedback and learning environment as predictors of intrinsic motivation in physical education. *Psychology of Sport and Exercise, 4,* 333–346.

Komaki, J., & Barnett, F. (1977). A behavioral approach to coaching football: Improving the play execution of the offensive backfield on a youth football team. *Journal of Applied Behavioral Analysis, 10,* 657–664.

Koop, S., & Martin, G.L. (1983). Evaluation of a coaching strategy to reduce swimming stroke errors with beginning age-group swimmers. *Journal of Applied Behavior Analysis, 16,* 447–460.

Koppen, J., & Raab, M. (2012). The hot and cold hand in volleyball: Individual expertise differences in a video-based playmaker decision test. *The Sport Psychologist, 26,* 167–185.

Kornspan, A.S. (2007a). E.W. Scripture and the Yale psychology laboratory: Studies related to athletes and physical activity. *The Sport Psychologist, 21,* 152–169.

Kornspan, A.S. (2007b). The early years of sport psychology: The work and influence of Pierre de Coubertin. *Journal of Sport Behavior, 30,* 77–93.

Kornspan, A.S. (2009). Enhancing performance in sport: The use of hypnosis and other psychological techniques in the 1950s and 1960s. In C.D. Green & L.T. Benjamin (Eds.). *Psychology gets in the game: Sport, mind and behavior* (pp. 253-294). Lincoln, Nebraska: University of Nebraska Press.

Kornspan, A.S. (2012). History of sport and performance psychology. In S.M. Murphy (Ed.), *The Oxford handbook of sport and performance psychology* (pp. 3–23). Oxford, UK: Oxford University Press.

Kornspan, A.S., & MacCracken, M.J. (2001). Psychology applied to sport in the 1940s: The work of Dorothy Hazeltine Yates. *The Sport Psychologist, 15,* 342–345.

Kosaba, S.C., Maddi, S.R., Puccetti, M.C., & Zola, M.A. (1985). Effectiveness of hardiness, exercise, and social support as resources against illness. *Journal of Psychosomatic Illness, 29,* 525–533.

Kramer, J., & Shaap, D. (1968). *Instant replay: The Green Bay diary of Jerry Kramer.* New York: Signet.

Kramer, R., & Lewicki, R. (2010). Repairing and enhancing trust: Approaches to reducing trust deficits. *The Academy of Management Annals, 4,* 245–277.

Krane, V., Greenleaf, C.A., & Snow, J. (1997). Reaching for gold and the price of glory: A motivational case study of an elite gymnast. *The Sport Psychologist, 11,* 53–71.

Krane, V., & Whaley, D.E. (2010). Quiet competence: Writing women into the history of U.S. sport and exercise psychology. *The Sport Psychologist, 24,* 349–372.

Krane, V., & Williams, J. (2010). Psychological characteristics of peak performance. In J.M. Williams (Ed.), *Applied sport psychology: Personal growth to peak performance* (6th ed., pp. 169–188). Mountain View, CA: Mayfield.

Kremer, J., & Moran, A. (2008). Swifter, higher, stronger: The history of sport psychology. *The Psychologist, 21*(8), 740–742.

Krentz, E., & Warschburger, P. (2011). Sports-related correlates of disordered eating: A comparison between aesthetic and ballgame sports. *International Journal of Sport Psychology, 42,* 548–564.

Kretchmar, R.S. (2001). Duty, habit, and meaning: Different faces of adherence. *Quest, 53,* 318–325.

Krivoschekov, S., & Lushnikov, O. (2011). Psychophysiology of sports addictions (exercise addiction). *Human Physiology, 37,* 135-140.

Kroll, W., & Lewis, G. (1970). America's first sport psychologist. *Quest, 13,* 1–4.

Kudlackova, K., Eccles, D., & Dieffenbach, K. (2013). Use of relaxation skills in differentially skilled athletes. *Psychology of Sport and Exercise, 14,* 468–475.

Kyllo, L.B., & Landers, D.M. (1995). Goal setting in sport and exercise: A research synthesis to resolve the controversy. *Journal of Sport and Exercise Psychology, 17,* 117–137.

Lacey, J.I. (1967). Somatic response patterning and stress: Some revision of activation theory. In M.H. Appley & R. Trumbell (Eds.), *Psychological stress: Issues in research* (pp. 170–179). New York: Appleton-Century-Crofts.

Lafreniere, M., Jowett, S., Vallerand, R.J., Donahue, E., & Lorimer, R. (2008). Passion in sport: On the quality of the coach-athlete relationship. *Journal of Sport and Exercise Psychology, 30,* 541–560.

Lai, C., & Wiggins, M.S. (2003). Burnout perceptions over time in NCAA Division I soccer players. *International Sports Journal, 7*(2), 120–127.

Lamarche, L., Gammage, K., & Strong, H. (2009). The effect of mirrored environments on self-presentational efficacy and social anxiety in women in a step aerobics class. *Psychology of Sport and Exercise, 10,* 67–71.

Lambert, S., Moore, D., & Dixon, R. (1999). Gymnasts in training: The differential effects of self- and coach-set goals as a function of locus of control. *Journal of Applied Sport Psychology, 11,* 72–82.

Land, W., & Tenenbaum, G. (2012). An outcome-and process-oriented examination of a golf-specific secondary task strategy to prevent choking in golf. *Journal of Applied Sport Psychology, 24,* 303–322.

Landers, D.M. (1985). Psychophysiological assessment and biofeedback: Applications for athletes in closed-skilled sports. In J.H. Sandweiss & S.L. Wolf (Eds.), *Biofeedback and sports science* (pp. 63–105). New York: Plenum Press.

Landers, D.M., & Arent, S.M. (2001). Physical activity and mental health. In R. Singer, H. Hausenblas, & C. Janelle (Eds.), *Handbook of sport psychology* (2nd ed., pp. 740–765). New York: Wiley.

Landers, D.M., & Arent, S.M. (2010). Arousal-performance relationships. In J.M. Williams (Ed.), *Applied sport psychology: Personal growth to peak performance* (6th ed., pp. 221–246). Dubuque, IA: McGraw-Hill.

Landers, D.M., Boutcher, S., & Wang, M.Q. (1986). A psychobiological study of archery performance. *Research Quarterly for Exercise and Sport, 57,* 236–244.

Landers, D.M., & Lueschen, G. (1974). Team performance outcome and cohesiveness of competitive coaching groups. *International Review of Sport Sociology, 2,* 57–69.

Landers, D.M., & Petruzzello, S.J. (1994). Physical activity, fitness, and anxiety. In C. Bouchard, R.J. Shepard, & T. Stevens (Eds.), *Physical activity, fitness, and health* (pp. 868–882). Champaign, IL: Human Kinetics.

Landers, D., Wang, M., & Courtet, P. (1985). Peripheral narrowing among experienced and inexperienced rifle shooters under low-and high-stress condition. *Research Quarterly, 56,*122-130.

Landers, D.M., Wilkinson, M.O., Hatfield, B.D., & Barber, H. (1982). Causality and the cohesion-performance relationship. *Journal of Sport Psychology, 4,* 170–183.

Landin, D., & Hebert, E. (1999). The influence of self-talk on the performance of skilled female tennis players. *Journal of Applied Sport Psychology, 11,* 263–282.

Landry, J.B., & Solmon, M.A. (2004). African American women's self-determination across the stages of change for exercise. *Journal of Sport and Exercise Psychology, 26,* 457–469.

Lang, P.J. (1977). Imagery in therapy: An information-processing analysis of fear. *Behavior Therapy, 8,* 862–886.

Lang, P.J. (1979). A bio-informational theory of emotional imagery. *Psychophysiology, 17,* 495–512.

Langan, E., Blake, C., & Longsdale, C. (2013). Systematic review of the effectiveness of interpersonal coach education interventions on athlete outcomes. *Psychology of Sport and Exercise, 14,* 37–49.

Larson, G.A., Starkey, C., & Zaichkowsky, L.D. (1996). Psychological aspects of athletic injuries as perceived by athletic trainers. *The Sport Psychologist, 10,* 37–47.

Larson, R.W. (2000). Toward a psychology of positive youth development. *American Psychologist, 55,* 170–183.

Lasco, R.A., Curry, R.H., Dickson, V.J., Powers, J., Menes, S., & Merritt, R.K. (1989). Participation rates, weight loss, and blood pressure changes among obese women in a nutrition-exercise program. *Public Health Reports, 104,* 640–646.

Latane, B., Williams, K.D., & Harkins, S.G. (1979). Many hands make light the work: The causes and consequences of social loafing. *Journal of Personality and Social Psychology, 37,* 823–832.

Latinjak, A., Torregrosa, M., & Renom, J. (2011). Combining self-talk and performance feedback: Their effectiveness with adult tennis players. *The Sport Psychologist, 25,* 18–31.

Lauer, L., & Paiement, C. (2009). The playing tough and clean hockey program. *The Sport Psychologist, 23,* 543–561.

Lausic, D., Tennebaum, G., Eccles, S., Jeong, A., & Johnson, T. (2009). Intrateam communication and performance in doubles tennis. *Research Quarterly for Exercise and Sport, 80,* 281–290.

Lavalle, D. (2005). The effect of a life development intervention in sports career transition adjustment. *The Sport Psychologist, 19,* 193–202.

Lavalle, D., Park, S., & Tod, D. (2013). Career termination. In S. Hanrahan & M. Andersen (Eds.), *Routledge handbook of applied sport psychology: A comprehensive guide for students and practitioners* (pp. 242–249). New York: Routledge.

LaVoi, N. (2007). Interpersonal communication and conflict in the coach-athlete relationship. In S. Jowett & D. LaValle (Eds.), *Social psychology of sport* (pp. 29–40). Champaign, IL: Human Kinetics.

Law, B., & Hall, C. (2009). Observational learning use and self-efficacy beliefs in adult sport novices. *Psychology of Sport and Exercise, 10,* 263–270.

Layden, T. (1995, April 3). Better education. *Sports Illustrated,* pp. 70–90.

Lazarus, L., Barkoukis, V., Rodafinos, A., & Tzorbatzoudis, H. (2010). Predictors of doping intentions in elite-level athletes: A social cognition approach. *Journal of Sport and Exercise Psychology, 32,* 694–710.

Lazarus, R. (2000). How emotions influence performance in competitive sports. *The Sport Psychologist, 4,* 229–252.

Lazarus, R.S. (1966). *Psychological stress and the coping process.* New York: McGraw-Hill.

Lazarus, R.S., & Folkman, S. (1984). *Stress, appraisal and coping.* New York: Springer-Verlag.

Leahy, T. (2008). Understanding and preventing sexual harassment and abuse in sport: Implications for the sport psychology profession. *International Journal of Sport and Exercise Psychology, 6,* 351–353.

Leffingwell, T., Durand-Bush, N., Wurzberger, D., & Cada, P. (2005). Psychological assessment. In J. Taylor & G. Wilson (Eds.), *Applying sport psychology: Four perspectives* (pp. 85–100). Champaign, IL: Human Kinetics.

Legrand, F., & Heuze, J. (2007). Antidepressant effects associated with different exercise conditions in participants with depression: A pilot study. *Journal of Sport and Exercise Psychology, 29,* 348–364.

Legwold, C. (1987). Incentives for fitness programs. *Fitness in Business, 2,* 131–133.

Leith, L.M., & Taylor, A.H. (1992). Behavior modification and exercise adherence: A literature review. *Journal of Sport Behavior, 15,* 60–74.

Lemyre, P., Hall, H.K., & Roberts, G.C. (2008). A social cognitive approach to burnout in elite athletes. *Scandinavian Journal of Medicine and Science in Sports, 18,* 221–234.

Lemyre, P., Roberts, G.C., & Stray-Gundersen, J. (2007). Motivation, overtraining, and burnout: Can self-determined motivation predict overtraining and burnout in elite athletes? *European Journal of Sport Sciences, 7,* 115–126.

Lemyre, P.N., Treasure, D.C., & Roberts, G.C. (2006). Influence of variability in motivation and effect on elite athlete burnout susceptibility. *Journal of Sport and Exercise Psychology, 28,* 32–48.

Lepper, M.R., & Greene, D. (1975). Turning play into work: Effects of adult surveillance and extrinsic rewards on children's intrinsic motivation. *Journal of Personality and Social Psychology, 31,* 479–486.

Lepper, M.R., Greene, D., & Nisbett, R.E. (1973). Undermining children's intrinsic interest with extrinsic rewards: A test of the overjustification hypothesis. *Journal of Personality and Social Psychology, 28,* 129–137.

LeUnes, A., & Nation, J. (2002). *Sport psychology* (3rd ed.). Pacific Grove, CA: Wadsworth.

Levy, A., Remco, C., Polman, J., Nicholls, A., & Marchant, D. (2009). Sport injury rehabilitation adherence: Perspectives of recreational athletes. *International Journal of Sport and Exercise Psychology, 7,* 212–229.

Levy, S., & Ebbeck, V. (2005). The exercise and self-esteem model in adult women: The inclusion of physical acceptance. *Psychology of Sport and Exercise, 6,* 571–584.

Lewis, M., & Sutton, A. (2011). Understanding exercise behavior: Examining the interaction of exercise motivation and personality in predicting exercise frequency. *Journal of Sport Behavior, 34,* 82–98.

Li, C., Wang, C.K.J., Pyun, D.Y., & Kee, Y.H. (2013). Burnout and its relations with basic psychological needs and motivation among athletes: A systematic review and meta-analysis. *Psychology, Sport and Exercise, 14,* 692–700.

Li, W., & Lee, A. (2004). A review of conceptions of ability and related motivational constructs in achievement motivation. *Quest, 56,* 439–461.

Lidor, R., & Singer, R. (2000). Teaching preperformance routines to beginners. *Journal of Physical Education, Recreation and Dance, 71,* 343–363.

Lind, E., Ekkekakis, P., & Vazou, S. (2008). The affective impact of exercise intensity that slightly exceeds preferred level: "Pain" for no additional "gain." *Journal of Health Psychology, 13,* 464–468.

Lind, E., Welch, A.S., & Ekkekakis, P. (2009). Do "mind over muscle" strategies work? *Sports Medicine, 39,* 743–765.

Lindsay, P., Maynard, I., & Thomas, O. (2005). Effects of hypnosis on flow states and cycling performance. *The Sport Psychologist, 19,* 164–177.

Lippke, S., Ziegelmann, J., & Schwarzer, R. (2005). Stage-specific adoption and maintenance of physical activity: Testing a three-stage model. *Psychology of Sport and Exercise, 6,* 585–603.

Lipsey, Z., Barton, S., Hulley, A., & Hill, A. (2006). "After a workout . . ." Beliefs about exercise, eating and appearance in female exercisers with and without eating disorder features. *Psychology of Sport and Exercise, 7,* 425–436.

Lirgg, C.D., & Feltz, D.L. (2001). Self-efficacy beliefs of athletes, teams, and coaches. In R. Singer, H. Hausenblas, & C. Janelle (Eds.), *Handbook of sport psychology* (2nd ed., pp. 340–361). New York: Wiley.

Liston, K., Reacher, D., Smith, T., & Waddington, I. (2006). Managing pain and injury in non-elite rugby union and rugby league: A case study of players at a British university. *Sport in Society, 9,* 388–402.

Little, D.E., & Watkins, M.N. (2004). Exploring variation in recreation activity leaders' experiences of leading. *Journal of Park and Recreation Administration, 22,* 75–95.

Lochbaum, M.R., Podlog, L., Litchfield, K., Surles, J., & Hillard, S. (2013). Stages of physical activity and approach-avoidance achievement goals in university students. *Psychology of Sport and Exercise, 14,* 161–168.

Lochbaum, M.R., Rhodes, R.E., Stevenson, S.J., Surles, J., Stevens, T., & Wang, C.K.J. (2010). Does gender moderate the exercising personality? An examination of continuous and stage-based exercise. *Psychology, Health, and Medicine, 15*(1), 50–60.

Locke, E.A. (1968). Toward a theory of task motivation incentives. *Organizational Behavior and Human Performance, 3,* 157–189.

Locke, E.A., & Latham, G.P. (1990). *A theory of goal setting and task performance.* Englewood Cliffs, NJ: Prentice Hall.

Locke, E.A., & Latham, G.P. (2002). Building a practically useful theory of goal setting and task motivation: A 35-year odyssey. *American Psychologist, 57*(9), 705–717.

Locke, E.A., Shaw, K.N., Saari, L.M., & Latham, G.P. (1981). Goal setting and task performance. *Psychological Bulletin, 90,* 125–152.

Loehr, J. (2005). Leadership: Full engagement for success. In S. Murphy (Ed.), *The sport psych handbook* (pp. 155–170). Champaign, IL: Human Kinetics.

Loehr, J., & Schwartz, T. (2001, January). The making of a corporate athlete. *Harvard Business Review,* pp. 120–128.

Lombard, D.N., Lombard, T.N., & Winett, R.A. (1995). Walking to meet health guidelines: The effect of prompting frequency and prompt structure. *Health Psychology, 14,* 164–179.

Long, B.C. (1984). Aerobic conditioning and stress inoculations: A comparison of stress management intervention. *Cognitive Therapy and Research, 8,* 517–542.

Long, B.C., & Haney, C.J. (1988). Coping strategies for working women: Aerobic exercise and relaxation interventions. *Behavior Therapy, 19,* 75–83.

Long, B.C., & Stavel, R.V. (1995). Effects of exercise training on anxiety: A meta-analysis. *Journal of Applied Sport Psychology, 7,* 167–189.

Long, T., Pantaleon, N., Bruant, G., & d'Arripe-Longueville, F. (2006). A qualitative study of moral reasoning of young athletes. *The Sport Psychologist, 20,* 330–347.

Lorimer, R. (2013). The development of empathetic accuracy in coaches. *Journal of Sport Psychology in Action, 4,* 26–33.

Lorimer, R., & Jowett, S. (2009a). Empathic accuracy in coach-athlete dyads who participate in team and individual sport. *Psychology of Sport and Exercise, 10,* 152–158.

Lorimer, R., & Jowett, S. (2009b). Feedback information in the empathic accuracy of sport coaches. *Psychology of Sport and Exercise, 10,* 1–6.

Lorimer, R., & Jowett, S. (2011). Empathetic accuracy, shared cognitive focus, and the assumptions of similarity made by coaches and athletes. *International Journal of Sport Psychology, 42,* 40–54.

Losoya, S.H., & Eisenberg, N. (2003). Affective empathy. In J.A. Hall & F.J. Bernieri (Eds.), *Interpersonal sensitivity: Theory and measurement* (pp. 21–43). Mahwah, NJ: Erlbaum.

Loughead, T., & Bloom, G. (2012). Team cohesion in sport: Critical overview and implications for team building J. Denison, P. Potrac, & W. Gilbert (Eds.), *The Routledge handbook of sports coaching* (pp.345-355). New York: Routledge.

Loughead, T., & Carron, A. (2004). The mediating role of cohesion in the leader behavior-satisfaction relationship. *Psychology of Sport and Exercise, 5,* 355–371.

Loughead, T., & Hardy, J. (2005). An examination of coach and peer leader behaviors in sport. *Psychology of Sport and Exercise, 6,* 303–312.

Loughead, T., Patterson, M., & Carron, A. (2008). The impact of fitness leader behavior and cohesion on an exerciser's affective state. *International Journal of Sport and Exercise Psychology, 6,* 53–68.

Lowe, R. (1971). Stress, arousal, and task performance of Little League baseball players. (Unpublished doctoral dissertation). Urbana, IL: University of Illinois.

Lox, C.L., McAuley, E., & Tucker, R.S. (1995). Exercise as an intervention for enhancing subjective well-being in an HIV-1 population. *Journal of Sport and Exercise Psychology, 17,* 345–362.

Loy, J.W. (1970). *Where the action is: A consideration of centrality in sport situations.* Paper presented at the meeting of the Second Canadian Psychomotor Learning and Sport Psychology Symposium, Windsor, ON.

Luiselli, J. (2012). Behavioral sport psychology consulting: A review of some practice concerns and recommendations. *Journal of Sport Psychology in Action, 3,* 41–51.

Luiselli, J., Woods, K., & Reed, D. (2011). Review of sports performance research with youth, collegiate, and elite athletes. *Journal of Applied Behavior Analysis, 44,* 999–1002.

Lundkvist, E., Gustafsson, H., Hjalm, S., & Hassmen, P. (2012). An interpretative phenomenological analysis of burnout and recovery in elite soccer coaches. *Qualitative Research in Sport, Exercise and Health, 4*(3), 400–419.

Lundquist, C. (2011). Well-being in competitive sports—The feel-good factor? A review of conceptual considerations of well-being. *International Review of Sport and Exercise Psychology, 4,* 109–127.

Luszczynska, A., Mazurkiewicz, M., Ziegelmann, J.P., & Schwarzer, R. (2007). Recovery self-efficacy and intention as predictors of running or jogging behavior: A cross-lagged panel analysis over a two-year period. *Psychology of Sport and Exercise, 8,* 247–269.

Luszczynska, A., & Tryburcy, M. (2008). Effects of a self-efficacy intervention on exercise: The moderating role of diabetes and cardiovascular disease. *Applied Psychology: An International Review, 57,* 644–659.

Luthje, P., Nurmi, I., Kataga, M., Belt, E., Helenius, P., & Kaukonen, J.P. (1996). Epidemiology and traumatology of injuries in elite soccer: A prospective study in Finland. *Scandinavian Journal of Medicine and Science in Sport, 6,* 601–605.

Machida, M., Ward, R., & Vealey, R. (2012). Predictors of self-confidence in collegiate athletes. *International Journal of Sport and Exercise Psychology, 10,* 172–185.

MacIntyre, T., & Moran, A. (2007). A qualitative investigation of imagery use and meta-imagery processes and imagery direction among elite canoe-slalom competitors. *Journal of Imagery Research in Sport and Physical Activity,* 2, Article 4. Available: www.bepress.com/jirspa/vol12/iss1/art4/.

MacIntyre, T., & Moran, A. (2010). Meta-imagery processes among elite sports performers. In A. Gullot & C. Collet (Eds.), *The neurophysiological foundation of mental and motor imagery* (pp. 227–244). Oxford, UK: Oxford University Press.

MacIntyre, T., Moran, A., Collet, C., & Guillot, A. (2013). An emerging paradigm: A strength-based approach to exploring mental imagery. *Frontiers in Human Neuroscience, 12,* 1–13.

Mack, M. (2001). Effects of time and movements on the pre-shot routine of free throw shooting. *Perceptual and Motor Skills, 93,* 567–573.

MacNamara, A., Button, A., & Collins, D. (2010a). The role of psychological characteristics in facilitating the pathway to elite performance. Part 1: Identifying mental skills and behaviors. *Journal of Applied Sport Psychology, 24,* 52–73.

MacNamara, A., Button, A., & Collins, D. (2010b). The role of psychological characteristics in facilitating the pathway to elite performance. Part 2: Examining environmental and stage-related differences in skills and behaviors. *Journal of Applied Sport Psychology, 24,* 74–96.

MacPherson, A., Collins, D., & Morriss, C. (2008). Is what you think what you get? Optimizing mental focus for technical performance. *The Sport Psychologist, 22,* 288–303.

Maddison, R., & Prapavessis, H. (2004). Using self-efficacy and intention to predict exercise compliance among patients with ischemic heart disease. *Journal of Sport and Exercise Psychology, 26,* 511–524.

Maddison, R., & Prapavessis, H. (2005). A psychological approach to the prediction and prevention of athletic injuries. *Journal of Sport and Exercise Psychology, 27,* 289–310.

Maddux, J. (1997). Health, habit, and happiness. *Journal of Sport and Exercise Psychology, 19,* 331–346.

Maddux, J., & Lewis, J. (1995). Self-efficacy and adjustment: Basic principles and issues. In J.E. Maddux (Ed.), *Self-efficacy, adaptation, and adjustment: Theory, research, and application* (pp. 37–68). New York: Plenum Press.

Maddux, J., & Meier, L. (1995). Self-efficacy and depression. In J.E. Maddux (Ed.), *Self-efficacy, adaptation, and adjustment: Theory, research, and application* (pp. 143–172). New York: Plenum Press.

Maehr, M., & Nicholls, J. (1980). Culture and achievement motivation: A second look. In N. Warren (Ed.), *Studies in cross-cultural psychology* (Vol. 2, pp. 53–75). New York: Academic Press.

Maganaris, C., Collins, D., & Sharp, M. (2000). Expectancy effects and strength training: Do steroids make a difference? *The Sport Psychologist, 14,* 272–278.

Magyar, M., Feltz, D., & Simpson, I. (2004). Individual and crew level determinants of collective efficacy in rowing. *Journal of Sport and Exercise Psychology, 26,* 136–153.

Magyar, T.M., & Duda, J.L. (2000). Confidence restoration following athletic injury. *The Sport Psychologist, 14,* 372–390.

Mahoney, M.J., & Avener, M. (1977). Psychology of the elite athlete: An exploratory study. *Cognitive Therapy and Research, 1,* 135–141.

Mahoney, M.J., Gabriel, T.J., & Perkins, T.S. (1987). Psychological skills and exceptional athletic performance. *The Sport Psychologist, 1,* 181–199.

Maitland, A., & Gervis, N. (2010). Goal-setting in youth football. Are coaches missing an opportunity? *Physical Education and Sport Pedagogy, 15*(4), 323–343.

Malcom, N. (2006). "Shaking it off" and "toughing it out": Socialization to pain and injury in girls' softball. *Journal of Contemporary Ethnography, 35,* 495–525.

Malete, L., & Feltz, D. (2000). The effect of a coaching education program on coaching efficacy. *The Sport Psychologist, 14,* 410–417.

Mallett, C. (2010). High performance coaches' careers and communities. In J. Lyle & C. Cushion (Eds.), *Sports coaching: Professionalism and practice* (pp. 119–133). London: Elsevier.

Mallett, C. (2013). Conflict management. In S. Hanrahan & M. Andersen (Eds.), *Routledge handbook of applied sport psychology: A comprehensive guide for students and practitioners* (pp. 335–344). New York: Routledge.

Mallett, C., & Coulter, T. (2011). Understanding and developing the will to win in sport: Perceptions of parents, coaches, and athletes. In D. Gucciardi & S. Gordon (Eds.), *Mental toughness in sport: Developments in theory and research* (pp. 187–211). New York: Routledge.

Mallett, C., & Hanrahan, S. (1997). Race modeling: An effective cognitive strategy for the 100 m sprinter. *The Sport Psychologist, 11,* 72–85.

Mallett, C., & Hanrahan, S. (2004). Elite athletes: Why does the fire burn so brightly? *Psychology of Sport and Exercise, 5,* 183–200.

Mamassis, G., & Doganis, G. (2004). The effects of a mental training program on juniors' pre-competitive anxiety, self-confidence, and tennis performance. *Journal of Applied Sport Psychology, 16,* 118–137.

Mann, B.J., Grana, W.A., Indelicato, P.A., O'Neil, D.F., & George, S.Z. (2007). A survey of sports medicine physicians regarding psychological issues in patient-athletes. *American Journal of Sports Medicine, 35,* 2140–2147.

Mann, D., Williams, M., Ward, P., & Janelle, C. (2007). Perceptual-cognitive expertise in sport: Meta-analysis. *Journal of Sport and Exercise Psychology, 29,* 457–478.

Marcus, B.H., Dubbert, P.M., Forsyth, L.H., McKenzie, T.L., Stone, E.J., Dunn, A.L., et al. (2000). Physical activity behavior change: Issues in adoption and maintenance. *Health Psychology, 19,* 42–56.

Marcus, B.H., Napolitano, M.A., King, A.C., Lewis, B.A., Whiteley, J.A., Albrecht, A., et al. (2007). Telephone versus print delivery of an individualized motivationally tailored physical activity intervention: Project STRIDE. *Health Psychology, 26,* 401–409.

Marcus, B.H., Pinto, B.M., Simkin, L.R., Audrain, J.E., & Taylor, E.R. (1994). Application of theoretical models to exercise behavior among employed women. *American Journal of Health Promotion, 9,* 49–55.

Marcus, B.H., Rossi, J.S., Selby, V.C., Niaura, R.S., & Abrams, D.B. (1992). The stages and processes of exercise adoption and maintenance in a worksite sample. *Health Psychology, 11,* 386–395.

Marcus, M.B. (2009). Cosmetic surgeries: What children will do to look "normal." Available: www.usatoday.com/news/health/2009-06-24-cosmetic-surgery-kids_N.htm.

Markowitz, S., & Arent, S. (2010). The exercise and affect relationship: Evidence for the dual-mode model and a modified opponent process theory. *Journal of Sport and Exercise Psychology, 32,* 711–730.

Marks, D.F. (1977). Imagery and consciousness: A theoretical review from an individual differences perspective. *Journal of Mental Imagery, 2,* 275–290.

Marsh, H.W. (1997). The measurement of physical self-concept: A construct validation approach. In K.R. Fox (Ed.), *The physical self: From motivation to well-being* (pp. 27–58). Champaign, IL: Human Kinetics.

Marsh, H.W., & Redmayne, R.S. (1994). A multidimensional physical self-concept and its relations to multiple components of physical fitness. *Journal of Sport and Exercise Psychology, 16,* 43–55.

Marsh, H.W., & Sonstroem, R.J. (1995). Importance ratings and specific components of physical self-concept: Relevance to predicting global components of self-concept and exercise. *Journal of Sport and Exercise Psychology, 17,* 84–104.

Marshall, S., & Biddle, S. (2001). The transtheoretical model of behavior change: A meta-analysis of applications to physical activity and exercise. *Annals of Behavioral Medicine, 23,* 229–246.

Martens, M., Dams-O'Connor, K., & Beck, R. (2006). Reducing heavy drinking in intercollegiate athletes: Evaluation of a web-based personalized feedback program. *The Sport Psychologist, 22,* 219–228.

Martens, M., Dams-O'Connor, K., & Duffy-Paiement, C. (2006). Comparing off-season with in-season alcohol consumption among intercollegiate athletes. *Journal of Sport and Exercise Psychology, 28,* 502–510.

Martens, M., Dams-O'Connor, K., & Kilmer, J. (2007). Alcohol and drug use among athletes. In G. Tenenbaum & R. Eklund (Eds.), *Handbook of sport psychology* (3rd ed., pp. 859–878). New York: Wiley.

Martens, R. (1975). *Social psychology of sport.* New York: Harper & Row.

Martens, R. (1976). *Competitiveness in sport.* Paper presented at the International Congress of Physical Activity Sciences, Quebec.

Martens, R. (1977). *Sport competition anxiety test.* Champaign, IL: Human Kinetics.

Martens, R. (1978). *Joy and sadness in children's sports.* Champaign, IL: Human Kinetics.

Martens, R. (1982). Kids' sports: A den of iniquity or land of promise. In R.A. Magill, M.J. Ash, & F.L. Smoll (Eds.), *Children in sport* (2nd ed., pp. 204–218). Champaign, IL: Human Kinetics.

Martens, R. (1987a). *Coaches' guide to sport psychology.* Champaign, IL: Human Kinetics.

Martens, R. (1987b). Science, knowledge and sport psychology. *The Sport Psychologist, 1,* 29–55.

Martens, R. (2004). *Successful coaching* (3rd ed.). Champaign, IL: Human Kinetics.

Martens, R., Burton, D., Vealey, R.S., Bump, L.A., & Smith, D. (1982, June). *Cognitive and somatic dimensions of competitive anxiety (CSAI-2).* Paper presented at NASPSPA Conference, University of Maryland, College Park.

Martens, R., Christina, R.W., Harvey, J.S., & Sharkey, B.J. (1981). *Coaching young athletes.* Champaign, IL: Human Kinetics.

Martens, R., Landers, D., & Loy, J. (1972). *Sports cohesiveness questionnaire.* Washington, DC: AAHPERD.

Martens, R., Vealey, R.S., & Burton, D. (Eds.). (1990). *Competitive anxiety in sport.* Champaign, IL: Human Kinetics.

Martin, F., & Lumsden, J. (1987). *Coaching: An effective behavioral approach.* St. Louis: Times Mirror/Mosby.

Martin, G.L., & Pear, J.J. (2003). *Behavior modification: What it is and how to do it* (7th ed.). Englewood Cliffs, NJ: Prentice Hall.

Martin, G., & Thompson, K. (2011). Overview of behavioral sport psychology. In J. Luisseli & D. Reed (Eds.), *Behavioral sport psychology: Evidence-based approaches to performance enhancement* (pp. 3–21). New York: Springer.

Martin, J. (2013). Athletes with physical disabilities. In S. Hanrahan & M. Andersen (Eds.), *Routledge handbook of applied sport psychology: A comprehensive guide for students and practitioners* (pp. 432–440). New York: Routledge.

Martin, J., Dubbert, P.M., Katell, A.D., Thompson, J.K., Raczynski, J.R., Lake, M., et al. (1984). The behavioral control of exercise in sedentary adults: Studies 1 through 6. *Journal of Consulting and Clinical Psychology, 52,* 795–811.

Martin, J., & Gill, D. (2002). Training and performance self-efficacy, affect, and performance in wheelchair road racers. *The Sport Psychologist, 16,* 384–395.

Martin, J., Martens, M., Serrao, H., & Rocha, T. (2008). Alcohol use and exercise dependence: Co-occurring behaviors among college students? *Journal of Clinical Sport Psychology, 2,* 381–393.

Martin, J., & McCaughtry, N. (2008). Using social cognitive theory to predict physical activity in inner-city African-American school children. *Journal of Sport and Exercise Psychology, 30,* 378–391.

Martin, J., McCaughtry, N., Hodges-Kulinna, P., Cothran, D., Dake, J., & Fahoome, G. (2005). Predicting physical activity and cardio-respiratory fitness in African-American children. *Journal of Sport and Exercise Psychology, 27,* 456–469.

Martin, J.J., Waldron, J.J., McCabe, A., & Yun, S.C. (2009). The impact of "Girls on the Run" on self-concept and fat attitudes. *Journal of Clinical Sport Psychology, 3,* 127–138.

Martin, K., Moritz, S., & Hall, C. (1999). Imagery use in sport: A literature review and applied model. *The Sport Psychologist, 13,* 245–268.

Martin, L., & Carron, A. (2012). Team attributions in sport: A meta-analysis. *Journal of Applied Sport Psychology, 24,* 157–174.

Martin, L., Carron, A., & Burke, S. (2009). Team building interventions in sport: A meta-analysis. *Sport and Exercise Psychology Review, 26,* 136–153.

Martin, L., Paradis, K., Eys, M., & Evans, B. (2013). Cohesion in sport: New directions for practitioners. *Journal of Sport Psychology in Action, 4,* 14–25.

Martin, S. (2005). High school and college athletes' attitudes toward sport psychology consulting. *Journal of Applied Sport Psychology, 17,* 127–139.

Martin, S., Jackson, A., Richardson, P., & Weiller, K. (1999). Coaching preferences of adolescent youths and their parents. *Journal of Applied Sport Psychology, 11,* 247–262.

Martin Ginis, K., Jung, M., & Gauvin, L. (2003). To see or not to see: Effects of exercising in mirrored environments on sedentary women's feeling states and self-efficacy. *Health Psychology, 22,* 354–361.

Martinek, T. (1988). Confirmation of a teacher-expectancy model: Student perceptions and causal attributions of teaching behaviors. *Research Quarterly for Exercise and Sport, 59,* 118–126.

Martinek, T., & Hellison, D.R. (1997). Fostering resiliency in underserved youth through physical activity. *Quest, 49*(1), 34–49.

Martinsen, E. (1993). Therapeutic implications of exercise for clinically anxious and depressed patients: Exercise and psychological well-being. *International Journal of Sport Psychology, 24,* 185–199.

Martinsen, E., & Stephens, T. (1994). Exercise and mental health in clinical and free-living populations. In R.K. Dishman (Ed.), *Advances in exercise adherence* (pp. 55–72). Champaign, IL: Human Kinetics.

Maslach, C., & Jackson, S.E. (1981). The measurement of experienced burnout. *Journal of Occupational Behavior, 2,* 99–113.

Masters, K., & Ogles, B. (1998). Associative and dissociative cognitive strategies in exercise and running 20 years later: What do we know? *The Sport Psychologist, 12,* 253–270.

Matson-Koffman, D., Brownstein, J., Neiner, J., & Greaney, M. (2005). A site-specific literature review of policy and environmental interventions that promote physical activity and nutrition for cardiovascular health: What works? *American Journal of Health Promotion, 19,* 167–183.

Mattie, P., & Munroe-Chandler, K. (2012). Examining the relationship between mental toughness and imagery use. *Journal of Applied Sport Psychology, 24,* 144–156.

Maxwell, J.P., Moores, E., & Chow, C.C.F. (2007). Anger rumination and self-reported aggression amongst British and Hong Kong Chinese athletes: A cross cultural comparison. *Journal of Sport and Exercise Psychology, 5,* 9–27.

Maxwell, J.P., Visek, A.J., & Moores, E. (2009). Anger and perceived legitimacy of aggression in male Hong Kong Chinese athletes: Effects of type of sport and competition. *Psychology of Sport and Exercise, 10,* 289–296.

Maynard, I.W., & Cotton, C.J. (1993). An investigation of two stress management techniques in a field setting. *The Sport Psychologist, 7,* 375–387.

Maynard, I.W., Hemmings, B., & Warwick-Evans, L. (1995). The effects of a somatic intervention strategy on competitive state anxiety and performance in semiprofessional soccer players. *The Sport Psychologist, 9,* 51–64.

Maynard, I.W., Smith, M.J., & Warwick-Evans, L. (1995). The effects of a cognitive intervention strategy on competitive state anxiety and performance in semiprofessional soccer players. *Journal of Sport and Exercise Psychology, 17,* 428–446.

Mazanov, J. (2013). Drug use and abuse by athletes. In S. Hanrahan & M. Andersen (Eds.), *Routledge handbook of applied sport psychology: A comprehensive guide for students and practitioners* (pp. 214–223). New York: Routledge.

Mazerolle, S.M., Monsma, E., Colin, D., & James, M. (2012). An assessment of burnout in graduate assistant certified athletic trainers. *Journal of Athletic Training, 47*(3), 320–328.

McAuley, E. (1985). Modeling and self-efficacy: A test of Bandura's model. *Journal of Sport Psychology, 7,* 283–295.

McAuley, E. (1992). The role of efficacy cognitions in the prediction of exercise behavior of middle-aged adults. *Journal of Behavioral Medicine, 15,* 65–88.

McAuley, E. (1993a). Self-efficacy and the maintenance of exercise participation in older adults. *Journal of Behavioral Medicine, 16,* 103–113.

McAuley, E. (1993b). Self-referent thought in sport and physical activity. In T.S. Horn (Ed.), *Advances in sport psychology* (pp. 101–118). Champaign, IL: Human Kinetics.

McAuley, E., & Blissmer, G. (2002). Self-efficacy and attributional processes in physical activity. In T. Horn (Ed.), *Advances in sport psychology* (2nd ed., pp. 185–206). Champaign, IL: Human Kinetics.

McAuley, E., Konopack, J., Motl, R., Morris, K., Doerksen, S., & Rosengren, K. (2006). Physical activity and quality of life in older adults: Influence of health status and self-efficacy. *Annuals of Behavioral Medicine, 31,* 99–103.

McAuley, E., Kramer, A.F., & Colcombe, S.J. (2004). Cardiovascular fitness and neurocognitive function in older adults: A brief review. *Brain, Behavior, and Immunity, 18,* 214–220.

McAuley, A., Mailey, E., Mullen, S., Szabo, A., Wojcicki, T., White, S., et al. (2011). Growth trajectories of exercise self-efficacy in older adults: Influence of measures and initial status. *Health Psychology, 30,* 75–83.

McAuley, E., Morris, K., Doerkson, S., Motl, R., Hu, L., White, S., et al. (2007). Effects of change in physical activity on physical function limitations in older women: Mediating roles of physical function performance and self-efficacy. *Journal of the American Geriatric Society, 55,* 1967–1973.

McAuley, E., Poag, K., & Gleason, A. (1990). Attrition from exercise programs: Attributional and affective perspectives. *Journal of Social Behavior and Personality, 5,* 591–602.

McAuley, E., & Tammen, V.V. (1989). The effects of subjective and objective competitive outcomes on intrinsic motivation. *Journal of Sport and Exercise Psychology, 11,* 84–93.

McCallum, J. (1991, November 11). For whom the Bull toils. *Sports Illustrated,* pp. 106–118.

McCallum, J. (2001, August 13). The gang's all here. *Sports Illustrated,* pp. 74–81.

McCallum, J., & Verducci, T. (2004, June). Hitting the skids: Serious slumps. *Sports Illustrated,* pp. 53–55.

McCann, S. (1995). Overtraining and burnout. In S.M. Murphy (Ed.), *Psychological interventions in sport* (pp. 347–368). Champaign, IL: Human Kinetics.

McCann, S. (2008). USOC sport psychology's "top ten" guiding principles for mental training. In *Coaches' guide—Mental training manual* (pp. 1–3). Colorado Springs.

McCarthy, P. (2009). Putting imagery to good affect: A case study among youth swimmers. *Sport and Exercise Psychology, 5,* 27–38.

McClelland, D. (1961). *The achieving society.* New York: Free Press.

McClure, B., & Foster, C. (1991). Group work as a method of promoting cohesiveness within a women's gymnastics team. *Perceptual and Motor Skills, 73,* 307–313.

McCullagh, P., Law, B., & St. Marie, D. (2012). Modeling and performance. In S. Murphy (Ed.) *The oxford handbook of sport and performance psychology* (pp. 250-272). New York: Routledge.

McCullagh, P., & Weiss, M. (2001). Modeling: Considerations for motor skill performance and psychological responses. In R. Singer, H. Hausenblas, & C. Janelle (Eds.), *Handbook of sport psychology* (pp. 205–238). New York: Wiley.

McCullagh, P., Weiss, M.R., & Ross, D. (1989). Modeling considerations in motor skill acquisition and performance: An integrated approach. *Exercise and Sport Sciences Reviews, 17,* 475–513.

McDonald, D.G., & Hodgdon, J.A. (1991). *The psychological effects of aerobic fitness training: Research and theory.* New York: Springer-Verlag.

McGannon, K., & Busanich, R. (2010). Rethinking subjectivity in sport and exercise psychology: A feminist post-structuralist perspective on women's embodied physical activity. In T. Ryba, R. Schinke, & G. Tenenbaum (Eds.), *The cultural turn in sport psychology* (pp. 203–229). Morgantown, WV: Fitness Information Technology.

McGhee, H., Hevey, D., & Horgan, J. (1999). Psychosocial outcome assessments for use in cardiac rehabilitation service evaluation: A 10-year systematic review. *Social Science and Medicine, 48,* 1373–1393.

McGrath, J.E. (1970). Major methodological issues. In J.E. McGrath (Ed.), *Social and psychological factors in stress* (pp. 19–49). New York: Holt, Rinehart & Winston.

McKay, B., & Wulf, G. (2012). A distal external focus enhances novice dart throwing performance. *International Journal of Sport and Exercise Psychology, 10,* 149–156.

McKay, J., Niven, A.G., Lavallee, D., & White, A. (2008). Sources of strain among elite UK track athletes. *The Sport Psychologist, 22,* 143–163.

McKenzie, T.L., & Rushall, B.S. (1974). Effects of self-recording on attendance and performance in a competitive swimming training environment. *Journal of Applied Behavior Analysis, 7,* 199–206.

McLachlan, S., & Hagger, M. (2011). Do people differentiate between intrinsic and extrinsic goals for physical activity? *Journal of Sport and Exercise Psychology, 33,* 273–288.

McNair, D., Lorr, M., & Droppleman, L. (1971). *Profile of mood states manual.* San Diego: Educational and Testing Service.

McNamara, J., & McCabe, M. (2012). Striving for success or addiction? Exercise dependence among elite Australian athletes. *Journal of Sport Sciences, 30,* 755–766.

McRae, R.R., & John, O.P. (1992). An introduction to the five-factor model and its applications. *Journal of Personality, 60,* 175–215.

Meehan, H.L., Bull, S.J., Wood, D.M., & James, D.V.B. (2004). The overtraining syndrome: A multicontextual assessment. *The Sport Psychologist, 18,* 154–171.

Meichenbaum, D. (1977). *Cognitive-behavior modification: An integrative approach.* New York: Plenum Press.

Meichenbaum, D. (1985). *Stress inoculation training.* New York: Pergamon Press.

Mellalieu, S.D., Hanton, S., & Fletcher, D. (2006). A competitive anxiety review: Recent directions in sport psychology research. In S. Hanton & S.D. Mellalieu (Eds.), *Literature reviews in sport psychology* (pp. 1–45). New York: Nova.

Mellalieu, S., Hanton, S., & Thomas, O. (2009). The effects of a motivational general-arousal imagery intervention upon pre-performance symptoms in male rugby union players. *Psychology of Sport and Exercise, 10,* 175–185.

Memmert, D. (2009). Pay attention! A review of visual attentional expertise in sport. *International Review of Sport and Exercise Psychology, 2,* 119–138.

Mendel, W., & Bradford, D. (1995). *Interagency cooperation: A regional model for overseas operations.* Washington, DC: Institute for National Strategic Studies.

Mento, A.J., Steel, R.P., & Karren, R.J. (1987). A meta-analytic study of the effects of goal-setting on task performance: 1966–1984. *Organizational Behavior and Human Decision Processes, 39,* 52–83.

Merritt, C.J., & Tharp, I.J. (2013). Personality, self-efficacy and risk-taking behavior in parkour (free running). *Psychology of Sport and Exercise, 14,* 608–611.

Mesagno, C., Harvey, J., & Janelle, C. (2011). Self-presentation origins of choking: Evidence from separate pressure manipulations. *Journal of Sport and Exercise Psychology, 33,* 441–459.

Mesagno, C., Marchant, D., & Morris, T. (2008). A pre-performance routine to alleviate choking in "choking-susceptible" athletes. *The Sport Psychologist, 22,* 439–457.

Meyer, B. (2000). The ropes and challenge course: A quasi-experimental investigation. *Perceptual and Motor Skills, 90,* 1249–1257.

Meyers, A.W., Whelan, J.P., & Murphy, S.M. (1996). Cognitive behavioral strategies in athletic performance enhancement. In M. Hersen, R.M. Miller, & A.S. Belack (Eds.), *Handbook of behavior modification* (Vol. 30, pp. 137–164). Pacific Grove, CA: Brooks/Cole.

Miche, S., Abraham, C., Whittington, C., McAteer, J., & Gupta, S. (2009). Effective techniques in healthy eating and physical activity interventions: A meta-regression. *Health Psychology, 28,* 690–701.

Michelson, P., & Koenig, O. (2002). On the relationship between imagery and visual perception: Evidence from priming studies. *European Journal of Cognitive Psychology, 14,* 161–184.

Michener, J. (1976). *Sports in America.* New York: Random House.

Mihoces, E. (1997, December 5). Player-coach battle stirs debate. *USA Today,* pp. C1–C2.

Mikes, J. (1987). *Basketball fundamentals: A complete mental training guide.* Champaign, IL: Leisure Press.

Milanese, C., Facci, G., Cesari, P., & Zancanzro, C. (2008). Amplification of error: A rapidly effective method for motor performance improvement. *The Sport Psychologist, 22,* 164–174.

Milani, R., & Lavie, C. (2007). Impact of cardiac rehabilitation on depression and its associated mortality. *American Journal of Medicine, 120,* 799–806.

Millar, S., Oldhan, A., & Donovan, M. (2011). Coaches' self-awareness of timing, nature, and intent of verbal instructions to athletes. *International Journal of Sports Science and Coaching, 6,* 503–515.

Miller, A., & Donohue, B. (2003). The development and controlled evaluation of athletic mental preparation strategies in high school distance runners. *Journal of Applied Sport Psychology, 15,* 321–334.

Miller, B.W., Roberts, G.C., & Ommundsen, Y. (2005). Effect of perceived motivational climate on moral functioning, team moral atmosphere perceptions, and the legitimacy of intentionally injurious acts among competitive youth football. *Psychology of Sport and Exercise, 6,* 461–477.

Miller, K., Barner, G., Sabo, D., Melnick, M., & Farrell, M. (2002). A comparison of health risk behavior in adolescent users of anabolic-androgenic steroids by gender and athletic status. *Sociology of Sport Journal, 19,* 385–402.

Miller, R.W. (1993, Spring). In search of peace: Peer conflict resolution. *Schools in the Middle,* pp. 11–13.

Miller, S.C., Bredemeier, B.J.L., & Shields, D.L.L. (1997). Sociomoral education through physical education with at-risk children. *Quest, 49,* 114–129.

Miller, S., & Weinberg, R. (1991). Perceptions of psychological momentum and their relationship to performance. *The Sport Psychologist, 5,* 211–222.

Miller, W., & Rollnick, S. (2009). Ten things that motivational interviewing is not. *Behavioral and Cognitive Psychotherapy, 37,* 129–140.

Milne, H., Wallman, K., Guilfoyle, A., Gordon, S., & Courneya, K. (2008). Self-determination theory and physical activity among breast cancer survivors. *Journal of Sport and Exercise Psychology, 30,* 23–38.

Milne, M., Rodgers, W., Hall, C., & Wilson, P. (2008). Starting up or starting over: The role of intentions to increase and maintain the behavior of exercise initiates. *Journal of Sport and Exercise Psychology, 30,* 286–301.

Ming, S., & Martin, G.L. (1996). Single-subject evaluation of a self-talk package for improving figure skating performance. *The Sport Psychologist, 10,* 227–238.

Moesch, K., & Apitzsch, E. (2012). How do coaches experience psychological momentum? A qualitative study of female elite handball teams. *The Sport Psychologist, 26,* 435–453.

Moore, W.E., & Stevenson, J.R. (1994). Training for trust in sport skills. *The Sport Psychologist, 8,* 1–12.

Moran, A. (1996). *The psychology of concentration in sport performance: A cognitive approach.* East Sussex, UK: Psychology Press.

Moran, A. (2003). Improving concentration skills in team-sport performers: Focusing techniques for soccer players. In R. Lidor & K. Henschen (Eds.), *The psychology of team sports* (pp. 161–190). Morgantown, WV: Fitness Information Technology.

Moran, A. (2004). *Sport and exercise psychology: A critical introduction.* London: Routledge.

Moran, A. (2012). Concentration: Attention and performance. In S. Murphy (Ed.), *The Oxford handbook of sport and performance psychology* (pp. 117–130). New York: Oxford University Press.

Moran, A. (2013). Concentration/attention. In S. Hanrahan & M. Andersen (Eds.), *Routledge handbook of applied sport psychology A comprehensive guide for students and practitioners* (pp. 500–509). New York: Routledge.

Moran, A., & MacIntyre, T. (1998). There's more to an image than meets the eye: A qualitative study of kinesthetic imagery among elite canoe-slalomists. *Irish Journal of Psychology, 19,* 406–423.

Moreno, J.A., Gonzales-Cutre, D., Sicilia, A., & Spray, C.M. (2010). Motivation in the exercise setting: Integrating some constructs from the approach-avoidance achievement goal framework and self-determination theory. *Psychology of Sport and Exercise, 11,* 542–550.

Morgan, P., Fletcher, D., & Sarkar, M. (2013). Defining and characterizing team resilience in elite sport. *Psychology of Sport and Exercise, 14,* 549–559.

Morgan, W.P. (1979a). Negative addiction in runners. *The Physician and Sportsmedicine, 7*(2), 56–63, 67–70.

Morgan, W.P. (1979b). Prediction of performance in athletics. In P. Klavora & J.V. Daniel (Eds.), *Coach, athlete, and the sport psychologist* (pp. 173–186). Champaign, IL: Human Kinetics.

Morgan, W.P. (1980). The trait psychology controversy. *Research Quarterly for Exercise and Sport, 51,* 50–76.

Morgan, W.P. (2001). Prescription of physical activity: A paradigm shift. *The Academy Papers: Adherence to Exercise and Physical Activity, 53,* 366–382.

Morgan, W.P., Brown, D.R., Raglin, J.S., O'Connor, P.J., & Ellickson, K.A. (1987). Psychological monitoring of overtraining and staleness. *British Journal of Sport Medicine, 21,* 107–114.

Morgan, W.P., & Dishman, R.K. (Eds.). (2001). The academy papers: Adherence to exercise and physical activity. *Quest, 53.*

Morgan, W.P., & Goldston, S.E. (1987). *Exercise and mental health.* Washington, DC: Hemisphere.

Morgan, W.P., O'Connor, P.J., Ellickson, K.A., & Bradley, P.W. (1988). Personality structure, mood states, and performance in elite distance runners. *International Journal of Sport Psychology, 19,* 247–269.

Morgan, W.P., O'Connor, P.J., Sparling, P.B., & Pate, R.R. (1987). Psychologic characterization of the elite female distance runner. *International Journal of Sports Medicine, 8,* 124–131.

Morgan, W.P., & Pollock, M. (1977). Psychologic characterization of the elite distance runner. *Annals of the New York Academy of Sciences, 301,* 382–403.

Moritz, S., Feltz, D., Fahrbach, K., & Mack, D. (2000). The relation of self-efficacy measures to sport performance: A meta-analytic review. *Research Quarterly for Exercise and Sport, 71,* 280–294.

Moritz, S.E., Hall, C.R., Martin, K.A., & Vadocz, E. (1996). What are confident athletes imaging? An examination of image content. *The Sport Psychologist, 10,* 171–179.

Morris, T. (2013). Imagery. In S. Hanrahan & M. Andersen (Eds.), *Routledge handbook of applied sport psychology: A comprehensive guide for students and practitioners* (pp. 481–489). New York: Routledge.

Morris, T., Spittle, M., & Perry, C. (2004). Mental imagery in sport. In T. Morris & J. Summers (Eds.), *Sport psychology: Theory, applications, and issues* (2nd ed., pp. 344–387). Queensland, Australia: Wiley.

Morris, T., Spittle, M., & Watt, P. (2005). *Imagery in sport.* Champaign, IL: Human Kinetics.

Morris, T., & Thomas, P. (2004). Applied sport psychology. In T. Morris & J. Summers (Eds.), *Sport psychology: Theory, applications, and issues* (2nd ed., pp. 235–277). Queensland, Australia: Wiley.

Motl, R., Dishman, R., Ward, D., Saunders, R., Dowda, M., Felton, G., et al. (2005). Comparison of barriers to self-efficacy and perceived behavioral control for explaining physical activity across 1 year among adolescent girls. *Health Psychology, 24,* 106–111.

Motl, R., Gappmaier, E., Nelson, K., & Benedict, R. (2011). Physical activity and cognitive function in multiple sclerosis. *Journal of Sport and Exercise Psychology, 33,* 734–741.

Motl, R., & McAuley, E. (2009). Pathways between physical activity and quality of life in adults with multiple sclerosis. *Health Psychology, 28,* 682–689.

Mouratidis, A., Lens, W., & Vansteenkiste, M. (2010). How you provide corrective feedback makes a difference: The motivating role of communicating in an autonomy-supportive way. *Journal of Sport and Exercise Psychology, 32,* 619–637.

Mouratidis, A., Vansteenkiste, M., Lens, W., & Sideridis, G. (2008). The motivating role of positive feedback in sport and physical education: Evidence for a motivational model. *Journal of Sport and Exercise Psychology, 30,* 240–268.

Mroczek, D.K., & Kolarz, C. (1998). The effect of age on positive and negative affect: A developmental perspective on happiness. *Journal of Personality and Social Psychology, 75,* 1333–1349.

Mueller, C.M., & Dweck, C.S. (1998). Praise for intelligence can undermine children's motivation and performance. *Journal of Personality and Social Psychology, 75,* 33–52.

Mullen, B., & Cooper, C. (1994). The relation between group cohesiveness and performance: An integration. *Psychological Bulletin, 115,* 210–227.

Mullen, R., & Hardy, L. (2010). Conscious processing and the process goal paradox. *Journal of Sport and Exercise Psychology, 32,* 275–297.

Mulvey, P., & Klein, H. (1998). The impact of perceived loafing and collective efficacy on group process and group performance. *Organizational Behavior and Human Decision Processes, 74,* 62–87.

Mumford, P., & Hall, C.R. (1985). The effects of internal and external imagery on performing figures in figure skating. *Canadian Journal of Applied Sport Science, 10,* 171–177.

Munroe, K., Estabrooks, P., Dennis, P., & Carron, A. (1999). A phenomenological analysis of group norms in sport teams. *The Sport Psychologist, 13,* 171–182.

Munroe, K., Giacobbi, P., Hall, C., & Weinberg, R. (2000). The 4 W's of imagery use: Where, when, why, and what. *The Sport Psychologist, 14,* 119–137.

Munroe-Chandler, K., & Morris, T. (2011). Imagery. In T. Morris & P. Terry (Eds.), *The new sport and exercise psychology companion* (pp. 275–308). Morgantown WV: Fitness Information Technology.

Munzert, J. (2008). Does level of expertise influence imagined durations in open skills? Played versus imagined durations of badminton sequences. *International Journal of Sport and Exercise Psychology, 6,* 24–38.

Murphy, S. (1990). Models of imagery in sport psychology: A review. *Journal of Mental Imagery, 14,* 153–172.

Murphy, S.M. (Ed.). (1995). *Sport psychology interventions.* Champaign, IL: Human Kinetics.

Murphy, S. (1996). *The achievement zone.* New York: Putnam's.

Murphy, S. (Ed.). (2005a). *The sport psychology handbook.* Champaign, IL: Human Kinetics.

Murphy, S. (2005b). Imagery: Inner theater becomes reality. In S. Murphy (Ed.), *The sport psych handbook* (pp. 128–151). Champaign. IL: Human Kinetics.

Murphy, S. (2009). Video games, competition and exercise: A new opportunity for sport psychologists. *The Sport Psychologist, 9*(23), 487–503.

Murphy, S.M., Fleck, S.J., Dudley, G., & Callister, R. (1990). Psychological and performance concomitants of increased volume training in athletes. *Journal of Applied Sport Psychology, 2,* 34–50.

Murphy, S., & Jowdy, D. (1992). Imagery and mental practice. In T. Horn (Ed.), *Advances in sport psychology.* Champaign, IL: Human Kinetics.

Murphy, S., Jowdy, D., & Durtschi, S. (1990). *Report on the U.S. Olympic Committee survey on imagery use in sport.* Colorado Springs: U.S. Olympic Training Center.

Murphy, S., & Martin, K. (2002). The use of imagery in sport. In T. Horn (Ed.), *Advances in sport psychology* (2nd ed., pp. 405–440). Champaign, IL: Human Kinetics.

Murphy, S., Nordin, S., & Cumming, J. (2008). Imagery in sport, exercise and dance. In T. Horn (Ed.), *Advances in sport psychology* (3rd ed., pp. 297–324). Champaign, IL: Human Kinetics.

Murray, C.J., & Lopez, A.D. (1997). Alternative projections of mortality and disability by cause 1990–2020: Global Burden of Disease Study. *Lancet, 349,* 1498–1504.

Murray, H.A. (1938). *Explorations in personality.* New York: Oxford University Press.

Muscat, A., & Long, B. (2008). Critical comments about body shape and weight: Disordered eating of female athletes and sport participants. *Journal of Applied Sport Psychology, 20,* 1–24.

Mutrie, N. (2001). The relationship between physical activity and clinically-defined depression. In S.J.H. Biddle, K.R. Fox, & S.H. Boutcher (Eds.), *Physical activity, mental health, and psychological well-being* (pp. 46–62). London: Routledge & Kegan Paul.

Mutrie, N., & Biddle, S.J.H. (1995). The effects of exercise on mental health of nonclinical populations. In S.J.H. Biddle (Ed.), *European perspectives on exercise and sport psychology* (pp. 50–70). Champaign, IL: Human Kinetics.

Mutrie, N., Kirk, A., & Hughes, A. (2011). Adherence and quality of life issues. In T. Morris & P. Terry (Eds.), *The new sport and exercise psychology companion* (pp. 461–481). Morgantown, WV: Fitness Information Technology.

Myers, N., Feltz, D., Chase, M., Reckase, M., & Hancock, D. (2008). The Coaching Efficacy Scale II—High school teams. *Educational and Psychological Measurement, 68,* 1059–1076.

Myers, N., Vargas-Tonsing, T., & Feltz, D. (2005). Coaching efficacy in intercollegiate coaches: Sources, coaching behavior and team variables. *Sport and Exercise Psychology, 6,* 129–143.

National Center on Addiction and Substance Abuse. (2000). *Winning at any cost: Doping in Olympic sports.* New York: The CASA National Commission on Sports and Substance Abuse.

National Collegiate Athletic Association. (1989). *Nutrition and eating disorders in collegiate athletics* [Videotape]. Kansas City, MO: National Collegiate Athletic Association.

National Collegiate Athletic Association. (2001). *NCAA study of substance use and habits of college student-athletes.* Indianapolis: AuthorHouse.

National Collegiate Athletic Association. (2004). *NCAA study finds sports wagering a problem among student-athletes.* Available: www.ncaa.org/releases/research/2004/2004051201re.htm.

National Collegiate Athletic Association (2009). *Sports-wagering study shows progression in education.* Available: www.ncaa.org/wps/portal/ncaahome?WCM_GLOBAL_CONTEXT=/ncaa/ncaa/ncaa+news/ncaa+news+online/2009/association-wide/sports-wagering+study+shows+progress+in+education_11_13_09_ncaa_news.

National Safe Kids Campaign. (2004). *Sports injury fact sheet.* Washington, DC: National Safe Kids Campaign and the American Academy of Pediatrics.

Nelson, L.R., & Furst, M.L. (1972). An objective study of the effects of expectation on competitive performance. *Journal of Psychology, 81,* 69–72.

Nelson, M.B. (1998). *Embracing victory: Life lessons in competition and compassion.* New York: Morrow.

Nelson, T., & Wechsler, H. (2001). Alcohol and college athletes. *Medicine and Science in Sports and Exercise, 33,* 43–47.

Ness, R.G., & Patton, R.W. (1979). The effects of beliefs on maximum weight-lifting performance. *Cognitive Therapy and Research, 3,* 205–211.

Netz, Y., Zeev, A., Arnon, M., & Tenenbaum, G. (2008). Reasons attributed to omitting exercising: A population-based study. *International Journal of Sport and Exercise Psychology, 6,* 9–23.

Newman, B.M., & Newman, P.R. (1991). *Development through life: A psychological approach.* Pacific Grove, CA: Brooks/Cole.

Newton, M., Fry, M., Watson, D., Gano-Overway, L., Kim, M., Magyar, M., et al. (2007). Psychometric properties of the caring climate scale in a physical activity setting. *Revisa de psicologia del Deporte, 16,* 67–84.

Nicholas, M., & Jebrane, A. (2009). Consistency of coping strategies and defense mechanisms during training sessions and sport competitions. *International Journal of Sport Psychology, 40,* 229–248.

Nicholls, A., Hemmings, B., & Clough, P. (2010). Stressors, coping, and emotion among international adolescent golfers. *Scandinavian Journal of Medicine and Science in Sports, 20,* 346–355.

Nicholls, A., Holt, N., & Polman, R. (2005). A phenomenological analysis of coping effectiveness in golf. *The Sport Psychologist, 19,* 111–130.

Nicholls, A., Holt, N., Polman, R., & Bloomfield, J. (2008). Stressors, coping, and coping effectiveness among professional rugby union players. *The Sport Psychologist, 20,* 314–329.

Nicholls, A., Perry, J., Jones, L., Morley, D., & Carson, F. (2013). Dispositional coping, coping effectiveness, and cognitive social maturity among adolescent athletes. *Journal of Sport and Exercise Psychology, 35,* 229–238.

Nicholls, A., & Polman, R. (2007). Coping in sport: A systematic review. *Journal of Sport Sciences, 25,* 11–31.

Nicholls, A., Polman, R., Levy, A., & Hulleman, J. (2012). An explanation for the fallacy of facilitative anxiety: Stress, emotions, coping and subjective performance in sport. *International Journal of Sport Psychology, 43,* 273–293.

Nicholls, A., Polman, R., Morley, D., & Taylor, N. (2009). Coping and coping effectiveness in relation to a competitive sport event: Pubertal status, chronological age, and gender among adolescent athletes. *Journal of Sport and Exercise Psychology, 31,* 299–317.

Nicholls, J. (1984). Concepts of ability and achievement motivation. In C. Ames & R. Ames (Eds.), *Research on motivation in education: Student motivation* (Vol. 1, pp. 39–73). New York: Academic Press.

Nicholson, N. (1989). The role of drug education. In S. Haynes & M. Anshel (Eds.), *Proceedings of the 1989 National Drugs in Sport Conference—treating the causes and symptoms* (pp. 48–57). Wollongong, NSW, Australia: University of Wollongong.

Nicklaus, J. (1974). *Golf my way.* New York: Heinemann.

Nicklaus, J. (1976). *Play better golf.* New York: King Features.

Nideffer, R.M. (1976a). *The inner athlete.* New York: Crowell.

Nideffer, R. (1976b). Test of attentional and interpersonal style. *Journal of Personality and Social Psychology, 34,* 394–404.

Nideffer, R. (1981). *The ethics and practice of applied sport psychology.* Ithaca, NY: Mouvement.

Nideffer, R.M., & Segal, M. (2001). Concentration and attention control training. In J.M. Williams (Ed.), *Applied sport psychology: Personal growth to peak performance* (4th ed., pp. 312–332). Mountain View, CA: Mayfield.

Nideffer, R.M., Segal, M.S., Lowry, M., & Bond, J. (2001). Identifying and developing world-class performers. In G. Tenenbaum (Ed.), *Reflections and experiences in sport and exercise psychology* (pp. 129–144). Morgantown, WV: Fitness Information Technology.

Nien, C.L., & Duda, J.L. (2008). Antecedents and consequences of approach and avoidance achievement goals: A test of gender invariance. *Psychology of Sport and Exercise, 9,* 352–372.

Nieuwenbuys, A., & Oudejans, R. (2010). Effects of anxiety on handgun shooting behavior of police officers: A pilot study. *Anxiety, Stress and Coping, 23,* 225–233.

Nieuwenhuys, A., Pijpers, J., Oudejans, R., & Bakker, F. (2008). The influence of anxiety on visual attention in climbing. *Journal of Sport and Exercise Psychology, 30,* 171–185.

Nigg, C., Borrelli, B., Maddock, J., & Dishman, R. (2008). A theory of physical activity maintenance. *Applied Psychology: An International Review, 57,* 544–560.

Ninedek, A., & Kolt, G.S. (2000). Sport physiotherapists' perceptions of psychological strategies in sport injury rehabilitation. *Journal of Sport Rehabilitation, 9,* 191–206.

Noblet, A.J., & Gifford, S.M. (2002). The sources of stress experienced by Australian professional footballers. *Journal of Applied Sport Psychology, 14,* 1–13.

Nordin, S., & Cumming, J. (2005). More than meets the eye: Investigating imagery type, direction, and outcome. *The Sport Psychologist, 19,* 1–17.

Nordin, S., & Cumming, J. (2008). Types and functions of athletes' imagery: Testing predictions from the applied model of imagery use by examining effectiveness. *International Journal of Sport and Exercise Psychology, 6,* 189–206.

North, T.C., McCullagh, P., & Tran, Z.V. (1990). Effects of exercise on depression. *Exercise and Sport Science Reviews, 18,* 379–415.

Northouse, P.G. (2010). *Leadership: Theory and practice* (5th ed.). Thousand Oaks, CA: Sage.

Ntoumanis, N., & Biddle, S.J.H. (1999). A review of psychological climate in physical activity settings with specific reference to motivation. *Journal of Sport Sciences, 17,* 643–665.

Ntoumanis, N., & Standage, M. (2009). Morality in sport: A self-determination theory perspective. *Journal of Applied Sport Psychology, 21*(4), 365–380.

Ntoumanis, N., Vazou, S., & Duda, J. (2007). Peer-created motivational climate. In S. Jowett & D. Lavelle (Eds.), *Social psychology in sport* (pp. 145–156). Champaign, IL: Human Kinetics.

O, J., & Hall, C. (2009). A quantitative analysis of athletes' voluntary use of slow motion, real-time and fast motion images. *Journal of Applied Sport Psychology, 21,* 15–30.

O, J., & Munroe-Chandler, K. (2008). The effects of image speed on the performance of a soccer task. *The Sport Psychologist, 22,* 1–17.

O'Brien, K.S., Kolt, G.S., Martens, M.P., Ruffman, T., Miller, P.G., & Lynott, D. (2012). Alcohol-related aggression and antisocial behavior in sportspeople/athletes. *Journal of Science & Medicine in Sport, 15,* 292-297.

O'Brien, M., Mellalieu, S., & Hanton, S. (2009). Goal-setting effects in elite and nonelite boxers. *Journal of Applied Sport Psychology, 21,* 293–306.

O'Brien, R.M., & Simek, T.C. (1983). A comparison of behavioral and traditional methods for teaching golf. In G.L. Martin & D. Hrycaiko (Eds.), *Behavior modification and coaching: Principles, procedures, and research.* Springfield, IL: Charles C Thomas.

O'Connor, P.J. (1997). Overtraining and staleness. In W.P. Morgan (Ed.), *Physical activity and mental health* (pp. 145–160). Philadelphia: Taylor & Francis.

O'Connor, P.J., Lewis, R.D., & Kirchner, E.M. (1995). Eating disorders in female college gymnasts. *Medicine and Science in Sports and Exercise, 27,* 550–555.

O'Connor, P., & Puetz, T. (2005). Chronic physical activity and feelings of energy and fatigue. *Medicine and Science in Sports and Exercise, 37,* 299–305.

Oldridge, N., & Jones, N. (1983). Improving patient compliance in cardiac exercise rehabilitation. *Journal of Cardiac Rehabilitation, 3,* 259-262.

Olusoga, P., Butt, J., Maynard, I., & Hays, K. (2010). Stress and coping: A study of world class coaches. *Journal of Applied Sport Psychology, 22,* 274–293.

Oman, R.F., & King, A.C. (2000). The effect of life events and exercise program format on the adoption and maintenance of exercise behavior. *Health Psychology, 19,* 605–612.

Opdenacker, J., Delecluse, C., & Boen, F. (2009). The longitudinal effects of a lifestyle physical activity intervention and a structured exercise intervention on physical self-perceptions and self-esteem in older adults. *Journal of Sport and Exercise Psychology, 31,* 743–760.

Orlick, T. (1978). *The cooperative sports and games book.* New York: Pantheon.

Orlick, T. (1986). *Psyching for sport: Mental training for athletes.* Champaign, IL: Human Kinetics.

Orlick, T. (1992). *Freeing children from stress: Focusing and stress control activities for children.* Willits, CA: ITA.

Orlick, T. (2000). *In pursuit of excellence: How to win in sport and life through mental training* (3rd ed.). Champaign, IL: Human Kinetics.

Orlick, T., & McCaffrey, N. (1991). Mental training with children for sport and life. *The Sport Psychologist, 5,* 322-334.

Orlick, T., McNally, J., & O'Hara, T. (1978). Cooperative games: Systematic analysis and cooperative impact. In F. Smoll & R.E. Smith (Eds.), *Psychological perspectives in youth sports* (pp. 203–228). New York: Hemisphere.

Orlick, T., & Partington, J. (1987). The sport psychology consultant: Analysis of critical components as viewed by Canadian Olympic athletes. *The Sport Psychologist, 1,* 4–17.

Orlick, T., & Partington, J. (1988). Mental links to excellence. *The Sport Psychologist, 2,* 105–130.

O'Rourke, D., Smith, R., Smoll, F., & Cumming, S. (2011). Trait anxiety in young athletes as a function of parental pressure and motivational climate: Is parental pressure always harmful? *Journal of Applied Sport Psychology, 23,* 398–412.

Ost, L.G. (1988). Applied relaxation: Description of an effective coping technique. *Scandinavian Journal of Behavior Therapy, 17,* 83–96.

Otis, C.L., Crespo, M., Flygare, C.T., Johnston, P., Keber, A., Lloyd-Koklin, D., et al. (2006). The Sony Ericsson WTA tour 10 year eligibility and professional development review. *British Journal of Sports Medicine, 40,* 464–468.

Otis, L., Maymí, J., Feliu, J., Vidal, J., Romero, E., Bassets, M., et al. (2007). Exercise motivation in university community members: A behavioural intervention. *Psichothema, 19*(2), 250–255.

Otten, M. (2009). Chocking versus clutch performance: A study of sport performance under pressure. *Journal of Sport and Exercise Psychology, 31,* 583–601.

Oudejans, R., & Pijpers, J. (2009). Training with anxiety has a positive effect on expert perceptual-motor performance under pressure. *Quarterly Journal of Experimental Psychology, 62,* 1631–1647.

Oudejans, R., & Pijpers, J. (2010). Training with mild anxiety may prevent choking under higher levels of anxiety. *Psychology of Sport and Exercise, 11,* 44–50.

Page, S. (2010). An overview of the effectiveness of motor imagery after a stroke: A neuroimaging approach. In A. Guillot & C. Collet (Eds.), *The neurophysiological foundations of mental and motor imagery* (pp. 145–160). Oxford, UK: Oxford University Press.

Page, S., Sime, W., & Nordell, K. (1999). The effects of imagery on female swimmers' perceptions of anxiety. *The Sport Psychologist, 13,* 458–469.

Pain, M., & Harwood, C. (2004). Knowledge and perceptions of sport psychology within English soccer. *Journal of Sport Sciences, 22,* 813–826.

Pain, M., & Harwood, C. (2008). The performance environment of the England youth soccer teams: A quantitative study. *Journal of Sports Sciences, 26,* 1157–1169.

Pain, M., & Harwood, C. (2009). Team building through mutual sharing and open discussion of team functioning. *The Sport Psychologist, 23,* 523–542.

Pain, M., Harwood, C., & Mullen, R. (2012). Improving the performance environment of a soccer team during a competitive season: An exploratory action research study. *The Sport Psychologist, 26,* 390–411.

Pan, J., & Nigg, C. (2011). Motivation for physical activity among Hawaiian, Japanese and Filipino university students in Hawaii. *Journal of Applied Sport Psychology, 23,* 1–15.

Paolucci, E., & Violato, C. (2004). A meta-analysis of the published research on the affective, cognitive, and behavioral effects of corporal punishment. *The Journal of Psychology, 138,* 197–221.

Papaioannou, A. (1995). Differential perceptual and motivational patterns when different goals are adopted. *Journal of Sport and Exercise Psychology, 17,* 18–34.

Papanek, J. (1977, October 31). The enforcers. *Sports Illustrated,* pp. 43–49.

Paradis, K., & Loughead, T. (2012). Examining the mediating role of cohesion between athlete leadership and athlete satisfaction in youth. *International Journal of Sport Psychology, 43,* 117–136.

Paradis, K., & Martin, L. (2012). Team building in sport: Linking theory and research to practical application. *Journal of Sport Psychology in Action, 3,* 179–190.

Paradis, K., Martin, L., & Carron, A. (2012). Examining the relationship between passion and perceptions of cohesion in athletes. *Sport and Exercise Psychology Review, 8,* 22–31.

Parcells, B., & Coplon, J. (1995). *Finding a way to win: The principles of leadership, teamwork, and motivation.* New York: Doubleday.

Park, D. (2007). Eating disorders: A call to arms. *American Psychologist, 62,* 158.

Parrott, M., Tennant, K., Olejnik, S., & Poudevigne, M. (2008). Theory of planned behavior: Implications for an e-mail based physical activity intervention. *Psychology of Sport and Exercise, 9,* 511–526.

Partington, J., & Orlick, T. (1987). The sport psychology consultant: Olympic coaches' views. *The Sport Psychologist, 1,* 95–102.

Partington, S., Partington, E., & Oliver, S. (2009). The dark side of flow: A qualitative study of dependence in big wave surfing. *The Sport Psychologist, 23,* 170–187.

Paskevich, D., Estabrooks, P., Brawley, L.R., & Carron, A.V. (2001). Group cohesion in sport and exercise. In R. Singer, H. Hausenblas, & C. Janelle (Eds.), *Handbook of sport psychology* (2nd ed., pp. 472–494). New York: Wiley.

Paternoster, R. (1987). The deterrent effect of the perceived certainty and severity of punishment: A review of the evidence and issues. *Justice Quarterly, 4,* 173–217.

Pates, J., Oliver, R., & Maynard, I. (2001). The effects of hypnosis on flow states and golf putting performance. *Journal of Applied Sport Psychology, 13,* 341-354.

Pavio, A. (1985). Cognitive and motivational functions of imagery in human performance. *Canadian Journal of Applied Sport Sciences, 10,* 22–28.

Pease, D.G., & Kozub, S. (1994). Perceived coaching behavior and team cohesion in high school girls' basketball teams. [Abstract]. *Journal of Sport and Exercise Psychology, 16*(Suppl.), S93.

Pegoraro, A. (2010). Look who's talking—Athletes on Twitter: A case study. *International Journal of Sport Communication, 4,* 501–515.

Pelletier, L.G., Fortier, M.S., Vallerand, R.J., Tuson, K.M. Briere, N.M., & Blais, M.R. (1995). Toward a new measure of intrinsic motivation, extrinsic motivation, and amotivation in sport: The Sport Motivation Scale (SMS). *Journal of Sport and Exercise Psychology, 17,* 35–53.

Penrod, S. (1986). *Social psychology* (2nd ed.). Englewood Cliffs, NJ: Prentice Hall.

Pensgaard, A.M., & Duda, J. (2003). Sydney 2000: The interplay between emotions, coping, and the performance of Olympic-level athletes. *The Sport Psychologist, 17,* 253–267.

Pensgaard, A.M., & Roberts, G.C. (2000). The relationship between motivational climate, perceived ability and sources of distress among elite athletes. *Journal of Sport Sciences, 18,* 191–200.

Perkos, S., Theodorakis, Y., & Chroni, S. (2002). Enhancing performance and skill acquisition in novice basketball players with instructional self-talk. *The Sport Psychologist, 16,* 368–383.

Perna, F.M., Antoni, M.H., Baum, A., Gordon, P., & Schneiderman, N. (2003). Cognitive behavioral stress management effects on injury and illness among competitive athletes: A randomized clinical trial. *Annuals of Behavioral Medicine, 25*(1), 66–73.

Perreault, S., Gaudreau, P., Lapointe, M.-C., & Lacrois, C. (2007). Does it take three to tango? Psychological need satisfaction and athlete burnout. *International Journal of Sport Psychology, 38,* 437–450.

Perreault, S., Vallerand, R., Montgomery, D., & Provencher, P. (1998). Coming from behind: On the effect of psychological momentum on sport performance. *Journal of Sport and Exercise Psychology, 20,* 421–436.

Perrow, C. (1970). *Organizational analysis: A sociological view.* Belmont, CA: Wadsworth.

Perry, C. (2005). Concentration: Focus under pressure. In S. Murphy (Ed.), *The sport psych handbook* (pp. 113–125). Champaign, IL: Human Kinetics.

Peters, H., & Williams, J. (2006). Moving cultural background to the foreground: An investigation of self-talk, performance, and persistence following feedback. *Journal of Applied Sport Psychology, 18,* 240–253.

Peterson, K., Brown, C., McCann, S., & Murphy, S. (2012). Sport and performance psychology: A look ahead. In S.M. Murphy (Ed.), *The Oxford handbook of sport and performance psychology* (pp. 741–753). Oxford, UK: Oxford University Press.

Petitpas, A., & Danish, S. (1995). Caring for injured athletes. In S. Murphy (Ed.), *Sport psychology interventions* (pp. 255–281). Champaign, IL: Human Kinetics.

Petitpas, A.J., Giges, B., & Danish, S. (1999). The sport psychologist-athlete relationship: Implications for training. *The Sport Psychologist, 13,* 344–357.

Petitpas, A., Tinsley, T., & Walker, A. (2012). Transitions: Ending active sport involvement in sports and other competitive endeavors. In S.M. Murphy (Ed.), *The Oxford handbook of sport and performance psychology* (pp. 513–523). New York: Oxford University Press.

Petlichkoff, L.M. (1996). The drop-out dilemma in youth sports. In O. Bar-Or (Ed.), *The child and adolescent athlete* (pp. 418–430). Cambridge, MA: Blackwell Science.

Petrie, T., & Greenleaf, C. (2007). Eating disorders in sport: From theory to research to intervention. In G. Tenenbaum & R. Eklund (Eds.), *Handbook of sport psychology* (3rd ed., pp. 352–378). Hoboken, NJ: Wiley.

Petrie, T., & Greenleaf, C. (2012). Eating disorders in sport. In S. Murphy (Ed.), *The Oxford handbook of sport and performance psychology* (pp. 635–659). New York: Oxford University Press.

Petrie, T., Greenleaf, C., Reel, J., & Carter, J. (2009). An examination of psychosocial correlates of eating disorders among female intercollegiate athletes. *Research Quarterly for Exercise and Sport, 80,* 621–632.

Petrie, T.A., & Perna, F. (2004). Psychology of injury: Theory, research and practice. In T. Morris & J. Summers (Eds.), *Sport psychology: Theory, application, and issues* (2nd ed., pp. 547–571). Milton, Australia: Wiley.

Pfeiffer, K.A., Dowda, M., Dishman, R.K., McIver, K.L., Sirard, J.R., Ward, D.S., et al. (2006). Sport participation and physical activity in adolescent females across a four-year period. *Journal of Adolescent Health, 39,* 523–529.

Philippen, P., & Lobinger, B. (2012). Understanding the yips in golf: Thoughts, feelings, and focus of attention in yips-affected golfers. *The Sport Psychologist, 26,* 325–340.

Phillippe, R.A., & Seiler, R. (2006). Closeness, co-orientation and complementarity in coach-athlete relationships: What male swimmers say about male coaches. *Psychology of Sport and Exercise, 7,* 159–171.

Piaget, J. (1936). *The moral judgment of the child.* New York: Harcourt & Brace.

Piedmont, R.L., Hill, D.C., & Blanco, S. (1999). Predicting athletic performance using the five-factor model of personality. *Personality and Individual Differences, 27,* 769–777.

Pijpers, J.R., Oudejans, R.R.D., Holsheimer, F., & Bakker, F.C. (2003). Anxiety-performance relationships in climbing: A process-oriented approach. *Psychology of Sport and Exercise, 4,* 283–304.

Pitino, R. (1998). *Success is a choice: Ten steps to overachieving in business and life.* New York: Broadway Books.

Plotnikoff, R., Lippke, S., Courneya, K., Birkett, N., & Sigal, R. (2008). Physical activity and social cognitive theory: A test in a population sample of adults with Type 1 or Type 2 diabetes. *Applied Psychology: An International Review, 57,* 628–643.

Poag-DuCharme, K.A., & Brawley, L.R. (1994). Perceptions of the behavioral influence of goals: A mediational relationship to exercise. *Journal of Applied Sport Psychology, 6,* 32–50.

Podlog, L., & Eklund, R.C. (2006). A longitudinal investigation of competitive athletes' return to sport following injury. *Journal of Applied Sport Psychology, 18,* 44–68.

Podlog, L., & Eklund, R. (2009). High level athletes' perceptions of success in returning to sport following injury. *Psychology of Sport and Exercise, 10,* 535–544.

Podlog, L., & Eklund, R. (2010). Returning to competition following a serious injury: The role of self-determination. *Journal of Sport Sciences, 28,* 819–831.

Pollock, M.L., Foster, C., Salisbury, R., & Smith, R. (1982). Effects of a YMCA starter fitness program. *The Physician and Sportsmedicine, 10,* 89–100.

Polman, R., Pieter, W., Bercades, L., & Ntoumanis, N. (2004). Relationship between psychological and biological factors and physical activity and exercise behavior in Filipino students. *International Journal of Sport and Exercise Psychology, 2,* 63–79.

Pop-Jordanova, N., & Demerdzieva, A. (2010). Biofeedback training for peak performance in sport: A case study. *Macadonian Journal of Medical Sciences, 3,* 115–118.

Post, P., Muncie, S., & Simpson, D. (2012). The effects of imagery training on swimming performance: An applied investigation. *Journal of Applied Sport Psychology, 24,* 323–337.

Post, P., & Wrisberg, C. (2012). A phenomenological investigation of gymnasts' lived experience of imagery. *The Sport Psychologist, 26,* 98–121.

Prapavessis, H. (2000). The POMS and sports performance: A review. *Journal of Applied Sport Psychology, 12,* 34–48.

Prapavessis, H., Carron, A.V., & Spink, K.S. (1997). Team building in sport groups. *International Journal of Sport Psychology, 27,* 269–285.

President's Council on Physical Fitness and Sport. (1996). What you need to know about the surgeon general's report on physical activity and health. *Physical Activity and Fitness Research, 2,* 1–8.

Prestwich, A., Perugini, M., & Hurling, R. (2009). Can implementation intentions and text messages promote brisk walking? A randomized trial. *Health Psychology, 29,* 40–49.

Price, M.S., & Weiss, M.R. (2000). Relationship among coach burnout, coach behaviors, and athletes' psychological responses. *The Sport Psychologist, 14,* 391–409.

Price, M.S., & Weiss, M.R. (2011). Peer leadership in sport: Relations among personal characteristics, leader behaviors, and team outcomes. *Journal of Applied Sport Psychology, 23,* 49–64.

Price, M.S., & Weiss, M.R. (2013). Relationships among coach leadership, peer leadership, and adolescent athletes' psychological and team outcomes: A test of transformational leadership theory. *Journal of Applied Sport Psychology, 25,* 265–279.

Prochaska, J.O., DiClemente, C.C., & Norcross, J.C. (1992). In search of how people change. *American Psychologist, 47,* 1102–1114.

Prochaska, J.O., & Velicer, W.F. (1997). Misinterpretations and misapplications of the transtheoretical model. *American Journal of Health Promotion, 12,* 11–12.

Prochaska, J., Wright, J., & Velicer, W. (2008). Evaluating theories of health behavior change: A hierarchy of criteria applied to the transtheoretical model. *Applied Psychology: An International Review, 57,* 561–588.

Proctor, S., & Boan-Lenzo, C. (2010). Prevalence of depressive symptoms in male intercollegiate student-athletes and non-athletes. *Journal of Clinical Sport Psychology, 4,* 204–220.

Puente, R., & Anshel, M. (2010). Exercisers' perceptions of their fitness instructor's interacting style, perceived competence, and autonomy as a function of self-determined regulation to exercise, enjoyment, affect, and exercise frequency. *Scandinavian Journal of Psychology, 51,* 38–45.

Quested, E., & Duda, J. (2011). Antecedents of burnout among elite dancers: A longitudinal test of basic needs theory. *Psychology of Sport and Exercise, 12,* 159–167.

Quinn, A.M., & Fallon, B.J. (1999). The changes in psychological characteristics and reactions of elite athletes from injury onset until full recovery. *Journal of Applied Sport Psychology, 11,* 210–229.

Rabin, C., Pinto, B., & Frierson, G. (2006). Mediators of a randomized controlled physical activity intervention for breast cancer survivors. *Journal of Sport and Exercise Psychology, 28,* 269–284.

Radzik, L. (2003). Do wrongdoers have a right to make amends? *Social Theory and Practice, 29,* 325–341.

Raedeke, T. (1997). Is athlete burnout more than just stress? A sport commitment perspective. *Journal of Sport and Exercise Psychology, 19*(4), 396–417.

Raedeke, T. (1998). Is athlete burnout more than just stress? A sport commitment perspective. *Journal of Sport and Exercise Psychology, 20*(4), 396–417.

Raedeke, T.D. (2004). Coach commitment and burnout: A one year follow-up. *Journal of Applied Sport Psychology, 16,* 333–349.

Raedeke, T. (2007). The relationship between enjoyment and affective responses to exercise. *Journal of Applied Sport Psychology, 19,* 105–115.

Raedeke, T.D., Granzyk, T.L., & Warren, A. (2000). Why coaches experience burnout: A commitment perspective. *Journal of Sport and Exercise Psychology, 22,* 85–105.

Raedeke, T.D., & Smith, A.L. (2001). Development and preliminary validation of an athlete burnout measure. *Journal of Sport and Exercise Psychology, 23,* 281–306.

Raedeke, T.D., & Smith, A.L. (2004). Coping resources and athlete burnout: An examination of stress: The mediation and moderation hypothesis. *Journal of Sport and Exercise Psychology, 26,* 525–541.

Raedeke, T.D., Smith, A.L., Kentta, G., Arce, C., & de Francisco, D. (2014). Burnout in sport: From theory to practice. In A. Rui Gomes, A. Albuquerque, & R. Resende (Eds.), *Positive human functioning from a multidimensional perspective. Vol. 1: Promoting stress adaptation* (pp. 131-141). Hauppague, NY: Nova.

Raglin, J.S. (1993). Overtraining and staleness: Psychometric monitoring of endurance athletes. In R. Singer, M. Murphey, & K. Tennant (Eds.), *Handbook of sport psychology* (pp. 840–850). New York: Macmillan.

Raglin, J. (2001a). Factors in exercise adherence: Influence of spouse participation. *The Academy Papers: Adherence to Exercise and Physical Activity, 53,* 356–361.

Raglin, J.S. (2001b). Psychological factors in sport performance: The mental health model revisited. *Sports Medicine, 31*(12), 875–890.

Raglin, J.S., Eksten, F., & Garl, T. (1995). Mood state responses to a pre-season conditioning program in male collegiate basketball players. *International Journal of Sport Psychology, 26,* 214–225.

Raglin, J.S., & Morgan, W.P. (1987). Influence of exercise and "distraction therapy" on state anxiety and blood pressure. *Medicine and Science in Sports and Exercise, 19,* 456–463.

Raglin, J.S., & Morgan, W.P. (1989). Development of a scale to measure training-induced distress. *Medicine and Science in Sports and Exercise, 21*(Suppl.), 60.

Raglin, J., Sawamura, S., Alexiou, S., Hassmen, P., & Kentta, G. (2000). Training practices and staleness in 13-18 year old swimmers: A cross-cultural study. *Pediatric Exercise Science, 12,* 61–70.

Raglin, J.S., Stager, J.M., Koceja, D.M., & Harms, C.A. (1996). Changes in mood state, neuromuscular function, and performance during a season of training in female collegiate swimmers. *Medicine and Science in Sports and Exercise, 28,* 372–377.

Ramsey, R., Cumming, J., & Edwards, M. (2008). Exploring a modified conceptualization of imagery direction and golf putting performance. *International Journal of Sport and Exercise Psychology, 6,* 207–223.

Ramsey, R., Cumming, J., Edwards, M., Williams, S., & Brunning, C. (2010). Examining the emotion aspect of PETTLEP-based imagery with penalty kicks in soccer. *Journal of Sport Behavior, 33,* 295–314.

Rata, G., Rata, B., Rata, M., Mares, G., & Melinte, M. (2012). Verbal and nonverbal communication during hammer throw training and competitions. *Ovidius University Annals Series Physical Education and Sport/Science Movement and Health,* Supplement, 370–377.

Rathschiag, M., & Memmert, D. (2013). The influence of self-generated emotions of physical performance: An investigation of happiness, anger, anxiety, and sadness. *Journal of Sport and Exercise Psychology, 35,* 197–210.

Ravizza, K. (2001). Reflections and insights from the field of performance enhancement consulting. In G. Tenenbaum (Ed.), *Reflections and experiences in sport and exercise psychology* (pp. 197–215). Morgantown, WV: Fitness Information Technology.

Reed, J., & Ones, D. (2006). The effect of acute aerobic exercise on positive activated affect: A meta-analysis. *Psychology of Sport and Exercise, 7,* 477–514.

Rees, D.I., & Schnepel, K.T. (2009). College football games and crime. *Journal of Sport Economics, 10*(1), 68–87.

Rees, T. (2007). Influence of social support on athletes. In S. Jowett & D. Lavelle (Eds.), *Social psychology of sport* (pp. 223–232). Champaign, IL: Human Kinetics.

Rees, T., & Hardy, L. (2000). An investigation of the social support experiences of high-level sport performers. *The Sport Psychologist, 14,* 327–347.

Rees, T., & Hardy, L. (2004). Matching social support with stressors: Effects on factors underlying performance in tennis. *Psychology of Sport and Exercise, 5,* 319–337.

Reeves, C., Nicholls, A., & McKenna, J. (2011). The effects of a coping intervention on coping self-efficacy, coping effectiveness, and subjective performance among adolescent soccer players. *International Journal of Sport and Exercise Psychology, 9,* 126–142.

Regier, D.A., Boyd, J.H., Burke, J.D., Rae, D.S., Meyers, J.K., Kramer, M., et al. (1988). One-month prevalence of mental health disorders in the United States. *Archives of General Psychiatry, 45,* 977–986.

Rejeski, W.J., & Brawley, L.R. (1988). Defining the boundaries of sport psychology. *The Sport Psychologist, 2,* 231–242.

Renger, R. (1993). A review of the profile of mood states (POMS) in the prediction of athletic success. *Journal of Applied Sport Psychology, 5,* 78–84.

Rest, J.R. (1984). The major components of morality. In W. Kurines & J. Gewirtz (Eds.), *Morality, moral behavior, and moral development* (pp. 356–429). New York: Wiley.

Rhind, D., & Jowett, S. (2010). Relationship maintenance strategies in the coach-athlete relationship: The development of the COMPASS model. *Journal of Applied Sport Psychology, 22,* 106–121.

Rhodes, R., & Courneya, K. (2005). Assessment of attitude, subjective norm, and perceived behavioral control for predicting exercise intention and behavior. *Psychology of Sport and Exercise, 6,* 349–361.

Rhodes, R.E., Courneya, K.S., & Hayduk, L.A. (2002). Does personality moderate the theory of planned behavior in the exercise domain? *Journal of Sport and Exercise Psychology, 24,* 120–132.

Rhodes, R.E., & Smith, N.E.I. (2006). Personality correlates of physical activity: A review and meta-analysis. *British Journal of Sports Medicine, 40,* 958–965.

Richardson, A. (1967a). Mental practice: A review and discussion (part 1). *Research Quarterly, 38,* 95–107.

Richardson, A. (1967b). Mental practice. A review and discussion (part 2). *Research Quarterly, 38,* 263–273.

Riemer, H., & Chelladurai, P. (1995). Leadership and satisfaction in athletes. *Journal of Sport and Exercise Psychology, 17,* 276–293.

Riley, A., & Anderson-Butcher, D. (2012). Participation in a summer sport-based youth development program for disadvantaged youth: Getting the parent perspective. *Children and Youth Services Review, 34,* 1367–1377.

Riley, P. (1993). *The winner within: A life plan for team players.* New York: Putnam.

Ripol, W. (1993). The psychology of the swimming taper. *Contemporary Psychology on Performance Enhancement, 2,* 22–64.

Roberts, G. (1993). Motivation in sport: Understanding and enhancing the motivation and achievement of children. In R.N. Singer, M. Murphey, & L.K. Tennant (Eds.), *Handbook of sport psychology* (pp. 405–420). New York: Macmillan.

Roberts, J.E. (2001). A philosophy of school sports. In V. Seefeldt, M.A. Clark, & E.W. Brown (Eds.), *Program for athletic coaches' education* (3rd ed., pp. 3–5). Traverse City, MI: Cooper.

Roberts, R., Callow, N., Hardy, L., Woodman, T., & Thomas, L. (2010). Interactive effects of different visual imagery perspectives and narcissism on motor performance. *Journal of Sport and Exercise Psychology, 32,* 499–517.

Roberts, R., Rotherman, M., Maynard, I., Thomas, O., & Woodman, T. (2013). Perfectionism and the "yips": An initial investigation. *The Sport Psychologist, 27,* 53–61.

Roberts, R., Woodman, T., Hardy, L., Davis, L., & Wallace, H. (2013). Psychological skills do not always help performance: The moderating rose of narcissism. *Journal of Applied Sport Psychology, 25,* 316–325.

Robin, N., Dominique, L., Toussaint, L., Blandin, Y., Guillot, A., & Le Her, M. (2007). Effects of motor imagery training on service return accuracy in tennis: The role of image ability. *International Journal of Sport and Exercise Psychology, 2,* 175–186.

Roche, P. (1995, August). Second gold medal for Smith. *Irish Times.*

Rodgers, W., Hall, C.R., & Buckholtz, E. (1991). The effect of an imagery training program on imagery ability, imagery use, and figure skating performance. *Journal of Applied Sport Psychology, 3,* 109–125.

Roese, N., Sanna, L., & Galinsky, A. (2005). The mechanics of imagination: Automaticity and control in counterfactual thinking. In R. Hassin, J. Uleman, & J. Baugh (Eds.), *The new unconscious* (pp. 138–170). New York: Oxford University Press.

Rojas, R., Schlicht, W., & Hautinger, M. (2003). Effects of exercise training on quality of life, psychological well-being, immune status, and cardiopulmonary fitness in an HIV-1 positive population. *Journal of Sport and Exercise Psychology, 25,* 440–455.

Romance, T.J., Weiss, M.R., & Bockoven, J. (1986). A program to promote moral development through elementary school physical education. *Journal of Teaching Physical Education, 5,* 126–136.

Ronglan, L. (2007). Building and communicating collective efficacy: A season-long in-depth study of an elite sport team. *The Sport Psychologist, 21,* 78–93.

Roper, E. (2012a). Gender, identity and sport. In S. Murphy (Ed.), *The Oxford handbook of sport and performance psychology* (pp. 384–399). New York: Oxford University Press.

Roper, E. (2012b). *Gender relations in sport.* Boston: Sense Publishers.

Rosen, C.S. (2000a). Integrating stage and continuum models to explain processing of exercise messages and exercise initiation. *Health Psychology, 19,* 172–180.

Rosen, C.S. (2000b). Is the sequencing of change processes by stage consistent across health problems? A meta-analysis. *Health Psychology, 19,* 593–604.

Rosenfeld, L.B., & Richman, J.M. (1997). Developing effective social support: Team building and the social support process. *The Sport Psychologist, 9,* 133–153.

Rosenfeld, L., & Wilder, L. (1990). Communication fundamentals: Active listening. *Sport Psychology Training Bulletin, 1*(5), 1–8.

Rosenthal, R., & Jacobson, L. (1968). *Pygmalion in the classroom: Teacher expectations and pupils' intellectual development.* New York: Holt, Rinehart & Winston.

Roseth, C., Johnson, D., & Johnson, R. (2008). Promoting early adolescents' achievement and peer relationships: The effects of cooperative, competitive and individualistic goal structures. *Psychological Bulletin, 134,* 223–246.

Ross, M.S. (1992, Summer). Good sports report. *Fantastic Flyer,* pp. 16–17.

Ross-Stewart, L., & Short, S. (2009). The frequency and perceived effectiveness of images used to build, maintain, and regain confidence. *Journal of Applied Sport Psychology, 21*(Suppl. 1), s34–s47.

Rotella, R., & Heyman, S. (1986). Stress, injury, and the psychological rehabilitation of athletes. In J.M. Williams (Ed.) *Applied sport psychology: Personal growth to peak performance* (pp. 343-364). Mountain View, CA: Palo Alto.

Rotheram, M., Maynard, I., Thomas, O., Bawden, M., & Francis, L. (2012). Preliminary evidence for the treatment of Type I "yips": The efficacy of the Emotional Freedom Technique. *The Sport Psychologist, 26,* 551–570.

Rottensteiner, C., Laakso, L., Pihlaja, T., & Konttinen, N. (2013). Personal reasons for withdrawal from team sports and the influence of significant others among youth athletes. *International Journal of Sports Science and Coaching, 8*(1), 19–32.

Rousseau, V., Aubé, C., & Savoie, A. (2006). Teamwork behaviors: A review and an integration of frameworks. *Small Group Research, 37,* 540–570.

Rovinak, L., Sallis, J., Saelens, B., Frank, L., Marshall, S., Norman, G., et al. (2010). Adults' physical activity patterns across life domains: Cluster analysis with replication. *Health Psychology, 29,* 496–505.

Rovio, E., Arviven-Barrow, M., Weigand, D., Eskola, J., & Lintunen, T. (2012). Using team building methods with an ice hockey team: An action research case study. *The Sport Psychologist, 26,* 584–603.

Rowley, A.J., Landers, D.M., Kyllo, L.B., & Etnier, J.L. (1995). Does the iceberg profile discriminate between successful and less successful athletes? A meta-analysis. *Journal of Sport and Exercise Psychology, 17,* 185–199.

Ruby, M., Dunn, E., Perrino, A., Gillis, R., & Viel, S. (2011). The invisible benefits of exercise. *Health Psychology, 30,* 67–74.

Rudd, A., & Gordon, B.S. (2009). An exploratory investigation of sportsmanship attitudes among college student basketball fans. *Journal of Sport Behavior, 33*(4), 466–488.

Ruffer, W.A. (1976a). Personality traits of athletes. *Physical Educator, 33*(1), 50–55.

Ruffer, W.A. (1976b). Personality traits of athletes. *Physical Educator, 33*(4), 211–214.

Rumbold, J., Fletcher, D., & Daniels, K. (2012). A systematic review of stress management interventions with sport performers. *Sport, Exercise, and Performance Psychology, 1,* 173–193.

Rushall, B.S., Hall, M., & Rushall, A. (1988). Effects of three types of thought content instructions on skiing performance. *The Sport Psychologist, 2,* 283–297.

Russell, G.W., & Arms, R.L. (1995). False consensus effect, physical aggression, anger, and a willingness to escalate a disturbance. *Aggressive Behavior, 21,* 381–386.

Ryan, E.D. (1977). Attribution, intrinsic motivation, and athletics. In L.I. Gedvilas & M.E. Kneer (Eds.), *Proceedings of the NAPECW/NCPEAM national conference* (pp. 346–353). Chicago: Office of Publications Services, University of Illinois at Chicago Circle.

Ryan, E.D. (1980). Attribution, intrinsic motivation, and athletics: A replication and extension. In C.H. Nadeau, W.R. Halliwell, K.M. Newell, & G.C. Roberts (Eds.), *Psychology of motor behavior and sport—1979* (pp. 19–26). Champaign, IL: Human Kinetics.

Ryan, J. (1995). *Little girls in pretty boxes: The making and breaking of elite gymnasts and figure skaters.* New York: Doubleday.

Ryan, R.M., & Deci, E.L. (2000). Self-determination theory and the facilitation of intrinsic motivation, social development and well-being. *American Psychologist, 55,* 68–78.

Ryan, R., & Deci, E. (2002). An overview of self-determination theory: An organismic-dialectical perspective. In E.L. Deci & R.M. Ryan (Eds.), *Handbook of self-determination research* (pp. 3–53). Rochester, NY: University of Rochester Press.

Ryba, T., Stambulova, N., & Wrisberg, C. (2005). The Russian origins of sport psychology: A translation of an early work of A.C. Puni. *Journal of Applied Sport Psychology, 17,* 156–169.

Sachs, M.L. (1980). On the trail of the runner's high—A descriptive and experimental investigation of characteristics of an elusive phenomenon. (Unpublished doctoral dissertation). Tallahassee, FL: Florida State University.

Sachs, M.L. (1981). Running addiction. In M.H. Sacks & M.L. Sachs (Eds.), *Psychology of running* (pp. 116–121). Champaign, IL: Human Kinetics.

Sachs, M.L. (1984). The runner's high. In M.L. Sachs & G.W. Buffone (Eds.), *Running as therapy: An integrated approach* (pp. 273–287). Lincoln: University of Nebraska Press.

Sachs, M.L., & Pargman, D. (1984). Running addiction. In M.L. Sachs & G.W. Buffone (Eds.), *Running as therapy: An integrated approach* (pp. 231–253). Lincoln: University of Nebraska Press.

Sackett, R.S. (1934). The influences of symbolic rehearsal upon the retention of a maze habit. *Journal of General Psychology, 13,* 113–128.

Sadeh, A., Keinan, G., & Daon, K. (2004). Effects of stress on sleep: The moderating role of coping style. *Health Psychology, 23,* 542–543.

Sage, G. (1977). *Introduction to motor behavior: A neuropsychological approach* (2nd ed.). Reading, MA: Addison-Wesley.

Sage, G. (1978). Humanistic psychology and coaching. In W.F. Straub (Ed.), *Sport psychology: An analysis of athlete behavior* (pp. 215–228). Ithaca, NY: Mouvement.

Sallis, J.F. (2000). Environmental influences on physical activity: Applying ecological models. *Journal of Sport and Exercise Psychology, 22,* 51.

Sallis, J.F., Haskell, W.L., Fortmann, S.P., Vranizan, K.M., Taylor, C.B., & Solomon, D.S. (1986). Predictors of adoption and maintenance of physical activity in a community sample. *Preventive Medicine, 15,* 331–341.

Sallis, J.F., & Owen, N. (1999). *Physical activity and behavioral medicine.* Thousand Oaks, CA: Sage.

Sallis, J.F., Prochaska, J.J., & Taylor, W.C. (2000). A review of correlates of physical activity of children and adolescents. *Medicine and Science in Sports and Exercise, 32,* 963–975.

Salmon, J., Hall, C., & Haslam, I. (1994). The use of imagery in soccer players. *Journal of Applied Sport Psychology, 6,* 116–133.

Sambolec, E., Kerr, N., & Messe, L. (2007). The role of competitiveness at social tasks: Can indirect cues enhance performance? *Journal of Applied Sport Psychology, 19,* 160–172.

Samson, A., & Solomon, M. (2011). Examining the sources of self-efficacy for physical activity within the sport and exercise domains. *International Review of Sport and Exercise Psychology, 4,* 70–89.

Sanford-Martens, T., Davidson, M., Yakushko, O., Martens, M., Hinton, P., & Beck, N. (2005). Clinical and subclinical eating disorders: An examination of collegiate athletes. *Journal of Applied Sport Psychology, 17,* 79–86.

Sarason, I.G. (1975). Test anxiety and the self-disclosing coping model. *Journal of Consulting and Clinical Psychology, 43,* 148-153.

Sathre, S., Olson, R.W., & Whitney, C.I. (1973). *Let's talk.* Glenview, IL: Scott, Foresman.

Savelsbergh, G.P., Whiting, H.T.A., & Pijpers, J.R. (1992). The control of catching. In J.J. Summers (Ed.), *Approaches to the study of motor control and learning* (pp. 313–342). Amsterdam: North-Holland.

Savvidou, I., Lazaras, L., & Tsorbatzoudia, H. (2012). Social cognitive predictors of exercise intentions among substance users in recovery. *Journal of Applied Sport Psychology, 24,* 48–58.

Scanlan, T.K. (1986). Competitive stress in children. In M.R. Weiss & D. Gould (Eds.), *Sport for children and youths* (pp. 113–118). Champaign, IL: Human Kinetics.

Scanlan, T.K. (1988). Social evaluation and the competition process: A developmental perspective. In F.L. Smoll, R.A. Magill, & M.J. Ash (Eds.), *Children in sport* (3rd ed., pp. 135–148). Champaign, IL: Human Kinetics.

Schachter, S. (1966). The interaction of cognitive and physiological determinants of emotional state. In C.D. Spielberger (Ed.), *Anxiety and behavior* (pp. 49–80). New York: Academic Press.

Schack, T., Whitmarsh, B., Pike, R., & Redden, C. (2005). Routines. In J. Taylor & G. Wilson (Eds.), *Applying sport psychology: Four perspectives* (pp. 137–150). Champaign, IL: Human Kinetics.

Scherf, J., & Franklin, B. (1987). Exercise compliance: A data documentation system. *Journal of Physical Education, Recreation and Dance, 58,* 26–28.

Scherzer, C.B., Brewer, B.W., Cornelius, A.E., Van Raalte, J.L., Petitpas, A.J., Sklar, J.H., et al. (2001). Psychological skills and adherence to rehabilitation after reconstruction of the anterior cruciate ligament. *Journal of Sport Rehabilitation, 10,* 165–172.

Schmid, A., Peper, E., & Wilson, V. (2001). Strategies for training concentration. In J.M. Williams (Ed.), *Applied sport psychology: Personal growth to peak performance* (4th ed., pp. 333–346). Mountain View, CA: Mayfield.

Schmidt, G.W., & Stein, G.L. (1991). Sport commitment: A model integrating enjoyment, dropout, and burnout. *Journal of Sport and Exercise Psychology, 8,* 254–265.

Schmidt, R.A., & Wrisberg, C. (2004). *Motor learning and performance* (4th ed.). Champaign, IL: Human Kinetics.

Schmidt, U., McGuire, R., Humphrey, S., Williams, G., & Grawer, B. (2005). Team cohesion. In J. Taylor & G. Wilson (Eds.), *Applying sport psychology: Four perspectives* (pp. 171–183). Champaign, IL: Human Kinetics.

Schneider, M., Dunton, G., & Cooper, D. (2008). Physical activity and physical self-concept among sedentary adolescent females: An intervention study. *Psychology of Sport and Exercise, 9,* 1–14.

Schroeder, P.J. (2010). Changing team culture: The perspectives of ten successful head coaches. *Journal of Sport Behavior, 33*(1), 63–87.

Schucker, L., Hagemann, N., Strauss, B., & Volker, K. (2009). The effect of attentional focus on economy of running. *Journal of Sport Sciences, 27,* 1241–1248.

Schultz, J., & Luthe, W. (1969). *Autogenic methods* (Vol. 1). New York: Grune & Stratton.

Schurr, K.T., Ashley, M.A., & Joy, K.L. (1977). A multivariate analysis of male athlete characteristics: Sport type and success. *Multivariate Experimental Clinical Research, 3,* 53–68.

Schwarzer, R. (1992). Self-efficacy in the adoption and maintenance of health behaviors: Theoretical approaches and a new model. In R. Schwarzer (Ed.), *Self-efficacy: Thought control of action* (pp. 217–243). Washington, DC: Hemisphere.

Scott, S. (1999, July). Out of the woods. *SportsWrite,* pp. 44–48.

Seabourne, T., Weinberg, R.S., Jackson, A., & Suinn, R.M. (1985). Effect of individualized, nonindividualized, and package intervention strategies on karate performance. *Journal of Sport Psychology, 7,* 40–50.

Sebire, S., Standage, M., Gillison, F., & Vanteenkiste, M. (2013). "Coveting thy neighbour's legs": A qualitative study of exercisers' experiences of intrinsic and extrinsic goal pursuit. *Journal of Sport and Exercise Psychology, 35,* 308–321.

Sebire, S., Standage, M., & Vansteenkiste, M. (2009). Examining intrinsic versus extrinsic exercise goals: Cognitive, affective, and behavioral outcomes. *Journal of Sport and Exercise Psychology, 31,* 189–210.

Sebire, S., Standage, M., & Vansteenkiste, M. (2012). Predicting objectively assessed physical activity from the content and regulation of exercise goals: Evidence for a meditational model. *Journal of Sport and Exercise Psychology, 33,* 175–197.

Sedula, M.K., Collins, M.E., & Williamson, D.F. (1993). Weight control practices of United States adolescents and adults. *Annals of Internal Medicine, 119,* 667–671.

Seefeldt, V.D., & Ewing, M.E. (1997). Youth sports in America. *President's Council on Physical Fitness and Sports Research Digest, 2*(11), 1–11.

Seifried, C. (2008). Examining punishment and discipline: Defending the use of punishment by coaches. *Quest, 60,* 370–386.

Selby, C., & Reel, J. (2011). A coach's guide to identifying and helping athletes with eating disorders. *Journal of Sport Psychology in Action, 2,* 100–112.

Seligman, M., & Csikszentmihalyi, M. (2002). Positive psychology: An introduction. *American Psychologist, 55*(1), 5–14.

Selk, J. (2009). *10-minute toughness.* New York: McGraw-Hill.

Senecal, J., Loughead, T.M., & Bloom, G.A. (2008). A season-long team-building intervention: Examining the effect of team goal setting on cohesion. *Journal of Sport and Exercise Psychology, 30,* 186–199.

Shambrook, C.J., & Bull, C.J. (1999). Adherence to psychological preparation in sport. In S.J. Bull (Ed.), *Adherence issues in sport and exercise* (pp. 169–196). West Sussex, UK: Wiley.

Shankly, B. (1981, Oct 4th). *Sunday Times,* UK.

Shanmugam, V., Jowett, S., & Meyer, C. (2012). Eating psychopathology amongst athletes: The importance of relationships with parents, coaches and teammates. *International Journal of Sport and Exercise Psychology, 11,* 24–38.

Shapcott, K.M., Carron, A.V., Greenlees, I., & Hakim, Y.E. (2010). Determinants of team-referent attributions: A multilevel analysis. *International Journal of Sport and Exercise Psychology, 8,* 227–244.

Sharp, L., & Hodge, K. (2011). Sport psychology consulting effectiveness: The sport psychology consultant's perspective. *Journal of Applied Sport Psychology, 23,* 360–376.

Sheard, M., & Golby, J. (2010). Personality hardiness differentiates elite-level sport performers. *International Journal of Sport and Exercise Psychology, 8,* 160–169.

Sheard, M., Golby, J., & van Wersch, A. (2009). Progress toward construct validation of the sports mental toughness questionnaire (SMTQ). *European Journal of Psychological Assessment, 25,* 186–193.

Shearer, D., Holmes, P., & Mellalieu, S. (2009). Collective efficacy in sport: The future from a social neuroscience perspective. *International Review of Sport and Exercise Psychology, 2,* 38–53.

Sheehan, G. (1979). Negative addiction: A runner's perspective. *The Physician and Sportsmedicine, 7*(6), 49.

Sheldon, J.P., & Aimar, C.M. (2001). The role aggression plays in successful and unsuccessful ice hockey behaviors. *Research Quarterly for Exercise and Sport, 72,* 304–309.

Shepard, R. (1996). Habitual physical activity and quality of life. *Quest, 48,* 354–365.

Sherif, M., & Sherif, C.W. (1969). *Social psychology.* New York: Harper & Row.

Sherman, R., & Thompson, R. (2001). Athletes and disordered eating: Four major issues for the professional psychologist. *Professional Psychology: Research and Practice, 32,* 1.

Shields, D.L.L., & Bredemeier, B.J.L. (1995). *Character development and physical activity.* Champaign, IL: Human Kinetics.

Shields, D.L.L., & Bredemeier, B.J.L. (2001). Moral development and behavior in sport. In R. Singer, H. Hausenblas, & C. Janelle (Eds.), *Handbook of sport psychology* (2nd ed., pp. 585–603). New York: Wiley.

Shields, D.L., & Bredemeier, B.L. (2007). Advances in sport morality research. In G. Tenenbaum and R.C. Eklund (Eds.). *Handbook of sport psychology* (pp. 662-684). Hoboken, NJ: John Wiley & Sons.

Shields, D., & Bredemeier, B. (2009). *True competition: A guide to pursuing excellence in sport and society.* Champaign, IL: Human Kinetics.

Shields, D.L., LaVoi, N.M., Bredemeier, B.J.L., & Power, F.C. (2005). The sport behavior of youth, parents and coaches: The good, the bad, and the ugly. *Journal of Research in Character Education, 3,* 43–59.

Shields, D.L., LaVoi, N.M., Bredemeier, B.J.L., & Power, F.C. (2007). Predictors of poor sportspersonship in youth sports: Personal attitudes and social influences. *Journal of Sport and Exercise Psychology, 29,* 747–763.

Shilts, M.K., Horowitz, M., & Townsend, M.S. (2004). An innovative approach to goal setting for adolescents: Guided goal setting. *Journal of Nutritional Education and Behavior, 36,* 155–156.

Shoenfelt, E. (2010). "Values added" teambuilding: A process to ensure understanding and commitment to team values. *Journal of Sport Psychology in Action, 1,* 150–160.

Short, S., Monsma, E., & Short, M. (2004). Is what you see really what you get? Athletes' perceptions of imagery's functions. *The Sport Psychologist, 18,* 341–349.

Short, S., & Short, M. (2005). Differences between high-and-low confident football players on imagery function: A consideration of the athletes' perceptions. *Journal of Applied Sport Psychology, 17,* 197–208.

Shumaker, S.A., & Brownell, A. (1984). Toward a theory of social support: Closing conceptual gaps. *Journal of Social Issues, 40,* 11–36.

Sibley, B., & Beilock, S. (2007). Exercise and working memory: An individual differences investigation. *Journal of Sport and Exercise Psychology, 29,* 783–791.

Siedentop, D. (1980). The management of practice behavior. In W.F. Straub (Ed.), *Sport psychology: An analysis of athlete behavior* (2nd ed.). Ithaca, NY: Mouvement.

Silva, J.M. (1980). Understanding aggressive behavior and its effects upon athletic performance. In W.F. Straub (Ed.), *Sport psychology: An analysis of athlete behavior* (2nd ed.). Ithaca, NY: Mouvement.

Silva, J.M. (1982). Competitive sport environments: Performance enhancement through cognitive intervention. *Behavior Modification, 6,* 443–463.

Silva, J.M. (1990). An analysis of the training stress syndrome in competitive athletics. *Journal of Applied Sport Psychology, 2,* 5–20.

Silva, J.M. (2001). Current trends and future directions in sport psychology. In R. Singer, H. Hausenblas, & C. Janelle (Eds.), *Handbook of sport psychology* (2nd ed., pp. 823–832). New York: Wiley.

Simek, T.C., O'Brien, R.M., & Figlerski, L.B. (1994). Contracting and chaining to improve the performance of a college golf team: Improvement and deterioration. *Perceptual and Motor Skills, 78,* 1099–1105.

Simon, J., & Martens, R. (1979). Children's anxiety in sport and nonsport evaluative activities. *Journal of Sport Psychology, 1*(1), 160–169.

Simonds, C. (1997). Classroom understanding: An expanded notion of teacher clarity. *Communication Research Reports, 14,* 279–290.

Simons, J. (2000). Doing imagery in the field. In M. Andersen (Ed.), *Doing sport psychology* (pp. 77–92). Champaign, IL: Human Kinetics.

Simons, J. (2013). The applied sport psychology intake. In S. Hanrahan & M. Andersen (Eds.), *Routledge handbook of applied sport psychology* (pp. 81–89). New York: Routledge.

Simonton, O.C., Matthews-Simonton, S., & Creighton, J.L. (1978). *Getting well again.* New York: Bantam.

Singer, R.N. (1988). Psychological testing: What value to coaches and athletes? *International Journal of Sport Psychology, 19,* 87–106.

Singer, R.N. (1996). Future of sport and exercise psychology. In J.L. Van Raalte & B.W. Brewer (Eds.), *Exploring sport and exercise psychology* (pp. 451–468). Washington, DC: American Psychological Association.

Singer, R.N. (2002). Preperformance state, routines, and automaticity: What does it take to realize expertise in self-paced events? *Journal of Sport and Exercise Psychology, 24,* 359–375.

Singer, R.N., & Anshel, M.H. (2006). An overview of interventions in sport. In J. Dosil (Ed.), *The sport psychologist's handbook: A guide for sport-specific performance enhancement* (pp. 63–88). New York: Wiley.

Singley, K.I., Hale, B.D., & Russell, D.M. (2012). Heart rate, anxiety, and hardiness (tandem) and experienced (Solo) Skydivers. *Journal of Sport Behavior, 35*(4), 453–469.

Sirard, J.R., Pfeiffer, K.A., & Pate, R.R. (2006). Motivational factors associated with sports program participation in middle school children. *Journal of Adolescent Health, 38,* 696–703.

Skinner, B.F. (1968). *The technology of teaching.* New York: Appleton-Century-Crofts.

Slade, J.M., Landers, D.M., & Martin, P.E. (2002). Muscular activity during real and imagined movements: A test of inflow explanations. *Journal of Sport and Exercise Psychology, 24,* 151–167.

Smith, A. (1997). Peer relationships in physical activity participation in early adolescence. (Unpublished doctoral dissertation). Eugene, OR: University of Oregon.

Smith, A. (1999). Perceptions of peer relationships and physical activity in early adolescence. *Journal Sport and Exercise Psychology, 21,* 329–350.

Smith, A. (2007). Youth peer relationships in sport. In S. Jowett & D. Lavallee (Eds.), *Social psychology in sport* (pp. 41–54). Champaign, IL: Human Kinetics.

Smith, A.L., Gustafsson, H., & Hassmen, P. (2010). Peer motivational climate and burnout perceptions of adolescent athletes. *Psychology of Sport and Exercise, 11,* 453–460.

Smith, D., & Holmes, P. (2004). The effect of imagery modality on golf putting performance. *Journal of Sport and Exercise Psychology, 26,* 385–395.

Smith, D., Wright, A., Allsopp, A., & Westhead, H. (2007). It's all in the mind: PETTLEP-based imagery and sports performance. *Journal of Applied Sport Psychology, 19,* 80–92.

Smith, D., Wright, C.J., & Cantwell, C. (2008). Beating the bunker: The effect of PETTLEP imagery on golf bunker shot performance. *Research Quarterly for Exercise and Sport, 79,* 1–7.

Smith, G. (2012, Dec.). Stand up, speak out. *Sports Illustrated,* pp. 66–76.

Smith, H.W. (1994). *The 10 natural laws of successful time and life management: Proven strategies for increased productivity and inner peace.* New York: Warner.

Smith, M.D. (1983). *Violence and sport.* Toronto, ON: Butterworths.

Smith, M.D. (1988). Interpersonal sources of violence in hockey: The influence of parents, coaches, and teammates. In F.L. Smoll, R.A. Magill, & M.J. Ash (Eds.), *Children in sport* (3rd ed., pp. 301–313). Champaign, IL: Human Kinetics.

Smith, R.A., & Biddle, S.J.H. (1995). Psychological factors in the promotion of physical activity. In S.J.H. Biddle (Ed.), *European perspectives on exercise and sport psychology* (pp. 85–108). Champaign, IL: Human Kinetics.

Smith, R.E. (1980). A cognitive-affective approach to stress management training for athletes. In C.H. Nadeau, W.R. Halliwell, K.M. Newell, & G.C. Roberts (Eds.), *Psychology of motor behavior and sport—1979* (pp. 54–72). Champaign, IL: Human Kinetics.

Smith, R.E. (1986). Toward a cognitive-affective model of athletic burnout. *Journal of Sport Psychology, 8,* 36–50.

Smith, R.E. (1989). Applied sport psychology in the age of accountability. *Journal of Applied Sport Psychology, 1,* 166–180.

Smith, R.E. (2006). Positive reinforcement, performance feedback, and performance enhancement. In J.M. Williams (Ed.), *Applied sport psychology: Personal growth to peak performance* (5th ed., pp. 40–56). Mountain View, CA: Mayfield.

Smith, R.E., & Christensen, D.S. (1995). Psychological skills as predictors of performance and survival in professional baseball. *Journal of Sport and Exercise Psychology, 17,* 399–415.

Smith, R.E., Ptacek, J.T., & Patterson, E. (2000). Moderator effects of cognitive and somatic trait anxiety on the relation between life stress and physical injuries. *Anxiety, Stress, and Coping, 13,* 269–288.

Smith, R., & Rohsenow, D. (2011). *Cognitive-affective stress management training: A treatment and resource manual.* (Unpublished document). Seattle: University of Washington.

Smith, R.E., Schutz, R.W., Smoll, F.L., & Ptacek, J.T. (1995). Development and validation of a multidimensional measure of sport-specific psychological skills: The Athletic Coping Skills Inventory-26. *Journal of Sport and Exercise Psychology, 17,* 379–398.

Smith, R.E., & Smoll, F.L. (1990). Athletic performance anxiety. In H. Leitenberg (Ed.), *Handbook of social and evaluation anxiety* (pp. 417–454). New York: Plenum Press.

Smith, R.E., & Smoll, F.L. (1996). *Way to go, coach: A scientifically-proven approach to coaching effectiveness.* Portola Valley, CA: Warde.

Smith, R.E., & Smoll, F.L. (1997). Coach-mediated team building in youth sports. *Journal of Applied Sport Psychology, 9,* 114–132.

Smith, R.E., Smoll, F.L., & Cumming, S.P. (2007). Effects of a motivational climate intervention for coaches on young athletes' sport performance anxiety. *Journal of Sport and Exercise Psychology, 29,* 39–59.

Smith, R.E., Smoll, F.L., Cumming, S.P., & Grossbard (2006). Measurement of multidimensional performance anxiety in children and adults: The Sport Anxiety Scale-2. *Journal of Sport and Exercise Psychology, 21,* 131–147.

Smith, R.E., Smoll, F.L., & Curtis, B. (1979). Coach effectiveness training: A cognitive-behavioral approach to enhancing relationship skills in youth sport coaches. *Journal of Sport Psychology, 1,* 59–75.

Smith, R., Smoll, F., & O'Rourke, D. (2011). Anxiety management. In T. Morris & P. Terry (Eds.), *The new sport and exercise psychology companion* (pp. 227–255). Morgantown, WV: Fitness Information Technology.

Smith, R.E., Smoll, F.L., & Ptacek, J.T. (1990). Conjunctive moderator variables in vulnerability and resiliency research: Life stress, social support and coping skills, and adolescent sport injuries. *Journal of Personality and Social Psychology, 58*(2), 360–369.

Smith, R.E., Smoll, F.L., & Schutz, R.W. (1990). Measurement and correlates of sport-specific cognitive and somatic trait anxiety: The Sport Anxiety Scale. *Anxiety Research, 2,* 263–280.

Smoll, F.L., & Smith, R.E. (1979). *Improving relationship skills in youth sport coaches.* East Lansing, MI: Michigan Institute for the Study of Youth Sports.

Smoll, F.L., & Smith, R.E. (1980). Psychologically oriented coach training programs: Design, implementation, and assessment. In C.H. Nadeau, W.R. Halliwell, K.M. Newell, & G.C. Roberts (Eds.), *Psychology of motor behavior and sport—1979* (pp. 112–129). Champaign, IL: Human Kinetics.

Smoll, F.L., & Smith, R.E. (1989). Leadership behaviors in sport: A theoretical model and research paradigm. *Journal of Applied Social Psychology, 19,* 1522–1551.

Smoll, F.L., & Smith, R.E. (1996). *Coaches who never lose: A 30-minute primer for coaching effectiveness.* Portola Valley, CA: Warde.

Smoll, F.L., & Smith, R.E. (2001). Conducting sport psychology training programs for coaches: Cognitive-behavioral principles and techniques. In J.M. Williams (Ed.), *Applied sport psychology: Personal growth to peak performance* (4th ed., pp. 378–400). Mountain View, CA: Mayfield.

Smoll, F., & Smith, R. (2009). *Mastery approach to coaching: A leadership guide for youth sports.* Seattle: Youth Enrichment in Sports.

Snyder, C.R. (1994). *The psychology of hope.* New York: Free Press.

Solberg, E., Berglund, K., Engen, O., Ekeberg, O., & Loeb, M. (1996). The effect of meditation on shooting performance. *British Journal of Sports Medicine, 30,* 342–346.

Solberg, E., Ingjer, F., Holen, A., Sundgot-Borgenm, J., Nilsson, S., & Holme, I. (2000). Stress reactivity to and recovery from a standardized exercise bout: A study of 31 runners practicing relaxation techniques. *British Journal of Sports Medicine, 34,* 268–272.

Solomon, G. (2008a). The assessment of athletic ability in intercollegiate sport: Instrument construction and validation. *International Journal of Sport Science and Coaching, 3,* 509–521.

Solomon, G. (2008b). Expectations and perceptions as predictors of coaches' feedback in three competitive contexts. *Journal for the Study of Sports and Athletics in Education, 2,* 161–189.

Solomon, G. (2010). The assessment of athletic ability at the junior college level. *International Journal of Sport Science and Coaching, 53,* 37–46.

Solomon, G., DiMarco, A., Ohlson, C., & Reese, S. (1998). Expectations and coaching experience: Is more better? *Journal of Sport Behavior, 21,* 444–455.

Solomon, G., Golden, A., Ciaponni, T., & Martin, A. (1998). Coach expectations and differential feedback: Perceptual flexibility revisited. *Journal of Sport Behavior, 21,* 298–310.

Solomon, G., Striegel, D., Eliot, J., Heon, S., & Maas, J. (1996). The self-fulfilling prophecy in college basketball: Implications for effective coaching. *Journal of Applied Sport Psychology, 8,* 44–59.

Sonstroem, R.J. (1984). Exercise and self-esteem. *Exercise and Sport Sciences Reviews, 12,* 123–155.

Sonstroem, R.J. (1997a). Physical activity and self-esteem. In W.P. Morgan (Ed.), *Physical activity and mental health* (pp. 127–143). Washington, DC: Hemisphere.

Sonstroem, R.J. (1997b). The physical self-system: A mediator of exercise and self-esteem. In K.R. Fox (Ed.), *The physical self: From motivation to well-being* (pp. 3–26). Champaign, IL: Human Kinetics.

Sonstroem, R.J., Harlow, L.L., & Josephs, L. (1994). Exercise and self-esteem: Validity of model expansion and exercise association. *Journal of Sport and Exercise Psychology, 16,* 29–42.

Sonstroem, R.J., & Morgan, W.P. (1989). Exercise and self-esteem: Rationale and model. *Medicine and Science in Sports and Exercise, 21,* 329–337.

Sordoni, C., Hall, C., & Forwell, L. (2000). The use of imagery by athletes during injury rehabilitation. *Journal of Sport Rehabilitation, 9,* 329–338.

Sorrentino, R.M., & Sheppard, B.H. (1978). Effects of affiliation-related motives on swimmers in individual versus group competition: A field experiment. *Journal of Personality and Social Psychology, 36*(7), 704–714.

Spence, J.C., McGannon, K., & Poon, P. (2005). The effect of exercise on global self-esteem: A quantitative review. *Journal of Sport and Exercise Psychology, 27,* 311–334.

Spence, J.T., & Spence, K.W. (1966). The motivational components of manifest anxiety: Drive and drive stimuli. In C.D. Spielberger (Ed.), *Anxiety and behavior* (pp. 291–326). New York: Academic Press.

Spencer, L., Adams, T., Malone, S., Roy, L., & Yost, E. (2006). Applying the transtheoretical model to exercise: A systematic and comprehensive review of the literature. *Health Promotion Practice, 7,* 428–443.

Spielberger, C.D. (1966). Theory and research on anxiety. In C.D. Spielberger (Ed.), *Anxiety and behavior* (pp. 3–22). New York: Academic Press.

Spink, K.S., & Carron, A.V. (1992). Group cohesion and adhesion in exercise classes. *Journal of Sport and Exercise Psychology, 14,* 78–86.

Spink, K.S., & Carron, A.V. (1993). The effects of team building on the adherence patterns of female exercise participants. *Journal of Sport and Exercise Psychology, 15,* 50–62.

Spino, M. (1971). Running as a spiritual experience. In J. Scott (Ed.), *The athletic revolution* (p. 222). New York: Free Press.

Spittle, M., & Morris, T. (2007). Internal and external imagery perspective measurement and use in imaging open and closed sport skills: An exploratory study. *Perceptual and Motor Skills, 104,* 387–404.

Stajkoviv, A., Lee, D., & Nyberg, A. (2009). Collective efficacy, group potency, and group performance: Meta-analyses of their relationships, and test of the mediation model. *Journal of Applied Psychology, 94,* 814–828.

Stambulova, N., Alfermann, D., Statler, T., & Cote, J. (2009). ISSP position stand: Career development and transitions of athletes. *International Journal of Sport and Exercise Psychology, 7,* 292–308.

Stambulova, N., Wrisberg, C.A., & Ryba, T.V. (2006). A tale of two traditions in applied sport psychology: The heyday of Soviet sport and wake-up calls for North America. *Journal of Applied Sport Psychology, 18,* 173–184.

Standage, M. (2012). Motivation: Self-determination theory and performance in sports. In S. Murphy (Ed.), *Oxford handbook of sport and performance psychology* (pp. 233–249). New York: Oxford Press.

Standage, M., Sebire, S., & Loney, T. (2008). Does exercise motivation predict engagement in objectively assessed bouts of moderate-intensity exercise? A self-determination theory perspective. *Journal of Sport and Exercise Psychology, 30,* 337–352.

Stanley, C., Pargman, D., & Tenenbaum, G. (2007). The effect of attentional coping strategies on perceived exertion in a cycling task. *Journal of Applied Sport Psychology, 19,* 352–363.

Stanley, D., & Cumming, J. (2010a). Not just how one feels, but what one images? The effects of imagery use on affective responses to moderate exercise. *International Journal of Sport and Exercise Psychology, 20,* 343–359.

Stanley, D., & Cumming, J. (2010b). Are we having fun yet? Testing the effects of imagery use on the affective and enjoyment responses to acute moderate exercise. *Psychology of Sport and Exercise, 11,* 582–590.

Stanley, D., Cumming, J., Standage, M., & Duda, J. (2012). Images of exercising: Exploring the links between exercise imagery use, autonomous and controlled motivation to exercise, and exercise intention and behavior. *Psychology of Sport and Exercise, 13,* 133–141.

State of Michigan. (1976). *Joint legislative study on youth sports programs. Phase 2.* East Lansing, MI: State of Michigan.

Stavrou, N., Jackson, S., Zervas, Y., & Karterouliotis. (2007). Flow experience and athletes' performance with reference to the orthogonal model of flow. *The Sport Psychologist, 21,* 438–457.

Steinberg, G., Grieve, F.G., & Glass, B. (2000). Achievement goals across the lifespan. *Journal of Sport Behavior, 23,* 298–306.

Steiner, I.D. (1972). *Group process and productivity.* New York: Academic Press.

Steinfeldt, M., & Steinfeldt, J. (2012). Athletic identity and conformity to masculine norms among college football players. *Journal of Applied Sport Psychology, 24,* 115–128.

Stephens, D.E. (2004). Moral atmosphere and aggression in collegiate intramural sport. *International Sports Journal, 8,* 65–75.

Stephens, D., & Bredemeier, B. (1996). Moral atmosphere and judgements about aggression in girls' soccer: Relationships among moral and motivational variables. *Journal of Sport and Exercise Psychology, 18,* 158–173.

Stephens, D.E., & Kavanagh, B. (2003). Aggression in Canadian youth ice hockey: The role of moral atmosphere. *International Sports Journal, 7*(2), 109–119.

Stephens, T. (1988). Physical activity and mental health in the United States and Canada: Evidence from four population surveys. *Preventive Medicine, 17,* 35–47.

Sternberg, R.J. (2007). A systems model of leadership. *American Psychologist, 62,* 34–42.

Stodolska, M., Acevedo, J.C., & Shinew, K.J. (2009). Gangs of Chicago: Perceptions of crime and its effects on the recreation behavior of Latino residents in urban communities. *Leisure Sciences, 31,* 466–482.

Stoeber, J., Uphill, M.A., & Hotham, S. (2009). Predicting race performance in triathlon: The role of perfectionism, achievement goals, and personal goal setting. *Journal of Sport and Exercise Psychology, 31,* 211–245.

Stogdill, R.M. (1948). Personal factors associated with leadership: Survey of literature. *Journal of Psychology, 25,* 35–71.

Stokes, J., Luselli, J., & Reed, D. (2010). A behavioral intervention for teaching tackling skills to high school football athletes. *Journal of Applied Behavior Analysis, 43,* 509–512.

Stokes, J., Luselli, J., Reed, D., & Fleming, R. (2010). Behavioral coaching to improve offensive line passing skills of high school football athletes. *Journal of Applied Behavior Analysis, 43,* 463–472.

Stoll, O., Lau, A., & Stoeber, J. (2008). Perfectionism and performance in a new basketball training task: Does striving for perfection enhance or undermine performance? *Psychology of Sport and Exercise, 9,* 620–629.

Stork, M., Stapelton, J., & Martin-Ginis, K. (2013). Social influence and physical activity among individuals with multiple sclerosis: A meta-analysis. *Journal of Sport and Exercise Psychology, 35,* S115.

Stracchan, L., Côté, J.M., & Deakin, J. (2009). "Specializers" versus "samplers" in youth sports: Comparing experiences and outcomes. *The Sport Psychologist, 1,* 77–92.

Strean, W.B. (1995). Youth sport contexts: Coaches' perceptions and implications for intervention. *Journal of Applied Sport Psychology, 7,* 23–37.

Strean, W.B., Senecal, K., Howlett, S., & Burgess, J. (1997). Xs and Os and what the coach knows: Improving team strategy through critical thinking. *The Sport Psychologist, 11,* 243–256.

Strean, W.B., & Strean, H.S. (1998). Applying psychodynamic concepts to sport psychology practice. *The Sport Psychologist, 12,* 208–222.

Strelan, P., & Boeckmann, R. (2003). A new model for understanding performance-enhancing drug use by elite athletes. *Journal of Applied Sport Psychology, 15,* 176–183.

Striegel-Moore, R., & Bulik, C. (2007). Risk factors for eating disorders. *American Psychologist, 62,* 181–198.

Strupp, J. (2006). Caught (not) looking. *Editor and Publisher, 139,* 42–47.

Stuart, M.E. (2003). Moral issues in sport: The child's perspective. *Research Quarterly for Exercise and Sport, 74*(4), 445–454.

Stuntz, C., & Garwood, K. (2012). Enhancing social goal involvement through cooperative instructions. *Journal of Applied Sport Psychology, 24,* 260–264.

Stuntz, C.P., & Weiss, M.R. (2003). Influence of social goal orientations and peers on unsportsmanlike play. *Research Quarterly for Exercise and Sport, 74*(4), 421–435.

Stuntz, C.P., & Weiss, M.R. (2009). Achievement goal orientations and motivational outcomes in youth sport: The role of social orientations. *Psychology of Sport and Exercise, 10,* 255–262.

Suinn, R.M. (1972). Behavior rehearsal training for ski racers. *Behavior Therapy, 3,* 519.

Suinn, R.M. (1976, July). Body thinking: Psychology for Olympic champs. *Psychology Today, pp.* 38–43.

Suinn, R.M. (1993). Imagery. In R.N. Singer, M. Murphey, & L.K. Tennant (Eds.), *Handbook of sport psychology* (pp. 492–510). New York: Macmillan.

Sullivan, P. (1993). Communication skills training for interactive sports. *The Sport Psychologist, 7,* 79–91.

Sullivan, P., & Kent, A. (2003). Coaching efficacy as a predictor of leadership style in intercollegiate athletics. *Journal of Applied Sport Psychology, 15,* 1–11.

Summers, J.J., & Ford, S. (1995). Attention in sport. In T. Morris & J. Summers (Eds.), *Sport psychology: Theory, applications, and issues* (pp. 63–89). Chichester, UK: Wiley.

Sutherland, G., Andersen, M., & Stoove, M. (2001). Can aerobic exercise training affect health-related quality of life for people with multiple sclerosis? *Journal of Sport and Exercise Psychology, 23,* 122–135.

Swain, A., & Jones, G. (1995). Effects of goal setting interventions on selected basketball skills: A single subject design. *Research Quarterly for Exercise and Sport, 66,* 51–63.

Swift, E.M. (1996, October 7). The good old days: What Mark Messier and Wayne Gretzky hope to recapture in New York. *Sports Illustrated, pp.* 54–60.

Swift, E.M. (1999, July 5). Drug pedaling. *Sports Illustrated,* pp. 60–65.

Swoap, R.A., & Murphy, S.M. (1995). Eating disorders and weight management in athletics. In S.M. Murphy (Ed.), *Psychological interventions in sport* (pp. 307–329). Champaign, IL: Human Kinetics.

Syer, J. (1986). *Team spirit.* London: Simon & Schuster.

Sysoeva, O.V., Kulikova, M.A., Malyuchenko, N.V., Tonevitskii, A.G., & Ivanitskii, A.M. (2010). Genetic and social factors in the development of aggression. *Human Physiology, 36*(1), 40–46.

Tamminen, K., & Holt, N. (2010). Female adolescent athletes' coping: A season-long investigation. *Journal of Sport Sciences, 28,* 101–114.

Tarshis, B. (1977). *Tennis and the mind.* New York: Tennis Magazine.

Tatum, J., & Kushner, B. (1980). *They call me assassin.* New York: Avon.

Taylor, A.H. (2001). Physical activity, anxiety, and stress. In S.J.H. Biddle, K.R. Fox, & S.H. Boutcher (Eds.), *Physical activity and psychological well-being* (pp. 10–45). London: Routledge & Kegan Paul.

Taylor, A.H., Daniel, J.V., Leith, L., & Burke, R.J. (1990). Perceived stress, psychological burnout and paths to turnover intentions among sport officials. *Journal of Applied Sport Psychology, 2,* 84–97.

Taylor, A.H., & Fox, K. (2005). Effectiveness of a primary care exercise referral intervention for changing physical self-perceptions over 9 months. *Health Psychology, 24,* 11–21.

Taylor, D. (2012). L.A. parks gang up for kids. *Parks and Recreation, 47*(1), 10–12.

Taylor, J. (1995). A conceptual model for integrating athletes' needs and sport demands in the development of competitive mental preparation strategies. *The Sport Psychologist, 9,* 339–357.

Taylor, J., & Demick, A. (1994). A multidimensional model of momentum in sports. *Journal of Applied Sport Psychology, 6,* 51–70.

Taylor, R., Brown, A., Ebrahim, S., Jolliffe, S., Noorani, H., & Rees, K. (2004). Exercise-based rehabilitation for patients with coronary heart disease: Systematic review and meta-analysis of randomized controlled trials. *American Journal of Medicine, 116,* 682–692.

Tenenbaum, G., & Connolly, C. (2008). Attention allocation under varied workload and effort perception in rowers. *Psychology of Sport and Exercise, 9,* 704–717.

Tenenbaum, G., Stewart, E., Singer, R.N., & Duda, J. (1997). Aggression and violence in sport: An ISSP position stand. *ISSP Newsletter, 1,* 14–17.

Tennant, C., Mihailidou, A., Scott, A., Smith, R., Kellow, J., Jones, M., et al. (1994). Psychological symptom profiles in patients with chest pain. *Journal of Psychosomatic Medicine, 38,* 365–371.

Terry, P. (1995). The efficacy of mood state profiling with elite performers: A review and synthesis. *The Sport Psychologist, 9,* 309–324.

Tharp, R.G., & Gallimore, R. (1976). What a coach can teach a teacher. *Psychology Today, 9,* 74–78.

Thayer, R.E., Newman, R., & McClain, T.M. (1994). Self-regulation of mood: Strategies for changing a bad mood, raising energy, and reducing tension. *Journal of Personality and Social Behavior, 67,* 910–925.

Thelwell, R.C., & Greenlees, I.A. (2001). The effects of a mental skills training package on gymnasium triathlon performance. *The Sport Psychologist, 15,* 127–141.

Thelwell, R., Greenlees, I., & Weston, N. (2010). Examining the use of psychological skills throughout soccer performance. *Journal of Sport Behavior, 33,* 109–126.

Thelwell, R., Lane, A., Weston, N., & Greenlees, I. (2008). Examining relationships between emotional intelligence and coaching efficacy. *International Journal of Sport and Exercise Psychology, 6,* 224–235.

Thelwell, R., Weston, N., & Greenlees, I. (2005). Defining and understanding mental toughness within soccer. *Journal of Applied Sport Psychology, 17,* 326–332.

Thelwell, R., Weston, N., Greenlees, I., & Hutchings, N. (2008). A qualitative exploration of psychological-skills use in coaches. *The Sport Psychologist, 22,* 38–53.

Theodorakis, L.N., & Gargalianos, D.G. (2003). The importance of internal and external motivation factors in physical education and sport. *International Journal of Physical Education, 40*(1), 21–26.

Theodorakis, Y., Malliou, P., Papaioannou, A., Beneca, A., & Filactakidou, A. (1996). The effect of personal goals, self-efficacy, and self-satisfaction on injury rehabilitation. *Journal of Sport Rehabilitation, 5,* 214–233.

Thirer, J. (1993). Aggression. In R.N. Singer, M. Murphey, & L.K. Tennant (Eds.), *Handbook of sport psychology* (pp. 365–378). New York: Macmillan.

Thogersen-Ntoumani, C., Fox, K., & Ntoumanis, N. (2005). Relationships between exercise and three components of mental well-being in corporate employees. *Psychology of Sport and Exercise, 6,* 609–627.

Thomas, J.R., Landers, D.M., Salazar, W.J., & Etnier, J. (1994). Exercise and cognitive functioning. In C. Bouchard, R.J. Shepard, & T. Stephens (Eds.), *Physical activity, fitness, and health* (pp. 521–529). Champaign, IL: Human Kinetics.

Thomas, K. (2003). *Intrinsic motivation at work: Building energy and commitment.* San Francisco: Berrett-Kohler.

Thomas, O., Hanton, S., & Maynard, I. (2007). Anxiety responses and psychological skill use during the time leading up to competition: Theory to practice I. *Journal of Applied Sport Psychology, 19,* 379–397.

Thomas, O., Lane, A., & Kingston, K. (2011) Defining and contextualizing robust sport-cpnfidence. *Journal of Applied Sport Psychology, 23,* 189-208.

Thomas, O., Maynard, I., & Hanton, S. (2004). Temporal aspects of competitive anxiety and self-confidence as a function of anxiety perceptions. *The Sport Psychologist, 18,* 172–187.

Thomas, O., Maynard, I., & Hanton, S. (2007). Intervening with athletes during the time leading up to competition: Theory to practice II. *Journal of Applied Sport Psychology, 19,* 398–418.

Thomas, P.R., Murphy, S.M., & Hardy, L. (1999). Test of performance strategies: Development and preliminary validation of a comprehensive measure of athletes' psychological skills. *Journal of Sport Sciences, 17*(9), 697–711.

Thompson, R.A. (1987). Management of the athlete with an eating disorder: Implications for the sport management team. *The Sport Psychologist, 1,* 114–126.

Thompson, R.A., & Sherman, R. (1993). *Helping athletes with eating disorders.* Champaign, IL: Human Kinetics.

Thompson, R.A., & Sherman, R. (1999). Athletes, athletic performance, and eating disorders: Healthier alternatives. *Journal of Social Issues, 55,* 317–337.

Tippett, S.R., & Voight, M.L. (1995). *Functional progressions for sport rehabilitation.* Champaign, IL: Human Kinetics.

Titley, R.W. (1976, September). The loneliness of a long-distance kicker. *Athletic Journal, 57,* 74–80.

Titze, S., Martin, B., Seiler, R., Stronegger, W., & Marti, B. (2001). Effects of a lifestyle physical activity intervention on stages of change and energy expenditure in sedentary employees. *Psychology of Sport and Exercise, 2,* 103–116.

Titze, S., Stonegger, W., & Owen, N. (2005). Prospective study of individual, social, and environmental predictors of physical activity: Women's leisure running. *Psychology of Sport and Exercise, 6,* 363–376.

Tkachuk, G., Leslie-Toogood, A., & Martin, G. (2003). Behavioral assessment in sport psychology. *The Sport Psychologist, 17,* 104–117.

Tobar, D.A. (2012). Trait anxiety and mood state responses to overtraining in men and women college swimmers. *International Journal of Sport and Exercise Psychology, 10*(2), 135–148.

Tod, D., Hardy, J., & Oliver, E. (2011). Effects of self-talk: A systematic review. *Journal of Sport and Exercise Psychology, 33,* 666–687.

Tolli, A., & Schmidt, A. (2008). The role of feedback, causal attributions, and self-efficacy in goal revision. *Journal of Applied Psychology, 93,* 692–701.

Toner, J., & Moran, A. (2012). The effects of conscious processing on golf putting proficiency and kinematics. *Journal of Sport Sciences, 30,* 673–683.

Traclet, A., Romand, P., Moret, O., & Kavussanu, M. (2011). Antisocial behavior in soccer: A qualitative study of moral disengagement. *International Journal of Sport and Exercise Psychology, 9*(2), 143–155.

Treasure, D.C., & Roberts, G.C. (1995). Applications of achievement goal theory to physical education: Implications for enhancing motivation. *Quest, 47,* 475–489.

Tricker, R., Cook, D.L., & McGuire, R. (1989). Issues related to drug use in college athletics: Athletes at risk. *The Sport Psychologist, 3,* 155–165.

Triplett, N. (1898). The dynamogenic factors in pacemaking and competition. *American Journal of Psychology, 9,* 507–553.

Trost, S., Owenm, N., Bauman, A., Sallis, J., & Brown, W. (2002). Correlates of adults' participation in physical activity: Review and update. *Medicine and Science in Sports and Exercise, 34,* 1996–2001.

Trudel, P., Lemyre, F., Werthner, P., & Camire, M. (2007). Character development in youth sport: The perspective of ice hockey and baseball coaches. *International Journal of Coaching Science, 1,* 21–35.

Trulson, M.E. (1986). Martial arts training: A novel cure for juvenile delinquency. *Human Relations, 39,* 1131–1140.

Tuckman, B.W. (1965). Developmental sequence in small groups. *Psychological Bulletin, 63,* 384–399.

Turman, P. (2003). Coaches and cohesion: The impact of coaching techniques on team cohesion in the small group sport setting. *Journal of Sport Behavior, 26,* 86–104.

Turner, S., Bethell, H., Evane, J., Goddard, J., & Mullee, M. (2002). Patient characteristics and outcomes of cardiac rehabilitation. *Journal of Cardiopulmonary Rehabilitation, 22,* 253–260.

Turnnidge, J., Vierimaa, M., & Cote, J. (2012). An in-depth investigation of a model sport program for athletes with a disability. *Psychology, 3,* 1131–1141.

Udry, E., Gould, D., Bridges, D., & Beck, L. (1997). Down but not out: Athlete responses to season-ending ski injuries. *Journal of Sport and Exercise Psychology, 3,* 229–248.

Ullrich-French, S., & Smith, A. (2006). Perceptions of relationships with parents and peers in youth sport: Independent and combined prediction of motivational outcomes. *Psychology of Sport and Exercise, 7,* 193–214.

Ullrich-French, S., & Smith, A. (2009). Social and motivational predictors of continued youth sport participation. *Psychology of Sport and Exercise, 10,* 87–95.

Unesthal, L. (1986). *Integrated mental training.* Stockholm/Orebro: Sisu/Veje.

U.S. Anti-Doping Agency. (2011). What sport means in America: A study of sport's role in society. *Journal of Coaching Education, 4*(1), 2–27.

U.S. Centers for Disease Control and Prevention. (1993). Prevalence of sedentary lifestyle-behavioral risk factor surveillance system. United States, 1991. *Morbidity and Mortality Weekly Report, 42,* 576–579.

U.S. Department of Health and Human Services. (1996). *Physical activity and health: A report of the Surgeon General.* Washington, DC: U.S. Department of Health and Human Services, Centers for Disease Control and Prevention, National Center for Chronic Disease Prevention and Health Promotion.

U.S. Department of Health and Human Services. (1999). *Promoting physical activity at the community level: A guide for action.* Champaign, IL: Human Kinetics.

U.S. Department of Health and Human Services. (2000). *Healthy people 2010: Understanding and improving health* (2nd ed.). Washington, DC: Government Printing Office.

U.S. Department of Health and Human Services, Public Health Service, and Centers for Disease Control and Prevention. (1997). Guidelines for school and community programs to promote lifelong physical activity among young people. *Morbidity and Mortality Weekly Report, 46,* 1–37.

U.S. Olympic Committee. (1998). Overtraining: The challenge of prediction. The second annual U.S. Olympic Committee/American College of Sports Medicine consensus statement. *Olympic Coach, 8*(4), 4–8.

Vadocz, E.A., Hall, C.R., & Moritz, S.E. (1997). The relationship between competitive anxiety and imagery use. *Journal of Applied Sport Psychology, 9,* 241–253.

VaezMousavi, S.M. (2005). Frequencies of aggressive behaviors in win, lose and tie situations. *International Journal of Applied Sport Sciences, 17,* 35–43.

Vainio, H., & Bianchini, F. (2002). *Weight control and physical activity: Vol. 6. IARC handbooks of cancer prevention.* Lyon, France: IARC Press.

Valiante, G., & Morris, D. (2013). The sources and maintenance of professional golfers' self-efficacy beliefs. *The Sport Psychologist, 27,* 130–142.

Vallee, C., & Bloom, G. (2005). Building a successful university program: Key and common elements of expert coaches. *Journal of Applied Sport Psychology, 17,* 179–196.

Vallerand, R.J. (1983). Effect of differential amounts of positive verbal feedback on the intrinsic motivation of male hockey players. *Journal of Sport Psychology, 5,* 100–107.

Vallerand, R.J. (1997). Toward a hierarchical model of intrinsic and extrinsic motivation. In M.P. Zanna (Ed.), *Advances in experimental social psychology* (Vol. 29, pp. 271–360). New York: Academic Press.

Vallerand, R. (2010). On passion for life activities: The dualistic model of passion. In M. Zanna (Ed.), *Advances in experimental social psychology* (Vol. 42, pp. 7–193). New York: Academic Press.

Vallerand, R.J., Briere, N.M., Blanchard, C., & Provencher, P. (1997). Development and validation of the multidimensional sportsperson-ship orientation scale. *Journal of Sport and Exercise Psychology, 19,* 197–206.

Vallerand, R.J., Deci, E., & Ryan, R.M. (1987). Intrinsic motivation in sport. *Exercise and Sport Sciences Reviews 15,* 389–425.

Vallerand, R.J., Deshaies, P., Cuerrier, J.P., Briere, N., & Pelletier, L.C. (1996). Towards a multidimensional definition of sportsmanship. *Journal of Applied Sport Psychology, 8,* 89–101.

Vallerand, R.J., Donahue, E., & Lafreniere, M. (2011). Passion in sport. In T. Morris & P. Terry (Eds.), *The new sport and exercise psychology companion* (pp. 583–607). Morgantown, WV: Fitness Information Technology.

Vallerand, R.J., Gauvin, L.I., & Halliwell, W.R. (1986a). Effects of zero-sum competition on children's intrinsic motivation and perceived competence. *Journal of Social Psychology, 126,* 465–472.

Vallerand, R.J., Gauvin, L.I., & Halliwell, W.R. (1986b). Negative effects of competition on children's intrinsic motivation. *Journal of Social Psychology, 126,* 649–657.

Vallerand, R.J., & Losier, G. (1999). An integrative analysis of intrinsic and extrinsic motivation in sport. *Journal of Applied Sport Psychology, 11,* 142–169.

Vallerand, R.J., & Reid, G. (1984). On the causal effects of perceived competence on intrinsic motivation: A test of cognitive evaluation theory. *Journal of Sport Psychology, 6,* 94–102.

Vallerand, R.J., & Rousseau, F.L. (2001). Intrinsic and extrinsic motivation in sport and exercise: A review using the hierarchical model of intrinsic and extrinsic motivation. In R. Singer, H. Hausenblas, & C. Janelle (Eds.), *Handbook of sport psychology* (2nd ed., pp. 389–416). New York: Wiley.

Vallerand, R.J., Rousseau, F., Grouzet, M., Dumais, A., Grenier, S., & Blanchard, C. (2006). Passion in sport: A look at determinants and affective experiences. *Journal of Sport and Exercise Psychology, 28,* 454–478.

Vallerand, R.J., Vanden Auweele, Y., Boen, F., Schapendonk, W., & Dornez, K. (2005). Promoting stair use among female employees: The effects of a health sign followed by an e-mail. *Journal of Sport and Exercise Psychology, 27,* 188–196.

Van Raalte, J.L., Brewer, B.W., Rivera, P.M., & Petitpas, A.J. (1994). The relationship between self-talk and performance of competitive junior tennis players. *NASPSPA Conference Abstracts, 16*(Suppl.), S118.

Van Schoyck, S.R., & Grasha, A.F. (1981). Attentional style variations and athletic ability: The advantages of a sports-specific test. *Journal of Sport Psychology, 3,* 149–165.

Vansteenkiste, M., & Deci, E. (2003). Competitively contingent rewards and intrinsic motivation: Can losers remain motivated? *Motivation and Emotion, 27,* 273–299.

VanYperen, N.W. (1995). Interpersonal stress, performance level, and parental support: A longitudinal study among highly skilled young soccer players. *The Sport Psychologist, 9,* 225–241.

Vargas-Tonsing, T., & Guan, J. (2007). Athletes' preferences for informational and emotional pre-game speech content. *International Journal of Sports Science and Coaching, 2,* 171–180.

Vazou, S., Gavrilou, P., Mamalaki, E., Papanastasiou, A., & Sioumala, N. (2012). Does integrating physical activity in the elementary school classroom influence academic motivation? *International Journal of Sport & Exercise Psychology, 10*(4), 251-263.

Veach, T., & May, J. (2005). Teamwork: For the good of the whole. In S. Murphy (Ed.), *The sport psych handbook* (pp. 171–189). Champaign, IL: Human Kinetics.

Vealey, R. (1986). Conceptualization of sport-confidence and competitive orientation: Preliminary investigation and instrument development. *Journal of Sport Psychology, 8,* 221–246.

Vealey, R. (1989). Sport personality: A paradigmatic and methodological analysis. *Journal of Sport and Exercise Psychology, 11,* 216–235.

Vealey, R. (2001). Understanding and enhancing self-confidence in athletes. In R. Singer, H. Hausenblas, & C. Janelle (Eds.), *Handbook of sport psychology* (2nd ed., pp. 550–565). New York: Wiley.

Vealey, R.S. (2002). Personality and sport behavior. In T.S. Horn (Ed.), *Advances in sport psychology* (pp. 43–82). Champaign, IL: Human Kinetics.

Vealey, R. (2005). *Coaching for the inner edge.* Morgantown, WV: Fitness Institute Technology.

Vealey, R.S. (2006). Smocks and jocks outside the box: The paradigmatic evolution of sport and exercise psychology. *Quest, 58,* 128–159.

Vealey, R. (2007). Mental skills training in sport. In G. Tenenbaum & R. Eklund (Eds.), *Handbook of sport psychology* (3rd ed., pp. 287–309). New York: Wiley.

Vealey, R., & Chase, M. (2008). Self-confidence in sport: Conceptual and research advances. In T. Horn (Ed.), *Advances in sport psychology* (3rd ed., pp. 65–97). Champaign, IL: Human Kinetics.

Vealey, R., & Greenleaf, C. (2010). Imagery training for performance enhancement and personal development. In J.M. Williams (Ed.), *Applied sport psychology: Personal growth to peak performance* (3rd ed., pp. 267–304). Mountain View, CA: Mayfield.

Vealey, R., & Knight, B. (2002, October). *Conceptualization and measurement of multidimensional sport-confidence.* Paper presented at the Association for the Advancement of Applied Sport Psychology Conference, Tucson, AZ.

Vealey, R., Udry, E., Zimmerman, V., & Soliday, J. (1992). Interpersonal and situational predictors of coaching burnout. *Journal of Sport and Exercise Psychology, 14,* 40–58.

Vealey, R., & Vernau, D. (2013). Confidence. In S. Hanrahan & M. Andersen (Eds.), *Routledge handbook of applied sport psychology: A comprehensive guide for students and practitioners* (pp. 518–527). New York: Routledge.

Velentzas, K., Heinen, T., & Schack, T. (2011). Routine integration strategies and their effects on volleyball serve performance and players' movement mental representation. *Journal of Applied Sport Psychology, 23,* 209–222.

Verducci, T. (2006). Going, going, gone. *Sports Illustrated, 105,* 24–25.

Veroff, J. (1969). Social comparison and the development of achievement motivation. In C.P. Smith (Ed.), *Achievement-related motives in children* (pp. 46–101). New York: Russell Sage Foundation.

Vidic, Z., & Burton, D. (2010). The roadmap: Examining the impact of a systematic goal-setting program for collegiate women's tennis. *The Sport Psychologist, 24*(4), 427–447.

Vine, S., & Wilson, M. (2010). Quiet eye training: Effects on learning and performance under pressure. *Journal of Applied Sport Psychology, 22,* 361–376.

Voelker, D.K., Gould, D., & Crawford, M.J. (2011). Understanding the experience of high school sport captains. *The Sport Psychologist, 25,* 47–66.

Voight, M. (2009). Sources of stress and coping strategies of U.S. soccer officials. *Stress and Health, 25,* 91–101.

Voight, M. (2012). A leadership development intervention program: A case study with two elite teams. *The Sport Psychologist, 26,* 604–623.

von Gunten, C., Ferris, F., & Emanuel, L. (2000). Ensuring the competency in end-of-life care. *Journal of the American Medical Association, 284,* 3051–3057.

Vose, J., Clark, R., & Sachs, M. (2013). Athletes who are blind/visually impaired or deaf/hard of hearing. In S. Hanrahan & M. Andersen (Eds.), *Routledge handbook of applied sport psychology: A comprehensive guide for students and practitioners* (pp. 450–459). New York: Routledge.

Vroom, V.H., & Jago, A.G. (2007). The role of the situation in leadership. *American Psychologist, 62,* 17–24.

Wadey, R., & Hanton, S. (2008). Basic psychological skills usage and competitive anxiety responses: Perceived underlying mechanisms. *Research Quarterly for Exercise and Sport, 79,* 363–373.

Wakefield, C., & Smith, D. (2011). From strength to strength: A single-case design study of PETTLEP imagery frequency. *The Sport Psychologist, 25,* 305–320.

Wakefield, C., & Smith, D. (2012). Perfecting practice: Applying the PETTLEP model of motor imagery. *Journal of Sport Psychology in Action, 3,* 1–11.

Wakefield, C., Smith, D., Moran, A., & Holmes, P. (2013). Functional equivalence or behavioral matching? A critical reflection on 15 years of research using the PETLEPP model of motor imagery. *International Review of Sport and Exercise Psychology, 6,* 105–121.

Waldron, J. (2012). A social norms approach to hazing prevention workshops. *Journal of Sport Psychology in Action, 3,* 12–20.

Waldron, J.J., & Kowalski, C.L. (2009). Crossing the line: Rites of passage, team aspects and the ambiguity of hazing. *Research Quarterly for Sport and Exercise, 80,* 291–302.

Walsh, A. (2000). Evolutionary psychology and the origins of justice. *Justice Quarterly, 17,* 841–864.

Walsh, A. (2012). Exercise intensity, affect, and adherence: A guide for the fitness professional. *Journal of Sport Psychology in Action, 3,* 193–207.

Walsh, S. (2011). The relaxation response: A strategy to address stress. *International Journal of Athletic Therapy and Training, 16,* 20–23.

Wang, C.K.J., Liu, W.C., Lochbaum, M.R., & Stevenson, S.J. (2009). Sport ability beliefs, 2 x 2 achievement goals, and intrinsic motivation: The moderating role of perceived competence in sport and exercise. *Research Quarterly for Exercise and Sport, 80,* 303–312.

Wankel, L.M. (1980). Involvement in vigorous physical activity: Considerations for enhancing self-motivation. In R.R. Danielson & K.F. Danielson (Eds.), *Fitness motivation: Proceedings of the Geneva Park workshop* (pp. 18–32). Toronto: Ontario Research Council on Leisure.

Wankel, L.M. (1984). Decision-making and social support structures for increasing exercise adherence. *Journal of Cardiac Rehabilitation, 4,* 124–128.

Wann, D.L., Culver, Z., Akanda, R., Daglar, M., De Divitiis, D., & Smith, A. (2005). The effects of team identification and game outcome on willingness to consider anonymous acts of hostile aggression. *Journal of Sport Behavior, 28,* 282–294.

Wann, D.L., Dunham, M.D., Byrd, M.L., & Keenan, B.L. (2004). The five-factor model of personality and the psychological health of highly identified sports fans. *International Sports Journal, 8,* 28–36.

Wann, D.L., Schrader, M.P., & Carlson, J.D. (2000). The verbal aggression of sport spectators: A comparison of hostile and instrumental motives. *International Sports Journal, 4,* 56–63.

Ward, P., & Carnes, M. (2002). Effects of posting self-set goals on collegiate football players' skill execution during practice and games. *Journal of Applied Behavior Analysis, 35,* 1–12.

Waters, B. (1981). Defining the runner's personality. *Runner's World, 33,* 48–51.

Watson, D., Clark, L., & Tellegen, A. (1988). Development and validation of brief measures of positive and negative affect: The PANAS scales. *Journal of Personality and Social Psychology, 54,* 1063–1070.

Watson, J., & Shannon, V. (2013). Individual and group observations: Purposes and processes. In S. Hanrahan & M. Andersen (Eds.), *Routledge handbook of applied sport psychology* (pp. 90–100). New York: Routledge.

Wegner, D.M. (1997). Why the mind wanders. In J.D. Cohen & J.W. Schooler (Eds.), *Scientific approaches to consciousness* (pp. 295–315). Hillsdale, NJ: Erlbaum.

Wegner, D.M., Ansfield, M., & Piloff, D. (1998). The putt and the pendulum: Ironic effects of the mental control of action. *Psychological Science, 9,* 196–199.

Weinberg, R.S. (1981). The relationship between mental preparation strategies and motor performance: A review and critique. *Quest, 42,* 195–213.

Weinberg, R.S. (1988). *The mental advantage: Developing your psychological skills in tennis.* Champaign, IL: Human Kinetics.

Weinberg, R.S. (1994). Goal setting and performance in sport and exercise settings: A synthesis and critique. *Medicine and Science in Sports and Exercise, 26,* 469–477.

Weinberg, R.S. (2000). Goal setting in sport and exercise: How research can inform practice. In B.A. Carlsson, U. Johnson, & F. Wettertrand (Eds.), *Sport psychology conference in the new millennium* (pp. 76–84). Sweden: Halmstead University.

Weinberg, R.S. (2002). *Tennis: Winning the mental game.* Boston: Zimman.

Weinberg, R.S. (2004). Goal setting practices for coaches and athletes. In T. Morris & J. Summers (Eds.), *Sport psychology: Theory, applications, and issues* (pp. 278–293). Queensland, Australia, Wiley.

Weinberg, R.S. (2008). Does imagery work? Effects on performance and mental skills. *Journal of Imagery Research in Sport and Exercise, 3,* 1–20.

Weinberg, R. (2010a). Making goals effective: A primer for coaches. *Journal of Sport Psychology in Action, 1,* 57–65.

Weinberg, R. (2010b). *Mental toughness for sport, business and life.* Indianapolis: AuthorHouse.

Weinberg, R.S., Burke, K., & Jackson, A. (1997). Coaches' and players' perceptions of goal setting in junior tennis: An exploratory investigation. *The Sport Psychologist, 11,* 426–439.

Weinberg, R.S., Burton, D., Yukelson, D., & Weigand, D. (1993). Goal setting in competitive sport: An exploratory investigation of practices of collegiate athletes. *The Sport Psychologist, 7,* 275–289.

Weinberg, R.S., Burton, D., Yukelson, D., & Weigand, D. (2000). Perceived goal setting practices of Olympic athletes: An exploratory investigation. *The Sport Psychologist, 14,* 279–295.

Weinberg, R.S., & Butt, J. (2005). Goal setting in sport and exercise domains: The theory and practice of effective goal setting. In D. Hackfort, J. Duda, & R. Lidor (Eds.), *Handbook of research in applied sport psychology* (pp. 129–146). Morgantown, WV: Fitness Information Technology.

Weinberg, R., & Butt, J. (2011). Building mental toughness. In D. Gucciardi & S. Gordon (Eds.), *Mental toughness in sport: Developments in theory and research* (pp. 121–229). New York: Routledge.

Weinberg, R., Butt, J., & Culp, B. (2011). Coaches' views of mental toughness and how it is built. *International Journal of Sport and Exercise Psychology, 9,* 156–172.

Weinberg, R.S., Butt, J., & Knight, B. (2001). High school coaches' perceptions of the process of goal setting. *The Sport Psychologist, 15,* 20–47.

Weinberg, R.S., Butt, J., Knight, B., Burke, K.L., & Jackson, A. (2003). The relationship between the use and effectiveness of imagery: An explanatory investigation. *Journal of Applied Sport Psychology, 15,* 26–40.

Weinberg, R.S., Butt, J., Knight, B., & Perritt, N. (2001). Collegiate coaches' perceptions of their goal setting practices: A qualitative investigation. *Journal of Applied Sport Psychology, 13,* 374–398.

Weinberg, R.S., & Comar, W. (1994). The effectiveness of psychological interventions in competitive sport. *Sports Medicine, 18,* 406–418.

Weinberg, R.S., Gould, D., & Jackson, A. (1979). Expectancies and performance: An empirical test of Bandura's self-efficacy theory. *Journal of Sport Psychology, 1,* 320–331.

Weinberg, R.S., Grove, R., & Jackson, A. (1992). Strategies for building self-efficacy in tennis players: A comparative analysis of American and Australian coaches. *The Sport Psychologist, 6,* 3–13.

Weinberg, R.S., & Hunt, V.V. (1976). The interrelationships between anxiety, motor performance, and electromyography. *Journal of Motor Behavior, 8*(3), 219–224.

Weinberg, R.S., & Jackson, A. (1979). Competition and extrinsic rewards: Effect on intrinsic motivation and attribution. *Research Quarterly, 50,* 494–502.

Weinberg, R.S., Miller, A., & Horn, T. (2012). The influence of a self-talk intervention on collegiate cross-country runners. *International Journal of Sport and Exercise Psychology, 10,* 123–134.

Weinberg, R.S., Neff, R., & Jurica, B. (2012). Online mental training: Making it available to the masses. *Journal of Sport Psychology in Action, 3,* 182–192.

Weinberg, R.S., & Ragan, J. (1979). Effects of competition, success/failure, and sex on intrinsic motivation. *Research Quarterly, 50,* 503–510.

Weinberg, R.S., & Richardson, P.A. (1990). *Psychology of officiating.* Champaign, IL: Human Kinetics.

Weinberg, R.S., Seabourne, T.G., & Jackson, A. (1981). Effects of visuo-motor behavior rehearsal, relaxation, and imagery on karate performance. *Journal of Sport Psychology, 3,* 228–238.

Weinberg, R.S., Stitcher, P., Richardson, P., & Jackson, A. (1994). Effects of a seasonal goal setting program on lacrosse performance. *The Sport Psychologist, 7,* 275–289.

Weinberg, R.S., & Williams, J. (2001). Integrating and implementing a psychological skills training program. In J. Williams (Ed.), *Applied sport psychology: Personal growth to peak performance* (4th ed., pp. 347–377). Mountain View, CA: Mayfield.

Weinberg, R.S., Yukelson, D., & Jackson, A. (1980). Effect of public versus private efficacy expectations on competitive performance. *Journal of Sport Psychology, 2,* 340–349.

Weiner, B. (1985). An attribution theory of achievement motivation and emotion. *Psychological Review, 92,* 548–573.

Weiner, B. (1986). *An attribution theory of motivation and emotion.* New York: Springer-Verlag.

Weinstock, J., Whelan, J.P., & Meyers, A.W. (2000). *Gambling among collegiate athletes and non-athletes: Is there much action off the field?* Paper presented at the 11th International Conference on Gambling and Risk Taking, Las Vegas, NV.

Weintraub, B. (2009). New weapons in the fight against gangs. *Parks and Recreation, 44*(11), 46–49.

Weir, K. (2011, December). The exercise effect. *Monitor on Psychology,* pp. 48–52.

Weir, K. (2012, December). Big kids. *Monitor on Psychology,* pp. 58–63.

Weiss, M.R. (1987). Teaching sportsmanship and values. In V. Seefeldt (Ed.), *Handbook for youth sports coaches* (pp. 137–151). Reston, VA: AAHPERD.

Weiss, M.R. (1991). Psychological skill development in children and adolescents. *The Sport Psychologist, 5,* 335–354.

Weiss, M.R. (1993). Psychological effects of intensive sport participation on children and youth: Self-esteem and motivation. In B.R. Cahill & A.J. Pearl (Eds.), *Intensive participation in children's sports* (pp. 39–69). Champaign, IL: Human Kinetics.

Weiss, M.R., & Ambrose, A.J. (2008). Motivational orientations and sport behavior. In T. Horn (Ed.), Advances in sport psychology (3rd ed.) (pp. 115–154). Champaign, IL: Human Kinetics.

Weiss, M.R., & Bredemeier, B.J. (1991). Moral development in sport. *Exercise and Sport Sciences Reviews, 18,* 331–378.

Weiss, M.R., & Chaumeton, N. (1992). Motivational orientations in sport. In T. Horn (Ed.), *Advances in sport psychology* (pp. 61–99). Champaign, IL: Human Kinetics.

Weiss, M.R., & Ferrer-Caja, E. (2002). Motivational orientations and sport behavior. In T. Horn (Ed.), *Advances in sport psychology* (pp. 101–184). Champaign, IL: Human Kinetics.

Weiss, M.R., & Friedrichs, W.D. (1986). The influence of leader behaviors, coach attributes, and institutional variables on performance and satisfaction of collegiate basketball teams. *Journal of Sport Psychology, 8,* 332–346.

Weiss, M.R., & Smith, A.L. (1999). Quality of youth sport friendships: Measurement development and validation. *Journal of Sport and Exercise Psychology, 21,* 145–166.

Weiss, M.R., & Smith, A.L. (2002). Moral development in sport and physical activity: Theory, research and intervention. In T.S. Horn (Ed.), *Advances in sport psychology* (pp. 243–280). Champaign, IL: Human Kinetics.

Weiss, M.R., Smith, A.L., & Theeboom, M. (1996). "That's what friends are for": Children's and teenagers' perceptions of peer relationships in the sport domain. *Journal of Sport and Exercise Psychology, 18,* 347–379.

Weiss, M.R., & Stuntz, C.P. (2004). A little friendly competition: Peer relationships in psychosocial development in youth sport and activity contexts. In M.R. Weiss (Ed.), *Developmental sport and exercise psychology: A lifespan perspective* (pp. 165–196). Morgantown, WV: Fitness Information Technology.

Welch, A., & Tschampl, M. (2012). Something to shout about: A simple quick performance enhancement technique improved strength in both experts and novices. *Journal of Applied Sport Psychology, 24,* 418–428.

Wells, C., Collins, D., & Hale, B. (1993). The self-efficacy–performance link in maximum strength performance. *Journal of Sports Sciences, 11,* 167–175.

Weston, N., Greenlees, I., & Thelwell, R. (2010). Applied sport psychology consultant perceptions of the usefulness and impacts of performance profiling. *International Journal of Sport Psychology, 41,* 360–368.

Weston, N., Greenlees, I., & Thelwell, R. (2011). Athlete perceptions of the impacts of performance profiling. *International Journal of Sport and Exercise Psychology, 9,* 173–188.

Westre, K.R., & Weiss, M.R. (1991). The relationship between perceived coaching behaviors and group cohesion in high school football teams. *The Sport Psychologist, 5,* 41–54.

Weyerer, S. (1992). Physical inactivity and depression in the community: Evidence from the Upper Batavia Field Study. *International Journal of Sports Medicine, 13,* 492–496.

Whaley, D.E., & Krane, V. (2012). Resilient excellence: Challenges faced by trailblazing women in U.S. sport psychology. *Research Quarterly for Exercise and Sport, 83,* 65–76.

Whaley, D., & Shrider, A. (2005). The process of adult exerciser adherence: Self-perceptions and competence. *The Sport Psychologist, 19,* 148–163.

Whetten, D., & Cameron, K. (1991). *Developing management skills* (2nd ed.). New York: HarperCollins.

White, A., & Hardy, L. (1995). Use of different imagery perspectives on the learning and performance of different motor skills. *British Journal of Psychology, 86,* 169–180.

White, S. (2007). Parent-created motivational climate. In S. Jowett & D. Lavelle (Eds.), *Social psychology in sport* (pp. 132–143). Champaign IL: Human Kinetics.

Whitehead, R., Chilla, S., & Elliott, D. (1992). Anabolic steroid use among adolescents in a rural state. *Journal of Family Practice, 35,* 401–405.

Whyte, W.F. (1943). *Street corner society: The social structure of an Italian slum.* Chicago: University of Chicago Press.

Widmeyer, W.N. (1984). Aggression-performance relationships in sport. In J.M. Silva & R.S. Weinberg (Eds.), *Psychological foundations of sport* (pp. 274–286). Champaign, IL: Human Kinetics.

Widmeyer, W.N. (2002). Reducing aggression in sport. In J.M. Silva & D.E. Stevens (Eds.), *Psychological foundations of sport* (pp. 380–395). Boston: Allyn & Bacon.

Widmeyer, W.N., Brawley, L.R., & Carron, A.V. (1985). *The measurement of cohesion in sport teams: The group environment questionnaire.* London, ON: Sports Dynamics.

Widmeyer, W.N., Bray, S.R., Dorsch, K.M., & McGuire, E.J. (2001). Explanations of the occurrence of aggression: Theories and research. In J.M. Silva & D.E. Stevens (Eds.), *Psychological foundations of sport* (pp. 352–279). Boston: Allyn & Bacon.

Widmeyer, W.N., Carron, A.V., & Brawley, L.R. (1993). Group cohesion in sport and exercise. In R.N. Singer, M. Murphey, & L.K. Tennant (Eds.), *Handbook of sport psychology* (pp. 672–692). New York: Macmillan.

Widmeyer, W.N., Dorsch, K.D., Bray, S.R., & McGuire, E.J. (2002). The nature, prevalence, and consequences of aggression in sport. In J.M. Silva & D.E. Stevens (Eds.), *Psychological foundations of sport* (pp. 328–351). Boston: Allyn & Bacon.

Widmeyer, W.N., & DuCharme, K. (1997). Team building through team goal setting. *Journal of Applied Sport Psychology, 9,* 61–72.

Widmeyer, W.N., & McGuire, E.J. (1997). Frequency of competition and aggression in professional ice hockey. *International Journal of Sport Psychology, 28,* 57–66.

Widmeyer, W.N., Silva, J.M., & Hardy, C. (1992, October). *The nature of group cohesion in sport teams: A phenomenological approach.* Paper presented at the annual meeting of the Association for the Advancement of Applied Sport Psychology, Colorado Springs.

Widmeyer, W.N., & Williams, J. (1991). Predicting cohesion in coacting teams. *Small Group Research, 22,* 548–557.

Wiese, D., & Weiss, M. (1987). Psychological rehabilitation and physical injury: Implications for the sports medicine team. *The Sport Psychologist, 1,* 318-330.

Wiese, D.M., Weiss, M.R., & Yukelson, D.P. (1991). Sport psychology in the training room: A survey of athletic trainers. *The Sport Psychologist, 5*(1), 15–24.

Wiese-Bjornstahl, D. (2010). Psychology and socioculture affect injury risk, response and recovery in high-intensity athletes: A consensus statement. *Scandianavian Journal of Medicine and Science in Sports, 20,* 103–111.

Wilkinson, M.O., Landers, D.M., & Daniels, F.S. (1981). Breathing patterns and their influence on rifle shooting. *American Marksman, 6,* 8–9.

Williams, A.M., & Elliott, D. (1999). Anxiety, expertise, and visual strategy in karate. *Journal of Sport and Exercise Psychology, 21,* 362–375.

Williams, A.M., & Ericsson, A. (2008). How do experts learn? *Journal of Applied Sport Psychology, 30,* 653–662.

Williams, A.M., Ward, P., & Smeeton, N. (2004). Perceptual and cognitive expertise in sport: Implications for skill acquisition and performance enhancement. In A.M. Williams & N.J. Hodges (Eds.), *Skill acquisition in sport: Research, theory, and practice* (pp. 328–347). London: Routledge.

Williams, D.M. (2007). Piloting a self-paced exercise program among previously sedentary women. *Journal of Women's Health, 16,* 1101.

Williams, D.M. (2008). Exercise, affect and adherence: An integrated model and a case for self-paced exercise. *Journal of Sport and Exercise Psychology, 30,* 471–496.

Williams, D., Papandonatos, G., Napolitano, M., Lewis, B., Whitley, J., & Marcus, B. (2006). Perceived enjoyment moderates the efficacy of an individually tailored physical activity intervention. *Journal of Sport and Exercise Psychology, 28,* 300–309.

Williams, J.M. (1980). Personality characteristics of the successful female athlete. In W.F. Straub (Ed.). *Sport psychology: An analysis of athlete behavior.* Ithaca, NY: Mouvement.

Williams, J.M., & Andersen, M.B. (1998). Psychosocial antecedents of sport and injury: Review and critique of the stress and injury model. *Journal of Sport and Exercise Psychology, 10,* 5–25.

Williams, J.M., & Andersen, M.B. (2007). Psychosocial antecedents of sport injury and interventions for risk reduction. In G. Tennebaum & R.C. Eklund (Eds.), *Handbook of sport psychology* (3rd ed., pp. 379–403). Hoboken, NJ: Wiley.

Williams, J.M., & Hacker, C.M. (1982). Causal relationships among cohesion, satisfaction, and performance in women's intercollegiate field hockey teams. *Journal of Sport Psychology, 4,* 324–337.

Williams, J.M., & Straub, W.F. (2006). Sport psychology: Past, present, and future. In J.M. Williams (Ed.), *Applied sport psychology: Personal growth to peak performance* (5th ed., pp. 1–14). Boston: McGraw-Hill.

Williams, J.M., Tonyman, P., & Andersen, M.B. (1991). The effects of stressors and coping resources on anxiety and peripheral narrowing. *Journal of Applied Sport Psychology, 3,* 126–141.

Williams, K., Harkins, S., & Latane, B. (1981). Identifiability and social loafing: Two cheering experiments. *Journal of Personality and Social Psychology, 40,* 303–311.

Williams, S., Cooley, S., Newell, E., Weibull, F., & Cummings, J. (2013). Seeing the difference: Developing effective imagery scripts for athletes. *Journal of Sport Psychology in Action, 4,* 109–121.

Williams, S., & Cumming, J. (2011). Measuring athlete imagery ability: The Sport Imagery Ability Questionnaire. *Journal of Sport and Exercise Psychology, 33,* 416–440.

Williams, S., & Cumming J. (2012). Challenge vs. threat: Investigating the effect of using imagery to manipulate stress appraisal of a dart throwing task. *Sport and Exercise Psychology Review, 8,* 4–21.

Williams, S., Cumming, J., & Balanos, G. (2010). The use of imagery to manipulate challenge and treat appraisal states in athletes. *Journal of Sport and Exercise Psychology, 32,* 339–358.

Willis, J.D., & Campbell, L.F. (1992). *Exercise psychology.* Champaign, IL: Human Kinetics.

Wilmore, J.H. (1992). Body weight standards and athletic performance. In K.D. Brownell, J. Rodin, & J.H. Wilmor (Eds.), *Eating, body weight, and performance* (pp. 315–333). Malvern, PA: Lea & Febiger.

Wilson, K., & Brookfield, D. (2009). Effect of goal setting on motivation and adherence in a six-week exercise program. *International Journal of Sport and Exercise Psychology, 6,* 89–100.

Wilson, M. (2008). From processing efficiency to attentional control: A mechanistic account of the anxiety-performance relationship. *International Review of Sport and Exercise Psychology, 1,* 184–201.

Wilson, M. (2010). Gaze and cognitive control in motor performance: Implications for skill training. *The Sport and Exercise Sciences, 23,* 29–30.

Wilson, M. (2012). Anxiety: attention, the brain, the body and performance. In S. Murphy (Ed.) *The oxford handbook of sport and performance psychology* (pp. 173–190). New York: Routledge.

Wilson, M., Vine, S., & Wood, G. (2009). The influence of anxiety on visual attentional control in basketball free-throw shooting. *Journal of Sport and Exercise Psychology, 31,* 152–168.

Wilson, P., Rodgers, W., Hall, C., & Gammage, K. (2003). Do autonomous exercise regulations underpin types of exercise imagery? *Journal of Applied Sport Psychology, 15,* 294–306.

Wipfli, B., Rethorst, C., & Landers, D. (2008). The anxiolytic effects of exercise: A meta-analysis of randomized trials and dose-response analysis. *Journal of Sport and Exercise Psychology, 30,* 392–419.

Wold, B., & Anderssen, N. (1992). Health promotion aspects of family and peer influences on sport participation. *International Journal of Sport Psychology, 23,* 343–359.

Wolff, A. (1996, July 22). Roadshow. *Sport Illustrated,* pp. 94–97.

Wolko, K.I., Hrycaiko, D.W., & Martin, G.L. (1993). A comparison of two self-management packages to standard coaching for improving performance of gymnasts. *Behavior Modification, 17,* 209–223.

Wolpe, J. (1958). *Psychotherapy by reciprocal inhibition.* Stanford, CA: Stanford University Press.

Wong, E.H., & Bridges, L.J. (1995). A model of motivational orientation for youth sport: Some preliminary work. *Adolescence, 30,* 437–452.

Woodcock, C., Duda, J., Cumming, J., Sharp, L., & Holland, M. (2012). Assessing mental skill and technique use in applied intervention: Recognizing and minimizing threats to psychometric properties of the TOPS. *The Sport Psychologist, 26,* 1–15.

Woodman, T., & Davis, P. (2008). The role of repression in the incidence of ironic errors. *The Sport Psychologist, 22,* 183–196.

Woodman, T., & Hardy, L. (2001a). A case study of organization stress in elite sport. *Journal of Applied Sport Psychology, 13,* 207–236.

Woodman, T., & Hardy, L. (2001b). Stress and anxiety. In R. Singer, H. Hausenblas, & C. Janelle (Eds.), *Handbook of sport psychology* (2nd ed., pp. 290–318). New York: Wiley.

Woolsey, C., Waigandt, A., & Beck, N. (2010). Athletes and energy drinks: Reported risk-taking and consequences from the combined use of alcohol and energy drinks. *Journal of Applied Sport Psychology, 22,* 65–71.

World Health Organization Group. (1995). The World Health Organization Quality of Life assessment (WHOQOL): Position paper from the World Health Organization. *Social Science and Medicine, 41,* 1403–1409.

Wright, A., & Côté, J. (2003). A retrospective analysis of leadership development through sport. *The Sport Psychologist, 17,* 268–291.

Wright, C., & Smith, D. (2007). The effect of a short-term PETTLEP imagery intervention on a cognitive task. *Journal of Imagery Research in Sport and Physical Activity, 2*(1), article 1.

Wright, C., & Smith, D. (2009). The effect of PETTLEP imagery on strength performance. *International Journal of Sport and Exercise Psychology, 7,* 18–31.

Wrisberg, C., Loberg, L., Simpson, D., Withycombe, J., & Reed, A. (2010). An exploratory investigation of NCAA Division-1 coaches' support of sport psychology consultants and willingness to seek mental training services. *The Sport Psychologist, 24,* 489–503.

Wrisberg, C., Simpson, D., Loberg, L., & Reed, A. (2009). NCAA division-I student-athletes' receptivity to mental skills training by sport psychology consultants. *The Sport Psychologist, 23,* 470–486.

Wrisberg, C., Withycombe, J., Simpson, D., Loberg, L., & Reed, A. (2012). NCAA Division-1 administrators' perceptions of the benefits of sport psychology services and possible roles for a consultant. *The Sport Psychologist, 26,* 16–28.

Wuerth, S., Lee, M.J., & Alfermann, D. (2004). Parental involvement and athletes' career in youth sports. *Psychology of Sport and Exercise, 5,* 21–33.

Wulf, G. (2013). Attentional focus and motor learning: A review of 15 years. *International Review of Sport and Exercise Psychology, 6,* 77–104.

Yan, J.H., & McCullagh, P. (2004). Cultural influence on youth's motivation of participation in physical activity. *Journal of Sport Behavior, 27*(4), 378–390.

Yates, D.H. (1943). A practical method of using set. *Journal of Applied Psychology, 27,* 512–519.

Young, B., Medic, N., & Starkes, J. (2009). Effects of self-monitoring training logs on behaviors and beliefs of swimmers. *Journal of Applied Sport Psychology, 21,* 413–428.

Yukelson, D. (1993). Communicating effectively. In J. Williams (Ed.), *Applied sport psychology: Personal growth to peak performance* (pp. 122–136). Palo Alto, CA: Mayfield.

Yukelson, D. (1997). Principles of effective team building interventions in sport: A direct services approach at Penn State University. *Journal of Applied Sport Psychology, 9,* 73–96.

Yukelson, D. (1998). Communicating effectively. In J. Williams (Ed.), *Sport psychology: Personal growth to peak performance* (3rd ed., pp. 142–157). Mountain View, CA: Mayfield.

Yukelson, D., Weinberg, R., & Jackson, A. (1984). A multidimensional group cohesion instrument for intercollegiate basketball teams. *Journal of Sport Psychology, 6,* 103–117.

Zaccaro, S.J. (2007). Trait-based perspectives of leadership. *American Psychologist, 62,* 6–16.

Zaichkowsky, L.D., & Fuchs, C.Z. (1988). Biofeedback applications in exercise and athletic performance. *Exercise and Sport Sciences Reviews, 16,* 381–421.

Zaichkowsky, L.D., & Takenaka, K. (1993). Optimizing arousal level. In R.N. Singer, M. Murphey, & L.K. Tennant (Eds.), *Handbook of sport psychology* (pp. 511–527). New York: Macmillan.

Zajonc, R.B. (1965). Social facilitation. *Science, 149,* 269–274.

Zakrajsek, R., Steinfeldt, J., Bodey, K., Martin, S., & Zizzi, S. (2013). NCAA Division I coaches' perceptions and preferred use of sport psychology services: A qualitative perspective. *The Sport Psychologist, 27,* 258–268.

Zander, A. (1982). *Making groups effective.* San Francisco: Jossey-Bass.

Zhang, J., Jensen, B.E., & Mann, B.L. (1997). Modification and revision of the Leadership Scale for Sport. *Journal of Sport Behavior, 20,* 105–121.

Zhang, T. & Solomon, M. (2013). Integrating self-determination theory with the social ecological model to understand students' physical activity behaviors. *International Review of Sport and Exercise Psychology, 6,* 54-76.

Zhang, T., Solomon, M., Gao, Z., & Kosma, M. (2012). Promoting school students' physical activity: A social ecological perspective. *Journal of Applied Sport Psychology, 24,* 92–105.

Zourbanos, N., Hatzigeorgiadis, A., Bardas, N., & Theodorakis, Y. (2013). The effects of self-talk on dominant and nondominant arm performance on a handball task in primary physical education students. *The Sport Psychologist, 27,* 171–176.

Zourbanos, N., Hatzigeorgiadis, A., Chroni, S., Theodorakis, Y., & Papaioannou, S. (2009). Automatic Self-Talk Questionnaire for Sports (ASTQS): Development and preliminary validation of a measure identifying the structure of athletes' self-talk. *The Sport Psychologist, 23,* 233–251.

Zourbanos, N., Hatzigeorgiadis, A., Goudas, M., Papaioannou, A., Chroni, S., & Theororakis, Y. (2011). The social side of self-talk: Relationships between perceptions of support received from the coach and athletes' self-talk. *Psychology of Sport and Exercise, 12,* 1–8.

Zourbanos, N., Hatzigeorgiadis, A., & Theodorakis, Y. (2007). A preliminary investigation of the relationship between athletes' self-talk and coaches' behaviour and statements. *International Journal of Sports Science and Coaching, 2,* 57–66.

Zourbanos, N., Hatzigeorgiadis, A.,Tsiakaras, N., Chroni, S., & Theodorakis, Y. (2010). A multimethod examination of the relationship between coaching behavior and athletes' inherent self-talk. *Journal of Sport and Exercise Psychology, 32,* 764–785.

Please note: The italicized *f* and *t* following page numbers refer to figures and tables, respectively.

Robert S. Weinberg, PhD, is a professor in kinesiology and health at Miami University in Oxford, Ohio. Weinberg has more than 30 years of experience in both the scholarly and applied aspects of sport psychology. He has written numerous research articles, including more than 150 refereed articles in scholarly journals, as well as books, book chapters, and applied articles for coaches, athletes, and exercisers.

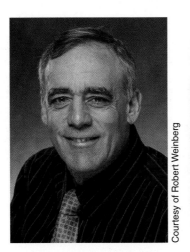

Courtesy of Robert Weinberg

Weinberg was voted one of the top 10 sport psychologists in North America by his peers. He is past president of the North American Society for Psychology of Sport and Physical Activity (NASPSPA) and of the Association for Applied Sport Psychology (AASP). He is also a certified AASP consultant, where he consults with athletes of all sports and ages.

Weinberg was named a Distinguished Scholar in Sport Psychology at Miami University in 2005. In addition, he was the editor of the *Journal of Applied Sport Psychology* and voted outstanding faculty member in the School of Education and Allied Professions at Miami University in 1998. In his leisure time, he enjoys playing tennis, traveling, and gardening.

Daniel Gould, **PhD,** is the director for the Institute for the Study of Youth Sports and professor in the department of kinesiology at Michigan State University. He has taught sport psychology for more than 35 years. An active researcher, Gould was the founding coeditor of *The Sport Psychologist* and has published more than 200 articles on sport psychology. He is best known for conducting applied research that links research and practice.

Courtesy of Dan Gould

Gould was voted one of the top 10 sport psychology specialists in North America and is internationally known, having presented his work in more than 30 countries. When on the faculty of the University of North Carolina at Greensboro, he received the university's coveted Alumni-Teaching Excellence Award, an all-campus teaching honor. He is an Association for Applied Sport Psychology (AASP) certified consultant and member of the United States Olympic Committee Sport Psychology Registry.

Gould is the former president of AASP and SHAPE America's Sport Psychology Academy. In addition to teaching sport psychology, he is extensively involved in coaching education from youth sports to Olympic competition. He also serves as mental skills training consultant for professional, Olympic, and world-class athletes, and in recent years he has served as an executive coach for business leaders interested in enhancing their organizations' performance.

He lives in Okemos, Michigan, with his wife, Deb. He is a proud father of two sons, Kevin and Brian. In his leisure time, he enjoys swimming, doing fitness activities, and spending time with his family.